The Oxford Colour German Dictionary

Also available

The Oxford Colour French Dictionary
The Oxford Colour Spanish Dictionary

The Oxford Colour German Dictionary

German–English
English–German

Deutsch–Englisch
Englisch–Deutsch

Gunhild Prowe
Jill Schneider

IAN KERR.
STREATHAM.
SW16 6RP.

Oxford New York

OXFORD UNIVERSITY PRESS

1995

Oxford University Press, Walton Street, Oxford OX2 6DP

Oxford New York
Athens Auckland Bangkok Bombay
Calcutta Cape Town Dar es Salaam Delhi
Florence Hong Kong Istanbul Karachi
Kuala Lumpur Madras Madrid Melbourne
Mexico City Nairobi Paris Singapore
Taipei Tokyo Toronto

and associated companies in
Berlin Ibadan

Oxford is a trade mark of Oxford University Press

First published 1993 as The Oxford German Minidictionary
First issued as an Oxford University Press paperback 1994
Two-colour edition first published 1995

British Library Cataloguing in Publication Data
Data available

Library of Congress Cataloging in Publication Data
Oxford colour German dictionary : German–English, English–German =
Deutsch–Englisch, Englisch–Deutsch / [editors], Gunhild Prowe,
Jill Schneider.
p.   cm.
1. German language—Dictionaries—English.   2. English language—
Dictionaries—German.   I. Prowe, Gunhild.   II. Schneider, Jill.
433'.21—dc20   PF3640.09 1995   95–10610
ISBN 0–19–8645414

Typeset by Latimer Trend & Company Ltd.
Printed in Spain by
Mateu Cromo Artes Graficas S.A.
Madrid

Preface

This dictionary is designed for both English and German users. It provides a handy and comprehensive reference work for tourists and business people, and covers the needs of the student for GCSE.

We should like to express our thanks to Dr Michael Clark of Oxford University Press for his advice and support, and to Roswitha and Neil Morris for reading the proofs.

G.P. & J.S.

Contents

Introduction

As an aid to easy reference all main headwords, compounds and derivatives in this dictionary are in blue.

A swung dash ∼ represents the headword or that part of the headword preceding a vertical bar |. The initial letter of a German headword is given to show whether or not it is a capital.

The vertical bar | follows the part of the headword which is not repeated in compounds or derivatives.

Square brackets [ ] are used for optional material.

Angled brackets ⟨ ⟩ are used after a verb translation to indicate the object; before a verb translation to indicate the subject; before an adjective to indicate a typical noun which it qualifies.

Round brackets ( ) are used for field or style labels (see list on page x) and for explanatory matter.

A ● indicates a new part of speech within an entry.

od (oder) and *or* denote that words or portions of a phrase are synonymous. An oblique stroke / is used where there is a difference in usage or meaning.

≈ is used where no exact equivalent exists in the other language.

A dagger † indicates that a German verb is irregular and that the parts can be found in the verb table on page 555. Compound verbs are not listed there as they follow the pattern of the basic verb.

The stressed vowel is marked in a German headword by – (long) or · (short). A phonetic transcription is only given for words which do not follow the normal rules of pronunciation. These rules can be found on page 551.

Phonetics are given for all English headwords and for derivatives where there is a change of pronunciation or stress. In blocks of compounds, if no stress is shown, it falls on the first element.

A change in pronunciation or stress shown within a block of compounds applies only to that particular word (subsequent entries revert to the pronunciation and stress of the headword).

German headword nouns are followed by the gender and, with the exception of compound nouns, by the genitive and plural. These are only given at compound nouns if they present some difficulty. Otherwise the user should refer to the final element.

Nouns that decline like adjectives are entered as follows: **-e(r)** *m/f,* **-e(s)** *nt.*

Adjectives which have no undeclined form are entered in the feminine form with the masculine and neuter in brackets **-e(r,s)**.

The reflexive pronoun **sich** is accusative unless marked (*dat*).

Note on proprietary status

This dictionary includes some words which have, or are asserted to have, proprietary status as trade marks or otherwise. Their inclusion does not imply that they have acquired for legal purposes a non-proprietary or general significance, nor any other judgement concerning their legal status. In cases where the editorial staff have some evidence that a word has proprietary status this is indicated by the symbol ® in the entry, but no judgement concerning the legal status of such words is made or implied thereby.

Abbreviations · Abkürzungen

adjective	a	Adjektiv
abbreviation	abbr	Abkürzung
accusative	acc	Akkusativ
Administration	Admin	Administration
adverb	adv	Adverb
American	Amer	amerikanisch
Anatomy	Anat	Anatomie
Archaeology	Archaeol	Archäologie
Architecture	Archit	Architektur
Astronomy	Astr	Astronomie
attributive	attrib	attributiv
Austrian	Aust	österreichisch
Motor vehicles	Auto	Automobil
Aviation	Aviat	Luftfahrt
Biology	Biol	Biologie
Botany	Bot	Botanik
Chemistry	Chem	Chemie
collective	coll	Kollektivum
Commerce	Comm	Handel
conjunction	conj	Konjunktion
Cookery	Culin	Kochkunst
dative	dat	Dativ
definite article	def art	bestimmter Artikel
demonstrative	dem	Demonstrativ-
dialect	dial	Dialekt
Electricity	Electr	Elektrizität
something	etw	etwas
feminine	f	Femininum
familiar	fam	familiär
figurative	fig	figurativ
genitive	gen	Genitiv
Geography	Geog	Geographie
Geology	Geol	Geologie
Geometry	Geom	Geometrie
Grammar	Gram	Grammatik
Horticulture	Hort	Gartenbau
impersonal	impers	unpersönlich
indefinite article	indef art	unbestimmter Artikel

indefinite pronoun	indef pron	unbestimmtes Pronomen
infinitive	inf	Infinitiv
inseparable	insep	untrennbar
interjection	int	Interjektion
invariable	inv	unveränderlich
irregular	irreg	unregelmäßig
someone	jd	jemand
someone	jdm	jemandem
someone	jdn	jemanden
someone's	jds	jemandes
Journalism	Journ	Journalismus
Law	Jur	Jura
Language	Lang	Sprache
literary	liter	dichterisch
masculine	m	Maskulinum
Mathematics	Math	Mathematik
Medicine	Med	Medizin
Meteorology	Meteorol	Meteorologie
Military	Mil	Militär
Mineralogy	Miner	Mineralogie
Music	Mus	Musik
noun	n	Substantiv
Nautical	Naut	nautisch
North German	N Ger	Norddeutsch
nominative	nom	Nominativ
neuter	nt	Neutrum
or	od	oder
Proprietary term	P	Warenzeichen
pejorative	pej	abwertend
Photography	Phot	Fotografie
Physics	Phys	Physik
plural	pl	Plural
Politics	Pol	Politik
possessive	poss	Possessiv-
past participle	pp	zweites Partizip
predicative	pred	prädikativ
prefix	pref	Präfix
preposition	prep	Präposition
present	pres	Präsens
present participle	pres p	erstes Partizip

pronoun	pron	Pronomen
Psychology	Psych	Psychologie
past tense	pt	Präteritum
Railway	Rail	Eisenbahn
reflexive	refl	reflexiv
regular	reg	regelmäßig
relative	rel	Relativ-
Religion	Relig	Religion
see	s.	siehe
School	Sch	Schule
separable	sep	trennbar
singular	sg	Singular
South German	S Ger	Süddeutsch
slang	sl	Slang
someone	s.o.	jemand
something	sth	etwas
Technical	Techn	Technik
Telephone	Teleph	Telefon
Textiles	Tex	Textilien
Theatre	Theat	Theater
Television	TV	Fernsehen
Typography	Typ	Typographie
University	Univ	Universität
auxiliary verb	v aux	Hilfsverb
intransitive verb	vi	intransitives Verb
reflexive verb	vr	reflexives Verb
transitive verb	vt	transitives Verb
vulgar	vulg	vulgär
Zoology	Zool	Zoologie

Pronunciation of the alphabet
Aussprache des Alphabets

English/Englisch		German/Deutsch
eɪ	a	aː
biː	b	beː
siː	c	ʦeː
diː	d	deː
iː	e	eː
ef	f	ɛf
dʒiː	g	geː
eɪtʃ	h	haː
aɪ	i	iː
dʒeɪ	j	jɔt
keɪ	k	kaː
el	l	ɛl
em	m	ɛm
en	n	ɛn
əʊ	o	oː
piː	p	peː
kjuː	q	kuː
aː(r)	r	ɛr
es	s	ɛs
tiː	t	teː
juː	u	uː
viː	v	faʊ
ˈdʌbljuː	w	veː
eks	x	ɪks
waɪ	y	ˈʏpsilɔn
zed	z	ʦɛt
eɪ umlaut	ä	ɛː
əʊ umlaut	ö	øː
juː umlaut	ü	yː
esˈzed	ß	ɛsˈʦɛt

GERMAN–ENGLISH

DEUTSCH–ENGLISCH

A

Aal *m* -[e]s,-e eel. **a~en (sich)** *vr* laze; (*ausgestreckt*) stretch out

Aas *nt* -es carrion; (*sl*) swine

ab *prep* (+ *dat*) from; **ab Montag** from Monday ● *adv* off; (*weg*) away; (*auf Fahrplan*) departs; **von jetzt ab** from now on; **ab und zu** now and then; **auf und ab** up and down

abändern *vt sep* alter; (*abwandeln*) modify

abarbeiten *vt sep* work off; **sich a~** slave away

Abart *f* variety. **a~ig** *a* abnormal

Abbau *m* dismantling; (*Kohlen-*) mining; (*fig*) reduction. **a~en** *vt sep* dismantle; mine ⟨*Kohle*⟩; (*fig*) reduce, cut

abbeißen† *vt sep* bite off

abbeizen *vt sep* strip

abberufen† *vt sep* recall

abbestellen *vt sep* cancel; **jdn a~** put s.o. off

abbiegen† *vi sep* (*sein*) turn off; **[nach] links a~** turn left

Abbild *nt* image. **a~en** *vt sep* depict, portray. **A~ung** *f* -,-en illustration

Abbitte *f* **A~ leisten** apologize

abblättern *vi sep* (*sein*) flake off

abblend|en *vt/i sep* (*haben*) **[die Scheinwerfer] a~en** dip one's headlights. **A~licht** *nt* dipped headlights *pl*

abbrechen† *v sep* ● *vt* break off; (*abreißen*) demolish ● *vi* (*sein/haben*) break off

abbrennen† *v sep* ● *vt* burn off; (*niederbrennen*) burn down; let off ⟨*Feuerwerkskörper*⟩ ● *vi* (*sein*) burn down

abbringen† *vt sep* dissuade (**von** from)

Abbruch *m* demolition; (*Beenden*) breaking off; **etw** (*dat*) **keinen A~ tun** do no harm to sth

abbuchen *vt sep* debit

abbürsten *vt sep* brush down; (*entfernen*) brush off

abdank|en *vi sep* (*haben*) resign; ⟨*Herrscher:*⟩ abdicate. **A~ung** *f* -,-en resignation; abdication

abdecken *vt sep* uncover; (*abnehmen*) take off; (*zudecken*) cover; **den Tisch a~** clear the table

abdichten *vt sep* seal

abdrehen *vt sep* turn off

Abdruck *m* (*pl* -e) impression; (*Finger-*) print; (*Nachdruck*) reprint. **a~en** *vt sep* print

abdrücken *vt/i sep* (*haben*) fire; **sich a~** leave an impression

Abend *m* -s,-e evening; **am A~** in the evening. **a~** *adv* **heute a~** this evening, tonight; **gestern a~** yesterday evening, last night. **A~brot** *nt* supper. **A~essen** *nt* dinner; (*einfacher*) supper. **A~kurs[us]** *m* evening class. **A~mahl** *nt* (*Relig*) [Holy] Communion. **a~s** *adv* in the evening

Abenteuer *nt* -s,- adventure; (*Liebes-*) affair. **a~lich** *a* fantastic; (*gefährlich*) hazardous

Abenteurer *m* -s,- adventurer

aber *conj* but; **oder a~** or else ● *adv* (*wirklich*) really; **a~ ja!** but of course! **Tausende und a~ Tausende** thousands upon thousands

Aber|glaube *m* superstition. **a~gläubisch** *a* superstitious

abermals *adv* once again

abfahr|en† *v sep* ● *vi* (*sein*) leave; ⟨*Auto:*⟩ drive off ● *vt* take away; (*entlangfahren*) drive along; use ⟨*Fahrkarte*⟩; **abgefahrene Reifen** worn tyres. **A~t** *f* departure; (*Talfahrt*) descent; (*Piste*) run; (*Ausfahrt*) exit

Abfall *m* refuse, rubbish, (*Amer*) garbage; (*auf der Straße*) litter;

(*Industrie-*) waste. **A~eimer** *m* rubbish-bin; litter-bin

abfallen† *vi sep* (*sein*) drop, fall; (*übrigbleiben*) be left (**für** for); (*sich neigen*) slope away; (*fig*) compare badly (**gegen** with); **vom Glauben a~** renounce one's faith. **a~d** *a* sloping

Abfallhaufen *m* rubbish-dump

abfällig *a* disparaging, *adv* -ly

abfangen† *vt sep* intercept; (*beherrschen*) bring under control

abfärben *vi sep* (*haben*) 〈*Farbe:*〉 run; 〈*Stoff:*〉 not be colour-fast; **a~ auf** (+ *acc*) (*fig*) rub off on

abfassen *vt sep* draft

abfertigen *vt sep* attend to; (*zollamtlich*) clear; **jdn kurz a~** (*fam*) give s.o. short shrift

abfeuern *vt sep* fire

abfind|en† *vt sep* pay off; (*entschädigen*) compensate; **sich a~en mit** come to terms with. **A~ung** *f* -,-**en** compensation

abflauen *vi sep* (*sein*) decrease

abfliegen† *vi sep* (*sein*) fly off; 〈*Aviat*〉 take off

abfließen† *vi sep* (*sein*) drain *or* run away

Abflug *m* 〈*Aviat*〉 departure

Abfluß *m* drainage; (*Öffnung*) drain. **A~rohr** *nt* drain-pipe

abfragen *vt sep* **jdn** *od* **jdm Vokabeln a~** test s.o. on vocabulary

Abfuhr *f* - removal; (*fig*) rebuff

abführ|en *vt sep* take *or* lead away. **a~end** *a* laxative. **A~mittel** *nt* laxative

abfüllen *vt sep* **auf** *od* **in Flaschen a~** bottle

Abgabe *f* handing in; (*Verkauf*) sale; (*Fußball*) pass; (*Steuer*) tax

Abgang *m* departure; (*Theat*) exit; (*Schul-*) leaving

Abgase *ntpl* exhaust fumes

abgeben† *vt sep* hand in; (*abliefern*) deliver; (*verkaufen*) sell; (*zur Aufbewahrung*) leave; (*Fußball*) pass; (*ausströmen*) give off; (*abfeuern*) fire; (*verlauten lassen*) give; cast 〈*Stimme*〉; **jdm etw a~** give s.o. a share of sth; **sich a~ mit** occupy oneself with

abgedroschen *a* hackneyed

abgehen† *v sep* ● *vi* (*sein*) leave; (*Theat*) exit; (*sich lösen*) come off; (*abgezogen werden*) be deducted; (*abbiegen*) turn off; (*verlaufen*) go off; **ihr geht jeglicher Humor ab** she totally lacks a sense of humour ● *vt* walk along

abgehetzt *a* harassed. **abgelegen** *a* remote. **abgeneigt** *a* etw (*dat*) **nicht a~ sein** not be averse to sth. **abgenutzt** *a* worn. **Abgeordnete(r)** *m/f* deputy; (*Pol*) Member of Parliament. **abgepackt** *a* pre-packed. **abgerissen** *a* ragged

abgeschieden *a* secluded. **A~heit** *f* - seclusion

abgeschlossen *a* (*fig*) complete; 〈*Wohnung*〉 self-contained. **abgeschmackt** *a* (*fig*) tasteless. **abgesehen** *prep* apart (from **von**). **abgespannt** *a* exhausted. **abgestanden** *a* stale. **abgestorben** *a* dead; 〈*Glied*〉 numb. **abgetragen** *a* worn. **abgewetzt** *a* threadbare

abgewinnen† *vt sep* win (**jdm** from s.o.); **etw** (*dat*) **Geschmack a~** get a taste for sth

abgewöhnen *vt sep* **jdm/sich das Rauchen a~** cure s.o. of/give up smoking

abgezehrt *a* emaciated

abgießen† *vt sep* pour off; drain 〈*Gemüse*〉

abgleiten† *vi sep* (*sein*) slip

Abgott *m* idol

abgöttisch *adv* **a~ lieben** idolize

abgrenz|en *vt sep* divide off; (*fig*) define. **A~ung** *f* - demarcation

Abgrund *m* abyss; (*fig*) depths *pl*

abgucken *vt sep* (*fam*) copy

Abguß *m* cast

abhacken *vt sep* chop off

abhaken *vt sep* tick off

abhalten† *vt sep* keep off; (*hindern*) keep, prevent (**von** from); (*veranstalten*) hold

abhanden *adv* **a~ kommen** get lost

Abhandlung *f* treatise

Abhang *m* slope

abhängen¹ *vt sep* (*reg*) take down; (*abkuppeln*) uncouple

abhäng|en²† *vi sep* (*haben*) depend (**von** on). **a~ig** *a* dependent (**von** on). **A~igkeit** *f* - dependence

abhärten *vt sep* toughen up

abhauen† *v sep* ● *vt* chop off ● *vi* (*sein*) (*fam*) clear off

abheben† *v sep* ● *vt* take off; (*vom Konto*) withdraw; **sich a~** stand out (**gegen** against) ● *vi* (*haben*) 〈*Cards*〉 cut [the cards]; 〈*Aviat*〉 take off; 〈*Rakete:*〉 lift off

abheften *vt sep* file

abhelfen† *vt sep* (+ *dat*) remedy

Abhilfe *f* remedy; **A~ schaffen** take [remedial] action

abholen *vt sep* collect; call for ⟨*Person*⟩; **jdn am Bahnhof a~** meet s.o. at the station

abhorchen *vt sep* (*Med*) sound

abhör|en *vt sep* listen to; (*überwachen*) tap; **jdn** *od* **jdm Vokabeln a~en** test s.o. on vocabulary. **A~gerät** *nt* bugging device

Abitur *nt* **-s** ≈ A levels *pl*. **A~ient(in)** *m* **-en,-en** (*f* **-,-nen**) pupil taking the 'Abitur'

abkanzeln *vt sep* (*fam*) reprimand

abkaufen *vt sep* buy (*dat* from)

abkehren (sich) *vr sep* turn away

abkette[l]n *vt/i sep* (*haben*) cast off

abklingen† *vi sep* (*sein*) die away; (*nachlassen*) subside

abkochen *vt sep* boil

abkommen† *vi sep* (*sein*) **a~ von** stray from; (*aufgeben*) give up; **vom Thema a~** digress. **A~** *nt* **-s,-** agreement

abkömmlich *a* available

Abkömmling *m* **-s,-e** descendant

abkratzen *v sep* ● *vt* scrape off ● *vi* (*sein*) (*sl*) die

abkühlen *vt/i sep* (*sein*) cool; **sich a~** cool [down]; ⟨*Wetter:*⟩ turn cooler

Abkunft *f* **-** origin

abkuppeln *vt sep* uncouple

abkürz|en *vt sep* shorten; abbreviate ⟨*Wort*⟩. **A~ung** *f* short cut; (*Wort*) abbreviation

abladen† *vt sep* unload

Ablage *f* shelf; (*für Akten*) tray

ablager|n *vt sep* deposit; **sich a~n** be deposited. **A~ung** *f* **-,-en** deposit

ablassen† *v sep* ● *vt* drain [off]; let off ⟨*Dampf*⟩; (*vom Preis*) knock off ● *vi* (*haben*) **a~ von** give up; **von jdm a~** leave s.o. alone

Ablauf *m* drain; (*Verlauf*) course; (*Ende*) end; (*einer Frist*) expiry. **a~en†** *v sep* ● *vi* (*sein*) run *or* drain off; (*verlaufen*) go off; (*enden*) expire; ⟨*Zeit:*⟩ run out; ⟨*Uhrwerk:*⟩ run down ● *vt* walk along; (*absuchen*) scour (**nach** for); (*abnutzen*) wear down

ableg|en *v sep* ● *vt* put down; discard ⟨*Karte*⟩; (*abheften*) file; (*ausziehen*) take off; (*aufgeben*) give up; sit, take ⟨*Prüfung*⟩; **abgelegte Kleidung** castoffs *pl* ● *vi* (*haben*) take off one's coat; (*Naut*) cast off. **A~er** *m* **-s,-** (*Bot*) cutting; (*Schößling*) shoot

ablehn|en *vt sep* refuse; (*mißbilligen*) reject. **A~ung** *f* **-,-en** refusal; rejection

ableit|en *vt sep* divert; **sich a~en** be derived (**von/aus** from). **A~ung** *f* derivation; (*Wort*) derivative

ablenk|en *vt sep* deflect; divert ⟨*Aufmerksamkeit*⟩; (*zerstreuen*) distract. **A~ung** *f* **-,-en** distraction

ablesen† *vt sep* read; (*absuchen*) pick off

ableugnen *vt sep* deny

ablicht|en *vt sep* photocopy. **A~ung** *f* photocopy

abliefern *vt sep* deliver

ablös|en *vt sep* detach; (*ablösen*) relieve; **sich a~en** come off; (*sich abwechseln*) take turns. **A~ung** *f* relief

abmach|en *vt sep* remove; (*ausmachen*) arrange; (*vereinbaren*) agree; **abgemacht!** agreed! **A~ung** *f* **-,-en** agreement

abmagern *vi sep* (*sein*) lose weight. **A~ungskur** *f* slimming diet

abmarschieren *vi sep* (*sein*) march off

abmelden *vt sep* cancel ⟨*Zeitung*⟩; **sich a~** report that one is leaving; (*im Hotel*) check out

abmess|en† *vt sep* measure. **A~ungen** *fpl* measurements

abmühen (sich) *vr sep* struggle

abnäh|en *vt sep* take in. **A~er** *m* **-s,-** dart

Abnahme *f* **-** removal; (*Kauf*) purchase; (*Verminderung*) decrease

abnehm|en† *v sep* ● *vt* take off, remove; pick up ⟨*Hörer*⟩; **jdm etw a~en** take-/(*kaufen*) buy sth from s.o. ● *vi* (*haben*) decrease; (*nachlassen*) decline; ⟨*Person:*⟩ lose weight; ⟨*Mond:*⟩ wane. **A~er** *m* **-s,-** buyer

Abneigung *f* dislike (**gegen** of)

abnorm *a* abnormal, *adv* -ly

abnutz|en *vt sep* wear out; **sich a~en** wear out. **A~ung** *f* - wear [and tear]

Abon|nement /abɔnə'mãː/ *nt* **-s,-s** subscription. **A~nent** *m* **-en,-en** subscriber. **a~nieren** *vt* take out a subscription to

Abordnung *f* **-,-en** deputation

abpassen *vt sep* wait for; **gut a~** time well

abprallen *vi sep* (*sein*) rebound; ⟨*Geschoß:*⟩ ricochet

abraten† *vi sep* (*haben*) **jdm von etw a~** advise s.o. against sth

abräumen *vt/i (haben)* clear away; clear ⟨Tisch⟩

abrechn|en *v sep* ● *vt* deduct ● *vi (haben)* settle up; *(fig)* get even. **A∼ung** *f* settlement [of accounts]; *(Rechnung)* account

Abreise *f* departure. **a∼n** *vi sep (sein)* leave

abreißen† *v sep* ● *vt* tear off; *(demolieren)* pull down ● *vi (sein)* come off; *(fig)* break off

abrichten *vt sep* train

abriegeln *vt sep* bolt; *(absperren)* seal off

Abriß *m* demolition; *(Übersicht)* summary

abrufen† *vt sep* call away; *(Computer)* retrieve

abrunden *vt sep* round off; **nach unten/oben a∼** round down/up

abrupt *a* abrupt, *adv* -ly

abrüst|en *vi sep (haben)* disarm. **A∼ung** *f* disarmament

abrutschen *vi sep (sein)* slip

Absage *f* -,-n cancellation; *(Ablehnung)* refusal. **a∼n** *v sep* ● *vt* cancel ● *vi (haben)* [jdm] **a∼n** cancel an appointment [with s.o.]; *(auf Einladung)* refuse [s.o.'s invitation]

absägen *vt sep* saw off; *(fam)* sack

Absatz *m* heel; *(Abschnitt)* paragraph; *(Verkauf)* sale

abschaff|en *vt sep* abolish; get rid of ⟨Auto, Hund⟩. **A∼ung** *f* abolition

abschalten *vt/i sep (haben)* switch off

abschätzig *a* disparaging, *adv* -ly

Abschaum *m (fig)* scum

Abscheu *m* - revulsion

abscheulich *a* revolting; *(fam)* horrible, *adv* -bly

abschicken *vt sep* send off

Abschied *m* -[e]s,-e farewell; *(Trennung)* parting; **A∼ nehmen** say goodbye (**von** to)

abschießen† *vt sep* shoot down; *(abtrennen)* shoot off; *(abfeuern)* fire; launch ⟨Rakete⟩

abschirmen *vt sep* shield

abschlagen† *vt sep* knock off; *(verweigern)* refuse; *(abwehren)* repel

abschlägig *a* negative; **a∼e Antwort** refusal

Abschlepp|dienst *m* breakdown service. **a∼en** *vt sep* tow away. **A∼seil** *nt* tow-rope. **A∼wagen** *m* breakdown vehicle

abschließen† *v sep* ● *vt* lock; *(beenden, abmachen)* conclude; make ⟨Wette⟩; balance ⟨Bücher⟩; **sich a∼** *(fig)* cut oneself off ● *vi (haben)* lock up; *(enden)* end. **a∼d** *adv* in conclusion

Abschluß *m* conclusion. **A∼prüfung** *f* final examination. **A∼zeugnis** *nt* diploma

abschmecken *vt sep* season

abschmieren *vt sep* lubricate

abschneiden† *v sep* ● *vt* cut off; **den Weg a∼** take a short cut ● *vi (haben)* **gut/schlecht a∼** do well/badly

Abschnitt *m* section; *(Stadium)* stage; *(Absatz)* paragraph; *(Kontroll-)* counterfoil

abschöpfen *vt sep* skim off

abschrauben *vt sep* unscrew

abschreck|en *vt sep* deter; *(Culin)* put in cold water ⟨Ei⟩. **a∼end** *a* repulsive, *adv* -ly; **a∼endes Beispiel** warning. **A∼ungsmittel** *nt* deterrent

abschreib|en† *v sep* ● *vt* copy; *(Comm & fig)* write off ● *vi (haben)* copy. **A∼ung** *f (Comm)* depreciation

Abschrift *f* copy

Abschuß *m* shooting down; *(Abfeuern)* firing; *(Raketen-)* launch

abschüssig *a* sloping; *(steil)* steep

abschwächen *vt sep* lessen; **sich a∼** lessen; *(schwächer werden)* weaken

abschweifen *vi sep (sein)* digress

abschwellen† *vi sep (sein)* go down

abschwören† *vi sep (haben)* (+ *dat*) renounce

abseh|bar *a* **in a∼barer Zeit** in the foreseeable future. **a∼en†** *vt/i sep (haben)* copy; *(voraussehen)* foresee; **a∼en von** disregard; *(aufgeben)* refrain from; **es abgesehen haben auf** (+ *acc*) have one's eye on; *(schikanieren)* have it in for

absein† *vi sep (sein) (fam)* have come off; *(erschöpft)* be worn out

abseits *adv* apart; *(Sport)* offside ● *prep* (+ *gen*) away from. **A∼** *nt* - *(Sport)* offside

absend|en† *vt sep* send off. **A∼er** *m* sender

absetzen *v sep* ● *vt* put *or* set down; *(ablagern)* deposit; *(abnehmen)* take off; *(absagen)* cancel; *(abbrechen)* stop; *(entlassen)* dismiss; *(verkaufen)* sell; *(abziehen)* deduct; **sich a∼** be deposited; *(fliehen)* flee ● *vi (haben)* pause

Absicht *f* -,-en intention; **mit A∼** intentionally, on purpose

absichtlich *a* intentional, *adv* -ly, deliberate, *adv* -ly

absitzen† *v sep* ● *vi (sein)* dismount ● *vt (fam)* serve ⟨*Strafe*⟩

absolut *a* absolute, *adv* -ly

Absolution /-'tsio:n/ *f* - absolution

absolvieren *vt* complete; (*bestehen*) pass

absonderlich *a* odd

absonder|n *vt sep* separate; (*ausscheiden*) secrete; **sich a~n** keep apart (**von** from). **A~ung** *f* -,-en secretion

absor|bieren *vt* absorb. **A~ption** /-'tsio:n/ *f* - absorption

abspeisen *vt sep* fob off (**mit** with)

abspenstig *a* **a~ machen** take (**jdm** from s.o.)

absperr|en *vt sep* cordon off; (*abstellen*) turn off; (*SGer*) lock. **A~ung** *f* -,-en barrier

abspielen *vt sep* play; (*Fußball*) pass; **sich a~** take place

Absprache *f* agreement

absprechen† *vt sep* arrange; **sich a~** agree; **jdm etw a~** deny s.o. sth

abspringen† *vi sep (sein)* jump off; (*mit Fallschirm*) parachute; (*abgehen*) come off; (*fam: zurücktreten*) back out

Absprung *m* jump

abspülen *vt sep* rinse; (*entfernen*) rinse off

abstamm|en *vi sep (haben)* be descended (**von** from). **A~ung** *f* - descent

Abstand *m* distance; (*zeitlich*) interval; **A~ halten** keep one's distance; **A~ nehmen von** (*fig*) refrain from

abstatten *vt sep* **jdm einen Besuch a~** pay s.o. a visit

abstauben *vt sep* dust

abstech|en† *vi sep (haben)* stand out. **A~er** *m* -s,- detour

abstehen† *vi sep (haben)* stick out; **a~ von** be away from

absteigen† *vi sep (sein)* dismount; (*niedersteigen*) descend; (*Fußball*) be relegated

abstell|en *vt sep* put down; (*lagern*) store; (*parken*) park; (*abschalten*) turn off; (*fig: beheben*) remedy. **A~gleis** *nt* siding. **A~raum** *m* boxroom

absterben† *vi sep (sein)* die; (*gefühllos werden*) go numb

Abstieg *m* -[e]s,-e descent; (*Fußball*) relegation

abstimm|en *v sep* ● *vi (haben)* vote (**über** + *acc* on) ● *vt* coordinate (**auf** + *acc* with). **A~ung** *f* vote

Abstinenz /-st-/ *f* - abstinence. **A~ler** *m* -s,- teetotaller

abstoßen† *vt sep* knock off; (*abschieben*) push off; (*verkaufen*) sell; (*fig: ekeln*) repel. **a~d** *a* repulsive, *adv* -ly

abstrakt /-st-/ *a* abstract

abstreifen *vt sep* remove; slip off ⟨*Kleidungsstück, Schuhe*⟩

abstreiten† *vt sep* deny

Abstrich *m* (*Med*) smear; (*Kürzung*) cut

abstufen *vt sep* grade

Absturz *m* fall; (*Aviat*) crash

abstürzen *vi sep (sein)* fall; (*Aviat*) crash

absuchen *vt sep* search; (*ablesen*) pick off

absurd *a* absurd

Abszeß *m* -sses,-sse abscess

Abt *m* -[e]s,̈-e abbot

abtasten *vt sep* feel; (*Techn*) scan

abtauen *vt/i sep (sein)* thaw; (*entfrosten*) defrost

Abtei *f* -,-en abbey

Abteil *nt* compartment

abteilen *vt sep* divide off

Abteilung *f* -,-en section; (*Admin, Comm*) department

abtragen† *vt sep* clear; (*einebnen*) level; (*abnutzen*) wear out; (*abzahlen*) pay off

abträglich *a* detrimental (*dat* to)

abtreib|en† *v sep* ● *vt (Naut)* drive off course; **ein Kind a~en lassen** have an abortion ● *vi (sein)* drift off course. **A~ung** *f* -,-en abortion

abtrennen *vt sep* detach; (*abteilen*) divide off

abtret|en† *v sep* ● *vt* cede (**an** + *acc* to); **sich** (*dat*) **die Füße a~en** wipe one's feet ● *vi (sein)* (*Theat*) exit; (*fig*) resign. **A~er** *m* -s,- doormat

abtrocknen *vt/i sep (haben)* dry; **sich a~** dry oneself

abtropfen *vi sep (sein)* drain

abtrünnig *a* renegade; **a~ werden** (+ *dat*) desert

abtun† *vt sep (fig)* dismiss

abverlangen *vt sep* demand (*dat* from)

abwägen† *vt sep (fig)* weigh

abwandeln *vt sep* modify

abwandern *vi sep (sein)* move away

abwarten *v sep* ● *vt* wait for ● *vi (haben)* wait [and see]

abwärts *adv* down[wards]

Abwasch *m* **-[e]s** washing-up; (*Geschirr*) dirty dishes *pl.* **a~en**† *v sep* ● *vt* wash; wash up ⟨*Geschirr*⟩; (*entfernen*) wash off ● *vi* (*haben*) wash up. **A~lappen** *m* dishcloth

Abwasser *nt* **-s,** ⁼ sewage. **A~kanal** *m* sewer

abwechseln *vi/r sep* (*haben*) **[sich]** **a~** alternate; ⟨*Personen:*⟩ take turns. **a~d** *a* alternate, *adv* -ly

Abwechslung *f* **-,-en** change; **zur A~** for a change. **a~sreich** *a* varied

Abweg *m* **auf A~e geraten** (*fig*) go astray. **a~ig** *a* absurd

Abwehr *f* - defence; (*Widerstand*) resistance; (*Pol*) counter-espionage. **a~en** *vt sep* ward off; (*Mil*) repel; (*zurückweisen*) dismiss. **A~system** *nt* immune system

abweich|en† *vi sep* (*sein*) deviate/ (*von Regel*) depart (**von** from); (*sich unterscheiden*) differ (**von** from). **a~end** *a* divergent; (*verschieden*) different. **A~ung** *f* **-,-en** deviation; difference

abweis|en† *vt sep* turn down; turn away ⟨*Person*⟩; (*abwehren*) repel. **a~end** *a* unfriendly. **A~ung** *f* rejection; (*Abfuhr*) rebuff

abwenden† *vt sep* turn away; (*verhindern*) avert; **sich a~** turn away; **den Blick a~** look away

abwerfen† *vt sep* throw off; throw ⟨*Reiter*⟩; (*Aviat*) drop; ⟨*Kartenspiel*⟩ discard; shed ⟨*Haut, Blätter*⟩; yield ⟨*Gewinn*⟩

abwert|en *vt sep* devalue. **a~end** *a* pejorative, *adv* -ly. **A~ung** *f* **-,-en** devaluation

abwesen|d *a* absent; (*zerstreut*) absent-minded. **A~heit** *f* - absence; absent-mindedness

abwickeln *vt sep* unwind; (*erledigen*) settle

abwischen *vt sep* wipe; (*entfernen*) wipe off

abwürgen *vt sep* stall ⟨*Motor*⟩

abzahlen *vt sep* pay off

abzählen *vt sep* count

Abzahlung *f* instalment

abzapfen *vt sep* draw

Abzeichen *nt* badge

abzeichnen *vt sep* copy; (*unterzeichnen*) initial; **sich a~** stand out

Abzieh|bild *nt* transfer. **a~en**† *v sep* ● *vt* pull off; take off ⟨*Laken*⟩; strip ⟨*Bett*⟩; (*häuten*) skin; (*Phot*) print; run off ⟨*Kopien*⟩; (*zurückziehen*)

withdraw; (*abrechnen*) deduct ● *vi* (*sein*) go away; ⟨*Rauch:*⟩ escape

abzielen *vi sep* (*haben*) **a~ auf** (+ *acc*) (*fig*) be aimed at

Abzug *m* withdrawal; (*Abrechnung*) deduction; (*Phot*) print; (*Korrektur-*) proof; (*am Gewehr*) trigger; (*A~söffnung*) vent; **A~e** *pl* deductions

abzüglich *prep* (+ *gen*) less

Abzugshaube *f* [cooker] hood

abzweig|en *v sep* ● *vi* (*sein*) branch off ● *vt* divert. **A~ung** *f* **-,-en** junction; (*Gabelung*) fork

ach *int* oh; **a~ je!** oh dear! **a~ so** I see; **mit A~ und Krach** (*fam*) by the skin of one's teeth

Achse *f* **-,-n** axis; (*Rad-*) axle

Achsel *f* **-,-n** shoulder; **die A~n zucken** shrug one's shoulders. **A~höhle** *f* armpit. **A~zucken** *nt* **-s** shrug

acht[1] *inv a*, **A~** *f* **-,-en** eight; **heute in a~ Tagen** a week today

acht[2] **außer a~ lassen** disregard; **sich in a~ nehmen** be careful

acht|e(r,s) *a* eighth. **a~eckig** *a* octagonal. **A~el** *nt* **-s,-** eighth. **A~elnote** *f* quaver, (*Amer*) eighth note

achten *vt* respect ● *vi* (*haben*) **a~ auf** (+ *acc*) pay attention to; (*aufpassen*) look after; **darauf a~, daß** take care that

ächten *vt* ban; ostracize ⟨*Person*⟩

Achter|bahn *f* roller-coaster. **a~n** *adv* (*Naut*) aft

achtgeben† *vi sep* (*haben*) be careful; **a~ auf** (+ *acc*) look after

achtlos *a* careless, *adv* -ly

achtsam *a* careful, *adv* -ly

Achtung *f* - respect (**vor** + *dat* for); **A~!** look out! (*Mil*) attention! **'A~ Stufe'** 'mind the step'

acht|zehn *inv a* eighteen. **a~zehnte(r,s)** *a* eighteenth. **a~zig** *a* *inv* eighty. **a~zigste(r,s)** *a* eightieth

ächzen *vi* (*haben*) groan

Acker *m* **-s,** ⁼ field. **A~bau** *m* agriculture. **A~land** *nt* arable land

addieren *vt/i* (*haben*) add; (*zusammenzählen*) add up

Addition /-'tsio:n/ *f* **-,-en** addition

ade *int* goodbye

Adel *m* **-s** nobility

Ader *f* **-,-n** vein; **künstlerische A~** artistic bent

Adjektiv *nt* **-s,-e** adjective

Adler *m* **-s,-** eagle

adlig *a* noble. **A~e(r)** *m* nobleman

ältest|e(r,s) *a* oldest; **der ä~e Sohn** the eldest son

althergebracht *a* traditional

altklug *a* precocious, *adv* -ly

ältlich *a* elderly

alt|modisch *a* old-fashioned ● *adv* in an old-fashioned way. **A~papier** *nt* waste paper. **A~stadt** *f* old [part of a] town. **A~warenhändler** *m* second-hand dealer. **A~weibermärchen** *nt* old wives' tale. **A~weibersommer** *m* Indian summer; (*Spinnfäden*) gossamer

Alufolie *f* [aluminium] foil

Aluminium *nt* -s aluminium, (*Amer*) aluminum

am *prep* = **an dem; am Montag** on Monday; **am Morgen** in the morning; **am besten/meisten** [the] best/ most; **am teuersten sein** be the most expensive

Amateur /-'tø:ɐ/ *m* -s,-e amateur

Ambition /-'tsio:n/ *f* -,-en ambition

Amboß *m* -sses,-sse anvil

ambulan|t *a* out-patient ... ● *adv* **a~t behandeln** treat as an out-patient. **A~z** *f* -,-en out-patients' department; (*Krankenwagen*) ambulance

Ameise *f* -,-n ant

amen *int*, **A~** *nt* -s amen

Amerika *nt* -s America

Amerikan|er(in) *m* -s,- (*f* -,-nen) American. **a~isch** *a* American

Ami *m* -s,-s (*fam*) Yank

Ammoniak *nt* -s ammonia

Amnestie *f* -,-n amnesty

amoralisch *a* amoral

Ampel *f* -,-n traffic lights *pl*; (*Blumen-*) hanging basket

Amphib|ie /-jə/ *f* -,-n amphibian. **a~isch** *a* amphibious

Amphitheater *nt* amphitheatre

Amput|ation /-'tsio:n/ *f* -,-en amputation. **a~ieren** *vt* amputate

Amsel *f* -,-n blackbird

Amt *nt* -[e]s,̈er office; (*Aufgabe*) task; (*Teleph*) exchange. **a~ieren** *vi* (*haben*) hold office; **a~ierend** acting. **a~lich** *a* official, *adv* -ly. **A~szeichen** *nt* dialling tone

Amulett *nt* -[e]s,-e [lucky] charm

amüs|ant *a* amusing, *adv* -ly. **a~ieren** *vt* amuse; **sich a~ieren** be amused (**über** + *acc* at); (*sich vergnügen*) enjoy oneself

an *prep* (+ *dat/acc*) at; (*haftend, berührend*) on; (*gegen*) against; (+ *acc*) ⟨*schicken*⟩ to; **an der/die Uni-** versität at/to university; **an dem Tag** on that day; **es ist an mir** it is up to me; **an [und für] sich** actually; **die Arbeit an sich** the work as such ● *adv* (*angeschaltet*) on; (*auf Fahrplan*) arriving; **an die zwanzig Mark/Leute** about twenty marks/ people; **von heute an** from today

analog *a* analogous; (*Computer*) analog. **A~ie** *f* -,-n analogy

Analphabet *m* -en,-en illiterate person. **A~entum** *nt* -s illiteracy

Analy|se *f* -,-n analysis. **a~sieren** *vt* analyse. **A~tiker** *m* -s,- analyst. **a~tisch** *a* analytical

Anämie *f* - anaemia

Ananas *f* -,-[se] pineapple

Anarch|ie *f* - anarchy. **A~ist** *m* -en,-en anarchist

Anat|omie *f* - anatomy. **a~omisch** *a* anatomical, *adv* -ly

anbahnen (sich) *vr sep* develop

Anbau *m* cultivation; (*Gebäude*) extension. **a~en** *vt sep* build on; (*anpflanzen*) cultivate, grow

anbehalten† *vt sep* keep on

anbei *adv* enclosed

anbeißen† *v sep* ● *vt* take a bite of ● *vi* (*haben*) ⟨*Fisch:*⟩ bite; (*fig*) take the bait

anbelangen *vt sep* = **anbetreffen**

anbellen *vt sep* bark at

anbeten *vt sep* worship

Anbetracht *m* **in A~** (+ *gen*) in view of

anbetreffen† *vt sep* **was mich/das anbetrifft** as far as I am/that is concerned

Anbetung *f* - worship

anbiedern (sich) *vr sep* ingratiate oneself (**bei** with)

anbieten† *vt sep* offer; **sich a~** offer (**zu** to)

anbinden† *vt sep* tie up

Anblick *m* sight. **a~en** *vt sep* look at

anbrechen† *v sep* ● *vt* start on; break into ⟨*Vorräte*⟩ ● *vi* (*sein*) begin; ⟨*Tag:*⟩ break; ⟨*Nacht:*⟩ fall

anbrennen† *v sep* ● *vt* light ● *vi* (*sein*) burn; (*Feuer fangen*) catch fire

anbringen† *vt sep* bring [along]; (*befestigen*) fix

Anbruch *m* (*fig*) dawn; **A~ des Tages/der Nacht** daybreak/nightfall

anbrüllen *vt sep* (*fam*) bellow at

Andacht *f* -,-en reverence; (*Gottesdienst*) prayers *pl*

andächtig *a* reverent, *adv* -ly; (*fig*) rapt, *adv* -ly

andauern *vi sep* (*haben*) last; (*anhalten*) continue. **a~d** *a* persistent, *adv* -ly; (*ständig*) constant, *adv* -ly

Andenken *nt* **-s,-** memory; (*Souvenir*) souvenir; **zum A~ an** (+ *acc*) in memory of

ander|e(r,s) *a* other; (*verschieden*) different; (*nächste*) next; **ein a~er, eine a~e** another ● *pron* **der a~e/die a~en** the other/others; **ein a~er** another [one]; (*Person*) someone else; **kein a~er** no one else; **einer nach dem a~en** one after the other; **alles a~e/ nichts a~es** everything/nothing else; **etwas ganz a~es** something quite different; **alles a~e als** anything but; **unter a~em** among other things. **a~enfalls** *adv* otherwise. **a~erseits** *adv* on the other hand. **a~mal** *adv* **ein a~mal** another time

ändern *vt* alter; (*wechseln*) change; **sich ä~** change

andernfalls *adv* otherwise

anders *pred a* different; **a~ werden** change ● *adv* differently; (*riechen, schmecken*) different; (*sonst*) else; **jemand/niemand/irgendwo a~** someone/no one/somewhere else

anderseits *adv* on the other hand

anders|herum *adv* the other way round. **a~wo** *adv* (*fam*) somewhere else

anderthalb *inv a* one and a half; **a~ Stunden** an hour and a half

Änderung *f* **-,-en** alteration; (*Wechsel*) change

anderweitig *a* other ● *adv* otherwise; (*anderswo*) elsewhere

andeut|en *vt sep* indicate; (*anspielen*) hint at. **A~ung** *f* **-,-en** indication; hint

andicken *vt sep* (*Culin*) thicken

Andrang *m* rush (**nach** for); (*Gedränge*) crush

andre *a & pron* = **andere**

andrehen *vt sep* turn on; **jdm etw a~** (*fam*) palm sth off on s.o.

andrerseits *adv* = **andererseits**

androhen *vt sep* **jdm etw a~** threaten s.o. with sth

aneignen *vt sep* **sich** (*dat*) **a~** appropriate; (*lernen*) learn

aneinander *adv & pref* together; (*denken*) of one another; **a~ vorbei** past one another. **a~geraten†** *vi sep* (*sein*) quarrel

Anekdote *f* **-,-n** anecdote

anekeln *vt sep* nauseate

anerkannt *a* acknowledged

anerkenn|en† *vt sep* acknowledge, recognize; (*würdigen*) appreciate. **a~end** *a* approving, *adv* -ly. **A~ung** *f* - acknowledgement, recognition; appreciation

anfahren† *v sep* ● *vt* deliver; (*streifen*) hit; (*schimpfen*) snap at ● *vi* (*sein*) start; **angefahren kommen** drive up

Anfall *m* fit, attack. **a~en†** *v sep* ● *vt* attack ● *vi* (*sein*) arise; (*Zinsen:*) accrue

anfällig *a* susceptible (**für** to); (*zart*) delicate. **A~keit** *f* - susceptibility (**für** to)

Anfang *m* **-s,¨e** beginning, start; **zu** *od* **am A~** at the beginning; (*anfangs*) at first. **a~en†** *vt/i sep* (*haben*) begin, start; (*tun*) do

Anfäng|er(in) *m* **-s,-** (*f* **-,-nen**) beginner. **a~lich** *a* initial, *adv* -ly

anfangs *adv* at first. **A~buchstabe** *m* initial letter. **A~gehalt** *nt* starting salary. **A~gründe** *mpl* rudiments

anfassen *vt sep* ● *vt* touch; (*behandeln*) treat; tackle (*Arbeit*); **jdn a~** take s.o.'s hand; **sich a~** hold hands; **sich weich a~** feel soft ● *vi* (*haben*) **mit a~** lend a hand

anfechten† *vt sep* contest; (*fig: beunruhigen*) trouble

anfeinden *vt sep* be hostile to

anfertigen *vt sep* make

anfeuchten *vt sep* moisten

anfeuern *vt sep* spur on

anflehen *vt sep* implore, beg

Anflug *m* (*Aviat*) approach; (*fig: Spur*) trace

anforder|n *vt sep* demand; (*Comm*) order. **A~ung** *f* demand

Anfrage *f* enquiry. **a~n** *vi sep* (*haben*) enquire, ask

anfreunden (sich) *vr sep* make friends (**mit** with); (*miteinander*) become friends

anfügen *vt sep* add

anfühlen *vt sep* feel; **sich weich a~** feel soft

anführ|en *vt sep* lead; (*zitieren*) quote; (*angeben*) give; **jdn a~en** (*fam*) have s.o. on. **A~er** *m* leader. **A~ungszeichen** *ntpl* quotation marks

Angabe f statement; (Anweisung) instruction; (Tennis) service; (fam: Angeberei) showing-off; **nähere A~n** particulars

angeb|en† v sep ● vt state; give (Namen, Grund); (anzeigen) indicate; set (Tempo) ● vi (haben) (Tennis) serve; (fam: protzen) show off. **A~er(in)** m **-s,-** (f -,-nen) (fam) show-off. **A~erei** f- (fam) showing-off

angeblich a alleged, adv -ly

angeboren a innate; (Med) congenital

Angebot nt offer; (Auswahl) range; **A~ und Nachfrage** supply and demand

angebracht a appropriate

angebunden a **kurz a~** curt

angegriffen a worn out; (Gesundheit) poor

angeheiratet a (Onkel, Tante) by marriage

angeheitert a (fam) tipsy

angehen† v sep ● vi (sein) begin, start; (Licht, Radio:) come on; (anwachsen) take root; **a~ gegen** fight ● vt attack; tackle (Arbeit); (bitten) ask (um for); (betreffen) concern; **das geht dich nichts an** it's none of your business. **a~d** a future; (Künstler) budding

angehör|en vi sep (haben) (+ dat) belong to. **A~ige(r)** m/f relative; (Mitglied) member

Angeklagte(r) m/f accused

Angel f -,-n fishing-rod; (Tür-) hinge

Angelegenheit f matter; **auswärtige A~en** foreign affairs

Angel|haken m fish-hook. **a~n** vi (haben) fish (**nach** for); **a~n gehen** go fishing ● vt (fangen) catch. **A~rute** f fishing-rod

angelsächsisch a Anglo-Saxon

angemessen a commensurate (dat with); (passend) appropriate, adv -ly

angenehm a pleasant, adv -ly; (bei Vorstellung) **a~!** delighted to meet you!

angenommen a (Kind) adopted; (Name) assumed

angeregt a animated, adv -ly

angesehen a respected; (Firma) reputable

angesichts prep (+ gen) in view of

angespannt a intent, adv -ly; (Lage) tense

Angestellte(r) m/f employee

angetan a **a~ sein von** be taken with

angetrunken a slightly drunk

angewandt a applied

angewiesen a dependent (**auf** + acc on); **auf sich selbst a~** on one's own

angewöhnen vt sep **jdm etw a~** get s.o. used to sth; **sich** (dat) **etw a~** get into the habit of doing sth

Angewohnheit f habit

Angina f - tonsillitis

angleichen† vt sep adjust (dat to)

Angler m -s,- angler

anglikanisch a Anglican

Anglistik f - English [language and literature]

Angorakatze f Persian cat

angreif|en† vt sep attack; tackle (Arbeit); (schädigen) damage; (anbrechen) break into; (anfassen) touch. **A~er** m **-s,-** attacker; (Pol) aggressor

angrenzen vi sep (haben) adjoin (**an etw** acc sth). **a~d** a adjoining

Angriff m attack; **in A~ nehmen** tackle. **a~slustig** a aggressive

Angst f -,"e fear; (Psych) anxiety; (Sorge) worry (**um** about); **A~ haben** be afraid (**vor** + dat of); (sich sorgen) be worried (**um** about) ● **jdm a~ machen** frighten s.o.; **mir ist a~** I am frightened; I am worried (**um** about)

ängstigen vt frighten; (Sorge machen) worry; **sich ä~** be frightened; be worried (**um** about)

ängstlich a nervous, adv -ly; (scheu) timid, adv -ly; (verängstigt) frightened, scared; (besorgt) anxious, adv -ly. **Ä~keit** f - nervousness; timidity; anxiety

angstvoll a anxious, adv -ly; (verängstigt) frightened

angucken vt sep (fam) look at

angurten (sich) vr sep fasten one's seat-belt

anhaben† vt sep have on; **er/es kann mir nichts a~** (fig) he/it cannot hurt me

anhalt|en† v sep ● vt stop; hold (Atem); **jdn zur Arbeit/Ordnung a~en** urge s.o. to work/be tidy ● vi (haben) stop; (andauern) continue. **a~end** a persistent, adv -ly; (Beifall) prolonged. **A~er(in)** m **-s,-** (f -,-nen) hitch-hiker; **per A~er fahren** hitch-hike. **A~spunkt** m clue

anhand prep (+ gen) with the aid of

Anhang m appendix; (fam: Angehörige) family

anhängen[1] *vt sep* (*reg*) hang up; (*befestigen*) attach; (*hinzufügen*) add

anhäng|en[2]†*vi* (*haben*) be a follower of. **A~er** *m* **-s,-** follower; (*Auto*) trailer; (*Schild*) [tie-on] label; (*Schmuck*) pendant; (*Aufhänger*) loop. **A~erin** *f* **-,-nen** follower. **A~erschaft** *f* - following, followers *pl.* **a~lich** *a* affectionate. **A~sel** *nt* **-s,-** appendage

anhäufen *vt sep* pile up; **sich a~** pile up, accumulate

anheben† *vt sep* lift; (*erhöhen*) raise

Anhieb *m* **auf A~** straight away

Anhöhe *f* hill

anhören *vt sep* listen to; **mit a~** overhear; **sich gut a~** sound good

animieren *vt* encourage (**zu** to)

Anis *m* **-es** aniseed

Anker *m* **-s,-** anchor; **vor A~ gehen** drop anchor. **a~n** *vi* (*haben*) anchor; (*liegen*) be anchored

anketten *vt sep* chain up

Anklage *f* accusation; (*Jur*) charge; (*Ankläger*) prosecution. **A~bank** *f* dock. **a~n** *vt sep* accuse (*gen* of); (*Jur*) charge (*gen* with)

Ankläger *m* accuser; (*Jur*) prosecutor

anklammern *vt sep* clip on; peg on the line (*Wäsche*); **sich a~** cling (**an** + *acc* to)

Anklang *m* **bei jdm A~ finden** meet with s.o.'s approval

ankleben *v sep* ● *vt* stick on ● *vi* (*sein*) stick (**an** + *dat* to)

Ankleide|kabine *f* changing cubicle; (*zur Anprobe*) fitting-room. **a~n** *vt sep* dress; **sich a~n** dress

anklopfen *vi sep* (*haben*) knock

anknipsen *vt sep* (*fam*) switch on

anknüpfen *v sep* ● *vt* tie on; (*fig*) enter into (*Gespräch, Beziehung*) ● *vi* (*haben*) refer (**an** + *acc* to)

ankommen† *vi sep* (*sein*) arrive; (*sich nähern*) approach; **gut a~** arrive safely; (*fig*) go down well (**bei** with); **nicht a~ gegen** (*fig*) be no match for; **a~ auf** (+ *acc*) depend on; **es a~ lassen auf** (+ *acc*) risk; **das kommt darauf an** it [all] depends

ankreuzen *vt sep* mark with a cross

ankündig|en *vt sep* announce. **A~ung** *f* announcement

Ankunft *f* - arrival

ankurbeln *vt sep* (*fig*) boost

anlächeln *vt sep* smile at

anlachen *vt sep* smile at

Anlage *f* **-,-n** installation; (*Industrie-*) plant; (*Komplex*) complex; (*Geld-*) investment; (*Plan*) layout; (*Beilage*) enclosure; (*Veranlagung*) aptitude; (*Neigung*) predisposition; **[öffentliche] A~n** [public] gardens; **als A~** enclosed

Anlaß *m* **-sses,-̈sse** reason; (*Gelegenheit*) occasion; **A~ geben zu** give cause for

anlass|en† *vt sep* (*Auto*) start; (*fam*) leave on (*Licht*); keep on (*Mantel*); **sich gut/schlecht a~en** start off well/badly. **A~er** *m* **-s,-** starter

anläßlich *prep* (+ *gen*) on the occasion of

Anlauf *m* (*Sport*) run-up; (*fig*) attempt. **a~en**† *v sep* ● *vi* (*sein*) start; (*beschlagen*) mist up; (*Metall:*) tarnish; **rot a~en** go red; (*erröten*) blush; **angelaufen kommen** come running up ● *vt* (*Naut*) call at

anlegen *v sep* ● *vt* put (**an** + *acc* against); put on (*Kleidung, Verband*); lay back (*Ohren*); aim (*Gewehr*); (*investieren*) invest; (*ausgeben*) spend (**für** on); (*erstellen*) build; (*gestalten*) lay out; draw up (*Liste*); **[mit] Hand a~** lend a hand; **es darauf a~** (*fig*) aim (**zu** to); **sich a~ mit** quarrel with ● *vi* (*haben*) (*Schiff:*) moor; **a~ auf** (+ *acc*) aim at

anlehnen *vt sep* lean (**an** + *acc* against); **sich a~** lean (**an** + *acc* on); **eine Tür angelehnt lassen** leave a door ajar

Anleihe *f* **-,-n** loan

anleinen *vt sep* put on a lead

anleit|en *vt sep* instruct. **A~ung** *f* instructions *pl*

anlernen *vt sep* train

Anliegen *nt* **-s,-** request; (*Wunsch*) desire

anlieg|en† *vi sep* (*haben*) **[eng] a~en** fit closely; **[eng] a~end** close-fitting. **A~er** *mpl* residents; **'A~er frei'** 'access for residents only'

anlocken *vt sep* attract

anlügen† *vt sep* lie to

anmachen *vt sep* (*fam*) fix; (*anschalten*) turn on; (*anzünden*) light; (*Culin*) dress (*Salat*)

anmalen *vt sep* paint

Anmarsch *m* (*Mil*) approach

anmaß|en *vt sep* **sich** (*dat*) **a~en** presume (**zu** to); **sich** (*dat*) **ein Recht a~en** claim a right. **a~end** *a* presumptuous, *adv* -ly; (*arrogant*) arrogant, *adv* -ly. **A~ung** *f* - presumption; arrogance

anmeld|en *vt sep* announce; (*Admin*) register; **sich a~en** say that one is coming; (*Admin*) register; (*Sch*) enrol; (*im Hotel*) check in; (*beim Arzt*) make an appointment. **A~ung** *f* announcement; (*Admin*) registration; (*Sch*) enrolment; (*Termin*) appointment

anmerk|en *vt sep* mark; **sich** (*dat*) **etw a~en lassen** show sth. **A~ung** *f* -,-en note

Anmut *f* - grace; (*Charme*) charm

anmuten *vt sep* **es mutet mich seltsam/vertraut an** it seems odd/familiar to me

anmutig *a* graceful, *adv* -ly; (*lieblich*) charming, *adv* -ly

annähen *vt sep* sew on

annäher|nd *a* approximate, *adv* -ly. **A~ungsversuche** *mpl* advances

Annahme *f* -,-n acceptance; (*Adoption*) adoption; (*Vermutung*) assumption

annehm|bar *a* acceptable. **a~en†** *vt sep* accept; (*adoptieren*) adopt; acquire ⟨*Gewohnheit*⟩; (*sich zulegen*, *vermuten*) assume; **sich a~en** (+ *gen*) take care of; **angenommen, daß** assuming that. **A~lichkeiten** *fpl* comforts

annektieren *vt* annex

Anno *adv* **A~ 1920** in the year 1920

Annon|ce /a'nõ:sə/ *f* -,-n advertisement. **a~cieren** /-'si:-/ *vt/i* (*haben*) advertise

annullieren *vt* annul; cancel ⟨*Flug*⟩

anöden *vt sep* (*fam*) bore

Anomalie *f* -,-n anomaly

anonym *a* anonymous, *adv* -ly

Anorak *m* -s,-s anorak

anordn|en *vt sep* arrange; (*befehlen*) order. **A~ung** *f* arrangement; order

anorganisch *a* inorganic

anormal *a* abnormal

anpacken *v sep* ● *vt* grasp; tackle ⟨*Arbeit, Problem*⟩ ● *vi* (*haben*) **mit a~** lend a hand

anpass|en *vt sep* try on; (*angleichen*) adapt (*dat* to); **sich a~en** adapt (*dat* to). **A~ung** *f* - adaptation. **a~ungsfähig** *a* adaptable. **A~ungsfähigkeit** *f* adaptability

Anpfiff *m* (*Sport*) kick-off; (*fam: Rüge*) reprimand

anpflanzen *vt sep* plant; (*anbauen*) grow

Anprall *m* -[e]s impact. **a~en** *vi sep* (*sein*) strike (**an etw** *acc* sth)

anprangern *vt sep* denounce

anpreisen† *vt sep* commend

Anprob|e *f* fitting. **a~ieren** *vt sep* try on

anrechnen *vt sep* count (**als** as); (*berechnen*) charge for; (*verrechnen*) allow ⟨*Summe*⟩; **ich rechne ihm seine Hilfe hoch an** I very much appreciate his help

Anrecht *nt* right (**auf** + *acc* to)

Anrede *f* [form of] address. **a~n** *vt sep* address; (*ansprechen*) speak to

anreg|en *vt sep* stimulate; (*ermuntern*) encourage (**zu** to); (*vorschlagen*) suggest. **a~end** *a* stimulating. **A~ung** *f* stimulation; (*Vorschlag*) suggestion

anreichern *vt sep* enrich

Anreise *f* journey; (*Ankunft*) arrival. **a~n** *vi sep* (*sein*) arrive

Anreiz *m* incentive

anrempeln *vt sep* jostle

Anrichte *f* -,-n sideboard. **a~n** *vt sep* (*Culin*) prepare; (*garnieren*) garnish (**mit** with); (*verursachen*) cause

anrüchig *a* disreputable

Anruf *m* call. **A~beantworter** *m* -s,- answering machine. **a~en†** *v sep* ● *vt* call to; (*bitten*) call on (**um** for); (*Teleph*) ring ● *vi* (*haben*) ring (**bei jdm** s.o.)

anrühren *vt sep* touch; (*verrühren*) mix

ans *prep* = **an das**

Ansage *f* announcement. **a~n** *vt sep* announce; **sich a~n** say that one is coming. **A~r(in)** *m* -s,- (*f* -,-nen) announcer

ansamm|eln *vt sep* collect; (*anhäufen*) accumulate; **sich a~eln** collect; (*sich häufen*) accumulate; ⟨*Leute*:⟩ gather. **A~lung** *f* collection; (*Menschen-*) crowd

ansässig *a* resident

Ansatz *m* beginning; (*Haar-*) hairline; (*Versuch*) attempt; (*Techn*) extension

anschaff|en *vt sep* **[sich** *dat*] **etw a~en** acquire/(*kaufen*) buy sth. **A~ung** *f* -,-en acquisition; (*Kauf*) purchase

anschalten *vt sep* switch on

anschau|en *vt sep* look at. **a~lich** *a* vivid, *adv* -ly. **A~ung** *f* -,-en (*fig*) view

Anschein *m* appearance; **den A~ haben** seem. **a~end** *adv* apparently

anschicken (sich) *vr sep* be about (**zu** to)

anschirren *vt sep* harness

Anschlag *m* notice; (*Vor-*) estimate; (*Überfall*) attack (**auf** + *acc* on); (*Mus*) touch; (*Techn*) stop; **240 A~e in der Minute** ≈ 50 words per minute. **A~brett** *nt* notice board. **a~en**† *v sep* ● *vt* put up ⟨*Aushang*⟩; strike ⟨*Note, Taste*⟩; cast on ⟨*Masche*⟩; (*beschädigen*) chip ● *vi* (*haben*) strike/(*stoßen*) knock (**an** + *acc* against); ⟨*Hund:*⟩ bark; (*wirken*) be effective ● *vi* (*sein*) knock (**an** + *acc* against); **mit dem Kopf a~en** hit one's head. **A~zettel** *m* notice

anschließen† *v sep* ● *vt* connect (**an** + *acc* to); (*zufügen*) add; **sich a~** (+ *acc*) (*anstoßen*) adjoin; (*folgen*) follow; (*sich anfreunden*) become friendly with; **sich jdm a~** join s.o. ● *vi* (*haben*) **a~ an** (+ *acc*) adjoin; (*folgen*) follow. **a~d** *a* adjoining; (*zeitlich*) following ● *adv* afterwards; **a~d an** (+ *acc*) after

Anschluß *m* connection; (*Kontakt*) contact; **A~ finden** make friends; **im A~ an** (+ *acc*) after

anschmieg|en (sich) *vr sep* snuggle up/⟨*Kleid:*⟩ cling (**an** + *acc* to). **a~sam** *a* affectionate

anschmieren *vt sep* smear; (*fam: täuschen*) cheat

anschnallen *vt sep* strap on; **sich a~** fasten one's seat-belt

anschneiden† *vt sep* cut into; broach ⟨*Thema*⟩

anschreiben† *vt sep* write (**an** + *acc* on); (*Comm*) put on s.o.'s account; (*sich wenden*) write to; **bei jdm gut/schlecht angeschrieben sein** be in s.o.'s good/bad books

anschreien† *vt sep* shout at

Anschrift *f* address

anschuldig|en *vt sep* accuse. **A~ung** *f* -,-en accusation

anschwellen† *vi sep* (*sein*) swell

anschwemmen *vt sep* wash up

anschwindeln *vt sep* (*fam*) lie to

ansehen† *vt sep* look at; (*einschätzen*) regard (**als** as); **[sich** *dat*] **etw a~** look at sth; (*TV*) watch sth. **A~** *nt* -s respect; (*Ruf*) reputation

ansehnlich *a* considerable

ansetzen *v sep* ● *vt* join (**an** + *acc* to); (*festsetzen*) fix; (*veranschlagen*) estimate; **Rost a~** get rusty; **sich a~**

form ● *vi* (*haben*) (*anbrennen*) burn; **zum Sprung a~** get ready to jump

Ansicht *f* view; **meiner A~ nach** in my view; **zur A~** (*Comm*) on approval. **A~s[post]karte** *f* picture postcard. **A~ssache** *f* matter of opinion

ansiedeln (sich) *vr sep* settle

ansonsten *adv* apart from that

anspannen *vt sep* hitch up; (*anstrengen*) strain; tense ⟨*Muskel*⟩

anspiel|en *vi sep* (*haben*) **a~en auf** (+ *acc*) allude to; (*versteckt*) hint at. **A~ung** *f* -,-en allusion; hint

Anspitzer *m* -s,- pencil-sharpener

Ansporn *m* (*fig*) incentive. **a~en** *vt sep* spur on

Ansprache *f* address

ansprechen† *v sep* ● *vt* speak to; (*fig*) appeal to ● *vi* (*haben*) respond (**auf** + *acc* to). **a~d** *a* attractive

anspringen† *v sep* ● *vt* jump at ● *vi* (*sein*) (*Auto*) start

Anspruch *m* claim/(*Recht*) right (**auf** + *acc* to); **A~ haben** be entitled (**auf** + *acc* to); **in A~ nehmen** make use of; (*erfordern*) demand; take up ⟨*Zeit*⟩; occupy ⟨*Person*⟩; **hohe A~e stellen** be very demanding. **a~slos** *a* undemanding; (*bescheiden*) unpretentious. **a~svoll** *a* demanding; (*kritisch*) discriminating; (*vornehm*) upmarket

anspucken *vt sep* spit at

anstacheln *vt sep* (*fig*) spur on

Anstalt *f* -,-en institution; **A~en/ keine A~en machen** prepare/make no move (**zu** to)

Anstand *m* decency; (*Benehmen*) [good] manners *pl*

anständig *a* decent, *adv* -ly; (*ehrbar*) respectable, *adv* -bly; (*fam: beträchtlich*) considerable, *adv* -bly; (*richtig*) proper, *adv* -ly

Anstands|dame *f* chaperon. **a~los** *adv* without any trouble; (*bedenkenlos*) without hesitation

anstarren *vt sep* stare at

anstatt *conj* & *prep* (+ *gen*) instead of; **a~ zu arbeiten** instead of working

anstechen† *vt sep* tap ⟨*Faß*⟩

ansteck|en *v sep* ● *vt* pin (**an** + *acc* to/on); put on ⟨*Ring*⟩; (*anzünden*) light; (*in Brand stecken*) set fire to; (*Med*) infect; **sich a~en** catch an infection (**bei** from) ● *vi* (*haben*) be infectious. **a~end** *a* infectious, (*fam*) catching. **A~ung** *f* -,-en infection

anstehen† *vi sep* (*haben*) queue, (*Amer*) stand in line

ansteigen† *vi sep* (*sein*) climb; ⟨*Gelände, Preise:*⟩ rise

anstelle *prep* (+ *gen*) instead of

anstell|en *vt sep* put, stand (**an** + *acc* against); (*einstellen*) employ; (*anschalten*) turn on; (*tun*) do; **sich a~en** queue [up], (*Amer*) stand in line; (*sich haben*) make a fuss. **A~ung** *f* employment; (*Stelle*) job

Anstieg *m* **-[e]s,-e** climb; (*fig*) rise

anstiften *vt sep* cause; (*anzetteln*) instigate; **jdn a~n** put s.o. up (**zu** to). **A~r** *m* instigator

Anstoß *m* (*Anregung*) impetus; (*Stoß*) knock; (*Fußball*) kick-off; **A~ erregen/nehmen** give/take offence (**an** + *dat* at). **a~en**† *v sep* ● *vt* knock; (*mit dem Ellbogen*) nudge ● *vi* (*sein*) knock (**an** + *acc* against) ● *vi* (*haben*) adjoin (**an etw** *acc* sth); **[mit den Gläsern] a~en** clink glasses; **a~en auf** (+ *acc*) drink to; **mit der Zunge a~en** lisp

anstößig *a* offensive, *adv* -ly

anstrahlen *vt sep* floodlight; (*anlachen*) beam at

anstreiche|n† *vt sep* paint; (*anmerken*) mark. **A~r** *m* **-s,-** painter

anstreng|en *vt sep* strain; (*ermüden*) tire; **sich a~en** exert oneself; (*sich bemühen*) make an effort (**zu** to). **a~end** *a* strenuous; (*ermüdend*) tiring. **A~ung** *f* **-,-en** strain; (*Mühe*) effort

Anstrich *m* coat [of paint]

Ansturm *m* rush; (*Mil*) assault

Ansuchen *nt* **-s,-** request

Antagonismus *m* - antagonism

Antarktis *f* - Antarctic

Anteil *m* share; **A~ nehmen** take an interest (**an** + *dat* in); (*mitfühlen*) sympathize. **A~nahme** *f* - interest (**an** + *dat* in); (*Mitgefühl*) sympathy

Antenne *f* **-,-n** aerial

Anthologie *f* **-,-n** anthology

Anthropologie *f* - anthropology

Antialkoholiker *m* teetotaller. **A~biotikum** *nt* **-s,-ka** antibiotic

antik *a* antique. **A~e** *f* - [classical] antiquity

Antikörper *m* antibody

Antilope *f* **-,-n** antelope

Antipathie *f* - antipathy

Antiquariat *nt* **-[e]s,-e** antiquarian bookshop. **a~quarisch** *a* & *adv* second-hand

Antiquitäten *fpl* antiques. **A~händler** *m* antique dealer

Antisemitismus *m* - anti-Semitism

Antisept|ikum *nt* **-s,-ka** antiseptic. **a~isch** *a* antiseptic

Antrag *m* **-[e]s,⁻e** proposal; (*Pol*) motion; (*Gesuch*) application. **A~steller** *m* **-s,-** applicant

antreffen† *vt sep* find

antreiben† *v sep* ● *vt* urge on; (*Techn*) drive; (*anschwemmen*) wash up ● *vi* (*sein*) be washed up

antreten† *v sep* ● *vt* start; take up ⟨*Amt*⟩ ● *vi* (*sein*) line up; (*Mil*) fall in

Antrieb *m* urge; (*Techn*) drive; **aus eigenem A~** of one's own accord

antrinken† *vt sep* **sich** (*dat*) **einen Rausch a~** get drunk; **sich** (*dat*) **Mut a~** give oneself Dutch courage

Antritt *m* start; **bei A~ eines Amtes** when taking office. **A~srede** *f* inaugural address

antun† *vt sep* **jdm etw a~** do sth to s.o.; **sich** (*dat*) **etwas a~** take one's own life; **es jdm angetan haben** appeal to s.o.

Antwort *f* **-,-en** answer, reply (**auf** + *acc* to). **a~en** *vt/i* (*haben*) answer (**jdm** s.o.)

anvertrauen *vt sep* entrust/(*mitteilen*) confide (**jdm** to s.o.); **sich jdm a~** confide in s.o.

anwachsen† *vi sep* (*sein*) take root; (*zunehmen*) grow

Anwalt *m* **-[e]s,⁻e, Anwältin** *f* **-,-nen** lawyer; (*vor Gericht*) counsel

Anwandlung *f* **-,-en** fit (**von** of)

Anwärter(in) *m(f)* candidate

anweis|en† *vt sep* assign (*dat* to); (*beauftragen*) instruct. **A~ung** *f* instruction; (*Geld-*) money order

anwend|en† *vt sep* apply (**auf** + *acc* to); (*gebrauchen*) use. **A~ung** *f* application; use

anwerben† *vt sep* recruit

Anwesen *nt* **-s,-** property

anwesen|d *a* present (**bei** at); **die A~den** those present. **A~heit** *f* - presence

anwidern *vt sep* disgust

Anwohner *mpl* residents

Anzahl *f* number

anzahl|en *vt sep* pay a deposit on; pay on account ⟨*Summe*⟩. **A~ung** *f* deposit

anzapfen *vt sep* tap

Anzeichen *nt* sign

Anzeige *f* **-,-n** announcement; (*Inserat*) advertisement; **A~ erstatten gegen jdn** report s.o. to the police. **a~n** *vt sep* announce; (*inserieren*) advertise; (*melden*) report [to the police]; (*angeben*) indicate, show. **A~r** *m* indicator

anzieh|en† *vt sep* ● *vt* attract; (*festziehen*) tighten; put on ⟨*Kleider, Bremse*⟩; draw up ⟨*Beine*⟩; (*ankleiden*) dress; **sich a~en** get dressed; **was soll ich a~en?** what shall I wear? **gut angezogen** well-dressed ● *vi* (*haben*) start pulling; ⟨*Preise:*⟩ go up. **a~end** *a* attractive. **A~ung** *f* - attraction. **A~ungskraft** *f* attraction; (*Phys*) gravity

Anzug *m* suit; **im A~ sein** (*fig*) be imminent

anzüglich *a* suggestive; ⟨*Bemerkung*⟩ personal

anzünden *vt sep* light; (*in Brand stecken*) set fire to

anzweifeln *vt sep* question

apart *a* striking, *adv* -ly

Apathie *f* - apathy

apathisch *a* apathetic, *adv* -ally

Aperitif *m* **-s,-s** aperitif

Apfel *m* **-s,-̈** apple. **A~mus** *nt* apple purée

Apfelsine *f* **-,-n** orange

Apostel *m* **-s,-** apostle

Apostroph *m* **-s,-e** apostrophe

Apotheke *f* **-,-n** pharmacy. **A~r(in)** *m* **-s,-** (*f* **-,-nen**) pharmacist, [dispensing] chemist

Apparat *m* **-[e]s,-e** device; (*Phot*) camera; (*Radio, TV*) set; (*Teleph*) telephone; **am A~!** speaking! **A~ur** *f* **-,-en** apparatus

Appell *m* **-s,-e** appeal; (*Mil*) rollcall. **a~ieren** *vi* (*haben*) appeal (**an** + *acc* to)

Appetit *m* **-s** appetite; **guten A~!** enjoy your meal! **a~lich** *a* appetizing, *adv* -ly

applaudieren *vi* (*haben*) applaud

Applaus *m* **-es** applause

Aprikose *f* **-,-n** apricot

April *m* **-[s]** April; **in den A~ schicken** (*fam*) make an April fool of

Aquarell *nt* **-s,-e** water-colour

Aquarium *nt* **-s,-ien** aquarium

Äquator *m* **-s** equator

Ära *f* **-** era

Araber(in) *m* **-s,-** (*f* **-,-nen**) Arab

arabisch *a* Arab; (*Geog*) Arabian; ⟨*Ziffer*⟩ Arabic

Arbeit *f* **-,-en** work; (*Anstellung*) employment, job; (*Aufgabe*) task; (*Sch*) [written] test; (*Abhandlung*) treatise; (*Qualität*) workmanship; **bei der A~** at work; **zur A~ gehen** go to work; **an die A~ gehen, sich an die A~ machen** set to work; **sich** (*dat*) **viel A~ machen** go to a lot of trouble. **a~en** *v sep* ● *vi* (*haben*) work (**an** + *dat* on) ● *vt* make; **einen Anzug a~en lassen** have a suit made; **sich durch etw a~en** work one's way through sth. **A~er(in)** *m* **-s,-** (*f* **-,-nen**) worker; (*Land-, Hilfs-*) labourer. **A~erklasse** *f* working class

Arbeit|geber *m* **-s,-** employer. **A~nehmer** *m* **-s,-** employee. **a~sam** *a* industrious

Arbeits|amt *nt* employment exchange. **A~erlaubnis, A~genehmigung** *f* work permit. **A~kraft** *f* worker; **Mangel an A~kräften** shortage of labour. **a~los** *a* unemployed; **a~los sein** be out of work. **A~lose(r)** *m/f* unemployed person; **die A~losen** the unemployed *pl*. **A~losenunterstützung** *f* unemployment benefit. **A~losigkeit** *f* - unemployment

arbeitsparend *a* labour-saving

Arbeits|platz *m* job. **A~tag** *m* working day. **A~zimmer** *nt* study

Archäo|loge *m* **-n,-n** archaeologist. **A~logie** *f* - archaeology. **a~logisch** *a* archaeological

Arche *f* **- die A~ Noah** Noah's Ark

Architekt(in) *m* **-en,-en** (*f* **-,-nen**) architect. **a~tonisch** *a* architectural. **A~tur** *f* - architecture

Archiv *nt* **-s,-e** archives *pl*

Arena *f* **-,-nen** arena

arg *a* (**ärger, ärgst**) bad; (*groß*) terrible; **sein ärgster Feind** his worst enemy ● *adv* badly; (*sehr*) terribly

Argentin|ien /-jən/ *nt* **-s** Argentina. **a~isch** *a* Argentinian

Ärger *m* **-s** annoyance; (*Unannehmlichkeit*) trouble. **ä~lich** *a* annoyed; (*leidig*) annoying; **ä~lich sein** be annoyed. **ä~n** *vt* annoy; (*necken*) tease; **sich ä~n** get annoyed (**über jdn/etw** with s.o./about sth). **Ä~nis** *nt* **-ses,-se** annoyance; **öffentliches Ä~nis** public nuisance

Arglist *f* **-** malice. **a~ig** *a* malicious, *adv* -ly

arglos *a* unsuspecting; (*unschuldig*) innocent, *adv* -ly

Argument *nt* -[e]s,-e argument. **a~ieren** *vi* (*haben*) argue (**daß** that)

Argwohn *m* -s suspicion

argwöhn|en *vt* suspect. **a~isch** *a* suspicious, *adv* -ly

Arie /'a:riə/ *f* -,-n aria

Aristo|krat *m* -en,-en aristocrat. **A~kratie** *f* - aristocracy. **a~kratisch** *a* aristocratic

Arithmetik *f* - arithmetic

Arkt|is *f* - Arctic. **a~isch** *a* Arctic

arm *a* (**ärmer, ärmst**) poor; **arm und reich** rich and poor

Arm *m* -[e]s,-e arm; **jdn auf den Arm nehmen** (*fam*) pull s.o.'s leg

Armaturenbrett *nt* instrument panel; (*Auto*) dashboard

Armband *nt* (*pl* -**bänder**) bracelet; (*Uhr*-) watch-strap. **A~uhr** *f* wristwatch

Arm|e(r) *m/f* poor man/woman; **die A~en** the poor *pl*; **du A~e** *od* **Ärmste!** you poor thing!

Armee *f* -,-n army

Ärmel *m* -s,- sleeve. **Ä~kanal** *m* [English] Channel. **ä~los** *a* sleeveless

Arm|lehne *f* arm. **A~leuchter** *m* candelabra

ärmlich *a* poor, *adv* -ly; (*elend*) miserable, *adv* -bly

armselig *a* miserable, *adv* -bly

Armut *f* - poverty

Arom|a *nt* -s,-men & -mas aroma; (*Culin*) essence. **a~atisch** *a* aromatic

Arran|gement /arãʒə'mã:/ *nt* -s,-s arrangement. **a~gieren** /-'ʒi:rən/ *vt* arrange; **sich a~gieren** come to an arrangement

Arrest *m* -[e]s (*Mil*) detention

arrogan|t *a* arrogant, *adv* -ly. **A~z** *f* - arrogance

Arsch *m* -[e]s,ˮe (*vulg*) arse

Arsen *nt* -s arsenic

Art *f* -,-en manner; (*Weise*) way; (*Natur*) nature; (*Sorte*) kind; (*Biol*) species; **auf diese Art** in this way. **a~en** *vi* (*sein*) **a~en nach** take after

Arterie /-iə/ *f* -,-n artery

Arthritis *f* - arthritis

artig *a* well-behaved; (*höflich*) polite, *adv* -ly; **sei a~!** be good!

Artikel *m* -s,- article

Artillerie *f* - artillery

Artischocke *f* -,-n artichoke

Artist(in) *m* -en,-en (*f* -,-nen) [circus] artiste

Arznei *f* -,-en medicine. **A~mittel** *nt* drug

Arzt *m* -[e]s,ˮe doctor

Ärzt|in *f* -,-nen [woman] doctor. **ä~lich** *a* medical

As *nt* -ses,-se ace

Asbest *m* -[e]s asbestos

Asche *f* - ash. **A~nbecher** *m* ashtray. **A~rmittwoch** *m* Ash Wednesday

Asiat|(in) *m* -en,-en (*f* -,-nen) Asian. **a~isch** *a* Asian

Asien /'a:ziən/ *nt* -s Asia

asozial *a* antisocial

Aspekt *m* -[e]s,-e aspect

Asphalt *m* -[e]s asphalt. **a~ieren** *vt* asphalt

Assistent(in) *m* -en,-en (*f* -,-nen) assistant

Ast *m* -[e]s,ˮe branch

ästhetisch *a* aesthetic

Asth|ma *nt* -s asthma. **a~matisch** *a* asthmatic

Astro|loge *m* -n,-n astrologer. **A~logie** *f* - astrology. **A~naut** *m* -en,-en astronaut. **A~nom** *m* -en,-en astronomer. **A~nomie** *f* - astronomy. **a~nomisch** *a* astronomical

Asyl *nt* -s,-e home; (*Pol*) asylum. **A~ant** *m* -en,-en asylum-seeker

Atelier /-'lie:/ *nt* -s,-s studio

Atem *m* -s breath; **tief A~ holen** take a deep breath. **a~beraubend** *a* breath-taking. **a~los** *a* breathless, *adv* -ly. **A~pause** *f* breather. **A~zug** *m* breath

Atheist *m* -en,-en atheist

Äther *m* -s ether

Äthiopien /-iən/ *nt* -s Ethiopia

Athlet|(in) *m* -en,-en (*f* -,-nen) athlete. **a~isch** *a* athletic

Atlant|ik *m* -s Atlantic. **a~isch** *a* Atlantic; **der A~ische Ozean** the Atlantic Ocean

Atlas *m* -lasses,-lanten atlas

atmen *vt/i* (*haben*) breathe

Atmosphär|e *f* -,-n atmosphere. **a~isch** *a* atmospheric

Atmung *f* - breathing

Atom *nt* -s,-e atom. **a~ar** *a* atomic. **A~bombe** *f* atom bomb. **A~krieg** *m* nuclear war

Atten|tat *nt* -[e]s,-e assassination attempt. **A~täter** *m* [would-be] assassin

Attest *nt* -[e]s,-e certificate

Attrak|tion /-'tsio:n/ *f* **-,-en** attraction. **a~tiv** *a* attractive, *adv* -ly

Attrappe *f* **-,-n** dummy

Attribut *nt* **-[e]s,-e** attribute. **a~iv** *a* attributive, *adv* -ly

ätzen *vt* corrode; (*Med*) cauterize; (*Kunst*) etch. **ä~d** *a* corrosive; (*Spott*) caustic

au *int* ouch; **au fein!** oh good!

Aubergine /obɛr'ʒi:nə/ *f* **-,-n** aubergine

auch *adv & conj* also, too; (*außerdem*) what's more; (*selbst*) even; **a~ wenn** even if; **ich mag ihn—ich a~** I like him—so do I; **ich bin nicht müde—ich a~ nicht** I'm not tired—nor *or* neither am I; **sie weiß es a~ nicht** she doesn't know either; **wer/wie/was a~ immer** whoever/however/whatever; **ist das a~ wahr?** is that really true?

Audienz *f* **-,-en** audience

audiovisuell *a* audio-visual

Auditorium *nt* **-s,-ien** (*Univ*) lecture hall

auf *prep* (+ *dat*) on; (+ *acc*) on [to]; (*bis*) until, till; (*Proportion*) to; **auf deutsch/englisch** in German/English; **auf einer/eine Party** at/to a party; **auf der Straße** in the street; **auf seinem Zimmer** in one's room; **auf einem Ohr taub** deaf in one ear; **auf einen Stuhl steigen** climb on [to] a chair; **auf die Toilette gehen** go to the toilet; **auf ein paar Tage verreisen** go away for a few days; **auf 10 Kilometer zu sehen** visible for 10 kilometres ● *adv* open; (*in die Höhe*) up; **auf und ab** up and down; **sich auf und davon machen** make off; **Tür auf!** open the door!

aufarbeiten *vt sep* do up; **Rückstände a~** clear arrears [of work]

aufatmen *vi sep* (*haben*) heave a sigh of relief

aufbahren *vt sep* lay out

Aufbau *m* construction; (*Struktur*) structure. **a~en** *v sep* ● *vt* construct, build; (*errichten*) erect; (*schaffen*) build up; (*arrangieren*) arrange; **sich a~en** (*fig*) be based (**auf** + *dat* on) ● *vi* (*haben*) be based (**auf** + *dat* on)

aufbäumen (sich) *vr sep* rear [up]. (*fig*) rebel

aufbauschen *vt sep* puff out; (*fig*) exaggerate

aufbehalten† *vt sep* keep on

aufbekommen† *vt sep* get open; (*Sch*) be given [as homework]

aufbessern *vt sep* improve; (*erhöhen*) increase

aufbewahr|en *vt sep* keep; (*lagern*) store. **A~ung** *f* - safe keeping; storage; (*Gepäck-*) left-luggage office

aufbieten† *vt sep* mobilize; (*fig*) summon up

aufblas|bar *a* inflatable. **a~en**† *vt sep* inflate; **sich a~en** (*fig*) give oneself airs

aufbleiben† *vi sep* (*sein*) stay open; (*Person:*) stay up

aufblenden *vt/i sep* (*haben*) (*Auto*) switch to full beam

aufblicken *vi sep* (*haben*) look up (**zu** at / (*fig*) to)

aufblühen *vi sep* (*sein*) flower; (*Knospe:*) open

aufbocken *vt sep* jack up

aufbraten† *vt sep* fry up

aufbrauchen *vt sep* use up

aufbrausen *vi sep* (*sein*) (*fig*) flare up. **a~d** *a* quick-tempered

aufbrechen† *v sep* ● *vt* break open ● *vi* (*sein*) (*Knospe:*) open; (*sich aufmachen*) set out, start

aufbringen† *vt sep* raise (*Geld*); find (*Kraft*); (*wütend machen*) infuriate

Aufbruch *m* start, departure

aufbrühen *vt sep* make (*Tee*)

aufbürden *vt sep* **jdm etw a~** (*fig*) burden s.o. with sth

aufdecken *vt sep* (*auflegen*) put on; (*abdecken*) uncover; (*fig*) expose

aufdrängen *vt sep* force (*dat* on); **sich jdm a~** force one's company on s.o.

aufdrehen *vt sep* turn on

aufdringlich *a* persistent

aufeinander *adv* one on top of the other; (*schießen*) at each other; (*warten*) for each other. **a~folgen** *vi sep* (*sein*) follow one another. **a~folgend** *a* successive; (*Tage*) consecutive

Aufenthalt *m* stay; **10 Minuten A~ haben** (*Zug:*) stop for 10 minutes. **A~serlaubnis, A~sgenehmigung** *f* residence permit. **A~sraum** *m* recreation room; (*im Hotel*) lounge

auferlegen *vt sep* impose (*dat* on)

aufersteh|en† *vi sep* (*sein*) rise from the dead. **A~ung** *f* - resurrection

aufessen† *vt sep* eat up

auffahr|en† *vi sep* (*sein*) drive up; (*aufprallen*) crash, run (**auf** + *acc* into); (*aufschrecken*) start up; (*aufbrausen*) flare up. **A~t** *f* drive; (*Autobahn-*) access road, slip road; (*Bergfahrt*) ascent

auffallen† *vi sep (sein)* be conspicuous; **unangenehm a~** make a bad impression; **jdm a~** strike s.o. **a~d** *a* striking, *adv* -ly

auffällig *a* conspicuous, *adv* -ly; (*grell*) gaudy, *adv* -ily

auffangen† *vt sep* catch; pick up ⟨*Funkspruch*⟩

auffass|en *vt sep* understand; (*deuten*) take; **falsch a~en** misunderstand. **A~ung** *f* understanding; (*Ansicht*) view. **A~ungsgabe** *f* grasp

aufforder|n *vt sep* ask; (*einladen*) invite; **jdn zum Tanz a~n** ask s.o. to dance. **A~ung** *f* request; invitation

auffrischen *v sep* ● *vt* freshen up; revive ⟨*Erinnerung*⟩; **seine Englischkenntnisse a~** brush up one's English

aufführ|en *vt sep* perform; (*angeben*) list; **sich a~en** behave. **A~ung** *f* performance

auffüllen *vt sep* fill up; **[wieder] a~** replenish

Aufgabe *f* task; (*Rechen-*) problem; (*Verzicht*) giving up; **A~n** (*Sch*) homework *sg*

Aufgang *m* way up; (*Treppe*) stairs *pl*; (*Astr*) rise

aufgeben† *v sep* ● *vt* give up; post ⟨*Brief*⟩; send ⟨*Telegramm*⟩; place ⟨*Bestellung*⟩; register ⟨*Gepäck*⟩; put in the paper ⟨*Annonce*⟩; **jdm eine Aufgabe/ein Rätsel a~** set s.o. a task/ a riddle; **jdm Suppe a~** serve s.o. with soup ● *vi (haben)* give up

aufgeblasen *a* (*fig*) conceited

Aufgebot *nt* contingent (**an** + *dat* of); (*Relig*) banns *pl*; **unter A~ aller Kräfte** with all one's strength

aufgebracht *a* (*fam*) angry

aufgedunsen *a* bloated

aufgehen† *vi sep (sein)* open; (*sich lösen*) come undone; ⟨*Teig, Sonne:*⟩ rise; ⟨*Saat:*⟩ come up; (*Math*) come out exactly; **in Flammen a~** go up in flames; **in etw** (*dat*) **a~** (*fig*) be wrapped up in sth; **ihm ging auf** (*fam*) he realized (**daß** that)

aufgelegt *a* **a~ sein zu** be in the mood for; **gut/schlecht a~ sein** be in a good/ bad mood

aufgelöst *a* (*fig*) distraught; **in Tränen a~** in floods of tears

aufgeregt *a* excited, *adv* -ly; (*erregt*) agitated, *adv* -ly

aufgeschlossen *a* (*fig*) open-minded

aufgesprungen *a* chapped

aufgeweckt *a* (*fig*) bright

aufgießen† *vt sep* pour on; (*aufbrühen*) make ⟨*Tee*⟩

aufgreifen† *vt sep* pick up; take up ⟨*Vorschlag, Thema*⟩

aufgrund *prep* (+ *gen*) on the strength of

Aufguß *m* infusion

aufhaben† *v sep* ● *vt* have on; **den Mund a~** have one's mouth open; **viel a~** (*Sch*) have a lot of homework ● *vi (haben)* be open

aufhalsen *vt sep* (*fam*) saddle with

aufhalten† *vt sep* hold up; (*anhalten*) stop; (*abhalten*) keep, detain; (*offenhalten*) hold open; hold out ⟨*Hand*⟩; **sich a~** stay; (*sich befassen*) spend one's time (**mit** on)

aufhäng|en *vt/i sep (haben)* hang up; (*henken*) hang; **sich a~en** hang oneself. **A~er** *m* -**s,**- loop. **A~ung** *f* - (*Auto*) suspension

aufheben† *vt sep* pick up; (*hochheben*) raise; (*aufbewahren*) keep; (*beenden*) end; (*rückgängig machen*) lift; (*abschaffen*) abolish; (*Jur*) quash ⟨*Urteil*⟩; repeal ⟨*Gesetz*⟩; (*ausgleichen*) cancel out; **sich a~** cancel each other out; **gut aufgehoben sein** be well looked after. **A~** *nt* -**s viel A~s machen** make a great fuss (**von** about)

aufheitern *vt sep* cheer up; **sich a~** ⟨*Wetter:*⟩ brighten up

aufhellen *vt sep* lighten; **sich a~** ⟨*Himmel:*⟩ brighten

aufhetzen *vt sep* incite

aufholen *v sep* ● *vt* make up ● *vi (haben)* catch up; (*zeitlich*) make up time

aufhorchen *vi sep (haben)* prick up one's ears

aufhören *vi sep (haben)* stop; **mit der Arbeit a~, a~ zu arbeiten** stop working

aufklappen *vt/i sep (sein)* open

aufklär|en *vt sep* solve; **jdn a~en** enlighten s.o.; (*sexuell*) tell s.o. the facts of life; **sich a~en** be solved; ⟨*Wetter:*⟩ clear up. **A~ung** *f* solution; enlightenment; (*Mil*) reconnaissance; **sexuelle A~ung** sex education

aufkleb|en vt sep stick on. **A~er** m **-s,-** sticker

aufknöpfen vt sep unbutton

aufkochen v sep • vt bring to the boil • vi (sein) come to the boil

aufkommen† vi sep (sein) start; ⟨Wind:⟩ spring up; ⟨Mode:⟩ come in; **a~ für** pay for

aufkrempeln vt sep roll up

aufladen† vt sep load; (Electr) charge

Auflage f impression; (Ausgabe) edition; (Zeitungs-) circulation; (Bedingung) condition; (Überzug) coating

auflassen† vt sep leave open; leave on ⟨Hut⟩

auflauern vi sep (haben) **jdm a~** lie in wait for s.o.

Auflauf m crowd; (Culin) ≈ soufflé. **a~en**† vi sep (sein) (Naut) run aground

auflegen v sep • vt apply (**auf** + acc to); put down ⟨Hörer⟩; **neu a~** reprint • vi (haben) ring off

auflehn|en (sich) vr sep (fig) rebel. **A~ung** f - rebellion

auflesen† vt sep pick up

aufleuchten vi sep (haben) light up

aufliegen† vi sep (haben) rest (**auf** + dat on)

auflisten vt sep list

auflockern vt sep break up; (entspannen) relax; (fig) liven up

auflös|en vt sep dissolve; close ⟨Konto⟩; **sich a~en** dissolve; ⟨Nebel:⟩ clear. **A~ung** f dissolution; (Lösung) solution

aufmach|en v sep • vt open; (lösen) undo; **sich a~en** set out (**nach** for); (sich schminken) make oneself up • vi (haben) open; **jdm a~en** open the door to s.o. **A~ung** f -,-en get-up; (Comm) presentation

aufmerksam a attentive, adv -ly; **a~ werden auf** (+ acc) notice; **jdn a~ machen auf** (+ acc) draw s.o.'s attention to. **A~keit** f -,-en attention; (Höflichkeit) courtesy

aufmucken vi sep (haben) rebel

aufmuntern vt sep cheer up

Aufnahme f -,-n acceptance; (Empfang) reception; (in Klub, Krankenhaus) admission; (Einbeziehung) inclusion; (Beginn) start; (Foto) photograph; (Film-) shot; (Mus) recording; (Band-) tape recording. **a~fähig** a receptive. **A~prüfung** f entrance examination

aufnehmen† vt sep pick up; (absorbieren) absorb; take ⟨Nahrung, Foto⟩; (fassen) hold; (annehmen) accept; (leihen) borrow; (empfangen) receive; (in Klub, Krankenhaus) admit; (beherbergen, geistig erfassen) take in; (einbeziehen) include; (beginnen) take up; (niederschreiben) take down; (filmen) film, shoot; (Mus) record; **auf Band a~** tape[-record]; **etw gelassen a~** take sth calmly; **es a~ können mit** (fig) be a match for

aufopfer|n vt sep sacrifice; **sich a~n** sacrifice oneself. **a~nd** a devoted, adv -ly. **A~ung** f self-sacrifice

aufpassen vi sep (haben) pay attention; (sich vorsehen) take care; **a~ auf** (+ acc) look after

aufpflanzen (sich) vr sep (fam) plant oneself

aufplatzen vi sep (sein) split open

aufplustern (sich) vr sep ⟨Vogel:⟩ ruffle up its feathers

Aufprall m -[e]s impact. **a~en** vi sep (sein) **a~en auf** (+ acc) hit

aufpumpen vt sep pump up, inflate

aufputsch|en vt sep incite; **sich a~en** take stimulants. **A~mittel** nt stimulant

aufquellen† vi sep (sein) swell

aufraffen vt sep pick up; **sich a~** pick oneself up; (fig) pull oneself together; (sich aufschwingen) find the energy (**zu** for)

aufragen vi sep (sein) rise [up]

aufräumen vt/i sep (haben) tidy up; (wegräumen) put away; **a~ mit** (fig) get rid of

aufrecht a & adv upright. **a~erhalten**† vt sep (fig) maintain

aufreg|en vt excite; (beunruhigen) upset; (ärgern) annoy; **sich a~en** get excited; (sich erregen) get worked up. **a~end** a exciting. **A~ung** f excitement

aufreiben† vt sep chafe; (fig) wear down; **sich a~** wear oneself out. **a~d** a trying, wearing

aufreißen† vt sep • vt tear open; dig up ⟨Straße⟩; open wide ⟨Augen, Mund⟩ • vi (sein) split open

aufreizend a provocative, adv -ly

aufrichten vt sep erect; (fig: trösten) comfort; **sich a~** straighten up; (sich setzen) sit up

aufrichtig a sincere, adv -ly. **A~keit** f - sincerity

aufriegeln vt sep unbolt

aufrollen vt sep roll up; (entrollen) unroll

aufrücken vi sep (sein) move up; (fig) be promoted

Aufruf m appeal (an + dat to). **a~en†** vt sep call out ⟨Namen⟩; **jdn a~en** call s.o.'s name; (fig) call on s.o. (**zu** to)

Aufruhr m -s,-e turmoil; (Empörung) revolt

aufrühr|en vt sep stir up. **A~er** m -s,- rebel. **a~erisch** a inflammatory; (rebellisch) rebellious

aufrunden vt sep round up

aufrüsten vi sep (haben) arm

aufs prep = **auf das**

aufsagen vt sep recite

aufsammeln vt sep gather up

aufsässig a rebellious

Aufsatz m top; (Sch) essay

aufsaugen† vt sep soak up

aufschauen vi sep (haben) look up (**zu** at/(fig) to)

aufschichten vt sep stack up

aufschieben† vt sep slide open; (verschieben) put off, postpone

Aufschlag m impact; (Tennis) service; (Hosen-) turn-up; (Ärmel-) upturned cuff; (Revers) lapel; (Comm) surcharge. **a~en†** v sep ● vt open; crack ⟨Ei⟩; (hochschlagen) turn up; (errichten) put up; (erhöhen) increase; cast on ⟨Masche⟩; **sich** (dat) **das Knie a~en** cut [open] one's knee ● vi (haben) hit (**auf etw** acc/dat sth); (Tennis) serve; (teurer werden) go up

aufschließen† v sep ● vt unlock ● vi (haben) unlock the door

aufschlitzen vt sep slit open

Aufschluß m **A~ geben** give information (**über** + acc on). **a~reich** a revealing; (lehrreich) informative

aufschneid|en† v sep ● vt cut open; (in Scheiben) slice; carve ⟨Braten⟩ ● vi (haben) (fam) exaggerate. **A~er** m -s,- (fam) show-off

Aufschnitt m sliced sausage, cold meat [and cheese]

aufschrauben vt sep screw on; (abschrauben) unscrew

aufschrecken v sep ● vt startle ● vi† (sein) start up; **aus dem Schlaf a~** wake up with a start

Aufschrei m [sudden] cry

aufschreiben† vt sep write down; (fam: verschreiben) prescribe; **jdn a~** ⟨Polizist:⟩ book s.o.

aufschreien† vi sep (haben) cry out

Aufschrift f inscription; (Etikett) label

Aufschub m delay; (Frist) grace

aufschürfen vt sep **sich** (dat) **das Knie a~** graze one's knee

aufschwatzen vt sep **jdm etw a~** talk s.o. into buying sth

aufschwingen† (sich) vr sep find the energy (**zu** for)

Aufschwung m (fig) upturn

aufsehen† vi sep (haben) look up (**zu** at/(fig) to). **A~** nt -s **A~ erregen** cause a sensation. **a~erregend** a sensational

Aufseher(in) m -s,- (f -,-nen) supervisor; (Gefängnis-) warder

aufsein† vi sep (sein) be open; ⟨Person:⟩ be up

aufsetzen vt sep put on; (verfassen) draw up; (entwerfen) draft; **sich a~** sit up

Aufsicht f supervision; (Person) supervisor. **A~srat** m board of directors

aufsitzen† vi sep (sein) mount

aufspannen vt sep put up

aufsparen vt sep save, keep

aufsperren vt sep open wide

aufspielen v sep ● vi (haben) play ● vr **sich a~** show off; **sich als Held a~** play the hero

aufspießen vt sep spear

aufspringen† vi sep (sein) jump up; (aufprallen) bounce; (sich öffnen) burst open; ⟨Haut:⟩ become chapped; **a~ auf** (+ acc) jump on

aufspüren vt sep track down

aufstacheln vt sep incite

aufstampfen vi sep (haben) **mit dem Fuß a~** stamp one's foot

Aufstand m uprising, rebellion

aufständisch a rebellious. **A~e(r)** m rebel, insurgent

aufstapeln vt sep stack up

aufstauen vt sep dam [up]

aufstehen† vi sep (sein) get up; (offen sein) be open; (fig) rise up

aufsteigen† vi sep (sein) get on; ⟨Reiter:⟩ mount; ⟨Bergsteiger:⟩ climb up; (hochsteigen) rise [up]; (fig: befördert werden) rise (**zu** to); (Sport) be promoted

aufstell|en vt sep put up; (Culin) put on; (postieren) post; (in einer Reihe) line up; (nominieren) nominate; (Sport) select ⟨Mannschaft⟩; make out ⟨Liste⟩; lay down ⟨Regel⟩; make ⟨Behauptung⟩; set up ⟨Rekord⟩; **sich**

a~en rise [up]; (*in einer Reihe*) line up. **A~ung** *f* nomination; (*Liste*) list

Aufstieg *m* ascent; (*fig*) rise; (*Sport*) promotion

aufstöbern *vt sep* flush out; (*fig*) track down

aufstoßen† *v sep* ● *vt* push open ● *vi* (*haben*) burp; **a~ auf** (+ *acc*) strike. **A~** *nt* **-s** burping

aufstrebend *a* (*fig*) ambitious

Aufstrich *m* [sandwich] spread

aufstützen *vt sep* rest (**auf** + *acc* on); **sich a~** lean (**auf** + *acc* on)

aufsuchen *vt sep* look for; (*besuchen*) go to see

Auftakt *m* (*fig*) start

auftauchen *vi sep* (*sein*) emerge; ⟨*U-Boot:*⟩ surface; (*fig*) turn up; ⟨*Frage:*⟩ crop up

auftauen *vt/i sep* (*sein*) thaw

aufteil|en *vt sep* divide [up]. **A~ung** *f* division

auftischen *vt sep* serve [up]

Auftrag *m* **-[e]s, ⁻e** task; (*Kunst*) commission; (*Comm*) order; **im A~** (+ *gen*) on behalf of. **a~en**† *v sep* ● *vt* apply; (*servieren*) serve; (*abtragen*) wear out; **jdm a~en** instruct s.o. (**zu** to) ● *vi* (*haben*) **dick a~en** (*fam*) exaggerate. **A~geber** *m* **-s,-** client

auftreiben† *vt sep* distend; (*fam: beschaffen*) get hold of

auftrennen *vt sep* unpick, undo

auftreten† *v sep* ● *vi* (*sein*) tread; (*sich benehmen*) behave, act; (*Theat*) appear; (*die Bühne betreten*) enter; (*vorkommen*) occur ● *vt* kick open. **A~** *nt* **-s** occurrence; (*Benehmen*) manner

Auftrieb *m* buoyancy; (*fig*) boost

Auftritt *m* (*Theat*) appearance; (*auf die Bühne*) entrance; (*Szene*) scene

auftun† *vt sep* **jdm Suppe a~** serve s.o. with soup; **sich** (*dat*) **etw a~** help oneself to sth; **sich a~** open

aufwachen *vi sep* (*sein*) wake up

aufwachsen† *vi sep* (*sein*) grow up

Aufwand *m* **-[e]s** expenditure; (*Luxus*) extravagance; (*Mühe*) trouble; **A~ treiben** be extravagant

aufwärmen *vt sep* heat up; (*fig*) rake up; **sich a~** warm oneself; (*Sport*) warm up

Aufwartefrau *f* cleaner

aufwärts *adv* upwards; (*bergauf*) uphill. **a~gehen**† *vi sep* (*sein*) **es geht a~ mit jdm/etw** s.o.'s/sth is improving

Aufwartung *f* - cleaner; **jdm seine A~ machen** call on s.o.

aufwaschen† *vt/i sep* (*haben*) wash up

aufwecken *vt sep* wake up

aufweichen *v sep* ● *vt* soften ● *vi* (*sein*) become soft

aufweisen† *vt sep* have, show

aufwend|en† *vt sep* spend; **Mühe a~en** take pains. **a~ig** *a* lavish, *adv* -ly; (*teuer*) expensive, *adv* -ly

aufwerfen† *vt sep* (*fig*) raise

aufwert|en *vt sep* revalue. **A~ung** *f* revaluation

aufwickeln *vt sep* roll up; (*auswickeln*) unwrap

aufwiegeln *vt sep* stir up

aufwiegen† *vt sep* compensate for

Aufwiegler *m* **-s,-** agitator

aufwirbeln *vt sep* **Staub a~** stir up dust; (*fig*) cause a stir

aufwisch|en *vt sep* wipe up; wash ⟨*Fußboden*⟩. **A~lappen** *m* floorcloth

aufwühlen *vt sep* churn up; (*fig*) stir up

aufzähl|en *vt sep* enumerate, list. **A~ung** *f* list

aufzeichn|en *vt sep* record; (*zeichnen*) draw. **A~ung** *f* recording; **A~ungen** notes

aufziehen† *v sep* ● *vt* pull up; hoist ⟨*Segel*⟩; (*öffnen*) open; draw ⟨*Vorhang*⟩; (*auftrennen*) undo; (*großziehen*) bring up; rear ⟨*Tier*⟩; mount ⟨*Bild*⟩; thread ⟨*Perlen*⟩; wind up ⟨*Uhr*⟩; (*arrangieren*) organize; (*fam: necken*) tease ● *vi* (*sein*) approach

Aufzucht *f* rearing

Aufzug *m* hoist; (*Fahrstuhl*) lift, (*Amer*) elevator; (*Prozession*) procession; (*Theat*) act; (*fam: Aufmachung*) get-up

Augapfel *m* eyeball

Auge *nt* **-s,-n** eye; (*Punkt*) spot; **vier A~n werfen** throw a four; **gute A~n** good eyesight; **unter vier A~n** in private; **aus den A~n verlieren** lose sight of; **im A~ behalten** keep in sight; (*fig*) bear in mind

Augenblick *m* moment; **im/jeden A~** at the/at any moment; **A~!** just a moment! **a~lich** *a* immediate; (*derzeitig*) present ● *adv* immediately; (*derzeit*) at present

Augen|braue *f* eyebrow. **A~höhle** *f* eye socket. **A~licht** *nt* sight. **A~lid** *nt* eyelid. **A~schein** *m* **in A~schein**

nehmen inspect. **A~zeuge** *m* eye-witness

August *m* **-[s]** August

Auktion /-'tsi̯o:n/ *f* **-,-en** auction. **A~ator** *m* **-s,-en** /-'to:rən/ auctioneer

Aula *f* **-,-len** (*Sch*) [assembly] hall

Au-pair-Mädchen /o'pɛːr-/ *nt* au-pair

aus *prep* (+ *dat*) out of; (*von*) from; (*bestehend*) [made] of; **aus Angst** from *or* out of fear; **aus Spaß** for fun ● *adv* out; ⟨*Licht, Radio*⟩ off; **aus und ein** in and out; **nicht mehr aus noch ein wissen** be at one's wits' end; **von … aus** from … ; **von sich aus** of one's own accord; **von mir aus** as far as I'm concerned

ausarbeiten *vt sep* work out

ausarten *vi sep* (*sein*) degenerate (**in** + *acc* into)

ausatmen *vt/i sep* (*haben*) breathe out

ausbaggern *vt sep* excavate; dredge ⟨*Fluß*⟩

ausbauen *vt sep* remove; (*vergrößern*) extend; (*fig*) expand

ausbedingen† *vt sep* **sich** (*dat*) **a~** insist on; (*zur Bedingung machen*) stipulate

ausbesser|n *vt sep* mend, repair. **A~ung** *f* repair

ausbeulen *vt sep* remove the dents from; (*dehnen*) make baggy

Ausbeut|e *f* yield. **a~en** *vt sep* exploit. **A~ung** *f* **-** exploitation

ausbild|en *vt sep* train; (*formen*) form; (*entwickeln*) develop; **sich a~en** train (**als/zu** as); (*entstehen*) develop. **A~er** *m* **-s,-** instructor. **A~ung** *f* training; (*Sch*) education

ausbitten† *vt sep* **sich** (*dat*) **a~** ask for; (*verlangen*) insist on

ausblasen† *vt sep* blow out

ausbleiben† *vi sep* (*sein*) fail to appear/⟨*Erfolg:*⟩ materialize; (*nicht heimkommen*) stay out; **es konnte nicht a~** it was inevitable. **A~** *nt* **-s** absence

Ausblick *m* view

ausbrech|en *vi sep* (*sein*) break out; ⟨*Vulkan:*⟩ erupt; (*fliehen*) escape; **in Tränen a~en** burst into tears. **A~er** *m* runaway

ausbreit|en *vt sep* spread [out]; **sich a~en** spread. **A~ung** *f* **-** spread

ausbrennen† *v sep* ● *vt* cauterize ● *vi* (*sein*) burn out; ⟨*Haus:*⟩ be gutted [by fire]

Ausbruch *m* outbreak; (*Vulkan-*) eruption; (*Wut-*) outburst; (*Flucht*) escape, break-out

ausbrüten *vt sep* hatch

Ausbund *m* **A~ der Tugend** paragon of virtue

ausbürsten *vt sep* brush; (*entfernen*) brush out

Ausdauer *f* perseverance; (*körperlich*) stamina. **a~nd** *a* persevering; (*unermüdlich*) untiring; (*Bot*) perennial ● *adv* with perseverance; untiringly

ausdehn|en *vt sep* stretch; (*fig*) extend; **sich a~en** stretch; (*Phys & fig*) expand; (*dauern*) last. **A~ung** *f* expansion; (*Umfang*) extent

ausdenken† *vt sep* **sich** (*dat*) **a~** think up; (*sich vorstellen*) imagine

ausdrehen *vt sep* turn off

Ausdruck *m* expression; (*Fach-*) term; (*Computer*) printout. **a~en** *vt sep* print

ausdrück|en *vt sep* squeeze out; squeeze ⟨*Zitrone*⟩; stub out ⟨*Zigarette*⟩; (*äußern*) express; **sich a~en** express oneself. **a~lich** *a* express, *adv* -ly

ausdrucks|los *a* expressionless. **a~voll** *a* expressive

auseinander *adv* apart; (*entzwei*) in pieces. **a~falten** *vt sep* unfold. **a~gehen†** *vi sep* (*sein*) part; ⟨*Linien, Meinungen:*⟩ diverge; ⟨*Menge:*⟩ disperse; ⟨*Ehe:*⟩ break up; (*entzweigehen*) come apart. **a~halten†** *vt sep* tell apart. **a~nehmen†** *vt sep* take apart *or* to pieces. **a~setzen** *vt sep* explain (**jdm** to s.o.); **sich a~setzen** have it out (**mit jdm** with s.o.); come to grips (**mit einem Problem** with a problem). **A~setzung** *f* **-,-en** discussion; (*Streit*) argument

auserlesen *a* select, choice

ausfahr|en† *v sep* ● *vt* take for a drive; take out ⟨*Baby*⟩ [in the pram] ● *vi* (*sein*) go for a drive. **A~t** *f* drive; (*Autobahn-, Garagen-*) exit

Ausfall *m* failure; (*Absage*) cancellation; (*Comm*) loss. **a~en†** *vi sep* (*sein*) fall out; (*versagen*) fail; (*abgesagt werden*) be cancelled; **gut/schlecht a~en** turn out to be good/poor

ausfallend, ausfällig *a* abusive

ausfertig|en *vt sep* make out. **A~ung** *f* **-,-en in doppelter/dreifacher A~ung** in duplicate/triplicate

ausfindig *a* **a~ machen** find

ausflippen *vi (sein)* freak out

Ausflucht *f* -,-̈e excuse

Ausflug *m* excursion, outing

Ausflügler *m* -s,- [day-]tripper

Ausfluß *m* outlet; (*Abfluß*) drain; (*Med*) discharge

ausfragen *vt sep* question

ausfransen *vi sep (sein)* fray

Ausfuhr *f* -,-en (*Comm*) export

ausführ|en *vt sep* take out; (*Comm*) export; (*durchführen*) carry out; (*erklären*) explain. **a∼lich** *a* detailed ● *adv* in detail. **A∼ung** *f* execution; (*Comm*) version; (*äußere*) finish; (*Qualität*) workmanship; (*Erklärung*) explanation

Ausgabe *f* issue; (*Buch-*) edition; (*Comm*) version

Ausgang *m* way out, exit; (*Flugsteig*) gate; (*Ende*) end; (*Ergebnis*) outcome, result; **A∼ haben** have time off. **A∼spunkt** *m* starting-point. **A∼ssperre** *f* curfew

ausgeben† *vt sep* hand out; issue ⟨*Fahrkarten*⟩; spend ⟨*Geld*⟩; buy ⟨*Runde Bier*⟩; **sich a∼ als** pretend to be

ausgebeult *a* baggy

ausgebildet *a* trained

ausgebucht *a* fully booked; ⟨*Vorstellung*⟩ sold out

ausgedehnt *a* extensive; (*lang*) long

ausgedient *a* worn out; ⟨*Person*⟩ retired

ausgefallen *a* unusual

ausgefranst *a* frayed

ausgeglichen *a* [well-]balanced; (*gelassen*) even-tempered

ausgeh|en† *vi sep (sein)* go out; ⟨*Haare:*⟩ fall out; ⟨*Vorräte, Geld:*⟩ run out; (*verblassen*) fade; (*herrühren*) come (**von** from); (*abzielen*) aim (**auf** + *acc* at); **gut/schlecht a∼en** end well/badly; **leer a∼en** come away empty-handed; **davon a∼en, daß** assume that. **A∼verbot** *nt* curfew

ausgelassen *a* high-spirited; **a∼ sein** be in high spirits

ausgelernt *a* [fully] trained

ausgemacht *a* agreed; (*fam: vollkommen*) utter

ausgenommen *conj* except; **a∼ wenn** unless

ausgeprägt *a* marked

ausgerechnet *adv* **a∼ heute** today of all days; **a∼ er/Rom** he of all people/ Rome of all places

ausgeschlossen *pred a* out of the question

ausgeschnitten *a* low-cut

ausgesprochen *a* marked ● *adv* decidedly

ausgestorben *a* extinct; **[wie] a∼** ⟨*Straße:*⟩ deserted

Ausgestoßene(r) *m/f* outcast

ausgewachsen *a* fully-grown

ausgewogen *a* [well-]balanced

ausgezeichnet *a* excellent, *adv* -ly

ausgiebig *a* extensive, *adv* -ly; (*ausgedehnt*) long; **a∼ Gebrauch machen von** make full use of; **a∼ frühstücken** have a really good breakfast

ausgießen† *vt sep* pour out; (*leeren*) empty

Ausgleich *m* -[e]s balance; (*Entschädigung*) compensation. **a∼en**† *v sep* ● *vt* balance; even out ⟨*Höhe*⟩; (*wettmachen*) compensate for; **sich a∼en** balance out ● *vi (haben)* (*Sport*) equalize. **A∼sgymnastik** *f* keep-fit exercises *pl*. **A∼streffer** *m* equalizer

ausgleiten† *vi sep (sein)* slip

ausgrab|en† *vt sep* dig up; (*Archaeol*) excavate. **A∼ung** *f* -,-en excavation

Ausguck *m* -[e]s,-e look-out post; (*Person*) look-out

Ausguß *m* [kitchen] sink

aushaben† *vt sep* have finished ⟨*Buch*⟩; **wann habt ihr Schule aus?** when do you finish school?

aushalten† *v sep* ● *vt* bear, stand; hold ⟨*Note*⟩; (*Unterhalt zahlen für*) keep; **nicht auszuhalten, nicht zum A∼** unbearable ● *vi (haben)* hold out

aushandeln *vt sep* negotiate

aushändigen *vt sep* hand over

Aushang *m* [public] notice

aushängen¹ *vt sep (reg)* display; take off its hinges ⟨*Tür*⟩

aushäng|en²† *vi sep (haben)* be displayed. **A∼eschild** *nt* sign

ausharren *vi sep (haben)* hold out

ausheben† *vt sep* excavate; take off its hinges ⟨*Tür*⟩

aushecken *vt sep (fig)* hatch

aushelfen† *vi sep (haben)* help out (**jdm** s.o.)

Aushilf|e *f* [temporary] assistant; **zur A∼e** to help out. **A∼skraft** *f* temporary worker. **a∼sweise** *adv* temporarily

aushöhlen *vt sep* hollow out

ausholen vi sep (haben) **[zum Schlag]** a~ raise one's arm [ready to strike]

aushorchen vt sep sound out

auskennen† (sich) vr sep know one's way around; **sich mit/in etw** (dat) a~ know all about sth

auskleiden vt sep undress; (Techn) line; **sich a~** undress

ausknipsen vi sep switch off

auskommen† vi sep (sein) manage (**mit/ohne** with/without); (sich vertragen) get on (**gut** well). A~ nt -s sein A~/ein gutes A~ haben get by/be well off

auskosten vt sep enjoy [to the full]

auskugeln vt sep **sich** (dat) **den Arm** a~ dislocate one's shoulder

auskühlen vt/i sep (sein) cool

auskundschaften vt sep spy out; (erfahren) find out

Auskunft f -,-̈e information; (A~stelle) information desk/ (Büro) bureau; (Teleph) enquiries pl; **eine A~** a piece of information. A~sbüro nt information bureau

auslachen vt sep laugh at

ausladen† vt sep unload; (fam: absagen) put off (Gast). a~d a projecting

Auslage f [window] display; A~n expenses

Ausland nt **im/ins A~** abroad

Ausländ|er(in) m -s,- (f -,-nen) foreigner. a~isch a foreign

Auslandsgespräch nt international call

auslass|en† vt sep let out; let down (Saum); (weglassen) leave out; (versäumen) miss; (Culin) melt; (fig) vent (Ärger) (**an** + dat on); **sich a~en über** (+ acc) go on about. A~ungszeichen nt apostrophe

Auslauf m run. a~en† vi sep (sein) run out; (Farbe:) run; (Naut) put to sea; (auslaufen) run dry; (enden) end; (Modell:) be discontinued

Ausläufer m (Geog) spur; (Bot) runner, sucker

ausleeren vt sep empty [out]

ausleg|en vt sep lay out; display (Waren); (bedecken) cover/(auskleiden) line (**mit** with); (bezahlen) pay; (deuten) interpret. A~ung f -,-en interpretation

ausleihen† vt sep lend; **sich** (dat) a~ borrow

auslernen vi sep (haben) finish one's training

Auslese f - selection; (fig) pick; (Elite) elite. a~n† vt sep finish reading (Buch); (auswählen) pick out, select

ausliefer|n vt sep hand over; (Jur) extradite; **ausgeliefert sein** (+ dat) be at the mercy of. A~ung f handing over; (Jur) extradition; (Comm) distribution

ausliegen† vi sep (haben) be on display

auslöschen vt sep extinguish; (abwischen) wipe off; (fig) erase

auslosen vt sep draw lots for

auslös|en vt sep set off, trigger; (fig) cause; arouse (Begeisterung); (einlösen) redeem; pay a ransom for (Gefangene). A~er m -s,- trigger; (Phot) shutter release

Auslosung f draw

auslüften vt/i sep (haben) air

ausmachen vt sep put out; (abschalten) turn off; (abmachen) arrange; (erkennen) make out; (betragen) amount to; (darstellen) represent; (wichtig sein) matter; **das macht mir nichts aus** I don't mind

ausmalen vt sep paint; (fig) describe; **sich** (dat) a~ imagine

Ausmaß nt extent; A~e dimensions

ausmerzen vt sep eliminate

ausmessen† vt sep measure

Ausnahm|e f -,-n exception. A~ezustand m state of emergency. a~slos adv without exception. a~sweise adv as an exception

ausnehmen† vt sep take out; gut (Fisch); draw (Huhn); (ausschließen) exclude; (fam: schröpfen) fleece; **sich gut a~** look good. a~d adv exceptionally

ausnutz|en, ausnütz|en vt sep exploit; make the most of (Gelegenheit). A~ung f exploitation

auspacken v sep ●vt unpack; (auswickeln) unwrap ●vi (haben) (fam) talk

auspeitschen vt sep flog

auspfeifen vt sep whistle and boo

ausplaudern vt sep let out, blab

ausplündern vt sep loot; rob (Person)

ausprobieren vt sep try out

Auspuff m -s exhaust [system]. A~gase ntpl exhaust fumes. A~rohr nt exhaust pipe

auspusten vt sep blow out

ausradieren vt sep rub out

ausrangieren vt sep (fam) discard

ausrauben vt sep rob

ausräuchern vt sep smoke out; fumigate ⟨Zimmer⟩

ausräumen vt sep clear out

ausrechnen vt sep work out, calculate

Ausrede f excuse. **a~n** v sep ● vi (haben) finish speaking; **laß mich a~n!** let me finish! ● vt jdm etw **a~n** talk s.o. out of sth

ausreichen vi sep (haben) be enough; **a~ mit** have enough. **a~d** a adequate, adv -ly; (Sch) ≈ pass

Ausreise f departure [from a country]. **a~n** vi sep (sein) leave the country. **A~visum** nt exit visa

ausreiß|en† v sep ● vt pull or tear out ● vi (sein) (fam) run away. **A~er** m (fam) runaway

ausrenken vt sep dislocate; **sich** (dat) **den Arm a~** dislocate one's shoulder

ausrichten vt sep align; (bestellen) deliver; (erreichen) achieve; **jdm a~** tell s.o. (**daß** that); **kann ich etwas a~?** can I take a message? **ich soll Ihnen Grüße von X a~** X sends [you] his regards

ausrotten vt sep exterminate; (fig) eradicate

ausrücken vi sep (sein) (Mil) march off; (fam) run away

Ausruf m exclamation. **a~en†** vt sep exclaim; call out ⟨Namen⟩; (verkünden) proclaim; call ⟨Streik⟩; **jdn a~en lassen** have s.o. paged. **A~ezeichen** nt exclamation mark

ausruhen vt/i sep (haben) rest; **sich a~** have a rest

ausrüst|en vt sep equip. **A~ung** f equipment; (Mil) kit

ausrutschen vi sep (sein) slip

Aussage f -,-n statement; (Jur) testimony, evidence; (Gram) predicate. **a~n** vt/i sep (haben) state; (Jur) give evidence, testify

Aussatz m leprosy

Aussätzige(r) m/f leper

ausschachten vt sep excavate

ausschalten vt sep switch or turn off; (fig) eliminate

Ausschank m sale of alcoholic drinks; (Bar) bar

Ausschau f - **A~ halten nach** look out for. **a~en** vi sep (haben) (SGer) look; **a~en nach** look out for

ausscheiden† v sep ● vi (sein) leave; (Sport) drop out; (nicht in Frage kommen) be excluded; **aus dem Dienst a~** retire ● vt eliminate; (Med) excrete

ausschenken vt sep pour out; (verkaufen) sell

ausscheren vi sep (sein) (Auto) pull out

ausschildern vt sep signpost

ausschimpfen vt sep tell off

ausschlachten vt sep (fig) exploit

ausschlafen† v sep ● vi/r (haben) [sich] **a~** get enough sleep; (morgens) sleep late; **nicht ausgeschlafen haben** od **sein** be still tired ● vt sleep off ⟨Rausch⟩

Ausschlag m (Med) rash; **den A~ geben** (fig) tip the balance. **a~en†** v sep ● vi (haben) kick [out]; (Bot) sprout; ⟨Baum:⟩ come into leaf ● vt knock out; (auskleiden) line; (ablehnen) refuse. **a~gebend** a decisive

ausschließ|en† vt sep lock out; (fig) exclude; (entfernen) expel. **a~lich** a exclusive, adv -ly

ausschlüpfen vi sep (sein) hatch

Ausschluß m exclusion; expulsion; **unter A~ der Öffentlichkeit** in camera

ausschmücken vt sep decorate; (fig) embellish

ausschneiden† vt sep cut out

Ausschnitt m excerpt, extract; (Zeitungs-) cutting; (Hals-) neckline

ausschöpfen vt sep ladle out; (Naut) bail out; exhaust ⟨Möglichkeiten⟩

ausschreiben† vt sep write out; (ausstellen) make out; (bekanntgeben) announce; put out to tender ⟨Auftrag⟩

Ausschreitungen fpl riots; (Exzesse) excesses

Ausschuß m committee; (Comm) rejects pl

ausschütten vt sep tip out; (verschütten) spill; (leeren) empty; **sich vor Lachen a~** (fam) be in stitches

ausschweif|end a dissolute. **A~ung** f -,-en debauchery; **A~ungen** excesses

ausschwenken vt sep rinse [out]

aussehen† vi sep (haben) look; **es sieht nach Regen aus** it looks like rain; **wie sieht er/es aus?** what does he/it look like? **A~** nt -s appearance

aussein† vi sep (sein) be out; ⟨Licht, Radio:⟩ be off; (zu Ende sein) be over; **a~ auf** (+ acc) be after; **mit ihm ist es aus** he's had it

außen adv [on the] outside; **nach a~** outwards. **A~bordmotor** m outboard motor. **A~handel** m foreign trade. **A~minister** m Foreign Minister. **A~politik** f foreign policy. **A~seite** f outside. **A~seiter** m **-s,-** outsider; (fig) misfit. **A~stände** mpl outstanding debts. **A~stehende(r)** m/f outsider

außer prep (+ dat) except [for], apart from; (außerhalb) out of; **a~ Atem/ Sicht** out of breath/sight; **a~ sich** (fig) beside oneself ● conj except; **a~ wenn** unless. **a~dem** adv in addition, as well ● conj moreover

äußer|e(r,s) a external; (Teil, Schicht) outer. **Ä~e(s)** nt exterior; (Aussehen) appearance

außer|ehelich a extramarital. **a~ gewöhnlich** a exceptional, adv -ly. **a~halb** prep (+ gen) outside ● adv **a~halb wohnen** live outside town

äußer|lich a external, adv -ly; (fig) outward, adv -ly. **ä~n** vt express; **sich ä~n** comment; (sich zeigen) manifest itself

außerordentlich a extraordinary, adv -ily; (außergewöhnlich) exceptional, adv -ly

äußerst adv extremely

außerstande adv unable (**zu** to)

äußerste|(r,s) a outermost; (weiteste) furthest; (höchste) utmost, extreme; (letzte) last; (schlimmste) worst; **am ä~n Ende** at the very end; **aufs ä~** extremely. **Ä~(s)** nt **das Ä~** the limit; (Schlimmste) the worst; **sein Ä~s tun** do one's utmost

Äußerung f **-,-en** comment; (Bemerkung) remark

aussetzen v sep ● vt expose (dat to); abandon (Kind, Hund); launch (Boot); offer (Belohnung); **etwas auszusetzen haben an** (+ dat) find fault with ● vi (haben) stop; (Motor:) cut out

Aussicht f **-,-en** view/(fig) prospect (**auf** + acc of); **in A~ stellen** promise; **weitere A~en** (Meteorol) further outlook sg. **a~slos** a hopeless, adv -ly. **a~sreich** a promising

aussöhnen vt sep reconcile; **sich a~** become reconciled

aussortieren vt sep pick out; (ausscheiden) eliminate

ausspann|en v sep ● vt spread out; unhitch (Pferd); (fam: wegnehmen) take (dat from) ● vi (haben) rest. **A~ung** f rest

aussperr|en vt sep lock out. **A~ung** f **-,-en** lock-out

ausspielen v sep ● vt play (Karte); (fig) play off (**gegen** against) ● vi (haben) (Kartenspiel) lead

Aussprache f pronunciation; (Sprechweise) diction; (Gespräch) talk

aussprechen† v sep ● vt pronounce; (äußern) express; **sich a~** talk; come out (**für/gegen** in favour of/against) ● vi (haben) finish [speaking]

Ausspruch m saying

ausspucken v sep ● vt spit out ● vi (haben) spit

ausspülen vt sep rinse out

ausstaffieren vt sep (fam) kit out

Ausstand m strike; **in den A~ treten** go on strike

ausstatt|en vt sep equip; **mit Möbeln a~en** furnish. **A~ung** f **-,-en** equipment; (Innen-) furnishings pl; (Theat) scenery and costumes pl; (Aufmachung) get-up

ausstehen† v sep ● vt suffer; **Angst a~** be frightened; **ich kann sie nicht a~** I can't stand her ● vi (haben) be outstanding

aussteig|en† vi sep (sein) get out; (aus Bus, Zug) get off; (fam: ausscheiden) opt out; (aus einem Geschäft) back out; **alles a~en!** all change! **A~er(in)** m **-s,-** (f **-,-nen**) (fam) drop-out

ausstell|en vt sep exhibit; (Comm) display; (ausfertigen) make out; issue (Paß). **A~er** m **-s,-** exhibitor. **A~ung** f exhibition; (Comm) display. **A~ungsstück** nt exhibit

aussterben† vi sep (sein) die out; (Biol) become extinct. **A~ nt -s** extinction

Aussteuer f trousseau

Ausstieg m **-[e]s,-e** exit

ausstopfen vt sep stuff

ausstoßen† vt sep emit; utter (Fluch); heave (Seufzer); (ausschließen) expel

ausstrahl|en vt/i sep (sein) radiate, emit; (Radio, TV) broadcast. **A~ung** f radiation; (fig) charisma

ausstrecken vt sep stretch out; put out (Hand); **sich a~** stretch out

ausstreichen† vt sep cross out

ausstreuen vt sep scatter; spread (Gerüchte)

ausströmen v sep ● vi (sein) pour out; (entweichen) escape ● vt emit; (ausstrahlen) radiate

aussuchen vt sep pick, choose

Austausch *m* exchange. **a∼bar** *a* interchangeable. **a∼en** *vt sep* exchange; (*auswechseln*) replace

austeilen *vt sep* distribute; (*ausgeben*) hand out

Auster *f* -,-n oyster

austoben (sich) *vr sep* ⟨*Sturm:*⟩ rage; ⟨*Person:*⟩ let off steam; ⟨*Kinder:*⟩ romp about

austragen† *vt sep* deliver; hold ⟨*Wettkampf*⟩; play ⟨*Spiel*⟩

Austral|ien /-jən/ *nt* -s Australia. **A∼ier(in)** *m* -s,- (*f* -,-nen) Australian. **a∼isch** *a* Australian

austreiben† *v sep* ● *vt* drive out; (*Relig*) exorcize ● *vi* (*haben*) (*Bot*) sprout

austreten† *v sep* ● *vt* stamp out; (*abnutzen*) wear down ● *vi* (*sein*) come out; (*ausscheiden*) leave (**aus etw** sth); **[mal] a∼** (*fam*) go to the loo; (*Sch*) be excused

austrinken† *vt/i sep* (*haben*) drink up; (*leeren*) drain

Austritt *m* resignation

austrocknen *vt/i sep* (*sein*) dry out

ausüben *vt sep* practise; carry on ⟨*Handwerk*⟩; exercise ⟨*Recht*⟩; exert ⟨*Druck, Einfluß*⟩; have ⟨*Wirkung*⟩

Ausverkauf *m* [clearance] sale. **a∼t** *a* sold out; **a∼tes Haus** full house

auswachsen† *vt sep* outgrow

Auswahl *f* choice, selection; (*Comm*) range; (*Sport*) team

auswählen *vt sep* choose, select

Auswander|er *m* emigrant. **a∼n** *vi sep* (*sein*) emigrate. **A∼ung** *f* emigration

auswärt|ig *a* non-local; (*ausländisch*) foreign. **a∼s** *adv* outwards; (*Sport*) away; **a∼s essen** eat out; **a∼s arbeiten** not work locally. **A∼sspiel** *nt* away game

auswaschen† *vt sep* wash out

auswechseln *vt sep* change; (*ersetzen*) replace; (*Sport*) substitute

Ausweg *m* (*fig*) way out. **a∼los** *a* (*fig*) hopeless

ausweich|en† *vi sep* (*sein*) get out of the way; **jdm/etw a∼en** avoid/(*sich entziehen*) evade s.o./sth. **a∼end** *a* evasive, *adv* -ly

ausweinen *vt sep* **sich** (*dat*) **die Augen a∼** cry one's eyes out; **sich a∼** have a good cry

Ausweis *m* -es,-e pass; (*Mitglieds-, Studenten-*) card. **a∼en**† *vt sep* deport; **sich a∼en** prove one's identity. **A∼papiere** *ntpl* identification papers. **A∼ung** *f* deportation

ausweiten *vt sep* stretch; (*fig*) expand

auswendig *adv* by heart

auswerten *vt sep* evaluate; (*nutzen*) utilize

auswickeln *vt sep* unwrap

auswirk|en (sich) *vr sep* have an effect (**auf** + *acc* on). **A∼ung** *f* effect; (*Folge*) consequence

auswischen *vt sep* wipe out; **jdm eins a∼** (*fam*) play a nasty trick on s.o.

auswringen *vt sep* wring out

Auswuchs *m* excrescence; **Auswüchse** (*fig*) excesses

auszahlen *vt sep* pay out; (*entlohnen*) pay off; (*abfinden*) buy out; **sich a∼** (*fig*) pay off

auszählen *vt sep* count; (*Boxen*) count out

Auszahlung *f* payment

auszeichn|en *vt sep* (*Comm*) price; (*ehren*) honour; (*mit einem Preis*) award a prize to; (*Mil*) decorate; **sich a∼en** distinguish oneself. **A∼ung** *f* honour; (*Preis*) award; (*Mil*) decoration; (*Sch*) distinction

ausziehen† *v sep* ● *vt* pull out; (*auskleiden*) undress; take off ⟨*Mantel, Schuhe*⟩; **sich a∼** take off one's coat; (*sich entkleiden*) undress ● *vi* (*sein*) move out; (*sich aufmachen*) set out

Auszubildende(r) *m/f* trainee

Auszug *m* departure; (*Umzug*) move; (*Ausschnitt*) extract, excerpt; (*Bank-*) statement

authentisch *a* authentic

Auto *nt* -s,-s car; **A∼ fahren** drive; (*mitfahren*) go in the car. **A∼bahn** *f* motorway, (*Amer*) freeway

Autobiographie *f* autobiography

Auto|bus *m* bus. **A∼fähre** *f* car ferry. **A∼fahrer(in)** *m(f)* driver, motorist. **A∼fahrt** *f* drive

Autogramm *nt* -s,-e autograph

autokratisch *a* autocratic

Automat *m* -en,-en automatic device; (*Münz-*) slot-machine; (*Verkaufs-*) vending-machine; (*Fahrkarten-*) machine; (*Techn*) robot. **A∼ik** *f* - automatic mechanism; (*Auto*) automatic transmission

Auto|mation /-'tsjo:n/ *f* - automation. **a∼matisch** *a* automatic, *adv* -ally

autonom *a* autonomous. **A∼ie** *f* - autonomy

Autonummer *f* registration number

Autopsie f -,-n autopsy
Autor m -s,-en /-'to:rən/ author
Auto|reisezug m Motorail. **A~rennen** nt motor race
Autorin f -,-nen author[ess]
Autori|sation /-'tsio:n/ f - authorization. **a~sieren** vt authorize. **a~tär** a authoritarian. **A~tät** f -,-en authority
Auto|schlosser m motor mechanic. **A~skooter** /-sku:tɐ/ m -s,- dodgem. **A~stopp** m -s per **A~stopp fahren** hitch-hike. **A~verleih** m car hire [firm]. **A~waschanlage** f car wash
autsch int ouch
Aversion f -,-en aversion (**gegen** to)
Axt f -,-̈e axe

B

B, b /be:/ nt - (Mus) B flat
Baby /'be:bi/ nt -s,-s baby. **B~ausstattung** f layette. **B~sitter** /-sItɐ/ m -s,- babysitter
Bach m -[e]s,-̈e stream
Backbord nt -[e]s port [side]
Backe f -,-n cheek
backen v ●vt/i † (haben) bake; (braten) fry ●vi (reg) (haben) (kleben) stick (**an** + dat to)
Backenzahn m molar
Bäcker m -s,- baker. **B~ei** f -,-en, **B~laden** m baker's shop
Back|form f baking tin. **B~obst** nt dried fruit. **B~ofen** m oven. **B~pfeife** f (fam) slap in the face. **B~pflaume** f prune. **B~pulver** nt baking-powder. **B~rohr** nt oven. **B~stein** m brick. **B~werk** nt cakes and pastries pl
Bad nt -[e]s,-̈er bath; (im Meer) bathe; (Zimmer) bathroom; (Schwimm-) pool; (Ort) spa
Bade|anstalt f swimming baths pl. **B~anzug** m swim-suit. **B~hose** f swimming trunks pl. **B~kappe** f bathing-cap. **B~mantel** m bathrobe. **B~matte** f bath-mat. **B~mütze** f bathing-cap. **b~n** vi (haben) have a bath; (im Meer) bathe ●vt bathe; (waschen) bathe. **B~ort** m seaside resort; (Kurort) spa. **B~tuch** nt bathtowel. **B~wanne** f bath[-tub]. **B~zimmer** nt bathroom
Bagatelle f -,-n trifle; (Mus) bagatelle

Bagger m -s,- excavator; (Naß-) dredger. **b~n** vt/i (haben) excavate; dredge. **B~see** m flooded gravel-pit
Bahn f -,-en path; (Astr) orbit; (Sport) track; (einzelne) lane; (Rodel-) run; (Stoff-, Papier-) width; (Rock-) panel; (Eisen-) railway; (Zug) train; (Straßen-) tram; **auf die schiefe B~ kommen** (fig) get into bad ways. **b~brechend** a (fig) pioneering. **b~en** vt sich (dat) **einen Weg b~en** clear a way (**durch** through). **B~hof** m [railway] station. **B~steig** m -[e]s,-e platform. **B~übergang** m level crossing, (Amer) grade crossing
Bahre f -,-n stretcher; (Toten-) bier
Baiser /bɛ'ze:/ nt -s,-s meringue
Bajonett nt -[e]s,-e bayonet
Bake f -,-n (Naut, Aviat) beacon
Bakterien /-jən/ fpl bacteria
Balanc|e /ba'lã:sə/ f - balance; **die B~e halten/verlieren** keep/lose one's balance. **b~ieren** vt/i (haben/sein) balance
bald adv soon; (fast) almost; **b~ ... b~ ...** now ... now ...
Baldachin /-xi:n/ m -s,-e canopy
bald|ig a early; (Besserung) speedy. **b~möglichst** adv as soon as possible
Balg nt & m -[e]s,-̈er (fam) brat. **b~en (sich)** vr tussle. **B~erei** f -,-en tussle
Balkan m -s Balkans pl
Balken m -s,- beam
Balkon /bal'kõ:/ m -s,-s balcony; (Theat) circle
Ball[1] m -[e]s,-̈e ball
Ball[2] m -[e]s,-̈e (Tanz) ball
Ballade f -,-n ballad
Ballast m -[e]s ballast. **B~stoffe** mpl roughage sg
ballen vt **die [Hand zur] Faust b~** clench one's fist; **sich b~** gather, mass. **B~** m -s,- bale; (Anat) ball of the hand/ (Fuß-) foot; (Med) bunion
Ballerina f -,-nen ballerina
Ballett nt -s,-e ballet
Balletttänzer(in) m(f) ballet dancer
ballistisch a ballistic
Ballon /ba'lõ:/ m -s,-s balloon
Ball|saal m ballroom. **B~ungsgebiet** nt conurbation. **B~wechsel** m (Tennis) rally
Balsam m -s balm
Balt|ikum nt -s Baltic States pl. **b~isch** a Baltic
Balustrade f -,-n balustrade
Bambus m -ses,-se bamboo

banal a banal. **B~ität** f -,-en banality

Banane f -,-n banana

Banause m -n,-n philistine

Band[1] nt -[e]s,¨er ribbon; ⟨Naht-, Ton-, Ziel-⟩ tape; ⟨Anat⟩ ligament; **auf B~ aufnehmen** tape; **laufendes B~** conveyor belt; **am laufenden B~** ⟨fam⟩ non-stop

Band[2] m -[e]s,¨e volume

Band[3] nt -[e]s,-e ⟨fig⟩ bond; **B~e der Freundschaft** bonds of friendship

Band[4] /bɛnt/ f -,-s [jazz] band

Bandag|e /ban'da:ʒə/ f -,-n bandage. **b~ieren** vt bandage

Bande f -,-n gang

bändigen vt control, restrain; ⟨zähmen⟩ tame

Bandit m -en,-en bandit

Band|maß nt tape-measure. **B~nudeln** fpl noodles. **B~scheibe** f ⟨Anat⟩ disc. **B~scheibenvorfall** m slipped disc. **B~wurm** m tapeworm

bang|[e] a (**bänger, bängst**) anxious; **jdm b~e machen** frighten s.o. **B~e** f **B~e haben** be afraid. **b~en** vi ⟨haben⟩ fear (**um** for); **mir b~t davor** I dread it

Banjo nt -s,-s banjo

Bank[1] f -,¨e bench

Bank[2] f -,-en ⟨Comm⟩ bank. **B~einzug** m direct debit

Bankett nt -s,-e banquet

Bankier /baŋ'kje:/ m -s,-s banker

Bank|konto nt bank account. **B~note** f banknote

Bankrott m -s,-s bankruptcy; **B~ machen** go bankrupt. **b~** a bankrupt

Bankwesen nt banking

Bann m -[e]s,-e ⟨fig⟩ spell; **in jds B~** under s.o.'s spell. **b~en** vt exorcize; ⟨abwenden⟩ avert; **[wie] gebannt** spellbound

Banner nt -s,- banner

Baptist(in) m -en,-en (f -,-nen) Baptist

bar a ⟨rein⟩ sheer; ⟨Gold⟩ pure; **b~es Geld** cash; **[in] b~ bezahlen** pay cash; **etw für b~e Münze nehmen** ⟨fig⟩ take sth as gospel

Bar f -,-s bar

Bär m -en,-en bear; **jdm einen B~en aufbinden** ⟨fam⟩ pull s.o.'s leg

Baracke f -,-n ⟨Mil⟩ hut

Barb|ar m -en,-en barbarian. **b~arisch** a barbaric

bar|fuß adv barefoot. **B~geld** nt cash

Bariton m -s,-e /-'to:nə/ baritone

Barkasse f -,-n launch

Barmann m (pl -**männer**) barman

barmherzig a merciful. **B~keit** f -mercy

barock a baroque. **B~** nt & m -[s] baroque

Barometer nt -s,- barometer

Baron m -s,-e baron. **B~in** f -,-nen baroness

Barren m -s,- ⟨Gold-⟩ bar, ingot; ⟨Sport⟩ parallel bars pl. **B~gold** nt gold bullion

Barriere f -,-n barrier

Barrikade f -,-n barricade

barsch a gruff, adv -ly; ⟨kurz⟩ curt, adv -ly

Barsch m -[e]s,-e ⟨Zool⟩ perch

Barschaft f - **meine ganze B~** all I have/had on me

Bart m -[e]s,¨e beard; ⟨der Katze⟩ whiskers pl

bärtig a bearded

Barzahlung f cash payment

Basar m -s,-e bazaar

Base[1] f -,-n [female] cousin

Base[2] f -,-n ⟨Chem⟩ alkali, base

Basel nt -s Basle

basieren vi ⟨haben⟩ be based (**auf** + dat on)

Basilikum nt -s basil

Basis f -,**Basen** base; ⟨fig⟩ basis

basisch a ⟨Chem⟩ alkaline

Bask|enmütze f beret. **b~isch** a Basque

Baß m -sses,¨sse bass; ⟨Kontra-⟩ double-bass

Bassin /ba'sɛ̃:/ nt -s,-s pond; ⟨Brunnen-⟩ basin; ⟨Schwimm-⟩ pool

Bassist m -en,-en bass player; ⟨Sänger⟩ bass

Baßstimme f bass voice

Bast m -[e]s raffia

basta int [**und damit**] **b~!** and that's that!

bast|eln vt make ● vi ⟨haben⟩ do handicrafts; ⟨herum-⟩ tinker (**an** + dat with). **B~ler** m -s,- amateur craftsman; ⟨Heim-⟩ do-it-yourselfer

Bataillon /batal'jo:n/ nt -s,-e battalion

Batterie f -,-n battery

Bau[1] m -[e]s,-e burrow; ⟨Fuchs-⟩ earth

Bau[2] m -[e]s,-ten construction; ⟨Gebäude⟩ building; ⟨Auf-⟩ structure; ⟨Körper-⟩ build; ⟨B~stelle⟩ building site; **im Bau** under construction. **B~arbeiten** fpl building work sg;

(*Straßen-*) roadworks. **B∼art** *f* design; (*Stil*) style

Bauch *m* -[e]s, **Bäuche** abdomen, belly; (*Magen*) stomach; (*Schmer-*) paunch; (*Bauchung*) bulge. **b∼ig** *a* bulbous. **B∼nabel** *m* navel. **B∼redner** *m* ventriloquist. **B∼schmerzen** *mpl* stomach-ache *sg*. **B∼speicheldrüse** *f* pancreas. **B∼weh** *nt* stomach-ache

bauen *vt* build; (*konstruieren*) construct; (*an-*) grow; **einen Unfall b∼** (*fam*) have an accident ● *vi* (*haben*) build (**an etw** *dat* sth); **b∼ auf** (+ *acc*) (*fig*) rely on

Bauer[1] *m* -s,- *n* farmer; (*Schach*) pawn
Bauer[2] *nt* -s,- [bird]cage
Bäuer|in *f* -,-nen farmer's wife. **b∼lich** *a* rustic

Bauern|haus *nt* farmhouse. **B∼hof** *m* farm

bau|fällig *a* dilapidated. **B∼genehmigung** *f* planning permission. **B∼gerüst** *nt* scaffolding. **B∼jahr** *nt* year of construction; **B∼jahr 1989** (*Auto*) 1989 model. **B∼kasten** *m* box of building bricks; (*Modell-*) model kit. **B∼klotz** *m* building brick. **B∼kunst** *f* architecture. **b∼lich** *a* structural, *adv* -ly. **B∼lichkeiten** *fpl* buildings

Baum *m* -[e]s, **Bäume** tree

baumeln *vi* (*haben*) dangle; **die Beine b∼ lassen** dangle one's legs

bäumen (sich) *vr* rear [up]

Baum|schule *f* [tree] nursery. **B∼stamm** *m* tree-trunk. **B∼wolle** *f* cotton. **b∼wollen** *a* cotton

Bauplatz *m* building plot

bäurisch *a* rustic; (*plump*) uncouth

Bausch *m* -[e]s, **Bäusche** wad; **in B∼ und Bogen** (*fig*) wholesale. **b∼en** *vt* puff out; **sich b∼en** billow [out]. **b∼ig** *a* puffed [out]; (*Ärmel*) full

Bau|sparkasse *f* building society. **B∼stein** *m* building brick; (*fig*) element. **B∼stelle** *f* building site; (*Straßen-*) roadworks *pl*. **B∼unternehmer** *m* building contractor. **B∼werk** *nt* building. **B∼zaun** *m* hoarding

Bayer|(in) *m* -s,-n (*f* -,-nen) Bavarian. **B∼n** *nt* -s Bavaria

bay[e]risch *a* Bavarian

Bazillus *m* -,-len bacillus; (*fam: Keim*) germ

beabsichtig|en *vt* intend. **b∼t** *a* intended; (*absichtlich*) intentional

beacht|en *vt* take notice of; (*einhalten*) observe; (*folgen*) follow; **nicht b∼en** ignore. **b∼lich** *a* considerable. **B∼ung** *f* - observance; **etw** (*dat*) **keine B∼ung schenken** take no notice of sth

Beamte(r) *m*, **Beamtin** *f* -,-nen official; (*Staats-*) civil servant; (*Schalter-*) clerk

beängstigend *a* alarming

beanspruchen *vt* claim; (*erfordern*) demand; (*brauchen*) take up; (*Techn*) stress; **die Arbeit beansprucht ihn sehr** his work is very demanding

beanstand|en *vt* take fault with; (*Comm*) make a complaint about. **B∼ung** *f* -,-en complaint

beantragen *vt* apply for

beantworten *vt* answer

bearbeiten *vt* work; (*weiter-*) process; (*behandeln*) treat (**mit** with); (*Admin*) deal with; (*redigieren*) edit; (*Theat*) adapt; (*Mus*) arrange; (*fam: bedrängen*) pester; (*fam: schlagen*) pummel

Beatmung *f* **künstliche B∼** artificial respiration. **B∼sgerät** *nt* ventilator

beaufsichtig|en *vt* supervise. **B∼ung** *f* - supervision

beauftrag|en *vt* instruct; commission (*Künstler*); **jdn mit einer Arbeit b∼en** assign a task to s.o. **B∼te(r)** *m/f* representative

bebauen *vt* build on; (*bestellen*) cultivate

beben *vi* (*haben*) tremble

bebildert *a* illustrated

Becher *m* -s,- beaker; (*Henkel-*) mug; (*Joghurt-, Sahne-*) carton

Becken *nt* -s,- basin; (*Schwimm-*) pool; (*Mus*) cymbals *pl*; (*Anat*) pelvis

bedacht *a* careful; **b∼ auf** (+ *acc*) concerned about; **darauf b∼** anxious (**zu** to)

bedächtig *a* careful, *adv* -ly; (*langsam*) slow, *adv* -ly

bedanken (sich) *vr* thank (**bei jdm** s.o.)

Bedarf *m* -s need/(*Comm*) demand (**an** + *dat* for); **bei B∼** if required. **B∼sartikel** *mpl* requisites. **B∼shaltestelle** *f* request stop

bedauer|lich *a* regrettable. **b∼licherweise** *adv* unfortunately. **b∼n** *vt* regret; (*bemitleiden*) feel sorry for; **bedaure!** sorry! **B∼n** *nt* -s regret; (*Mitgefühl*) sympathy. **b∼nswert** *a* pitiful; (*bedauerlich*) regrettable

bedeck|en *vt* cover; **sich b~en** ⟨*Himmel:*⟩ cloud over. **b~t** *a* covered; ⟨*Himmel*⟩ overcast

bedenken† *vt* consider; (*überlegen*) think over; **jdn b~** give s.o. a present; **sich b~** consider. **B~** *pl* misgivings; **ohne B~** without hesitation. **b~los** *a* unhesitating, *adv* -ly

bedenklich *a* doubtful; (*verdächtig*) dubious; (*bedrohlich*) worrying; (*ernst*) serious

bedeut|en *vi* (*haben*) mean; **jdm viel/nichts b~en** mean a lot/nothing to s.o.; **es hat nichts zu b~en** it is of no significance. **b~end** *a* important; (*beträchtlich*) considerable. **b~sam** *a* = **b~ungsvoll**. **B~ung** *f* -,-en meaning; (*Wichtigkeit*) importance. **b~ungslos** *a* meaningless; (*unwichtig*) unimportant. **b~ungsvoll** *a* significant; (*vielsagend*) meaningful, *adv* -ly

bedien|en *vt* serve; (*betätigen*) operate; **sich [selbst] b~en** help oneself. **B~ung** *f* -,-en service; (*Betätigung*) operation; (*Kellner*) waiter; (*Kellnerin*) *f* waitress. **B~ungsgeld** *nt*, **B~ungszuschlag** *m* service charge

bedingt *a* conditional; (*eingeschränkt*) qualified

Bedingung *f* -,-en condition; **B~en** conditions; (*Comm*) terms. **b~slos** *a* unconditional, *adv* -ly; (*unbedingt*) unquestioning, *adv* -ly

bedrängen *vt* press; (*belästigen*) pester

bedroh|en *vt* threaten. **b~lich** *a* threatening. **B~ung** *f* threat

bedrück|en *vt* depress. **b~end** *a* depressing. **b~t** *a* depressed

bedruckt *a* printed

bedürf|en† *vi* (*haben*) (+ *gen*) need. **B~nis** *nt* -ses,-se need. **B~nisanstalt** *f* public convenience. **b~tig** *a* needy

Beefsteak /'bi:fste:k/ *nt* -s,-s steak; **deutsches B~** hamburger

beeil|en (sich) *vr* hurry; hasten (**zu** to); **beeilt euch!** hurry up!

beeindrucken *vt* impress

beeinflussen *vt* influence

beeinträchtigen *vt* mar; (*schädigen*) impair

beend[ig]en *vt* end

beengen *vt* restrict; **beengt wohnen** live in cramped conditions

beerben *vt* **jdn b~** inherit s.o.'s property

beerdig|en *vt* bury. **B~ung** *f* -,-en funeral

Beere *f* -,-n berry

Beet *nt* -[e]s,-e ⟨*Hort*⟩ bed

Beete *f* -,-n **rote B~** beetroot

befähig|en *vt* enable; (*qualifizieren*) qualify. **B~ung** *f* - qualification; (*Fähigkeit*) ability

befahr|bar *a* passable. **b~en†** *vt* drive along; **stark b~ene Straße** busy road

befallen† *vt* attack; ⟨*Angst:*⟩ seize

befangen *a* shy; (*gehemmt*) self-conscious; (*Jur*) biased. **B~heit** *f* - shyness; self-consciousness; bias

befassen (sich) *vr* concern oneself/ (*behandeln*) deal (**mit** with)

Befehl *m* -[e]s,-e order; (*Leitung*) command (**über** + *acc* of). **b~en†** *vt* **jdm etw b~en** order s.o. to do sth ● *vi* (*haben*) give the orders. **b~igen** *vt* (*Mil*) command. **B~sform** *f* (*Gram*) imperative. **B~shaber** *m* -s,- commander

befestig|en *vt* fasten (**an** + *dat* to); (*stärken*) strengthen; (*Mil*) fortify. **B~ung** *f* -,-en fastening; (*Mil*) fortification

befeuchten *vt* moisten

befind|en† **(sich)** *vr* be. **B~** *nt* -s [state of] health

beflecken *vt* stain

beflissen *a* assiduous, *adv* -ly

befolgen *vt* follow

beförder|n *vt* transport; (*im Rang*) promote. **B~ung** *f* -,-en transport; promotion

befragen *vt* question

befrei|en *vt* free; (*räumen*) clear (**von** of); (*freistellen*) exempt (**von** from); **sich b~en** free oneself. **B~er** *m* -s,- liberator. **b~t** *a* (*erleichtert*) relieved. **B~ung** *f* - liberation; exemption

befremd|en *vt* disconcert. **B~en** *nt* -s surprise. **b~lich** *a* strange

befreunden (sich) *vr* make friends; **befreundet sein** be friends

befriedig|en *vt* satisfy. **b~end** *a* satisfying; (*zufriedenstellend*) satisfactory. **B~ung** *f* - satisfaction

befrucht|en *vt* fertilize. **B~ung** *f* - fertilization; **künstliche B~ung** artificial insemination

Befug|nis *f* -,-se authority. **b~t** *a* authorized

Befund *m* result

befürcht|en vt fear. **B~ung** f -,-en fear

befürworten vt support

begab|t a gifted. **B~ung** f -,-en gift, talent

begatten (sich) vr mate

begeben† **(sich)** vr go; (liter: geschehen) happen; **sich in Gefahr b~** expose oneself to danger. **B~heit** f -,-en incident

begegn|en vi (sein) **jdm/etw b~en** meet s.o./sth; **sich b~en** meet. **B~ung** f -,-en meeting; (Sport) encounter

begehen† vt walk along; (verüben) commit; (feiern) celebrate

begehr|en vt desire. **b~enswert** a desirable. **b~t** a sought-after

begeister|n vt **jdn b~n** arouse s.o.'s enthusiasm; **sich b~n** be enthusiastic (**für** about). **b~t** a enthusiastic, adv -ally; (eifrig) keen. **B~ung** f - enthusiasm

Begier|de f -,-n desire. **b~ig** a eager (**auf** + acc for)

begießen† vt water; (Culin) baste; (fam: feiern) celebrate

Beginn m -s beginning; **zu B~** at the beginning. **b~en†** vt/i (haben) start, begin; (anstellen) do

beglaubigen vt authenticate

begleichen† vt settle

begleit|en vt accompany. **B~er** m -s,-, **B~erin** f -,-nen companion; (Mus) accompanist. **B~ung** f -,-en company; (Gefolge) entourage; (Mus) accompaniment

beglück|en vt make happy. **b~t** a happy. **b~wünschen** vt congratulate (**zu** on)

begnadig|en vt (Jur) pardon. **B~ung** f -,-en (Jur) pardon

begnügen (sich) vr content oneself (**mit** with)

Begonie /-iə/ f -,-n begonia

begraben† vt bury

Begräbnis n -ses,-se burial; (Feier) funeral

begreif|en† vt understand; **nicht zu b~en** incomprehensible. **b~lich** a understandable; **jdm etw b~lich machen** make s.o. understand sth. **b~licherweise** adv understandably

begrenz|en vt form the boundary of; (beschränken) restrict. **b~t** a limited. **B~ung** f -,-en restriction; (Grenze) boundary

Begriff m -[e]s,-e concept; (Ausdruck) term; (Vorstellung) idea; **für meine**

B~e to my mind; **im B~ sein** od **stehen** be about (**zu** to); **schwer von B~** (fam) slow on the uptake. **b~sstutzig** a obtuse

begründ|en vt give one's reason for; (gründen) establish. **b~et** a justified. **B~ung** f -,-en reason

begrüß|en vt greet; (billigen) welcome. **b~enswert** a welcome. **B~ung** f - greeting; welcome

begünstigen vt favour; (fördern) encourage

begutachten vt give an opinion on; (fam: ansehen) look at

begütert a wealthy

begütigen vt placate

behaart a hairy

behäbig a portly; (gemütlich) comfortable, adv -bly

behag|en vi (haben) please (**jdm** s.o.). **B~en** nt -s contentment; (Genuß) enjoyment. **b~lich** a comfortable, adv -bly. **B~lichkeit** f - comfort

behalten† vt keep; (sich merken) remember; **etw für sich b~** (verschweigen) keep sth to oneself

Behälter m -s,- container

behand|eln vt treat; (sich befassen) deal with. **B~lung** f treatment

beharr|en vi (haben) persist (**auf** + dat in). **b~lich** a persistent, adv -ly; (hartnäckig) dogged, adv -ly. **B~lichkeit** f - persistence

behaupt|en vt maintain; (vorgeben) claim; (sagen) say; (bewahren) retain; **sich b~en** hold one's own. **B~ung** f -,-en assertion; claim; (Äußerung) statement

beheben† vt remedy; (beseitigen) remove

behelf|en† **(sich)** vr make do (**mit** with). **b~smäßig** a makeshift ● adv provisionally

behelligen vt bother

behende a nimble, adv -bly

beherbergen vt put up

beherrsch|en vt rule over; (dominieren) dominate; (meistern, zügeln) control; (können) know; **sich b~en** control oneself. **b~t** a self-controlled. **B~ung** f - control; (Selbst-) self-control; (Können) mastery

beherz|igen vt heed. **b~t** a courageous, adv -ly

behilflich a **jdm b~ sein** help s.o.

behinder|n vt hinder; (blockieren) obstruct. **b~t** a handicapped;

(*schwer*) disabled. **B∼te(r)** *m/f* handicapped/disabled person. **B∼ung** *f* **-,-en** obstruction; (*Med*) handicap; disability

Behörde *f* **-,-n** [public] authority

behüte|n *vt* protect; **Gott behüte!** heaven forbid! **b∼t** *a* sheltered

behutsam *a* careful, *adv* -ly; (*zart*) gentle, *adv* -ly

bei *prep* (+ *dat*) near; (*dicht*) by; at ⟨*Firma, Veranstaltung*⟩; **bei der Hand nehmen** take by the hand; **bei sich haben** have with one; **bei mir** at my place; (*in meinem Fall*) in my case; **Herr X bei Meyer** Mr X c/o Meyer; **bei Regen** when/(*falls*) if it rains; **bei Feuer** in case of fire; **bei Tag/Nacht** by day/night; **bei der Ankunft** on arrival; **bei Tisch/der Arbeit** at table/work; **bei guter Gesundheit** in good health; **bei der hohen Miete** [what] with the high rent; **bei all seiner Klugheit** for all his cleverness

beibehalten† *vt sep* keep

beibringen† *vt sep* **jdm etw b∼** teach s.o. sth; (*mitteilen*) break sth to s.o.; (*zufügen*) inflict sth on s.o.

Beicht|e *f* **-,-n** confession. **b∼en** *vt/i* (*haben*) confess. **B∼stuhl** *m* confessional

beide *a & pron* both; **die b∼n Brüder** the two brothers; **b∼s** both; **dreißig b∼** (*Tennis*) thirty all. **b∼rseitig** *a* mutual. **b∼rseits** *adv & prep* (+ *gen*) on both sides (of)

beidrehen *vi sep* (*haben*) heave to

beieinander *adv* together

Beifahrer|(in) *m(f)* [front-seat] passenger; (*Lkw*) driver's mate; (*Motorrad*) pillion passenger. **B∼sitz** *m* passenger seat

Beifall *m* **-[e]s** applause; (*Billigung*) approval; **B∼ klatschen** applaud

beifällig *a* approving, *adv* -ly

beifügen *vt sep* add; (*beilegen*) enclose

beige /beːʒ/ *inv a* beige

beigeben† *v sep* ● *vt* add ● *vi* (*haben*) **klein b∼** give in

Beigeschmack *m* [slight] taste

Beihilfe *f* financial aid; (*Studien-*) grant; (*Jur*) aiding and abetting

beikommen† *vi sep* (*sein*) **jdm b∼** get the better of s.o.

Beil *nt* **-[e]s,-e** hatchet, axe

Beilage *f* supplement; (*Gemüse*) vegetable; **als B∼ Reis** (*Culin*) served with rice

beiläufig *a* casual, *adv* -ly

beilegen *vt sep* enclose; (*schlichten*) settle

beileibe *adv* **b∼ nicht** by no means

Beileid *nt* condolences *pl*. **B∼sbrief** *m* letter of condolence

beiliegend *a* enclosed

beim *prep* = **bei dem**; **b∼ Militär** in the army; **b∼ Frühstück** at breakfast; **b∼ Lesen** when reading; **b∼ Lesen sein** be reading

beimessen† *vt sep* (*fig*) attach (*dat* to)

Bein *nt* **-[e]s,-e** leg; **jdm ein B∼ stellen** trip s.o. up

beinah[e] *adv* nearly, almost

Beiname *m* epithet

beipflichten *vi sep* (*haben*) agree (*dat* with)

Beirat *m* advisory committee

beirren *vt* **sich nicht b∼ lassen** not let oneself be put off

beisammen *adv* together. **b∼sein†** *vi sep* (*sein*) be together. **B∼sein** *nt* **-s** get-together

Beisein *nt* presence

beiseite *adv* aside; (*abseits*) apart; **b∼ legen** put aside; (*sparen*) put by; **Spaß** *od* **Scherz b∼** joking apart

beisetz|en *vt sep* bury. **B∼ung** *f* **-,-en** funeral

Beispiel *nt* example; **zum B∼** for example. **b∼haft** *a* exemplary. **b∼los** *a* unprecedented. **b∼sweise** *adv* for example

beispringen† *vi sep* (*sein*) **jdm b∼** come to s.o.'s aid

beiß|en† *vt & i* (*haben*) bite; (*brennen*) sting; **sich b∼en** ⟨*Farben:*⟩ clash. **b∼end** *a* (*fig*) biting; ⟨*Bemerkung*⟩ caustic. **B∼zange** *f* pliers *pl*

Bei|stand *m* **-[e]s** help; **jdm B∼stand leisten** help s.o. **b∼stehen†** *vi sep* (*haben*) **jdm b∼stehen** help s.o.

beisteuern *vt sep* contribute

beistimmen *vi sep* (*haben*) agree

Beistrich *m* comma

Beitrag *m* **-[e]s,⸚e** contribution; (*Mitglieds-*) subscription; (*Versicherungs-*) premium; (*Zeitungs-*) article. **b∼en†** *vt/i sep* (*haben*) contribute

bei|treten† *vi sep* (*sein*) (+ *dat*) join. **B∼tritt** *m* joining

beiwohnen *vi sep* (*haben*) (+ *dat*) be present at

Beize *f* **-,-n** (*Holz-*) stain; (*Culin*) marinade

beizeiten *adv* in good time

beizen vt stain ⟨Holz⟩

bejahen vt answer in the affirmative; (billigen) approve of

bejahrt a aged, old

bejubeln vt cheer

bekämpf|en vt fight. **B~ung** f - fight (gen against)

bekannt a well-known; (vertraut) familiar; **jdm b~ sein** be known to s.o.; **jdn b~ machen** introduce s.o. **B~e(r)** m/f acquaintance; (Freund) friend. **B~gabe** f announcement. **b~geben†** vt sep announce. **b~lich** adv as is well known. **b~machen** vt sep announce. **B~machung** f -,-en announcement. **B~schaft** f - (Anschlag) notice. acquaintance; (Leute) acquaintances pl; (Freunde) friends pl. **b~werden†** vi sep (sein) become known

bekehr|en vt convert; **sich b~en** become converted. **B~ung** f -,-en conversion

bekenn|en† vt confess; profess ⟨Glauben⟩; **sich [für] schuldig b~en** admit one's guilt; **sich b~en zu** confess to ⟨Tat⟩; profess ⟨Glauben⟩; (stehen zu) stand by. **B~tnis** nt -ses,-se confession; (Konfession) denomination

beklag|en vt lament; (bedauern) deplore; **sich b~en** complain. **b~enswert** a unfortunate. **B~te(r)** m/f (Jur) defendant

beklatschen vt applaud

bekleid|en vt hold ⟨Amt⟩. **b~et** a dressed (**mit** in). **B~ung** f clothing

Beklemmung f -,-en feeling of oppression

beklommen a uneasy; (ängstlich) anxious, adv -ly

bekommen† vt get; have ⟨Baby⟩; catch ⟨Erkältung⟩; **Angst/Hunger b~** get frightened/hungry; **etw geliehen b~** be lent sth ● vi (sein) **jdm gut b~** do s.o. good; ⟨Essen:⟩ agree with s.o.

bekömmlich a digestible

beköstig|en vt feed; **sich selbst b~en** cater for oneself. **B~ung** f - board; (Essen) food

bekräftigen vt reaffirm; (bestätigen) confirm

bekreuzigen (sich) vr cross oneself

bekümmert a troubled; (besorgt) worried

bekunden vt show; (bezeugen) testify

belächeln vt laugh at

beladen† vt load ● a laden

Belag m -[e]s,‥e coating; (Fußboden-) covering; (Brot-) topping; (Zahn-) tartar; (Brems-) lining

belager|n vt besiege. **B~ung** f -,-en siege

Belang m von/ohne **B~** of/of no importance; **B~e** pl interests. **b~en** vt (Jur) sue. **b~los** a irrelevant; (unwichtig) trivial. **B~losigkeit** f -,-en triviality

belassen† vt leave; **es dabei b~** leave it at that

belasten vt load; (fig) burden; (beanspruchen) put a strain on; (Comm) debit; (Jur) incriminate

belästigen vt bother; (bedrängen) pester; (unsittlich) molest

Belastung f -,-en load; (fig) strain; (Last) burden; (Comm) debit. **B~smaterial** nt incriminating evidence. **B~szeuge** m prosecution witness

belaufen† (sich) vr amount (auf + acc to)

belauschen vt eavesdrop on

beleb|en vt (fig) revive; (lebhaft machen) enliven; **B~en** revive; ⟨Stadt:⟩ come to life. **b~t** a lively; ⟨Straße⟩ busy

Beleg m -[e]s,-e evidence; (Beispiel) instance (**für** of); (Quittung) receipt. **b~en** vt cover/(garnieren) garnish (**mit** with); (besetzen) reserve; (Univ) enrol for; (nachweisen) provide evidence for; **den ersten Platz b~en** (Sport) take first place. **B~schaft** f -,-en work-force. **b~t** a occupied; ⟨Zunge⟩ coated; ⟨Stimme⟩ husky; **b~te Brote** open sandwiches; **der Platz ist b~t** this seat is taken

belehren vt instruct; (aufklären) inform

beleibt a corpulent

beleidig|en vt offend; (absichtlich) insult. **B~ung** f -,-en insult

belesen a well-read

beleucht|en vt light; (anleuchten) illuminate. **B~ung** f -,-en illumination; (elektrisch) lighting; (Licht) light

Belg|ien /-jən/ nt -s Belgium. **B~ier(in)** m -s,- (f -,-nen) Belgian. **b~isch** a Belgian

belicht|en vt (Phot) expose. **B~ung** f - exposure

Belieb|en nt -s nach **B~en** [just] as one likes; (Culin) if liked. **b~ig** a eine **b~ige Zahl/Farbe** any number/ colour you like ● adv **b~ig lange/oft** as

long/often as one likes. **b~t** *a* popular.
B~theit *f* - popularity
beliefern *vt* supply (**mit** with)
bellen *vi (haben)* bark
belohn|en *vt* reward. **B~ung** *f* -,-en
reward
belüften *vt* ventilate
belügen† *vt* lie to; **sich [selbst] b~**
deceive oneself
belustig|en *vt* amuse. **B~ung** *f* -,-en
amusement
bemächtigen (sich) *vr* (+ *gen*) seize
bemalen *vt* paint
bemängeln *vt* criticize
bemannt *a* manned
bemerk|bar *a* **sich b~bar machen**
attract attention; ⟨*Ding:*⟩ become noticeable. **b~en** *vt* notice; (*äußern*) remark. **b~enswert** *a* remarkable,
adv -bly. **B~ung** *f* -,-en remark
bemitleiden *vt* pity
bemittelt *a* well-to-do
bemüh|en *vt* trouble; **sich b~en** try
(**zu** to; **um etw** to get sth); (*sich kümmern*) attend (**um** to); **b~t sein** endeavour (**zu** to). **B~ung** *f* -,-en effort;
(*Mühe*) trouble
bemuttern *vt* mother
benachbart *a* neighbouring
benachrichtig|en *vt* inform; (*amt-
lich*) notify. **B~ung** *f* -,-en notification
benachteilig|en *vt* discriminate
against; (*ungerecht sein*) treat un-
fairly. **B~ung** *f* -,-en discrimination
(*gen* against)
benehmen† **(sich)** *vr* behave. **B~** *nt*
-s behaviour
beneiden *vt* envy (**um etw** sth).
b~swert *a* enviable
Bengel *m* **-s,-** boy; (*Rüpel*) lout
benommen *a* dazed
benötigen *vt* need
benutz|en, (*SGer*) **benütz|en** *vt* use;
take ⟨*Bahn*⟩. **B~er** *m* **-s,-** user. **b~er-
freundlich** *a* user-friendly. **B~ung** *f*
use
Benzin *nt* **-s** petrol, (*Amer*) gasoline.
B~tank *m* petrol tank
beobacht|en *vt* observe. **B~er** *m* **-s,-**
observer. **B~ung** *f* -,-en observation
bepacken *vt* load (**mit** with)
bepflanzen *vt* plant (**mit** with)
bequem *a* comfortable, *adv* -bly;
(*mühelos*) easy, *adv* -ily; (*faul*) lazy.
b~en (sich) *vr* deign (**zu** to). **B~-
lichkeit** *f* -,-en comfort; (*Faulheit*)
laziness

berat|en† *vt* advise; (*überlegen*) dis-
cuss; **sich b~en** confer; **sich b~en
lassen** get advice ● *vi (haben)* discuss
(**über etw** *acc* sth); (*beratschlagen*)
confer. **B~er** *m* **-s,-**, **B~erin** *f* -,-nen
adviser. **b~schlagen** *vi (haben)* confer. **B~ung** *f* -,-en guidance; (*Rat*)
advice; (*Besprechung*) discussion; (*Med,
Jur*) consultation. **B~ungsstelle** *f* advice centre
berauben *vt* rob (*gen* of)
berauschen *vt* intoxicate. **b~d** *a*
intoxicating, heady
berechn|en *vt* calculate; (*anrechnen*)
charge for; (*abfordern*) charge.
b~end *a* (*fig*) calculating. **B~ung** *f*
calculation
berechtig|en *vt* entitle; (*befugen*)
authorize; (*fig*) justify. **b~t** *a*
justified, justifiable. **B~ung** *f* -,-en
authorization; (*Recht*) right; (*Rechtmä-
ßigkeit*) justification
bered|en *vt* talk about; (*klatschen*)
gossip about; (*überreden*) talk round;
sich b~en talk. **B~samkeit** *f* - elo-
quence
beredt *a* eloquent, *adv* -ly
Bereich *m* **-[e]s,-e** area; (*fig*) realm;
(*Fach-*) field
bereichern *vi* enrich; **sich b~** grow
rich (**an** + *dat* on)
Bereifung *f* - tyres *pl*
bereinigen *vt* (*fig*) settle
bereit *a* ready. **b~en** *vt* prepare;
(*verursachen*) cause; give ⟨*Über-
raschung*⟩. **b~halten**† *vt sep* have/
(*ständig*) keep ready. **b~legen** *vt sep*
put out [ready]. **b~machen** *vt sep* get
ready; **sich b~machen** get ready. **b~s**
adv already
Bereitschaft *f* -,-en readiness;
(*Einheit*) squad. **B~sdienst** *m* **B~s-
dienst haben** (*Mil*) be on stand-by;
⟨*Arzt:*⟩ be on call; ⟨*Apotheke:*⟩ be open for
out-of-hours dispensing. **B~s-
polizei** *f* riot police
bereit|stehen† *vi sep (haben)* be
ready. **b~stellen** *vt sep* put out
ready; (*verfügbar machen*) make
available. **B~ung** *f* - preparation.
b~willig *a* willing, *adv* -ly. **B~-
willigkeit** *f* - willingness
bereuen *vt* regret
Berg *m* **-[e]s,-e** mountain; (*Anhöhe*)
hill; **in den B~en** in the mountains.
b~ab *adv* downhill. **b~an** *adv* uphill. **B~arbeiter** *m* miner. **b~auf**

Bett|vorleger *m* bedside rug. **B~wäsche** *f* bed linen. **B~zeug** *nt* bedding

betupfen *vt* dab (**mit** with)

beug|en *vt* bend; (*Gram*) decline; conjugate ⟨*Verb*⟩; **sich b~en** bend; (*lehnen*) lean; (*sich fügen*) submit (*dat* to). **B~ung** *f* -,-en (*Gram*) declension; conjugation

Beule *f* -,-n bump; (*Delle*) dent

beunruhig|en *vt* worry; **sich b~en** worry. **B~ung** *f* - worry

beurlauben *vt* give leave to; (*des Dienstes entheben*) suspend

beurteil|en *vt* judge. **B~ung** *f* -,-en judgement; (*Ansicht*) opinion

Beute *f* - booty, haul; (*Jagd-*) bag; (*B~tier*) quarry; (*eines Raubtiers*) prey

Beutel *m* -s,- bag; (*Geld-*) purse; (*Tabak- & Zool*) pouch. **B~tier** *nt* marsupial

bevölker|n *vt* populate. **B~ung** *f* -,-en population

bevollmächtig|en *vt* authorize. **B~te(r)** *m/f* [authorized] agent

bevor *conj* before; **b~ nicht** until

bevormunden *vt* treat like a child

bevorstehen† *vi sep* (*haben*) approach; (*unmittelbar*) be imminent; **jdm b~** be in store for s.o. **b~d** *a* approaching, forthcoming; **unmittelbar b~d** imminent

bevorzug|en *vt* prefer; (*begünstigen*) favour. **b~t** *a* privileged; ⟨*Behandlung*⟩ preferential; (*beliebt*) favoured

bewachen *vt* guard; **bewachter Parkplatz** car park with an attendant

bewachsen *a* covered (**mit** with)

Bewachung *f* - guard; **unter B~** under guard

bewaffn|en *vt* arm. **b~et** *a* armed. **B~ung** *f* - armament; (*Waffen*) arms *pl*

bewahren *vt* protect (**vor** + *dat* from); (*behalten*) keep; **die Ruhe b~** keep calm; **Gott bewahre!** heaven forbid!

bewähren (sich) *vr* prove one's/ ⟨*Ding:*⟩ its worth; (*erfolgreich sein*) prove a success

bewahrheiten (sich) *vr* prove to be true

bewähr|t *a* reliable; (*erprobt*) proven. **B~ung** *f* - (*Jur*) probation. **B~ungsfrist** *f* [period of] probation. **B~ungsprobe** *f* (*fig*) test

bewaldet *a* wooded

bewältigen *vt* cope with; (*überwinden*) overcome; (*schaffen*) manage

bewandert *a* knowledgeable

bewässer|n *vt* irrigate. **B~ung** *f* - irrigation

bewegen[1] *vt* (*reg*) move; **sich b~** move; (*körperlich*) take exercise

bewegen†[2] *vt* jdn dazu b~, etw zu tun induce s.o. to do sth

Beweg|grund *m* motive. **b~lich** *a* movable, mobile; (*wendig*) agile. **B~lichkeit** *f* - mobility; agility. **b~t** *a* moved; (*ereignisreich*) eventful; ⟨*See*⟩ rough. **B~ung** *f* -,-en movement; (*Phys*) motion; (*Rührung*) emotion; (*Gruppe*) movement; **körperliche B~ung** physical exercise; **sich in B~ung setzen** [start to] move. **B~ungsfreiheit** *f* freedom of movement/(*fig*) of action. **b~ungslos** *a* motionless

beweinen *vt* mourn

Beweis *m* -es,-e proof; (*Zeichen*) token; **B~e** evidence *sg*. **b~en**† *vt* prove; (*zeigen*) show; **sich b~en** prove oneself/⟨*Ding:*⟩ itself. **B~material** *nt* evidence

bewenden *vi* **es dabei b~ lassen** leave it at that

bewerb|en† **(sich)** *vr* apply (**um** for; **bei** to). **B~er(in)** *m* -s,- (*f* -,-nen) applicant. **B~ung** *f* -,-en application

bewerkstelligen *vt* manage

bewerten *vt* value; (*einschätzen*) rate; (*Sch*) mark, grade

bewilligen *vt* grant

bewirken *vt* cause; (*herbeiführen*) bring about; (*erreichen*) achieve

bewirt|en *vt* entertain. **B~ung** *f* - hospitality

bewohn|bar *a* habitable. **b~en** *vt* inhabit, live in. **B~er(in)** *m* -s,- (*f* -,-nen) resident, occupant; (*Einwohner*) inhabitant

bewölk|en (sich) *vr* cloud over; **b~t** *a* cloudy. **B~ung** *f* - clouds *pl*

bewunder|n *vt* admire. **b~nswert** *a* admirable. **B~ung** *f* - admiration

bewußt *a* conscious (*gen* of); (*absichtlich*) deliberate, *adv* -ly; (*besagt*) said; **sich** (*dat*) **etw** (*gen*) **b~ sein/ werden** be/become aware of sth. **b~los** *a* unconscious. **B~losigkeit** *f* - unconsciousness. **B~sein** *n* -s consciousness; (*Gewißheit*) awareness; **bei [vollem] B~sein** [fully] conscious; **mir kam zum B~sein** I realized (**daß** that)

bez. *abbr* (**bezahlt**) paid; (**bezüglich**) re

bezahl|en *vt/i (haben)* pay; pay for ⟨*Ware, Essen*⟩; **sich b∼t machen** *(fig)* pay off. **B∼ung** *f* - payment; *(Lohn)* pay

bezähmen *vt* control; *(zügeln)* restrain; **sich b∼** restrain oneself

bezaubern *vt* enchant. **b∼d** *a* enchanting

bezeichn|en *vt* mark; *(bedeuten)* denote; *(beschreiben, nennen)* describe (**als** as). **b∼end** *a* typical. **B∼ung** *f* marking; *(Beschreibung)* description (**als** as); *(Ausdruck)* term; *(Name)* name

bezeugen *vt* testify to

bezichtigen *vt* accuse *(gen* of)

bezieh|en† *vt* cover; *(einziehen)* move into; *(beschaffen)* obtain; *(erhalten)* get, receive; take ⟨*Zeitung*⟩; *(in Verbindung bringen)* relate (**auf** + *acc* to); **sich b∼en** *(bewölken)* cloud over; **sich b∼en auf** (+ *acc)* refer to; **das Bett frisch b∼en** put clean sheets on the bed. **B∼ung** *f* -,-en relation; *(Verhältnis)* relationship; *(Bezug)* respect; **in dieser B∼ung** in this respect; **[gute] B∼ungen haben** have [good] connections. **b∼ungsweise** *adv* respectively; *(vielmehr)* or rather

beziffern (sich) *vr* amount (**auf** + *acc* to)

Bezirk *m* -[e]s,-e district

Bezug *m* cover; *(Kissen-)* case; *(Beschaffung)* obtaining; *(Kauf)* purchase; *(Zusammenhang)* reference; **B∼̃e** *pl* earnings; **B∼ nehmen** refer (**auf** + *acc* to); **in b∼ auf** (+ *acc)* regarding, concerning

bezüglich *prep* (+ *gen)* regarding, concerning ● *a* relating (**auf** + *acc* to); *(Gram)* relative

bezwecken *vt (fig)* aim at

bezweifeln *vt* doubt

bezwingen† *vt* conquer

BH /be:'ha:/ *m* -[s],-[s] bra

bibbern *vi (haben)* tremble; *(vor Kälte)* shiver

Bibel *f* -,-n Bible

Biber[1] *m* -s,- beaver

Biber[2] *m & nt* -s flannelette

Biblio|graphie *f* -,-n bibliography. **B∼thek** *f* -,-en library. **B∼thekar(in)** *m* -s,- *(f* -,-nen) librarian

biblisch *a* biblical

bieder *a* honest, upright; *(ehrenwert)* worthy; *(einfach)* simple

bieg|en† *vt* bend; **sich b∼en** bend; **sich vor Lachen b∼en** *(fam)* double up with laughter ● *vi (sein)* curve (**nach** to); **um die Ecke b∼en** turn the corner. **b∼sam** *a* flexible, supple. **B∼ung** *f* -,-en bend

Biene *f* -,-n bee. **B∼nhonig** *m* natural honey. **B∼nstock** *m* beehive. **B∼nwabe** *f* honeycomb

Bier *nt* -s,-e beer. **B∼deckel** *m* beermat. **B∼krug** *m* beer-mug

Biest *nt* -[e]s,-er *(fam)* beast

bieten† *vt* offer; *(bei Auktion)* bid; *(zeigen)* present; **das lasse ich mir nicht b∼** I won't stand for that

Bifokalbrille *f* bifocals *pl*

Biga|mie *f* - bigamy. **B∼mist** *m* -en,-en bigamist

bigott *a* over-pious

Bikini *m* -s,-s bikini

Bilanz *f* -,-en balance sheet; *(fig)* result; **die B∼ ziehen** *(fig)* draw conclusions *(aus* from)

Bild *nt* -[e]s,-er picture; *(Theat)* scene; **jdn ins B∼ setzen** put s.o. in the picture

bilden *vt* form; *(sein)* be; *(erziehen)* educate; **sich b∼** form; *(geistig)* educate oneself

Bild|erbuch *nt* picture-book. **B∼ergalerie** *f* picture gallery. **B∼fläche** *f* screen; **von der B∼fläche verschwinden** disappear from the scene. **B∼hauer** *m* -s,- sculptor. **B∼hauerei** *f* - sculpture. **b∼hübsch** *a* very pretty. **b∼lich** *a* pictorial; *(figurativ)* figurative, *adv* -ly. **B∼nis** *nt* -ses,-se portrait. **B∼schirm** *m (TV)* screen. **B∼schirmgerät** *nt* visual display unit, VDU. **b∼schön** *a* very beautiful

Bildung *f* - formation; *(Erziehung)* education; *(Kultur)* culture

Billard /'bɪljart/ *nt* -s billiards *sg*. **B∼tisch** *m* billiard table

Billett /bɪl'jɛt/ *nt* -[e]s,-e & -s ticket

Billiarde *f* -,-n thousand million million

billig *a* cheap, *adv* -ly; *(dürftig)* poor; *(gerecht)* just; **recht und b∼** right and proper. **b∼en** *vt* approve. **B∼ung** *f* - approval

Billion /br'ljo:n/ *f* -,-en million million, billion

bimmeln *vi (haben)* tinkle

Bimsstein *m* pumice stone

bin *s.* **sein; ich bin** I am

Binde *f* -,-n band; *(Verband)* bandage; *(Damen-)* sanitary towel. **B∼hautentzündung** *f* conjunctivitis. **b∼n**† *vt* tie (**an** + *acc* to); make

⟨*Strauß*⟩; bind ⟨*Buch*⟩; (*fesseln*) tie up; (*Culin*) thicken; **sich b~en** commit oneself. **b~nd** *a* (*fig*) binding. **B~strich** *m* hyphen. **B~wort** *nt* (*pl* **-wörter**) (*Gram*) conjunction

Bind|faden *m* string; **ein B~faden** a piece of string. **B~ung** *f* **-,-en** (*fig*) tie, bond; (*Beziehung*) relationship; (*Verpflichtung*) commitment; (*Ski-*) binding; (*Tex*) weave

binnen *prep* (+ *dat*) within; **b~ kurzem** shortly. **B~handel** *m* home trade

Binse *f* **-,-n** (*Bot*) rush. **B~nwahrheit, B~nweisheit** *f* truism

Bio- *pref* organic

Bio|chemie *f* biochemistry. **b~dynamisch** *m* organic

Biographie *f* **-,-n** biography

Bio|hof *m* organic farm. **B~laden** *m* health-food store

Biolog|e *m* **-n,-n** biologist. **B~ie** *f* **-** biology. **b~isch** *a* biological, *adv* -ly; **b~ischer Anbau** organic farming; **b~isch angebaut** organically grown

Birke *f* **-,-n** birch [tree]

Birm|a *nt* **-s** Burma. **b~anisch** *a* Burmese

Birn|baum *m* pear-tree. **B~e** *f* **-,-n** pear; (*Electr*) bulb

bis *prep* (+ *acc*) as far as, [up] to; (*zeitlich*) until, till; (*spätestens*) by; **bis zu** up to; **bis jetzt** up to now, so far; **bis dahin** until/(*spätestens*) by then; **bis auf** (+ *acc*) (*einschließlich*) [down] to; (*ausgenommen*) except [for]; **drei bis vier Mark** three to four marks; **bis morgen!** see you tomorrow! ● *conj* until

Bischof *m* **-s,̈ e** bishop

bisher *adv* so far, up to now. **b~ig** *attrib a* (*Präsident*) outgoing; **meine b~igen Erfahrungen** my experiences so far

Biskuit|rolle /bɪsˈkviːt-/ *f* Swiss roll. **B~teig** *m* sponge mixture

bislang *adv* so far, up to now

Biß *m* **-sses,-sse** bite

bißchen *inv pron* **ein b~** a bit, a little; **ein b~ Brot** a bit of bread; **kein b~** not a bit

Biss|en *m* **-s,-** bite, mouthful. **b~ig** *a* vicious; (*fig*) caustic

bist *s.* **sein; du b~** you are

Bistum *nt* **-s,̈ er** diocese, see

bisweilen *adv* from time to time

bitt|e *adv* please; (*nach Klopfen*) come in; (*als Antwort auf 'danke'*)

don't mention it, you're welcome; **wie b~e?** pardon? (*empört*) I beg your pardon? **möchten Sie Kaffee?—ja b~e** would you like some coffee?—yes please. **B~e** *f* **-,-n** request/(*dringend*) plea (**um** for). **b~en†** *vt/i* (*haben*) ask/(*dringend*) beg (**um** for); (*einladen*) invite, ask; **ich b~e dich!** I beg [of] you! (*empört*) I ask you! **b~end** *a* pleading, *adv* -ly

bitter *a* bitter, *adv* -ly. **B~keit** *f* **-** bitterness. **b~lich** *adv* bitterly

Bittschrift *f* petition

bizarr *a* bizarre, *adv* -ly

bläh|en *vt* swell; puff out ⟨*Vorhang*⟩; **sich b~en** swell; ⟨*Vorhang, Segel:*⟩ billow ● *vi* (*haben*) cause flatulence. **B~ungen** *fpl* flatulence *sg*, (*fam*) wind *sg*

Blamage /blaˈmaːʒə/ *f* **-,-n** humiliation; (*Schande*) disgrace

blamieren *vt* disgrace; **sich b~** disgrace oneself; (*sich lächerlich machen*) make a fool of oneself

blanchieren /blãˈʃiːrən/ *vt* (*Culin*) blanch

blank *a* shiny; (*nackt*) bare; **b~ sein** (*fam*) be broke. **B~oscheck** *m* blank cheque

Blase *f* **-,-n** bubble; (*Med*) blister; (*Anat*) bladder. **B~balg** *m* **-[e]s,̈ e** bellows *pl.* **b~n†** *vt/i* (*haben*) blow; play ⟨*Flöte*⟩. **B~nentzündung** *f* cystitis

Bläser *m* **-s,-** (*Mus*) wind player; **die B~** the wind section *sg*

blasiert *a* blasé

Blas|instrument *nt* wind instrument. **B~kapelle** *f* brass band

Blasphemie *f* **-** blasphemy

blaß *a* (**blasser, blassest**) pale; (*schwach*) faint; **b~ werden** turn pale

Blässe *f* **-** pallor

Blatt *nt* **-[e]s,̈ er** (*Bot*) leaf; (*Papier*) sheet; (*Zeitung*) paper; **kein B~ vor den Mund nehmen** (*fig*) not mince one's words

blätter|n *vi* (*haben*) **b~n in** (+ *dat*) leaf through. **B~teig** *m* puff pastry

Blattlaus *f* greenfly

blau *a*, **B~** *nt* **-s,-** blue; **b~er Fleck** bruise; **b~es Auge** black eye; **b~ sein** (*fam*) be tight; **Fahrt ins B~e** mystery tour. **B~beere** *f* bilberry. **B~licht** *nt* blue flashing light. **b~machen** *vi sep* (*haben*) (*fam*) skive off work

Blech *nt* **-[e]s,-e** sheet metal; (*Weiß-*) tin; (*Platte*) metal sheet; (*Back-*) baking sheet; (*Mus*) brass; (*fam: Unsinn*) rubbish. **b~en** *vt/i* (*haben*) (*fam*) pay. **B~[blas]instrument** *nt* brass instrument. **B~schaden** *m* (*Auto*) damage to the bodywork

Blei *nt* **-[e]s** lead

Bleibe *f* - place to stay. **b~n†** *vi* (*sein*) remain, stay; (*übrig-*) be left; **ruhig b~n** keep calm; **bei etw b~n** (*fig*) stick to sth; **b~n Sie am Apparat** hold the line. **b~nd** *a* permanent; (*anhaltend*) lasting. **b~nlassen†** *vt sep* **etw b~nlassen** not do sth; (*aufhören*) stop doing sth

bleich *a* pale. **b~en†** *vi* (*sein*) bleach; (*ver-*) fade ● *vt* (*reg*) bleach. **B~mittel** *nt* bleach

blei|ern *a* leaden. **b~frei** *a* unleaded. **B~stift** *m* pencil. **B~stiftabsatz** *m* stiletto heel. **B~stiftspitzer** *m* **-s,-** pencil-sharpener

Blende *f* **-,-n** shade, shield; (*Sonnen-*) [sun] visor; (*Phot*) diaphragm; (*Öffnung*) aperture; (*an Kleid*) facing. **b~n** *vt* dazzle, blind. **b~nd** *a* (*fig*) dazzling; (*prima*) marvellous, *adv* -ly

Blick *m* **-[e]s,-e** look; (*kurz*) glance; (*Aussicht*) view; **auf den ersten B~** at first sight; **einen B~ für etw haben** (*fig*) have an eye for sth. **b~en** *vi* (*haben*) look/(*kurz*) glance (**auf** + *acc* at). **B~punkt** *m* (*fig*) point of view

blind *a* blind; (*trübe*) dull; **b~er Alarm** false alarm; **b~er Passagier** stowaway. **B~darm** *m* appendix. **B~darmentzündung** *f* appendicitis. **B~e(r)** *m/f* blind man/woman; **die B~en** the blind *pl*. **B~enhund** *m* guide-dog. **B~enschrift** *f* braille. **B~gänger** *m* **-s,-** (*Mil*) dud. **B~heit** *f* - blindness. **b~lings** *adv* (*fig*) blindly

blink|en *vi* (*haben*) flash; (*funkeln*) gleam; (*Auto*) indicate. **B~er** *m* **-s,-** (*Auto*) indicator. **B~licht** *nt* flashing light

blinzeln *vi* (*haben*) blink

Blitz *m* **-es,-e** [flash of] lightning; (*Phot*) flash; **ein B~ aus heiterem Himmel** (*fig*) a bolt from the blue. **B~ableiter** *m* lightning-conductor. **b~artig** *a* lightning ... ● *adv* like lightning. **B~birne** *f* flashbulb. **b~en** *vi* (*haben*) flash; (*funkeln*) sparkle; **es hat geblitzt** there was a flash of lightning. **B~gerät** *nt* flash [unit]. **B~licht** *nt* (*Phot*) flash. **b~sauber** *a*

spick and span. **b~schnell** *a* lightning ... ● *adv* like lightning. **B~strahl** *m* flash of lightning

Block *m* **-[e]s,̈e** block ● **-[e]s,-s** & **̈e** (*Schreib-*) [note-]pad; (*Häuser-*) block; (*Pol*) bloc

Blockade *f* **-,-n** blockade

Blockflöte *f* recorder

blockieren *vt* block; (*Mil*) blockade

Blockschrift *f* block letters *pl*

blöd[e] *a* feeble-minded; (*dumm*) stupid, *adv* -ly

Blödsinn *m* **-[e]s** idiocy; (*Unsinn*) nonsense. **b~ig** *a* feeble-minded; (*verrückt*) idiotic

blöken *vi* (*haben*) bleat

blond *a* fair-haired; ⟨*Haar*⟩ fair. **B~ine** *f* **-,-n** blonde

bloß *a* bare; (*alleinig*) mere; **mit b~em Auge** with the naked eye ● *adv* only, just; **was mache ich b~?** whatever shall I do?

Blöße *f* **-,-n** nakedness; **sich** (*dat*) **eine B~ geben** (*fig*) show a weakness

bloß|legen *vt sep* uncover; **b~stellen** *vt sep* compromise; **sich b~stellen** show oneself up

Bluff *m* **-s,-s** bluff. **b~en** *vt/i* (*haben*) bluff

blühen *vi* (*haben*) flower; (*fig*) flourish. **b~d** *a* flowering; (*fig*) flourishing, thriving; ⟨*Phantasie*⟩ fertile

Blume *f* **-,-n** flower; (*vom Wein*) bouquet. **B~nbeet** *nt* flower-bed. **B~ngeschäft** *nt* flower-shop, florist's [shop]. **B~nkohl** *m* cauliflower. **B~nmuster** *nt* floral design. **B~nstrauß** *m* bunch of flowers. **B~ntopf** *m* flowerpot; (*Pflanze*) [flowering] pot plant. **B~nzwiebel** *f* bulb

blumig *a* (*fig*) flowery

Bluse *f* **-,-n** blouse

Blut *nt* **-[e]s** blood. **b~arm** *a* anaemic. **B~bahn** *f* bloodstream. **b~befleckt** *a* blood-stained. **B~bild** *nt* blood count. **B~buche** *f* copper beech. **B~druck** *m* blood pressure. **b~dürstig** *a* bloodthirsty

Blüte *f* **-,-n** flower, bloom; (*vom Baum*) blossom; (*B~zeit*) flowering period; (*Baum-*) blossom time; (*fig*) flowering; (*Höhepunkt*) peak, prime; (*fam: Banknote*) forged note, (*fam*) dud

Blut|egel *m* **-s,-** leech. **b~en** *vi* (*haben*) bleed

Blüten|blatt *nt* petal. **B~staub** *m* pollen

Blut|er *m* **-s,-** haemophiliac. **B~erguß** *m* bruise. **B~gefäß** *nt* blood-vessel. **B~gruppe** *f* blood group. **B~hund** *m* bloodhound. **b~ig** *a* bloody. **b~jung** *a* very young. **B~körperchen** *nt* **-s,-** [blood] corpuscle. **B~probe** *f* blood test. **b~rünstig** *a* (*fig*) bloody, gory; ⟨*Person*⟩ bloodthirsty. **B~schande** *f* incest. **B~spender** *m* blood donor. **B~sturz** *m* haemorrhage. **B~sverwandte(r)** *m/f* blood relation. **B~transfusion, B~übertragung** *f* blood transfusion. **B~ung** *f* **-,-en** bleeding; (*Med*) haemorrhage; (*Regel-*) period. **b~unterlaufen** *a* bruised; ⟨*Auge*⟩ bloodshot. **B~vergießen** *nt* **-s** bloodshed. **B~vergiftung** *f* blood-poisoning. **B~wurst** *f* black pudding

Bö *f* **-,-en** gust; (*Regen-*) squall

Bob *m* **-s,-s** bob[-sleigh]

Bock *m* **-[e]s,¨e** buck; (*Ziege*) billy goat; (*Schaf*) ram; (*Gestell*) support; **einen B~ schießen** (*fam*) make a blunder. **b~en** *vi* (*haben*) ⟨*Pferd:*⟩ buck; ⟨*Kind:*⟩ be stubborn. **b~ig** *a* (*fam*) stubborn. **B~springen** *nt* leap-frog

Boden *m* **-s,¨** ground; (*Erde*) soil; (*Fuß-*) floor; (*Grundfläche*) bottom; (*Dach-*) loft, attic. **B~kammer** *f* attic [room]. **b~los** *a* bottomless; (*fam*) incredible. **B~satz** *m* sediment. **B~schätze** *mpl* mineral deposits. **B~see (der)** Lake Constance

Bogen *m* **-s,- &** ¨ curve; (*Geom*) arc; (*beim Skilauf*) turn; (*Archit*) arch; (*Waffe, Geigen-*) bow; (*Papier*) sheet; **einen großen B~ um jdn/etw machen** (*fam*) give s.o./sth a wide berth. **B~gang** *m* arcade. **B~schießen** *nt* archery

Bohle *f* **-,-n** [thick] plank

Böhm|en *nt* **-s** Bohemia. **b~isch** *a* Bohemian

Bohne *f* **-,-n** bean; **grüne B~n** French beans. **B~nkaffee** *m* real coffee

bohner|n *vt* polish. **B~wachs** *nt* floor-polish

bohr|en *vt/i* (*haben*) drill (**nach** for); drive ⟨*Tunnel*⟩; sink ⟨*Brunnen*⟩; ⟨*Insekt:*⟩ bore; **in der Nase b~en** pick one's nose. **B~er** *m* **-s,-** drill. **B~insel** *f* [offshore] drilling rig. **B~maschine** *f* electric drill. **B~turm** *m* derrick

Boje *f* **-,-n** buoy

Böllerschuß *m* gun salute

Bolzen *m* **-s,-** bolt; (*Stift*) pin

bombardieren *vt* bomb; (*fig*) bombard (**mit** with)

bombastisch *a* bombastic

Bombe *f* **-,-n** bomb. **B~nangriff** *m* bombing raid. **B~nerfolg** *m* huge success. **B~r** *m* **-s,-** (*Aviat*) bomber

Bon /bɔŋ/ *m* **-s,-s** voucher; (*Kassen-*) receipt

Bonbon /bɔŋ'bɔŋ/ *m & nt* **-s,-s** sweet

Bonus *m* **-[sses],-[sse]** bonus

Boot *nt* **-[e]s,-e** boat. **B~ssteg** *m* landing-stage

Bord¹ *nt* **-[e]s,-e** shelf

Bord² *m* (*Naut*) **an B~** aboard, on board; **über B~** overboard. **B~buch** *nt* log[-book]

Bordell *nt* **-s,-e** brothel

Bord|karte *f* boarding-pass. **B~stein** *m* kerb

borgen *vt* borrow; **jdm etw b~** lend s.o. sth

Borke *f* **-,-n** bark

borniert *a* narrow-minded

Börse *f* **-,-n** purse; (*Comm*) stock exchange. **B~nmakler** *m* stockbroker

Borst|e *f* **-,-n** bristle. **b~ig** *a* bristly

Borte *f* **-,-n** braid

bösartig *a* vicious; (*Med*) malignant

Böschung *f* **-,-en** embankment; (*Hang*) slope

böse *a* wicked, evil; (*unartig*) naughty; (*schlimm*) bad, *adv* -ly; (*zornig*) cross; **jdm** *od* **auf jdn b~ sein** be cross with s.o. **B~wicht** *m* **-[e]s,-e** villain; (*Schlingel*) rascal

bos|haft *a* malicious, *adv* -ly; (*gehässig*) spiteful, *adv* -ly. **B~heit** *f* **-,-en** malice; spite; (*Handlung*) spiteful act/(*Bemerkung*) remark

böswillig *a* malicious, *adv* -ly. **B~keit** *f* -malice

Botani|k *f* - botany. **B~ker(in)** *m* **-s,-** (*f* **-,-nen**) botanist. **b~sch** *a* botanical

Bot|e *m* **-n,-n** messenger. **B~engang** *m* errand. **B~schaft** *f* **-,-en** message; (*Pol*) embassy. **B~schafter** *m* **-s,-** ambassador

Bottich *m* **-[e]s,-e** vat; (*Wasch-*) tub

Bouillon /bʊl'jɔŋ/ *f* **-,-s** clear soup. **B~würfel** *m* stock cube

Bowle /'boːlə/ *f* **-,-n** punch

box|en *vi* (*haben*) box ● *vt* punch. **B~en** *nt* **-s** boxing. **B~er** *m* **-s,-** boxer. **B~kampf** *m* boxing match; (*Boxen*) boxing

Boykott *m* **-[e]s,-s** boycott. **b~ieren** *vt* boycott; (*Comm*) black

brachliegen† *vi sep* (*haben*) lie fallow

Branche /'brãːʃə/ *f* -**,-n** [line of] business. **B~nverzeichnis** *nt* (*Teleph*) classified directory

Brand *m* -**[e]s,-̈e** fire; (*Med*) gangrene; (*Bot*) blight; **in B~** *geraten* catch fire; **in B~** *setzen od* **stecken** set on fire. **B~bombe** *f* incendiary bomb

branden *vi* (*haben*) surge; (*sich brechen*) break

Brand|geruch *m* smell of burning. **b~marken** *vt* (*fig*) brand. **B~stifter** *m* arsonist. **B~stiftung** *f* arson

Brandung *f* - surf. **B~sreiten** *nt* surfing

Brand|wunde *f* burn. **B~zeichen** *nt* brand

Branntwein *m* spirit; (*coll*) spirits *pl*. **B~brennerei** *f* distillery

bras|ilianisch *a* Brazilian. **B~ilien** /-jən/ *nt* -**s** Brazil

Brat|apfel *m* baked apple. **b~en**† *vt/i* (*haben*) roast; (*in der Pfanne*) fry. **B~en** *m* -**s,-** roast; (*B~stück*) joint. **B~ensoße** *f* gravy. **b~fertig** *a* oven-ready. **B~hähnchen, B~huhn** *nt* roast/(*zum Braten*) roasting chicken. **B~kartoffeln** *fpl* fried potatoes. **B~klops** *m* rissole. **B~pfanne** *f* frying-pan

Bratsche *f* -**,-n** (*Mus*) viola

Brat|spieß *m* spit. **B~wurst** *f* sausage for frying; (*gebraten*) fried sausage

Brauch *m* -**[e]s, Bräuche** custom. **b~bar** *a* usable; (*nützlich*) useful. **b~en** *vt* need; (*ge-, verbrauchen*) use; take (*Zeit*); **er b~t es nur zu sagen** he only has to say; **du b~st nicht zu gehen** you needn't go

Braue *f* -**,-n** eyebrow

brau|en *vt* brew. **B~er** *m* -**s,-** brewer. **B~erei** *f* -**,-en** brewery

braun *a*, **B~** *nt* -**s,-** brown; **b~ werden** (*Person.*) get a tan

Bräune *f* - [sun-]tan. **b~n** *vt/i* (*haben*) brown; (*in der Sonne*) tan

braungebrannt *a* [sun-]tanned

Braunschweig *nt* -**s** Brunswick

Brause *f* -**,-n** (*Dusche*) shower; (*an Gießkanne*) rose; (*B~limonade*) fizzy drink. **b~n** *vi* (*haben*) roar; (*duschen*) shower ● *vi* (*sein*) rush [along] ● *vr* **sich b~n** shower. **b~nd** *a* roaring; (*sprudelnd*) effervescent

Braut *f* -**,-̈e** bride; (*Verlobte*) fiancée

Bräutigam *m* -**s,-e** bridegroom; (*Verlobter*) fiancé

Brautkleid *nt* wedding dress

bräutlich *a* bridal

Brautpaar *nt* bridal couple; (*Verlobte*) engaged couple

brav *a* good, well-behaved; (*redlich*) honest ● *adv* dutifully; (*redlich*) honestly

bravo *int* bravo!

BRD *abbr* (**Bundesrepublik Deutschland**) FRG

Brech|eisen *nt* jemmy; (*B~stange*) crowbar. **b~en**† *vt* break; (*Phys*) refract (*Licht*); (*erbrechen*) vomit; **sich b~en** (*Wellen:*) break; (*Licht:*) be refracted; **sich** (*dat*) **den Arm b~en** break one's arm ● *vi* (*sein*) break ● *vi* (*haben*) vomit, be sick; **mit jdm b~en** (*fig*) break with s.o. **B~er** *m* -**s,-** breaker. **B~reiz** *m* nausea. **B~stange** *f* crowbar

Brei *m* -**[e]s,-e** paste; (*Culin*) purée; (*Grieß-*) pudding; (*Hafer-*) porridge. **b~ig** *a* mushy

breit *a* wide; (*Schultern, Grinsen*) broad ● *adv* **b~ grinsen** grin broadly. **b~beinig** *a & adv* with legs apart. **B~e** *f* -**,-n** width; breadth; (*Geog*) latitude. **b~en** *vt* spread (**über** + *acc* over). **B~engrad** *m* [degree of] latitude. **B~enkreis** *m* parallel. **B~seite** *f* long side; (*Naut*) broadside

Bremse¹ *f* -**,-n** horsefly

Bremse² *f* -**,-n** brake. **b~n** *vt* slow down; (*fig*) restrain ● *vi* (*haben*) brake

Bremslicht *nt* brake-light

brenn|bar *a* combustible; **leicht b~bar** highly [in]flammable. **b~en**† *vi* (*haben*) burn; (*Licht:*) be on; (*Zigarette:*) be alight; (*weh tun*) smart, sting; **es b~t in X** there's a fire in X; **darauf b~en, etw zu tun** be dying to do sth ● *vt* burn; (*rösten*) roast; (*im Brennofen*) fire; (*destillieren*) distil. **b~end** *a* burning; (*angezündet*) lighted; (*fig*) fervent ● *adv* **ich würde b~end gern . . .** I'd love to . . . **B~erei** *f* -**,-en** distillery

Brennessel *f* -**,-n** stinging nettle

Brenn|holz *nt* firewood. **B~ofen** *m* kiln. **B~punkt** *m* (*Phys*) focus; **im B~punkt des Interesses stehen** be the focus of attention. **B~spiritus** *m* methylated spirits. **B~stoff** *m* fuel

brenzlig *a* (*fam*) risky; **b~er Geruch** smell of burning

Bresche f -,-n (fig) breach
Bretagne /bre'tanjə/ **(die)** - Brittany
Brett nt -[e]s,-er board; (im Regal) shelf; **schwarzes B~** notice board. **B~chen** nt -s,- slat; (Frühstücks-) small board (used as plate). **B~spiel** nt board game
Brezel f -,-n pretzel
Bridge /brɪtʃ/ nt - (Spiel) bridge
Brief m -[e]s,-e letter. **B~beschwerer** m -s,- paperweight. **B~block** m writing pad. **B~freund(in)** m(f) pen-friend. **B~kasten** m letter-box, (Amer) mailbox. **B~kopf** m letter-head. **b~lich** a & adv by letter. **B~marke** f [postage] stamp. **B~öffner** m paper-knife. **B~papier** nt notepaper. **B~porto** nt letter rate. **B~tasche** f wallet. **B~träger** m postman, (Amer) mailman. **B~umschlag** m envelope. **B~wahl** f postal vote. **B~wechsel** m correspondence
Brigade f -,-n brigade
Brikett nt -s,-s briquette
brillan|t /brɪl'jant/ a brilliant, adv -ly. **B~t** m -en,-en [cut] diamond. **B~z** f - brilliance
Brille f -,-n glasses pl, spectacles pl; (Schutz-) goggles pl; (Klosett-) toilet seat
bringen† vt bring; (fort-) take; (ein-) yield; (veröffentlichen) publish; (im Radio) broadcast; show (Film); **ins Bett b~** put to bed; **jdn nach Hause b~** take/(begleiten) see s.o. home; **an sich (acc) b~** get possession of; **mit sich b~** entail; **um etw b~** deprive of sth; **etw hinter sich (acc) b~** get sth over [and done] with; **jdn dazu b~, etw zu tun** get s.o. to do sth; **es weit b~** (fig) go far
brisant a explosive
Brise f -,-n breeze
Brit|e m -n,-n, **B~in** f -,-nen Briton. **b~isch** a British
Bröck|chen nt -s,- (Culin) crouton. **b~elig** a crumbly; (Gestein) friable. **b~eln** vt/i (haben/sein) crumble
Brocken m -s,- chunk; (Erde, Kohle) lump; **ein paar B~ Englisch** (fam) a smattering of English
Brokat m -[e]s,-e brocade
Brokkoli pl broccoli sg
Brombeer|e f blackberry. **B~strauch** m bramble [bush]
Bronchitis f - bronchitis
Bronze /'brõːsə/ f -,-n bronze
Brosch|e f -,-n brooch. **b~iert** a paperback. **B~üre** f -,-n brochure; (Heft) booklet

Brösel mpl (Culin) breadcrumbs
Brot n -[e]s,-e bread; **ein B~** a loaf [of bread]; (Scheibe) a slice of bread; **sein B~ verdienen** (fig) earn one's living (mit by)
Brötchen n -s,- [bread] roll
Brot|krümel m breadcrumb. **B~verdiener** m breadwinner
Bruch m -[e]s,ːe break; (Brechen) breaking; (Rohr-) burst; (Med) fracture; (Eingeweide-) rupture, hernia; (Math) fraction; (fig) breach; (in Beziehung) break-up
brüchig a brittle
Bruch|landung f crash-landing. **B~rechnung** f fractions pl. **B~stück** nt fragment. **b~stückhaft** a fragmentary. **B~teil** m fraction
Brücke f -,-n bridge; (Teppich) rug
Bruder m -s,ː brother
brüderlich a brotherly, fraternal
Brügge nt -s Bruges
Brüh|e f -,-n broth; (Knochen-) stock; **klare B~e** clear soup. **b~en** vt scald; (auf-) make (Kaffee). **B~würfel** m stock cube
brüllen vt/i (haben) roar; (Kuh:) moo; (fam: schreien) bawl
brumm|eln vt/i (haben) mumble. **b~en** vi (haben) (Insekt:) buzz; (Bär:) growl; (Motor:) hum; (murren) grumble ● vt mutter. **B~er** m -s,- (fam) bluebottle. **b~ig** a (fam) grumpy, adv -ily
brünett a dark-haired. **B~e** f -,-n brunette
Brunnen m -s,- well; (Spring-) fountain; (Heil-) spa water. **B~kresse** f watercress
brüsk a brusque, adv -ly. **b~ieren** vt snub
Brüssel nt -s Brussels
Brust f -,ːe chest; (weibliche, Culin: B~stück) breast. **B~bein** nt breastbone. **B~beutel** m purse worn round the neck
brüsten (sich) vr boast
Brust|fellentzündung f pleurisy. **B~schwimmen** nt breast-stroke
Brüstung f -,-en parapet
Brustwarze f nipple
Brut f -,-en incubation; (Junge) brood; (Fisch-) fry
brutal a brutal, adv -ly. **B~ität** f -,-en brutality
brüten vi (haben) sit (on eggs); (fig) ponder (über + dat over); **b~de Hitze** oppressive heat

Brutkasten *m* (*Med*) incubator
brutto *adv*, **B~-** *pref* gross
brutzeln *vi* (*haben*) sizzle ● *vt* fry
Bub *m* **-en,-en** (*SGer*) boy. **B~e** *m* **-n,-n**
(*Karte*) jack, knave
Bubikopf *m* bob
Buch *nt* **-[e]s,¨er** book; **B~ führen** keep
a record (**über**+*acc* of); **die B~er**
führen keep the accounts. **B~drucker**
m printer
Buche *f* **-,-n** beech
buchen *vt* book; (*Comm*) enter
Bücher|bord, **B~brett** *nt* book-
shelf. **B~ei** *f* **-,-n** library. **B~regal**
nt bookcase, bookshelves *pl*. **B~-**
schrank *m* bookcase. **B~wurm** *m*
bookworm
Buchfink *m* chaffinch
Buch|führung *f* bookkeeping.
B~halter(in) *m* **-s,-** (*f* **-,-nen**) book-
keeper, accountant. **B~haltung** *f*
bookkeeping, accountancy; (*Abtei-*
lung) accounts department. **B~händ-**
ler(in) *m*(*f*) bookseller. **B~hand-**
lung *f* bookshop. **B~macher** *m* **-s,-**
bookmaker. **B~prüfer** *m* auditor
Büchse *f* **-,-n** box; (*Konserven-*) tin, can;
(*Gewehr*) [sporting] gun. **B~nmilch** *f*
evaporated milk. **B~nöffner** *m* tin
or can opener
Buch|stabe *m* **-ns,-n** letter. **b~sta-**
bieren *vt* spell [out]. **b~stäblich** *adv*
literally
Buchstützen *fpl* book-ends
Bucht *f* **-,-en** (*Geog*) bay
Buchung *f* **-,-en** booking, reservation;
(*Comm*) entry
Buckel *m* **-s,-** hump; (*Beule*) bump;
(*Hügel*) hillock; **einen B~ machen**
⟨*Katze:*⟩ arch its back
bücken (sich) *vr* bend down
bucklig *a* hunchbacked. **B~e(r)** *m/f*
hunchback
Bückling *m* **-s,-e** smoked herring;
(*fam: Verbeugung*) bow
buddeln *vt/i* (*haben*) (*fam*) dig
Buddhi|smus *m* - Buddhism. **B~t(in)**
m **-en,-en** (*f* **-,-nen**) Buddhist. **b~t-**
isch *a* Buddhist
Bude *f* **-,-n** hut; (*Kiosk*) kiosk; (*Markt-*)
stall; (*fam: Zimmer*) room; (*Studen-*
ten-) digs *pl*
Budget /by'dʒe:/ *nt* **-s,-s** budget
Büfett *nt* **-[e]s,-e** sideboard; (*Theke*)
bar; **kaltes B~** cold buffet
Büffel *m* **-s,-** buffalo. **b~n** *vt/i*
(*haben*) (*fam*) swot
Bug *m* **-[e]s,-e** (*Naut*) bow[s *pl*]

Bügel *m* **-s,-** frame; (*Kleider-*) coat-
hanger; (*Steig-*) stirrup; (*Brillen-*) side-
piece. **B~brett** *nt* ironing-board.
B~eisen *nt* iron. **B~falte** *f* crease.
b~frei *a* non-iron. **b~n** *vt/i* (*haben*)
iron
bugsieren *vt* (*fam*) manœuvre
buhen *vi* (*haben*) (*fam*) boo
Buhne *f* **-,-n** breakwater
Bühne *f* **-,-n** stage. **B~nbild** *nt* set.
B~neingang *m* stage door
Buhrufe *mpl* boos
Bukett *nt* **-[e]s,-e** bouquet
Bulette *f* **-,-n** [meat] rissole
Bulgarien /-ɪən/ *nt* **-s** Bulgaria
Bull|auge *nt* (*Naut*) porthole.
B~dogge *f* bulldog. **B~dozer**
/-do:zɐ/ *m* **-s,-** bulldozer. **B~e** *m* **-n,-n**
bull; (*sl: Polizist*) cop
Bummel|I *m* **-s,-** (*fam*) stroll. **B~lant**
m **-en,-en** (*fam*) dawdler; (*Faulenzer*)
loafer. **B~lei** *f* **-** (*fam*) dawdling;
(*Nachlässigkeit*) carelessness
bummel|ig *a* (*fam*) slow; (*nach-*
lässig) careless. **b~n** *vi* (*sein*) (*fam*)
stroll ● *vi* (*haben*) (*fam*) dawdle.
B~streik *m* go-slow. **B~zug** *m* (*fam*)
slow train
Bums *m* **-es,-e** (*fam*) bump, thump
Bund¹ *nt* **-[e]s,-e** bunch; (*Stroh-*) bundle
Bund² *m* **-[e]s,¨e** association; (*Bündnis*)
alliance; (*Pol*) federation; (*Rock-,*
Hosen-) waistband; **im B~e sein** be in
league (**mit** with); **der B~** the Federal
Government; (*fam: Bundeswehr*) the
[German] Army
Bündel *nt* **-s,-** bundle. **b~n** *vt* bundle
[up]
Bundes|- *pref* Federal. **B~genosse**
m ally. **B~kanzler** *m* Federal Chan-
cellor. **B~land** *nt* [federal] state;
(*Aust*) province. **B~liga** *f* German
national league. **B~rat** *m* Upper
House of Parliament. **B~regierung**
f Federal Government. **B~republik**
f **die B~republik Deutschland** the
Federal Republic of Germany.
B~straße *f* ≈ A road. **B~tag** *m*
Lower House of Parliament.
B~wehr *f* [Federal German] Army
bündig *a* & *adv* **kurz und b~ig** short
and to the point. **B~nis** *nt* **-sses,-sse**
alliance
Bunker *m* **-s,-** bunker; (*Luftschutz-*)
shelter
bunt *a* coloured; (*farbenfroh*) col-
ourful; (*grell*) gaudy; (*gemischt*) varied; (*wirr*) confused; **b~er Abend**

social evening; **b~e Platte** assorted cold meats ● *adv* **b~ durcheinander** higgledy-piggledy; **es zu b~ treiben** (*fam*) go too far. **B~stift** *m* crayon

Bürde *f* **-,-n** (*fig*) burden

Burg *f* **-,-en** castle

Bürge *m* **-n,-n** guarantor. **b~n** *vi* (*haben*) **b~n für** vouch for; (*fig*) guarantee

Bürger|(in) *m* **-s,-** (*f* **-,-nen**) citizen. **B~krieg** *m* civil war. **b~lich** *a* civil; ⟨*Pflicht*⟩ civic; (*mittelständisch*) middle-class; **b~liche Küche** plain cooking. **B~liche(r)** *m/f* commoner. **B~meister** *m* mayor. **B~rechte** *npl* civil rights. **B~steig** *m* **-[e]s,-e** pavement, (*Amer*) sidewalk

Burggraben *m* moat

Bürgschaft *f* **-,-en** surety; **B~ leisten** stand surety

Burgunder *m* **-s,-** (*Wein*) Burgundy

Burleske *f* **-,-n** burlesque

Büro *nt* **-s,-s** office. **B~angestellte(r)** *m/f* office-worker. **B~klammer** *f* paper-clip. **B~krat** *m* **-en,-en** bureaucrat. **B~kratie** *f* **-,-n** bureaucracy. **b~kratisch** *a* bureaucratic

Bursch|e *m* **-n,-n** lad, youth; (*fam: Kerl*) fellow. **b~ikos** *a* hearty; (*männlich*) mannish

Bürste *f* **-,-n** brush. **b~n** *vt* brush. **B~nschnitt** *m* crew cut

Bus *m* **-ses,-se** bus; (*Reise-*) coach. **B~bahnhof** *m* bus and coach station

Busch *m* **-[e]s,¨e** bush

Büschel *nt* **-s,-** tuft

buschig *a* bushy

Busen *m* **-s,-** bosom

Bussard *m* **-s,-e** buzzard

Buße *f* **-,-n** penance; (*Jur*) fine

büßen *vt/i* (*haben*) **[für] etw b~** atone for sth; (*fig: bezahlen*) pay for sth

buß|fertig *a* penitent. **B~geld** *nt* (*Jur*) fine

Büste *f* **-,-n** bust; (*Schneider-*) dummy. **B~nhalter** *m* **-s,-** bra

Butter *f* **-** butter. **B~blume** *f* buttercup. **B~brot** *nt* slice of bread and butter. **B~brotpapier** *nt* greaseproof paper. **B~faß** *nt* churn. **B~milch** *f* buttermilk. **b~n** *vi* (*haben*) make butter ● *vt* butter

b.w. *abbr* (**bitte wenden**) PTO

bzgl. *abbr s.* **bezüglich**

bzw. *abbr s.* **beziehungsweise**

C

ca. *abbr* (**circa**) about

Café /ka'fe:/ *nt* **-s,-s** café

Cafeteria /kafete'ri:a/ *f* **-,-s** cafeteria

camp|en /'kɛmpən/ *vi* (*haben*) go camping. **C~ing** *nt* **-s** camping. **C~ingplatz** *m* campsite

Cape /ke:p/ *nt* **-s,-s** cape

Caravan /'ka[:]ravan/ *m* **-s,-s** (*Auto*) caravan; (*Kombi*) estate car

Cassette /ka'sɛtə/ *f* **-,-n** cassette. **C~nrecorder** /-rekɔrdɐ/ *m* **-s,-** cassette recorder

CD /tse:'de:/ *f* **-,-s** compact disc, CD

Cell|ist(in) /tʃɛ'lıst(ın)/ *m* **-en,-en** (*f* **-,-nen**) cellist. **C~o** /'tʃɛlo/ *nt* **-,-los &** **-li** cello

Celsius /'tsɛlzjʊs/ *inv* Celsius, centigrade

Cembalo /'tʃɛmbalo/ *nt* **-s,-los &** **-li** harpsichord

Champagner /ʃam'panjɐ/ *m* **-s** champagne

Champignon /'ʃampınjɔŋ/ *m* **-s,-s** [field] mushroom

Chance /'ʃã:s[ə]/ *f* **-,-n** chance

Chaos /'ka:ɔs/ *nt* **-** chaos

chaotisch /ka'o:tıʃ/ *a* chaotic

Charakter /ka'raktɐ/ *m* **-s,-e** /-'te:rə/ character. **c~isieren** *vt* characterize. **c~istisch** *a* characteristic (**für** of), *adv* -ally

Charism|a /ka'rısma/ *nt* **-s** charisma. **c~atisch** *a* charismatic

charm|ant /ʃar'mant/ *a* charming, *adv* -ly. **C~e** /ʃarm/ *m* **-s** charm

Charter|flug /'tʃ-, 'ʃartɐ-/ *m* charter flight. **c~n** *vt* charter

Chassis /ʃa'si:/ *nt* **-,-** /-'si:[s], -'si:s/ chassis

Chauffeur /ʃɔ'fø:ɐ/ *m* **-s,-e** chauffeur; (*Taxi-*) driver

Chauvinis|mus /ʃovi'nısmʊs/ *m* **-** chauvinism. **C~t** *m* **-en,-en** chauvinist

Chef /ʃɛf/ *m* **-s,-s** head; (*fam*) boss

Chem|ie /çe'mi:/ *f* **-** chemistry. **C~ikalien** /-jən/ *fpl* chemicals

Chem|iker(in) /'çe:-/ *m* **-s,-** (*f* **-,-nen**) chemist. **c~isch** *a* chemical, *adv* -ly; **c~ische Reinigung** dry-cleaning; (*Geschäft*) dry-cleaner's

Chicorée /'ʃıkore:/ *m* **-s** chicory

Chiffr|e /'ʃɪfə, 'ʃɪfrə/ f -,-n cipher; (bei Annonce) box number. **c~iert** a coded

Chile /'çi:le/ nt -s Chile

Chin|a /'çi:na/ nt -s China. **C~ese** m -n,-n, **C~esin** f -,-nen Chinese. **c~esisch** a Chinese. **C~esisch** nt -[s] (Lang) Chinese

Chip /tʃɪp/ m -s,-s [micro]chip. **C~s** pl crisps, (Amer) chips

Chirurg /çi'rʊrk/ m -en,-en surgeon. **C~ie** /-'gi:/ f - surgery. **c~isch** /-g-/ a surgical, adv -ly

Chlor /klo:ɐ/ nt -s chlorine. **C~o-form** /kloro'fɔrm/ nt -s chloroform

Choke /tʃo:k/ m -s,-s (Auto) choke

Cholera /'ko:lera/ f - cholera

cholerisch /ko'le:rɪʃ/ a irascible

Cholesterin /ço-, kolɛste'ri:n/ nt -s cholesterol

Chor /ko:ɐ/ m -[e]s,"e choir; (Theat) chorus; **im C~** in chorus

Choral /ko'ra:l/ m -[e]s,"e chorale

Choreographie /koreogra'fi:/ f -,-n choreography

Chor|knabe /'ko:ɐ-/ m choirboy. **C~musik** f choral music

Christ /krɪst/ m -en,-en Christian. **C~baum** m Christmas tree. **C~entum** nt -s Christianity. **C~in** f -,-nen Christian. **C~kind** nt Christ-child; (als Geschenkbringer) ≈ Father Christmas. **c~lich** a Christian

Christus /'krɪstʊs/ m -ti Christ

Chrom /kro:m/ nt -s chromium

Chromosom /kromo'zo:m/ nt -s,-en chromosome

Chronik /'kro:nɪk/ f -,-en chronicle

chron|isch /'kro:nɪʃ/ a chronic, adv -ally. **c~ologisch** a chronological, adv -ly

Chrysantheme /kryzan'te:mə/ f -,-n chrysanthemum

circa /'tsɪrka/ adv about

Clique /'klɪka/ f -,-n clique

Clou /klu:/ m -s,-s highlight, (fam) high spot

Clown /klaʊn/ m -s,-s clown. **c~en** vi (haben) clown

Club /klʊp/ m -s,-s club

Cocktail /'kɔkte:l/ m -s,-s cocktail

Code /ko:t/ m -s,-s code

Cola /'ko:la/ f -,- (fam) Coke (P)

Comic-Heft /'kɔmɪk-/ nt comic

Computer /kɔm'pju:tɐ/ m -s,- computer. **c~isieren** vt computerize

Conférencier /kõferã'sje:/ m -s,-s compère

Cord /kɔrt/ m -s, **C~samt** m corduroy. **C~[samt]hose** f cords pl

Couch /kaʊtʃ/ f -,-es settee. **C~tisch** m coffee-table

Coupon /ku'põ:/ m -s,-s = **Kupon**

Cousin /ku'zɛ̃:/ m -s,-s [male] cousin. **C~e** /-'zi:nə/ f -,-n [female] cousin

Creme /kre:m/ f -s,-s cream; (Speise) cream dessert. **c~farben** a cream

cremig /'kre:mɪç/ a creamy

Curry /'kari, 'kœri/ nt & m -s curry powder ● nt -s,-s (Gericht) curry

D

da adv there; (hier) here; (zeitlich) then; (in dem Fall) in that case; **von da an** from then on ● conj as, since

dabehalten† vt sep keep there

dabei (emphatic: **dabei**) adv nearby; (daran) with it; (eingeschlossen) included; (hinsichtlich) about it; (während dem) during this; (gleichzeitig) at the same time; (doch) and yet; **dicht d~** close by; **d~ bleiben** (fig) remain adamant; **was ist denn d~?** (fam) so what? **d~sein†** vi sep (sein) be present; (mitmachen) be involved; **d~sein, etw zu tun** be just doing sth

dableiben† vi sep (sein) stay there

Dach nt -[e]s,"er roof. **D~boden** m loft. **D~gepäckträger** m roof-rack. **D~kammer** f attic room. **D~luke** f skylight. **D~rinne** f gutter

Dachs m -es,-e badger

Dach|sparren m -s,- rafter. **D~ziegel** m [roofing] tile

Dackel m -s,- dachshund

dadurch (emphatic: **dadurch**) adv through it/them; (Ursache) by it; (deshalb) because of that; **d~, daß** because

dafür (emphatic: **dafür**) adv for it/them; (anstatt) instead; (als Ausgleich) but [on the other hand]; (angesichts) considering that. **d~können†** vi sep (haben) **ich kann nichts dafür** it's not my fault

dagegen (emphatic: **dagegen**) adv against it/them; (Mittel, Tausch) for it; (verglichen damit) by comparison; (jedoch) however; **hast du was d~?** do you mind? **d~halten†** vt sep argue (daß that)

daheim adv at home

daher (emphatic: **daher**) adv from there; (deshalb) for that reason; **das**

kommt d~, weil that's because; **d~ meine Eile** hence my hurry ● *conj* that is why

dahin (*emphatic:* **dahin**) *adv* there; **bis d~** up to there; (*bis dann*) until/ (*Zukunft*) by then; **jdn d~ bringen, daß er etw tut** get s.o. to do sth; **d~ sein** (*fam*) be gone. **d~gehen**† *vi sep* (*sein*) walk along; ⟨*Zeit:*⟩ pass. **d~gestellt** *a* **d~gestellt lassen** (*fig*) leave open; **das bleibt d~gestellt** that remains to be seen

dahinten *adv* back there

dahinter (*emphatic:* **dahinter**) *adv* behind it/them. **d~kommen**† *vi sep* (*sein*) (*fig*) get to the bottom of it

Dahlie /-iə/ *f* -,-n dahlia

dalassen† *vt sep* leave there

daliegen† *vi sep* (*haben*) lie there

damalig *a* at that time; **der d~e Minister** the then minister

damals *adv* at that time

Damast *m* -es,-e damask

Dame *f* -,-n lady; (*Karte, Schach*) queen; (*D~spiel*) draughts *sg*, (*Amer*) checkers *sg*; (*Doppelstein*) king. **D~n- pref** ladies'/lady's ... **d~nhaft** *a* ladylike

damit (*emphatic:* **damit**) *adv* with it/ them; (*dadurch*) by it; **hör auf d~!** stop it! ● *conj* so that

dämlich *a* (*fam*) stupid, *adv* -ly

Damm *m* -[e]s,˙-e dam; (*Insel-*) causeway; **nicht auf dem D~** (*fam*) under the weather

dämmer|ig *a* dim; **es wird d~ig** dusk is falling. **D~licht** *nt* twilight. **d~n** *vi* (*haben*) ⟨*Morgen:*⟩ dawn; **der Abend d~t** dusk is falling; **es d~t** it is getting light; (*abends*) dark. **D~ung** *f* - dawn; (*Abend-*) dusk

Dämon *m* -s,-en /-'mo:nən/ demon

Dampf *m* -es,˙-e steam; (*Chem*) vapour. **d~en** *vi* (*haben*) steam

dämpfen *vt* (*Culin*) steam; (*fig*) muffle ⟨*Ton*⟩; lower ⟨*Stimme*⟩; dampen ⟨*Enthusiasmus*⟩

Dampf|er *m* -s,- steamer. **D~koch- topf** *m* pressure-cooker. **D~ maschine** *f* steam engine. **D~ walze** *f* steamroller

Damwild *nt* fallow deer *pl*

danach (*emphatic:* **danach**) *adv* after it/them; ⟨*suchen*⟩ for it/them; ⟨*riechen*⟩ of it; (*später*) afterwards; (*entsprechend*) accordingly; **es sieht d~ aus** it looks like it

Däne *m* -n,-n Dane

daneben (*emphatic:* **daneben**) *adv* beside it/them; (*außerdem*) in addition; (*verglichen damit*) by comparison. **d~gehen**† *vi sep* (*sein*) miss; (*scheitern*) fail

Dän|emark *nt* -s Denmark. **D~in** *f* -,-nen Dane. **d~isch** *a* Danish

Dank *m* -es thanks *pl*; **vielen D~!** thank you very much! **d~** *prep* (+ *dat or gen*) thanks to. **d~bar** *a* grateful, *adv* -ly; (*erleichtert*) thankful, *adv* -ly; (*lohnend*) rewarding. **D~barkeit** *f* - gratitude. **d~e** *adv* **d~e [schön od sehr]!** thank you [very much]! **[nein] d~e!** no thank you! **d~en** *vi* (*haben*) thank ⟨*jdm* s.o.⟩; (*ablehnen*) decline; **ich d~e!** no thank you! **nichts zu d~en!** don't mention it!

dann *adv* then; **d~ und wann** now and then; **nur/selbst d~, wenn** only/ even if

daran (*emphatic:* **daran**) *adv* on it/ them; at it/them; ⟨*denken*⟩ of it; **nahe d~** on the point (**etw zu tun** of doing sth); **denkt d~!** remember! **d~gehen**† *vi sep* (*sein*), **d~machen (sich)** *vr sep* set about (**etw zu tun** doing sth). **d~setzen** *vt sep* alles **d~setzen** do one's utmost (**zu** to)

darauf (*emphatic:* **darauf**) *adv* on it/ them; ⟨*warten*⟩ for it; ⟨*antworten*⟩ to it; (*danach*) after that; (*d~hin*) as a result; **am Tag d~** the day after. **d~folgend** *a* following. **d~hin** *adv* as a result

daraus (*emphatic:* **daraus**) *adv* out of or from it/them; **er macht sich nichts d~** he doesn't care for it; **was ist d~ geworden?** what has become of it?

Darbietung *f* -,-en performance; (*Nummer*) item

darin (*emphatic:* **darin**) *adv* in it/them

darlegen *vt sep* expound; (*erklären*) explain

Darlehen *nt* -s,- loan

Darm *m* -[e]s,˙-e intestine; (*Wurst-*) skin. **D~grippe** *f* gastric flu

darstell|en *vt sep* represent; (*bildlich*) portray; (*Theat*) interpret; (*spielen*) play; (*schildern*) describe. **D~er** *m* -s,- actor. **D~erin** *f* -,-nen actress. **D~ung** *f* representation; interpretation; description; (*Bericht*) account

darüber (*emphatic:* **darüber**) *adv* over it/them; (*höher*) above it/them; ⟨*sprechen, lachen, sich freuen*⟩ about it;

(*mehr*) more; (*inzwischen*) in the meantime; **d~ hinaus** beyond [it]; (*dazu*) on top of that

darum (*emphatic:* **darum**) *adv* round it/them; ⟨*bitten, kämpfen*⟩ for it; (*deshalb*) that is why; **d~, weil** because

darunter (*emphatic:* **darunter**) *adv* under it/them; (*tiefer*) below it/them; (*weniger*) less; (*dazwischen*) among them

das *def art & pron s.* **der**

dasein† *vi sep* (*sein*) be there/(*hier*) here; (*existieren*) exist; **wieder d~** be back; **noch nie dagewesen** unprecedented. **D~** *nt* **-s** existence

dasitzen† *vi sep* (*haben*) sit there

dasjenige *pron s.* **derjenige**

daß *conj* that; **daß du nicht fällst!** mind you don't fall!

dasselbe *pron s.* **derselbe**

dastehen† *vi sep* (*haben*) stand there; **allein d~** (*fig*) be alone

Daten|sichtgerät *nt* visual display unit, VDU. **D~verarbeitung** *f* data processing

datieren *vt/i* (*haben*) date

Dativ *m* **-s,-e** dative. **D~objekt** *nt* indirect object

Dattel *f* **-,-n** date

Datum *nt* **-s,-ten** date; **Daten** (*Angaben*) data

Dauer *f* **-** duration, length; (*Jur*) term; **von D~** lasting; **auf die D~** in the long run. **D~auftrag** *m* standing order. **d~haft** *a* lasting, enduring; (*fest*) durable. **D~karte** *f* season ticket. **D~lauf** *m* **im D~lauf** at a jog. **D~milch** *f* long-life milk. **d~n** *vi* (*haben*) last; **lange d~n** take a long time. **d~nd** *a* lasting; (*ständig*) constant, *adv* -ly; **d~nd fragen** keep asking. **D~stellung** *f* permanent position. **D~welle** *f* perm. **D~wurst** *f* salami-type sausage

Daumen *m* **-s,-** thumb; **jdm den D~ drücken** *od* **halten** keep one's fingers crossed for s.o.

Daunen *fpl* down *sg.* **D~decke** *f* [down-filled] duvet

davon (*emphatic:* **davon**) *adv* from it/them; (*dadurch*) by it; (*damit*) with it/them; (*darüber*) about it; (*Menge*) of it/them; **die Hälfte d~** half of it/them; **das kommt d~!** it serves you right! **d~kommen†** *vi sep* (*sein*) escape (**mit dem Leben** with one's life). **d~laufen†** *vi sep* (*sein*) run away. **d~machen (sich)** *vr sep* (*fam*) make

off. **d~tragen†** *vt sep* carry off; (*erleiden*) suffer; (*gewinnen*) win

davor (*emphatic:* **davor**) *adv* in front of it/them; ⟨*sich fürchten*⟩ of it; (*zeitlich*) before it/them

dazu (*emphatic:* **dazu**) *adv* to it/them; (*damit*) with it/them; (*dafür*) for it; **noch d~** in addition to that; **jdn d~ bringen, etw zu tun** get s.o. to do sth; **ich kam nicht d~** I didn't get round to [doing] it. **d~gehören** *vi sep* (*haben*) belong to it/them; **alles, was d~gehört** everything that goes with it. **d~kommen†** *vi sep* (*sein*) arrive [on the scene]; (*hinzukommen*) be added; **d~ kommt, daß er krank ist** on top of that he is ill. **d~rechnen** *vt sep* add to it/them

dazwischen (*emphatic:* **dazwischen**) *adv* between them; in between; (*darunter*) among them. **d~fahren†** *vi sep* (*sein*) (*fig*) intervene. **d~kommen†** *vi sep* (*sein*) (*fig*) crop up; **wenn nichts d~kommt** if all goes well. **d~reden** *vi sep* (*haben*) interrupt. **d~treten†** *vi sep* (*sein*) (*fig*) intervene

DDR *f* **-** *abbr* (**Deutsche Demokratische Republik**) GDR

Debat|te *f* **-,-n** debate; **zur D~te stehen** be at issue. **d~tieren** *vt/i* (*haben*) debate

Debüt /de'by:/ *nt* **-s,-s** début

dechiffrieren /deʃɪ'fri:rən/ *vt* decipher

Deck *nt* **-[e]s,-s** (*Naut*) deck; **an D~** on deck. **D~bett** *nt* duvet

Decke *f* **-,-n** cover; (*Tisch-*) table-cloth; (*Bett-*) blanket; (*Reise-*) rug; (*Zimmer-*) ceiling; **unter einer D~ stecken** (*fam*) be in league

Deckel *m* **-s,-** lid; (*Flaschen-*) top; (*Buch-*) cover

decken *vt* cover; tile ⟨*Dach*⟩; lay ⟨*Tisch*⟩; (*schützen*) shield; (*Sport*) mark; meet ⟨*Bedarf*⟩; **jdn d~** (*fig*) cover up for s.o.; **sich d~** (*fig*) cover oneself (**gegen** against); (*übereinstimmen*) coincide

Deck|mantel *m* (*fig*) pretence. **D~name** *m* pseudonym

Deckung *f* **-** (*Mil*) cover; (*Sport*) defence; (*Mann-*) marking; (*Boxen*) guard; (*Sicherheit*) security; **in D~ gehen** take cover

Defekt *m* **-[e]s,-e** defect. **d~** *a* defective

defensiv *a* defensive. **D~e** *f* - defensive

defilieren *vi* (*sein/haben*) file past

definieren *vt* define. **D~ition** /-'tsio:n/ *f* -,-en definition. **d~itiv** *a* definite, *adv* -ly

Defizit *nt* -s,-e deficit

Deflation /-'tsio:n/ *f* - deflation

deformiert *a* deformed

deftig *a* (*fam*) ⟨*Mahlzeit*⟩ hearty; ⟨*Witz*⟩ coarse

Degen *m* -s,- sword; (*Fecht-*) épée

degenerier|en *vi* (*sein*) degenerate. **d~t** *a* (*fig*) degenerate

degradieren *vt* (*Mil*) demote; (*fig*) degrade

dehn|bar *a* elastic. **d~en** *vt* stretch; lengthen ⟨*Vokal*⟩; **sich d~en** stretch

Deich *m* -[e]s,-e dike

Deichsel *f* -,-n pole; (*Gabel-*) shafts *pl*

dein *poss pron* your. **d~e(r,s)** *poss pron* yours; **die D~en** *pl* your family *sg*. **d~erseits** *adv* for your part. **d~etwegen** *adv* for your sake; (*wegen dir*) because of you, on your account. **d~etwillen** *adv* **um d~etwillen** for your sake. **d~ige** *poss pron* **der/die/das d~ige** yours. **d~s** *poss pron* yours

Deka *nt* -[s],- (*Aust*) = **Dekagramm**

dekaden|t *a* decadent. **D~z** *f* - decadence

Dekagramm *nt* (*Aust*) 10 grams; **10 D~** 100 grams

Dekan *m* -s,-e dean

Deklin|ation /-'tsio:n/ *f* -,-en declension. **d~ieren** *vt* decline

Dekolleté /dekɔl'te:/ *nt* -s,-s low neckline

Dekor *m* & *nt* -s decoration. **D~ateur** /-'tø:ɐ/ *m* -s,-e interior decorator; (*Schaufenster-*) window-dresser. **D~ation** /-'tsio:n/ *f* -,-en decoration; (*Schaufenster-*) window-dressing; (*Auslage*) display; **D~ationen** (*Theat*) scenery *sg*. **d~ativ** *a* decorative. **d~ieren** *vt* decorate; dress ⟨*Schaufenster*⟩

Deleg|ation /-'tsio:n/ *f* -,-en delegation. **d~ieren** *vt* delegate. **D~ierte(r)** *m/f* delegate

delikat *a* delicate; (*lecker*) delicious; (*taktvoll*) tactful, *adv* -ly. **D~esse** *f* -,-n delicacy. **D~essengeschäft** *nt* delicatessen

Delikt *nt* -[e]s,-e offence

Delinquent *m* -en,-en offender

Delirium *nt* -s delirium

Delle *f* -,-n dent

Delphin *m* -s,-e dolphin

Delta *nt* -s,-s delta

dem *def art & pron* s. **der**

Dement|i *nt* -s,-s denial. **d~ieren** *vt* deny

dem|entsprechend *a* corresponding; (*passend*) appropriate ● *adv* accordingly; (*passend*) appropriately. **d~gemäß** *adv* accordingly. **d~nach** *adv* according to that; (*folglich*) consequently. **d~nächst** *adv* soon; (*in Kürze*) shortly

Demokrat *m* -en,-en democrat. **D~ie** *f* -,-n democracy. **d~isch** *a* democratic, *adv* -ally

demolieren *vt* wreck

Demonstr|ant *m* -en,-en demonstrator. **D~ation** /-'tsio:n/ *f* -,-en demonstration. **d~ativ** *a* pointed, *adv* -ly; (*Gram*) demonstrative. **D~ativpronomen** *nt* demonstrative pronoun. **d~ieren** *vt/i* (*haben*) demonstrate

demontieren *vt* dismantle

demoralisieren *vt* demoralize

Demoskopie *f* - opinion research

Demut *f* - humility

demütig *a* humble, *adv* -bly. **d~en** *vt* humiliate; **sich d~en** humble oneself. **D~ung** *f* -,-en humiliation

demzufolge *adv* = **demnach**

den *def art & pron* s. **der**. **d~en** *pron* s. **der**

denk|bar *a* conceivable. **d~en†** *vt/i* (*haben*) think (**an** + *acc* of); (*sich erinnern*) remember (**an etw** *acc* sth); **für jdn gedacht** meant for s.o.; **das kann ich mir d~en** I can imagine [that]; **ich d~e nicht daran** I have no intention of doing it; **d~t daran!** don't forget! **D~mal** *nt* memorial; (*Monument*) monument. **d~würdig** *a* memorable. **D~zettel** *m* **jdm einen D~zettel geben** (*fam*) teach s.o. a lesson

denn *conj* for; **besser/mehr d~ je** better/more than ever ● *adv* **wie/wo d~?** but how/where? **warum d~ nicht?** why ever not? **es sei d~ [, daß]** unless

dennoch *adv* nevertheless

Denunz|iant *m* -en,-en informer. **d~ieren** *vt* denounce

Deodorant *nt* -s,-s deodorant

deplaciert /-'tsi:ɐt/ *a* (*fig*) out of place

Deponie *f* -,-n dump. **d~ren** *vt* deposit

deportieren *vt* deport

Depot /de'po:/ *nt* **-s,-s** depot; (*Lager*) warehouse; (*Bank-*) safe deposit

Depression *f* **-,-en** depression

deprimieren *vt* depress. **d∼d** *a* depressing

Deputation /-'tsio:n/ *f* **-,-en** deputation

der, die, das, *pl* **die** *def art* (*acc* **den, die, das,** *pl* **die;** *gen* **des, der, des,** *pl* **der;** *dat* **dem, der, dem,** *pl* **den**) the; **der Mensch** man; **die Natur** nature; **das Leben** life; **das Lesen/Tanzen** reading/dancing; **sich** (*dat*) **das Gesicht/die Hände waschen** wash one's face/hands; **5 Mark das Pfund** 5 marks a pound ● *pron* (*acc* **den, die, das,** *pl* **die;** *gen* **dessen, deren, dessen,** *pl* **deren;** *dat* **dem, der, dem,** *pl* **denen**) ● *dem pron* that; (*pl*) those; (*substantivisch*) he, she, it; (*Ding*) it; (*betont*) that; (*d∼jenige*) the one; (*pl*) they, those; (*Dinge*) those; (*diejenigen*) the ones; **der und der** such and such; **um die und die Zeit** at such and such a time; **das waren Zeiten!** those were the days! ● *rel pron* who; (*Ding*) which, that

derart *adv* so; (*so sehr*) so much. **d∼ig** *a* such ● *adv* = **derart**

derb *a* tough; (*kräftig*) strong; (*grob*) coarse, *adv* -ly; (*unsanft*) rough, *adv* -ly

deren *pron s.* **der**

dergleichen *inv a* such ● *pron* such a thing/such things; **nichts d∼** nothing of the kind; **und d∼** and the like

der-/die-/dasjenige, *pl* **diejenigen** *pron* the one; (*Person*) he, she; (*Ding*) it; (*pl*) those, the ones

dermaßen *adv* = **derart**

der-/die-/dasselbe, *pl* **dieselben** *pron* the same; **ein- und dasselbe** one and the same thing

derzeit *adv* at present

des *def art s.* **der**

Desert|eur /-'tø:ɐ̯/ *m* **-s,-e** deserter. **d∼ieren** *vi* (*sein/haben*) desert

desgleichen *adv* likewise ● *pron* the like

deshalb *adv* for this reason; (*also*) therefore

Designer(in) /di'zaɪnɐ, -nərɪn/ *m* **-s,- (**∼**-,-nen)** designer

Desin|fektion /dɛs?ɪnfɛk'tsio:n/ *f* - disinfecting. **D∼fektionsmittel** *nt* disinfectant. **d∼fizieren** *vt* disinfect

Desodorant *nt* **-s,-s** deodorant

Despot *m* **-en,-en** despot

dessen *pron s.* **der**

Dessert /dɛ'se:ɐ̯/ *nt* **-s,-s** dessert, sweet. **D∼löffel** *m* dessertspoon

Destill|ation /-'tsio:n/ *f* - distillation. **d∼ieren** *vt* distil

desto *adv* **je mehr/eher, d∼ besser** the more/sooner the better

destruktiv *a* (*fig*) destructive

deswegen *adv* = **deshalb**

Detail /de'taɪ/ *nt* **-s,-s** detail

Detektiv *m* **-s,-e** detective. **D∼roman** *m* detective story

Deton|ation /-'tsio:n/ *f* **-,-en** explosion. **d∼ieren** *vi* (*sein*) explode

deut|en *vt* interpret; predict ⟨*Zukunft*⟩ ● *vi* (*haben*) point (**auf** + *acc* at/(*fig*) to). **d∼lich** *a* clear, *adv* -ly; (*eindeutig*) plain, *adv* -ly. **D∼lichkeit** *f* - clarity

deutsch *a* German; **auf d∼** in German. **D∼** *nt* **-[s]** (*Lang*) German. **D∼e(r)** *m/f* German. **D∼land** *nt* **-s** Germany

Deutung *f* **-,-en** interpretation

Devise *f* **-,-n** motto. **D∼n** *pl* foreign currency *or* exchange *sg*

Dezember *m* **-s,-** December

dezent *a* unobtrusive, *adv* -ly; (*diskret*) discreet, *adv* -ly

Dezernat *nt* **-[e]s,-e** department

Dezimal|system *nt* decimal system. **D∼zahl** *f* decimal

dezimieren *vt* decimate

dgl. *abbr s.* **dergleichen**

d.h. *abbr* (**das heißt**) i.e.

Dia *nt* **-s,-s** (*Phot*) slide

Diabet|es *m* - diabetes. **D∼iker** *m* **-s,-** diabetic

Diadem *nt* **-s,-e** tiara

Diagnos|e *f* **-,-n** diagnosis. **d∼tizieren** *vt* diagnose

diagonal *a* diagonal, *adv* -ly. **D∼e** *f* **-,-n** diagonal

Diagramm *nt* **-s,-e** diagram; (*Kurven-*) graph

Diakon *m* **-s,-e** deacon

Dialekt *m* **-[e]s,-e** dialect

Dialog *m* **-[e]s,-e** dialogue

Diamant *m* **-en,-en** diamond

Diameter *m* **-s,-** diameter

Diapositiv *nt* **-s,-e** (*Phot*) slide

Diaprojektor *m* slide projector

Diät *f* **-,-en** (*Med*) diet. **d∼** *adv* **d∼ leben** be on a diet. **D∼assistent(in)** *m(f)* dietician

dich *pron* (*acc of* **du**) you; (*refl*) yourself

dicht *a* dense; (*dick*) thick; (*undurchlässig*) airtight; (*wasser-*) watertight ● *adv* densely; thickly; (*nahe*) close (**bei** to). **D~e** *f* - density. **d~en**[1] *vt* make watertight; (*ab-*) seal

d**icht|en**[2] *vi (haben)* write poetry. ● *vt* write, compose. **D~er(in)** *m* **-s,-** (*f* **-,-nen**) poet. **d~erisch** *a* poetic. **D~ung**[1] *f* **-,-en** poetry; (*Gedicht*) poem

Dichtung[2] *f* **-,-en** seal; (*Ring*) washer; (*Auto*) gasket

d**ick** *a* thick, *adv* -ly; (*beleibt*) fat; (*geschwollen*) swollen; (*fam: eng*) close; **d~ werden** get fat; **d~ machen** be fattening; **ein d~es Fell haben** (*fam*) be thick-skinned. **D~e** *f* **-,-n** thickness; (*D~leibigkeit*) fatness. **d~fellig** *a* (*fam*) thick-skinned. **d~flüssig** *a* thick; (*Phys*) viscous. **D~kopf** *m* (*fam*) stubborn person; **einen D~kopf haben** be stubborn. **d~köpfig** *a* (*fam*) stubborn

di**daktisch** *a* didactic

d**ie** *def art & pron s.* der

D**ieb|(in)** *m* **-[e]s,-e** (*f* **-,-nen**) thief. **d~isch** *a* thieving; (*Freude*) malicious. **D~stahl** *m* **-[e]s,̈e** theft; (*geistiger*) plagiarism

die**jenige** *pron s.* derjenige

D**iele** *f* **-,-n** floorboard; (*Flur*) hall

d**ien|en** *vi (haben)* serve. **D~er** *m* **-s,-** servant; (*Verbeugung*) bow. **D~erin** *f* **-,-nen** maid, servant. **d~lich** *a* helpful

D**ienst** *m* **-[e]s,-e** service; (*Arbeit*) work; (*Amtsausübung*) duty; **außer D~** off duty; (*pensioniert*) retired; **D~ haben** work; (*Soldat, Arzt:*) be on duty; **jdm einen schlechten D~ erweisen** do s.o. a disservice

D**ienstag** *m* Tuesday. **d~s** *adv* on Tuesdays

D**ienst|alter** *nt* seniority. **d~bereit** *a* obliging; (*Apotheke*) open. **D~bote** *m* servant. **d~eifrig** *a* zealous, *adv* - ly. **d~frei** *a* **d~freier Tag** day off; **d~frei haben** have time off; (*Soldat, Arzt:*) be off duty. **D~grad** *m* rank. **d~habend** *a* duty ... **D~leistung** *f* service. **d~lich** *a* official ● *adv* **d~lich verreist** away on business. **D~mädchen** *nt* maid. **D~reise** *f* business trip. **D~stelle** *f* office. **D~stunden** *fpl* office hours. **D~weg** *m* official channels *pl*

d**ies** *inv pron* this. **d~bezüglich** *a* relevant ● *adv* regarding this matter. **d~e(r,s)** *pron* this; (*pl*) these; (*substantivisch*) this [one]; (*pl*) these; **d~e Nacht** tonight; (*letzte*) last night

D**iesel** *m* **-[s],-** (*fam*) diesel

die**selbe** *pron s.* derselbe

D**iesel|kraftstoff** *m* diesel [oil]. **D~motor** *m* diesel engine

d**iesig** *a* hazy, misty

d**ies|mal** *adv* this time. **d~seits** *adv* & *prep* (+ *gen*) this side (of)

D**ietrich** *m* **-s,-e** skeleton key

D**iffam|ation** /-'tsio:n/ *f* - defamation. **d~ierend** *a* defamatory

D**ifferential** /-'tsia:l/ *nt* **-s,-e** differential

D**ifferenz** *f* **-,-en** difference. **d~ieren** *vt/i (haben)* differentiate (**zwischen** + *dat* between)

D**igital-** *pref* digital. **D~uhr** *f* digital clock/watch

D**ikt|at** *nt* **-[e]s,-e** dictation. **D~ator** *m* **-s,-en** /-'to:rən/ dictator. **d~atorisch** *a* dictatorial. **D~atur** *f* **-,-en** dictatorship. **d~ieren** *vt/i (haben)* dictate

D**ilemma** *nt* **-s,-s** dilemma

D**ilettant|(in)** *m* **-en,-en** (*f* **-,-nen**) dilettante. **d~isch** *a* amateurish

D**ill** *m* **-s** dill

D**imension** *f* **-,-en** dimension

D**ing** *nt* **-[e]s,-e** & (*fam*) thing; **guter D~e sein** be cheerful; **vor allen D~en** above all

D**inghi** /'dɪŋgi/ *nt* **-s,-s** dinghy

D**inosaurier** /-iɐ̯/ *m* **-s,-** dinosaur

D**iözese** *f* **-,-n** diocese

D**iphtherie** *f* - diphtheria

D**iplom** *nt* **-s,-e** diploma; (*Univ*) degree

D**iplomat** *m* **-en,-en** diplomat. **D~ie** *f* - diplomacy. **d~isch** *a* diplomatic, *adv* -ally

d**ir** *pron* (*dat of* **du**) [to] you; (*refl*) yourself; **ein Freund von dir** a friend of yours

d**irekt** *a* direct ● *adv* directly; (*wirklich*) really. **D~ion** /-'tsio:n/ *f* - management; (*Vorstand*) board of directors. **D~or** *m* **-s,-en** /-'to:rən/, **D~orin** *f* **-,-nen** director; (*Bank-, Theater-*) manager; (*Sch*) head; (*Gefängnis*) governor. **D~übertragung** *f* live transmission

D**irig|ent** *m* **-en,-en** (*Mus*) conductor. **d~ieren** *vt* direct; (*Mus*) conduct

D**irndl** *nt* **-s,-** dirndl [dress]

D**irne** *f* **-,-n** prostitute

D**iskant** *m* **-s,-e** (*Mus*) treble

D**iskette** *f* **-,-n** floppy disc

D**isko** *f* **-,-s** (*fam*) disco. **D~thek** *f* **-,-en** discothèque

D**iskrepanz** *f* **-,-en** discrepancy

diskret a discreet, adv -ly. **D~ion** /-'tsio:n/ f - discretion

diskriminier|en vt discriminate against. **D~ung** f - discrimination

Diskus m -,-se & **Disken** discus

Disku|ssion f -,-en discussion. **d~tieren** vt/i (haben) discuss

disponieren vi (haben) make arrangements; **d~ [können] über** (+ acc) have at one's disposal

Disput m -[e]s,-e dispute

Disqualifi|kation /-'tsio:n/ f disqualification. **d~zieren** vt disqualify

Dissertation /-'tsio:n/ f -,-en dissertation

Dissident m -en,-en dissident

Dissonanz f -,-en dissonance

Distanz f -,-en distance. **d~ieren (sich)** vr dissociate oneself (**von** from). **d~iert** a aloof

Distel f -,-n thistle

distinguiert /dıstıŋ'gi:ɐt/ a distinguished

Disziplin f -,-en discipline. **d~arisch** a disciplinary. **d~iert** a disciplined

dito adv ditto

diverse attrib a pl various

Divid|ende f -,-n dividend. **d~ieren** vt divide (**durch** by)

Division f -,-en division

DJH abbr (**Deutsche Jugendherberge**) [German] youth hostel

DM abbr (**Deutsche Mark**) DM

doch conj & adv but; (dennoch) yet; (trotzdem) after all; **wenn d~ ...!** if only ...! **nicht d~!** don't [do that]! **er kommt d~?** he is coming, isn't he? **kommst du nicht?— d~!** aren't you coming?—yes, I am!

Docht m -[e]s,-e wick

Dock nt -s,-s dock. **d~en** vt/i (haben) dock

Dogge f -,-n Great Dane

Dogm|a nt -s,-men dogma. **d~atisch** a dogmatic, adv -ally

Dohle f -,-n jackdaw

Doktor m -s,-en /-'to:rən/ doctor. **D~arbeit** f [doctoral] thesis. **D~würde** f doctorate

Doktrin f -,-en doctrine

Dokument nt -[e]s,-e document. **D~arbericht** m documentary. **D~arfilm** m documentary film

Dolch m -[e]s,-e dagger

doll a (fam) fantastic; (schlimm) awful ● adv beautifully; (sehr) very; (schlimm) badly

Dollar m -s,- dollar

dolmetsch|en vt/i (haben) interpret. **D~er(in)** m -s,- (f -,-nen) interpreter

Dom m -[e]s,-e cathedral

domin|ant a dominant. **d~ieren** vi (haben) dominate; (vorherrschen) predominate

Domino nt -s,-s dominoes sg. **D~stein** m domino

Dompfaff m -en,-en bullfinch

Donau f - Danube

Donner m -s thunder. **d~n** vi (haben) thunder

Donnerstag m Thursday. **d~s** adv on Thursdays

Donnerwetter nt (fam) telling-off; (Krach) row ● int /'--'--/ wow! (Fluch) damn it!

doof a (fam) stupid, adv -ly

Doppel nt -s,- duplicate; (Tennis) doubles pl. **D~bett** nt double bed. **D~decker** m -s,- double-decker [bus]. **d~deutig** a ambiguous. **D~gänger** m -s,- double. **D~kinn** nt double chin. **D~name** m double-barrelled name. **D~punkt** m (Gram) colon. **D~schnitte** f sandwich. **d~sinnig** a ambiguous. **D~stecker** m two-way adaptor. **d~t** a double; 〈Boden〉 false; **in d~ter Ausfertigung** in duplicate; **die d~te Menge** twice the amount ● adv doubly; (zweimal) twice; **d~t so viel** twice as much. **D~zimmer** nt double room

Dorf nt -[e]s,-̈er village. **D~bewohner** m villager

dörflich a rural

Dorn m -[e]s,-en thorn. **d~ig** a thorny

Dörrobst nt dried fruit

Dorsch m -[e]s,-e cod

dort adv there; **d~ drüben** over there. **d~her** adv [**von**] **d~her** from there. **d~hin** adv there. **d~ig** a local

Dose f -,-n tin, can; (Schmuck-) box

dösen vi (haben) doze

Dosen|milch f evaporated milk. **D~öffner** m tin or can opener

dosieren vt measure out

Dosis f -, **Dosen** dose

Dotter m & nt -s,- [egg] yolk

Dozent(in) m -en,-en (f -,-nen) (Univ) lecturer

Dr. abbr (**Doktor**) Dr

Drache m -n,-n dragon. **D~n** m -s,- kite; (fam: Frau) dragon. **D~nfliegen**

nt hang-gliding. **D~nflieger** *m* hang-glider

Draht *m* **-[e]s,~e** wire; **auf D~** (*fam*) on the ball. **d~ig** *a* (*fig*) wiry. **D~seilbahn** *f* cable railway

drall *a* plump; ⟨*Frau*⟩ buxom

Dram|a *nt* **-s,-men** drama. **D~atik** *f* - drama. **D~atiker** *m* **-s,-** dramatist. **d~atisch** *a* dramatic, *adv* -ally. **d~atisieren** *vt* dramatize

dran *adv* (*fam*) = **daran; gut/schlecht d~ sein** be well off/in a bad way; **ich bin d~** it's my turn

Dränage /-'na:ʒə/ *f* - drainage

Drang *m* **-[e]s** urge; ⟨*Druck*⟩ pressure

dräng|eln *vt/i* (*haben*) push; (*bedrängen*) pester. **d~en** *vt* push; (*bedrängen*) urge; **sich d~en** crowd (**um** round) ● *vi* (*haben*) push; (*eilen*) be urgent; ⟨*Zeit:*⟩ press; **d~en auf** (+ *acc*) press for

dran|halten† (**sich**) *vr sep* hurry. **d~kommen**† *vi sep* (*sein*) have one's turn; **wer kommt dran?** whose turn is it?

drapieren *vt* drape

drastisch *a* drastic, *adv* -ally

drauf *adv* (*fam*) = **darauf; d~ und dran sein** be on the point (**etw zu tun** of doing sth). **D~gänger** *m* **-s,-** daredevil. **d~gängerisch** *a* reckless

draus *adv* (*fam*) = **daraus**

draußen *adv* outside; (*im Freien*) out of doors

drechseln *vt* (*Techn*) turn

Dreck *m* **-s** dirt; ⟨*Morast*⟩ mud; (*fam: Kleinigkeit*) trifle; **in den D~ ziehen** (*fig*) denigrate. **d~ig** *a* dirty; muddy

Dreh *m* **-s** (*fam*) knack; **den D~ heraushaben** have got the hang of it. **D~bank** *f* lathe. **D~bleistift** *m* propelling pencil. **D~buch** *nt* screenplay, script. **d~en** *vt* turn; (*im Kreis*) rotate; (*verschlingen*) twist; roll ⟨*Zigarette*⟩; shoot ⟨*Film*⟩; **lauter/ leiser d~en** turn up/down; **sich d~en** turn; (*im Kreis*) rotate; (*schnell*) spin; ⟨*Wind:*⟩ change; **sich d~en um** revolve around; (*sich handeln*) be about ● *vi* (*haben*) turn; ⟨*Wind:*⟩ change; **an etw** (*dat*) **d~en** turn sth. **D~orgel** *f* barrel organ. **D~stuhl** *m* swivel chair. **D~tür** *f* revolving door. **D~ung** *f* **-,-en** turn; (*im Kreis*) rotation. **D~zahl** *f* number of revolutions

drei *inv a*, **D~** *f* **-,-en** three; ⟨*Sch*⟩ ≈ pass. **D~eck** *nt* **-[e]s,-e** triangle. **d~eckig** *a* triangular. **D~einigkeit**

f - **die [Heilige] D~einigkeit** the [Holy] Trinity. **d~erlei** *inv a* three kinds of ● *pron* three things. **d~fach** *a* triple; **in d~facher Ausfertigung** in triplicate. **D~faltigkeit** *f* - = **D~einigkeit. d~mal** *adv* three times. **D~rad** *nt* tricycle

dreißig *inv a* thirty. **d~ste(r,s)** *a* thirtieth

dreist *a* impudent, *adv* -ly; (*verwegen*) audacious, *adv* -ly. **D~igkeit** *f* - impudence; audacity

dreiviertel *inv a* three-quarter. **D~stunde** *f* three-quarters of an hour

dreizehn *inv a* thirteen. **d~te(r,s)** *a* thirteenth

dreschen† *vt* thresh

dress|ieren *vt* train. **D~ur** *f* - training

dribbeln *vi* (*haben*) dribble

Drill *m* **-[e]s** (*Mil*) drill. **d~en** *vt* drill

Drillinge *mpl* triplets

drin *adv* (*fam*) = **darin**; (*drinnen*) inside

dring|en† *vi* (*sein*) penetrate (**in** + *acc* into; **durch etw** sth); (*heraus-*) come (**aus** out of); **d~en auf** (+ *acc*) insist on. **d~end** *a* urgent, *adv* -ly. **d~lich** *a* urgent. **D~lichkeit** *f* - urgency

Drink *m* **-[s],-s** [alcoholic] drink

drinnen *adv* inside; (*im Haus*) indoors

dritt *adv* **zu d~** in threes; **wir waren zu d~** there were three of us. **d~e(r,s)** *a* third; **ein D~er** a third person. **D~el** *nt* **-s,-** third. **d~ens** *adv* thirdly. **d~rangig** *a* third-rate

Drog|e *f* **-,-n** drug. **D~enabhängige(r)** *m/f* drug addict. **D~erie** *f* **-,-n** chemist's shop, (*Amer*) drugstore. **D~ist** *m* **-en,-en** chemist

drohen *vi* (*haben*) threaten (**jdm** s.o.). **d~d** *a* threatening; ⟨*Gefahr*⟩ imminent

dröhnen *vi* (*haben*) resound; (*tönen*) boom

Drohung *f* **-,-en** threat

drollig *a* funny; (*seltsam*) odd

Drops *m* **-,-** [fruit] drop

Droschke *f* **-,-n** cab

Drossel *f* **-,-n** thrush

drosseln *vt* (*Techn*) throttle; (*fig*) cut back

drüb|en *adv* over there. **d~er** *adv* (*fam*) = **darüber**

Druck¹ *m* **-[e]s,~e** pressure; **unter D~ setzen** (*fig*) pressurize

Druck[2] *m* **-[e]s,-e** printing; (*Schrift, Re-produktion*) print. **D~buchstabe** *m* block letter

Drückeberger *m* **-s,-** shirker

drucken *vt* print

drücken *vt/i* (*haben*) press; (*aus-*) squeeze; (*Schuh:*) pinch; (*umarmen*) hug; (*fig: belasten*) weigh down; **Preise d~** force down prices; (*an Tür*) **d~** push; **sich d~** (*fam*) make one-self scarce; **sich d~ vor** (+ *dat*) (*fam*) shirk. **d~d** *a* heavy; (*schwül*) oppressive

Drucker *m* **-s,-** printer

Drücker *m* **-s,-** push-button; (*Tür-*) door knob

Druckerei *f* **-,-en** printing works

Druck|fehler *m* misprint. **D~knopf** *m* press-stud; (*Drücker*) push-button. **D~luft** *f* compressed air. **D~sache** *f* printed matter. **D~schrift** *f* type; (*Veröffentlichung*) publication; **in D~schrift** in block letters *pl*

drucksen *vi* (*haben*) hum and haw

Druck|stelle *f* bruise. **D~taste** *f* push-button. **D~topf** *m* pressure-cooker

drum *adv* (*fam*) = **darum**

drunter *adv* (*fam*) = **darunter**; **alles geht d~ und drüber** (*fam*) everything is topsy-turvy

Drüse *f* **-,-n** (*Anat*) gland

Dschungel *m* **-s,-** jungle

du *pron* (*familiar address*) you; **auf du und du** on familiar terms

Dübel *m* **-s,-** plug

duck|en *vt* duck; (*fig: demütigen*) humiliate; **sich d~en** duck; (*fig*) cringe. **D~mäuser** *m* **-s,-** moral coward

Dudelsack *m* bagpipes *pl*

Duell *nt* **-s,-e** duel

Duett *nt* **-s,-e** [vocal] duet

Duft *m* **-[e]s,-̈e** fragrance, scent; (*Aroma*) aroma. **d~en** *vi* (*haben*) smell (**nach** of). **d~ig** *a* fine; (*zart*) delicate

duld|en *vt* tolerate; (*erleiden*) suffer • *vi* (*haben*) suffer. **d~sam** *a* tolerant

dumm *a* (**dümmer, dümmst**) stupid, *adv* -ly; (*unklug*) foolish, *adv* -ly; (*fam: lästig*) awkward; **wie d~!** what a nuisance! **der D~e sein** (*fig*) be the loser. **d~erweise** *adv* stupidly; (*leider*) unfortunately. **D~heit** *f* **-,-en** stupidity; (*Torheit*) foolishness; (*Handlung*) folly. **D~kopf** *m* (*fam*) fool.

dumpf *a* dull, *adv* -y; (*muffig*) musty. **d~ig** *a* musty

Düne *f* **-,-n** dune

Dung *m* **-s** manure

Dünge|mittel *nt* fertilizer. **d~en** *vt* fertilize. **D~er** *m* **-s,-** fertilizer

dunk|el *a* dark; (*vage*) vague, *adv* -ly; (*fragwürdig*) shady; **d~les Bier** brown ale; **im D~eln** in the dark

Dünkel *m* **-s** conceit

dunkel|blau *a* dark blue. **d~braun** *a* dark brown

dünkelhaft *a* conceited

Dunkel|heit *f* - darkness. **D~kammer** *f* dark-room. **d~n** *vi* (*haben*) get dark. **d~rot** *a* dark red

dünn *a* thin, *adv* -ly; (*Buch*) slim; (*spärlich*) sparse; (*schwach*) weak

Dunst *m* **-es,-̈e** mist, haze; (*Dampf*) vapour

dünsten *vt* steam

dunstig *a* misty, hazy

Dünung *f* - swell

Duo *nt* **-s,-s** [instrumental] duet

Duplikat *nt* **-[e]s,-e** duplicate

Dur *nt* - (*Mus*) major [key]; **in A-Dur** in A major

durch *prep* (+ *acc*) through; (*mittels*) by; **[geteilt] d~** (*Math*) divided by • *adv* **die Nacht d~** throughout the night; **sechs Uhr d~** (*fam*) gone six o'clock; **d~ und d~ naß** wet through

durcharbeiten *vt sep* work through; **sich d~** work one's way through

durchaus *adv* absolutely; **d~ nicht** by no means

durchbeißen† *vt sep* bite through

durchblättern *vt sep* leaf through

durchblicken *vi sep* (*haben*) look through; **d~ lassen** (*fig*) hint at

Durchblutung *f* circulation

durchbohren *vt insep* pierce

durchbrechen[1]**†** *vt/i sep* (*haben*) break [in two]

durchbrechen[2]**†** *vt insep* break through; break (*Schallmauer*)

durchbrennen† *vi sep* (*sein*) burn through; (*Sicherung:*) blow; (*fam: weglaufen*) run away

durchbringen† *vt sep* get through; (*verschwenden*) squander; (*versorgen*) support; **sich d~ mit** make a living by

Durchbruch *m* breakthrough

durchdacht *a* **gut d~** well thought out

durchdrehen *v sep* • *vt* mince • *vi* (*haben/sein*) (*fam*) go crazy

durchdringen[1]† *vt insep* penetrate

durchdringen[2]† *vi sep (sein)* penetrate; (*sich durchsetzen*) get one's way. **d~d** *a* penetrating; ⟨*Schrei*⟩ piercing

durcheinander *adv* in a muddle; ⟨*Person*⟩ confused. **D~** *nt* **-s** muddle. **d~bringen**† *vt sep* muddle [up]; confuse ⟨*Person*⟩. **d~geraten**† *vi sep (sein)* get mixed up. **d~reden** *vi sep (haben)* all talk at once

durchfahren[1]† *vi sep (sein)* drive through; ⟨*Zug:*⟩ go through

durchfahren[2]† *vt insep* drive/go through; **jdn d~** ⟨*Gedanke:*⟩ flash through s.o.'s mind

Durchfahrt *f* journey/drive through; **auf der D~** passing through; **'D~ verboten'** 'no thoroughfare'

Durchfall *m* diarrhoea; (*fam: Versagen*) flop. **d~en**† *vi sep (sein)* fall through; (*fam: versagen*) flop; (*bei Prüfung*) fail

durchfliegen[1]† *vi sep (sein)* fly through; (*fam: durchfallen*) fail

durchfliegen[2]† *vt insep* fly through; (*lesen*) skim through

durchfroren *a* frozen

Durchfuhr *f* - (*Comm*) transit

durchführ|bar *a* feasible. **d~en** *vt sep* carry out

Durchgang *m* passage; (*Sport*) round; **'D~ verboten'** 'no entry'. **D~sverkehr** *m* through traffic

durchgeben† *vt sep* pass through; (*übermitteln*) transmit; (*Radio, TV*) broadcast

durchgebraten *a* **gut d~** well done

durchgehen† *v sep* ● *vi (sein)* go through; (*davonlaufen*) run away; ⟨*Pferd:*⟩ bolt; **jdm etw d~ lassen** let s.o. get away with sth ● *vt* go through. **d~d** *a* continuous, *adv* -ly; **d~d geöffnet** open all day; **d~der Wagen/Zug** through carriage/train

durchgreifen† *vi sep (haben)* reach through; (*vorgehen*) take drastic action. **d~d** *a* drastic

durchhalte|n† *v sep* (*fig*) ● *vi (haben)* hold out ● *vt* keep up. **D~vermögen** *nt* stamina

durchhängen† *vi sep (haben)* sag

durchkommen† *vi sep (sein)* come through; (*gelangen, am Telefon*) get through; (*bestehen*) pass; (*überleben*) pull through; (*finanziell*) get by (**mit** on)

durchkreuzen *vt insep* thwart

durchlassen† *vt sep* let through

durchlässig *a* permeable; (*undicht*) leaky

durchlaufen[1]† *v sep* ● *vi (sein)* run through ● *vt* wear out

durchlaufen[2]† *vt insep* pass through

Durchlauferhitzer *m* **-s,-** geyser

durchleben *vt insep* live through

durchlesen† *vt sep* read through

durchleuchten *vt insep* X-ray

durchlöchert *a* riddled with holes

durchmachen *vt sep* go through; (*erleiden*) undergo; have ⟨*Krankheit*⟩

Durchmesser *m* **-s,-** diameter

durchnäßt *a* wet through

durchnehmen† *vt sep (Sch)* do

durchnumeriert *a* numbered consecutively

durchpausen *vt sep* trace

durchqueren *vt insep* cross

Durchreiche *f* **-,-n** [serving] hatch. **d~n** *vt sep* pass through

Durchreise *f* journey through; **auf der D~** passing through. **d~n** *vi sep (sein)* pass through

durchreißen† *vt/i sep (sein)* tear

durchs *adv* = **durch das**

Durchsage *f* **-,-n** announcement. **d~n** *vt sep* announce

durchschauen *vt insep* (*fig*) see through

durchscheinend *a* translucent

Durchschlag *m* carbon copy; (*Culin*) colander. **d~en**[1]† *v sep* ● *vt (Culin)* rub through a sieve; **sich d~en** (*fig*) struggle through ● *vi (sein)* ⟨*Sicherung:*⟩ blow

durchschlagen[2]† *vt insep* smash

durchschlagend *a* (*fig*) effective; ⟨*Erfolg*⟩ resounding

durchschneiden† *vt sep* cut

Durchschnitt *m* average; **im D~** on average. **d~lich** *a* average ● *adv* on average. **D~s-** *pref* average

Durchschrift *f* carbon copy

durchsehen† *v sep* ● *vi (haben)* see through ● *vt* look through

durchseihen *vt sep* strain

durchsetzen[1] *vt sep* force through; **sich d~** assert oneself; ⟨*Mode:*⟩ catch on

durchsetzen[2] *vt insep* intersperse; (*infiltrieren*) infiltrate

Durchsicht *f* check

durchsichtig *a* transparent

durchsickern *vi sep (sein)* seep through; ⟨*Neuigkeit:*⟩ leak out

durchsprechen† *vt sep* discuss

durchstehen† *vt sep* (*fig*) come through

durchstreichen† *vt sep* cross out

durchsuch|en *vt insep* search. **D~ung** *f* -,-en search

durchtrieben *a* cunning

durchwachsen *a* ⟨*Speck*⟩ streaky; (*fam:gemischt*) mixed

durchwacht *a* sleepless ⟨*Nacht*⟩

durchwählen *vi sep* (*haben*) (*Teleph*) dial direct

durchweg *adv* without exception

durchweicht *a* soggy

durchwühlen *vt insep* rummage through; ransack ⟨*Haus*⟩

durchziehen† *v sep* ● *vt* pull through ● *vi* (*sein*) pass through

durchzucken *vt insep* (*fig*) shoot through; **jdn d~** ⟨*Gedanke*⟩ flash through s.o.'s mind

Durchzug *m* through draught

dürfen† *vt & v aux* **etw [tun] d~** be allowed to do sth; **darf ich?** may I? **sie darf es nicht sehen** she must not see it; **ich hätte es nicht tun/sagen d~** I ought not to have done/said it; **das dürfte nicht allzu schwer sein** that should not be too difficult

dürftig *a* poor; ⟨*Mahlzeit*⟩ scanty

dürr *a* dry; ⟨*Boden*⟩ arid; (*mager*) skinny. **D~e** *f* -,-n drought

Durst *m* -[e]s thirst; **D~ haben** be thirsty. **d~en** *vi* (*haben*) be thirsty. **d~ig** *a* thirsty

Dusche *f* -,-n shower. **d~n** *vi/r* (*haben*) [**sich**] **d~n** have a shower

Düse *f* -,-n nozzle. **D~nflugzeug** *nt* jet

düster *a* gloomy, *adv* -ily; (*dunkel*) dark

Dutzend *nt* -s,-e dozen. **d~weise** *adv* by the dozen

duzen *vt* **jdn d~** call s.o. 'du'

Dynam|ik *f* - dynamics *sg*; (*fig*) dynamism. **d~isch** *a* dynamic; ⟨*Rente*⟩ index-linked

Dynamit *nt* -es dynamite

Dynamo *m* -s,-s dynamo

Dynastie *f* -,-n dynasty

D-Zug /'de:-/ *m* express [train]

E

Ebbe *f* -,-n low tide

eben *a* level; (*glatt*) smooth; **zu e~er Erde** on the ground floor ● *adv* just; (*genau*) exactly; **e~ noch** only just;

(*gerade vorhin*) just now; **das ist es e~!** that's just it! [**na**] **e~!** exactly! **E~bild** *nt* image. **e~bürtig** *a* equal; **jdm e~bürtig sein** be s.o.'s equal

Ebene *f* -,-n (*Geog*) plain; (*Geom*) plane; (*fig: Niveau*) level

eben|falls *adv* also; **danke, e~falls** thank you, [the] same to you. **E~holz** *nt* ebony. **e~mäßig** *a* regular, *adv* -ly. **e~so** *adv* just the same; (*eben-sosehr*) just as much. **e~so gut/teuer** just as good/expensive. **e~sogut** *adv* just as well. **e~sosehr** *adv* just as much. **e~soviel** *adv* just as much/many. **e~sowenig** *adv* just as little/few; (*noch*) no more

Eber *m* -s,- boar. **E~esche** *f* rowan

ebnen *vt* level; (*fig*) smooth

Echo *nt* -s,-s echo. **e~en** *vt/i* (*haben*) echo

echt *a* genuine, real; (*authentisch*) authentic; ⟨*Farbe*⟩ fast; (*typisch*) typical ● *adv* (*fam*) really; typically. **E~heit** *f* - authenticity

Eck|ball *m* (*Sport*) corner. **E~e** *f* -,-n corner; **um die E~e bringen** (*fam*) bump off. **e~ig** *a* angular; ⟨*Klammern*⟩ square; (*unbeholfen*) awkward. **E~stein** *m* corner-stone. **E~stoß** *m* = **E~ball**. **E~zahn** *m* canine tooth

Ecu, ECU /e'ky:/ *m* -[s],-[s] ecu

edel *a* noble, *adv* -bly; (*wertvoll*) precious; (*fein*) fine. **E~mann** *m* (*pl* -**leute**) nobleman. **E~mut** *m* magnanimity. **e~mütig** *a* magnanimous, *adv* -ly. **E~stahl** *m* stainless steel. **E~stein** *m* precious stone

Efeu *m* -s ivy

Effekt *m* -[e]s,-e effect. **E~en** *pl* securities. **e~iv** *a* actual, *adv* -ly; (*wirksam*) effective, *adv* -ly. **e~voll** *a* effective

EG *f* - *abbr* (**Europäische Gemeinschaft**) EC

egal *a* **das ist mir e~** (*fam*) it's all the same to me ● *adv* **e~ wie/wo** no matter how/where. **e~itär** *a* egalitarian

Egge *f* -,-n harrow

Ego|ismus *m* - selfishness. **E~ist(in)** *m* -**en,-en** (*f* -,-**nen**) egoist. **e~istisch** *a* selfish, *adv* -ly. **e~zentrisch** *a* egocentric

eh *adv* (*Aust fam*) anyway; **seit eh und je** from time immemorial

ehe *conj* before; **ehe nicht** until

Ehe *f* -,-n marriage. **E~bett** *nt* double bed. **E~bruch** *m* adultery. **E~frau** *f*

wife. **E∼leute** pl married couple sg.
e∼lich a marital; ⟨Recht⟩ conjugal;
⟨Kind⟩ legitimate
ehemal|ig a former. **e∼s** adv formerly
Ehe|mann m (pl **-männer**) husband.
E∼paar nt married couple
eher adv earlier, sooner; (lieber,
vielmehr) rather; (mehr) more
Ehering m wedding ring
ehr|bar a respectable. **E∼e** f -,-ri
honour; **jdm E∼e machen** do credit to
s.o. **e∼en** vt honour. **e∼enamtlich** a
honorary ● adv in an honorary
capacity. **E∼endoktorat** nt
honorary doctorate. **E∼engast** m
guest of honour. **e∼enhaft** a honourable, adv -bly. **E∼enmann** m (pl
-männer) man of honour. **E∼enmitglied** nt honorary member. **e∼enrührig** a defamatory. **E∼enrunde**
f lap of honour. **E∼ensache** f point
of honour. **e∼enwert** a honourable.
E∼enwort nt word of honour. **e∼erbietig** a deferential, adv -ly. **E∼erbietung** f - deference. **E∼furcht** f
reverence; ⟨Scheu⟩ awe. **e∼fürchtig**
a reverent, adv -ly. **E∼gefühl** nt
sense of honour. **E∼geiz** m ambition.
e∼geizig a ambitious. **e∼lich** a
honest, adv -ly; **e∼lich gesagt** to be
honest. **E∼lichkeit** f - honesty. **e∼los**
a dishonourable. **e∼sam** a respectable. **e∼würdig** a venerable;
(als Anrede) Reverend
Ei nt -[e]s,-er egg
Eibe f -,-n yew
Eiche f -,-n oak. **E∼l** f -,-n acorn.
E∼lhäher m -s,- jay
eichen vt standardize
Eichhörnchen nt -s,- squirrel
Eid m -[e]s,-e oath
Eidechse f -,-n lizard
eidlich a sworn ● adv on oath
Eidotter m & nt egg yolk
Eier|becher m egg-cup. **E∼kuchen**
m pancake; (Omelett) omelette. **E∼schale** f eggshell. **E∼schnee** m
beaten egg-white. **E∼stock** m ovary.
E∼uhr f egg-timer
Eifer m -s eagerness; (Streben) zeal.
E∼sucht f jealousy. **e∼süchtig** a
jealous, adv -ly
eiförmig a egg-shaped; (oval) oval
eifrig a eager, adv -ly; (begeistert)
keen, adv -ly
Eigelb nt -[e]s,-e [egg] yolk

eigen a own; (typisch) characteristic
(dat of); (seltsam) odd, adv -ly;
(genau) particular. **E∼art** f peculiarity. **e∼artig** a peculiar, adv -ly;
(seltsam) odd. **E∼brötler** m -s,- crank.
e∼händig a personal, adv
-ly; ⟨Unterschrift⟩ own. **E∼heit** f -,
-en peculiarity. **e∼mächtig** a highhanded; (unbefugt) unauthorized
● adv high-handedly; without authority. **E∼name** m proper name.
E∼nutz m self-interest. **e∼nützig** a
selfish, adv -ly. **e∼s** adv specially.
E∼schaft f -,-en quality; (Phys) property; (Merkmal) characteristic;
(Funktion) capacity. **E∼schaftswort**
nt (pl **-wörter**) adjective. **E∼sinn** m
obstinacy. **e∼sinnig** a obstinate,
adv -ly
eigentlich a actual, real; (wahr) true
● adv actually, really; (streng genommen) strictly speaking; **wie geht es
ihm e∼?** by the way, how is he?
Eigen|tor nt own goal. **E∼tum** nt
-s property. **E∼tümer(in)** m -s,- (f
-,-nen) owner. **e∼tümlich** a odd, adv
-ly; (typisch) characteristic. **E∼tumswohnung** f freehold flat. **e∼willig** a self-willed; ⟨Stil⟩ highly
individual
eign|en (sich) vr be suitable. **E∼ung**
f - suitability
Eil|brief m express letter. **E∼e** f -
hurry; **E∼e haben** be in a hurry;
⟨Sache:⟩ be urgent. **e∼en** vi (sein)
hurry ● (haben) (drängen) be urgent.
e∼ends adv hurriedly. **e∼ig** a hurried, adv -ly; (dringend) urgent, adv -
ly; **es e∼ig haben** be in a hurry. **E∼zug** m semi-fast train
Eimer m -s,- bucket; (Abfall-) bin
ein[1] adj one; **e∼es Tages/Abends** one
day/evening; **mit jdm in einem
Zimmer schlafen** sleep in the same
room as s.o. ● indef art a, (vor Vokal)
an; **so ein** such a; **was für ein** (Frage)
what kind of a? (Ausruf) what a!
ein[2] adv **ein und aus** in and out; **nicht
mehr ein noch aus wissen** (fam) be at
one's wits' end
einander pron one another
einarbeiten vt sep train
einäscher|n vt sep reduce to ashes;
cremate ⟨Leiche⟩. **E∼ung** f -,-en
cremation
einatmen vt/i sep (haben) inhale,
breathe in

ein|äugig *a* one-eyed. **E~bahnstraße** *f* one-way street
einbalsamieren *vt sep* embalm
Einband *m* binding
Einbau *m* installation; (*Montage*) fitting. **e~en** *vt sep* install; (*montieren*) fit. **E~küche** *f* fitted kitchen
einbegriffen *pred a* included
einberuf|en† *vt sep* convene; (*Mil*) call up, (*Amer*) draft. **E~ung** *f* call-up, (*Amer*) draft
Einbettzimmer *nt* single room
einbeulen *vt sep* dent
einbeziehen† *vt sep* **[mit]** **e~** include; (*berücksichtigen*) take into account
einbiegen† *vi sep* (*sein*) turn
einbild|en *vt sep* **sich** (*dat*) **etw e~en** imagine sth; **sich** (*dat*) **viel e~en** be conceited. **E~ung** *f* imagination; (*Dünkel*) conceit. **E~ungskraft** *f* imagination
einblenden *vt sep* fade in
einbleuen *vt sep* **jdm etw e~** (*fam*) drum sth into s.o.
Einblick *m* insight
einbrech|en† *vi sep* (*haben/sein*) break in; **bei uns ist eingebrochen worden** we have been burgled ● (*sein*) set in; ⟨*Nacht:*⟩ fall. **E~er** *m* burglar
einbring|en† *vt sep* get in; bring in ⟨*Geld*⟩; **das bringt nichts ein** it's not worth while. **e~lich** *a* profitable
Einbruch *m* burglary; **bei E~ der Nacht** at nightfall
einbürger|n *vt sep* naturalize; **sich e~n** become established. **E~ung** *f* naturalization
Ein|buße *f* loss (**an**+ *dat* of). **e~büßen** *vt sep* lose
einchecken /-tʃɛkən/ *vt/i sep* (*haben*) check in
eindecken (sich) *vr sep* stock up
eindeutig *a* unambiguous; (*deutlich*) clear, *adv* -ly
eindicken *vt sep* (*Culin*) thicken
eindring|en† *vi sep* (*sein*) **e~en in** (+ *acc*) penetrate into; (*mit Gewalt*) force one's/⟨*Wasser:*⟩ its way into; (*Mil*) invade; **auf jdn e~en** (*fig*) press s.o.; (*bittend*) plead with s.o. **e~lich** *a* urgent, *adv* -ly. **E~ling** *m* -s,-e intruder
Eindruck *m* impression; **E~ machen** impress (**auf jdn** s.o.)
eindrücken *vt sep* crush
eindrucksvoll *a* impressive
ein|e(r,s) *pron* one; (*jemand*) someone; (*man*) one, you; **e~er von uns** one of us; **es macht e~en müde** it makes you tired
einebnen *vt sep* level
eineiig *a* ⟨*Zwillinge*⟩ identical
eineinhalb *inv a* one and a half; **e~ Stunden** an hour and a half
Einelternfamilie *f* one-parent family
einengen *vt sep* restrict
Einer *m* -s,- (*Math*) unit. **e~** *pron s.* **eine(r,s)**. **e~lei** *inv a* ● *attrib a* one kind of; (*eintönig, einheitlich*) the same ● *pred a* (*fam*) immaterial; **es ist mir e~lei** it's all the same to me. **E~lei** *nt* -s monotony. **e~seits** *adv* on the one hand
einfach *a* simple, *adv* -ly; ⟨*Essen*⟩ plain; ⟨*Faden, Fahrt, Fahrkarte*⟩ single; **e~er Soldat** private. **E~heit** *f* - simplicity
einfädeln *vt sep* thread; (*fig: arrangieren*) arrange; **sich e~** (*Auto*) filter in
einfahr|en† *v sep* ● *vi* (*sein*) arrive; ⟨*Zug:*⟩ pull in ● *vt* (*Auto*) run in; **die Ernte e~en** get in the harvest. **E~t** *f* arrival; (*Eingang*) entrance, way in; (*Auffahrt*) drive; (*Autobahn-*) access road; **keine E~t** no entry
Einfall *m* idea; (*Mil*) invasion. **e~en†** *vi sep* (*sein*) collapse; (*eindringen*) invade; (*einstimmen*) join in; **jdm e~en** occur to s.o.; **sein Name fällt mir nicht ein** I can't think of his name; **was fällt ihm ein!** what does he think he is doing! **e~sreich** *a* imaginative
Einfalt *f* - naïvety
einfältig *a* simple; (*naiv*) naïve
Einfaltspinsel *m* simpleton
einfangen† *vt sep* catch
einfarbig *a* of one colour; ⟨*Stoff, Kleid*⟩ plain
einfass|en *vt sep* edge; set ⟨*Edelstein*⟩. **E~ung** *f* border, edging
einfetten *vt sep* grease
einfinden† (sich) *vr sep* turn up
einfließen† *vi sep* (*sein*) flow in
einflößen *vt sep* **jdm etw e~** give s.o. sips of sth; **jdm Angst e~** (*fig*) frighten s.o.
Einfluß *m* influence. **e~reich** *a* influential
einförmig *a* monotonous, *adv* -ly. **E~keit** *f* - monotony
einfried[ig]en *vt sep* enclose. **E~ung** *f* -,-en enclosure
einfrieren† *vt/i sep* (*sein*) freeze

einfügen

einfügen vt sep insert; (einschieben) interpolate; **sich e~** fit in
einfühl|en (sich) vr sep empathize (**in** + acc with). **e~sam** a sensitive
Einfuhr f -,-en import
einführ|en vt sep introduce; (einstecken) insert; (einweisen) initiate; (Comm) import. **e~end** a introductory. **E~ung** f introduction; (Einweisung) initiation
Eingabe f petition; (Computer) input
Eingang m entrance, way in; (Ankunft) arrival
eingebaut a built-in; (Schrank) fitted
eingeben† vt sep hand in; (einflößen) give (**jdm** s.o.); (Computer) feed in
eingebildet a imaginary; (überheblich) conceited
Eingeborene(r) m/f native
Eingebung f -,-en inspiration
eingedenk prep (+ gen) mindful of
eingefleischt a **e~er Junggeselle** confirmed bachelor
eingehakt adv arm in arm
eingehen† v sep ● vi (sein) come in; (ankommen) arrive; (einlaufen) shrink; (sterben) die; (Zeitung, Firma:) fold; **auf etw** (acc) **e~** go into sth; (annehmen) agree to sth ● vt enter into; contract (Ehe); make (Wette); take (Risiko). **e~d** a detailed; (gründlich) thorough, adv -ly
eingelegt a inlaid; (Culin) pickled; (mariniert) marinaded
eingemacht a (Culin) bottled
eingenommen pred a (fig) taken (**von** with); prejudiced (**gegen** against); **von sich e~** conceited
eingeschneit a snowbound
eingeschrieben a registered
Einge|ständnis nt admission. **e~stehen**† vt sep admit
eingetragen a registered
Eingeweide pl bowels, entrails
eingewöhnen (sich) vr sep settle in
eingießen† vt sep pour in; (einschenken) pour
eingleisig a single-track
einglieder|n vt sep integrate. **E~ung** f integration
eingraben† vt sep bury
eingravieren vt sep engrave
eingreifen† vi sep (haben) intervene. **E~** nt -s intervention
Eingriff m intervention; (Med) operation

einhaken vt/r sep **jdn e~** od **sich bei jdm e~** take s.o.'s arm
einhalten† v sep ● vt keep; (befolgen) observe ● vi (haben) stop
einhändigen vt sep hand in
einhängen v sep ● vt hang; put down (Hörer); **sich bei jdm e~** take s.o.'s arm ● vi (haben) hang up
einheimisch a local; (eines Landes) native; (Comm) home-produced. **E~e(r)** m/f local; native
Einheit f -,-en unity; (Maß-, Mil) unit. **e~lich** a uniform, adv -ly; (vereinheitlicht) standard. **E~spreis** m standard price; (Fahrpreis) flat fare
einhellig a unanimous, adv -ly
einholen vt sep catch up with; (aufholen) make up for; (erbitten) seek; (einkaufen) buy; **e~ gehen** go shopping
einhüllen vt sep wrap
einhundert inv a one hundred
einig a united; [**sich** (dat)] **e~ werden/sein** come to an/be in agreement
einig|e(r,s) pron some; (ziemlich viel) quite a lot of; (substantivisch) **e~e** pl some; (mehrere) several; (ziemlich viele) quite a lot; **e~es** sg some things; **vor e~er Zeit** some time ago. **e~emal** adv a few times
einigen vt unite; unify (Land); **sich e~** come to an agreement; (ausmachen) agree (**auf** + acc on)
einigermaßen adv to some extent; (ziemlich) fairly; (ziemlich gut) fairly well
Einig|keit f - unity; (Übereinstimmung) agreement. **E~ung** f - unification; (Übereinkunft) agreement
einjährig a one-year-old; (ein Jahr dauernd) one year's...; **e~e Pflanze** annual
einkalkulieren vt sep take into account
einkassieren vt sep collect
Einkauf m purchase; (Einkaufen) shopping; **Einkäufe machen** do some shopping. **e~en** vt sep buy; **e~en gehen** go shopping. **E~skorb** m shopping/(im Geschäft) wire basket. **E~stasche** f shopping bag. **E~swagen** m shopping trolley. **E~szentrum** nt shopping centre
einkehren vi sep (sein) **[in einem Lokal] e~** stop for a meal/drink [at an inn]
einklammern vt sep bracket

Einklang *m* harmony; **in E~ stehen** be in accord (**mit** with)

einkleben *vt sep* stick in

einkleiden *vt sep* fit out

einklemmen *vt sep* clamp; **sich** (*dat*) **den Finger in der Tür e~** catch one's finger in the door

einkochen *v sep* ● *vi* (*sein*) boil down ● *vt* preserve, bottle

Einkommen *nt* **-s** income. **E~[s]-steuer** *f* income tax

einkreisen *vt sep* encircle; **rot e~** ring in red

Einkünfte *pl* income *sg*; (*Einnahmen*) revenue *sg*

einlad|en† *vt sep* load; (*auffordern*) invite; (*bezahlen für*) treat. **e~end** *a* inviting. **E~ung** *f* invitation

Einlage *f* enclosure; (*Schuh-*) arch support; (*Zahn-*) temporary filling; (*Programm-*) interlude; (*Comm*) investment; (*Bank-*) deposit; **Suppe mit E~** soup with noodles/ dumplings

Ein|laß *m* **-sses** admittance. **e~lassen**† *vt sep* let in; run ⟨*Bad, Wasser*⟩; **sich auf etw** (*acc*)/**mit jdm e~lassen** get involved in sth/with s.o.

einlaufen† *vi sep* (*sein*) come in; (*ankommen*) arrive; ⟨*Wasser:*⟩ run in; (*schrumpfen*) shrink; **[in den Hafen] e~** enter port

einleben (sich) *vr sep* settle in

Einlege|arbeit *f* inlaid work. **e~n** *vt sep* put in; lay in ⟨*Vorrat*⟩; lodge ⟨*Protest, Berufung*⟩; (*einfügen*) insert; (*Auto*) engage ⟨*Gang*⟩; (*verzieren*) inlay; (*Culin*) pickle; (*marinieren*) marinade; **eine Pause e~n** have a break. **E~sohle** *f* insole

einleit|en *vt sep* initiate; (*eröffnen*) begin. **e~end** *a* introductory. **E~ung** *f* introduction

einlenken *vi sep* (*haben*) (*fig*) relent

einleuchten *vi sep* (*haben*) be clear (*dat* to). **e~d** *a* convincing

einliefer|n *vt sep* take (**ins Krankenhaus** to hospital). **E~ung** *f* admission

einlösen *vt sep* cash ⟨*Scheck*⟩; redeem ⟨*Pfand*⟩; (*fig*) keep

einmachen *vt sep* preserve

einmal *adv* once; (*eines Tages*) one or some day; **noch/schon e~** again/ before; **noch e~ so teuer** twice as expensive; **auf e~** at the same time; (*plötzlich*) suddenly; **nicht e~** not even; **es geht nun e~ nicht** it's just not possible. **E~eins** *nt* - [multiplication]

tables *pl*. **e~ig** *a* single; (*einzigartig*) unique; (*fam: großartig*) fantastic, *adv* -ally

einmarschieren *vi sep* (*sein*) march in

einmisch|en (sich) *vr sep* interfere. **E~ung** *f* interference

einmütig *a* unanimous, *adv* -ly

Einnahme *f* **-,-n** taking; (*Mil*) capture; **E~n** *pl* income *sg*; (*Einkünfte*) revenue *sg*; (*Comm*) receipts; (*eines Ladens*) takings

einnehmen† *vt sep* take; have ⟨*Mahlzeit*⟩; (*Mil*) capture; take up ⟨*Platz*⟩; (*fig*) prejudice (**gegen** against); **jdn für sich e~** win s.o. over. **e~d** *a* engaging

einnicken *vi sep* (*sein*) nod off

Einöde *f* wilderness

einordnen *vt sep* put in its proper place; (*klassifizieren*) classify; **sich e~** fit in; (*Auto*) get in lane

einpacken *vt sep* pack; (*einhüllen*) wrap

einparken *vt sep* park

einpauken *vt sep* **jdm etw e~** (*fam*) drum sth into s.o.

einpflanzen *vt sep* plant; implant ⟨*Organ*⟩

einplanen *vt sep* allow for

einpräg|en *vt sep* impress (**jdm** [up]on s.o.); **sich** (*dat*) **etw e~en** memorize sth. **e~sam** *a* easy to remember; ⟨*Melodie*⟩ catchy

einquartieren *vt sep* (*Mil*) billet (**bei** on); **sich in einem Hotel e~** put up at a hotel

einrahmen *vt sep* frame

einrasten *vi sep* (*sein*) engage

einräumen *vt sep* put away; (*zugeben*) admit; (*zugestehen*) grant

einrechnen *vt sep* include

einreden *v sep* ● *vt* **jdm/sich** (*dat*) **etw e~** persuade s.o./oneself of sth ● *vi* (*haben*) **auf jdn e~** talk insistently to s.o.

einreib|en† *vt sep* rub (**mit** with). **E~-mittel** *nt* liniment

einreichen *vt sep* submit; **die Scheidung e~** file for divorce

Einreih|er *m* **-s,-** single-breasted suit. **e~ig** *a* single-breasted

Einreise *f* entry. **e~n** *vi sep* (*sein*) enter (**nach Irland** Ireland). **E~visum** *nt* entry visa

einreißen† *v sep* ● *vt* tear; (*abreißen*) pull down ● *vi* (*sein*) tear; ⟨*Sitte:*⟩ become a habit

adv -ly. **E~resultat** *nt* final result.
E~spiel *nt* final. **E~spurt** *m* **-[e]s**
final spurt. **E~station** *f* terminus.
E~ung *f* -,-en (*Gram*) ending
Energie *f* - energy
energisch *a* resolute, *adv* -ly;
(*nachdrücklich*) vigorous, *adv* -ly;
e~ werden put one's foot down
eng *a* narrow; (*beengt*) cramped;
(*anliegend*) tight; (*nah*) close, *adv* -ly
Enga|gement /āgaʒə'mā:/ *nt* **-s,-s**
(*Theat*) engagement; (*fig*) commitment.
e~gieren /-'ʒi:rən/ *vt* (*Theat*) engage; **sich e~gieren** become involved;
e~giert committed
eng|anliegend *a* tight-fitting. **E~e** *f*
- narrowness; **in die E~e treiben** (*fig*)
drive into a corner
Engel *m* **-s,-** angel. **e~haft** *a* angelic
engherzig *a* petty
England *nt* -s England
Engländer *m* **-s,-** Englishman; (*Techn*)
monkey-wrench; **die E~** the English *pl*.
E~in *f* -,-nen Englishwoman
englisch *a* English; **auf e~** in English. **E~** *nt* **-[s]** (*Lang*) English
Engpaß *m* (*fig*) bottle-neck
en gros /ã'gro:/ *adv* wholesale
engstirnig *a* (*fig*) narrow-minded
Enkel *m* **-s,-** grandson; **E~** *pl* grandchildren. **E~in** *f* -,-nen granddaughter. **E~kind** *nt* grandchild.
E~sohn *m* grandson. **E~tochter** *f*
granddaughter
enorm *a* enormous, *adv* -ly; (*fam:
großartig*) fantastic
Ensemble /ã'sā:bəl/ *nt* **-s,-s** ensemble; (*Theat*) company
entart|en *vi* (*sein*) degenerate. **e~et**
a degenerate
entbehr|en *vt* do without; (*ver-
missen*) miss. **e~lich** *a* dispensable;
(*überflüssig*) superfluous. **E~ung** *f*
-,-en privation
entbind|en† *vt* release (**von** from);
(*Med*) deliver (**von** of) ● *vi* (*haben*) give
birth. **E~ung** *f* delivery. **E~ungs-
station** *f* maternity ward
entblöß|en *vt* bare. **e~t** *a* bare
entdeck|en *vt* discover. **E~er** *m* **-s,-**
discoverer; (*Forscher*) explorer.
E~ung *f* -,-en discovery
Ente *f* -,-n duck
entehren *vt* dishonour
enteignen *vt* dispossess; expro-
priate (*Eigentum*)
enterben *vt* disinherit
Enterich *m* **-s,-e** drake

entfachen *vt* kindle
entfallen† *vi* (*sein*) not apply; **jdm
e~** slip from s.o.'s hand; (*aus dem Gedächtnis*) slip s.o.'s mind; **auf jdn e~** be
s.o.'s share
entfalt|en *vt* unfold; (*entwickeln*) de-
velop; (*zeigen*) display; **sich e~en** unfold; develop. **E~ung** *f* - development
entfern|en *vt* remove; **sich e~en**
leave. **e~t** *a* distant; (*schwach*)
vague, *adv* -ly; **2 Kilometer e~t** 2 kilometres away; **e~t verwandt** distantly
related; **nicht im e~testen** not in
the least. **E~ung** *f* -,-en removal;
(*Abstand*) distance; (*Reichweite*) range.
E~ungsmesser *m* range- finder
entfesseln *vt* (*fig*) unleash
entfliehen† *vi* (*sein*) escape
entfremd|en *vt* alienate. **E~ung** *f* -
alienation
entfrosten *vt* defrost
entführ|en *vt* abduct, kidnap; hijack
(*Flugzeug*). **E~er** *m* abductor,
kidnapper; hijacker. **E~ung** *f* abduction, kidnapping; hijacking
entgegen *adv* towards ● *prep*
(+ *dat*) contrary to. **e~gehen**† *vi sep*
(*sein*) (+ *dat*) go to meet; (*fig*) be
heading for. **e~gesetzt** *a* opposite;
(*gegensätzlich*) opposing. **e~-
halten**† *vt sep* (*fig*) object. **e~-
kommen**† *vi sep* (*sein*) (+ *dat*) come
to meet; (*zukommen auf*) come
towards; (*fig*) oblige. **E~kommen**
nt **-s** helpfulness; (*Zugeständnis*)
concession. **e~kommend** *a* approaching; (*Verkehr*) oncoming; (*fig*)
obliging. **e~nehmen**† *vt sep* accept.
e~sehen† *vi sep* (*haben*) (+ *dat*)
(*fig*) await; (*freudig*) look forward to.
e~setzen *vt sep* **Widerstand e~-
setzen** (+ *dat*) resist. **e~treten**† *vi
sep* (*sein*) (+ *dat*) (*fig*) confront; (*bekämpfen*) fight. **e~wirken** *vi sep* (*haben*) (+ *dat*) counteract; (*fig*) oppose
entgegn|en *vt* reply (**auf** + *acc* to).
E~ung *f* -,-en reply
entgehen† *vi sep* (*sein*) (+ *dat*) escape; **jdm e~** (*unbemerkt bleiben*) escape s.o.'s notice; **sich** (*dat*) **etw e~
lassen** miss sth
entgeistert *a* flabbergasted
Entgelt *nt* **-[e]s** payment; **gegen E~**
for money. **e~en** *vt* **jdn etw e~en
lassen** (*fig*) make s.o. pay for sth
entgleis|en *vi* (*sein*) be derailed;
(*fig*) make a gaffe. **E~ung** *f* -,-en de-
railment; (*fig*) gaffe

entgleiten† vi (sein) **jdm e~** slip from s.o.'s grasp

entgräten vt fillet, bone

Enthaarungsmittel nt depilatory

enthalt|en† vt contain; **in etw** (dat) **e~en sein** be contained/(eingeschlossen) included in sth; **sich der Stimme e~en** (Pol) abstain. **E~sam** a abstemious. **E~samkeit** f - abstinence. **E~ung** f (Pol) abstention

enthaupten vt behead

entheben† vt **jdn seines Amtes e~** relieve s.o. of his post

enthüll|en vt unveil; (fig) reveal. **E~ung** f -,-en revelation

Enthusias|mus m - enthusiasm. **E~t** m -en,-en enthusiast. **e~tisch** a enthusiastic, adv -ally

entkernen vt stone; core (Apfel)

entkleid|en vt undress; **sich e~en** undress. **E~ungsnummer** f striptease [act]

entkommen† vi (sein) escape

entkorken vt uncork

entkräft|en vt weaken; (fig) invalidate. **E~ung** f - debility

entkrampfen vt relax; **sich e~** relax

entlad|en† vt unload; (Electr) discharge; **sich e~** discharge; (Gewitter:) break; (Zorn:) explode

entlang adv & prep (+ preceding acc or following dat) along; **die Straße e~, e~ der Straße** along the road; **an etw** (dat) **e~** along sth. **e~fahren**† vi sep (sein) drive along. **e~gehen**† vi sep (sein) walk along

entlarven vt unmask

entlass|en† vt dismiss; (aus Krankenhaus) discharge; (aus der Haft) release; **aus der Schule e~en werden** leave school. **E~ung** f -,-en dismissal; discharge; release

entlast|en vt relieve the strain on; ease (Gewissen, Verkehr); relieve (von of); (Jur) exonerate. **E~ung** f - relief; exoneration. **E~ungszug** m relief train

entlaufen† vi (sein) run away

entledigen (sich) vr (+ gen) rid oneself of; (ausziehen) take off; (erfüllen) discharge

entleeren vt empty

entlegen a remote

entleihen† vt borrow (**von** from)

entlocken vt coax (dat from)

entlohnen vt pay

entlüft|en vt ventilate. **E~er** m -s,- extractor fan. **E~ung** f ventilation

entmündigen vt declare incapable of managing his own affairs

entmutigen vt discourage

entnehmen† vt take (dat from); (schließen) gather (dat from)

Entomologie f - entomology

entpuppen (sich) vr (fig) turn out (**als etw** to be sth)

entrahmt a skimmed

entreißen† vt snatch (dat from)

entrichten vt pay

entrinnen† vi (sein) escape

entrollen vt unroll; unfurl (Fahne); **sich e~** unroll; unfurl

entrüst|en vt fill with indignation; **sich e~en** be indignant (**über** + acc at). **e~et** a indignant, adv -ly. **E~ung** f - indignation

entsaft|en vt extract the juice from. **E~er** m -s,- juice extractor

entsag|en vi (haben) (+ dat) renounce. **E~ung** f - renunciation

entschädig|en vt compensate. **E~ung** f -,-en compensation

entschärfen vt defuse

entscheid|en† vt/i (haben) decide; **sich e~en** decide; (Sache:) be decided. **e~end** a decisive, adv -ly; (kritisch) crucial. **E~ung** f decision

entschieden a decided, adv -ly; (fest) firm, adv -ly

entschlafen† vi (sein) (liter) pass away

entschließen† (sich) vr decide, make up one's mind; **sich anders e~** change one's mind

entschlossen a determined; (energisch) resolute, adv -ly; **kurz e~** without hesitation; (spontan) on the spur of the moment. **E~heit** f - determination

Entschluß m decision; **einen E~ fassen** make a decision

entschlüsseln vt decode

entschuld|bar a excusable. **e~igen** vt excuse; **sich e~igen** apologize (**bei** to); **e~igen Sie [bitte]!** sorry! (bei Frage) excuse me. **E~igung** f -,-en apology; (Ausrede) excuse; **[jdn] um E~igung bitten** apologize [to s.o.]; **E~igung!** sorry! (bei Frage) excuse me

entsetz|en vt horrify. **E~en** nt -s horror. **e~lich** a horrible, adv -bly; (schrecklich) terrible, adv -bly. **e~t** a horrified

entsinnen† (sich) vr (+ gen) remember

Entsorgung f - waste disposal

entspann|en vt relax; sich e~en relax; ⟨Lage:⟩ ease. E~ung f - relaxation; easing; (Pol) détente

entsprech|en† vi (haben) (+ dat) correspond to; (übereinstimmen) agree with; (nachkommen) comply with. e~end a corresponding; (angemessen) appropriate; (zuständig) relevant ● adv correspondingly; appropriately; (demgemäß) accordingly ● prep (+ dat) in accordance with. E~ung f -,-en equivalent

entspringen† vi (sein) ⟨Fluß:⟩ rise; (fig) arise, spring (dat from); (entfliehen) escape

entstammen vi (sein) come/(abstammen) be descended (dat from)

entsteh|en† vi (sein) come into being; (sich bilden) form; (sich entwickeln) develop; ⟨Brand:⟩ start; (stammen) originate/(sich ergeben) result (aus from). E~ung f - origin; formation; development; (fig) birth

entsteinen vt stone

entstell|en vt disfigure; (verzerren) distort. E~ung f disfigurement; distortion

entstört a (Electr) suppressed

enttäusch|en vt disappoint. E~ung f disappointment

entvölkern vt depopulate

entwaffnen vt disarm. e~d a (fig) disarming

Entwarnung f all-clear [signal]

entwässer|n vt drain. E~ung f - drainage

entweder conj & adv either

entweichen† vi (sein) escape

entweih|en vt desecrate. E~ung f - desecration

entwenden vt steal (dat from)

entwerfen† vt design; (aufsetzen) draft; (skizzieren) sketch

entwert|en vt devalue; (ungültig machen) cancel. E~er m -s,- ticket-cancelling machine. E~ung f devaluation; cancelling

entwick|eln vt develop; sich e~eln develop. E~lung f -,-en development; (Biol) evolution. E~lungsland nt developing country

entwinden† vt wrench (dat from)

entwirren vt disentangle; (fig) unravel

entwischen vi (sein) jdm e~ (fam) give s.o. the slip

entwöhnen vt wean (gen from); cure ⟨Süchtige⟩

entwürdigend a degrading

Entwurf m design; (Konzept) draft; (Skizze) sketch

entwurzeln vt uproot

entzieh|en† vt take away (dat from); jdm den Führerschein e~hen disqualify s.o. from driving; sich e~hen (+ dat) withdraw from; (entgehen) evade. E~hungskur f treatment for drug/alcohol addiction

entziffern vt decipher

entzücken vt delight. E~ nt -s delight. e~d a delightful

Entzug m withdrawal; (Vorenthaltung) deprivation. E~serscheinungen fpl withdrawal symptoms

entzünd|en vt ignite; (anstecken) light; (fig: erregen) inflame; sich e~en ignite; (Med) become inflamed. e~et a (Med) inflamed. e~lich a inflammable. E~ung f (Med) inflammation

entzwei a broken. e~en (sich) vr quarrel. e~gehen† vi sep (sein) break

Enzian m -s,-e gentian

Enzyklo|pädie f -,-en encyclopaedia. e~pädisch a encyclopaedic

Enzym nt -s,-e enzyme

Epidemie f -,-n epidemic

Epi|lepsie f - epilepsy. E~leptiker(in) m -s,- (f -,-nen) epileptic. e~leptisch a epileptic

Epilog m -s,-e epilogue

episch a epic

Episode f -,-n episode

Epitaph nt -s,-e epitaph

Epoche f -,-n epoch. e~machend a epoch-making

Epos nt -,Epen epic

er pron he; (Ding, Tier) it

erachten vt consider (für nötig necessary). E~ nt -s meines E~s in my opinion

erbarmen (sich) vr have pity/⟨Gott:⟩ mercy (gen on). E~ nt -s pity; mercy

erbärmlich a wretched, adv -ly; (stark) terrible, adv -bly

erbarmungslos a merciless, adv -ly

erbau|en vt build; (fig) edify; sich e~en be edified (an + dat by); nicht e~t von (fam) not pleased about. e~lich a edifying

Erbe¹ m -n,-n heir

Erbe² nt -s inheritance; (fig) heritage. e~n vt inherit

erbeuten vt get; (Mil) capture

Erbfolge f (Jur) succession
erbieten† **(sich)** vr offer (**zu** to)
Erbin f **-,-nen** heiress
erbitten† vt ask for
erbittert a bitter; (heftig) fierce, adv -ly
erblassen vi (sein) turn pale
erblich a hereditary
erblicken vt catch sight of
erblinden vi (sein) go blind
erbost a angry, adv -ily
erbrechen† vt vomit ● vi/r **[sich] e~** vomit. **E~** nt **-s** vomiting
Erbschaft f **-,-en** inheritance
Erbse f **-,-n** pea
Erb|stück nt heirloom. **E~teil** nt inheritance
Erd|apfel m (Aust) potato. **E~beben** nt **-s,-** earthquake. **E~beere** f strawberry. **E~boden** m ground
Erde f **-,-n** earth; (Erdboden) ground; (Fußboden) floor; **auf der E~** on earth; (auf dem Boden) on the ground/floor. **e~n** vt (Electr) earth
erdenklich a imaginable
Erd|gas nt natural gas. **E~geschoß** nt ground floor, (Amer) first floor. **e~ig** a earthy. **E~kugel** f globe. **E~kunde** f geography. **E~nuß** f peanut. **E~öl** nt [mineral] oil. **E~reich** nt soil
erdreisten (sich) vr have the audacity (**zu** to)
erdrosseln vt strangle
erdrücken vt crush to death. **e~d** a (fig) overwhelming
Erd|rutsch m landslide. **E~teil** m continent
erdulden vt endure
ereifern (sich) vr get worked up
ereignen (sich) vr happen
Ereignis nt **-ses,-se** event. **e~los** a uneventful. **e~reich** a eventful
Eremit m **-en,-en** hermit
ererbt a inherited
erfahr|en† vt learn, hear; (erleben) experience ● a experienced. **E~ung** f **-,-en** experience; **in E~ung bringen** find out
erfassen vt seize; (begreifen) grasp; (einbeziehen) include; (aufzeichnen) record; **von einem Auto erfaßt werden** be struck by a car
erfind|en† vt invent. **E~er** m **-s,-inventor. e~erisch** a inventive. **E~ung** f **-,-en** invention
Erfolg m **-[e]s,-e** success; (Folge) result; **E~ haben** be successful. **e~en**

vi (sein) take place; (geschehen) happen. **e~los** a unsuccessful, adv -ly. **e~reich** a successful, adv -ly. **e~versprechend** a promising
erforder|lich a required, necessary. **e~n** vt require, demand. **E~nis** nt **-ses,-se** requirement
erforsch|en vt explore; (untersuchen) investigate. **E~ung** f exploration; investigation
erfreu|en vt please; **sich guter Gesundheit e~en** enjoy good health. **e~lich** a pleasing, gratifying; (willkommen) welcome. **e~licherweise** adv happily. **e~t** a pleased
erfrier|en† vi (sein) freeze to death; ⟨Glied:⟩ become frostbitten; ⟨Pflanze:⟩ be killed by the frost. **E~ung** f **-,-en** frostbite
erfrisch|en vt refresh; **sich e~en** refresh onself. **e~end** a refreshing. **E~ung** f **-,-en** refreshment
erfüll|en vt fill; (nachkommen) fulfil; serve ⟨Zweck⟩; discharge ⟨Pflicht⟩; **sich e~en** come true. **E~ung** f fulfilment; **in E~ung gehen** come true
erfunden invented; (fiktiv) fictitious
ergänz|en vt complement; (nachtragen) supplement; (auffüllen) replenish; (vervollständigen) complete; (hinzufügen) add; **sich e~en** complement each other. **E~ung** f complement; supplement; (Zusatz) addition. **E~ungsband** m supplement
ergeb|en† vt produce; (zeigen) show, establish; **sich e~en** result; ⟨Schwierigkeit:⟩ arise; (kapitulieren) surrender; (sich fügen) submit; **es ergab sich** it turned out (**daß** that) ● a devoted, adv -ly; (resigniert) resigned, adv -ly. **E~enheit** f - devotion
Ergebnis nt **-ses,-se** result. **e~los** a fruitless, adv -ly
ergehen† vi (sein) be issued; **etw über sich** (acc) **e~ lassen** submit to sth; **wie ist es dir ergangen?** how did you get on? ● vr **sich e~ in** (+ dat) indulge in
ergiebig a productive; (fig) rich
ergötzen vt amuse
ergreifen† vt seize; take ⟨Maßnahme, Gelegenheit⟩; take up ⟨Beruf⟩; (rühren) move; **die Flucht e~** flee. **e~d** a moving
ergriffen a deeply moved. **E~heit** f - emotion

Fenster nt -s,- window. **F∼brett** nt window-sill. **F∼laden** m [window] shutter. **F∼leder** nt chamois [-leather]. **F∼putzer** m -s,- window-cleaner. **F∼scheibe** f [window-]pane

Ferien /'fe:riən/ pl holidays; (Univ) vacation sg; **F∼ haben** be on holiday. **F∼ort** m holiday resort

Ferkel nt -s,- piglet

fern a distant; **der F∼e Osten** the Far East ● adv far away; **von f∼** from a distance ● prep (+ dat) far [away] from. **F∼bedienung** f remote control. **f∼bleiben**† vi sep (sein) stay away (dat from). **F∼e** f - distance; **in/aus der F∼e** in the/from a distance; **in weiter F∼e** far away; (zeitlich) in the distant future. **f∼er** a further ● adv (außerdem) furthermore; (in Zukunft) in future. **f∼gelenkt** a remote-controlled; ⟨Rakete⟩ guided. **F∼gespräch** nt long-distance call. **f∼gesteuert** a = **f∼gelenkt**. **F∼glas** nt binoculars pl. **f∼halten**† vt sep keep away; **sich f∼halten** keep away. **F∼kopierer** m -s,- fax machine. **F∼kurs[us]** m correspondence course. **F∼lenkung** f remote control. **F∼licht** nt (Auto) full beam. **F∼meldewesen** nt telecommunications pl. **F∼rohr** nt telescope. **F∼schreiben** nt telex. **F∼schreiber** m -s,- telex [machine]

Fernseh|apparat m television set. **f∼en**† vi sep (haben) watch television. **F∼en** nt -s television. **F∼er** m -s,- [television] viewer; (Gerät) television set. **F∼gerät** nt television set

Fernsprech|amt nt telephone exchange; (Amer) central. **F∼er** m telephone. **F∼nummer** f telephone number. **F∼zelle** f telephone box

Fernsteuerung f remote control

Ferse f -,-n heel. **F∼ngeld** nt **F∼ngeld geben** (fam) take to one's heels

fertig a finished; (bereit) ready; (Comm) ready-made; ⟨Gericht⟩ ready-to-serve; **f∼ werden mit** finish; (bewältigen) cope with; **f∼ sein** have finished; (fig) be through (**mit jdm** with s.o.); (fam: erschöpft) be all in/(seelisch) shattered ● adv **f∼ essen/lesen** eating/reading. **F∼bau** m (pl -bauten) prefabricated building. **f∼bringen**† vt sep manage to do; (beenden) finish; **ich bringe es nicht f∼** I can't bring myself to do it. **f∼en** vt make. **F∼gericht** nt ready-to-serve meal.

F∼haus nt prefabricated house. **F∼keit** f -,-en skill. **f∼kriegen** vt sep (fam) = **f∼bringen**. **f∼machen** vt sep finish; (bereitmachen) get ready; (fam: erschöpfen) wear out; (seelisch) shatter; (fam: abkanzeln) carpet; **sich f∼machen** get ready. **f∼stellen** vt sep complete. **F∼stellung** f completion. **F∼ung** f - manufacture

fesch a (fam) attractive; (flott) smart; (Aust: nett) kind

Fessel f -,-n ankle

fesseln vt tie up; tie (**an** + acc to); (fig) fascinate; **ans Bett gefesselt** confined to bed. **F∼** fpl bonds. **f∼d** a (fig) fascinating; (packend) absorbing

fest a firm; (nicht flüssig) solid; (erstarrt) set; (haltbar) strong; (nicht locker) tight; (feststehend) fixed; (ständig) steady; ⟨Anstellung⟩ permanent; ⟨Schlaf⟩ sound; ⟨Blick, Stimme⟩ steady; **f∼ werden** harden; ⟨Gelee:⟩ set; **f∼e Nahrung** solids pl ● adv firmly; tightly; steadily; soundly; (kräftig, tüchtig) hard; **f∼ schlafen** be fast asleep

Fest nt -[e]s,-e celebration; (Party) party; (Relig) festival; **frohes F∼!** happy Christmas!

fest|angestellt a permanent. **f∼binden**† vt sep tie (**an** + dat to). **f∼bleiben**† vi sep (sein) (fig) remain firm. **f∼e** adv (fam) hard. **F∼essen** nt = **F∼mahl**. **f∼fahren**† vi/r sep (sein) [sich] ⟨Verhandlungen:⟩ reach deadlock. **f∼halten**† v sep ● vt hold on to; (aufzeichnen) record; **sich f∼halten** hold on ● vi (haben) **f∼halten an** (+ dat) (fig) stick to; cling to ⟨Tradition⟩. **f∼igen** vt strengthen; **sich f∼igen** grow stronger. **F∼iger** m -s,- styling lotion/(Schaum-) mousse. **F∼igkeit** f - (s. fest) firmness; solidity; strength; steadiness. **f∼klammern** vt sep clip (**an** + dat to); **sich f∼klammern** cling (**an** + dat to). **F∼land** nt mainland; (Kontinent) continent. **f∼legen** vt sep (fig) fix, settle; lay down ⟨Regeln⟩; tie up ⟨Geld⟩; **sich f∼legen** commit oneself

festlich a festive, adv -ly. **F∼keiten** fpl festivities

fest|liegen† vi sep (haben) be fixed, settled. **f∼machen** v sep ● vt fasten/(binden) tie (**an** + dat to); (f∼legen) fix, settle ● vi (haben) (Naut) moor.

F∼**mahl** *nt* feast; (*Bankett*) banquet.
F∼**nahme** *f* -,-**n** arrest. f∼**nehmen**†
vt sep arrest. F∼**ordner** *m* steward.
f∼**setzen** *vt sep* fix, settle; (*inhaftieren*) gaol; **sich f∼setzen** collect.
f∼**sitzen**† *vi sep* (*haben*) be firm/
⟨*Schraube:*⟩ tight; (*haften*) stick;
(*nicht weiterkommen*) be stuck. F∼
spiele *npl* festival *sg.* f∼**stehen**† *vi
sep* (*haben*) be certain. f∼**stellen** *vt
sep* fix; (*ermitteln*) establish; (*bemerken*) notice; (*sagen*) state.
F∼**stellung** *f* establishment; (*Aussage*) statement; (*Erkenntnis*) realization. F∼**tag** *m* special day
Festung *f* -,-**en** fortress
Fest|zelt *nt* marquee. f∼**ziehen**† *vt
sep* pull tight. F∼**zug** *m* [grand] procession
Fete /'fe:tə, 'fɛ:tə/ *f* -,-**n** party
fett *a* fat; (*f∼reich*) fatty; (*fettig*)
greasy; (*üppig*) rich; ⟨*Druck*⟩ bold.
F∼ *nt* -[e]s,-e fat; (*flüssig*) grease.
f∼**arm** *a* low-fat. f∼**en** *vt* grease ● *vi*
(*haben*) be greasy. F∼**fleck** *m* grease
mark. f∼**ig** *a* greasy. f∼**leibig** *a*
obese. F∼**näpfchen** *nt* **ins F∼näpf-
chen treten** (*fam*) put one's foot in it
Fetzen *m* -**s,**- scrap; (*Stoff*) rag; **in F∼**
in shreds
feucht *a* damp, moist; ⟨*Luft*⟩ humid.
f∼**heiß** *a* humid. F∼**igkeit** *f* - damp-
ness; (*Nässe*) moisture; (*Luft-*) humid-
ity. F∼**igkeitscreme** *f* moisturizer
feudal *a* (*fam: vornehm*) sumptuous,
adv -ly. F∼**ismus** *m* - feudalism
Feuer *nt* -**s,**- fire; (*für Zigarette*) light;
(*Begeisterung*) passion; F∼ **machen**
light a fire; F∼ **fangen** catch fire; (*fam:
sich verlieben*) be smitten; **jdm F∼
geben** give s.o. a light. F∼**alarm**
m fire alarm. F∼**bestattung** *f*
cremation. f∼**gefährlich** *a* [in]
flammable. F∼**leiter** *f* fire-escape.
F∼**löscher** *m* -**s,**- fire extinguisher.
F∼**melder** *m* -**s,**- fire alarm. f∼**n** *vi*
(*haben*) fire (**auf** + *acc* on) ● *vt* (*fam*)
(*schleudern*) fling; (*entlassen*) fire.
F∼**probe** *f* (*fig*) test. f∼**rot** *a* crimson. f∼**speiend** *a* f∼**speiender Berg**
volcano. F∼**stein** *m* flint. F∼**stelle** *f*
hearth. F∼**treppe** *f* fire-escape.
F∼**wache** *f* fire station. F∼**waffe**
f firearm. F∼**wehr** *f* -,-**en** fire brigade. F∼**wehrauto** *nt* fire-engine.
F∼**wehrmann** *m* (*pl* -**männer** &
-**leute**) fireman. F∼**werk** *nt* firework

display, fireworks *pl.* F∼**werkskör-
per** *m* firework. F∼**zeug** *nt* lighter
feurig *a* fiery; (*fig*) passionate
Fiaker *m* -**s,**- (*Aust*) horse-drawn cab
Fichte *f* -,-**n** spruce
fidel *a* cheerful
Fieber *nt* -**s** [raised] temperature; F∼
haben have a temperature. f∼**haft** *a*
(*fig*) feverish, *adv* -ly. f∼**n** *vi* (*haben*)
be feverish. F∼**thermometer** *nt*
thermometer
fiebrig *a* feverish
fies *a* (*fam*) nasty, *adv* -ily
Figur *f* -,-**en** figure; (*Roman-, Film-*)
character; (*Schach-*) piece
Fik|tion /-'tsio:n/ *f* -,-**en** fiction. f∼**tiv**
a fictitious
Filet /fi'le:/ *nt* -**s,**-**s** fillet
Filial|e *f* -,-**n,** F∼**geschäft** *nt* (*Comm*)
branch
Filigran *nt* -**s** filigree
Film *m* -[e]s,-e film; (*Kino-*) film, (*Amer*)
movie; (*Schicht*) coating. f∼**en** *vt/i*
(*haben*) film. F∼**kamera** *f* cine-/(*für
Kinofilm*) film camera
Filt|er *m* & (*Techn*) *nt* -**s,**- filter;
(*Zigaretten-*) filter-tip. f∼**ern** *vt* filter.
F∼**erzigarette** *f* filter-tipped cigarette. f∼**rieren** *vt* filter
Filz *m* -**es** felt. f∼**en** *vi* (*haben*) become
matted ● *vt* (*fam*) (*durch- suchen*)
frisk; (*stehlen*) steal. F∼**schreiber** *m*
-**s,**-, F∼**stift** *m* felt-tipped pen
Fimmel *m* -**s,**- (*fam*) obsession
Fina|le *nt* -**s,**- (*Mus*) finale; (*Sport*) final.
F∼**list(in)** *m* -**en,**-**en** (*f* -,-**nen**) finalist
Finanz *f* -,-**en** finance. F∼**amt** *nt* tax
office. f∼**iell** *a* financial, *adv* -ly.
f∼**ieren** *vt* finance. F∼**minister** *m*
minister of finance
find|en† *vt* find; (*meinen*) think; **den
Tod f∼en** meet one's death; **wie f∼est
du das?** what do you think of that?
f∼est du? do you think so? **es wird
sich f∼en** it'll turn up; (*fig*) it'll be all
right ● *vi* (*haben*) find one's way. F∼**er**
m -**s,**- finder. F∼**erlohn** *m* reward.
f∼**ig** *a* resourceful. F∼**ling** *m* -**s,**-**e**
boulder
Finesse *f* -,-**n** (*Kniff*) trick; F∼**n**
(*Techn*) refinements
Finger *m* -**s,**- finger; **die F∼ lassen von**
(*fam*) leave alone; **etw im kleinen
F∼ haben** (*fam*) have sth at one's
fingertips. F∼**abdruck** *m* finger-
mark; (*Admin*) fingerprint. F∼**hut**
m thimble. F∼**nagel** *m* finger-nail.

F∼ring *m* ring. **F∼spitze** *f* finger-tip. **F∼zeig** *m* **-[e]s,-e** hint

fingier|en *vt* fake. **f∼t** *a* fictitious

Fink *m* **-en,-en** finch

Finn|e *m* **-n,-n, F∼in** *f* **-,-nen** Finn. **f∼isch** *a* Finnish. **F∼land** *nt* **-s** Finland

finster *a* dark; (*düster*) gloomy; (*unheildrohend*) sinister; **im F∼n** in the dark. **F∼nis** *f* **-** darkness; (*Astr*) eclipse

Finte *f* **-,-n** trick; (*Boxen*) feint

Firma *f* **-,-men** firm, company

firmen *vt* (*Relig*) confirm

Firmen|wagen *m* company car. **F∼zeichen** *nt* trade mark, logo

Firmung *f* **-,-en** (*Relig*) confirmation

Firnis *m* **-ses,-se** varnish. **f∼sen** *vt* varnish

First *m* **-[e]s,-e** [roof] ridge

Fisch *m* **-[e]s,-e** fish; **F∼e** (*Astr*) Pisces. **F∼dampfer** *m* trawler. **f∼en** *vt/i* (*haben*) fish; **aus dem Wasser f∼en** (*fam*) fish out of the water. **F∼er** *m* **-s,-** fisherman. **F∼erei** *f* **-, F∼fang** *f* fishing. **F∼gräte** *f* fishbone. **F∼händler** *m* fishmonger. **F∼otter** *m* otter. **F∼reiher** *m* heron. **F∼stäbchen** *nt* **-s,-** fish finger. **F∼teich** *m* fish-pond

Fiskus *m* **- der F∼** the Treasury

Fisole *f* **-,-n** (*Aust*) French bean

fit *a* fit. **F∼neß** *f* **-** fitness

fix *a* (*fam*) quick, *adv* -ly; (*geistig*) bright; **f∼e Idee** obsession; **fix und fertig** all finished; (*bereit*) all ready; (*fam: erschöpft*) shattered. **F∼er** *m* **-s,-** (*sl*) junkie

fixieren *vt* stare at; (*Phot*) fix

Fjord *m* **-[e]s,-e** fiord

FKK *abbr* (**Freikörperkultur**) naturism

flach *a* flat; (*eben*) level; (*niedrig*) low; (*nicht tief*) shallow; **F∼er Teller** dinner plate; **die f∼e Hand** the flat of the hand

Fläche *f* **-,-n** area; (*Ober-*) surface; (*Seite*) face. **F∼nmaß** *nt* square measure

Flachs *m* **-es** flax. **f∼blond** *a* flaxen-haired; (*Haar*) flaxen

flackern *vi* (*haben*) flicker

Flagg|e *f* **-,-n** flag

flagrant *a* flagrant

Flair /flɛː̞/ *nt* **-s** air, aura

Flak *f* **-,-[s]** anti-aircraft artillery//(*Geschütz*) gun

flämisch *a* Flemish

Flamme *f* **-,-n** flame; (*Koch-*) burner; **in F∼n** in flames

Flanell *m* **-s** (*Tex*) flannel

Flank|e *f* **-,-n** flank. **f∼ieren** *vt* flank

Flasche *f* **-,-n** bottle. **F∼nbier** *nt* bottled beer. **F∼nöffner** *m* bottle-opener

flatter|haft *a* fickle. **f∼n** *vi* (*sein/haben*) flutter; (*Segel:*) flap

flau *a* (*schwach*) faint; (*Comm*) slack; **mir ist f∼** I feel faint

Flaum *m* **-[e]s** down. **f∼ig** *a* downy; **f∼ig rühren** (*Aust Culin*) cream

flauschig *a* fleecy; (*Spielzeug*) fluffy

Flausen *fpl* (*fam*) silly ideas; (*Ausflüchte*) silly excuses

Flaute *f* **-,-n** (*Naut*) calm; (*Comm*) slack period; (*Schwäche*) low

fläzen (sich) *vr* (*fam*) sprawl

Flechte *f* **-,-n** (*Med*) eczema; (*Bot*) lichen; (*Zopf*) plait. **f∼n†** *vt* plait; weave (*Korb*)

Fleck *m* **-[e]s,-e[n]** spot; (*größer*) patch; (*Schmutz-*) stain, mark; **blauer F∼** bruise; **nicht vom F∼ kommen** (*fam*) make no progress. **f∼en** *vi* (*haben*) stain. **F∼en** *m* **-s,- = Fleck**; (*Ortschaft*) small town. **f∼enlos** *a* spotless. **F∼entferner** *m* **-s,-** stain remover. **f∼ig** *a* stained; (*Haut*) blotchy

Fledermaus *f* bat

Flegel *m* **-s,-** lout. **f∼haft** *a* loutish. **F∼jahre** *npl* (*fam*) awkward age *sg*. **f∼n (sich)** *vr* loll

flehen *vi* (*haben*) beg (**um** for). **f∼tlich** *a* pleading, *adv* -ly

Fleisch *nt* **-[e]s** flesh; (*Culin*) meat; (*Frucht-*) pulp. **F∼er** *m* **-s,-** butcher. **F∼erei** *f* **-,-en, F∼erladen** *m* butcher's shop. **f∼fressend** *a* carnivorous. **F∼fresser** *m* **-s,-** carnivore. **F∼hauer** *m* **-s,-** (*Aust*) butcher. **f∼ig** *a* fleshy. **f∼lich** *a* carnal. **F∼wolf** *m* mincer. **F∼wunde** *f* flesh-wound

Fleiß *m* **-es** diligence; **mit F∼** diligently; (*absichtlich*) on purpose. **f∼ig** *a* diligent, *adv* -ly; (*arbeitsam*) industrious, *adv* -ly

flektieren *vt* (*Gram*) inflect

fletschen *vt* **die Zähne f∼** (*Tier:*) bare its teeth

flex|ibel *a* flexible; (*Einband*) limp. **F∼ibilität** *f* **-** flexibility. **F∼ion** *f* **-,-en** (*Gram*) inflexion

flicken *vt* mend; (*mit Flicken*) patch. **F∼** *m* **-s,-** patch

Flieder *m* **-s** lilac. **f∼farben** *a* lilac

Fliege *f* **-,-n** fly; (*Schleife*) bow-tie; **zwei F∼n mit einer Klappe schlagen** kill

two birds with one stone. **f~n†** vi
(sein) fly; (geworfen werden) be
thrown; (fam: fallen) fall; (fam: entlassen werden) be fired/(von der
Schule) expelled; **in die Luft f~n** blow
up ● vt fly. **f~nd** a flying; ⟨Händler⟩
itinerant; **in f~nder Eile** in great
haste. **F~r** m **-s,-** airman; (Pilot) pilot;
(fam: Flugzeug) plane. **F~rangriff** m
air raid

flieh|en† vi (sein) flee (**vor**+ dat
from); (entweichen) escape ● vt shun.
f~end a fleeing; ⟨Kinn, Stirn⟩ re-
ceding. **F~kraft** f centrifugal force

Fliese f **-,-n** tile

Fließ|band nt assembly line. **f~en†**
vi (sein) flow; (aus Wasserhahn) run.
f~end a flowing; ⟨Wasser⟩ running;
⟨Verkehr⟩ moving; (geläufig) fluent,
adv -ly. **F~heck** nt fastback. **F~-
wasser** nt running water

flimmern vi (haben) shimmer; (TV)
flicker; **es flimmert mir vor den
Augen** everything is dancing in front
of my eyes

flink a nimble, adv -bly; (schnell)
quick, adv -ly

Flinte f **-,-n** shotgun

Flirt /flœɐt/ m **-s,-s** flirtation. **f~en** vi
(haben) flirt

Flitter m **-s** sequins pl; (F~schmuck)
tinsel. **F~wochen** fpl honeymoon sg

flitzen vi (sein) (fam) dash; ⟨Auto:⟩
whizz

Flock|e f **-,-n** flake; (Wolle) tuft. **f~ig** a
fluffy

Floh m **-[e]s,⁻e** flea. **F~markt** m flea
market. **F~spiel** nt tiddly-winks sg

Flor m **-s** gauze; (Trauer-) crape; (Samt-,
Teppich-) pile

Flora f **-** flora

Florett nt **-[e]s,-e** foil

florieren vi (haben) flourish

Floskel f **-,-n** [empty] phrase

Floß nt **-es,⁻e** raft

Flosse f **-,-n** fin; (Seehund-, Gummi-)
flipper; (sl: Hand) paw

Flöt|e f **-,-n** flute; (Block-) recorder.
f~en vi (haben) play the flute/
recorder; (fam: pfeifen) whistle
● vt play on the flute/recorder.
F~ist(in) m **-en,-en** (f **-,-nen**) flautist

flott a quick, adv -ly; (lebhaft) lively;
(schick) smart, adv -ly; **f~ leben** live
it up

Flotte f **-,-n** fleet

flottmachen vt sep **wieder f~** (Naut)
refloat; get going again ⟨Auto⟩; put back
on its feet ⟨Unternehmen⟩

Flöz nt **-es,-e** [coal] seam

Fluch m **-[e]s,⁻e** curse. **f~en** vi
(haben) curse, swear

Flucht¹ f **-,-en** (Reihe) line; (Zimmer-)
suite

Flucht² f **-** flight; (Entweichen) escape;
die F~ ergreifen take flight. **f~artig**
a hasty, adv -ily

flücht|en vi (sein) flee (**vor**+ dat
from); (entweichen) escape ● vr **sich
f~en** take refuge. **f~ig** a fugitive;
(kurz) brief, adv -ly; ⟨Blick, Gedanke⟩
fleeting; ⟨Bekanntschaft⟩ passing;
(oberflächlich) cursory, adv -ily;
(nicht sorgfältig) careless, adv -ly;
(Chem) volatile; **f~ig sein** be on the
run; **f~ig kennen** know slightly.
F~igkeitsfehler m slip. **F~ling** m
-s,-e fugitive; (Pol) refugee

Fluchwort nt (pl **-wörter**) swearword

Flug m **-[e]s,⁻e** flight. **F~abwehr** f
anti-aircraft defence. **F~ball** m
(Tennis) volley. **F~blatt** nt pamphlet

Flügel m **-s,-** wing; (Fenster-) casement;
(Mus) grand piano

Fluggast m [air] passenger

flügge a fully-fledged

Flug|gesellschaft f airline. **F~-
hafen** m airport. **F~lotse** m air-traf-
fic controller. **F~platz** m airport;
(klein) airfield. **F~preis** m air fare.
F~schein m air ticket. **F~schneise**
f flight path. **F~schreiber** m **-s,-**
flight recorder. **F~schrift** f pamphlet.
F~steig m **-[e]s,-e** gate. **F~wesen** nt
aviation. **F~zeug** nt **-[e]s,-e** aircraft,
plane

Fluidum nt **-s** aura

Flunder f **-,-n** flounder

flunkern vi (haben) (fam) tell fibs;
(aufschneiden) tell tall stories

Flunsch m **-[e]s,-e** pout

fluoreszierend a fluorescent

Flur m **-[e]s,-e** [entrance] hall; (Gang)
corridor

Flusen fpl fluff sg

Fluß m **-sses,⁻sse** river; (Fließen) flow;
im F~ (fig) in a state of flux. **f~ab-
wärts** adv downstream. **f~auf-
wärts** adv upstream. **F~bett** nt
river-bed

flüssig a liquid; ⟨Lava⟩ molten;
(fließend) fluent, adv -ly; ⟨Verkehr⟩
freely moving. **F~keit** f **-,-en** liquid;
(Anat) fluid

Flußpferd nt hippopotamus

flüstern vt/i (haben) whisper

Flut f -,-en high tide; (fig) flood; **F~en** waters. **F~licht** nt floodlight. **F~welle** f tidal wave

Föderation /-'tsio:n/ f -,-en federation

Fohlen nt -s,- foal

Föhn m -s föhn [wind]

Folg|e f -,-n consequence; (Reihe) succession; (Fortsetzung) instalment; (Teil) part; **F~e leisten** (+ dat) accept ⟨Einladung⟩; obey ⟨Befehl⟩. **f~en** vi (sein) follow ⟨jdm/etw s.o./sth⟩; (zuhören) listen ⟨dat to⟩; **daraus f~t, daß** it follows that; **wie f~t** as follows ● (haben) (gehorchen) obey ⟨jdm s.o.⟩. **f~end** a following; **f~endes** the following. **f~endermaßen** adv as follows

folger|n vt conclude (**aus** from). **F~ung** f -,-en conclusion

folg|lich adv consequently. **f~sam** a obedient, adv -ly

Folie /'fo:liə/ f -,-n foil; (Plastik-) film

Folklore f - folklore

Folter f -,-n torture; **auf die F~ spannen** (fig) keep on tenterhooks. **f~n** vt torture

Fön(P) m -s,-e hair-drier

Fonds /fõ:/ m -,- /-[s],-s/ fund

fönen vt [blow-]dry

Fontäne f -,-n jet; (Brunnen) fountain

Förder|band nt (pl -bänder) conveyor belt. **f~lich** a beneficial

fordern vt demand; (beanspruchen) claim; (zum Kampf) challenge; **gefordert werden** (fig) be stretched

fördern vt promote; (unterstützen) encourage; (finanziell) sponsor; (gewinnen) extract

Forderung f -,-en demand; (Anspruch) claim

Förderung f - (s. fördern) promotion; encouragement; (Techn) production

Forelle f -,-n trout

Form f -,-en form; (Gestalt) shape; (Culin, Techn) mould; (Back-) tin; **[gut] in F~** in good form

Formalität f -,-en formality

Format nt -[e]s,-e format; (Größe) size; (fig: Bedeutung) stature

Formation /-'tsio:n/ f -,-en formation

Formel f -,-n formula

formell a formal, adv -ly

formen vt shape, mould; (bilden) form; **sich f~** take shape

förmlich a formal, adv -ly; (regelrecht) virtual, adv -ly. **F~keit** f -,-en formality

form|los a shapeless; (zwanglos) informal, adv -ly. **F~sache** f formality

Formular nt -s,-e [printed] form

formulier|en vt formulate, word. **F~ung** f -,-en wording

forsch a brisk, adv -ly; (schneidig) dashing, adv -ly

forsch|en vi (haben) search (**nach** for). **f~end** a searching. **F~er** m -s,- research scientist; (Reisender) explorer. **F~ung** f -,-en research. **F~ungsreisende(r)** m explorer

Forst m -[e]s,-e forest

Förster m -s,- forester

Forstwirtschaft f forestry

Forsythie /-tsiə/ f -,-n forsythia

Fort nt -s,-s (Mil) fort

fort adv away; **f~ sein** be away; (gegangen/verschwunden) have gone; **und so f~** and so on; **in einem f~** continuously. **f~bewegen** vt sep move; **sich f~bewegen** move. **F~bewegung** f locomotion. **F~bildung** f further education/training. **f~bleiben†** vi sep (sein) stay away. **f~bringen†** vt sep take away. **f~fahren†** vi sep (sein) go away ● (haben/sein) continue (**zu** to). **f~fallen†** vi sep (sein) be dropped/ (ausgelassen) omitted; (entfallen) no longer apply; (aufhören) cease. **f~führen** vt sep continue. **F~gang** m departure; (Verlauf) progress. **f~gehen†** vi sep (sein) leave, go away; (ausgehen) go out; (andauern) go on. **f~geschritten** a advanced; (spät) late. **F~geschrittene(r)** m/f advanced student. **f~gesetzt** a constant, adv -ly. **f~jagen** vt sep chase away. **f~lassen†** vt sep let go; (auslassen) omit. **f~laufen†** vi sep (sein) run away; (sich f~setzen) continue. **f~laufend** a consecutive, adv -ly. **f~nehmen†** vt sep take away. **f~pflanzen (sich)** vr sep reproduce; ⟨Ton, Licht:⟩ travel. **F~pflanzung** f - reproduction. **F~pflanzungsorgan** nt reproductive organ. **f~reißen†** vt sep carry away; (entreißen) tear away. **f~schaffen** vt sep take away. **f~schicken** vt sep send away; (abschicken) send off. **f~schreiten†** vi sep (sein) continue; (Fortschritte machen) progress, advance. **f~schreitend** a progressive; ⟨Alter⟩ advancing. **F~schritt** m progress; **F~schritte machen** make progress.

f~schrittlich a progressive. **f~setzen** vt sep continue; **sich f~setzen** continue. **F~setzung** f -,-en continuation; (Folge) instalment; **F~setzung folgt** to be continued. **F~setzungsroman** m serialized novel, serial. **f~während** a constant, adv -ly. **f~werfen†** vt sep throw away. **f~ziehen†** v sep ● vt pull away ● vi (sein) move away

Fossil nt -,-ien /-jən/ fossil

Foto nt -s,-s photo. **F~apparat** m camera. **f~gen** a photogenic

Fotograf|(in) m -en,-en (f -,-nen) photographer. **F~ie** f -,-n photography; (Bild) photograph. **f~ieren** vt take a photo[graph] of; **sich f~ie- ren lassen** have one's photo[graph] taken ● vi (haben) take photographs. **f~isch** a photographic

Fotokopie f photocopy. **f~ren** vt photocopy. **F~rgerät** nt photocopier

Fötus m -,-ten foetus

Foul /faul/ nt -s,-s (Sport) foul. **f~en** vt foul

Foyer /foa'je:/ nt -s,-s foyer

Fracht f -,-en freight. **F~er** m -s,- freighter. **F~gut** nt freight. **F~schiff** nt cargo boat

Frack m -[e]s,ˮe & -s tailcoat; **im F~** in tails pl

Frage f -,-n question; **eine F~ stellen** ask a question; **etw in F~ stellen** question sth; (ungewiß machen) make sth doubtful; **ohne F~** undoubtedly; **nicht in F~ kommen** be out of the question. **F~bogen** m questionnaire. **f~n** vt/i (haben) ask; **sich f~n** wonder (ob whether). **f~nd** a questioning, adv -ly; (Gram) interrogative. **F~zeichen** nt question mark

frag|lich a doubtful; (Person, Sache) in question. **f~los** adv undoubtedly

Fragment nt -[e]s,-e fragment. **f~a- risch** a fragmentary

fragwürdig a questionable; (verdächtig) dubious

fraisefarben /'frɛ:s-/ a strawberry-pink

Fraktion /-'tsjo:n/ f -,-en parliamentary party

Franken[1] m -s,- (Swiss) franc

Franken[2] nt -s Franconia

Frankfurter f -,- frankfurter

frankieren vt stamp, frank

Frankreich nt -s France

Fransen fpl fringe sg

Franz|ose m -n,-n Frenchman; **die F~osen** the French pl. **F~ösin** f -,-nen Frenchwoman. **f~ösisch** a French. **F~ösisch** nt -[s] (Lang) French

frapp|ant a striking. **f~ieren** vt (fig) strike; **f~ierend** striking

fräsen vt (Techn) mill

Fraß m -es feed; (pej: Essen) muck

Fratze f -,-n grotesque face; (Grimasse) grimace; (pej: Gesicht) face; **F~n schneiden** pull faces

Frau f -,-en woman; (Ehe-) wife; **F~ Thomas** Mrs/(unverheiratet) Miss/ (Admin) Ms Thomas; **Unsere Liebe F~** (Relig) Our Lady. **F~chen** nt -s,- mistress

Frauen|arzt m, **F~ärztin** f gynaecologist. **F~rechtlerin** f -,-nen feminist. **F~zimmer** nt woman

Fräulein nt -s,- single woman; (jung) young lady; (Anrede) Miss

fraulich a womanly

frech a cheeky, adv -ily; (unverschämt) impudent, adv -ly. **F~dachs** m (fam) cheeky monkey. **F~heit** f -,-en cheekiness; impudence; (Äußerung, Handlung) impertinence

frei a free; (freischaffend) freelance; ⟨Künstler⟩ independent; (nicht besetzt) vacant; (offen) open; (bloß) bare; **f~er Tag** day off; **sich** (dat) **f~ nehmen** take time off; **f~ machen** (räumen) clear; vacate ⟨Platz⟩; (befreien) liberate; (entkleiden) bare; **f~ lassen** leave free; **jdm f~e Hand lassen** give s.o. a free hand; **ist dieser Platz f~?** is this seat taken? **'Zimmer f~'** 'vacancies' ● adv freely; (ohne Notizen) without notes; (umsonst) free

Frei|bad nt open-air swimming pool. **f~bekommen†** vt sep get released; **einen Tag f~bekommen** get a day off. **f~beruflich** a & adv freelance. **F~e** nt im F~en in the open air, out of doors. **F~frau** f baroness. **F~gabe** f release. **f~geben†** v sep ● vt release; (eröffnen) open; **jdm einen Tag f~geben** give s.o. a day off ● vi (haben) **jdm f~geben** give s.o. time off. **f~gebig** a generous, adv -ly. **F~gebigkeit** f -, generosity. **f~haben†** v sep ● vt **eine Stunde f~haben** have an hour off; (Sch) have a free period ● vi (haben) be off work/(Sch) school; (beurlaubt sein) have time off. **f~halten†** vt sep keep clear; (belegen) keep; **einen Tag/sich f~halten** keep a day/

oneself free; **jdn f~halten** treat s.o.
[to a meal/ drink]. **F~handelszone**
f free-trade area. **f~händig** *adv*
without holding on
Freiheit *f* -,-en freedom, liberty; **sich**
(*dat*) **F~en erlauben** take liberties.
F~sstrafe *f* prison sentence
freiheraus *adv* frankly
Frei|herr *m* baron. **F~karte** *f* free
ticket. **F~körperkultur** *f* naturism.
f~lassen† *vt sep* release, set free.
F~lassung *f* - release. **f~lauf** *m*
free-wheel. **f~legen** *vt sep* expose.
f~lich *adv* admittedly; (*natürlich*) of
course. **F~lichttheater** *nt* open-air
theatre. **f~machen** *v sep* ● *vt*
(*frankieren*) frank ● *vi/r* (*haben*)
[**sich**] **f~machen** take time off.
F~marke *f* [postage] stamp.
F~maurer *m* Freemason. **f~mütig**
a candid, *adv* -ly. **F~platz** *m* free
seat; (*Sch*) free place. **f~schaffend** *a*
freelance. **f~schwimmen**† (**sich**) *vr*
sep pass one's swimming test. **f~set-**
zen *vt sep* release; (*entlassen*) make
redundant. **f~sprechen**† *vt sep*
acquit. **F~spruch** *m* acquittal.
f~stehen† *vi sep* (*haben*) stand
empty; **es steht ihm f~** (*fig*) he is free
(**zu** to). **f~stellen** *vt sep* exempt (**von**
from); **jdm etw f~stellen** leave sth up
to s.o. **f~stempeln** *vt sep* frank.
F~stil *m* freestyle. **F~stoß** *m* free
kick. **F~stunde** *f* (*Sch*) free period
Freitag *m* Friday. **f~s** *adv* on Fri-
days
Frei|tod *m* suicide. **F~übungen** *fpl*
[physical] exercises. **F~umschlag** *m*
stamped envelope. **f~weg** *adv*
freely; (*offen*) openly. **f~willig** *a* voluntary, *adv* -ily. **F~willige(r)** *m/f*
volunteer. **F~zeichen** *nt* ringing
tone; (*Rufzeichen*) dialling tone.
F~zeit *f* free *or* spare time; (*Muße*)
leisure; (*Tagung*) [weekend/holi-
day] course. **F~zeit-** *pref* leisure ...
F~zeitbekleidung *f* casual wear.
f~zügig *a* unrestricted; (*großzügig*)
liberal; (*moralisch*) permissive
fremd *a* foreign; (*unbekannt, unge-*
wohnt) strange; (*nicht das eigene*)
other people's; **ein f~er Mann** *a*
stranger; **f~e Leute** strangers; **unter**
f~em Namen under an assumed
name; **jdm f~ sein** be unknown/
(*wesens-*) alien to s.o.; **ich bin hier f~**
I'm a stranger here. **f~artig** *a*
strange, *adv* -ly; (*exotisch*) exotic.

F~e *f* - **in der F~e** away from home;
(*im Ausland*) in a foreign country.
F~e(r) *m/f* stranger; (*Ausländer*)
foreigner; (*Tourist*) tourist. **F~en-**
führer *m* [tourist] guide. **F~en-**
verkehr *m* tourism. **F~enzimmer** *nt*
room [to let]; (*Gäste-*) guest room.
f~gehen† *vi sep* (*sein*) (*fam*) be unfaithful. **F~körper** *m* foreign body.
f~ländisch *a* foreign; (*exotisch*)
exotic. **F~ling** *m* **-s,-e** stranger.
F~sprache *f* foreign language. **F~**
wort *nt* (*pl -wörter*) foreign word
frenetisch *a* frenzied
frequentieren *vt* frequent. **F~enz**
f -,-en frequency
Freske *f* -,-n, **Fresko** *nt* **-s,-ken** fresco
Fresse *f* -,-n (*sl*) (*Mund*) gob; (*Gesicht*)
mug; **halt die F~!** shut your trap!
f~n† *vt/i* (*haben*) eat. **F~n** *nt* **-s**
feed; (*sl: Essen*) grub
Freßnapf *m* feeding bowl
Freud|e *f* -,-n pleasure; (*innere*) joy;
mit F~en with pleasure; **jdm eine F~e**
machen please s.o. **f~ig** *a* joyful, *adv*
-ly; **f~iges Ereignis** (*fig*) happy event.
f~los *a* cheerless; (*traurig*) sad
freuen *vt* please; **sich f~** be pleased
(**über** + *acc* about); **sich f~ auf** (+ *acc*)
look forward to; **es freut mich, ich**
freue mich I'm glad *or* pleased (**daß**
that)
Freund *m* **-es,-e** friend; (*Verehrer*) boy-
friend; (*Anhänger*) lover (*gen* of). **F~in**
f -,-nen friend; (*Liebste*) girlfriend;
(*Anhängerin*) lover (*gen* of). **f~lich** *a*
kind, *adv* -ly; (*umgänglich*) friendly;
(*angenehm*) pleasant; **wären Sie so**
f~lich? would you be so kind? **f~**
licherweise *adv* kindly. **F~lichkeit**
f -,-en kindness; friendliness; pleas-
antness
Freundschaft *f* -,-en friendship; **F~**
schließen become friends. **f~lich** *a*
friendly
Frevel /'fre:fəl/ *m* **-s,-** (*liter*) outrage.
f~haft *a* (*liter*) wicked
Frieden *m* **-s** peace; **F~ schließen**
make peace; **im F~** in peacetime; **laß**
mich in F~! leave me alone! **F~s-**
richter *m* ≈ magistrate. **F~svertrag**
m peace treaty
fried|fertig *a* peaceable. **F~hof** *m*
cemetery. **f~lich** *a* peaceful, *adv* -ly;
(*verträglich*) peaceable. **f~liebend** *a*
peace-loving
frieren† *vi* (*haben*) ⟨*Person:*⟩ be cold;
impers **es friert/hat gefroren** it is

freezing/there has been a frost; **frierst du? friert [es] dich?** are you cold? ● (*sein*) (*gefrieren*) freeze

Fries *m* **-es,-e** frieze

Frikadelle *f* **-,-n** [meat] rissole

frisch *a* fresh; (*sauber*) clean; (*leuchtend*) bright; (*munter*) lively; (*rü- stig*) fit; **sich f~ machen** freshen up ● *adv* freshly, newly; **f~ gelegte Eier** new-laid eggs; **ein Bett f~ beziehen** put clean sheets on a bed; **f~ gestrichen!** wet paint! **F~e** *f* - freshness; brightness; liveliness; fitness. **F~haltepackung** *f* vacuum pack. **F~käse** *m* ≈ cottage cheese. **f~weg** *adv* freely

Fri|seur /fri'zø:ɐ̯/ *m* **-s,-e** hairdresser; (*Herren-*) barber. **F~seursalon** *m* hairdressing salon. **F~seuse** /-'zø:zə/ *f* **-,-n** hairdresser

frisier|en *vt* **jdn/sich f~en** do s.o.'s/ one's hair; **die Bilanz/einen Motor f~en** (*fam*) fiddle the accounts/soup up an engine. **F~kommode** *f* dressing-table. **F~salon** *m* = **Friseursalon**. **F~tisch** *m* dressing-table

Frisör *m* **-s,-e** = **Friseur**

Frist *f* **-,-en** period; (*Termin*) deadline; (*Aufschub*) time; **drei Tage F~** three days' grace. **f~en** *vt* **sein Leben f~en** eke out an existence. **f~los** *a* instant, *adv* -ly

Frisur *f* **-,-en** hairstyle

fritieren *vt* deep-fry

frivol /fri'vo:l/ *a* frivolous, *adv* -ly; (*schlüpfrig*) smutty

froh *a* happy; (*freudig*) joyful; (*erleichtert*) glad; **f~e Ostern!** happy Easter!

fröhlich *a* cheerful, *adv* -ly; (*vergnügt*) merry, *adv* -ily; **f~e Weihnachten!** merry Christmas! **F~keit** *f* - cheerfulness; merriment

frohlocken *vi* (*haben*) rejoice; (*schadenfroh*) gloat

Frohsinn *m* - cheerfulness

fromm *a* (**frömmer, frömmst**) devout, *adv* -ly; (*gutartig*) docile, *adv* -ly; **f~er Wunsch** idle wish

Frömm|igkeit *f* - devoutness, piety. **f~lerisch** *a* sanctimonious, *adv* -ly

frönen *vi* (*haben*) indulge (*dat* in)

Fronleichnam *m* Corpus Christi

Front *f* **-,-en** front. **f~al** *a* frontal; ⟨*Zusammenstoß*⟩ head-on ● *adv* from the front; ⟨*zusammenstoßen*⟩ head-on. **F~alzusammenstoß** *m* head-on collision

Frosch *m* **-[e]s,:̈e** frog. **F~laich** *m* frog-spawn. **F~mann** *m* (*pl* **-männer**) frogman

Frost *m* **-[e]s,:̈e** frost. **F~beule** *f* chilblain

frösteln *vi* (*haben*) shiver; **mich fröstelte [es]** I shivered/(*fror*) felt chilly

frost|ig *a* frosty, *adv* -ily. **F~schutzmittel** *nt* antifreeze

Frottee *nt* & *m* **-s** towelling

frottier|en *vt* rub down. **F~[hand]tuch** *nt* terry towel

frotzeln *vt/i* (*haben*) **[über] jdn f~** make fun of s.o.

Frucht *f* **-,:̈e** fruit; **F~ tragen** bear fruit. **f~bar** *a* fertile; (*fig*) fruitful. **F~barkeit** *f* - fertility. **f~en** *vi* (*haben*) **wenig/nichts f~en** have little/ no effect. **f~ig** *a* fruity. **f~los** *a* fruitless, *adv* -ly. **f~saft** *m* fruit juice

frugal *a* frugal, *adv* -ly

früh *a* early ● *adv* early; (*morgens*) in the morning; **heute/gestern/morgen f~** this/yesterday/tomorrow morning; **von f~ an** from an early age. **f~auf** *adv* **von f~auf** from an early age. **F~aufsteher** *m* **-s,-** early riser. **F~e** *f* **- in aller F~e** bright and early; **in der F~e** (*SGer*) in the morning. **f~er** *adv* earlier; (*eher*) sooner; (*ehemals*) formerly; (*vor langer Zeit*) in the old days; **f~er oder später** sooner or later; **ich wohnte f~er in X** I used to live in X. **f~ere(r,s)** *a* earlier; (*ehemalig*) former; (*vorige*) previous; **in f~eren Zeiten** in former times. **f~estens** *adv* at the earliest. **F~geburt** *f* premature birth/(*Kind*) baby. **F~jahr** *nt* spring. **F~jahrsputz** *m* spring-cleaning. **F~kartoffeln** *fpl* new potatoes. **F~ling** *m* **-s,-e** spring. **f~morgens** *adv* early in the morning. **f~reif** *a* precocious

Frühstück *nt* breakfast. **f~en** *vi* (*haben*) have breakfast

frühzeitig *a* & *adv* early; (*vorzeitig*) premature, *adv* -ly

Frustr|ation /-'tsĭo:n/ *f* **-,-en** frustration. **f~ieren** *vt* frustrate; **f~ierend** frustrating

Fuchs *m* **-es,:̈e** fox; (*Pferd*) chestnut. **f~en** *vt* (*fam*) annoy

Füchsin *f* **-,-nen** vixen

fuchteln *vi* (*haben*) **mit etw f~** (*fam*) wave sth about

Fuder *nt* **-s,-** cart-load

Fuge[1] *f* **-,-n** joint; **aus den F~n gehen** fall apart

Fuge[2] *f* **-,-n** (*Mus*) fugue

füg|en *vt* fit (**in**+ *acc* into); (*an-*) join (**an**+ *acc* on to); (*dazu-*) add (**zu** to); (*fig: bewirken*) ordain; **sich f~en** fit (**in**+ *acc* into); adjoin/(*folgen*) follow (**an etw** *acc* sth); (*fig: gehorchen*) submit (*dat* to); **sich in sein Schicksal f~en** resign oneself to one's fate; **es f~te sich** it so happened (**daß** that). **f~sam** *a* obedient, *adv* -ly. **F~ung** *f* **-,-en eine F~ung des Schicksals** a stroke of fate

fühl|bar *a* noticeable. **f~en** *vt/i* (*haben*) feel; **sich f~en** feel (**krank/ einsam** ill/lonely); (*fam: stolz sein*) fancy oneself; **sich [nicht] wohl f~en** [not] feel well. **F~er** *m* **-s,-** feeler. **F~ung** *f* **-** contact; **F~ung aufnehmen** get in touch

Fuhre *f* **-,-n** load

führ|en *vt* lead; guide (*Tourist*); (*geleiten*) take; (*leiten*) run; (*befehligen*) command; (*verkaufen*) stock; bear (*Namen, Titel*); keep (*Liste, Bücher, Tagebuch*); **bei** *od* **mit sich f~en** carry; **sich gut/schlecht f~en** conduct oneself well/badly ● *vi* (*haben*) lead; (*verlaufen*) go, run; **zu etw f~en** lead to sth. **f~end** *a* leading. **F~er** *m* **-s,-** leader; (*Fremden-*) guide; (*Buch*) guide[book]. **F~erhaus** *nt* driver's cab. **F~erschein** *m* driving licence; **den F~erschein machen** take one's driving test. **F~erscheinentzug** *m* disqualification from driving. **F~ung** *f* **-,-en** leadership; (*Leitung*) management; (*Mil*) command; (*Betragen*) conduct; (*Besichtigung*) guided tour; (*Vorsprung*) lead; **in F~ung gehen** go into the lead

Fuhr|unternehmer *m* haulage contractor. **F~werk** *nt* cart

Fülle *f* **-,-n** abundance, wealth (**an**+ *dat* of); (*Körper-*) plumpness. **f~n** *vt* fill; (*Culin*) stuff; **sich f~n** fill [up]

Füllen *nt* **-s,-** foal

Füll|er *m* **-s,-** (*fam*), **F~federhalter** *m* fountain pen. **f~ig** *a* plump; (*Busen*) ample. **F~ung** *f* **-,-en** filling; (*Kissen-, Braten-*) stuffing; (*Pralinen-*) centre

fummeln *vi* (*haben*) fumble (**an**+ *dat* with)

Fund *m* **-[e]s,-e** find

Fundament *nt* **-[e]s,-e** foundations *pl*. **f~al** *a* fundamental

Fund|büro *nt* lost-property office. **F~grube** *f* (*fig*) treasure trove. **F~sachen** *fpl* lost property *sg*

fünf *inv a*, **F~** *f* **-,-en** five; (*Sch*) ≈ fail mark. **F~linge** *mpl* quintuplets. **f~te(r,s)** *a* fifth. **f~zehn** *inv a* fifteen. **f~zehnte(r,s)** *a* fifteenth. **f~zig** *inv a* fifty. **F~ziger** *m* **-s,-** man in his fifties; (*Münze*) 50-pfennig piece. **f~zigste(r,s)** *a* fiftieth

fungieren *vi* (*haben*) act (**als** as)

Funk *m* **-s** radio; **über F~** over the radio. **F~e** *m* **-n,-n** spark. **f~eln** *vi* (*haben*) sparkle; (*Stern:*) twinkle. **f~elnagelneu** *a* (*fam*) brand-new. **F~en** *m* **-s,-** spark. **f~en** *vt* radio. **F~er** *m* **-s,-** radio operator. **F~sprechgerät** *nt* walkie-talkie. **F~spruch** *m* radio message. **F~streife** *f* [police] radio patrol

Funktion /-'tsio:n/ *f* **-,-en** function; (*Stellung*) position; (*Funktionieren*) working; **außer F~** out of action. **F~är** *m* **-s,-e** official. **f~ieren** *vi* (*haben*) work

für *prep* (+ *acc*) for; **Schritt für Schritt** step by step; **was für [ein]** what [a]! (*fragend*) what sort of [a]? **für sich** by oneself/(*Ding:*) itself. **Für** *nt* **das Für und Wider** the pros and cons *pl*. **F~bitte** *f* intercession

Furche *f* **-,-n** furrow

Furcht *f* **-** fear (**vor**+ *dat* of). **f~bar** *a* terrible, *adv* -bly

fürcht|en *vt/i* (*haben*) fear; **sich f~en** be afraid (**vor**+ *dat* of); **ich f~e, das geht nicht** I'm afraid that's impossible. **f~erlich** *a* dreadful, *adv* -ly

furcht|erregend *a* terrifying. **f~los** *a* fearless, *adv* -ly. **f~sam** *a* timid, *adv* -ly

füreinander *adv* for each other

Furnier *nt* **-s,-e** veneer. **f~t** *a* veneered

fürs *prep* = **für das**

Fürsorg|e *f* care; (*Admin*) welfare; (*fam: Geld*) ≈ social security. **F~er(in)** *m* **-s,-** (*f* **-,-nen**) social worker. **f~lich** *a* solicitous

Fürsprache *f* intercession; **F~ einlegen** intercede

Fürsprecher *m* (*fig*) advocate

Fürst *m* **-en,-en** prince. **F~entum** *nt* **-s,¨er** principality. **F~in** *f* **-,-nen** princess. **f~lich** *a* princely; (*üppig*) lavish, *adv* -ly

Furt *f* **-,-en** ford

Furunkel *m* **-s,-** (*Med*) boil

Fürwort *nt* (*pl* **-wörter**) pronoun

Furz *m* **-es,-e** (*vulg*) fart. **f~en** *vi* (*haben*) (*vulg*) fart

Fusion f -,-en fusion; (*Comm*) merger.
f~ieren vi (haben) (*Comm*) merge
Fuß m -es,¨e leg; (*Aust: Bein*) leg;
(*Lampen-*) base; (*von Weinglas*) stem; **zu
Fuß** on foot; **zu Fuß gehen** walk; **auf
freiem Fuß** free; **auf freundschaft-
lichem/großem Fuß** on friendly
terms/in grand style. **F~abdruck** m
footprint. **F~abtreter** m -s,- door-
mat. **F~bad** nt foot-bath. **F~ball** m
football. **F~ballspieler** m footballer.
F~balltoto nt football pools pl.
F~bank f footstool. **F~boden** m
floor. **F~bremse** f footbrake
Fussel f -,-n & m -s,-[n] piece of fluff;
F~n fluff sg. **f~n** vi (haben) shed fluff
fuß|en vi (haben) be based (**auf** + dat
on). **F~ende** nt foot
Fußgänger|(in) m -s,- (f -,-nen) ped-
estrian. **F~brücke** f footbridge.
F~überweg m pedestrian crossing.
F~zone f pedestrian precinct
Fußgeher m -s,- (*Aust*) = **F~gänger.**
F~gelenk nt ankle. **F~hebel** m
pedal. **F~nagel** m toenail. **F~note** f
footnote. **F~pflege** f chiropody.
F~pfleger(in) m(f) chiropodist.
F~rücken m instep. **F~sohle** f sole
of the foot. **F~stapfen** pl **in jds
F~stapfen treten** (*fig*) follow in s.o.'s
footsteps. **F~tritt** m kick. **F~weg** m
footpath; **eine Stunde F~weg** an
hour's walk
futsch pred a (*fam*) gone
Futter[1] nt -s feed; (*Trocken-*) fodder
Futter[2] nt -s,- (*Kleider-*) lining
Futteral nt -s,-e case
füttern[1] vt feed
füttern[2] vt line
Futur nt -s (*Gram*) future; **zweites F~**
future perfect. **f~istisch** a futuristic

G

Gabe f -,-n gift; (*Dosis*) dose
Gabel f -,-n fork. **g~n (sich)** vr fork.
G~stapler m -s,- fork-lift truck.
G~ung f -,-en fork (*in road*)
gackern vi (haben) cackle
gaffen vi (haben) gape, stare
Gag /gɛk/ m -s,-s (*Theat*) gag
Gage /'ga:ʒə/ f -,-n (*Theat*) fee
gähnen vi (haben) yawn. **G~** nt -s
yawn; (*wiederholt*) yawning
Gala f - ceremonial dress
galant a gallant, adv -ly

Galavorstellung f gala performance
Galerie f -,-n gallery
Galgen m -s,- gallows sg. **G~frist** f
(*fam*) reprieve
Galionsfigur f figurehead
Galle f - bile; (*G~nblase*) gall-bladder.
G~nblase f gall-bladder. **G~nstein**
m gallstone
Gallert nt -[e]s,-e, **Gallerte** f -,-n
[meat] jelly
Galopp m -s gallop; **im G~** at a gallop.
g~ieren vi (sein) gallop
galvanisieren vt galvanize
gamm|eln vi (haben) (*fam*) loaf
around. **G~ler(in)** m -s,- (f -,-nen)
drop-out
Gams f -,¨e (*Aust*) chamois
gäng pred a **g~ und gäbe** quite usual
Gang m -[e]s,¨e walk; (*Gangart*) gait;
(*Boten-*) errand; (*Funktionieren*) running; (*Verlauf, Culin*) course; (*Durch-*)
passage; (*Korridor*) corridor; (*zwischen
Sitzreihen*) aisle, gangway; (*Anat*) duct;
(*Auto*) gear; **in G~ bringen/halten**
get/keep going; **in G~ kommen** get
going/(*fig*) under way; **im G~e/in vollem G~e sein** be in progress/in full
swing; **Essen mit vier G~en** four-
course meal. **G~art** f gait
gängig a common; (*Comm*) popular
Gangschaltung f gear change
Gangster /'gɛŋstɐ/ m -s,- gangster
Gangway /'gɛŋwe:/ f -,-s gangway
Ganove m -n,-n (*fam*) crook
Gans f -,¨e goose
Gänse|blümchen nt -s,- daisy.
G~füßchen ntpl inverted commas.
G~haut f goose-pimples pl. **G~-
marsch** m **im G~marsch** in single file.
G~rich m -s,-e gander
ganz a whole, entire; (*vollständig*)
complete; (*fam: heil*) undamaged, intact; **die g~e Zeit** all the time, the
whole time; **eine g~e Weile/Menge**
quite a while/lot; **g~e zehn Mark** all
of ten marks; **meine g~en Bücher** all
my books; inv **g~ Deutschland** the
whole of Germany; **g~ bleiben** (*fam*)
remain mend; **wieder g~ machen**
(*fam*) mend; **im g~en** in all, altogether; **im großen und g~en** on the
whole ● adv quite; (*völlig*) completely,
entirely; (*sehr*) very; **nicht g~** not
quite; **g~ allein** all on one's own; **ein
g~ alter Mann** a very old man; **g~ wie
du willst** just as you like; **es war g~**

nett it was quite nice; **g~ und gar** completely, totally; **g~ und gar nicht** not at all. **G~e(s)** nt whole; **es geht ums G~e** it's all or nothing. **g~jährig** adv all the year round

gänzlich adv completely, entirely

ganz|tägig a & adv full-time; ⟨geöffnet⟩ all day. **g~tags** adv all day; ⟨arbeiten⟩ full-time

gar¹ a done, cooked

gar² adv **gar nicht/nichts/niemand** not/nothing/no one at all; **oder gar** or even

Garage /ga'ra:ʒə/ f -,-n garage

Garantie f -,-n guarantee. **g~ren** vt/i (haben) [**für**] etw **g~ren** guarantee sth; **er kommt g~rt zu spät** (fam) he's sure to be late. **G~schein** m guarantee

Garbe f -,-n sheaf

Garderobe f -,-n ⟨Kleider⟩ wardrobe; ⟨Ablage⟩ cloakroom, (Amer) checkroom; ⟨Flur-⟩ coat-rack; ⟨Künstler-⟩ dressing-room. **G~nfrau** f cloakroom attendant

Gardine f -,-n curtain. **G~nstange** f curtain rail

garen vt/i (haben) cook

gären† vi (haben) ferment; (fig) seethe

Garn nt -[e]s,-e yarn; ⟨Näh-⟩ cotton

Garnele f -,-n shrimp; ⟨rote⟩ prawn

garnieren vt decorate; ⟨Culin⟩ garnish

Garnison f -,-en garrison

Garnitur f -,-en set; ⟨Wäsche⟩ set of matching underwear; ⟨Möbel-⟩ suite; **erste/zweite G~ sein** (fam) be first-rate/second best

garstig a nasty

Garten m -s,- garden; **botanischer G~** botanical gardens pl. **G~arbeit** f gardening. **G~bau** m horticulture. **G~haus** nt, **G~laube** f summerhouse. **G~lokal** nt open-air café. **G~schere** f secateurs pl

Gärtner|(in) m -s,- (f -,-nen) gardener. **G~ei** f -,-en nursery; (fam: Gartenarbeit) gardening

Gärung f - fermentation

Gas nt -es,-e gas; **Gas geben** (fam) accelerate. **G~herd** m gas cooker. **G~maske** f gas mask. **G~pedal** nt (Auto) accelerator

Gasse f -,-n alley; (Aust) street

Gast m -[e]s,-e guest; ⟨Hotel-, Urlaubs-⟩ visitor; (im Lokal) patron; **zum Mittag G~e haben** have people to lunch; **bei**

jdm zu G~ sein be staying with s.o. **G~arbeiter** m foreign worker. **G~bett** nt spare bed

Gäste|bett nt spare bed. **G~buch** nt visitors' book. **G~zimmer** nt [hotel] room; (privat) spare room; (Aufenthaltsraum) residents' lounge

gast|frei, g~freundlich a hospitable, adv -bly. **G~freundschaft** f hospitality. **G~geber** m -s,- host. **G~geberin** f -,-nen hostess. **G~haus** nt, **G~hof** m inn, hotel

gastieren vi (haben) make a guest appearance; ⟨Truppe, Zirkus:⟩ perform (**in** + dat in)

gastlich a hospitable, adv -bly. **G~keit** f - hospitality

Gastro|nomie f - gastronomy. **g~nomisch** a gastronomic

Gast|spiel nt guest performance. **G~spielreise** f ⟨Theat⟩ tour. **G~stätte** f restaurant. **G~stube** f bar; ⟨Restaurant⟩ restaurant. **G~wirt** m landlord. **G~wirtin** f landlady. **G~wirtschaft** f restaurant

Gas|werk nt gasworks sg. **G~zähler** m gas-meter

Gatte m -n,-n husband

Gatter nt -s,- gate; ⟨Gehege⟩ pen

Gattin f -,-nen wife

Gattung f -,-en kind; ⟨Biol⟩ genus; ⟨Kunst⟩ genre. **G~sbegriff** m generic term

Gaudi f - ⟨Aust, fam⟩ fun

Gaul m -[e]s, Gäule [old] nag

Gaumen m -s,- palate

Gauner m -s,- crook, swindler. **G~ei** f -,-en swindle

Gaze /'ga:zə/ f - gauze

Gazelle f -,-n gazelle

geachtet a respected

geädert a veined

geartet a **gut g~** good-natured; **anders g~** different

Gebäck nt -s [cakes and] pastries pl; ⟨Kekse⟩ biscuits pl

Gebälk nt -s timbers pl

geballt a ⟨Faust⟩ clenched

Gebärde f -,-n gesture. **g~n (sich)** vr behave (**wie** like)

Gebaren nt -s behaviour

gebär|en† vt give birth to, bear; **geboren werden** be born. **G~mutter** f womb, uterus

Gebäude nt -s,- building

Gebeine ntpl [mortal] remains

Gebell nt -s barking

geben† *vt* give; *(tun, bringen)* put; *(Karten)* deal; *(aufführen)* perform; *(unterrichten)* teach; **etw verloren g~** give sth up as lost; **von sich g~** utter; *(fam: erbrechen)* bring up; **viel/ wenig g~ auf** (+ *acc*) set great/ little store by; **sich g~** *(nachlassen)* wear off; *(besser werden)* get better; *(sich verhalten)* behave; **sich geschlagen g~** admit defeat ● *impers* **es gibt** there is/ are; **was gibt es Neues/ zum Mittag/ im Kino?** what's the news/for lunch/ on at the cinema? **es wird Regen g~** it's going to rain; **das gibt es nicht** there's no such thing ● *vi (haben) (Karten)* deal

Gebet *nt* **-[e]s,-e** prayer

Gebiet *nt* **-[e]s,-e** area; *(Hoheits-)* territory; *(Sach-)* field

gebieten|en† *vt* command; *(erfordern)* demand ● *vi (haben)* rule. **G~er** *m* **-s,-** master; *(Herrscher)* ruler. **g~erisch** *a* imperious, *adv* -ly; *⟨Ton⟩* peremptory

Gebilde *nt* **-s,-** structure

gebildet *a* educated; *(kultiviert)* cultured

Gebirg|e *nt* **-s,-** mountains *pl.* **g~ig** *a* mountainous

Gebiß *nt* **-sses,-sse** teeth *pl;* *(künstliches)* false teeth *pl,* dentures *pl;* *(des Zaumes)* bit

geblümt *a* floral, flowered

gebogen *a* curved

geboren *a* born; **g~er Deutscher** German by birth; **Frau X, g~e Y** Mrs X, née Y

geborgen *a* safe, secure. **G~heit** *f* -security

Gebot *nt* **-[e]s,-e** rule; *(Relig)* commandment; *(bei Auktion)* bid

gebraten *a* fried

Gebrauch *m* use; *(Sprach-)* usage; **Gebräuche** customs; **in G~** in use; **G~ machen von** make use of. **g~en** *vt* use; **ich kann es nicht/gut g~en** I have no use for/can make good use of it; **zu nichts zu g~en** useless

gebräuchlich *a* common; *⟨Wort⟩* in common use

Gebrauch|sanleitung, G~sanweisung *f* directions *pl* for use. **g~t** *a* used; *(Comm)* secondhand. **G~twagen** *m* used car

gebrechlich *a* frail, infirm

gebrochen *a* broken ● *adv* **g~ Englisch sprechen** speak broken English

Gebrüll *nt* **-s** roaring; *(fam: Schreien)* bawling

Gebrumm *nt* **-s** buzzing; *(Motoren-)* humming

Gebühr *f* **-,-en** charge, fee; **über G~** excessively. **g~en** *vi (haben)* **ihm g~t Respekt** he deserves respect; **wie es sich g~t** as is right and proper. **g~end** *a* due, *adv* duly; *(geziemend)* proper, *adv* -ly. **g~enfrei** *a* free ● *adv* free of charge. **g~enpflichtig** *a* & *adv* subject to a charge; **g~enpflichtige Straße** toll road

gebunden *a* bound; *⟨Suppe⟩* thickened

Geburt *f* **-,-en** birth; **von G~** by birth. **G~enkontrolle, G~enregelung** *f* birth-control. **G~enziffer** *f* birthrate

gebürtig *a* native (**aus** of); **g~er Deutscher** German by birth

Geburts|datum *nt* date of birth. **G~helfer** *m* obstetrician. **G~hilfe** *f* obstetrics *sg.* **G~ort** *m* place of birth. **G~tag** *m* birthday. **G~urkunde** *f* birth certificate

Gebüsch *nt* **-[e]s,-e** bushes *pl*

Gedächtnis *nt* **-ses** memory; **aus dem G~** from memory

gedämpft *a* *⟨Ton⟩* muffled; *⟨Stimme⟩* hushed; *⟨Musik⟩* soft; *⟨Licht, Stimmung⟩* subdued

Gedanke *m* **-ns,-n** thought (**an** + *acc* of); *(Idee)* idea; **sich** *(dat)* **G~n machen** worry (**über** + *acc* about). **G~nblitz** *m* brainwave. **g~nlos** *a* thoughtless, *adv* -ly; *(zerstreut)* absent-minded, *adv* -ly. **G~nstrich** *m* dash. **G~nübertragung** *f* telepathy. **g~nvoll** *a* pensive, *adv* -ly

Gedärme *ntpl* intestines; *(Tier-)* entrails

Gedeck *nt* **-[e]s,-e** place setting; *(auf Speisekarte)* set meal; **ein G~ auflegen** set a place. **g~t** *a* covered; *⟨Farbe⟩* muted

gedeihen† *vi (sein)* thrive, flourish

gedenken† *vi (haben)* propose (**etw zu tun** to do sth); **jds/etw g~** remember s.o./sth. **G~** *nt* **-s** memory; **zum G~ an** (+ *acc*) in memory of

Gedenk|feier *f* commemoration. **G~gottesdienst** *m* memorial service. **G~stätte** *f* memorial. **G~tafel** *f* commemorative plaque. **G~tag** *m* day of remembrance; *(Jahrestag)* anniversary

Gedicht *nt* **-[e]s,-e** poem

g~**wenig** adv just as little/few; (noch) no more

Gendarm /ʒã'darm/ m -en,-en (Aust) policeman

Genealogie f - genealogy

genehmig|en vt grant; approve ⟨Plan⟩. **G~ung** f -,-en permission; (Schein) permit

geneigt a sloping, inclined; (fig) well-disposed (dat towards); [nicht] g~ sein (fig) [not] feel inclined (zu to)

General m -s,-̈e general. **G~direktor** m managing director. **g~isieren** vi (haben) generalize. **G~probe** f dress rehearsal. **G~streik** m general strike. **g~überholen** vt insep (inf & pp only) completely overhaul

Generation /-'tsjo:n/ f -,-en generation

Generator m -s,-en /-'to:rən/ generator

generell a general, adv -ly

genes|en† vi (sein) recover. **G~ung** f - recovery; (Erholung) convalescence

Genet|ik f - genetics sg. **g~isch** a genetic, adv -ally

Genf nt -s Geneva. **G~er** a Geneva...; **G~er See** Lake Geneva

genial a brilliant, adv -ly; **ein g~er Mann** a man of genius. **G~ität** f - genius

Genick nt -s,-e [back of the] neck; **sich** (dat) **das G~ brechen** break one's neck

Genie /ʒe'ni:/ nt -s,-s genius

genieren /ʒe'ni:rən/ vt embarrass; **sich g~** feel or be embarrassed

genieß|bar a fit to eat/drink. **g~en†** vt enjoy; (verzehren) eat/drink. **G~er** m -s,- gourmet. **g~erisch** a appreciative ● adv with relish

Genitiv m -s,-e genitive

Genosse m -n,-n (Pol) comrade. **G~nschaft** f -,-en co-operative

Genre /'ʒã:rə/ nt -s,-s genre

Gentechnologie f genetic engineering

genug inv a & adv enough

Genüge f **zur G~** sufficiently. **g~n** vi (haben) be enough; **jds Anforderungen g~n** meet s.o.'s requirements. **g~nd** inv a sufficient, enough; (Sch) fair ● adv sufficiently, enough

genügsam a frugal, adv -ly; (bescheiden) modest, adv -ly

Genugtuung f - satisfaction

Genuß m -sses,-̈sse enjoyment; (Vergnügen) pleasure; (Verzehr) consumption. **genüßlich** a pleasurable ● adv with relish

geöffnet a open

Geo|graphie f - geography. **g~graphisch** a geographical, adv -ly. **G~loge** m -n,-n geologist. **G~logie** f - geology. **g~logisch** a geological, adv -ly. **G~meter** m -s,- surveyor. **G~metrie** f - geometry. **g~metrisch** a geometric[al]

geordnet a well-ordered; (stabil) stable; **alphabetisch g~** in alphabetical order

Gepäck nt -s luggage, baggage. **G~ablage** f luggage-rack. **G~aufbewahrung** f left-luggage office. **G~schalter** m luggage office. **G~schein** m left-luggage ticket; (Aviat) baggage check. **G~stück** nt piece of luggage. **G~träger** m porter; (Fahrrad-) luggage carrier; (Dach-) roof-rack. **G~wagen** m luggage-van

Gepard m -s,-e cheetah

gepflegt a well-kept; ⟨Person⟩ well-groomed; ⟨Hotel⟩ first-class

Gepflogenheit f -,-en practice; (Brauch) custom

Gepolter nt -s [loud] noise

gepunktet a spotted

gerade a straight; (direkt) direct; (aufrecht) upright; (aufrichtig) straightforward; ⟨Zahl⟩ even ● adv straight; directly; (eben) just; (genau) exactly; (besonders) especially; **nicht g~ billig** not exactly cheap; **g~ erst** only just; **g~ an dem Tag** on that very day. **G~** f -,-n straight line. **g~aus** adv straight ahead/on

gerade|biegen† vt sep straighten; (fig) straighten out. **g~halten†** (sich) vr sep hold oneself straight. **g~heraus** adv (fig) straight out. **g~sitzen†** vi sep (haben) sit [up] straight. **g~so** adv just the same; **g~so gut** just as good. **g~sogut** adv just as well. **g~stehen†** vi sep (haben) stand up straight; (fig) accept responsibility (**für** for). **g~wegs** adv directly, straight. **g~zu** adv virtually; (wirklich) absolutely

Geranie /-jə/ f -,-n geranium

Gerät nt -[e]s,-e tool; (Acker-) implement; (Küchen-) utensil; (Elektro-) appliance; (Radio-, Fernseh-) set;

(*Turn-*) piece of apparatus; (*coll*) equipment

geraten† *vi (sein)* get; **in Brand g~** catch fire; **in Wut g~** get angry; **in Streit g~** start quarrelling; **gut/ schlecht g~** turn out well/badly; **nach jdm g~** take after s.o.

Geratewohl *nt* **aufs G~** at random

geräuchert *a* smoked

geräumig *a* spacious, roomy

Geräusch *nt* -[e]s,-e noise. **g~los** *a* noiseless, *adv* -ly. **g~voll** *a* noisy, *adv* -ily

gerben *vt* tan

gerecht *a* just, *adv* -ly; (*fair*) fair, *adv* -ly; **g~ werden** (+ *dat*) do justice to. **g~fertigt** *a* justified. **G~igkeit** *f* - justice; fairness

Gerede *nt* -s talk; (*Klatsch*) gossip

geregelt *a* regular

gereift *a* mature

gereizt *a* irritable, *adv* -bly. **G~heit** *f* - irritability

gereuen *vt* **es gereut mich nicht** I don't regret it

Geriatrie *f* - geriatrics *sg*

Gericht[1] *nt* -[e]s,-e (*Culin*) dish

Gericht[2] *nt* -[e]s,-e court [of law]; **vor G~** in court; **das Jüngste G~** the Last Judgement; **mit jdm ins G~ gehen** take s.o. to task. **g~lich** *a* judicial; ⟨*Verfahren*⟩ legal ● *adv* **g~lich vorgehen** take legal action. **G~sbarkeit** *f* - jurisdiction. **G~shof** *m* court of justice. **G~smedizin** *f* forensic medicine. **G~ssaal** *m* courtroom. **G~svollzieher** *m* -s,- bailiff

gerieben *a* grated; (*fam: schlau*) crafty

gering *a* small; (*niedrig*) low; (*g~fügig*) slight. **g~achten** *vt sep* have little regard for; (*verachten*) despise. **g~fügig** *a* slight, *adv* -ly. **g~schätzig** *a* contemptuous, *adv* -ly; ⟨*Bemerkung*⟩ disparaging. **g~ste(r,s)** *a* least; **nicht im g~sten** not in the least

gerinnen† *vi (sein)* curdle; ⟨*Blut:*⟩ clot

Gerippe *nt* -s,- skeleton; (*fig*) framework

gerissen *a* (*fam*) crafty

Germ *m* -[e]s & (*Aust*) *f* - yeast

German|e *m* -n,-n [ancient] German. **g~isch** *a* Germanic. **G~ist(in)** *m* -en,-en (*f* -,-nen) Germanist. **G~istik** *f* - German [language and literature]

gern[e] *adv* gladly; **g~ haben** like; (*lieben*) be fond of; **ich tanze/schwimme**

g~ I like dancing/swimming; **das kannst du g~ tun** you're welcome to do that; **willst du mit?—g~!** do you want to come?—I'd love to!

gerötet *a* red

Gerste *f* - barley. **G~nkorn** *nt* (*Med*) stye

Geruch *m* -[e]s,¨e smell (**von/nach** of). **g~los** *a* odourless. **G~ssinn** *m* sense of smell

Gerücht *nt* -[e]s,-e rumour

geruhen *vi (haben)* deign (**zu** to)

gerührt *a* (*fig*) moved, touched

Gerümpel *nt* -s lumber, junk

Gerüst *nt* -[e]s,-e scaffolding; (*fig*) framework

gesalzen *a* salted; (*fam: hoch*) steep

gesammelt *a* collected; (*gefaßt*) composed

gesamt *a* entire, whole. **G~ausgabe** *f* complete edition. **G~betrag** *m* total amount. **G~eindruck** *m* overall impression. **G~heit** *f* - whole. **G~schule** *f* comprehensive school. **G~summe** *f* total

Gesandte(r) *m/f* envoy

Gesang *m* -[e]s,¨e singing; (*Lied*) song; (*Kirchen-*) hymn. **G~buch** *nt* hymnbook. **G~verein** *m* choral society

Gesäß *nt* -es buttocks *pl.* **G~tasche** *f* hip pocket

Geschäft *nt* -[e]s,-e business; (*Laden*) shop, (*Amer*) store; (*Transaktion*) deal; (*fam: Büro*) office; **schmutzige G~e** shady dealings; **ein gutes G~ machen** do very well (**mit** out of); **sein G~ verstehen** know one's job. **g~ehalber** *adv* on business. **g~ig** *a* busy, *adv* -ily; ⟨*Treiben*⟩ bustling. **G~igkeit** *f* - activity. **g~lich** *a* business ... ● *adv* on business

Geschäfts|brief *m* business letter. **G~führer** *m* manager; (*Vereins-*) secretary. **G~mann** *m* (*pl* **-leute**) businessman. **G~reise** *f* business trip. **G~stelle** *f* office; (*Zweigstelle*) branch. **g~tüchtig** *a* **g~tüchtig sein** be a good businessman/-woman. **G~viertel** *nt* shopping area. **G~zeiten** *fpl* hours of business

geschehen† *vi (sein)* happen (*dat* to); **es ist ein Unglück g~** there has been an accident; **es ist um uns g~** we are done for; **das geschieht dir recht!** it serves you right! **gern g~!** you're welcome! **G~** *nt* -s events *pl*

gescheit *a* clever; **daraus werde ich nicht g~** I can't make head or tail of it

Geschenk nt -[e]s,-e present, gift. **G~korb** m gift hamper

Geschicht|e f -,-n history; (*Erzählung*) story; (*fam: Sache*) business. **g~lich** a historical, adv -ly

Geschick nt -[e]s fate; (*Talent*) skill; **G~ haben** be good (**zu** at). **G~lichkeit** f - skilfulness, skill. **g~t** a skilful, adv -ly; (*klug*) clever, adv -ly

geschieden a divorced. **G~e(r)** m/f divorcee

Geschirr nt -s,-e (*coll*) crockery; (*Porzellan*) china; (*Service*) service; (*Pferde-*) harness; **schmutziges G~** dirty dishes pl. **G~spülmaschine** f dishwasher. **G~tuch** nt tea-towel

Geschlecht nt -[e]s,-er sex; (*Gram*) gender; (*Familie*) family; (*Generation*) generation. **g~lich** a sexual, adv -ly. **G~skrankheit** f venereal disease. **G~steile** ntpl genitals. **G~sverkehr** m sexual intercourse. **G~swort** nt (pl -**wörter**) article

geschliffen a (*fig*) polished

geschlossen a closed ● adv unanimously; (*vereint*) in a body

Geschmack m -[e]s,-̈e taste; (*Aroma*) flavour; (*G~ssinn*) sense of taste; **einen guten G~ haben** (*fig*) have good taste; **G~ finden an** (+ dat) acquire a taste for. **g~los** a tasteless, adv -ly; **g~los sein** (*fig*) be in bad taste. **G~ssache** f matter of taste. **g~voll** a (*fig*) tasteful, adv -ly

geschmeidig a supple; (*weich*) soft

Geschöpf nt -[e]s,-e creature

Geschoß nt -sses,-sse missile; (*Stockwerk*) storey, floor

geschraubt a (*fig*) stilted

Geschrei nt -s screaming; (*fig*) fuss

Geschütz nt -es,-e gun, cannon

geschützt a protected; ⟨Stelle⟩ sheltered

Geschwader nt -s,- squadron

Geschwätz nt -es talk. **g~ig** a garrulous

geschweift a curved

geschweige conj **g~ denn** let alone

geschwind a quick, adv -ly

Geschwindigkeit f -,-en speed; (*Phys*) velocity. **G~sbegrenzung**, **G~sbeschränkung** f speed limit

Geschwister pl brother[s] and sister[s]; siblings

geschwollen a swollen; (*fig*) pompous, adv -ly

Geschworene|(r) m/f juror; **die G~n** the jury sg

Geschwulst f -,-̈e swelling; (*Tumor*) tumour

geschwungen a curved

Geschwür nt -s,-e ulcer

Geselle m -n,-n fellow; (*Handwerks-*) journeyman

gesellig a sociable; (*Zool*) gregarious; (*unterhaltsam*) convivial; **g~er Abend** social evening. **G~keit** f -,-en entertaining; **die G~keit lieben** love company

Gesellschaft f -,-en company; (*Veranstaltung*) party; **die G~** society; **jdm G~ leisten** keep s.o. company. **g~lich** a social, adv -ly. **G~sreise** f group tour. **G~sspiel** nt party game

Gesetz nt -es,-e law. **G~entwurf** m bill. **g~gebend** a legislative. **G~gebung** f - legislation. **g~lich** a legal, adv -ly. **g~los** a lawless. **g~mäßig** a lawful, adv -ly; (*gesetzlich*) legal, adv -ly

gesetzt a staid; (*Sport*) seeded ● conj **g~ den Fall** supposing

gesetzwidrig a illegal, adv -ly

gesichert a secure

Gesicht nt -[e]s,-er face; (*Aussehen*) appearance; **zu G~ bekommen** set eyes on. **G~sausdruck** m [facial] expression. **G~sfarbe** f complexion. **G~spunkt** m point of view. **G~szüge** mpl features

Gesindel nt -s riff-raff

gesinnt a **gut/übel g~** well/ill disposed (dat towards)

Gesinnung f -,-en mind; (*Einstellung*) attitude; **politische G~** political convictions pl

gesittet a well-mannered; (*zivilisiert*) civilized

gesondert a separate, adv -ly

Gespann nt -[e]s,-e team; (*Wagen*) horse and cart/carriage

gespannt a taut; (*fig*) tense, adv -ly; ⟨Beziehungen⟩ strained; (*neugierig*) eager, adv -ly; (*erwartungsvoll*) expectant, adv -ly; **g~ sein, ob** wonder whether; **auf etw/jdn g~ sein** look forward eagerly to sth/to seeing s.o.

Gespenst nt -[e]s,-er ghost. **g~isch** a ghostly; (*unheimlich*) eerie

Gespött nt -[e]s mockery; **zum G~ werden** become a laughing-stock

Gespräch nt -[e]s,-e conversation; (*Telefon-*) call; **ins G~ kommen** get talking; **im G~ sein** be under discussion. **g~ig** a talkative. **G~sgegenstand** m, **G~sthema** nt topic of conversation

gesprenkelt a speckled

Gespür nt -s feeling; (Instinkt) instinct

Gestalt f -,-en figure; (Form) shape, form; **G∼ annehmen** (fig) take shape. **g∼en** vt shape; (organisieren) arrange; (schaffen) create; (entwerfen) design; **sich g∼en** turn out

geständ|ig a confessed; **g∼ig sein** have confessed. **G∼nis** nt -ses,-se confession

Gestank m -s stench, [bad] smell

gestatten vt allow, permit; **nicht gestattet** prohibited; **g∼ Sie?** may I?

Geste /' gɛ-, 'geːstə/ f -,-n gesture

Gesteck nt -[e]s,-e flower arrangement

gestehen† vt/i (haben) confess; confess to ⟨Verbrechen⟩; **offen gestanden** to tell the truth

Gestein nt -[e]s,-e rock

Gestell nt -[e]s,-e stand; (Flaschen-) rack; (Rahmen) frame

gestellt a **gut/schlecht g∼** well/badly off; **auf sich** (acc) **selbst g∼ sein** be thrown on one's own resources

gestelzt a (fig) stilted

gesteppt a quilted

gestern adv yesterday; **g∼ nacht** last night

Gestik /'gɛstɪk/ f - gestures pl. **g∼ulieren** vi (haben) gesticulate

gestrandet a stranded

gestreift a striped

gestrichelt a ⟨Linie⟩ dotted

gestrichen a **g∼er Teelöffel** level teaspoon[ful]

gestrig /'gɛstrɪç/ a yesterday's; **am g∼en Tag** yesterday

Gestrüpp nt -s,-e undergrowth

Gestüt nt -[e]s,-e stud [farm]

Gesuch nt -[e]s,-e request; (Admin) application. **g∼t** a sought-after; (gekünstelt) contrived

gesund a healthy, adv -ily; **g∼ sein** be in good health; ⟨Sport, Getränk:⟩ be good for one; **wieder g∼ werden** get well again

Gesundheit f - health; **G∼!** (bei Niesen) bless you! **g∼lich** a health ...; **g∼licher Zustand** state of health ● adv **es geht ihm g∼lich gut/schlecht** he is in good/poor health. **g∼shalber** adv for health reasons. **g∼sschädlich** a harmful. **G∼szustand** m state of health

getäfelt a panelled

getigert a tabby

Getöse nt -s racket, din

getragen a solemn, adv -ly

Getränk nt -[e]s,-e drink. **G∼ekarte** f wine-list

getrauen vt sich (dat) etw g∼ dare [to] do sth; **sich g∼** dare

Getreide nt -s (coll) grain

getrennt a separate, adv -ly; **g∼ leben** live apart. **g∼schreiben**† vt sep write as two words

getreu a faithful, adv -ly ● prep (+ dat) true to; **der Wahrheit g∼** truthfully. **g∼lich** adv faithfully

Getriebe nt -s,- bustle; (Techn) gear; (Auto) transmission; (Gehäuse) gearbox

getrost adv with confidence

Getto nt -s,-s ghetto

Getue nt -s (fam) fuss

Getümmel nt -s tumult

getüpfelt a spotted

geübt a skilled; ⟨Auge, Hand⟩ practised

Gewächs nt -es,-e plant; (Med) growth

gewachsen a jdm/etw g∼ sein be a match for s.o./be equal to sth

Gewächshaus nt greenhouse; (Treibhaus) hothouse

gewagt a daring

gewählt a refined

gewahr a g∼ werden become aware (acc/gen of)

Gewähr f - guarantee

gewahren vt notice

gewähr|en vt grant; (geben) offer; **jdn g∼en lassen** let s.o. have his way. **g∼leisten** vt guarantee

Gewahrsam m -s safekeeping; (Haft) custody

Gewährsmann m (pl -männer & -leute) informant, source

Gewalt f -,-en power; (Kraft) force; (Brutalität) violence; **mit G∼** by force; **G∼ anwenden** use force; **sich in der G∼ haben** be in control of oneself. **G∼herrschaft** f tyranny. **g∼ig** a powerful; (fam: groß) enormous, adv -ly; (stark) tremendous, adv -ly. **g∼sam** a forcible, adv -bly; ⟨Tod⟩ violent. **g∼tätig** a violent. **G∼tätigkeit** f -,-en violence; (Handlung) act of violence

Gewand nt -[e]s,¨-er robe

gewandt a skilful, adv -ly; (flink) nimble, adv -bly. **G∼heit** f - skill; nimbleness

Gewässer nt -s,- body of water; **G∼** pl waters

Gewebe nt -s,- fabric; (Anat) tissue

Gewehr nt -s,-e rifle, gun
Geweih nt -[e]s,-e antlers pl
Gewerb|e nt -s,- trade. **g~lich** a commercial, adv -ly. **g~smäßig** a professional, adv -ly
Gewerkschaft f -,-en trade union. **G~ler(in)** m -s,- (f -,-nen) trade unionist
Gewicht nt -[e]s,-e weight; (Bedeutung) importance. **G~heben** nt -s weight-lifting. **g~ig** a important
gewieft a (fam) crafty
gewillt a **g~ sein** be willing
Gewinde nt -s,- [screw] thread
Gewinn m -[e]s,-e profit; (fig) gain, benefit; (beim Spiel) winnings pl; (Preis) prize; (Los) winning ticket. **G~beteiligung** f profit-sharing. **g~bringend** a profitable, adv -bly. **g~en†** vt win; (erlangen) gain; (fördern) extract; **jdn für sich g~en** win s.o. over ● vi (haben) win; **g~en an** (+ dat) gain in. **g~end** a engaging. **G~er(in)** m -s,- (f -,-nen) winner
Gewirr nt -s,-e tangle; (Straßen-) maze; **G~ von Stimmen** hubbub of voices
gewiß a (gewisser, gewissest) certain, adv -ly
Gewissen nt -s,- conscience. **g~haft** a conscientious, adv -ly. **g~los** a unscrupulous. **G~sbisse** mpl pangs of conscience
gewissermaßen adv to a certain extent; (sozusagen) as it were
Gewißheit f - certainty
Gewitt|er nt -s,- thunderstorm. **g~ern** vi (haben) **es g~ert** it is thundering. **g~rig** a thundery
gewogen a (fig) well-disposed (dat towards)
gewöhnen vt jdn/sich g~ an (+ acc) get s.o. used to/get used to; **[an] jdn/ etw gewöhnt sein** be used to s.o./sth
Gewohnheit f -,-en habit. **g~smäßig** a habitual, adv -ly. **G~srecht** nt common law
gewöhnlich a ordinary, adv -ily; (üblich) usual, adv -ly; (ordinär) common
gewohnt a customary; (vertraut) familiar; (üblich) usual; **etw** (acc) **g~ sein** be used to sth
Gewöhnung f - getting used (**an** + acc to); (Süchtigkeit) addiction
Gewölb|e nt -s,- vault. **g~t** a curved; (Archit) vaulted
gewollt a forced
Gewühl nt -[e]s crush

gewunden a winding
gewürfelt a check[ed]
Gewürz nt -es,-e spice. **G~nelke** f clove
gezackt a serrated
gezähnt a serrated; (Säge) toothed
Gezeiten fpl tides
gezielt a specific; (Frage) pointed
geziemend a proper, adv -ly
geziert a affected, adv -ly
gezwungen a forced ● adv **g~ lachen** give a forced laugh. **g~ermaßen** adv of necessity; **etw g~ermaßen tun** be forced to do sth
Gicht f - gout
Giebel m -s,- gable
Gier f - greed (**nach** for). **g~ig** a greedy, adv -ily
gießen† vt pour; water (Blumen, Garten); (Techn) cast ● v impers **es g~t** it is pouring [with rain]. **G~erei** f -,-en foundry. **G~kanne** f watering-can
Gift nt -[e]s,-e poison; (Schlangen-) venom; (Biol, Med) toxin. **g~ig** a poisonous; (Schlange) venomous; (Med, Chem) toxic; (fig) spiteful, adv -ly. **G~müll** m toxic waste. **G~pilz** m poisonous fungus, toadstool. **G~zahn** m [poison] fang
gigantisch a gigantic
Gilde f -,-n guild
Gimpel m -s,- bullfinch; (fam: Tölpel) simpleton
Gin /dʒɪn/ m -s gin
Ginster m -s (Bot) broom
Gipfel m -s,- summit, top; (fig) peak. **G~konferenz** f summit conference. **g~n** vi (haben) culminate (**in** + dat in)
Gips m -es plaster. **G~abguß** m plaster cast. **G~er** m -s,- plasterer. **G~verband** m (Med) plaster cast
Giraffe f -,-n giraffe
Girlande f -,-n garland
Girokonto /ˈʒiːro-/ nt current account
Gischt m -[e]s & f -spray
Gitar|re f -,-n guitar. **G~rist(in)** m -en,-en (f -,-nen) guitarist
Gitter nt -s,- bars pl; (Rost) grating, grid; (Geländer, Zaun) railings pl; (Fenster-) grille; (Draht-) wire screen; **hinter G~n** (fam) behind bars. **G~netz** nt grid
Glanz m -es shine; (von Farbe, Papier) gloss; (Seiden-) sheen; (Politur) polish; (fig) brilliance; (Pracht) splendour

glänzen vi (haben) shine. **g~d** a shining; bright; ⟨Papier, Haar⟩ glossy; (fig) brilliant, adv -ly

glanz|los a dull. **G~stück** nt masterpiece; (einer Sammlung) showpiece. **g~voll** a (fig) brilliant, adv -ly; (prachtvoll) splendid, adv -ly. **G~zeit** f heyday

Glas nt -es,-̈er glass; (Brillen-) lens; (Fern-) binoculars pl; (Marmeladen-) [glass] jar. **G~er** m -s,- glazier

gläsern a glass …

Glashaus nt greenhouse

glasieren vt glaze; ice ⟨Kuchen⟩

glas|ig a glassy; (durchsichtig) transparent. **G~scheibe** f pane

Glasur f -,-en glaze; (Culin) icing

glatt a smooth; (eben) even; ⟨Haar⟩ straight; (rutschig) slippery; (einfach) straightforward; (eindeutig) downright; ⟨Absage⟩ flat ● adv smoothly; evenly; (fam: völlig) completely; (gerade) straight; (leicht) easily; ⟨ablehnen⟩ flatly; **g~ verlaufen** go off smoothly; **das ist g~ gelogen** it's a downright lie

Glätte f - smoothness; (Rutschigkeit) slipperiness

Glatteis nt [black] ice; **aufs G~ führen** (fam) take for a ride

glätten vt smooth; **sich g~** become smooth; ⟨Wellen:⟩ subside

glatt|gehen† vi sep (sein) (fig) go off smoothly. **g~rasiert** a cleanshaven. **g~streichen**† vt sep smooth out. **g~weg** adv (fam) outright

Glatz|e f -,-n bald patch; (Voll-) bald head; **eine G~e bekommen** go bald. **g~köpfig** a bald

Glaube m -ns belief (an + acc in); (Relig) faith; **in gutem G~n** in good faith; **G~n schenken** (+ dat) believe. **g~n** vt/i (haben) believe (an + acc in); (vermuten) think; **jdm g~n** believe s.o.; **nicht zu g~n** unbelievable, incredible. **G~nsbekenntnis** nt creed

glaubhaft a credible; (überzeugend) convincing, adv -ly

gläubig a religious; (vertrauend) trusting, adv -ly. **G~e(r)** m/f (Relig) believer; **die G~en** the faithful. **G~er** m -s,- (Comm) creditor

glaub|lich a **kaum g~lich** scarcely believable. **g~würdig** a credible; ⟨Person⟩ reliable. **G~würdigkeit** f - credibility; reliability

gleich a same; (identisch) identical; (g~wertig) equal; **2 mal 5 [ist] g~ 10** two times 5 equals 10; **das ist mir g~** it's all the same to me; **ganz g~, wo/wer** no matter where/who ● adv equally; (übereinstimmend) identically, the same; (sofort) immediately; (in Kürze) in a minute; (fast) nearly; (direkt) right; **g~ alt/schwer sein** be the same age/weight. **g~altrig** a [of] the same age. **g~artig** a similar. **g~bedeutend** a synonymous. **g~berechtigt** a equal. **G~berechtigung** f equality. **g~bleibend** a constant

gleichen† vi (haben) **jdm/etw g~** be like or resemble s.o./sth; **sich g~** be alike

gleich|ermaßen adv equally. **g~falls** adv also, likewise; **danke g~falls** thank you, the same to you. **g~förmig** a uniform, adv -ly; (eintönig) monotonous, adv -ly. **G~förmigkeit** f - uniformity; monotony. **g~gesinnt** a like-minded. **G~gewicht** nt balance; (Phys & fig) equilibrium. **g~gültig** a indifferent, adv -ly; (unwichtig) unimportant. **G~gültigkeit** f indifference. **G~heit** f - equality; (Ähnlichkeit) similarity. **g~machen** vt sep make equal; **dem Erdboden g~machen** raze to the ground. **g~mäßig** a even, adv -ly, regular, adv -ly; (beständig) constant, adv -ly. **G~mäßigkeit** f - regularity. **G~mut** m equanimity. **g~mütig** a calm, adv -ly

Gleichnis nt -ses,-se parable

gleich|sam adv as it were. **G~schritt** m **im G~schritt** in step. **g~sehen**† vi sep (haben) **jdm g~sehen** look like s.o.; (fam: typisch sein) be just like s.o. **g~setzen** vt sep equate/(g~stellen) place on a par (dat/mit with). **g~stellen** vt sep place on a par (dat with). **G~strom** m direct current. **g~tun**† vi sep (haben) **es jdm g~tun** emulate s.o.

Gleichung f -,-en equation

gleich|viel adv no matter (ob/wer whether/who). **g~wertig** a of equal value. **g~zeitig** a simultaneous, adv -ly

Gleis nt -es,-e track; (Bahnsteig) platform; **G~ 5** platform 5

gleiten† vi (sein) glide; (rutschen) slide. **g~d** a sliding; **g~de Arbeitszeit** flexitime

Gleitzeit f flexitime

Gletscher *m* **-s,-** glacier. **G~spalte** *f* crevasse

Glied *nt* **-[e]s,-er** limb; (*Teil*) part; (*Ketten-*) link; (*Mitglied*) member; (*Mil*) rank. **g~ern** *vt* arrange; (*einteilen*) divide; **sich g~ern** be divided (**in** + *acc* into). **G~maßen** *fpl* limbs

glimmen† *vi* (*haben*) glimmer

glimpflich *a* lenient, *adv* -ly; **g~ davonkommen** get off lightly

glitschig *a* slippery

glitzern *vi* (*haben*) glitter

global *a* global, *adv* -ly

Globus *m* **-** & **-busses, -ben** & **-busse** globe

Glocke *f* **-,-n** bell. **G~nturm** *m* belltower, belfry

glorifizieren *vt* glorify

glorreich *a* glorious

Glossar *nt* **-s,-e** glossary

Glosse *f* **-,-n** comment

glotzen *vi* (*haben*) stare

Glück *nt* **-[e]s** [good] luck; (*Zufriedenheit*) happiness; **G~/kein G~ haben** be lucky/unlucky; **zum G~** luckily, fortunately; **auf gut G~** on the off chance; (*wahllos*) at random. **g~bringend** *a* lucky. **g~en** *vi* (*sein*) succeed; **es ist mir geglückt** I succeeded

gluckern *vi* (*haben*) gurgle

glücklich *a* lucky, fortunate; (*zufrieden*) happy; (*sicher*) safe ● *adv* happily; safely; (*fam: endlich*) finally. **g~erweise** *adv* luckily, fortunately

glückselig *a* blissfully happy. **G~keit** *f* bliss

glucksen *vi* (*haben*) gurgle

Glücksspiel *nt* game of chance; (*Spielen*) gambling

Glückwunsch *m* good wishes *pl*; (*Gratulation*) congratulations *pl*; **herzlichen G~!** congratulations! (*zum Geburtstag*) happy birthday! **G~karte** *f* greetings card

Glüh|birne *f* light-bulb. **g~en** *vi* (*haben*) glow. **g~end** *a* glowing; (*rot-*) red-hot; (*Hitze*) scorching; (*leidenschaftlich*) fervent, *adv* -ly. **G~faden** *m* filament. **G~wein** *m* mulled wine. **G~würmchen** *nt* **-s,-** glow-worm

Glukose *f* **-** glucose

Glut *f* **-** embers *pl*; (*Röte*) glow; (*Hitze*) heat; (*fig*) ardour

Glyzinie /-iə/ *f* **-,-n** wisteria

GmbH *abbr* (**Gesellschaft mit beschränkter Haftung**) ≈ plc

Gnade *f* **-** mercy; (*Gunst*) favour; (*Relig*) grace. **G~nfrist** *f* reprieve. **g~nlos** *a* merciless, *adv* -ly

gnädig *a* gracious, *adv* -ly; (*mild*) lenient, *adv* -ly; **g~e Frau** Madam

Gnom *m* **-en,-en** gnome

Gobelin /gobaˈlɛ̃:/ *m* **-s,-s** tapestry

Gold *nt* **-[e]s** gold. **g~en** *a* gold . . .; (*g~farben*) golden; **g~ene Hochzeit** golden wedding. **G~fisch** *m* goldfish. **G~grube** *f* gold-mine. **g~ig** *a* sweet, lovely. **G~lack** *m* wallflower. **G~regen** *m* laburnum. **G~schmied** *m* goldsmith

Golf[1] *m* **-[e]s,-e** (*Geog*) gulf

Golf[2] *nt* **-s** golf. **G~platz** *m* golfcourse. **G~schläger** *m* golf-club. **G~spieler(in)** *m(f)* golfer

Gondel *f* **-,-n** gondola; (*Kabine*) cabin

Gong *m* **-s,-s** gong

gönnen *vt* **jdm etw g~** not begrudge s.o. sth; **jdm etw nicht g~** begrudge s.o. sth; **sie gönnte sich** (*dat*) **keine Ruhe** she allowed herself no rest

Gönner *m* **-s,-** patron. **g~haft** *a* patronizing, *adv* -ly

Gör *nt* **-s,-en**, **Göre** *f* **-,-n** (*fam*) kid

Gorilla *m* **-s,-s** gorilla

Gosse *f* **-,-n** gutter

Got|ik *f* **-** Gothic. **g~isch** *a* Gothic

Gott *m* **-[e]s,¨er** God; (*Myth*) god

Götterspeise *f* jelly

Gottes|dienst *m* service. **g~lästerlich** *a* blasphemous, *adv* -ly. **G~lästerung** *f* blasphemy

Gottheit *f* **-,-en** deity

Göttin *f* **-,-nen** goddess

göttlich *a* divine, *adv* -ly

gott|los *a* ungodly; (*atheistisch*) godless. **g~verlassen** *a* God-forsaken

Götze *m* **-n,-n**, **G~nbild** *nt* idol

Gouver|nante /guvɛrˈnantə/ *f* **-,-n** governess. **G~neur** /-ˈnøːɐ̯/ *m* **-s,-e** governor

Grab *nt* **-[e]s,¨er** grave

graben† *vi* (*haben*) dig

Graben *m* **-s,¨** ditch; (*Mil*) trench

Grab|mal *nt* tomb. **G~stein** *m* gravestone, tombstone

Grad *m* **-[e]s,-e** degree

Graf *m* **-en,-en** count

Grafik *f* **-,-en** graphics *sg*; (*Kunst*) graphic arts *pl*; (*Druck*) print

Gräfin *f* **-,-nen** countess

grafisch *a* graphic; **g~e Darstellung** diagram

Grafschaft f -,-en county
Gram m -s grief
grämen (sich) vr grieve
grämlich a morose, adv -ly
Gramm nt -s,-e gram
Gram|matik f -,-en grammar.
g~matikalisch, g~matisch a
grammatical, adv -ly
Granat m -[e]s,-e (Miner) garnet.
G~apfel m pomegranate. **G~e** f -,-
shell; (Hand-) grenade
Granit m -s,-e granite
Graph|ik f, **g~isch** a = **Grafik,
grafisch**
Gras nt -es,¨er grass. **g~en** vi (haben)
graze. **G~hüpfer** m -s,- grasshopper
grassieren vi (haben) be rife
gräßlich a dreadful, adv -ly
Grat m -[e]s,-e [mountain] ridge
Gräte f -,-n fishbone
Gratifikation /-'tsio:n/ f -,-en bonus
gratis adv free [of charge]. **G~probe**
f free sample
Gratu|lant(in) m -en,-en (f -,-nen)
well-wisher. **G~lation** /-'tsio:n/ f
-,-en congratulations pl; (Glück-
wünsche) best wishes pl. **g~lieren** vi
(haben) jdm **g~lieren** congratulate
s.o. (**zu** on); (zum Geburtstag) wish s.o.
happy birthday; **[ich] g~liere!** congratulations!
grau a, **G~** nt -s,- grey. **G~brot** nt
mixed rye and wheat bread
grauen¹ vi (haben) **der Morgen** od **es
graut** dawn is breaking
grauen² v impers **mir graut [es] davor**
I dread it. **G~** nt -s dread. **g~haft,
g~voll** a gruesome; (gräßlich) horrible, adv -bly
gräulich a greyish
Graupeln fpl soft hail sg
grausam a cruel, adv -ly. **G~keit** f
-,-en cruelty
graus|en v impers **mir graust davor**
I dread it. **G~en** nt -s horror, dread.
g~ig a gruesome
gravieren vt engrave. **g~d** a (fig)
serious
Grazie /'gra:tsiə/ f - grace
graziös a graceful, adv -ly
greifbar a tangible; **in g~er Nähe**
within reach
greifen† vt take hold of; (fangen)
catch ● vi (haben) reach (**nach** for);
g~ zu (fig) turn to; **um sich g~** (fig)
spread. **G~** nt **G~ spielen** play tag
Greis m -es,-e old man. **G~enalter** nt
extreme old age. **g~enhaft** a old.
G~in f -,-nen old woman

grell a glaring; (Farbe) garish;
(schrill) shrill, adv -y
Gremium nt -s,-ien committee
Grenz|e f -,-n border; (Staats-) fron-
tier; (Grundstücks-) boundary; (fig)
limit. **g~en** vi (haben) border
(**an** + acc on). **g~enlos** a boundless;
(maßlos) infinite, adv -ly. **G~fall** m
borderline case
Greuel m -s,- horror. **G~tat** f
atrocity
greulich a horrible, adv -bly
Griech|e m -n,-n Greek. **G~enland**
nt -s Greece. **G~in** f -,-nen Greek
woman. **g~isch** a Greek. **G~isch** nt
-[s] (Lang) Greek
griesgrämig a (fam) grumpy
Grieß m -es semolina
Griff m -[e]s,-e grasp, hold; (Hand-)
movement of the hand; (Tür-, Messer-)
handle; (Schwert-) hilt. **g~bereit** a
handy
Grill m -s,-s grill; (Garten-) barbecue
Grille f -,-n (Zool) cricket; (fig: Laune)
whim
grill|en vt grill; (im Freien) barbecue
● vi (haben) have a barbecue. **G~-
fest** nt barbecue. **G~gericht** nt grill
Grimasse f -,-n grimace; **G~n
schneiden** pull faces
grimmig a furious; (Kälte) bitter
grinsen vi (haben) grin. **G~** nt -s grin
Grippe f -,-n influenza, (fam) flu
grob a (gröber, gröbst) coarse, adv
-ly; (unsanft, ungefähr) rough, adv -ly;
(unhöflich) rude, adv -ly; (schwer) gross,
adv -ly; (Fehler) bad; **g~e Arbeit** rough
work; **g~ geschätzt** roughly. **G~ian**
m -s,-e brute
gröblich a gross, adv -ly
grölen vt/i (haben) bawl
Groll m -[e]s resentment; **einen G~
gegen jdn hegen** bear s.o. a grudge.
g~en vi (haben) be angry (dat with);
(Donner:) rumble
Grönland nt -s Greenland
Gros¹ nt -ses,- (Maß) gross
Gros² /gro:/ nt - majority, bulk
Groschen m -s,- (Aust) groschen;
(fam) ten-pfennig piece; **der G~ ist gefallen** (fam) the penny's dropped
groß a (größer, größt) big; (Anzahl,
Summe) large; (bedeutend, stark) great;
(g~artig) grand; (Buchstabe) capital;
g~e Ferien summer holidays; **g~e
Angst haben** be very frightened; **der
größte Teil** the majority or bulk; **g~
werden** (Person:) grow up; **g~ in etw**

(*dat*) **sein** be good at sth; **g~ und klein** young and old; **im g~en und ganzen** on the whole ● *adv* ⟨*feiern*⟩ in style; (*fam: viel*) much; **jdn g~ ansehen** look at s.o. in amazement

groß|artig *a* magnificent, *adv* -ly. **G~aufnahme** *f* close-up. **G~britannien** *nt* -s Great Britain. **G~buchstabe** *m* capital letter. **G~e(r)** *m/f* **unser G~er** our eldest; **die G~en** the grown-ups; (*fig*) the great *pl*

Größe *f* -,-n size; (*Ausmaß*) extent; (*Körper-*) height; (*Bedeutsamkeit*) greatness; (*Math*) quantity; (*Person*) great figure

Groß|eltern *pl* grandparents. **g~enteils** *adv* largely

Größenwahnsinn *m* megalomania

Groß|handel *m* wholesale trade. **G~händler** *m* wholesaler. **g~herzig** *a* magnanimous, *adv* -ly. **G~macht** *f* superpower. **G~mut** *f* - magnanimity. **g~mütig** *a* magnanimous, *adv* -ly. **G~mutter** *f* grandmother. **G~onkel** *m* great-uncle. **G~reinemachen** *nt* -s spring-clean. **G~schreibung** *f* capitalization. **g~sprecherisch** *a* boastful. **g~spurig** *a* pompous, *adv* -ly; (*überheblich*) arrogant, *adv* -ly. **G~stadt** *f* [large] city. **g~städtisch** *a* city ... **G~tante** *f* great-aunt. **G~teil** *m* large proportion; (*Hauptteil*) bulk

größtenteils *adv* for the most part

groß|tun† (**sich**) *vr sep* brag. **G~vater** *m* grandfather. **g~ziehen†** *vt sep* bring up; rear ⟨*Tier*⟩. **g~zügig** *a* generous, *adv* -ly; (*weiträumig*) spacious. **G~zügigkeit** *f* - generosity

grotesk *a* grotesque, *adv* -ly

Grotte *f* -,-n grotto

Grübchen *nt* -s,- dimple

Grube *f* -,-n pit

grübeln *vi* (*haben*) brood

Gruft *f* -,-̈e [burial] vault

grün *a* green; **im G~en** out in the country; **die G~en** the Greens. **G~** *nt* -s,- green; (*Laub, Zweige*) greenery

Grund *m* -[e]s,-̈e ground; (*Boden*) bottom; (*Hinter-*) background; (*Ursache*) reason; **auf G~** (+ *gen*) on the strength of; **aus diesem G~e** for this reason; **von G~ auf** (*fig*) radically; **im G~e [genommen]** basically; **auf G~ laufen** (*Naut*) run aground. **G~begriffe** *mpl* basics. **G~besitz** *m* landed property. **G~besitzer** *m* landowner

gründ|en *vt* found, set up; start ⟨*Familie*⟩; (*fig*) base (**auf** + *acc* on); **sich g~en** be based (**auf** + *acc* on). **G~er(in)** *m* -s,- (*f* -,-nen) founder

Grund|farbe *f* primary colour. **G~form** *f* (*Gram*) infinitive. **G~gesetz** *nt* (*Pol*) constitution. **G~lage** *f* basis, foundation. **g~legend** *a* fundamental, *adv* -ly

gründlich *a* thorough, *adv* -ly. **G~keit** *f* - thoroughness

grund|los *a* bottomless; (*fig*) groundless ● *adv* without reason. **G~mauern** *fpl* foundations

Gründonnerstag *m* Maundy Thursday

Grund|regel *f* basic rule. **G~riß** *m* ground-plan; (*fig*) outline. **G~satz** *m* principle. **g~sätzlich** *a* fundamental, *adv* -ly; (*im allgemeinen*) in principle; (*prinzipiell*) on principle. **G~schule** *f* primary school. **G~stein** *m* foundation-stone. **G~stück** *nt* plot [of land]

Gründung *f* -,-en foundation

grün|en *vi* (*haben*) become green. **G~gürtel** *m* green belt. **G~span** *m* verdigris. **G~streifen** *m* grass verge; (*Mittel-*) central reservation, (*Amer*) median strip

grunzen *vi* (*haben*) grunt

Gruppe *f* -,-n group; (*Reise-*) party

gruppieren *vt* group; **sich g~** form a group/groups

Grusel|geschichte *f* horror story. **g~ig** *a* creepy

Gruß *m* -es,-̈e greeting; (*Mil*) salute; **einen schönen G~ an X** give my regards to X; **viele/herzliche G~e** regards; **Mit freundlichen G~en** Yours sincerely/(*Comm*) faithfully

grüßen *vt/i* (*haben*) say hallo (**jdn** to s.o.); (*Mil*) salute; **g~ Sie X von mir** give my regards to X; **jdn g~ lassen** send one's regards to s.o.; **grüß Gott!** (*SGer, Aust*) good morning/afternoon/ evening!

guck|en *vi* (*haben*) (*fam*) look. **G~loch** *nt* peep-hole

Guerilla /ge'rɪlja/ *f* - guerrilla warfare. **G~kämpfer** *m* guerrilla

Gulasch *nt & m* -[e]s goulash

gültig *a* valid, *adv* -ly. **G~keit** *f* - validity

Gummi *m & nt* -s,-[s] rubber; (*Harz*) gum. **G~band** *nt* (*pl* -bänder) elastic or rubber band; (*G~zug*) elastic

gummiert *a* gummed

Gummi|knüppel *m* truncheon.
G~stiefel *m* gumboot, wellington.
G~zug *m* elastic

Gunst *f* - favour; **zu jds G~en** in s.o.'s favour

günstig *a* favourable, *adv* -bly; (*passend*) convenient, *adv* -ly

Günstling *m* **-s,-e** favourite

Gurgel *f* **-,-n** throat. **g~n** *vi* (*haben*) gargle. **G~wasser** *nt* gargle

Gurke *f* **-,-n** cucumber; (*Essig-*) gherkin

gurren *vi* (*haben*) coo

Gurt *m* **-[e]s,-e** strap; (*Gürtel*) belt; (*Auto*) safety-belt. **G~band** *nt* (*pl* **-bänder**) waistband

Gürtel *m* **-s,-** belt. **G~linie** *f* waistline. **G~rose** *f* shingles *sg*

GUS *abbr* (**Gemeinschaft Unabhängiger Staaten**) CIS

Guß *m* **-sses,-̈sse** (*Techn*) casting; (*Strom*) stream; (*Regen-*) downpour; (*Torten-*) icing. **G~eisen** *nt* cast iron. **g~eisern** *a* cast-iron

gut *a* (**besser, best**) good; (*Gewissen*) clear; (*gütig*) kind (**zu** to); **jdm gut sein** be fond of s.o.; **im g~en** amicably; **zu g~er Letzt** in the end; **schon gut** that's all right ● *adv* well; (*schmecken, riechen*) good; (*leicht*) easily; **es gut haben** be well off; (*Glück haben*) be lucky; **gut zu sehen** clearly visible; **gut drei Stunden** a good three hours; **du hast gut reden** it's easy for you to talk

Gut *nt* **-[e]s,-̈er** possession, property; (*Land-*) estate; **Gut und Böse** good and evil; **Güter** (*Comm*) goods

Gutacht|en *nt* **-s,-** expert's report. **G~er** *m* **-s,-** expert

gut|artig *a* good-natured; (*Med*) benign. **g~aussehend** *a* good-looking. **g~bezahlt** *a* well-paid. **G~dünken** *nt* **-s nach eigenem G~dünken** at one's own discretion

Gute|(s) *nt* **etwas/nichts G~s** something/nothing good; **G~s tun** do good; **das G~ daran** the good thing about it all; **alles G~!** all the best!

Güte *f* **-,-n** goodness, kindness; (*Qualität*) quality; **du meine G~!** my goodness!

Güterzug *m* goods/(*Amer*) freight train

gut|gehen† *vi sep* (*sein*) go well; **es geht mir gut** I am well/(*geschäftlich*) doing well. **g~gehend** *a* flourishing, thriving. **g~gemeint** *a* well-meant. **g~gläubig** *a* trusting. **g~haben†**

vt sep **fünfzig Mark g~haben** have fifty marks credit (**bei** with). **g~haben** *nt* **-s,-** [credit] balance; (*Kredit*) credit. **g~heißen†** *vt sep* approve of

gütig *a* kind, *adv* -ly

gütlich *a* amicable, *adv* -bly

gut|machen *vt sep* make up for; make good (*Schaden*). **g~mütig** *a* good-natured, *adv* -ly. **G~mütigkeit** *f* - good nature. **G~schein** *m* credit note; (*Bon*) voucher; (*Geschenk-*) gift token. **g~schreiben†** *vt sep* credit. **G~schrift** *f* credit

Guts|haus *nt* manor house. **G~hof** *m* manor

gut|situiert *a* well-to-do. **g~tun†** *vi sep* (*haben*) **jdm/etw g~tun** do s.o./sth good. **g~willig** *a* willing, *adv* -ly

Gymnasium *nt* **-s,-ien** ≈ grammar school

Gymnast|ik *f* - [keep-fit] exercises *pl*; (*Turnen*) gymnastics *sg*. **g~isch** *a* **g~ische Übung** exercise

Gynäko|loge *m* **-n,-n** gynaecologist. **G~logie** *f* - gynaecology. **g~logisch** *a* gynaecological

H

H, h /ha:/ *nt* **-,-** (*Mus*) B, b

Haar *nt* **-[e]s,-e** hair; **sich** (*dat*) **die Haare** *od* **das H~ waschen** wash one's hair; **um ein H~** (*fam*) very nearly. **H~bürste** *f* hairbrush. **h~en** *vi* (*haben*) shed hairs; (*Tier:*) moult ● *vr* **sich h~en** moult. **h~ig** *a* hairy; (*fam*) tricky. **H~klammer, H~klemme** *f* hair-grip. **H~nadel** *f* hairpin. **H~nadelkurve** *f* hairpin bend. **H~schleife** *f* bow. **H~schnitt** *m* haircut. **H~spange** *f* slide. **h~sträubend** *a* hair-raising; (*empörend*) shocking. **H~trockner** *m* **-s,-** hair-drier. **H~waschmittel** *nt* shampoo

Habe *f* - possessions *pl*

haben† *vt* have; **Angst/Hunger/Durst h~** be frightened/hungry/ thirsty; **ich hätte gern** I'd like; **sich h~** (*fam*) make a fuss; **es gut/schlecht h~** be well/badly off; **etw gegen jdn h~** have sth against s.o.; **was hat er?** what's the matter with him? ● *v aux* have; **ich habe/hatte geschrieben** I have/had written; **er hätte ihr geholfen** he would have helped her

Habgier f greed. **h⁓ig** a greedy
Habicht m -[e]s,-e hawk
Hab|seligkeiten fpl belongings.
H⁓sucht f = **Habgier**
Hachse f -,-n (Culin) knuckle
Hack|beil nt chopper. **H⁓braten** m meat loaf
Hacke¹ f -,-n hoe; (Spitz-) pick
Hacke² f -,-n, **Hacken** m -s,- heel
hack|en vt hoe; (schlagen, zerkleinern) chop; (Vogel:) peck; **gehacktes Rindfleisch** minced/(Amer) ground beef. **H⁓fleisch** nt mince, (Amer) ground meat
Hafen m -s,⁓ harbour; (See-) port. **H⁓arbeiter** m docker. **H⁓damm** m mole. **H⁓stadt** f port
Hafer m -s oats pl. **H⁓flocken** fpl [rolled] oats. **H⁓mehl** nt oatmeal
Haft f - (Jur) custody; (H⁓strafe) imprisonment. **h⁓bar** a (Jur) liable. **H⁓befehl** m warrant [of arrest]
haften vi (haben) cling; (kleben) stick; (bürgen) vouch/(Jur) be liable (**für** for)
Häftling m -s,-e detainee
Haftpflicht f (Jur) liability. **H⁓versicherung** f (Auto) third-party insurance
Haftstrafe f imprisonment
Haftung f - (Jur) liability
Hagebutte f -,-n rose-hip
Hagel m -s hail. **H⁓korn** nt hailstone. **h⁓n** vi (haben) hail
hager a gaunt
Hahn m -[e]s,⁓e cock; (Techn) tap, (Amer) faucet
Hähnchen nt -s,- (Culin) chicken
Hai[fisch] m -[e]s,-e shark
Häkchen nt -s,- tick
häkel|n vt/i (haben) crochet. **H⁓nadel** f crochet-hook
Haken m -s,- hook; (Häkchen) tick; (fam: Schwierigkeit) snag. **h⁓** vt hook (**an** + acc to). **H⁓kreuz** nt swastika. **H⁓nase** f hooked nose
halb a half; **eine h⁓e Stunde** half an hour; **zum h⁓en Preis** at half price; **auf h⁓em Weg** half-way ● adv half; **h⁓ drei** half past two; **fünf [Minuten] vor/nach h⁓ vier** twenty-five [minutes] past three/to four; **h⁓ und h⁓** half and half; (fast ganz) more or less. **H⁓blut** nt half-breed. **H⁓dunkel** nt semidarkness. **H⁓e(r,s)** f/m/nt half [a litre]
halber prep (+ gen) for the sake of; **Geschäfte h⁓** on business

Halb|finale nt semifinal. **H⁓heit** f -,-en (fig) half-measure
halbieren vt halve, divide in half; (Geom) bisect
Halb|insel f peninsula. **H⁓kreis** m semicircle. **H⁓kugel** f hemisphere. **h⁓laut** a low ● adv in an undertone. **h⁓mast** adv at half-mast. **H⁓messer** m -s,- radius. **H⁓mond** m half moon. **H⁓pension** f halfboard. **h⁓rund** a semicircular. **H⁓schuh** m [flat] shoe. **h⁓stündlich** a & adv half-hourly. **h⁓tags** adv [for] half a day; **h⁓tags arbeiten** ≈ work part-time. **H⁓ton** m semitone. **h⁓wegs** adv half-way; (ziemlich) more or less. **h⁓wüchsig** a adolescent. **H⁓zeit** f (Sport) half-time; (Spielzeit) half
Halde f -,-n dump, tip
Hälfte f -,-n half; **zur H⁓** half
Halfter¹ m & nt -s,- halter
Halfter² f -,-n & nt -s,- holster
Hall m -[e]s,-e sound
Halle f -,-n hall; (Hotel-) lobby; (Bahnhofs-) station concourse
hallen vi (haben) resound; (wider-) echo
Hallen- pref indoor
hallo int hallo
Halluzination /-'tsi̯o:n/ f -,-en hallucination
Halm m -[e]s,-e stalk; (Gras-) blade
Hals m -es,⁓e neck; (Kehle) throat; **aus vollem H⁓e** at the top of one's voice; (lachen) one's head off. **H⁓ausschnitt** m neckline. **H⁓band** nt (pl -bänder) collar. **H⁓kette** f necklace. **H⁓schmerzen** mpl sore throat sg. **h⁓starrig** a stubborn. **H⁓tuch** nt scarf
halt¹ adv (SGer) just; **es geht h⁓ nicht** it's just not possible
halt² int stop! (Mil) halt! (fam) wait a minute!
Halt m -[e]s,-e hold; (Stütze) support; (innerer) stability; (Anhalten) stop. **h⁓bar** a durable; (Tex) hard- wearing; (fig) tenable; **h⁓bar bis ...** (Comm) use by ...
halten† vt hold; make (Rede); give (Vortrag); (einhalten, bewahren) keep; [sich (dat)] **etw h⁓** keep (Hund); take (Zeitung); run (Auto); **warm h⁓** keep warm; **h⁓ für** regard as; **viel/nicht viel h⁓ von** think highly/little of; **sich h⁓** hold on (**an** + dat to); (fig) hold out; (Geschäft:) keep going; (haltbar sein) keep; (Wetter:) hold; (Blumen:) last;

sich links h∼ keep left; **sich gerade h∼** hold oneself upright; **sich h∼ an** (+ *acc*) (*fig*) keep to ● *vi* (*haben*) hold; (*haltbar sein, bestehen bleiben*) keep; 〈*Freundschaft, Blumen:*〉 last; (*haltmachen*) stop; **h∼ auf** (+ *acc*) (*fig*) set great store by; **auf sich** (*acc*) **h∼** take pride in oneself; **an sich** (*acc*) **h∼** contain oneself; **zu jdm h∼** be loyal to s.o.

Halter *m* **-s,-** holder

Halte|stelle *f* stop. **H∼verbot** *nt* waiting restriction; **'H∼verbot**' 'no waiting'

halt|los *a* (*fig*) unstable; (*unbegründet*) unfounded. **h∼machen** *vi sep* (*haben*) stop

Haltung *f* **-,-en** (*Körper-*) posture; (*Verhalten*) manner; (*Einstellung*) attitude; (*Fassung*) composure; (*Halten*) keeping; **H∼ annehmen** (*Mil*) stand to attention

Halunke *m* **-n,-n** scoundrel

Hamburger *m* **-s,-** hamburger

hämisch *a* malicious, *adv* -ly

Hammel *m* **-s,-** ram; (*Culin*) mutton. **H∼fleisch** *nt* mutton

Hammer *m* **-s,.̈** hammer

hämmern *vt/i* (*haben*) hammer; 〈*Herz:*〉 pound

Hämorrhoiden /hɛmɔroˈiːdən/ *fpl* haemorrhoids

Hamster *m* **-s,-** hamster. **h∼n** *vt/i* (*fam*) hoard

Hand *f* **-,.̈e** hand; **jdm die H∼ geben** shake hands with s.o.; **rechter/linker H∼** on the right/left; **[aus] zweiter H∼** second-hand; **unter der H∼** unofficially; (*geheim*) secretly; **an H∼ von** with the aid of; **H∼ und Fuß haben** (*fig*) be sound. **H∼arbeit** *f* manual work; (*handwerklich*) handicraft; (*Nadelarbeit*) needlework; (*Gegenstand*) hand-made article. **H∼ball** *m* [German] handball. **H∼besen** *m* brush. **H∼bewegung** *f* gesture. **H∼bremse** *f* handbrake. **H∼buch** *nt* handbook, manual

Händedruck *m* handshake

Handel *m* **-s** trade, commerce; (*Unternehmen*) business; (*Geschäft*) deal; **H∼ treiben** trade. **h∼n** *vi* (*haben*) act; (*Handel treiben*) trade (**mit** in); **von etw** *od* **über etw** (*acc*) **h∼n** deal with sth; **sich h∼n um** be about, concern. **H∼smarine** *f* merchant navy. **H∼sschiff** *nt* merchant vessel. **H∼sschule** *f* commercial college.

h∼süblich *a* customary. **H∼sware** *f* merchandise

Hand|feger *m* **-s,-** brush. **H∼fertigkeit** *f* dexterity. **h∼fest** *a* sturdy; (*fig*) solid. **H∼fläche** *f* palm. **h∼gearbeitet** *a* hand-made. **H∼gelenk** *nt* wrist. **h∼gemacht** *a* handmade. **H∼gemenge** *nt* **-s,-** scuffle. **H∼gepäck** *nt* hand-luggage. **h∼geschrieben** *a* hand-written. **H∼granate** *f* hand-grenade. **h∼greiflich** *a* tangible; **h∼greiflich werden** become violent. **H∼griff** *m* handle; **mit einem H∼griff** with a flick of the wrist

handhaben *vt insep* (*reg*) handle

Handikap /ˈhɛndikɛp/ *nt* **-s,-s** handicap

Hand|kuß *m* kiss on the hand. **H∼lauf** *m* handrail

Händler *m* **-s,-** dealer, trader

handlich *a* handy

Handlung *f* **-,-en** act; (*Handeln*) action; (*Roman-*) plot; (*Geschäft*) shop. **H∼sweise** *f* conduct

Hand|schellen *fpl* handcuffs. **H∼schlag** *m* handshake. **H∼schrift** *f* handwriting; (*Text*) manuscript. **H∼schuh** *m* glove. **H∼schuhfach** *nt* glove compartment. **H∼stand** *m* handstand. **H∼tasche** *f* handbag. **H∼tuch** *nt* towel. **H∼voll** *f* **-,-** handful

Handwerk *nt* craft, trade; **sein H∼ verstehen** know one's job. **H∼er** *m* **-s,-** craftsman; (*Arbeiter*) workman

Hanf *m* **-[e]s** hemp

Hang *m* **-[e]s,.̈e** slope; (*fig*) inclination, tendency

Hänge|brücke *f* suspension bridge. **H∼lampe** *f* [light] pendant. **H∼matte** *f* hammock

hängen[1] *vt* (*reg*) hang

hängen[2]† *vi* (*haben*) hang; **h∼ an** (+ *dat*) (*fig*) be attached to. **h∼bleiben**† *vi sep* (*sein*) stick (**an** + *dat* to); 〈*Kleid:*〉 catch (**an** + *dat* on). **h∼lassen**† *vt sep* leave; **den Kopf h∼lassen** be downcast

Hannover *nt* **-s** Hanover

hänseln *vt* tease

hantieren *vi* (*haben*) busy oneself

hapern *vi* (*haben*) **es hapert** there's a lack (**an** + *dat* of)

Happen *m* **-s,-** mouthful; **einen H∼ essen** have a bite to eat

Harfe *f* **-,-n** harp

Harke f -,-n rake. **h~n** vt/i (haben) rake

harmlos a harmless; (arglos) innocent, adv -ly. **H~igkeit** f - harmlessness; innocence

Harmonie f -,-n harmony. **h~ren** vi (haben) harmonize; (gut auskommen) get on well

Harmonika f -,-s accordion; (Mund-) mouth-organ

harmonisch a harmonious, adv -ly

Harn m -[e]s urine. **H~blase** f bladder

Harpune f -,-n harpoon

hart (härter, härtest) a hard; (heftig) violent; (streng) harsh ● adv hard; (streng) harshly

Härte f -,-n hardness; (Strenge) harshness; (Not) hardship. **h~n** vt harden

Hart|faserplatte f hardboard. **h~gekocht** a hard-boiled. **h~herzig** a hard-hearted. **h~näckig** a stubborn, adv -ly; (ausdauernd) persistent, adv -ly. **H~näckigkeit** f - stubbornness; persistence

Harz nt -es,-e resin

Haschee nt -s,-s (Culin) hash

haschen vi (haben) **h~ nach** try to catch

Haschisch nt & m -[s] hashish

Hase m -n,-n hare; **falscher H~** meat loaf

Hasel f -,-n hazel. **H~maus** f dormouse. **H~nuß** f hazel-nut

Hasenfuß m (fam) coward

Haß m -sses hatred

hassen vt hate

häßlich a ugly; (unfreundlich) nasty, adv -ily. **H~keit** f - ugliness; nastiness

Hast f - haste. **h~en** vi (sein) hasten, hurry. **h~ig** a hasty, adv -ily, hurried, adv -ly

hast, hat, hatte, hätte s. **haben**

Haube f -,-n cap; (Trocken-) drier; (Kühler-) bonnet, (Amer) hood

Hauch m -[e]s breath; (Luft-) breeze; (Duft) whiff; (Spur) tinge. **h~dünn** a very thin; ⟨Strümpfe⟩ sheer. **h~en** vt/i (haben) breathe

Haue f -,-n pick; (fam: Prügel) beating. **h~n†** vt beat; (hämmern) knock; (meißeln) hew; **sich h~n** fight; **übers Ohr h~n** (fam) cheat ● vi (haben) bang (**auf**+acc on); **jdm ins Gesicht h~n** hit s.o. in the face

Haufen m -s,- heap, pile; (Leute) crowd

häufen vt heap or pile [up]; **sich h~** pile up; (zunehmen) increase

haufenweise adv in large numbers; **h~ Geld** pots of money

häufig a frequent, adv -ly. **H~keit** f - frequency

Haupt nt -[e]s, **Häupter** head. **H~bahnhof** m main station. **H~darsteller** m, **H~darstellerin** f male/female lead. **H~fach** nt main subject. **H~gericht** nt main course. **H~hahn** m mains tap; (Wasser-) stopcock

Häuptling m -s,-e chief

Haupt|mahlzeit f main meal. **H~mann** m (pl -leute) captain. **H~person** f most important person; (Theat) principal character. **H~post** f main post office. **H~quartier** nt headquarters pl. **H~rolle** f lead; (fig) leading role. **H~sache** f main thing; **in der H~sache** in the main. **h~sächlich** a main, adv -ly. **H~satz** m main clause. **H~schlüssel** m master key. **H~stadt** f capital. **H~straße** f main street. **H~verkehrsstraße** f main road. **H~verkehrszeit** f rush-hour. **H~wort** nt (pl -wörter) noun

Haus nt -es, **Häuser** house; (Gebäude) building; (Schnecken-) shell; **zu H~e** at home; **nach H~e** home. **H~angestellte(r)** m/f domestic servant. **H~arbeit** f housework; (Sch) homework. **H~arzt** m family doctor. **H~aufgaben** fpl homework sg. **H~besetzer** m -s,- squatter. **H~besuch** m house-call

hausen vi (haben) live; (wüten) wreak havoc

Haus|frau f housewife. **H~gehilfin** f domestic help. **h~gemacht** a home-made. **H~halt** m -[e]s,-e household; (Pol) budget. **h~halten†** vi sep (haben) **h~halten mit** manage carefully; conserve ⟨Kraft⟩. **H~hälterin** f -,-nen housekeeper. **H~haltsgeld** nt housekeeping [money]. **H~haltsplan** m budget. **H~herr** m head of the household; (Gastgeber) host. **h~hoch** a huge; (fam) big ● adv (fam) vastly; (verlieren) by a wide margin

hausier|en vi (haben) **h~en mit** hawk. **H~er** m -s,- hawker

Hauslehrer m [private] tutor. **H~in** f governess

häuslich a domestic; ⟨Person⟩ domesticated

Haus|meister m caretaker. **H~nummer** f house number.

H∼ordnung f house rules pl.
H∼putz m cleaning. H∼rat m -[e]s
household effects pl. H∼schlüssel m
front-door key. H∼schuh m slipper.
H∼stand m household. H∼suchung
f [police] search. H∼suchungs-
befehl m search-warrant. H∼tier nt
domestic animal; (Hund, Katze) pet.
H∼tür f front door. H∼wart m
-[e]s,-e caretaker. H∼wirt m landlord. H∼wirtin f landlady

Haut f -, Häute skin; (Tier-) hide; aus
der H∼ fahren (fam) fly off the handle.
H∼arzt m dermatologist

häuten vt skin; sich h∼ moult

haut|eng a skin-tight. H∼farbe f
colour; (Teint) complexion

Haxe f -,-n = Hachse

Hbf. abbr s. Hauptbahnhof

Hebamme f -,-n midwife

Hebel m -s,- lever. H∼kraft, H∼-
wirkung f leverage

heben† vt lift; (hoch-, steigern) raise;
sich h∼ rise; (Nebel:) lift; (sich verbessern) improve

hebräisch a Hebrew

hecheln vi (haben) pant

Hecht m -[e]s,-e pike

Heck nt -s,-s (Naut) stern; (Aviat) tail;
(Auto) rear

Hecke f -,-n hedge. H∼nschütze m
sniper

Heck|fenster nt rear window.
H∼motor m rear engine. H∼tür f
hatchback

Heer nt -[e]s,-e army

Hefe f - yeast. H∼teig m yeast dough.
H∼teilchen nt Danish pastry

Heft¹ nt -[e]s,-e haft, handle

Heft² nt -[e]s,-e booklet; (Sch) exercise
book; (Zeitschrift) issue. h∼en vt
(nähen) tack; (stecken) pin/(klammern) clip/(mit Heftmaschine) staple
(an+acc to). H∼er m -s,- file

heftig a fierce, adv -ly, violent, adv
-ly; (Schlag, Regen) heavy, adv -ily;
(Schmerz, Gefühl) intense, adv -ly;
(Person) quick-tempered. H∼keit f -
fierceness, violence; intensity

Heft|klammer f staple; (Büro-)
paper-clip. H∼maschine f stapler.
H∼pflaster nt sticking plaster.
H∼zwecke f -,-n drawing-pin

hegen vt care for; (fig) cherish
(Hoffnung); harbour (Verdacht)

Hehl nt & m kein[en] H∼ machen aus
make no secret of. H∼er m -s,- re-
ceiver, fence

Heide¹ m -n,-n heathen

Heide² f -,-n heath; (Bot) heather.
H∼kraut nt heather

Heidelbeere f bilberry, (Amer) blue-
berry

Heid|in f -,-nen heathen. h∼nisch a
heathen

heikel a difficult, tricky; (delikat)
delicate; (dial) (Person) fussy

heil a undamaged, intact; (Person)
unhurt; (gesund) well; mit h∼er
Haut (fam) unscathed

Heil nt -s salvation; sein H∼ versuchen
try one's luck

Heiland m -s (Relig) Saviour

Heil|anstalt f sanatorium; (Nerven-)
mental hospital. H∼bad nt spa.
h∼bar a curable

Heilbutt m -[e]s,-e halibut

heilen vt cure; heal (Wunde) ● vi
(sein) heal

heilfroh a (fam) very relieved

Heilgymnastik f physiotherapy

heilig a holy; (geweiht) sacred; der
H∼e Abend Christmas Eve; die h∼e
Anna Saint Anne. H∼abend m
Christmas Eve. H∼e(r) m/f saint.
h∼en vt keep, observe. H∼enschein
m halo. h∼halten† vt sep hold sacred; keep (Feiertag). H∼keit f - sanctity, holiness. h∼sprechen† vt sep
canonize. H∼tum nt -s,-̈er shrine

heil|kräftig a medicinal. H∼kräu-
ter ntpl medicinal herbs. h∼los a
unholy. H∼mittel nt remedy.
H∼praktiker m -s,- practitioner of
alternative medicine. h∼sam a (fig)
salutary. H∼sarmee f Salvation
Army. H∼ung f - cure

Heim nt -[e]s,-e home; (Studenten-)
hostel. h∼ adv home

Heimat f -,-en home; (Land) native
land. H∼abend m folk evening.
h∼los a homeless. H∼stadt f home
town

heim|begleiten vt sep see home.
h∼bringen† vt sep bring home; (begleiten) see home. H∼computer m
home computer. h∼fahren† v sep
● vi (sein) go/drive home ● vt take/
drive home. H∼fahrt f way home.
h∼gehen† vi sep (sein) go home;
(sterben) die

heimisch a native, indigenous; (Pol)
domestic; h∼ sein/sich h∼ fühlen be/
feel at home

Heim|kehr f - return [home].
h∼kehren vi sep (sein) return home.

h∼**kommen**† vi sep (sein) come home

heimlich a secret, adv -ly. **H∼keit** f -,-en secrecy; **H∼keiten** secrets. **H∼tuerei** f - secretiveness

Heim|reise f journey home. h∼**reisen** vi sep (sein) go home. **H∼spiel** nt home game. **h∼suchen** vt sep afflict. **h∼tückisch** a treacherous; ⟨Krankheit⟩ insidious. **h∼wärts** adv home. **H∼weg** m way home. **H∼weh** nt -s homesickness; **H∼weh haben** be homesick. **H∼werker** m -s,- [home] handyman. **h∼zahlen** vt sep **jdm etw h∼zahlen** (fig) pay s.o. back for sth

Heirat f -,-en marriage. h∼en vt/i (haben) marry. **H∼santrag** m proposal; **jdm einen H∼santrag machen** propose to s.o. **h∼sfähig** a marriageable

heiser a hoarse, adv -ly. **H∼keit** f - hoarseness

heiß a hot, adv -ly; ⟨hitzig⟩ heated; ⟨leidenschaftlich⟩ fervent, adv -ly; **mir ist h∼** I am hot

heißen† vi (haben) be called; ⟨bedeuten⟩ mean; **ich heiße ...** my name is ...; **wie h∼ Sie?** what is your name? **wie heißt ... auf englisch?** what's the English for ...? **es heißt** it says; ⟨man sagt⟩ it is said; **das heißt** that is [to say]; **was soll das h∼?** what does it mean? ⟨empört⟩ what is the meaning of this? ● vt call; **jdn etw tun h∼** tell s.o. to do sth

heiß|geliebt a beloved. **h∼hungrig** a ravenous. **H∼wasserbereiter** m -s,- water heater

heiter a cheerful, adv -ly; ⟨Wetter⟩ bright; ⟨amüsant⟩ amusing; **aus h∼em Himmel** (fig) out of the blue. **H∼keit** f - cheerfulness; ⟨Gelächter⟩ mirth

Heiz|anlage f heating; ⟨Auto⟩ heater. **H∼decke** f electric blanket. **h∼en** vt heat; light ⟨Ofen⟩ ● vi (haben) put the heating on; ⟨Ofen:⟩ give out heat. **H∼gerät** nt heater. **H∼kessel** m boiler. **H∼körper** m radiator. **H∼lüfter** m -s,- fan heater. **H∼material** nt fuel. **H∼ofen** m heater. **H∼ung** f -,-en heating; ⟨Heizkörper⟩ radiator

Hektar nt & m -s,- hectare

hektisch a hectic

Held m -en,-en hero. **h∼enhaft** a heroic, adv -ally. **H∼enmut** m heroism. **h∼enmütig** a heroic, adv -ally.

H∼entum nt -s heroism. **H∼in** f -,-nen heroine

helf|en† vi (haben) help (**jdm** s.o.); ⟨nützen⟩ be effective; **sich** ⟨dat⟩ **nicht zu h∼en wissen** not know what to do; **es hilft nichts** it's no use. **H∼er(in)** m -s,- (f -,-nen) helper, as- sistant. **H∼ershelfer** m accomplice

hell a light; ⟨Licht ausstrahlend, klug⟩ bright; ⟨Stimme⟩ clear; ⟨fam: völlig⟩ utter; **h∼es Bier** ≈ lager ● adv brightly; **h∼ begeistert** absolutely delighted. **h∼hörig** a poorly soundproofed; **h∼hörig werden** (fig) sit up and take notice

hellicht a **h∼er Tag** broad daylight

Hell|igkeit f - brightness. **H∼seher(in)** m -s,- (f -,-nen) clairvoyant. **h∼wach** a wide awake

Helm m -[e]s,-e helmet

Hemd nt -[e]s,-en vest, (Amer) undershirt; ⟨Ober-⟩ shirt. **H∼bluse** f shirt

Hemisphäre f -,-n hemisphere

hemm|en vt check; ⟨verzögern⟩ impede; ⟨fig⟩ inhibit. **H∼ung** f -,-en ⟨fig⟩ inhibition; ⟨Skrupel⟩ scruple; **H∼ungen haben** be inhibited. **h∼ungslos** a unrestrained, adv -ly

Hendl nt -s,-[n] (Aust) chicken

Hengst m -[e]s,-e stallion. **H∼fohlen** nt colt

Henkel m -s,- handle

henken vt hang

Henne f -,-n hen

her adv here; ⟨zeitlich⟩ ago; **her mit ...!** give me ...! **von oben/unten/Norden/weit her** from above/below/the north/far away; **vor/hinter jdm/etw her** in front of/behind s.o./sth; **von der Farbe/vom Thema her** as far as the colour/subject is concerned

herab adv down [here]; **von oben h∼** from above; ⟨fig⟩ condescending, adv -ly. **h∼blicken** vi sep (haben) = **h∼sehen**

herablass|en† vt sep let down; **sich h∼en** condescend (**zu** to). **h∼end** a condescending, adv -ly. **H∼ung** f - condescension

herab|sehen† vi sep (haben) look down (**auf** + acc on). **h∼setzen** vt sep reduce, cut; ⟨fig⟩ belittle. **h∼setzend** a disparaging, adv -ly. **h∼würdigen** vt sep belittle, disparage

Heraldik f - heraldry

heran adv near; **[bis] h∼ an** (+ acc) up to. **h∼bilden** vt sep train.

h~gehen† *vi sep* (*sein*) **h~gehen an** (+ *acc*) go up to; get down to ⟨*Arbeit*⟩. **h~kommen**† *vi sep* (*sein*) approach; **h~kommen an** (+ *acc*) come up to; (*erreichen*) get at; (*fig*) measure up to. **h~machen (sich)** *vr sep* **sich h~machen an** (+ *acc*) approach; get down to ⟨*Arbeit*⟩. **h~reichen** *vi sep* (*haben*) **h~reichen an** (+ *acc*) reach; (*fig*) measure up to. **h~wachsen**† *vi sep* (*sein*) grow up. **h~ziehen** *v sep* ● *vt* pull up (**an** + *acc* to); (*züchten*) raise; (*h~bilden*) train; (*hinzuziehen*) call in ● *vi* (*sein*) approach

herauf *adv* up [here]; **die Treppe h~** up the stairs. **h~beschwören** *vt sep* evoke; (*verursachen*) cause. **h~kommen**† *vi sep* (*sein*) come up. **h~setzen** *vt sep* raise, increase

heraus *adv* out (**aus** of); **h~ damit** *od* **mit der Sprache!** out with it! **h~bekommen**† *vt sep* get out; (*ausfindig machen*) find out; (*lösen*) solve; **Geld h~bekommen** get change. **h~bringen**† *vt sep* bring out; (*fam*) get out. **h~finden**† *v sep* ● *vt* find out ● *vi* (*haben*) find one's way out. **H~forderer** *m* -s,- challenger. **h~fordern** *vt sep* provoke; challenge ⟨*Person*⟩. **H~forderung** *f* provocation; challenge. **H~gabe** *f* handing over; (*Admin*) issue; (*Veröffentlichung*) publication. **h~geben**† *vt sep* hand over; (*Admin*) issue; (*veröffentlichen*) publish; edit ⟨*Zeitschrift*⟩; **jdm Geld h~geben** give s.o. change ● *vi* (*haben*) give change (**auf** + *acc* for). **H~geber** *m* -s,- publisher; editor. **h~gehen**† *vi sep* (*Fleck:*) come out; **aus sich h~gehen** (*fig*) come out of one's shell. **h~halten**† **(sich)** *vr sep* (*fig*) keep out (**aus** of). **h~holen** *vt sep* get out. **h~kommen**† *vi sep* (*sein*) come out; (*aus Schwierigkeit, Takt*) get out; **auf eins** *od* **dasselbe h~kommen** (*fam*) come to the same thing. **h~lassen**† *vt sep* let out. **h~machen** *vt sep* get out; **sich gut h~machen** (*fig*) do well. **h~nehmen**† *vt sep* take out; **sich zuviel h~nehmen** (*fig*) take liberties. **h~platzen** *vi sep* (*haben*) (*fam*) burst out laughing. **h~putzen (sich)** *vr sep* doll oneself up. **h~ragen** *vi sep* (*haben*) jut out; (*fig*) stand out. **h~reden (sich)** *vr sep* make excuses. **h~rücken** *v sep* ● *vt* move out; (*hergeben*) hand over ● *vi* (*sein*)

h~rücken mit hand over; (*fig: sagen*) come out with. **h~rutschen** *vi sep* (*sein*) slip out. **h~schlagen**† *vt sep* knock out; (*fig*) gain. **h~stellen** *vt sep* put out; **sich h~stellen** turn out (**als** to be; **daß** that). **h~suchen** *vt sep* pick out. **h~ziehen**† *vt sep* pull out

herb *a* sharp; ⟨*Wein*⟩ dry; ⟨*Landschaft*⟩ austere; (*fig*) harsh

herbei *adv* here. **h~führen** *vt sep* (*fig*) bring about. **h~lassen**† **(sich)** *vr sep* condescend (**zu** to). **h~schaffen** *vt sep* get. **h~sehnen** *vt sep* long for

Herberg|e *f* -,-n [youth] hostel; (*Unterkunft*) lodging. **H~svater** *m* warden

herbestellen *vt sep* summon

herbitten† *vt sep* ask to come

herbringen† *vt sep* bring [here]

Herbst *m* -[e]s,-e autumn. **h~lich** *a* autumnal

Herd *m* -[e]s,-e stove, cooker; (*fig*) focus

Herde *f* -,-n herd; (*Schaf-*) flock

herein *adv* in [here]; **h~!** come in! **h~bitten**† *vt sep* ask in. **h~brechen**† *vi sep* (*sein*) burst in; (*fig*) set in; ⟨*Nacht:*⟩ fall; **h~brechen über** (+ *acc*) overtake. **h~fallen**† *vi sep* (*sein*) (*fam*) be taken in (**auf** + *acc* by). **h~kommen**† *vi sep* (*sein*) come in. **h~lassen**† *vt sep* let in. **h~legen** *vt sep* (*fam*) take for a ride. **h~rufen**† *vt sep* call in

Herfahrt *f* journey/drive here

herfallen† *vi sep* (*sein*) **h~ über** (+ *acc*) attack; fall upon ⟨*Essen*⟩

hergeben† *vt sep* hand over; (*fig*) give up; **sich h~ zu** (*fig*) be a party to

hergebracht *a* traditional

hergehen† *vi sep* (*sein*) **h~ vor/ neben/hinter** (+ *dat*) walk along in front of/beside/behind; **es ging lustig her** (*fam*) there was a lot of merriment

herhalten† *vt sep* (*haben*) hold out; **h~ müssen** be the one to suffer

herholen *vt sep* fetch; **weit hergeholt** (*fig*) far-fetched

Hering *m* -s,-e herring; (*Zeltpflock*) tent-peg

her|kommen† *vi sep* (*sein*) come here; **wo kommt das her?** where does it come from? **h~kömmlich** *a* traditional. **H~kunft** *f* - origin

herlaufen† *vi sep* (*sein*) **h~ vor/ neben/hinter** (+ *dat*) run/(*gehen*) walk along in front of/beside/behind

herleiten *vt sep* derive

hermachen *vt sep* **viel/wenig h~** be impressive/unimpressive; (*wichtig nehmen*) make a lot of/little fuss (**von** of); **sich h~ über** (+ *acc*) fall upon; tackle ⟨*Arbeit*⟩

Hermelin[1] *nt* **-s,-e** (*Zool*) stoat

Hermelin[2] *m* **-s,-e** (*Pelz*) ermine

hermetisch *a* hermetic, *adv* -ally

Hernie /'hɛrnjə/ *f* **-,-n** hernia

Heroin *nt* **-s** heroin

heroisch *a* heroic, *adv* -ally

Herr *m* **-n,-en** gentleman; (*Gebieter*) master (**über** + *acc* of); **[Gott,] der H~** the Lord [God]; **H~ Meier** Mr Meier; **Sehr geehrte H~en** Dear Sirs. **H~chen** *nt* **-s,-** master. **H~enhaus** *nt* manor [house]. **h~enlos** *a* ownerless; ⟨*Tier*⟩ stray. **H~ensitz** *m* manor

Herrgott *m* **der H~** the Lord; **H~ [noch mal]!** damn it!

herrichten *vt sep* prepare; **wieder h~** renovate

Herrin *f* **-,-nen** mistress

herrisch *a* imperious, *adv* -ly; ⟨*Ton*⟩ peremptory; (*herrschsüchtig*) overbearing

herrlich *a* marvellous, *adv* -ly; (*großartig*) magnificent, *adv* -ly. **H~keit** *f* **-,-en** splendour

Herrschaft *f* **-,-en** rule; (*Macht*) power; (*Kontrolle*) control; **meine H~en!** ladies and gentlemen!

herrsch|en *vi* (*haben*) rule; (*verbreitet sein*) prevail; **es h~te Stille/ große Aufregung** there was silence/ great excitement. **H~er(in)** *m* **-s,-** (*f* **-,-nen**) ruler. **h~süchtig** *a* domineering

herrühren *vi sep* (*haben*) stem (**von** from)

hersein† *vi sep* (*sein*) come (**von** from); **h~ hinter** (+ *dat*) be after; **es ist schon lange/drei Tage her** it was a long time/three days ago

herstammen *vi sep* (*haben*) come (**aus/von** from)

herstell|en *vt sep* establish; (*Comm*) manufacture, make. **H~er** *m* **-s,-** manufacturer, maker. **H~ung** *f* - establishment; manufacture

herüber *adv* over [here]. **h~kommen**† *vi sep* (*sein*) come over [here]

herum *adv* **im Kreis h~** [round] in a circle; **falsch h~** the wrong way round; **um ... h~** round ...; (*ungefähr*) [round] about ... **h~albern** *vi sep*

(*haben*) fool around. **h~drehen** *vt sep* turn round/(*wenden*) over; turn ⟨*Schlüssel*⟩; **sich h~drehen** turn round/over. **h~gehen**† *vi sep* (*sein*) walk around; ⟨*Zeit:*⟩ pass; **h~gehen um** go round. **h~kommen**† *vi sep* (*sein*) get about; **h~kommen um** get round; come round ⟨*Ecke*⟩; **um etw [nicht] h~kommen** (*fig*) [not] get out of sth. **h~kriegen** *vt sep* **jdn h~kriegen** (*fam*) talk s.o. round. **h~liegen**† *vi sep* (*sein*) lie around. **h~lungern** *vi sep* (*haben*) loiter. **h~schnüffeln** *vi sep* (*haben*) (*fam*) nose about. **h~sitzen**† *vi sep* (*haben*) sit around; **h~sitzen um** sit round. **h~sprechen**† (**sich**) *vr sep* ⟨*Gerücht:*⟩ get about. **h~stehen**† *vi sep* (*haben*) stand around; **h~stehen um** stand round. **h~treiben**† (**sich**) *vr sep* hang around. **h~ziehen**† *vi sep* (*sein*) move around; (*ziellos*) wander about

herunter *adv* down [here]; **die Treppe h~** down the stairs. **h~fallen**† *vi* fall off. **h~gehen**† *vi sep* (*sein*) come down; (*sinken*) go/come down. **h~gekommen** *a* (*fig*) rundown; ⟨*Gebäude*⟩ dilapidated; ⟨*Person*⟩ down-at-heel. **h~kommen**† *vi sep* (*sein*) come down; (*fig*) go to rack and ruin; ⟨*Firma, Person:*⟩ go downhill; (*gesundheitlich*) get run down. **h~lassen**† *vt sep* let down, lower. **h~machen** *vt sep* (*fam*) reprimand; (*herabsetzen*) run down. **h~spielen** *vt sep* (*fig*) play down. **h~ziehen**† *vt sep* pull down

hervor *adv* out (**aus** of). **h~bringen**† *vt sep* produce; utter ⟨*Wort*⟩. **h~gehen**† *vi sep* (*sein*) come/(*sich ergeben*) emerge/(*folgen*) follow (**aus** from). **h~heben**† *vt sep* (*fig*) stress, emphasize. **h~quellen**† *vi sep* (*sein*) stream out; (*h~treten*) bulge. **h~ragen** *vi sep* (*haben*) jut out; (*fig*) stand out. **h~ragend** *a* (*fig*) outstanding. **h~rufen**† *vt sep* (*fig*) cause. **h~stehen**† *vi sep* (*haben*) protrude. **h~treten**† *vi sep* (*sein*) protrude, bulge; (*fig*) stand out. **h~tun**† (**sich**) *vr sep* (*fig*) distinguish oneself; (*angeben*) show off

Herweg *m* way here

Herz *nt* **-ens,-en** heart; (*Kartenspiel*) hearts *pl*; **sich** (*dat*) **ein H~ fassen** pluck up courage. **H~anfall** *m* heart attack

herzeigen *vt sep* show

herz|en *vt* hug. **H~enslust** *f* **nach H~enslust** to one's heart's content. **h~haft** *a* hearty, *adv* -ily; (*würzig*) savoury

herziehen† *v sep* ● *vt* **hinter sich** (*dat*) **h~** pull along [behind one] ● *vi* (*sein*) **hinter jdm h~** follow along behind s.o.; **über jdn h~** (*fam*) run s.o. down

herz|ig *a* sweet, adorable. **H~infarkt** *m* heart attack. **H~klopfen** *nt* -s palpitations *pl*; **ich hatte H~klopfen** my heart was pounding

herzlich *a* cordial, *adv* -ly; (*warm*) warm, *adv* -ly; (*aufrichtig*) sincere, *adv* -ly; **h~en Dank!** many thanks! **h~e Grüße** kind regards; **h~ wenig** precious little. **H~keit** *f* - cordiality; warmth; sincerity

herzlos *a* heartless

Herzog *m* **-s,-̈e** duke. **H~in** *f* **-,-nen** duchess. **H~tum** *nt* **-s,-̈er** duchy

Herz|schlag *m* heartbeat; (*Med*) heart failure. **h~zerreißend** *a* heart-breaking

Hessen *nt* -s Hesse

heterosexuell *a* heterosexual

Hetze *f* - rush; (*Kampagne*) virulent campaign (**gegen** against). **h~n** *vt* chase; **sich h~n** hurry ● *vi* (*haben*) agitate; (*sich beeilen*) hurry ● *vi* (*sein*) rush

Heu *nt* -s hay; **Geld wie Heu haben** (*fam*) have pots of money

Heuchelei *f* - hypocrisy

heuch|eln *vt* feign ● *vi* (*haben*) pretend. **H~ler(in)** *m* **-s,-** (*f* **-,-nen**) hypocrite. **h~lerisch** *a* hypocritical, *adv* -ly

heuer *adv* (*Aust*) this year

Heuer *f* **-,-n** (*Naut*) pay. **h~n** *vt* hire; sign on (*Matrosen*)

heulen *vi* (*haben*) howl; (*fam: weinen*) cry; (*Sirene:*) wail

Heurige(r) *m* (*Aust*) new wine

Heu|schnupfen *m* hay fever. **H~schober** *m* **-s,-** haystack. **H~schrecke** *f* **-,-n** grasshopper; (*Wander-*) locust

heut|e *adv* today; (*heutzutage*) nowadays; **h~e früh** *od* **morgen** this morning; **von h~e auf morgen** from one day to the next. **h~ig** *a* today's ...; (*gegenwärtig*) present; **der h~ige Tag** today. **h~zutage** *adv* nowadays

Hexe *f* **-,-n** witch. **h~n** *vi* (*haben*) work magic; **ich kann nicht h~n** (*fam*) I can't perform miracles.

H~njagd *f* witch-hunt. **H~nschuß** *m* lumbago. **H~rei** *f* - witchcraft

Hieb *m* **-[e]s,-e** blow; (*Peitschen-*) lash; **H~e** hiding *sg*

hier *adv* here; **h~ und da** here and there; (*zeitlich*) now and again

Hierarchie /hierar'çi:/ *f* **-,-n** hierarchy

hier|auf *adv* on this/these; (*antworten*) to this; (*zeitlich*) after this. **h~aus** *adv* out of *or* from this/these. **h~behalten**† *vt* sep keep here. **h~bleiben**† *vi sep* (*sein*) stay here. **h~durch** *adv* through this/these; (*Ursache*) as a result of this. **h~für** *adv* for this/these. **h~her** *adv* here. **h~hin** *adv* here. **h~in** *adv* in this/these. **h~lassen**† *vt sep* leave here. **h~mit** *adv* with this/these; (*Comm*) herewith; (*Admin*) hereby. **h~nach** *adv* after this/these; (*demgemäß*) according to this/these. **h~sein**† *vi sep* (*sein*) be here. **h~über** *adv* over/(*höher*) above this/these; (*sprechen, streiten*) about this/these. **h~unter** *adv* under/(*tiefer*) below this/these; (*dazwischen*) among these. **h~von** *adv* from this/these; (*h~über*) about this/these; (*Menge*) of this/these. **h~zu** *adv* to this/these; (*h~für*) for this/these. **h~zulande** *adv* here

hiesig *a* local. **H~e(r)** *m/f* local

Hilf|e *f* **-,-n** help, aid; **um H~e rufen** call for help; **jdm zu H~e kommen** come to s.o.'s aid. **h~los** *a* helpless, *adv* -ly. **H~losigkeit** *f* - helplessness. **h~reich** *a* helpful

Hilfs|arbeiter *m* unskilled labourer. **h~bedürftig** *a* needy; **h~bedürftig sein** be in need of help. **h~bereit** *a* helpful, *adv* -ly. **H~kraft** *f* helper. **H~mittel** *nt* aid. **H~verb, H~zeitwort** *nt* auxiliary verb

Himbeere *f* raspberry

Himmel *m* **-s,-** sky; (*Relig & fig*) heaven; (*Bett-*) canopy; **am H~** in the sky; **unter freiem H~** in the open air. **H~bett** *nt* four-poster [bed]. **H~fahrt** *f* Ascension; **Mariä H~fahrt** Assumption. **h~schreiend** *a* scandalous. **H~srichtung** *f* compass point; **in alle H~srichtungen** in all directions. **h~weit** *a* (*fam*) vast

himmlisch *a* heavenly

hin *adv* there; **hin und her** to and fro; **hin und zurück** there and back; (*Rail*) return; **hin und wieder** now and again; **an** (+ *dat*) ... **hin** along; **auf** (+ *acc*) ...

hin in reply to 〈*Brief, Anzeige*〉; on 〈*jds Rat*〉; **zu** *od* **nach ... hin** towards; **vor sich hin reden** talk to oneself
hinab *adv* down [there]
hinauf *adv* up [there]; **die Treppe/ Straße h~** up the stairs/road.
h~gehen† *vi sep (sein)* go up.
h~setzen *vt sep* raise
hinaus *adv* out [there]; (*nach draußen*) outside; **zur Tür h~** out of the door; **auf Jahre h~** for years to come; **über etw** (*acc*) **h~** beyond sth; (*Menge*) [over and] above sth. **h~fliegen**† *v sep* ● *vi (sein)* fly out; (*fam*) get the sack ● *vt* fly out. **h~gehen**† *vi sep (sein)* go out; 〈*Zimmer:*〉 face (**nach Norden** north); **h~gehen über** (+ *acc*) go beyond, exceed. **h~kommen**† *vi sep (sein)* get out; **h~kommen über** (+ *acc*) get beyond. **h~laufen**† *vi sep (sein)* run out; **h~laufen auf** (+ *acc*) (*fig*) amount to. **h~lehnen** (**sich**) *vr sep* lean out. **h~ragen** *vi sep (haben)* **h~ragen über** (+ *acc*) project beyond; (*in der Höhe*) rise above; (*fig*) stand out above. **h~schicken** *vt sep* send out. **h~schieben**† *vt sep* push out; (*fig*) put off. **h~sehen**† *vi sep (haben)* look out. **h~sein**† *vi sep (sein)* **über etw** (*acc*) **h~sein** (*fig*) be past sth. **h~werfen**† *vt sep* throw out; (*fam: entlassen*) fire. **h~wollen**† *vi sep (haben)* want to go out; **h~wollen auf** (+ *acc*) (*fig*) aim at; **hoch h~wollen** (*fig*) be ambitious. **h~ziehen**† *v sep* ● *vt* pull out; (*in die Länge ziehen*) drag out; (*verzö- gern*) delay; **sich h~ziehen** drag on; be delayed ● *vi (sein)* move out. **h~zögern** *vt sep* delay; **sich h~zögern** be delayed
Hinblick *m* **im H~ auf** (+ *acc*) in view of; (*hinsichtlich*) regarding
hinbringen† *vt sep* take there; (*verbringen*) spend
hinder|lich *a* awkward; **jdm h~lich sein** hamper s.o. **h~n** *vt* hamper; (*verhindern*) prevent. **H~nis** *nt* **-ses,-se** obstacle. **H~nisrennen** *nt* steeplechase
hindeuten *vi sep (haben)* point (**auf** + *acc*)
Hindu *m* **-s,-s** Hindu. **H~ismus** *m* - Hinduism
hindurch *adv* through it/them; **den Sommer h~** throughout the summer
hinein *adv* in [there]; (*nach drinnen*) inside; **h~ in** (+ *acc*) into. **h~fallen**†

vi sep (sein) fall in. **h~gehen**† *vi sep (sein)* go in; **h~gehen in** (+ *acc*) go into. **h~laufen**† *vi sep (sein)* run in; **h~laufen in** (+ *acc*) run into. **h~reden** *vi sep (haben)* **jdm h~reden** interrupt s.o.; (*sich einmischen*) interfere in s.o.'s affairs. **h~versetzen** (**sich**) *vr sep* **sich in jds Lage h~versetzen** put oneself in s.o.'s position. **h~ziehen**† *vt sep* pull in; **h~ziehen in** (+ *acc*) pull into; **in etw** (*acc*) **h~gezogen werden** (*fig*) become involved in sth
hin|fahren† *v sep* ● *vi (sein)* go/drive there ● *vt* take/drive there. **H~fahrt** *f* journey/drive there; (*Rail*) outward journey. **h~fallen**† *vi sep (sein)* fall. **h~fällig** *a* (*gebrechlich*) frail; (*ungültig*) invalid. **h~fliegen**† *v sep* ● *vi (sein)* fly there; (*fam*) fall ● *vt* fly there. **H~flug** *m* flight there; (*Admin*) outward flight. **H~gabe** *f* - devotion; (*Eifer*) dedication
hingeb|en† *vt sep* give up; **sich h~en** (*fig*) devote oneself (**einer Aufgabe** to a task); abandon oneself (**dem Vergnügen** to pleasure). **H~ung** *f* - devotion. **h~ungsvoll** *a* devoted, *adv* -ly
hingegen *adv* on the other hand
hingehen† *vi sep (sein)* go/(*zu Fuß*) walk there; (*vergehen*) pass; **h~ zu** go up to; **wo gehst du hin?** where are you going? **etw h~ lassen** (*fig*) let sth pass
hingerissen *a* rapt, *adv* -ly; **h~ sein** be carried away (**von** by)
hin|halten† *vt sep* hold out; (*warten lassen*) keep waiting. **h~hocken** (**sich**) *vr sep* squat down. **h~kauern** (**sich**) *vr sep* crouch down
hinken *vi (haben/sein)* limp
hin|knien (**sich**) *vr sep* kneel down. **h~kommen**† *vi sep (sein)* get there; (*h~gehören*) belong, go; (*fam: auskommen*) manage (**mit** with); (*fam: stimmen*) be right. **h~länglich** *a* adequate, *adv* -ly. **h~laufen**† *vi sep (sein)* run/(*gehen*) walk there. **h~legen** *vt sep* lay *or* put down; **sich h~legen** lie down. **h~nehmen**† *vt sep* (*fig*) accept
hinreichen *v sep* ● *vt* hand (*dat* to) ● *vi (haben)* extend (**bis** to); (*ausreichen*) be adequate. **h~d** *a* adequate, *adv* -ly
Hinreise *f* journey there; (*Rail*) outward journey

hinreißen† *vt sep* (*fig*) carry away; **sich h~ lassen** get carried away. **h~d** *a* ravishing, *adv* -ly

hinricht|en *vt sep* execute. **H~ung** *f* execution

hinschicken *vt sep* send there

hinschleppen *vt sep* drag there; (*fig*) drag out; **sich h~** drag oneself along; (*fig*) drag on

hinschreiben† *vt sep* write there; (*aufschreiben*) write down

hinsehen† *vi sep* (*haben*) look

hinsein† *vi sep* (*sein*) (*fam*) be gone; (*kaputt, tot*) have had it; **[ganz] h~ von** be overwhelmed by; **es ist noch/ nicht mehr lange hin** it's a long time yet/not long to go

hinsetzen *vt sep* put down; **sich h~** sit down

Hinsicht *f* - **in dieser/gewisser H~** in this respect/in a certain sense; **in finanzieller H~** financially. **h~lich** *prep* (+ *gen*) regarding

hinstellen *vt sep* put *or* set down; park (*Auto*); (*fig*) make out (**als** to be); **sich h~** stand

hinstrecken *vt sep* hold out; **sich h~** extend

hintan|setzen, h~stellen *vt sep* ignore; (*vernachlässigen*) neglect

hinten *adv* at the back; **dort h~** back there; **nach/von h~** to the back/ from behind. **h~herum** *adv* round the back; (*fam*) by devious means; (*erfahren*) in a roundabout way

hinter *prep* (+ *dat/acc*) behind; (*nach*) after; **h~ jdm/etw herlaufen** run after s.o./sth; **h~ etw** (*dat*) **stecken** (*fig*) be behind sth; **h~ etw** (*acc*) **kommen** (*fig*) get to the bottom of sth; **etw h~ sich** (*acc*) **bringen** get sth over [and done] with. **H~bein** *nt* hind leg

Hinterbliebene *pl* (*Admin*) surviving dependants; **die H~n** the bereaved family *sg*

hinterbringen† *vt* tell (**jdm** s.o.)

hintere|(r,s) *a* back, rear; **h~s Ende** far end

hintereinander *adv* one behind/ (*zeitlich*) after the other; **dreimal h~** three times in succession/(*fam*) in a row

Hintergedanke *m* ulterior motive

hintergehen† *vt* deceive

Hinter|grund *m* background. **H~halt** *m* -[e]s,-e ambush; **aus dem H~halt überfallen** ambush. **h~hältig** *a* underhand

hinterher *adv* behind, after; (*zeitlich*) afterwards. **h~gehen**† *vi sep* (*sein*) follow (**jdm** s.o.). **h~kommen**† *vi sep* (*sein*) follow [behind]. **h~laufen**† *vi sep* (*sein*) run after (**jdm** s.o.)

Hinter|hof *m* back yard. **H~kopf** *m* back of the head

hinterlassen† *vt* leave [behind]; (*Jur*) leave, bequeath (*dat* to). **H~schaft** *f* -,-en (*Jur*) estate

hinterlegen *vt* deposit

Hinter|leib *m* (*Zool*) abdomen. **H~list** *f* deceit. **h~listig** *a* deceitful, *adv* -ly. **h~m** *prep* = **hinter dem. H~mann** *m* (*pl* -**männer**) person behind. **h~n** *prep* = **hinter den. H~n** *m* -**s,-** (*fam*) bottom, backside. **H~rad** *nt* rear *or* back wheel. **h~rücks** *adv* from behind. **h~s** *prep* = **hinter das. h~- ste(r,s)** *a* last; **h~ste Reihe** back row. **H~teil** *nt* (*fam*) behind

hintertreiben† *vt* (*fig*) block

Hinter|treppe *f* back stairs *pl*. **H~tür** *f* back door; (*fig*) loophole

hinterziehen† *vt* (*Admin*) evade

Hinterzimmer *nt* back room

hinüber *adv* over *or* across [there]. **h~gehen**† *vi sep* (*sein*) go over *or* across; **h~gehen über** (+ *acc*) cross

hinunter *adv* down [there]; **die Treppe/Straße h~** down the stairs/ road. **h~gehen**† *vi sep* (*sein*) go down. **h~schlucken** *vt sep* swallow

Hinweg *m* way there

hinweg *adv* away, off; **h~ über** (+ *acc*) over; **über eine Zeit h~** over a period. **h~gehen**† *vi sep* (*sein*) **h~gehen über** (+ *acc*) (*fig*) pass over. **h~kommen**† *vi sep* (*sein*) **h~kommen über** (+ *acc*) (*fig*) get over. **h~sehen**† *vi sep* (*haben*) **h~sehen über** (+ *acc*) see over; (*fig*) overlook. **h~setzen** (**sich**) *vr sep* **sich h~setzen über** (+ *acc*) ignore

Hinweis *m* -**es,-e** reference; (*Andeutung*) hint; (*Anzeichen*) indication; **unter H~ auf** (+ *acc*) with reference to. **h~en**† *v sep* ●*vi* (*haben*) point (**auf** + *acc* to) ● *vt* **jdn auf etw** (*acc*) **h~en** point sth out to s.o. **h~end** *a* (*Gram*) demonstrative

hin|wenden† *vt sep* turn; **sich h~wenden** turn (**zu** to). **h~werfen**† *vt sep* throw down; drop ⟨*Bemerkung*⟩; (*schreiben*) jot down; (*zeichnen*) sketch; (*fam: aufgeben*) pack in

hinwieder *adv* on the other hand

hin|zeigen *vi sep* (*haben*) point (**auf** + *acc* to). **h∼ziehen**† *vt sep* pull; (*fig: in die Länge ziehen*) drag out; (*verzögern*) delay; **sich h∼ziehen** drag on; be delayed; **sich h∼gezogen fühlen zu** (*fig*) feel drawn to

hinzu *adv* in addition. **h∼fügen** *vt sep* add. **h∼kommen**† *vi sep (sein)* be added; (*ankommen*) arrive [on the scene]; join (**zu jdm** s.o.). **h∼rechnen** *vt sep* add. **h∼ziehen**† *vt sep* call in

Hiobsbotschaft *f* bad news *sg*

Hirn *nt* **-s** brain; (*Culin*) brains *pl*. **H∼gespinst** *nt* **-[e]s,-e** figment of the imagination. **H∼hautentzündung** *f* meningitis. **h∼verbrannt** *a* (*fam*) crazy

Hirsch *m* **-[e]s,-e** deer; (*männlich*) stag; (*Culin*) venison

Hirse *f* - millet

Hirt *m* **-en,-en, Hirte** *m* **-n,-n** shepherd

hissen *vt* hoist

Histor|iker *m* **-s,-** historian. **h∼isch** *a* historical; (*bedeutend*) historic

Hit *m* **-s,-s** (*Mus*) hit

Hitz|e *f* - heat. **H∼ewelle** *f* heat wave. **h∼ig** *a* (*fig*) heated, *adv* -ly; ⟨*Person*⟩ hot-headed; (*jähzornig*) hot-tempered. **H∼kopf** *m* hothead. **H∼schlag** *m* heat-stroke

H-Milch /'ha:-/ *f* long-life milk

Hobby *nt* **-s,-s** hobby

Hobel *m* **-s,-** (*Techn*) plane; (*Culin*) slicer. **h∼n** *vt/i* (*haben*) plane. **H∼späne** *mpl* shavings

hoch *a* (**höher, höchst**; *attrib* **hohe(r,s)**) high; ⟨*Baum, Mast*⟩ tall; ⟨*Offizier*⟩ high-ranking; ⟨*Alter*⟩ great; ⟨*Summe*⟩ large; ⟨*Strafe*⟩ heavy; **hohe Schuhe** ankle boots ● *adv* high; (*sehr*) highly; **die Treppe/den Berg h∼** up the stairs/ hill; **sechs Mann h∼** six of us/them. **H∼** *nt* **-s,-s** cheer; (*Meteorol*) high

Hoch|achtung *f* high esteem. **H∼achtungsvoll** *adv* Yours faithfully. **H∼amt** *nt* High Mass. **h∼arbeiten (sich)** *vr sep* work one's way up. **h∼begabt** *attrib a* highly gifted. **H∼betrieb** *m* great activity; **in den Geschäften herrscht H∼betrieb** the shops are terribly busy. **H∼burg** *f* (*fig*) stronghold. **H∼deutsch** *nt*

High German. **H∼druck** *m* high pressure. **H∼ebene** *f* plateau. **h∼fahren**† *vi sep (sein)* go up; (*auffahren*) start up; (*aufbrausen*) flare up. **h∼fliegend** *a* (*fig*) ambitious. **h∼gehen**† *vi sep (sein)* go up; (*explodieren*) blow up; (*aufbrausen*) flare up. **h∼gestellt** *attrib a* high-ranking; ⟨*Zahl*⟩ superior. **h∼gewachsen** *a* tall. **H∼glanz** *m* high gloss. **h∼gradig** *a* extreme, *adv* -ly. **h∼hackig** *a* high-heeled. **h∼halten**† *vt sep* hold up; (*fig*) uphold. **H∼haus** *nt* high-rise building. **h∼heben**† *vt sep* lift up; raise ⟨*Kopf, Hand*⟩. **h∼herzig** *a* magnanimous, *adv* -ly. **h∼kant** *adv* on end. **h∼kommen**† *vi sep (sein)* come up; (*aufstehen*) get up; (*fig*) get on [in the world]. **H∼konjunktur** *f* boom. **h∼krempeln** *vt sep* roll up. **h∼leben** *vi sep (haben)* **h∼leben lassen** give three cheers for; **... lebe hoch!** three cheers for ...! **H∼mut** *m* pride, arrogance. **h∼mütig** *a* arrogant, *adv* -ly. **h∼näsig** *a* (*fam*) snooty. **h∼nehmen**† *vt sep* pick up; (*fam*) tease. **H∼ofen** *m* blast-furnace. **h∼ragen** *vi sep* rise [up]; ⟨*Turm:*⟩ soar. **H∼ruf** *m* cheer. **H∼saison** *f* high season. **H∼schätzung** *f* high esteem. **h∼schlagen**† *vt sep* turn up ⟨*Kragen*⟩. **h∼schrecken** *vi sep (sein)* start up. **H∼schule** *f* university; (*Musik-, Kunst-*) academy. **h∼sehen**† *vi sep (haben)* look up. **H∼sommer** *m* midsummer. **H∼spannung** *f* high/(*fig*) great tension. **h∼spielen** *vt sep* (*fig*) magnify. **H∼sprache** *f* standard language. **H∼sprung** *m* high jump

höchst *adv* extremely, most

Hochstapler *m* **-s,-** confidence trickster

höchst|e(r,s) *a* highest; ⟨*Baum, Turm*⟩ tallest; (*oberste, größte*) top; **es ist h∼e Zeit** it is high time. **h∼ens** *adv* at most; (*es sei denn*) except perhaps. **H∼fall** *m* **im H∼fall** at most. **H∼geschwindigkeit** *f* top *or* maximum speed. **H∼maß** *nt* maximum. **h∼persönlich** *adv* in person. **H∼preis** *m* top price. **H∼temperatur** *f* maximum temperature. **h∼wahrscheinlich** *adv* most probably

hoch|trabend *a* pompous, *adv* -ly. **h∼treiben**† *vt sep* push up ⟨*Preis*⟩. **H∼verrat** *m* high treason.

H~wasser nt high tide; (Über-schwemmung) floods pl. **H~würden** m -s Reverend; (Anrede) Father

Hochzeit f -,-en wedding; **H~ feiern** get married. **H~skleid** nt wedding dress. **H~sreise** f honeymoon [trip]. **H~stag** m wedding day/(Jahrestag) anniversary

hochziehen† vt sep pull up; (hissen) hoist; raise ⟨Augenbrauen⟩

Hocke f - **in der H~ sitzen** squat; **in die H~ gehen** squat down. **h~n** vi (haben) squat ● vr **sich h~n** squat down

Hocker m -s,- stool

Höcker m -s,- bump; (Kamel-) hump

Hockey /'hɔki/ nt -s hockey

Hode f -,-n, **Hoden** m -s,- testicle

Hof m -[e]s,¨e [court]yard; (Bauern-) farm; (Königs-) court; (Schul-) play-ground; (Astr) halo

hoffen vt/i (haben) hope (**auf** + acc for). **h~tlich** adv I hope, let us hope; (als Antwort) **h~tlich/h~tlich nicht** let's hope so/not

Hoffnung f -,-en hope. **h~slos** a hopeless, adv -ly. **h~svoll** a hopeful, adv -ly

höflich a polite, adv -ly, courteous, adv -ly. **H~keit** f -,-en politeness, courtesy; (Äußerung) civility

hohe(r,s) a s. **hoch**

Höhe f -,-n height; (Aviat, Geog) altitude; (Niveau) level; (einer Summe) size; (An-) hill; **in die H~ gehen** rise, go up; **nicht auf der H~** (fam) under the weather; **das ist die H~!** (fam) that's the limit!

Hoheit f -,-en (Staats-) sovereignty; (Titel) Highness. **H~sgebiet** nt [sovereign] territory. **H~szeichen** nt national emblem

Höhe|nlinie f contour line. **H~nsonne** f sun-lamp. **H~nzug** m mountain range. **H~punkt** m (fig) climax, peak; (einer Vorstellung) highlight. **h~r** a & adv higher; **h~re Schule** secondary school

hohl a hollow; (leer) empty

Höhle f -,-n cave; (Tier-) den; (Hohlraum) cavity; (Augen-) socket

Hohl|maß nt measure of capacity. **H~raum** m cavity

Hohn m -s scorn, derision

höhn|en vt deride ● vi (haben) jeer. **h~isch** a scornful, adv -ly

holen vt fetch, get; (kaufen) buy; (nehmen) take (**aus** from); **h~ lassen**

send for; **[tief] Atem** od **Luft h~** take a [deep] breath; **sich** (dat) **etw h~** get sth; catch ⟨Erkältung⟩

Holland nt -s Holland

Holländ|er m -s,- Dutchman; **die H~er** the Dutch pl. **H~erin** f -,-nen Dutchwoman. **h~isch** a Dutch

Höll|e f - hell. **h~isch** a infernal; (schrecklich) terrible, adv -bly

holpern vi (sein) jolt or bump along ● vi (haben) be bumpy

holp[e]rig a bumpy

Holunder m -s (Bot) elder

Holz nt -es,¨er wood; (Nutz-) timber. **H~blasinstrument** nt woodwind instrument

hölzern a wooden

Holz|hammer m mallet. **h~ig** a woody. **H~kohle** f charcoal. **H~schnitt** m woodcut. **H~schuh** m [wooden] clog. **H~wolle** f wood shavings pl. **H~wurm** m woodworm

homogen a homogeneous

Homöopathie f - homoeopathy

homosexuell a homosexual. **H~e(r)** m/f homosexual

Honig m -s honey. **H~wabe** f honeycomb

Hono|rar nt -s,-e fee. **h~rieren** vt remunerate; (fig) reward

Hopfen m -s hops pl; (Bot) hop

hopsen vi (sein) jump

Hör|apparat m hearing-aid. **h~bar** a audible, adv -bly

horchen vi (haben) listen (**auf** + acc to); (heimlich) eavesdrop

Horde f -,-n horde; (Gestell) rack

hören vt hear; (an-) listen to ● vi (haben) hear; (horchen) listen; (ge-horchen) obey; **h~ auf** (+ acc) listen to. **H~sagen** nt **vom H~sagen** from hearsay

Hör|er m -s,- listener; (Teleph) receiver. **H~funk** m radio. **H~gerät** nt hear-ing-aid

Horizon|t m -[e]s horizon. **h~tal** a horizontal, adv -ly

Hormon nt -s,-e hormone

Horn nt -s,¨er horn. **H~haut** f hard skin; (Augen-) cornea

Hornisse f -,-n hornet

Horoskop nt -[e]s,-e horoscope

Hörrohr nt stethoscope

Horrorfilm m horror film

Hör|saal m (Univ) lecture hall. **H~spiel** nt radio play

Hort m -[e]s,-e (Schatz) hoard; (fig) refuge. **h~en** vt hoard

Hortensie /·iə/ f **-,-n** hydrangea

Hörweite f **in/außer H~** within/out of earshot

Hose f **-,-n, Hosen** pl trousers pl. **H~nrock** m culottes pl. **H~nschlitz** m fly, flies pl. **H~nträger** mpl braces, (Amer) suspenders

Hostess, Hosteß f **-,-tessen** hostess; (Aviat) air hostess

Hostie /'hɔstiə/ f **-,-n** (Relig) host

Hotel nt **-s,-s** hotel; **H~ garni** /gar'ni:/ bed-and-breakfast hotel. **H~ier** /·'lie:/ m **-s,-s** hotelier

hübsch a pretty, adv -ily; (nett) nice, adv -ly; (Summe) tidy

Hubschrauber m **-s,-** helicopter

huckepack adv **jdn h~ tragen** give s.o. a piggyback

Huf m **-[e]s,-e** hoof. **H~eisen** nt horseshoe

Hüft|e f **-,-n** hip. **H~gürtel, H~halter** m **-s,-** girdle

Hügel m **-s,-** hill. **h~ig** a hilly

Huhn nt **-s,ˉer** chicken; (Henne) hen

Hühn|chen nt **-s,-** chicken. **H~erauge** nt corn. **H~erbrühe** f chicken broth. **H~erstall** m henhouse, chicken-coop

huldig|en vi (haben) pay homage (dat to). **H~ung** f - homage

Hülle f **-,-n** cover; (Verpackung) wrapping; (Platten-) sleeve; **in H~ und Fülle** in abundance. **h~n** vt wrap

Hülse f **-,-n** (Bot) pod; (Etui) case. **H~nfrüchte** fpl pulses

human a humane, adv -ly. **h~itär** a humanitarian. **H~ität** f - humanity

Hummel f **-,-n** bumble-bee

Hummer m **-s,-** lobster

Hum|or m **-s** humour; **H~or haben** have a sense of humour. **h~oristisch** a humorous. **h~orvoll** a humorous, adv -ly

humpeln vi (sein/haben) hobble

Humpen m **-s,-** tankard

Hund m **-[e]s,-e** dog; (Jagd-) hound. **H~ehalsband** nt dog-collar. **H~ehütte** f kennel. **H~eleine** f dog lead

hundert inv a one/a hundred. **H~** nt **-s,-e** hundred; **H~e von** hundreds of. **H~jahrfeier** f centenary, (Amer) centennial. **h~prozentig** a & adv one hundred per cent. **h~ste(r,s)** a hundredth. **H~stel** nt **-s,-** hundredth

Hündin f **-,-nen** bitch

Hüne m **-n,-n** giant

Hunger m **-s** hunger; **H~ haben** be hungry. **h~n** vi (haben) starve; **h~n**

nach (fig) hunger for. **H~snot** f famine

hungrig a hungry, adv -ily

Hupe f **-,-n** (Auto) horn. **h~n** vi (haben) sound one's horn

hüpf|en vi (sein) skip; (Vogel, Frosch:) hop; (Grashüpfer:) jump. **H~er** m **-s,-** skip, hop

Hürde f **-,-n** (Sport & fig) hurdle; (Schaf-) pen, fold

Hure f **-,-n** whore

hurra int hurray. **H~** nt **-s,-s** hurray; (Beifallsruf) cheer

Husche f **-,-n** [short] shower. **h~n** vi (sein) slip; (Eidechse:) dart; (Maus:) scurry; (Lächeln:) flit

hüsteln vi (haben) give a slight cough

husten vi (haben) cough. **H~** m **-s** cough. **H~saft** m cough mixture

Hut¹ m **-[e]s,ˉe** hat; (Pilz-) cap

Hut² f **- auf der H~ sein** be on one's guard (**vor** + dat against)

hüten vt watch over; tend (Tiere); (aufpassen) look after; **das Bett h~ müssen** be confined to bed; **sich h~** be on one's guard (**vor** + dat against); **sich h~, etw zu tun** take care not to do sth

Hütte f **-,-n** hut; (Hunde-) kennel; (Techn) iron and steel works. **H~nkäse** m cottage cheese. **H~nkunde** f metallurgy

Hyäne f **-,-n** hyena

Hybride f **-,-n** hybrid

Hydrant m **-en,-en** hydrant

hydraulisch a hydraulic, adv -ally

hydroelektrisch /hydro⁹e'lɛktrɪʃ/ a hydroelectric

Hygien|e /hy'giə:nə/ f - hygiene. **h~isch** a hygienic, adv -ally

hypermodern a ultra-modern

Hypno|se f - hypnosis. **h~tisch** a hypnotic. **H~tiseur** /·'zø:ɐ̯/ m **-s,-e** hypnotist. **h~tisieren** vt hypnotize

Hypochonder /hypo'xɔndɐ/ m **-s,-** hypochondriac

Hypothek f **-,-en** mortgage

Hypothe|se f **-,-n** hypothesis. **h~tisch** a hypothetical, adv -ly

Hys|terie f - hysteria. **h~terisch** a hysterical, adv -ly

I

ich pron I; **ich bin's** it's me. **Ich** nt **-[s],-[s]** self; (Psych) ego

IC-Zug /i'tse:-/ m inter-city train

ideal a ideal. **I~** nt **-s,-e** ideal. **i~i-sieren** vt idealize. **I~ismus** m - idealism. **I~ist(in)** m **-en,-en** (f **-,-nen**) idealist. **i~istisch** a idealistic

Idee f **-,-n** idea; **fixe I~** obsession; **eine I~** (fam: wenig) a tiny bit

identifizieren vt identify

identi|sch a identical. **I~tät** f **-,-en** identity

Ideo|logie f **-,-n** ideology. **i~logisch** a ideological

idiomatisch a idiomatic

Idiot m **-en,-en** idiot. **i~isch** a idiotic, adv -ally

Idol nt **-s,-e** idol

idyllisch /i'dylɪʃ/ a idyllic

Igel m **-s,-** hedgehog

ignorieren vt ignore

ihm pron (dat of **er, es**) [to] him; (Ding, Tier) [to] it; **Freunde von ihm** friends of his

ihn pron (acc of **er**) him; (Ding, Tier) it. **I~en** pron (dat of **sie** pl) [to] them; **Freunde von i~en** friends of theirs. **I~en** pron (dat of **Sie**) [to] you; **Freunde von I~en** friends of yours

ihr pron (2nd pers pl) you ● (dat of **sie** sg) [to] her; (Ding, Tier) [to] it; **Freunde von ihr** friends of hers ● poss pron her; (Ding, Tier) its; (pl) their. **Ihr** poss pron your. **i~e(r,s)** poss pron hers; (pl) theirs. **I~e(r,s)** poss pron yours. **i~erseits** adv for her/(pl) their part. **I~erseits** adv on your part. **i~etwegen** adv for her/(Ding, Tier) its/(pl) their sake; (wegen) because of her/it/them, on her/its/their account. **I~etwegen** adv for your sake; (wegen) because of you, on your account. **i~etwillen** adv **um i~etwillen** for her/(Ding, Tier) its/(pl) their sake. **I~etwillen** adv **um I~etwillen** for your sake. **i~ige** poss pron **der/die/das i~ige** hers; (pl) theirs. **I~ige** poss pron **der/die/das I~ige** yours. **i~s** poss pron hers; (pl) theirs. **I~s** poss pron yours

Ikone f **-,-n** icon

illegal a illegal, adv -ly

Illus|ion f **-,-en** illusion; **sich** (dat) **I~ionen machen** delude oneself. **i~o-risch** a illusory

Illustr|ation /-'tsio:n/ f **-,-en** illustration. **i~ieren** vt illustrate. **I~ierte** f **-n,-[n]** [illustrated] magazine

Iltis m **-ses,-se** polecat

im prep = **in dem; im Mai** in May; **im Kino** at the cinema

Image /'ɪmɪdʒ/ nt **-[s],-s** /-ɪs/ [public] image

Imbiß m snack. **I~halle, I~stube** f snack-bar

Imitation /-'tsio:n/ f **-,-en** imitation. **i~ieren** vt imitate

Imker m **-s,-** bee-keeper

Immatrikul|ation /-'tsio:n/ f - (Univ) enrolment. **i~ieren** vt (Univ) enrol; **sich i~ieren** enrol

immer adv always; **für i~** for ever; (endgültig) for good; **i~ noch** still; **i~ mehr/weniger/wieder** more and more/less and less/again and again; **wer/was [auch] i~** whoever/whatever. **i~fort** adv = **i~zu**. **i~grün** a evergreen. **i~hin** adv (wenigstens) at least; (trotzdem) all the same; (schließlich) after all. **i~zu** adv all the time

Immobilien /-jən/ pl real estate sg. **I~händler, I~makler** m estate agent, (Amer) realtor

immun a immune (**gegen** to). **i~isieren** vt immunize. **I~ität** f - immunity

Imperativ m **-s,-e** imperative

Imperfekt nt **-s,-e** imperfect

Imperialismus m - imperialism

impf|en vt vaccinate, inoculate. **I~stoff** m vaccine. **I~ung** f **-,-en** vaccination, inoculation

Implantat nt **-[e]s,-e** implant

imponieren vi (haben) impress (**jdm** s.o.)

Impor|t m **-[e]s,-e** import. **I~teur** /-'tø:ɐ/ m **-s,-e** importer. **i~tieren** vt import

imposant a imposing

impoten|t a (Med) impotent. **I~z** f - (Med) impotence

imprägnieren vt waterproof

Impressionismus m - impressionism

improvisieren vt/i (haben) improvise

Impuls m **-es,-e** impulse. **i~iv** a impulsive, adv -ly

imstande pred a able (**zu** to); capable (**etw zu tun** of doing sth)

in prep (+ dat) in; (+ acc) into, in; (bei Bus, Zug) on; **in der Schule/Oper** at school/the opera; **in die Schule** to school ● a **in sein** be in

Inbegriff m embodiment. **i~en** pred a included

Inbrunst f - fervour

inbrünstig a fervent, adv -ly

indem *conj* (*während*) while; (*dadurch*) by (+ -ing)

Inder(in) *m* **-s,-** (*f* **-,-nen**) Indian

indessen *conj* while ● *adv* (*un-
terdessen*) meanwhile; (*jedoch*) however

Indian *m* **-s,-e** (*Aust*) turkey

Indian|er(in) *m* **-s,-** (*f* **-,-nen**)
(American) Indian. **i~isch** *a* Indian

Indien /'mdiən/ *nt* **-s** India

indignier t *a* indignant, *adv* -ly

Indikativ *m* **-s,-e** indicative

indirekt *a* indirect, *adv* -ly

indisch *a* Indian

indiskre|t *a* indiscreet. **I~tion**
/-'tsio:n/ *f* **-,-en** indiscretion

indiskutabel *a* out of the question

indisponiert *a* indisposed

Individu|alist *m* **-en,-en** indiv-
idualist. **I~alität** *f* - individuality. **i~
ell** *a* individual, *adv* -ly. **I~um** /-'vi:
duʊm/ *nt* **-s,-duen** individual

Indizienbeweis /ɪn'di:tsiən-/ *m* cir-
cumstantial evidence

indoktrinieren *vt* indoctrinate

industr|ialisiert *a* industrialized.
I~ie *f* **-,-n** industry. **i~iell** *a* industrial. **I~ielle(r)** *m* industrialist

ineinander *adv* in/into one another

Infanterie *f* - infantry

Infektion /-'tsio:n/ *f* **-,-en** infection.
I~skrankheit *f* infectious disease

Infinitiv *m* **-s,-e** infinitive

inf izieren *vt* infect; **sich i~** become;
⟨*Person:*⟩ be infected

Inflation /-'tsio:n/ *f* - inflation. **i~är**
a inflationary

infolge *prep* (+ *gen*) as a result of.
i~dessen *adv* consequently

Inform|atik *f* - information science.
I~ation /-'tsio:n/ *f* **-,-en** information;
I~ationen information *sg*. **i~ieren**
vt inform; **sich i~ieren** find out
(**über** + *acc* about)

infrarot *a* infra-red

Ingenieur /ɪnʒe'niø:ɐ/ *m* **-s,-e** engineer

Ingwer *m* **-s** ginger

Inhaber(in) *m* **-s,-** (*f* **-,-nen**) holder;
(*Besitzer*) proprietor; (*Scheck-*) bearer

inhaftieren *vt* take into custody

inhalieren *vt/i* (*haben*) inhale

Inhalt *m* **-[e]s,-e** contents *pl*; (*Bedeutung, Gehalt*) content; (*Geschichte*)
story. **I~sangabe** *f* summary.
I~sverzeichnis *nt* list/(*in Buch*)
table of contents

Initiale /-'tsia:lə/ *f* **-,-n** initial

Initiative /initsia'ti:və/ *f* **-,-n** initiative

Injektion /-'tsio:n/ *f* **-,-en** injection.
injizieren *vt* inject

inklusive *prep* (+ *gen*) including
● *adv* inclusive

inkognito *adv* incognito

inkonsequen|t *a* inconsistent, *adv*
-ly. **I~z** *f* **-,-en** inconsistency

inkorrekt *a* incorrect, *adv* -ly

Inkubationszeit /-'tsio:ns-/ *f* (*Med*)
incubation period

Inland *nt* **-[e]s** home country;
(*Binnenland*) interior. **I~sgespräch**
nt inland call

inmitten *prep* (+ *gen*) in the middle
of; (*unter*) amongst ● *adv* **i~ von**
amongst, amidst

inne|haben† *vt sep* hold, have. **i~
halten†** *vi sep* (*haben*) pause

innen *adv* inside; **nach i~** inwards.
I~architekt(in) *m(f)* interior de-
signer. **I~minister** *m* Minister of the
Interior; (*in UK*) Home Secretary.
I~politik *f* domestic policy. **I~stadt**
f town centre

inner|e(r,s) *a* inner; (*Med, Pol*) in-
ternal. **I~e(s)** *nt* interior; (*Mitte*)
centre; (*fig: Seele*) inner being. **I~ei-
en** *fpl* (*Culin*) offal *sg*. **i~halb** *prep*
(+ *gen*) inside; (*zeitlich & fig*) within;
(*während*) during ● *adv* **i~halb von**
within. **i~lich** *a* internal; (*seelisch*)
inner; (*besinnlich*) intro- spective
● *adv* internally; (*im Inneren*) inwardly. **i~ste(r,s)** innermost; **im I~
sten** (*fig*) deep down

innig *a* sincere, *adv* -ly; (*tief*) deep,
adv -ly; (*eng*) intimate, *adv* -ly

Innung *f* **-,-en** guild

inoffiziell *a* unofficial, *adv* -ly

ins *prep* = **in das; ins Kino/Büro** to the
cinema/office

Insasse *m* **-n,-n** inmate; (*im Auto*)
occupant; (*Passagier*) passenger

insbesondere *adv* especially

Inschrift *f* inscription

Insekt *nt* **-[e]s,-en** insect. **I~en-
vertilgungsmittel** *nt* insecticide

Insel *f* **-,-n** island

Inser|at *nt* **-[e]s,-e** [newspaper]
advertisement. **I~ent** *m* **-en,-en**
advertiser. **i~ieren** *vt/i* (*haben*) advertise

insge|heim *adv* secretly. **i~samt**
adv [all] in all

Insignien /-iən/ *pl* insignia

insofern, insoweit adv /-'zo:-/ in this respect; **i~ als** in as much as ● conj /-zo'fɛrn, -'vait/ **i~ als** in so far as

Insp|ektion /ɪnspɛk'tsi̯o:n/ f **-,-en** inspection. **l~ektor** m **-en,-en** /-'to:ran/ inspector

Inspir|ation /ɪnspira'tsi̯o:n/ f **-,-en** inspiration. **i~ieren** vt inspire

inspizieren /-sp-/ vt inspect

Install|ateur /ɪnstala'tø:ɐ̯/ m **-s,-e** fitter; (Klempner) plumber. **i~ieren** vt install

instand adv **i~ halten** maintain; (pflegen) look after; **i~ setzen** restore; (reparieren) repair. **l~haltung** f - maintenance, upkeep

inständig a urgent, adv -ly

Instandsetzung f - repair

Instant- /'ɪnstant-/ pref instant

Instanz /-st-/ f **-,-en** authority

Instinkt /-st-/ m **-[e]s,-e** instinct. **i~iv** a instinctive, adv -ly

Institu|t /-st-/ nt **-[e]s,-e** institute. **l~tion** /-'tsi̯o:n/ f **-,-en** institution

Instrument /-st-/ nt **-[e]s,-e** instrument. **l~almusik** f instrumental music

Insulin nt **-s** insulin

inszenier|en vt (Theat) produce. **l~ung** f **-,-en** production

Integr|ation /-'tsi̯o:n/ f - integration. **i~ieren** vt integrate; **sich i~ieren** integrate. **l~ität** f - integrity

Intellekt m **-[e]s** intellect. **i~uell** a intellectual

intelligen|t a intelligent, adv -ly. **l~z** f - intelligence; (Leute) intelligentsia

Intendant m **-en,-en** director

Intens|ität f - intensity. **i~iv** a intensive, adv -ly. **i~ivieren** vt intensify. **l~ivstation** f intensive-care unit

inter|essant a interesting. **l~esse** nt **-s,-n** interest; **l~esse haben** be interested **(an** + dat in). **l~essengruppe** f pressure group. **l~essent** m **-en,-en** interested party; (Käufer) prospective buyer. **i~essieren** vt interest; **sich i~essieren** be interested **(für** in)

intern a (fig) internal, adv -ly

Inter|nat nt **-[e]s,-e** boarding school. **i~national** a international, adv -ly. **i~nieren** vt intern. **l~nierung** f - internment. **l~nist** m **-en,-en** specialist in internal diseases. **l~pretation**

/-'tsi̯o:n/ f **-,-en** interpretation. **i~pretieren** vt interpret. **l~punktion** /-'tsi̯o:n/ f - punctuation. **l~rogativpronomen** nt interrogative pronoun. **l~vall** nt **-s,-e** interval. **l~vention** /-'tsi̯o:n/ f **-,-en** intervention

Interview /'ɪntɛvju:/ nt **-s,-s** interview. **i~en** /-'vju:ən/ vt interview

intim a intimate, adv -ly. **l~ität** f -, **-en** intimacy

intoleran|t a intolerant. **l~z** f - intolerance

intransitiv a intransitive, adv -ly

intravenös a intravenous, adv -ly

Intrig|e f **-,-n** intrigue. **i~ieren** vi (haben) plot

introvertiert a introverted

Intui|tion /-'tsi̯o:n/ f **-,-en** intuition. **i~tiv** a intuitive, adv -ly

Invalidenrente f disability pension

Invasion f **-,-en** invasion

Inven|tar nt **-s,-e** furnishings and fittings pl; (Techn) equipment; (Bestand) stock; (Liste) inventory. **l~tur** f **-,-en** stock-taking

investieren vt invest

inwendig a & adv inside

inwie|fern adv in what way. **i~weit** adv how far, to what extent

Inzest m **-[e]s** incest

inzwischen adv in the meantime

Irak (der) -[s] Iraq. **i~isch** a Iraqi

Iran (der) -[s] Iran. **i~isch** a Iranian

irdisch a earthly

Ire m **-n,-n** Irishman; **die l~n** the Irish pl

irgend adv **i~ jemand/etwas** someone/something; (fragend, verneint) anyone/anything; **wer/was/wann i~** whoever/whatever/whenever; **wenn i~ möglich** if at all possible. **i~ein** indef art some/any; **i~ein anderer** someone/anyone else. **i~eine(r,s)** pron any one; (jemand) someone/anyone. **i~wann** pron at some time [or other]/at any time. **i~was** pron (fam) something [or other]/anything. **i~welche(r,s)** pron any. **i~wer** pron someone/anyone. **i~wie** adv somehow [or other]. **i~wo** adv somewhere/anywhere; **i~wo anders** somewhere else

Irin f **-,-nen** Irishwoman

Iris f **-,-** (Anat, Bot) iris

irisch a Irish

Irland nt **-s** Ireland

Ironie f - irony

ir̲onisch *a* ironic, *adv* -ally

irr *a* = **irre**

irrational *a* irrational

ir̲re *a* mad, crazy; (*fam: gewaltig*) incredible, *adv* -bly; **i∼ werden** get confused. **I∼(r)** *m/f* lunatic. **i∼führen** *vt sep* (*fig*) mislead. **i∼gehen**† *vi sep* (*sein*) lose one's way; (*sich täuschen*) be wrong

irrelevant *a* irrelevant

ir̲re|machen *vt sep* confuse. **i∼n** *vi/r* (*haben*) **[sich] i∼n** be mistaken; **wenn ich mich nicht i∼** if I am not mistaken ● *vi (sein)* wander. **I∼nanstalt** *f*, **I∼nhaus** *nt* lunatic asylum. **i∼reden** *vi sep* (*haben*) ramble

Irr̲|garten *m* maze. **i∼ig** *a* erroneous

irritieren *vt* irritate

Irr̲|sinn *m* madness, lunacy. **i∼sinnig** *a* mad; (*fam: gewaltig*) incredible, *adv* -bly. **I∼tum** *m* **-s,-̈er** mistake. **i∼tümlich** *a* mistaken, *adv* -ly

Ischias *m & nt* - sciatica

Islam (der) **-[s]** Islam. **islamisch** *a* Islamic

Island *nt* **-s** Iceland

Isolier̲|band *nt* insulating tape. **i∼en** *vt* isolate; (*Phys, Electr*) insulate; (*gegen Schall*) soundproof. **I∼ung** *f* - isolation; insulation; soundproofing

Isra̲el /'ɪsraeːl/ *nt* **-s** Israel. **I∼eli** *m* **-[s],-s** & *f* **-,-[s]** Israeli. **i∼elisch** *a* Israeli

ist *s.* **sein; er ist** he is

Ital̲|ien /-jən/ *nt* **-s** Italy. **I∼iener(in)** *m* **-s,-** (*f* **-,-nen**) Italian. **i∼ienisch** *a* Italian. **I∼ienisch** *nt* **-[s]** (*Lang*) Italian

J

ja *adv* yes; **ich glaube ja** I think so; '**ja nicht!** not on any account! **seid 'ja vorsichtig!** whatever you do, be careful! **da seid ihr ja!** there you are! **das ist es ja** that's just it; **das mag ja wahr sein** that may well be true

Jacht *f* **-,-en** yacht

Jacke *f* **-,-n** jacket; (*Strick-*) cardigan

Jackett /ʒa'kɛt/ *nt* **-s,-s** jacket

Jade *m* **-[s]** & *f* - jade

Jagd *f* **-,-en** hunt; (*Schießen*) shoot; (*Jagen*) hunting; shooting; (*fig*) pursuit (**nach** of); **auf die J∼ gehen** go hunting/shooting. **J∼flugzeug** *nt* fighter aircraft. **J∼gewehr** *nt* sporting gun. **J∼hund** *m* gun-dog; (*Hetzhund*) hound

jagen *vt* hunt; (*schießen*) shoot; (*verfolgen, wegjagen*) chase; (*treiben*) drive; **sich j∼** chase each other; **in die Luft j∼** blow up ● *vi (haben)* hunt, go hunting/shooting; (*fig*) chase (**nach** after) ● *vi (sein)* race, dash

Jäger *m* **-s,-** hunter

jäh *a* sudden, *adv* -ly; (*steil*) steep, *adv* -ly

Jahr *nt* **-[e]s,-e** year. **J∼buch** *nt* yearbook. **j∼elang** *adv* for years. **J∼estag** *m* anniversary. **J∼eszahl** *f* year. **J∼eszeit** *f* season. **J∼gang** *m* year; (*Wein*) vintage. **J∼hundert** *nt* century. **J∼hundertfeier** *f* centenary. (*Amer*) centennial

jährlich *a* annual, yearly ● *adv* annually, yearly

Jahr̲|markt *m* fair. **J∼tausend** *nt* millennium. **J∼zehnt** *nt* **-[e]s,-e** decade

Jähzorn *m* violent temper. **j∼ig** *a* hot-tempered

Jalousie /ʒalu'ziː/ *f* **-,-n** venetian blind

Jammer *m* **-s** misery; (*Klagen*) lamenting; **es ist ein J∼** it is a shame

jämmerlich *a* miserable, *adv* -bly; (*mitleiderregend*) pitiful, *adv* -ly

jammer̲|n *vi (haben)* lament ● *vt* **jdn j∼n** arouse s.o.'s pity. **j∼schade** *a* **j∼schade sein** (*fam*) be a terrible shame

Jänner *m* **-s,-** (*Aust*) January

Januar *m* **-s,-e** January

Jap̲|an *nt* **-s** Japan. **J∼aner(in)** *m* **-s,-** (*f* **-,-nen**) Japanese. **j∼anisch** *a* Japanese. **J∼anisch** *nt* **-[s]** (*Lang*) Japanese

Jargon /ʒar'gõː/ *m* **-s** jargon

jäten *vt/i (haben)* weed

jauchzen *vi (haben)* (*liter*) exult

jaulen *vi (haben)* yelp

Jause *f* **-,-n** (*Aust*) snack

jawohl *adv* yes

Jawort *nt* **jdm sein J∼ geben** accept s.o.'s proposal [of marriage]

Jazz /jats, dʒɛs/ *m* - jazz

je *adv* (*jemals*) ever; (*jeweils*) each; (*pro*) per; **je nach** according to; **seit eh und je** always; **besser denn je** better than ever ● *conj* **je mehr, desto** *od* **um so besser** the more the better ● *prep* (+ *acc*) per

Jeans /dʒiːns/ *pl* jeans

jed|e(r,s) *pron* every; (*j~er einzelne*) each; (*j~er beliebige*) any; (*substantivisch*) everyone; each one; anyone; **ohne j~en Grund** without any reason. **j~enfalls** *adv* in any case; (*wenigstens*) at least. **j~ermann** *pron* everyone. **j~erzeit** *adv* at any time. **j~esmal** *adv* every time; **j~esmal wenn** whenever

jedoch *adv & conj* however

jeher *adv* **von** *od* **seit j~** always

jemals *adv* ever

jemand *pron* someone, somebody; (*fragend, verneint*) anyone, anybody

jen|e(r,s) *pron* that; (*pl*) those; (*substantivisch*) that one; (*pl*) those. **j~seits** *prep* (+ *gen*) [on] the other side of

jetzig *a* present; (*Preis*) current

jetzt *adv* now. **J~zeit** *f* present

jeweil|ig *a* respective. **j~s** *adv* at a time

jiddisch *a*, **J~** *nt* -[s] Yiddish

Job /dʒɔp/ *m* -s,-s job. **j~ben** *vi* (*haben*) (*fam*) work

Joch *nt* -[e]s,-e yoke

Jockei, Jockey /'dʒɔki/ *m* -s,-s jockey

Jod *nt* -[e]s iodine

jodeln *vi* (*haben*) yodel

Joga *m & nt* -[s] yoga

jogg|en /'dʒɔgən/ *vi* (*haben/sein*) jog. **J~ing** *nt* -[s] jogging

Joghurt *m & nt* -[s] yoghurt

Johannisbeere *f* redcurrant; **schwarze J~** blackcurrant

johlen *vi* (*haben*) yell; (*empört*) jeer

Joker *m* -s,- (*Karte*) joker

Jolle *f* -,-n dinghy

Jongl|eur /ʒõ'glø:ɐ/ *m* -s,-e juggler. **j~ieren** *vi* (*haben*) juggle

Joppe *f* -,-n [thick] jacket

Jordanien /-jən/ *nt* -s Jordan

Journalis|mus /ʒʊrna'lɪsmʊs/ *m* - journalism. **J~t(in)** *m* -en,-en (*f* -,-nen) journalist

Jubel *m* -s rejoicing, jubilation. **j~n** *vi* (*haben*) rejoice

Jubil|ar(in) *m* -s,-e (*f* -,-nen) person celebrating an anniversary. **J~äum** *nt* -s,-äen jubilee; (*Jahrestag*) anniversary

juck|en *vi* (*haben*) itch; **sich j~en** scratch; **es j~t mich** I have an itch; (*fam: möchte*) I'm itching (**zu** to). **J~reiz** *m* itch[ing]

Jude *m* -n,-n Jew. **J~ntum** *nt* -s Judaism; (*Juden*) Jewry

Jüd|in *f* -,-nen Jewess. **j~isch** *a* Jewish

Judo *nt* -[s] judo

Jugend *f* - youth; (*junge Leute*) young people *pl*. **J~herberge** *f* youth hostel. **J~klub** *m* youth club. **J~kriminalität** *f* juvenile delinquency. **j~lich** *a* youthful. **J~liche(r)** *m/f* young man/woman; (*Admin*) juvenile; **J~liche** *pl* young people. **J~stil** *m* art nouveau. **J~zeit** *f* youth

Jugoslaw|ien /-jən/ *nt* -s Yugoslavia. **j~isch** *a* Yugoslav

Juli *m* -[s],-s July

jung *a* (**jünger, jüngst**) young; (*Wein*) new ● *pron* **j~ und alt** young and old. **J~e** *m* -n,-n boy. **J~e(s)** *nt* young animal/bird; (*Katzen-*) kitten; (*Baren-, Löwen-*) cub; (*Hunde-, Seehund-*) pup; **die J~en** the young *pl*. **j~enhaft** *a* boyish

Jünger *m* -s,- disciple

Jungfer *f* -,-n **alte J~** old maid. **J~nfahrt** *f* maiden voyage

Jung|frau *f* virgin; (*Astr*) Virgo. **j~fräulich** *a* virginal. **J~geselle** *m* bachelor

Jüngling *m* -s,-e youth

jüngst|e(r,s) *a* youngest; (*neueste*) latest; **in j~er Zeit** recently

Juni *m* -[s],-s June

Junior *m* -s,-en /-'o:rən/ junior

Jura *pl* law *sg*

Jurist|(in) *m* -en,-en (*f* -,-nen) lawyer. **j~isch** *a* legal, *adv* -ly

Jury /ʒy'ri:/ *f* -,-s jury; (*Sport*) judges *pl*

justieren *vt* adjust

Justiz *f* - **die J~** justice. **J~irrtum** *m* miscarriage of justice. **J~minister** *m* Minister of Justice

Juwel *nt* -s,-en & (*fig*) -e jewel. **J~ier** *m* -s,-e jeweller

Jux *m* -es,-e (*fam*) joke; **aus Jux** for fun

K

Kabarett *nt* -s,-s & -e cabaret

kabbelig *a* choppy

Kabel *nt* -s,- cable. **K~fernsehen** *nt* cable television

Kabeljau *m* -s,-e & -s cod

Kabine *f* -,-n cabin; (*Umkleide-*) cubicle; (*Telefon-*) booth; (*einer K~nbahn*) car. **K~nbahn** *f* cable-car

Kabinett *nt* -s,-e (*Pol*) Cabinet

Kabriolett *nt* -s,-s convertible

Kachel f -,-n tile. **k~n** vt tile

Kadaver m -s,- carcass

Kadenz f -,-en (Mus) cadence; (für Solisten) cadenza

Kadett m -en,-en cadet

Käfer m -s,- beetle

Kaff nt -s,-s (fam) dump

Kaffee /'kafe:, ka'fe:/ m -s,-s coffee; (Mahlzeit) afternoon coffee. **K~grund** m = **K~satz**. **K~kanne** f coffee-pot. **K~maschine** f coffee-maker. **K~mühle** f coffee-grinder. **K~satz** m coffee-grounds pl

Käfig m -s,-e cage

kahl a bare; (haarlos) bald. **k~geschoren** a shaven. **k~köpfig** a bald-headed

Kahn m -s,-e boat; (Last-) barge

Kai m -s,-s quay

Kaiser m -s,- emperor. **K~in** f -,-nen empress. **k~lich** a imperial. **K~reich** nt empire. **K~schnitt** m Caesarean [section]

Kajüte f -,-n (Naut) cabin

Kakao /ka'kau/ m -s cocoa

Kakerlak m -s & -en,-en cockroach

Kaktee /kak'te:ə/ f -,-n, **Kaktus** m -,-teen /-'te:ən/ cactus

Kalb nt -[e]s,-er calf. **K~fleisch** nt veal

Kalender m -s,- calendar; (Taschen-, Termin-) diary

Kaliber nt -s,- calibre; (Gewehr-) bore

Kalium nt -s potassium

Kalk m -[e]s,-e lime; (Kalzium) calcium. **k~en** vt whitewash. **K~stein** m limestone

Kalkulation /-'tsio:n/ f -,-en calculation. **k~ieren** vt/i (haben) calculate

Kalorie f -,-n calorie

kalt a (kälter, kältest) cold; **es ist k~** it is cold; **mir ist k~** I am cold. **k~blütig** a cold-blooded, adv -ly; (ruhig) cool, adv -ly

Kälte f - cold; (Gefühls-) coldness; **10 Grad K~** 10 degrees below zero. **K~welle** f cold spell

kalt|herzig a cold-hearted. **k~schnäuzig** a (fam) cold, adv -ly

Kalzium nt -s calcium

Kamel nt -s,-e camel; (fam: Idiot) fool

Kamera f -,-s camera

Kamerad|(in) m -en,-en (f -,-nen) companion; (Freund) mate; (Mil, Pol) comrade. **K~schaft** f - comradeship

Kameramann m (pl -männer & -leute) cameraman

Kamille f - camomile

Kamin m -s,-e fireplace; (SGer: Schornstein) chimney. **K~feger** m -s,- (SGer) chimney-sweep

Kamm m -[e]s,-e comb; (Berg-) ridge; (Zool, Wellen-) crest

kämmen vt comb; **jdn/sich k~** comb s.o.'s/one's hair

Kammer f -,-n small room; (Techn, Biol, Pol) chamber. **K~diener** m valet. **K~musik** f chamber music

Kammgarn nt (Tex) worsted

Kampagne /kam'panjə/ f -,-n (Pol, Comm) campaign

Kampf m -es,-e fight; (Schlacht) battle; (Wett-) contest; (fig) struggle; **schwere K~e** heavy fighting sg; **den K~ ansagen** (+ dat) (fig) declare war on

kämpf|en vi (haben) fight; **sich k~en durch** fight one's way through. **K~er(in)** m -s,- (f -,-nen) fighter

kampf|los adv without a fight. **K~richter** m (Sport) judge

kampieren vi (haben) camp

Kanada nt -s Canada

Kanad|ier(in) /-iɐ, -iərin/ m -s,- (f -, -nen) Canadian. **k~isch** a Canadian

Kanal m -s,-e canal; (Abfluß-) drain, sewer; (Radio, TV) channel; **der K~** the [English] Channel

Kanalis|ation /-'tsio:n/ f - sewerage system, drains pl. **k~ieren** vt canalize; (fig: lenken) channel

Kanarienvogel /-iən-/ m canary

Kanarisch a **K~e Inseln** Canaries

Kandi|dat(in) m -en,-en (f -,-nen) candidate. **k~dieren** vi (haben) stand (für for)

kandiert a candied

Känguruh nt -s,-s kangaroo

Kaninchen nt -s,- rabbit

Kanister m -s,- canister; (Benzin-) can

Kännchen nt -s,- [small] jug; (Kaffee-) pot

Kanne f -,-n jug; (Kaffee-, Tee-) pot; (Öl-) can; (große Milch-) churn; (Gieß-) watering-can

Kannibal|e m -n,-n cannibal. **K~ismus** m - cannibalism

Kanon m -s,-s canon; (Lied) round

Kanone f -,-n cannon, gun; (fig: Könner) ace

kanonisieren vt canonize

Kantate f -,-n cantata

Kante f -,-n edge; **auf die hohe K~ legen** (fam) put by

Kanten m -s,- crust [of bread]

Kanter m -s,- canter

kantig *a* angular

Kantine *f* -,-n canteen

Kanton *m* -s,-e (*Swiss*) canton

Kantor *m* -s,-en /-'to:rən/ choir-master and organist

Kanu *nt* -s,-s canoe

Kanzel *f* -,-n pulpit; (*Aviat*) cockpit

Kanzleistil *m* officialese

Kanzler *m* -s,- chancellor

Kap *nt* -s,-s (*Geog*) cape

Kapazität *f* -,-en capacity; (*Experte*) authority

Kapelle *f* -,-n chapel; (*Mus*) band

Kaper *f* -,-n (*Culin*) caper

kapern *vt* (*Naut*) seize

kapieren *vt* (*fam*) understand, (*fam*) get

Kapital *nt* -s capital; **K~ schlagen aus** (*fig*) capitalize on. **K~ismus** *m* - capitalism. **K~ist** *m* -en,-en capitalist. **k~istisch** *a* capitalist

Kapitän *m* -s,-e captain

Kapitel *nt* -s,- chapter

Kapitulation /-'tsio:n/ *f* - capit-ulation. **k~ieren** *vi* (*haben*) ca-pitulate

Kaplan *m* -s,-e curate

Kappe *f* -,-n cap. **k~n** *vt* cut

Kapsel *f* -,-n capsule; (*Flaschen-*) top

kaputt *a* (*fam*) broken; (*zerrissen*) torn; (*defekt*) out of order; (*rui-niert*) ruined; (*erschöpft*) worn out. **k~gehen†** *vi sep* (*sein*) (*fam*) break; (*zerreißen*) tear; (*defekt werden*) pack up; (*Ehe, Freundschaft:*) break up. **k~lachen (sich)** *vr sep* (*fam*) be in stitches. **k~machen** *vt sep* (*fam*) break; (*zerreißen*) tear; (*defekt machen*) put out of order; (*er-schöpfen*) wear out; **sich k~machen** wear oneself out

Kapuze *f* -,-n hood

Kapuzinerkresse *f* nasturtium

Karaffe *f* -,-n carafe; (*mit Stöpsel*) de-canter

Karambolage /karambo'la:ʒə/ *f* -,-n collision

Karamel *m* -s caramel. **K~bonbon** *m* & *nt* ≈ toffee

Karat *nt* -[e]s,-e carat

Karawane *f* -,-n caravan

Kardinal *m* -s,-̈e cardinal. **K~zahl** *f* cardinal number

Karfiol *m* -s (*Aust*) cauliflower

Karfreitag *m* Good Friday

karg *a* (**kärger, kärgst**) meagre; (*frugal*) frugal; (*spärlich*) sparse; (*un-fruchtbar*) barren; (*gering*) scant.

k~en *vi* (*haben*) be sparing (**mit** with)

kärglich *a* poor, meagre; (*gering*) scant

Karibik *f* - Caribbean

kariert *a* check[ed]; (*Papier*) squared; **schottisch k~** tartan

Karik|atur *f* -,-en caricature; (*Journ*) cartoon. **k~ieren** *vt* caricature

karitativ *a* charitable

Karneval *m* -s,-e & -s carnival

Karnickel *nt* -s,- (*dial*) rabbit

Kärnten *nt* -s Carinthia

Karo *nt* -s,- (*Raute*) diamond; (*Viereck*) square; (*Muster*) check; (*Kartenspiel*) diamonds *pl*. **K~muster** *nt* check

Karosserie *f* -,-n bodywork

Karotte *f* -,-n carrot

Karpfen *m* -s,- carp

Karre *f* -,-n = **Karren**

Karree *nt* -s,-s square; **ums K~** round the block

Karren *m* -s,- cart; (*Hand-*) barrow. **k~** *vt* cart

Karriere /ka'rie:rə/ *f* -,-n career; **K~ machen** get to the top

Karte *f* -,-n card; (*Eintritts-, Fahr-*) ticket; (*Speise-*) menu; (*Land-*) map

Kartei *f* -,-en card index. **K~karte** *f* index card

Karten|spiel *nt* card-game; (*Spiel-karten*) pack/(*Amer*) deck of cards. **K~vorverkauf** *m* advance booking

Kartoffel *f* -,-n potato. **K~brei** *m*, **K~püree** *nt* mashed potatoes *pl*. **K~salat** *m* potato salad

Karton /kar'tɔŋ/ *m* -s,-s cardboard; (*Schachtel*) carton, cardboard box

Karussell *nt* -s,-s & -e roundabout

Karwoche *f* Holy Week

Käse *m* -s,- cheese. **K~kuchen** *m* cheesecake

Kaserne *f* -,-n barracks *pl*

Kasino *nt* -s,-s casino

Kasperle *nt* & *m* -s,- Punch. **K~-theater** *nt* Punch and Judy show

Kasse *f* -,-n till; (*Registrier-*) cash re-gister; (*Zahlstelle*) cash desk; (*im Su-permarkt*) check-out; (*Theater-*) box-office; (*Geld*) pool [of money], (*fam*) kitty; (*Kranken-*) health insurance scheme; (*Spar-*) savings bank; **knapp/gut bei K~ sein** (*fam*) be short of cash/be flush. **K~npatient** *m* ≈ NHS patient. **K~nschlager** *m* box-office hit. **K~nwart** *m* -[e]s,-e treasurer. **K~nzettel** *m* receipt

Kasserolle *f* -,-n saucepan [with one handle]

Kassette *f* -,-n cassette; (*Film-, Farbband-*) cartridge; (*Schmuck-*) case; (*Geld-*) money-box. **K~nrecorder** /-rəkɔrdɐ/ *m* -s,- cassette recorder

kassieren *vi* (haben) collect the money;(*im Bus*) the fares ● *vt* collect. **K~er(in)** *m* -s,- (*f* -,-nen) cashier

Kastagnetten /kastan'jɛtən/ *pl* castanets

Kastanie /kas'ta:niə/ *f* -,-n [horse] chestnut, (*fam*) conker. **k~nbraun** *a* chestnut

Kaste *f* -,-n caste

Kasten *m* -s,⸗ box; (*Brot-*) bin; (*Flaschen-*) crate; (*Brief-*) letter-box; (*Aust: Schrank*) cupboard; (*Kleider-*) wardrobe

kastrieren *vt* castrate; neuter ⟨*Tier*⟩

Kasus *m* -,- /-u:s/ (*Gram*) case.

Katalog *m* -[e]s,-e catalogue. **k~isieren** *vt* catalogue

Katalysator *m* -s,-en /-'to:rən/ catalyst; (*Auto*) catalytic converter

Katapult *nt* -[e]s,-e catapult. **k~ieren** *vt* catapult

Katarrh *m* -s,-e catarrh

katastrophal *a* catastrophic. **K~ophe** *f* -,-n catastrophe

Katechismus *m* - catechism

Kategorie *f* -,-n category. **k~orisch** *a* categorical, *adv* -ly

Kater *m* -s,- tom-cat; (*fam: Katzenjammer*) hangover

Katheder *nt* -s,- [teacher's] desk

Kathedrale *f* -,-n cathedral

Kath|olik(in) *m* -en,-en (*f* -,-nen) Catholic. **k~olisch** *a* Catholic. **K~olizismus** *m* - Catholicism

Kätzchen *nt* -s,- kitten; (*Bot*) catkin

Katze *f* -,-n cat. **K~njammer** *m* (*fam*) hangover. **K~nsprung** *m* ein **K~nsprung** (*fam*) a stone's throw

Kauderwelsch *nt* -[s] gibberish

kauen *vt/i* (haben) chew; bite ⟨*Nägel*⟩

kauern *vi* (haben) crouch; **sich k~** crouch down

Kauf *m* -[e]s, Käufe purchase; **guter K~** bargain; **in K~ nehmen** (*fig*) put up with. **k~en** *vt/i* (haben) buy; **k~en bei** shop at

Käufer(in) *m* -s,- (*f* -,-nen) buyer; (*im Geschäft*) shopper

Kauf|haus *nt* department store. **K~kraft** *f* purchasing power. **K~laden** *m* shop

käuflich *a* saleable; (*bestechlich*) corruptible; **k~ sein** be for sale; **k~ erwerben** buy

Kauf|mann *m* (*pl* -leute) businessman; (*Händler*) dealer; (*dial*) grocer. **k~männisch** *a* commercial. **K~preis** *m* purchase price

Kaugummi *m* chewing-gum

Kaulquappe *f* -,-n tadpole

kaum *adv* hardly; **k~ glaublich** *od* **zu glauben** hard to believe

kauterisieren *vt* cauterize

Kaution /-'tsio:n/ *f* -,-en surety; (*Jur*) bail; (*Miet-*) deposit

Kautschuk *m* -s rubber

Kauz *m* -es, Käuze owl; **komischer K~** (*fam*) odd fellow

Kavalier *m* -s,-e gentleman

Kavallerie *f* - cavalry

Kaviar *m* -s caviare

keck *a* bold; (*frech*) cheeky

Kegel *m* -s,- skittle; (*Geom*) cone; **mit Kind und K~** (*fam*) with all the family. **K~bahn** *f* skittle-alley. **k~förmig** *a* conical. **k~n** *vi* (haben) play skittles

Kehl|e *f* -,-n throat; **aus voller K~e** at the top of one's voice; **etw in die falsche K~e bekommen** (*fam*) take sth the wrong way. **K~kopf** *m* larynx. **K~kopfentzündung** *f* laryngitis

Kehr|e *f* -,-n [hairpin] bend. **k~en** *vi* (haben) (*fegen*) sweep ● *vt* sweep; (*wenden*) turn; **den Rücken k~en** turn one's back (*dat* on); **sich k~en** turn; **sich nicht k~en an** (+ *acc*) not care about. **K~icht** *m* -[e]s sweepings *pl*. **K~reim** *m* refrain. **K~seite** *f* (*fig*) drawback; **die K~seite der Medaille** the other side of the coin. **k~tmachen** *vi sep* (haben) turn back; (*sich umdrehen*) turn round. **K~twendung** *f* about-turn; (*fig*) U-turn

keifen *vi* (haben) scold

Keil *m* -[e]s,-e wedge

Keile *f* - (*fam*) hiding. **k~n (sich)** *vr* (*fam*) fight. **K~rei** *f* -,-en (*fam*) punch-up

Keil|kissen *nt* [wedge-shaped] bolster. **K~riemen** *m* fan belt

Keim *m* -[e]s,-e (*Bot*) sprout; (*Med*) germ; **im K~ ersticken** (*fig*) nip in the bud. **k~en** *vi* (haben) germinate; (*austreiben*) sprout. **K~frei** *a* sterile

kein *pron* no; not a; **auf k~en Fall** on no account; **k~e fünf Minuten** less than five minutes. **k~e(r,s)** *pron* no one, nobody; (*Ding*) none, not one. **k~esfalls** *adv* on no account.

k~**eswegs** *adv* by no means. **k~mal** *adv* not once. **k~s** *pron* none, not one

Keks *m* **-[es], -[e]** biscuit, (*Amer*) cookie

Kelch *m* **-[e]s, -e** goblet, cup; (*Relig*) chalice; (*Bot*) calyx

Kelle *f* **-, -n** ladle; (*Maurer-, Pflanz-*) trowel

Keller *m* **-s, -** cellar. **K~ei** *f* **-, -en** winery. **K~geschoß** *nt* cellar; (*bewohnbar*) basement. **K~wohnung** *f* basement flat

Kellner *m* **-s, -** waiter. **K~in** *f* **-, -nen** waitress

keltern *vt* press

keltisch *a* Celtic

Kenia *nt* **-s** Kenya

kenn|en† *vt* know. **k~enlernen** *vt sep* get to know; (*treffen*) meet; **sich k~enlernen** meet; (*näher*) get to know one another. **K~er** *m* **-s, -**, **K~erin** *f* **-, -nen** connoisseur; (*Experte*) expert. **K~melodie** *f* signature tune. **k~tlich** *a* recognizable; **k~tlich machen** mark. **K~tnis** *f* **-, -se** knowledge; **zur K~tnis nehmen** take note of; **in K~tnis setzen** inform (**von** of). **K~wort** *nt* (*pl* **-wörter**) reference; (*geheimes*) password. **K~zeichen** *nt* distinguishing mark *or* feature; (*Merkmal*) characteristic; (*Markierung*) mark, marking; (*Abzeichen*) badge; (*Auto*) registration. **k~zeichnen** *vt* distinguish; (*markieren*) mark. **k~zeichnend** *a* typical (**für** of). **K~ziffer** *f* reference number

kentern *vi* (*sein*) capsize

Keramik *f* **-, -en** pottery, ceramics *sg*; (*Gegenstand*) piece of pottery

Kerbe *f* **-, -n** notch

Kerbholz *nt* **etwas auf dem K~ haben** (*fam*) have a record

Kerker *m* **-s, -** dungeon; (*Gefängnis*) prison

Kerl *m* **-s, -e & -s** (*fam*) fellow, bloke

Kern *m* **-s, -e** pip; (*Kirsch-*) stone; (*Nuß-*) kernel; (*Techn*) core; (*Atom-, Zell- & fig*) nucleus; (*Stadt-*) centre; (*einer Sache*) heart. **K~energie** *f* nuclear energy. **K~gehäuse** *nt* core. **k~gesund** *a* perfectly healthy. **k~ig** *a* robust; (*Ausspruch*) pithy. **k~los** *a* seedless. **K~physik** *f* nuclear physics *sg*

Kerze *f* **-, -n** candle. **k~ngerade** *a* & *adv* straight. **K~nhalter** *m* **-s, -** candlestick

keß *a* (**kesser, kessest**) pert

Kessel *m* **-s, -** kettle; (*Heiz-*) boiler. **K~stein** *m* fur

Kette *f* **-, -n** chain; (*Hals-*) necklace. **k~n** *vt* chain (**an +** *acc* to). **K~nladen** *m* chain store. **K~nraucher** *m* chainsmoker. **K~nreaktion** *f* chain reaction

Ketze|r(in) *m* **-s, -** (*f* **-, -nen**) heretic. **K~rei** *f* **-** heresy

keuch|en *vi* (*haben*) pant. **K~husten** *m* whooping cough

Keule *f* **-, -n** club; (*Culin*) leg; (*Hühner-*) drumstick

keusch *a* chaste. **K~heit** *f* **-** chastity

Kfz *abbr s.* **Kraftfahrzeug**

Khaki *nt* **-** khaki. **k~farben** *a* khaki

kichern *vi* (*haben*) giggle

Kiefer[1] *f* **-, -n** pine[-tree]

Kiefer[2] *m* **-s, -** jaw

Kiel *m* **-s, -e** (*Naut*) keel. **K~wasser** *nt* wake

Kiemen *fpl* gills

Kies *m* **-es** gravel. **K~el** *m* **-s, -**, **K~elstein** *m* pebble. **K~grube** *f* gravel pit

Kilo *nt* **-s, -[s]** kilo. **K~gramm** *nt* kilogram. **K~hertz** *nt* kilohertz. **K~meter** *m* kilometre. **K~meterstand** *m* ≈ mileage. **K~watt** *nt* kilowatt

Kind *nt* **-es, -er** child; **von K~ auf** from childhood

Kinder|arzt *m*, **K~ärztin** *f* paediatrician. **K~bett** *nt* child's cot. **K~ei** *f* **-, -en** childish prank. **K~garten** *m* nursery school. **K~gärtnerin** *f* nursery-school teacher. **K~geld** *nt* child benefit. **K~gottesdienst** *m* Sunday school. **K~lähmung** *f* polio. **k~leicht** *a* very easy. **k~los** *a* childless. **K~mädchen** *nt* nanny. **k~reich** *a* **k~reiche Familie** large family. **K~reim** *m* nursery rhyme. **K~spiel** *nt* children's game; **das ist ein/kein K~spiel** that is dead easy/not easy. **K~tagesstätte** *f* day nursery. **K~teller** *m* children's menu. **K~wagen** *m* pram, (*Amer*) baby carriage. **K~zimmer** *nt* child's/children's room; (*für Baby*) nursery

Kind|heit *f* **-** childhood. **k~isch** *a* childish, puerile. **k~lich** *a* childlike

kinetisch *a* kinetic

Kinn *nt* **-[e]s, -e** chin. **K~lade** *f* jaw

Kino *nt* **-s, -s** cinema

Kiosk *m* **-[e]s, -e** kiosk

Kippe *f* **-, -n** (*Müll-*) dump; (*fam:* *Zigaretten-*) fag-end; **auf der K~ stehen**

(*fam*) be in a precarious position; (*unsicher sein*) hang in the balance. **k~lig** *a* wobbly. **k~ln** *vi* (*haben*) wobble. **k~n** *vt* tilt; (*schütten*) tip (**in** + *acc* into) ● *vi* (*sein*) topple

Kirch|e *f* -,-n church. **K~enbank** *f* pew. **K~endiener** *m* verger. **K~enlied** *nt* hymn. **K~enschiff** *nt* nave. **K~hof** *m* churchyard. **k~lich** *a* church ... ● *adv* **k~lich getraut werden** be married in church. **K~turm** *m* church tower, steeple. **K~weih** *f* -,-en [village] fair

Kirmes *f* -,-sen = **Kirchweih**

Kirsch|e *f* -,-n cherry. **K~wasser** *nt* kirsch

Kissen *nt* -s,- cushion; (*Kopf-*) pillow

Kiste *f* -,-n crate; (*Zigarren-*) box

Kitsch *m* -es sentimental rubbish; (*Kunst*) kitsch. **k~ig** *a* slushy; (*Kunst*) kitschy

Kitt *m* -s [adhesive] cement; (*Fenster-*) putty

Kittel *m* -s,- overall, smock; (*Arzt-, Labor-*) white coat

kitten *vt* stick; (*fig*) cement

Kitz *nt* -es,-e (*Zool*) kid

Kitz|el *m* -s,- tickle; (*Nerven-*) thrill. **k~eln** *vt/i* (*haben*) tickle. **k~lig** *a* ticklish

Kladde *f* -,-n notebook

klaffen *vi* (*haben*) gape

kläffen *vi* (*haben*) yap

Klage *f* -,-n lament; (*Beschwerde*) complaint; (*Jur*) action. **k~n** *vi* (*haben*) lament; (*sich beklagen*) complain; (*Jur*) sue

Kläger(in) *m* -s,- (*f* -,-nen) (*Jur*) plaintiff

kläglich *a* pitiful, *adv* -ly; (*erbärmlich*) miserable, *adv* -bly

klamm *a* cold and damp; (*steif*) stiff. **K~** *f* -,-en (*Geog*) gorge

Klammer *f* -,-n (*Wäsche-*) peg; (*Büro-*) paper-clip; (*Heft-*) staple; (*Haar-*) grip; (*für Zähne*) brace; (*Techn*) clamp; (*Typ*) bracket. **k~n (sich)** *vr* cling (**an** + *acc* to)

Klang *m* -[e]s,-̈e sound; (*K~farbe*) tone. **k~voll** *a* resonant; ⟨*Stimme*⟩ sonorous

Klapp|bett *nt* folding bed. **K~e** *f* -,-n flap; (*fam: Mund*) trap. **k~en** *vt* fold; (*hoch-*) tip up ● *vi* (*haben*) (*fam*) work out. **K~entext** *m* blurb

Klapper *f* -,-n rattle. **k~n** *vi* (*haben*) rattle. **K~schlange** rattlesnake

klapp|rig *a* rickety; (*schwach*) decrepit. **K~stuhl** *m* folding chair. **K~tisch** *m* folding table

Klaps *m* -es,-e pat; (*strafend*) smack. **k~en** *vt* smack

klar *a* clear; (*dat*) **k~** *od* **im k~en sein** realize ● *adv* clearly; (*fam: natürlich*) of course. **K~e(r)** *m* (*fam*) schnapps

klären *vt* clarify; **sich k~** clear; (*fig: sich lösen*) resolve itself

Klarheit *f* - clarity

Klarinette *f* -,-n clarinet

klar|machen *vt sep* make clear (*dat* to); **sich** (*dat*) **etw k~machen** understand sth. **K~sichtfolie** *f* transparent/(*haftend*) cling film. **k~stellen** *vt sep* clarify

Klärung *f* - clarification

klarwerden† *vi sep* (*sein*) (*fig*) become clear (*dat* to); **sich** (*dat*) **k~** make up one's mind; (*erkennen*) realize

Klasse *f* -,-n class; (*Sch*) class, form, (*Amer*) grade; (*Zimmer*) classroom; **erster/zweiter K~** first/second class. **k~** *inv a* (*fam*) super. **K~narbeit** *f* [written] test. **K~nbuch** *nt* ≈ register. **K~nkamerad(in)** *m*(*f*) class-mate. **K~nkampf** *m* class struggle. **K~nzimmer** *nt* classroom

klassifizier|en *vt* classify. **K~ung** *f* -,-en classification

Klass|ik *f* - classicism; (*Epoche*) classical period. **K~iker** *m* -s,- classical author/(*Mus*) composer. **k~isch** *a* classical; (*mustergültig, typisch*) classic

Klatsch *m* -[e]s gossip. **K~base** *f* (*fam*) gossip. **k~en** *vt* slap; **Beifall k~en** applaud ● *vi* (*haben*) make a slapping sound; (*im Wasser*) splash; (*tratschen*) gossip; (*applaudieren*) clap; **[in die Hände] k~en** clap one's hands ● *vi* (*haben/sein*) slap (**gegen** against). **K~maul** *nt* gossip. **k~naß** *a* (*fam*) soaking wet

klauben *vt* pick

Klaue *f* -,-n claw; (*fam: Schrift*) scrawl. **k~n** *vt/i* (*haben*) (*fam*) steal

Klausel *f* -,-n clause

Klaustrophobie *f* - claustrophobia

Klausur *f* -,-en (*Univ*) [examination] paper; (*Sch*) written test

Klaviatur *f* -,-en keyboard

Klavier *nt* -s,-e piano. **K~spieler(in)** *m*(*f*) pianist

kleb|en *vt* stick/(*mit Klebstoff*) glue (**an** + *acc* to) ● *vi* (*haben*) stick (**an**

+ *dat* to). **k~rig** *a* sticky. **K~stoff** *m* adhesive, glue. **K~streifen** *m* adhesive tape

kleckern *vi (haben) (fam)* = **klecksen**

Klecks *m* **-es,-e** stain; (*Tinten-*) blot; (*kleine Menge*) dab. **k~en** *vi (haben)* make a mess

Klee *m* **-s** clover. **K~blatt** *nt* clover leaf

Kleid *nt* **-[e]s,-er** dress; **K~er** dresses; (*Kleidung*) clothes. **k~en** *vt* dress; (*gut stehen*) suit; **sich k~en** dress. **K~erbügel** *m* coat-hanger. **K~erbürste** *f* clothes-brush. **K~erhaken** *m* coat-hook. **K~errock** *m* pinafore dress. **K~erschrank** *m* wardrobe, (*Amer*) clothes closet. **k~sam** *a* becoming. **K~ung** *f* - clothes *pl*, clothing. **K~ungsstück** *nt* garment

Kleie *f* - bran

klein *a* small, little; (*von kleinem Wuchs*) short; **von k~ auf** from childhood. **K~arbeit** *f* painstaking work. **K~bus** *m* minibus. **K~e(r,s)** *m/f/nt* little one. **K~geld** *nt* [small] change. **k~hacken** *vt sep* chop up small. **K~handel** *m* retail trade. **K~heit** *f* - smallness; (*Wuchs*) short stature. **K~holz** *nt* firewood. **K~igkeit** *f* **-,-en** trifle; (*Mahl*) snack. **K~kind** *nt* infant. **K~kram** *m* (*fam*) odds and ends *pl*; (*Angelegenheiten*) trivia *pl*. **k~laut** *a* subdued. **k~lich** *a* petty. **K~lichkeit** *f* - pettiness. **k~mütig** *a* faint-hearted

Kleinod *nt* **-[e]s,-e** jewel

klein|schneiden† *vt sep* cut into small pieces. **K~stadt** *f* small town. **k~städtisch** *a* provincial. **K~wagen** *m* small car

Kleister *m* **-s** paste. **k~n** *vt* paste

Klemme *f* **-,-n** [hair-]grip; **in der K~ sitzen** (*fam*) be in a fix. **k~n** *vt* jam; **sich** (*dat*) **den Finger k~n** get one's finger caught ● *vi (haben)* jam, stick

Klempner *m* **-s,-** plumber

Klerus (der) - the clergy

Klette *f* **-,-n** burr; **wie eine K~** (*fig*) like a limpet

kletter|n *vi (sein)* climb. **K~pflanze** *f* climber. **K~rose** *f* climbing rose

Klettverschluß *m* Velcro (P) fastening

klicken *vi (haben)* click

Klient(in) /kli'ɛnt(ɪn)/ *m* **-en,-en** (*f* **-,-nen**) (*Jur*) client

Kliff *nt* **-[e]s,-e** cliff

Klima *nt* **-s** climate. **K~anlage** *f* air-conditioning

klimat|isch *a* climatic. **k~isiert** *a* air-conditioned

klimpern *vi (haben)* jingle; **k~ auf** (+ *dat*) tinkle on ⟨*Klavier*⟩; strum ⟨*Gitarre*⟩

Klinge *f* **-,-n** blade

Klingel *f* **-,-n** bell. **k~n** *vi (haben)* ring; **es k~t** there's a ring at the door

klingen† *vi (haben)* sound

Klinik *f* **-,-en** clinic. **k~sch** *a* clinical, *adv* -ly

Klinke *f* **-,-n** [door] handle

klipp *pred a* **k~ und klar** quite plain, *adv* -ly

Klipp *m* **-s,-s** = **Klips**

Klippe *f* **-,-n** [submerged] rock

Klips *m* **-es,-e** clip; (*Ohr-*) clip-on earring

klirren *vi (haben)* rattle; ⟨*Geschirr, Glas:*⟩ chink

Klischee *nt* **-s,-s** cliché

Klo *nt* **-s,-s** (*fam*) loo, (*Amer*) john

klobig *a* clumsy

klönen *vi (haben)* (*NGer fam*) chat

klopf|en *vi (haben)* knock; (*leicht*) tap; ⟨*Herz:*⟩ pound; **es k~te** there was a knock at the door ● *vt* beat; (*ein-*) knock

Klops *m* **-es,-e** meatball; (*Brat-*) rissole

Klosett *nt* **-s,-s** lavatory

Kloß *m* **-es,-e** dumpling; **ein K~ im Hals** (*fam*) a lump in one's throat

Kloster *nt* **-s,-** monastery; (*Nonnen-*) convent

klösterlich *a* monastic

Klotz *m* **-es,-e** block

Klub *m* **-s,-s** club

Kluft[1] *f* **-,-e** cleft; (*fig: Gegensatz*) gulf

Kluft[2] *f* **-,-en** outfit; (*Uniform*) uniform

klug *a* (**klüger, klügst**) intelligent, *adv* -ly; (*schlau*) clever, *adv* -ly; **nicht k~ werden aus** not understand. **K~heit** *f* - cleverness

Klump|en *m* **-s,-** lump. **k~en** *vi (haben)* go lumpy. **k~ig** *a* lumpy

knabbern *vt/i (haben)* nibble

Knabe *m* **-n,-n** boy. **k~nhaft** *a* boyish

Knäckebrot *nt* crispbread

knack|en *vt/i (haben)* crack. **K~s** *m* **-es,-e** crack; **einen K~s haben** be cracked; (*fam: verrückt sein*) be crackers

Knall *m* **-[e]s,-e** bang. **K~bonbon** *m* cracker. **k~en** *vi (haben)* go bang; ⟨*Peitsche:*⟩ crack ● *vt* (*fam: werfen*) chuck; **jdm eine k~en** (*fam*) clout s.o.

k∼ig a (fam) gaudy. k∼rot a bright red

knapp a (gering) scant; (kurz) short; (mangelnd) scarce; (gerade ausreichend) bare; (eng) tight; **ein k∼es Pfund** just under a pound. k∼halten† vt sep (fam) keep short (**mit** of). K∼heit f - scarcity

Knarre f -,-n rattle. k∼n vi (haben) creak

Knast m -[e]s (fam) prison

knattern vi (haben) crackle; ⟨Gewehr:⟩ stutter

Knäuel m & nt -s,- ball

Knauf m -[e]s, Knäufe knob

knauser|ig a (fam) stingy. k∼n vi (haben) (fam) be stingy

knautschen vt (fam) crumple ● vi (haben) crumple

Knebel m -s,- gag. k∼n vt gag

Knecht m -[e]s,-e farm-hand; (fig) slave. k∼en vt (fig) enslave. K∼schaft f - (fig) slavery

kneif|en† vt pinch ● vi (haben) pinch; (fam: sich drücken) chicken out. K∼zange f pincers pl

Kneipe f -,-n (fam) pub, (Amer) bar

knet|en vt knead; (formen) mould. K∼masse f Plasticine (P)

Knick m -[e]s,-e bend; (im Draht) kink; (Kniff) crease. k∼en vt bend; (kniffen) fold; **geknickt sein** (fam) be dejected. k∼[e]rig a (fam) stingy

Knicks m -es,-e curtsy. k∼en vi (haben) curtsy

Knie nt -s,- /'kni:ə/ knee. K∼bundhose f knee-breeches pl. K∼kehle f hollow of the knee

knien /'kni:ən/ vi (haben) kneel ● vr sich k∼ kneel [down]

Knie|scheibe f kneecap. K∼strumpf m knee-length sock

Kniff m -[e]s,-e pinch; (Falte) crease; (fam: Trick) trick. k∼en vt fold. k∼[e]lig a (fam) tricky

knipsen vt (lochen) punch; (Phot) photograph ● vi (haben) take a photograph/photographs

Knirps m -es,-e (fam) little chap; (P) (Schirm) telescopic umbrella

knirschen vi (haben) grate; ⟨Schnee, Kies:⟩ crunch; **mit den Zähnen k∼** grind one's teeth

knistern vi (haben) crackle; ⟨Papier:⟩ rustle

Knitter|falte f crease. k∼frei a crease-resistant. k∼n vi (haben) crease

knobeln vi (haben) toss (**um** for); (fam: überlegen) puzzle

Knoblauch m -s garlic

Knöchel m -s,- ankle; (Finger-) knuckle

Knochen m -s,- bone. K∼mark nt bone marrow. k∼trocken a bone-dry

knochig a bony

Knödel m -s,- (SGer) dumpling

Knoll|e f -,-n tuber. k∼ig a bulbous

Knopf m -[e]s,¨e button; (Kragen-) stud; (Griff) knob

knöpfen vt button

Knopfloch nt buttonhole

Knorpel m -s gristle; (Anat) cartilage

knorrig a gnarled

Knospe f bud

Knötchen nt -s,- nodule

Knoten m -s,- knot; (Med) lump; (Haar-) bun, chignon. k∼ vt knot. K∼punkt m junction

knotig a knotty; ⟨Hände⟩ gnarled

knuffen vt poke

knüll|en vt crumple ● vi (haben) crease. K∼er m -s,- (fam) sensation

knüpfen vt knot; (verbinden) attach (**an** + acc to)

Knüppel m -s,- club; (Gummi-) truncheon

knurr|en vi (haben) growl; ⟨Magen:⟩ rumble; (fam: schimpfen) grumble. k∼ig a grumpy

knusprig a crunchy, crisp

knutschen vi (haben) (fam) smooch

k.o. /ka'ʔo:/ a k.o. **schlagen** knock out; **k.o. sein** (fam) be worn out. **K.o.** m -s,-s knock-out

Koalition /koali'tsio:n/ f -,-en coalition

Kobold m -[e]s,-e goblin, imp

Koch m -[e]s,¨e cook; (im Restaurant) chef. K∼buch nt cookery book, (Amer) cookbook. k∼en vt cook; (sieden) boil; make ⟨Kaffee, Tee⟩ ● vi (haben) cook; (sieden) boil; (fam) seethe (**vor** + dat with). K∼en nt -s cooking; (Sieden) boiling; **zum K∼en bringen/kommen** bring/come to the boil. k∼end a boiling ● adv k∼end **heiß** boiling hot. K∼er m -s,- cooker. K∼gelegenheit f cooking facilities pl. K∼herd m cooker, stove

Köchin f -,-nen [woman] cook

Koch|kunst f cookery. K∼löffel m wooden spoon. K∼nische f kitchenette. K∼platte f hotplate. K∼topf m saucepan

Kode /koːt/ m **-s,-s** code
Köder m **-s,-** bait
Koexist|enz /ˈkoːʔɛksɪstɛnts/ f coexistence. **k~ieren** vi (haben) coexist
Koffein /kɔfeˈiːn/ nt **-s** caffeine. **k~frei** a decaffeinated
Koffer m **-s,-** suitcase. **K~kuli** m luggage trolley. **K~radio** nt portable radio. **K~raum** m (Auto) boot, (Amer) trunk
Kognak /ˈkɔnjak/ m **-s,-s** brandy
Kohl m **-[e]s** cabbage
Kohle f **-,-n** coal. **K~[n]hydrat** nt **-[e]s,-e** carbohydrate. **K~nbergwerk** nt coal-mine, colliery. **K~ndioxyd** nt carbon dioxide. **K~ngrube** f = **K~nbergwerk. K~nherd** m [kitchen] range. **K~nsäure** f carbon dioxide. **K~nstoff** m carbon. **K~papier** nt carbon paper
Kohl|kopf m cabbage. **K~rabi** m **-[s],-[s]** kohlrabi. **K~rübe** f swede
Koje f **-,-n** (Naut) bunk
Kokain /kokaˈiːn/ nt **-s** cocaine
kokett a flirtatious. **k~ieren** vi (haben) flirt
Kokon /koˈkõ/ m **-s,-s** cocoon
Kokosnuß f coconut
Koks m **-es** coke
Kolben m **-s,-** (Gewehr-) butt; (Mais-) cob; (Techn) piston; (Chem) flask
Kolibri m **-s,-s** humming-bird
Kolik f **-,-en** colic
Kollabora|teur /-ˈtøːɐ̯/ m **-s,-e** collaborator. **K~tion** /-ˈtsi̯oːn/ f - collaboration
Kolleg nt **-s,-s** & **-ien** /-i̯ən/ (Univ) course of lectures
Kolleg|e m **-n,-n**, **K~in** f **-,-nen** colleague. **K~ium** nt **-s,-ien** staff
Kollek|te f **-,-n** (Relig) collection. **K~tion** /-ˈtsi̯oːn/ f **-,-en** collection. **k~tiv** a collective. **K~tivum** nt **-s,-va** collective noun
kolli|dieren vi (sein) collide. **K~sion** f **-,-en** collision
Köln nt **-s** Cologne. **K~ischwasser, K~isch Wasser** nt eau-de-Cologne
Kolonialwaren fpl groceries
Kolon|ie f **-,-n** colony. **k~isieren** vt colonize
Kolonne f **-,-n** column; (Mil) convoy
Koloß m **-sses** giant
kolossal a enormous, adv -ly
Kolumne f **-,-n** (Journ) column
Koma nt **-s,-s** coma

Kombi m **-s,-s** = **K~wagen. K~nation** /-ˈtsi̯oːn/ f **-,-en** combination; (Folgerung) deduction; (Kleidung) coordinating outfit. **k~nieren** vt combine; (fig) reason; (folgern) deduce. **K~wagen** m estate car, (Amer) station-wagon
Kombüse f **-,-n** (Naut) galley
Komet m **-en,-en** comet. **k~enhaft** a (fig) meteoric
Komfort /kɔmˈfoːɐ̯/ m **-s** comfort; (Luxus) luxury. **k~abel** /-ˈtaːbəl/ a comfortable, adv -bly; (luxuriös) luxurious, adv -ly
Komik f - humour. **K~er** m **-s,-** comic, comedian
komisch a funny; (Oper) comic; (sonderbar) odd, funny ● adv funnily; oddly. **k~erweise** adv funnily enough
Komitee nt **-s,-s** committee
Komma nt **-s,-s** & **-ta** comma; (Dezimal-) decimal point; **drei K~ fünf** three point five
Komman|dant m **-en,-en** commanding officer. **K~deur** /-ˈdøːɐ̯/ m **-s,-e** commander. **k~dieren** vt command; (befehlen) order; (fam: herum-) order about ● vi (haben) give the orders
Kommando nt **-s,-s** order; (Befehlsgewalt) command; (Einheit) detachment. **K~brücke** f bridge
kommen† vi (sein) come; (eintreffen) arrive; (gelangen) get (**nach** to); **k~ lassen** send for; **auf/hinter etw** (acc) **k~** think of/find out about sth; **um/zu etw k~** lose/acquire sth; **wieder zu sich k~** come round; **wie kommt das?** why is that? **K~** nt **-s** coming; **K~ und Gehen** coming and going. **k~d** a coming; **k~den Montag** next Monday
Kommen|tar m **-s,-e** commentary; (Bemerkung) comment. **K~tator** m **-s, -en** /-ˈtoːrən/ commentator. **k~tieren** vt comment on
kommer|zialisieren vt commercialize. **k~ziell** a commercial, adv -ly
Kommili|tone m **-n,-n**, **K~tonin** f **-,-nen** fellow student
Kommiß m **-sses** (fam) army
Kommissar m **-s,-e** commissioner; (Polizei-) superintendent
Kommission f **-,-en** commission; (Gremium) committee
Kommode f **-,-n** chest of drawers
Kommunalwahlen fpl local elections

Kommunikation /-'tsi̯o:n/ f -,-en
communication

Kommunion f -,-en [Holy] Communion

Kommuniqué /kɔmyni'ke:/ nt -s,-s
communiqué

Kommun|ismus m - Communism.
K~ist(in) m -en,-en (f -,-nen) Communist. **k~istisch** a Communist

kommunizieren vi (haben) receive
[Holy] Communion

Komödie /ko'mø:di̯ə/ f -,-n comedy

Kompagnon /'kɔmpanjõ:/ m -s,-s
(Comm) partner

kompakt a compact. **K~schall-
platte** f compact disc

Kompanie f -,-n (Mil) company

Komparativ m -s,-e comparative

Komparse m -n,-n (Theat) extra

Kompaß m -sses,-sse compass

kompatibel a compatible

kompeten|t a competent. **K~z** f
-,-en competence

komplett a complete, adv -ly

Komplex m -es,-e complex. **k~** a
complex

Komplikation /-'tsi̯o:n/ f -,-en com-
plication

Kompliment nt -[e]s,-e compliment

Komplize m -n,-n accomplice

komplizier|en vt complicate. **k~t** a
complicated

Komplott nt -[e]s,-e plot

kompo|nieren vt/i (haben) com-
pose. **K~nist** m -en,-en composer.
K~sition /-'tsi̯o:n/ f -,-en composition

Kompositum nt -s,-ta compound

Kompost m -[e]s compost

Kompott nt -[e]s,-e stewed fruit

Kompresse f -,-n compress

komprimieren vt compress

Kompromiß m -sses,-sse compromise; **einen K~ schließen** compromise. **k~los** a uncompromising

kompromittieren vt compromise

Konden|sation /-'tsi̯o:n/ f - con-
densation. **k~sieren** vt condense

Kondensmilch f evaporated/(ge-
süßt) condensed milk

Kondition /-'tsi̯o:n/ f - (Sport) fitness;
in K~ in form. **K~al** m -s,-e (Gram)
conditional

Konditor m -s,-en /-'to:rən/ confectioner. **K~ei** f -,-en patisserie

Kondo|lenzbrief m letter of con-
dolence. **k~lieren** vi (haben) express
one's condolences

Kondom nt & m -s,-e condom

Konfekt nt -[e]s confectionery; (Pra-
linen) chocolates pl

Konfektion /-'tsi̯o:n/ f - ready-to-
wear clothes pl

Konferenz f -,-en conference; (Besprechung) meeting

Konfession f -,-en [religious] denomination. **k~ell** a denominational.
k~slos a non-denominational

Konfetti nt -s confetti

Konfirm|and(in) m -en,-en (f
-,-nen) candidate for confirmation.
K~ation /-'tsi̯o:n/ f -,-en (Relig) confirmation. **k~ieren** vt (Relig) confirm

Konfitüre f -,-n jam

Konflikt m -[e]s,-e conflict

Konföderation /-'tsi̯o:n/ f confederation

Konfront|ation /-'tsi̯o:n/ f -,-en con-
frontation. **k~ieren** vt confront

konfus a confused

Kongreß m -sses,-sse congress

König m -s,-e king. **K~in** f -,-nen
queen. **k~lich** a royal, adv -ly;
(hoheitsvoll) regal, adv -ly; (großzügig) handsome, adv -ly; (fam:
groß) tremendous, adv -ly. **K~reich**
nt kingdom

konisch a conical

Konjug|ation /-'tsi̯o:n/ f -,-en con-
jugation. **k~ieren** vt conjugate

Konjunktion /-'tsi̯o:n/ f -,-en
(Gram) conjunction

Konjunktiv m -s,-e subjunctive

Konjunktur f - economic situation;
(Hoch-) boom

konkav a concave

konkret a concrete

Konkurren|t(in) m -en,-en (f -,-nen)
competitor, rival. **K~z** f - competition;
jdm K~z machen compete with s.o.
k~zfähig a (Comm) competitive.
K~zkampf m competition, rivalry

konkurrieren vi (haben) compete

Konkurs m -es,-e bankruptcy; **K~
machen** go bankrupt

können† vt/i (haben) etw k~ be able
to do sth; (beherrschen) know sth; **k~
Sie Deutsch?** do you know any German? **das kann ich nicht** I can't do that;
er kann nicht mehr he can't go on; **für
etw nichts k~** not be to blame for sth
● v aux **lesen/schwimmen k~** be able
to read/swim; **er kann/konnte es tun**
he can/could do it; **das kann** od **könnte
[gut] sein** that may [well] be. **K~** nt -s
ability; (Wissen) knowledge

Könner(in) m -s,- (f -,-nen) expert

konsequen|t a consistent, adv -ly; (logisch) logical, adv -ly. **K~z** f -,-en consequence

konservativ a conservative

Konserv|en fpl tinned or canned food sg. **K~enbüchse, K~endose** f tin, can. **k~ieren** vt preserve; (in Dosen) tin, can. **K~ierungsmittel** nt preservative

Konsistenz f - consistency

konsolidieren vt consolidate

Konsonant m -en,-en consonant

konsterniert a dismayed

Konstitution /-'tsio:n/ f -,-en constitution. **k~ell** a constitutional

konstruieren vt construct; (entwerfen) design

Konstruk|tion /-'tsio:n/ f -,-en construction; (Entwurf) design. **k~tiv** a constructive

Konsul m -s,-n consul. **K~at** nt -[e]s,-e consulate

Konsult|ation /-'tsio:n/ f -,-en consultation. **k~ieren** vt consult

Konsum m -s consumption. **K~ent** m -en,-en consumer. **K~güter** npl consumer goods

Kontakt m -[e]s,-e contact. **K~linsen** fpl contact lenses. **K~person** f contact

kontern vt/i (haben) counter

Kontinent /'kon-, konti'nɛnt/ m -s,-e continent

Kontingent nt -[e]s,-e (Comm) quota; (Mil) contingent

Kontinuität f - continuity

Konto nt -s,-s account. **K~auszug** m [bank] statement. **K~nummer** f account number. **K~stand** m [bank] balance

Kontrabaß m double-bass

Kontrast m -[e]s,-e contrast

Kontroll|abschnitt m counterfoil. **K~e** f -,-n control; (Prüfung) check. **K~eur** /-'lø:ɐ/ m -s,-e [ticket] inspector. **k~ieren** vt check; inspect ⟨Fahrkarten⟩; (beherrschen) control

Kontroverse f -,-n controversy

Kontur f -,-en contour

Konvention /-'tsio:n/ f -,-en convention. **k~ell** a conventional, adv -ly

Konversation /-'tsio:n/ f -,-en conversation. **K~slexikon** nt encyclopaedia

konvert|ieren vi (haben) (Relig) convert. **K~it** m -en,-en convert

konvex a convex

Konvoi /kon'voy/ m -s,-s convoy

Konzentration /-'tsio:n/ f -,-en concentration. **K~slager** nt concentration camp

konzentrieren vt concentrate; **sich k~** concentrate (**auf** + acc on)

Konzept nt -[e]s,-e [rough] draft; **jdn aus dem K~ bringen** put s.o. off his stroke. **K~papier** nt rough paper

Konzern m -s,-e (Comm) group [of companies]

Konzert nt -[e]s,-e concert; (Klavier-, Geigen-) concerto. **K~meister** m leader, (Amer) concert-master

Konzession f -,-en licence; (Zugeständnis) concession

Konzil nt -s,-e (Relig) council

Kooperation /ko'ɔpera'tsio:n/ f co-operation

Koordin|ation /ko'ɔrdina'tsio:n/ f - co-ordination. **k~ieren** vt coordinate

Kopf m -[e]s,"-e head; **ein K~ Kohl/ Salat** a cabbage/lettuce; **aus dem K~** from memory; (auswendig) by heart; **auf dem K~** (verkehrt) upside down; **K~ an K~** neck and neck; ⟨stehen⟩ shoulder to shoulder; **sich** (dat) **den K~ waschen** wash one's hair; **sich** (dat) **den K~ zerbrechen** rack one's brains. **K~ball** m header. **K~bedeckung** f head-covering

Köpf|chen nt -s,- little head; **K~chen haben** (fam) be clever. **k~en** vt behead; (Fußball) head

Kopf|ende nt head. **K~haut** f scalp. **K~hörer** m headphones pl. **K~kissen** nt pillow. **K~kissenbezug** m pillow-case. **k~los** a panic-stricken. **K~nicken** nt -s nod. **K~rechnen** nt mental arithmetic. **K~salat** m lettuce. **K~schmerzen** mpl headache sg. **K~schütteln** nt -s shake of the head. **K~sprung** m header, dive. **K~stand** m headstand. **K~steinpflaster** nt cobble-stones pl. **K~stütze** f head-rest. **K~tuch** nt headscarf. **k~über** adv head first; (fig) headlong. **K~wäsche** f shampoo. **K~weh** nt headache. **K~zerbrechen** nt -s sich (dat) **K~zerbrechen machen** rack one's brains; (sich sorgen) worry

Kopie f -,-n copy. **k~ren** vt copy

Koppel f -,-n enclosure; (Pferde-) paddock

Koppel[2] *nt* **-s,-** (*Mil*) belt. **k∼n** *vt* couple

Koralle *f* **-,-n** coral

Korb *m* **-[e]s,¨e** basket; **jdm einen K∼ geben** (*fig*) turn s.o. down. **K∼ball** *m* [kind of] netball. **K∼stuhl** *m* wicker chair

Kord *m* **-s** (*Tex*) corduroy

Kordel *f* **-,-n** cord

Korinthe *f* **-,-n** currant

Kork *m* **-s** cork. **K∼en** *m* **-s,-** cork. **K∼enzieher** *m* **-s,-** corkscrew

Korn[1] *nt* **-[e]s,¨er** grain; (*Samen-*) seed; (*coll: Getreide*) grain, corn; (*am Visier*) front sight

Korn[2] *m* **-[e]s,-** (*fam*) grain schnapps

Körn|chen *nt* **-s,-** granule. **k∼ig** *a* granular

Körper *m* **-s,-** body; (*Geom*) solid. **K∼bau** *m* build, physique. **k∼behindert** *a* physically disabled. **k∼lich** *a* physical, *adv* -ly; ⟨*Strafe*⟩ corporal. **K∼pflege** *f* personal hygiene. **K∼puder** *m* talcum powder. **K∼schaft** *f* **-,-en** corporation, body. **K∼strafe** *f* corporal punishment. **K∼teil** *m* part of the body

Korps /koːɐ̯/ *nt* **-,-** /-[s],-s/ corps

korpulent *a* corpulent

korrekt *a* correct, *adv* -ly. **K∼or** *m* **-s,-en** /-'toːrən/ proof-reader. **K∼ur** *f* **-,-en** correction. **K∼urabzug, K∼urbogen** *m* proof

Korrespon|dent(in) *m* **-en,-en** (*f* **-,-nen**) correspondent. **K∼denz** *f* **-,-en** correspondence. **k∼dieren** *vi* (*haben*) correspond

Korridor *m* **-s,-e** corridor

korrigieren *vt* correct

Korrosion *f* **-** corrosion

korrumpieren *vt* corrupt

korrup|t *a* corrupt. **K∼tion** /-'tsioːn/ *f* **-** corruption

Korsett *nt* **-[e]s,-e** corset

koscher *a* kosher

Kose|name *m* pet name. **K∼wort** *nt* (*pl* **-wörter**) term of endearment

Kosmet|ik *f* **-** beauty culture. **K∼ika** *ntpl* cosmetics. **K∼ikerin** *f* **-,-nen** beautician. **k∼isch** *a* cosmetic; ⟨*Chirurgie*⟩ plastic

kosm|isch *a* cosmic. **K∼onaut(in)** *m* **-en,-en** (*f* **-,-nen**) cosmonaut. **k∼opolitisch** *a* cosmopolitan

Kosmos *m* **-** cosmos

Kost *f* **-** food; (*Ernährung*) diet; (*Verpflegung*) board

kostbar *a* precious. **K∼keit** *f* **-,-en** treasure

kosten[1] *vt/i* (*haben*) **[von] etw k∼** taste sth

kosten[2] *vt* cost; (*brauchen*) take; **wieviel kostet es?** how much is it? **K∼** *pl* expense *sg*, cost *sg*; (*Jur*) costs; **auf meine K∼** at my expense. **K∼[vor]anschlag** *m* estimate. **k∼los** *a* free ● *adv* free [of charge]

Kosthappen *m* taste

köstlich *a* delicious; (*entzückend*) delightful. **K∼keit** *f* **-,-en** (*fig*) gem; (*Culin*) delicacy

Kost|probe *f* taste; (*fig*) sample. **k∼spielig** *a* expensive, costly

Kostüm *nt* **-s,-e** (*Theat*) costume; (*Verkleidung*) fancy dress; (*Schneider-*) suit. **K∼fest** *nt* fancy-dress party. **k∼iert** *a* **k∼iert sein** be in fancy dress

Kot *m* **-[e]s** excrement; (*Schmutz*) dirt

Kotelett /kɔt'lɛt/ *nt* **-s,-s** chop, cutlet. **K∼en** *pl* sideburns

Köter *m* **-s,-** (*pej*) dog

Kotflügel *m* (*Auto*) wing, (*Amer*) fender

kotzen *vi* (*haben*) (*sl*) throw up; **es ist zum K∼** it makes you sick

Krabbe *f* **-,-n** crab; (*Garnele*) shrimp; (*rote*) prawn

krabbeln *vi* (*sein*) crawl

Krach *m* **-[e]s,¨e** din, racket; (*Knall*) crash; (*fam: Streit*) row; (*fam: Ruin*) crash. **k∼en** *vi* (*haben*) crash; **es hat gekracht** there was a bang/(*fam: Unfall*) a crash ● (*sein*) break, crack; (*auftreffen*) crash (**gegen** into)

krächzen *vi* (*haben*) croak

Kraft *f* **-,¨e** strength; (*Gewalt*) force; (*Arbeits-*) worker; **in/außer K∼** in/no longer in force; **in K∼ treten** come into force. **k∼** *prep* (+ *gen*) by virtue of. **K∼ausdruck** *m* swear-word. **K∼fahrer** *m* driver. **K∼fahrzeug** *nt* motor vehicle. **K∼fahrzeugbrief** *m* [vehicle] registration document

kräftig *a* strong; (*gut entwickelt*) sturdy; (*nahrhaft*) nutritious; (*heftig*) hard ● *adv* strongly; (*heftig*) hard. **k∼en** *vt* strengthen

kraft|los *a* weak. **K∼post** *f* post bus service. **K∼probe** *f* trial of strength. **K∼rad** *nt* motorcycle. **K∼stoff** *m* (*Auto*) fuel. **k∼voll** *a* strong, powerful. **K∼wagen** *m* motor car. **K∼werk** *nt* power station

Kragen *m* **-s,-** collar

Krähe *f* **-,-n** crow

krähen *vi (haben)* crow

krakeln *vt/i (haben)* scrawl

Kralle *f* -,-n claw. **k~n (sich)** *vr* clutch (**an jdn/etw** s.o./sth); ⟨*Katze:*⟩ dig its claws (**in** + *acc* into)

Kram *m* -s (*fam*) things *pl*, (*fam*) stuff; (*Angelegenheiten*) business; **wertloser K~** junk. **k~en** *vi (haben)* rummage about (**in** + *dat* in; **nach** for). **K~laden** *m* [small] general store

Krampf *m* -[e]s,⁓e cramp. **K~adern** *fpl* varicose veins. **k~haft** *a* convulsive, *adv* -ly; (*verbissen*) desperate, *adv* -ly

Kran *m* -[e]s,⁓e (*Techn*) crane

Kranich *m* -s,-e (*Zool*) crane

krank *a* (**kränker, kränkst**) sick; ⟨*Knie, Herz:*⟩ bad; **k~ sein/werden/machen** be/fall/make ill; **sich k~ melden** report sick. **K~e(r)** *m/f* sick man/woman, invalid; **die K~en** the sick *pl*

kränkeln *vi (haben)* be in poor health. **k~d** *a* ailing

kranken *vi (haben)* (*fig*) suffer (**an** + *dat* from)

kränken *vt* offend, hurt

Kranken|bett *nt* sick-bed. **K~geld** *nt* sickness benefit. **K~gymnast(in)** *m* -en,-en (*f* -,-nen) physiotherapist. **K~gymnastik** *f* physiotherapy. **K~haus** *nt* hospital. **K~kasse** *f* health insurance scheme/(*Amt*) office. **K~pflege** *f* nursing. **K~pfleger(in)** *m(f)* nurse. **K~saal** *m* [hospital] ward. **K~schein** *m* certificate of entitlement to medical treatment. **K~schwester** *f* nurse. **K~urlaub** *m* sick-leave. **K~versicherung** *f* health insurance. **K~wagen** *m* ambulance. **K~zimmer** *nt* sick-room

krank|haft *a* morbid; (*pathologisch*) pathological. **K~heit** *f* -,-en illness, disease

kränk|lich *a* sickly. **K~ung** *f* -,-en slight

Kranz *m* -es,⁓e wreath; (*Ring*) ring

Krapfen *m* -s,- doughnut

kraß *a* (**krasser, krassest**) glaring; (*offensichtlich*) blatant; (*stark*) gross; rank (*Außenseiter*)

Krater *m* -s,- crater

kratz|bürstig *a* (*fam*) prickly. **k~en** *vt/i (haben)* scratch; **sich k~en** scratch oneself/⟨*Tier:*⟩ itself. **K~er** *m* -s,- scratch; (*Werkzeug*) scraper

Kraul *nt* -s (*Sport*) crawl. **k~en**¹ *vi (haben/sein)* (*Sport*) do the crawl

kraulen² *vt* tickle; **sich am Kopf k~** scratch one's head

kraus *a* wrinkled; ⟨*Haar:*⟩ frizzy; (*verworren*) muddled; **k~ ziehen** wrinkle. **K~e** *f* -,-n frill, ruffle; (*Haar-*) frizziness

kräuseln *vt* wrinkle; frizz ⟨*Haar*⟩; gather ⟨*Stoff*⟩; ripple ⟨*Wasser*⟩; **sich k~** wrinkle; (*sich kringeln*) curl; ⟨*Haar:*⟩ go frizzy; ⟨*Wasser:*⟩ ripple

krausen *vt* wrinkle; frizz ⟨*Haar*⟩; gather ⟨*Stoff*⟩; **sich k~** wrinkle; ⟨*Haar:*⟩ go frizzy

Kraut *nt* -[e]s, **Kräuter** herb; (*SGer*) cabbage; (*Sauer-*) sauerkraut; **wie K~ und Rüben** (*fam*) higgledy-piggledy

Krawall *m* -s,-e riot; (*Lärm*) row

Krawatte *f* -,-n [neck]tie

kraxeln *vi (sein)* (*fam*) clamber

krea|tiv /krea'ti:f/ *a* creative. **K~tur** *f* -,-en creature

Krebs *m* -es,-e crayfish; (*Med*) cancer; (*Astr*) Cancer. **k~ig** *a* cancerous

Kredit *m* -s,-e credit; (*Darlehen*) loan; **auf K~** on credit. **K~karte** *f* credit card

Kreid|e *f* - chalk. **k~ebleich** *a* deathly pale. **k~ig** *a* chalky

kreieren /kre'i:rən/ *vt* create

Kreis *m* -es,-e circle; (*Admin*) district

kreischen *vt/i (haben)* screech; (*schreien*) shriek

Kreisel *m* -s,- [spinning] top; (*fam: Kreisverkehr*) roundabout

kreis|en *vi (haben)* circle; revolve (**um** around). **k~förmig** *a* circular. **K~lauf** *m* cycle; (*Med*) circulation. **k~rund** *a* circular. **K~säge** *f* circular saw. **K~verkehr** *m* [traffic] roundabout, (*Amer*) traffic circle

Krem *f* -,-s & *m* -s,-e cream

Krematorium *nt* -s,-ien crematorium

Krempe *f* -,-n [hat] brim

Krempel *m* -s (*fam*) junk

krempeln *vt* turn (**nach oben** up)

Kren *m* -[e]s (*Aust*) horseradish

krepieren *vi (sein)* explode; (*sl: sterben*) die

Krepp *m* -s,-s & -e crêpe

Kreppapier *nt* crêpe paper

Kresse *f* -,-n cress; (*Kapuziner-*) nasturtium

Kreta *nt* -s Crete

Kreuz *nt* -es,-e cross; (*Kreuzung*) intersection; (*Mus*) sharp; (*Kartenspiel*) clubs *pl*; (*Anat*) small of the back; **über K~** crosswise; **das K~ schlagen** cross oneself. **k~** *adv* **k~ und quer** in all directions. **k~en** *vt* cross; **sich k~en** cross; ⟨*Straßen:*⟩ intersect; ⟨*Meinungen:*⟩ clash ● *vi (haben/sein)* cruise; ⟨*Segelschiff:*⟩ tack. **K~er** *m* **-s,-** cruiser. **K~fahrt** *f (Naut)* cruise; *(K~zug)* crusade. **K~feuer** *nt* crossfire. **K~gang** *m* cloister

kreuzig|en *vt* crucify. **K~ung** *f* **-,-en** crucifixion

Kreuz|otter *f* adder, common viper. **K~ung** *f* **-,-en** intersection; *(Straßen-)* crossroads *sg*; *(Hybride)* cross. **K~verhör** *nt* cross-examination; **ins K~verhör nehmen** cross-examine. **K~weg** *m* crossroads *sg; (Relig)* Way of the Cross. **k~weise** *adv* crosswise. **K~worträtsel** *nt* crossword [puzzle]. **K~zug** *m* crusade

kribbel|ig *a (fam)* edgy. **k~n** *vi (haben)* tingle; *(kitzeln)* tickle

kriech|en† *vi (sein)* crawl; *(fig)* grovel (**vor** + *dat* to). **k~erisch** *a* grovelling. **K~spur** *f (Auto)* crawler lane. **K~tier** *nt* reptile

Krieg *m* **-[e]s,-e** war

kriegen *vt (fam)* get; **ein Kind k~** have a baby

Krieger|denkmal *nt* war memorial. **k~isch** *a* warlike; *(militärisch)* military

kriegs|beschädigt *a* war-disabled. **K~dienstverweigerer** *m* **-s,-** conscientious objector. **K~gefangene(r)** *m* prisoner of war. **K~gefangenschaft** *f* captivity. **K~gericht** *nt* court martial. **K~list** *f* stratagem. **K~rat** *m* council of war. **K~recht** *nt* martial law. **K~schiff** *nt* warship. **K~verbrechen** *nt* war crime

Krimi *m* **-s,-s** *(fam)* crime story/film. **K~nalität** *f* **-** crime; *(Vorkommen)* crime rate. **K~nalpolizei** *f* criminal investigation department. **K~nalroman** *m* crime novel. **k~nell** *a* criminal. **K~nelle(r)** *m* criminal

kringeln (sich) *vr* curl [up]; *(vor Lachen)* fall about

Kripo *f* **-** = **Kriminalpolizei**

Krippe *f* **-,-n** manger; *(Weihnachts-)* crib; *(Kinder-)* crèche. **K~nspiel** *nt* Nativity play

Krise *f* **-,-n** crisis

Kristall[1] *nt* **-s** *(Glas)* crystal; *(geschliffen)* cut glass

Kristall[2] *m* **-s,-e** crystal. **k~isieren** *vi/r (haben)* **[sich] k~isieren** crystallize

Kriterium *nt* **-s,-ien** criterion

Kritik *f* **-,-en** criticism; *(Rezension)* review; **unter aller K~** *(fam)* abysmal

Kriti|ker *m* **-s,-** critic; *(Rezensent)* reviewer. **k~sch** *a* critical, *adv* -ly. **k~sieren** *vt* criticize; review

kritteln *vi (haben)* find fault (**an** + *acc* with)

kritzeln *vt/i (haben)* scribble

Krokette *f* **-,-n** *(Culin)* croquette

Krokodil *nt* **-s,-e** crocodile

Krokus *m* **-,-[se]** crocus

Krone *f* **-,-n** crown; *(Baum-)* top

krönen *vt* crown

Kron|leuchter *m* chandelier. **K~prinz** *m* crown prince

Krönung *f* **-,-en** coronation; *(fig: Höhepunkt)* crowning event/*(Leistung)* achievement

Kropf *m* **-[e]s,-̈e** *(Zool)* crop; *(Med)* goitre

Kröte *f* **-,-n** toad

Krücke *f* **-,-n** crutch; *(Stock-)* handle; **an K~n** on crutches

Krug *m* **-[e]s,-̈e** jug; *(Bier-)* tankard

Krume *f* **-,-n** soft part [of loaf]; *(Krümel)* crumb; *(Acker-)* topsoil

Krümel *m* **-s,-** crumb. **k~ig** *a* crumbly. **k~n** *vt* crumble ● *vi (haben)* be crumbly; ⟨*Person:*⟩ drop crumbs

krumm *a* crooked; *(gebogen)* curved; *(verbogen)* bent. **k~beinig** *a* bow-legged

krümmen *vt* bend; crook ⟨*Finger*⟩; **sich k~** bend; *(sich winden)* writhe; *(vor Schmerzen/Lachen)* double up

krummnehmen† *vt sep (fam)* take amiss

Krümmung *f* **-,-en** bend; *(Kurve)* curve

Krüppel *m* **-s,-** cripple

Kruste *f* **-,-n** crust; *(Schorf)* scab

Kruzifix *nt* **-es,-e** crucifix

Krypta /'krypta/ *f* **-,-ten** crypt

Kuba *nt* **-s** Cuba. **k~anisch** *a* Cuban

Kübel *m* **-s,-** tub; *(Eimer)* bucket; *(Techn)* skip

Kubik- *pref* cubic. **K~meter** *m & nt* cubic metre

Küche *f* **-,-n** kitchen; *(Kochkunst)* cooking; **kalte/warme K~** cold/hot food; **französische K~** French cuisine

Kuchen *m* **-s,-** cake

Küchen|herd *m* cooker, stove. **K~maschine** *f* food processor, mixer. **K~schabe** *f* **-,-n** cockroach. **K~zettel** *m* menu

Kuckuck *m* **-s,-e** cuckoo; **zum K~!** (*fam*) hang it! **K~suhr** *f* cuckoo clock

Kufe *f* **-,-n** [sledge] runner

Kugel *f* **-,-n** ball; (*Geom*) sphere; (*Gewehr-*) bullet; (*Sport*) shot. **k~förmig** *a* spherical. **K~lager** *nt* ball-bearing. **k~n** *vt/i* (*haben*) roll; **sich k~n** roll/ (*vor Lachen*) fall about. **k~rund** *a* spherical; (*fam: dick*) tubby. **K~schreiber** *m* **-s,-** ballpoint [pen]. **k~sicher** *a* bullet-proof. **K~stoßen** *nt* **-s** shot-putting

Kuh *f* **-,-e** cow

kühl *a* cool, *adv* -ly; (*kalt*) chilly. **K~box** *f* **-,-en** cool-box. **K~e** *f* - coolness; chilliness. **k~en** *vt* cool; refrigerate (*Lebensmittel*); chill (*Wein*). **K~er** *m* **-s,-** ice-bucket; (*Auto*) radiator. **K~erhaube** *f* bonnet, (*Amer*) hood. **K~fach** *nt* frozen-food compartment. **K~raum** *m* cold store. **K~schrank** *m* refrigerator. **K~truhe** *f* freezer. **K~ung** *f* - cooling; (*Frische*) coolness. **K~wasser** *nt* [radiator] water

Kuhmilch *f* cow's milk

kühn *a* bold, *adv* -ly; (*wagemutig*) daring. **K~heit** *f* - boldness

Kuhstall *m* cowshed

Küken *nt* **-s,-** chick; (*Enten-*) duckling

Kukuruz *m* **-[es]** (*Aust*) maize

kulant *a* obliging

Kuli *m* **-s,-s** (*fam: Kugelschreiber*) ballpoint [pen], Biro (P)

kulinarisch *a* culinary

Kulissen *fpl* (*Theat*) scenery *sg*; (*seitlich*) wings; **hinter den K~** (*fig*) behind the scenes

kullern *vt/i* (*sein*) (*fam*) roll

Kult *m* **-[e]s,-e** cult

kultivier|en *vt* cultivate. **k~t** *a* cultured

Kultur *f* **-,-en** culture; **K~en** plantations. **K~beutel** *m* toilet-bag. **k~ell** *a* cultural. **K~film** *m* documentary film

Kultusminister *m* Minister of Education and Arts

Kümmel *m* **-s** caraway; (*Getränk*) kümmel

Kummer *m* **-s** sorrow, grief; (*Sorge*) worry; (*Ärger*) trouble

kümmer|lich *a* puny; (*dürftig*) meagre; (*armselig*) wretched. **k~n** *vt* concern; **sich k~n um** look after; (*sich befassen*) concern oneself with; (*beachten*) take notice of; **ich werde mich darum k~n** I shall see to it; **k~e dich**

um deine eigenen Angelegenheiten! mind your own business!

kummervoll *a* sorrowful

Kumpel *m* **-s,-** (*fam*) mate

Kunde *m* **-n,-n** customer. **K~ndienst** *m* [after-sales] service

Kund|gebung *f* **-,-en** (*Pol*) rally. **k~ig** *a* knowledgeable; (*sach-*) expert

kündig|en *vt* cancel (*Vertrag*); give notice of withdrawal for (*Geld*); give notice to quit (*Wohnung*); **seine Stellung k~en** (*in one's*) notice ● *vi* (*haben*) give [in one's] notice; **jdm k~en** give s.o. notice [of dismissal/ (*Vermieter:*) to quit]. **K~ung** *f* **-,-en** cancellation; notice [of withdrawal/dismissal/to quit]; (*Entlassung*) dismissal. **K~ungsfrist** *f* period of notice

Kund|in *f* **-,-nen** [woman] customer. **K~machung** *f* **-,-en** (*Aust*) [public] notice. **K~schaft** *f* - clientele, customers *pl*

künftig *a* future ● *adv* in future

Kunst *f* **-,-̈e** art; (*Können*) skill. **K~dünger** *m* artificial fertilizer. **K~faser** *f* synthetic fibre. **k~fertig** *a* skilful. **K~fertigkeit** *f* skill. **K~galerie** *f* art gallery. **k~gerecht** *a* expert, *adv* -ly. **K~geschichte** *f* history of art. **K~gewerbe** *nt* arts and crafts *pl*. **K~griff** *m* trick. **K~händler** *m* art dealer

Künstler *m* **-s,-** artist; (*Könner*) master. **K~in** *f* **-,-nen** [woman] artist. **k~isch** *a* artistic, *adv* -ally. **K~name** *m* pseudonym; (*Theat*) stage name

künstlich *a* artificial, *adv* -ly

kunst|los *a* simple. **K~maler** *m* painter. **K~stoff** *m* plastic. **K~stopfen** *nt* invisible mending. **K~stück** *nt* trick; (*große Leistung*) feat. **k~voll** *a* artistic; (*geschickt*) skilful, *adv* -ly; (*kompliziert*) elaborate, *adv* -ly. **K~werk** *nt* work of art

kunterbunt *a* multicoloured; (*gemischt*) mixed ● *adv* **k~durcheinander** higgledy-piggledy

Kupfer *nt* **-s** copper. **k~n** *a* copper

kupieren *vt* crop

Kupon /ku'põ:/ *m* **-s,-s** voucher; (*Zins-*) coupon; (*Stoff-*) length

Kuppe *f* **-,-n** [rounded] top; (*Finger-*) end, tip

Kuppel *f* **-,-n** dome

kupp|eln *vt* couple (**an** + *acc* **to**) ● *vi* (*haben*) (*Auto*) operate the clutch. **K~lung** *f* **-,-en** coupling; (*Auto*) clutch

Kur *f* **-,-en** course of treatment; (*im Kurort*) cure

Kür *f* **-,-en** (*Sport*) free exercise; (*Eislauf*) free programme

Kurbel *f* **-,-n** crank. **k~n** *vt* wind (**nach oben/unten** up/down). **K~welle** *f* crankshaft

Kürbis *m* **-ses,-se** pumpkin; (*Flaschen-*) marrow

Kurgast *m* health-resort visitor

Kurier *m* **-s,-e** courier

kurieren *vt* cure

kurios *a* curious, odd. **K~ität** *f* **-,-en** oddness; (*Objekt*) curiosity; (*Kunst*) curio

Kur|ort *m* health resort; (*Badeort*) spa. **K~pfuscher** *m* quack

Kurs *m* **-es,-e** course; (*Aktien-*) price. **K~buch** *nt* timetable

kursieren *vi* (*haben*) circulate

kursiv *a* italic ● *adv* in italics. **K~schrift** *f* italics *pl*

Kursus *m* **-,Kurse** course

Kurswagen *m* through carriage

Kurtaxe *f* visitors' tax

Kurve *f* **-,-n** curve; (*Straßen-*) bend

kurz *a* (**kürzer, kürzest**) short; (*knapp*) brief; (*rasch*) quick; (*schroff*) curt; **k~e Hosen** shorts; **vor k~em** a short time ago; **seit k~em** lately; **binnen k~em** shortly; **den kürzeren ziehen** get the worst of it ● *adv* briefly; quickly; curtly; **k~ vor/nach** a little way/(*zeitlich*) shortly before/after; **sich k~ fassen** be brief; **k~ und gut** in short; **über k~ oder lang** sooner or later; **zu k~ kommen** get less than one's fair share. **K~arbeit** *f* short-time working. **k~ärmelig** *a* short-sleeved. **k~atmig** *a* **k~atmig sein** be short of breath

Kürze *f* **-** shortness; (*Knappheit*) brevity; **in K~** shortly. **k~n** *vt* shorten; (*verringern*) cut

kurz|erhand *adv* without further ado. **k~fristig** *a* short-term ● *adv* at short notice. **K~geschichte** *f* short story. **k~lebig** *a* short-lived

kürzlich *adv* recently

Kurz|meldung *f* newsflash. **K~nachrichten** *fpl* news headlines. **K~schluß** *m* short circuit; (*fig*) brainstorm. **K~schrift** *f* shorthand. **K~sichtig** *a* short-sighted. **K~sichtigkeit** *f* - short-sightedness. **K~streckenrakete** *f* short-range missile. **k~um** *adv* in short

Kürzung *f* **-,-en** shortening; (*Verringerung*) cut (*gen* in)

Kurz|waren *fpl* haberdashery *sg*, (*Amer*) notions. **k~weilig** *a* amusing. **K~welle** *f* short wave

kuscheln (sich) *vr* snuggle (**an** + *acc* up to)

Kusine *f* **-,-n** [female] cousin

Kuß *m* **-sses,-̈sse** kiss

küssen *vt/i* (*haben*) kiss; **sich k~** kiss

Küste *f* **-,-n** coast. **K~nwache, K~nwacht** *f* coastguard

Küster *m* **-s,-** verger

Kustos *m* **-,-oden** /-'to:/ curator

Kutsch|e *f* **-,-n** [horse-drawn] carriage/(*geschlossen*) coach. **K~er** *m* **-s,-** coachman, driver. **k~ieren** *vt/i* (*haben*) drive

Kutte *f* **-,-n** (*Relig*) habit

Kutter *m* **-s,-** (*Naut*) cutter

Kuvert /ku've:ɐ̯/ *nt* **-s,-s** envelope

KZ /ka:'tsɛt/ *nt* **-[s],-[s]** concentration camp

L

labil *a* unstable

Labo|r *nt* **-s,-s** & **-e** laboratory. **L~rant(in)** *m* **-en,-en** (*f* **-,-nen**) laboratory assistant. **L~ratorium** *nt* **-s,-ien** laboratory

Labyrinth *nt* **-[e]s,-e** maze, labyrinth

Lache *f* **-,-n** puddle; (*Blut-*) pool

lächeln *vi* (*haben*) smile. **L~** *nt* **-s** smile. **l~d** *a* smiling

lachen *vi* (*haben*) laugh. **L~** *nt* **-s** laugh; (*Gelächter*) laughter

lächerlich *a* ridiculous, *adv* **-ly**; **sich l~ machen** make a fool of oneself. **L~keit** *f* **-,-en** ridiculousness; (*Kleinigkeit*) triviality

lachhaft *a* laughable

Lachs *m* **-es,-e** salmon. **l~farben, l~rosa** *a* salmon-pink

Lack *m* **-[e]s,-e** varnish; (*Japan-*) lacquer; (*Auto*) paint. **l~en** *vt* varnish. **l~ieren** *vt* varnish; (*spritzen*) spray. **L~schuhe** *mpl* patent-leather shoes

Lade *f* **-,-n** drawer

laden† *vt* load; (*Electr*) charge; (*Jur: vor-*) summons

Laden *m* **-s,-̈** shop, (*Amer*) store; (*Fenster-*) shutter. **L~dieb** *m* shoplifter. **L~diebstahl** *m* shop-lifting. **L~schluß** *m* [shop] closing-time. **L~tisch** *m* counter

Laderaum m (Naut) hold
lädieren vt damage
Ladung f -,-en load; (Naut, Aviat) cargo; (elektrische, Spreng-) charge; (Jur: Vor-) summons
Lage f -,-n position; (Situation) situation; (Schicht) layer; (fam: Runde) round; **nicht in der L~ sein** not be in a position (**zu** to)
Lager nt -s,- camp; (L~haus) warehouse; (Vorrat) stock; (Techn) bearing; (Erz-, Ruhe-) bed; (eines Tieres) lair; **[nicht] auf L~** [not] in stock. **L~haus** nt warehouse. **l~n** vt store; (legen) lay; **sich l~n** settle; (sich legen) lie down ●vi (haben) camp; (liegen) lie; ⟨Waren:⟩ be stored. **L~raum** m storeroom. **L~stätte** f (Geol) deposit. **L~ung** f - storage
Lagune f -,-n lagoon
lahm a lame. **l~en** vi (haben) be lame
lähmen vt paralyse
lahmlegen vt sep (fig) paralyse
Lähmung f -,-en paralysis
Laib m -[e]s,-e loaf
Laich m -[e]s (Zool) spawn. **l~en** vi (haben) spawn
Laie m -n,-n layman; (Theat) amateur. **l~nhaft** a amateurish. **L~nprediger** m lay preacher
Lake f -,-n brine
Laken nt -s,- sheet
lakonisch a laconic, adv -ally
Lakritze f - liquorice
lallen vt/i (haben) mumble; ⟨Baby:⟩ babble
Lametta nt -s tinsel
Lamm nt -[e]s,-er lamb
Lampe f -,-n lamp; (Decken-, Wand-) light; (Glüh-) bulb. **L~nfieber** nt stage fright. **L~nschirm** m lampshade
Lampion /lamˈpiɔŋ/ m -s,-s Chinese lantern
lancieren /lãˈsiːrən/ vt (Comm) launch
Land nt -[e]s,-̈er country; (Fest-) land; (Bundes-) state, Land; (Aust) province; **Stück L~** piece of land; **auf dem L~e** in the country; **an L~ gehen** (Naut) go ashore. **L~arbeiter** m agricultural worker. **L~ebahn** f runway. **l~einwärts** adv inland. **l~en** vt/i (sein) land; (fam: gelangen) end up
Ländereien pl estates
Länderspiel nt international
Landesteg m landing-stage
Landesverrat m treason

Land|karte f map. **l~läufig** a popular
ländlich a rural
Land|maschinen fpl agricultural machinery sg. **L~schaft** f -,-en scenery; (Geog, Kunst) landscape; (Gegend) country[side]. **l~schaftlich** a scenic; (regional) regional. **L~smann** m (pl -leute) fellow countryman, compatriot. **L~smännin** f -,-nen fellow countrywoman. **L~straße** f country road; (Admin) ≈ B road. **L~streicher** m -s,- tramp. **L~tag** m state-/(Aust) provincial parliament
Landung f -,-en landing. **L~sbrücke** f landing-stage
Land|vermesser m -s,- surveyor. **L~weg** m country lane; **auf dem L~weg** overland. **L~wirt** m farmer. **L~wirtschaft** f agriculture; (Hof) farm. **l~wirtschaftlich** a agricultural
lang[1] adv & prep (+ preceding acc or preceding an + dat) along; **den od am Fluß l~** along the river
lang[2] a (länger, längst) long; (groß) tall; **seit l~em** for a long time ●adv **eine Stunde/Woche l~** for an hour/a week; **mein Leben l~** all my life. **l~ärmelig** a long-sleeved. **l~atmig** a long-winded. **l~e** adv a long time; ⟨schlafen⟩ late; **wie/zu l~e** how/too long; **schon l~e** [for] a long time; (zurückliegend) a long time ago; **l~e nicht** not for a long time; (bei weitem nicht) nowhere near
Länge f -,-n length; (Geog) longitude; **der L~ nach** lengthways; ⟨liegen, fallen⟩ full length
langen vt hand (dat to) ●vi (haben) reach (**an etw** acc sth; **nach** for); (genügen) be enough
Läng|engrad m degree of longitude. **L~enmaß** nt linear measure. **l~er** a & adv longer; (längere Zeit) [for] some time
Langeweile f - boredom; **L~ haben** be bored
lang|fristig a long-term; ⟨Vorhersage⟩ long-range. **l~jährig** a long-standing; ⟨Erfahrung⟩ long. **l~lebig** a long-lived
länglich a oblong. **l~rund** a oval
langmütig a long-suffering
längs adv & prep (+ gen/dat) along; (der Länge nach) lengthways
lang|sam a slow, adv -ly. **L~samkeit** f - slowness. **L~schläfer(in)** m(f)

los|werden† *vt sep* get rid of. **l~ziehen†** *vi sep (sein)* set off; **l~ziehen gegen** *od* **über** (+ *acc*) *(beschimpfen)* run down

Lot *nt* **-[e]s,-e** perpendicular; *(Blei-)* plumb[-bob]; **im Lot sein** *(fig)* be all right. **l~en** *vt* plumb

löt|en *vt* solder. **L~lampe** *f* blow-lamp, *(Amer)* blowtorch. **L~metall** *nt* solder

lotrecht *a* perpendicular, *adv* -ly

Lotse *m* **-n,-n** *(Naut)* pilot. **l~n** *vt* *(Naut)* pilot; *(fig)* guide

Lotterie *f* **-,-n** lottery

Lotto *nt* **-s,-s** lotto; *(Lotterie)* lottery

Löw|e *m* **-n,-n** lion; *(Astr)* Leo. **L~enanteil** *m* *(fig)* lion's share. **L~enzahn** *m* *(Bot)* dandelion. **L~in** *f* **-,-nen** lioness

loyal /loa'jaːl/ *a* loyal. **L~ität** *f* **-** loyalty

Luchs *m* **-es,-e** lynx

Lücke *f* **-,-n** gap. **L~nbüßer** *m* **-s,-** stopgap. **l~nhaft** *a* incomplete; *(Wissen)* patchy. **l~nlos** *a* complete; *(Folge)* unbroken

Luder *nt* **-s,-** *(sl)* *(Frau)* bitch; **armes L~** poor wretch

Luft *f* **-,ˑe** air; **tief L~ holen** take a deep breath; **in die L~ gehen** explode. **L~angriff** *m* air raid. **L~aufnahme** *f* aerial photograph. **L~ballon** *m* balloon. **L~bild** *nt* aerial photograph. **L~blase** *f* air bubble

Lüftchen *nt* **-s,-** breeze

luft|dicht *a* airtight. **L~druck** *m* atmospheric pressure

lüften *vt* air; raise *(Hut)*; reveal *(Geheimnis)*

Luft|fahrt *f* aviation. **L~fahrtgesellschaft** *f* airline. **L~gewehr** *nt* airgun. **L~hauch** *m* breath of air. **l~ig** *a* airy; *(Kleid)* light. **L~kissenfahrzeug** *nt* hovercraft. **L~krieg** *m* aerial warfare. **L~kurort** *m* climatic health resort. **l~leer** *a* **l~leerer Raum** vacuum. **L~linie** *f* **100 km L~linie** 100 km as the crow flies. **L~loch** *nt* air-hole; *(Aviat)* air pocket. **L~matratze** *f* air-bed, inflatable mattress. **L~pirat** *m* [air-craft] hijacker. **L~post** *f* airmail. **L~pumpe** *f* air pump; *(Fahrrad-)* bicycle-pump. **L~röhre** *f* windpipe. **L~schiff** *nt* airship. **L~schlange** *f* [paper] streamer. **L~schlösser** *ntpl* castles in the air. **L~schutzbunker** *m* air-raid shelter

Lüftung *f* **-** ventilation

Luft|veränderung *f* change of air. **L~waffe** *f* air force. **L~weg** *m* **auf dem L~weg** by air. **L~zug** *m* draught

Lüg|e *f* **-,-n** lie. **l~en†** *vt/i (haben)* lie. **L~ner(in)** *m* **-s,-** *(f* **-,-nen)** liar. **l~nerisch** *a* untrue; *(Person)* untruthful

Luke *f* **-,-n** hatch; *(Dach-)* skylight

Lümmel *m* **-s,-** lout; *(fam: Schelm)* rascal. **l~n (sich)** *vr* loll

Lump *m* **-en,-en** scoundrel. **L~en** *m* **-s,-** rag; **in L~en** in rags. **l~en** *vt* **sich nicht l~en lassen** be generous. **L~engesindel, L~enpack** *nt* riff-raff. **L~ensammler** *m* rag-and-bone man. **l~ig** *a* mean, shabby; *(gering)* measly

Lunchpaket /'lan[t]ʃ-/ *nt* packed lunch

Lunge *f* **-,-n** lungs *pl*; *(L~nflügel)* lung. **L~nentzündung** *f* pneumonia

lungern *vi (haben)* loiter

Lunte *f* **L~ riechen** *(fam)* smell a rat

Lupe *f* **-,-n** magnifying glass

Lurch *m* **-[e]s,-e** amphibian

Lust *f* **-,ˑe** pleasure; *(Verlangen)* desire; *(sinnliche Begierde)* lust; **L~ haben** feel like **(auf etw** *acc* sth); **ich habe keine L~** I don't feel like it; *(will nicht)* I don't want to

Lüster *m* **-s,-** lustre; *(Kronleuchter)* chandelier

lüstern *a* greedy **(auf** + *acc* for); *(sinnlich)* lascivious; *(geil)* lecherous

lustig *a* jolly; *(komisch)* funny; **sich l~ machen über** (+ *acc*) make fun of

Lüstling *m* **-s,-e** lecher

lust|los *a* listless, *adv* -ly. **L~mörder** *m* sex killer. **L~spiel** *nt* comedy

lutherisch *a* Lutheran

lutsch|en *vt/i (haben)* suck. **L~er** *m* **-s,-** lollipop; *(Schnuller)* dummy, *(Amer)* pacifier

lütt *a* *(NGer)* little

Lüttich *nt* **-s** Liège

Luv *f* & *nt* **- nach Luv** *(Naut)* to windward

luxuriös *a* luxurious, *adv* -ly

Luxus *m* **-** luxury. **L~artikel** *m* luxury article. **L~ausgabe** *f* de luxe edition. **L~hotel** *nt* luxury hotel

Lymph|drüse /'lymf-/ *f*, **L~knoten** *m* lymph gland

lynchen /'lynçən/ *vt* lynch

Lyr|ik f - lyric poetry. **L~iker** m -s,- lyric poet. **l~isch** a lyrical; ⟨Dichtung⟩ lyric

M

Mach|art f style. **m~bar** a feasible. **m~en** vt make; get ⟨Mahlzeit⟩; take ⟨Foto⟩; (ausführen, tun, in Ordnung bringen) do; (Math: ergeben) be; (kosten) come to; **sich** (dat) **etw m~en lassen** have sth made; **was m~st du da?** what are you doing? **was m~t die Arbeit?** how is work? **das m~t 6 Mark [zusammen]** that's 6 marks [altogether]; **das m~t nichts** it doesn't matter; **sich** (dat) **wenig/nichts m~en aus** care little/nothing for ● vr **sich m~en** do well; **sich an die Arbeit m~en** get down to work ● vi (haben) **ins Bett m~en** (fam) wet the bed; **schnell m~en** hurry. **M~enschaften** fpl machinations

Macht f -,-̈e power; **mit aller M~** with all one's might. **M~haber** m -s,- ruler

mächtig a powerful; (groß) enormous ● adv (fam) terribly

macht|los a powerless. **M~wort** nt **ein M~wort sprechen** put one's foot down

Mädchen nt -s,- girl; (Dienst-) maid. **m~haft** a girlish. **M~name** m girl's name; (vor der Ehe) maiden name

Made f -,-n maggot

Mädel nt -s,- girl

madig a maggoty; **jdn m~ machen** (fam) run s.o. down

Madonna f -,-nen madonna

Magazin nt -s,-e magazine; (Lager) warehouse; (Raum) store-room

Magd f -,-̈e maid

Magen m -s,-̈ stomach. **M~schmerzen** mpl stomach-ache sg. **M~verstimmung** f stomach upset

mager a thin; ⟨Fleisch⟩ lean; ⟨Boden⟩ poor; (dürftig) meagre. **M~keit** f - thinness; leanness. **M~sucht** f anorexia

Magie f - magic

Mag|ier /'ma:giɐ/ m -s,- magician. **m~isch** a magic; (geheimnisvoll) magical

Magistrat m -s,-e city council

Magnesia f - magnesia

Magnet m -en & -[e]s,-e magnet. **m~isch** a magnetic. **m~isieren** vt magnetize. **M~ismus** m - magnetism

Mahagoni nt -s mahogany

Mäh|drescher m -s,- combine harvester. **m~en** vt/i (haben) mow

Mahl nt -[e]s,-̈er meal

mahlen† vt grind

Mahlzeit f meal; **M~!** enjoy your meal!

Mähne f -,-n mane

mahn|en vt/i (haben) remind (**wegen** about); (ermahnen) admonish; (auffordern) urge (**zu** to); **zur Vorsicht/ Eile m~en** urge caution/haste. **M~ung** f -,-en reminder; admonition; (Aufforderung) ex-hortation

Mai m -[e]s,-e May; **der Erste Mai** May Day. **M~glöckchen** nt -s,- lily of the valley. **M~käfer** m cockchafer

Mailand nt -s Milan

Mais m -es maize; (Amer) corn; (Culin) sweet corn. **M~kolben** m corn-cob

Majestät f -,-en majesty. **m~isch** a majestic, adv -ally

Major m -s,-e major

Majoran m -s marjoram

Majorität f -,-en majority

makaber a macabre

Makel m -s,- blemish; (Defekt) flaw; (fig) stain. **m~los** a flawless; (fig) unblemished

mäkeln vi (haben) grumble

Makkaroni pl macaroni sg

Makler m -s,- (Comm) broker

Makrele f -,-n mackerel

Makrone f -,-n macaroon

mal adv (Math) times; (bei Maßen) by; (fam: einmal) once; (eines Tages) one day; **schon mal** once before; (jemals) ever; **nicht mal** not even; **hört/seht mal!** listen!/look!

Mal¹ nt -[e]s,-e time; **zum ersten Mal** for the first time; **mit einem Mal** all at once; **ein für alle Mal** once and for all

Mal² nt -[e]s,-e mark; (auf der Haut) mole; (Mutter-) birthmark

Mal|buch nt colouring book. **m~en** vt/i (haben) paint. **M~er** m -s,- painter. **M~erei** f -,-en painting. **M~erin** f -,-nen painter. **m~erisch** a picturesque

Malheur /ma'lø:ɐ/ nt -s,-e & -s (fam) mishap; (Ärger) trouble

Mallorca /ma'lɔrka, -'jɔrka/ nt -s Majorca

malnehmen† vt sep multiply (**mit** by)

Mithilfe f assistance

mitkommen† vi sep (sein) come [along] too; (fig: folgen können) keep up; (verstehen) follow

Mitlaut m consonant

Mitleid nt pity, compassion. **M~enschaft** f **in M~enschaft ziehen** affect. **m~erregend** a pitiful. **m~ig** a pitying; (mitfühlend) compassionate. **m~slos** a pitiless

mitmachen v sep ● vt take part in; (erleben) go through ● vi (haben) join in

Mitmensch m fellow man

mitnehmen† vt sep take along; (mitfahren lassen) give a lift to; (fig: schädigen) affect badly; (erschöpfen) exhaust; **'zum M~'** 'to take away', (Amer) 'to go'

mitnichten adv not at all

mitreden vi sep (haben) join in [the conversation]; (mit entscheiden) have a say (**bei** in)

mitreißen† vt sep sweep along; (fig: begeistern) carry away; **m~d** rousing

mitsamt prep (+ dat) together with

mitschneiden† vt sep record

mitschreiben† vt sep (haben) take down

Mitschuld f partial blame. **m~ig** a **m~ig sein** be partly to blame

Mitschüler(in) m(f) fellow pupil

mitspiel|en vi sep (haben) join in; (Theat) be in the cast; (beitragen) play a part; **jdm übel m~en** treat s.o. badly. **M~er** m fellow player; (Mitwirkender) participant

Mittag m midday, noon; (Mahlzeit) lunch; (Pause) lunch-break; **[zu] M~ essen** have lunch. **m~** adv **heute m~** at lunch-time today. **M~essen** nt lunch. **m~s** adv at noon; (als Mahlzeit) for lunch; **um 12 Uhr m~s** at noon. **M~spause** f lunch-hour; (Pause) lunch-break. **M~sschlaf** m after-lunch nap. **M~stisch** m lunch table; (Essen) lunch. **M~szeit** f lunch-time

Mittäter|(in) m(f) accomplice. **M~schaft** f - complicity

Mitte f -,-n middle; (Zentrum) centre; **die goldene M~** the golden mean; **M~ Mai** in mid-May; **in unserer M~** in our midst

mitteil|en vt sep **jdm etw m~en** tell s.o. sth; (amtlich) inform s.o. of sth. **m~sam** a communicative. **M~ung** f -,-en communication; (Nachricht) piece of news

Mittel nt -s,- means sg; (Heil-) remedy; (Medikament) medicine; (M~wert) mean; (Durchschnitt) average; **M~** pl (Geld-) funds, resources. **m~** pred a medium; (m~mäßig) middling. **M~alter** nt Middle Ages pl. **m~alterlich** a medieval. **m~bar** a indirect, adv -ly. **M~ding** nt (fig) cross. **m~europäisch** a Central European. **M~finger** m middle finger. **m~groß** a medium-sized; ⟨Person⟩ of medium height. **M~klasse** f middle range. **m~los** a destitute. **m~mäßig** a middling; **[nur] m~mäßig** mediocre. **M~meer** nt Mediterranean. **M~punkt** m centre; (fig) centre of attention

mittels prep (+ gen) by means of

Mittel|schule f = **Realschule.** **M~smann** m (pl -männer), **M~sperson** f intermediary, go-between. **M~stand** m middle class. **m~ste(r,s)** a middle. **M~streifen** m (Auto) central reservation, (Amer) median strip. **M~stürmer** m centre-forward. **M~weg** m (fig) middle course; **goldener M~weg** happy medium. **M~welle** f medium wave. **M~wort** nt (pl -wörter) participle

mitten adv **m~ in/auf** (dat/acc) in the middle of; **m~ unter** (dat/acc) amidst. **m~durch** adv [right] through the middle

Mitternacht f midnight

mittler|e(r,s) a middle; ⟨Größe, Qualität⟩ medium; (durchschnittlich) mean, average. **m~weile** adv meanwhile; (seitdem) by now

Mittwoch m -s,-e Wednesday. **m~s** adv on Wednesdays

mitunter adv now and again

mitwirk|en vi sep (haben) take part; (helfen) contribute. **M~ung** f participation

mix|en vt mix. **M~er** m -s,- (Culin) liquidizer, blender. **M~tur** f -,-en (Med) mixture

Möbel pl furniture sg. **M~stück** nt piece of furniture. **M~tischler** m cabinet-maker. **M~wagen** m removal van

mobil a mobile; (fam: munter) lively; (nach Krankheit) fit [and well]; **m~ machen** mobilize

Mobile nt -s,-s mobile

Mobiliar nt -s furniture

mobilisier|en vt mobilize. **M~ung** f - mobilization

Mobilmachung f - mobilization
möblier|en vt furnish; **m~tes Zimmer** furnished room
mochte, möchte s. **mögen**
Modalverb nt modal auxiliary
Mode f -,-n fashion; **M~ sein** be fashionable
Modell nt -s,-e model; **M~ stehen** pose (**jdm** for s.o.).**m~ieren** vt model
Modenschau f fashion show
Modera|tor m -s,-en /-'to:rən/, **M~torin** f -,-nen (TV) presenter
modern[1] vi (haben) decay
modern[2] a modern; (modisch) fashionable.**m~isieren** vt modernize
Mode|schmuck m costume jewellery. **M~schöpfer** m fashion designer
Modifi|kation /-'tsio:n/ f -,-en modification.**m~zieren** vt modify
modisch a fashionable
Modistin f -,-nen milliner
modrig a musty
modulieren vt modulate
Mofa nt -s,-s moped
mogeln vi (haben) (fam) cheat
mögen† vt like; **lieber m~** prefer● v aux **ich möchte** I'd like; **möchtest du nach Hause?** do you want to go home? **ich mag nicht mehr** I've had enough; **ich hätte weinen m~** I could have cried; **ich mag mich irren** I may be wrong; **wer/was mag das sein?** whoever/whatever can it be? **wie mag es ihm ergangen sein?** I wonder how he got on; **[das] mag sein** that may well be; **mag kommen, was da will** come what may
möglich a possible; **alle m~en** all sorts of. **m~erweise** adv possibly. **M~keit** f -,-en possibility. **M~keitsform** f subjunctive. **m~st** adv if possible; **m~st viel/früh** as much/early as possible
Mohammedan|er(in) m -s,- (f-,-nen) Muslim.**m~isch** a Muslim
Mohn m -s poppy; (Culin) poppy-seed. **M~blume** f poppy
Möhre, Mohrrübe f -,-n carrot
mokieren (sich) vr make fun (**über** + acc of)
Mokka m -s mocha; (Geschmack) coffee
Molch m -[e]s,-e newt
Mole f -,-n (Naut) mole
Molekül nt -s,-e molecule
Molkerei f -,-en dairy
Moll nt - (Mus) minor

mollig a cosy; (warm) warm; (rundlich) plump
Moment m -s,-e moment; **im/jeden M~** at the/any moment; **M~ [mal]!** just a moment! **m~an** a momentary, adv -ily; (gegenwärtig) at the moment
Momentaufnahme f snapshot
Monarch m -en,-en monarch. **M~ie** f -,-n monarchy
Monat m -s,-e month. **m~elang** adv for months. **m~lich** a & adv monthly. **M~skarte** f monthly season ticket
Mönch m -[e]s,-e monk
Mond m -[e]s,-e moon
mondän a fashionable, adv -bly
Mond|finsternis f lunar eclipse. **m~hell** a moonlit.**M~sichel** f crescent moon.**M~schein** m moonlight
monieren vt criticize
Monitor m -s,-en /-'to:rən/ (Techn) monitor
Monogramm nt -s,-e monogram
Mono|log m -s,-e monologue. **M~pol** nt -s,-e monopoly. **m~polisieren** vt monopolize. **m~ton** a monotonous, adv -ly. **M~tonie** f - monotony
Monster nt -s,- monster
monstr|ös a monstrous. **M~osität** f -,-en monstrosity
Monstrum nt -s,-stren monster
Monsun m -s,-e monsoon
Montag m Monday
Montage /mɔn'ta:ʒə/ f -,-n fitting; (Zusammenbau) assembly; (Film-) editing; (Kunst) montage
montags adv on Mondays
Montanindustrie f coal and steel industry
Monteur /mɔn'tø:ɐ/ m -s,-e fitter. **M~anzug** m overalls pl
montieren vt fit; (zusammenbauen) assemble
Monument nt -[e]s,-e monument. **m~al** a monumental
Moor nt -[e]s,-e bog; (Heide-) moor
Moos nt -es,-e moss.**m~ig** a mossy
Mop m -s,-s mop
Moped nt -s,-s moped
Mops m -es,̈-e pug [dog]
Moral f - morals pl; (Selbstvertrauen) morale; (Lehre) moral. **m~isch** a moral, adv -ly.**m~isieren** vi (haben) moralize
Morast m -[e]s,-e morass; (Schlamm) mud

Nacht|essen nt (SGer) supper. **N~falter** m moth. **N~hemd** nt nightdress; (Männer-) night-shirt
Nachtigall f -,-en nightingale
Nachtisch m dessert
Nacht|klub m night-club. **N~leben** nt night-life
nächtlich a nocturnal, night...
Nacht|lokal nt night-club. **N~mahl** nt (Aust) supper
Nachtrag m postscript; (Ergänzung) supplement. **n~en**† vt sep add; **jdm etw n~en** walk behind s.o. carrying sth; (fig) bear a grudge against s.o. for sth. **n~end** a vindictive; **n~end sein** bear grudges
nachträglich a subsequent, later; (verspätet) belated ● adv later; (nachher) afterwards; (verspätet) belatedly
nachtrauern vi sep (haben) (+ dat). mourn the loss of
Nacht|ruhe f night's rest; **angenehme N~ruhe!** sleep well! **n~s** adv at night; **2 Uhr n~s** 2 o'clock in the morning. **N~schicht** f night-shift. **N~tisch** m bedside table. **N~tischlampe** f bedside lamp. **N~topf** m chamber-pot. **N~wächter** m night-watchman. **N~zeit** f nighttime
Nachuntersuchung f check-up
nachwachsen† vi sep (sein) grow again
Nachwahl f by-election
Nachweis m -es,-e proof. **n~bar** a demonstrable. **n~en**† vt sep prove; (aufzeigen) show; (vermitteln) give details of; **jdm nichts n~en können** have no proof against s.o. **n~lich** a demonstrable, adv -bly
Nachwelt f posterity
Nachwirkung f after-effect
Nachwort nt (pl -e) epilogue
Nachwuchs m new generation; (fam: Kinder) offspring. **N~spieler** m young player
nachzahlen vt/i sep (haben) pay extra; (später zahlen) pay later; **Steuern n~** pay tax arrears
nachzählen vt/i sep (haben) count again; (prüfen) check
Nachzahlung f extra/later payment; (Gehalts-) back-payment
nachzeichnen vt sep copy
Nachzügler m -s,- late-comer; (Zurückgebliebener) straggler
Nacken m -s,- nape or back of the neck

nackt a naked; (bloß, kahl) bare; (Wahrheit) plain. **N~baden** nt nude bathing. **N~heit** f - nakedness, nudity. **N~kultur** f nudism. **N~schnecke** f slug
Nadel f -,-n needle; (Häkel-) hook; (Schmuck-, Hut-) pin. **N~arbeit** f needlework. **N~baum** m conifer. **N~kissen** nt pincushion. **N~stich** m stitch; (fig) pinprick. **N~wald** m coniferous forest
Nagel m -s," nail. **N~bürste** f nailbrush. **N~feile** f nail-file. **N~haut** f cuticle. **N~lack** m nail varnish. **n~n** vt nail. **n~neu** a brand-new. **N~schere** f nail scissors pl
nagen vt/i (haben) gnaw (**an** + dat at); **n~d** (fig) nagging
Nagetier nt rodent
nah a, adv & prep = **nahe; von nah und fern** from far and wide
Näharbeit f sewing; **eine N~** a piece of sewing
Nahaufnahme f close-up
nahe a (näher, nächst) nearby; (zeitlich) imminent; (eng) close; **der N~ Osten** the Middle East; **in n~r Zukunft** in the near future; **von n~m** [from] close to; **n~ sein** be close (dat to); **den Tränen n~** close to tears ● adv near, close; (verwandt) closely; **n~ an** (+ acc/dat) near [to], close to; **n~ daran sein, etw zu tun** nearly do sth; **jdm zu n~ treten** (fig) offend s.o. ● prep (+ dat) near [to], close to
Nähe f - nearness, proximity; **aus der N~** [from] close to; **in der N~** near or close by; **in der N~ der Kirche** near the church
nahebei adv near or close by
nahe|gehen† vi sep (sein) **jdm n~gehen** (fig) affect s.o. deeply. **n~kommen**† vi sep (sein) (fig) come close (dat to); (vertraut werden) get close (dat to). **n~legen** vt sep recommend (dat to); **jdm n~legen, etw zu tun** urge s.o. to do sth. **n~liegen**† vi sep (haben) (fig) be highly likely. **n~liegend** a obvious
nahen vi (sein) (liter) approach
nähen vt/i (haben) sew; (anfertigen) make; (Med) stitch [up]
näher a closer; (Weg) shorter; (Einzelheiten) further ● adv closer; (genauer) more closely; **sich n~ erkundigen** make further enquiries; **n~ an** (+ acc/dat) nearer [to], closer to ● prep (+ dat) nearer [to], closer to.

N~e[s] *nt* [further] details *pl.* **n~kommen**† *vi sep (sein)* come closer, approach; *(fig)* get closer (*dat* to). **n~n (sich)** *vr* approach

nahestehen† *vi sep (haben) (fig)* be close (*dat* to)

nahezu *adv* almost

Nähgarn *nt* [sewing] cotton

Nahkampf *m* close combat

Näh|maschine *f* sewing machine. **N~nadel** *f* sewing-needle

nähren *vt* feed; *(fig)* nurture; **sich n~ von** live on ● *vi (haben)* be nutritious

nahrhaft *a* nutritious

Nährstoff *m* nutrient

Nahrung *f* -, food, nourishment. **N~smittel** *nt* food

Nährwert *m* nutritional value

Naht *f* -,ä̈e seam; *(Med)* suture. **n~los** *a* seamless

Nahverkehr *m* local service. **N~szug** *m* local train

Nähzeug *nt* sewing; *(Zubehör)* sewing kit

naiv /na'iːf/ *a* naïve, *adv* -ly. **N~ität** /-viˈtɛːt/ *f* - naïvety

Name *m* -ns,-n name; **im N~n** (+ *gen*) in the name of; *(handeln)* on behalf of; **das Kind beim rechten N~n nennen** *(fam)* call a spade a spade. **n~nlos** *a* nameless; *(unbekannt)* unknown, anonymous. **n~ns** *adv* by the name of ● *prep* (+ *gen*) on behalf of. **N~nstag** *m* name-day. **N~nsvetter** *m* namesake. **N~nszug** *m* signature. **n~ntlich** *adv* by name; *(besonders)* especially

namhaft *a* noted; *(ansehnlich)* considerable; **n~ machen** name

nämlich *adv* (*und zwar*) namely; *(denn)* because

nanu *int* hallo

Napf *m* -[e]s,ä̈e bowl

Narbe *f* -,-n scar

Narkose *f* -,-n general anaesthetic. **N~arzt** *m* anaesthetist. **N~mittel** *nt* anaesthetic

Narkot|ikum *nt* -s,-ka narcotic; *(Narkosemittel)* anaesthetic. **n~isieren** *vt* anaesthetize

Narr *m* -en,-en fool; **zum N~en haben** *od* **halten** make a fool of. **n~en** *vt* fool. **n~ensicher** *a* foolproof. **N~heit** *f* -,-en folly

Närr|in *f* -,-nen fool. **n~isch** *a* foolish; *(fam: verrückt)* crazy (**auf** + *acc* about)

Narzisse *f* -,-n narcissus; **gelbe N~** daffodil

nasal *a* nasal

nasch|en *vt/i (haben)* nibble (**an** + *dat* at); **wer hat vom Kuchen genascht?** who's been at the cake? **n~haft** *a* sweet-toothed

Nase *f* -,-n nose; **an der N~ herumführen** *(fam)* dupe

näseln *vi (haben)* speak through one's nose; **n~d** nasal

Nasen|bluten *nt* -s nosebleed. **N~loch** *nt* nostril. **N~rücken** *m* bridge of the nose

Naseweis *m* -es,-e *(fam)* know-all

Nashorn *nt* rhinoceros

naß *a* (**nasser, nassest**) wet

Nässe *f* - wet; *(Naßsein)* wetness. **n~n** *vt* wet

naßkalt *a* cold and wet

Nation /na'tsjoːn/ *f* -,-en nation. **n~al** *a* national. **N~alhymne** *f* national anthem. **N~alismus** *m* - nationalism. **N~alität** *f* -,-en nationality. **N~alsozialismus** *m* National Socialism. **N~alspieler** *m* international

Natrium *nt* -s sodium

Natron *nt* -s **doppeltkohlensaures N~** bicarbonate of soda

Natter *f* -,-n snake; *(Gift-)* viper

Natur *f* -,-en nature; **von N~ aus** by nature. **N~alien** /-jən/ *pl* natural produce *sg.* **n~alisieren** *vt* naturalize. **N~alisierung** *f* -,-en naturalization

Naturell *nt* -s,-e disposition

Natur|erscheinung *f* natural phenomenon. **n~farben** *a* natural-coloured. **N~forscher** *m* naturalist. **N~kunde** *f* natural history. **N~lehrpfad** *m* nature trail

natürlich *a* natural ● *adv* naturally; *(selbstverständlich)* of course. **N~keit** *f* - naturalness

natur|rein *a* pure. **N~schutz** *m* nature conservation; **unter N~schutz stehen** be protected. **N~schutzgebiet** *nt* nature reserve. **N~wissenschaft** *f* [natural] science. **N~wissenschaftler** *m* scientist. **n~wissenschaftlich** *a* scientific; *(Sch)* science ...

nautisch *a* nautical

Navigation /-'tsjoːn/ *f* - navigation

Nazi *m* -s,-s Nazi

n.Chr. *abbr* (**nach Christus**) AD

Nebel *m* **-s,-** fog; (*leicht*) mist. **n∼haft** *a* hazy. **N∼horn** *nt* fog-horn. **n∼ig** *a* = **neblig**

neben *prep* (+ *dat/acc*) next to, beside; (+ *dat*) (*außer*) apart from; **n∼ mir** next to me. **n∼an** *adv* next door

Neben|anschluß *m* (*Teleph*) extension. **N∼ausgaben** *fpl* incidental expenses

nebenbei *adv* in addition; (*beiläufig*) casually; **n∼ bemerkt** incidentally

Neben|bemerkung *f* passing remark. **N∼beruf** *m* second job. **N∼beschäftigung** *f* spare-time occupation. **N∼buhler(in)** *m* **-s,-** (*f* **-,-nen**) rival

nebeneinander *adv* next to each other, side by side

Neben|eingang *m* side entrance. **N∼fach** *nt* (*Univ*) subsidiary subject. **N∼fluß** *m* tributary. **N∼gleis** *nt* siding. **N∼haus** *nt* house next door

nebenher *adv* in addition. **n∼ gehen**† *vi sep* (*sein*) walk alongside **nebenhin** *adv* casually

Neben|höhle *f* sinus. **N∼kosten** *pl* additional costs. **N∼mann** *m* (*pl* **-männer**) person next to one. **N∼ produkt** *nt* by-product. **N∼rolle** *f* supporting role; (*kleine*) minor role; **eine N∼rolle spielen** (*fig*) be unimportant. **N∼sache** *f* unimportant matter. **n∼sächlich** *a* unimportant. **N∼satz** *m* subordinate clause. **N∼ straße** *f* minor road; (*Seiten-*) side street. **N∼verdienst** *m* additional earnings *pl*. **N∼wirkung** *f* sideeffect. **N∼zimmer** *nt* room next door

neblig *a* foggy; (*leicht*) misty

nebst *prep* (+ *dat*) [together] with

Necessaire /nesɛˈsɛːɐ̯/ *nt* **-s,-s** toilet bag; (*Näh-, Nagel-*) set

neck|en *vt* tease. **N∼erei** *f* **-** teasing. **n∼isch** *a* teasing; (*keß*) saucy

nee *adv* (*fam*) no

Neffe *m* **-n,-n** nephew

negativ *a* negative. **N∼** *nt* **-s,-e** (*Phot*) negative

Neger *m* **-s,-** Negro

nehmen† *vt* take (*dat* from); **sich** (*dat*) **etw n∼** take sth; help oneself to ⟨*Essen*⟩; **jdn zu sich n∼** have s.o. to live with one

Neid *m* **-[e]s** envy, jealousy. **n∼en** *vt* **jdm den Erfolg n∼en** be jealous of

s.o.'s success. **n∼isch** *a* envious, jealous (**auf** + *acc* of); **auf jdn n∼isch sein** envy s.o.

neig|en *vt* incline; (*zur Seite*) tilt; (*beugen*) bend; **sich n∼en** incline; ⟨*Boden:*⟩ slope; ⟨*Person:*⟩ bend (**über** + *acc* over) ● *vi* (*haben*) **n∼en zu** (*fig*) have a tendency towards; be prone to ⟨*Krankheit*⟩; incline towards ⟨*Ansicht*⟩; **dazu n∼en, etw zu tun** tend to do sth. **N∼ung** *f* **-,-en** inclination; (*Gefälle*) slope; (*fig*) tendency; (*Hang*) leaning; (*Herzens-*) affection

nein *adv*, **N∼** *nt* **-s** no

Nektar *m* **-s** nectar

Nelke *f* **-,-n** carnation; (*Feder-*) pink; (*Culin*) clove

nenn|en† *vt* call; (*taufen*) name; (*angeben*) give; (*erwähnen*) mention; **sich n∼en** call oneself. **n∼enswert** *a* significant. **N∼ung** *f* **-,-en** mention; (*Sport*) entry. **N∼wert** *m* face value

Neofaschismus *m* neofascism

Neon *nt* **-s** neon. **N∼beleuchtung** *f* fluorescent lighting

neppen *vt* (*fam*) rip off

Nerv *m* **-s,-en** /-fən/ nerve; **die N∼en verlieren** lose control of oneself. **n∼en** *vt* **jdn n∼en** (*sl*) get on s.o.'s nerves. **N∼enarzt** *m* neurologist. **n∼enaufreibend** *a* nerve-racking. **N∼enbündel** *nt* (*fam*) bundle of nerves. **N∼enkitzel** *m* (*fam*) thrill. **N∼ensystem** *nt* nervous system. **N∼enzusammenbruch** *m* nervous breakdown

nervös *a* nervy, edgy; (*Med*) nervous; **n∼ sein** be on edge

Nervosität *f* **-** nerviness, edginess

Nerz *m* **-es,-e** mink

Nessel *f* **-,-n** nettle

Nest *nt* **-[e]s,-er** nest; (*fam: Ort*) small place

nesteln *vi* (*haben*) fumble (**an** + *dat* with)

Nesthäkchen *nt* **-s,-** (*fam*) baby of the family

nett *a* nice, *adv* -ly; (*freundlich*) kind, *adv* -ly

netto *adv* net. **N∼gewicht** *nt* net weight

Netz *nt* **-es,-e** net; (*Einkaufs-*) string bag; (*Spinnen-*) web; (*auf Landkarte*) grid; (*System*) network; (*Electr*) mains *pl*. **N∼haut** *f* retina. **N∼karte** *f* area season-ticket. **N∼werk** *nt* network

neu *a* new; (*modern*) modern; **wie neu** as good as new; **das ist mir neu** it's news to me; **aufs n~e** [once] again; **von n~em** all over again ● *adv* newly; (*gerade erst*) only just; (*erneut*) again; **etw neu schreiben/streichen** rewrite/ repaint sth. **N~ankömmling** *m* **-s,-e** newcomer. **N~anschaffung** *f* recent acquisition. **n~artig** *a* new [kind of]. **N~auflage** *f* new edition; (*unverändert*) reprint. **N~bau** *m* (*pl* **-ten**) new house/building

Neu|e(r) *m/f* new person, newcomer; (*Schüler*) new boy/girl. **N~e(s)** *nt* **das N~e** the new; **etwas N~es** something new; (*Neuigkeit*) a piece of news; **was gibt's N~es?** what's the news?

neuer|dings *adv* [just] recently. **n~ lich** *a* renewed, new ● *adv* again. **N~ung** *f* **-,-en** innovation

neuest|e(r,s) *a* newest; (*letzte*) latest; **seit n~em** just recently. **N~e** *nt* **das N~e** the latest thing; (*Neuigkeit*) the latest news *sg*

neugeboren *a* newborn

Neugier, Neugierde *f* - curiosity; (*Wißbegierde*) inquisitiveness

neugierig *a* curious (**auf** + *acc* about), *adv* -ly; (*wißbegierig*) inquisitive, *adv* -ly

Neuheit *f* **-,-en** novelty; (*Neusein*) newness; **die letzte N~** the latest thing

Neuigkeit *f* **-,-en** piece of news; **N~en** news *sg*

Neujahr *nt* New Year's Day; **über N~** over the New Year

neulich *adv* the other day

Neu|ling *m* **-s,-e** novice. **n~modisch** *a* newfangled. **N~mond** *m* new moon

neun *inv a*, **N~** *f* **-,-en** nine. **N~mal- kluge(r)** *m* (*fam*) clever Dick. **n~te(r,s)** *a* ninth. **n~zehn** *inv a* nineteen. **n~zehnte(r,s)** *a* nine- teenth. **n~zig** *inv a* ninety. **n~zig- ste(r,s)** *a* ninetieth

Neuralgie *f* **-,-n** neuralgia

neureich *a* nouveau riche

Neurologe *m* **-n,-n** neurologist

Neuro|se *f* **-,-n** neurosis. **n~tisch** *a* neurotic

Neuschnee *m* fresh snow

Neuseeland *nt* **-s** New Zealand

neuste(r,s) *a* = **neueste(r,s)**

neutral *a* neutral. **n~isieren** *vt* neutralize. **N~ität** *f* - neutrality

Neutrum *nt* **-s,-tra** neuter noun

neu|vermählt *a* **n~vermähltes Paar** newly-weds *pl*. **N~zeit** *f* modern times *pl*

nicht *adv* not; **ich kann n~** I cannot *or* can't; **er ist n~ gekommen** he hasn't come; **n~ mehr/besser als** no more/ better than; **bitte n~!** please don't! **n~ berühren!** do not touch! **du kommst doch auch, ~ [wahr]?** you are coming too, aren't you? **du kennst ihn doch, n~?** you know him, don't you?

Nichtachtung *f* disregard; (*Ge- ringschätzung*) disdain

Nichte *f* **-,-n** niece

nichtig *a* trivial; (*Jur*) [null and] void

Nichtraucher *m* non-smoker. **N~ abteil** *nt* non-smoking compartment

nichts *pron* & *a* nothing; **n~ ande- res/Besseres** nothing else/better; **n~ mehr** no more; **ich weiß n~** I know nothing *or* don't know anything. **N~** *nt* - nothingness; (*fig: Leere*) void; (*Person*) nonentity. **n~ahnend** *a* un- suspecting

Nichtschwimmer *m* non-swimmer

nichtsdesto|trotz *adv* all the same. **n~weniger** *adv* nevertheless

nichts|nutzig *a* good-for-nothing; (*fam: unartig*) naughty. **n~sagend** *a* meaningless; (*uninteressant*) non- descript. **N~tun** *nt* **-s** idleness

Nickel *nt* **-s** nickel

nicken *vi* (*haben*) nod. **N~** *nt* **-s** nod

Nickerchen *nt* **-s,-** (*fam*) nap; **ein N~ machen** have forty winks

nie *adv* never

nieder *a* low ● *adv* down. **n~ brennen†** *vt/i sep* (*sein*) burn down. **N~deutsch** *nt* Low German. **N~gang** *m* (*fig*) decline. **n~ge- drückt** *a* (*fig*) depressed. **n~gehen†** *vi sep* (*sein*) come down. **n~ge- schlagen** *a* dejected, despondent. **N~geschlagenheit** *f* - dejection, despondency. **N~kunft** *f* **-,̈e** con- finement. **N~lage** *f* defeat

Niederlande (die) *pl* the Netherlands

Niederländ|er *m* **-s,-** Dutchman; **die N~er** the Dutch *pl*. **N~erin** *f* **-,-nen** Dutchwoman. **n~isch** *a* Dutch

nieder|lassen† *vt sep* let down; **sich n~lassen** settle; (*sich setzen*) sit down. **N~lassung** *f* **-,-en** settlement; (*Zweig- stelle*) branch. **n~legen** *vt sep* put or lay down; resign (*Amt*); **die Arbeit n~legen** go on strike; **sich n~legen** lie down. **n~machen, n~metzeln** *vt sep* massacre. **n~reißen†** *vt sep* tear down. **N~sachsen** *nt* Lower Saxony. **N~schlag** *m* precipitation; (*Regen*) rainfall; (*radioaktiver*) fall-out; (*Boxen*) knock-down. **n~schlagen**† *vt sep* knock down; lower ⟨*Augen*⟩; (*unterdrücken*) crush. **n~schmettern** *vt sep* (*fig*) shatter. **n~schreiben**† *vt sep* write down. **n~schreien**† *vt sep* shout down. **n~setzen** *vt sep* put *or* set down; **sich n~setzen** sit down. **n~strecken** *vt sep* fell; (*durch Schuß*) gun down

niederträchtig *a* base, vile

Niederung *f* -,-en low ground

nieder|walzen *vt sep* flatten. **n~werfen**† *vt sep* throw down; (*unterdrücken*) crush; **sich n~werfen** prostrate oneself

niedlich *a* pretty; (*goldig*) sweet; (*Amer*) cute

niedrig *a* low; (*fig: gemein*) base ● *adv* low

niemals *adv* never

niemand *pron* nobody, no one

Niere *f* -,-n kidney; **künstliche N~** kidney machine

niesel|n *vi* (*haben*) drizzle; **es n~t** it is drizzling. **N~regen** *m* drizzle

niesen *vi* (*haben*) sneeze. **N~** *nt* -s sneezing; (*Nieser*) sneeze

Niet *m & nt* -[e]s,-e, **Niete**[1] *f* -,-n rivet; (*an Jeans*) stud

Niete[2] *f* -,-n blank; (*fam*) failure

nieten *vt* rivet

Nikotin *nt* -s nicotine

Nil *m* -[s] Nile. **N~pferd** *nt* hippopotamus

nimmer *adv* (*SGer*) not any more; **nie und n~** never. **n~müde** *a* tireless. **n~satt** *a* insatiable. **N~wiedersehen** *nt* **auf N~wiedersehen** (*fam*) for good

nippen *vi* (*haben*) take a sip (**an** + *dat* of)

nirgend|s, n~wo *adv* nowhere

Nische *f* -,-n recess, niche

nisten *vi* (*haben*) nest

Nitrat *nt* -[e]s,-e nitrate

Niveau /ni'voː/ *nt* -s,-s level; (*geistig, künstlerisch*) standard

nix *adv* (*fam*) nothing

Nixe *f* -,-n mermaid

nobel *a* noble; (*fam: luxuriös*) luxurious; (*fam: großzügig*) generous

noch *adv* still; (*zusätzlich*) as well; (*mit Komparativ*) even; **n~ nicht** not yet; **gerade n~** only just; **n~ immer** *od* **immer n~** still; **n~ letzte Woche** only last week; **es ist n~ viel Zeit** there's plenty of time yet; **wer/was/** **wo n~?** who/what/where else? **n~ jemand/etwas** someone/something else; (*Frage*) anyone/anything else? **n~ einmal** again; **n~ ein Bier** another beer; **n~ größer** even bigger; **n~ so sehr/schön** however much/beautiful ● *conj* **weder ... n~** neither ... nor

nochmal|ig *a* further. **n~s** *adv* again

Nomad|e *m* -n,-n nomad. **n~isch** *a* nomadic

Nominativ *m* -s,-e nominative

nominell *a* nominal, *adv* -ly

nominier|en *vt* nominate. **N~ung** *f* -,-en nomination

nonchalant /nōʃaˈlãː/ *a* nonchalant, *adv* -ly

Nonne *f* -,-n nun. **N~nkloster** *nt* convent

Nonstopflug *m* direct flight

Nord *m* -[e]s north. **N~amerika** *nt* North America. **n~deutsch** *a* North German

Norden *m* -s north; **nach N~** north

nordisch *a* Nordic

nördlich *a* northern; ⟨*Richtung*⟩ northerly ● *adv & prep* (+ *gen*) **n~ [von] der Stadt** [to the] north of the town

Nordosten *m* north-east

Nord|pol *m* North Pole. **N~see** *f* - North Sea. **n~wärts** *adv* northwards. **N~westen** *m* north-west

Nörgelei *f* -,-en grumbling

nörgeln *vi* (*haben*) grumble

Norm *f* -,-en norm; (*Techn*) standard; (*Soll*) quota

normal *a* normal, *adv* -ly. **n~erweise** *adv* normally. **n~isieren** *vt* normalize; **sich n~isieren** return to normal

normen, normieren *vt* standardize

Norwe|gen *nt* -s Norway. **N~ger(in)** *m* -s,- (*f* -,-nen) Norwegian. **n~gisch** *a* Norwegian

Nost|algie *f* - nostalgia. **n~algisch** *a* nostalgic

Not *f* -,-̈e need; (*Notwendigkeit*) necessity; (*Entbehrung*) hardship; (*seelisch*) trouble; **Not leiden** be in need, suffer hardship; **mit knapper Not** only just; **zur Not** if need be; (*äußerstenfalls*) at a pinch

Notar *m* -s,-e notary public

Not|arzt *m* emergency doctor. **N~ausgang** *m* emergency exit. **N~behelf** *m* -[e]s,-e makeshift. **N~bremse** *f* emergency brake. **N~dienst** *m* **N~dienst haben** be on call. **n~dürftig** _a_ scant; _(behelfsmäßig)_ makeshift

Note _f_ **-,-n** note; _(Zensur)_ mark; **ganze/ halbe N~** _(Mus)_ semibreve/minim, _(Amer)_ whole/half note; **N~n lesen** read music; **persönliche N~** personal touch. **N~nblatt** _nt_ sheet of music. **N~nschlüssel** _m_ clef. **N~nständer** _m_ music-stand

Notfall _m_ emergency; **im N~** in an emergency; _(notfalls)_ if need be; **für den N~** just in case. **n~s** _adv_ if need be

not|gedrungen _adv_ of necessity. **N~groschen** _m_ nest-egg

notieren _vt_ note down; _(Comm)_ quote; **sich** _(dat)_ **etw n~** make a note of sth

nötig _a_ necessary; **n~ haben** need; **das N~ste** the essentials _pl_ ● _adv_ urgently. **n~en** _vt_ force; _(auffordern)_ press; **laßt euch nicht n~en** help yourselves. **n~enfalls** _adv_ if need be. **N~ung** _f_ -coercion

Notiz _f_ **-,-en** note; _(Zeitungs-)_ item; **[keine] N~ nehmen von** take [no] notice of. **N~buch** _nt_ notebook. **N~-kalender** _m_ diary

Not|lage _f_ plight. **n~landen** _vi (sein)_ make a forced landing. **N~landung** _f_ forced landing. **n~-leidend** _a_ needy. **N~lösung** _f_ stopgap. **N~lüge** _f_ white lie

notorisch _a_ notorious

Not|ruf _m_ emergency call; _(Naut, Aviat)_ distress call; _(Nummer)_ emergency services number. **N~signal** _nt_ distress signal. **N~stand** _m_ state of emergency. **N~unterkunft** _f_ emergency accommodation. **N~wehr** _f_ -_(Jur)_ self-defence

notwendig _a_ necessary; _(unerläßlich)_ essential ● _adv_ urgently. **N~keit** _f_ -,-en necessity

Notzucht _f_ - _(Jur)_ rape

Nougat /'nu:gat/ _m_ & _nt_ **-s** nougat

Novelle _f_ **-,-n** novella; _(Pol)_ amendment

November _m_ **-s,-** November

Novität _f_ **-,-en** novelty

Novize _m_ **-n,-n**, **Novizin** _f_ **-,-nen** _(Relig)_ novice

Nu _m_ **im Nu** _(fam)_ in a flash

Nuance /'nyิ̃ã:sə/ _f_ **-,-n** nuance; _(Spur)_ shade

nüchtern _a_ sober; _(sachlich)_ matter-of-fact; _(schmucklos)_ bare; _(ohne_ _Würze)_ bland; **auf n~en Magen** on an empty stomach ● _adv_ soberly

Nudel _f_ **-,-n** piece of pasta; **N~n** pasta _sg_; _(Band-)_ noodles. **N~holz** _nt_ rolling-pin

Nudist _m_ **-en,-en** nudist

nuklear _a_ nuclear

null _inv_ _a_ zero, nought; _(Teleph)_ 0; _(Sport)_ nil; _(Tennis)_ love; **n~ Fehler** no mistakes; **n~ und nichtig** _(Jur)_ null and void. **N~** _f_ **-,-en** nought, zero; _(fig: Person)_ nonentity; **drei Grad unter N~** three degrees below zero. **N~punkt** _m_ zero

numerieren _vt_ number

numerisch _a_ numerical

Nummer _f_ **-,-n** number; _(Ausgabe)_ issue; _(Darbietung)_ item; _(Zirkus-)_ act; _(Größe)_ size. **N~nschild** _nt_ number-/ _(Amer)_ license-plate

nun _adv_ now; _(na)_ well; _(halt)_ just; **von nun an** from now on; **nun gut!** very well then! **das Leben ist nun mal so** life's like that

nur _adv_ only, just; **wo kann sie nur sein?** wherever can she be? **alles, was ich nur will** everything I could possibly want; **er soll es nur versuchen!** _(drohend)_ just let him try! **könnte/ hätte ich nur …!** if only I could/had …! **nur Geduld!** just be patient!

Nürnberg _nt_ **-s** Nuremberg

nuscheln _vt/i (haben)_ mumble

Nuß _f_ **-, Nüsse** nut. **N~baum** _m_ walnut tree. **N~knacker** _m_ **-s,-** nutcrackers _pl_. **N~schale** _f_ nutshell

Nüstern _fpl_ nostrils

Nut _f_ **-,-en**, **Nute** _f_ **-,-n** groove

Nutte _f_ **-,-n** _(sl)_ tart _(sl)_

nutz|bar _a_ usable; **n~bar machen** utilize; cultivate ⟨_Boden_⟩. **n~-bringend** _a_ profitable, _adv_ -bly

nütze _a_ **zu etwas/nichts n~ sein** be useful/useless

nutzen _vt_ use, utilize; _(aus-)_ take advantage of ● _vi (haben)_ = **nützen**. **N~** _m_ **-s** benefit; _(Comm)_ profit; **N~ ziehen aus** benefit from; **von N~ sein** be useful

nützen _vi (haben)_ be useful _or_ of use _(dat_ to); ⟨_Mittel:_⟩ be effective; **nichts n~** be useless _or_ no use; **was nützt mir das?** what good is that to me? ● _vt_ = **nutzen**

Nutzholz _nt_ timber

nützlich _a_ useful; **sich n~ machen** make oneself useful. **N~keit** _f_ - usefulness

nutz|los *a* useless; (*vergeblich*) vain. **N~losigkeit** *f* - uselessness. **N~nießer** *m* **-s,-** beneficiary. **N~ung** *f* - use, utilization
Nylon /'nailɔn/ *nt* **-s** nylon
Nymphe /'nʏmfə/ *f* **-,-n** nymph

O

o *int* **o ja/nein!** oh yes/no! **o weh!** oh dear!
Oase *f* **-,-n** oasis
ob *conj* whether; **ob reich, ob arm** rich or poor; **ob sie wohl krank ist?** I wonder whether she is ill; **und ob!** (*fam*) you bet!
Obacht *f* **O~ geben** pay attention; **O~ geben auf** (+ *acc*) look after; **O~!** look out!
Obdach *nt* **-[e]s** shelter. **o~los** *a* homeless. **O~lose(r)** *m/f* homeless person; **die O~losen** the homeless *pl*
Obduktion /-'tsio:n/ *f* **-,-en** postmortem
O-Beine *ntpl* (*fam*) bow-legs, bandy legs. **O-beinig** *a* bandy-legged
oben *adv* at the top; (*auf der Oberseite*) on top; (*eine Treppe hoch*) upstairs; **da o~** up there; **o~ im Norden** up in the north; **siehe o~** see above; **o~ auf** (+ *acc/dat*) on top of; **nach o~** up[wards]; (*die Treppe hinauf*) upstairs; **von o~** from above/upstairs; **von o~ bis unten** from top to bottom/ ⟨*Person*⟩ to toe; **jdn von o~ bis unten mustern** look s.o. up and down. **o~an** *adv* at the top. **o~auf** *adv* on top; **o~auf sein** (*fig*) be cheerful. **o~drein** *adv* on top of that. **o~erwähnt, o~genannt** *a* above-mentioned. **o~hin** *adv* casually
Ober *m* **-s,-** waiter
Ober|arm *m* upper arm. **O~arzt** *m* ≈ senior registrar. **O~befehlshaber** *m* commander-in-chief. **O~begriff** *m* generic term. **O~deck** *nt* upper deck. **o~e(r,s)** *a* upper; (*höhere*) higher. **O~fläche** *f* surface. **o~flächlich** *a* superficial, *adv* -ly. **O~geschoß** *nt* upper storey. **o~halb** *adv* & *prep* (+ *gen*) above; **o~halb vom Dorf/des Dorfes** above the village. **O~hand** *f* **die O~hand gewinnen** gain the upper hand. **O~haupt** *nt* (*fig*) head. **O~haus** *nt* (*Pol*) upper house; (*in UK*) House of Lords. **O~hemd** *nt* [man's] shirt

Oberin *f* **-,-nen** matron; (*Relig*) mother superior
ober|irdisch *a* surface ... ● *adv* above ground. **O~kellner** *m* head waiter. **O~kiefer** *m* upper jaw. **O~körper** *m* upper part of the body. **O~leutnant** *m* lieutenant. **O~licht** *nt* overhead light; (*Fenster*) skylight; (*über Tür*) fanlight. **O~lippe** *f* upper lip
Obers *nt* - (*Aust*) cream
Ober|schenkel *m* thigh. **O~schicht** *f* upper class. **O~schule** *f* grammar school. **O~schwester** *f* (*Med*) sister. **O~seite** *f* upper-/(*rechte Seite*) right side
Oberst *m* **-en** & **-s,-en** colonel
oberste(r,s) *a* top; (*höchste*) highest; ⟨*Befehlshaber, Gerichtshof*⟩ supreme; (*wichtigste*) first
Ober|stimme *f* treble. **O~stufe** *f* upper school. **O~teil** *nt* top. **O~weite** *f* chest-/(*der Frau*) bust size
obgleich *conj* although
Obhut *f* - care; **in guter O~ sein** be well looked after
obig *a* above
Objekt *nt* **-[e]s,-e** object; (*Haus, Grundstück*) property; **O~ der Forschung** subject of research
Objektiv *nt* **-s,-e** lens. **o~** *a* objective, *adv* -ly. **O~ität** *f* - objectivity
Oblate *f* **-,-n** (*Relig*) wafer
obliga|t *a* (*fam*) inevitable. **O~tion** /-'tsio:n/ *f* **-,-en** obligation; (*Comm*) bond. **o~torisch** *a* obligatory
Obmann *m* (*pl* **-männer**) [jury] foreman; (*Sport*) referee
Oboe /o'bo:ə/ *f* **-,-n** oboe
Obrigkeit *f* - authorities *pl*
obschon *conj* although
Observatorium *nt* **-s,-ien** observatory
obskur *a* obscure; (*zweifelhaft*) dubious
Obst *nt* **-es** (*coll*) fruit. **O~baum** *m* fruit-tree. **O~garten** *m* orchard. **O~händler** *m* fruiterer. **O~kuchen** *m* fruit flan. **O~salat** *m* fruit salad
obszön *a* obscene. **O~ität** *f* **-,-en** obscenity
O-Bus *m* trolley bus
obwohl *conj* although
Ochse *m* **-n,-n** ox. **o~n** *vi* (*haben*) (*fam*) swot. **O~nschwanzsuppe** *f* oxtail soup

öde *a* desolate; (*unfruchtbar*) barren; (*langweilig*) dull. **Öde** *f* - desolation; barrenness; dullness; (*Gegend*) waste

oder *conj* or; **du kennst ihn doch, o∼?** you know him, don't you?

Ofen *m* **-s,** stove; (*Heiz-*) heater; (*Back-*) oven; (*Techn*) furnace

offen *a* open, *adv* -ly; (*Haar*) loose; (*Flamme*) naked; (*o∼herzig*) frank, *adv* -ly; (*o∼ gezeigt*) overt, *adv* -ly; (*unentschieden*) unsettled; **o∼e Stelle** vacancy; **Tag der o∼en Tür** open day; **Wein o∼ verkaufen** sell wine by the glass; *adv* **o∼ gesagt** *od* **gestanden** to be honest. **o∼bar** *a* obvious ● *adv* apparently. **o∼baren** *vt* reveal. **O∼barung** *f* **-,-en** revelation. **o∼bleiben†** *vi sep* (*sein*) remain open. **o∼halten†** *vt sep* hold open (*Tür*); keep open (*Mund, Augen*). **O∼heit** *f* - frankness, openness. **o∼herzig** *a* frank, *adv* -ly. **O∼herzigkeit** *f* - frankness. **o∼kundig** *a* manifest, *adv* -ly. **o∼lassen†** *vt sep* leave open; leave vacant (*Stelle*). **o∼sichtlich** *a* obvious, *adv* -ly

offensiv *a* offensive. **O∼e** *f* **-,-n** offensive

offenstehen† *vi sep* (*haben*) be open; (*Rechnung:*) be outstanding; **jdm o∼** (*fig*) be open to s.o.

öffentlich *a* public, *adv* -ly. **Ö∼keit** *f* - public; **an die Ö∼keit gelangen** become public; **in aller Ö∼keit** in public, publicly

Offerte *f* **-,-n** (*Comm*) offer

offiziell *a* official, *adv* -ly

Offizier *m* **-s,-e** (*Mil*) officer

öffnen *vt/i* (*haben*) open; **sich ö∼en** open. **Ö∼er** *m* **-s,-** opener. **Ö∼ung** *f* **-,-en** opening. **Ö∼ungszeiten** *fpl* opening hours

oft *adv* often

öfter *adv* quite often. **ö∼e(r,s)** *a* frequent; **des ö∼en** frequently. **ö∼s** *adv* (*fam*) quite often

oftmals *adv* often

oh *int* oh!

ohne *prep* (+ *acc*) without; **o∼ mich!** count me out! **oben o∼** topless; **nicht o∼ sein** (*fam*) be not bad; (*nicht harmlos*) be quite nasty ● *conj* **o∼ zu überlegen** without thinking; **o∼ daß ich es merkte** without my noticing it. **o∼dies** *adv* anyway. **o∼gleichen** *pred a* unparalleled; **eine Frechheit o∼gleichen** a piece of unprecedented insolence. **o∼hin** *adv* anyway

Ohn|macht *f* **-,-en** faint; (*fig*) powerlessness; **in O∼macht fallen** faint. **o∼mächtig** *a* unconscious; (*fig*) powerless; **o∼mächtig werden** faint

Ohr *nt* **-[e]s,-en** ear; **übers Ohr hauen** (*fam*) cheat

Öhr *nt* **-[e]s,-e** eye

ohren|betäubend *a* deafening. **O∼schmalz** *nt* ear-wax. **O∼schmerzen** *mpl* earache *sg*. **O∼sessel** *m* wing-chair. **O∼tropfen** *mpl* ear drops

Ohrfeige *f* slap in the face; **jdm eine O∼ geben** slap s.o.'s face. **o∼n** *vt* **jdn o∼n** slap s.o.'s face

Ohr|läppchen *nt* **-s,-** ear-lobe. **O∼ring** *m* ear-ring. **O∼wurm** *m* earwig

oje *int* oh dear!

okay /o'ke:/ *a & adv* (*fam*) OK

okkult *a* occult

Öko|logie *f* - ecology. **ö∼logisch** *a* ecological. **Ö∼nomie** *f* - economy; (*Wissenschaft*) economics *sg*. **ö∼nomisch** *a* economic; (*sparsam*) economical

Oktave *f* **-,-n** octave

Oktober *m* **-s,-** October

Okular *nt* **-s,-e** eyepiece

okulieren *vt* graft

ökumenisch *a* ecumenical

Öl *nt* **-[e]s,-e** oil; **in Öl malen** paint in oils. **Ölbaum** *m* olive-tree. **ölen** *vt* oil; **wie ein geölter Blitz** (*fam*) like greased lightning. **Ölfarbe** *f* oil-paint. **Ölfeld** *nt* oilfield. **Ölgemälde** *nt* oil-painting. **ölig** *a* oily

Olive *f* **-,-n** olive. **O∼enöl** *nt* olive oil. **o∼grün** *a* olive[-green]

oll *a* (*fam*) old; (*fam: häßlich*) nasty

Ölmeßstab *m* dip-stick. **Ölsardinen** *fpl* sardines in oil. **Ölstand** *m* oil-level. **Öltanker** *m* oil-tanker. **Ölteppich** *m* oil-slick

Olympiade *f* **-,-n** Olympic Games *pl*, Olympics *pl*

Olymp|iasieger(in) /o'lympia-/ *m(f)* Olympic champion. **o∼isch** *a* Olympic; **O∼ische Spiele** Olympic Games

Ölzeug *nt* oilskins *pl*

Oma *f* **-,-s** (*fam*) granny

Omelett *nt* **-[e]s,-e** & **-s** omelette

Omen *nt* **-s,-** omen

ominös *a* ominous

Omnibus *m* bus; (*Reise-*) coach

onanieren *vi* (*haben*) masturbate

Onkel *m* **-s,-** uncle

Opa *m* **-s,-s** (*fam*) grandad

Opal *m* **-s,-e** opal

Oper *f* **-,-n** opera

Operation /-'tsi̯o:n/ *f* **-,-en** operation. **O~ssaal** *m* operating-theatre

Operette *f* **-,-n** operetta

operieren *vt* operate on ⟨*Patient, Herz*⟩; **sich o~ lassen** have an operation.● *vi (haben)* operate

Opern|glas *nt* opera-glasses *pl*. **O~haus** *nt* opera-house. **O~sänger(in)** *m(f)* opera-singer

Opfer *nt* **-s,-** sacrifice; (*eines Unglücks*) victim; **ein O~ bringen** make a sacrifice; **jdm/etw zum O~ fallen** fall victim to s.o./sth. **o~n** *vt* sacrifice. **O~ung** *f* **-,-en** sacrifice

Opium *nt* **-s** opium

opponieren *vi (haben)* **o~ gegen** oppose

Opportunist *m* **-en,-en** opportunist. **o~isch** *a* opportunist

Opposition /-'tsi̯o:n/ *f* **-** opposition. **O~spartei** *f* opposition party

Optik *f* **-** optics *sg*; (*fam: Objektiv*) lens. **O~er** *m* **-s,-** optician

optimal *a* optimum

Optimis|mus *m* **-** optimism. **O~t** *m* **-en,-en** optimist. **o~tisch** *a* optimistic, *adv* -ally

Optimum *nt* **-s,-ma** optimum

Option /ɔp'tsi̯o:n/ *f* **-,-en** option

optisch *a* optical; ⟨*Eindruck*⟩ visual

Orakel *nt* **-s,-** oracle

Orange /o'rã:ʒə/ *f* **-,-n** orange. **o~** *inv a* orange. **O~ade** /orã'ʒa:də/ *f* **-,-n** orangeade. **O~nmarmelade** *f* [orange] marmalade. **O~nsaft** *m* orange juice

Oratorium *nt* **-s,-ien** oratorio

Orchest|er /ɔr'kɛstɐ/ *nt* **-s,-** orchestra. **o~rieren** *vt* orchestrate

Orchidee /ɔrçi'de:ə/ *f* **-,-n** orchid

Orden *m* **-s,-** (*Ritter-, Kloster-*) order; (*Auszeichnung*) medal, decoration; **jdm einen O~ verleihen** decorate s.o. **O~stracht** *f* (*Relig*) habit

ordentlich *a* neat, tidy; (*anständig*) respectable; (*ordnungsgemäß, fam: richtig*) proper; ⟨*Mitglied, Versammlung*⟩ ordinary; (*fam: gut*) decent; (*fam: gehörig*) good ● *adv* neatly, tidily; respectably; properly; (*fam: gut, gehörig*) well; (*sehr*) very; (*regelrecht*) really

Order *f* **-,-s** & **-n** order

ordinär *a* common

Ordin|ation /-'tsi̯o:n/ *f* **-,-en** (*Relig*) ordination; (*Aust*) surgery. **o~ieren** *vt* (*Relig*) ordain

ordn|en *vt* put in order; (*aufräumen*) tidy; (*an-*) arrange; **sich zum Zug o~en** form a procession. **O~er** *m* **-s,-** steward; (*Akten-*) file

Ordnung *f* **-** order; **O~ halten** keep order; **O~ machen** tidy up; **in O~ bringen** put in order; (*aufräumen*) tidy; (*reparieren*) mend; (*fig*) put right; **in O~ sein** be in order; (*ordentlich sein*) be tidy; (*fig*) be all right; **ich bin mit dem Magen** *od* **mein Magen ist nicht ganz in O~** I have a slight stomach upset; **[geht] in O~!** OK! **o~sgemäß** *a* proper, *adv* -ly. **O~sstrafe** *f* (*Jur*) fine. **o~swidrig** *a* improper, *adv* -ly

Ordonnanz *f* **-,-en** (*Mil*) orderly

Organ *nt* **-s,-e** organ; (*fam: Stimme*) voice

Organi|sation /-'tsi̯o:n/ *f* **-,-en** organization. **O~sator** *m* **-s,-en** /-'to:rən/ organizer

organisch *a* organic, *adv* -ally

organisieren *vt* organize; (*fam: beschaffen*) get [hold of]

Organismus *m* **-,-men** organism; (*System*) system

Organist *m* **-en,-en** organist

Organspenderkarte *f* donor card

Orgasmus *m* **-,-men** orgasm

Orgel *f* **-,-n** (*Mus*) organ. **O~pfeife** *f* organ-pipe

Orgie /'ɔrgi̯ə/ *f* **-,-n** orgy

Orien|t /'o:ri̯ɛnt/ *m* **-s** Orient. **o~talisch** *a* Oriental

orientier|en /ori̯ɛn'ti:rən/ *vt* inform (**über** + *acc* about); **sich o~en** get one's bearings, orientate oneself; (*unterrichten*) inform oneself (**über** + *acc* about). **O~ung** *f* **-** orientation; **die O~ung verlieren** lose one's bearings

original *a* original. **O~** *nt* **-s,-e** original; (*Person*) character. **O~ität** *f* **-** originality. **O~übertragung** *f* live transmission

originell *a* original; (*eigenartig*) unusual

Orkan *m* **-s,-e** hurricane

Ornament *nt* **-[e]s,-e** ornament

Ornat *m* **-[e]s,-e** robes *pl*

Ornithologie *f* **-** ornithology

Ort *m* **-[e]s,-e** place; (*Ortschaft*) [small] town; **am Ort** locally; **am Ort des Verbrechens** at the scene of the crime; **an Ort und Stelle** in the right place; (*sofort*) on the spot. **o~en** *vt* locate

ortho|dox a orthodox. **O~graphie** f - spelling. **o~graphisch** a spelling . . . **O~päde** m **-n,-n** orthopaedic specialist. **o~pädisch** a orthopaedic
örtlich a local, adv -ly. **Ö~keit** f **-,-en** locality
Qrtschaft f **-,-en** [small] town; (Dorf) village; **geschlossene O~** (Auto) built-up area
orts|fremd a **o~fremd sein** be a stranger. **O~gespräch** nt (Teleph) local call. **O~name** m place-name. **O~sinn** m sense of direction. **O~verkehr** m local traffic. **O~zeit** f local time
Öse f **-,-n** eyelet; (Schlinge) loop; **Haken und Öse** hook and eye
Ost m **-[e]s** east. **o~deutsch** a Eastern/(Pol) East German
Osten m **-s** east; **nach O~** east
ostentativ a pointed, adv -ly
Osteopath m **-en,-en** osteopath
Oster|ei /'o:stɐ⁹aj/ nt Easter egg. **O~fest** nt Easter. **O~glocke** f daffodil. **O~montag** m Easter Monday. **O~n** nt **-,-** Easter; **frohe O~n!** happy Easter!
Österreich nt **-s** Austria. **Ö~er** m **-s,-,** **Ö~erin** f **-,-nen** Austrian. **ö~isch** a Austrian
östlich a eastern; ⟨Richtung⟩ easterly ● adv & prep (+gen) **ö~ [von] der Stadt** [to the] east of the town
Qst|see f Baltic [Sea]. **o~wärts** adv eastwards
oszillieren vi (haben) oscillate
Qtter¹ m **-s,-** otter
Qtter² f **-,-n** adder
Ouverture /uvɛr'ty:rə/ f **-,-n** overture
oval a oval. **O~** nt **-s,-e** oval
Ovation /-'tsjo:n/ f **-,-en** ovation
Ovulation /-'tsjo:n/ f **-,-en** ovulation
Oxid, Oxyd nt **-[e]s,-e** oxide
Ozean m **-s,-e** ocean
Ozon nt **-s** ozone. **O~loch** nt hole in the ozone layer. **O~schicht** f ozone layer

P

paar pron inv **ein p~** a few; **alle p~ Tage** every few days. **P~** nt **-[e]s,-e** pair; (Ehe-, Liebes-, Tanz-) couple. **p~en** vt mate; (verbinden) combine; **sich p~en** mate. **P~ung** f **-,-en** mating. **p~weise** adv in pairs, in twos

Pacht f **-,-en** lease; (P~summe) rent. **p~en** vt lease
Pächter m **-s,-** lessee; (eines Hofes) tenant
Pachtvertrag m lease
Pack¹ m **-[e]s,-e** bundle
Pack² nt **-[e]s** (sl) rabble
Päckchen nt **-s,-** package, small packet
pack|en vt/i (haben) pack; (ergreifen) seize; (fig: fesseln) grip; **p~ dich!** (sl) beat it! **P~en** m **-s,-** bundle. **p~end** a (fig) gripping. **P~papier** nt [strong] wrapping paper. **P~ung** f **-,-en** packet; (Med) pack
Pädagog|e m **-n,-n** educationalist; (Lehrer) teacher. **P~ik** f - educational science. **p~isch** a educational
Paddel nt **-s,-** paddle. **P~boot** nt canoe. **p~n** vt/i (haben/sein) paddle. **P~sport** m canoeing
Page /'pa:ʒə/ m **-n,-n** page
Paillette /paj'jɛtə/ f **-,-n** sequin
Paket nt **-[e]s,-e** packet; (Post-) parcel
Pakist|an nt **-s** Pakistan. **P~aner(in)** m **-s,-** (f **-,-nen**) Pakistani. **p~anisch** a Pakistani
Pakt m **-[e]s,-e** pact
Palast m **-[e]s,ˆe** palace
Paläst|ina nt **-s** Palestine. **P~inenser(in)** m **-s,-** (f **-,-nen**) Palestinian. **p~inensisch** a Palestinian
Palette f **-,-n** palette
Palm|e f **-,-n** palm[-tree]; **jdn auf die P~e bringen** (fam) drive s.o. up the wall. **P~sonntag** m Palm Sunday
Pampelmuse f **-,-n** grapefruit
Panier|mehl nt (Culin) breadcrumbs pl. **p~ta** (Culin) breaded
Panik f - panic; **in P~ geraten** panic
panisch a **p~e Angst** panic
Panne f **-,-n** breakdown; (Reifen-) flat tyre; (Mißgeschick) mishap. **P~ndienst** m breakdown service
Panorama nt **-s** panorama
panschen vt adulterate ● vi (haben) splash about
Pantine f **-,-n** [wooden] clog
Pantoffel m **-s,-n** slipper; (ohne Ferse) mule. **P~held** m (fam) henpecked husband
Pantomime¹ f **-,-n** mime
Pantomime² m **-n,-n** mime artist
pantschen vt/i = **panschen**
Panzer m **-s,-** armour; (Mil) tank; (Zool) shell. **p~n** vt armour-plate. **P~schrank** m safe
Papa /'papa, pa'pa:/ m **-s,-s** daddy
Papagei m **-s** & **-en,-en** parrot

Papier nt -[e]s,-e paper. **P~korb** m waste-paper basket. **P~schlange** f streamer. **P~waren** fpl stationery sg

Pappe f - cardboard; (dial: Kleister) glue

Pappel f -,-n poplar

pappen vt/i (haben) (fam) stick

pappig a (fam) sticky

Papp|karton m, **P~schachtel** f cardboard box

Paprika m -s,-[s] [sweet] pepper; (Gewürz) paprika

Papst m -[e]s,-̈e pope

päpstlich a papal

Parade f -,-n parade

Paradeiser m -s,- (Aust) tomato

Paradies nt -es,-e paradise. **p~isch** a heavenly

Paradox nt -es,-e paradox. **p~** a paradoxical

Paraffin nt -s paraffin

Paragraph m -en,-en section

parallel a & adv parallel. **P~e** f -,-n parallel

Paranuß f Brazil nut

Parasit m -en,-en parasite

parat a ready

Pärchen nt -s,- pair; (Liebes-) couple

Parcours /par'ku:ɐ̯/ m -,- /-[s],-s/ (Sport) course

Pardon /par'dõ:/ int sorry!

Parfüm nt -s,-e & -s perfume, scent. **p~iert** a perfumed, scented

parieren[1] vt parry

parieren[2] vi (haben) (fam) obey

Parität f - parity; (in Ausschuß) equal representation

Park m -s,-s park. **p~en** vt/i (haben) park. **P~en** nt -s parking; **'P~en verboten'** 'no parking'

Parkett nt -[e]s,-e parquet floor; (Theat) stalls pl

Park|haus nt multi-storey car park. **P~lücke** f parking space. **P~platz** m car park, (Amer) parking-lot; (für ein Auto) parking space; (Autobahn-) lay-by. **P~scheibe** f parking-disc. **P~schein** m car-park ticket. **P~uhr** f parking-meter. **P~verbot** nt parking ban; **'P~verbot'** 'no parking'

Parlament nt -[e]s,-e parliament. **p~arisch** a parliamentary

Parodie f -,-n parody. **p~ren** vt parody

Parole f -,-n slogan; (Mil) password

Part m -s,-s (Theat, Mus) part

Partei f -,-en (Pol, Jur) party; (Miet-) tenant; **für jdn P~ ergreifen** take s.o.'s part. **p~isch** a biased. **p~los** a independent

Parterre /par'tɛr/ nt -s,-s ground floor, (Amer) first floor; (Theat) rear stalls pl. **p~** adv on the ground floor

Partie f -,-n part; (Tennis, Schach) game; (Golf) round; (Comm) batch; **eine gute P~ machen** marry well

Partikel[1] nt -s,- particle

Partikel[2] f -,-n (Gram) particle

Partitur f -,-en (Mus) full score

Partizip nt -s,-ien /-i̯ən/ participle; **erstes/zweites P~** present/past participle

Partner|(in) m -s,- (f -,-nen) partner. **P~schaft** f -,-en partnership. **P~stadt** f twin town

Party /'pa:ɐ̯ti/ f -,-s party

Parzelle f -,-n plot [of ground]

Paß m -sses,-̈sse passport; (Geog, Sport) pass

passabel a passable

Passage /pa'sa:ʒə/ f -,-n passage; (Einkaufs-) shopping arcade

Passagier /pasa'ʒi:ɐ̯/ m -s,-e passenger

Paßamt nt passport office

Passant(in) m -en,-en (f -,-nen) passer-by

Paßbild nt passport photograph

Passe f -,-n yoke

passen vi (haben) fit; (geeignet sein) be right (für for); (Sport) pass the ball; (aufgeben) pass; **p~ zu** go [well] with; (übereinstimmen) match; **jdm p~** fit s.o.; (gelegen sein) suit s.o.; **seine Art paßt mir nicht** I don't like his manner; **[ich] passe** pass. **p~d** a suitable; (angemessen) appropriate; (günstig) convenient; (übereinstimmend) matching

passier|bar a passable. **p~en** vt pass; cross (Grenze); (Culin) rub through a sieve ● vi (sein) happen (jdm to s.o.); **es ist ein Unglück p~t** there has been an accident. **P~schein** m pass

Passion f -,-en passion. **p~iert** a very keen (Jäger, Angler)

passiv a passive. **P~** nt -s,-e (Gram) passive

Paß|kontrolle f passport control. **P~straße** f pass

Paste f -,-n paste

Pastell nt -[e]s,-e pastel. **P~farbe** f pastel colour

Pastet|chen nt -s,- [individual] pie; (Königin-) vol-au-vent. **P~e** f -,-n pie; (Gänseleber-) pâté

pasteurisieren /pastøri'zi:rən/ vt pasteurize

Pastille f -,-n pastille

Pastinake f -,-n parsnip

Pastor m -s,-en /-'to:rən/ pastor

Pate m -n,-n godfather; (fig) sponsor; **P~n** godparents. **P~nkind** nt godchild. **P~nschaft** f - sponsorship. **P~nsohn** m godson

Patent nt -[e]s,-e patent; (Offiziers-) commission. **p~** a (fam) clever, adv -ly; (Person) resourceful. **p~ieren** vt patent

Patentochter f god-daughter

Pater m -s,- (Relig) Father

pathetisch a emotional ●adv with emotion

Patholog|e m -n,-n pathologist. **p~isch** a pathological, adv -ly

Pathos nt - emotion, feeling

Patience /pa'sjā:s/ f -,-n patience

Patient(in) /pa'tsiɛnt(m)/ m -en,-en (f -,-nen) patient

Patin f -,-nen godmother

Patriot|(in) m -en,-en (f -,-nen) patriot. **p~isch** a patriotic. **P~ismus** m - patriotism

Patrone f -,-n cartridge

Patrouille /pa'trʊljə/ f -,-n patrol. **p~ieren** /-'ji:rən/ vi (haben/sein) patrol

Patsch|e f **in der P~e sitzen** (fam) be in a jam. **p~en** vi (haben/sein) splash ●vt slap. **p~naß** a (fam) soaking wet

Patt nt -s stalemate

Pätz|er m -s,- (fam) slip. **p~ig** a (fam) insolent

Pauk|e f -,-n kettledrum; **auf die P~e hauen** (fam) have a good time; (prahlen) boast. **p~en** vt/i (haben) (fam) swot. **P~er** m -s,- (fam: Lehrer) teacher

pausbäckig a chubby-cheeked

pauschal a all-inclusive; (einheitlich) flat-rate; (fig) sweeping (Urteil); **p~e Summe** lump sum ●adv in a lump sum; (fig) wholesale. **P~e** f -,-n lump sum. **P~reise** f package tour. **P~summe** f lump sum

Pause [1] f -,-n break; (beim Sprechen) pause; (Theat) interval; (im Kino) intermission; (Mus) rest; **P~ machen** have a break

Pause [2] f -,-n tracing. **p~n** vt trace

pausenlos a incessant, adv -ly

pausieren vi (haben) have a break; (ausruhen) rest

Pauspapier nt tracing-paper

Pavian m -s,-e baboon

Pavillon /'pavɪljõ/ m -s,-s pavilion

Pazifi|k m -s Pacific [Ocean]. **p~sch** a Pacific

Pazifist m -en,-en pacifist

Pech nt -s pitch; (Unglück) bad luck; **P~ haben** be unlucky. **p~schwarz** a pitch-black; (Haare, Augen) jet-black. **P~strähne** f run of bad luck. **P~vogel** m (fam) unlucky devil

Pedal nt -s,-e pedal

Pedant m -en,-en pedant. **p~isch** a pedantic, adv -ally

Pediküre f -,-n pedicure

Pegel m -s,- level; (Gerät) water-level indicator. **P~stand** m [water] level

peilen vt take a bearing on; **über den Daumen gepeilt** (fam) at a rough guess

Pein f - (liter) torment. **p~igen** vt torment

peinlich a embarrassing, awkward; (genau) scrupulous, adv -ly; **es war mir sehr p~** I was very embarrassed

Peitsche f -,-n whip. **p~n** vt whip; (fig) lash ●vi (sein) lash (an + acc against). **P~nhieb** m lash

pekuniär a financial, adv -ly

Pelikan m -s,-e pelican

Pell|e f -,-n skin. **p~en** vt peel; shell (Ei); **sich p~en** peel. **P~kartoffeln** fpl potatoes boiled in their skins

Pelz m -es,-e fur. **P~mantel** m fur coat

Pendel nt -s,- pendulum. **p~n** vi (haben) swing ●vi (sein) commute. **P~verkehr** m shuttle-service; (für Pendler) commuter traffic

Pendler m -s,- commuter

penetrant a penetrating; (fig) obtrusive, adv -ly

penibel a fastidious, fussy; (pedantisch) pedantic

Penis m -,-se penis

Penne f -,-n (fam) school. **p~n** vi (haben) (fam) sleep. **P~r** m -s,- (sl) tramp

Pension /pã'zjo:n/ f -,-en pension; (Hotel) guest-house; **bei voller/halber P~** with full/half board. **P~är(in)** m -s,-e (f -,-nen) pensioner. **P~at** nt -[e]s,-e boarding-school. **p~ieren** vt retire. **p~iert** a retired. **P~ierung** f - retirement

Pistole *f* -,-n pistol
pitschnaß *a (fam)* soaking wet
pittoresk *a* picturesque
Pizza *f* -,-s pizza
Pkw /'pe:kave:/ *m* -s,-s (=**Personenkraftwagen**) [private] car
placieren /-'tsi:rən/ *vt* = **plazieren**
Plackerei *f* - *(fam)* drudgery
plädieren *vi (haben)* plead (**für** for); **auf Freispruch p~** *(Jur)* ask for an acquittal
Plädoyer /plɛdŏa'je:/ *nt* -s,-s *(Jur)* closing speech; *(fig)* plea
Plage *f* -,-n [hard] labour; *(Mühe)* trouble; *(Belästigung)* nuisance. **p~n** *vt* torment, plague; *(bedrängen)* pester; **sich p~n** struggle; *(arbeiten)* work hard
Plagi|at *nt* -[e]s,-e plagiarism. **p~ieren** *vt* plagiarize
Plakat *nt* -[e]s,-e poster
Plakette *f* -,-n badge
Plan *m* -[e]s,-e plan
Plane *f* -,-n tarpaulin; *(Boden-)* groundsheet
planen *vt/i (haben)* plan
Planet *m* -en,-en planet
planier|en *vt* level. **P~raupe** *f* bulldozer
Planke *f* -,-n plank
plan|los *a* unsystematic, *adv* -ally. **p~mäßig** *a* systematic; *(Ankunft)* scheduled ● *adv* systematically; *(nach Plan)* according to plan; *(ankommen)* on schedule
Plansch|becken *nt* paddling pool. **p~en** *vi (haben)* splash about
Plantage /plan'ta:ʒə/ *f* -,-n plantation
Planung *f* - planning
Plapper|maul *nt (fam)* chatterbox. **p~n** *vi (haben)* chatter ● *vt* talk *(Unsinn)*
plärren *vi (haben)* bawl; *(Radio:)* blare
Plasma *nt* -s plasma
Plastik[1] *f* -,-en sculpture
Plast|ik[2] *nt* -s plastic. **p~isch** *a* three-dimensional; *(formbar)* plastic; *(anschaulich)* graphic, *adv* -ally; **p~ische Chirurgie** plastic surgery
Platane *f* -,-n plane [tree]
Plateau /pla'to:/ *nt* -s,-s plateau
Platin *nt* -s platinum
Platitüde *f* -,-n platitude
platonisch *a* platonic
plätschen *vi (sein)* splash

plätschern *vi (haben)* splash; *(Bach:)* babble ● *vi (sein) (Bach:)* babble along
platt *a* & *adv* flat; **p~ sein** *(fam)* be flabbergasted. **P~** *nt* -[s] *(Lang)* Low German
Plättbrett *nt* ironing-board
Platte *f* -,-n slab; *(Druck-)* plate; *(Metall-, Glas-)* sheet; *(Fliese)* tile; *(Koch-)* hotplate; *(Tisch-)* top; *(Auszieh-)* leaf; *(Schall-)* record, disc; *(zum Servieren)* [flat] dish, platter; **kalte P~** assorted cold meats and cheeses *pl*
Plätt|eisen *nt* iron. **p~en** *vt/i (haben)* iron
Plattenspieler *m* record-player
Platt|form *f* -,-en platform. **P~füße** *mpl* flat feet. **P~heit** *f* -,-en platitude
Platz *m* -es,-e place; *(von Häusern umgeben)* square; *(Sitz-)* seat; *(Sport-)* ground; *(Fußball-)* pitch; *(Tennis-)* court; *(Golf-)* course; *(freier Raum)* room, space; **P~ nehmen** take a seat; **P~ machen/lassen** make/leave room; **vom P~ stellen** *(Sport)* send off. **P~angst** *f* agoraphobia; *(Klaustrophobie)* claustrophobia. **P~anweiserin** *f* -,-nen usherette
Plätzchen *nt* -s,- spot; *(Culin)* biscuit
platzen *vi (sein)* burst; *(auf-)* split; *(fam: scheitern)* fall through; *(Verlobung:)* be off; **vor Neugier p~** be bursting with curiosity
Platz|karte *f* seat reservation ticket. **P~konzert** *nt* open-air concert. **P~mangel** *m* lack of space. **P~patrone** *f* blank. **P~regen** *m* downpour. **P~verweis** *m (Sport)* sending off. **P~wunde** *f* laceration
Plauderei *f* -,-en chat
plaudern *vi (haben)* chat
Plausch *m* -[e]s,-e *(SGer)* chat. **p~en** *vi (haben) (SGer)* chat
plausibel *a* plausible
plazieren *vt* place, put; **sich p~** *(Sport)* be placed
pleite *a (fam)* **p~ sein** be broke; *(Firma:)* be bankrupt; **p~ gehen** go bankrupt. **P~** *f* -,-n *(fam)* bankruptcy; *(Mißerfolg)* flop; **P~ machen** go bankrupt
plissiert *a* [finely] pleated
Plomb|e *f* -,-n seal; *(Zahn-)* filling. **p~ieren** *vt* seal; fill *(Zahn)*
plötzlich *a* sudden, *adv* -ly
plump *a* plump; *(ungeschickt)* clumsy, *adv* -ily
plumpsen *vi (sein) (fam)* fall

Plunder *m* **-s** (*fam*) junk, rubbish
plündern *vt/i* (*haben*) loot
Plunderstück *nt* Danish pastry
Plural *m* **-s,-e** plural
plus *adv, conj & prep* (+ *dat*) plus. **P~
nt** - surplus; (*Gewinn*) profit; (*Vorteil*)
advantage, plus. **P~punkt** *m* (*Sport*)
point; (*fig*) plus. **P~quamperfekt** *nt*
pluperfect. **P~zeichen** *nt* plus sign
Po *m* **-s,-s** (*fam*) bottom
Pöbel *m* **-s** mob, rabble. **p~haft** *a*
loutish
pochen *vi* (*haben*) knock; ⟨*Herz:*⟩
pound; **p~ auf** (+ *acc*) (*fig*) insist on
pochieren /po'ʃiːrən/ *vt* poach
Pocken *pl* smallpox *sg*
Podest *nt* **-[e]s,-e** rostrum
Podium *nt* **-s,-ien** /-jən/ platform;
(*Podest*) rostrum
Poesie /poe'ziː/ *f* - poetry
poetisch *a* poetic
Pointe /'poɛ̃ːtə/ *f* -,-**n** point (*of a joke*)
Pokal *m* **-s,-e** goblet; (*Sport*) cup
pökeln *vt* (*Culin*) salt
Poker *nt* **-s** poker
Pol *m* **-s,-e** pole. **p~ar** *a* polar
polarisieren *vt* polarize
Polarstern *m* pole-star
Pole *m* **-n,-n** Pole. **P~n** *nt* **-s** Poland
Police /po'liːsə/ *f* -,-**n** policy
Polier *m* **-s,-e** foreman
polieren *vt* polish
Polin *f* -,-**nen** Pole
Politesse *f* -,-**n** [woman] traffic war-
den
Politik *f* - politics *sg*; (*Vorgehen, Maß-
nahme*) policy
Polit|iker(in) *m* **-s,-** (*f* -,-**nen**) poli-
tician. **p~isch** *a* political, *adv* -ly
Politur *f* -,-**en** polish
Polizei *f* - police *pl*. **P~beamte(r)** *m*
police officer. **p~lich** *a* police ...
● *adv* by the police; ⟨*sich anmelden*⟩
with the police. **P~streife** *f* police
patrol. **P~stunde** *f* closing time.
P~wache *f* police station
Polizist *m* **-en,-en** policeman. **P~in** *f*
-,-**nen** policewoman
Pollen *m* **-s** pollen
polnisch *a* Polish
Polohemd *nt* polo shirt
Polster *nt* **-s,-** pad; (*Kissen*) cushion;
(*Möbel-*) upholstery; (*fam: Rücklage*)
reserves *pl*. **P~er** *m* **-s,-** upholsterer.
P~möbel *pl* upholstered furniture
sg. **p~n** *vt* pad; upholster ⟨*Möbel*⟩.
P~ung *f* - padding; upholstery

Polter|abend *m* wedding-eve party.
p~n *vi* (*haben*) thump, bang;
(*schelten*) bawl ● *vi* (*sein*) crash
down; (*gehen*) clump [along];
(*fahren*) rumble [along]
Polyäthylen *nt* **-s** polythene
Polyester *m* **-s** polyester
Polyp *m* **-en,-en** polyp; (*sl: Polizist*)
copper; **P~en** adenoids *pl*
Pomeranze *f* -,-**n** Seville orange
Pommes *pl* (*fam*) French fries
Pommes frites /pom'friːt/ *pl* chips;
(*dünner*) French fries
Pomp *m* **-s** pomp
Pompon /põ'põː/ *m* **-s,-s** pompon
pompös *a* ostentatious, *adv* -ly
Pony[1] *nt* **-s,-s** pony
Pony[2] *m* **-s,-s** fringe
Pop *m* **-[s]** pop. **P~musik** *f* pop music
Popo *m* **-s,-s** (*fam*) bottom
popul|är *a* popular. **P~arität** *f* - pop-
ularity
Pore *f* -,-**n** pore
Porno|graphie *f* - pornography. **p~-
graphisch** *a* pornographic
porös *a* porous
Porree *m* **-s** leeks *pl*; **eine Stange P~**
a leek
Portal *nt* **-s,-e** portal
Portemonnaie /portmo'neː/ *nt* **-s,-s**
purse
Portier /por'tieː/ *m* **-s,-s** doorman,
porter
Portion /-'tsioːn/ *f* -,-**en** helping, por-
tion
Porto *nt* **-s** postage. **p~frei** *adv* post
free, post paid
Porträ|t /por'trɛː/ *nt* **-s,-s** portrait.
p~tieren *vt* paint a portrait of
Portugal *nt* **-s** Portugal
Portugies|e *m* **-n,-n**, **P~in** *f* -,-**nen**
Portuguese. **p~isch** *a* Portuguese
Portwein *m* port
Porzellan *nt* **-s** china, porcelain
Posaune *f* -,-**n** trombone
Pose *f* -,-**n** pose
posieren *vi* (*haben*) pose
Position /-'tsioːn/ *f* -,-**en** position
positiv *a* positive, *adv* -ly. **P~** *nt* **-s,-e**
(*Phot*) positive
Posse *f* -,-**n** (*Theat*) farce. **P~n** *m* **-s,-**
prank; **P~n** *pl* tomfoolery *sg*
Possessivpronomen *nt* possessive
pronoun
possierlich *a* cute
Post *f* - post office; (*Briefe*) mail, post;
mit der P~ by post
postalisch *a* postal

Post|amt nt post office. **P~anwei-sung** f postal money order. **P~bote** m postman

Posten m -s,- post; (Wache) sentry; (Waren-) batch; (Rechnungs-) item, entry; **P~ stehen** stand guard; **nicht auf dem P~** (fam) under the weather

Poster nt & m -s,- poster

Postfach nt post-office or PO box

postieren vt post, station; **sich p~** station oneself

Post|karte f postcard. **p~lagernd** adv poste restante. **P~leitzahl** f postcode, (Amer) Zip code. **P~scheckkonto** nt ≈ National Giro-bank account. **P~stempel** m postmark

postum a posthumous, adv -ly

post|wendend adv by return of post. **P~wertzeichen** nt [postage] stamp

Poten|tial /-'tsi̯a:l/ nt -s,-e potential. **p~tiell** /-'tsi̯ɛl/ a potential, adv -ly

Potenz f -,-en potency; (Math & fig) power

Pracht f - magnificence, splendour. **P~exemplar** nt magnificent specimen

prächtig a magnificent, adv -ly; (prima) splendid, adv -ly

prachtvoll a magnificent, adv -ly

Prädikat nt -[e]s,-e rating; (Comm) grade; (Gram) predicate. **p~iv** a (Gram) predicative, adv -ly. **P~s-wein** m high-quality wine

präge|n vt stamp (**auf** + acc on); emboss (Leder, Papier); mint (Münze); coin ⟨Wort, Ausdruck⟩; (fig) shape. **P~stempel** m die

pragmatisch a pragmatic, adv -ally

prägnant a succinct, adv -ly

prähistorisch a prehistoric

prahl|en vi (haben) boast, brag (**mit** about). **p~erisch** a boastful, adv -ly

Prakti|k f -,-en practice. **P~kant(in)** m -en,-en (f -,-nen) trainee

Prakti|kum nt -s,-ka practical training. **p~sch** a practical; (nützlich) handy; (tatsächlich) virtual; **p~scher Arzt** general practitioner ● adv practically; virtually; (in der Praxis) in practice; **p~sch arbeiten** do practical work. **p~zieren** vt/i (haben) practise; (anwenden) put into practice; (fam: bekommen) get

Praline f -,-n chocolate; **Schachtel P~n** box of chocolates

prall a bulging; (dick) plump; ⟨Sonne⟩ blazing ● adv **p~ gefüllt** full to bursting. **p~en** vi (sein) **p~ auf** (+ acc)/**gegen** collide with, hit; ⟨Sonne:⟩ blaze down on

Prämie /-i̯ə/ f -,-n premium; (Preis) award

präm[i]ieren vt award a prize to

Pranger m -s,- pillory

Pranke f -,-n paw

Präpar|at nt -[e]s,-e preparation. **p~ieren** vt prepare; (zerlegen) dissect; (ausstopfen) stuff

Präposition /-'tsi̯o:n/ f -,-en preposition

Präsens nt - (Gram) present

präsentieren vt present; **sich p~** present itself/⟨Person:⟩ oneself

Präsenz f - presence

Präservativ nt -s,-e condom

Präsident|(in) m -en,-en (f -,-nen) president. **P~schaft** f - presidency

Präsidium nt -s presidency; (Gremium) executive committee; (Polizei-) headquarters pl

prasseln vi (haben) ⟨Regen:⟩ beat down; ⟨Feuer:⟩ crackle ● vi (sein) **p~ auf** (+ acc)/**gegen** beat down on/beat against

prassen vi (haben) live extravagantly; (schmausen) feast

Präteritum nt -s imperfect

präventiv a preventive

Praxis f -,-xen practice; (Erfahrung) practical experience; (Arzt-) surgery; **in der P~** in practice

Präzedenzfall m precedent

präzis[e] a precise, adv -ly

Präzision f - precision

predig|en vt/i (haben) preach. **P~er** m -s,- preacher. **P~t** f -,-en sermon

Preis m -es,-e price; (Belohnung) prize; **um jeden/keinen P~** at any/not at any price. **P~ausschreiben** nt competition

Preiselbeere f (Bot) cowberry; (Culin) ≈ cranberry

preisen† vt praise; **sich glücklich p~** count oneself lucky

preisgeben† vt sep abandon (dat to); reveal ⟨Geheimnis⟩

preis|gekrönt a award-winning. **P~gericht** nt jury. **p~günstig** a reasonably priced ● adv at a reasonable price. **P~lage** f price range. **p~lich** a price ... ● adv in price. **P~richter** m judge. **P~schild** nt price-tag. **P~träger(in)** *m(f)* prize-winner. **p~wert** *a* reasonable, *adv* -bly; (*billig*) inexpensive, *adv* -ly

prekär *a* difficult; (*heikel*) delicate

Prell|bock *m* buffers *pl*. **p~en** *vt* bounce; (*verletzen*) bruise; (*fam: betrügen*) cheat. **P~ung** *f* -,-en bruise

Premiere /prə'mie:rə/ *f* -,-n première

Premierminister(in) /prə'mie:-/ *m(f)* Prime Minister

Presse *f* -,-n press. **p~n** *vt* press; **sich p~n** press (**an** + *acc* against)

pressieren *vi* (*haben*) (*SGer*) be urgent

Preßluft *f* compressed air. **P~bohrer** *m* pneumatic drill

Prestige /prɛs'ti:ʒə/ *nt* -s prestige

Preußen *nt* -s Prussia. **p~isch** *a* Prussian

prickeln *vi* (*haben*) tingle

Priester *m* -s,- priest

prima *inv* *a* first-class, first-rate; (*fam: toll*) fantastic, *adv* fantastically well

primär *a* primary, *adv* -ily

Primel *f* -,-n primula; (*Garten-*) polyanthus

primitiv *a* primitive

Prinz *m* -en,-en prince. **P~essin** *f* -,-nen princess

Prinzip *nt* -s,-ien /-iən/ principle; **im/aus P~** in/on principle. **p~iell** *a* ⟨*Frage*⟩ of principle ● *adv* on principle; (*im Prinzip*) in principle

Priorität *f* -,-en priority

Prise *f* -,-n **P~ Salz** pinch of salt

Prisma *nt* -s,-men prism

privat *a* private, *adv* -ly; (*persönlich*) personal. **P~adresse** *f* home address. **p~isieren** *vt* privatize

Privat|leben *nt* private life. **P~lehrer** *m* private tutor. **P~lehrerin** *f* governess. **P~patient(in)** *m(f)* private patient

Privileg *nt* -[e]s,-ien /-iən/ privilege. **p~iert** *a* privileged

pro *prep* (+ *dat*) per. **Pro** *nt* - **das Pro und Kontra** the pros and cons *pl*

Probe *f* -,-n test, trial; (*Menge, Muster*) sample; (*Theat*) rehearsal; **auf die P~ stellen** put to the test. **P~fahrt** *f* test drive. **p~n** *vt/i* (*haben*) (*Theat*) rehearse. **p~weise** *adv* on a trial basis. **P~zeit** *f* probationary period

probieren *vt/i* (*haben*) try; (*kosten*) taste; (*proben*) rehearse

Problem *nt* -s,-e problem. **p~atisch** *a* problematic

problemlos *a* problem-free ● *adv* without any problems

Produkt *nt* -[e]s,-e product

Produk|tion /-'tsio:n/ *f* -,-en production. **p~tiv** *a* productive. **P~tivität** *f* - productivity

Produ|zent *m* -en,-en producer. **p~zieren** *vt* produce; **sich p~zieren** (*fam*) show off

professionell *a* professional, *adv* -ly

Professor *m* -s,-en /-'so:rən/ professor

Profi *m* -s,-s (*Sport*) professional

Profil *nt* -s,-e profile; (*Reifen-*) tread; (*fig*) image. **p~iert** *a* (*fig*) distinguished

Profit *m* -[e]s,-e profit. **p~ieren** *vi* (*haben*) profit (**von** from)

Prognose *f* -,-n forecast; (*Med*) prognosis

Programm *nt* -s,-e programme; (*Computer-*) program; (*TV*) channel; (*Comm: Sortiment*) range. **p~ieren** *vt/i* (*haben*) (*Computer*) program. **P~ierer(in)** *m* -s,- (*f* -,-nen) [computer] programmer

progressiv *a* progressive

Projekt *nt* -[e]s,-e project

Projektor *m* -s,-en /-'to:rən/ projector

projizieren *vt* project

Proklam|ation /-'tsio:n/ *f* -,-en proclamation. **p~ieren** *vt* proclaim

Prolet *m* -en,-en boor. **P~ariat** *nt* -[e]s proletariat. **P~arier** /-iɐ/ *m* -s,- proletarian

Prolog *m* -s,-e prologue

Promenade *f* -,-n promenade. **P~nmischung** *f* (*fam*) mongrel

Promille *pl* (*fam*) alcohol level *sg* in the blood; **zuviel P~ haben** (*fam*) be over the limit

prominen|t *a* prominent. **P~z** *f* - prominent figures *pl*

Promiskuität *f* - promiscuity

promovieren *vi* (*haben*) obtain one's doctorate

prompt *a* prompt, *adv* -ly; (*fam: natürlich*) of course

Pronomen *nt* -s,- pronoun

Propag|anda *f* - propaganda; (*Reklame*) publicity. **p~ieren** *vt* propagate

Propeller *m* -s,- propeller

Prophet *m* -en,-en prophet. **p~isch** *a* prophetic

prophezei|en *vt* prophesy. **P~ung** *f*
-,-en prophecy
Proportion /-'tsjo:n/ *f* **-,-en** proportion. **p~al** *a* proportional. **p~iert**
a **gut p~iert** well proportioned
Prosa *f* - prose
prosaisch *a* prosaic, *adv* -ally
prosit *int* cheers!
Prospekt *m* **-[e]s,-e** brochure; (*Comm*)
prospectus
prost *int* cheers!
Prostitu|ierte *f* **-n,-n** prostitute. **P~**
tion /-'tsjo:n/ *f* - prostitution
Protest *m* **-[e]s,-e** protest
Protestant|(in) *m* **-en,-en** (*f* **-,-nen**)
(*Relig*) Protestant. **p~isch** *a* (*Relig*)
Protestant
protestieren *vi* (*haben*) protest
Prothese *f* **-,-n** artificial limb; (*Zahn-*)
denture
Protokoll *nt* **-s,-e** record; (*Sitzungs-*)
minutes *pl*; (*diplomatisches*) protocol;
(*Strafzettel*) ticket
Prototyp *m* **-s,-en** prototype
protz|en *vi* (*haben*) show off (**mit etw**
sth). **p~ig** *a* ostentatious
Proviant *m* **-s** provisions *pl*
Provinz *f* **-,-en** province. **p~iell** *a*
provincial
Provision *f* **-,-en** (*Comm*) commission
provisorisch *a* provisional, *adv* -ly,
temporary, *adv* -ily
Provokation /-'tsjo:n/ *f* **-,-en** provocation
provozieren *vt* provoke. **p~d** *a*
provocative, *adv* -ly
Prozedur *f* **-,-en** [lengthy] business
Prozent *nt* **-[e]s,-e** & - per cent; **5 P~**
5 per cent. **P~satz** *m* percentage.
p~ual *a* percentage ...
Prozeß *m* **-sses,-sse** process; (*Jur*)
lawsuit; (*Kriminal-*) trial
Prozession *f* **-,-en** procession
prüde *a* prudish
prüf|en *vt* test/(*über-*) check
(**auf** + *acc* for); audit ⟨*Bücher*⟩; (*Sch*) examine; **p~ender Blick** searching look.
P~er *m* **-s,-** inspector; (*Buch-*) auditor;
(*Sch*) examiner. **P~ling** *m* **-s,-e** examination candidate. **P~ung** *f* **-,-en**
examination; (*Test*) test; (*Bücher-*)
audit; (*fig*) trial
Prügel *m* **-s,-** cudgel; **P~** *pl* hiding *sg*,
beating *sg*. **P~ei** *f* **-,-en** brawl, fight.
p~n *vt* beat, thrash; **sich p~n** fight,
brawl
Prunk *m* **-[e]s** magnificence, splendour.
p~en *vi* (*haben*) show off (**mit etw**
sth). **p~voll** *a* magnificent, *adv* -ly

prusten *vi* (*haben*) splutter;
(*schnauben*) snort
Psalm *m* **-s,-en** psalm
Pseudonym *nt* **-s,-e** pseudonym
pst *int* shush!
Psychi|ater *m* **-s,-** psychiatrist. **P~a-**
trie *f* - psychiatry. **p~atrisch** *a* psychiatric
psychisch *a* psychological, *adv* -ly;
(*Med*) mental, *adv* -ly
Psycho|analyse *f* psychoanalysis.
P~loge *m* **-n,-n** psychologist. **P~**
logie *f* - psychology. **p~logisch** *a*
psychological, *adv* -ly
Pubertät *f* - puberty
publik *a* **p~ werden/machen** be-
come/make public
Publi|kum *nt* **-s** public; (*Zuhörer*)
audience; (*Zuschauer*) spectators *pl*.
p~zieren *vt* publish
Pudding *m* **-s,-s** blancmange; (*im
Wasserbad gekocht*) pudding
Pudel *m* **-s,-** poodle
Puder *m* & (*fam*) *nt* **-s,-** powder;
(*Körper-*) talcum [powder]. **P~dose** *f*
[powder] compact. **p~n** *vt* powder.
P~zucker *m* icing sugar
Puff¹ *m* **-[e]s,ͤe** push, poke
Puff² *m* & *nt* **-s,-s** (*sl*) brothel
puffen *vt* (*fam*) poke ● *vi* (*sein*) puff
along
Puffer *m* **-s,-** (*Rail*) buffer; (*Culin*) pan-
cake. **P~zone** *f* buffer zone
Pull|i *m* **-s,-s** jumper. **P~over** *m* **-s,-**
jumper; (*Herren-*) pullover
Puls *m* **-es** pulse. **P~ader** *f* artery.
p~ieren *vi* (*haben*) pulsate
Pult *nt* **-[e]s,-e** desk; (*Lese-*) lectern
Pulver *nt* **-s,-** powder. **p~ig** *a* pow-
dery. **p~isieren** *vt* pulverize
Pulver|kaffee *m* instant coffee.
P~schnee *m* powder snow
pummelig *a* (*fam*) chubby
Pump *m* **auf P~** (*fam*) on tick
Pumpe *f* **-,-n** pump. **p~n** *vt/i* (*haben*)
pump; (*fam: leihen*) lend; [**sich** (*dat*)]
etw p~n (*fam: borgen*) borrow sth
Pumps /pœmps/ *pl* court shoes
Punkt *m* **-[e]s,-e** dot; (*Tex*) spot; (*Geom,
Sport* & *fig*) point; (*Gram*) full stop,
period; **P~ sechs Uhr** at six o'clock
sharp; **nach P~en siegen** win on
points. **p~iert** *a* ⟨*Linie, Note*⟩ dotted
pünktlich *a* punctual, *adv* -ly.
P~keit *f* - punctuality
Punsch *m* **-[e]s,-e** [hot] punch
Pupille *f* **-,-n** (*Anat*) pupil

Puppe f -,-n doll; (*Marionette*) puppet; (*Schaufenster-, Schneider-*) dummy; (*Zool*) chrysalis

pur a pure; (*fam: bloß*) sheer; **Whisky pur** neat whisky

Püree nt -s,-s purée; (*Kartoffel-*) mashed potatoes pl

puritanisch a puritanical

purpurrot a crimson

Purzel|baum m (*fam*) somersault. **p~n** vi (*sein*) (*fam*) tumble

pusseln vi (*haben*) (*fam*) potter

Puste f - (*fam*) breath; **aus der P~** out of breath. **p~n** vt/i (*haben*) (*fam*) blow

Pute f -,-n turkey; (*Henne*) turkey hen. **P~r** m -s,- turkey cock

Putsch m -[e]s,-e coup

Putz m -es plaster; (*Staat*) finery. **p~en** vt clean; (*Aust*) dry-clean; (*zieren*) adorn; **sich p~en** dress up; **sich** (*dat*) **die Zähne/Nase p~en** clean one's teeth/blow one's nose. **P~frau** f cleaner, charwoman. **p~ig** a (*fam*) amusing, cute; (*seltsam*) odd. **P~macherin** f -,-nen milliner

Puzzlespiel /'pazl-/ nt jigsaw

Pyramide f -,-n pyramid

Q

Quacksalber m -s,- quack

Quadrat nt -[e]s,-e square. **q~isch** a square. **Q~meter** m & nt square metre

quaken vi (*haben*) quack; (*Frosch:*) croak

quäken vi (*haben*) screech; (*Baby:*) whine

Quäker(in) m -s,- (f -,-nen) Quaker

Qual f -,-en torment; (*Schmerz*) agony

quälen vt torment; (*foltern*) torture; (*bedrängen*) pester; **sich q~** torment oneself; (*leiden*) suffer; (*sich mühen*) struggle. **q~d** a agonizing

Quälerei f -,-en torture; (*Qual*) agony

Quälgeist m (*fam*) pest

Qualifi|kation /-'tsio:n/ f -,-en qualification. **q~zieren** vt qualify; **sich q~zieren** qualify. **q~ziert** a qualified; (*fähig*) competent; (*Arbeit*) skilled

Qualität f -,-en quality

Qualle f -,-n jellyfish

Qualm m -s [thick] smoke. **q~en** vi

Quantität f -,-en quantity

Quantum nt -s,-ten quantity; (*Anteil*) share, quota

Quarantäne f - quarantine

Quark m -s quark, ≈ curd cheese; (*fam: Unsinn*) rubbish

Quartal nt -s,-e quarter

Quartett nt -[e]s,-e quartet

Quartier nt -s,-e accommodation; (*Mil*) quarters pl; **ein Q~ suchen** look for accommodation

Quarz m -es quartz

quasseln vi (*haben*) (*fam*) jabber

Quaste f -,-n tassel

Quatsch m -[e]s (*fam*) nonsense, rubbish; **Q~ machen** (*Unfug machen*) fool around; (*etw falsch machen*) do a silly thing. **q~en** (*fam*) vi (*haben*) talk; (*schwatzen*) natter; (*Wasser, Schlamm:*) squelch ● vt talk. **q~naß** a (*fam*) soaking wet

Quecksilber nt mercury

Quelle f -,-n spring; (*Fluß- & fig*) source. **q~n†** vi (*sein*) well [up]/ (*fließen*) pour (*aus* from); (*aufquellen*) swell; (*hervortreten*) bulge

quengeln vi (*fam*) whine; (*Baby:*) grizzle

quer adv across, crosswise; (*schräg*) diagonally

Quere f - **der Q~ nach** across, crosswise; **jdm in die Q~ kommen** get in s.o.'s way

querfeldein adv across country

quer|gestreift a horizontally striped. **Q~latte** f crossbar. **q~köpfig** a (*fam*) awkward. **Q~schiff** nt transept. **Q~schnitt** m crosssection. **q~schnittsgelähmt** a paraplegic. **Q~straße** f side-street; **die erste Q~straße links** the first turning on the left. **Q~verweis** m crossreference

quetsch|en vt squash; (*drücken*) squeeze; (*zerdrücken*) crush; (*Culin*) mash; **sich q~en in** (+ *acc*) squeeze into; **sich** (*dat*) **den Arm q~en** bruise one's arm. **Q~ung** f -,-en, **Q~wunde** f bruise

Queue /kø:/ nt -s,-s cue

quicklebendig a very lively

quieken vi (*haben*) squeal; (*Maus:*) squeak

quietschen vi (*haben*) squeal; (*Tür, Dielen:*) creak

Quintett nt -[e]s,-e quintet

quitt *a* **q∼ sein** *(fam)* be quits
Quitte *f -,-n* quince
quittieren *vt* receipt ⟨*Rechnung*⟩; sign for ⟨*Geldsumme, Sendung*⟩; *(reagieren auf)* greet **(mit** with); **den Dienst q∼** resign
Quittung *f -,-en* receipt
Quiz /kvɪs/ *nt -,-* quiz
Quote *f -,-n* proportion

R

Rabatt *m -[e]s,-e* discount
Rabatte *f -,-n* *(Hort)* border
Rabattmarke *f* trading stamp
Rabbiner *m -s,-* rabbi
Rabe *m -n,-n* raven. **r∼nschwarz** *a* pitch-black
rabiat *a* violent, *adv* -ly; *(wütend)* furious, *adv* -ly
Rache *f -* revenge, vengeance
Rachen *m -s,-* pharynx; *(Maul)* jaws *pl*
rächen *vt* avenge; **sich r∼** take revenge **(an+** *dat* on); ⟨*Fehler, Leichtsinn:*⟩ cost s.o. dear
Racker *m -s,-* *(fam)* rascal
Rad *nt -[e]s,¨er* wheel; *(Fahr-)* bicycle, *(fam)* bike
Radar *m & nt -s* radar
Radau *m -s* *(fam)* din, racket
radebrechen *vt/i (haben)* **[Deutsch/ Englisch] r∼** speak broken German/ English
radeln *vi (sein) (fam)* cycle
Rädelsführer *m* ringleader
radfahr|en† *vi sep (sein)* cycle; **ich fahre gern Rad** I like cycling. **R∼er(in)** *m(f) -s,- (-,-nen)* cyclist
radier|en *vt/i (haben)* rub out; *(Kunst)* etch. **R∼gummi** *m* eraser, rubber. **R∼ung** *f -,-en* etching
Radieschen /-'diːsçən/ *nt -s,-* radish
radikal *a* radical, *adv* -ly; *(drastisch)* drastic, *adv* -ally. **R∼e(r)** *m/f (Pol)* radical
Radio *nt -s,-s* radio
radioaktiv *a* radioactive. **R∼ität** *f -* radioactivity
Radioapparat *m* radio [set]
Radius *m -,-ien* /-jən/ radius
Rad|kappe *f* hub-cap. **R∼ler** *m -s,-* cyclist; *(Getränk)* shandy. **R∼weg** *m* cycle track
raff|en *vt* grab; *(kräuseln)* gather; *(kürzen)* condense. **r∼gierig** *a* avaricious

Raffin|ade *f -* refined sugar. **R∼erie** *f -,-n* refinery. **R∼esse** *f -,-n* refinement; *(Schlauheit)* cunning. **r∼ieren** *vt* refine. **r∼iert** *a* ingenious, *adv* -ly; *(durchtrieben)* crafty, *adv* -ily
Rage /'raːʒə/ *f -* *(fam)* fury
ragen *vi (haben)* rise [up]
Rahm *m -s (SGer)* cream
rahmen *vt* frame. **R∼** *m -s,-* frame; *(fig)* framework; *(Grenze)* limits *pl*; *(einer Feier)* setting
Rain *m -[e]s,-e* grass verge
räkeln *v = rekeln
Rakete *f -,-n* rocket; *(Mil)* missile
Rallye /'rali/ *nt -s,-s* rally
rammen *vt* ram
Rampe *f -,-n* ramp; *(Theat)* front of the stage. **R∼nlicht** *nt* **im R∼nlicht stehen** *(fig)* be in the limelight
ramponier|en *vt (fam)* damage; *(ruinieren)* ruin; **r∼t** battered
Ramsch *m -[e]s* junk. **R∼laden** *m* junk-shop
ran *adv = heran
Rand *m -[e]s,¨er* edge; *(Teller-, Gläser-, Brillen-)* rim; *(Zier-)* border, edging; *(Buch-, Brief-)* margin; *(Stadt-)* outskirts *pl*; *(Ring)* ring; **am R∼e des Ruins** on the brink of ruin; **am R∼e erwähnen** mention in passing; **zu R∼e kommen mit** *(fam)* cope with; **außer R∼ und Band** *(fam: ausgelassen)* very boisterous
randalieren *vi (haben)* rampage
Rand|bemerkung *f* marginal note. **R∼streifen** *m (Auto)* hard shoulder
Rang *m -[e]s,¨e* rank; *(Theat)* tier; **erster/zweiter R∼** *(Theat)* dress/ upper circle; **ersten R∼es** first-class
rangieren /raŋ'ʒiːrən/ *vt* shunt ● *vi (haben)* rank **(vor+** *dat* before); **an erster Stelle r∼** come first
Rangordnung *f* order of importance; *(Hierarchie)* hierarchy
Ranke *f -,-n* tendril; *(Trieb)* shoot
ranken (sich) *vr (Bot)* trail; *(in die Höhe)* climb; **sich r∼ um** twine around
Ranzen *m -s,- (Sch)* satchel
ranzig *a* rancid
Rappe *m -n,-n* black horse
rappeln *v (fam)* ● *vi (haben)* rattle ● *vr* **sich r∼** pick oneself up; *(fig)* rally
Raps *m -es (Bot)* rape
rar *a* rare; **er macht sich rar** *(fam)* we don't see much of him. **R∼ität** *f -,-en* rarity
rasant *a* fast; *(schnittig, schick)* stylish ● *adv* fast; stylishly

rasch a quick, adv -ly
rascheln vi (haben) rustle
Rasen m -s,- lawn
rasen vi (sein) tear [along]; ⟨Puls:⟩ race; ⟨Zeit:⟩ fly; **gegen eine Mauer r∼** career into a wall ● vi (haben) rave; ⟨Sturm:⟩ rage; **vor Begeisterung r∼** go wild with enthusiasm. **r∼d** a furious; (tobend) raving; ⟨Sturm, Durst⟩ raging; ⟨Schmerz⟩ excruciating; ⟨Beifall⟩ tumultuous ● adv terribly
Rasenmäher m lawn-mower
Raserei f - speeding; (Toben) frenzy
Rasier|apparat m razor. **r∼en** vt shave; **sich r∼en** shave. **R∼klinge** f razor blade. **R∼pinsel** m shaving-brush. **R∼wasser** nt aftershave [lotion]
Raspel f -,-n rasp; (Culin) grater. **r∼n** vt grate
Rasse f -,-n race. **R∼hund** m pedigree dog
Rassel f -,-n rattle. **r∼n** vi (haben) rattle; ⟨Schlüssel:⟩ jangle; ⟨Kette:⟩ clank ● vi (sein) rattle [along]
Rassen|diskriminierung f racial discrimination. **R∼trennung** f racial segregation
Rassepferd nt thoroughbred
rassisch a racial
Rassis|mus m - racism. **r∼tisch** a racist
Rast f -,-en rest. **r∼en** vi (haben) rest. **R∼haus** nt motorway restaurant. **r∼los** a restless, adv -ly; (ununterbrochen) ceaseless, adv -ly. **R∼platz** m picnic area. **R∼stätte** f motorway restaurant [and services]
Rasur f -,-en shave
Rat[1] m -[e]s [piece of] advice; **guter Rat** good advice; **zu Rat[e] ziehen** consult; **sich** (dat) **keinen Rat wissen** not know what to do
Rat[2] m -[e]s, ̈-e (Admin) council; (Person) councillor
Rate f -,-n instalment
raten† vt guess; (empfehlen) advise ● vi (haben) guess; **jdm r∼** advise s.o.
Ratenzahlung f payment by instalments
Rat|geber m -s,- adviser; (Buch) guide. **R∼haus** nt town hall
ratifizier|en vt ratify. **R∼ung** f -,-en ratification
Ration /ra'tsio:n/ f -,-en ration; **eiserne R∼** iron rations pl. **r∼al** a rational, adv -ly. **r∼alisieren** vt/i

(haben) rationalize. **r∼ell** a efficient, adv -ly. **r∼ieren** vt ration
rat|los a helpless, adv -ly; **r∼los sein** not know what to do. **r∼sam** pred a advisable; (klug) prudent. **R∼schlag** m piece of advice; **R∼schläge** advice sg
Rätsel nt -s,- riddle; (Kreuzwort-) puzzle; (Geheimnis) mystery. **r∼haft** a puzzling, mysterious. **r∼n** vi (haben) puzzle
Ratte f -,-n rat
rattern vi (haben) rattle ● vi (sein) rattle [along]
Raub m -[e]s robbery; (Menschen-) abduction; (Beute) loot, booty. **r∼en** vt steal; abduct ⟨Menschen⟩; **jdm etw r∼en** rob s.o. of sth
Räuber m -s,- robber
Raub|mord m robbery with murder. **R∼tier** nt predator. **R∼überfall** m robbery. **R∼vogel** m bird of prey
Rauch m -[e]s smoke. **r∼en** vt/i (haben) smoke. **R∼en** nt -s smoking; **'R∼en verboten'** 'no smoking'. **R∼er** m -s,- smoker. **R∼erabteil** nt smoking compartment
Räucher|lachs m smoked salmon. **r∼n** vt (Culin) smoke
Rauch|fang m (Aust) chimney. **r∼ig** a smoky. **R∼verbot** nt smoking ban
räudig a mangy
rauf adv = herauf, hinauf
rauf|en vt pull; **sich** (dat) **die Haare r∼en** (fig) tear one's hair ● vr/i (haben) **[sich] r∼en** fight. **R∼erei** f -,-en fight
rauh a rough, adv -ly; (unfreundlich) gruff, adv -ly; ⟨Klima, Wind⟩ harsh, raw; ⟨Landschaft⟩ rugged; (heiser) husky; ⟨Hals⟩ sore
Rauheit f - (s. rauh) roughness; gruffness; harshness; ruggedness
rauh|haarig a wire-haired. **R∼reif** m hoar-frost
Raum m -[e]s, Räume room; (Gebiet) area; (Welt-) space
räumen vt clear; vacate ⟨Wohnung⟩; evacuate ⟨Gebäude, Gebiet, Mil Stellung⟩; (bringen) put (**in/auf** + acc into/on); (holen) get (**aus** out of); **beiseite r∼** move/put to one side; **aus dem Weg r∼** (fam) get rid of
Raum|fahrer m astronaut. **R∼fahrt** f space travel. **R∼fahrzeug** nt spacecraft. **R∼flug** m space flight. **R∼inhalt** m volume

räumlich *a* spatial. **R~keiten** *fpl* rooms

Raum|pflegerin *f* cleaner.

R~schiff *nt* spaceship

Räumung *f* **-** *(s.* **räumen)** clearing; vacating; evacuation. **R~sverkauf** *m* clearance/closing-down sale

raunen *vt/i (haben)* whisper

Raupe *f* **-,-n** caterpillar

raus *adv* = **heraus, hinaus**

Rausch *m* **-[e]s, Räusche** intoxication; *(fig)* exhilaration; **einen R~ haben** be drunk

rauschen *vi (haben)* ⟨*Wasser, Wind:*⟩ rush; ⟨*Bäume, Blätter:*⟩ rustle ● *vi (sein)* rush [along]; **aus dem Zimmer r~** sweep out of the room. **r~d** *a* rushing; rustling; ⟨*Applaus*⟩ tumultuous

Rauschgift *nt* [narcotic] drug; *(coll)* drugs *pl.* **R~süchtige(r)** *m/f* drug addict

räuspern (sich) *vr* clear one's throat

rausschmeiß|en† *vt sep (fam)* throw out; *(entlassen)* sack. **R~er** *m* **-s,-** *(fam)* bouncer

Raute *f* **-,-n** diamond

Razzia *f* **-,-ien** /-iən/ [police] raid

Reagenzglas *nt* test-tube

reagieren *vi (haben)* react (**auf**+ *acc* to)

Reaktion /-'tsio:n/ *f* **-,-en** reaction. **r~är** *a* reactionary

Reaktor *m* **-s,-en** /-'to:rən/ reactor

real *a* real; *(gegenständlich)* tangible; *(realistisch)* realistic, *adv* -ally. **r~i-sieren** *vt* realize

Realis|mus *m* **-** realism. **R~t** *m* **-en,-en** realist. **r~tisch** *a* realistic, *adv* -ally

Realität *f* **-,-en** reality

Realschule *f* ≈ secondary modern school

Rebe *f* **-,-n** vine

Rebell *m* **-en,-en** rebel. **r~ieren** *vi (haben)* rebel. **R~ion** *f* **-,-en** rebellion

rebellisch *a* rebellious

Rebhuhn *nt* partridge

Rebstock *m* vine

Rechen *m* **-s,-** rake. **r~** *vt/i (haben)* rake

Rechen|aufgabe *f* arithmetical problem; *(Sch)* sum. **R~fehler** *m* arithmetical error. **R~maschine** *f* calculator

Rechenschaft *f* **-** **R~ ablegen** give account (**über**+ *acc* of); **jdn zur R~ ziehen** call s.o. to account

recherchieren /refɛr'ʃi:rən/ *vt/i (haben)* investigate; *(Journ)* research

rechnen *vi (haben)* do arithmetic; *(schätzen)* reckon; *(zählen)* count (**zu** among; **auf**+ *acc* on); **r~ mit** reckon with; *(erwarten)* expect; **gut r~ können** be good at figures ● *vt* calculate, work out; do ⟨*Aufgabe*⟩; *(dazu-)* add (**zu** to); *(fig)* count (**zu** among). **R~nt -s** arithmetic

Rechner *m* **-s,-** calculator; *(Computer)* computer; **ein guter R~ sein** be good at figures

Rechnung *f* **-,-en** bill, *(Amer)* check; *(Comm)* invoice; *(Berechnung)* calculation; **R~ führen über** (+ *acc*) keep account of; **etw** *(dat)* **R~ tragen** *(fig)* take sth into account. **R~sjahr** *nt* financial year. **R~sprüfer** *m* auditor

Recht *nt* **-[e]s,-e** law; *(Berechtigung)* right (**auf**+ *acc* to); **im R~ sein** be in the right; **mit** *od* **zu R~** rightly; **von R~s wegen** by right; *(eigentlich)* by rights

recht *a* right; *(wirklich)* real; **ich habe keine r~e Lust** I don't really feel like it; **es jdm r~ machen** please s.o.; **jdm r~ sein** be all right with s.o. ● **r~ haben/behalten** be right; **r~ bekommen** be proved right; **jdm r~ geben** agree with s.o. ● *adv* correctly; *(ziemlich)* quite; *(sehr)* very; **r~ vielen Dank** many thanks

Recht|e *f* **-n,-[n]** right side; *(Hand)* right hand; *(Boxen)* right; **die R~e** *(Pol)* the right; **zu meiner R~en** on my right. **r~e(r,s)** *a* right; *(Pol)* right-wing; **r~e Masche** plain stitch. **R~e(r)** *m/f* **der/die R~e** the right man/woman; **du bist mir der/die R~e!** you're a fine one! **R~e(s)** *nt* **das R~e** the right thing; **etwas R~es lernen** learn something useful; **nach dem R~en sehen** see that everything is all right

Rechteck *nt* **-[e]s,-e** rectangle. **r~ig** *a* rectangular

rechtfertig|en *vt* justify; **sich r~en** justify oneself. **R~ung** *f* - justification

recht|haberisch *a* opinionated. **r~lich** *a* legal, *adv* -ly. **r~mäßig** *a* legitimate, *adv* -ly

rechts *adv* on the right; *(bei Stoff)* on the right side; **von/nach r~** from/to the right; **zwei r~, zwei links stricken** knit two, purl two. **R~-anwalt** *m,* **R~-anwältin** *f* lawyer

rechtschaffen *a* upright; (*ehrlich*) honest, *adv* -ly; **r~ müde** thoroughly tired

rechtschreib|en *vi* (*inf only*) spell correctly. **R~fehler** *m* spelling mistake. **R~ung** *f* - spelling

Rechts|händer(in) *m* -s,- (*f* -,-nen) right-hander. **r~händig** *a & adv* right-handed. **r~kräftig** *a* legal, *adv* -ly. **R~streit** *m* law suit. **R~verkehr** *m* driving on the right. **r~widrig** *a* illegal, *adv* -ly. **R~wissenschaft** *f* jurisprudence

recht|winklig *a* right-angled. **r~zeitig** *a & adv* in time

Reck *nt* -[e]s,-e horizontal bar

recken *vt* stretch; **sich r~** stretch; **den Hals r~** crane one's neck

Redakteur /redak'tø:ɐ̯/ *m* -s,-e editor; (*Radio, TV*) producer

Redaktion /-'tsio:n/ *f* -,-en editing; (*Radio, TV*) production; (*Abteilung*) editorial/production department. **r~ell** *a* editorial

Rede *f* -,-n speech; **zur R~ stellen** demand an explanation from; **davon ist keine R~** there's no question of it; **nicht der R~ wert** not worth mentioning. **r~gewandt** *a* eloquent, *adv* -ly

reden *vi* (*haben*) talk (**von** about; **mit** to); (*eine Rede halten*) speak ● *vt* talk; speak (*Wahrheit*); **kein Wort r~** not say a word. **R~sart** *f* saying; (*Phrase*) phrase

Redewendung *f* idiom

redigieren *vt* edit

redlich *a* honest, *adv* -ly

Red|ner *m* -s,- speaker. **r~selig** *a* talkative

reduzieren *vt* reduce

Reeder *m* -s,- shipowner. **R~ei** *f* -,-en shipping company

reell *a* real; (*ehrlich*) honest, *adv* -ly; (*Preis, Angebot*) fair

Refer|at *nt* -[e]s,-e report; (*Abhandlung*) paper; (*Abteilung*) section. **R~ent(in)** *m* -en,-en (*f* -,-nen) speaker; (*Sachbearbeiter*) expert. **R~enz** *f* -,-en reference. **r~ieren** *vi* (*haben*) deliver a paper; (*berichten*) report (**über** + *acc* on)

reflektieren *vt/i* (*haben*) reflect (**über** + *acc* on)

Reflex *m* -es,-e reflex; (*Widerschein*) reflection. **R~ion** *f* -,-en reflection. **r~iv** *a* reflexive. **R~ivpronomen** *nt* reflexive pronoun

Reform *f* -,-en reform. **R~ation** /-'tsio:n/ *f* - (*Relig*) Reformation

Reform|haus *nt* health-food shop. **r~ieren** *vt* reform

Refrain /rə'frɛ̃:/ *m* -s,-s refrain

Regal *nt* -s,-e [set of] shelves *pl*

Regatta *f* -,-ten regatta

rege *a* active; (*lebhaft*) lively; (*geistig*) alert; (*Handel*) brisk ● *adv* actively

Regel *f* -,-n rule; (*Monats-*) period; **in der R~** as a rule. **r~mäßig** *a* regular, *adv* -ly. **r~n** *vt* regulate; direct (*Verkehr*); (*erledigen*) settle. **r~recht** *a* real, proper ● *adv* really. **R~ung** *f* -,-en regulation; settlement. **r~widrig** *a* irregular, *adv* -ly

regen *vt* move; **sich r~** move; (*wach werden*) stir

Regen *m* -s,- rain. **R~bogen** *m* rainbow. **R~bogenhaut** *f* iris

Regener|ation /-'tsio:n/ *f* - regeneration. **r~ieren** *vt* regenerate; **sich r~ieren** regenerate

Regen|mantel *m* raincoat. **R~schirm** *m* umbrella. **R~tag** *m* rainy day. **R~tropfen** *m* raindrop. **R~wetter** *nt* wet weather. **R~wurm** *m* earthworm

Regie /re'ʒi:/ *f* - direction; **R~ führen** direct

regier|en *vt/i* (*haben*) govern, rule; (*Monarch:*) reign [over]; (*Gram*) take. **r~end** *a* ruling; reigning. **R~ung** *f* -,-en government; (*Herrschaft*) rule; (*eines Monarchen*) reign

Regime /re'ʒi:m/ *nt* -s,- /-mə/ regime

Regiment *nt* -[e]s,-er regiment

Regiment *nt* -[e]s,-e rule

Region *f* -,-en region. **r~al** *a* regional, *adv* -ly

Regisseur /reʒɪ'sø:ɐ̯/ *m* -s,-e director

Register *nt* -s,- register; (*Inhaltsverzeichnis*) index; (*Orgel-*) stop

registrier|en *vt* register; (*Techn*) record. **R~kasse** *f* cash register

Regler *m* -s,- regulator

reglos *a & adv* motionless

regn|en *vi* (*haben*) rain; **es r~et** it is raining. **r~erisch** *a* rainy

regul|är *a* normal, *adv* -ly; (*rechtmäßig*) legitimate, *adv* -ly. **r~ieren** *vt* regulate

Regung *f* -,-en movement; (*Gefühls-*) emotion. **r~slos** *a & adv* motionless

Reh *nt* -[e]s,-e roe-deer; (*Culin*) venison

Rehabilit|ation /-'tsio:n/ *f* - rehabilitation. **r~ieren** *vt* rehabilitate

Rehbock *m* roebuck

Reib|e *f* -,-n grater. **r~en**† *vt* rub; (*Culin*) grate; **blank r~en** polish ● *vi* (*haben*) rub. **R~ereien** *fpl* (*fam*) friction *sg*. **R~ung** *f* - friction. **r~ungslos** *a* (*fig*) smooth, *adv* -ly

reich *a* rich (**an** + *dat* in), *adv* -ly; (*r~haltig*) abundant, *adv* -ly

Reich *nt* -[e]s,-e empire; (*König*-) kingdom; (*Bereich*) realm

Reich|e(r) *m/f* rich man/woman; **die R~en** the rich *pl*

reichen *vt* reach; (*anbieten*) offer ● *vi* (*haben*) be enough; (*in der Länge*) be long enough; **r~ bis zu** reach [up to]; (*sich erstrecken*) extend to; **mit dem Geld r~** have enough money; **mir reicht's!** I've had enough!

reich|haltig *a* extensive, large; ⟨*Mahlzeit*⟩ substantial. **r~lich** *a* ample; ⟨*Vorrat*⟩ abundant, plentiful; **eine r~liche Stunde** a good hour ● *adv* amply; abundantly; (*fam: sehr*) very. **R~tum** *m* -s,-tümer wealth (**an** + *dat* of); **R~tümer** riches. **R~weite** *f* reach; (*Techn, Mil*) range

Reif *m* -[e]s [hoar-]frost

reif *a* ripe; (*fig*) mature; **r~ für** ready for. **R~e** *f* - ripeness; (*fig*) maturity. **r~en** *vi* (*sein*) ripen; ⟨*Wein, Käse & fig*⟩ mature

Reifen *m* -s,- hoop; (*Arm*-) bangle; (*Auto*-) tyre. **R~druck** *m* tyre pressure. **R~panne** *f* puncture, flat tyre

Reifeprüfung *f* ≈ A levels *pl*

reiflich *a* careful, *adv* -ly

Reihe *f* -,-n row; (*Anzahl & Math*) series; **der R~ nach** in turn; **außer der R~** out of turn; **wer ist an der** *od* **kommt an die R~?** whose turn is it? **r~n** (**sich**) *vr* **sich r~n an** (+ *acc*) follow. **R~nfolge** *f* order. **R~nhaus** *nt* terraced house. **r~nweise** *adv* in rows; (*fam*) in large numbers

Reiher *m* -s,- heron

Reim *m* -[e]s,-e rhyme. **r~en** *vt* rhyme; **sich r~en** rhyme

rein¹ *a* pure; (*sauber*) clean; ⟨*Unsinn, Dummheit*⟩ sheer; **ins r~e schreiben** make a fair copy of; **ins r~e bringen** (*fig*) sort out ● *adv* purely; (*fam*) absolutely

rein² *adv* = **herein, hinein**

Reinfall *m* (*fam*) let-down; (*Mißerfolg*) flop. **r~en**† *vi sep* (*sein*) fall in; (*fam*) be taken in (**auf** + *acc* by)

Rein|gewinn *m* net profit. **R~heit** *f* - purity

reinig|en *vt* clean; (*chemisch*) dryclean. **R~ung** *f* -,-en cleaning; (*chemische*) dry-cleaning; (*Geschäft*) dry cleaner's

Reinkarnation /re'ɪnkarna'tsɪon:/ *f* -,-en reincarnation

reinlegen *vt sep* put in; (*fam*) dupe; (*betrügen*) take for a ride

reinlich *a* clean. **R~keit** *f* - cleanliness

Rein|machefrau *f* cleaner. **R~schrift** *f* fair copy. **r~seiden** *a* pure silk

Reis *m* -es rice

Reise *f* -,-n journey; (*See*-) voyage; (*Urlaubs*-, *Geschäfts*-) trip. **R~andenken** *nt* souvenir. **R~büro** *nt* travel agency. **R~bus** *m* coach. **R~führer** *m* tourist guide; (*Buch*) guide. **R~gesellschaft** *f* tourist group. **R~leiter(in)** *m(f)* courier. **r~n** *vi* (*sein*) travel. **R~nde(r)** *m/f* traveller. **R~paß** *m* passport. **R~scheck** *m* traveller's cheque. **R~unternehmer, R~veranstalter** *m* -s,- tour operator. **R~ziel** *nt* destination

Reisig *nt* -s brushwood

Reißaus *m* **R~ nehmen** (*fam*) run away

Reißbrett *nt* drawing-board

reißen† *vt* tear; (*weg*-) snatch; (*töten*) kill; **Witze r~** crack jokes; **aus dem Schlaf r~** awaken rudely; **an sich** (*acc*) **r~** snatch; seize ⟨*Macht*⟩; **mit sich r~** sweep away; **sich r~ um** (*fam*) fight for; (*gern mögen*) be keen on; **hin und her gerissen sein** (*fig*) be torn ● *vi* (*sein*) tear; ⟨*Seil, Faden*:⟩ break ● *vi* (*haben*) **r~ an** (+ *dat*) pull at. **r~d** *a* raging; ⟨*Tier*⟩ ferocious; ⟨*Schmerz*⟩ violent

Reißer *m* -s,- (*fam*) thriller; (*Erfolg*) big hit. **r~isch** *a* (*fam*) sensational

Reiß|nagel *m* = **R~zwecke**. **R~verschluß** *m* zip [fastener]. **R~wolf** *m* shredder. **R~zwecke** *f* -,-n drawing-pin, (*Amer*) thumbtack

reit|en† *vt/i* (*sein*) ride. **R~er(in)** *m* -s,- (*f* -,-nen) rider. **R~hose** *f* riding breeches *pl*. **R~pferd** *nt* saddlehorse. **R~schule** *f* riding-school. **R~weg** *m* bridle-path

(Charme) charm. r~bar *a* irritable. R~barkeit *f* - irritability. r~en *vt* provoke; *(Med)* irritate; *(interessieren, locken)* appeal to, attract; arouse ⟨*Neugier*⟩; *(beim Kartenspiel)* bid. r~end *a* charming, *adv* -ly; *(entzückend)* delightful. R~ung *f* -,-en *(Med)* irritation. r~voll *a* attractive

rekapitulieren *vt/i (haben)* recapitulate

rekeln (sich) *vr* stretch; *(lümmeln)* sprawl

Reklamation /-'tsio:n/ *f* -,-en *(Comm)* complaint

Reklam|e *f* -,-n advertising, publicity; *(Anzeige)* advertisement; *(TV, Radio)* commercial; R~e machen advertise (für etw sth). r~ieren *vt* complain about; *(fordern)* claim ● *vi (haben)* complain

rekonstruieren *vt* reconstruct. R~ktion /-'tsio:n/ *f* -,-en reconstruction

Rekonvaleszenz *f* - convalescence

Rekord *m* -[e]s,-e record

Rekrut *m* -en,-en recruit. r~ieren *vt* recruit

Rek|tor *m* -s,-en /-'to:rən/ *(Sch)* head[master]; *(Univ)* vice-chancellor. R~torin *f* -,-nen head[mistress]; vice-chancellor

Relais /rə'lɛ:/ *nt* -,- /-s,-s/ *(Electr)* relay

relativ *a* relative, *adv* -ly. R~pronomen *nt* relative pronoun

relevan|t *a* relevant (für to). R~z *f* - relevance

Relief /rə'ljɛf/ *nt* -s,-s relief

Religi|on *f* -,-en religion; *(Sch)* religious education. r~ös *a* religious

Reling *f* -,-s *(Naut)* rail

Reliquie /re'li:kvjə/ *f* -,-n relic

Remouladensoße /remu'la:dən-/ *f* ≈ tartar sauce

rempeln *vt* jostle; *(stoßen)* push

Ren *nt* -s,-s reindeer

Reneklode *f* -,-n greengage

Renn|auto *nt* racing car. R~bahn *f* race-track; *(Pferde-)* racecourse. R~boot *nt* speedboat. r~en† *vt/i (sein)* run; um die Wette r~en have a race. R~en *nt* -s,- race. R~pferd *nt* racehorse. R~sport *m* racing. R~wagen *m* racing car

renommiert *a* renowned; ⟨*Hotel, Firma*⟩ of repute

renovier|en *vt* renovate; redecorate ⟨*Zimmer*⟩. R~ung *f* - renovation; redecoration

rentabel *a* profitable, *adv* -bly

Rente *f* -,-n pension; in R~ gehen *(fam)* retire. R~nversicherung *f* pension scheme

Rentier *nt* reindeer

rentieren (sich) *vr* be profitable; *(sich lohnen)* be worth while

Rentner(in) *m* -s,- *(f -,-nen)* [old-age] pensioner

Reparatur *f* -,-en repair. R~werkstatt *f* repair workshop; *(Auto)* garage

reparieren *vt* repair, mend

repatriieren *vt* repatriate

Repertoire /repɛr'toa:ɐ̯/ *nt* -s,-s repertoire

Reportage /-'ta:ʒə/ *f* -,-n report

Reporter(in) *m* -s,- *(f -,-nen)* reporter

repräsent|ativ *a* representative (für of); *(eindrucksvoll)* imposing; *(Prestige verleihend)* prestigious. r~ie- ren *vt* represent ● *vi (haben)* perform official/social duties

Repress|alie /-ljə/ *f* -,-n reprisal. r~iv *a* repressive

Reprodu|ktion /-'tsio:n/ *f* -,-en reproduction. R~zieren *vt* reproduce

Reptil *nt* -s,-ien /-jən/ reptile

Republik *f* -,-en republic. r~anisch *a* republican

requirieren *vt (Mil)* requisition

Requisiten *pl (Theat)* properties, *(fam)* props

Reservat *nt* -[e]s,-e reservation

Reserve *f* -,-n reserve; *(Mil, Sport)* reserves *pl.* R~rad *nt* spare wheel. R~spieler *m* reserve. R~tank *m* reserve tank

reservier|en *vt* reserve; r~en lassen book. r~t a reserved. R~ung *f* -,-en reservation

Reservoir /rezɛr'voa:ɐ̯/ *nt* -s,-s reservoir

Resid|enz *f* -,-en residence. r~ieren *vi (haben)* reside

Resign|ation /-'tsio:n/ *f* - resignation. r~ieren *vi (haben) (fig)* give up. r~iert *a* resigned, *adv* -ly

resolut *a* resolute, *adv* -ly

Resolution /-'tsio:n/ *f* -,-en resolution

Resonanz *f* -,-en resonance; *(fig: Widerhall)* response

Respekt /-sp-, -ʃp-/ *m* -[e]s respect (vor + *dat* for). r~abel *a* respectable. r~ieren *vt* respect

respekt|los *a* disrespectful, *adv* -ly. r~voll *a* respectful, *adv* -ly

Ressort /rɛ'so:ɐ̯/ nt **-s,-s** department

Rest m **-[e]s,-e** remainder, rest; **R~e** remains; (Essens-) leftovers

Restaurant /rɛsto'rã:/ nt **-s,-s** restaurant

Restaur|ation /rɛstaura'tsio:n/ f - restoration. **r~ieren** vt restore

Rest|betrag m balance. **r~lich** a remaining. **r~los** a utter, adv -ly

Resultat nt **-[e]s,-e** result

Retorte f **-,-n** (Chem) retort. **R~n-baby** nt (fam) test-tube baby

rett|en vt save (**vor** + dat from); (aus Gefahr befreien) rescue; **sich r~en** save oneself; (flüchten) escape. **R~er** m **-s,-** rescuer; (fig) saviour

Rettich m **-s,-e** white radish

Rettung f **-,-en** rescue; (fig) salvation; **jds letzte R~** s.o.'s last hope. **R~sboot** nt lifeboat. **R~sdienst** m rescue service. **R~sgürtel** m lifebelt. **r~slos** adv hopelessly. **R~sring** m lifebelt. **R~swagen** m ambulance

retuschieren vt (Phot) retouch

Reu|e f - remorse; (Relig) repentance. **r~en** vt fill with remorse; **es reut mich nicht** I don't regret it. **r~ig** a penitent. **r~mütig** a contrite, adv -ly

Revanch|e /re'vã:ʃə/ f **-,-n** revenge; **R~e fordern** (Sport) ask for a return match. **r~ieren (sich)** vr take revenge; (sich erkenntlich zeigen) reciprocate (**mit** with); **sich für eine Einladung r~ieren** return an invitation

Revers /re've:ɐ̯/ nt **-,- /**-[s],-s/ lapel

revidieren vt revise; (prüfen) check

Revier nt **-s,-e** district; (Zool & fig) territory; (Polizei-) [police] station

Revision f **-,-en** revision; (Prüfung) check; (Bücher-) audit; (Jur) appeal

Revolte f **-,-n** revolt

Revolution /-'tsio:n/ f **-,-en** revolution. **r~är** a revolutionary. **r~ieren** vt revolutionize

Revolver m **-s,-** revolver

Revue /rə'vy:/ f **-,-n** revue

Rezen|sent m **-en,-en** reviewer. **r~sieren** vt review. **R~sion** f **-,-en** review

Rezept nt **-[e]s,-e** prescription; (Culin) recipe

Rezeption /-'tsio:n/ f **-,-en** reception

Rezession f **-,-en** recession

rezitieren vt recite

R-Gespräch nt reverse-charge call, (Amer) collect call

Rhabarber m **-s** rhubarb

Rhapsodie f **-,-n** rhapsody

Rhein m **-s** Rhine. **R~land** nt **-s** Rhineland. **R~wein** m hock

Rhetori|k f - rhetoric. **r~sch** a rhetorical

Rheum|a nt **-s** rheumatism. **r~atisch** a rheumatic. **R~atismus** m - rheumatism

Rhinozeros nt **-[ses],-se** rhinoceros

rhyth|misch /'ryt-/ a rhythmic[al], adv -ally. **R~mus** m **-,-men** rhythm

Ribisel f **-,-n** (Aust) redcurrant

richten vt direct (**auf** + acc at); address (Frage, Briefe) (**an** + acc to); aim, train (Waffe) (**auf** + acc at); (einstellen) set; (vorbereiten) prepare; (reparieren) mend; (hinrichten) execute; (SGer: ordentlich machen) tidy; **in die Höhe r~** raise [up]; **das Wort an jdn r~** address s.o.; **sich r~** be directed (**auf** + acc at; **gegen** against); (Blick:) turn (**auf** + acc on); **sich r~ nach** comply with (Vorschrift, jds Wünschen); fit in with (jds Plänen); (befolgen) go by; (abhängen) depend on ● vi (haben) **r~ über** (+ acc) judge

Richter m **-s,-** judge

Richtfest nt topping-out ceremony

richtig a right, correct; (wirklich, echt) real; **das R~e** the right thing ● adv correctly; really; **die Uhr geht r~** the clock is right. **R~keit** f - correctness. **r~stellen** vt sep (fig) correct

Richtlinien fpl guidelines

Richtung f **-,-en** direction; (fig) trend

riechen† vt/i (haben) smell (**nach** of; **an etw** dat sth)

Riegel m **-s,-** bolt; (Seife) bar

Riemen m **-s,-** strap; (Ruder) oar

Riese m **-n,-n** giant

rieseln vi (sein) trickle; (Schnee:) fall lightly

Riesen|erfolg m huge success. **r~groß** a huge, enormous

riesig a huge; (gewaltig) enormous ● adv (fam) terribly

Riff nt **-[e]s,-e** reef

rigoros a rigorous, adv -ly

Rille f **-,-n** groove

Rind nt **-es,-er** ox; (Kuh) cow; (Stier) bull; (R~fleisch) beef; **R~er** cattle pl

Rinde f **-,-n** bark; (Käse-) rind; (Brot-) crust

Rinderbraten m roast beef

Rind|fleisch nt beef. **R~vieh** nt cattle pl; (fam: Idiot) idiot

Ring m **-[e]s,-e** ring

ringeln (sich) vr curl; ⟨Schlange:⟩ coil itself (**um** round)

ring|en† vi (haben) wrestle; (fig) struggle (**um/nach** for) • vt wring ⟨Hände⟩. **R~en** nt -s wrestling. **R~er** m -s,- wrestler. **R~kampf** m wrestling match; (als Sport) wrestling. **R~richter** m referee

rings adv **r~ im Kreis** in a circle; **r~ um jdn/etw** all around s.o./sth. **r~herum, r~um** adv all around

Rinn|e f -,-n channel; (Dach-) gutter. **r~en†** vi (sein) run; ⟨Sand:⟩ trickle. **R~stein** m gutter

Rippe f -,-n rib. **R~nfellentzündung** f pleurisy. **R~nstoß** m dig in the ribs

Risiko nt -s,-s & -ken risk; **ein R~ eingehen** take a risk

risk|ant a risky. **r~ieren** vt risk

Riß m -sses,-sse tear; (Mauer-) crack; (fig) rift

rissig a cracked; ⟨Haut⟩ chapped

Rist m -[e]s,-e instep

Ritt m -[e]s,-e ride

Ritter m -s,- knight. **r~lich** a chivalrous, adv -ly. **R~lichkeit** f - chivalry

rittlings adv astride

Ritu|al nt -s,-e ritual. **r~ell** a ritual

Ritz m -es,-e scratch. **R~e** f -,-n crack; (Fels-) cleft; ⟨zwischen Betten, Vorhängen⟩ gap. **r~en** vt scratch

Rival|e m -n,-n, **R~in** f -,-nen rival. **r~isieren** vi (haben) compete (**mit** with). **r~isierend** a rival ... **R~ität** f -,-en rivalry

Robbe f -,-n seal. **r~n** vi (sein) crawl

Robe f -,-n gown; (Talar) robe

Roboter m -s,- robot

robust a robust

röcheln vi (haben) breathe stertorously

Rochen m -s,- (Zool) ray

Rock¹ m -[e]s,-̈e skirt; (Jacke) jacket

Rock² m -[s] (Mus) rock

Rodel|bahn f toboggan run. **r~n** vi (sein/haben) toboggan. **R~schlitten** m toboggan

roden vt clear ⟨Land⟩; grub up ⟨Stumpf⟩

Rogen m -s,- [hard] roe

Roggen m -s rye

roh a rough; (ungekocht) raw; ⟨Holz⟩ bare; (brutal) brutal; **r~e Gewalt** brute force • adv roughly; brutally. **R~bau** m -[e]s,-ten shell. **R~kost** f raw [vegetarian] food. **R~ling** m

-s,-e brute. **R~material** nt raw material. **R~öl** nt crude oil

Rohr nt -[e]s,-e pipe; (Geschütz-) barrel; (Bot) reed; (Zucker-, Bambus-) cane

Röhr|chen nt -s,- [drinking] straw; (Auto, fam) breathalyser (P). **R~e** f -,-n tube; (Radio-) valve; (Back-) oven

Rohstoff m raw material

Rokoko nt -s rococo

Rolladen m roller shutter

Rollbahn f taxiway; (Start-/Landebahn) runway

Rolle f -,-n roll; (Garn-) reel; (Draht-) coil; (Techn) roller; (Seil-) pulley; (Wäsche-) mangle; (Lauf-) castor; (Schrift-) scroll; (Theat) part, role; **das spielt keine R~** (fig) that doesn't matter. **r~n** vt roll; (auf-) roll up; roll out ⟨Teig⟩; put through the mangle ⟨Wäsche⟩; **sich r~n** roll; (sich ein-) curl up • vi (sein) roll; ⟨Flugzeug:⟩ taxi • vi (haben) ⟨Donner:⟩ rumble. **R~r** m -s,- scooter

Roll|feld nt airfield. **R~kragen** m polo-neck. **R~mops** m rollmop[s] sg

Rollo nt -s,-s [roller] blind

Roll|schuh m roller-skate; **R~schuh laufen** roller-skate. **R~splitt** m -s loose chippings pl. **R~stuhl** m wheelchair. **R~treppe** f escalator

Rom nt -s Rome

Roman m -s,-e novel. **r~isch** a Romanesque; ⟨Sprache⟩ Romance. **R~schriftsteller(in)** m(f) novelist

Romant|ik f - romanticism. **r~isch** a romantic, adv -ally

Romanze f -,-n romance

Röm|er(in) m -s,- (f -,-nen) Roman. **r~isch** a Roman

Rommé /'rɔme:/ nt -s rummy

röntgen vt X-ray. **R~aufnahme** f, **R~bild** nt X-ray. **R~strahlen** mpl X-rays

rosa inv a, **R~** nt -[s],- pink

Rose f -,-n rose. **R~nkohl** m [Brussels] sprouts pl. **R~nkranz** m (Relig) rosary. **R~nmontag** m Monday before Shrove Tuesday

Rosette f -,-n rosette

rosig a rosy

Rosine f -,-n raisin

Rosmarin m -s rosemary

Roß nt Rosses, Rösser horse. **R~kastanie** f horse-chestnut

Rost¹ m -[e]s,-e grating; (Kamin-) grate; (Brat-) grill

Rost² m -[e]s rust. **r~en** vi (haben) rust

röst|en vt roast; toast ⟨*Brot*⟩. **R∼er** m
-s,- toaster

rostfrei a stainless

rostig a rusty

rot a (**röter, rötest**), **Rot** nt -s,- red; **rot
werden** turn red; (*erröten*) go red,
blush

Rotation /-'tsio:n/ f -,-en rotation

Röte f - redness; (*Scham-*) blush

Röteln pl German measles sg

röten vt redden; **sich r∼** turn red

rothaarig a red-haired

rotieren vi (*haben*) rotate

Rot|kehlchen nt -s,- robin. **R∼kohl**
m red cabbage

rötlich a reddish

Rot|licht nt red light. **R∼wein** m red
wine

Rou|lade /ru'la:də/ f -,-n beef olive.
R∼leau /-'lo:/ nt -s,-s [roller] blind

Route /'ru:tə/ f -,-n route

Routin|e /ru'ti:nə/ f -,-n routine;
(*Erfahrung*) experience. **r∼emäßig** a
routine ... ● adv routinely. **r∼iert** a
experienced

Rowdy /'raudi/ m -s,-s hooligan

Rübe f -,-n beet; **rote R∼** beetroot;
gelbe R∼ (*SGer*) carrot

rüber adv = herüber, hinüber

Rubin m -s,-e ruby

Rubrik f -,-en column; (*Kategorie*)
category

Ruck m -[e]s,-e jerk

Rückantwort f reply

ruckartig a jerky, adv -ily

rück|bezüglich a (*Gram*) reflexive.
R∼blende f flashback. **R∼blick** m
(*fig*) review (**auf** + acc of). **r∼-
blickend** adv in retrospect. **r∼da-
tieren** vt (*inf & pp only*) backdate

rücken vt/i (*sein/haben*) move; **an
etw** (*dat*) **r∼** move sth

Rücken m -s,- back; (*Buch-*) spine;
(*Berg-*) ridge. **R∼lehne** f back.
R∼mark nt spinal cord.
R∼schwimmen nt backstroke. **R∼-
wind** m following wind; (*Aviat*) tail
wind

rückerstatten vt (*inf & pp only*)
refund

Rückfahr|karte f return ticket. **R∼t**
f return journey

Rück|fall m relapse. **r∼fällig** a **r∼-
fällig werden** (*Jur*) re-offend. **R∼flug**
m return flight. **R∼frage** f [further]
query. **r∼fragen** vi (*haben*) (*inf & pp
only*) check (**bei** with). **R∼gabe** f

drop, fall. **r∼gängig** a **r∼gängig
machen** cancel; break off ⟨*Verlobung*⟩.
R∼grat nt -[e]s,-e spine, backbone.
R∼halt m (*fig*) support. **R∼hand** f
backhand. **R∼kehr** return. **R∼-
lagen** fpl reserves. **R∼licht** nt rear-
light. **r∼lings** adv backwards; (*von
hinten*) from behind. **R∼reise** f return journey

Rucksack m rucksack

Rück|schau f review. **R∼schlag** m
(*Sport*) return; (*fig*) set-back. **R∼-
schluß** m conclusion. **R∼schritt** m
(*fig*) retrograde step. **r∼schrittlich**
a retrograde. **R∼seite** f back; (*einer
Münze*) reverse

Rücksicht f -,-en consideration; **R∼
nehmen auf** (+ acc) show consideration for; (*berücksichtigen*) take
into consideration. **R∼nahme** f - consideration. **r∼slos** a inconsiderate,
adv -ly; (*schonungslos*) ruthless, adv
-ly. **r∼svoll** a considerate, adv -ly

Rück|sitz m back seat; (*Sozius*) pil-
lion. **R∼spiegel** m rear-view mirror.
R∼spiel nt return match. **R∼-
sprache** f consultation; **R∼sprache
nehmen mit** consult. **R∼stand** m
(*Chem*) residue; (*Arbeits-*) backlog;
R∼stände arrears; **im R∼stand sein**
be behind. **r∼ständig** a (*fig*) backward. **R∼stau** m (*Auto*) tailback.
R∼strahler m -s,- reflector. **R∼tritt**
m resignation; (*Fahrrad*) back ped-
alling. **r∼vergüten** vt (*inf & pp only*)
refund. **R∼wanderer** m repatriate

rückwärt|ig a back ..., rear ... **r∼s**
adv backwards. **R∼sgang** m reverse
[gear]

Rückweg m way back

ruckweise adv jerkily

rück|wirkend a retrospective, adv
-ly. **R∼wirkung** f retrospective
force; **mit R∼wirkung vom** backdated
to. **R∼zahlung** f repayment. **R∼zug**
m retreat

Rüde m -n,-n [male] dog

Rudel nt -s,- herd; (*Wolfs-*) pack;
(*Löwen-*) pride

Ruder nt -s,- oar; (*Steuer-*) rudder; **am
R∼** (*Naut & fig*) at the helm. **R∼boot**
nt rowing boat. **R∼er** m -s,- oarsman.
r∼n vt/i (*haben/sein*) row

Ruf m -[e]s,-e call; (*laut*) shout; (*Telefon*) telephone number; (*Ansehen*) reputation; **Künstler von Ruf** artist of
repute. **r∼en†** vt/i (*haben*) call (**nach**

Rüffel *m* -s,- *(fam)* telling-off. **r~n** *vt* *(fam)* tell off

Ruf|name *m* forename by which one is known. **R~nummer** *f* telephone number. **R~zeichen** *nt* dialling tone

Rüge *f* -,-n reprimand. **r~n** *vt* reprimand; *(kritisieren)* criticize

Ruhe *f* - rest; *(Stille)* quiet; *(Frieden)* peace; *(innere)* calm; *(Gelassenheit)* composure; **die R~ bewahren** keep calm; **in R~ lassen** leave in peace; **sich zur R~ setzen** retire; **R~ [da]!** quiet! **R~gehalt** *nt* [retirement] pension. **r~los** *a* restless, *adv* -ly. **r~n** *vi (haben)* rest **(auf**+ *dat* on); *(Arbeit, Verkehr:)* have stopped; **hier ruht ...** here lies ... **R~pause** *f* rest, break. **R~stand** *m* retirement; **in den R~stand treten** retire; **im R~stand** retired. **R~störung** *f* disturbance of the peace. **R~tag** *m* day of rest; **'Montag R~tag'** 'closed on Mondays'

ruhig *a* quiet, *adv* -ly; *(erholsam)* restful; *(friedlich)* peaceful, *adv* -ly; *(unbewegt, gelassen)* calm, *adv* -ly; **r~ bleiben** remain calm; **sehen Sie sich r~ um** you're welcome to look round; **man kann r~ darüber sprechen** there's no harm in talking about it

Ruhm *m* -[e]s fame; *(Ehre)* glory

rühmen *vt* praise; **sich r~** boast *(gen* about)

ruhmreich *a* glorious

Ruhr *f* - *(Med)* dysentery

Rühr|ei *nt* scrambled eggs *pl.* **r~en** *vt* move; *(Culin)* stir; **sich r~en** move; **zu Tränen r~en** move to tears; **r~t euch!** *(Mil)* at ease! ● *vi (haben)* stir; **r~en an** (+ *acc)* touch; *(fig)* touch on; **r~en von** *(fig)* come from. **r~end** *a* touching, *adv* -ly

rühr|ig *a* active. **r~selig** *a* sentimental. **R~ung** *f* - emotion

Ruin *m* -s ruin. **R~e** *f* -,-n ruin; ruins *pl (gen* of). **r~ieren** *vt* ruin

rülpsen *vi (haben) (fam)* belch

Rum *m* -s rum

rum *adv* = **herum**

Rumän|ien /-iən/ *nt* -s Romania. **r~isch** *a* Romanian

Rummel *m* -s *(fam)* hustle and bustle; *(Jahrmarkt)* funfair. **R~platz** *m* fairground

rumoren *vi (haben)* make a noise; *(Magen:)* rumble

Rumpel|kammer *f* junk-room. **r~n** *vi (haben/sein)* rumble

Rumpf *m* -[e]s,-̈e body, trunk; *(Schiffs-)* hull; *(Aviat)* fuselage

rümpfen *vt* **die Nase r~** turn up one's nose **(über** + *acc* at)

rund *a* round ● *adv* approximately; **r~ um** [a]round. **R~blick** *m* panoramic view. **R~brief** *m* circular [letter]

Runde *f* -,-n round; *(Kreis)* circle; *(eines Polizisten)* beat; *(beim Rennen)* lap; **eine R~ Bier** a round of beer. **r~n** *vt* round; **sich r~n** become round; *(Backen:)* fill out

Rund|fahrt *f* tour. **R~frage** *f* poll

Rundfunk *m* radio; **im R~** on the radio. **R~gerät** *nt* radio [set]

Rund|gang *m* round; *(Spaziergang)* walk **(durch** round). **r~heraus** *adv* straight out. **r~herum** *adv* all around. **r~lich** *a* rounded; *(mollig)* plump. **R~reise** *f* [circular] tour. **R~schreiben** *nt* circular. **r~um** *adv* all round. **R~ung** *f* -,-en curve. **r~weg** *adv* ⟨*ablehnen*⟩ flatly

runter *adv* = **herunter, hinunter**

Runzel *f* -,-n wrinkle. **r~n** *vt* **die Stirn r~n** frown

runzlig *a* wrinkled

Rüpel *m* -s,- *(fam)* lout. **r~haft** *a* *(fam)* loutish

rupfen *vt* pull out; pluck ⟨*Geflügel*⟩; *(fam: schröpfen)* fleece

ruppig *a* rude, *adv* -ly

Rüsche *f* -,-n frill

Ruß *m* -es soot

Russe *m* -n,-n Russian

Rüssel *m* -s,- *(Zool)* trunk

ruß|en *vi (haben)* smoke. **r~ig** *a* sooty

Russ|in *f* -,-nen Russian. **r~isch** *a* Russian. **R~isch** *nt* -[s] *(Lang)* Russian

Rußland *nt* -s Russia

rüsten *vi (haben)* prepare **(zu/für** for) ● *vr* **sich r~** get ready; **gerüstet sein** be ready

rüstig *a* sprightly

rustikal *a* rustic

Rüstung *f* -,-en armament; *(Harnisch)* armour. **R~skontrolle** *f* arms control

Rute *f* -,-n twig; *(Angel-, Wünschel-)* rod; *(zur Züchtigung)* birch; *(Schwanz)* tail

Rutsch *m* -[e]s,-e slide. **R~bahn** *f* slide. **R~e** *f* -,-n chute. **r~en** *vt* slide;

(*rücken*) move ● *vi* (*sein*) slide; (*aus-, ab-*) slip; (*Auto*) skid; (*rücken*) move [along]. **r~ig** *a* slippery
rütteln *vt* shake ● *vi* (*haben*) **r~ an** (+ *dat*) rattle

S

Saal *m* **-[e]s, Säle** hall; (*Theat*) auditorium; (*Kranken-*) ward
Saat *f* **-,-en** seed; (*Säen*) sowing; (*Gesätes*) crop. **S~gut** *nt* seed
sabbern *vi* (*haben*) (*fam*) slobber; (*Baby:*) dribble; (*reden*) jabber
Säbel *m* **-s,-** sabre
Sabo|tage /zabo'taːʒə/ *f* - sabotage. **S~teur** /-'tøːɐ̯/ *m* **-s,-e** saboteur. **s~tieren** *vt* sabotage
Sach|bearbeiter *m* expert. **S~buch** *nt* non-fiction book. **s~dienlich** *a* relevant
Sache *f* **-,-n** matter, business; (*Ding*) thing; (*fig*) cause; **zur S~ kommen** come to the point
Sach|gebiet *nt* (*fig*) area, field. **s~gemäß** *a* proper, *adv* -ly. **S~kenntnis** *f* expertise. **s~kundig** *a* expert, *adv* -ly. **s~lich** *a* factual, *adv* -ly; (*nüchtern*) matter-of-fact, *adv* -ly; (*objektiv*) objective, *adv* -ly; (*schmucklos*) functional
sächlich *a* (*Gram*) neuter
Sachse *m* **-n,-n** Saxon. **S~n** *nt* **-s** Saxony
sächsisch *a* Saxon
sacht *a* gentle, *adv* -ly
Sach|verhalt *m* **-[e]s** facts *pl.* **s~verständig** *a* expert, *adv* -ly. **S~verständige(r)** *m/f* expert
Sack *m* **-[e]s,¨e** sack; **mit S~ und Pack** with all one's belongings
sacken *vi* (*sein*) sink; (*zusammen-*) go down; (*Person:*) slump
Sack|gasse *f* cul-de-sac; (*fig*) impasse. **S~leinen** *nt* sacking
Sadis|mus *m* - sadism. **S~t** *m* **-en,-en** sadist. **s~tisch** *a* sadistic, *adv* -ally
säen *vt/i* (*haben*) sow
Safe /zeːf/ *m* **-s,-s** safe
Saft *m* **-[e]s,¨e** juice; (*Bot*) sap. **s~ig** *a* juicy; (*Wiese*) lush; (*Preis, Rechnung*) hefty; (*Witz*) coarse. **s~los** *a* dry
Sage *f* **-,-n** legend
Säge *f* **-,-n** saw. **S~mehl** *nt* sawdust

sagen *vt* say; (*mitteilen*) tell; (*bedeuten*) mean; **das hat nichts zu s~** it doesn't mean anything
sägen *vt/i* (*haben*) saw
sagenhaft *a* legendary; (*fam: unglaublich*) fantastic, *adv* -ally
Säge|späne *mpl* wood shavings. **S~werk** *nt* sawmill
Sahn|e *f* - cream. **S~ebonbon** *m* & *nt* ≈ toffee. **s~ig** *a* creamy
Saison /zɛ'zõ:/ *f* **-,-s** season
Saite *f* **-,-n** (*Mus, Sport*) string. **S~ninstrument** *nt* stringed instrument
Sakko *m* & *nt* **-s,-s** sports jacket
Sakrament *nt* **-[e]s,-e** sacrament
Sakrileg *nt* **-s,-e** sacrilege
Sakrist|an *m* **-s,-e** verger. **S~ei** *f* **-,-en** vestry
Salat *m* **-[e]s,-e** salad; **ein Kopf S~** a lettuce. **S~soße** *f* salad-dressing
Salbe *f* **-,-n** ointment
Salbei *m* **-s** & *f* **-** sage
salben *vt* anoint
Saldo *m* **-s,-dos** & **-den** balance
Salon /za'lõ:/ *m* **-s,-s** salon; (*Naut*) saloon
salopp *a* casual, *adv* -ly; (*Benehmen*) informal, *adv* -ly; (*Ausdruck*) slangy
Salto *m* **-s,-s** somersault
Salut *m* **-[e]s,-e** salute. **s~ieren** *vi* (*haben*) salute
Salve *f* **-,-n** volley; (*Geschütz-*) salvo; (*von Gelächter*) burst
Salz *nt* **-es,-e** salt. **s~en†** *vt* salt. **S~faß** *nt* salt-cellar. **s~ig** *a* salty. **S~kartoffeln** *fpl* boiled potatoes. **S~säure** *f* hydrochloric acid
Samen *m* **-s,-** seed; (*Anat*) semen, sperm
sämig *a* (*Culin*) thick
Sämling *m* **-s,-e** seedling
Sammel|becken *nt* reservoir. **S~begriff** *m* collective term. **s~n** *vt/i* (*haben*) collect; (*suchen, versammeln*) gather; **sich s~n** collect; (*sich versammeln*) gather; (*sich fassen*) collect oneself. **S~name** *m* collective noun
Samm|ler(in) *m* **-s,-** (*f* **-,-nen**) collector. **S~lung** *f* **-,-en** collection; (*innere*) composure
Samstag *m* **-s,-e** Saturday. **s~s** *adv* on Saturdays
samt *prep* (+ *dat*) together with ● *adv* **s~ und sonders** without exception
Samt *m* **-[e]s** velvet. **s~ig** *a* velvety

sämtlich *indef pron inv* all. **s∼e(r,s)** *indef pron* all the; **s∼e Werke** complete works; **meine s∼en Bücher** all my books

Sanatorium *nt* **-s,-ien** sanatorium

Sand *m* **-[e]s** sand

Sandal|e *f* **-,-n** sandal. **S∼ette** *f* **-,-n** high-heeled sandal

Sand|bank *f* sandbank. **S∼burg** *f* sand-castle. **s∼ig** *a* sandy. **S∼kasten** *m* sand-pit. **S∼kuchen** *m* Madeira cake. **S∼papier** *nt* sandpaper. **S∼stein** *m* sandstone

sanft *a* gentle, *adv* -ly. **s∼mütig** *a* meek

Sänger(in) *m* **-s,-** (*f*-,**-nen**) singer

sanieren *vt* clean up; redevelop ⟨*Gebiet*⟩; (*modernisieren*) modernize; make profitable ⟨*Industrie, Firma*⟩; **sich s∼** become profitable

sanitär *a* sanitary

Sanität|er *m* **-s,-** first-aid man; (*Fahrer*) ambulance man; (*Mil*) medical orderly. **S∼swagen** *m* ambulance

Sanktion /zaŋk'tsjo:n/ *f* **-,-en** sanction. **s∼ieren** *vt* sanction

Saphir *m* **-s,-e** sapphire

Sardelle *f* **-,-n** anchovy

Sardine *f* **-,-n** sardine

Sarg *m* **-[e]s,-e** coffin

Sarkas|mus *m* **-** sarcasm. **s∼tisch** *a* sarcastic, *adv* -ally

Sat|an *m* **-s** Satan; (*fam: Teufel*) devil. **s∼anisch** *a* satanic

Satellit *m* **-en,-en** satellite. **S∼enfernsehen** *nt* satellite television

Satin /za'tɛŋ/ *m* **-s** satin

Satir|e *f* **-,-n** satire. **s∼isch** *a* satirical, *adv* -ly

satt *a* full; ⟨*Farbe*⟩ rich; **s∼ sein** have had enough [to eat]; **sich s∼ essen** eat as much as one wants; **s∼ machen** feed; ⟨*Speise:*⟩ be filling; **etw s∼ haben** (*fam*) be fed up with sth

Sattel *m* **-s,-** saddle. **s∼n** *vt* saddle. **S∼schlepper** *m* tractor unit. **S∼zug** *m* articulated lorry

sättigen *vt* satisfy; (*Chem & fig*) saturate ●*vi* (*haben*) be filling. **s∼d** *a* filling

Satz *m* **-es,-e** sentence; (*Teil-*) clause; (*These*) proposition; (*Math*) theorem; (*Mus*) movement; (*Tennis, Zusammengehöriges*) set; (*Boden-*) sediment; (*Kaffee-*) grounds *pl*; (*Steuer-, Zins-*)

(*Sprung*) leap, bound. **S∼aussage** *f* predicate. **S∼gegenstand** *m* subject. **S∼zeichen** *nt* punctuation mark

Sau *f* **-, Säue** sow; (*sl: schmutziger Mensch*) dirty pig

sauber *a* clean; (*ordentlich*) neat, *adv* -ly; (*anständig*) decent, *adv* -ly; (*fam: nicht anständig*) fine. **s∼halten**† *vt sep* keep clean. **S∼keit** *f* - cleanliness; neatness; decency

säuberlich *a* neat, *adv* -ly

saubermachen *vt/i sep* (*haben*) clean

säuber|n *vt* clean; (*befreien*) rid/ (*Pol*) purge (**von** of). **S∼ungsaktion** *f* (*Pol*) purge

Sauce /'zo:sə/ *f* **-,-n** sauce; (*Braten-*) gravy

Saudi-Arabien /-jən/ *nt* **-s** Saudi Arabia

sauer *a* sour; (*Chem*) acid; (*eingelegt*) pickled; (*schwer*) hard; **saurer Regen** acid rain; **s∼ sein** (*fam*) be annoyed

Saurerei *f* **-,-en = Schweinerei**

Sauerkraut *nt* sauerkraut

säuerlich *a* slightly sour

Sauerstoff *m* oxygen

saufen† *vt/i* (*haben*) drink; (*sl*) booze

Säufer *m* **-s,-** (*sl*) boozer

saugen† *vt/i* (*haben*) suck; (*staub-*) vacuum, hoover; **sich voll Wasser s∼** soak up water

säugen *vt* suckle

Sauger *m* **-s,-** [baby's] dummy, (*Amer*) pacifier; (*Flaschen-*) teat

Säugetier *nt* mammal

saugfähig *a* absorbent

Säugling *m* **-s,-e** infant

Säule *f* **-,-n** column

Saum *m* **-[e]s, Säume** hem; (*Rand*) edge

säumen¹ *vt* hem; (*fig*) line

säum|en² *vi* (*haben*) delay. **s∼ig** *a* dilatory

Sauna *f* **-,-nas & -nen** sauna

Säure *f* **-,-n** acidity; (*Chem*) acid

säuseln *vi* (*haben*) rustle [softly]

sausen *vi* (*haben*) rush; (*Ohren:*) buzz ● *vi* (*sein*) rush [along]

Sauwetter *nt* (*sl*) lousy weather

Saxophon *nt* **-s,-e** saxophone

SB- /ɛs'be:-/ *pref* (= **Selbstbedienung**) self-service...

S-Bahn *f* city and suburban railway

sch *int* shush! (*fort*) shoo!

Schabe *f* **-,-n** cockroach

schäbig *a* shabby, *adv* -ily

Schablone *f* -,-n stencil; (*Muster*) pattern; (*fig*) stereotype

Schach *nt* -s chess; **S~!** check! **in S~ halten** (*fig*) keep in check. **S~brett** *nt* chessboard

schachern *vi* (*haben*) haggle

Schachfigur *f* chess-man

schachmatt *a* **s~ setzen** checkmate; **s~!** checkmate!

Schachspiel *nt* game of chess

Schacht *m* -[e]s,¨e shaft

Schachtel *f* -,-n box; (*Zigaretten-*) packet

Schachzug *m* move

schade *a* **s~ sein** be a pity *or* shame; **zu s~ für** too good for; **[wie] s~!** [what a] pity *or* shame!

Schädel *m* -s,- skull. **S~bruch** *m* fractured skull

schaden *vi* (*haben*) (+ *dat*) damage; (*nachteilig sein*) hurt; **das schadet nichts** that doesn't matter. **S~** *m* -s,¨ damage; (*Defekt*) defect; (*Nachteil*) disadvantage; **zu S~ kommen** be hurt. **S~ersatz** *m* damages *pl.* **S~freude** *f* malicious glee. **s~froh** *a* gloating

schadhaft *a* defective

schädigen *vt* damage, harm. **S~ung** *f* -,-en damage

schädlich *a* harmful

Schädling *m* -s,-e pest. **S~sbekämpfungsmittel** *nt* pesticide

Schaf *nt* -[e]s,-e sheep; (*fam: Idiot*) idiot. **S~bock** *m* ram

Schäfchen *nt* -s,- lamb

Schäfer *m* -s,- shepherd. **S~hund** *m* sheepdog; **Deutscher S~hund** German shepherd, alsatian

Schaffell *nt* sheepskin

schaffen[1]† *vt* create; (*herstellen*) establish; make (*Platz*); **wie geschaffen für** made for

schaffen[2] *v* (*reg*) ● *vt* manage [to do]; pass (*Prüfung*); catch (*Zug*); (*bringen*) take; **jdm zu s~ machen** trouble s.o.; **sich** (*dat*) **zu s~ machen** busy oneself (**an** + *dat* with) ● *vi* (*haben*) (*SGer: arbeiten*) work. **S~** *nt* -s work

Schaffner *m* -s,- conductor; (*Zug-*) ticket-inspector

Schaffung *f* - creation

Schaft *m* -[e]s,¨e shaft; (*Gewehr-*) stock; (*Stiefel-*) leg. **S~stiefel** *m* high boot

Schal *m* -s,-s scarf

schal *a* insipid; (*abgestanden*) flat; (*fig*) stale

Schale *f* -,-n skin; (*abgeschält*) peel; (*Eier-, Nuß-, Muschel-*) shell; (*Schüssel*) dish

schälen *vt* peel; **sich s~** peel

schalkhaft *a* mischievous, *adv* -ly

Schall *m* -[e]s sound. **S~dämpfer** *m* silencer. **s~dicht** *a* soundproof. **s~en** *vi* (*haben*) ring out; (*nachhallen*) resound; **s~end lachen** roar with laughter. **S~mauer** *f* sound barrier. **S~platte** *f* record, disc

schalt|en *vt* switch ● *vi* (*haben*) switch/⟨*Ampel:*⟩ turn (**auf** + *acc* to); (*Auto*) change gear; (*fam: begreifen*) catch on. **S~er** *m* -s,- switch; (*Post-, Bank-*) counter; (*Fahrkarten-*) ticket window. **S~hebel** *m* switch; (*Auto*) gear-lever. **S~jahr** *nt* leap year. **S~kreis** *m* circuit. **S~ung** *f* -,-en circuit; (*Auto*) gear change

Scham *f* - shame; (*Anat*) private parts *pl*; **falsche S~** false modesty

schämen (sich) *vr* be ashamed; **schämt euch!** you should be ashamed of yourselves!

scham|haft *a* modest, *adv* -ly; (*schüchtern*) bashful, *adv* -ly. **s~los** *a* shameless, *adv* -ly

Schampon *nt* -s shampoo. **s~ieren** *vt* shampoo

Schande *f* - disgrace, shame; **S~ machen** (+ *dat*) bring shame on

schänd|en *vt* dishonour; (*fig*) defile; (*Relig*) desecrate; (*sexuell*) violate. **s~lich** *a* disgraceful, *adv* -ly. **S~ung** *f* -,-en defilement; desecration; violation

Schanktisch *m* bar

Schanze *f* -,-n [ski-]jump

Schar *f* -,-en crowd; (*Vogel-*) flock; **in [hellen] S~en** in droves

Scharade *f* -,-n charade

scharen *vt* um sich s~ gather round one; **sich s~ um** flock round. **s~weise** *adv* in droves

scharf *a* (**schärfer, schärfst**) sharp; (*stark*) strong; (*stark gewürzt*) hot; ⟨*Geruch*⟩ pungent; ⟨*Frost, Wind, Augen, Verstand*⟩ keen; ⟨*streng*⟩ harsh; ⟨*Galopp, Ritt*⟩ hard; ⟨*Munition*⟩ live; ⟨*Hund*⟩ fierce; **s~ einstellen** (*Phot*) focus; **s~ sein** (*Phot*) be in focus; **s~ sein auf** (+ *acc*) (*fam*) be keen on ● *adv* sharply; ⟨*hinsehen, nachdenken, bremsen, reiten*⟩ hard; (*streng*) harshly; **s~ schießen** fire live ammunition

Scharfblick m perspicacity
Schärfe f - (s. **scharf**) sharpness; strength; hotness; pungency; keenness; harshness. s∼n vt sharpen
scharf|machen vt sep (fam) incite. S∼richter m executioner. S∼schütze m marksman. s∼sichtig a perspicacious. S∼sinn m astuteness. s∼sinnig a astute, adv -ly
Scharlach m -s scarlet fever
Scharlatan m -s,-e charlatan
Scharnier nt -s,-e hinge
Schärpe f -,-n sash
scharren vi (haben) scrape; ⟨Huhn:⟩ scratch; ⟨Pferd:⟩ paw the ground ● vt scrape
Schart|e f -,-n nick. s∼ig a jagged
Schaschlik m & nt -s,-s kebab
Schatten m -s,- shadow; ⟨schattige Stelle⟩ shade; **im S∼** in the shade. s∼haft a shadowy. S∼riß m silhouette. S∼seite f shady side; (fig) disadvantage
schattier|en vt shade. S∼ung f -,-en shading; (fig: Variante) shade
schattig a shady
Schatz m -es,-̈e treasure; (Freund, Freundin) sweetheart; (Anrede) darling
Schätzchen nt -s,- darling
schätzen vt estimate; (taxieren) value; (achten) esteem; (würdigen) appreciate; (fam: vermuten) reckon; **sich glücklich s∼** consider oneself lucky
Schätzung f -,-en estimate; (Taxierung) valuation. s∼sweise adv approximately
Schau f -,-en show; **zur S∼ stellen** display. S∼bild nt diagram
Schauder m -s shiver; (vor Abscheu) shudder. s∼haft a dreadful, adv -ly. s∼n vi (haben) shiver; (vor Abscheu) shudder; **mich s∼te** I shivered/ shuddered
schauen vi (haben) (SGer, Aust) look; s∼, **daß** make sure that
Schauer m -s,- shower; (Schauder) shiver. S∼geschichte f horror story. s∼lich a ghastly. s∼n vi (haben) shiver; **mich s∼te** I shivered
Schaufel f -,-n shovel; (Kehr-) dustpan. s∼n vt shovel; (graben) dig
Schaufenster nt shop-window. S∼bummel m window-shopping. S∼puppe f dummy
Schaukasten m display case
Schaukel f -,-n swing. s∼n vt rock ● vi (haben) rock; (auf einer

Schaukel) swing; (schwanken) sway. S∼pferd nt rocking-horse. S∼stuhl m rocking-chair
schaulustig a curious
Schaum m -[e]s foam; (Seifen-) lather; (auf Bier) froth; (als Frisier-, Rasiermittel) mousse
schäumen vi (haben) foam, froth; ⟨Seife:⟩ lather
Schaum|gummi m foam rubber. s∼ig a frothy; **s∼ig rühren** (Culin) cream. S∼krone f white crest; (auf Bier) head. S∼speise f mousse. S∼stoff m [synthetic] foam. S∼wein m sparkling wine
Schauplatz m scene
schaurig a dreadful, adv -ly; (unheimlich) eerie, adv eerily
Schauspiel nt play; (Anblick) spectacle. S∼er m actor. S∼erin f actress. s∼ern vi (haben) act; (sich verstellen) play-act
Scheck m -s,-s cheque, (Amer) check. S∼buch, S∼heft nt cheque-book. S∼karte f cheque card
Scheibe f -,-n disc; (Schieß-) target; (Glas-) pane; (Brot-, Wurst-) slice. S∼nwaschanlage f windscreen washer. S∼nwischer m -s,- windscreen-wiper
Scheich m -s,-e & -s sheikh
Scheide f -,-n sheath; (Anat) vagina
scheid|en† vt separate; (unterscheiden) distinguish; dissolve ⟨Ehe⟩; **sich s∼en lassen** get divorced; **sich s∼en** diverge; ⟨Meinungen:⟩ differ ● vi (sein) leave; (voneinander) part. S∼ung f -,-en divorce
Schein m -[e]s,-e light; (Anschein) appearance; (Bescheinigung) certificate; (Geld-) note; **etw nur zum S∼ tun** only pretend to do sth. s∼bar a apparent, adv -ly. s∼en† vi (haben) shine; (den Anschein haben) seem, appear; **mir s∼t** it seems to me
scheinheilig a hypocritical, adv -ly. S∼keit f hypocrisy
Scheinwerfer m -s,- floodlight; (Such-) searchlight; (Auto) headlight; (Theat) spotlight
Scheiß-, scheiß- pref (vulg) bloody. S∼e f - (vulg) shit. s∼en† vi (haben) (vulg) shit
Scheit nt -[e]s,-e log
Scheitel m -s,- parting. s∼n vt part ⟨Haar⟩
scheitern vi (sein) fail

Schelle f -,-n bell. **s~n** vi (haben) ring

Schellfisch m haddock

Schelm m -s,-e rogue. **s~isch** a mischievous, adv -ly

Schelte f - scolding. **s~n†** vi (haben) grumble (**über** + acc about); **mit jdm s~n** scold s.o. ● vt scold; (bezeichnen) call

Schema nt -s,-mata model, pattern; (Skizze) diagram

Schemel m -s,- stool

Schenke f -,-n tavern

Schenkel m -s,- thigh; (Geom) side

schenken vt give [as a present]; **jdm Vertrauen/Glauben s~** trust/believe s.o.; **sich (dat) etw s~** give sth a miss

scheppern vi (haben) clank

Scherbe f -,-n [broken] piece

Schere f -,-n scissors pl; (Techn) shears pl; (Hummer-) claw. **s~n†** vt shear; crop ⟨Haar⟩; clip ⟨Hund⟩

scheren² vt (reg) (fam) bother; **sich nicht s~ um** not care about; **scher dich zum Teufel!** go to hell!

Scherenschnitt m silhouette

Schererei[en fpl (fam) trouble sg

Scherz m -es,-e joke; **im/zum S~** as a joke. **s~en** vi (haben) joke. **S~frage** f riddle. **s~haft** a humorous

scheu a shy, adv -ly; ⟨Tier⟩ timid; **s~ werden** ⟨Pferd:⟩ shy; **s~ machen** startle. **S~** f - shyness; timidity; (Ehrfurcht) awe

scheuchen vt shoo

scheuen vt be afraid of; (meiden) shun; **keine Mühe/Kosten s~** spare no effort/expense; **sich s~** be afraid (**vor** + dat of); shrink (**etw zu tun** from doing sth) ● vi (haben) ⟨Pferd:⟩ shy

Scheuer|lappen m floor-cloth. **s~n** vt scrub; (mit Scheuerpulver) scour; (reiben) rub; **[wund] s~n** chafe ● vi (haben) rub, chafe. **S~tuch** nt floorcloth

Scheuklappen fpl blinkers

Scheune f -,-n barn

Scheusal nt -s,-e monster

scheußlich a horrible, adv -bly

Schi m -s,-er ski; **S~ fahren** od **laufen** ski

Schicht f -,-en layer; (Geol) stratum; (Gesellschafts-) class; (Arbeits-) shift. **S~arbeit** f shift work. **s~en** vt stack [up]

schick a stylish, adv -ly; ⟨Frau⟩ chic; (fam: prima) great. **S~** m -[e]s style

schicken vt/i (haben) send; **s~ nach** send for; **sich s~ in** (+ acc) resign oneself to

schicklich a fitting, proper

Schicksal nt -s,-e fate. **s~haft** a fateful. **S~sschlag** m misfortune

Schieb|edach nt (Auto) sun-roof. **s~en†** vt push; (gleitend) slide; (fam: handeln mit) traffic in; **etw s~en auf** (+ acc) (fig) put sth down to; shift ⟨Schuld, Verantwortung⟩ on to ● vi (haben) push. **S~er** m -s,- slide; (Person) black marketeer. **S~etür** f sliding door. **S~ung** f -,-en (fam) illicit deal; (Betrug) rigging, fixing

Schieds|gericht nt panel of judges; (Jur) arbitration tribunal. **S~richter** m referee; (Tennis) umpire; (Jur) arbitrator

schief a crooked; (unsymmetrisch) lopsided; (geneigt) slanting, sloping; (nicht senkrecht) leaning; (Winkel) oblique; (fig) false; (mißtrauisch) suspicious ● adv not straight; **jdn s~ ansehen** look at s.o. askance

Schiefer m -s slate

schief|gehen† vi sep (sein) (fam) go wrong. **s~lachen (sich)** vr sep double up with laughter

schielen vi (haben) squint

Schienbein nt shin; (Knochen) shinbone

Schiene f -,-n rail; (Gleit-) runner; (Med) splint. **s~n** vt (Med) put in a splint

schier¹ adv almost

schier² a pure; ⟨Fleisch⟩ lean

Schießbude f shooting-gallery. **s~en†** vt shoot; fire ⟨Kugel⟩; score ⟨Tor⟩ ● vi (haben) shoot, fire (**auf** + acc at) ● vi (sein) shoot [along]; (strömen) gush; **in die Höhe s~en** shoot up. **S~erei** f -,-en shooting. **S~scheibe** f target. **S~stand** m shooting-range

Schifahr|en nt skiing. **S~er(in)** m(f) skier

Schiff nt -[e]s,-e ship; (Kirchen-) nave; (Seiten-) aisle

Schiffahrt f shipping

schiff|bar a navigable. **S~bau** m shipbuilding. **S~bruch** m shipwreck. **s~brüchig** a shipwrecked. **S~chen** nt -s,- small boat; (Tex) shuttle. **S~er** m -s,- skipper

Schikan|e f -,-n harassment; **mit allen S~en** (fam) with every refinement. **s~ieren** vt harass; (tyrannisieren) bully

Schi|laufen nt -s skiing. **S~läufer(in)** m(f) -s,- (f-,-nen) skier

Schild[1] m -[e]s,-e shield; **etw im S~e führen** (fam) be up to sth

Schild[2] nt -[e]s,-er sign; (Namens-, Nummern-) plate; (Mützen-) badge; (Etikett) label

Schilddrüse f thyroid [gland]

schilder|n vt describe. **S~ung** f -,-en description

Schild|kröte f tortoise; (See-) turtle. **S~patt** nt -[e]s tortoiseshell

Schilf nt -[e]s reeds pl

schillern vi (haben) shimmer

Schimmel m -s,- mould; (Pferd) white horse. **s~ig** a mouldy. **s~n** vi (haben/sein) go mouldy

Schimmer m -s gleam; (Spur) glimmer. **s~n** vi (haben) gleam

Schimpanse m -n,-n chimpanzee

schimpf|en vi (haben) grumble (**mit** at; **über** + acc about); scold (**mit jdm** s.o.) ● vt call. **S~name** m term of abuse. **S~wort** nt (pl -wörter) swearword; (Beleidigung) insult

schind|en† vt work or drive hard; (quälen) ill-treat; **sich s~en** slave [away]; **Eindruck s~en** (fam) try to impress. **S~er** m -s,- slave-driver. **S~erei** f - slave-driving; (Plackerei) hard slog

Schinken m -s,- ham. **S~speck** m bacon

Schippe f -,-n shovel. **s~n** vt shovel

Schirm m -[e]s,-e umbrella; (Sonnen-) sunshade; (Lampen-) shade; (Augen-) visor; (Mützen-) peak; (Ofen-, Bild-) screen; (fig: Schutz) shield. **S~herr** m patron. **S~herrschaft** f patronage. **S~mütze** f peaked cap

schizophren a schizophrenic. **S~ie** f - schizophrenia

Schlacht f -,-en battle

schlachten vt slaughter, kill

Schlächter, Schlächter m -s,- (NGer) butcher

Schlacht|feld nt battlefield. **S~haus** nt, **S~hof** m abattoir. **S~platte** f plate of assorted cooked meats and sausages. **S~schiff** nt battleship

Schlacke f -,-n slag

Schlaf m -[e]s sleep; **im S~** in one's sleep. **S~anzug** m pyjamas pl, (Amer) pajamas pl. **S~couch** f sofa bed

Schläfe f -,-n (Anat) temple

schlafen† vi (haben) sleep; (fam: nicht aufpassen) be asleep; **s~ gehen**

go to bed; **er schläft noch** he is still asleep. **S~szeit** f bedtime

Schläfer(in) m -s,- (f-,-nen) sleeper

schlaff a limp, adv -ly; (Seil) slack; (Muskel) flabby

Schlaf|lied nt lullaby. **s~los** a sleepless. **S~losigkeit** f - insomnia. **S~mittel** nt sleeping drug

schläfrig a sleepy, adv -ily

Schlaf|saal m dormitory. **S~sack** m sleeping-bag. **S~tablette** f sleeping-pill. **s~trunken** a [still] half asleep. **S~wagen** m sleeping-car, sleeper. **s~wandeln** vi (haben/sein) sleepwalk. **S~zimmer** nt bedroom

Schlag m -[e]s,¨e blow; (Faust-) punch; (Herz-, Puls-, Trommel-) beat; (einer Uhr) chime; (Glocken-, Gong- & Med) stroke; (elektrischer) shock; (Portion) helping; (Art) type; (Aust) whipped cream; **S~e bekommen** get a beating; **S~ auf S~** in rapid succession. **S~ader** f artery. **S~anfall** m stroke. **s~artig** a sudden, adv -ly. **S~baum** m barrier

schlagen† vt hit, strike; (fällen) fell; knock (Loch, Nagel) (**in** + acc into); (prügeln, besiegen) beat; (Culin) whisk (Eiweiß); whip (Sahne); (legen) throw; (wickeln) wrap; (hinzufügen) add (**zu** to); **sich s~** fight; (sich) **geschlagen geben** admit defeat ● vi (haben) beat; (Tür:) bang; (Uhr:) strike; (melodisch) chime; **mit den Flügeln s~** flap its wings; **um sich s~** lash out; **es schlug sechs** the clock struck six ● vi (sein) **in etw** (acc) **s~** (Blitz, Kugel:) strike sth; **s~ an** (+ acc) knock against; **nach jdm s~** (fig) take after s.o. **S~d** a (fig) conclusive, adv -ly

Schlager m -s,- pop song; (Erfolg) hit

Schläger m -s,- racket; (Tischtennis-) bat; (Golf-) club; (Hockey-) stick; (fam: Raufbold) thug. **S~ei** f -,-en fight, brawl

schlag|fertig a quick-witted. **S~instrument** nt percussion instrument. **S~loch** nt pot-hole. **S~sahne** f whipped cream; (ungeschlagen) whipping cream. **S~seite** f (Naut) list. **S~stock** m truncheon. **S~wort** nt (pl -worte) slogan. **S~zeile** f headline. **S~zeug** nt (Mus) percussion. **S~zeuger** m -s,- percussionist; (in Band) drummer

schlaksig a gangling

Schlamassel m & nt -s (fam) mess

Schlamm m -[e]s mud. **s~ig** a muddy

Schlampe f -,-n (fam) slut. **s~en**
vi (haben) (fam) be sloppy (**bei**
in). **S~erei** f -,-en sloppiness; (Unordnung) mess. **s~ig** a slovenly; ⟨Ar-
beit⟩ sloppy ● adv in a slovenly way;
sloppily

Schlange f -,-n snake; (Menschen-,
Auto-) queue; **S~ stehen** queue, (Amer)
stand in line

schlängeln (sich) vr wind; ⟨Person:⟩
weave (**durch** through)

Schlangen|biß m snakebite. **S~**
linie f wavy line

schlank a slim. **S~heit** f slimness.
S~heitskur f slimming diet

schlapp a tired; (schlaff) limp, adv
-ly. **S~e** f -,-n (fam) setback

schlau a clever, adv -ly; (gerissen)
crafty, adv -ily; **ich werde nicht s~**
daraus I can't make head or tail of it

Schlauch m -[e]s, **Schläuche** tube;
(Wasser-) hose[pipe]. **S~boot** nt rubber dinghy. **s~en** vt (fam) exhaust

Schlaufe f -,-n loop

schlecht a bad; (böse) wicked; (unzulänglich) poor; **s~ werden** go bad;
⟨Wetter:⟩ turn bad; **s~er werden** get
worse; **s~ aussehen** look bad/⟨Person:⟩
unwell; **mir ist s~** I feel sick ● adv
badly; poorly; (kaum) not really.
s~gehen† vi sep (sein) (+ dat) **es**
geht ihm s~ he's doing badly; (gesundheitlich) he's not well. **s~gelaunt**
attrib a bad-tempered. **s~hin** adv
quite simply. **S~igkeit** f - wicked-
ness. **s~machen** vt sep (fam) run
down

schlecken vt/i (haben) lick (**an etw**
dat sth); (auf-) lap up

Schlegel m -s,- mallet; (Trommel-)
stick; (SGer: Keule) leg; (Hühner-) drumstick

schleichen† vi (sein) creep; (langsam
gehen/fahren) crawl ● vr **sich s~**
creep. **s~d** a creeping; ⟨Krankheit⟩
insidious

Schleier m -s,- veil; (fig) haze. **s~haft**
a **es ist mir s~haft** (fam) it's a mystery
to me

Schleife f -,-n bow; (Fliege) bow-tie;
(Biegung) loop

schleifen¹ v (reg) ● vt drag; (zerstören)
raze to the ground ● vi (haben) trail,
drag

schleifen²† vt grind; (schärfen)
sharpen; cut ⟨Edelstein, Glas⟩;

Schleim m -[e]s slime; (Anat) mucus;
(Med) phlegm. **s~ig** a slimy

schlemm|en vi (haben) feast ● vt
feast on. **S~er** m -s,- gourmet

schlendern vi (sein) stroll

schlenkern vt/i (haben) swing; **s~**
mit swing; dangle ⟨Beine⟩

Schlepp|dampfer m tug. **S~e** f -,-n
train. **s~en** vt drag; (tragen) carry;
(ziehen) tow; **sich s~en** drag oneself;
(sich hinziehen) drag on; **sich s~en mit**
carry. **s~end** a slow, adv -ly. **S~er** m
-s,- tug; (Traktor) tractor. **S~kahn** m
barge. **S~lift** m T-bar lift. **S~tau** nt
tow-rope; **ins S~tau nehmen** take in
tow

Schleuder f -,-n catapult; (Wäsche-)
spin-drier. **s~n** vt hurl; spin ⟨Wäsche⟩;
extract ⟨Honig⟩ ● vi (sein) skid; **ins**
S~n geraten skid. **S~preise** mpl
knock-down prices. **S~sitz** m ejector
seat

schleunigst adv hurriedly; (sofort)
at once

Schleuse f -,-n lock; (Sperre) sluice
[-gate]. **s~n** vt steer

Schliche pl tricks; **jdm auf die S~**
kommen (fam) get on to s.o.

schlicht a plain, adv -ly; (einfach)
simple, adv -ply

schlicht|en vt settle ● vi (haben)
arbitrate. **S~ung** f - settlement;
(Jur) arbitration

Schlick m -[e]s silt

Schließe f -,-n clasp; (Schnalle) buckle

schließen† vt close; (ab-) lock; fasten
⟨Kleid, Verschluß⟩; (stillegen) close
down; (beenden, folgern) conclude;
enter into ⟨Vertrag⟩; **sich s~** close; **in**
die Arme s~ embrace; **etw s~ an**
(+ acc) connect sth to; **sich s~ an**
(+ acc) follow ● vi (haben) close; (den
Betrieb einstellen) close down; (den
Schlüssel drehen) turn the key; (enden,
folgern) conclude; **s~ lassen auf**
(+ acc) suggest

Schließ|fach nt locker. **s~lich** adv
finally, in the end; (immerhin) after
all. **S~ung** f -,-en closure

Schliff m -[e]s cut; (Schleifen) cutting;
(fig) polish; **der letzte S~** the finishing
touches pl

schlimm a bad, adv -ly; **s~er werden**
get worse; **nicht so s~!** it doesn't matter! **s~stenfalls** adv if the worst
comes to the worst

Schlinge f -,-n loop; (Henkers-) noose;

Schlingel *m* **-s,-** (*fam*) rascal

schling|en† *vt* wind, wrap; tie ⟨*Knoten*⟩; **sich s~en um** coil around ● *vi* (*haben*) bolt one's food. **S~pflanze** *f* climber

Schlips *m* **-es,-e** tie

Schlitten *m* **-s,-** sledge; (*Rodel-*) toboggan; (*Pferde-*) sleigh; **S~ fahren** toboggan

schlittern *vi* (*haben/sein*) slide

Schlittschuh *m* skate; **S~ laufen** skate. **S~läufer(in)** *m(f)* skater

Schlitz *m* **-es,-e** slit; (*für Münze*) slot; (*Jacken-*) vent; (*Hosen-*) flies *pl.* **s~en** *vt* slit

Schloß *nt* **-sses,̈-sser** lock; (*Vorhänge-*) padlock; (*Verschluß*) clasp; (*Gebäude*) castle; (*Palast*) palace

Schlosser *m* **-s,-** locksmith; (*Auto-*) mechanic; (*Maschinen-*) fitter

Schlot *m* **-[e]s,-e** chimney

schlottern *vi* (*haben*) shake, tremble; ⟨*Kleider:*⟩ hang loose

Schlucht *f* **-,-en** ravine, gorge

schluchz|en *vi* (*haben*) sob. **S~er** *m* **-s,-** sob

Schluck *m* **-[e]s,-e** mouthful; (*klein*) sip

Schluckauf *m* **-s** hiccups *pl*

schlucken *vt/i* (*haben*) swallow. **S~** *m* **-s** hiccups *pl*

schlud|ern *vi* (*haben*) be sloppy (**bei** in). **s~rig** *a* sloppy, *adv* -ily; ⟨*Arbeit*⟩ slipshod

Schlummer *m* **-s** slumber. **s~n** *vi* (*haben*) slumber

Schlund *m* **-[e]s** [back of the] throat; (*fig*) mouth

schlüpf|en *vi* (*sein*) slip; **[aus dem Ei] s~en** hatch. **S~er** *m* **-s,-** knickers *pl.* **s~rig** *a* slippery; (*anstößig*) smutty

schlurfen *vi* (*sein*) shuffle

schlürfen *vt/i* (*haben*) slurp

Schluß *m* **-sses,̈-sse** end; (*S~folgerung*) conclusion; **zum S~** finally; **S~ machen** stop (**mit etw** sth); finish (**mit jdm** with s.o.)

Schlüssel *m* **-s,-** key; (*Schrauben-*) spanner; (*Geheim-*) code; (*Mus*) clef. **S~bein** *nt* collar-bone. **S~bund** *m & nt* bunch of keys. **S~loch** *nt* keyhole. **S~ring** *m* key-ring

Schlußfolgerung *f* conclusion

schlüssig *a* conclusive, *adv* -ly; **sich** (*dat*) **s~ werden** make up one's mind

Schluß|licht *nt* rear-light. **S~verkauf** *m* [end of season] sale

Schmach *f* **-** disgrace

schmachten *vi* (*haben*) languish

schmächtig *a* slight

schmackhaft *a* tasty

schmal *a* narrow; (*dünn*) thin; (*schlank*) slender; (*karg*) meagre

schmälern *vt* diminish; (*herabsetzen*) belittle

Schmalz¹ *nt* **-es** lard; (*Ohren-*) wax

Schmalz² *m* **-es** (*fam*) schmaltz. **s~ig** *a* (*fam*) schmaltzy, slushy

schmarotz|en *vi* (*haben*) be parasitic (**auf** + *acc* on); ⟨*Person:*⟩ sponge (**bei** on). **S~er** *m* **-s,-** parasite; (*Person*) sponger

Schmarren *m* **-s,-** (*Aust*) pancake [torn into strips]; (*fam: Unsinn*) rubbish

schmatzen *vi* (*haben*) eat noisily

schmausen *vi* (*haben*) feast

schmecken *vi* (*haben*) taste (**nach** of); **[gut] s~** taste good; **hat es dir geschmeckt?** did you enjoy it? ● *vt* taste

Schmeichelei *f* **-,-en** flattery; (*Kompliment*) compliment

schmeichel|haft *a* complimentary, flattering. **s~n** *vi* (*haben*) (+ *dat*) flatter

schmeißen† *vt/i* (*haben*) **s~ [mit]** (*fam*) chuck

Schmeißfliege *f* bluebottle

schmelz|en† *vt/i* (*sein*) melt; smelt ⟨*Erze*⟩. **S~wasser** *nt* melted snow

Schmerbauch *m* (*fam*) paunch

Schmerz *m* **-es,-en** pain; (*Kummer*) grief; **S~en haben** be in pain. **s~en** *vt* hurt; (*fig*) grieve ● *vi* (*haben*) hurt, be painful. **S~ensgeld** *nt* compensation for pain and suffering. **s~haft** *a* painful. **s~lich** *a* (*fig*) painful; (*traurig*) sad, *adv* -ly. **s~los** *a* painless, *adv* -ly. **s~stillend** *a* pain-killing; **s~stillendes Mittel** analgesic, pain-killer. **S~tablette** *f* pain-killer

Schmetterball *m* (*Tennis*) smash

Schmetterling *m* **-s,-e** butterfly

schmettern *vt* hurl; (*Tennis*) smash; (*singen*) sing; (*spielen*) blare out ● *vi* (*haben*) sound; ⟨*Trompeten:*⟩ blare

Schmied *m* **-[e]s,-e** blacksmith

Schmiede *f* **-,-n** forge. **S~eisen** *nt* wrought iron. **s~n** *vt* forge; (*fig*) hatch; **Pläne s~n** make plans

schmieg|en *vt* press; **sich s~en an** (+ *acc*) nestle or snuggle up to; ⟨*Kleid:*⟩ cling to. **s~sam** *a* supple

Schmier|e *f* **-,-n** grease; (*Schmutz*) mess. **s~en** *vt* lubricate; (*streichen*) spread; (*schlecht schreiben*) scrawl;

(*sl: bestechen*) bribe ● *vi (haben)* smudge; (*schreiben*) scrawl. **S~fett** *nt* grease. **S~geld** *nt (fam)* bribe. **s~ig** *a* greasy; (*schmutzig*) grubby; (*anstößig*) smutty; (*Person*) slimy. **S~mittel** *nt* lubricant

Schminke *f -,-n* make-up. **s~n** *vt* make up; **sich s~n** put on make-up; **sich** (*dat*) **die Lippen s~n** put on lipstick

schmirgel|n *vt* sand down. **S~papier** *nt* emery-paper

schmökern *vt/i (haben) (fam)* read

schmollen *vi (haben)* sulk; (*s~d den Mund verziehen*) pout

schmor|en *vt/i (haben)* braise; (*fam: schwitzen*) roast. **S~topf** *m* casserole

Schmuck *m -[e]s* jewellery; (*Verzierung*) ornament, decoration

schmücken *vt* decorate, adorn; **sich s~** adorn oneself

schmuck|los *a* plain. **S~stück** *nt* piece of jewellery; (*fig*) jewel

schmuddelig *a* grubby

Schmuggel *m -s* smuggling. **s~n** *vt* smuggle. **S~ware** *f* contraband

Schmuggler *m -s,-* smuggler

schmunzeln *vi (haben)* smile

schmusen *vi (haben)* cuddle

Schmutz *m -es* dirt; **in den S~ ziehen** (*fig*) denigrate. **s~en** *vi (haben)* get dirty. **S~fleck** *m* dirty mark. **s~ig** *a* dirty

Schnabel *m -s,-̈* beak, bill; (*eines Kruges*) lip; (*Tülle*) spout

Schnake *f -,-n* mosquito; (*Kohl-*) daddy-long-legs

Schnalle *f -,-n* buckle. **s~n** *vt* strap; (*zu-*) buckle; **den Gürtel enger s~n** tighten one's belt

schnalzen *vi (haben)* **mit der Zunge/ den Fingern s~** click one's tongue/ snap one's fingers

schnapp|en *vi (haben)* **s~en nach** snap at; gasp for (*Luft*) ● *vt* snatch, grab; (*fam: festnehmen*) nab. **S~schloß** *nt* spring lock. **S~schuß** *m* snapshot

Schnaps *m -es,-̈e* schnapps

schnarchen *vi (haben)* snore

schnarren *vi (haben)* rattle; (*Klingel:*) buzz

schnattern *vi (haben)* cackle

schnauben *vi (haben)* snort ● *vt* **sich** (*dat*) **die Nase s~** blow one's nose

schnaufen *vi (haben)* puff, pant

Schnauze *f -,-n* muzzle; (*eines Kruges*) lip; (*Tülle*) spout

Schnecke *f -,-n* snail; (*Nackt-*) slug; (*Spirale*) scroll; (*Gebäck*) ≈ Chelsea bun. **S~nhaus** *nt* snail-shell

Schnee *m -s* snow; (*Eier-*) beaten egg-white. **S~ball** *m* snowball. **S~besen** *m* whisk. **S~brille** *f* snow-goggles *pl.* **S~fall** *m* snowfall. **S~flocke** *f* snowflake. **S~glöckchen** *nt -s,-* snowdrop. **S~kette** *f* snow chain. **S~mann** *m (pl -männer)* snow- man. **S~pflug** *m* snow-plough. **S~schläger** *m* whisk. **S~sturm** *m* snowstorm, blizzard. **S~wehe** *f -,-n* snow-drift

Schneid *m -[e]s (SGer)* courage

Schneide *f -,-n* [cutting] edge; (*Klinge*) blade

schneiden† *vt* cut; (*in Scheiben*) slice; (*kreuzen*) cross; (*nicht beachten*) cut dead; **Gesichter s~** pull faces; **sich s~** cut oneself; (*über-*) intersect; **sich** (*dat/acc*) **in den Finger s~** cut one's finger. **s~d** *a* cutting; (*kalt*) biting

Schneider *m -s,-* tailor. **S~in** *f -,-nen* dressmaker. **s~n** *vt* make (*Anzug, Kostüm*)

Schneidezahn *m* incisor

schneidig *a* dashing, *adv* -ly

schneien *vi (haben)* snow; **es schneit** it is snowing

Schneise *f -,-n* path; (*Feuer-*) firebreak

schnell *a* quick; (*Auto, Tempo*) fast ● *adv* quickly; (*in s~em Tempo*) fast; (*bald*) soon; **mach s~!** hurry up! **s~en** *vi (sein)* **in die Höhe s~en** shoot up. **S~igkeit** *f -* rapidity; (*Tempo*) speed. **S~imbiß** *m* snack-bar. **S~kochtopf** *m* pressure-cooker. **S~reinigung** *f* express cleaners. **s~stens** *adv* as quickly as possible. **S~zug** *m* express [train]

schnetzeln *vt* cut into thin strips

schneuzen (sich) *vr* blow one's nose

schnippen *vt/i*

schnippisch *a* pert, *adv* -ly

Schnipsel *m & nt -s,-* scrap

Schnitt *m -[e]s,-e* cut; (*Film-*) cutting; (*S~muster*) [paper] pattern; **im S~** (*durchschnittlich*) on average

Schnitte *f -,-n* slice [of bread]; (*belegt*) open sandwich

schnittig *a* stylish; (*stromlinienförmig*) streamlined

Schnitt|käse *m* hard cheese. **S~lauch** *m* chives *pl.* **S~muster** *nt*

[paper] pattern. **S~punkt** *m* [point of] intersection. **S~wunde** *f* cut

Schnitzel *nt* **-s,-** scrap; (*Culin*) escalope. **s~n** *vt* shred

schnitz|en *vt/i (haben)* carve. **S~er** *m* **-s,-** carver; (*fam: Fehler*) blunder. **S~erei** *f* **-,-en** carving

schnodderig *a (fam)* brash

schnöde *a* despicable, *adv* -bly; (*verächtlich*) contemptuous, *adv* -ly

Schnorchel *m* **-s,-** snorkel

Schnörkel *m* **-s,-** flourish; (*Kunst*) scroll. **s~ig** *a* ornate

schnorren *vt/i (haben) (fam)* scrounge

schnüffeln *vi (haben)* sniff (**an etw** *dat* sth); (*fam: spionieren*) snoop [around]

Schnuller *m* **-s,-** [baby's] dummy, (*Amer*) pacifier

schnupf|en *vt* sniff; **Tabak s~en** take snuff. **S~en** *m* **-s,-** [head] cold. **S~tabak** *m* snuff

schnuppern *vt/i (haben)* sniff (**an etw** *dat* sth)

Schnur *f* **-,⁀e** string; (*Kordel*) cord; (*Besatz-*) braid; (*Electr*) flex; **eine S~** a piece of string

Schnür|chen *nt* **-s,- wie am S~chen** (*fam*) like clockwork. **s~en** *vt* tie; lace [up] ⟨*Schuhe*⟩

schnurgerade *a & adv* dead straight

Schnurr|bart *m* moustache. **s~en** *vi (haben)* hum; ⟨*Katze:*⟩ purr

Schnür|schuh *m* lace-up shoe. **S~senkel** *m* [shoe-]lace

schnurstracks *adv* straight

Schock *m* **-[e]s,-s** shock. **s~en** *vt* (*fam*) shock; **geschockt sein** be shocked. **s~ieren** *vt* shock; **s~ierend** shocking

Schöffe *m* **-n,-n** lay judge

Schokolade *f* - chocolate

Scholle *f* **-,-n** clod [of earth]; (*Eis-*) [ice-]floe; (*Fisch*) plaice

schon *adv* already; (*allein*) just; (*sogar*) even; (*ohnehin*) anyway; **s~ ein- mal** before; (*jemals*) ever; **s~ immer/ oft/wieder** always/often/again; **hast du ihn s~ gesehen?** have you seen him yet? **s~ der Gedanke daran** the mere thought of it; **s~ deshalb** for that reason alone; **das ist s~ möglich** that's quite possible; **ja s~, aber** well yes, but; **nun geh/komm s~!** go/come on then!

schön *a* beautiful; ⟨*Wetter*⟩ fine; (*angenehm, nett*) nice; (*gut*) good; (*fam:*

thank you very much! **na s~** all right then ●*adv* beautifully; nicely; (*gut*) well; **s~ langsam** nice and slowly

schonen *vt* spare; (*gut behandeln*) look after; **sich s~** take things easy. **s~d** *a* gentle, *adv* -tly

Schönheit *f* **-,-en** beauty. **S~sfehler** *m* blemish. **S~skonkurrenz** *f*, **S~swettbewerb** *m* beauty contest

schönmachen *vt sep* smarten up; **sich s~** make oneself look nice

Schonung *f* **-,-en** gentle care; (*nach Krankheit*) rest; (*Baum-*) plantation. **s~slos** *a* ruthless, *adv* -ly

Schonzeit *f* close season

schöpf|en *vt* scoop [up]; ladle ⟨*Suppe*⟩; **Mut s~en** take heart; **frische Luft s~en** get some fresh air. **S~er** *m* **-s,-** creator; (*Kelle*) ladle. **s~erisch** *a* creative. **S~kelle** *f*, **S~löffel** *m* ladle. **S~ung** *f* **-,-en** creation

Schoppen *m* **-s,-** ⟨*SGer*⟩ ≈ pint

Schorf *m* **-[e]s** scab

Schornstein *m* chimney; (*Naut*) funnel. **S~feger** *m* **-s,-** chimney-sweep

Schoß *m* **-es,⁀e** lap; (*Frack-*) tail

Schote *f* **-,-n** pod; (*Erbse*) pea

Schotte *m* **-n,-n** Scot, Scotsman

Schotter *m* **-s** gravel; (*für Gleise*) ballast

schott|isch *a* Scottish, Scots. **S~land** *nt* **-s** Scotland

schraffieren *vt* hatch

schräg *a* diagonal, *adv* -ly; (*geneigt*) sloping; **s~ halten** tilt. **S~e** *f* **-,-n** slope. **S~strich** *m* oblique stroke

Schramme *f* **-,-n** scratch. **s~n** *vt* scrape, scratch

Schrank *m* **-[e]s,⁀e** cupboard; (*Kleider-*) wardrobe; (*Akten-, Glas-*) cabinet

Schranke *f* **-,-n** barrier

Schraube *f* **-,-n** screw; (*Schiffs-*) propeller. **s~n** *vt* screw; (*ab-*) unscrew; (*drehen*) turn; **sich in die Höhe s~n** spiral upwards. **S~nmutter** *f* nut. **S~nschlüssel** *m* spanner. **S~n- zieher** *m* **-s,-** screwdriver

Schraubstock *m* vice

Schrebergarten *m* ≈ allotment

Schreck *m* **-[e]s,-e** fright; **jdm einen S~ einjagen** give s.o. a fright. **S~en** *m* **-s,-** fright; (*Entsetzen*) horror. **s~en** *vt* (*reg*) frighten; (*auf-*) startle ●*vi†* (*sein*) **in die Höhe s~en** start up

Schreck|gespenst *nt* spectre. **s~haft** *a* easily frightened; (*nervös*) jumpy. **s~lich** *a* terrible, *adv* -bly.

Schrei m -[e]s,-e cry, shout; (*gellend*) scream; **der letzte S~** (*fam*) the latest thing

Schreib|block m writing-pad. **s~en†** vt/i (haben) write; (*auf der Maschine*) type; **richtig/falsch s~en** spell right/wrong; **sich s~en** ⟨*Wort:*⟩ be spelt; (*korrespondieren*) correspond; **sich krank s~en lassen** get a doctor's certificate. **S~en** nt -s,- writing; (*Brief*) letter. **S~fehler** m spelling mistake. **S~heft** nt exercise book. **S~kraft** f clerical assistant; (*für Maschineschreiben*) typist. **S~maschine** f typewriter. **S~papier** nt writing-paper. **S~schrift** f script. **S~tisch** m desk. **S~ung** f -,-en spelling. **S~waren** fpl stationery sg. **S~weise** f spelling

schreien† vt/i (haben) cry; (*gellend*) scream; (*rufen, laut sprechen*) shout; **zum S~** (*fam*) be a scream. **s~d** a (*fig*) glaring; (*grell*) garish

Schreiner m -s,- joiner

schreiten† vi (sein) walk

Schrift f -,-en writing; (*Druck-*) type; (*Abhandlung*) paper; **die Heilige S~** the Scriptures pl. **S~führer** m secretary. **s~lich** a written ● adv in writing. **S~sprache** f written language. **S~steller(in)** m -s,- (f -,-nen) writer. **S~stück** nt document. **S~zeichen** nt character

schrill a shrill, adv -y

Schritt m -[e]s,-e step; (*Entfernung*) pace; (*Gangart*) walk; (*der Hose*) crotch; **im S~** in step; (*langsam*) at walking pace; **S~ halten mit** (*fig*) keep pace with. **S~macher** m -s,- pace-maker. **s~weise** adv step by step

schroff a precipitous, adv -ly; (*abweisend*) brusque, adv -ly; (*unvermittelt*) abrupt, adv -ly; ⟨*Gegensatz*⟩ stark

schröpfen vt (fam) fleece

Schrot m & nt -[e]s coarse meal; (*Blei-*) small shot. **s~en** vt grind coarsely. **S~flinte** f shotgun

Schrott m -[e]s scrap[-metal]; **zu S~ fahren** (*fam*) write off. **S~platz** m scrap-yard. **s~reif** a ready for the scrap-heap

schrubb|en vt/i (haben) scrub. **S~er** m -s,- [long-handled] scrubbing-brush

Schrulle f -,-n whim; **alte S~e** (*fam*) old crone. **s~ig** a cranky

schrumpfen vi (sein) shrink; ⟨*Obst:*⟩ shrivel

schrump[e]lig a wrinkled

Schrunde f -,-n crack; (*Spalte*) crevasse

Schub m -[e]s,-̈e (*Phys*) thrust; (*S~fach*) drawer; (*Menge*) batch. **S~fach** nt drawer. **S~karre** f, **S~karren** m wheelbarrow. **S~lade** f drawer

Schubs m -es,-e push, shove. **s~en** vt push, shove

schüchtern a shy, adv -ly; (*zaghaft*) tentative, adv -ly. **S~heit** f - shyness

Schuft m -[e]s,-e (*pej*) swine. **s~en** vi (haben) (fam) slave away

Schuh m -[e]s,-e shoe. **S~anzieher** m -s,- shoehorn. **S~band** nt (pl -bänder) shoe-lace. **S~creme** f shoe-polish. **S~löffel** m shoehorn. **S~macher** m -s,- shoemaker; (*zum Flicken*) [shoe] mender. **S~werk** nt shoes pl

Schul|abgänger m -s,- school-leaver. **S~arbeiten, S~aufgaben** fpl homework sg. **S~buch** nt schoolbook

Schuld f -,-en guilt; (*Verantwortung*) blame; (*Geld-*) debt; **S~en machen** get into debt; **S~ haben an** (+ dat) to be to blame for ● **s~ haben** od **sein** to be to blame (**an** + dat for); **jdm s~ geben** blame s.o. **s~en** vt owe

schuldig a guilty (gen of); (*gebührend*) due; **jdm etw s~ sein** owe s.o. sth. **S~keit** f - duty

schuld|los a innocent. **S~ner** m -s,- debtor. **S~spruch** m guilty verdict

Schule f -,-n school; **in der/die S~** at/ to school. **s~n** vt train

Schüler|(in) m -s,- (f -,-nen) pupil. **S~lotse** m pupil acting as crossing warden

schul|frei a **s~freier Tag** day without school; **wir haben morgen s~frei** there's no school tomorrow. **S~hof** m [school] playground. **S~jahr** nt school year; (*Klasse*) form. **S~junge** m schoolboy. **S~kind** nt schoolchild. **S~leiter(in)** m(f) head [teacher]. **S~mädchen** nt schoolgirl. **S~stunde** f lesson

Schulter f -,-n shoulder. **S~blatt** nt shoulder-blade. **s~n** vt shoulder. **S~tuch** nt shawl

Schulung f - training

schummeln vi (haben) (fam) cheat

Schund m -[e]s trash. **S~roman** m trashy novel

Schuppe f -,-n scale; **S~n** pl dandruff sg. **s~n (sich)** vr flake [off]

Schuppen m -s,- shed

Schur f - shearing

Schür|eisen nt poker. **s~en** vt poke; (fig) stir up

schürf|en vt mine; **sich** (dat) **das Knie s~en** graze one's knee ● vi (haben) **s~en nach** prospect for. **S~wunde** f abrasion, graze

Schürhaken m poker

Schurke m -n,-n villain

Schürze f -,-n apron. **s~n** vt (raffen) gather [up]; tie ⟨Knoten⟩; purse ⟨Lippen⟩. **S~njäger** m (fam) womanizer

Schuß m -sses,"-sse shot; (kleine Menge) dash

Schüssel f -,-n bowl; (TV) dish

schusselig a (fam) scatter-brained

Schuß|fahrt f (Ski) schuss. **S~-waffe** f firearm

Schuster m -s,- = **Schuhmacher**

Schutt m -[e]s rubble. **S~ablade-platz** m rubbish dump

Schüttel|frost m shivering fit. **s~n** vt shake; **sich s~n** shake oneself/itself; (vor Ekel) shudder; **jdm die Hand s~n** shake s.o.'s hand

schütten vt pour; (kippen) tip; (ver-) spill ● vi (haben) **es schüttet** it is pouring [with rain]

Schutthaufen m pile of rubble

Schutz m -es protection; (Zuflucht) shelter; (Techn) guard; **S~ suchen** take refuge; **unter dem S~ der Dunkelheit** under cover of darkness. **S~anzug** m protective suit. **S~blech** nt mud-guard. **S~brille** goggles pl

Schütze m -n,-n marksman; (Tor-) scorer; (Astr) Sagittarius; **guter S~** good shot

schützen vt protect/(Zuflucht gewähren) shelter (**vor** + dat from) ● vi (haben) give protection/shelter (**vor** + dat from). **s~d** a protective, adv -ly

Schützenfest nt fair with shooting competition

Schutz|engel m guardian angel. **S~heilige(r)** m/f patron saint

Schützling m -s,-e charge; (Protegé) protégé

schutz|los a defenceless, helpless. **S~mann** m (pl -**männer** & -**leute**) policeman. **S~umschlag** m dust-jacket

Schwaben nt -s Swabia

schwäbisch a Swabian

schwach a (**schwächer, schwächst**) weak, adv -ly; (nicht gut; gering) poor, adv -ly; (leicht) faint, adv -ly

Schwäche f -,-n weakness. **s~n** vt weaken

Schwach|heit f - weakness. **S~kopf** m (fam) idiot

schwäch|lich a delicate. **S~ling** m -s,-e weakling

Schwachsinn m mental deficiency. **s~ig** a mentally deficient; (fam) idiotic

Schwächung f - weakening

schwafeln (fam) vi (haben) waffle ● vt talk

Schwager m -s,"- brother-in-law

Schwägerin f -,-nen sister-in-law

Schwalbe f -,-n swallow

Schwall m -[e]s torrent

Schwamm m -[e]s,"-e sponge; (SGer: Pilz) fungus; (eßbar) mushroom. **s~ig** a spongy; (aufgedunsen) bloated

Schwan m -[e]s,"-e swan

schwanen vi (haben) (fam) **mir schwante, daß** I had a nasty feeling that

schwanger a pregnant

schwängern vt make pregnant

Schwangerschaft f -,-en pregnancy

Schwank m -[e]s,"-e (Theat) farce

schwank|en vi (haben) sway; ⟨Boot:⟩ rock; (sich ändern) fluctuate; (unentschieden sein) be undecided ● (sein) stagger. **S~ung** f -,-en fluctuation

Schwanz m -es,"-e tail

schwänzen vt (fam) skip; **die Schule s~** play truant

Schwarm m -[e]s,"-e swarm; (Fisch-) shoal; (fam: Liebe) idol

schwärmen vi (haben) swarm; **s~ für** (fam) adore; (verliebt sein) have a crush on; **s~ von** (fam) rave about

Schwarte f -,-n (Speck-) rind; (fam: Buch) tome

schwarz a (**schwärzer, schwärzest**) black; (fam: illegal) illegal, adv -ly; **s~er Markt** black market; **s~ geklei-det** dressed in black; **s~ auf weiß** in black and white; **ins S~e treffen** score a bull's-eye. **S~** nt -[e]s,- black. **S~-arbeit** f moonlighting. **s~arbei-ten** vi sep (haben) moonlight. **S~-brot** nt black bread. **S~e(r)** m/f black

Schwärze f - blackness. **s~n** vt blacken

Schwarz|fahrer m fare-dodger. **S~handel** m black market (**mit** in).

S~händler m black marketeer.
S~markt m black market. **s~sehen**† vi sep (haben) watch television without a licence; (fig) be pessimistic. **S~wald** m Black Forest. **s~weiß** a black and white

Schwatz m **-es** (fam) chat

schwatzen, (SGer) **schwätzen** vi (haben) chat; (klatschen) gossip; (Sch) talk [in class] ● vt talk

schwatzhaft a garrulous

Schwebe f - **in der S~** (fig) undecided. **S~bahn** f cable railway. **s~n** vi (haben) float; (fig) be undecided; ⟨Verfahren:⟩ be pending; **in Gefahr s~n** be in danger ● (sein) float

Schwed|e m **-n,-n** Swede. **S~en** nt **-s** Sweden. **S~in** f **-,-nen** Swede. **s~isch** a Swedish

Schwefel m **-s** sulphur. **S~säure** f sulphuric acid

schweigen† vi (haben) be silent; **ganz zu s~ von** to say nothing of, let alone. **S~** nt **-s** silence; **zum S~ bringen** silence. **s~d** a silent, adv -ly

schweigsam a silent; (wortkarg) taciturn

Schwein nt **-[e]s,-e** pig; (Culin) pork; (sl) (schmutziger Mensch) dirty pig; (Schuft) swine; **S~ haben** (fam) be lucky. **S~ebraten** m roast pork. **S~efleisch** nt pork. **S~ehund** m (sl) swine. **S~erei** f **-,-en** (sl) [dirty] mess; (Gemeinheit) dirty trick. **S~estall** m pigsty. **s~isch** a lewd. **S~sleder** nt pigskin

Schweiß m **-es** sweat

schweiß|en vt weld. **S~er** m **-s,-welder**

Schweiz (die) - Switzerland. **S~er** a & m **-s,-,** **S~erin** f **-,-nen** Swiss. **s~erisch** a Swiss

schwelen vi (haben) smoulder

schwelgen vi (haben) feast; **s~ in** (+ dat) wallow in

Schwelle f **-,-n** threshold; (Eisenbahn-) sleeper

schwell|en† vi (sein) swell. **S~ung** f **-,-en** swelling

Schwemme f **-,-n** watering-place; (fig: Überangebot) glut. **s~n** vt wash; **an Land s~n** wash up

Schwenk m **-[e]s** swing. **s~en** vt swing; (schwingen) wave; (spülen) rinse; **in Butter s~en** toss in butter ● vi (sein) turn

schwer a heavy; (schwierig) difficult; (mühsam, streng) hard; (ernst) serious; (schlimm) bad; **3 Pfund s~ sein** weigh 3 pounds ● adv heavily; with difficulty; (mühsam, streng) hard; (schlimm, sehr) badly, seriously; **s~ hören** be hard of hearing; **s~ arbeiten** work hard; **s~ zu sagen** difficult or hard to say

Schwere f - heaviness; (Gewicht) weight; (Schwierigkeit) difficulty; (Ernst) gravity. **S~losigkeit** f - weightlessness

schwer|fallen† vi sep (sein) be hard (dat for). **s~fällig** a ponderous, adv -ly; (unbeholfen) clumsy, adv -ily. **S~gewicht** nt heavyweight. **s~hörig** a **s~hörig sein** be hard of hearing. **S~kraft** f (Phys) gravity. **s~krank** a seriously ill. **s~lich** adv hardly. **s~machen** vt sep make difficult (dat for). **s~mütig** a melancholic. **s~nehmen**† vt sep take seriously. **S~punkt** m centre of gravity; (fig) emphasis

Schwert nt **-[e]s,-er** sword. **S~lilie** f iris

schwer|tun† (sich) vr sep have difficulty (**mit** with). **S~verbrecher** m serious offender. **s~verdaulich** a indigestible. **s~verletzt** a seriously injured. **s~wiegend** a weighty

Schwester f **-,-n** sister; (Kranken-) nurse. **s~lich** a sisterly

Schwieger|eltern pl parents-in-law. **S~mutter** f mother-in-law. **S~sohn** m son-in-law. **S~tochter** f daughter-in-law. **S~vater** m father-in-law

Schwiele f **-,-n** callus

schwierig a difficult. **S~keit** f **-,-en** difficulty

Schwimm|bad nt swimming-baths pl. **S~becken** nt swimming-pool. **s~en**† vt/i (sein/haben) swim; (auf dem Wasser treiben) float. **S~er** m **-s,-** swimmer; (Techn) float. **S~-weste** f life-jacket

Schwindel m **-s** dizziness, vertigo; (fam: Betrug) fraud; (Lüge) lie. **S~anfall** m dizzy spell. **s~frei** a **s~frei sein** have a good head for heights. **s~n** vi (haben) (lügen) lie; **mir od mich s~t** I feel dizzy

schwinden† vi (sein) dwindle; (vergehen) fade; (nachlassen) fail

Schwindl|er m **-s,-** liar; (Betrüger) fraud, con-man. **s~ig** a dizzy; **mir ist** od **wird s~ig** I feel dizzy

schwing|en† vi (haben) swing; (Phys) oscillate; (vibrieren) vibrate

● *vt* swing; wave ⟨*Fahne*⟩; ⟨*drohend*⟩ brandish. **S~tür** *f* swing-door. **S~ung** *f* -,-en oscillation; vibration

Schwips *m* -es,-e **einen S~ haben** (*fam*) be tipsy

schwirren *vi* (*haben/sein*) buzz; (*surren*) whirr

Schwitz|e *f* -,-n (*Culin*) roux. **s~en** *vi* (*haben*) sweat; **ich s~e** *od* **mich s~t** I am hot ● *vt* (*Culin*) sweat

schwören† *vt/i* (*haben*) swear (**auf** + *acc* by); **Rache s~** swear revenge

schwul *a* (*fam: homosexuell*) gay

schwül *a* close. **S~e** *f* - closeness

schwülstig *a* bombastic, *adv* -ally

Schwung *m* -[e]s,ˇe swing; (*Bogen*) sweep; (*Schnelligkeit*) momentum; (*Kraft*) vigour; (*Feuer*) verve; (*fam: Anzahl*) batch; **in S~ kommen** gather momentum; (*fig*) get going. **S~haft** *a* brisk, *adv* -ly. **s~los** *a* dull. **s~voll** *a* vigorous, *adv* -ly; ⟨*Bogen, Linie*⟩ sweeping; (*mitreißend*) spirited, lively

Schwur *m* -[e]s,ˇe vow; (*Eid*) oath. **S~gericht** *nt* jury [court]

sechs *inv a*, **S~** *f* -,-en six; (*Sch*) ≈ fail mark. **s~eckig** *a* hexagonal. **s~te(r,s)** *a* sixth

sech|zehn *inv a* sixteen. **s~ zehnte(r,s)** *a* sixteenth. **s~zig** *inv a* sixty. **s~zigste(r,s)** *a* sixtieth

sedieren *vt* sedate

See[1] *m* -s,-n /'ze:ən/ lake

See[2] *f* - sea; **an die/der See** to/at the seaside; **auf See** at sea. **S~bad** *nt* seaside resort. **S~fahrt** *f* [sea] voyage; (*Schiffahrt*) navigation. **S~gang** *m* **schwerer S~gang** rough sea. **S~hund** *m* seal. **S~krank** *a* seasick

Seele *f* -,-n soul. **s~nruhig** *a* calm, *adv* -ly

seelisch *a* psychological, *adv* -ly; (*geistig*) mental, *adv* -ly

Seelsorger *m* -s,- pastor

See|luft *f* sea air. **S~macht** *f* maritime power. **S~mann** *m* (*pl* **-leute**) seaman, sailor. **S~not** *f* **in S~not** in distress. **S~räuber** *m* pirate. **S~reise** *f* [sea] voyage. **S~rose** *f* water-lily. **S~sack** *m* kitbag. **S~stern** *m* starfish. **S~tang** *m* seaweed. **s~tüchtig** *a* seaworthy. **S~weg** *m* sea route; **auf dem S~weg** by sea. **S~zunge** *f* sole

Segel *nt* -[e]s,- sail. **S~boot** *nt* sailing-

glider. **s~n** *vt/i* (*sein/haben*) sail. **S~schiff** *nt* sailing-ship. **S~sport** *m* sailing. **S~tuch** *nt* canvas

Segen *m* -s blessing. **s~sreich** *a* beneficial; (*gesegnet*) blessed

Segler *m* -s,- yachtsman

Segment *nt* -[e]s,-e segment

segnen *vt* bless; **gesegnet mit** blessed with

sehen† *vt* see; watch ⟨*Fernsehsendung*⟩; **sich s~ lassen** show oneself ● *vi* (*haben*) see; (*blicken*) look (**auf** + *acc* at); (*ragen*) show (**aus** above); **gut/schlecht s~** have good/bad eyesight; **vom S~ kennen** know by sight; **s~ nach** keep an eye on; (*betreuen*) look after; (*suchen*) look for; **darauf s~, daß** see [to it] that. **s~swert**, **s~swürdig** *a* worth seeing. **S~swürdigkeit** *f* -,-en sight

Sehkraft *f* sight, vision

Sehne *f* -,-n tendon; (*eines Bogens*) string

sehnen (sich) *vr* long (**nach** for)

sehnig *a* sinewy; (*zäh*) stringy

sehn|lich[st] *a* ⟨*Wunsch*⟩ dearest ● *adv* longingly. **S~sucht** *f* - longing (**nach** for). **s~süchtig** *a* longing, *adv* -ly; ⟨*Wunsch*⟩ dearest

sehr *adv* very; (*mit Verb*) very much

seicht *a* shallow

seid *s.* **sein**[1]; **ihr s~** you are

Seide *f* -,-n silk

Seidel *nt* -s,- beer-mug

seiden *a* silk … **S~papier** *nt* tissue paper. **S~raupe** *f* silkworm. **s~weich** *a* silky-soft

seidig *a* silky

Seife *f* -,-n soap. **S~npulver** *nt* soap powder. **S~nschaum** *m* lather

seifig *a* soapy

seihen *vt* strain

Seil *nt* -[e]s,-e rope; (*Draht-*) cable. **S~bahn** *f* cable railway. **s~springen**† *vi* (*sein*) (*inf & pp only*) skip. **S~tänzer(in)** *m*(*f*) tightrope walker

sein[1]† *vi* (*sein*) be; **er ist Lehrer** he is a teacher; **sei still!** be quiet! **mir ist kalt/ schlecht** I am cold/feel sick; **wie dem auch sei** be that as it may ● *v aux* have; **angekommen/gestorben s~** have arrived/died; **er war/wäre gefallen** he had/would have fallen; **es ist/war viel zu tun/nichts zu sehen** there is/was a lot to be done/nothing to be seen

sein[2] *poss pron* his; (*Ding, Tier*) its;

pron his; (*nach man*) one's own; **das S~e tun** do one's share. **s~erseits** *adv* for his part. **s~erzeit** *adv* in those days. **s~etwegen** *adv* for his sake; (*wegen ihm*) because of him, on his account. **s~etwillen** *adv* **um s~etwillen** for his sake. **s~ige** *poss pron* **der/die/das s~ige** his

seinlassen† *vt sep* leave; (*aufhören mit*) stop

seins *poss pron* his; (*nach man*) one's own

seit *conj & prep* (+ *dat*) since; **s~ wann?** since when? **s~ einiger Zeit** for some time [past]; **ich wohne s~ zehn Jahren hier** I've lived here for ten years. **s~dem** *conj* since ● *adv* since then

Seite *f* -,-n side; (*Buch-*) page; **S~ an S~** side by side; **zur S~ legen/treten** put/step aside; **jds starke S~** s.o.'s strong point; **von S~n** (+ *gen*) on the part of; **auf die einen/anderen S~** (*fig*) on the one/other hand

seitens *prep* (+ *gen*) on the part of

Seiten|schiff *nt* [side] aisle. **S~sprung** *m* infidelity; **einen S~sprung machen** be unfaithful. **S~stechen** *nt* -s (*Med*) stitch. **S~straße** *f* side-street. **S~streifen** *m* verge; (*Autobahn-*) hard shoulder

seither *adv* since then

seit|lich *a* side ... ● *adv* at/on the side; **s~lich von** to one side of ● *prep* (+ *gen*) to one side of. **s~wärts** *adv* on/to one side; (*zur Seite*) sideways

Sekret *nt* -[e]s,-e secretion

Sekret|är *m* -s,-e secretary; (*Schrank*) bureau. **S~ariat** *nt* -[e]s,-e secretary's office. **S~ärin** *f* -,-nen secretary

Sekt *m* -[e]s [German] sparkling wine

Sekte *f* -,-n sect

Sektion /-'tsio:n/ *f* -,-en section; (*Sezierung*) autopsy

Sektor *m* -s,-en /-'to:rən/ sector

Sekundant *m* -en,-en (*Sport*) second

sekundär *a* secondary

Sekunde *f* -,-n second

selber *pron* (*fam*) = **selbst**

selbst *pron* oneself; **ich/du/er/sie s~** I myself/you yourself/he him- self/she herself; **wir/ihr/sie s~** we ourselves/ you yourselves/they themselves; **ich schneide mein Haar s~** I cut my own hair; **von s~** of one's own accord; (*automatisch*) automatically ● *adv* even. **S~achtung** *f* self-esteem, self-respect

selbständig *a* independent, *adv* -ly; self-employed (*Handwerker*); **sich s~ machen** set up on one's own. **S~keit** *f* - independence

Selbstaufopferung *f* self-sacrifice

Selbstbedienung *f* self-service. **S~srestaurant** *nt* self-service restaurant, cafeteria

Selbst|befriedigung *f* masturbation. **S~beherrschung** *f* self-control. **S~bestimmung** *f* self-determination. **S~bewußt** *a* self-confident. **S~bewußtsein** *nt* self-confidence. **S~bildnis** *nt* self-portrait. **S~erhaltung** *f* self-preservation. **s~gefällig** *a* self-satisfied, smug, *adv* -ly. **s~gemacht** *a* home-made. **s~gerecht** *a* self-righteous. **S~gespräch** *nt* soliloquy; **S~gespräche führen** talk to oneself. **s~haftend** *a* self-adhesive. **s~herrlich** *a* autocratic, *adv* -ally. **S~hilfe** *f* self-help. **s~klebend** *a* self-adhesive. **S~kostenpreis** *m* cost price. **S~laut** *m* vowel. **s~los** *a* selfless, *adv* -ly. **S~mitleid** *nt* self-pity. **S~mord** *m* suicide. **S~mörder(in)** *m(f)* suicide. **s~mörderisch** *a* suicidal. **S~porträt** *nt* self-portrait. **s~sicher** *a* self-assured. **S~sicherheit** *f* self-assurance. **s~süchtig** *a* selfish, *adv* -ly. **S~tanken** *nt* self-service (*for petrol*). **s~tätig** *a* automatic, *adv* -ally. **S~versorgung** *f* self-catering

selbstverständlich *a* natural, *adv* -ly; **etw für s~ halten** take sth for granted; **das ist s~** that goes without saying; **s~!** of course! **S~keit** *f* - matter of course; **das ist eine S~keit** that goes without saying

Selbst|verteidigung *f* self-defence. **S~vertrauen** *nt* self-confidence. **S~verwaltung** *f* self-government. **s~zufrieden** *a* complacent, *adv* -ly

selig *a* blissfully happy; (*Relig*) blessed; (*verstorben*) late. **S~keit** *f* - bliss

Sellerie *m* -s,-s & *f* -,- celeriac; (*Stangen-*) celery

selten *a* rare ● *adv* rarely, seldom; (*besonders*) exceptionally. **S~heit** *f* -,-en rarity

Selterswasser *nt* seltzer [water]

seltsam *a* odd, *adv* -ly, strange, *adv* -ly. **s~erweise** *adv* oddly/strangely enough

Semester *nt* -s,- (*Univ*) semester

Semikolon *nt* **-s,-s** semicolon

Seminar *nt* **-s,-e** seminar; (*Institut*) department; (*Priester-*) seminary

Semmel *f* **-,-n** [bread] roll. **S~brösel** *pl* breadcrumbs

Senat *m* **-[e]s,-e** senate. **S~or** *m* **-s,-en** /-'to:rən/ senator

senden[1] *vt* send

senden[2] *vt* (*reg*) broadcast; (*über Funk*) transmit, send. **S~r** *m* **-s,-** [broadcasting] station; (*Anlage*) transmitter. **S~reihe** *f* series

Sendung *f* **-,-en** consignment, shipment; (*Auftrag*) mission; (*Radio, TV*) programme

Senf *m* **-s** mustard

sengend *a* scorching

senil *a* senile. **S~ität** *f* - senility

Senior *m* **-s,-en** /-'o:rən/ senior; **S~en** senior citizens. **S~enheim** *nt* old people's home. **S~enteller** *m* senior citizen's menu

Senke *f* **-,-n** dip, hollow

Senkel *m* **-s,-** [shoe-]lace

senken *vt* lower; bring down (*Fieber, Preise*); bow (*Kopf*); **sich s~** come down, fall; (*absinken*) subside; (*abfallen*) slope down

senkrecht *a* vertical, *adv* -ly. **S~e** *f* **-n,-n** perpendicular

Sensation /-'tsio:n/ *f* **-,-en** sensation. **s~ell** *a* sensational, *adv* -ly

Sense *f* **-,-n** scythe

sensib|el *a* sensitive, *adv* -ly. **S~ilität** *f* - sensitivity

sentimental *a* sentimental. **S~ität** *f* - sentimentality

separat *a* separate, *adv* -ly

September *m* **-s,-** September

Serenade *f* **-,-n** serenade

Serie /'ze:riə/ *f* **-,-n** series; (*Briefmarken*) set; (*Comm*) range. **S~nnummer** *f* serial number

seriös *a* respectable, *adv* -bly; (*zuverlässig*) reliable, *adv* -bly; (*ernstgemeint*) serious

Serpentine *f* **-,-n** winding road; (*Kehre*) hairpin bend

Serum *nt* **-s, Sera** serum

Service[1] /zɛr'vi:s/ *nt* **-[s],-** /-'vi:s[əs], -'vi:sə/ service, set

Service[2] /'zø:ɐvɪs/ *m* & *nt* **-s** /-vɪs[əs]/ (*Comm, Tennis*) service

servier|en *vt/i* (*haben*) serve. **S~erin** *f* **-,-nen** waitress. **S~wagen** *m* trolley

Serviette *f* **-,-n** napkin, serviette

Servus *int* (*Aust*) cheerio; (*Begrüßung*) hallo

Sessel *m* **-s,-** armchair. **S~bahn** *f*, **S~lift** *m* chair-lift

seßhaft *a* settled; **s~ werden** settle down

Set /zɛt/ *nt* & *m* **-[s],-s** set; (*Deckchen*) place-mat

setz|en *vt* put; (*abstellen*) set down; (*hin-*) sit down (*Kind*); move (*Spielstein*); (*pflanzen*) plant; (*schreiben, wetten*) put; **sich s~en** sit down; (*sinken*) settle ● *vi* (*sein*) leap ● *vi* (*haben*) **s~en auf** (+ *acc*) back. **S~ling** *m* **-s,-e** seedling

Seuche *f* **-,-n** epidemic

seufz|en *vi* (*haben*) sigh. **S~er** *m* **-s,-** sigh

Sex /zɛks/ *m* **-[es]** sex. **s~istisch** *a* sexist

Sexu|alität *f* - sexuality. **s~ell** *a* sexual, *adv* -ly

sexy /'zɛksi/ *inv a* sexy

sezieren *vt* dissect

Shampoo /ʃam'pu:/, **Shampoon** /ʃam'po:n/ *nt* **-s** shampoo

siamesisch *a* Siamese

sich *refl pron* oneself; (*mit er/sie/es*) himself/herself/itself; (*mit sie pl*) themselves; (*mit Sie*) yourself; (*pl*) yourselves; (*einander*) each other; **s~ kennen** know oneself/(*einander*) each other; **s~ waschen** have a wash; **s~** (*dat*) **die Zähne putzen/die Haare kämmen** clean one's teeth/comb one's hair; **s~** (*dat*) **das Bein brechen** break a leg; **s~ wundern/schämen** be surprised/ashamed; **s~ gut lesen/verkaufen** read/sell well; **von s~ aus** of one's own accord

Sichel *f* **-,-n** sickle

sicher *a* safe; (*gesichert*) secure; (*gewiß*) certain; (*zuverlässig*) reliable; sure (*Urteil, Geschmack*); steady (*Hand*); (*selbstbewußt*) self-confident; **sich** (*dat*) **etw** (*gen*) **s~ sein** be sure of sth; **bist du s~?** are you sure? ● *adv* safely; securely; certainly; reliably; self-confidently; (*wahrscheinlich*) most probably; **er kommt s~** he is sure to come; **s~!** certainly! **s~gehen**[†] *vi sep* (*sein*) be sure

Sicherheit *f* - safety; (*Pol, Psych, Comm*) security; (*Gewißheit*) certainty; (*Zuverlässigkeit*) reliability; (*des Urteils, Geschmacks*) surety; (*Selbstbewußtsein*) self-confidence.

S~**sgurt** *m* safety-belt; (*Auto*) seat-belt. s~**shalber** *adv* to be on the safe side. S~**snadel** *f* safety-pin

sicherlich *adv* certainly; (*wahrscheinlich*) most probably

sicher|n *vt* secure; (*garantieren*) safeguard; (*schützen*) protect; put the safety-catch on 〈*Pistole*〉; **sich** (*dat*) **etw s~n** secure sth. s~**stellen** *vt sep* safeguard; (*beschlagnahmen*) seize. S~**ung** *f* -,**-en** safeguard, protection; (*Gewehr-*) safety-catch; (*Electr*) fuse

Sicht *f* - view; (S~*weite*) visibility; **in S~ kommen** come into view; **auf lange S~** in the long term. s~**bar** *a* visible, *adv* -bly. s~**en** *vt* sight; (*durchsehen*) sift through. s~**lich** *a* obvious, *adv* -ly. S~**vermerk** *m* visa. S~**weite** *f* visibility; **in/außer S~weite** within/out of sight

sickern *vi* (*sein*) seep

sie *pron* (*nom*) (*sg*) she; (*Ding, Tier*) it; (*pl*) they; (*acc*) (*sg*) her; (*Ding, Tier*) it; (*pl*) them

Sie *pron* you; **gehen/warten Sie!** go/wait!

Sieb *nt* **-[e]s,-e** sieve; (*Tee-*) strainer. s~**en¹** *vt* sieve, sift

sieben² *inv a,* S~ *f* -,**-en** seven. S~**sachen** *fpl* (*fam*) belongings. s~**te(r,s)** *a* seventh

sieb|te(r,s) *a* seventh. s~**zehn** *inv a* seventeen. s~**zehnte(r,s)** *a* seventeenth. s~**zig** *inv a* seventy. s~**zigste(r,s)** *a* seventieth

siede|n† *vt/i* (*haben*) boil. S~**punkt** *m* boiling point

Siedl|er *m* -s,- settler. S~**ung** *f* -,**-en** [housing] estate; (*Niederlassung*) settlement

Sieg *m* **-[e]s,-e** victory

Siegel *nt* -s,- seal. S~**ring** *m* signet-ring

sieg|en *vi* (*haben*) win. S~**er(in)** *m* **-s,-** (*f* -,**-nen**) winner. s~**reich** *a* victorious

siezen *vt* **jdn s~** call s.o. 'Sie'

Signal *nt* **-s,-e** signal. s~**isieren** *vt* signal

signieren *vt* sign

Silbe *f* -,**-n** syllable. S~**ntrennung** *f* word-division

Silber *nt* -s silver. S~**hochzeit** *f* silver wedding. s~**n** *a* silver. S~**papier** *nt* silver paper

Silhouette /zɪ'lŭɛtə/ *f* -,**-n** silhouette

Silizium *nt* -s silicon

Silo *m* & *nt* **-s,-s** silo

Silvester *nt* **-s** New Year's Eve

simpel *a* simple, *adv* -ply; (*einfältig*) simple-minded

Simplex *nt* -,**-e** simplex

Sims *m* & *nt* **-es,-e** ledge; (*Kamin-*) mantelpiece

Simul|ant *m* **-en,-en** malingerer. s~**ieren** *vt* feign; (*Techn*) simulate ● *vi* (*haben*) pretend; (*sich krank stellen*) malinger

simultan *a* simultaneous, *adv* -ly

sind *s.* **sein¹; wir/sie s~** we/they are

Sinfonie *f* -,**-n** symphony

singen† *vt/i* (*haben*) sing

Singular *m* **-s,-e** singular

Singvogel *m* songbird

sinken† *vi* (*sein*) sink; (*nieder-*) drop; (*niedriger werden*) go down, fall; **den Mut s~ lassen** lose courage

Sinn *m* **-[e]s,-e** sense; (*Denken*) mind; (*Zweck*) point; **im S~ haben** have in mind; **in gewissem S~e** in a sense; **es hat keinen S~** it is pointless; **nicht bei S~en sein** be out of one's mind. S~**bild** *nt* symbol. s~**en†** *vi* (*haben*) think; **auf Rache s~en** plot one's revenge

sinnlich *a* sensory; (*sexuell*) sensual; 〈*Genüsse*〉 sensuous. S~**keit** *f* - sensuality; sensuousness

sinn|los *a* senseless, *adv* -ly; (*zwecklos*) pointless, *adv* -ly. s~**voll** *a* meaningful; (*vernünftig*) sensible, *adv* -bly

Sintflut *f* flood

Siphon /'zi:fõ/ *m* **-s,-s** siphon

Sippe *f* -,**-n** clan. S~**schaft** *f* - clan; (*Pack*) crowd

Sirene *f* -,**-n** siren

Sirup *m* **-s,-e** syrup; (*schwarzer*) treacle

Sitte *f* -,**-n** custom; S~**n** manners. s~**nlos** *a* immoral

sittlich *a* moral, *adv* -ly. S~**keit** *f* - morality. S~**keitsverbrecher** *m* sex offender

sittsam *a* well-behaved; (*züchtig*) demure, *adv* -ly

Situ|ation /-'tsi̯o:n/ *f* -,**-en** situation. s~**iert** *a* **gut/schlecht s~iert** well/badly off

Sitz *m* **-es,-e** seat; (*Paßform*) fit

sitzen† *vi* (*haben*) sit; (*sich befinden*) be; (*passen*) fit; (*fam: treffen*) hit home; **s~ bleiben** remain seated; **[im Gefängnis] s~** (*fam*) be in jail. s~**bleiben†** *vi sep* (*sein*) (*fam*) (*Sch*) stay or be kept down; (*nicht heiraten*) be left on the shelf; **s~bleiben auf** (+ *dat*) be

Sitz|gelegenheit *f* seat. **S~platz** *m* seat. **S~ung** *f* -,-en session

Sizilien /-iən/ *nt* -s Sicily

Skala *f* -,-len scale; (*Reihe*) range

Skalpell *nt* -s,-e scalpel

skalpieren *vt* scalp

Skandal *m* -s,-e scandal. **s~ös** *a* scandalous

skandieren *vt* scan ⟨*Verse*⟩; chant ⟨*Parolen*⟩

Skandinav|ien /-iən/ *nt* -s Scandinavia. **s~isch** *a* Scandinavian

Skat *m* -s skat

Skelett *nt* -[e]s,-e skeleton

Skep|sis *f* - scepticism. **s~tisch** *a* sceptical, *adv* -ly; (*mißtrauisch*) doubtful, *adv* -ly

Ski /ʃiː/ *m* -s,-er ski; **Ski fahren** *od* **laufen** ski. **S~fahrer(in)**, **S~läufer(in)** *m(f)* skier. **S~sport** *m* skiing

Skizz|e *f* -,-n sketch. **s~enhaft** *a* sketchy, *adv* -ily. **s~ieren** *vt* sketch

Sklav|e *m* -n,-n slave. **S~erei** *f* - slavery. **S~in** *f* -,-nen slave. **s~isch** *a* slavish, *adv* -ly

Skorpion *m* -s,-e scorpion; (*Astr*) Scorpio

Skrupel *m* -s,- scruple. **s~los** *a* unscrupulous

Skulptur *f* -,-en sculpture

skurril *a* absurd, *adv* -ly

Slalom *m* -s,-s slalom

Slang /slɛŋ/ *m* -s slang

Slaw|e *m* -n,-n, **S~in** *f* -,-nen Slav. **s~isch** *a* Slav; (*Lang*) Slavonic

Slip *m* -s,-s briefs *pl*

Smaragd *m* -[e]s,-e emerald

Smoking *m* -s,-s dinner jacket, (*Amer*) tuxedo

Snob *m* -s,-s snob. **S~ismus** *m* - snobbery. **s~istisch** *a* snobbish

so *adv* so; (*so sehr*) so much; (*auf diese Weise*) like this/that; (*solch*) such; (*fam: sowieso*) anyway; (*fam: umsonst*) free; (*fam: ungefähr*) about; **nicht so schnell** not so fast; **so gut/bald wie** as good/soon as; **so ein Mann** a man like that; **so ein Zufall!** what a coincidence! **so nicht** not like that; **mir ist so, als ob** I feel as if; **so oder so** in any case; **eine Stunde oder so** an hour or so; **so um zehn Mark** (*fam*) about ten marks; **[es ist] gut so** that's fine; **so, das ist geschafft** there, that's done; **so?**

really? **so kommt doch!** come on then! ● *conj* (*also*) so; (*dann*) then; **so daß** so that; **so gern ich auch käme** as much as I would like to come

sobald *conj* as soon as

Söckchen *nt* -s,- [ankle] sock

Socke *f* -,-n sock

Sockel *m* -s,- plinth, pedestal

Socken *m* -s,- sock

Soda *nt* -s soda. **S~wasser** *nt* soda water

Sodbrennen *nt* -s heartburn

soeben *adv* just [now]

Sofa *nt* -s,-s settee, sofa

sofern *adv* provided [that]

sofort *adv* at once, immediately; (*auf der Stelle*) instantly. **s~ig** *a* immediate

Software /'zɔftvɛːɐ/ *f* - software

sogar *adv* even

sogenannt *a* so-called

sogleich *adv* at once

Sohle *f* -,-n sole; (*Tal-*) bottom

Sohn *m* -[e]s,ˉe son

Sojabohne *f* soya bean

solange *conj* as long as

solch *inv pron* such; **s~ ein(e)** such a; **s~ einer/eine/eins** one/ (*Person*) someone like that. **s~e(r,s)** *pron* such; **ein s~er Mann/eine s~e Frau** a man/ woman like that; **ich habe s~e Angst** I am so afraid ● *a* (*substantivisch*) **ein s~er/eine s~e/ein s~es** one/ (*Person*) someone like that; **s~e** (*pl*) those; (*Leute*) people like that

Sold *m* -[e]s (*Mil*) pay

Soldat *m* -en,-en soldier

Söldner *m* -s,- mercenary

solidarisch *a* **s~e Handlung** act of solidarity; **sich s~ erklären** declare one's solidarity

Solidarität *f* - solidarity

solide *a* solid, *adv* -ly; (*haltbar*) sturdy, *adv* -ily; (*sicher*) sound, *adv* -ly; (*anständig*) respectable, *adv* -bly

Solist(in) *m* -en,-en (*f* -,-nen) soloist

Soll *nt* -s (*Comm*) debit; (*Produktions-*) quota

sollen† *v aux* **er soll warten** he is to wait; (*möge*) let him wait; **was soll ich machen?** what shall I do? **du sollst nicht lügen** you shouldn't tell lies; **du sollst nicht töten** (*liter*) thou shalt not kill; **ihr sollt jetzt still sein!** will you be quiet now! **du solltest dich schämen** you ought to/ ought to be ashamed of yourself; **es hat nicht sein s~** it was not to be; **ich hätte es nicht tun s~** I ought

---

(left column, top)

left with. **s~d** *a* seated; ⟨*Tätigkeit*⟩ sedentary. **s~lassen†** *vt sep* (*fam*) (*nicht heiraten*) jilt; (*im Stich lassen*) leave in the lurch; (*Sch*) keep down not to *or* should not have done it; **er soll sehr nett/reich sein** he is supposed to be very nice/rich; **sollte es regnen, so ...** if it should rain then ...; **das soll man nicht [tun]** you're not supposed to [do that]; **soll ich [mal versuchen]?** shall I [try]? **soll er doch!** let him! **was soll's!** so what!

Solo *nt* **-s,-los & -li** solo. **s∼** *adv* solo

somit *adv* therefore, so

Sommer *m* **-s,-** summer. **S∼ferien** *pl* summer holidays. **s∼lich** *a* summery; (*Sommer-*) summer ... • *adv* **s∼lich warm** as warm as summer. **S∼schlußverkauf** *m* summer sale. **S∼sprossen** *fpl* freckles. **s∼sprossig** *a* freckled

Sonate *f* **-,-n** sonata

Sonde *f* **-,-n** probe

Sonder|angebot *nt* special offer. **s∼bar** *a* odd, *adv* -ly. **S∼fahrt** *f* special excursion. **S∼fall** *m* special case. **s∼gleichen** *adv* **eine Gemeinheit/Grausamkeit s∼gleichen** unparalleled meanness/cruelty. **s∼lich** *a* particular, *adv* -ly; (*sonderbar*) odd, *adv* -ly. **S∼ling** *m* **-s,-e** crank. **S∼marke** *f* special stamp

sondern *conj* but; **nicht nur ... s∼ auch** not only ... but also

Sonder|preis *m* special price. **S∼schule** *f* special school. **S∼zug** *m* special train

sondieren *vt* sound out

Sonett *nt* **-[e]s,-e** sonnet

Sonnabend *m* **-s,-e** Saturday. **s∼s** *adv* on Saturdays

Sonne *f* **-,-n** sun. **s∼n (sich)** *vr* sun oneself; (*fig*) bask (**in** + *dat* in)

Sonnen|aufgang *m* sunrise. **s∼baden** *vi* (*haben*) sunbathe. **S∼bank** *f* sun-bed. **S∼blume** *f* sunflower. **S∼brand** *m* sunburn. **S∼brille** *f* sun-glasses *pl*. **S∼energie** *f* solar energy. **S∼finsternis** *f* solar eclipse. **S∼milch** *f* sun-tan lotion. **S∼öl** *nt* sun-tan oil. **S∼schein** *m* sunshine. **S∼schirm** *m* sunshade. **S∼stich** *m* sunstroke. **S∼uhr** *f* sundial. **S∼untergang** *m* sunset. **S∼wende** *f* solstice

sonnig *a* sunny

Sonntag *m* **-s,-e** Sunday. **s∼s** *adv* on Sundays

sonst *adv* (*gewöhnlich*) usually; (*im übrigen*) apart from that; (*andernfalls*) otherwise, or [else]; **wer**

where else? **s∼ niemand/nichts** no one/nothing else; **s∼ noch jemand/ etwas?** anyone/anything else? **s∼ noch Fragen?** any more questions? **s∼ig** *a* other. **s∼jemand** *pron* (*fam*) someone/(*fragend, verneint*) anyone else. **s∼wer** *pron* = **s∼jemand.** **s∼wie** *adv* (*fam*) some/any other way. **s∼wo** *adv* (*fam*) somewhere/ anywhere else

sooft *conj* whenever

Sopran *m* **-s,-e** soprano

Sorge *f* **-,-n** worry (**um** about); (*Fürsorge*) care; **in S∼ sein** be worried; **sich** (*dat*) **S∼n machen** worry; **keine S∼!** don't worry! **s∼n** *vi* (*haben*) **s∼n für** look after, care for; (*vorsorgen*) provide for; (*sich kümmern*) see to; **dafür s∼n, daß** see [to it] *or* make sure that ● *vr* **sich s∼n** worry. **s∼nfrei** *a* carefree. **s∼nvoll** *a* worried, *adv* -ly. **S∼recht** *nt* (*Jur*) custody

Sorg|falt *f* - care. **s∼fältig** *a* careful, *adv* -ly. **s∼los** *a* careless, *adv* -ly; (*unbekümmert*) carefree. **s∼sam** *a* careful, *adv* -ly

Sorte *f* **-,-n** kind, sort; (*Comm*) brand

sort|ieren *vt* sort [out]; (*Comm*) grade. **S∼iment** *nt* **-[e]s,-e** range

sosehr *conj* however much

Soße *f* **-,-n** sauce; (*Braten-*) gravy; (*Salat-*) dressing

Souffl|eur /zuˈfløːɐ̯/ *m* **-s,-e,** **S∼euse** /-ˈøːzə/ *f* **-,-n** prompter. **s∼ieren** *vi* (*haben*) prompt

Souvenir /zuvəˈniːɐ̯/ *nt* **-s,-s** souvenir

souverän /zuvəˈrɛːn/ *a* sovereign; (*fig: überlegen*) expert, *adv* -ly. **S∼ität** *f* - sovereignty

soviel *conj* however much; **s∼ ich weiß** as far as I know ● *adv* as much (**wie** as); **s∼ wie möglich** as much as possible

soweit *conj* as far as; (*insoweit*) [in] so far as ● *adv* on the whole; **s∼ wie möglich** as far as possible; **s∼ sein** be ready; **es ist s∼** the time has come

sowenig *conj* however little ● *adv* no more (**wie** than); **s∼ wie möglich** as little as possible

sowie *conj* as well as; (*sobald*) as soon as

sowieso *adv* anyway, in any case

sowjet|isch *a* Soviet. **S∼union** *f* - Soviet Union

sowohl *adv* **s∼ ... als** *od* **wie auch ...** as well as ... **s∼ er als auch seine**

sozial a social, adv -ly; ⟨Einstellung, Beruf⟩ caring. **S∼arbeit** f social work. **S∼arbeiter(in)** m(f) social worker. **S∼demokrat** m social democrat. **S∼hilfe** f social security

Sozialis|mus m - socialism. **S∼t** m -en,-en socialist. **s∼tisch** a socialist

Sozial|versicherung f National Insurance. **S∼wohnung** f ≈ council flat

Soziol|oge m -n,-n sociologist. **S∼ogie** f - sociology

Sozius m -,-se (Comm) partner; (Beifahrersitz) pillion

sozusagen adv so to speak

Spachtel m -s,- & f -,-n spatula

Spagat m -[e]s,-e (Aust) string; **S∼ machen** do the splits pl

Spaghetti pl spaghetti sg

spähen vi (haben) peer

Spalier nt -s,-e trellis; **S∼ stehen** line the route

Spalt m -[e]s,-e crack; (im Vorhang) chink

Spalt|e f -,-n crack, crevice; (Gletscher-) crevasse; (Druck-) column; (Orangen-) segment. **s∼en**† vt split; **sich s∼en** split. **S∼ung** f -,-en splitting; (Kluft) split; (Phys) fission

Span m -[e]s,¨e [wood] chip; (Hobel-) shaving

Spange f -,-n clasp; (Haar-) slide; (Zahn-) brace; (Arm-) bangle

Span|ien /-jən/ nt -s Spain. **S∼ier** m -s,-, **S∼ierin** f -,-nen Spaniard. **s∼isch** a Spanish. **S∼isch** nt -[s] (Lang) Spanish

Spann m -[e]s instep

Spanne f -,-n span; (Zeit-) space; (Comm) margin

spann|en vt stretch; put up ⟨Leine⟩; (straffen) tighten; (an-) harness (**an** + acc to); **den Hahn s∼en** cock the gun; **sich s∼en** tighten ● vi (haben) be too tight. **s∼end** a exciting. **S∼er** m -s,- (fam) Peeping Tom. **S∼ung** f -,-en tension; (Erwartung) suspense; (Electr) voltage

Spar|buch nt savings book. **S∼büchse** f money-box. **s∼en** vt/i (haben) save; (sparsam sein) economize (**mit/an** + dat on); **sich** (dat) **die Mühe s∼en** save oneself the trouble. **S∼er** m -s,- saver

Spargel m -s,- asparagus

Spar|kasse f savings bank. **S∼konto** nt deposit account

spärlich a sparse, adv -ly; (dürftig) meagre; (knapp) scanty, adv -ily

Sparren m -s,- rafter

sparsam a economical, adv -ly; ⟨Person⟩ thrifty. **S∼keit** f - economy; thrift

Sparschwein nt piggy bank

spartanisch a Spartan

Sparte f -,-n branch; (Zeitungs-) section; (Rubrik) column

Spaß m -es,¨e fun; (Scherz) joke; **im/aus/zum S∼** for fun; **S∼ machen** be fun; ⟨Person:⟩ be joking; **es macht mir keinen S∼** I don't enjoy it; **viel S∼!** have a good time! **s∼en** vi (haben) joke. **s∼ig** a amusing, funny. **S∼vogel** m joker

Spast|iker m -s,- spastic. **s∼isch** a spastic

spät a & adv late; **wie s∼ ist es?** what time is it? **zu s∼** too late; **zu s∼ kommen** be late. **s∼abends** adv late at night

Spatel m -s,- & f -,-n spatula

Spaten m -s,- spade

später a later; (zukünftig) future ● adv later

spätestens adv at the latest

Spatz m -en,-en sparrow

Spätzle pl (Culin) noodles

spazieren vi (sein) stroll. **s∼gehen**† vi sep (sein) go for a walk

Spazier|gang m walk; **einen S∼gang machen** go for a walk. **S∼gänger(in)** m -s,- (f -,-nen) walker. **S∼stock** m walking-stick

Specht m -[e]s,-e woodpecker

Speck m -s bacon; (fam: Fettpolster) fat. **s∼ig** a greasy

Spedi|teur /ʃpedi'tøːɐ/ m -s,-e haulage/(für Umzüge) removals contractor. **S∼tion** /-'tsioːn/ f -,-en carriage, haulage; (Firma) haulage/(für Umzüge) removals firm

Speer m -[e]s,-e spear; (Sport) javelin

Speiche f -,-n spoke

Speichel m -s saliva

Speicher m -s,- warehouse; (dial: Dachboden) attic; (Computer) memory. **s∼n** vt store

speien† vt spit; (erbrechen) vomit

Speise f -,-n food; (Gericht) dish; (Pudding) blancmange. **S∼eis** nt ice-cream. **S∼kammer** f larder. **S∼karte** f menu. **s∼n** vi (haben) eat; **zu Abend s∼n** have dinner ● vt feed. **S∼röhre** f oesophagus. **S∼saal** m dining-room. **S~wagen** *m* dining-car

Spektakel *m* **-s** (*fam*) noise

spektakulär *a* spectacular

Spektrum *nt* **-s,-tra** spectrum

Spekul|ant *m* **-en,-en** speculator. **S~ation** /-ˈtsi̯oːn/ *f* **-,-en** speculation. **s~ieren** *vi* (*haben*) speculate; **s~ieren auf** (+ *acc*) (*fam*) hope to get

Spelze *f* **-,-n** husk

spendabel *a* generous

Spende *f* **-,-n** donation. **s~n** *vt* donate; give ⟨*Blut, Schatten*⟩; **Beifall s~n** applaud. **S~r** *m* **-s,-** donor; (*Behälter*) dispenser

spendieren *vt* pay for; **jdm etw/ein Bier s~** treat s.o. to sth/stand s.o. a beer

Spengler *m* **-s,-** (*SGer*) plumber

Sperling *m* **-s,-e** sparrow

Sperre *f* **-,-n** barrier; (*Verbot*) ban; (*Comm*) embargo. **s~n** *vt* close; (*ver-*) block; (*verbieten*) ban; cut off ⟨*Strom, Telefon*⟩; stop ⟨*Scheck, Kredit*⟩; **s~n in** (+ *acc*) put in ⟨*Gefängnis, Käfig*⟩; **sich s~n** balk (**gegen** at); **gesperrt gedruckt** (*Typ*) spaced

Sperr|holz *nt* plywood. **s~ig** *a* bulky. **S~müll** *m* bulky refuse. **S~stunde** *f* closing time

Spesen *pl* expenses

spezial|isieren (sich) *vr* specialize (**auf** + *acc* in). **S~ist** *m* **-en,-en** specialist. **S~ität** *f* **-,-en** speciality

speziell *a* special, *adv* -ly

spezifisch *a* specific, *adv* -ally

Sphäre /ˈsfɛːrə/ *f* **-,-n** sphere

spicken *vt* (*Culin*) lard; **gespickt mit** (*fig*) full of ● *vi* (*haben*) (*fam*) crib (**bei** from)

Spiegel *m* **-s,-** mirror; (*Wasser-, Alkohol-*) level. **S~bild** *nt* reflection. **S~ei** *nt* fried egg. **s~n** *vt* reflect; **sich s~n** be reflected ● *vi* (*haben*) reflect [the light]; (*glänzen*) gleam. **S~ung** *f* **-,-en** reflection

Spiel *nt* **-[e]s,-e** game; (*Spielen*) playing; (*Glücks-*) gambling; (*Schau-*) play; (*Satz*) set; **ein S~ Karten** a pack/ (*Amer*) deck of cards; **auf dem S~ stehen** be at stake; **aufs S~ setzen** risk. **S~art** *f* variety. **S~automat** *m* fruit machine. **S~bank** *f* casino. **S~dose** *f* musical box. **s~en** *vt/i* (*haben*) play; (*im Glücksspiel*) gamble; (*vortäuschen*) act; ⟨*Roman:*⟩ be set (**in** + *dat* in); **s~en mit** (*fig*) toy with. **s~end** *a* (*mühelos*) effortless, *adv* -ly

Spieler|(in) *m* **-s,-** (*f* **-,-nen**) player; (*Glücks-*) gambler. **S~ei** *f* **-,-en** amusement; (*Kleinigkeit*) trifle

Spiel|feld *nt* field, pitch. **S~gefährte** *m*, **S~gefährtin** *f* playmate. **S~karte** *f* playing-card. **S~marke** *f* chip. **S~plan** *m* programme. **S~platz** *m* playground. **S~raum** *m* (*fig*) scope; (*Techn*) clearance. **S~regeln** *fpl* rules [of the game]. **S~sachen** *fpl* toys. **S~verderber** *m* **-s,-** spoilsport. **S~waren** *fpl* toys. **S~warengeschäft** *nt* toyshop. **S~zeug** *nt* toy; (*S~sachen*) toys *pl*

Spieß *m* **-es,-e** spear; (*Brat-*) spit; (*für Schaschlik*) skewer; (*Fleisch-*) kebab; **den S~ umkehren** turn the tables on s.o. **S~bürger** *m* [petit] bourgeois. **s~bürgerlich** *a* bourgeois. **s~en** *vt* **etw auf etw** (*acc*) **s~en** spear sth with sth. **S~er** *m* **-s,-** [petit] bourgeois. **s~ig** *a* bourgeois. **S~ruten** *fpl* **S~ruten laufen** run the gauntlet

Spike[s]reifen /ˈʃpaɪk[s]-/ *m* studded tyre

Spinat *m* **-s** spinach

Spind *m* & *nt* **-[e]s,-e** locker

Spindel *f* **-,-n** spindle

Spinne *f* **-,-n** spider

spinn|en† *vt/i* (*haben*) spin; **er spinnt** (*fam*) he's crazy. **S~ennetz** *nt* spider's web. **S~[en]gewebe** *nt*, **S~webe** *f* **-,-n** cobweb

Spion *m* **-s,-e** spy

Spionage /ʃpi̯oˈnaːʒə/ *f* - espionage, spying; **S~ treiben** spy. **S~abwehr** *f* counter-espionage

spionieren *vi* (*haben*) spy

Spionin *f* **-,-nen** [woman] spy

Spirale *f* **-,-n** spiral. **s~ig** *a* spiral

Spiritismus *m* - spiritualism. **s~tisch** *a* spiritualist

Spirituosen *pl* spirits

Spiritus *m* - alcohol; (*Brenn-*) methylated spirits *pl*. **S~kocher** *m* spirit stove

Spital *nt* **-s,-̈er** (*Aust*) hospital

spitz *a* pointed; (*scharf*) sharp; (*schrill*) shrill; ⟨*Winkel*⟩ acute; **s~e Bemerkung** dig. **S~bube** *m* scoundrel; (*Schlingel*) rascal. **s~bübisch** *a* mischievous, *adv* -ly

Spitze *f* **-,-n** point; (*oberer Teil*) top; (*vorderer Teil*) front; (*Pfeil-, Finger-, Nasen-*) tip; (*Schuh-, Strumpf-*) toe; (*Zigarren-, Zigaretten-*) holder; (*Höchstleistung*) maximum; (*Tex*) lace;

(*fam: Anspielung*) dig; **an der S~
liegen** be in the lead
Spitzel *m* **-s,-** informer
spitzen *vt* sharpen; purse ⟨*Lippen*⟩;
prick up ⟨*Ohren*⟩; **sich s~ auf** (+ *acc*)
(*fam*) look forward to. **S~ge-
schwindigkeit** *f* top speed
spitz|findig *a* over-subtle. **S~hacke**
f pickaxe. **S~name** *m* nickname
Spleen /ʃpliːn/ *m* **-s,-e** obsession;
einen S~ haben be crazy. **s~ig** *a*
eccentric
Splitter *m* **-s,-** splinter. **s~n** *vi* (*sein*)
shatter. **s~[faser]nackt** *a* (*fam*)
stark naked
sponsern *vt* sponsor
spontan *a* spontaneous, *adv* -ly
sporadisch *a* sporadic, *adv* -ally
Spore *f* **-,-n** (*Biol*) spore
Sporn *m* **-[e]s, Sporen** spur; **einem
Pferd die Sporen geben** spur a horse
Sport *m* **-[e]s** sport; (*Hobby*) hobby.
S~art *f* sport. **S~fest** *nt* sports day.
S~ler *m* **-s,-** sportsman. **S~lerin** *f*
-,-nen sportswoman. **s~lich** *a* sports
...; (*fair*) sporting, *adv* -ly; (*flott,
schlank*) sporty. **S~platz** *m* sports
ground. **S~verein** *m* sports club.
S~wagen *m* sports car; (*Kinder-*)
push-chair, (*Amer*) stroller
Spott *m* **-[e]s** mockery. **s~billig** *a* &
adv dirt cheap
spötteln *vi* (*haben*) mock; **s~ über**
(+ *acc*) poke fun at
spotten *vi* (*haben*) mock; **s~ über**
(+ *acc*) make fun of; (*höhnend*) ridicule
spöttisch *a* mocking, *adv* -ly
Sprach|e *f* **-,-n** language; (*Sprech-
fähigkeit*) speech; **zur S~e bringen**
bring up. **S~fehler** *m* speech defect.
S~labor *nt* language laboratory.
s~lich *a* linguistic, *adv* -ally. **s~los**
a speechless
Spray /ʃpreː/ *nt* & *m* **-s,-s** spray.
S~dose *f* aerosol [can]
Sprech|anlage *f* intercom. **S~chor**
m chorus; **im S~chor rufen** chant
sprechen† *vi* (*haben*) speak/(*sich
unterhalten*) talk (**über** + *acc*/**von**
about/of); **deutsch/englisch s~** speak
German/English ● *vt* speak; (*sagen,
aufsagen*) say; pronounce ⟨*Urteil*⟩;
schuldig s~ find guilty; **jdn s~** speak
to s.o.; **Herr X ist nicht zu s~** Mr X is
not available
Sprecher(in) *m* **-s,-** (*f* **-,-nen**) speaker;
(*Radio, TV*) announcer; (*Wortführer*)
spokesman, *f* spokeswoman

Sprechstunde *f* consulting hours
pl; (*Med*) surgery. **S~nhilfe** *f* (*Med*)
receptionist
Sprechzimmer *nt* consulting room
spreizen *vt* spread
Sprengel *m* **-s,-** parish
spreng|en *vt* blow up; blast ⟨*Felsen*⟩;
(*fig*) burst; (*begießen*) water; (*mit
Sprenger*) sprinkle; dampen ⟨*Wäsche*⟩
. **S~er** *m* **-s,-** sprinkler. **S~kopf** *m*
warhead. **S~körper** *m* explosive device. **S~stoff** *m* explosive
Spreu *f* - chaff
Sprich|wort *nt* (*pl* **-wörter**) proverb.
s~wörtlich *a* proverbial
sprießen† *vi* (*sein*) sprout
Springbrunnen *m* fountain
spring|en† *vi* (*sein*) jump; (*Schwimm-
sport*) dive; ⟨*Ball:*⟩ bounce; (*spritzen*)
spurt; (*zer-*) break; (*rissig werden*)
crack; (*SGer: laufen*) run. **S~er** *m* **-s,-**
jumper; (*Kunst-*) diver; (*Schach*) knight.
S~reiten *nt* show-jumping. **S~seil**
nt skipping-rope
Sprint *m* **-s,-s** sprint
Sprit *m* **-s** (*fam*) petrol
Spritz|e *f* **-,-n** syringe; (*Injektion*) in-
jection; (*Feuer-*) hose. **s~en** *vt* spray;
(*be-, ver-*) splash; (*Culin*) pipe; (*Med*)
inject ● *vi* (*haben*) splash; (*Fett:*) spit
● *vi* (*sein*) splash; (*hervor-*) spurt;
(*fam: laufen*) dash. **S~er** *m* **-s,-**
splash; (*Schuß*) dash. **s~ig** *a* lively;
⟨*Wein, Komödie*⟩ sparkling. **S~tour** *f*
(*fam*) spin
spröde *a* brittle; (*trocken*) dry;
(*rissig*) chapped; ⟨*Stimme*⟩ harsh;
(*abweisend*) aloof
Sproß *m* **-sses,-sse** shoot
Sprosse *f* **-,-n** rung. **S~nkohl** *m*
(*Aust*) Brussels sprouts *pl*
Sprotte *f* **-,-n** sprat
Spruch *m* **-[e]s,-̈e** saying; (*Denk-*)
motto; (*Zitat*) quotation. **S~band** *nt*
(*pl* **-bänder**) banner
Sprudel *m* **-s,-** sparkling mineral
water. **s~n** *vi* (*haben/sein*) bubble
Sprüh|dose *f* aerosol [can]. **s~en** *vt*
spray ● *vi* (*sein*) ⟨*Funken:*⟩ fly; (*fig*)
sparkle. **S~regen** *m* fine drizzle
Sprung *m* **-[e]s,-̈e** jump, leap;
(*Schwimmsport*) dive; (*fam: Katzen-*)
stone's throw; (*Riß*) crack; **auf einen
S~** (*fam*) for a moment. **S~brett** *nt*
springboard. **s~haft** *a* erratic;
(*plötzlich*) sudden, *adv* -ly. **S~-
schanze** *f* ski-jump. **S~seil** *nt* skipping-rope

Spucke f - spit. **s~n** vt/i (haben) spit; (sich übergeben) be sick

Spuk m -[e]s,-e [ghostly] apparition. **s~en** vi (haben) ⟨Geist:⟩ walk; **in diesem Haus s~t es** this house is haunted

Spülbecken nt sink

Spule f -,-n spool

Spüle f -,-n sink unit; (Becken) sink

spulen vt spool

spülen vt rinse; (schwemmen) wash; **Geschirr s~en** wash up ● vi (haben) flush [the toilet]. **S~kasten** m cistern. **S~mittel** nt washing-up liquid. **S~tuch** nt dishcloth

Spur f -,-en track; (Fahr-) lane; (Fährte) trail; (Anzeichen) trace; (Hinweis) lead; **keine** od **nicht die S~** (fam) not in the least

spürbar a noticeable, adv -bly

spuren vi (haben) (fam) toe the line

spür|en vt feel; (seelisch) sense. **S~hund** m tracker dog

spurlos adv without trace

spurten vi (sein) put on a spurt; (fam: laufen) sprint

sputen (sich) vr hurry

Staat m -[e]s,-en state; (Land) country; (Putz) finery. **s~lich** a state ... ● adv by the state

Staatsangehörig|e(r) m/f national. **S~keit** f - nationality

Staats|anwalt m state prosecutor. **S~beamte(r)** m civil servant. **S~besuch** m state visit. **S~bürger(in)** m(f) national. **S~mann** m (pl -männer) statesman. **S~streich** m coup

Stab m -[e]s,-e rod; (Gitter-) bar; (Sport) baton; (Mitarbeiter-) team; (Mil) staff

Stäbchen ntpl chopsticks

Stabhochsprung m pole-vault

stabil a stable; (gesund) robust; (solide) sturdy, adv -ily. **s~isieren** vt stabilize; **sich s~isieren** stabilize. **S~ität** f - stability

Stachel m -s,- spine; (Gift-) sting; (Spitze) spike. **S~beere** f gooseberry. **S~draht** m barbed wire. **s~ig** a prickly. **S~schwein** nt porcupine

Stadion nt -s,-ien stadium

Stadium nt -s,-ien stage

Stadt f -,-e town; (Groß-) city

Städt|chen nt -s,- small town. **s~isch** a urban; (kommunal) municipal

Stadt|mauer f city wall. **S~mitte** f town centre. **S~plan** m street map.

S~teil m district. **S~zentrum** nt town centre

Staffel f -,-n team; (S~lauf) relay; (Mil) squadron

Staffelei f -,-en easel

Staffel|lauf m relay race. **s~n** vt stagger; (abstufen) grade

Stagn|ation /-'tsio:n/ f - stagnation. **s~ieren** vi (haben) stagnate

Stahl m -s steel. **S~beton** m reinforced concrete

Stall m -[e]s,-e stable; (Kuh-) shed; (Schweine-) sty; (Hühner-) coop; (Kaninchen-) hutch

Stamm m -[e]s,-e trunk; (Sippe) tribe; (Kern) core; (Wort-) stem. **S~baum** m family tree; (eines Tieres) pedigree

stammeln vt/i (haben) stammer

stammen vi (haben) come/(zeitlich) date (**von/aus** from); **das Zitat stammt von Goethe** the quotation is from Goethe

Stamm|gast m regular. **S~halter** m son and heir

stämmig a sturdy

Stamm|kundschaft f regulars pl. **S~lokal** nt favourite pub. **S~tisch** m table reserved for the regulars; (Treffen) meeting of the regulars

stampf|en vi (haben) stamp; ⟨Maschine:⟩ pound; **mit den Füßen s~en** stamp one's feet ● vi (sein) tramp ● vt pound; mash ⟨Kartoffeln⟩. **S~kartoffeln** fpl mashed potatoes

Stand m -[e]s,-e standing position; (Zustand) state; (Spiel-) score; (Höhe) level; (gesellschaftlich) class; (Verkaufs-) stall; (Messe-) stand; (Taxi-) rank; **auf den neuesten S~ bringen** update

Standard m -s,-s standard. **s~isieren** vt standardize

Standarte f -,-n standard

Standbild nt statue

Ständchen nt -s,- serenade; **jdm ein S~ bringen** serenade s.o.

Ständer m -s,- stand; (Geschirr-, Platten-) rack; (Kerzen-) holder

Standes|amt nt registry office. **S~beamte(r)** m registrar. **S~unterschied** m class distinction

stand|haft a steadfast, adv -ly. **s~halten†** vi sep (haben) stand firm; **etw** (dat) **s~halten** stand up to sth

ständig a constant, adv -ly; (fest) permanent, adv -ly

Stand|licht nt sidelights pl. **S~ort** m position; (Firmen-) location; (Mil) garrison. S~**pauke** f (fam) dressing-down. S~**punkt** m point of view. S~**spur** f hard shoulder. S~**uhr** f grandfather clock

Stange f -,-n bar; (Holz-) pole; (Gardinen-) rail; (Hühner-) perch; (Zimt-) stick; **von der S~** (fam) off the peg. S~**nbohne** f runner bean. S~**nbrot** nt French bread

Stanniol nt -s tin foil. S~**papier** nt silver paper

stanzen vt stamp; (aus-) stamp out; punch ⟨Loch⟩

Stapel m -s,- stack, pile; **vom S~ laufen** be launched. S~**lauf** m launch[ing]. s~**n** vt stack or pile up; **sich s~n** pile up

stapfen vi (sein) tramp, trudge

Star[1] m -[e]s,-e starling

Star[2] m -[e]s (Med) **[grauer] S~** cataract; **grüner S~** glaucoma

Star[3] m -s,-s (Theat, Sport) star

stark a (**stärker, stärkst**) strong; ⟨Motor⟩ powerful; ⟨Verkehr, Regen⟩ heavy; ⟨Hitze, Kälte⟩ severe; (groß) big; (schlimm) bad; (dick) thick; (korpulent) stout ● adv strongly; heavily; badly; (sehr) very much

Stärk|e f -,-n (s. **stark**) strength; power; thickness; stoutness; ⟨Größe⟩ size; (Mais-, Wäsche-) starch. S~**emehl** nt cornflour. s~**en** vt strengthen; starch ⟨Wäsche⟩; **sich s~en** fortify oneself. S~**ung** f -,-en strengthening; (Erfrischung) refreshment

starr a rigid, adv -ly; (steif) stiff, adv -ly; ⟨Blick⟩ fixed; (unbeugsam) inflexible, adv -bly

starren vi (haben) stare; **vor Schmutz s~** be filthy

starr|köpfig a stubborn. S~**sinn** m obstinacy. s~**sinnig** a obstinate, adv -ly

Start m -s,-s start; (Aviat) take-off. S~**bahn** f runway. s~**en** vi (sein) start; (Aviat) take off; (aufbrechen) set off; (teilnehmen) compete ● vt start; (fig) launch

Station /-'tsio:n/ f -,-en station; (Haltestelle) stop; (Abschnitt) stage; (Med) ward; **S~ machen** break one's journey; **bei freier S~** all found. S~**är** adv as an in-patient. s~**ieren** vt station

statisch a static

Statist(in) m -en,-en (f -,-nen) (Theat) extra

Statisti|k f -,-en statistics sg; (Aufstellung) statistics pl. s~**sch** a statistical, adv -ly

Stativ nt -s,-e (Phot) tripod

statt prep (+ gen) instead of; **s~ dessen** instead ● conj **s~ etw zu tun** instead of doing sth

Stätte f -,-n place

statt|finden† vi sep (haben) take place. s~**haft** a permitted

stattlich a imposing; (beträchtlich) considerable

Statue /'∫ta:tuə/ f -,-n statue

Statur f - build, stature

Status m - status. S~**symbol** nt status symbol

Statut nt -[e]s,-en statute

Stau m -[e]s,-e congestion; (Auto) [traffic] jam; (Rück-) tailback

Staub m -[e]s dust; S~ **wischen** dust; S~ **saugen** vacuum, hoover

Staubecken nt reservoir

staub|en vi (haben) raise dust; **es s~t** it's dusty. s~**ig** a dusty. s~**saugen** vt/i (haben) vacuum, hoover. S~**sauger** m vacuum cleaner, Hoover (P). S~**tuch** nt duster

Staudamm m dam

Staude f -,-n shrub

stauen vt dam up; **sich s~** accumulate; ⟨Autos:⟩ form a tailback

staunen vi (haben) be amazed or astonished. S~ nt -s amazement, astonishment

Stau|see m reservoir. S~**ung** f -,-en congestion; (Auto) [traffic] jam

Steak /∫te:k, ste:k/ nt -s,-s steak

stechen† vt stick (**in** + acc in); (verletzen) prick; (mit Messer) stab; ⟨Insekt:⟩ sting; ⟨Mücke:⟩ bite; (gravieren) engrave ● vi (haben) prick; ⟨Insekt:⟩ sting; ⟨Mücke:⟩ bite; (mit Stechuhr) clock in/out; **in See s~** put to sea. s~**d** a stabbing; ⟨Geruch⟩ pungent

Stech|ginster m gorse. S~**kahn** m punt. S~**mücke** f mosquito. S~**palme** f holly. S~**uhr** f time clock

Steck|brief m 'wanted' poster. S~**dose** f socket. s~**en** vt put; (mit Nadel, Reißzwecke) pin; (pflanzen) plant ● vi (haben) be; (fest-) be stuck; **hinter etw** (dat) **s~en** (fig) be behind sth

Stecken m -s,- (SGer) stick

stecken|bleiben† vi sep (sein) get stuck. s~**lassen**† vt sep leave. S~**pferd** nt hobby-horse

Steck|er m -s,- (Electr) plug. S~**ling** m -s,-e cutting. S~**nadel** f pin. S~**rübe** f swede

Steg m -[e]s,-e foot-bridge; (*Boots-*) landing-stage; (*Brillen-*) bridge. **S~reif** m **aus dem S~reif** extempore

stehen† vi (haben) stand; (*sich befinden*) be; (*still-*) be stationary; (*Maschine, Uhr:*) have stopped; **vor dem Ruin s~** face ruin; **zu jdm/etw s~** (*fig*) stand by s.o./sth; **gut s~** (*Getreide, Aktien:*) be doing well; (*Chancen:*) be good; **jdm [gut] s~** suit s.o.; **sich gut s~** be on good terms; **es steht 3 zu 1** the score is 3 – 1; **es steht schlecht um ihn** he is in a bad way. **S~** nt -s standing; **zum S~ bringen/kommen** bring/come to a standstill. **s~bleiben**† vi sep (sein) stop; (*Motor:*) stall; (*Zeit:*) stand still; (*Gebäude:*) be left standing. **s~d** a standing; (*sich nicht bewegend*) stationary; (*Gewässer:*) stagnant. **s~lassen**† vt sep leave; **sich** (dat) **einen Bart s~lassen** grow a beard

Steh|lampe f standard lamp. **S~leiter** f step-ladder

stehlen† vt/i (haben) steal; **sich s~** steal, creep

Steh|platz m standing place. **S~vermögen** nt stamina, staying-power

steif a stiff, adv -ly. **S~heit** f - stiffness

Steig|bügel m stirrup. **S~eisen** nt crampon

steigen† vi (sein) climb; (*hochgehen*) rise, go up; (*Schulden, Spannung:*) mount; **s~ auf** (+ acc) climb on [to] (*Stuhl*); climb (*Berg, Leiter*); get on (*Pferd, Fahrrad*); **s~ in** (+ acc) climb into; get in (*Auto*); get on (*Bus, Zug*); **s~ aus** climb out of; get out of (*Bus, Zug*); **einen Drachen s~ lassen** fly a kite; **s~de Preise** rising prices

steiger|n vt increase; **sich s~n** increase; (*sich verbessern*) improve. **S~ung** f -,-en increase; improvement; (*Gram*) comparison

Steigung f -,-en gradient; (*Hang*) slope

steil a steep, adv -ly. **S~küste** f cliffs pl

Stein m -[e]s,-e stone; (*Ziegel-*) brick; (*Spiel-*) piece. **s~alt** a ancient. **S~bock** m ibex; (*Astr*) Capricorn. **S~bruch** m quarry. **S~garten** m rockery. **S~gut** nt earthenware. **s~hart** a rock-hard. **s~ig** a stony. **s~igen** vt stone. **S~kohle** f [hard]

coal. **s~reich** a (*fam*) very rich. **S~schlag** m rock fall

Stelle f -,-n place; (*Fleck*) spot; (*Abschnitt*) passage; (*Stellung*) job, post; (*Büro*) office; (*Behörde*) authority; **kahle S~** bare patch; **auf der S~** immediately; **an deiner S~** in your place

stellen vt put; (*aufrecht*) stand; set (*Wecker, Aufgabe*); ask (*Frage*); make (*Antrag, Forderung, Diagnose*); **zur Verfügung s~** provide; **lauter/leiser s~** turn up/down; **kalt/warm s~** chill/keep hot; **sich s~** [go and] stand; give oneself up (**der Polizei** to the police); **sich tot/schlafend s~** pretend to be dead/asleep; **gut gestellt sein** be well off

Stellen|anzeige f job advertisement. **S~vermittlung** f employment agency. **s~weise** adv in places

Stellung f -,-en position; (*Arbeit*) job; **S~ nehmen** make a statement (**zu** on). **s~slos** a jobless. **S~suche** f jobhunting

stellvertret|end a deputy … ●adv as a deputy; **s~end für jdn** on s.o.'s behalf. **S~er** m deputy

Stellwerk nt signal-box

Stelzen fpl stilts. **s~** vi (sein) stalk

stemmen vt press; lift (*Gewicht*); **sich s~ gegen** brace oneself against

Stempel m -s,- stamp; (*Post-*) postmark; (*Präge-*) die; (*Feingehalts-*) hallmark. **s~n** vt stamp; hallmark (*Silber*); cancel (*Marke*)

Stengel m -s,- stalk, stem

Steno f - (*fam*) shorthand

Steno|gramm nt -[e]s,-e shorthand text. **S~graphie** f - shorthand. **s~graphieren** vt take down in shorthand ●vi (haben) do shorthand. **S~typistin** f -,-nen shorthand typist

Steppdecke f quilt

Steppe f -,-n steppe

Steptanz m tap-dance

sterben† vi (sein) die (**an** + dat of); **im S~ liegen** be dying

sterblich a mortal. **S~e(r)** m/f mortal. **S~keit** f - mortality

stereo adv in stereo. **S~anlage** f stereo [system]

stereotyp a stereotyped

steril a sterile. **s~isieren** vt sterilize. **S~ität** f - sterility

Stern m -[e]s,-e star. **S~bild** nt constellation. **S~chen** nt -s,- asterisk.

S~kunde f astronomy. **S~-schnuppe** f -,-n shooting star. **S~-warte** f -,-n observatory

stetig a steady, adv -ily

stets adv always

Steuer[1] nt -s,- steering-wheel; (Naut) helm; **am S~** at the wheel

Steuer[2] f -,-n tax

Steuer|bord nt -[e]s starboard [side]. **S~erklärung** f tax return. **s~frei** a & adv tax-free. **S~mann** m (pl -leute) helmsman; (beim Rudern) cox. **s~n** vt steer; (Aviat) pilot; (Techn) control • vi (haben) be at the wheel/ (Naut) helm • (sein) head (**nach** for). **s~pflichtig** a taxable. **S~rad** nt steering-wheel. **S~ruder** nt helm. **S~ung** f - steering; (Techn) controls pl.**S~zahler** m -s,- taxpayer

Stewardeß /ˈstjuːədɛs/ f -,-dessen air hostess, stewardess

Stich m -[e]s,-e prick; (Messer-) stab; (S~wunde) stab wound; (Bienen-) sting; (Mücken-) bite; (Schmerz) stabbing pain; (Näh-) stitch; (Kupfer-) engraving; (Kartenspiel) trick; **S~ ins Rötliche** tinge of red; **jdn im S~ lassen** leave s.o. in the lurch; (Gedächtnis:) fail s.o. **s~eln** vi (haben) make snide remarks

Stich|flamme f jet of flame. **s~haltig** a valid. **S~probe** f spot check. **S~wort** nt (pl -wörter) headword; (pl -worte) (Theat) cue; **S~worte** notes

stick|en vt/i (haben) embroider. **S~erei** f - embroidery

stickig a stuffy

Stickstoff m nitrogen

Stiefbruder m stepbrother

Stiefel m -s,- boot

Stief|kind nt stepchild. **S~mutter** f stepmother. **S~mütterchen** nt -s,- pansy. **S~schwester** f stepsister. **S~sohn** m stepson. **S~tochter** f stepdaughter. **S~vater** m stepfather

Stiege f -,-n stairs pl

Stiel m -[e]s,-e handle; (Blumen-, Gläser-) stem; (Blatt-) stalk

Stier m -[e]s,-e bull; (Astr) Taurus

stieren vi (haben) stare

Stier|kampf m bullfight

Stift[1] m -[e]s,-e pin; (Nagel) tack; (Blei-) pencil; (Farb-) crayon

Stift[2] nt -[e]s,-e endowed foundation. **s~en** vt endow; (spenden) donate; create (Unheil, Verwirrung); bring about (Frieden). **S~er** m -s,- founder;

(Spender) donor.**S~ung** f -,-en foundation; (Spende) donation

Stigma nt -s (fig) stigma

Stil m -[e]s,-e style; **in großem S~** in style.**s~isiert** a stylized.**s~istisch** a stylistic, adv -ally

still a quiet, adv -ly; (reglos, ohne Kohlensäure) still; (heimlich) secret, adv -ly; **der S~e Ozean** the Pacific; **im s~en** secretly; (bei sich) inwardly.**S~e** f - quiet; (Schweigen) silence

Stilleben nt still life

stilleg|en vt sep close down. **S~ung** f -,-en closure

stillen vt satisfy; quench (Durst); stop (Schmerzen, Blutung); breast-feed (Kind)

stillhalten† vi sep (haben) keep still

Stillschweigen nt silence. **s~d** a silent, adv -ly; (fig) tacit, adv -ly

still|sitzen† vi sep (haben) sit still. **S~stand** m standstill; **zum S~stand bringen** stop. **S~stehen**† vi sep (haben) stand still; (anhalten) stop; (Verkehr:) be at a standstill

Stil|möbel pl reproduction furniture sg.**s~voll** a stylish, adv -ly

Stimm|bänder ntpl vocal cords. **s~berechtigt** a entitled to vote. **S~bruch** m **er ist im S~bruch** his voice is breaking

Stimme f -,-n voice; (Wahl-) vote

stimmen vi (haben) be right; (wählen) vote; **stimmt das?** is that right/ (wahr) true? • vt tune; **jdn traurig/ fröhlich s~** make s.o. feel sad/happy

Stimm|enthaltung f abstention. **S~recht** nt right to vote

Stimmung f -,-en mood; (Atmosphäre) atmosphere. **s~svoll** a full of atmosphere

Stimmzettel m ballot-paper

stimulieren vt stimulate

stink|en† vi (haben) smell/(stark) stink (**nach** of).**S~tier** nt skunk

Stipendium nt -s,-ien scholarship; (Beihilfe) grant

Stirn f -,-en forehead; **die S~ bieten** (+ dat) (fig) defy. **S~runzeln** nt -s frown

stöbern vi (haben) rummage

stochern vi (haben) **s~ in** (+ dat) poke (Feuer); pick at (Essen); pick (Zähne)

Stock[1] m -[e]s,"-e stick; (Ski-) pole; (Bienen-) hive; (Rosen-) bush; (Reb-) vine

Stock[2] m -[e]s,- storey, floor. **S~bett** nt bunk-beds pl. **s~dunkel** a (fam) pitch-dark

stock|en vi (haben) stop; ⟨Verkehr:⟩ come to a standstill; ⟨Person:⟩ falter. **s∼end** a hesitant, adv -ly. **s∼taub** a (fam) stone-deaf. **S∼ung** f -,-en hold-up

Stockwerk nt storey, floor

Stoff m -[e]s,-e substance; (Tex) fabric, material; (Thema) subject [matter]; (Gesprächs-) topic. **S∼tier** nt soft toy. **S∼wechsel** m metabolism

stöhnen vi (haben) groan, moan. **S∼** nt -s groan, moan

stoisch a stoic, adv -ally

Stola f -,-len stole

Stollen m -s,- gallery; (Kuchen) stollen

stolpern vi (sein) stumble; **s∼ über** (+ acc) trip over

stolz a proud (**auf** + acc of), adv -ly. **S∼** m -es pride

stolzieren vi (sein) strut

stopfen vt stuff; (stecken) put; (ausbessern) darn ●vi (haben) be constipating; (fam: essen) guzzle

Stopp m -s,-s stop. **s∼** int stop!

stoppel|ig a stubbly. **S∼n** fpl stubble sg

stopp|en vt stop; (Sport) time ●vi (haben) stop. **S∼schild** nt stop sign. **S∼uhr** f stop-watch

Stöpsel m -s,- plug; (Flaschen-) stopper

Storch m -[e]s,ːe stork

Store /ʃtoːɐ̯/ m -s,-s net curtain

stören vt disturb; disrupt ⟨Rede, Sitzung⟩; jam ⟨Sender⟩; (mißfallen) bother; **stört es Sie, wenn ich rauche?** do you mind if I smoke? ●vi (haben) be a nuisance; **entschuldigen Sie, daß ich störe** I'm sorry to bother you

stornieren vt cancel

störrisch a stubborn, adv -ly

Störung f -,-en (s. **stören**) disturbance; disruption; (Med) trouble; (Radio) interference; **technische S∼** technical fault

Stoß m -es,ːe push, knock; (mit Ellbogen) dig; (Hörner-) butt; (mit Waffe) thrust; (Schwimm-) stroke; (Ruck) jolt; (Erd-) shock; (Stapel) stack, pile. **S∼dämpfer** m -s,- shock absorber

stoßen† vt push, knock; (mit Füßen) kick; (mit Kopf, Hörnern) butt; (an-) poke, nudge; (treiben) thrust; **sich s∼** knock oneself; **sich** (dat) **den Kopf s∼** hit one's head ●vi (haben) push; **s∼ an** (+ acc) knock against; (angrenzen) adjoin ●vi (sein) **s∼ gegen** knock against; bump into ⟨Tür⟩; **s∼ auf** (+ acc) bump into; (entdecken) come

across; strike ⟨Öl⟩; (fig) meet with ⟨Ablehnung⟩

Stoß|stange f bumper. **S∼verkehr** m rush-hour traffic. **S∼zahn** m tusk. **S∼zeit** f rush-hour

stottern vt/i (haben) stutter, stammer

Str. abbr (**Straße**) St

Straf|anstalt f prison. **S∼arbeit** f (Sch) imposition. **s∼bar** a punishable; **sich s∼bar machen** commit an offence

Strafe f -,-n punishment; (Jur & fig) penalty; (Geld-) fine; (Freiheits-) sentence. **s∼n** vt punish

straff a tight, taut. **s∼en** vt tighten; **sich s∼en** tighten

Strafgesetz nt criminal law

sträf|lich a criminal, adv -ly. **S∼ling** m -s,-e prisoner

Straf|mandat nt (Auto) [parking/speeding] ticket. **S∼porto** nt excess postage. **S∼predigt** f (fam) lecture. **S∼raum** m penalty area. **S∼stoß** m penalty. **S∼tat** f crime. **S∼zettel** m (fam) = **S∼mandat**

Strahl m -[e]s,-en ray; (einer Taschenlampe) beam; (Wasser-) jet. **s∼en** vi (haben) shine; (funkeln) sparkle; (lächeln) beam. **S∼enbehandlung** f radiotherapy. **s∼end** a shining; sparkling; beaming; radiant ⟨Schönheit⟩. **S∼entherapie** f radiotherapy. **S∼ung** f - radiation

Strähn|e f -,-n strand. **s∼ig** a straggly

stramm a tight, adv -ly; (kräftig) sturdy; (gerade) upright

Strampel|höschen nt -s,- rompers pl. **s∼n** vi (haben) ⟨Baby:⟩ kick

Strand m -[e]s,ːe beach. **s∼en** vi (sein) run aground; (fig) fail. **S∼korb** m wicker beach-chair. **S∼promenade** f promenade

Strang m -[e]s,ːe rope

Strapaz|e f -,-n strain. **s∼ieren** vt be hard on; tax ⟨Nerven, Geduld⟩. **s∼ierfähig** a hard-wearing. **s∼iös** a exhausting

Straß m - & -sses paste

Straße f -,-n road; (in der Stadt auch) street; (Meeres-) strait; **auf der S∼** in the road/street. **S∼nbahn** f tram, (Amer) streetcar. **S∼nkarte** f roadmap. **S∼nlaterne** f street lamp. **S∼nsperre** f road-block

Strat|egie f -,-n strategy. **s∼egisch** a strategic, adv -ally

sträuben vt ruffle up ⟨Federn⟩; **sich s∼** ⟨Fell, Haar:⟩ stand on end; (fig) resist

Strauch m -[e]s, **Sträucher** bush

straucheln vi (sein) stumble

Strauß¹ m -es, **Sträuße** bunch [of flowers]; (Bukett) bouquet

Strauß² m -es, -e ostrich

Strebe f -, -n brace, strut

streben vi (haben) strive (**nach** for) ● vi (sein) head (**nach/zu** for)

Streb|er m -s, - pushy person; (Sch) swot. **s∼sam** a industrious

Strecke f -, -n stretch, section; (Entfernung) distance; (Rail) line; (Route) route

strecken vt stretch; (aus-) stretch out; (gerade machen) straighten; (Culin) thin down; **sich s∼** stretch; (sich aus-) stretch out; **den Kopf aus dem Fenster s∼** put one's head out of the window

Streich m -[e]s, -e prank, trick; **jdm einen S∼ spielen** play a trick on s.o.

streicheln vt stroke

streichen† vt spread; (weg-) smooth; (an-) paint; (aus-) delete; (kürzen) cut ● vi (haben) **s∼ über** (+ acc) stroke

Streicher m -s, - string-player; **die S∼** the strings

Streichholz nt match. **S∼schachtel** f matchbox

Streich|instrument nt stringed instrument. **S∼käse** m cheese spread. **S∼orchester** nt string orchestra. **S∼ung** f -, -en deletion; (Kürzung) cut

Streife f -, -n patrol

streifen vt brush against; (berühren) touch; (verletzen) graze; (fig) touch on ⟨Thema⟩; (ziehen) slip (**über** + acc over); **mit dem Blick s∼** glance at ● vi (sein) roam

Streifen m -s, - stripe; (Licht-) streak; (auf der Fahrbahn) line; (schmales Stück) strip

Streif|enwagen m patrol car. **s∼ig** a streaky. **S∼schuß** m glancing shot; (Wunde) graze

Streik m -s, -s strike; **in den S∼ treten** go on strike. **S∼brecher** m strikebreaker, (pej) scab. **s∼en** vi (haben) strike; (fam) refuse; (versagen) pack up. **S∼ende(r)** m striker. **S∼posten** m picket

Streit m -[e]s, -e quarrel; (Auseinandersetzung) dispute. **s∼en**† vr/i (haben) [sich] s∼en quarrel. **s∼ig** a **jdm etw s∼ig machen** dispute s.o.'s

right to sth. **S∼igkeiten** fpl quarrels. **S∼kräfte** fpl armed forces. **s∼süchtig** a quarrelsome

streng a strict, adv -ly; ⟨Blick, Ton⟩ stern, adv -ly; (rauh, nüchtern) severe, adv -ly; ⟨Geschmack⟩ sharp. **S∼e** f - strictness; sternness; severity. **s∼genommen** adv strictly speaking. **s∼gläubig** a strict; (orthodox) orthodox. **s∼stens** adv strictly

Streß m -sses, -sse stress

streßig a (fam) stressful

streuen vt spread; (ver-) scatter; sprinkle ⟨Zucker, Salz⟩; **die Straßen s∼** grit the roads

streunen vi (sein) roam; **s∼der Hund** stray dog

Strich m -[e]s, -e line; (Feder-, Pinsel-) stroke; (Morse-, Gedanken-) dash; **gegen den S∼** the wrong way; (fig) against the grain. **S∼kode** m bar code. **S∼punkt** m semicolon

Strick m -[e]s, -e cord; (Seil) rope; (fam: Schlingel) rascal

strick|en vt/i (haben) knit. **S∼jacke** f cardigan. **S∼leiter** f rope-ladder. **S∼nadel** f knitting-needle. **S∼waren** fpl knitwear sg. **S∼zeug** nt knitting

striegeln vt groom

strikt a strict, adv -ly

strittig a contentious

Stroh nt -[e]s straw. **S∼blumen** fpl everlasting flowers. **S∼dach** nt thatched roof. **s∼gedeckt** a thatched. **S∼halm** m straw

Strolch m -[e]s, -e (fam) rascal

Strom m -[e]s, ∼e river; (Menschen-, Auto-, Blut-) stream; (Tränen-) flood; (Schwall) torrent; (Electr) current, power; **gegen den S∼** (fig) against the tide; **es regnet in Strömen** it is pouring with rain. **s∼abwärts** adv downstream. **s∼aufwärts** adv upstream

strömen vi (sein) flow; ⟨Menschen, Blut:⟩ stream, pour; **s∼der Regen** pouring rain

Strom|kreis m circuit. **s∼linienförmig** a streamlined. **S∼sperre** f power cut

Strömung f -, -en current

Strophe f -, -n verse

strotzen vi (haben) be full (**vor** + dat of); **vor Gesundheit s∼d** bursting with health

Strudel m -s, - whirlpool; (SGer Culin) strudel

Struktur f -,-en structure; (*Tex*) texture

Strumpf m -[e]s,¨e stocking; (*Knie-*) sock. **S~band** nt (*pl* -**bänder**) suspender,(*Amer*) garter. **S~bandgürtel** m suspender/(*Amer*) garter belt. **S~halter** m = **S~band**. **S~hose** f tights *pl*, (*Amer*) pantyhose

Strunk m -[e]s,¨e stalk; (*Baum-*) stump

struppig a shaggy

Stube f -,-n room. s~**rein** a housetrained

Stuck m -s stucco

Stück nt -[e]s,-e piece; (*Zucker-*) lump; (*Seife*) tablet; (*Theater-*) play; (*Gegenstand*) item; (*Exemplar*) specimen; **20 S~ Vieh** 20 head of cattle; **ein S~** (*Entfernung*) some way; **aus freien S~en** voluntarily. **S~chen** nt -s,-[little] bit. **s~weise** adv bit by bit; (*einzeln*) singly

Student|(in) m -en,-en (f -,-nen) student. **s~isch** a student ...

Studie /-jə/ f -,-n study

studier|en vt/i (*haben*) study. **S~zimmer** nt study

Studio nt -s,-s studio

Studium nt -s,-ien studies *pl*

Stufe f -,-n step; (*Treppen-*) stair; (*Raketen-*) stage; (*Niveau*) level. s~**n** vt terrace; (*staffeln*) grade

Stuhl m -[e]s,¨e chair; (*Med*) stools *pl.* **S~gang** m bowel movement

stülpen vt put (**über** + acc over)

stumm a dumb; (*schweigsam*) silent, adv -ly

Stummel m -s,- stump; (*Zigaretten-*) butt; (*Bleistift-*) stub

Stümper m -s,- bungler. s~**haft** a incompetent, adv -ly

stumpf a blunt; (*Winkel*) obtuse; (*glanzlos*) dull; (*fig*) apathetic, adv - ally. **S~** m -[e]s,¨e stump

Stumpfsinn m apathy; (*Langweiligkeit*) tedium. s~**ig** a apathetic, adv -ally; (*langweilig*) tedious

Stunde f -,-n hour; (*Sch*) lesson

stunden vt **jdm eine Schuld s~** give s.o. time to pay a debt

Stunden|kilometer mpl kilometres per hour. s~**lang** adv for hours. **S~lohn** m hourly rate. **S~plan** m timetable. **s~weise** adv by the hour

stündlich a & adv hourly

Stups m -es,-e nudge; (*Schubs*) push. s~**en** vt nudge; (*schubsen*) push. **S~nase** f snub nose

stur a pigheaded; (*phlegmatisch*) stolid, adv -ly; (*unbeirrbar*) dogged, adv -ly

Sturm m -[e]s,¨e gale; (*schwer*) storm; (*Mil*) assault

stürm|en vi (*haben*) ⟨*Wind:*⟩ blow hard; **es s~t** it's blowing a gale ●vi (*sein*) rush ●vt storm; (*bedrängen*) besiege. **S~er** m -s,- forward. s~**isch** a stormy; ⟨*Überfahrt*⟩ rough; (*fig*) tumultuous, adv -ly; (*ungestüm*) tempestuous, adv -ly

Sturz m -es,¨e [heavy] fall; (*Preis-, Kurs-*) sharp drop; (*Pol*) overthrow

stürzen vi (*sein*) fall [heavily]; (*in die Tiefe*) plunge; ⟨*Preise, Kurse:*⟩ drop sharply; ⟨*Regierung:*⟩ fall; (*eilen*) rush ●vt throw; (*umkippen*) turn upside down; turn out ⟨*Speise, Kuchen*⟩; (*Pol*) overthrow, topple; **sich s~** throw oneself (**aus/in** + acc out of/ into); **sich s~ auf** (+ acc) pounce on

Sturz|flug m (*Aviat*) dive. **S~helm** m crash-helmet

Stute f -,-n mare

Stütze f -,-n support; (*Kopf-, Arm-*) rest

stutzen vi (*haben*) stop short ●vt trim; (*Hort*) cut back; (*kupieren*) crop

stützen vt support; (*auf-*) rest; **sich s~ auf** (+ acc) lean on; (*beruhen*) be based on

Stutzer m -s,- dandy

stutzig a puzzled; (*mißtrauisch*) suspicious

Stützpunkt m (*Mil*) base

Subjekt nt -[e]s,-e subject. s~**iv** a subjective, adv -ly

Subskription /-'tsio:n/ f -,-en subscription

Substantiv nt -s,-e noun

Substanz f -,-en substance

subtil a subtle, adv -tly

subtra|hieren vt subtract. **S~ktion** /-'tsio:n/ f -,-en subtraction

Subvention /-'tsio:n/ f -,-en subsidy. s~**ieren** vt subsidize

subversiv a subversive

Such|e f - search; **auf der S~e nach** looking for. **s~en** vt look for; (*intensiv*) search for; seek ⟨*Hilfe, Rat*⟩; **'Zimmer gesucht'** 'room wanted' ●vi (*haben*) look, search (**nach** for). **S~er** m -s,- (*Phot*) viewfinder

Sucht f -,¨e addiction; (*fig*) mania

süchtig a addicted. **S~e(r)** m/f addict

Süd m -[e]s south. **S~afrika** nt South Africa. **S~amerika** nt South America. s~**deutsch** a South German

Süden *m* **-s** south; **nach S**∼ south
Süd|frucht *f* tropical fruit. **s**∼**lich** *a* southern; ⟨*Richtung*⟩ southerly ● *adv & prep* (+ *gen*) **s**∼**lich [von] der Stadt** [to the] south of the town. **S**∼**osten** *m* south-east. **S**∼**pol** *m* South Pole. **s**∼**wärts** *adv* southwards. **S**∼**westen** *m* south-west
süffisant *a* smug, *adv* -ly
suggerieren *vt* suggest (*dat* to)
Suggest|ion /-'tio:n/ *f* **-,-en** suggestion. **s**∼**iv** *a* suggestive
Sühne *f* **-,-n** atonement; (*Strafe*) penalty. **s**∼**n** *vt* atone for
Sultanine *f* **-,-n** sultana
Sülze *f* **-,-n** [meat] jelly; (*Schweinskopf-*) brawn
Summe *f* **-,-n** sum
summ|en *vi* (*haben*) hum; ⟨*Biene:*⟩ buzz ● *vt* hum. **S**∼**er** *m* **-s,-** buzzer
summieren (sich) *vr* add up; (*sich häufen*) increase
Sumpf *m* **-[e]s,ˑe** marsh, swamp. **s**∼**ig** *a* marshy
Sünd|e *f* **-,-n** sin. **S**∼**enbock** *m* scapegoat. **S**∼**er(in)** *m* **-s,-** (*f* -,-**nen**) sinner. **s**∼**haft** *a* sinful. **s**∼**igen** *vi* (*haben*) sin
super *inv a* (*fam*) great. **S**∼**lativ** *m* **-s,-e** superlative. **S**∼**markt** *m* supermarket
Suppe *f* **-,-n** soup. **S**∼**nlöffel** *m* soupspoon. **S**∼**nteller** *m* soup-plate. **S**∼**nwürfel** *m* stock cube
Surf|brett /'sœrf-/ *nt* surfboard. **S**∼**en** *nt* **-s** surfing
surren *vi* (*haben*) whirr
süß *a* sweet, *adv* -ly. **S**∼**e** *f* - sweetness. **s**∼**en** *vt* sweeten. **S**∼**igkeit** *f* **-,-en** sweet. **s**∼**lich** *a* sweetish; (*fig*) sugary. **S**∼**speise** *f* sweet. **S**∼**stoff** *m* sweetener. **S**∼**waren** *fpl* confectionery *sg*, sweets *pl*. **S**∼**wasser-** *pref* freshwater . . .
Sylvester *nt* **-s** = **Silvester**
Symbol *nt* **-s,-e** symbol. **S**∼**ik** *f* - symbolism. **s**∼**isch** *a* symbolic, *adv* -ally. **s**∼**isieren** *vt* symbolize
Sym|metrie *f* - symmetry. **s**∼**metrisch** *a* symmetrical, *adv* -ly
Sympathie *f* **-,-n** sympathy
sympath|isch *a* agreeable; ⟨*Person*⟩ likeable. **S**∼**isieren** *vi* (*haben*) be sympathetic (**mit** to)
Symphonie *f* -,-n = **Sinfonie**
Symptom *nt* **-s,-e** symptom. **s**∼**a-tisch** *a* symptomatic
Synagoge *f* **-,-n** synagogue

synchronisieren /zʏnkroni'zi:rən/ *vt* synchronize; dub ⟨*Film*⟩
Syndikat *nt* **-[e]s,-e** syndicate
Syndrom *nt* **-s,-e** syndrome
synonym *a* synonymous, *adv* -ly. **S**∼ *nt* **-s,-e** synonym
Syntax /'zʏntaks/ *f* - syntax
Synthe|se *f* **-,-n** synthesis. **S**∼**tik** *nt* **-s** synthetic material. **s**∼**tisch** *a* synthetic, *adv* -ally
Syrien /-jən/ *nt* **-s** Syria
System *nt* **-s,-e** system. **s**∼**atisch** *a* systematic, *adv* -ally
Szene *f* **-,-n** scene. **S**∼**rie** *f* scenery

T

Tabak *m* **-s,-e** tobacco
Tabelle *f* **-,-n** table; (*Sport*) league table
Tablett *nt* **-[e]s,-s** tray
Tablette *f* **-,-n** tablet
tabu *a* taboo. **T**∼ *nt* **-s,-s** taboo
Tacho *m* **-s,-s**, **Tachometer** *m & nt* speedometer
Tadel *m* **-s,-** reprimand; (*Kritik*) censure; (*Sch*) black mark. **t**∼**los** *a* impeccable, *adv* -bly. **t**∼**n** *vt* reprimand; censure. **t**∼**nswert** *a* reprehensible
Tafel *f* **-,-n** (*Tisch, Tabelle*) table; (*Platte*) slab; (*Anschlag-, Hinweis-*) board; (*Gedenk-*) plaque; (*Schiefer-*) slate; (*Wand-*) blackboard; (*Bild-*) plate; (*Schokolade*) bar. **t**∼**n** *vi* (*haben*) feast
Täfelung *f* - panelling
Tag *m* **-[e]s,-e** day; **Tag für Tag** day by day; **am T**∼**e** in the daytime; **eines T**∼**es** one day; **unter T**∼**e** underground; **es wird Tag** it is getting light; **guten Tag!** good morning/afternoon! **t**∼**aus** *adv* **t**∼**aus, t**∼**ein** day in, day out
Tage|buch *nt* diary. **t**∼**lang** *adv* for days
tagen *vi* (*haben*) meet; ⟨*Gericht:*⟩ sit; **es tagt** day is breaking
Tages|anbruch *m* daybreak. **T**∼**ausflug** *m* day trip. **T**∼**decke** *f* bedspread. **T**∼**karte** *f* day ticket; (*Speise-*) menu of the day. **T**∼**licht** *nt* daylight. **T**∼**mutter** *f* child-minder. **T**∼**ordnung** *f* agenda. **T**∼**rückfahrkarte** *f* day return [ticket]. **T**∼**zeit** *f* time of the day. **T**∼**zeitung** *f* daily [news]paper
täglich *a & adv* daily; **zweimal t**∼ twice a day

tagsadv by day; **t~ zuvor/darauf** the day before/after

tagsüberadv during the day

tag|täglich a daily ●adv every single day. **T~traum** m daydream. **T~undnachtgleiche** f -,-n equinox. **T~ung** f -,-en meeting; (Konferenz) conference

Taill|e /'taljə/ f -,-n waist. **t~iert** /ta'ji:ɐt/ a fitted

Takt m -[e]s,-e tact; (Mus) bar; (Tempo) time; (Rhythmus) rhythm; **im T~** in time [to the music]. **T~gefühl** nt tact

Takt|ik f - tactics pl. **t~isch** a tactical, adv -ly

takt|los a tactless, adv -ly. **T~losigkeit** f - tactlessness. **T~stock** m baton. **t~voll** a tactful, adv -ly

Tal nt -[e]s,ˮer valley

Talar m -s,-e robe; (Univ) gown

Talent nt -[e]s,-e talent. **t~iert** a talented

Talg m -s tallow; (Culin) suet

Talsperre f dam

Tampon /tam'põ:/ m -s,-s tampon

Tang m -s seaweed

Tangente f -,-n tangent; (Straße) by-pass

Tank m -s,-s tank. **t~en** vt fill up with ⟨Benzin⟩ ●vi (haben) fill up with petrol; (Aviat) refuel; **ich muß t~en** I need petrol. **T~er** m -s,- tanker. **T~stelle** f petrol/(Amer) gas station. **T~wart** m -[e]s,-e petrol-pump attendant

Tanne f -,-n fir [tree]. **T~nbaum** m fir tree; (Weihnachtsbaum) Christmas tree. **T~nzapfen** m fir cone

Tante f -,-n aunt

Tantiemen /tan'tje:mən/ pl royalties

Tanz m -es,ˮe dance. **t~en** vt/i (haben) dance

Tänzer(in) m -s,- (f -,-nen) dancer

Tanz|lokal nt dance-hall. **T~musik** f dance music

Tapete f -,-n wallpaper. **T~nwechsel** m (fam) change of scene

tapezier|en vt paper. **T~er** m -s,- paperhanger, decorator

tapfer a brave, adv -ly. **T~keit** f - bravery

tappen vi (sein) walk hesitantly; (greifen) grope (**nach** for)

Tarif m -s,-e rate; (Verzeichnis) tariff

tarn|en vt disguise; (Mil) camouflage; **sich t~en** disguise/camouflage oneself. **T~ung** f - disguise; camouflage

Tasche f -,-n bag; (Hosen-, Mantel-) pocket. **T~nbuch** nt paperback. **T~ndieb** m pickpocket. **T~ngeld** nt pocket-money. **T~nlampe** f torch, (Amer) flashlight. **T~nmesser** nt penknife. **T~ntuch** nt handkerchief

Tasse f -,-n cup

Tastatur f -,-en keyboard

tast|bar a palpable. **T~e** f -,-n key; (Druck-) push-button. **t~en** vi (haben) feel, grope (**nach** for) ●vt key in ⟨Daten⟩; **sich t~en** feel one's way (**zu** to). **t~end** a tentative, adv -ly

Tat f -,-en action; (Helden-) deed; (Straf-) crime; **in der Tat** indeed; **auf frischer Tat ertappt** caught in the act. **t~enlos** adv passively

Täter(in) m -s,- (f -,-nen) culprit; (Jur) offender

tätig a active, adv -ly; **t~ sein** work. **T~keit** f -,-en activity; (Funktionieren) action; (Arbeit) work, job

Tatkraft f energy

tätlich a physical, adv -ly; **t~ werden** become violent. **T~keiten** fpl violence sg

Tatort m scene of the crime

tätowier|en vt tattoo. **T~ung** f -,-en tattooing; (Bild) tattoo

Tatsache f fact. **T~nbericht** m documentary

tatsächlich a actual, adv -ly

tätscheln vt pat

Tatze f -,-n paw

Tau¹ m -[e]s dew

Tau² nt -[e]s,-e rope

taub a deaf; (gefühllos) numb; ⟨Nuß⟩ empty; ⟨Gestein⟩ worthless

Taube f -,-n pigeon; (Turtel- & fig) dove. **T~nschlag** m pigeon-loft

Taub|heit f - deafness; (Gefühllosigkeit) numbness. **t~stumm** a deaf and dumb

tauch|en vt dip, plunge; (unter-) duck ●vi (haben/sein) dive/(ein-) plunge (**in** + acc into); (auf-) appear (**aus** out of). **T~er** m -s,- diver. **T~eranzug** m diving-suit. **T~sieder** m -s,- [small, portable] immersion heater

tauen vi (sein) melt, thaw ●impers **es taut** it is thawing

Tauf|becken nt font. **T~e** f -,-n christening, baptism. **t~en** vt christen, baptize. **T~pate** m godfather. **T~stein** m font

tauge|n vi (haben) **etwas/nichts t~n** be good/no good; **zu etw t~n/nicht**

t~n be good/no good for sth. **T~nichts** *m* **-es,-e** good-for-nothing
tauglich *a* suitable; (*Mil*) fit. **T~keit** *f* - suitability; fitness
Taumel *m* **-s** daze; **wie im T~** in a daze. **t~n** *vi (sein)* stagger
Tausch *m* **-[e]s,-e** exchange, (*fam*) swap. **t~en** *vt* exchange/(*handeln*) barter (**gegen** for); **die Plätze t~en** change places ● *vi (haben)* swap (**mit etw** sth; **mit jdm** with s.o.)
täuschen *vt* deceive, fool; betray ⟨*Vertrauen*⟩; **sich t~** delude oneself; (*sich irren*) be mistaken ● *vi (haben)* be deceptive. **t~d** *a* deceptive; ⟨*Ähnlichkeit*⟩ striking
Tausch|geschäft *nt* exchange. **T~handel** *m* barter; (*T~geschäft*) exchange
Täuschung *f* **-,-en** deception; (*Irrtum*) mistake; (*Illusion*) delusion
tausend *inv a* one/a thousand. **T~** *nt* **-s,-e** thousand. **T~füßler** *m* **-s,-** centipede. **t~ste(r,s)** *a* thousandth. **T~stel** *nt* **-s,-** thousandth
Tau|tropfen *m* dewdrop. **T~wetter** *nt* thaw. **T~ziehen** *nt* **-s** tug of war
Taxe *f* **-,-n** charge; (*Kur-*) tax; (*Taxi*) taxi
Taxi *nt* **-s,-s** taxi, cab
taxieren *vt* estimate/(*im Wert*) value (**auf** + *acc* at); (*fam: mustern*) size up
Taxi|fahrer *m* taxi driver. **T~stand** *m* taxi rank
Teakholz /'ti:k-/ *nt* teak
Team /ti:m/ *nt* **-s,-s** team
Technik *f* **-,-en** technology; (*Methode*) technique. **T~ker** *m* **-s,-** technician. **t~sch** *a* technical, *adv* -ly; (*technologisch*) technological, *adv* -ly; **T~sche Hochschule** Technical University
Techno|logie *f* **-,-n** technology. **t~logisch** *a* technological
Teckel *m* **-s,-** dachshund
Teddybär *m* teddy bear
Tee *m* **-s,-s** tea. **T~beutel** *m* tea-bag. **T~kanne** *f* teapot. **T~kessel** *m* kettle. **T~löffel** *m* teaspoon
Teer *m* **-s** tar. **t~en** *vt* tar
Tee|sieb *nt* tea-strainer. **T~tasse** *f* teacup. **T~wagen** *m* [tea] trolley
Teich *m* **-[e]s,-e** pond
Teig *m* **-[e]s,-e** pastry; (*Knet-*) dough; (*Rühr-*) mixture; (*Pfannkuchen-*) batter. **T~rolle** *f*, **T~roller** *m* rolling-pin. **T~waren** *fpl* pasta *sg*
Teil *m* **-[e]s,-e** part; (*Bestand-*) component; (*Jur*) party; **der vordere T~**

the front part; **zum T~** partly; **zum großen/größten T~** for the most part ● *m & nt* **-[e]s** (*Anteil*) share; **sein[en] T~ beitragen** do one's share; **für mein[en] T~** for my part ● *nt* **-[e]s,-e** part; (*Ersatz-*) spare part; (*Anbau-*) unit
teil|bar *a* divisible. **T~chen** *nt* **-s,-** particle. **t~en** *vt* divide; (*auf-*) share out; (*gemeinsam haben*) share; (*Pol*) partition ⟨*Land*⟩; **sich** (*dat*) **etw [mit jdm] t~en** share sth [with s.o.]; **sich t~en** divide; (*sich gabeln*) fork; ⟨*Vorhang:*⟩ open; ⟨*Meinungen:*⟩ differ ● *vi (haben)* share
teilhab|en† *vi sep (haben)* share (**an etw** *dat* sth). **T~er** *m* **-s,-** (*Comm*) partner
Teilnahm|e *f* - participation; (*innere*) interest; (*Mitgefühl*) sympathy. **t~slos** *a* apathetic, *adv* -ally
teilnehm|en† *vi sep (haben)* **t~en an** (+ *dat*) take part in; (*mitfühlen*) share [in]. **T~er(in)** *m* **-s,-** (*f* **-,-nen**) participant; (*an Wettbewerb*) competitor
teil|s *adv* partly. **T~ung** *f* **-,-en** division; (*Pol*) partition. **t~weise** *a* partial ● *adv* partially, partly; (*manchmal*) in some cases. **T~zahlung** *f* part-payment; (*Rate*) instalment. **T~zeitbeschäftigung** *f* part-time job
Teint /tɛ̃:/ *m* **-s,-s** complexion
Telefax *nt* fax
Telefon *nt* **-s,-e** [tele]phone. **T~anruf** *m*, **T~at** *nt* **-[e]s,-e** [tele]phone call. **T~buch** *nt* [tele]phone book. **t~ieren** *vi (haben)* [tele]phone
telefon|isch *a* [tele]phone . . . ● *adv* by [tele]phone. **T~ist(in)** *m* **-en,-en** (*f* **-,-nen**) telephonist. **T~karte** *f* phone card. **T~nummer** *f* [tele] phone number. **T~zelle** *f* [tele] phone box
Telegraf *m* **-en,-en** telegraph. **T~enmast** *m* telegraph pole. **t~ieren** *vi (haben)* send a telegram. **t~isch** *a* telegraphic ● *adv* by telegram
Telegramm *nt* **-s,-e** telegram
Telegraph *m* **-en,-en** = **Telegraf**
Teleobjektiv *nt* telephoto lens
Telepathie *f* - telepathy
Telephon *nt* **-s,-e** = **Telefon**
Teleskop *nt* **-s,-e** telescope. **t~isch** *a* telescopic
Telex *nt* **-,-[e]** telex. **t~en** *vt* telex
Teller *m* **-s,-** plate
Tempel *m* **-s,-** temple

Temperament nt **-s,-e** temperament; (Lebhaftigkeit) vivacity. **t~los** a dull. **t~voll** a vivacious; ⟨Pferd⟩ spirited

Temperatur f **-,-en** temperature

Tempo nt **-s,-s** speed; (Mus: pl **-pi**) tempo; **T~ [T~]!** hurry up!

Tend|enz f **-,-en** trend; (Neigung) tendency. **t~ieren** vi (haben) tend (**zu** towards)

Tennis nt **-** tennis. **T~platz** m tennis-court. **T~schläger** m tennis-racket

Tenor m **-s,ˉe** (Mus) tenor

Teppich m **-s,-e** carpet. **T~boden** m fitted carpet

Termin m **-s,-e** date; (Arzt-) appointment; **[letzter] T~** deadline. **T~kalender** m [appointments] diary

Terminologie f **-,-n** terminology

Terpentin nt **-s** turpentine

Terrain /tɛˈrɛ̃:/ nt **-s,-s** terrain

Terrasse f **-,-n** terrace

Terrier /'tɛrjɐ/ m **-s,-** terrier

Terrine f **-,-n** tureen

Territorium nt **-s,-ien** territory

Terror m **-s** terror. **t~isieren** vt terrorize. **T~ismus** m **-** terrorism. **T~ist** m **-en,-en** terrorist

Terzett nt **-[e]s,-e** [vocal] trio

Tesafilm (P) m ≈ Sellotape (P)

Test m **-[e]s,-s** & **-e** test

Testament nt **-[e]s,-e** will; **Altes/ Neues T~** Old/New Testament. **T~svollstrecker** m **-s,-** executor

testen vt test

Tetanus m **-** tetanus

teuer a expensive, adv -ly; (lieb) dear; **wie t~?** how much? **T~ung** f **-,-en** rise in prices

Teufel m **-s,-** devil; **zum T~!** (sl) damn [it]! **T~skreis** m vicious circle

teuflisch a fiendish

Text m **-[e]s,-e** text; (Passage) passage; (Bild-) caption; (Lied-) lyrics pl, words pl; (Opern-) libretto. **T~er** m **-s,-** copywriter; (Schlager-) lyricist

Textil|ien /-jən/ pl textiles; (Textilwaren) textile goods. **T~industrie** f textile industry

Textverarbeitungssystem nt word processor

TH abbr = **Technische Hochschule**

Theater nt **-s,-** theatre; (fam: Getue) fuss, to-do; **T~ spielen** act; (fam) put on an act. **T~kasse** f box-office. **T~stück** nt play

theatralisch a theatrical, adv -ly

Theke f **-,-n** bar; (Ladentisch) counter

Thema nt **-s,-men** subject; (Mus) theme

Themse f **-** Thames

Theolo|ge m **-n,-n** theologian. **T~gie** f **-** theology

theor|etisch a theoretical, adv -ly. **T~ie** f **-,-n** theory

Therapeut|(in) m **-en,-en** (f **-,-nen**) therapist. **t~isch** a therapeutic

Therapie f **-,-n** therapy

Thermal|bad nt thermal bath; (Ort) thermal spa. **T~quelle** f thermal spring

Thermometer nt **-s,-** thermometer

Thermosflasche (P) f Thermos flask (P)

Thermostat m **-[e]s,-e** thermostat

These f **-,-n** thesis

Thrombose f **-,-n** thrombosis

Thron m **-[e]s,-e** throne. **t~en** vi (haben) sit [in state]. **T~folge** f succession. **T~folger** m **-s,-** heir to the throne

Thunfisch m tuna

Thymian m **-s** thyme

Tick m **-s,-s** (fam) quirk; **einen T~ haben** be crazy

ticken vi (haben) tick

tief a deep; (t~liegend, niedrig) low; (t~gründig) profound; **t~er Teller** soup-plate; **im t~sten Winter** in the depths of winter ● adv deep; low; (sehr) deeply, profoundly; ⟨schlafen⟩ soundly. **T~** nt **-s,-s** (Meteorol) depression. **T~bau** m civil engineering. **T~e** f **-,-n** depth

Tief|ebene f [lowland] plain. **T~garage** f underground car park. **t~gekühlt** a [deep-]frozen. **t~greifend** a radical, adv -ly. **t~gründig** a (fig) profound

Tiefkühl|fach nt freezer compartment. **T~kost** f frozen food. **T~truhe** f deep-freeze

Tief|land nt lowlands pl. **T~punkt** m (fig) low. **t~schürfend** a (fig) profound. **t~sinnig** a (fig) profound; (trübsinnig) melancholy. **T~stand** m (fig) low

Tiefsttemperatur f minimum temperature

Tier nt **-[e]s,-e** animal. **T~arzt** m, **T~ärztin** f vet, veterinary surgeon. **T~garten** m zoo. **t~isch** a animal ...; (fig: roh) bestial. **T~kreis** m zodiac. **T~kreiszeichen** nt sign of the zodiac. **T~kunde** f zoology. **T~quälerei** f cruelty to animals

Tiger *m* -s, - tiger

tilgen *vt* pay off ⟨*Schuld*⟩; ⟨streichen⟩ delete; (*fig: auslöschen*) wipe out

Tinte *f* -,-n ink. **T~nfisch** *m* squid

Tip *m* -s, -s (*fam*) tip

tipp|en *vt* (*fam*) type ● *vi* (*haben*) (*berühren*) touch (**auf/an etw** *acc* sth); (*fam: maschineschreiben*) type; **t~en auf** (+*acc*) (*fam: wetten*) bet on. **T~fehler** *m* (*fam*) typing error. **T~schein** *m* pools/lottery coupon

tipptopp *a* (*fam*) immaculate, *adv* -ly

Tirol *nt* -s [the] Tyrol

Tisch *m* -[e]s,-e table; (*Schreib-*) desk; **nach T~** after the meal. **T~decke** *f* table-cloth. **T~gebet** *nt* grace. **T~ler** *m* -s,- joiner; (*Möbel-*) cabinet-maker. **T~rede** *f* after-dinner speech. **T~tennis** *nt* table tennis. **T~tuch** *nt* table-cloth

Titel *m* -s,- title. **T~rolle** *f* title-role

Toast /to:st/ *m* -[e]s,-e toast; (*Scheibe*) piece of toast; **einen T~ ausbringen** propose a toast (**auf** + *acc* to). **T~er** *m* -s,- toaster

tob|en *vi* (*haben*) rave; ⟨*Sturm:*⟩ rage; ⟨*Kinder:*⟩ play boisterously ● *vi* (*sein*) rush. **t~süchtig** *a* raving mad

Tochter *f* -,- daughter. **T~gesellschaft** *f* subsidiary

Tod *m* -es death. **t~ernst** *a* deadly serious, *adv* -ly

Todes|angst *f* mortal fear. **T~anzeige** *f* death announcement; (*Zeitungs-*) obituary. **T~fall** *m* death. **T~opfer** *nt* fatality, casualty. **T~strafe** *f* death penalty. **T~urteil** *nt* death sentence

Tod|feind *m* mortal enemy. **t~krank** *a* dangerously ill

tödlich *a* fatal, *adv* -ly; ⟨*Gefahr*⟩ mortal, *adv* -ly; (*groß*) deadly; **t~ gelangweilt** bored to death

tod|müde *a* dead tired. **t~sicher** *a* (*fam*) dead certain ● *adv* for sure. **T~sünde** *f* deadly sin. **t~unglücklich** *a* desperately unhappy

Toilette /toaˈlɛtə/ *f* -,-n toilet. **T~npapier** *nt* toilet paper

toler|ant *a* tolerant. **T~anz** *f* - tolerance. **t~ieren** *vt* tolerate

toll *a* crazy, mad; (*fam: prima*) fantastic; (*schlimm*) awful ● *adv* beautifully; (*sehr*) very; (*schlimm*) badly. **t~en** *vi* (*haben/sein*) romp. **t~kühn** *a* foolhardy. **t~wut** *f* rabies. **t~wütig** *a* rabid

tolpatschig *a* clumsy, *adv* -ily

Tölpel *m* -s,- fool

Tomate *f* -,-n tomato. **T~nmark** *nt* tomato purée

Tombola *f* -,-s raffle

Ton[1] *m* -[e]s clay

Ton[2] *m* -[e]s,-e tone; (*Klang*) sound; (*Note*) note; (*Betonung*) stress; (*Farb-*) shade; **der gute Ton** (*fig*) good form. **T~abnehmer** *m* -s,- pick-up. **t~angebend** *a* (*fig*) leading. **T~art** *f* tone [of voice]; (*Mus*) key. **T~band** *nt* (*pl* -bänder) tape. **T~bandgerät** *nt* tape recorder

tönen *vi* (*haben*) sound ● *vt* tint

Ton|fall *m* tone [of voice]; (*Akzent*) intonation. **T~leiter** *f* scale. **t~los** *a* toneless, *adv* -ly

Tonne *f* -,-n barrel, cask; (*Müll-*) bin; (*Maß*) tonne, metric ton

Topf *m* -[e]s,-e pot; (*Koch-*) pan

Topfen *m* -s (*Aust*) ≈ curd cheese

Töpfer|(in) *m* -s,- (*f* -,-nen) potter. **T~ei** *f* -,-en pottery

Töpferwaren *fpl* pottery *sg*

Topf|lappen *m* oven-cloth. **T~pflanze** *f* potted plant

Tor[1] *m* -en,-en fool

Tor[2] *nt* -[e]s,-e gate; (*Einfahrt*) gateway; (*Sport*) goal. **T~bogen** *m* archway

Torf *m* -s peat

Torheit *f* -,-en folly

Torhüter *m* -s,- goalkeeper

töricht *a* foolish, *adv* -ly

torkeln *vi* (*sein/haben*) stagger

Tornister *m* -s,- knapsack; (*Sch*) satchel

torp|edieren *vt* torpedo. **T~edo** *m* -s,-s torpedo

Torpfosten *m* goal-post

Torte *f* -,-n gâteau; (*Obst-*) flan

Tortur *f* -,-en torture

Torwart *m* -s,-e goalkeeper

tosen *vi* (*haben*) roar; ⟨*Sturm:*⟩ rage

tot *a* dead; **einen t~en Punkt haben** (*fig*) be at a low ebb

total *a* total, *adv* -ly. **t~itär** *a* totalitarian. **T~schaden** *m* ≈ write-off

Tote(r) *m/f* dead man/woman; (*Todesopfer*) fatality; **die T~n** the dead *pl*

töten *vt* kill

toten|blaß *a* deathly pale. **T~gräber** *m* -s,- grave-digger. **T~kopf** *m* skull. **T~schein** *m* death certificate. **T~stille** *f* deathly silence

tot|fahren † *vt* run over and kill. **t~geboren** *a* stillborn. **t~lachen (sich)** *vr sep* (*fam*) be in stitches

Toto *nt* & *m* **-s** football pools *pl.* **T~schein** *m* pools coupon

tot|schießen† *vt sep* shoot dead. **T~schlag** *m* (*Jur*) manslaughter. **t~schlagen†** *vt sep* kill. **t~schweigen†** *vt sep* (*fig*) hush up. **t~stellen (sich)** *vr sep* pretend to be dead

Tötung *f* **-,-en** killing; **fahrlässige T~** (*Jur*) manslaughter

Toup|et /tu'pe:/ *nt* **-s,-s** toupee. **t~ieren** *vt* back-comb

Tour /tu:ɐ̯/ *f* **-,-en** tour; (*Ausflug*) trip; (*Auto-*) drive; (*Rad-*) ride; (*Strecke*) distance; (*Techn*) revolution; (*fam: Weise*) way; **auf vollen T~en** at full speed; (*fam*) flat out

Touris|mus /tu'rɪsmʊs/ *m* **-** tourism. **T~t** *m* **-en,-en** tourist

Tournee /tʊr'ne:/ *f* **-,-n** tour

Trab *m* **-[e]s** trot

Trabant *m* **-en,-en** satellite

traben *vi* (*haben/sein*) trot

Tracht *f* **-,-en** [national] costume; **eine T~ Prügel** a good hiding

trachten *vi* (*haben*) strive (**nach** for); **jdm nach dem Leben t~** be out to kill s.o.

trächtig *a* pregnant

Tradition /-'tsio:n/ *f* **-,-en** tradition. **t~ell** *a* traditional, *adv* -ly

Trafik *f* **-,-en** (*Aust*) tobacconist's

Trag|bahre *f* stretcher. **t~bar** *a* portable; (*Kleidung*) wearable; (*erträglich*) bearable

träge *a* sluggish, *adv* -ly; (*faul*) lazy, *adv* -ily; (*Phys*) inert

tragen† *vt* carry; (*an-/aufhaben*) wear; (*fig*) bear ● *vi* (*haben*) carry; **gut t~** ⟨*Baum:*⟩ produce a good crop; **schwer t~** carry a heavy load; (*fig*) be deeply affected (**an** + *dat* by). **t~d** *a* (*Techn*) load-bearing; (*trächtig*) pregnant

Träger *m* **-s,-** porter; (*Inhaber*) bearer; (*eines Ordens*) holder; (*Bau-*) beam; (*Stahl-*) girder; (*Achsel-*) [shoulder] strap. **T~kleid** *nt* pinafore dress

Trag|etasche *f* carrier bag. **T~fläche** *f* (*Aviat*) wing; (*Naut*) hydrofoil. **T~flächenboot,** **T~flügelboot** *nt* hydrofoil

Trägheit *f* **-** sluggishness; (*Faulheit*) laziness; (*Phys*) inertia

Trag|ik *f* **-** tragedy. **t~isch** *a* tragic, *adv* -ally

Tragödie /-iə/ *f* **-,-n** tragedy

Tragweite *f* range; (*fig*) consequence

Train|er /'trɛ:nɐ/ *m* **-s,-** trainer; (*Tennis-*) coach. **t~ieren** *vt/i* (*haben*) train

Training /'trɛ:nɪŋ/ *nt* **-s** training. **T~sanzug** *m* tracksuit. **T~sschuhe** *mpl* trainers

Trakt *m* **-[e]s,-e** section; (*Flügel*) wing

traktieren *vi* (*haben*) **mit Schlägen/ Tritten t~** hit/kick

Traktor *m* **-s,-en** /-'to:rən/ tractor

trampeln *vi* (*haben*) stamp one's feet ● *vi* (*sein*) trample (**auf** + *acc* on) ● *vt* trample

trampen /'trɛmpən/ *vi* (*sein*) (*fam*) hitch-hike

Trance /'trã:sə/ *f* **-,-n** trance

Tranchier|messer /trã'ʃi:ɐ̯-/ *nt* carving-knife. **t~en** *vt* carve

Träne *f* **-,-n** tear. **t~n** *vi* (*haben*) water. **T~ngas** *nt* tear-gas

Tränke *f* **-,-n** watering-place; (*Trog*) drinking-trough. **t~n** *vt* water ⟨*Pferd*⟩; (*nässen*) soak (**mit** with)

Trans|aktion *f* transaction. **T~fer** *m* **-s,-s** transfer. **T~formator** *m* **-s,-en** /-'to:rən/ transformer. **T~fusion** *f* **-,-en** [blood] transfusion

Transistor *m* **-,-en** /-'to:rən/ transistor

Transit /tran'zi:t/ *m* **-s** transit

transitiv *a* transitive, *adv* -ly

Transparent *nt* **-[e]s,-e** banner; (*Bild*) transparency

transpirieren *vi* (*haben*) perspire

Transplantation /-'tsio:n/ *f* **-,-en** transplant

Transport *m* **-[e]s,-e** transport; (*Güter-*) consignment. **t~ieren** *vt* transport. **T~mittel** *nt* means of transport

Trapez *nt* **-es,-e** trapeze; (*Geom*) trapezium

Tratsch *m* **-[e]s** (*fam*) gossip. **t~en** *vi* (*haben*) (*fam*) gossip

Tratte *f* **-,-n** (*Comm*) draft

Traube *f* **-,-n** bunch of grapes; (*Beere*) grape; (*fig*) cluster. **T~nzucker** *m* glucose

trauen *vi* (*haben*) (+ *dat*) trust; **ich traute kaum meinen Augen** I could hardly believe my eyes ● *vt* marry; **sich t~** dare (**etw zu tun** [to] do sth); venture (**in** + *acc*/**aus** into/out of)

Trauer *f* **-** mourning; (*Schmerz*) grief (**um** for); **T~ tragen** be [dressed] in mourning. **T~fall** *m* bereavement. **T~feier** *f* funeral service. **T~marsch** *m* funeral march. **t~n** *vi* (*haben*) grieve; **t~n um** mourn [for].

T~spiel nt tragedy. T~weide f weeping willow

traulich a cosy, adv -ily

Traum m -[e]s, Träume dream

Trau|ma nt -s, -men trauma. t~matisch a traumatic

träumen vt/i (haben) dream

traumhaft a dreamlike; (schön) fabulous, adv -ly

traurig a sad, adv -ly; (erbärmlich) sorry. T~keit f - sadness

Trau|ring m wedding-ring. T~schein m marriage certificate. T~ung f -,-en wedding [ceremony]

Treck m -s, -s trek

Trecker m -s, - tractor

Treff nt -s, -s (Karten) spades pl

treff|en† vt hit; (Blitz:) strike; (fig: verletzen) hurt; (zusammenkommen mit) meet; take ⟨Maßnahme⟩; sich t~en meet (mit jdm s.o.); sich gut t~en be convenient; es traf sich, daß it so happened that; es gut/schlecht t~en be lucky/unlucky ● vi (haben) hit the target; t~en auf (+ acc) meet; (fig) meet with. T~en nt -s, - meeting. t~end a apt, adv -ly; ⟨Ähnlichkeit⟩ striking. T~er m -s, - hit; (Los) winner. T~punkt m meeting-place

treiben† vt drive; (sich befassen mit) do; carry on ⟨Gewerbe⟩; indulge in ⟨Luxus⟩; get up to ⟨Unfug⟩; Handel t~ trade; Blüten/Blätter t~ come into flower/leaf; zur Eile t~ hurry [up]; was treibt ihr da? (fam) what are you up to? ● vi (sein) drift; (schwimmen) float ● vi (haben) (Bot) sprout. T~ nt -s activity; (Getriebe) bustle

Treib|haus nt hothouse. T~hauseffekt m greenhouse effect. T~holz nt driftwood. T~riemen m transmission belt. T~sand m quicksand. T~stoff m fuel

Trend m -s, -s trend

trenn|bar a separable. t~en vt separate/(abmachen) detach (von from); divide, split ⟨Wort⟩; sich t~en separate; (auseinandergehen) part; sich t~en von leave; (fortgeben) part with. T~ung f -,-en separation; (Silben-) division. T~ungsstrich m hyphen. T~wand f partition

trepp|ab adv downstairs. t~auf adv upstairs

Treppe f -,-n stairs pl; (Außen-) steps pl; eine T~ a flight of stairs/steps. T~nflur m landing. T~ngeländer

nt banisters pl. T~nhaus nt stairwell. T~nstufe f stair, step

Tresor m -s, -e safe

Tresse f -,-n braid

Treteimer m pedal bin

treten† vi (sein/haben) step; (versehentlich) tread; (ausschlagen) kick (nach at); in Verbindung t~ get in touch ● vt tread; (mit Füßen) kick

treu a faithful, adv -ly; (fest) loyal, adv -ly. T~e f - faithfulness; loyalty; (eheliche) fidelity. T~händer m -s,- trustee. t~herzig a trusting, adv -ly; (arglos) innocent, adv -ly. t~los a disloyal, adv -ly; (untreu) unfaithful

Tribüne f -,-n platform; (Zuschauer-) stand

Tribut m -[e]s, -e tribute; (Opfer) toll

Trichter m -s,- funnel; (Bomben-) crater

Trick m -s, -s trick. T~film m cartoon. t~reich a clever

Trieb m -[e]s, -e drive, urge; (Instinkt) instinct; (Bot) shoot. T~täter, T~verbrecher m sex offender. T~werk nt (Aviat) engine; (Uhr-) mechanism

trief|en† vi (haben) drip; (naß sein) be dripping (von/vor + dat with). t~naß a dripping wet

triftig a valid

Trigonometrie f - trigonometry

Trikot /tri'ko:/ m -s (Tex) jersey

Trikot nt -s,-s (Sport) jersey; (Fußball-) shirt

Trimester nt -s,- term

Trimm-dich nt -s keep-fit

trimmen vt trim; (fam) train; tune ⟨Motor⟩; sich t~ keep fit

trink|bar a drinkable. t~en† vt/i (haben) drink. T~er(in) m -s,- (f -,-nen) alcoholic. T~geld nt tip. T~halm m [drinking-]straw. T~spruch m toast. T~wasser nt drinking-water

Trio nt -s,-s trio

trippeln vi (sein) trip along

trist a dreary

Tritt m -[e]s, -e step; (Fuß-) kick. T~brett nt step. T~leiter f stepladder

Triumph m -s, -e triumph. t~ieren vi (haben) rejoice; t~ieren über (+ acc) triumph over. t~ierend a triumphant, adv -ly

trocken a dry, adv drily. T~haube f drier. T~heit f -,-en dryness; (Dürre) drought. t~legen vt sep change ⟨Baby⟩; drain ⟨Sumpf⟩. T~milch f powdered milk

trockn|en vt/i (sein) dry. T~er m **-s,-** drier

Troddel f **-,-n** tassel

Trödel m **-s** (fam) junk. T~laden m (fam) junk-shop. T~markt m (fam) flea market. t~n vi (haben) dawdle

Trödler m **-s,-** (fam) slowcoach; (Händler) junk-dealer

Trog m **-[e]s,"e** trough

Trommel f **-,-n** drum. T~fell nt eardrum. t~n vi (haben) drum

Trommler m **-s,-** drummer

Trompete f **-,-n** trumpet. T~r m **-s,-** trumpeter

Tropen pl tropics

Tropf m **-[e]s,-e** (Med) drip

tröpfeln vt/i (sein/haben) drip; **es tröpfelt** it's spitting with rain

tropfen vt/i (sein/haben) drip. T~m **-s,-** drop; (fallend) drip. t~weise adv drop by drop

tropf|naß a dripping wet. T~stein m stalagmite; (hängend) stalactite

Trophäe /tro'fɛ:ə/ f **-,-n** trophy

tropisch a tropical

Trost m **-[e]s** consolation, comfort

tröst|en vt console, comfort; **sich t~en** console oneself. t~lich a comforting

trost|los a desolate; (elend) wretched; (reizlos) dreary. T~preis m consolation prize. t~reich a comforting

Trott m **-s** amble; (fig) routine

Trottel m **-s,-** (fam) idiot

trotten vi (sein) traipse; (Tier:) amble

Trottoir /trɔ'tŏa:ɐ̯/ nt **-s,-s** pavement, (Amer) sidewalk

trotz prep (+ gen) despite, in spite of. T~ m **-es** defiance. t~dem adv nevertheless. t~en vi (haben) (+ dat) defy. t~ig a defiant, adv -ly; (Kind) stubborn

trübe a dull; (Licht) dim; (Flüssigkeit) cloudy; (fig) gloomy

Trubel m **-s** bustle

trüben vt dull; make cloudy (Flüssigkeit); (fig) spoil; strain (Verhältnis); **sich t~** (Flüssigkeit:) become cloudy; (Himmel:) cloud over; (Augen:) dim; (Verhältnis, Erinnerung:) deteriorate

Trüb|sal f - misery; T~sal blasen (fam) mope. t~selig a miserable; (trübe) gloomy, adv -ily. T~sinn m melancholy. t~sinnig a melancholy

Trugbild nt illusion

trüg|en† vt deceive ● vi (haben) be deceptive. t~erisch a false; (täuschend) deceptive

Trugschluß m fallacy

Truhe f **-,-n** chest

Trümmer pl rubble sg; (T~teile) wreckage sg; (fig) ruins. T~haufen m pile of rubble

Trumpf m **-[e]s,"e** trump [card]; T~ sein be trumps. t~en vi (haben) play trumps

Trunk m **-[e]s** drink. T~enbold m **-[e]s,-e** drunkard. T~enheit f - drunkenness; T~enheit am Steuer drunken driving. T~sucht f alcoholism

Trupp m **-s,-s** group; (Mil) squad. T~e f **-,-n** (Mil) unit; (Theat) troupe; T~en troops

Truthahn m turkey

Tschech|e m **-n,-n**, T~in f **-,-nen** Czech. t~isch a Czech. T~oslowakei (die) - Czechoslovakia

tschüs int bye, cheerio

Tuba f **-,-ben** (Mus) tuba

Tube f **-,-n** tube

Tuberkulose f - tuberculosis

Tuch nt **-[e]s,"er** cloth; (Hals-, Kopf-) scarf; (Schulter-) shawl

Tuch nt **-[e]s,-e** (Stoff) cloth

tüchtig a competent; (reichlich, beträchtlich) good; (groß) big ● adv competently; (ausreichend) well; (regnen, schneien) hard. T~keit f - competence

Tück|e f **-,-n** malice; T~en haben be temperamental; (gefährlich sein) be treacherous. t~isch a malicious, adv -ly; (gefährlich) treacherous

tüfteln vi (haben) (fam) fiddle (an + dat with); (geistig) puzzle (an + dat over)

Tugend f **-,-en** virtue. t~haft a virtuous

Tülle f **-,-n** spout

Tulpe f **-,-n** tulip

tummeln (sich) vr romp [about]; (sich beeilen) hurry [up]

Tümmler m **-s,-** porpoise

Tumor m **-s,-en** /-'mo:rən/ tumour

Tümpel m **-s,-** pond

Tumult m **-[e]s,-e** commotion; (Aufruhr) riot

tun† vt do; take (Schritt, Blick); work (Wunder); (bringen) put (in + acc into); **sich tun** happen; **jdm etwas tun** hurt s.o.; **viel zu tun haben** have a lot to do; **das tut man nicht** it isn't done; **das tut nichts** it doesn't matter ● vi (*haben*) act (**als ob** as if); **überrascht tun** pretend to be surprised; **er tut nur so** he's just pretending; **zu tun haben** have things/work to do; **[es] zu tun haben mit** have to deal with; **[es] mit dem Herzen zu tun haben** have heart trouble. **Tun** *nt* **-s** actions *pl*

Tünche *f* **-,-n** whitewash; (*fig*) veneer. **t~n** *vt* whitewash

Tunesien /-iən/ *nt* **-s** Tunisia

Tunke *f* **-,-n** sauce. **t~n** *vt/i* (*haben*) (*fam*) dip (**in** + *acc* into)

Tunnel *m* **-s,-** tunnel

tupf|en *vt* dab ● *vi* (*haben*) **t~en an/ auf** (+ *acc*) touch. **T~en** *m* **-s,-** spot. **T~er** *m* **-s,-** spot; (*Med*) swab

Tür *f* **-,-en** door

Turban *m* **-s,-e** turban

Turbine *f* **-,-n** turbine

turbulen|t *a* turbulent. **T~z** *f* **-,-en** turbulence

Türk|e *m* **-n,-n** Turk. **T~ei (die)** - Turkey. **T~in** *f* **-,-nen** Turk

türkis *inv a* turquoise. **T~** *m* **-es,-e** turquoise

türkisch *a* Turkish

Turm *m* **-[e]s,ˁe** tower; (*Schach*) rook, castle

Türm|chen *nt* **-s,-** turret. **t~en** *vt* pile [up]; **sich t~en** pile up ● *vi* (*sein*) (*fam*) escape

Turmspitze *f* spire

turn|en *vi* (*haben*) do gymnastics. **T~en** *nt* **-s** gymnastics *sg*; (*Sch*) physical education, (*fam*) gym. **T~er(in)** *m* **-s,-** (*f* **-,-nen**) gymnast. **T~halle** *f* gymnasium

Turnier *nt* **-s,-e** tournament; (*Reit-*) show

Turnschuhe *mpl* gym shoes

Türschwelle *f* doorstep, threshold

Tusch *m* **-[e]s,-e** fanfare

Tusche *f* **-,-n** [drawing] ink; (*Wasserfarbe*) watercolour

tuscheln *vt/i* (*haben*) whisper

Tüte *f* **-,-n** bag; (*Comm*) packet; (*Eis-*) cornet; **in die T~ blasen** (*fam*) be breathalysed

tuten *vi* (*haben*) hoot; ⟨*Schiff:*⟩ sound its hooter; ⟨*Sirene:*⟩ sound

TÜV *m* **-** ≈ MOT [test]

Typ *m* **-s,-en** type; (*fam: Kerl*) bloke. **T~e** *f* **-,-n** type; (*fam: Person*) character

Typhus *m* **-** typhoid

typisch *a* typical, *adv* -ly; (**für** of)

Typographie *f* **-** typography

Typus *m* **-, Typen** type

Tyrann *m* **-en,-en** tyrant. **T~ei** *f* - tyranny. **t~isch** *a* tyrannical. **t~i- sieren** *vt* tyrannize

U

u.a. *abbr* (**unter anderem**) amongst other things

U-Bahn *f* underground, (*Amer*) subway

übel *a* bad; (*häßlich*) nasty, *adv* -ily; **mir ist/wird ü~** I feel sick. **Ü~** *nt* **-s,-** evil. **Ü~keit** *f* - nausea. **ü~neh- men**† *vt sep* take amiss; **jdm etw ü~- nehmen** hold sth against s.o. **Ü~täter** *m* culprit

üben *vt/i* (*haben*) practise; **sich in etw** (*dat*) **ü~** practise sth

über *prep* (+ *dat/acc*) over; (*höher als*) above; (*betreffend*) about; ⟨*Buch, Vortrag*⟩ on; ⟨*Scheck, Rechnung*⟩ for; (*quer ü~*) across; **ü~ Köln fahren** go via Cologne; **ü~ Ostern** over Easter; **die Woche ü~** during the week; **heute ü~ eine Woche** a week today; **Fehler ü~ Fehler** mistake after mistake ● *adv* **ü~ und ü~** all over; **jdm ü~ sein** be better/(*stärker*) stronger than s.o. ● *a* (*fam*) **ü~ sein** be left over; **etw ü~ sein** be fed up with sth

überall *adv* everywhere

überanstrengen *vt insep* overtax; strain ⟨*Augen*⟩; **sich ü~** overexert oneself

überarbeit|en *vt insep* revise; **sich ü~en** overwork. **Ü~ung** *f* - revision; overwork

überaus *adv* extremely

überbewerten *vt insep* overrate

überbieten† *vt insep* outbid; (*fig*) outdo; (*übertreffen*) surpass

Überblick *m* overall view; (*Abriß*) summary

überblicken *vt insep* overlook; (*abschätzen*) assess

überbringen† *vt insep* deliver

überbrücken *vt insep* (*fig*) bridge

überdauern *vt insep* survive

überdenken† *vt insep* think over

überdies *adv* moreover

überdimensional *a* oversized

Überdosis *f* overdose

Überdruß *m* **-sses** surfeit; **bis zum Ü~** ad nauseam

überdrüssig *a* **ü~ sein/werden** be/ grow tired (*gen* of)

übereignen *vt insep* transfer

übereilt *a* over-hasty, *adv* -ily
übereinander *adv* one on top of/ above the other; ⟨*sprechen*⟩ about each other. **ü~schlagen†** *vt sep* cross ⟨*Beine*⟩; fold ⟨*Arme*⟩
überein|kommen† *vi sep (sein)* agree. **Ü~kunft** *f* - agreement. **ü~stimmen***vi sep (haben)* agree; ⟨*Zahlen:*⟩ tally; ⟨*Ansichten:*⟩ coincide; ⟨*Farben:*⟩ match. **Ü~stimmung** *f* agreement
überempfindlich *a* over-sensitive; (*Med*) hypersensitive
überfahren†*vt insep* run over
Überfahrt*f* crossing
Überfall*m* attack; (*Bank-*) raid
überfallen† *vt insep* attack; raid ⟨*Bank*⟩; ⟨*bestürmen*⟩ bombard (**mit** with); ⟨*überkommen*⟩ come over; (*fam: besuchen*) surprise
überfällig*a* overdue
überfliegen† *vt insep* fly over; (*lesen*) skim over
überflügeln*vt insep* outstrip
Überfluß*m* abundance; (*Wohlstand*) affluence
überflüssig*a* superfluous
überfluten*vt insep* flood
überfordern*vt insep* overtax
überführ|en*vt insep* transfer; (*Jur*) convict (*gen* of). **Ü~ung** *f* transfer; (*Straße*) flyover; (*Fußgänger-*) footbridge
überfüllt*a* overcrowded
Übergabe *f* (*s.* **übergeben**) handing over; transfer
Übergang *m* crossing; (*Wechsel*) transition. **Ü~sstadium** *nt* transitional stage
übergeben† *vt insep* hand over; (*übereignen*) transfer; **sich ü~** be sick
übergehen¹† *vi sep (sein)* pass (**an** + *acc* to); (*überwechseln*) go over (**zu** to); (*werden zu*) turn (**in** + *acc* into); **zum Angriff ü~** start the attack
übergehen²†*vt insep* (*fig*) pass over; (*nicht beachten*) ignore; (*auslassen*) leave out
Übergewicht*nt* excess weight; (*fig*) predominance; **Ü~ haben** be overweight
übergießen†*vt insep* **mit Wasser ü~** pour water over
überglücklich*a* overjoyed
über|greifen† *vi sep (haben)* spread (**auf** + *acc* to). **Ü~griff** *m* infringement

übergroß *a* outsize; (*übertrieben*) exaggerated. **Ü~größe***f* outsize
überhaben† *vt sep* have on; (*fam: satthaben*) be fed up with
überhandnehmen† *vi sep (haben)* increase alarmingly
überhängen *v sep* ●*vi†* (*haben*) overhang ●*vt (reg)* **sich** (*dat*) **etw ü~** sling over one's shoulder ⟨*Gewehr*⟩; put round one's shoulders ⟨*Jacke*⟩
überhäufen *vt insep* inundate (**mit** with)
überhaupt *adv* (*im allgemeinen*) altogether; (*eigentlich*) anyway; (*überdies*) besides; **ü~ nicht/nichts** not/nothing at all
überheblich *a* arrogant, *adv* -ly. **Ü~keit** *f* - arrogance
überhol|en *vt insep* overtake; (*reparieren*) overhaul. **ü~t** *a* outdated. **Ü~ung** *f* -,-en overhaul. **Ü~verbot** *nt* '**Ü~verbot**' 'no overtaking'
überhören *vt insep* fail to hear; (*nicht beachten*) ignore
überirdisch*a* supernatural
überkochen*vi sep (sein)* boil over
überladen† *vt insep* overload ●*a* over-ornate
überlassen† *vt insep* **jdm etw ü~** leave sth to s.o.; (*geben*) let s.o. have sth; **sich seinem Schmerz ü~** abandon oneself to one's grief; **sich** (*dat*) **selbst ü~ sein** be left to one's own devices
überlasten *vt insep* overload; overtax ⟨*Person*⟩
Überlauf*m* overflow
überlaufen¹† *vi sep (sein)* overflow; (*Mil, Pol*) defect
überlaufen²† *vt insep* **jdn ü~** ⟨*Gefühl:*⟩ come over s.o. ●*a* overrun; ⟨*Kursus*⟩ over-subscribed
Überläufer*m* defector
überleben *vt/i insep (haben)* survive. **Ü~de(r)***m/f*survivor
überlegen¹*vt sep* put over
überlegen² *v insep* ●*vt* [**sich** *dat*] **ü~** think over, consider; **es sich** (*dat*) **anders ü~** change one's mind ●*vi* (*haben*) think, reflect; **ohne zu ü~** without thinking
überlegen³ *a* superior; (*herablassend*) supercilious, *adv* -ly. **Ü~heit** *f* - superiority
Überlegung*f* -,-en reflection
überliefer|n *vt insep* hand down. **Ü~ung***f*tradition
überlisten*vt insep* outwit

überm *prep* = **über dem**

Über|macht *f* superiority. **ü~-mächtig** *a* superior; ⟨*Gefühl*⟩ overpowering

übermạnnen *vt insep* overcome

Über|maß *nt* excess. **ü~mäßig** *a* excessive, *adv* -ly

Übermẹnsch *m* superman. **ü~lich** *a* superhuman

übermịtteln *vt insep* convey; (*senden*) transmit

übermọrgen *adv* the day after tomorrow

übermüdet *a* overtired

Über|mut *m* high spirits *pl.* **ü~-mütig** *a* high-spirited ● *adv* in high spirits

übern *prep* = **über den**

übernächst|e(r,s) *a* next ... but one; **ü~es Jahr** the year after next

übernạcht|en *vi insep* (*haben*) stay overnight. **Ü~ung** *f* -,-en overnight stay; **Ü~ung und Frühstück** bed and breakfast

Übernahme *f* - taking over; (*Comm*) take-over

übernatürlich *a* supernatural

übernẹhmen† *vt insep* take over; (*annehmen*) take on; **sich ü~** overdo things; (*finanziell*) overreach oneself

überprüf|en *vt insep* check. **Ü~ung** *f* check

überquẹren *vt insep* cross

überrạgen *vt insep* tower above; (*fig*) surpass. **ü~d** *a* outstanding

überrạsch|en *vt insep* surprise. **ü~end** *a* surprising, *adv* -ly; (*unerwartet*) unexpected, *adv* -ly. **Ü~ung** *f* -,-en surprise

überrẹden *vt insep* persuade

überreichen *vt insep* present

überreizt *a* overwrought

überrẹnnen† *vt insep* overrun

Überreste *mpl* remains

überrụmpeln *vt insep* take by surprise

übers *prep* = **über das**

Überschall- *pref* supersonic

überschạtten *vt insep* overshadow

überschätzen *vt insep* overestimate

Überschlag *m* rough estimate; (*Sport*) somersault

überschlagen¹† *vt sep* cross ⟨*Beine*⟩

überschlagen²† *vt insep* estimate roughly; (*auslassen*) skip; **sich ü~** somersault; ⟨*Ereignisse:*⟩ happen fast ● *a* tepid

überschnạppen *vi sep* (*sein*) (*fam*) go crazy

überschneiden† **(sich)** *vr insep* intersect, cross; (*zusammenfallen*) overlap

überschreiben† *vt insep* entitle; (*übertragen*) transfer

überschreiten† *vt insep* cross; (*fig*) exceed

Überschrift *f* heading; (*Zeitungs-*) headline

Über|schuß *m* surplus. **ü~schüssig** *a* surplus

überschütten *vt insep* **ü~ mit** cover with; (*fig*) shower with

überschwẹmm|en *vt insep* flood; (*fig*) inundate. **Ü~ung** *f* -,-en flood

überschwenglich *a* effusive, *adv* -ly

Übersee in/nach Ü~ overseas; **aus/von Ü~** from overseas. **Ü~dampfer** *m* ocean liner. **ü~isch** *a* overseas

übersẹhen† *vt insep* look out over; (*abschätzen*) assess; (*nicht sehen*) overlook, miss; (*ignorieren*) ignore

übersẹnden† *vt insep* send

übersẹtzen¹ *vi sep* (*haben/sein*) cross [over]

übersẹtz|en² *vt insep* translate. **Ü~er(in)** *m* -s,- (*f* -,-nen) translator. **Ü~ung** *f* -,-en translation

Übersicht *f* overall view; (*Abriß*) summary; (*Tabelle*) table. **ü~lich** *a* clear, *adv* -ly

übersied|eln *vi sep* (*sein*), **übersiedeln** *vi insep* (*sein*) move (**nach** to). **Ü~lung** *f* move

übersịnnlich *a* supernatural

überspạnnt *a* exaggerated; (*verschroben*) eccentric

überspielen *vt insep* (*fig*) cover up; **auf Band ü~** tape

überspịtzt *a* exaggerated

überspringen† *vt insep* jump [over]; (*auslassen*) skip

überstehen¹† *vi sep* (*haben*) project, jut out

überstehen²† *vt insep* come through; get over ⟨*Krankheit*⟩; (*überleben*) survive

übersteigen† *vt insep* climb [over]; (*fig*) exceed

überstimmen *vt insep* outvote

überstreifen *vt sep* slip on

Überstunden *fpl* overtime *sg*; **ü~ machen** work overtime

überstürz|en *vt insep* rush; **sich**

ü~en ⟨*Ereignisse:*⟩ happen fast; ⟨*Worte:*⟩ tumble out. **ü~t** *a* hasty, *adv* -ily

übertölpeln *vt insep* dupe

übertönen *vt insep* drown [out]

übertrag|bar *a* transferable; (*Med*) infectious. **ü~en**† *vt insep* transfer; (*übergeben*) assign (**dat** to); (*Techn, Med*) transmit; (*Radio, TV*) broadcast; (*übersetzen*) translate; (*anwenden*) apply (**auf** + *acc* to) ● *a* transferred, figurative. **Ü~ung** *f* **-,-en** transfer; transmission; broadcast; translation; application

übertreffen† *vt insep* surpass; (*übersteigen*) exceed; **sich selbst ü~** excel oneself

übertreib|en† *vt insep* exaggerate; (*zu weit treiben*) overdo. **Ü~ung** *f* **-,-en** exaggeration

übertreten[1]† *vi sep* (*sein*) step over the line; (*Pol*) go over/(*Relig*) convert (**zu** to)

übertret|en[2]† *vt insep* infringe; break ⟨*Gesetz*⟩. **Ü~ung** *f* **-,-en** infringement

übertrieben *a* exaggerated; (*übermäßig*) excessive, *adv* -ly

übervölkert *a* overpopulated

übervorteilen *vt insep* cheat

überwachen *vt insep* supervise; (*kontrollieren*) monitor; (*bespitzeln*) keep under surveillance

überwachsen *a* overgrown

überwältigen *vt insep* overpower; (*fig*) overwhelm. **ü~d** *a* overwhelming

überweis|en† *vt insep* transfer; refer ⟨*Patienten*⟩. **Ü~ung** *f* transfer; (*ärztliche*) referral

überwerfen[1]† *vt sep* throw on ⟨*Mantel*⟩

überwerfen[2]† (**sich**) *vr insep* fall out (**mit** with)

überwiegen† *v insep* ● *vi* (*haben*) predominate ● *vt* outweigh. **ü~d** *a* predominant, *adv* -ly

überwind|en† *vt insep* overcome; **sich ü~en** force oneself. **Ü~ung** *f* effort

Überwurf *m* wrap; (*Bett-*) bedspread

Über|zahl *f* majority. **ü~zählig** *a* spare

überzeug|en *vt insep* convince; **sich [selbst] ü~en** satisfy oneself. **ü~end** *a* convincing, *adv* -ly. **Ü~ung** *f* **-,-en** conviction

überziehen[1]† *vt sep* put on

überziehen[2]† *vt insep* cover; overdraw ⟨*Konto*⟩

Überzug *m* cover; (*Schicht*) coating

üblich *a* usual; (*gebräuchlich*) customary

U-Boot *nt* submarine

übrig *a* remaining; (*andere*) other; **alles ü~e** [all] the rest; **im ü~en** besides; (*ansonsten*) apart from that; **ü~ sein** be left [over]; **etw ü~ haben** have sth left [over]. **ü~behalten**† *vt sep* have sth left [over]. **ü~bleiben**† *vi sep* (*sein*) be left [over]; **uns blieb nichts anderes ü~** we had no choice. **ü~ens** *adv* by the way. **ü~lassen**† *vt sep* leave [over]

Übung *f* **-,-en** exercise; (*Üben*) practice; **außer** *od* **aus der Ü~** out of practice

UdSSR *f* - USSR

Ufer *nt* **-s,-** shore; (*Fluß-*) bank

Uhr *f* **-,-en** clock; (*Armband-*) watch; (*Zähler*) meter; **um ein U~** at one o'clock; **wieviel U~ ist es?** what's the time? **U~armband** *nt* watch-strap. **U~macher** *m* **-s,-** watch and clockmaker. **U~werk** *nt* clock/watch mechanism. **U~zeiger** *m* [clock-/watch-]hand. **U~zeigersinn** *m* **im/ entgegen dem U~zeigersinn** clockwise/anticlockwise. **U~zeit** *f* time

Uhu *m* **-s,-s** eagle owl

UKW *abbr* (**Ultrakurzwelle**) VHF

Ulk *m* **-s** fun; (*Streich*) trick. **u~en** *vi* (*haben*) joke. **u~ig** *a* funny; (*seltsam*) odd, *adv* -ly

Ulme *f* **-,-n** elm

Ultimatum *nt* **-s,-ten** ultimatum

Ultrakurzwelle *f* very high frequency

Ultraschall *m* ultrasound

ultraviolett *a* ultraviolet

um *prep* (+ *acc*) [a]round; (*Uhrzeit*) at; ⟨*bitten, kämpfen*⟩ for; ⟨*streiten*⟩ over; ⟨*sich sorgen*⟩ about; ⟨*betrügen*⟩ out of; (*bei Angabe einer Differenz*) by; **um [... herum]** around, [round] about; **Tag um Tag** day after day; **einen Tag um den andern** every other day; **um seinetwillen** for his sake ● *adv* (*ungefähr*) around, about ● *conj* **um zu** to; (*Absicht*) [in order] to; **zu müde, um zu ...** too tired to ...; **um so besser** all the better

umändern *vt sep* alter

umarbeiten *vt sep* alter; (*bearbeiten*) revise

umarm|en *vt insep* embrace, hug. **U~ung** *f* -,**-en** embrace, hug
Umbau*m* rebuilding; conversion (**zu** into). **u~en** *vt sep* rebuild; convert (**zu** into)
umbild|en *vt sep* change; (*umgestalten*) reorganize; reshuffle ⟨*Kabinett*⟩. **U~ung** *f* reorganization; (*Pol*) reshuffle
umbinden†*vt sep* put on
umblättern *v sep* ●*vt* turn [over] ●*vi (haben)* turn the page
umblicken (sich) *vr sep* look round; (*zurück-*) look back
umbringen†*vt sep* kill; **sich u~** kill oneself
Umbruch*m* (*fig*) radical change
umbuchen *v sep* ●*vt* change; (*Comm*) transfer ●*vi (haben)* change one's booking
umdrehen *v sep* ●*vt* turn round/ (*wenden*) over; turn ⟨*Schlüssel*⟩; (*umkrempeln*) turn inside out; **sich u~** turn round; (*im Liegen*) turn over ●*vi (haben/sein)* turn back
Umdrehung *f* turn; (*Motor-*) revolution
umeinander*adv* around each other; **sich u~ sorgen** worry about each other
umfahren¹†*vt sep* run over
umfahren²†*vt insep* go round; by-pass ⟨*Ort*⟩
umfallen† *vi sep (sein)* fall over; (*Person:*) fall down
Umfang *m* girth; (*Geom*) circumference; (*Größe*) size; (*Ausmaß*) extent; (*Mus*) range
umfangen† *vt insep* embrace; (*fig*) envelop
umfangreich*a* extensive; (*dick*) big
umfassen *vt insep* consist of, comprise; (*umgeben*) surround. **u~d** *a* comprehensive
Umfrage*f* survey, poll
umfüllen*vt sep* transfer
umfunktionieren*vt sep* convert
Umgang *m* [social] contact; (*Umgehen*) dealing (**mit** with); **U~ haben mit** associate with
umgänglich*a* sociable
Umgangs|formen *fpl* manners. **U~sprache** *f* colloquial language. **u~sprachlich***a* colloquial, *adv* -ly
umgeb|en† *vt/i insep (haben)* surround ●*a* **u~en von** surrounded by. **U~ung***f* -,**-en** surroundings *pl*

umgehen¹† *vi sep (sein)* go round; **u~ mit** treat, handle; (*verkehren*) associate with; **in dem Schloß geht ein Gespenst um** the castle is haunted
umgehen²† *vt insep* avoid; (*nicht beachten*) evade; ⟨*Straße:*⟩ bypass
umgehend*a* immediate, *adv* -ly
Umgehungsstraße*f* bypass
umgekehrt *a* inverse; ⟨*Reihenfolge*⟩ reverse; **es war u~** it was the other way round ●*adv* conversely; **und u~** and vice versa
umgraben†*vt sep* dig [over]
umhaben†*vt sep* have on
Umhang*m* cloak
umhauen† *vt sep* knock down; (*fällen*) chop down
umher *adv* **weit u~** all around. **u~gehen**†*vi sep (sein)* walk about
umhören (sich)*vr sep* ask around
Umkehr*f* - turning back. **u~en** *v sep* ●*vi (sein)* turn back ●*vt* turn round; turn inside out ⟨*Tasche*⟩; (*fig*) reverse. **U~ung***f* - reversal
umkippen *v sep* ●*vt* tip over; (*versehentlich*) knock over ●*vi (sein)* fall over; ⟨*Boot:*⟩ capsize; (*fam: ohnmächtig werden*) faint
Umkleide|kabine *f* changing-cubicle. **u~n (sich)** *vr sep* change. **U~raum***m* changing-room
umknicken *v sep* ●*vt* bend; (*falten*) fold ●*vi (sein)* bend; (*mit dem Fuß*) go over on one's ankle
umkommen† *vi sep (sein)* perish; **u~ lassen** waste ⟨*Lebensmittel*⟩
Umkreis *m* surroundings *pl*; **im U~ von** within a radius of
umkreisen *vt insep* circle; (*Astr*) revolve around; ⟨*Satellit:*⟩ orbit
umkrempeln *vt sep* turn up; (*von innen nach außen*) turn inside out; (*ändern*) change radically
Umlauf *m* circulation; (*Astr*) revolution. **U~bahn***f* orbit
Umlaut*m* umlaut
umlegen*vt sep* lay *or* put down; flatten ⟨*Getreide*⟩; turn down ⟨*Kragen*⟩; put on ⟨*Schal*⟩; throw ⟨*Hebel*⟩; (*verlegen*) transfer; (*fam: niederschlagen*) knock down; (*töten*) kill
umleit|en *vt sep* divert. **U~ung** *f* diversion
umliegend*a* surrounding
umpflanzen*vt sep* transplant
umrahmen*vt insep* frame
umranden*vt insep* edge
umräumen*vt sep* rearrange

u~end *a* enterprising. **U~er** *m* **-s,-** employer; (*Bau-*) contractor; (*Industrieller*) industrialist. **U~ung** *f* **-,-en** undertaking; (*Comm*) venture.

u~ungslustig *a* enterprising; (*abenteuerlustig*) adventurous

Unteroffizier *m* non-commissioned officer

unterordnen *vt sep* subordinate; **sich u~** accept a subordinate role

Unterredung *f* **-,-en** talk

Unterricht *m* **-[e]s** teaching; (*Privat-*) tuition; (*U~sstunden*) lessons *pl*; **U~ geben/nehmen** give/have lessons

unterrichten *vt/i insep* (*haben*) teach; (*informieren*) inform; **sich u~** inform oneself

Unterrock *m* slip

unters *prep* = **unter das**

untersagen *vt insep* forbid

Untersatz *m* mat; (*mit Füßen*) stand; (*Gläser-*) coaster

unterschätzen *vt insep* underestimate

unterscheid|en† *vt/i insep* (*haben*) distinguish; (*auseinanderhalten*) tell apart; **sich u~en** differ. **U~ung** *f* **-,-en** distinction

Unterschied *m* **-[e]s,-e** difference; (*Unterscheidung*) distinction; **im U~ zu ihm** unlike him. **u~lich** *a* different; (*wechselnd*) varying; **das ist u~lich** it varies. **u~slos** *a* equal, *adv* -ly

unterschlag|en† *vt insep* embezzle; (*verheimlichen*) suppress. **U~ung** *f* **-,-en** embezzlement; suppression

Unterschlupf *m* **-[e]s** shelter; (*Versteck*) hiding-place

unterschreiben† *vt/i insep* (*haben*) sign

Unter|schrift *f* signature; (*Bild-*) caption. **U~seeboot** *nt* submarine. **U~setzer** *m* **-s,-** = **Untersatz**

untersetzt *a* stocky

Unterstand *m* shelter

unterste(r,s) *a* lowest, bottom

unterstehen¹† *vi sep* (*haben*) shelter

unterstehen²† *v insep* ● *vi* (*haben*) be answerable (*dat* to); (*unterliegen*) be subject (*dat* to) ● *vr* **sich u~** dare; **untersteh dich!** don't you dare!

unterstellen¹ *vt sep* put underneath; (*abstellen*) store; **sich u~** shelter

unterstellen² *vt insep* place under the control (*dat* of); (*annehmen*) assume; (*fälschlich zuschreiben*) impute (*dat* to)

unterstreichen† *vt insep* underline

unterstütz|en *vt insep* support; (*helfen*) aid. **U~ung** *f* **-,-en** support; (*finanziell*) aid; (*regelmäßiger Betrag*) allowance; (*Arbeitslosen-*) benefit

untersuch|en *vt insep* examine; (*Jur*) investigate; (*prüfen*) test; (*überprüfen*) check; (*durchsuchen*) search. **U~ung** *f* **-,-en** examination; investigation; test; check; search. **U~ungshaft** *f* detention on remand; **in U~ungshaft** on remand. **U~ungsrichter** *m* examining magistrate

Untertan *m* **-s** & **-en,-en** subject

Untertasse *f* saucer

untertauchen *v sep* ● *vt* duck ● *vi* (*sein*) go under; (*fig*) disappear

Unterteil *nt* bottom (part)

unterteilen *vt insep* subdivide; (*aufteilen*) divide

Untertitel *m* subtitle

Unterton *m* undertone

untervermieten *vt/i insep* (*haben*) sublet

unterwandern *vt insep* infiltrate

Unterwäsche *f* underwear

Unterwasser- *pref* underwater

unterwegs *adv* on the way; (*außer Haus*) out; (*verreist*) away

unterweisen† *vt insep* instruct

Unterwelt *f* underworld

unterwerfen† *vt insep* subjugate; **sich u~en** submit (*dat* to); **etw** (*dat*) **unterworfen sein** be subject to sth

unterwürfig *a* obsequious, *adv* -ly

unterzeichnen *vt insep* sign

unterziehen¹† *vt sep* put on underneath; (*Culin*) fold in

unterziehen²† *vt insep* **etw einer Untersuchung/Überprüfung u~** examine/check sth; **sich einer Operation/Prüfung u~** have an operation/take a test

Untier *nt* monster

untragbar *a* intolerable

untrennbar *a* inseparable

untreu *a* disloyal; (*in der Ehe*) unfaithful. **U~e** *f* disloyalty; infidelity

untröstlich *a* inconsolable

untrüglich *a* infallible

Untugend *f* bad habit

unüberlegt *a* rash, *adv* -ly

unüber|sehbar *a* obvious; (*groß*) immense. **u~troffen** *a* unsurpassed

unum|gänglich *a* absolutely necessary. **u~schränkt** *a* absolute. **u~wunden** *adv* frankly

ununterbrochen *a* incessant, *adv* -ly

unveränderlich *a* invariable; (*gleichbleibend*) unchanging
unverändert *a* unchanged
unverantwortlich *a* irresponsible, *adv* -bly
unverbesserlich *a* incorrigible
unverbindlich *a* non-committal; (*Comm*) not binding ● *adv* without obligation
unverblümt *a* blunt ● *adv* -ly
unverdaulich *a* indigestible
unver|einbar *a* incompatible. **u~geßlich** *a* unforgettable. **u~gleichlich** *a* incomparable
unver|hältnismäßig *adv* disproportionately. **u~heiratet** *a* unmarried. **u~hofft** *a* unexpected, *adv* -ly. **u~hohlen** *a* undisguised ● *adv* openly. **u~käuflich** *a* not for sale; (*Muster*) free
unverkennbar *a* unmistakable, *adv* -bly
unverletzt *a* unhurt
unvermeidlich *a* inevitable
unver|mindert *a* & *adv* undiminished. **u~mittelt** *a* abrupt, *adv* -ly. **u~mutet** *a* unexpected, *adv* -ly
Unver|nunft *f* folly. **u~nünftig** *a* foolish, *adv* -ly
unverschämt *a* insolent, *adv* -ly; (*fam: ungeheuer*) outrageous, *adv* -ly. **U~heit** *f* -,-en insolence
unver|sehens *adv* suddenly. **u~sehrt** *a* unhurt; (*unbeschädigt*) intact. **u~söhnlich** *a* irreconcilable; (*Gegner*) implacable
unverständ|lich *a* incomprehensible; (*undeutlich*) indistinct. **U~nis** *nt* lack of understanding
unverträglich *a* incompatible; (*Person*) quarrelsome; (*unbekömmlich*) indigestible
unverwandt *a* fixed, *adv* -ly
unver|wundbar *a* invulnerable. **u~wüstlich** *a* indestructible; (*Person, Humor*) irrepressible; (*Gesundheit*) robust. **u~zeihlich** *a* unforgivable
unverzüglich *a* immediate, *adv* -ly
unvollendet *a* unfinished
unvollkommen *a* imperfect; (*unvollständig*) incomplete. **U~heit** *f* -,-en imperfection
unvollständig *a* incomplete
unvor|bereitet *a* unprepared. **u~eingenommen** *a* unbiased. **u~hergesehen** *a* unforeseen

unvorsichtig *a* careless, *adv* -ly. **U~keit** *f* - carelessness
unvorstellbar *a* unimaginable, *adv* -bly
unvorteilhaft *a* unfavourable; (*nicht hübsch*) unattractive; (*Kleid, Frisur*) unflattering
unwahr *a* untrue. **U~heit** *f* -,-en untruth. **u~scheinlich** *a* unlikely; (*unglaublich*) improbable; (*fam: groß*) incredible, *adv* -bly
unweigerlich *a* inevitable, *adv* -bly
unweit *adv* & *prep* (+ *gen*) not far; **u~ vom Fluß/des Flusses** not far from the river
unwesentlich *a* unimportant ● *adv* slightly
Unwetter *nt* -s,- storm
unwichtig *a* unimportant
unwider|legbar *a* irrefutable. **u~ruflich** *a* irrevocable, *adv* -bly. **u~stehlich** *a* irresistible
Unwill|e *m* displeasure. **u~ig** *a* angry, *adv* -ily; (*widerwillig*) reluctant, *adv* -ly. **u~kürlich** *a* involuntary, *adv* -ily; (*instinktiv*) instinctive, *adv* -ly
unwirklich *a* unreal
unwirksam *a* ineffective
unwirsch *a* irritable, *adv* -bly
unwirtlich *a* inhospitable
unwirtschaftlich *a* uneconomic, *adv* -ally
unwissen|d *a* ignorant. **U~heit** *f* - ignorance
unwohl *a* unwell; (*unbehaglich*) uneasy. **U~sein** *nt* -s indisposition
unwürdig *a* unworthy (*gen* of); (*würdelos*) undignified
Unzahl *f* vast number. **unzählig** *a* innumerable, countless
unzerbrechlich *a* unbreakable
unzerstörbar *a* indestructible
unzertrennlich *a* inseparable
Unzucht *f* sexual offence; **gewerbsmäßige U~** prostitution
unzüchtig *a* indecent, *adv* -ly; (*Schriften*) obscene
unzufrieden *a* dissatisfied; (*innerlich*) discontented. **U~heit** *f* dissatisfaction; (*Pol*) discontent
unzulänglich *a* inadequate, *adv* -ly
unzulässig *a* inadmissible
unzumutbar *a* unreasonable
unzurechnungsfähig *a* insane. **U~keit** *f* insanity
unzusammenhängend *a* incoherent

unzutreffend *a* inapplicable; (*falsch*) incorrect

unzuverlässig *a* unreliable

unzweckmäßig *a* unsuitable, *adv* -bly

unzweideutig *a* unambiguous

unzweifelhaft *a* undoubted, *adv* -ly

üppig *a* luxuriant, *adv* -ly; (*überreichlich*) lavish, *adv* -ly; (*Busen, Figur*) voluptuous

uralt *a* ancient

Uran *nt* -s uranium

Uraufführung *f* first performance

urbar **u~ machen** cultivate

Ureinwohner *mpl* native inhabitants

Urenkel *m* great-grandson; (*pl*) great-grandchildren

Urgroß|mutter *f* great-grandmother. **U~vater** *m* great-grandfather

Urheber *m* -s,- originator; (*Verfasser*) author. **U~recht** *nt* copyright

Urin *m* -s,-e urine

Urkunde *f* -,-n certificate; (*Dokument*) document

Urlaub *m* -s holiday; (*Mil, Admin*) leave; **auf U~** on holiday/leave; **U~ haben** be on holiday/leave. **U~er(in)** *m* -s,- (*f* -,-nen) holiday- maker. **U~sort** *m* holiday resort

Urne *f* -,-n urn; (*Wahl-*) ballot-box

Ursache *f* cause; (*Grund*) reason; **keine U~!** don't mention it!

Ursprung *m* origin

ursprünglich *a* original, *adv* -ly; (*anfänglich*) initial, *adv* -ly; (*natürlich*) natural

Urteil *nt* -s,-e judgement; (*Meinung*) opinion; (*U~sspruch*) verdict; (*Strafe*) sentence. **u~en** *vi* (*haben*) judge. **U~svermögen** *nt* [power of] judgement

Urwald *m* primeval forest; (*tropischer*) jungle

urwüchsig *a* natural; (*derb*) earthy

Urzeit *f* primeval times *pl*; **seit U~en** from time immemorial

USA *pl* USA *sg*

usw. *abbr* (**und so weiter**) etc.

Utensilien /-jən/ *ntpl* utensils

utopisch *a* Utopian

V

vage /'va:gə/ *a* vague, *adv* -ly

Vakuum /'va:kuʊm/ *nt* -s vacuum. **v~verpackt** *a* vacuum-packed

Vanille /va'nɪljə/ *f* - vanilla

vari|abel /va'rja:bəl/ *a* variable. **V~ante** *f* -,-n variant. **V~ation** /-'tsjo:n/ *f* -,-en variation. **v~ieren** *vt/i* (*haben*) vary

Vase /'va:zə/ *f* -,-n vase

Vater *m* -s,: father. **V~land** *nt* fatherland

väterlich *a* paternal; (*fürsorglich*) fatherly. **V~erseits** *adv* on one's/the father's side

Vater|schaft *f* - fatherhood; (*Jur*) paternity. **V~unser** *nt* -s,- Lord's Prayer

Vati *m* -s,-s (*fam*) daddy

v. Chr. *abbr* (**vor Christus**) BC

Vegetar|ier(in) /vege'ta:rjɐ, -jərɪn/ *m*(*f*) -s,- (*f*-,-nen) vegetarian. **v~isch** *a* vegetarian

Vegetation /vegeta'tsjo:n/ *f* -,-en vegetation

Veilchen *nt* -s,- violet

Vene /'ve:nə/ *f* -,-n vein

Venedig /ve'ne:dɪç/ *nt* -s Venice

Ventil /vɛn'ti:l/ *nt* -s,-e valve. **V~ator** *m* -s,-en /-'to:rən/ fan

verabred|en *vt* arrange; **sich [mit jdm] v~en** arrange to meet [s.o.]. **V~ung** *f* -,-en arrangement; (*Treffen*) appointment

verabreichen *vt* administer

verabscheuen *vt* detest, loathe

verabschieden *vt* say goodbye to; (*aus dem Dienst*) retire; pass (*Gesetz*); **sich v~** say goodbye

verachten *vt* despise. **v~swert** *a* contemptible

verächtlich *a* contemptuous, *adv* -ly; (*unwürdig*) contemptible

Verachtung *f* - contempt

verallgemeiner|n *vt/i* (*haben*) generalize. **V~ung** *f* -,-en generalization

veralte|n *vi* (*sein*) become obsolete. **v~t** *a* obsolete

Veranda /ve'randa/ *f* -,-den veranda

veränder|lich *a* changeable; (*Math*) variable. **v~n** *vt* change; **sich v~n** change; (*beruflich*) change one's job. **V~ung** *f* change

verängstigt *a* frightened, scared

verankern *vt* anchor

veranlag|t *a* **künstlerisch/musikalisch v~t sein** have an artistic/a musical bent; **praktisch v~t** practically minded. **V~ung** *f* -,-en disposition; (*Neigung*) tendency; (*künstlerisch*) bent

veranlass|en *vt* (*reg*) arrange for; (*einleiten*) institute; **jdn v~en** prompt s.o. (**zu** to). V~**ung** *f* - reason; **auf meine V~ung** at my suggestion; (*Befehl*) on my orders

veranschaulichen *vt* illustrate

veranschlagen *vt (reg)* estimate

veranstalt|en *vt* organize; hold, give ⟨*Party*⟩; make ⟨*Lärm*⟩. V~**er** *m* **-s,-** organizer. V~**ung** *f* **-,-en** event

verantwort|en *vt* take responsibility for; **sich v~en** answer (**für** for). v~**lich** *a* responsible; v~**lich machen** hold responsible. V~**ung** *f* - responsibility. v~**ungsbewußt** *a* responsible, *adv* -bly. v~**ungslos** *a* irresponsible, *adv* -bly. v~**ungsvoll** *a* responsible

verarbeiten *vt* use; (*Techn*) process; (*verdauen & fig*) digest; **v~ zu** make into

verärgern *vt* annoy

verarmt *a* impoverished

verästeln (sich) *vr* branch out

verausgaben (sich) *vr* spend all one's money; (*körperlich*) wear oneself out

veräußern *vt* sell

Verb /vɛrp/ *nt* **-s,-en** verb. v~**al** /vɛrˈbaːl/ *a* verbal, *adv* -ly

Verband *m* **-[e]s,-̈e** association; (*Mil*) unit; (*Med*) bandage; (*Wund-*) dressing. V~**szeug** *nt* first-aid kit

verbann|en *vt* exile; (*fig*) banish. V~**ung** *f* - exile

verbarrikadieren *vt* barricade

verbeißen† *vt* suppress; **ich konnte mir kaum das Lachen v~** I could hardly keep a straight face

verbergen† *vt* hide; **sich v~** hide

verbesser|n *vt* improve; (*berichtigen*) correct. V~**ung** *f* **-,-en** improvement; correction

verbeug|en (sich) *vr* bow. V~**ung** *f* bow

verbeulen *vt* dent

verbiegen† *vt* bend; **sich v~** bend

verbieten† *vt* forbid; (*Admin*) prohibit, ban

verbillig|en *vt* reduce [in price]. v~**t** *a* reduced

verbinden† *vt* connect (**mit** to); (*zusammenfügen*) join; (*verknüpfen*) combine; (*in Verbindung bringen*) associate; (*Med*) bandage; dress ⟨*Wunde*⟩; **sich v~** combine; (*sich zusammentun*) join together; **jdm die Augen v~** blindfold s.o.; **jdm verbunden sein** (*fig*) be obliged to s.o.

verbindlich *a* friendly; (*bindend*) binding. V~**keit** *f* **-,-en** friendliness; V~**keiten** obligations; (*Comm*) liabilities

Verbindung *f* connection; (*Verknüpfung*) combination; (*Kontakt*) contact; (*Vereinigung*) association; **chemische V~** chemical compound; **in V~ stehen/sich in V~ setzen** be/get in touch

verbissen *a* grim, *adv* -ly; (*zäh*) dogged, *adv* -ly

verbitten† *vt* **sich** (*dat*) **etw v~** not stand for sth

verbitter|n *vt* make bitter. v~**t** *a* bitter. V~**ung** *f* - bitterness

verblassen *vi (sein)* fade

Verbleib *m* **-s** whereabouts *pl.* v~**en†** *vi (sein)* remain

verbleichen† *vi (sein)* fade

verbleit *a* ⟨*Benzin*⟩ leaded

verblüff|en *vt* amaze, astound. V~**ung** *f* - amazement

verblühen *vi (sein)* wither, fade

verbluten *vi (sein)* bleed to death

verborgen¹ *a* hidden

verborgen² *vt* lend

Verbot *nt* **-[e]s,-e** ban. v~**en** *a* forbidden; (*Admin*) prohibited; '**Rauchen v~en**' 'no smoking'

Verbrauch *m* **-[e]s** consumption. v~**en** *vt* use; consume ⟨*Lebensmittel*⟩; (*erschöpfen*) use up, exhaust. V~**er** *m* **-s,-** consumer. v~**t** *a* worn; ⟨*Luft*⟩ stale

verbrechen† *vt* (*fam*) perpetrate. V~ *nt* **-s,-** crime

Verbrecher *m* **-s,-** criminal. v~**isch** *a* criminal

verbreit|en *vt* spread; **sich v~en** spread. v~**ern** *vt* widen; **sich v~ern** widen. v~**et** *a* widespread. V~**ung** *f* - spread; (*Verbreiten*) spreading

verbrenn|en† *vt/i (sein)* burn; cremate ⟨*Leiche*⟩. V~**ung** *f* **-,-en** burning; cremation; (*Wunde*) burn

verbringen† *vt* spend

verbrühen *vt* scald

verbuchen *vt* enter; (*fig*) notch up ⟨*Erfolg*⟩

verbünd|en (sich) *vr* form an alliance. V~**ete(r)** *m/f* ally

verbürgen *vt* guarantee; **sich v~ für** vouch for

verbüßen *vt* serve ⟨*Strafe*⟩

Verdacht *m* **-[e]s** suspicion; **in** *or* **im V~ haben** suspect

verdächtig a suspicious, adv -ly. **v~en** vt suspect (gen of). **V~te(r)** m/f suspect

verdamm|en vt condemn; (Relig) damn. **V~nis** f - damnation. **v~t** a & adv (sl) damned; **v~t!** damn!

verdampfen vt/i (sein) evaporate

verdanken vt owe (dat to)

verdau|en vt digest. **v~lich** a digestible. **V~ung** f - digestion

Verdeck nt -[e]s,-e hood; (Oberdeck) top deck. **v~en** vt cover; (verbergen) hide, conceal

verdenken† vt **das kann man ihm nicht v~** you can't blame him for it

verderb|en† vi (sein) spoil; (Lebensmittel:) go bad ● vt spoil; (zerstören) ruin; (moralisch) corrupt; **ich habe mir den Magen verdorben** I have an upset stomach. **V~en** nt -s ruin. **v~lich** a perishable; (schädlich) pernicious

verdeutlichen vt make clear

verdichten vt compress; **sich v~** (Nebel:) thicken

verdien|en vt/i (haben) earn; (fig) deserve. **V~er** m -s,- wage-earner

Verdienst¹ m -[e]s earnings pl

Verdienst² nt -[e]s,-e merit

verdient a well-deserved; (Person) of outstanding merit. **v~ermaßen** adv deservedly

verdoppeln vt double; (fig) redouble; **sich v~** double

verdorben a spoilt, ruined; (Magen) upset; (moralisch) corrupt; (verkommen) depraved

verdorren vi (sein) wither

verdrängen vt force out; (fig) displace; (psychisch) repress

verdreh|en vt twist; roll (Augen); (fig) distort. **v~t** a (fam) crazy

verdreifachen vt treble, triple

verdreschen† vt (fam) thrash

verdrießlich a morose, adv -ly

verdrücken vt crumple; (fam: essen) polish off; **sich v~** (fam) slip away

Verdruß m -sses annoyance

verdunk|eln vt darken; black out (Zimmer); **sich v~eln** darken. **V~[e]-lung** f - black-out

verdünnen vt dilute; **sich v~** taper off

verdunst|en vi (sein) evaporate. **V~ung** f - evaporation

verdursten vi (sein) die of thirst

verdutzt a baffled

veredeln vt refine; (Hort) graft

verehr|en vt revere; (Relig) worship; (bewundern) admire; (schenken) give. **V~er(in)** m -s,- (f -,-nen) admirer. **V~ung** f - veneration; worship; admiration

vereidigen vt swear in

Verein m -s,-e society; (Sport-) club

vereinbar a compatible. **v~en** vt arrange; **nicht zu v~en** incompatible. **V~ung** f -,-en agreement

vereinen vt unite; **sich v~** unite

vereinfachen vt simplify

vereinheitlichen vt standardize

vereinig|en vt unite; merge (Firmen); **sich v~en** unite; **V~te Staaten [von Amerika]** United States sg [of America]. **V~ung** f -,-en union; (Organisation) organization

vereinsamt a lonely

vereinzelt a isolated ● adv occasionally

vereist a frozen; (Straße) icy

vereiteln vt foil, thwart

vereitert a septic

verenden vi (sein) die

verengen vt restrict; **sich v~** narrow; (Pupille:) contract

vererb|en vt leave (dat to); (Biol & fig) pass on (dat to). **V~ung** f - heredity

verewigen vt immortalize; **sich v~** (fam) leave one's mark

verfahren† vi (sein) proceed; **v~ mit** deal with ● vr **sich v~** lose one's way ● a muddled. **V~** nt -s,- procedure; (Techn) process; (Jur) proceedings pl

Verfall m decay; (eines Gebäudes) dilapidation; (körperlich & fig) decline; (Ablauf) expiry. **v~en†** vi (sein) decay; (Person, Sitten:) decline; (ablaufen) expire; **v~en in** (+ acc) lapse into; **v~en auf** (+ acc) hit on (Idee); **jdm/etw v~en sein** be under the spell of s.o./sth; be addicted to (Alkohol)

verfälschen vt falsify; adulterate (Wein, Lebensmittel)

verfänglich a awkward

verfärben (sich) vr change colour; (Stoff:) discolour

verfass|en vt write; (Jur) draw up; (entwerfen) draft. **V~er** m -s,- author. **V~ung** f (Pol) constitution; (Zustand) state

verfaulen vi (sein) rot, decay

verfechten† vt advocate

verfehlen vt miss

verfeinde|n (sich) vr become enemies; **v~t sein** be enemies

verfeinern vt refine; (verbessern) improve

verfilmen vt film

verfilzt a matted

verfliegen† vi (sein) evaporate; (Zeit:) fly

verflixt a (fam) awkward; (verdammt) blessed; **v~!** damn!

verfluch|en vt curse. **v~t** a & adv (fam) damned; **v~t!** damn!

verflüchtigen (sich) vr evaporate

verflüssigen vt liquefy

verfolg|en vt pursue; (folgen) follow; (bedrängen) pester; (Pol) persecute; **strafrechtlich v~en** prosecute. **V~er** m -s,- pursuer. **V~ung** f - pursuit; persecution

verfrachten vt ship

verfrüht a premature

verfügbar a available

verfüg|en vt order; (Jur) decree ● vi (haben) **v~en über** (+ acc) have at one's disposal. **V~ung** f -,-en order; (Jur) decree; **jdm zur V~ung stehen/stellen** be/place at s.o.'s disposal

verführ|en vt seduce; (verlocken) tempt. **V~er** m seducer. **v~erisch** a seductive; tempting. **V~ung** f seduction; temptation

vergammelt a rotten; (Gebäude) decayed; (Person) scruffy

vergangen a past; (letzte) last. **V~heit** f - past; (Gram) past tense

vergänglich a transitory

vergas|en vt gas. **V~er** m -s,- carburettor

vergeb|en† vt award (**an** + dat to); (weggeben) give away; (verzeihen) forgive. **v~ens** adv in vain. **v~lich** a futile, vain ● adv in vain. **V~ung** f - forgiveness

vergehen† vi (sein) pass; **v~ vor** (+ dat) nearly die of; **sich v~** violate (**gegen etw** sth); (sexuell) sexually assault (**an jdm** s.o.). **V~** nt -s,- offence

vergelt|en† vt repay. **V~ung** f - retaliation; (Rache) revenge. **V~ungsmaßnahme** f reprisal

vergessen† vt forget; (liegenlassen) leave behind. **V~heit** f - oblivion; **in V~heit geraten** be forgotten

vergeßlich a forgetful. **V~keit** f - forgetfulness

vergeuden vt waste, squander

vergewaltig|en vt rape. **V~ung** f -,-en rape

vergewissern (sich) vr make sure (gen of)

vergießen† vt spill; shed (Tränen, Blut)

vergift|en vt poison. **V~ung** f -,-en poisoning

Vergißmeinnicht nt -[e]s,-[e] forget-me-not

vergittert a barred

verglasen vt glaze

Vergleich m -[e]s,-e comparison; (Jur) settlement. **v~bar** a comparable. **v~en**† vt compare (**mit** with/to). **v~sweise** adv comparatively

vergnüg|en (sich) vr enjoy oneself. **V~en** nt -s,- pleasure; (Spaß) fun; **viel V~en!** have a good time! **v~lich** a enjoyable. **v~t** a cheerful, adv -ly; (zufrieden) happy, adv -ily; (vergnüglich) enjoyable. **V~ungen** fpl entertainments

vergolden vt gild; (plattieren) gold-plate

vergönnen vt grant

vergöttern vt idolize

vergraben† vt bury

vergreifen† (sich) vr **sich v~ an** (+ dat) assault; (stehlen) steal

vergriffen a out of print

vergrößer|n vt enlarge; (Linse:) magnify; (vermehren) increase; (erweitern) extend; expand (Geschäft); **sich v~n** grow bigger; (Firma:) expand; (zunehmen) increase. **V~ung** f -,-en magnification; increase; expansion; (Phot) enlargement. **V~ungsglas** nt magnifying glass

Vergünstigung f -,-en privilege

vergüt|en vt pay for; **jdm etw v~en** reimburse s.o. for sth. **V~ung** f -,-en remuneration; (Erstattung) reimbursement

verhaft|en vt arrest. **V~ung** f -,-en arrest

verhalten† (sich) vr behave; (handeln) act; (beschaffen sein) be; **sich still v~** keep quiet. **V~** nt -s behaviour, conduct

Verhältnis nt -ses,-se relationship; (Liebes-) affair; (Math) ratio; **V~se** circumstances; (Bedingungen) conditions; **über seine V~se leben** live beyond one's means. **v~mäßig** adv comparatively, relatively

verhand|eln vt discuss; (Jur) try ● vi (haben) negotiate; **v~eln gegen** (Jur) try. **V~lung** f (Jur) trial; **V~lungen** negotiations

verhängen vt cover; (fig) impose

Verhängnis nt -ses fate, doom.
v∼volla fatal, disastrous
verharmlosenvt play down
verharrenvi (haben) remain
verhärtenvt/i (sein) harden; **sich v∼** harden
verhaßta hated
verhätschelnvt spoil, pamper
verhauen† vt (fam) beat; make a mess of ⟨Prüfung⟩
verheerend a devastating; (fam) terrible
verhehlenvt conceal
verheilenvi (sein) heal
verheimlichenvt keep secret
verheirat|en (sich) vr get married (**mit** to). **v∼et**a married
verhelfen† vi (haben) **jdm zu etw v∼** help s.o. get sth
verherrlichenvt glorify
verhexen vt bewitch; **es ist wie verhext** (fam) there is a jinx on it
verhinder|n vt prevent; **v∼t sein** be unable to come. **V∼ung**f - prevention
verhöhnenvt deride
Verhör nt -s,-e interrogation; **ins V∼ nehmen** interrogate. **v∼en** vt interrogate; **sich v∼en** mishear
verhüllen vt cover; (fig) disguise.
v∼da euphemistic, adv -ally
verhungernvi (sein) starve
verhüt|envt prevent. **V∼ung**f - prevention. **V∼ungsmittel** nt contraceptive
verhutzelta wizened
verirren (sich)vr get lost
verjagenvt chase away
verjüngen vt rejuvenate; **sich v∼** taper
verkalkta (fam) senile
verkalkulieren (sich) vr miscalculate
Verkauf m sale; **zum V∼** for sale.
v∼envt sell; **zu v∼en**for sale
Verkäufer(in) m(f) seller; (im Geschäft) shop assistant
Verkehr m -s traffic; (Kontakt) contact; (Geschlechts-) intercourse; **aus dem V∼ ziehen** take out of circulation.
v∼envi (haben) operate; ⟨Bus, Zug:⟩ run; (Umgang haben) associate, mix (**mit** with); ⟨Gast sein⟩ visit (**bei jdm** s.o.); frequent (**in einem Lokal** a restaurant); **brieflich v∼en** correspond
● vt **ins Gegenteil v∼** turn round
Verkehrs|ampel f traffic lights pl.
V∼büro nt = **V∼verein. V∼funk** m

[radio] traffic information. **V∼unfall** m road accident. **V∼verein** m tourist office. **V∼zeichen** nt traffic sign
verkehrt a wrong, adv -ly.
v∼herumadv the wrong way round; (links) inside out
verkennen†vt misjudge
verklagenvt sue (**auf** + acc for)
verkleid|envt disguise; (Techn) line; **sich v∼en** disguise oneself; (für Kostümfest) dress up. **V∼ung** f -,-en disguise; (Kostüm) fancy dress; (Techn) lining
verkleiner|n vt reduce [in size].
V∼ungf - reduction. **V∼ungsform**f diminutive
verklemmt a jammed; (psychisch) inhibited
verkneifen† vt **sich** (dat) **etw v∼** do without sth; (verbeißen) suppress sth
verknitternvt/i (sein) crumple
verknüpfen vt knot together; (verbinden) connect, link; (zugleich tun) combine
verkommen† vi (sein) be neglected; (sittlich) go to the bad; (verfallen) decay; ⟨Haus:⟩ fall into disrepair; ⟨Gegend:⟩ become run-down; ⟨Lebensmittel:⟩ go bad ● a neglected; (sittlich) depraved; ⟨Haus⟩ dilapidated; ⟨Gegend⟩ run-down
verkörper|n vt embody, personify.
V∼ung f -,-en embodiment, personification
verkraftenvt cope with
verkrampfta (fig) tense
verkriechen† (**sich**) vr hide
verkrümmta crooked, bent
verkrüppelt a crippled; ⟨Glied⟩ deformed
verkühl|en (sich) vr catch a chill.
V∼ungf -,-en chill
verkümmer|n vi (sein) waste/ ⟨Pflanze:⟩ wither away. **v∼t** a stunted
verkünd|envt announce; pronounce ⟨Urteil⟩. **v∼igen** vt announce; (predigen) preach
verkürzen vt shorten; (verringern) reduce; (abbrechen) cut short; while away ⟨Zeit⟩
verladen†vt load
Verlag m -[e]s,-e publishing firm
verlangen vt ask for; (fordern) demand; (berechnen) charge; **am Telefon verlangt werden** be wanted

on the telephone. **V∼** *nt* **-s** desire; (*Bitte*) request; **auf V∼** on demand

verlänger|n *vt* extend; lengthen ⟨*Kleid*⟩; (*zeitlich*) prolong; renew ⟨*Paß, Vertrag*⟩; (*Culin*) thin down. **V∼ung** *f* **-,-en** extension; renewal. **V∼ungsschnur** *f* extension cable

verlangsamen *vt* slow down

Verlaß *m* **-sses auf ihn ist kein V∼** you cannot rely on him

verlassen† *vt* leave; (*im Stich lassen*) desert; **sich v∼ auf** (+ *acc*) rely or depend on ● *a* deserted. **V∼heit** *f* - desolation

verläßlich *a* reliable

Verlauf *m* course; **im V∼** (+ *gen*) in the course of. **v∼en**† *vi* (*sein*) run; (*ablaufen*) go; (*zerlaufen*) melt; **gut v∼en** go [off] well ● *vr* **sich v∼en** lose one's way; ⟨*Menge:*⟩ disperse; ⟨*Wasser:*⟩ drain away

verleben *vt* spend

verlegen *vt* move; (*verschieben*) postpone; (*vor-*) bring forward; (*verlieren*) mislay; (*versperren*) block; (*legen*) lay ⟨*Teppich, Rohre*⟩; (*veröffentlichen*) publish; **sich v∼ auf** (+ *acc*) take up ⟨*Beruf, Fach*⟩; resort to ⟨*Taktik, Bitten*⟩ ● *a* embarrassed; **nie v∼ um** never at a loss for. **V∼heit** *f* - embarrassment

Verleger *m* **-s,-** publisher

verleihen† *vt* lend; (*gegen Gebühr*) hire out; (*überreichen*) award, confer; (*fig*) give

verleiten *vt* induce/(*verlocken*) tempt (**zu** to)

verlernen *vt* forget

verlesen¹† *vt* read out; **ich habe mich v∼** I misread it

verlesen²† *vt* sort out

verletz|en *vt* injure; (*kränken*) hurt; (*verstoßen gegen*) infringe; violate ⟨*Grenze*⟩. **v∼end** *a* hurtful, wounding. **v∼lich** *a* vulnerable. **V∼te(r)** *m/f* injured person; (*bei Unfall*) casualty. **V∼ung** *f* **-,-en** injury; (*Verstoß*) infringement; violation

verleugnen *vt* deny; disown ⟨*Freund*⟩

verleumd|en *vt* slander; (*schriftlich*) libel. **v∼erisch** *a* slanderous; libellous. **V∼ung** *f* **-,-en** slander; (*schriftlich*) libel

verlieben (sich) *vr* fall in love (**in** + *acc* with); **verliebt sein** be in love (**in** + *acc* with)

verlier|en† *vt* lose; shed ⟨*Laub*⟩; **sich v∼en** disappear; ⟨*Weg:*⟩ peter out ● *vi* (*haben*) lose (**an etw** *dat* sth). **V∼er** *m* **-s,-** loser

verlob|en (sich) *vr* get engaged (**mit** to); **v∼t sein** be engaged. **V∼te** *f* fiancée. **V∼te(r)** *m* fiancé. **V∼ung** *f* **-,-en** engagement

verlock|en *vt* tempt; **v∼end** tempting. **V∼ung** *f* **-,-en** temptation

verlogen *a* lying

verloren *a* lost; **v∼e Eier** poached eggs. **v∼gehen**† *vi sep* (*sein*) get lost

verlos|en *vt* raffle. **V∼ung** *f* **-,-en** raffle; (*Ziehung*) draw

verlottert *a* run-down; ⟨*Person*⟩ scruffy; (*sittlich*) dissolute

Verlust *m* **-[e]s,-e** loss

vermachen *vt* leave, bequeath

Vermächtnis *nt* **-ses,-se** legacy

vermähl|en (sich) *vr* marry. **V∼ung** *f* **-,-en** marriage

vermehren *vt* increase; propagate ⟨*Pflanzen*⟩; **sich v∼** increase; (*sich fortpflanzen*) breed, multiply

vermeiden† *vt* avoid

vermeintlich *a* supposed, *adv* -ly

Vermerk *m* **-[e]s,-e** note. **v∼en** *vt* note [down]; **übel v∼en** take amiss

vermess|en† *vt* measure; survey ⟨*Gelände*⟩ ● *a* presumptuous. **V∼enheit** *f* - presumption. **V∼ung** *f* measurement; (*Land-*) survey

vermiet|en *vt* let, rent [out]; hire out ⟨*Boot, Auto*⟩; **zu v∼en** to let; ⟨*Boot:*⟩ for hire. **V∼er** *m* landlord. **V∼erin** *f* landlady

verminder|n *vt* reduce, lessen. **V∼ung** *f* - reduction, decrease

vermischen *vt* mix; **sich v∼** mix

vermissen *vt* miss

vermißt *a* missing. **V∼e(r)** *m* missing person/(*Mil*) soldier

vermittel|n *vi* (*haben*) mediate ● *vt* arrange; (*beschaffen*) find; place ⟨*Arbeitskräfte*⟩; impart ⟨*Wissen*⟩; convey ⟨*Eindruck*⟩. **v∼s** *prep* (+ *gen*) by means of

Vermittl|er *m* **-s,-** agent; (*Schlichter*) mediator. **V∼ung** *f* **-,-en** arrangement; (*Agentur*) agency; (*Teleph*) exchange; (*Schlichtung*) mediation

vermögen† *vt* be able (**zu** to). **V∼** *nt* **-s,-** fortune. **v∼d** *a* wealthy

vermut|en *vt* suspect; (*glauben*) presume. **v∼lich** *a* probable ● *adv* presumably. **V∼ung** *f* **-,-en** supposition;

(*Verdacht*) suspicion; (*Mutmaßung*) conjecture

vernachlässig|en *vt* neglect. **V∼ung** *f* - neglect

vernehm|en† *vt* hear; (*verhören*) question; (*Jur*) examine. **V∼ung** *f* -,-en questioning

verneig|en (sich) *vr* bow. **V∼ung** *f* -,-en bow

vernein|en *vt* answer in the negative; (*ablehnen*) reject. **v∼end** *a* negative. **V∼ung** *f* -,-en negative answer; (*Gram*) negative

vernicht|en *vt* destroy; (*ausrotten*) exterminate. **v∼end** *a* devastating; (*Niederlage*) crushing. **V∼ung** *f* - destruction; extermination

Vernunft *f* - reason; **V∼ annehmen** see reason

vernünftig *a* reasonable, sensible; (*fam: ordentlich*) decent ● *adv* sensibly; (*fam*) properly

veröffentlich|en *vt* publish. **V∼ung** *f* -,-en publication

verordn|en *vt* prescribe (*dat* for). **V∼ung** *f* -,-en prescription; (*Verfügung*) decree

verpachten *vt* lease [out]

verpack|en *vt* pack; (*einwickeln*) wrap. **V∼ung** *f* packaging; wrapping

verpassen *vt* miss; (*fam: geben*) give

verpfänden *vt* pawn

verpflanzen *vt* transplant

verpfleg|en *vt* feed; **sich selbst v∼en** cater for oneself. **V∼ung** *f* - board; (*Essen*) food; **Unterkunft und V∼ung** board and lodging

verpflicht|en *vt* oblige; (*einstellen*) engage; (*Sport*) sign; **sich v∼en** undertake/(*versprechen*) promise (**zu** to); (*vertraglich*) sign a contract; **jdm v∼et sein** be indebted to s.o. **V∼ung** *f* -,-en obligation, commitment

verpfuschen *vt* make a mess of

verpönt *a* **v∼ sein** be frowned upon

verprügeln *vt* beat up, thrash

Verputz *m* -es plaster. **v∼en** *vt* plaster; (*fam: essen*) polish off

Verrat *m* -[e]s betrayal, treachery. **v∼en†** *vt* betray; give away (*Geheimnis*); (*fam: sagen*) tell; **sich v∼en** give oneself away

Verräter *m* -s,- traitor. **v∼isch** *a* treacherous; (*fig*) revealing

verräuchert *a* smoky

verrech|nen *vt* settle; clear (*Scheck*); **sich v∼nen** make a mistake; (*fig*) miscalculate. **V∼nungsscheck** *m* crossed cheque

verregnet *a* spoilt by rain; (*Tag*) rainy, wet

verreisen *vi (sein)* go away; **verreist sein** be away

verreißen† *vt (fam)* pan, slate

verrenken *vt* dislocate; **sich v∼** contort oneself

verricht|en *vt* perform, do; say (*Gebet*). **V∼ung** *f* -,-en task

verriegeln *vt* bolt

verringer|n *vt* reduce; **sich v∼n** decrease. **V∼ung** *f* - reduction; decrease

verrost|en *vi (sein)* rust. **v∼et** *a* rusty

verrücken *vt* move

verrückt *a* crazy, mad; **v∼ werden/ machen** go/drive crazy. **V∼e(r)** *m/f* lunatic. **V∼heit** *f* -,-en madness; (*Torheit*) folly

Verruf *m* disrepute. **v∼en** *a* disreputable

verrühren *vt* mix

verrunzelt *a* wrinkled

verrutschen *vi (sein)* slip

Vers /fɛrs/ *m* -es,-e verse

versag|en *vi (haben)* fail ● *vt* jdm/ **sich etw v∼en** deny s.o./oneself sth. **V∼en** *nt* -s,- failure. **V∼er** *m* -s,- failure

versalzen† *vt* put too much salt in/ on; (*fig*) spoil

versamm|eln *vt* assemble; **sich v∼eln** assemble, meet. **V∼lung** *f* assembly, meeting

Versand *m* -[e]s dispatch. **V∼haus** *nt* mail-order firm

versäum|en *vt* miss; lose (*Zeit*); (*unterlassen*) neglect; **[es] v∼en, etw zu tun** fail *or* neglect to do sth. **V∼nis** *nt* -ses,-se omission

verschaffen *vt* get; **sich** (*dat*) **v∼** obtain; gain (*Respekt*)

verschämt *a* bashful, *adv* -ly

verschandeln *vt* spoil

verschärfen *vt* intensify; tighten (*Kontrolle*); increase (*Tempo*); aggravate (*Lage*); **sich v∼** intensify; increase; (*Lage:*) worsen

verschätzen (sich) *vr* **sich v∼ in** (+ *dat*) misjudge

verschenken *vt* give away

verscheuchen *vt* shoo/(*jagen*) chase away

verschicken vt send; (Comm) dispatch

verschieb|en† vt move; (aufschieben) put off, postpone; (sl: handeln mit) traffic in; **sich v~en** move, shift; (verrutschen) slip; (zeitlich) postponed. **V~ung** f shift; postponement

verschieden a different; **v~e** (pl) different; (mehrere) various; **v~es** some things; (dieses und jenes) various things; **die v~sten Farben** a whole variety of colours; **das ist v~** it varies ● adv differently; **v~ groß/lang** of different sizes/lengths. **v~artig** a diverse. **V~heit** f - difference; (Vielfalt) diversity. **v~tlich** adv several times

verschimmel|n vi (sein) go mouldy. **v~t** a mouldy

verschlafen† vi (haben) oversleep ● vt sleep through ⟨Tag⟩; (versäumen) miss ⟨Zug, Termin⟩; **sich v~** oversleep ● a sleepy; **noch v~** still half asleep

Verschlag m -[e]s, :e shed

verschlagen† vt lose ⟨Seite⟩; **jdm die Sprache/den Atem v~** leave s.o. speechless/take s.o.'s breath away; **nach X v~ werden** end up in X ● a sly, adv -ly

verschlechter|n vt make worse; **sich v~n** get worse, deteriorate. **V~ung** f -,-en deterioration

verschleiern vt veil; (fig) hide

Verschleiß m -es wear and tear; (Verbrauch) consumption. **v~en**† vt/i (sein) wear out

verschleppen vt carry off; (entführen) abduct; spread ⟨Seuche⟩; neglect ⟨Krankheit⟩; (hinausziehen) delay

verschleudern vt sell at a loss; (verschwenden) squander

verschließen† vt close; (abschließen) lock; (einschließen) lock up

verschlimmer|n vt make worse; aggravate ⟨Lage⟩; **sich v~n** get worse, deteriorate. **V~ung** f -,-en deterioration

verschlingen† vt intertwine; (fressen) devour; (fig) swallow

verschlissen a worn

verschlossen a reserved. **V~heit** f - reserve

verschlucken vt swallow; **sich v~** choke (**an** + dat on)

Verschluß m -sses, :sse fastener, clasp; (Fenster-, Koffer-) catch; (Flaschen-) top;

(luftdicht) seal; (Phot) shutter; **unter V~** under lock and key

verschlüsselt a coded

verschmähen vt spurn

verschmelzen† vt/i (sein) fuse

verschmerzen vt get over

verschmutz|en vt soil; pollute ⟨Luft⟩ ● vi (sein) get dirty. **V~ung** f - pollution

verschnaufen vi/r (haben) **[sich] v~** get one's breath

verschneit a snow-covered

verschnörkelt a ornate

verschnüren vt tie up

verschollen a missing

verschonen vt spare

verschönern vt brighten up; (verbessern) improve

verschossen a faded

verschrammt a scratched

verschränken vt cross

verschreiben† vt prescribe; **sich v~** make a slip of the pen

verschrie[e]n a notorious

verschroben a eccentric

verschrotten vt scrap

verschulden vt be to blame for. **V~nt** -s fault

verschuldet a **v~ sein** be in debt

verschütten vt spill; (begraben) bury

verschweigen† vt conceal, hide

verschwend|en vt waste. **v~erisch** a extravagant, adv -ly; (üppig) lavish, adv -ly. **V~ung** f - extravagance; (Vergeudung) waste

verschwiegen a discreet; ⟨Ort⟩ secluded. **V~heit** f - discretion

verschwimmen† vi (sein) become blurred

verschwinden† vi (sein) disappear; **[mal] v~** (fam) spend a penny. **V~** nt -s disappearance

verschwommen a blurred

verschwör|en (sich) vr conspire. **V~ung** f -,-en conspiracy

versehen† vt perform; hold ⟨Posten⟩; keep ⟨Haushalt⟩; **v~ mit** provide with; **sich v~** make a mistake; **ehe man sich's versieht** before you know where you are. **V~** nt -s,- oversight; (Fehler) slip; **aus V~** by mistake. **v~tlich** adv by mistake

Versehrte(r) m disabled person

versenden† vt send [out]

versengen vt singe; (stärker) scorch

versenken vt sink; **sich v~ in** (+ acc) immerse oneself in

versessen a keen (**auf** + acc on)

versetz|en vt move; transfer ⟨Person⟩; (Sch) move up; (verpfänden) pawn; (verkaufen) sell; (vermischen) blend; (antworten) reply; **jdn v~en** (fam: warten lassen) stand s.o. up; **jdm einen Stoß/Schreck v~en** give s.o. a push/fright; **jdn in Angst/Erstaunen v~en** frighten/astonish s.o.; **sich in jds Lage v~en** put oneself in s.o.'s place. **V~ung** f -,-en move; transfer; (Sch) move to a higher class

verseuch|en vt contaminate. **V~ung** f - contamination

versicher|n vt insure; (bekräftigen) affirm; **jdm v~n** assure s.o. (**daß** that). **V~ung** f -,-en insurance; assurance

versiegeln vt seal

versiegen vi (sein) dry up

versiert /vɛrˈziːɐt/ a experienced

versilbert a silver-plated

versinken† vi (sein) sink; **in Gedanken versunken** lost in thought

Version /vɛrˈzioːn/ f -,-en version

Versmaß /ˈfɛrs-/ nt metre

versöhn|en vt reconcile; **sich v~en** become reconciled. **v~lich** a conciliatory. **V~ung** f -,-en reconciliation

versorg|en vt provide, supply (**mit** with); provide for ⟨Familie⟩; (betreuen) look after; keep ⟨Haushalt⟩. **V~ung** f - provision, supply; (Betreuung) care

verspät|en (sich) vr be late. **v~et** a late; ⟨Zug⟩ delayed; ⟨Dank, Glückwunsch⟩ belated ● adv late; belatedly. **V~ung** f - lateness; **V~ung haben** be late

versperren vt block; bar ⟨Weg⟩

verspiel|en vt gamble away; **sich v~en** play a wrong note. **v~t** a playful, adv -ly

verspotten vt mock, ridicule

versprech|en† vt promise; **sich v~en** make a slip of the tongue; **sich** (dat) **viel v~en von** have high hopes of. **V~en** nt -s,- promise. **V~ungen** fpl promises

verspüren vt feel

verstaatlich|en vt nationalize. **V~ung** f - nationalization

Verstand m -[e]s mind; (Vernunft) reason; **den V~ verlieren** go out of one's mind. **v~esmäßig** a rational, adv -ly

verständig a sensible, adv -bly; (klug) intelligent, adv -ly. **v~en** vt

notify, inform; **sich v~en** communicate; (sich verständlich machen) make oneself understood; (sich einigen) reach agreement. **V~ung** f - notification; communication; (Einigung) agreement

verständlich a comprehensible, adv -bly; (deutlich) clear, adv -ly; (begreiflich) understandable; **sich v~ machen** make oneself understood. **v~erweise** adv understandably

Verständnis nt -ses understanding. **v~los** a uncomprehending, adv -ly. **v~voll** a understanding, adv -ly

verstärk|en vt strengthen, reinforce; (steigern) intensify, increase; amplify ⟨Ton⟩; **sich v~en** intensify. **V~er** m -s,- amplifier. **V~ung** f reinforcement; increase; amplification; (Truppen) reinforcements pl

verstaubt a dusty

verstauchen vt sprain

verstauen vt stow

Versteck nt -[e]s,-e hiding-place; **V~ spielen** play hide-and-seek. **v~en** vt hide; **sich v~en** hide. **v~t** a hidden; (heimlich) secret; (verstohlen) furtive, adv -ly

verstehen† vt understand; (können) know; **falsch v~** misunderstand; **sich v~** understand one another; (auskommen) get on; **das versteht sich von selbst** that goes without saying

versteif|en vt stiffen; **sich v~** stiffen; (fig) insist (**auf** + acc on)

versteiger|n vt auction. **V~ung** f auction

versteinert a fossilized

verstell|bar a adjustable. **v~en** vt adjust; (versperren) block; (verändern) disguise; **sich v~en** pretend. **V~ung** f - pretence

versteuern vt pay tax on

verstiegen a (fig) extravagant

verstimm|t a disgruntled; ⟨Magen⟩ upset; (Mus) out of tune. **V~ung** f - ill humour; (Magen-) upset

verstockt a stubborn, adv -ly

verstohlen a furtive, adv -ly

verstopf|en vt plug; (versperren) block; **v~t** a blocked; ⟨Person⟩ constipated. **V~ung** f -,-en blockage; (Med) constipation

verstorben a late, deceased. **V~e(r)** m/f deceased

verstört a bewildered

Verstoß m infringement. **v~en†** vt disown ● vi (haben) **v~en gegen** contravene, infringe; offend against ⟨Anstand⟩

verstreichen† vt spread ● vi (sein) pass

verstreuen vt scatter

verstümmeln vt mutilate; garble ⟨Text⟩

verstummen vi (sein) fall silent; ⟨Gespräch, Lärm:⟩ cease

Versuch m -[e]s,-e attempt; (Experiment) experiment. **v~en** vt/i (haben) try; **sich v~en in** (+ dat) try one's hand at; **v~t sein** be tempted (**zu** to). **V~skaninchen** nt (fig) guinea-pig. **v~sweise** adv as an experiment. **V~ung** f -,-en temptation

versündigen (sich) vr sin (**an**+ dat against)

vertagen vt adjourn; (aufschieben) postpone; **sich v~** adjourn

vertauschen vt exchange; (verwechseln) mix up

verteidig|en vt defend. **V~er** m -s,- defender; (Jur) defence counsel. **V~ung** f -,-en defence

verteil|en vt distribute; (zuteilen) allocate; (ausgeben) hand out; (verstreichen) spread; **sich v~en** spread out. **V~ung** f - distribution; allocation

vertief|en vt deepen; (zuteilen) **v~t sein in** (+ acc) be engrossed in. **V~ung** f -,-en hollow, depression

vertikal /vɛrtiˈkaːl/ a vertical, adv -ly

vertilgen vt exterminate; kill [off] ⟨Unkraut⟩; (fam: essen) demolish

vertippen (sich) vr make a typing mistake

vertonen vt set to music

Vertrag m -[e]s,ᵉe contract; (Pol) treaty

vertragen† vt tolerate, stand; take ⟨Kritik, Spaß⟩; **sich v~** get on; (passen) go (**mit** with); **sich wieder v~** make it up ● a worn

vertraglich a contractual

verträglich a good-natured; (bekömmlich) digestible

vertrauen vi (haben) trust (**jdm/etw** s.o./sth; **auf**+ acc in). **V~** nt -s trust, confidence (**zu** in); **im V~** in confidence. **V~smann** m (pl -**leute**) representative; (Sprecher) spokesman. **v~svoll** a trusting, adv -ly. **v~swürdig** a trustworthy

vertraulich a confidential, adv -ly; (intim) familiar, adv -ly

vertraut a intimate; (bekannt) familiar; **sich v~ machen mit** familiarize oneself with. **V~heit** f - intimacy; familiarity

vertreib|en† vt drive away; drive out ⟨Feind⟩; (Comm) sell; **sich** (dat) **die Zeit v~en** pass the time. **V~ung** f -,-en expulsion

vertret|en† vt represent; (einspringen für) stand in or deputize for; (verfechten) support; hold ⟨Meinung⟩; **sich** (dat) **den Fuß v~en** twist one's ankle; **sich** (dat) **die Beine v~en** stretch one's legs. **V~er** m -s,- representative; deputy; (Arzt-) locum; (Verfechter) supporter, advocate. **V~ung** f -,-en representation; (Person) deputy; (eines Arztes) locum; (Handels-) agency

Vertrieb m -[e]s (Comm) sale. **V~ene(r)** m/f displaced person

vertrocknen vi (sein) dry up

vertrösten vt **jdn auf später v~** put s.o. off until later

vertun† vt waste; **sich v~** (fam) make a mistake

vertuschen vt hush up

verübeln vt **jdm etw v~** hold sth against s.o.

verüben vt commit

verunglimpfen vt denigrate

verunglücken vi (sein) be involved in an accident; (fam: mißglücken) go wrong; **tödlich v~** be killed in an accident

verunreinigen vt pollute; (verseuchen) contaminate; (verschmutzen) soil

verunstalten vt disfigure

veruntreu|en vt embezzle. **V~ung** f - embezzlement

verursachen vt cause

verurteil|en vt condemn; (Jur) convict (**wegen** of); sentence (**zum Tode** to death). **V~ung** f - condemnation; (Jur) conviction

vervielfachen vt multiply

vervielfältigen vt duplicate

vervollkommnen vt perfect

vervollständigen vt complete

verwachsen a deformed

verwählen (sich) vr misdial

verwahren vt keep; (verstauen) put away; **sich v~** (fig) protest

verwahrlost a neglected; ⟨Haus⟩ dilapidated; (sittlich) depraved

Verwahrung *f* - keeping; **in V~ neh-men** take into safe keeping

verwaist *a* orphaned

verwalt|en *vt* administer; (*leiten*) manage; govern ⟨*Land*⟩. **V~er** *m* **-s,-** administrator; manager. **V~ung** *f* **-,-en** administration; management; government

verwand|eln *vt* transform, change (**in** + *acc* into); **sich v~eln** change, turn (**in** + *acc* into). **V~lung** *f* transformation

verwandt *a* related (**mit** to). **V~e(r)** *m/f* relative. **V~schaft** *f* - relationship; (*Menschen*) relatives *pl*

verwarn|en *vt* warn, caution. **V~ung** *f* warning, caution

verwaschen *a* washed out, faded

verwechs|eln *vt* mix up, confuse; (*halten für*) mistake (**mit** for). **V~lung** *f* **-,-en** mix-up

verwegen *a* audacious, *adv* -ly

Verwehung *f* **-,-en** [snow-]drift

verweichlicht *a* (*fig*) soft

verweiger|n *vt/i* (*haben*) refuse (**jdm etw** s.o sth); **den Gehorsam v~n** refuse to obey. **V~ung** *f* refusal

verweilen *vi* (*haben*) stay

Verweis *m* **-es,-e** reference (**auf** + *acc* to); (*Tadel*) reprimand. **v~en†** *vt* refer (**auf/an** + *acc* to); (*tadeln*) reprimand; **von der Schule v~en** expel

verwelken *vi* (*sein*) wilt

verwend|en† *vt* use; spend ⟨*Zeit, Mühe*⟩. **V~ung** *f* use

verwerf|en† *vt* reject; **sich v~en** warp. **v~lich** *a* reprehensible

verwert|en *vt* utilize, use; (*Comm*) exploit. **V~ung** *f* - utilization; exploitation

verwesen *vi* (*sein*) decompose

verwick|eln *vt* involve (**in** + *acc* in); **sich v~eln** get tangled up; **in etw** (*acc*) **v~elt sein** (*fig*) be involved *or* mixed up in sth. **v~elt** *a* complicated

verwildert *a* wild; ⟨*Garten*⟩ overgrown; ⟨*Aussehen*⟩ unkempt

verwinden† *vt* (*fig*) get over

verwirken *vt* forfeit

verwirklichen *vt* realize; **sich v~** be realized

verwirr|en *vt* tangle up; (*fig*) confuse; **sich v~en** get tangled; (*fig*) become confused. **v~t** *a* confused. **V~ung** *f* - confusion

verwischen *vt* smudge

verwittert *a* weathered; ⟨*Gesicht*⟩ weather-beaten

verwitwet *a* widowed

verwöhn|en *vt* spoil. **v~t** *a* spoilt; (*anspruchsvoll*) discriminating

verworren *a* confused

verwund|bar *a* vulnerable. **v~en** *vt* wound

verwunder|lich *a* surprising. **v~n** *vt* surprise; **sich v~n** be surprised. **V~ung** *f* - surprise

Verwundete(r) *m* wounded soldier; **die V~eten** the wounded *pl*. **V~ung** *f* **-,-en** wound

verwünsch|en *vt* curse. **v~t** *a* confounded

verwüst|en *vt* devastate, ravage. **V~ung** *f* **-,-en** devastation

verzagen *vi* (*haben*) lose heart

verzählen (sich) *vr* miscount

verzärteln *vt* mollycoddle

verzaubern *vt* bewitch; (*fig*) enchant; **v~ in** (+ *acc*) turn into

Verzehr *m* **-s** consumption. **v~en** *vt* eat; (*aufbrauchen*) use up; **sich v~en** (*fig*) pine away

verzeich|nen *vt* list; (*registrieren*) register. **V~nis** *nt* **-ses,-se** list; (*Inhalts-*) index

verzeih|en† *vt* forgive; **v~en Sie!** excuse me! **V~ung** *f* - forgiveness; **um V~ung bitten** apologize; **V~ung!** sorry! (*bei Frage*) excuse me!

verzerren *vt* distort; contort ⟨*Gesicht*⟩; pull ⟨*Muskel*⟩

Verzicht *m* **-[e]s** renunciation (**auf** + *acc* of). **v~en** *vi* (*haben*) do without; **v~en auf** (+ *acc*) give up; renounce ⟨*Recht, Erbe*⟩

verziehen† *vt* pull out of shape; (*verwöhnen*) spoil; **sich v~** lose shape; ⟨*Holz:*⟩ warp; ⟨*Gesicht:*⟩ twist; (*verschwinden*) disappear; ⟨*Nebel:*⟩ disperse; ⟨*Gewitter:*⟩ pass; **das Gesicht v~** pull a face ● *vi* (*sein*) move [away]

verzier|en *vt* decorate. **V~ung** *f* **-,-en** decoration

verzinsen *vt* pay interest on

verzöger|n *vt* delay; (*verlangsamen*) slow down; **sich v~n** be delayed. **V~ung** *f* **-,-en** delay

verzollen *vt* pay duty on; **haben Sie etwas zu v~?** have you anything to declare?

verzück|t *a* ecstatic, *adv* -ally. **V~ung** *f* - rapture, ecstasy

Verzug *m* delay; **in V~** in arrears

verzweif|eln *vi* (*sein*) despair. **v~elt** *a* desperate, *adv* -ly; **v~elt sein** be in despair; (*ratlos*) be desperate. **V~lung** *f* - despair; (*Ratlosigkeit*) desperation

verzweigen (sich) *vr* branch [out]

verzwickt *a* (*fam*) tricky

Veto /'ve:to/ *nt* **-s,-s** veto

Vetter *m* **-s,-n** cousin. **V~nwirtschaft** *f* nepotism

vgl. *abbr* (**vergleiche**) cf.

Viadukt /via'dʊkt/ *nt* **-[e]s,-e** viaduct

vibrieren /vi'bri:rən/ *vi* (*haben*) vibrate

Video /'vi:deo/ *nt* **-s,-s** video. **V~kassette** *f* video cassette. **V~recorder** /-rəkɔrdə/ *m* **-s,-** video recorder

Vieh *nt* **-[e]s** livestock; (*Rinder*) cattle *pl*; (*fam: Tier*) creature. **v~isch** *a* brutal, *adv* -ly

viel *pron* a great deal/(*fam*) a lot of; (*pl*) many, (*fam*) a lot of; (*substantivisch*) **v~[es]** much, (*fam*) a lot; **nicht/zu v~** not/too much; **v~e** *pl* many; **das v~e Geld/Lesen** all that money/reading ● *adv* much, (*fam*) a lot; **v~ mehr/weniger** much more/less; **v~ zu groß/klein** much *or* far too big/small

viel|deutig *a* ambiguous. **v~erlei** *inv a* many kinds of ● *pron* many things. **v~fach** *a* multiple ● *adv* many times; (*fam: oft*) frequently. **V~falt** *f* - diversity, [great] variety. **v~fältig** *a* diverse, varied

vielleicht *adv* perhaps, maybe; (*fam: wirklich*) really

vielmals *adv* very much; **danke v~!** thank you very much!

viel|mehr *adv* rather; (*im Gegenteil*) on the contrary. **v~sagend** *a* meaningful, *adv* -ly

vielseitig *a* varied; (*Person*) versatile ● *adv* **v~ begabt** versatile. **V~keit** *f* - versatility

vielversprechend *a* promising

vier *inv a;* **V~** *f* -, **-e** four; (*Sch*) **I** fair. **V~eck** *nt* **-[e]s,-e** oblong, rectangle; (*Quadrat*) square. **v~eckig** *a* oblong, rectangular; square. **v~fach** *a* quadruple. **V~linge** *mpl* quadruplets

Viertel /'fɪrtl/ *nt* **-s,-** quarter; (*Wein*) quarter litre. **v~ vor/nach sechs** [a] quarter to/past six; **V~ neun** [a] quarter past eight; **drei V~ neun** [a] quarter to nine. **V~finale** *nt* quarter-final. **V~jahr** *nt* three months *pl*; (*Comm*) quarter. **v~jährlich** *a & adv* quarterly. **v~n** *vt* quarter. **V~note** *f* crotchet, (*Amer*) quarter note. **V~stunde** *f* quarter of an hour

vier|zehn /'fɪr-/ *inv a* fourteen. **v~zehnte(r,s)** *a* fourteenth. **v~zig** *inv a* forty. **v~zigste(r,s)** *a* fortieth

Villa /'vɪla/ *f* -, **-len** villa

violett /vio'lɛt/ *a* violet

Vio|line /vio'li:nə/ *f* -, **-n** violin. **V~linschlüssel** *m* treble clef. **V~loncello** /-lɔn'tʃɛlo/ *nt* cello

Virtuose /vɪr'tuo:zə/ *m* **-n,-n** virtuoso

Virus /'vi:rʊs/ *nt* -, **-ren** virus

Visier /vi'zi:ɐ/ *nt* **-s,-e** visor

Vision /vi'zio:n/ *f* -, **-en** vision

Visite /vi'zi:tə/ *f* -, **-n** round; **V~ machen** do one's round

visuell /vi'zuɛl/ *a* visual, *adv* -ly

Visum /'vi:zʊm/ *nt* **-s,-sa** visa

vital /vi'ta:l/ *a* vital; (*Person*) energetic. **V~ität** *f* - vitality

Vitamin /vita'mi:n/ *nt* **-s,-e** vitamin

Vitrine /vi'tri:nə/ *f* -, **-n** display cabinet/(*im Museum*) case

Vizepräsident /'fi:tsə-/ *m* vice president

Vogel *m* **-s,-̈** bird; **einen V~ haben** (*fam*) have a screw loose. **V~scheuche** *f* -, **-n** scarecrow

Vokab|eln /vo'ka:bəln/ *fpl* vocabulary *sg*. **V~ular** *nt* **-s,-e** vocabulary

Vokal /vo'ka:l/ *m* **-s,-e** vowel

Volant /vo'lã:/ *m* **-s,-s** flounce; (*Auto*) steering-wheel

Volk *nt* **-[e]s,-̈er** people *sg*; (*Bevölkerung*) people *pl*; (*Bienen-*) colony

Völker|kunde *f* ethnology. **V~mord** *m* genocide. **V~recht** *nt* international law

Volks|abstimmung *f* plebiscite. **V~fest** *nt* public festival. **V~hochschule** *f* adult education classes *pl*/(*Gebäude*) centre. **V~lied** *nt* folksong. **V~tanz** *m* folk-dance. **v~tümlich** *a* popular. **V~wirt** *m* economist. **V~wirtschaft** *f* economics *sg*. **V~zählung** *f* [national] census

voll *a* full (**von** *od* **mit** of); (*Haar*) thick; (*Erfolg, Ernst*) complete; (*Wahrheit*) whole; **v~ machen** fill up; **die Uhr schlug v~** (*fam*) the clock struck the hour ● *adv* (*ganz*) completely; (*arbeiten*) full-time; (*auszahlen*) in full; **v~ und ganz** completely

vollauf *adv* fully, completely

Voll|beschäftigung *f* full employment. **V~blut** *nt* thoroughbred

vollbringen† *vt insep* accomplish; work (*Wunder*)

vollende|n *vt insep* complete. **v~t** *a* perfect, *adv* -ly; **v~te Gegenwart/ Vergangenheit** perfect/pluperfect
vollends *adv* completely
Vollendung *f* completion; (*Vollkommenheit*) perfection
voller *inv a* full of; **v~ Angst/Freude** filled with fear/joy; **v~ Flecken** covered with stains
Völlerei *f* - gluttony
Volleyball /'vɔli-/ *m* volleyball
vollführen *vt insep* perform
vollfüllen *vt sep* fill up
Vollgas *nt* **V~ geben** put one's foot down; **mit V~** flat out
völlig *a* complete, *adv* -ly
volljährig *a* **v~ sein** (*Jur*) be of age. **V~keit** *f* - (*Jur*) majority
Vollkaskoversicherung *f* fully comprehensive insurance
vollkommen *a* perfect, *adv* -ly; (*völlig*) complete, *adv* -ly. **V~heit** *f* - perfection
Voll|kornbrot *nt* wholemeal bread. **V~macht** *f* -,-en authority; (*Jur*) power of attorney. **V~mond** *m* full moon. **V~pension** *f* full board. **v~schlank** *a* with a fuller figure
vollständig *a* complete, *adv* -ly
vollstrecken *vt insep* execute; carry out (*Urteil*)
volltanken *vi sep* (*haben*) (*Auto*) fill up [with petrol]
Volltreffer *m* direct hit
vollzählig *a* complete; **sind wir v~?** are we all here?
vollziehen† *vt insep* carry out; perform (*Handlung*); consummate (*Ehe*); **sich v~** take place
Volt /vɔlt/ *nt* **-[s],-** volt
Volumen /vo'luːmən/ *nt* **-s,-** volume
vom *prep* = **von dem; vom Rauchen** from smoking
von *prep* (+ *dat*) of; (*über*) about; (*Ausgangspunkt, Ursache*) from; (*beim Passiv*) by; **Musik von Mozart** music by Mozart; **einer von euch** one of you; **von hier/heute an** from here/today; **von mir aus** I don't mind
voneinander *adv* from each other; (*abhängig*) on each other
vonstatten *adv* **v~ gehen** take place; **gut v~ gehen** go [off] well
vor *prep* (+ *dat/acc*) in front of; (*zeitlich, Reihenfolge*) before; (+ *dat*) (*bei Uhrzeit*) to; (*warnen, sich fürchten/ schämen*) of; (*schützen, davonlaufen*) from; (*Respekt haben*) for; **vor Angst/**

Kälte zittern tremble with fear/cold; **vor drei Tagen/Jahren** three days/ years ago; **vor sich** (*acc*) **hin murmeln** mumble to oneself; **vor allen Dingen** above all ● *adv* forward; **vor und zurück** backwards and forwards
Vor|abend *m* eve. **V~ahnung** *f* premonition
voran *adv* at the front; (*voraus*) ahead; (*vorwärts*) forward. **v~gehen†** *vi sep* (*sein*) lead the way; (*Fortschritte machen*) make progress; **jdm/etw v~gehen** precede s.o./sth. **v~kommen†** *vi sep* (*sein*) make progress; (*fig*) get on
Vor|anschlag *m* estimate. **V~anzeige** *f* advance notice. **V~arbeit** *f* preliminary work. **V~arbeiter** *m* foreman
voraus *adv* ahead (*dat* of); (*vorn*) at the front; (*vorwärts*) forward ● **im voraus** in advance. **v~bezahlen** *vt sep* pay in advance. **v~gehen†** *vi sep* (*sein*) go on ahead; **jdm/etw v~gehen** precede s.o./sth. **V~sage** *f* -,-n prediction. **v~sagen** *vt sep* predict. **v~sehen†** *vt sep* foresee
voraussetz|en *vt sep* take for granted; (*erfordern*) require; **vorausgesetzt, daß** provided that. **V~ung** *f* -,-en assumption; (*Erfordernis*) prerequisite; **unter der V~ung, daß** on condition that
Voraussicht *f* foresight; **aller V~ nach** in all probability. **v~lich** *a* anticipated, expected ● *adv* probably
Vorbehalt *m* -[e]s,-e reservation. **v~en†** *vt sep* **sich** (*dat*) **v~en** reserve (*Recht*); **jdm v~en sein/bleiben** be left to s.o. **v~los** *a* unreserved, *adv* -ly
vorbei *adv* past (**an jdm/etw** s.o./ sth); (*zu Ende*) over. **v~fahren†** *vi sep* (*sein*) drive/go past. **v~gehen†** *vi sep* (*sein*) go past; (*verfehlen*) miss; (*vergehen*) pass; (*fam: besuchen*) drop in (**bei** on). **v~kommen†** *vi sep* (*sein*) pass/(**v~können**) get past (**an jdm/etw** s.o./sth); (*fam: besuchen*) drop in (**bei** on)
vorbereit|en *vt sep* prepare; prepare for (*Reise*); **sich v~en** prepare [oneself] (**auf** + *acc* for). **V~ung** *f* -,-en preparation
vorbestellen *vt sep* order/(*im Theater, Hotel*) book in advance
vorbestraft *a* **v~ sein** have a [criminal] record

vorbeug|en v sep ● vt bend forward; **sich v~en** bend or lean forward ● vi (haben) prevent (**etw** dat sth); **v~end** preventive. **V~ung** f - prevention

Vorbild nt model. **v~lich** a exemplary, model ● adv in an exemplary manner

vorbringen† vt sep put forward; offer ⟨Entschuldigung⟩

vordatieren vt sep post-date

Vorder|bein nt foreleg. **v~e(r,s)** a front. **V~grund** m foreground. **V~mann** m (pl **-männer**) person in front; **auf V~mann bringen** (fam) lick into shape; (aufräumen) tidy up. **V~rad** nt front wheel. **V~seite** f front; (einer Münze) obverse. **v~ste(r,s)** a front, first. **V~teil** nt front

vor|drängeln (sich) vr sep (fam) jump the queue. **v~drängen (sich)** vr sep push forward. **v~dringen**† vi sep (sein) advance

vor|ehelich a pre-marital. **v~eilig** a rash, adv -ly

voreingenommen a biased, prejudiced. **V~heit** f - bias

vorenthalten† vt sep withhold

vorerst adv for the time being

Vorfahr m **-en,-en** ancestor

vorfahren† vi sep (sein) drive up; (vorwärts-) move forward; (voraus-) drive on ahead

Vorfahrt f right of way; **'V~ beachten'** 'give way'. **V~sstraße** f ≈ major road

Vorfall m incident. **v~en**† vi sep (sein) happen

vorfinden† vt sep find

Vorfreude f [happy] anticipation

vorführ|en vt sep present, show; (demonstrieren) demonstrate; (aufführen) perform. **V~ung** f presentation; demonstration; performance

Vor|gabe f (Sport) handicap. **V~gang** m occurrence; (Techn) process. **V~gänger(in)** m **-s,-** (f **-,-nen**) predecessor. **V~garten** m front garden

vorgeben† vt sep pretend

vor|gefaßt a preconceived. **v~gefertigt** a prefabricated

vorgehen† vi sep (sein) go forward; (voraus-) go on ahead; ⟨Uhr:⟩ be fast; (wichtig sein) take precedence; (verfahren) act, proceed; (geschehen) happen, go on. **V~** nt **-s** action

vor|geschichtlich a prehistoric. **V~geschmack** m foretaste. **V~gesetzte(r)** m/f superior. **v~gestern** adv the day before yesterday

vorhaben† vt sep propose, intend (**zu** to); **etw v~** have sth planned; **nichts v~** have no plans. **V~** nt **-s,-** plan; (Projekt) project

vorhalt|en† v sep ● vt hold up; **jdm etw v~en** reproach s.o. for sth ● vi (haben) last. **V~ungen** fpl **jdm V~ungen machen** reproach s.o. (**wegen** for)

Vorhand f (Sport) forehand

vorhanden a existing; **v~ sein** exist; (verfügbar sein) be available. **V~sein** nt **-s** existence

Vorhang m curtain

Vorhängeschloß nt padlock

vorher adv before[hand]

vorhergehend a previous

vorherig a prior; (vorhergehend) previous

Vorherrsch|aft f supremacy. **v~en** vi sep (haben) predominate. **v~end** a predominant

Vorher|sage f **-,-n** prediction; (Wetter-) forecast. **v~sagen** vt sep predict; forecast ⟨Wetter⟩. **v~sehen**† vt sep foresee

vorhin adv just now

vorige(r,s) a last, previous

Vor|kämpfer m (fig) champion. **V~kehrungen** fpl precautions. **V~kenntnisse** fpl previous knowledge sg

vorkommen† vi sep (sein) happen; (vorhanden sein) occur; (nach vorn kommen) come forward; (hervorkommen) come out; (zu sehen sein) show; **jdm bekannt/verdächtig v~** seem familiar/suspicious to s.o.; **sich** (dat) **dumm/alt v~** feel stupid/old. **V~** nt **-s,-** occurrence; (Geol) deposit

Vorkriegszeit f pre-war period

vorlad|en† vt sep (Jur) summons. **V~ung** f summons

Vorlage f model; (Muster) pattern; (Gesetzes-) bill

vorlassen† vt sep admit; **jdn v~** (fam) let s.o. pass; (den Vortritt lassen) let s.o. go first

Vor|lauf m (Sport) heat. **V~läufer** m forerunner. **V~läufig** a provisional, adv -ly; (zunächst) for the time being. **v~laut** a forward. **V~leben** nt past

vorleg|en vt sep put on ⟨Kette⟩; (unterbreiten) present; (vorzeigen)

show; **jdm Fleisch v~en** serve s.o. with meat. **V~er** *m* **-s,-** mat; (*Bett-*) rug
vorles|en† *vt sep* read [out]; **jdm v~en** read to s.o. **V~ung** *f* lecture
vorletzt|e(r,s) *a* last ... but one; ⟨*Silbe*⟩ penultimate; **v~es Jahr** the year before last
Vorliebe *f* preference
vorliebnehmen† *vt sep* make do (**mit** with)
vorliegen† *vi sep* (*haben*) be present/(*verfügbar*) available; (*bestehen*) exist, be; **es muß ein Irrtum v~** there must be some mistake. **v~d** *a* present; ⟨*Frage*⟩ at issue
vorlügen† *vt sep* lie (*dat* to)
vorm *prep* = **vor dem**
vormachen *vt sep* put up; put on ⟨*Kette*⟩; push ⟨*Riegel*⟩; (*zeigen*) demonstrate; **jdm etwas v~** (*fam: täuschen*) kid s.o.
Vormacht *f* supremacy
vormals *adv* formerly
Vormarsch *m* (*Mil & fig*) advance
vormerken *vt sep* make a note of; (*reservieren*) reserve
Vormittag *m* morning. **v~** *adv* **gestern/heute v~** yesterday/this morning. **v~s** *adv* in the morning
Vormund *m* **-[e]s,-munde** & **-münder** guardian
vorn *adv* at the front; **nach v~** to the front; **von v~** from the front/(*vom Anfang*) beginning; **von v~ anfangen** start afresh
Vorname *m* first name
vorne *adv* = **vorn**
vornehm *a* distinguished; (*elegant*) smart, *adv* -ly
vornehmen† *vt sep* carry out; **sich** (*dat*) **v~, etw zu tun** plan/(*beschließen*) resolve to do sth
vorn|herein *adv* **von v~herein** from the start. **v~über** *adv* forward
Vor|ort *m* suburb. **V~rang** *m* priority, precedence (**vor** + *dat* over). **V~rat** *m* **-[e]s,-e** supply, stock (**an** + *dat* of). **v~rätig** *a* available; **v~rätig haben** have in stock. **V~ratskammer** *f* larder. **V~raum** *m* anteroom. **V~recht** *nt* privilege. **V~richtung** *f* device
vorrücken *vt/i sep* (*sein*) move forward; (*Mil*) advance
Vorrunde *f* qualifying round
vors *prep* = **vor das**
vorsagen *vt/i sep* (*haben*) recite; **jdm [die Antwort] v~** tell s.o. the answer

Vor|satz *m* resolution. **v~sätzlich** *a* deliberate, *adv* -ly; (*Jur*) premeditated
Vorschau *f* preview; (*Film-*) trailer
Vorschein *m* **zum V~ kommen** appear
vorschießen† *vt sep* advance ⟨*Geld*⟩
Vorschlag *m* suggestion, proposal. **v~en**† *vt sep* suggest, propose
vorschnell *a* rash, *adv* -ly
vorschreiben† *vt sep* lay down; dictate (*dat* to); **vorgeschriebene Dosis** prescribed dose
Vorschrift *f* regulation; (*Anweisung*) instruction; **jdm v~en machen** tell s.o. what to do; **Dienst nach V~** work to rule. **v~smäßig** *a* correct, *adv* -ly
Vorschule *f* nursery school
Vorschuß *m* advance
vorschützen *vt sep* plead [as an excuse]; feign ⟨*Krankheit*⟩
vorseh|en† *v sep* ● *vt* intend (**für/als** for/as); (*planen*) plan; **sich v~en** be careful (**vor** + *dat* of) ● *vi* (*haben*) peep out. **V~ung** *f* - providence
vorsetzen *vt sep* move forward; **jdm etw v~** serve s.o. sth
Vorsicht *f* - care; (*bei Gefahr*) caution; **V~!** careful! (*auf Schild*) 'caution'. **v~ig** *a* careful, *adv* -ly; cautious, *adv* -ly. **v~shalber** *adv* to be on the safe side. **V~smaßnahme** *f* precaution
Vorsilbe *f* prefix
Vorsitz *m* chairmanship; **den V~ führen** be in the chair. **v~en**† *vi sep* (*haben*) preside (*dat* over). **V~ende(r)** *m/f* chairman
Vorsorge *f* **V~ treffen** take precautions; make provisions (**für** for). **v~n** *vi sep* (*haben*) provide (**für** for). **V~untersuchung** *f* check-up
vorsorglich *adv* as a precaution
Vorspeise *f* starter
Vorspiel *nt* prelude. **v~en** *v sep* ● *vt* perform/(*Mus*) play (*dat* for) ● *vi* (*haben*) audition
vorsprechen† *v sep* ● *vt* recite; (*zum Nachsagen*) say (*dat* to) ● *vi* (*haben*) (*Theat*) audition; **bei jdm v~** call on s.o.
vorspringen† *vi sep* (*sein*) jut out; **v~des Kinn** prominent chin
Vor|sprung *m* projection; (*Fels-*) ledge; (*Vorteil*) lead (**vor** + *dat* over). **V~stadt** *f* suburb. **v~städtisch** *a* suburban. **V~stand** *m* board [of

directors]; (*Vereins-*) committee; (*Partei-*) executive

vorsteh|en† *vi sep (haben)* project, protrude; **einer Abteilung v~en** be in charge of a department; **v~end** protruding; ⟨*Augen*⟩ bulging. **V~er** *m* -s,- head; ((*Gemeinde-*) chairman

vorstell|bar *a* imaginable, conceivable. **v~en** *vt sep* put forward ⟨*Bein, Uhr*⟩; (*darstellen*) represent; (*bekanntmachen*) introduce; **sich v~en** introduce oneself; (*als Bewerber*) go for an interview; **sich** (*dat*) **etw v~en** imagine sth. **V~ung** *f* introduction; (*bei Bewerbung*) interview; (*Aufführung*) performance; (*Idee*) idea; (*Phantasie*) imagination. **V~ungsgespräch** *nt* interview. **V~ungskraft** *f* imagination

Vorstoß *m* advance

Vorstrafe *f* previous conviction

Vortag *m* day before

vortäuschen *vt sep* feign, fake

Vorteil *m* advantage. **v~haft** *a* advantageous, *adv* -ly; ⟨*Kleidung, Farbe*⟩ flattering

Vortrag *m* -[e]s,"e talk; (*wissenschaftlich*) lecture; ⟨*Klavier-, Gedicht-*⟩ recital. **v~en**† *vt sep* perform; (*aufsagen*) recite; (*singen*) sing; (*darlegen*) present (*dat* to); express ⟨*Wunsch*⟩

vortrefflich *a* excellent, *adv* -ly

vortreten† *vi sep (sein)* step forward; (*hervor-*) protrude

Vortritt *m* precedence; **jdm den V~ lassen** let s.o. go first

vorüber *adv* **v~ sein** be over; **an etw** (*dat*) **v~** past sth. **v~gehen**† *vi sep (sein)* walk past; (*vergehen*) pass. **v~gehend** *a* temporary, *adv* -ily

Vor|urteil *nt* prejudice. **V~verkauf** *m* advance booking

vorverlegen *vt sep* bring forward

Vor|wahl[nummer] *f* dialling code. **V~wand** *m* -[e]s,"e pretext; (*Ausrede*) excuse

vorwärts *adv* forward[s]. **v~kommen**† *vi sep (sein)* make progress; (*fig*) get on

vorweg *adv* beforehand; (*vorn*) in front; (*voraus*) ahead. **v~nehmen**† *vt sep* anticipate

vorweisen† *vt sep* show

vorwerfen† *vt sep* throw (*dat* to); **jdm etw v~** reproach s.o. with sth; (*beschuldigen*) accuse s.o. of sth

vorwiegend *adv* predominantly

Vorwort *nt* (*pl* **-worte**) preface

Vorwurf *m* reproach; **jdm Vorwürfe machen** reproach s.o. **v~svoll** *a* reproachful, *adv* -ly

Vorzeichen *nt* sign; (*fig*) omen

vorzeigen *vt sep* show

vorzeitig *a* premature, *adv* -ly

vorziehen† *vt sep* pull forward; draw ⟨*Vorhang*⟩; (*vorverlegen*) bring forward; (*lieber mögen*) prefer; (*bevorzugen*) favour

Vor|zimmer *nt* ante-room; (*Büro*) outer office. **V~zug** *m* preference; (*gute Eigenschaft*) merit, virtue; (*Vorteil*) advantage

vorzüglich *a* excellent, *adv* -ly

vorzugsweise *adv* preferably

vulgär /vʊlˈgɛːɐ̯/ *a* vulgar ● *adv* in a vulgar way

Vulkan /vʊlˈkaːn/ *m* -s,-e volcano

W

Waage *f* -,-n scales *pl*; (*Astr*) Libra. **w~recht** *a* horizontal, *adv* -ly

Wabe *f* -,-n honeycomb

wach *a* awake; (*aufgeweckt*) alert; **w~ werden** wake up

Wach|e *f* -,-n guard; (*Posten*) sentry; (*Dienst*) guard duty; (*Naut*) watch; (*Polizei-*) station; **W~e halten** keep watch; **W~e stehen** stand guard. **w~en** *vi (haben)* be awake; **w~en über** (+ *acc*) watch over. **W~hund** *m* guard-dog

Wacholder *m* -s juniper

Wachposten *m* sentry

Wachs *nt* -es wax

wachsam *a* vigilant, *adv* -ly. **W~keit** *f* - vigilance

wachsen¹† *vi (sein)* grow

wachsen² *vt (reg)* wax. **W~figur** *f* waxwork. **W~tuch** *nt* oilcloth

Wachstum *nt* -s growth

Wächter *m* -s,- guard; (*Park-*) keeper; (*Parkplatz-*) attendant

Wacht|meister *m* [police] constable. **W~posten** *m* sentry

Wachturm *m* watch-tower

wackel|ig *a* wobbly; ⟨*Stuhl*⟩ rickety; ⟨*Person*⟩ shaky. **W~kontakt** *m* loose connection. **w~n** *vi (haben)* wobble; (*zittern*) shake ● *vi (sein)* totter

wacklig *a* = **wackelig**

Wade *f* -,-n (*Anat*) calf

Waffe *f* -,-n weapon; **W~n** arms

Waffel *f* -,-n waffle; (*Eis-*) wafer

Waffen|ruhe f cease-fire. **W~schein** m firearms licence. **W~stillstand** m armistice

Wagemut m daring. **w~ig** a daring, adv -ly

wagen vt risk; **es w~, etw zu tun** dare [to] do sth; **sich w~** (gehen) venture

Wagen m -s,- cart; (Eisenbahn-) carriage, coach; (Güter-) wagon; (Kinder-) pram; (Auto) car. **W~heber** m -s,- jack

Waggon /va'gõ:/ m -s,-s wagon

waghalsig a daring, adv -ly

Wagnis nt -ses,-se risk

Wahl f -,-en choice; (Pol, Admin) election; (geheime) ballot; **zweite W~** (Comm) seconds pl

wähl|en vt/i (haben) choose; (Pol, Admin) elect; (stimmen) vote; (Teleph) dial. **W~er(in)** m -s,- (f -,-nen) voter. **w~erisch** a choosy, fussy

Wahl|fach nt optional subject. **w~frei** a optional. **W~kampf** m election campaign. **W~kreis** m constituency. **W~lokal** nt polling-station. **w~los** a indiscriminate, adv -ly. **W~recht** nt [right to] vote

Wählscheibe f (Teleph) dial

Wahl|spruch m motto. **W~urne** f ballot-box

Wahn m -[e]s delusion; (Manie) mania

wähnen vt believe

Wahnsinn m madness. **w~ig** a mad, insane; (fam: unsinnig) crazy; (fam: groß) terrible; **w~ig werden** go mad ● adv (fam) terribly. **W~ige(r)** m/f maniac

wahr a true; (echt) real; **w~ werden** come true; **du kommst doch, nicht w~?** you are coming, aren't you?

wahren vt keep; (verteidigen) safeguard; **den Schein w~** keep up appearances

währen vi (haben) last

während prep (+ gen) during ● conj while; (wohingegen) whereas. **W~dessen** adv in the meantime

wahrhaben vt **etw nicht w~ wollen** refuse to admit sth

wahrhaftig adv really, truly

Wahrheit f -,-en truth. **w~sgemäß** a truthful, adv -ly

wahrnehm|bar a perceptible. **w~en†** vt sep notice; (nutzen) take advantage of; exploit (Vorteil); look after (Interessen). **W~ung** f -,-en perception

wahrsag|en v sep ● vt predict ● vi (haben) **jdm w~en** tell s.o.'s fortune. **W~erin** f -,-nen fortune-teller

wahrscheinlich a probable, adv -bly. **W~keit** f - probability

Währung f -,-en currency

Wahrzeichen nt symbol

Waise f -,-n orphan. **W~nhaus** nt orphanage. **W~nkind** nt orphan

Wal m -[e]s,-e whale

Wald m -[e]s,¨-er wood; (groß) forest. **w~ig** a wooded

Walis|er m -s,- Welshman. **w~isch** a Welsh

Wall m -[e]s,¨-e mound; (Mil) rampart

Wallfahr|er(in) m(f) pilgrim. **W~t** f pilgrimage

Walnuß f walnut

Walze f -,-n roller. **w~n** vt roll

wälzen vt roll; pore over (Bücher); mull over (Probleme); **sich w~** roll [about]; (schlaflos) toss and turn

Walzer m -s,- waltz

Wand f -,¨-e wall; (Trenn-) partition; (Seite) side; (Fels-) face

Wandel m -s change. **w~bar** a changeable. **w~n** vi (sein) stroll ● vr **sich w~n** change

Wander|er m -s,-, **W~in** f -,-nen hiker, rambler. **w~n** vi (sein) hike, ramble; (ziehen) travel; (gemächlich gehen) wander; (ziellos) roam. **W~schaft** f - travels pl. **W~ung** f -,-en hike, ramble; (länger) walking tour. **W~weg** m footpath

Wandgemälde nt mural

Wandlung f -,-en change, transformation

Wand|malerei f mural. **W~tafel** f blackboard. **W~teppich** m tapestry

Wange f -,-n cheek

wank|elmütig a fickle. **w~en** vi (haben) sway; (Person:) stagger; (fig) waver ● vi (sein) stagger

wann adv when

Wanne f -,-n tub

Wanze f -,-n bug

Wappen nt -s,- coat of arms. **W~kunde** f heraldry

war, wäre s. **sein**[1]

Ware f -,-n article; (Comm) commodity; (coll) merchandise; **W~n** goods. **W~nhaus** nt department store. **W~nprobe** f sample. **W~nzeichen** nt trademark

warm a (wärmer, wärmst) warm; (Mahlzeit) hot; **w~ machen** heat ● adv warmly; **w~ essen** have a hot meal

Wärm|e f - warmth; (Phys) heat; **10 Grad W~e** 10 degrees above zero. **w~en** vt warm; heat ⟨Essen, Wasser⟩. **W~flasche** f hot-water bottle

warmherzig a warm-hearted

Warn|blinkanlage f hazard [warning] lights pl. **w~en** vt/i (haben) warn (**vor**+ dat of). **W~ung** f -,-en warning

Warteliste f waiting list

warten vi (haben) wait (**auf**+ acc for); **auf sich** (acc) **w~ lassen** take one's/ its time ● vt service

Wärter(in) m -s,- (f -,-nen) keeper; (Museums-) attendant; (Gefängnis-) warder, (Amer) guard; (Kranken-) orderly

Warte|raum, W~saal m waiting-room. **W~zimmer** nt (Med) waiting-room

Wartung f - (Techn) service

warum adv why

Warze f -,-n wart

was pron what; **was für [ein]?** what kind of [a]? **was für ein Pech!** what bad luck! **das gefällt dir, was?** you like that, don't you? ● rel pron what; **alles, was ich brauche** all [that] I need ● indef pron (fam: etwas) something; (fragend, verneint) anything; **was zu essen** something to eat; **so was Ärgerliches!** what a nuisance! ● adv (fam) (warum) why; (wie) how

wasch|bar a washable. **W~becken** nt wash-basin. **W~beutel** m sponge-bag

Wäsche f - washing; (Unter-) underwear; **in der W~** in the wash

waschecht a colour-fast; (fam) genuine

Wäsche|klammer f clothes-peg. **W~leine** f clothes-line

waschen† vt wash; **sich w~** have a wash; **sich** (dat) **die Hände w~** wash one's hands; **W~ und Legen** shampoo and set ● vi (haben) do the washing

Wäscherei f -,-en laundry

Wäsche|schleuder f spin-drier. **W~trockner** m tumble-drier

Wasch|küche f laundry-room. **W~lappen** m face-flannel, (Amer) washcloth; (fam: Feigling) sissy. **W~maschine** f washing machine. **W~mittel** nt detergent. **W~pulver** nt washing-powder. **W~raum** m wash-room. **W~salon** m launderette. **W~zettel** m blurb

Wasser nt -s water; (Haar-) lotion; **ins W~ fallen** (fam) fall through; **mir lief das W~ im Mund zusammen** my mouth was watering. **W~ball** m beach-ball; (Spiel) water polo. **w~dicht** a watertight; ⟨Kleidung⟩ waterproof. **W~fall** m waterfall. **W~farbe** f watercolour. **W~hahn** m tap, (Amer) faucet. **W~kasten** m cistern. **W~kraft** f water-power. **W~kraftwerk** nt hydroelectric power-station. **W~leitung** f watermain; **aus der W~leitung** from the tap. **W~mann** m (Astr) Aquarius

wässern vt soak; (begießen) water ● vi (haben) water

Wasser|scheide f watershed. **W~ski** nt -s water-skiing. **W~stoff** m hydrogen. **W~straße** f waterway. **W~waage** f spirit-level. **W~werfer** m -s,- water-cannon. **W~zeichen** nt watermark

wäßrig a watery

waten vi (sein) wade

watscheln vi (sein) waddle

Watt¹ nt -[e]s mud-flats pl

Watt² nt -s,- (Phys) watt

Watt|e f - cotton wool. **w~iert** a padded; (gesteppt) quilted

WC /ve'tse:/ nt -s,-s WC

web|en vt/i (haben) weave. **W~er** m -s,- weaver. **W~stuhl** m loom

Wechsel m -s,- change; (Tausch) exchange; (Comm) bill of exchange. **W~geld** nt change. **w~haft** a changeable. **W~jahre** npl menopause sg. **W~kurs** m exchange rate. **w~n** vt change; (tauschen) exchange ● vi (haben) change; (ab-) alternate; (verschieden sein) vary. **w~nd** a changing; (verschieden) varying. **w~seitig** a mutual, adv -ly. **W~strom** m alternating current. **W~stube** f bureau de change. **w~weise** adv alternately. **W~wirkung** f interaction

weck|en vt wake [up]; (fig) awaken ● vi (haben) ⟨Wecker:⟩ go off. **W~er** m -s,- alarm [clock]

wedeln vi (haben) wave; **mit dem Schwanz w~** wag its tail

weder conj **w~ ... noch** neither ... nor

Weg m -[e]s,-e way; (Fuß-) path; (Fahr-) track; (Gang) errand; **auf dem Weg** on the way (**nach** to); **sich auf den Weg machen** set off; **im Weg sein** be in the way

weg *adv* away, off; (*verschwunden*) gone; **weg sein** be away; (*gegangen/verschwunden*) have gone; (*fam: schlafen*) be asleep; **Hände weg!** hands off! **w~bleiben**† *vi sep (sein)* stay away. **w~bringen**† *vt sep* take away.

wegen *prep* (+ *gen*) because of; (*um … willen*) for the sake of; (*bezüglich*) about

weg|fahren† *vi sep (sein)* go away; (*abfahren*) leave. **w~fallen**† *vi sep (sein)* be dropped/(*ausgelassen*) omitted; (*entfallen*) no longer apply; (*aufhören*) cease. **w~geben**† *vt sep* give away; send to the laundry (*Wäsche*). **w~gehen**† *vi sep (sein)* leave, go away; (*ausgehen*) go out; ⟨*Fleck:*⟩ come out. **w~jagen** *vt sep* chase away. **w~kommen**† *vi sep (sein)* get away; (*verlorengehen*) disappear. **w~lassen**† *vt sep* let go; (*auslassen*) omit. **w~laufen**† *vi sep (sein)* run away. **w~machen** *vt sep* remove. **w~nehmen**† *vt sep* take away. **w~räumen** *vt sep* put away; (*entfernen*) clear away. **w~schicken**† *vt sep* send away; (*abschicken*) send off. **w~tun**† *vt sep* put away; (*wegwerfen*) throw away

Wegweiser *m* **-s,-** signpost

weg|werfen† *vt sep* throw away. **w~ziehen**† *v sep* ● *vt* pull away ● *vi (sein)* move away

weh *a* sore; **weh tun** hurt; ⟨*Kopf, Rücken:*⟩ **jdm weh tun** hurt s.o. ● *int* **oh weh!** oh dear!

wehe *int* alas; **w~ [dir/euch]!** (*drohend*) don't you dare!

wehen *vi (haben)* blow; (*flattern*) flutter ● *vt* blow

Wehen *fpl* contractions; **in den W~ liegen** be in labour

weh|leidig *a* soft; (*weinerlich*) whining. **W~mut** *f* - wistfulness. **w~mutig** *a* wistful, *adv* -ly

Wehr[1] *nt* **-[e]s,-e** weir

Wehr[2] *f* **sich zur W~ setzen** resist. **W~dienst** *m* military service. **W~dienstverweigerer** *m* **-s,-** conscientious objector

wehren (sich) *vr* resist; (*gegen Anschuldigung*) protest; (*sich sträuben*) refuse

wehr|los *a* defenceless. **W~macht** *f* armed forces *pl*. **W~pflicht** *f* conscription

Weib *nt* **-[e]s,-er** woman; (*Ehe-*) wife. **W~chen** *nt* **-s,-** (*Zool*) female.

W~erheld *m* womanizer. **w~isch** *a* effeminate. **w~lich** *a* feminine; (*Biol*) female. **W~lichkeit** *f* - femininity

weich *a* soft, *adv* -ly; (*gar*) done; ⟨*Ei*⟩ soft-boiled; ⟨*Mensch*⟩ soft-hearted; **w~ werden** (*fig*) relent

Weiche *f* **-,-n** (*Rail*) points *pl*

weichen[1] *vi (sein) (reg)* soak

weichen[2] *vi (sein)* give way (*dat* to); **nicht von jds Seite w~** not leave s.o.'s side

Weich|heit *f* - softness. **w~herzig** *a* soft-hearted. **w~lich** *a* soft; ⟨*Charakter*⟩ weak. **W~spüler** *m* **-s,-** (*Tex*) conditioner. **W~tier** *nt* mollusc

Weide[1] *f* **-,-n** (*Bot*) willow

Weide[2] *f* **-,-n** pasture. **w~n** *vt/i (haben)* graze; **sich w~n an** (+ *dat*) enjoy; (*schadenfroh*) gloat over

weiger|n (sich) *vr* refuse. **W~ung** *f* **-,-en** refusal

Weihe *f* **-,-n** consecration; (*Priester-*) ordination. **w~n** *vt* consecrate; (*zum Priester*) ordain; dedicate ⟨*Kirche*⟩ (*dat* to)

Weiher *m* **-s,-** pond

Weihnacht|en *nt* **-s** ● *pl* Christmas. **w~lich** *a* Christmassy. **W~sbaum** *m* Christmas tree. **W~sfest** *nt* Christmas. **W~slied** *nt* Christmas carol. **W~smann** *m* (*pl* **-männer**) Father Christmas. **W~stag** *m* **erster/zweiter W~stag** Christmas Day/ Boxing Day

Weih|rauch *m* incense. **W~wasser** *nt* holy water

weil *conj* because; (*da*) since

Weile *f* - while

Wein *m* **-[e]s,-e** wine; (*Bot*) vines *pl*; (*Trauben*) grapes *pl*. **W~bau** *m* wine-growing. **W~beere** *f* grape. **W~berg** *m* vineyard. **W~brand** *m* **-[e]s** brandy

wein|en *vt/i (haben)* cry, weep. **w~erlich** *a* tearful, *adv* -ly

Wein|glas *nt* wineglass. **W~karte** *f* wine-list. **W~keller** *m* wine-cellar. **W~lese** *f* grape harvest. **W~liste** *f* wine-list. **W~probe** *f* wine-tasting. **W~rebe** *f*, **W~stock** *m* vine. **W~stube** *f* wine-bar. **W~traube** *f* bunch of grapes; (*W~beere*) grape

weise *a* wise, *adv* -ly

Weise *f* **-,-n** way; (*Melodie*) tune; **auf diese W~** in this way

weisen† *vt* show; **von sich w~** (*fig*) reject ● *vi (haben)* point (**auf** + *acc* at)

Weisheit f -,-en wisdom. **W~zahn** m wisdom tooth

weiß a, **W~**nt -,- white

weissag|en vt/i insep (haben) prophesy. **W~ung** f -,-en prophecy

Weiß|brot nt white bread. **W~e(r)** m/f white man/woman. **w~en** vt whitewash. **W~wein** m white wine

Weisung f -,-en instruction; (Befehl) order

weit a wide; (ausgedehnt) extensive; (lang) long ● adv widely; (offen, öffnen) wide; (lang) far; **von w~em** from a distance; **bei w~em** by far; **w~ und breit** far and wide; **ist es noch w~?** is it much further? **ich bin so w~** I'm ready; **zu w~ gehen** (fig) go too far. **w~aus** adv far. **W~blick** m (fig) far-sightedness. **w~blickend** a (fig) far-sighted

Weite f -,-n expanse; (Entfernung) distance; (Größe) width. **w~n** vt widen; stretch (Schuhe); **sich w~n** widen; stretch; (Pupille) dilate

weiter a further ● adv further; (außerdem) in addition; (anschließend) then; **etw w~ tun** go on doing sth; **w~ nichts/niemand** nothing/no one else; **und so w~** and so on. **w~arbeiten** vi sep (haben) go on working

weiter|e(r,s) a further; **im w~en Sinne** in a wider sense; **ohne w~es** just like that; (leicht) easily; **bis auf w~es** until further notice; (vorläufig) for the time being

weiter|erzählen vt sep go on with; (w~sagen) repeat. **w~fahren**† vi sep (sein) go on. **w~geben**† vt sep pass on. **w~gehen**† vi sep (sein) go on. **w~hin** adv (immer noch) still; (in Zukunft) in future; (außerdem) furthermore; **etw w~hin tun** go on doing sth. **w~kommen**† vi sep (sein) get on. **w~machen** vi sep (haben) carry on. **w~sagen** vt sep pass on; (verraten) repeat

weit|gehend a extensive ● adv to a large extent. **w~hin** adv a long way; (fig) widely. **w~läufig** a spacious; (entfernt) distant, adv -ly; (ausführlich) lengthy, adv at length. **w~reichend** a far-reaching. **w~schweifig** a long-winded. **w~sichtig** a long-sighted; (fig) far-sighted. **W~sprung** m long jump. **w~verbreitet** a widespread

Weizen m -s wheat

welch inv pron what; **w~ ein(e)** what a. **w~e(r,s)** pron which; **um w~e Zeit?** at what time? ● rel pron which; (Person) who ● indef pron some; (fragend) any; **was für w~e?** what sort of?

welk a wilted; (Laub) dead. **w~en** vi (haben) wilt; (fig) fade

Wellblech nt corrugated iron

Well|e f -,-n wave; (Techn) shaft. **W~enlänge** f wavelength. **W~enlinie** f wavy line. **W~enreiten** nt surfing. **W~ensittich** m -s,-e budgerigar. **w~ig** a wavy

Welt f -,-en world; **auf der W~** in the world; **auf die** od **zur W~ kommen** be born. **W~all** nt universe. **w~berühmt** a world-famous. **w~fremd** a unworldly. **w~gewandt** a sophisticated. **W~kugel** f globe. **w~lich** a worldly; (nicht geistlich) secular

Weltmeister|(in) m(f) world champion. **W~schaft** f world championship

Weltraum m space. **W~fahrer** m astronaut

Welt|rekord m world record. **w~weit** a & adv world-wide

wem pron (dat of wer) to whom

wen pron (acc of wer) whom

Wende f -,-n change. **W~kreis** m (Geog) tropic

Wendeltreppe f spiral staircase

wenden[1] vt (reg) turn; **sich zum Guten w~** take a turn for the better ● vi (haben) turn [round]

wenden[2]† (& reg) vt turn; **sich w~** turn; **sich an jdn w~** turn/(schriftlich) write to s.o.

Wend|epunkt m (fig) turning-point. **w~ig** a nimble; (Auto) manœuvrable. **W~ung** f -,-en turn; (Biegung) bend; (Veränderung) change

wenig pron little; (pl) few; **w~e** pl few ● adv little; (kaum) not much. **w~er** pron less; (pl) fewer; **immer w~er** less and less ● adv & conj less. **w~ste(r,s)** least; **am w~sten** least [of all]. **w~stens** adv at least

wenn conj if; (sobald) when; **immer w~** whenever; **w~ nicht** od **außer w~** unless; **w~ auch** even though

wer pron who; (fam: jemand) someone; (fragend) anyone; **ist da wer?** is anyone there?

Werbe|agentur f advertising agency. **w~n**† vt recruit; attract

⟨*Kunden, Besucher*⟩ ● *vi (haben)*
w∼n für advertise; canvass for
⟨*Partei*⟩; **w∼n um** try to attract ⟨*Besucher*⟩; court ⟨*Frau, Gunst*⟩.
W∼spot /-sp-/ *m* **-s,-s** commercial
Werbung *f* - advertising
werden† *vi (sein)* become; ⟨*müde, alt, länger*⟩ get, grow; ⟨*blind, wahnsinnig*⟩ go; **blaß w∼** turn pale; **krank w∼** fall ill; **es wird warm/dunkel** it is getting warm/dark; **mir wurde schlecht/schwindlig** I felt sick/dizzy; **er will Lehrer w∼** he wants to be a teacher; **was ist aus ihm geworden?** what has become of him? ● *v aux* ⟨*Zukunft*⟩ shall; **wir w∼ sehen** we shall see; **es wird bald regnen** it's going to rain soon; **würden Sie so nett sein?** would you be so kind? ● ⟨*Passiv; pp* **worden**⟩ be; **geliebt/geboren w∼** be loved/born; **es wurde gemunkelt** it was rumoured
werfen† *vt* throw; cast ⟨*Blick, Schatten*⟩; **sich w∼** ⟨*Holz:*⟩ warp ● *vi (haben)* **mit** throw
Werft *f* **-,-en** shipyard
Werk *nt* **-[e]s,-e** work; ⟨*Fabrik*⟩ works *sg*, factory; ⟨*Trieb-*⟩ mechanism. **W∼en** *nt* **-s** ⟨*Sch*⟩ handicraft. **W∼statt** *f* **-,-ˈen** workshop; ⟨*Auto-*⟩ garage; ⟨*Künstler-*⟩ studio. **W∼tag** *m* weekday. **w∼tags** *adv* on weekdays. **w∼tätig** *a* working. **W∼unterricht** *m* ⟨*Sch*⟩ handicraft
Werkzeug *nt* tool; ⟨*coll*⟩ tools *pl*. **W∼maschine** *f* machine tool
Wermut *m* **-s** vermouth
wert *a* **viel/50 Mark w∼** worth a lot/50 marks; **nichts w∼ sein** be worthless; **jds/etw** ⟨*gen*⟩ **w∼ sein** be worthy of s.o./sth. **W∼** *m* **-[e]s,-e** value; ⟨*Nenn-*⟩ denomination; **im W∼ von** worth; **W∼ legen auf** (+ *acc*) set great store by. **w∼en** *vt* rate
Wert|gegenstand *m* object of value; **W∼gegenstände** valuables. **w∼los** *a* worthless. **W∼minderung** *f* depreciation. **W∼papier** *nt* ⟨*Comm*⟩ security. **W∼sachen** *fpl* valuables. **w∼voll** *a* valuable
Wesen *nt* **-s,-** nature; ⟨*Lebe-*⟩ being; ⟨*Mensch*⟩ creature
wesentlich *a* essential; ⟨*grundlegend*⟩ fundamental; ⟨*erheblich*⟩ considerable; **im w∼en** essentially ● *adv* considerably, much
weshalb *adv* why
Wespe *f* **-,-n** wasp

wessen *pron* ⟨*gen of* **wer**⟩ whose
westdeutsch *a* West German
Weste *f* **-,-n** waistcoat, ⟨*Amer*⟩ vest
Westen *m* **-s** west; **nach W∼** west
Western *m* **-[s],-** western
Westfalen *nt* **-s** Westphalia
Westindien *nt* West Indies *pl*
west|lich *a* western; ⟨*Richtung*⟩ westerly ● *adv* & *prep* (+ *gen*) **w∼lich [von] der Stadt** [to the] west of the town. **w∼wärts** *adv* westwards
weswegen *adv* why
wett *a* **w∼ sein** be quits
Wett|bewerb *m* **-s,-e** competition. **W∼büro** *nt* betting shop
Wette *f* **-,-n** bet; **um die W∼ laufen** race ⟨**mit jdm** s.o.⟩
wetteifern *vi (haben)* compete
wetten *vt/i (haben)* bet ⟨**auf** + *acc* on⟩; **mit jdm w∼** have a bet with s.o.
Wetter *nt* **-s,-** weather; ⟨*Un-*⟩ storm. **W∼bericht** *m* weather report. **W∼hahn** *m* weathercock. **W∼lage** *f* weather conditions *pl*. **W∼vorhersage** *f* weather forecast. **W∼warte** *f* **-,-n** meteorological station
Wett|kampf *m* contest. **W∼kämpfer(in)** *m(f)* competitor. **W∼lauf** *m* race. **w∼machen** *vt sep* make up for. **W∼rennen** *nt* race. **W∼streit** *m* contest
wetzen *vt* sharpen ● *vi (sein)* ⟨*fam*⟩ dash
Whisky *m* **-s** whisky
wichsen *vt* polish
wichtig *a* important; **w∼ nehmen** take seriously. **W∼keit** *f* - importance. **w∼tuerisch** *a* self-important
Wicke *f* **-,-n** sweet pea
Wickel *m* **-s,-** compress
wick|eln *vt* wind; ⟨*ein-*⟩ wrap; ⟨*bandagieren*⟩ bandage; **ein Kind frisch w∼eln** change a baby. **W∼ler** *m* **-s,-** curler
Widder *m* **-s,-** ram; ⟨*Astr*⟩ Aries
wider *prep* (+ *acc*) against; ⟨*entgegen*⟩ contrary to; **w∼ Willen** against one's will
widerfahren† *vi insep (sein)* **jdm w∼** happen to s.o.
widerhallen *vi sep (haben)* echo
widerlegen *vt insep* refute
wider|lich *a* repulsive; ⟨*unangenehm*⟩ nasty, *adv* -ily. **W∼rechtlich** *a* unlawful, *adv* -ly. **W∼rede** *f* contradiction; **keine W∼rede!** don't argue!

widerrufen† *vt/i insep (haben)* retract; revoke ⟨*Befehl*⟩

Widersacher *m* **-s,-** adversary

widersetzen (sich) *vr insep* resist (**jdm/etw** s.o./sth)

wider|sinnig *a* absurd. **w∼spenstig** *a* unruly; (*störrisch*) stubborn

widerspiegeln *vt sep* reflect; **sich w∼** be reflected

widersprechen† *vi insep (haben)* contradict (**jdm/etw** s.o./sth)

Wider|spruch *m* contradiction; (*Protest*) protest. **w∼sprüchlich** *a* contradictory. **w∼spruchslos** *adv* without protest

Widerstand *m* resistance; **W∼ leisten** resist. **w∼sfähig** *a* resistant; (*Bot*) hardy

widerstehen† *vi insep (haben)* resist (**jdm/etw** s.o./sth); (*anwidern*) be repugnant (**jdm** to s.o.)

widerstreben *vi insep (haben)* **es widerstrebt mir** I am reluctant (**zu** to). **W∼** *nt* **-s** reluctance. **w∼d** *a* reluctant, *adv* -ly

widerwärtig *a* disagreeable, unpleasant; (*ungünstig*) adverse

Widerwill|e *m* aversion, repugnance. **w∼ig** *a* reluctant, *adv* -ly

widmen *vt* dedicate (*dat* to); (*verwenden*) devote (*dat* to); **sich w∼en** (+ *dat*) devote oneself to. **W∼ung** *f* **-,-en** dedication

widrig *a* adverse, unfavourable

wie *adv* how; **wie viele?** how many? **wie ist Ihr Name?** what is your name? **wie ist das Wetter?** what is the weather like? ● *conj* as; (*gleich wie*) like; (*sowie*) as well as; (*als*) when, as; **genau wie du** just like you; **so gut/ reich wie** as good/rich as; **nichts wie** nothing but; **größer wie ich** (*fam*) bigger than me

wieder *adv* again; **er ist w∼ da** he is back

Wiederaufbau *m* reconstruction. **w∼en** *vt sep* reconstruct

wieder|aufnehmen† *vt sep* resume. **W∼aufrüstung** *f* rearmament

wieder|bekommen† *vt sep* get back. **w∼beleben** *vt sep* revive. **W∼belebung** *f* - resuscitation. **w∼bringen**† *vt sep* bring back. **w∼erkennen**† *vt sep* recognize. **W∼gabe** *f* (*s.* **w∼geben**) return; portrayal; rendering; reproduction. **w∼geben**† *vt sep* give back, return;

(*darstellen*) portray; (*ausdrücken, übersetzen*) render; (*zitieren*) quote; (*Techn*) reproduce. **W∼geburt** *f* reincarnation

wiedergutmach|en *vt sep* (*fig*) make up for; redress ⟨*Unrecht*⟩; (*bezahlen*) pay for. **W∼ung** *f* - reparation; (*Entschädigung*) compensation

wiederher|stellen *vt sep* reestablish; restore ⟨*Gebäude*⟩; restore to health ⟨*Kranke*⟩; **w∼gestellt sein** be fully recovered. **W∼stellung** *f* re-establishment; restoration; (*Genesung*) recovery

wiederholen¹ *vt sep* get back

wiederhol|en² *vt insep* repeat; (*Sch*) revise; **sich w∼en** recur; ⟨*Person:*⟩ repeat oneself. **w∼t** *a* repeated, *adv* -ly. **W∼ung** *f* **-,-en** repetition; (*Sch*) revision

Wieder|hören *nt* **auf W∼hören!** goodbye! **W∼käuer** *m* **-s,-** ruminant. **W∼kehr** *f* - return; (*W∼holung*) recurrence. **w∼kehren** *vi sep (sein)* return; (*sich wiederholen*) recur. **w∼kommen**† *vi sep (sein)* come back

wiedersehen† *vt sep* see again. **W∼** *nt* **-s,-** reunion; **auf W∼!** goodbye!

wiederum *adv* again; (*andererseits*) on the other hand

wiedervereinig|en *vt sep* reunify ⟨*Land*⟩. **W∼ung** *f* reunification

wieder|verheiraten (sich) *vr sep* remarry. **w∼verwenden**† *vt sep* reuse. **w∼verwerten** *vt sep* recycle. **w∼wählen** *vt sep* re-elect

Wiege *f* **-,-n** cradle

wiegen¹† *vt/i (haben)* weigh

wiegen² *vt (reg)* rock; **sich w∼** sway; (*schaukeln*) rock. **W∼lied** *nt* lullaby

wiehern *vi (haben)* neigh

Wien *nt* **-s** Vienna. **W∼er** *a* Viennese; **W∼er Schnitzel** Wiener schnitzel ● *m* **-s,-** Viennese ● *f* **-,-** ≈ frankfurter. **w∼erisch** *a* Viennese

Wiese *f* **-,-n** meadow

Wiesel *nt* **-s,-** weasel

wieso *adv* why

wieviel *pron* how much/(*pl*) many; **um w∼ Uhr?** at what time? **w∼te(r,s)** *a* which; **der W∼te ist heute?** what is the date today?

wieweit *adv* how far

wild *a* wild, *adv* -ly; ⟨*Stamm*⟩ savage; **w∼er Streik** wildcat strike; **w∼ wachsen** grow wild. **W∼** *nt* **-[e]s**

game; (*Rot-*) deer; (*Culin*) venison. **W~dieb** *m* poacher. **W~e(r)** *m/f* savage
Wilder|er *m* **-s,-** poacher. **w~n** *vt/i* (*haben*) poach
wildfremd *a* totally strange; **w~e Leute** total strangers
Wild|heger, W~hüter *m* **-s,-** gamekeeper. **W~leder** *nt* suede. **w~ledern** *a* suede. **W~nis** *f* - wilderness. **W~schwein** *nt* wild boar. **W~westfilm** *m* western
Wille *m* **-ns** will; **Letzter W~** will; **seinen W~n durchsetzen** get one's [own] way; **mit W~n** intentionally
willen *prep* (+ *gen*) **um . . . w~** for the sake of . . .
Willens|kraft *f* will-power. **w~stark** *a* strong-willed
willig *a* willing, *adv* -ly
willkommen *a* welcome; **w~ heißen** welcome. **W~** *nt* **-s** welcome
willkürlich *a* arbitrary, *adv* -ily
wimmeln *vi* (*haben*) swarm
wimmern *vi* (*haben*) whimper
Wimpel *m* **-s,-** pennant
Wimper *f* **-,-n** [eye]lash; **nicht mit der W~ zucken** (*fam*) not bat an eyelid. **W~ntusche** *f* mascara
Wind *m* **-[e]s,-e** wind
Winde *f* **-,-n** (*Techn*) winch
Windel *f* **-,-n** nappy, (*Amer*) diaper
winden† *vt* wind; make (*Kranz*); **in die Höhe w~** winch up; **sich w~** wind (**um** round); (*sich krümmen*) writhe
Wind|hund *m* greyhound. **w~ig** *a* windy. **W~mühle** *f* windmill. **W~pocken** *fpl* chickenpox *sg.* **W~schutzscheibe** *f* windscreen, (*Amer*) windshield. **w~still** *a* calm. **W~stille** *f* calm. **W~stoß** *m* gust of wind. **W~surfen** *nt* windsurfing
Windung *f* **-,-en** bend; (*Spirale*) spiral
Wink *m* **-[e]s,-e** sign; (*Hinweis*) hint
Winkel *m* **-s,-** angle; (*Ecke*) corner. **W~messer** *m* **-s,-** protractor
winken *vi* (*haben*) wave; **jdm w~** wave/(*herbei~*) beckon to s.o.
winseln *vi* (*haben*) whine
Winter *m* **-s,-** winter. **w~lich** *a* wintry; (*Winter-*) winter . . . **W~schlaf** *m* hibernation; **W~schlaf halten** hibernate. **W~sport** *m* winter sports *pl*
Winzer *m* **-s,-** winegrower
winzig *a* tiny, minute
Wipfel *m* **-s,-** [tree-]top
Wippe *f* **-,-n** see-saw. **w~n** *vi* (*haben*) bounce; (*auf Wippe*) play on the seesaw

wir *pron* we; **wir sind es** it's us
Wirbel *m* **-s,-** eddy; (*Drehung*) whirl; (*Trommel-*) roll; (*Anat*) vertebra; (*Haar-*) crown; (*Aufsehen*) fuss. **w~n** *vt/i* (*sein/haben*) whirl. **W~säule** *f* spine. **W~sturm** *m* cyclone. **W~tier** *nt* vertebrate. **W~wind** *m* whirlwind
wird *s.* **werden**
wirken *vi* (*haben*) have an effect (**auf** + *acc* on); (*zur Geltung kommen*) be effective; (*tätig sein*) work; (*scheinen*) seem ● *vt* (*Tex*) knit; **Wunder w~** work miracles
wirklich *a* real, *adv* -ly. **W~keit** *f* **-,-en** reality
wirksam *a* effective, *adv* -ly. **W~keit** *f* - effectiveness
Wirkung *f* **-,-en** effect. **w~slos** *a* ineffective, *adv* -ly. **w~svoll** *a* effective, *adv* -ly
wirr *a* tangled; (*Haar*) tousled; (*verwirrt, verworren*) confused. **W~warr** *m* **-s** tangle; (*fig*) confusion; (*von Stimmen*) hubbub
Wirt *m* **-[e]s,-e** landlord. **W~in** *f* **-,-nen** landlady
Wirtschaft *f* **-,-en** economy; (*Gast-*) restaurant; (*Kneipe*) pub. **w~en** *vi* (*haben*) manage one's finances; (*sich betätigen*) busy oneself; **sie kann nicht w~en** she's a bad manager. **W~erin** *f* **-,-nen** housekeeper. **w~lich** *a* economic, *adv* -ally; (*sparsam*) economical, *adv* -ly. **W~sgeld** *nt* housekeeping [money]. **W~sprüfer** *m* auditor
Wirtshaus *nt* inn; (*Kneipe*) pub
Wisch *m* **-[e]s,-e** (*fam*) piece of paper
wisch|en *vt/i* (*haben*) wipe; wash (*Fußboden*) ● *vi* (*sein*) slip; (*Maus:*) scurry. **W~lappen** *m* cloth; (*Aufwisch-*) floor-cloth
wispern *vt/i* (*haben*) whisper
wissen† *vt/i* (*haben*) know; **weißt du noch?** do you remember? **nichts w~ wollen von** not want anything to do with. **W~** *nt* **-s** knowledge; **meines W~s** to my knowledge
Wissenschaft *f* **-,-en** science. **W~ler** *m* **-s,-** academic; (*Natur-*) scientist. **w~lich** *a* academic, *adv* -ally; scientific, *adv* -ally
wissens|wert *a* worth knowing. **w~tlich** *a* deliberate ● *adv* knowingly
witter|n *vt* scent; (*ahnen*) sense. **W~ung** *f* - scent; (*Wetter*) weather

Witwe *f* -,-n widow. **W∼r** *m* -s,- widower

Witz *m* -es,-e joke; (*Geist*) wit. **W∼bold** *m* -[e]s,-e joker. **w∼ig** *a* funny; (*geistreich*) witty

wo *adv* where; (*als*) when; (*irgendwo*) somewhere; **wo immer** wherever ● *conj* seeing that; (*obwohl*) although; (*wenn*) if

woanders *adv* somewhere else

wobei *adv* how; (*relativ*) during the course of which

Woche *f* -,-n week. **W∼nende** *nt* weekend. **W∼nkarte** *f* weekly ticket. **w∼nlang** *adv* for weeks. **W∼ntag** *m* day of the week; (*Werktag*) weekday. **w∼ntags** *adv* on weekdays

wöchentlich *a & adv* weekly

Wodka *m* -s vodka

wodurch *adv* how; (*relativ*) through/ (*Ursache*) by which; (*Folge*) as a result of which

wofür *adv* what ... for; (*relativ*) for which

Woge *f* -,-n wave

wogegen *adv* what ... against; (*relativ*) against which ● *conj* whereas. **woher** *adv* where from; **woher weißt du das?** how do you know that? **wohin** *adv* where [to]; **wohin gehst du?** where are you going? **wohingegen** *conj* whereas

wohl *adv* well; (*vermutlich*) probably; (*etwa*) about; (*zwar*) perhaps; **w∼ kaum** hardly; **w∼ oder übel** willy-nilly; **sich w∼ fühlen** feel well/ (*behaglich*) comfortable; **der ist w∼ verrückt!** he must be mad! **W∼** *nt* -[e]s welfare, well-being; **auf jds W∼ trinken** drink s.o.'s health; **zum W∼** (+*gen*) for the good of; **zum W∼!** cheers!

wohlauf *a* **w∼ sein** be well

Wohl|befinden *nt* well-being. **W∼behagen** *nt* feeling of well-being. **w∼behalten** *a* safe, *adv* -ly. **W∼ergehen** *nt* -s welfare. **w∼erzogen** *a* well brought-up

Wohlfahrt *f* - welfare. **W∼sstaat** *m* Welfare State

Wohl|gefallen *nt* -s pleasure. **W∼geruch** *m* fragrance. **w∼gesinnt** *a* well disposed (*dat* towards). **w∼habend** *a* prosperous, well-to-do. **w∼ig** *a* comfortable, *adv* -bly. **w∼klingend** *a* melodious. **w∼riechend** *a* fragrant. **w∼schmeckend** *a* tasty

Wohlstand *m* prosperity. **W∼s-gesellschaft** *f* affluent society

Wohltat *f* [act of] kindness; (*Annehmlichkeit*) treat; (*Genuß*) bliss

Wohltät|er *m* benefactor. **w∼ig** *a* charitable

wohl|tuend *a* agreeable, *adv* -bly. **w∼tun**† *vi sep* (*haben*) **jdm w∼tun** do s.o. good. **w∼verdient** *a* well-deserved. **w∼weislich** *adv* deliberately

Wohlwollen *nt* -s goodwill; (*Gunst*) favour. **w∼d** *a* benevolent, *adv* -ly

Wohn|anhänger *m* = **Wohnwagen**. **W∼block** *m* block of flats. **w∼en** *vi* (*haben*) live; (*vorübergehend*) stay. **W∼gegend** *f* residential area. **w∼haft** *a* resident. **W∼haus** *nt* [dwelling-]house. **W∼heim** *nt* hostel; (*Alten-*) home. **w∼lich** *a* comfortable, *adv* -bly. **W∼mobil** *nt* -s,-e camper. **W∼ort** *m* place of residence. **W∼raum** *m* living space; (*Zimmer*) living-room. **W∼sitz** *m* place of residence

Wohnung *f* -,-en flat, (*Amer*) apartment; (*Unterkunft*) accommodation. **W∼snot** *f* housing shortage

Wohn|wagen *m* caravan, (*Amer*) trailer. **W∼zimmer** *nt* living-room

wölb|en *vt* curve; arch ⟨*Rücken*⟩. **W∼ung** *f* -,-en curve; (*Archit*) vault

Wolf *m* -[e]s,¨e wolf; (*Fleisch-*) mincer; (*Reiß-*) shredder

Wolk|e *f* -,-n cloud. **W∼enbruch** *m* cloudburst. **W∼enkratzer** *m* sky-scraper. **w∼enlos** *a* cloudless. **w∼ig** *a* cloudy

Woll|decke *f* blanket. **W∼e** *f* -,-n wool

wollen¹† *vt/i* (*haben*) & *v aux* want; **etw tun w∼** want to do sth; (*beabsichtigen*) be going to do sth; **ich will nach Hause** I want to go home; **wir wollten gerade gehen** we were just going; **ich wollte, ich könnte dir helfen** I wish I could help you; **der Motor will nicht anspringen** the engine won't start

woll|en² *a* woollen. **w∼ig** *a* woolly. **W∼sachen** *fpl* woollens

wollüstig *a* sensual, *adv* -ly

womit *adv* what ... with; (*relativ*) with which. **womöglich** *adv* possibly. **wonach** *adv* what ... after/⟨*suchen*⟩ for/⟨*riechen*⟩ of; (*relativ*) after/ for/of which

Wonn|e f -,-n bliss; (*Freude*) joy.
w~ig a sweet

woran adv what ... on/⟨*denken, sterben*⟩ of; (*relativ*) on/of which; **woran hast du ihn erkannt?** how did you recognize him? **worauf** adv what ... on/⟨*warten*⟩ for; (*relativ*) on/for which; (*woraufhin*) whereupon.

woraufhin adv whereupon. **woraus** adv what ... from; (*relativ*) from which. **worin** adv what ... in; (*relativ*) in which

Wort nt -[e]s,"er & -e word; **jdm ins W~ fallen** interrupt s.o.; **ein paar W~e sagen** say a few words. **w~brüchig** a **w~brüchig werden** break one's word

Wörterbuch nt dictionary

Wort|führer m spokesman. **w~getreu** a & adv word-for-word. **w~gewandt** a eloquent, adv -ly. **w~karg** a taciturn. **W~laut** m wording

wörtlich a literal, adv -ly; (*wortgetreu*) word-for-word

wort|los a silent ● adv without a word. **W~schatz** m vocabulary. **W~spiel** nt pun, play on words. **W~wechsel** m exchange of words; (*Streit*) argument. **w~wörtlich** a & adv = **wörtlich**

worüber adv what ... over/⟨*lachen, sprechen*⟩ about; (*relativ*) over/about which. **worum** adv what ... round/⟨*bitten, kämpfen*⟩ for; (*relativ*) round/for which; **worum geht es?** what is it about? **worunter** adv what ... under/⟨*wozwischen*⟩ among; (*relativ*) under/among which. **wovon** adv what ... from/⟨*sprechen*⟩ about; (*relativ*) from/about which. **wovor** adv what ... in front of; ⟨*sich fürchten*⟩ what ... of; (*relativ*) in front of/what of which. **wozu** adv what ... to/⟨*brauchen, benutzen*⟩ for; (*relativ*) to/for which; **wozu?** what for?

Wrack nt -s,-s wreck

wringen† vt wring

wucher|n vi (haben/sein) grow profusely. **W~preis** m extortionate price. **W~ung** f -,-en growth

Wuchs m -es growth; (*Gestalt*) stature

Wucht f - force. **w~en** vt heave. **w~ig** a massive

wühlen vi (haben) rummage; (*in der Erde*) burrow ● vt dig

Wulst m -[e]s,"e bulge; (*Fett-*) roll. **w~ig** a bulging; ⟨*Lippen*⟩ thick

wund a sore; **w~ reiben** chafe. **W~brand** m gangrene

Wunde f -,-n wound

Wunder nt -s,- wonder, marvel; (*übernatürliches*) miracle; **kein W~!** no wonder! **w~bar** a miraculous; (*herrlich*) wonderful, adv -ly, marvellous, adv -ly. **W~kind** nt infant prodigy. **w~lich** a odd, adv -ly. **w~n** vt surprise; **sich w~n** be surprised (**über** + acc at). **w~schön** a beautiful, adv -ly. **w~voll** a wonderful, adv -ly

Wundstarrkrampf m tetanus

Wunsch m -[e]s,"e wish; (*Verlangen*) desire; (*Bitte*) request

wünschen vt want; **sich** (*dat*) **etw w~** want sth; (*bitten um*) ask for sth; **jdm Glück/gute Nacht w~** wish s.o. luck/good night; **ich wünschte, ich könnte ...** I wish I could ...; **Sie w~?** can I help you? **w~swert** a desirable

Wunsch|konzert nt musical request programme. **W~traum** m (*fig*) dream

wurde, würde s. **werden**

Würde f -,-n dignity; (*Ehrenrang*) honour. **w~los** a undignified. **W~nträger** m dignitary. **w~voll** a dignified ● adv with dignity

würdig a dignified; (*wert*) worthy. **w~en** vt recognize; (*schätzen*) appreciate; **keines Blickes w~en** not deign to look at

Wurf m -[e]s,"e throw; (*Junge*) litter

Würfel m -s,- cube; (*Spiel-*) dice; (*Zucker-*) lump. **w~n** vi (haben) throw the dice; **w~n um** play dice for ● vt throw; (*in Würfel schneiden*) dice. **W~zucker** m cube sugar

würgen vt choke ● vi (haben) retch; choke (**an** + dat on)

Wurm m -[e]s,"er worm; (*Made*) maggot. **w~en** vi (haben) **jdn w~en** (*fam*) rankle [with s.o.]. **w~stichig** a worm-eaten

Wurst f -,"e sausage; **das ist mir W~** (*fam*) I couldn't care less

Würstchen nt -s,- small sausage; **Frankfurter W~** frankfurter

Würze f -,-n spice; (*Aroma*) aroma

Wurzel f -,-n root; **W~n schlagen** take root. **w~n** vi (haben) root

würz|en vt season. **w~ig** a tasty; (*aromatisch*) aromatic; (*pikant*) spicy

wüst a chaotic; (wirr) tangled; (öde) desolate; (wild) wild, adv -ly; (schlimm) terrible, adv -bly
Wüste f -,-n desert
Wut f - rage, fury. **W∼anfall** m fit of rage
wüten vi (haben) rage. **w∼d** a furious, adv -ly; **w∼d machen** infuriate

X

x /ɪks/ inv a (Math) x; (fam) umpteen. **X-Beine** ntpl knock-knees. **x-beinig** a knock-kneed. **x-beliebig** a (fam) any; **eine x-beliebige Zahl** any number [you like]. **x-mal** adv (fam) umpteen times

Y

Yoga /'jo:ga/ m & nt -[s] yoga

Z

Zack|e f -,-n point; (Berg-) peak; (Gabel-) prong. **z∼ig** a jagged; (gezackt) serrated; (fam: schneidig) smart, adv -ly
zaghaft a timid, adv -ly; (zögernd) tentative, adv -ly
zäh a tough; (hartnäckig) tenacious, adv -ly; (zähflüssig) viscous; (schleppend) sluggish, adv -ly. **z∼flüssig** a viscous; (Verkehr) slow-moving. **Z∼igkeit** f - toughness; tenacity
Zahl f -,-en number; (Ziffer, Betrag) figure
zahl|bar a payable. **z∼en** vt/i (haben) pay; (bezahlen) pay for; **bitte z∼en!** the bill please!
zählen vi (haben) count; **z∼ zu** (fig) be one/(pl) some of; **z∼ auf** (+ acc) count on ● vt count; **z∼ zu** add to; (fig) count among; **die Stadt zählt 5000 Einwohner** the town has 5000 inhabitants
zahlenmäßig a numerical, adv -ly
Zähler m -s,- meter
Zahl|grenze f fare-stage. **Z∼karte** f paying-in slip. **z∼los** a countless. **z∼reich** a numerous; ⟨Anzahl, Gruppe⟩ large ● adv in large numbers. **Z∼ung** f -,-en payment; **in Z∼ung nehmen** take in part-exchange

Zählung f -,-en count
zahlungsunfähig a insolvent
Zahlwort nt (pl -wörter) numeral
zahm a tame
zähmen vt tame; (fig) restrain
Zahn m -[e]s,-̈e tooth; (am Zahnrad) cog. **Z∼arzt** m, **Z∼ärztin** f dentist. **Z∼belag** m plaque. **Z∼bürste** f toothbrush. **z∼en** vi (haben) be teething. **Z∼fleisch** nt gums pl. **z∼los** a toothless. **Z∼pasta** f -,-en toothpaste. **Z∼rad** nt cog-wheel. **Z∼schmelz** m enamel. **Z∼schmerzen** mpl toothache sg. **Z∼spange** f brace. **Z∼stein** m tartar. **Z∼stocher** m -s,- toothpick
Zange f -,-n pliers pl; (Kneif-) pincers pl; (Kohlen-, Zucker-) tongs pl; (Geburts-) forceps pl
Zank m -[e]s squabble. **z∼en** vr **sich z∼en** squabble ● vi (haben) scold (**mit jdm** s.o.)
zänkisch a quarrelsome
Zäpfchen nt -s,- (Anat) uvula; (Med) suppository
Zapfen m -s,- (Bot) cone; (Stöpsel) bung; (Eis-) icicle. **z∼** vt tap, draw. **Z∼streich** m (Mil) tattoo
Zapf|hahn m tap. **Z∼säule** f petrol-pump
zappel|ig a fidgety; (nervös) jittery. **z∼n** vi (haben) wriggle; ⟨Kind:⟩ fidget
zart a delicate, adv -ly; (weich, zärtlich) tender, adv -ly; (sanft) gentle, adv -ly. **Z∼gefühl** nt tact. **Z∼heit** f - delicacy; tenderness; gentleness
zärtlich a tender, adv -ly; (liebevoll) loving, adv -ly. **Z∼keit** f -,-en tenderness; (Liebkosung) caress
Zauber m -s magic; (Bann) spell. **Z∼er** m -s,- magician. **z∼haft** a enchanting. **Z∼künstler** m con- juror. **Z∼kunststück** nt = **Z∼trick**. **z∼n** vi (haben) do magic; (Zaubertricks ausführen) do conjuring tricks ● vt produce as if by magic. **Z∼stab** m magic wand. **Z∼trick** m conjuring trick
zaudern vi (haben) delay; (zögern) hesitate
Zaum m -[e]s, Zäume bridle; **im Z∼ halten** (fig) restrain
Zaun m -[e]s, Zäune fence. **Z∼könig** m wren
z.B. abbr (**zum Beispiel**) e.g.
Zebra nt -s,-s zebra. **Z∼streifen** m zebra-crossing
Zeche f -,-n bill; (Bergwerk) pit

zechen vi (haben) (fam) drink

Zeder f -,-n cedar

Zeh m -[e]s,-en toe. **Z~e** f -,-n toe; (Knoblauch-) clove. **Z~ennagel** m toenail

zehn inv a, **Z~** f -,-en ten. **z~te(r,s)** a tenth. **Z~tel** nt -s,- tenth

Zeichen nt -s,- sign; (Signal) signal. **Z~setzung** f - punctuation. **Z~trickfilm** m cartoon [film]

zeichn|en vt/i (haben) draw; (kenn-) mark; (unter-) sign. **Z~er** m -s,- draughtsman. **Z~ung** f -,-en drawing; (auf Fell) markings pl

Zeige|finger m index finger. **z~n** vt show; **sich z~n** appear; (sich herausstellen) become clear; **das wird sich z~n** we shall see • vi (haben) point (**auf** + acc to). **Z~r** m -s,- pointer; (Uhr-) hand

Zeile f -,-n line; (Reihe) row

zeit prep (+ gen) **z~ meines/seines Lebens** all my/his life

Zeit f -,-en time; **sich** (dat) **Z~ lassen** take one's time; **es hat Z~** there's no hurry; **mit der Z~** in time; **in nächster Z~** in the near future; **die erste Z~** at first; **von Z~ zu Z~** from time to time; **zur Z~** at present; (rechtzeitig) in time; **[ach] du liebe Z~!** (fam) good heavens!

Zeit|alter nt age, era. **Z~arbeit** f temporary work. **Z~bombe** f time bomb. **z~gemäß** a modern, up-to-date. **Z~genosse** m, **Z~genossin** f contemporary. **z~genössisch** a contemporary. **z~ig** a & adv early. **Z~lang** f **eine Z~lang** for a time or while. **z~lebens** adv all one's life

zeitlich a (Dauer) in time; (Folge) chronological • adv **z~ begrenzt** for a limited time

zeit|los a timeless. **Z~lupe** f slow motion. **Z~punkt** m time. **z~raubend** a time-consuming. **Z~raum** m period. **Z~schrift** f magazine, periodical

Zeitung f -,-en newspaper. **Z~spapier** nt newspaper

Zeit|verschwendung f waste of time. **Z~vertreib** m pastime; **zum Z~vertreib** to pass the time. **z~weilig** a temporary • adv temporarily; (hin und wieder) at times. **z~weise** adv at times. **Z~wort** nt (pl -wörter) verb. **Z~zünder** m time fuse

Zelle f -,-n cell; (Telefon-) box

Zelt nt -[e]s,-e tent; (Fest-) marquee. **z~en** vi (haben) camp. **Z~en** nt -s camping. **Z~plane** f tarpaulin. **Z~platz** m campsite

Zement m -[e]s cement. **z~ieren** vt cement

zen|sieren vt (Sch) mark; censor (Presse, Film). **Z~sur** f -,-en (Sch) mark, (Amer) grade; (Presse-) censorship

Zentimeter m & nt centimetre. **Z~maß** nt tape-measure

Zentner m -s,- [metric] hundredweight (50 kg)

zentral a central, adv -ly. **Z~e** f -,-n central office; (Partei-) headquarters pl; (Teleph) exchange. **Z~heizung** f central heating. **z~isieren** vt centralize

Zentrum nt -s,-tren centre

zerbrech|en† vt/i (sein) break; **sich** (dat) **den Kopf z~en** rack one's brains. **z~lich** a fragile

zerdrücken vt crush; mash (Kartoffeln)

Zeremonie f -,-n ceremony

Zeremoniell nt -s,-e ceremonial. **z~** a ceremonial, adv -ly

Zerfall m disintegration; (Verfall) decay. **z~en**† vi (sein) disintegrate; (verfallen) decay; **in drei Teile z~en** be divided into three parts

zerfetzen vt tear to pieces

zerfließen† vi (sein) melt; (Tinte:) run

zergehen† vi (sein) melt; (sich auflösen) dissolve

zergliedern vt dissect

zerkleinern vt chop/(schneiden) cut up; (mahlen) grind

zerknirscht a contrite

zerknüllen vt crumple [up]

zerkratzen vt scratch

zerlassen† vt melt

zerlegen vt take to pieces, dismantle; (zerschneiden) cut up; (tranchieren) carve

zerlumpt a ragged

zermalmen vt crush

zermürb|en vt (fig) wear down. **Z~ungskrieg** m war of attrition

zerplatzen vi (sein) burst

zerquetschen vt squash; crush; mash (Kartoffeln)

Zerrbild nt caricature

zerreißen† vt tear; (in Stücke) tear up; break (Faden, Seil) • vi (sein) tear; break

zerren *vt* drag; pull ⟨*Muskel*⟩ ● *vi* (*haben*) pull (**an** + *dat* at)

zerrinnen† *vi* (*sein*) melt

zerrissen *a* torn

zerrütten *vt* ruin, wreck; shatter ⟨*Nerven*⟩; **zerrüttete Ehe** broken marriage

zerschlagen† *vt* smash; smash up ⟨*Möbel*⟩; **sich z∼** (*fig*) fall through; ⟨*Hoffnung:*⟩ be dashed ● *a* (*erschöpft*) worn out

zerschmettern *vt/i* (*sein*) smash

zerschneiden† *vt* cut; (*in Stücke*) cut up

zersetzen *vt* corrode; undermine ⟨*Moral*⟩; **sich z∼** decompose

zersplittern *vi* (*sein*) splinter; ⟨*Glas:*⟩ shatter ● *vt* shatter

zerspringen† *vi* (*sein*) shatter; (*bersten*) burst

Zerstäuber *m* **-s,-** atomizer

zerstör|en *vt* destroy; (*zunichte machen*) wreck. **Z∼er** *m* **-s,-** destroyer. **Z∼ung** *f* destruction

zerstreu|en *vt* scatter; disperse ⟨*Menge*⟩; dispel ⟨*Zweifel*⟩; **sich z∼en** disperse; (*sich unterhalten*) amuse oneself. **z∼t** *a* absent-minded, *adv* -ly. **Z∼ung** *f* **-,-en** (*Unterhaltung*) entertainment

zerstückeln *vt* cut up into pieces

zerteilen *vt* divide up

Zertifikat *nt* **-[e]s,-e** certificate

zertreten† *vt* stamp on; (*zerdrücken*) crush

zertrümmern *vt* smash [up]; wreck ⟨*Gebäude, Stadt*⟩

zerzaus|en *vt* tousle. **z∼t** *a* dishevelled; ⟨*Haar:*⟩ tousled

Zettel *m* **-s,-** piece of paper; (*Notiz*) note; (*Bekanntmachung*) notice; (*Reklame-*) leaflet

Zeug *nt* **-s** (*fam*) stuff; (*Sachen*) things *pl*; (*Ausrüstung*) gear; **dummes Z∼** nonsense; **das Z∼ haben zu** have the makings of

Zeuge *m* **-n,-n** witness. **z∼n** *vi* (*haben*) testify; **z∼n von** (*fig*) show ● *vt* father. **Z∼naussage** *f* testimony. **Z∼nstand** *m* witness box/ (*Amer*) stand

Zeugin *f* **-,-nen** witness

Zeugnis *nt* **-ses,-se** certificate; (*Sch*) report; (*Referenz*) reference; (*fig: Beweis*) evidence

Zickzack *m* **-[e]s,-e** zigzag

Ziege *f* **-,-n** goat

Ziegel *m* **-s,-** brick; (*Dach-*) tile. **Z∼stein** *m* brick

ziehen† *vt* pull; (*sanfter; zücken; zeichnen*) draw; (*heraus-*) pull out; extract ⟨*Zahn*⟩; raise ⟨*Hut*⟩; put on ⟨*Bremse*⟩; move ⟨*Schachfigur*⟩; put up ⟨*Leine, Zaun*⟩; (*dehnen*) stretch; make ⟨*Grimasse, Scheitel*⟩; (*züchten*) breed; grow ⟨*Rosen, Gemüse*⟩; **nach sich z∼** (*fig*) entail ● *vr* **sich z∼** (*sich erstrecken*) run; (*sich verziehen*) warp ● *vi* (*haben*) pull (**an** + *dat* on/at); ⟨*Tee, Ofen:*⟩ draw; (*Culin*) simmer; **es zieht** there is a draught; **solche Filme z∼ nicht mehr** films like that are no longer popular ● *vi* (*sein*) (*um-*) move (**nach** to); ⟨*Menge:*⟩ march; ⟨*Vögel:*⟩ migrate; ⟨*Wolken, Nebel:*⟩ drift. **Z∼** *nt* **-s** ache

Ziehharmonika *f* accordion

Ziehung *f* **-,-en** draw

Ziel *nt* **-[e]s,-e** destination; (*Sport*) finish; (*Z∼scheibe & Mil*) target; (*Zweck*) aim, goal. **z∼bewußt** *a* purposeful, *adv* -ly. **z∼en** *vi* (*haben*) aim (**auf** + *acc* at). **z∼end** *a* (*Gram*) transitive. **z∼los** *a* aimless, *adv* -ly. **Z∼scheibe** *f* target; (*fig*) butt. **z∼strebig** *a* single-minded, *adv* -ly

ziemen (sich) *vr* be seemly

ziemlich *a* (*fam*) fair ● *adv* rather, fairly; (*fast*) pretty well

Zier|de *f* **-,-n** ornament. **z∼en** *vt* adorn; **sich z∼en** make a fuss; (*sich bitten lassen*) need coaxing

zierlich *a* dainty, *adv* -ily; (*fein*) delicate, *adv* -ly; ⟨*Frau*⟩ petite

Ziffer *f* **-,-n** figure, digit; (*Zahlzeichen*) numeral. **Z∼blatt** *nt* dial

zig *inv a* (*fam*) umpteen

Zigarette *f* **-,-n** cigarette

Zigarre *f* **-,-n** cigar

Zigeuner(in) *m* **-s,-** (*f* **-,-nen**) gypsy

Zimmer *nt* **-s,-** room. **Z∼mädchen** *nt* chambermaid. **Z∼mann** *m* (*pl* **-leute**) carpenter. **z∼n** *vt* make ● *vi* (*haben*) do carpentry. **Z∼nachweis** *m* accommodation bureau. **Z∼pflanze** *f* house plant

zimperlich *a* squeamish; (*wehleidig*) soft; (*prüde*) prudish

Zimt *m* **-[e]s** cinnamon

Zink *nt* **-s** zinc

Zinke *f* **-,-n** prong; (*Kamm-*) tooth

Zinn *m* **-s** tin; (*Gefäße*) pewter

Zins|en *mpl* interest *sg*; **Z∼en tragen** earn interest. **Z∼eszins** *m* **-es,-en** compound interest. **Z∼fuß, Z∼satz** *m* interest rate

Zipfel *m* -s,- corner; (*Spitze*) point; (*Wurst-*) [tail-]end

zirka *adv* about

Zirkel *m* -s,- [pair of] compasses *pl*; (*Gruppe*) circle

Zirkul|ation /-'tsio:n/ *f* - circulation. **z~ieren** *vi* (*sein*) circulate

Zirkus *m* -,-**se** circus

zirpen *vi* (*haben*) chirp

zischen *vi* (*haben*) hiss; (*Fett:*) sizzle ● *vt* hiss

Zit|at *nt* -[e]s,-e quotation. **z~ieren** *vt/i* (*haben*) quote; (*rufen*) summon

Zitr|onat *nt* -[e]s candied lemon-peel. **Z~one** *f* -,-n lemon. **Z~onen-limonade** *f* lemonade

zittern *vi* (*haben*) tremble; (*vor Kälte*) shiver; (*beben*) shake

zittrig *a* shaky, *adv* -ily

Zitze *f* -,-n teat

zivil *a* civilian; (*Ehe, Recht, Luftfahrt*) civil; (*mäßig*) reasonable. **Z~** *nt* -**s** civilian clothes *pl*. **Z~courage** /-'ku:-ʒə/ *f* - courage of one's convictions. **Z~dienst** *m* community service

Zivili|sation /-'tsio:n/ *f* -,-en civilization. **z~sieren** *vt* civilize. **z~siert** *a* civilized ● *adv* in a civilized manner

Zivilist *m* -en,-en civilian

zögern *vi* (*haben*) hesitate. **Z~** *nt* -**s** hesitation. **z~d** *a* hesitant, *adv* -ly

Zoll¹ *m* -[e]s,- inch

Zoll² *m* -[e]s,⸚e [customs] duty; (*Behörde*) customs *pl*. **Z~abfertigung** *f* customs clearance. **Z~beamte(r)** *m* customs officer. **z~frei** *a & adv* duty-free. **Z~kontrolle** *f* customs check

Zone *f* -,-n zone

Zoo *m* -s,-s zoo

Zoo|loge /tsoo'lo:gə/ *m* -n,-n zoologist. **Z~logie** *f* - zoology. **z~lo-gisch** *a* zoological

Zopf *m* -[e]s,⸚e plait

Zorn *m* -[e]s anger. **z~ig** *a* angry, *adv* -ily

zotig *a* smutty, dirty

zottig *a* shaggy

z.T. *abbr* (**zum Teil**) partly

zu *prep* (+ *dat*) to; (*dazu*) with; (*zeitlich, preislich*) at; (*Zweck*) for; (*über*) about; **zu ... hin** towards; **zu Hause** at home; **zu Fuß/Pferde** on foot/horseback; **zu beiden Seiten** on both sides; **zu Ostern** at Easter; **zu diesem Zweck** for this purpose; **zu meinem Erstaunen/Entsetzen** to my surprise/

horror; **zu Dutzenden** by the dozen; **eine Marke zu 60 Pfennig** a 60-pfennig stamp; **das Stück zu zwei Mark** at two marks each; **wir waren zu dritt/viert** there were three/four of us; **es steht 5 zu 3** the score is 5–3; **zu etw werden** turn into sth ● *adv* (*allzu*) too; (*Richtung*) towards; (*geschlossen*) closed; (*an Schalter, Hahn*) off; **zu groß/weit** too big/far; **nach dem Fluß zu** towards the river; **Augen zu!** close your eyes! **Tür zu!** shut the door! **nur zu!** go on! **mach zu!** (*fam*) hurry up! ● *conj* to; **etwas zu essen** something to eat; **nicht zu glauben** unbelievable; **zu erörternde Probleme** problems to be discussed

zuallererst *adv* first of all. **z~letzt** *adv* last of all

Zubehör *nt* -**s** accessories *pl*

zubereit|en *vt sep* prepare. **Z~ung** *f* - preparation; (*in Rezept*) method

zubilligen *vt sep* grant

zubinden† *vt sep* tie [up]

zubring|en† *vt sep* spend. **Z~er** *m* -**s**,- access road; (*Bus*) shuttle

Zucchini /tsu'ki:ni/ *pl* courgettes

Zucht *f* -,-en breeding; (*Pflanzen-*) cultivation; (*Art, Rasse*) breed; (*von Pflanzen*) strain; (*Z~farm*) farm; (*Pferde-*) stud; (*Disziplin*) discipline

zücht|en *vt* breed; cultivate, grow (*Rosen, Gemüse*). **Z~er** *m* -**s**,- breeder; grower

Zuchthaus *nt* prison

züchtigen *vt* chastise

Züchtung *f* -,-en breeding; (*Pflanzen-*) cultivation; (*Art, Rasse*) breed; (*von Pflanzen*) strain

zucken *vi* (*haben*) twitch; (*sich z~d bewegen*) jerk; (*Blitz:*) flash; (*Flamme:*) flicker ● *vt* **die Achseln z~** shrug one's shoulders

zücken *vt* draw (*Messer*)

Zucker *m* -**s** sugar. **Z~dose** *f* sugar basin. **Z~guß** *m* icing. **z~krank** *a* diabetic. **Z~krankheit** *f* diabetes. **z~n** *vt* sugar. **Z~rohr** *nt* sugar cane. **Z~rübe** *f* sugar beet. **z~süß** *a* sweet; (*fig*) sugary. **Z~watte** *f* candyfloss. **Z~zange** *f* sugar tongs *pl*

zuckrig *a* sugary

zudecken *vt sep* cover up; (*im Bett*) tuck up; cover (*Topf*)

zudem *adv* moreover

zudrehen *vt sep* turn off; **jdm den Rücken z~** turn one's back on s.o.

zudringlich *a* pushing, (*fam*) pushy

zudrücken *vt sep* press *or* push shut; close ⟨*Augen*⟩

zueinander *adv* to one another; **z∼ passen** go together. **z∼halten**† *vi sep* (*haben*) (*fig*) stick together

zuerkennen† *vt sep* award (*dat* to)

zuerst *adv* first; (*anfangs*) at first; **mit dem Kopf z∼** head first

zufahr|en† *vi sep* (*sein*) **z∼en auf** (+ *acc*) drive towards. **Z∼t** *f* access; (*Einfahrt*) drive

Zufall *m* chance; (*Zusammentreffen*) coincidence; **durch Z∼** by chance/ coincidence. **z∼en**† *vi sep* (*sein*) close, shut; **jdm z∼en** ⟨*Aufgabe:*⟩ fall/ ⟨*Erbe:*⟩ go to s.o.

zufällig *a* chance, accidental ● *adv* by chance; **ich war z∼ da** I happened to be there

Zuflucht *f* refuge; (*Schutz*) shelter. **Z∼sort** *m* refuge

zufolge *prep* (+ *dat*) according to

zufrieden *a* contented, *adv* -ly; (*befriedigt*) satisfied. **z∼geben**† (**sich**) *vr sep* be satisfied. **Z∼heit** *f* - contentment; satisfaction. **z∼lassen**† *vt sep* leave in peace. **z∼stellen** *vt sep* satisfy. **z∼stellend** *a* satisfactory, *adv* -ily

zufrieren† *vi sep* (*sein*) freeze over

zufügen *vt sep* inflict (*dat* on); do ⟨*Unrecht*⟩ (*dat* to)

Zufuhr *f* - supply

zuführen *vt sep* ● *vt* supply ● *vi* (*haben*) **z∼ auf** (+ *acc*) lead to

Zug *m* **-[e]s, ̈e** train; (*Kolonne*) column; (*Um-*) procession; (*Mil*) platoon; (*Vogelschar*) flock; (*Ziehen, Zugkraft*) pull; (*Wandern, Ziehen*) migration; (*Schluck, Luft-*) draught; (*Atem-*) breath; (*beim Rauchen*) puff; (*Schach-*) move; (*beim Schwimmen, Rudern*) stroke; (*Gesichts-*) feature; (*Wesens-*) trait; **etw in vollen Zügen genießen** enjoy sth to the full; **in einem Zug[e]** at one go

Zugabe *f* (*Geschenk*) [free] gift; (*Mus*) encore

Zugang *m* access

zugänglich *a* accessible; ⟨*Mensch:*⟩ approachable; (*fig*) amenable (*dat/ für* to)

Zugbrücke *f* drawbridge

zugeben† *vt sep* add; (*gestehen*) admit; (*erlauben*) allow. **zugegebenermaßen** *adv* admittedly

zugegen *a* **z∼ sein** be present

zugehen† *vi sep* (*sein*) close; **jdm z∼** be sent to s.o.; **z∼ auf** (+ *acc*) go towards; **dem Ende z∼** draw to a

close; ⟨*Vorräte:*⟩ run low; **auf der Party ging es lebhaft zu** the party was pretty lively

Zugehörigkeit *f* - membership

Zügel *m* **-s, -** rein

zugelassen *a* registered

zügel|los *a* unrestrained, *adv* -ly; (*sittenlos*) licentious. **z∼n** *vt* rein in; (*fig*) curb

Zuge|ständnis *nt* concession. **z∼stehen**† *vt sep* grant

zugetan *a* fond (*dat* of)

zugig *a* draughty

zügig *a* quick, *adv* -ly

Zug|kraft *f* pull; (*fig*) attraction. **z∼kräftig** *a* effective; (*anreizend*) popular; ⟨*Titel*⟩ catchy

zugleich *adv* at the same time

Zug|luft *f* draught. **Z∼pferd** *nt* draught-horse; (*fam*) draw

zugreifen† *vi sep* (*haben*) grab it/ them; (*bei Tisch*) help oneself; (*bei Angebot*) jump at it; (*helfen*) lend a hand

zugrunde *adv* **z∼ richten** destroy; **z∼ gehen** be destroyed; ⟨*Ehe:*⟩ founder; (*sterben*) die; **z∼ liegen** form the basis (*dat* of)

zugucken *vi sep* (*haben*) = **zusehen**

zugunsten *prep* (+ *gen*) in favour of; ⟨*Sammlung*⟩ in aid of

zugute *adv* **jdm/etw z∼ kommen** benefit s.o./sth; **jdm seine Jugend z∼ halten** make allowances for s.o.'s youth

Zugvogel *m* migratory bird

zuhalten† *v sep* ● *vt* keep closed; (*bedecken*) cover; **sich** (*dat*) **die Nase z∼** hold one's nose ● *vi* (*haben*) **z∼ auf** (+ *acc*) head for

Zuhälter *m* **-s, -** pimp

Zuhause *nt* **-s, -** home

zuhör|en *vi sep* (*haben*) listen (*dat* to). **Z∼er(in)** *m(f)* listener

zujubeln *vi sep* (*haben*) **jdm z∼** cheer s.o.

zukehren *vt sep* turn (*dat* to)

zukleben *vt sep* seal

zuknallen *vt/i sep* (*sein*) slam

zuknöpfen *vt sep* button up

zukommen† *vi sep* (*sein*) **z∼ auf** (+ *acc*) come towards; (*sich nähern*) approach; **z∼ lassen** send (**jdm** s.o.); devote ⟨*Pflege*⟩ (*dat* to); **jdm z∼** be s.o.'s right

Zukunft *f* - future. **zukünftig** *a* future ● *adv* in future

zulächeln *vi sep* (*haben*) smile (*dat* at)

Zulage f -,-n extra allowance

zulangen vi sep (haben) help oneself; **tüchtig z~** tuck in

zulassen† vt sep allow, permit; (teilnehmen lassen) admit; (Admin) license, register; (geschlossen lassen) leave closed; leave unopened ⟨Brief⟩

zulässig a permissible

Zulassung f -,-en admission; registration; (Lizenz) licence

zulaufen† vi sep (sein) **z~ auf** (+ acc) run towards; **spitz z~** taper to a point

zulegen vt sep add; **sich** (dat) **etw z~** get sth; grow ⟨Bart⟩

zuleide adv **jdm etwas z~ tun** hurt s.o.

zuletzt adv last; (schließlich) in the end; **nicht z~** not least

zuliebe adv **jdm/etw z~** for the sake of s.o./sth

zum prep = **zu dem; zum Spaß** for fun; **etw zum Lesen** sth to read

zumachen v sep ● vt close, shut; do up ⟨Jacke⟩; seal ⟨Umschlag⟩; turn off ⟨Hahn⟩; (stillegen) close down ● vi (haben) close, shut; (stillgelegt werden) close down

zumal adv especially ● conj especially since

zumeist adv for the most part

zumindest adv at least

zumutbar a reasonable

zumute adv **mir ist traurig/elend z~** I feel sad/wretched; **mir ist nicht danach z~** I don't feel like it

zumut|en vt sep **jdm etw z~en** ask or expect sth of s.o.; **sich** (dat) **zuviel z~en** overdo things. **Z~ung** f - imposition; **eine Z~ung sein** be unreasonable

zunächst adv first [of all]; (anfangs) at first; (vorläufig) for the moment ● prep (+ dat) nearest to

Zunahme f -,-n increase

Zuname m surname

zünd|en vt/i (haben) ignite; **z~ende Rede** rousing speech. **Z~er** m **-s,-** detonator, fuse. **Z~holz** nt match. **Z~kerze** f sparking-plug. **Z~schlüssel** m ignition key. **Z~schnur** f fuse. **Z~ung** f -,-en ignition

zunehmen† vi sep (haben) increase (**an** + dat in); ⟨Mond:⟩ wax; (an Gewicht) put on weight. **z~d** a increasing, adv -ly

Zuneigung f - affection

Zunft f -,¨e guild

zünftig a proper, adv -ly

Zunge f -,-n tongue. **Z~nbrecher** m tongue-twister

zunichte a **z~ machen** wreck; **z~ werden** come to nothing

zunicken vi sep (haben) nod (dat to)

zunutze a **sich** (dat) **etw z~ machen** make use of sth; (ausnutzen) take advantage of sth

zuoberst adv right at the top

zuordnen vt sep assign (dat to)

zupfen vt/i (haben) pluck (**an** + dat at); pull out ⟨Unkraut⟩

zur prep = **zu der; zur Schule/Arbeit** to school/work; **zur Zeit** at present

zurechnungsfähig a of sound mind

zurecht|finden† (sich) vr sep find one's way. **z~kommen†** vi sep (sein) cope (**mit** with); (rechtzeitig kommen) be in time. **z~legen** vt sep put out ready; **sich** (dat) **eine Ausrede z~legen** have an excuse all ready. **z~machen** vt sep get ready; **sich z~machen** get ready. **z~weisen†** vt sep reprimand. **Z~weisung** f reprimand

zureden vi sep (haben) **jdm z~** try to persuade s.o.

zurichten vt sep prepare; (beschädigen) damage; (verletzen) injure

zuriegeln vt sep bolt

zurück adv back; **Berlin, hin und z~** return to Berlin. **z~behalten†** vt sep keep back; be left with ⟨Narbe⟩. **z~bekommen†** vt sep get back; **20 Pfennig z~bekommen** get 20 pfennigs change. **z~bleiben†** vi sep (sein) stay behind; (nicht mithalten) lag behind. **z~blicken** vi sep (haben) look back. **z~bringen†** vt sep bring back; (wieder hinbringen) take back. **z~erobern** vt sep recapture; (fig) regain. **z~erstatten** vt sep refund. **z~fahren†** v sep ● vt drive back ● vi (sein) return, go back; (im Auto) drive back; (z~weichen) recoil. **z~finden†** vi sep (haben) find one's way back. **z~führen** v sep ● vt take back; (fig) attribute (**auf** + acc to) ● vi (haben) lead back. **z~geben†** vt sep give back, return. **z~geblieben** a retarded. **z~gehen†** vi sep (sein) go back, return; (abnehmen) go down; **z~gehen auf** (+ acc) (fig) go back to

zurückgezogen a secluded. **Z~heit** f - seclusion

zurückhalt|en† vt sep hold back; (abhalten) stop; **sich z~en** restrain oneself. **z~end** a reserved. **Z~ung** f - reserve

zurück|kehren vi sep (sein) return.
z~kommen† vi sep (sein) come
back, return; (ankommen) get back;
z~kommen auf (+ acc) (fig) come
back to. **z~lassen†** vt sep leave behind; (z~kehren lassen) allow back.
z~legen vt sep put back; (reservieren) keep; (sparen) put by; cover
⟨Strecke⟩. **z~lehnen (sich)** vr sep
lean back. **z~liegen†** vi sep (haben)
be in the past; (Sport) be behind; **das
liegt lange zurück** that was long ago.
z~melden (sich) vr sep report back.
z~nehmen† vt sep take back. **z~
rufen†** vt/i sep (haben) call back.
z~scheuen vi sep (sein) shrink
(**vor** + dat from). **z~schicken** vt sep
send back. **z~schlagen†** v sep ●vi
(haben) hit back ●vt hit back;
(abwehren) beat back; (umschlagen)
turn back. **z~schneiden†** vt sep cut
back. **z~schrecken†** vi sep (sein)
shrink back, recoil; (fig) shrink
(**vor** + dat from). **z~setzen** v sep ●vt
put back; (Auto) reverse, back; (herabsetzen) reduce; (fig) neglect ●vi
(haben) reverse, back. **z~stellen** vt
sep put back; (reservieren) keep; (fig)
put aside; (aufschieben) postpone.
z~stoßen† v sep ●vt push back ●vi
(sein) reverse, back. **z~treten†** vi
sep (sein) step back; (vom Amt)
resign; (verzichten) withdraw.
z~weichen† vi sep (sein) draw back;
(z~schrecken) shrink back. **z~
weisen†** vt sep turn away; (fig) reject. **z~werfen†** vt sep throw back;
(reflektieren) reflect. **z~zahlen** vt sep
pay back. **z~ziehen†** vt sep draw
back; (fig) withdraw; **sich z~ziehen**
withdraw; (vom Beruf) retire; (Mil) retreat
Zuruf m shout. **z~en†** vt sep shout
(dat to)
Zusage f -,-n acceptance; (Versprechen) promise. **z~n** v sep ●vt
promise ●vi (haben) accept; **jdm
z~n** appeal to s.o.
zusammen adv together; (insgesamt) altogether. **Z~arbeit** f co-
operation. **z~arbeiten** vi sep
(haben) co-operate. **z~bauen** vt sep
assemble. **z~beißen†** vt sep **die
Zähne z~beißen** clench/(fig) grit
one's teeth. **z~bleiben†** vi sep (sein)
stay together. **z~brechen†** vi sep
(sein) collapse. **z~bringen†** vt sep
bring together; (beschaffen) raise.

Z~bruch m collapse; (Nerven- & fig)
breakdown. **z~fahren†** vi sep (sein)
collide; (z~zucken) start. **z~fallen†**
vi sep (sein) collapse; (zeitlich) coincide. **z~falten** vt sep fold up.
z~fassen vt sep summarize, sum up.
Z~fassung f summary. **z~fügen** vt
sep fit together. **z~führen** vt sep
bring together. **z~gehören** vi sep
(haben) belong together; (z~passen)
go together. **z~gesetzt** a (Gram)
compound. **z~halten†** v sep ●vt
hold together; (beisammenhalten)
keep together ●vi (haben) (fig) stick
together. **Z~hang** m connection;
(Kontext) context. **z~hängen†** vi sep
(haben) be connected. **z~hanglos** a
incoherent, adv -ly. **z~klappen** v sep
●vt fold up ●vi (sein) collapse.
z~kommen† vi sep (sein) meet; (sich
sammeln) accumulate. **Z~kunft** f
-,-̈e meeting. **z~laufen†** vi sep (sein)
gather; ⟨Flüssigkeit:⟩ collect;
⟨Linien:⟩ converge. **z~leben** vi sep
(haben) live together. **z~legen** v sep
●vt put together; (z~falten) fold up;
(vereinigen) amalgamate; pool ⟨Geld⟩
●vi (haben) club together. **z~neh-
men†** vt sep gather up; summon up
⟨Mut⟩; collect ⟨Gedanken⟩; **sich
z~nehmen** pull oneself together.
z~passen vi sep (haben) go together,
match; ⟨Personen:⟩ be well matched.
Z~prall m collision. **z~prallen** vi
sep (sein) collide. **z~rechnen** vt sep
add up. **z~reißen†** (sich) vr sep
(fam) pull oneself together. **z~rol-
len** vt sep roll up; **sich z~rollen** curl
up. **z~schlagen†** vt sep smash up;
(prügeln) beat up. **z~schließen†**
(sich) vr sep join together; ⟨Firmen:⟩
merge. **Z~schluß** m union; (Comm)
merger. **z~schreiben†** vt sep write
as one word
zusammensein† vi sep (sein) be together. **Z~nt -s** get-together
zusammensetz|en vt sep put to-
gether; (Techn) assemble; **sich z~en**
sit [down] together; (bestehen) be made
up (**aus** from). **Z~ung** f -,-en composition; (Techn) assembly; (Wort) compound
zusammen|stellen vt sep put to-
gether; (gestalten) compile. **Z~stoß**
m collision; (fig) clash. **z~stoßen†**
vi sep (sein) collide. **z~treffen†** vi
sep (sein) meet; (zeitlich) coincide.
Z~treffen nt meeting; coincidence.

z~zählen vt sep add up. **z~ziehen**† v sep ● vt draw together; (addieren) add up; (konzentrieren) mass; **sich z~ziehen** contract; ⟨Gewitter:⟩ gather ● vi (sein) move in together; move in (**mit** with). **z~zucken** vi sep (sein) start; (vor Schmerz) wince

Zusatz m addition; (Jur) rider; (Lebensmittel-) additive. **Z~gerät** nt attachment. **zusätzlich** a additional ● adv in addition

zuschanden adv **z~ machen** ruin, wreck; **z~ fahren** wreck

zuschauen vi sep (haben) watch. **Z~er(in)** m -s,- (f -,-nen) spectator; (TV) viewer. **Z~erraum** m auditorium

zuschicken vt sep send (dat to)

Zuschlag m surcharge; (D-Zug-) supplement. **z~en**† v sep ● vt shut; (heftig) slam; (bei Auktion) knock down (**jdm** to s.o.) ● vi (haben) hit out; ⟨Feind:⟩ strike ● vi (sein) slam shut. **z~pflichtig** a for which a supplement is payable

zuschließen† v sep ● vt lock ● vi (haben) lock up

zuschneiden† vt sep cut out; cut to size ⟨Holz⟩

zuschreiben† vt sep attribute (dat to); **jdm die Schuld z~** blame s.o.

Zuschrift f letter; (auf Annonce) reply

zuschulden adv **sich** (dat) **etwas z~ kommen lassen** do wrong

Zuschuß m contribution; (staatlich) subsidy

zusehen† vi sep (haben) watch; **z~, daß** see [to it] that

zusehends adv visibly

zusein† vi sep (sein) be closed

zusenden† vt sep send (dat to)

zusetzen v sep ● vt add; (einbüßen) lose ● vi (haben) **jdm z~** pester s.o.; ⟨Hitze:⟩ take it out of s.o.

zusicher|n vt sep promise. **Z~ung** f promise

Zuspätkommende(r) m/f latecomer

zuspielen vt sep (Sport) pass

zuspitzen (sich) vr sep (fig) become critical

zusprechen† v sep ● vt award (**jdm** s.o.); **jdm Trost/Mut z~** comfort/encourage s.o. ● vi (haben) **dem Essen z~** eat heartily

Zustand m condition, state

zustande adv **z~ bringen/kommen** bring/come about

zuständig a competent; (verantwortlich) responsible. **Z~keit** f -competence; responsibility

zustehen† vi sep (haben) **jdm z~** be s.o.'s right; ⟨Urlaub:⟩ be due to s.o.; **es steht ihm nicht zu** he is not entitled to it; (gebührt) it is not for him (**zu** to)

zusteigen† vi sep (sein) get on; **noch jemand zugestiegen?** tickets please; (im Bus) any more fares please?

zustell|en vt sep block; (bringen) deliver. **Z~ung** f delivery

zusteuern v sep ● vi (sein) head (**auf** + acc for) ● vt contribute

zustimm|en vi sep (haben) agree; (billigen) approve (dat of). **Z~ung** f consent; approval

zustoßen† vi sep (sein) happen (dat to)

Zustrom m influx

zutage adv **z~ treten** od **kommen/ bringen** come/bring to light

Zutat f (Culin) ingredient

zuteil|en vt sep allocate; assign ⟨Aufgabe⟩. **Z~ung** f allocation

zutiefst adv deeply

zutragen† vt sep carry/(fig) report (dat to); **sich z~** happen

zutrau|en vt sep **jdm etw z~** believe s.o. capable of sth. **Z~en** nt -s confidence. **z~lich** a trusting, adv -ly; ⟨Tier⟩ friendly

zutreffen† vi sep (haben) be correct; **z~ auf** (+ acc) apply to. **z~d** a applicable (**auf** + acc to); (richtig) correct, adv -ly

zutrinken† vi sep (haben) **jdm z~** drink to s.o.

Zutritt m admittance

zuunterst adv right at the bottom

zuverlässig a reliable, adv -bly. **Z~keit** f - reliability

Zuversicht f - confidence. **z~lich** a confident, adv -ly

zuviel pron & adv too much; (pl) too many

zuvor adv before; (erst) first

zuvorkommen† vi sep (sein) (+ dat) anticipate; **jdm z~** beat s.o. to it. **z~d** a obliging, adv -ly

Zuwachs m -es increase

zuwege adv **z~ bringen** achieve

zuweilen adv now and then

zuweisen† vt sep assign; (zuteilen) allocate

zuwend|en† vt sep turn (dat to); **sich z~en** (+ dat) turn to; (fig) devote oneself to. **Z~ung** f donation; (Fürsorge) care

zuwenig pron & adv too little; (pl) too few

zuwerfen† vt sep slam ⟨Tür⟩; **jdm etw z~** throw s.o. sth; give s.o. ⟨Blick, Lächeln⟩

zuwider adv **jdm z~ sein** be repugnant to s.o. ● prep (+ dat) contrary to. **z~handeln** vi sep (haben) contravene (**etw** dat sth)

zuzahlen vt sep pay extra

zuziehen† v sep ● vt pull tight; draw ⟨Vorhänge⟩; (hinzu-) call in; **sich** (dat) **etw z~** contract ⟨Krankheit⟩; sustain ⟨Verletzung⟩; incur ⟨Zorn⟩ ● vi (sein) move into the area

zuzüglich prep (+ gen) plus

Zwang m -[e]s,⁻e compulsion; (Gewalt) force; (Verpflichtung) obligation

zwängen vt squeeze

zwanglos a informal, adv -ly; ⟨Benehmen⟩ free and easy. **Z~igkeit** f - informality

Zwangs|jacke f straitjacket. **Z~lage** f predicament. **z~läufig** a inevitable, adv -bly

zwanzig inv a twenty. **z~ste(r,s)** a twentieth

zwar adv admittedly; **und z~** to be precise

Zweck m -[e]s,-e purpose; (Sinn) point; **es hat keinen Z~** there is no point. **z~dienlich** a appropriate; ⟨Information⟩ relevant. **z~los** a pointless. **z~mäßig** a suitable, adv -bly; (praktisch) functional, adv -ly. **z~s** prep (+ gen) for the purpose of

zwei inv a, **Z~** f -,-en two; (Sch) ≈ B. **Z~bettzimmer** nt twinbedded room

zweideutig a ambiguous, adv -ly; (schlüpfrig) suggestive, adv -ly. **Z~keit** f -,-en ambiguity

zwei|erlei inv a two kinds of ● pron two things. **z~fach** a double

Zweifel m -s,- doubt. **z~haft** a doubtful; (fragwürdig) dubious. **z~los** adv undoubtedly. **z~n** vi (haben) doubt (**an etw** dat sth)

Zweig m -[e]s,-e branch. **Z~geschäft** nt branch. **Z~stelle** f branch [office]

Zwei|kampf m duel. **z~mal** adv twice. **z~reihig** a double-breasted. **z~sprachig** a bilingual

zweit adv **zu z~** in twos; **wir waren zu z~** there were two of us. **z~beste(r,s)** a second-best. **z~e(r,s)** a second

zwei|teilig a two-piece; ⟨Film, Programm⟩ two-part. **z~tens** adv secondly

zweitklassig a second-class

Zwerchfell nt diaphragm

Zwerg m -[e]s,-e dwarf

Zwetsch[g]e f -,-n quetsche

Zwickel m -s,- gusset

zwicken vt/i (haben) pinch

Zwieback m -[e]s,⁻e rusk

Zwiebel f -,-n onion; (Blumen-) bulb

Zwielicht nt half-light; (Dämmerlicht) twilight. **z~ig** a shady

Zwie|spalt m conflict. **z~spältig** a conflicting. **Z~tracht** f - discord

Zwilling m -s,-e twin; **Z~e** (Astr) Gemini

zwingen† vt force; **sich z~** force oneself. **z~d** a compelling

Zwinger m -s,- run; (Zucht-) kennels pl

zwinkern vi (haben) blink; (als Zeichen) wink

Zwirn m -[e]s button thread

zwischen prep (+ dat/acc) between; (unter) among[st]. **Z~bemerkung** f interjection. **Z~ding** nt (fam) cross. **z~durch** adv in between; (in der Z~zeit) in the meantime; (ab und zu) now and again. **Z~fall** m incident. **Z~händler** m middleman. **Z~landung** f stop-over. **Z~raum** m gap, space. **Z~ruf** m interjection. **Z~stecker** m adaptor. **Z~wand** f partition. **Z~zeit** f **in der Z~zeit** in the meantime

Zwist m -[e]s,-e discord; (Streit) feud. **Z~igkeiten** fpl quarrels

zwitschern vi (haben) chirp

zwo inv a two

zwölf inv a twelve. **z~te(r,s)** a twelfth

zwote(r,s) a second

Zyklus m -,-klen cycle

Zylind|er m -s,- cylinder; (Hut) top hat. **z~risch** a cylindrical

Zyn|iker m -s,- cynic. **z~isch** a cynical, adv -ly. **Z~ismus** m - cynicism

Zypern nt -s Cyprus

Zypresse f -,-n cypress

Zyste /ˈtsʏstə/ f -,-n cyst

z.Zt. abbr (**zur Zeit**) at present

ENGLISH–GERMAN

ENGLISCH–DEUTSCH

A

a /ə, *betont* eɪ/ (*vor einem Vokal* **an**) *indef art* ein(e); (*each*) pro; **not a** kein(e)

aback /ə'bæk/ *adv* **be taken ~** verblüfft sein

abandon /ə'bændən/ *vt* verlassen; (*give up*) aufgeben ● *n* Hingabe *f*. **~ed** *a* verlassen; ⟨*behaviour*⟩ hemmungslos

abase /ə'beɪs/ *vt* demütigen

abashed /ə'bæʃt/ *a* beschämt, verlegen

abate /ə'beɪt/ *vi* nachlassen

abattoir /'æbətwɑ:(r)/ *n* Schlachthof *m*

abb|ey /'æbɪ/ *n* Abtei *f*. **~ot** *n* Abt *m*

abbreviat|e /ə'bri:vɪeɪt/ *vt* abkürzen. **~ion** /-'eɪʃn/ *n* Abkürzung *f*

abdicat|e /'æbdɪkeɪt/ *vi* abdanken. **~ion** /-'keɪʃn/ *n* Abdankung *f*

abdom|en /'æbdəmən/ *n* Unterleib *m*. **~inal** /-'dɒmml/ *a* Unterleibs-

abduct /əb'dʌkt/ *vt* entführen. **~ion** /-ʌkʃn/ *n* Entführung *f*. **~or** *n* Entführer *m*

aberration /æbə'reɪʃn/ *n* Abweichung *f*; (*mental*) Verwirrung *f*

abet /ə'bet/ *vt* (*pt/pp* **abetted**) **aid and ~** (*Jur*) Beihilfe leisten (+ *dat*)

abeyance /ə'beɪəns/ *n* **in ~** [zeitweilig] außer Kraft; **fall into ~** außer Kraft kommen

abhor /əb'hɔ:(r)/ *vt* (*pt/pp* **abhorred**) verabscheuen. **~rence** /-'hɒrəns/ *n* Abscheu *f*. **~rent** /-'hɒrənt/ *a* abscheulich

abid|e /ə'baɪd/ *vt* (*pt/pp* **abided**) (*tolerate*) aushalten; ausstehen ⟨*person*⟩ ● *vi* **~e by** sich halten an (+ *acc*). **~ing** *a* bleibend

ability /ə'bɪlətɪ/ *n* Fähigkeit *f*; (*talent*) Begabung *f*

abject /'æbdʒekt/ *a* erbärmlich; (*humble*) demütig

ablaze /ə'bleɪz/ *a* in Flammen; **be ~** in Flammen stehen

able /'eɪbl/ *a* (**-r, -st**) fähig; **be ~ to do sth** etw tun können. **~-'bodied** *a* körperlich gesund; (*Mil*) tauglich

ably /'eɪblɪ/ *adv* gekonnt

abnormal /æb'nɔ:ml/ *a* anormal; (*Med*) abnorm. **~ity** /-'mælətɪ/ *n* Abnormität *f*. **~ly** *adv* ungewöhnlich

aboard /ə'bɔ:d/ *adv* & *prep* an Bord (+ *gen*)

abode /ə'bəʊd/ *n* Wohnsitz *m*

abol|ish /ə'bɒlɪʃ/ *vt* abschaffen. **~ition** /æbə'lɪʃn/ *n* Abschaffung *f*

abominable /ə'bɒmɪnəbl/ *a*, **-bly** *adv* abscheulich

abominate /ə'bɒmɪneɪt/ *vt* verabscheuen

aborigines /æbə'rɪdʒəni:z/ *npl* Ureinwohner *pl*

abort /ə'bɔ:t/ *vt* abtreiben. **~ion** /-ɔ:ʃn/ *n* Abtreibung *f*; **have an ~ion** eine Abtreibung vornehmen lassen. **~ive** /-tɪv/ *a* ⟨*attempt*⟩ vergeblich

abound /ə'baʊnd/ *vi* reichlich vorhanden sein; **~ in** reich sein an (+ *dat*)

about /ə'baʊt/ *adv* umher, herum; (*approximately*) ungefähr; **be ~** (*in circulation*) umgehen; (*in existence*) vorhanden sein; **be up and ~** auf den Beinen sein; **be ~ to do sth** im Begriff sein, etw zu tun; **there are a lot ~** es gibt viele; **there was no one ~** es war kein Mensch da; **run/play ~** herumlaufen/-spielen ● *prep* um (+ *acc*) [... herum]; (*concerning*) über (+ *acc*); **what is it ~?** worum geht es? ⟨*book:*⟩ wovon handelt es? **I know nothing ~ it** ich weiß nichts davon; **talk/know ~** reden/wissen von

about: **~-'face** *n*, **-'turn** *n* Kehrtwendung *f*

above /ə'bʌv/ *adv* oben ● *prep* über (+ *dat/acc*); **~ all** vor allem

above: **~-'board** *a* legal. **~-mentioned** *a* obenerwähnt

abrasion /ə'breɪʒn/ *n* Schürfwunde *f*

abrasive /ə'breɪsɪv/ *a* Scheuer-; ⟨*remark*⟩ verletzend ● *n* Scheuermittel *nt*; (*Techn*) Schleifmittel *nt*

abreast /ə'brest/ *adv* nebeneinander; **keep ～ of** Schritt halten mit

abridge /ə'brɪdʒ/ *vt* kürzen

abroad /ə'brɔːd/ *adv* im Ausland; **go ～** ins Ausland fahren

abrupt /ə'brʌpt/ *a*, **-ly** *adv* abrupt; (*sudden*) plötzlich; (*curt*) schroff

abscess /'æbsɪs/ *n* Abszeß *m*

abscond /əb'skɒnd/ *vi* entfliehen

absence /'æbsəns/ *n* Abwesenheit *f*

absent[1] /'æbsənt/ *a*, **-ly** *adv* abwesend; **be ～** fehlen

absent[2] /æb'sent/ *vt* **～ oneself** fernbleiben

absentee /æbsən'tiː/ *n* Abwesende(r) *m/f*

absent-minded /æbsənt'maɪndɪd/ *a*, **-ly** *adv* geistesabwesend; (*forgetful*) zerstreut

absolute /'æbsəluːt/ *a*, **-ly** *adv* absolut

absolution /æbsə'luːʃn/ *n* Absolution *f*

absolve /əb'zɒlv/ *vt* lossprechen

absorb /əb'sɔːb/ *vt* absorbieren, aufsaugen; **～ed in** vertieft in (+ *acc*). **～ent** /-ənt/ *a* saugfähig

absorption /əb'sɔːpʃn/ *n* Absorption *f*

abstain /əb'steɪn/ *vi* sich enthalten (**from** *gen*); **～ from voting** sich der Stimme enthalten

abstemious /əb'stiːmɪəs/ *a* enthaltsam

abstention /əb'stenʃn/ *n* (*Pol*) [Stimm]enthaltung *f*

abstinence /'æbstɪnəns/ *n* Enthaltsamkeit *f*

abstract[1] /'æbstrækt/ *a* abstrakt ● *n* (*summary*) Abriß *m*

absurd /əb'sɜːd/ *a*, **-ly** *adv* absurd. **～ity** *n* Absurdität *f*

abundan|ce /ə'bʌndəns/ *n* Fülle *f* (**of** an + *dat*). **～t** *a* reichlich

abuse[1] /ə'bjuːz/ *vt* mißbrauchen; (*insult*) beschimpfen

abus|e[2] /ə'bjuːs/ *n* Mißbrauch *m*; (*insults*) Beschimpfungen *pl*. **～ive** /-ɪv/ *a* ausfallend

abut /ə'bʌt/ *vi* (*pt/pp* **abutted**) angrenzen (**on to** an + *acc*)

abysmal /ə'bɪzml/ *a* (*fam*) katastrophal

abyss /ə'bɪs/ *n* Abgrund *m*

academic /ækə'demɪk/ *a*, **-ally** *adv* akademisch ● *n* Akademiker(in) *m(f)*

academy /ə'kædəmɪ/ *n* Akademie *f*

accede /ək'siːd/ *vi* **～ to** zustimmen (+ *dat*); besteigen ⟨*throne*⟩

accelerat|e /ək'seləreɪt/ *vt* beschleunigen ● *vi* die Geschwindigkeit erhöhen. **～ion** /-'reɪʃn/ *n* Beschleunigung *f*. **～or** *n* (*Auto*) Gaspedal *nt*

accent[1] /'æksənt/ *n* Akzent *m*

accent[2] /æk'sent/ *vt* betonen

accentuate /æk'sentjʊeɪt/ *vt* betonen

accept /ək'sept/ *vt* annehmen; (*fig*) akzeptieren ● *vi* zusagen. **～able** /-əbl/ *a* annehmbar. **～ance** *n* Annahme *f*; (*of invitation*) Zusage *f*

access /'ækses/ *n* Zugang *m*; (*road*) Zufahrt *f*. **～ible** /ək'sesəbl/ *a* zugänglich

accession /ək'seʃn/ *n* (*to throne*) Thronbesteigung *f*

accessor|y /ək'sesərɪ/ *n* (*Jur*) Mitschuldige(r) *m/f*; **～ies** *pl* (*fashion*) Accessoires *pl*; (*Techn*) Zubehör *nt*

accident /'æksɪdənt/ *n* Unfall *m*; (*chance*) Zufall *m*; **by ～** zufällig; (*unintentionally*) versehentlich. **～al** /-'dentl/ *a*, **-ly** *adv* zufällig; (*unintentional*) versehentlich

acclaim /ə'kleɪm/ *n* Beifall *m* ● *vt* feiern (**as** als)

acclimate /'æklɪmeɪt/ *vt* (*Amer*) = **acclimatize**

acclimatize /ə'klaɪmətaɪz/ *vt* **become ～d** sich akklimatisieren

accolade /'ækəleɪd/ *n* Auszeichnung *f*

accommodat|e /ə'kɒmədeɪt/ *vt* unterbringen; (*oblige*) entgegenkommen (+ *dat*). **～ing** *a* entgegenkommend. **～ion** /-'deɪʃn/ *n* (*rooms*) Unterkunft *f*

accompan|iment /ə'kʌmpənɪmənt/ *n* Begleitung *f*. **～ist** *n* (*Mus*) Begleiter(in) *m(f)*

accompany /ə'kʌmpənɪ/ *vt* (*pt/pp* **-ied**) begleiten

accomplice /ə'kʌmplɪs/ *n* Komplize/-zin *m/f*

accomplish /ə'kʌmplɪʃ/ *vt* erfüllen ⟨*task*⟩; (*achieve*) erreichen. **～ed** *a* fähig. **～ment** *n* Fertigkeit *f*; (*achievement*) Leistung *f*

accord /ə'kɔːd/ *n* (*treaty*) Abkommen *nt*; **of one ～** einmütig; **of one's own ～** aus eigenem Antrieb ● *vt* gewähren. **～ance** *n* **in ～ance with** entsprechend (+ *dat*)

according /ə'kɔːdɪŋ/ *adv* **～ to** nach (+ *dat*). **～ly** *adv* entsprechend

accordion /əˈkɔːdɪən/ n Akkordeon nt

accost /əˈkɒst/ vt ansprechen

account /əˈkaʊnt/ n Konto nt; (bill) Rechnung f; (description) Darstellung f; (report) Bericht m; **~s** pl (Comm) Bücher pl; **on ~ of** wegen (+ gen); **on no ~** auf keinen Fall; **on this ~** deshalb; **on my ~** meinetwegen; **of no ~** ohne Bedeutung; **take into ~** in Betracht ziehen, berücksichtigen ● vi **~ for** Rechenschaft ablegen für; (explain) erklären

accountant /əˈkaʊntənt/ n Buchhalter(in) m(f); (chartered) Wirtschaftsprüfer m; (for tax) Steuerberater m

accoutrements /əˈkuːtrəmənts/ npl Ausrüstung f

accredited /əˈkredɪtɪd/ a akkreditiert

accrue /əˈkruː/ vi sich ansammeln

accumulat|e /əˈkjuːmjʊleɪt/ vt ansammeln, anhäufen ● vi sich ansammeln, sich anhäufen. **~ion** /-ˈleɪʃn/ n Ansammlung f, Anhäufung f. **~or** n (Electr) Akkumulator m

accura|cy /ˈækjʊrəsɪ/ n Genauigkeit f. **~te** /-rət/ a, **-ly** adv genau

accusation /ækjuːˈzeɪʃn/ n Anklage f

accusative /əˈkjuːzətɪv/ a & n **~ [case]** (Gram) Akkusativ m

accuse /əˈkjuːz/ vt (Jur) anklagen (of gen); **~ s.o. of doing sth** jdn beschuldigen, etw getan zu haben. **~d** n **the ~d** der/die Angeklagte

accustom /əˈkʌstəm/ vt gewöhnen (to an + dat); **grow** or **get ~ed to** sich gewöhnen an (+ acc). **~ed** a gewohnt

ace /eɪs/ n (Cards, Sport) As nt

ache /eɪk/ n Schmerzen pl ● vi weh tun, schmerzen

achieve /əˈtʃiːv/ vt leisten; (gain) erzielen; (reach) erreichen. **~ment** n (feat) Leistung f

acid /ˈæsɪd/ a sauer; (fig) beißend ● n Säure f. **~ity** /əˈsɪdətɪ/ n Säure f. **~ 'rain** n saurer Regen m

acknowledge /əkˈnɒlɪdʒ/ vt anerkennen; (admit) zugeben; erwidern ⟨greeting⟩; **~ receipt of** den Empfang bestätigen (+ gen). **~ment** n Anerkennung f; (of letter) Empfangsbestätigung f

acne /ˈæknɪ/ n Akne f

acorn /ˈeɪkɔːn/ n Eichel f

acoustic /əˈkuːstɪk/ a, **-ally** adv akustisch. **~s** npl Akustik f

acquaint /əˈkweɪnt/ vt **~ s.o. with** jdn bekannt machen mit; **be ~ed with** kennen; vertraut sein mit ⟨fact⟩. **~ance** n Bekanntschaft f; (person) Bekannte(r) m/f; **make s.o.'s ~ance** jdn kennenlernen

acquiesce /ækwɪˈes/ vi einwilligen (to in + acc). **~nce** n Einwilligung f

acquire /əˈkwaɪə(r)/ vt erwerben

acquisit|ion /ækwɪˈzɪʃn/ n Erwerb m; (thing) Erwerbung f. **~ive** /əˈkwɪzətɪv/ a habgierig

acquit /əˈkwɪt/ vt (pt/pp acquitted) freisprechen; **~ oneself well** seiner Aufgabe gerecht werden. **~tal** n Freispruch m

acre /ˈeɪkə(r)/ n ≈ Morgen m

acrid /ˈækrɪd/ a scharf

acrimon|ious /ækrɪˈməʊnɪəs/ a bitter. **~y** /ˈækrɪmənɪ/ n Bitterkeit f

acrobat /ˈækrəbæt/ n Akrobat(in) m(f). **~ic** /-ˈbætɪk/ a akrobatisch

across /əˈkrɒs/ adv hinüber/herüber; (wide) breit; (not lengthwise) quer; (in crossword) waagerecht; **come ~ sth** auf etw (acc) stoßen; **go ~** hinübergehen; **bring ~** herüberbringen ● prep über (+ acc); (crosswise) quer über (+ acc/dat); (on the other side of) auf der anderen Seite (+ gen)

act /ækt/ n Tat f; (action) Handlung f; (law) Gesetz nt; (Theat) Akt m; (item) Nummer f; **put on an ~** (fam) sich verstellen ● vi handeln; (behave) sich verhalten; (Theat) spielen; (pretend) sich verstellen; **~ as** fungieren als ● vt spielen ⟨role⟩. **~ing** a (deputy) stellvertretend ● n (Theat) Schauspielerei f. **~ing profession** n Schauspielerberuf m

action /ˈækʃn/ n Handlung f; (deed) Tat f; (Mil) Einsatz m; (Jur) Klage f; (effect) Wirkung f; (Techn) Mechanismus m; **out of ~** ⟨machine:⟩ außer Betrieb; **take ~** handeln; **killed in ~** gefallen. **~ 'replay** n (TV) Wiederholung f

activate /ˈæktɪveɪt/ vt betätigen; (Chem, Phys) aktivieren

activ|e /ˈæktɪv/ a, **-ly** adv aktiv; **on ~e service** im Einsatz. **~ity** /-ˈtɪvətɪ/ n Aktivität f

act|or /ˈæktə(r)/ n Schauspieler m. **~ress** n Schauspielerin f

actual /'æktʃʊəl/ a, **-ly** adv eigentlich; (real) tatsächlich. ~**ity** /-'æləti/ n Wirklichkeit f

acumen /'ækjʊmən/ n Scharfsinn m

acupuncture /'ækjʊ-/ n Akupunktur f

acute /ə'kju:t/ a scharf; ⟨angle⟩ spitz; ⟨illness⟩ akut. ~**ly** adv sehr

ad /æd/ n (fam) = **advertisement**

AD abbr (**Anno Domini**) n.Chr.

adamant /'ædəmənt/ a **be** ~ **that** darauf bestehen, daß

adapt /ə'dæpt/ vt anpassen; bearbeiten ⟨play⟩ ● vi sich anpassen. ~**ability** /-ə'bɪləti/ n Anpassungsfähigkeit f. ~**able** /-əbl/ a anpassungsfähig

adaptation /ædæp'teɪʃn/ n (Theat) Bearbeitung f

adapter, adaptor /ə'dæptə(r)/ n (Techn) Adapter m; (Electr) (two-way) Doppelstecker m

add /æd/ vt hinzufügen; (Math) addieren ● vi zusammenzählen, addieren; ~ **to** hinzufügen zu; (fig: increase) steigern; (compound) verschlimmern. ~ **up** vt zusammenzählen ⟨figures⟩ ● vi zusammenzählen, addieren; ~ **up to** machen; **it doesn't** ~ **up** (fig) da stimmt etwas nicht

adder /'ædə(r)/ n Kreuzotter f

addict /'ædɪkt/ n Süchtige(r) m/f

addict|ed /ə'dɪktɪd/ a süchtig; ~**ed to drugs** drogensüchtig. ~**ion** /-'ɪkʃn/ n Sucht f. ~**ive** /-ɪv/ a **be** ~**ive** zur Süchtigkeit führen

addition /ə'dɪʃn/ n Hinzufügung f; (Math) Addition f; (thing added) Ergänzung f; **in** ~ zusätzlich. ~**al** a, **-ly** adv zusätzlich

additive /'ædɪtɪv/ n Zusatz m

address /ə'dres/ n Adresse f, Anschrift f; (speech) Ansprache f; **form of** ~ Anrede f ● vt adressieren (**to** an + acc); (speak to) anreden ⟨person⟩; sprechen vor (+ dat) ⟨meeting⟩. ~**ee** /ædre'si:/ n Empfänger m

adenoids /'ædənɔɪdz/ npl [Rachen]-polypen pl

adept /'ædept/ a geschickt (**at** in + dat)

adequate /'ædɪkwət/ a, **-ly** adv ausreichend

adhere /əd'hɪə(r)/ vi kleben/⟨fig⟩ festhalten (**to** an + dat). ~**nce** n Festhalten nt

adhesive /əd'hi:sɪv/ a klebend ● n Klebstoff m

adjacent /ə'dʒeɪsnt/ a angrenzend

adjective /'ædʒɪktɪv/ n Adjektiv nt

adjoin /ə'dʒɔɪn/ vt angrenzen an (+ acc). ~**ing** a angrenzend

adjourn /ə'dʒɜ:n/ vt vertagen (**until** auf + acc) ● vi sich vertagen. ~**ment** n Vertagung f

adjudicate /ə'dʒu:dɪkeɪt/ vi entscheiden; (in competition) Preisrichter sein

adjust /ə'dʒʌst/ vt einstellen; (alter) verstellen ● vi sich anpassen (**to** dat). ~**able** /-əbl/ a verstellbar. ~**ment** n Einstellung f; Anpassung f

ad lib /æd'lɪb/ adv aus dem Stegreif ● vi (pt/pp **ad libbed**) (fam) improvisieren

administer /əd'mɪnɪstə(r)/ vt verwalten; verabreichen ⟨medicine⟩

administrat|ion /ədmɪnɪ'streɪʃn/ n Verwaltung f; (Pol) Regierung f. ~**or** /əd'mɪnɪstreɪtə(r)/ n Verwaltungsbeamte(r) m/-beamtin f

admirable /'ædmərəbl/ a bewundernswert

admiral /'ædmərəl/ n Admiral m

admiration /ædmə'reɪʃn/ n Bewunderung f

admire /əd'maɪə(r)/ vt bewundern. ~**r** n Verehrer(in) m(f)

admissible /əd'mɪsəbl/ a zulässig

admission /əd'mɪʃn/ n Eingeständnis nt; (entry) Eintritt m

admit /əd'mɪt/ vt (pt/pp **admitted**) (let in) hereinlassen; (acknowledge) zugeben; ~ **to sth** etw zugeben. ~**tance** n Eintritt m. ~**tedly** adv zugegebenermaßen

admoni|sh /əd'mɒnɪʃ/ vt ermahnen. ~**tion** /ædmə'nɪʃn/ n Ermahnung f

ado /ə'du:/ n **without more** ~ ohne weiteres

adolescen|ce /ædə'lesns/ n Jugend f, Pubertät f. ~**t** a Jugend-; ⟨boy, girl⟩ halbwüchsig ● n Jugendliche(r) m/f

adopt /ə'dɒpt/ vt adoptieren; ergreifen ⟨measure⟩; (Pol) annehmen ⟨candidate⟩. ~**ion** /-ɒpʃn/ n Adoption f. ~**ive** /-ɪv/ a Adoptiv-

ador|able /ə'dɔ:rəbl/ a bezaubernd. ~**ation** /ædə'reɪʃn/ n Anbetung f

adore /ə'dɔ:(r)/ vt ⟨worship⟩ anbeten; (fam: like) lieben

adorn /ə'dɔ:n/ vt schmücken. ~**ment** n Schmuck m

adrenalin /ə'drenəlm/ n Adrenalin nt

Adriatic /eɪdrɪ'ætɪk/ a & n ~ **[Sea]** Adria f

adrift /ə'drɪft/ a **be** ~ treiben; **come** ~ sich losreißen

adroit /ə'drɔɪt/ a, **-ly** adv gewandt, geschickt

adulation /ædjʊ'leɪʃn/ n Schwärmerei f

adult /'ædʌlt/ n Erwachsene(r) m/f

adulterate /ə'dʌltəreɪt/ vt verfälschen; panschen ⟨wine⟩

adultery /ə'dʌltərɪ/ n Ehebruch m

advance /əd'vɑːns/ n Fortschritt m; (Mil) Vorrücken nt; (payment) Vorschuß m; **in** ~ im voraus ●vi vorankommen; (Mil) vorrücken; (make progress) Fortschritte machen ●vt fördern ⟨cause⟩; vorbringen ⟨idea⟩; vorschießen ⟨money⟩. ~ **booking** n Kartenvorverkauf m. ~**d** a fortgeschritten; (progressive) fortschrittlich. ~**ment** n Förderung f; (promotion) Beförderung f

advantage /əd'vɑːntɪdʒ/ n Vorteil m; **take** ~ **of** ausnutzen. ~**ous** /ædvən'teɪdʒəs/ a vorteilhaft

advent /'ædvent/ n Ankunft f; **A**~ (season) Advent m

adventur|e /əd'ventʃə(r)/ n Abenteuer nt. ~**er** n Abenteurer m. ~**ous** /-rəs/ a abenteuerlich; ⟨person⟩ abenteuerlustig

adverb /'ædvɜːb/ n Adverb nt

adversary /'ædvəsərɪ/ n Widersacher m

advers|e /'ædvɜːs/ a ungünstig. ~**ity** /əd'vɜːsətɪ/ n Not f

advert /'ædvɜːt/ n (fam) = **advertisement**

advertise /'ædvətaɪz/ vt Reklame machen für; (by small ad) inserieren ●vi Reklame machen; inserieren; ~ **for** per Anzeige suchen

advertisement /əd'vɜːtɪsmənt/ n Anzeige f; (publicity) Reklame f; (small ad) Inserat nt

advertis|er /'ædvətaɪzə(r)/ n Inserent m. ~**ing** n Werbung f ●attrib Werbe-

advice /əd'vaɪs/ n Rat m. ~ **note** n Benachrichtigung f

advisable /əd'vaɪzəbl/ a ratsam

advis|e /əd'vaɪz/ vt raten (**s.o.** jdm); (counsel) beraten; (inform) benachrichtigen; ~**e s.o. against sth** jdm

von etw abraten ●vi raten. ~**er** n Berater(in) m(f). ~**ory** a beratend

advocate[1] /'ædvəkət/ n [Rechts]-anwalt m/-anwältin f; (supporter) Befürworter m

advocate[2] /'ædvəkeɪt/ vt befürworten

aerial /'eərɪəl/ a Luft- ● n Antenne f

aerobics /eə'rəʊbɪks/ n Aerobic nt

aero|drome /'eərədrəʊm/ n Flugplatz m. ~**plane** n Flugzeug nt

aerosol /'eərəsɒl/ n Spraydose f

aesthetic /iːs'θetɪk/ a ästhetisch

afar /ə'fɑː(r)/ adv **from** ~ aus der Ferne

affable /'æfəbl/ a, **-bly** adv freundlich

affair /ə'feə(r)/ n Angelegenheit f, Sache f; (scandal) Affäre f; **[love-]** ~ [Liebes]verhältnis nt

affect /ə'fekt/ vt sich auswirken auf (+ acc); (concern) betreffen; (move) rühren; (pretend) vortäuschen. ~**ation** /æfek'teɪʃn/ n Affektiertheit f. ~**ed** a affektiert

affection /ə'fekʃn/ n Liebe f. ~**ate** /-ət/ a, **-ly** adv liebevoll

affiliated /ə'fɪlɪeɪtɪd/ a angeschlossen (**to** dat)

affinity /ə'fɪnətɪ/ n Ähnlichkeit f; (attraction) gegenseitige Anziehung f

affirm /ə'fɜːm/ vt behaupten; (Jur) eidesstattlich erklären

affirmative /ə'fɜːmətɪv/ a bejahend ● n Bejahung f

affix /ə'fɪks/ vt anbringen (**to** dat); (stick) aufkleben (**to** auf + acc); setzen ⟨signature⟩ (**to** unter + acc)

afflict /ə'flɪkt/ vt **be** ~**ed with** behaftet sein mit. ~**ion** /-ɪkʃn/ n Leiden nt

affluen|ce /'æflʊəns/ n Reichtum m. ~**t** a wohlhabend. ~**t society** n Wohlstandsgesellschaft f

afford /ə'fɔːd/ vt (provide) gewähren; **be able to** ~ **sth** sich (dat) etw leisten können. ~**able** /-əbl/ a erschwinglich

affray /ə'freɪ/ n Schlägerei f

affront /ə'frʌnt/ n Beleidigung f ● vt beleidigen

afield /ə'fiːld/ adv **further** ~ weiter weg

afloat /ə'fləʊt/ a **be** ~ ⟨ship:⟩ flott sein; **keep** ~ ⟨person:⟩ sich über Wasser halten

afoot /ə'fʊt/ a im Gange

aforesaid /əˈfɔːˌsed/ a (Jur) obenerwähnt

afraid /əˈfreɪd/ a be ∼ Angst haben
(of vor + dat); I'm ∼ not leider nicht;
I'm ∼ so [ja] leider; I'm ∼ I can't help
you ich kann Ihnen leider nicht helfen

afresh /əˈfreʃ/ adv von vorne

Africa /ˈæfrɪkə/ n Afrika nt. ∼n a
afrikanisch ● n Afrikaner(in) m(f)

after /ˈɑːftə(r)/ adv danach ● prep
nach (+ dat); ∼ that danach; ∼ all
schließlich; the day ∼ tomorrow
übermorgen; be ∼ aussein auf (+ acc)
● conj nachdem

after: ∼-effect n Nachwirkung f.
∼math /-mɑːθ/ n Auswirkungen pl.
∼noon n Nachmittag m; good
∼noon! guten Tag! ∼sales service n
Kundendienst m. ∼shave n
Rasierwasser nt. ∼thought n
nachträglicher Einfall m. ∼wards
adv nachher

again /əˈgeɪn/ adv wieder; (once more)
noch einmal; (besides) außerdem; ∼
and ∼ immer wieder

against /əˈgeɪnst/ prep gegen (+ acc)

age /eɪdʒ/ n Alter nt; (era) Zeitalter
nt; ∼s (fam) ewig; under ∼ minderjährig; ∼ volljährig; two years of ∼
zwei Jahre alt ● v (pres p ageing) ● vt
älter machen ● vi altern; (mature)
reifen

aged[1] /eɪdʒd/ a ∼ two zwei Jahre alt

aged[2] /ˈeɪdʒɪd/ a betagt ● n the ∼ pl
die Alten

ageless /ˈeɪdʒlɪs/ a ewig jung

agency /ˈeɪdʒənsɪ/ n Agentur f; (office) Büro nt; have the ∼ for die Ver-
tretung haben für

agenda /əˈdʒendə/ n Tagesordnung
f; on the ∼ auf dem Programm

agent /ˈeɪdʒənt/ n Agent(in) m(f);
(Comm) Vertreter(in) m(f); (substance) Mittel nt

aggravat|e /ˈægrəveɪt/ vt ver-
schlimmern; (fam: annoy) ärgern.
∼ion /-ˈveɪʃn/ n (fam) Ärger m

aggregate /ˈægrɪgət/ a gesamt ● n
Gesamtzahl f; (sum) Gesamtsumme
f

aggress|ion /əˈgreʃn/ n Aggression
f. ∼ive /-sɪv/ a, -ly adv aggressiv. ∼
iveness n Aggressivität f. ∼or n An-
greifer(in) m(f)

aggrieved /əˈgriːvd/ a verletzt

aggro /ˈægrəʊ/ n (fam) Ärger m

aghast /əˈgɑːst/ a entsetzt

agil|e /ˈædʒaɪl/ a flink, behende;
⟨mind⟩ wendig. ∼ity /əˈdʒɪlətɪ/ n
Flinkheit f, Behendigkeit f

agitat|e /ˈædʒɪteɪt/ vt bewegen;
(shake) schütteln ● vi (fig) ∼ for agi-
tieren für. ∼ed a, -ly adv erregt. ∼ion
/-ˈteɪʃn/ n Erregung f; (Pol) Agi-
tation f. ∼or n Agitator m

agnostic /ægˈnɒstɪk/ n Agnostiker
m

ago /əˈgəʊ/ adv vor (+ dat); a month
∼ vor einem Monat; a long time ∼ vor
langer Zeit; how long ∼ is it? wie lange
ist es her?

agog /əˈgɒg/ a gespannt

agoniz|e /ˈægənaɪz/ vi [innerlich]
ringen. ∼ing a qualvoll

agony /ˈægənɪ/ n Qual f; be in ∼
furchtbare Schmerzen haben

agree /əˈgriː/ vt vereinbaren;
(admit) zugeben; ∼ to do sth sich bereit erklären, etw zu tun ● vi ⟨people,
figures:⟩ übereinstimmen; (reach
agreement) sich einigen; (get on) gut
miteinander auskommen; (consent)
einwilligen (to in + acc); I ∼ der Meinung bin ich auch; ∼ with s.o. jdm
zustimmen; ⟨food:⟩ jdm bekommen; ∼
with sth (approve of) mit etw einverstanden sein

agreeable /əˈgriːəbl/ a angenehm;
be ∼ einverstanden sein (to mit)

agreed /əˈgriːd/ a vereinbart

agreement /əˈgriːmənt/ n Übereinstimmung f; (consent) Einwilligung f; (contract) Abkommen
nt; reach ∼ sich einigen

agricultur|al /ægrɪˈkʌltʃərəl/ a
landwirtschaftlich. ∼e /ˈægrɪ-
kʌltʃə(r)/ n Landwirtschaft f

aground /əˈgraʊnd/ a gestrandet;
run ∼ ⟨ship:⟩ stranden

ahead /əˈhed/ adv straight ∼ geradeaus; be ∼ of s.o./sth vor jdm/etw
sein; (fig) voraus sein; draw ∼ nach
vorne ziehen; go on ∼ vorgehen; get ∼
vorankommen; go ∼! (fam) bitte!
look/plan ∼ vorausblicken/ -planen

aid /eɪd/ n Hilfe f; (financial) Unterstützung f; in ∼ of zugunsten
(+ gen) ● vt helfen (+ dat)

aide /eɪd/ n Berater m

Aids /eɪdz/ n Aids nt

ail|ing /ˈeɪlɪŋ/ a kränkelnd. ∼ment
n Leiden nt

aim /eɪm/ n Ziel nt; take ∼ zielen ● vt
richten (at auf + acc) ● vi zielen (at auf

+ *acc*); ~ **to do sth** beabsichtigen, etw zu tun. ~**less** *a*, **-ly** *adv* ziellos

air /eə(r)/ *n* Luft *f*; (*tune*) Melodie *f*; (*expression*) Miene *f*; (*appearance*) Anschein *m*; **be on the** ~ ⟨*programme:*⟩ gesendet werden; ⟨*person:*⟩ senden, auf Sendung sein; **put on** ~**s** vornehm tun; **by** ~ auf dem Luftweg; (*airmail*) mit Luftpost ● *vt* lüften; vorbringen ⟨*views*⟩

air: ~**-bed** *n* Luftmatratze *f*. ~**-conditioned** *a* klimatisiert. ~**-conditioning** *n* Klimaanlage *f*. ~**craft** *n* Flugzeug *nt*. ~ **fare** *n* Flugpreis *m*. ~**field** *n* Flugplatz *m*. ~ **force** *n* Luftwaffe *f*. ~ **freshener** *n* Raumspray *nt*. ~**gun** *n* Luftgewehr *nt*. ~ **hostess** *n* Stewardeß *f*. ~ **letter** *n* Aerogramm *nt*. ~**line** *n* Fluggesellschaft *f*. ~**lock** *n* Luftblase *f*. ~**mail** *n* Luftpost *f*. ~**man** *n* Flieger *m*. ~**plane** *n* (*Amer*) Flugzeug *nt*. ~ **pocket** *n* Luftloch *nt*. ~**port** *n* Flughafen *m*. ~ **raid** *n* Luftangriff *m*. ~**-raid shelter** *n* Luftschutzbunker *m*. ~**ship** *n* Luftschiff *nt*. ~ **ticket** *n* Flugschein *m*. ~**tight** *a* luftdicht. ~ **traffic** *n* Luftverkehr *m*. ~**-traffic controller** *n* Fluglotse *m*. ~**worthy** *a* flugtüchtig

airy /ˈeərɪ/ *a* (**-ier, -iest**) luftig; ⟨*manner*⟩ nonchalant

aisle /aɪl/ *n* Gang *m*

ajar /əˈdʒɑː(r)/ *a* angelehnt

akin /əˈkɪn/ *a* ~ **to** verwandt mit; (*similar*) ähnlich (**to** *dat*)

alabaster /ˈæləbɑːstə(r)/ *n* Alabaster *m*

alacrity /əˈlækrətɪ/ *n* Bereitfertigkeit *f*

alarm /əˈlɑːm/ *n* Alarm *m*; (*device*) Alarmanlage *f*; (*clock*) Wecker *m*; (*fear*) Unruhe *f* ● *vt* erschrecken; alarmieren. ~ **clock** *n* Wecker *m*

alas /əˈlæs/ *int* ach!

album /ˈælbəm/ *n* Album *nt*

alcohol /ˈælkəhɒl/ *n* Alkohol *m*. ~**ic** /-ˈhɒlɪk/ *a* alkoholisch ● *n* Alkoholiker(in) *m(f)*. ~**ism** *n* Alkoholismus *m*

alcove /ˈælkəʊv/ *n* Nische *f*

alert /əˈlɜːt/ *a* aufmerksam ● *n* Alarm *m*; **on the** ~ auf der Hut ● *vt* alarmieren

algae /ˈældʒiː/ *npl* Algen *pl*

algebra /ˈældʒɪbrə/ *n* Algebra *f*

Algeria /ælˈdʒɪərɪə/ *n* Algerien *nt*

alias /ˈeɪlɪəs/ *n* Deckname *m* ● *adv* alias

alibi /ˈælɪbaɪ/ *n* Alibi *nt*

alien /ˈeɪlɪən/ *a* fremd ● *n* Ausländer(in) *m(f)*

alienat|e /ˈeɪlɪəneɪt/ *vt* entfremden. ~**ion** /-ˈneɪʃn/ *n* Entfremdung *f*

alight[1] /əˈlaɪt/ *vi* aussteigen (**from** aus); ⟨*bird:*⟩ sich niederlassen

alight[2] *a* **be** ~ brennen; **set** ~ anzünden

align /əˈlaɪn/ *vt* ausrichten. ~**ment** *n* Ausrichtung *f*; **out of** ~**ment** nicht richtig ausgerichtet

alike /əˈlaɪk/ *a & adv* ähnlich; (*same*) gleich; **look** ~ sich (*dat*) ähnlich sehen

alimony /ˈælɪmənɪ/ *n* Unterhalt *m*

alive /əˈlaɪv/ *a* lebendig; **be** ~ leben; **be** ~ **with** wimmeln von

alkali /ˈælkəlaɪ/ *n* Base *f*, Alkali *nt*

all /ɔːl/ *a* alle *pl*; (*whole*) ganz; ~ **[the] children** alle Kinder; ~ **our children** alle unsere Kinder; ~ **the others** alle anderen; ~ **day** den ganzen Tag; ~ **the wine** der ganze Wein; **for** ~ **that** (*nevertheless*) trotzdem; **in** ~ **innocence** in aller Unschuld ● *pron* alle *pl*; (*everything*) alles; ~ **of you/them** Sie/sie alle; ~ **of the town** die ganze Stadt; **not at** ~ gar nicht; **in** ~ insgesamt; ~ **in** ~ alles in allem; **most of** ~ am meisten; **once and for** ~ ein für allemal ● *adv* ganz; ~ **but** fast; ~ **at once** auf einmal; ~ **too soon** viel zu früh; ~ **the same** (*nevertheless*) trotzdem; ~ **the better** um so besser; **be** ~ **in** (*fam*) völlig erledigt sein; **four** ~ (*Sport*) vier zu vier

allay /əˈleɪ/ *vt* zerstreuen

allegation /ælɪˈgeɪʃn/ *n* Behauptung *f*

allege /əˈledʒ/ *vt* behaupten. ~**d** *a*, **-ly** /-ɪdlɪ/ *adv* angeblich

allegiance /əˈliːdʒəns/ *n* Treue *f*

allegor|ical /ælɪˈgɒrɪkl/ *a* allegorisch. ~**y** /ˈælɪgərɪ/ *n* Allegorie *f*

allerg|ic /əˈlɜːdʒɪk/ *a* allergisch (**to** gegen). ~**y** /ˈælədʒɪ/ *n* Allergie *f*

alleviate /əˈliːvɪeɪt/ *vt* lindern

alley /ˈælɪ/ *n* Gasse *f*; (*for bowling*) Bahn *f*

alliance /əˈlaɪəns/ *n* Verbindung *f*; (*Pol*) Bündnis *nt*

allied /ˈælaɪd/ *a* alliiert; (*fig: related*) verwandt (**to** mit)

alligator /ˈælɪgeɪtə(r)/ *n* Alligator *m*

allocat|e /ˈæləkeɪt/ *vt* zuteilen; (*share out*) verteilen. ~**ion** /-ˈkeɪʃn/ *n* Zuteilung *f*

allot /əˈlɒt/ vt (pt/pp **allotted**) zu-teilen (**s.o.** jdm). **~ment** n ≈ Schrebergarten m

allow /əˈlaʊ/ vt erlauben; (give) geben; (grant) gewähren; (reckon) rechnen; (agree, admit) zugeben; **~ for** berücksichtigen; **~ s.o. to do sth** jdm erlauben, etw zu tun; **be ~ed to do sth** etw tun dürfen

allowance /əˈlaʊəns/ n [finanzielle] Unterstützung f; **~ for petrol** Benzingeld nt; **make ~s for** berücksichtigen

alloy /ˈælɔɪ/ n Legierung f

allude /əˈluːd/ vi anspielen (**to** auf + acc)

allure /əˈlʊə(r)/ n Reiz m

allusion /əˈluːʒn/ n Anspielung f

ally[1] /ˈælaɪ/ n Verbündete(r) m/f; **the Allies** pl die Alliierten

ally[2] /əˈlaɪ/ vt (pt/pp **-ied**) verbinden; **~ oneself with** sich verbünden mit

almighty /ɔːlˈmaɪtɪ/ a allmächtig; (fam: big) Riesen-. ● n **the A~** der Allmächtige

almond /ˈɑːmənd/ n (Bot) Mandel f

almost /ˈɔːlməʊst/ adv fast, beinahe

alms /ɑːmz/ npl (liter) Almosen pl

alone /əˈləʊn/ a & adv allein; **leave me ~** laß mich in Ruhe; **leave that ~!** laß die Finger davon! **let ~** ganz zu schweigen von

along /əˈlɒŋ/ prep entlang (+ acc); **~ the river** den Fluß entlang ● adv **~ with** zusammen mit; **all ~** die ganze Zeit; **come ~** komm doch; **I'll bring it ~** ich bringe es mit; **move ~** weiter-gehen

along'side adv daneben ● prep neben (+ dat)

aloof /əˈluːf/ a distanziert

aloud /əˈlaʊd/ adv laut

alphabet /ˈælfəbet/ n Alphabet nt. **~ical** /-ˈbetɪkl/ a, **-ly** adv alphabetisch

alpine /ˈælpaɪn/ a alpin; **A~** Alpen-

Alps /ælps/ npl Alpen pl

already /ɔːlˈredɪ/ adv schon

Alsace /ælˈsæs/ n Elsaß nt

Alsatian /ælˈseɪʃn/ n (dog) [deutscher] Schäferhund m

also /ˈɔːlsəʊ/ adv auch

altar /ˈɔːltə(r)/ n Altar m

alter /ˈɔːltə(r)/ vt ändern ● vi sich verändern. **~ation** /-ˈreɪʃn/ n Än-derung f

alternate[1] /ˈɔːltəneɪt/ vi [sich] abwechseln ● vt abwechseln

alternate[2] /ɔːlˈtɜːnət/ a, **-ly** adv abwechselnd; (Amer: alternative) an-dere(r,s); **on ~ days** jeden zweiten Tag

'alternating current n Wechsel-strom m

alternative /ɔːlˈtɜːnətɪv/ a andere(r, s) ● n Alternative f. **~ly** adv oder aber

although /ɔːlˈðəʊ/ conj obgleich, obwohl

altitude /ˈæltɪtjuːd/ n Höhe f

altogether /ɔːltəˈgeðə(r)/ adv ins-gesamt; (on the whole) alles in allem

altruistic /æltruˈɪstɪk/ altruistisch

aluminium /æljʊˈmɪnɪəm/ n, (Amer) **aluminum** /əˈluːmɪnəm/ n Alumi-nium nt

always /ˈɔːlweɪz/ adv immer

am /æm/ see **be**

a.m. abbr (**ante meridiem**) vormittags

amalgamate /əˈmælgəmeɪt/ vt ver-einigen; (Chem) amalgamieren ● vi sich vereinigen; (Chem) sich amal-gamieren

amass /əˈmæs/ vt anhäufen

amateur /ˈæmətə(r)/ n Amateur m ● attrib Amateur-; (Theat) Laien-. **~ish** a laienhaft

amaze /əˈmeɪz/ vt erstaunen. **~d** a erstaunt. **~ment** n Erstaunen nt

amazing /əˈmeɪzɪŋ/ a, **-ly** adv er-staunlich

ambassador /æmˈbæsədə(r)/ n Bot-schafter m

amber /ˈæmbə(r)/ n Bernstein m ● a (colour) gelb

ambidextrous /æmbɪˈdekstrəs/ a **be ~** mit beiden Händen gleich geschickt sein

ambience /ˈæmbɪəns/ n Atmos-phäre f

ambigu|ity /æmbɪˈgjuːətɪ/ n Zwei-deutigkeit f. **~ous** /-ˈbɪgjʊəs/ a, **-ly** adv zweideutig

ambiti|on /æmˈbɪʃn/ n Ehrgeiz m; (aim) Ambition f. **~ous** /-ʃəs/ a ehrgeizig

ambivalent /æmˈbɪvələnt/ a zwie-spältig; **be/feel ~** im Zwiespalt sein

amble /ˈæmbl/ vi schlendern

ambulance /ˈæmbjʊləns/ n Kran-kenwagen m. **~ man** n Sanitäter m

ambush /ˈæmbʊʃ/ n Hinterhalt m ● vt aus dem Hinterhalt überfallen

amen /ɑːˈmen/ int amen

amenable /əˈmiːnəbl/ a **~ to** zu-gänglich (**to** dat)

amend /ə'mend/ *vt* ändern. **∼ment** *n* Änderung *f*. **∼s** *npl* **make ∼s for sth** etw wiedergutmachen

amenities /ə'mi:nətɪz/ *npl* Einrichtungen *pl*

America /ə'merɪkə/ *n* Amerika *nt*. **∼n** *a* amerikanisch ● *n* Amerikaner(in) *m(f)*. **∼nism** *n* Amerikanismus *m*

amiable /'eɪmɪəbl/ *a* nett

amicable /'æmɪkəbl/ *a*, **-bly** *adv* freundschaftlich; ⟨*agreement*⟩ gütlich

amid[st] /ə'mɪd[st]/ *prep* inmitten (+ *gen*)

amiss /ə'mɪs/ *a* **be ∼** nicht stimmen ● *adv* **not come ∼** nicht unangebracht sein; **take sth ∼** etw übelnehmen

ammonia /ə'məʊnɪə/ *n* Ammoniak *nt*

ammunition /æmjʊ'nɪʃn/ *n* Munition *f*

amnesia /æm'ni:zɪə/ *n* Amnesie *f*

amnesty /'æmnəstɪ/ *n* Amnestie *f*

among[st] /ə'mʌŋ[st]/ *prep* unter (+ *dat/acc*); **∼ yourselves** untereinander

amoral /eɪ'mɒrəl/ *a* amoralisch

amorous /'æmərəs/ *a* zärtlich

amount /ə'maʊnt/ *n* Menge *f*; (*sum of money*) Betrag *m*; (*total*) Gesamtsumme *f* ● *vi* **∼ to** sich belaufen auf (+ *acc*); (*fig*) hinauslaufen auf (+ *acc*)

amp /æmp/ *n* Ampere *nt*

amphibi|an /æm'fɪbɪən/ *n* Amphibie *f*. **∼ous** /-ɪəs/ *a* amphibisch

amphitheatre /'æmfɪ-/ *n* Amphitheater *nt*

ample /'æmpl/ *a* (**-r, -st**), **-ly** *adv* reichlich; (*large*) füllig

amplif|ier /'æmplɪfaɪə(r)/ *n* Verstärker *m*. **∼y** /-faɪ/ *vt* (*pt/pp* **-ied**) weiter ausführen; verstärken ⟨*sound*⟩

amputat|e /'æmpjʊteɪt/ *vt* amputieren. **∼ion** /-'teɪʃn/ *n* Amputation *f*

amuse /ə'mju:z/ *vt* amüsieren, belustigen; (*entertain*) unterhalten. **∼ment** *n* Belustigung *f*; Unterhaltung *f*. **∼ment arcade** *n* Spielhalle *f*

amusing /ə'mju:zɪŋ/ *a* amüsant

an /ən/, *betont* æn/ *see* **a**

anaem|ia /ə'ni:mɪə/ *n* Blutarmut *f*, Anämie *f*. **∼ic** *a* blutarm

anaesthesia /ænəs'θi:zɪə/ *n* Betäubung *f*

anaesthetic /ænəs'θetɪk/ *n* Narkosemittel *nt*, Betäubungsmittel *nt*; **under [an] ∼** in Narkose; **give s.o. an ∼** jdm eine Narkose geben

anaesthet|ist /ə'ni:sθətɪst/ *n* Narkosearzt *m*. **∼ize** /-taɪz/ *vt* betäuben

analog[ue] /'ænəlɒg/ *n* Analog-

analogy /ə'nælədʒɪ/ *n* Analogie *f*

analyse /'ænəlaɪz/ *vt* analysieren

analysis /ə'næləsɪs/ *n* Analyse *f*

analyst /'ænəlɪst/ *n* Chemiker(in) *m(f)*; (*Psych*) Analytiker *m*

analytical /ænə'lɪtɪkl/ *a* analytisch

anarch|ist /'ænəkɪst/ *n* Anarchist *m*. **∼y** *n* Anarchie *f*

anathema /ə'næθəmə/ *n* Greuel *m*

anatom|ical /ænə'tɒmɪkl/ *a*, **-ly** *adv* anatomisch. **∼y** /ə'nætəmɪ/ *n* Anatomie *f*

ancest|or /'ænsestə(r)/ *n* Vorfahr *m*. **∼ry** *n* Abstammung *f*

anchor /'æŋkə(r)/ *n* Anker *m* ● *vi* ankern ● *vt* verankern

anchovy /'æntʃəvɪ/ *n* Sardelle *f*

ancient /'eɪnʃənt/ *a* alt

ancillary /æn'sɪlərɪ/ *a* Hilfs-

and /ənd, *betont* ænd/ *conj* und; **∼ so on** und so weiter; **six hundred ∼ two** sechshundertzwei; **more ∼ more** immer mehr; **nice ∼ warm** schön warm; **try ∼ come** versuche zu kommen

anecdote /'ænɪkdəʊt/ *n* Anekdote *f*

anew /ə'nju:/ *adv* von neuem

angel /'eɪndʒl/ *n* Engel *m*. **∼ic** /æn'dʒelɪk/ *a* engelhaft

anger /'æŋgə(r)/ *n* Zorn *m* ● *vt* zornig machen

angle[1] /'æŋgl/ *n* Winkel *m*; (*fig*) Standpunkt *m*; **at an ∼** schräg

angle[2] *vi* angeln; **∼ for** (*fig*) fischen nach. **∼r** *n* Angler *m*

Anglican /'æŋglɪkən/ *a* anglikanisch ● *n* Anglikaner(in) *m(f)*

Anglo-Saxon /æŋgləʊ'sæksn/ *a* angelsächsisch ● *n* Angelsächsisch *nt*

angry /'æŋgrɪ/ *a* (**-ier, -iest**), **-ily** *adv* zornig; **be ∼ with** böse sein auf (+ *acc*)

anguish /'æŋgwɪʃ/ *n* Qual *f*

angular /'æŋgjʊlə(r)/ *a* eckig; ⟨*features*⟩ kantig

animal /'ænɪml/ *n* Tier *nt* ● *a* tierisch

animate[1] /'ænɪmət/ *a* lebendig

animat|e[2] /'ænɪmeɪt/ *vt* beleben. **∼ed** *a* lebhaft. **∼ion** /-'meɪʃn/ *n* Lebhaftigkeit *f*

animosity /ænɪ'mɒsətɪ/ *n* Feindseligkeit *f*

aniseed /'ænɪsi:d/ *n* Anis *m*

ankle /'æŋkl/ n [Fuß]knöchel m

annex /ə'neks/ vt annektieren

annex[e] √'æneks/ n Nebengebäude nt; (extension) Anbau m

annihilat|e /ə'naɪəleɪt/ vt vernichten. **~ion** /-'leɪʃn/ n Vernichtung f

anniversary /ænɪ'vɜːsərɪ/ n Jahrestag m

annotate /'ænəteɪt/ vt kommentieren

announce /ə'naʊns/ vt bekanntgeben; (over loudspeaker) durchsagen; (at reception) ankündigen; (Radio, TV) ansagen; (in newspaper) anzeigen. **~ment** n Bekanntgabe f, Bekanntmachung f; Durchsage f; Ansage f; Anzeige f. **~r** n Ansager(in) m(f)

annoy /ə'nɔɪ/ vt ärgern; (pester) belästigen; **get ~ed** sich ärgern. **~ance** n Ärger m. **~ing** a ärgerlich

annual /'ænjʊəl/ a, **-ly** adv jährlich ● n (Bot) einjährige Pflanze f; (book) Jahresalbum nt

annuity /ə'nju:ətɪ/ n [Leib]rente f

annul /ə'nʌl/ vt (pt/pp **annulled**) annullieren

anoint /ə'nɔɪnt/ vt salben

anomaly /ə'nɒməlɪ/ n Anomalie f

anonymous /ə'nɒnɪməs/ a, **-ly** adv anonym

anorak /'ænəræk/ n Anorak m

anorexia /ænə'reksɪə/ n Magersucht f

another /ə'nʌðə(r)/ a & pron ein anderer/eine andere/ein anderes; (additional) noch ein(e); **~ [one]** noch einer/eine/eins; **~ day** an einem anderen Tag; **in ~ way** auf andere Weise; **~ time** ein andermal; **one ~** einander

answer /'ɑːnsə(r)/ n Antwort f; (solution) Lösung f ● vt antworten (jdm); beantworten ⟨question, letter⟩; **~ the door/telephone** an die Tür/ans Telefon gehen ● vi antworten; (Teleph) sich melden; **~ back** eine freche Antwort geben; **~ for** verantwortlich sein für. **~able** /-əbl/ a verantwortlich. **~ing machine** n (Teleph) Anrufbeantworter m

ant /ænt/ n Ameise f

antagonis|m /æn'tægənɪzm/ n Antagonismus m. **~tic** /-'nɪstɪk/ a feindselig

antagonize /æn'tægənaɪz/ vt gegen sich aufbringen

Antarctic /ænt'ɑːktɪk/ n Antarktis f

antelope /'æntɪləʊp/ n Antilope f

antenatal /æntɪ'neɪtl/ a **~ care** Schwangerschaftsfürsorge f

antenna /æn'tenə/ n Fühler m; (Amer: aerial) Antenne f

ante-room /'æntɪ-/ n Vorraum m

anthem /'ænθəm/ n Hymne f

anthology /æn'θɒlədʒɪ/ n Anthologie f

anthropology /ænθrə'pɒlədʒɪ/ n Anthropologie f

anti-'aircraft /ænti-/ a Flugabwehr-

antibiotic /æntɪbaɪ'ɒtɪk/ n Antibiotikum nt

'antibody n Antikörper m

anticipat|e /æn'tɪsɪpeɪt/ vt vorhersehen; (forestall) zuvorkommen (+ dat); (expect) erwarten. **~ion** /-'peɪʃn/ n Erwartung f

anti'climax n Enttäuschung f

anti'clockwise a & adv gegen den Uhrzeigersinn

antics /'æntɪks/ npl Mätzchen pl

anti'cyclone n Hochdruckgebiet nt

antidote /'æntɪdəʊt/ n Gegengift nt

'antifreeze n Frostschutzmittel nt

antipathy /æn'tɪpəθɪ/ n Abneigung f, Antipathie f

antiquarian /æntɪ'kweərɪən/ a antiquarisch. **~ bookshop** n Antiquariat nt

antiquated /'æntɪkweɪtɪd/ a veraltet

antique /æn'tiːk/ a antik ● n Antiquität f. **~ dealer** n Antiquitätenhändler m

antiquity /æn'tɪkwətɪ/ n Altertum nt

anti-Semitic /æntɪsɪ'mɪtɪk/ a antisemitisch

anti'septic a antiseptisch ● n Antiseptikum nt

anti'social a asozial; (fam) ungesellig

antithesis /æn'tɪθəsɪs/ n Gegensatz m

antlers /'æntləz/ npl Geweih nt

anus /'eɪnəs/ n After m

anvil /'ænvɪl/ n Amboß m

anxiety /æŋ'zaɪətɪ/ n Sorge f

anxious /'æŋkʃəs/ a, **-ly** adv ängstlich; (worried) besorgt; **be ~ to do sth** etw gerne machen wollen

any /'enɪ/ a irgendein(e); pl irgendwelche; (every) jede(r,s); pl alle; (after negative) kein(e); pl keine; **~ colour/**

number you like eine beliebige Farbe/ Zahl; **have you ~ wine/apples?** haben Sie Wein/Äpfel? **for ~ reason** aus irgendeinem Grund ● *pron* [irgend] einer/eine/eins; *pl* [irgend]welche; (*some*) welche(r,s); *pl* welche; (*all*) alle *pl*; (*negative*) keiner/keine/keins; *pl* keine; **I don't want ~ of it** ich will nichts davon; **there aren't ~** es gibt eine; **I need wine/apples/ money—have we ~?** ich brauche Wein/Äpfel/Geld—haben wir welchen/welche/welches? ● *adv* noch; **~ quicker/slower** noch schneller/langsamer; **is it ~ better?** geht es etwas besser? **would you like ~ more?** möchten Sie noch [etwas]? **I can't eat ~ more** ich kann nichts mehr essen; **I can't go ~ further** ich kann nicht mehr weiter

'anybody *pron* [irgend] jemand; (*after negative*) niemand; **~ can do that** das kann jeder

'anyhow *adv* jedenfalls; (*nevertheless*) trotzdem; (*badly*) irgendwie

'anyone *pron* = **anybody**

'anything *pron* [irgend] etwas; (*after negative*) nichts; (*everything*) alles

'anyway *adv* jedenfalls; (*in any case*) sowieso

'anywhere *adv* irgendwo; (*after negative*) nirgendwo; ⟨*be, live*⟩ überall; **I'd go ~** ich würde überallhin gehen

apart /ə'pɑːt/ *adv* auseinander; **live ~** getrennt leben; **~ from** abgesehen von

apartment /ə'pɑːtmənt/ *n* Zimmer *nt*; (*Amer: flat*) Wohnung *f*

apathy /'æpəθɪ/ *n* Apathie *f*

ape /eɪp/ *n* [Menschen]affe *m* ● *vt* nachäffen

aperitif /ə'perətiːf/ *n* Aperitif *m*

aperture /'æpətʃə(r)/ *n* Öffnung *f*; (*Phot*) Blende *f*

apex /'eɪpeks/ *n* Spitze *f*; (*fig*) Gipfel *m*

apiece /ə'piːs/ *adv* pro Person; (*thing*) pro Stück

apologetic /əpɒlə'dʒetɪk/ *a*, **-ally** *adv* entschuldigend; **be ~** sich entschuldigen

apologize /ə'pɒlədʒaɪz/ *vi* sich entschuldigen (**to** bei)

apology /ə'pɒlədʒɪ/ *n* Entschuldigung *f*

apostle /ə'pɒsl/ *n* Apostel *m*

apostrophe /ə'pɒstrəfɪ/ *n* Apostroph *m*

appal /ə'pɔːl/ *vt* (*pt/pp* **appalled**) entsetzen. **~ling** *a* entsetzlich

apparatus /æpə'reɪtəs/ *n* Apparatur *f*; (*Sport*) Geräte *pl*; (*single piece*) Gerät *nt*

apparel /ə'pærəl/ *n* Kleidung *f*

apparent /ə'pærənt/ *a* offenbar; (*seeming*) scheinbar. **~ly** *adv* offenbar, anscheinend

apparition /æpə'rɪʃn/ *n* Erscheinung *f*

appeal /ə'piːl/ *n* Appell *m*, Aufruf *m*; (*request*) Bitte *f*; (*attraction*) Reiz *m*; (*Jur*) Berufung *f* ● *vi* appellieren (**to** an + *acc*); (*ask*) bitten (**for** um); (*be attractive*) zusagen (**to** *dat*); (*Jur*) Berufung einlegen. **~ing** *a* ansprechend

appear /ə'pɪə(r)/ *vi* erscheinen; (*seem*) scheinen; (*Theat*) auftreten. **~ance** *n* Erscheinen *nt*; (*look*) Aussehen *nt*; **to all ~ances** allem Anschein nach

appease /ə'piːz/ *vt* beschwichtigen

append /ə'pend/ *vt* nachtragen; setzen ⟨*signature*⟩ (**to** unter + *acc*). **~age** /-ɪdʒ/ *n* Anhängsel *nt*

appendicitis /əpendɪ'saɪtɪs/ *n* Blinddarmentzündung *f*

appendix /ə'pendɪks/ *n* (*pl* **-ices** /-ɪsiːz/) (*of book*) Anhang *m* ● (*pl* **-es**) (*Anat*) Blinddarm *m*

appertain /æpə'teɪn/ *vi* **~ to** betreffen

appetite /'æpɪtaɪt/ *n* Appetit *m*

appetizing /'æpɪtaɪzɪŋ/ *a* appetitlich

applau|d /ə'plɔːd/ *vt/i* Beifall klatschen (+ *dat*). **~se** *n* Beifall *m*

apple /'æpl/ *n* Apfel *m*

appliance /ə'plaɪəns/ *n* Gerät *nt*

applicable /'æplɪkəbl/ *a* anwendbar (**to** auf + *acc*); (*on form*) **not ~** nicht zutreffend

applicant /'æplɪkənt/ *n* Bewerber(in) *m(f)*

application /æplɪ'keɪʃn/ *n* Anwendung *f*; (*request*) Antrag *m*; ⟨*for job*⟩ Bewerbung *f*; (*diligence*) Fleiß *m*

applied /ə'plaɪd/ *a* angewandt

apply /ə'plaɪ/ *vt* (*pt/pp* **-ied**) auftragen ⟨*paint*⟩; anwenden ⟨*force, rule*⟩ ● *vi* zutreffen (**to** auf + *acc*); **~ for** beantragen; sich bewerben um ⟨*job*⟩

appoint /ə'pɔɪnt/ *vt* ernennen; (*fix*) festlegen; **well ~ed** gut ausgestattet. **~ment** *n* Ernennung *f*; (*meeting*)

Verabredung *f*; (*at doctor's, hairdresser's*) Termin *m*; (*job*) Posten *m*; **make an ～ment** sich anmelden

apposite /'æpəzɪt/ *a* treffend

appraise /ə'preɪz/ *vt* abschätzen

appreciable /ə'priːʃəbl/ *a* merklich; (*considerable*) beträchtlich

appreciat|e /ə'priːʃɪeɪt/ *vt* zu schätzen wissen; (*be grateful for*) dankbar sein für; (*enjoy*) schätzen; (*understand*) verstehen ● *vi* (*increase in value*) im Wert steigen. ～ion /-'eɪʃn/ *n* (*gratitude*) Dankbarkeit *f*; **in ～ion** als Dank (**of** für). ～ive /-ətɪv/ *a* dankbar

apprehend /æprɪ'hend/ *vt* festnehmen

apprehens|ion /æprɪ'henʃn/ *n* Festnahme *f*; (*fear*) Angst *f*. ～ive /-sɪv/ *a* ängstlich

apprentice /ə'prentɪs/ *n* Lehrling *m*. ～ship *n* Lehre *f*

approach /ə'prəʊtʃ/ *n* Näherkommen *nt*; (*of time*) Nahen *nt*; (*access*) Zugang *m*; (*road*) Zufahrt *f* ● *vi* sich nähern; (*time:*) nahen ● *vt* sich nähern (+ *dat*); (*with request*) herantreten an (+ *acc*); (*set about*) sich heranmachen an (+ *acc*). ～able /-əbl/ *a* zugänglich

approbation /æprə'beɪʃn/ *n* Billigung *f*

appropriate[1] /ə'prəʊprɪət/ *a* angebracht, angemessen

appropriate[2] /ə'prəʊprɪeɪt/ *vt* sich (*dat*) aneignen

approval /ə'pruːvl/ *n* Billigung *f*; **on ～** zur Ansicht

approv|e /ə'pruːv/ *vt* billigen ● *vi* ～**e of sth/s.o.** mit etw/jdm einverstanden sein. ～**ing** *a*, **-ly** *adv* anerkennend

approximate[1] /ə'prɒksɪmeɪt/ *vi* ～ **to** nahekommen (+ *dat*)

approximate[2] /ə'prɒksɪmət/ *a* ungefähr. ～**ly** *adv* ungefähr, etwa

approximation /əprɒksɪ'meɪʃn/ *n* Schätzung *f*

apricot /'eɪprɪkɒt/ *n* Aprikose *f*

April /'eɪprəl/ *n* April *m*; **make an ～ fool of** sb im April schicken

apron /'eɪprən/ *n* Schürze *f*

apropos /'æprəpəʊ/ *adv* ～ **[of]** betreffs (+ *gen*)

apt /æpt/ *a*, **-ly** *adv* passend; (*pupil*) begabt; **be ～ to do sth** dazu neigen, etw zu tun

aptitude /'æptɪtjuːd/ *n* Begabung *f*

aqualung /'ækwəlʌŋ/ *n* Tauchgerät *nt*

aquarium /ə'kweərɪəm/ *n* Aquarium *nt*

Aquarius /ə'kweərɪəs/ *n* (*Astr*) Wassermann *m*

aquatic /ə'kwætɪk/ *a* Wasser-

Arab /'ærəb/ *a* arabisch ● *n* Araber(in) *m(f)*. ～**ian** /ə'reɪbɪən/ *a* arabisch

Arabic /'ærəbɪk/ *a* arabisch

arable /'ærəbl/ *a* ～ **land** Ackerland *nt*

arbitrary /'ɑːbɪtrərɪ/ *a*, **-ily** *adv* willkürlich

arbitrat|e /'ɑːbɪtreɪt/ *vi* schlichten. ～**ion** /-'treɪʃn/ *n* Schlichtung *f*

arc /ɑːk/ *n* Bogen *m*

arcade /ɑː'keɪd/ *n* Laubengang *m*; (*shops*) Einkaufspassage *f*

arch /ɑːtʃ/ *n* Bogen *m*; (*of foot*) Gewölbe *nt* ● *vt* ～ **its back** (*cat:*) einen Buckel machen

archaeological /ɑːkɪə'lɒdʒɪkl/ *a* archäologisch

archaeolog|ist /ɑːkɪ'ɒlədʒɪst/ *n* Archäologe *m*/-login *f*. ～**y** *n* Archäologie *f*

archaic /ɑː'keɪɪk/ *a* veraltet

arch'bishop /ɑːtʃ-/ *n* Erzbischof *m*

arch-'enemy *n* Erzfeind *m*

archer /'ɑːtʃə(r)/ *n* Bogenschütze *m*. ～**y** *n* Bogenschießen *nt*

architect /'ɑːkɪtekt/ *n* Architekt(in) *m(f)*. ～**ural** /ɑːkɪ'tektʃərəl/ *a*, **-ly** *adv* architektonisch

architecture /'ɑːkɪtektʃə(r)/ *n* Architektur *f*

archives /'ɑːkaɪvz/ *npl* Archiv *nt*

archway /'ɑːtʃweɪ/ *n* Torbogen *m*

Arctic /'ɑːktɪk/ *a* arktisch ● *n* **the ～** die Arktis

ardent /'ɑːdənt/ *a*, **-ly** *adv* leidenschaftlich

ardour /'ɑːdə(r)/ *n* Leidenschaft *f*

arduous /'ɑːdjʊəs/ *a* mühsam

are /ɑː(r)/ *see* **be**

area /'eərɪə/ *n* (*surface*) Fläche *f*; (*Geom*) Flächeninhalt *m*; (*region*) Gegend *f*; (*fig*) Gebiet *nt*. ～ **code** *n* Vorwahlnummer *f*

arena /ə'riːnə/ *n* Arena *f*

aren't /ɑːnt/ = **are not.** *See* **be**

Argentina /ɑːdʒən'tiːnə/ *n* Argentinien *nt*

Argentin|e /'ɑːdʒəntaɪn/, ～**ian** /-'tɪnɪən/ *a* argentinisch

argue /'ɑːgjuː/ *vi* streiten (**about** über + *acc*); (*two people:*) sich streiten;

(*debate*) diskutieren; **don't ~!** keine Widerrede! ● *vt* (*debate*) diskutieren; (*reason*) ~ **that** argumentieren, daß

argument /ˈɑːgjʊmənt/ *n* Streit *m*, Auseinandersetzung *f*; (*reasoning*) Argument *nt*; **have an ~** sich streiten. **~ative** /-ˈmentətɪv/ *a* streitlustig

aria /ˈɑːrɪə/ *n* Arie *f*

arid /ˈærɪd/ *a* dürr

Aries /ˈeəriːz/ *n* (*Astr*) Widder *m*

arise /əˈraɪz/ *vi* (*pt* **arose**, *pp* **arisen**) sich ergeben (**from** aus)

aristocracy /ærɪˈstɒkrəsɪ/ *n* Aristokratie *f*

aristocrat /ˈærɪstəkræt/ *n* Aristokrat(in) *m(f)*. **~ic** /-ˈkrætɪk/ *a* aristokratisch

arithmetic /əˈrɪθmətɪk/ *n* Rechnen *nt*

ark /ɑːk/ *n* **Noah's A~** die Arche Noah

arm /ɑːm/ *n* Arm *m*; (*of chair*) Armlehne *f*; **~s** *pl* (*weapons*) Waffen *pl*; (*Heraldry*) Wappen *nt*; **up in ~s** (*fam*) empört ● *vt* bewaffnen

armament /ˈɑːməmənt/ *n* Bewaffnung *f*; **~s** *pl* Waffen *pl*

'armchair *n* Sessel *m*

armed /ɑːmd/ *a* bewaffnet; **~ forces** Streitkräfte *pl*

armistice /ˈɑːmɪstɪs/ *n* Waffenstillstand *m*

armour /ˈɑːmə(r)/ *n* Rüstung *f*. **~ed** *a* Panzer-

'armpit *n* Achselhöhle *f*

army /ˈɑːmɪ/ *n* Heer *nt*; (*specific*) Armee *f*; **join the ~** zum Militär gehen

aroma /əˈrəʊmə/ *n* Aroma *nt*, Duft *m*. **~tic** /ærəˈmætɪk/ *a* aromatisch

arose /əˈrəʊz/ *see* **arise**

around /əˈraʊnd/ *adv* **[all]** ~ rings herum; **he's not** ~ er ist nicht da; **look/turn** ~ sich umsehen/umdrehen; **travel** ~ herumreisen ● *prep* um (+ *acc*) ... herum; (*approximately*) gegen

arouse /əˈraʊz/ *vt* aufwecken; (*excite*) erregen

arrange /əˈreɪndʒ/ *vt* arrangieren; anordnen (*furniture, books*); (*settle*) abmachen; **I have ~d to go there** ich habe abgemacht, daß ich dahingehe. **~ment** *n* Anordnung *f*; (*agreement*) Vereinbarung *f*; (*of flowers*) Gesteck *nt*; **make ~ments** Vorkehrungen treffen

arrears /əˈrɪəz/ *npl* Rückstände *pl*; **in** ~ im Rückstand

arrest /əˈrest/ *n* Verhaftung *f*; **under** ~ verhaftet ● *vt* verhaften

arrival /əˈraɪvl/ *n* Ankunft *f*; **new ~s** *pl* Neuankömmlinge *pl*

arrive /əˈraɪv/ *vi* ankommen; ~ **at** (*fig*) gelangen zu

arrogan|ce /ˈærəgəns/ *n* Arroganz *f*. **~t** *a*, **-ly** *adv* arrogant

arrow /ˈærəʊ/ *n* Pfeil *m*

arse /ɑːs/ *n* (*vulg*) Arsch *m*

arsenic /ˈɑːsənɪk/ *n* Arsen *nt*

arson /ˈɑːsn/ *n* Brandstiftung *f*. **~ist** /-sənɪst/ *n* Brandstifter *m*

art /ɑːt/ *n* Kunst *f*; **work of ~** Kunstwerk *nt*; **~s and crafts** *pl* Kunstgewerbe *nt*; **A~s** *pl* (*Univ*) Geisteswissenschaften *pl*

artery /ˈɑːtərɪ/ *n* Schlagader *f*, Arterie *f*

artful /ˈɑːtfl/ *a* gerissen

'art gallery *n* Kunstgalerie *f*

arthritis /ɑːˈθraɪtɪs/ *n* Arthritis *f*

artichoke /ˈɑːtɪtʃəʊk/ *n* Artischocke *f*

article /ˈɑːtɪkl/ *n* Artikel *m*; (*object*) Gegenstand *m*; ~ **of clothing** Kleidungsstück *nt*

articulate[1] /ɑːˈtɪkjʊlət/ *a* deutlich; **be ~** sich gut ausdrücken können

articulate[2] /ɑːˈtɪkjʊleɪt/ *vt* aussprechen. **~d lorry** *n* Sattelzug *m*

artifice /ˈɑːtɪfɪs/ *n* Arglist *f*

artificial /ɑːtɪˈfɪʃl/ *a*, **-ly** *adv* künstlich

artillery /ɑːˈtɪlərɪ/ *n* Artillerie *f*

artist /ˈɑːtɪst/ *n* Künstler(in) *m(f)*

artiste /ɑːˈtiːst/ *n* (*Theat*) Artist(in) *m(f)*

artistic /ɑːˈtɪstɪk/ *a*, **-ally** *adv* künstlerisch

artless /ˈɑːtlɪs/ *a* unschuldig

as /æz/ *conj* (*because*) da; (*when*) als; (*while*) während ● *prep* als; **as a child/foreigner** als Kind/Ausländer ● *adv* **as well** auch; **as soon as** sobald; **as much as** soviel wie; **as quick as you** so schnell wie du; **as you know** wie Sie wissen; **as far as I'm concerned** mich betrifft

asbestos /æzˈbestɒs/ *n* Asbest *m*

ascend /əˈsend/ *vi* [auf]steigen ● *vt* besteigen (*throne*)

Ascension /əˈsenʃn/ *n* (*Relig*) [Christi] Himmelfahrt *f*

ascent /əˈsent/ *n* Aufstieg *m*

ascertain /æsəˈteɪn/ *vt* ermitteln

ascribe /əˈskraɪb/ *vt* zuschreiben (**to** *dat*)

ash[1] /æʃ/ n (*tree*) Esche *f*

ash[2] n Asche *f*

ashamed /ə'ʃeɪmd/ a beschämt; **be ~** sich schämen (**of** über + *acc*)

ashore /ə'ʃɔː(r)/ *adv* an Land

ash: ~tray n Aschenbecher *m*. **A~ 'Wednesday** n Aschermittwoch *m*

Asia /'eɪʃə/ n Asien *nt*. **~n** a asiatisch ● n Asiat(in) *m(f)*. **~tic** /eɪʃɪ'ætɪk/ a asiatisch

aside /ə'saɪd/ *adv* beiseite; **~ from** (*Amer*) außer (+ *dat*)

ask /ɑːsk/ *vt/i* fragen; stellen (*question*); (*invite*) einladen; **~ for** bitten um; verlangen (*s.o.*); **~ after** sich erkundigen nach; **~ s.o. in** jdn hereinbitten; **~ s.o. to do sth** jdn bitten, etw zu tun

askance /ə'skɑːns/ *adv* **look ~ at** schief ansehen

askew /ə'skjuː/ a & *adv* schief

asleep /ə'sliːp/ a **be ~** schlafen; **fall ~** einschlafen

asparagus /ə'spærəgəs/ n Spargel *m*

aspect /'æspekt/ n Aspekt *m*

aspersions /ə'spɜːʃnz/ *npl* **cast ~ on** schlechtmachen

asphalt /'æsfælt/ n Asphalt *m*

asphyxia /æ'sfɪksɪə/ n Erstickung *f*. **~te** /æ'sfɪksɪeɪt/ *vt/i* ersticken. **~tion** /-'eɪʃn/ n Erstickung *f*

aspirations /æspə'reɪʃnz/ *npl* Streben *nt*

aspire /ə'spaɪə(r)/ *vi* **~ to** streben nach

ass /æs/ n Esel *m*

assail /ə'seɪl/ *vt* bestürmen. **~ant** n Angreifer(in) *m(f)*

assassin /ə'sæsɪn/ n Mörder(in) *m(f)*. **~ate** *vt* ermorden. **~ation** /-'neɪʃn/ n [politischer] Mord *m*

assault /ə'sɔːlt/ n (*Mil*) Angriff *m*; (*Jur*) Körperverletzung *f* ● *vt* [tätlich] angreifen

assemble /ə'sembl/ *vi* sich versammeln ● *vt* versammeln; (*Techn*) montieren

assembly /ə'semblɪ/ n Versammlung *f*; (*Sch*) Andacht *f*; (*Techn*) Montage *f*. **~ line** n Fließband *nt*

assent /ə'sent/ n Zustimmung *f* ● *vi* zustimmen (**to** *dat*)

assert /ə'sɜːt/ *vt* behaupten; **~ oneself** sich durchsetzen. **~ion** /-ʃn/ n Behauptung *f*. **~ive** /-tɪv/ a **be ~ive** sich durchsetzen können

assess /ə'ses/ *vt* bewerten; (*fig & for tax purposes*) einschätzen; schätzen

(*value*). **~ment** n Einschätzung *f*; (*of tax*) Steuerbescheid *m*

asset /'æset/ n Vorteil *m*; **~s** *pl* (*money*) Vermögen *nt*; (*Comm*) Aktiva *pl*

assiduous /ə'sɪdjʊəs/ a, **-ly** *adv* fleißig

assign /ə'saɪn/ *vt* zuweisen (**to** *dat*). **~ment** n (*task*) Aufgabe *f*

assimilate /ə'sɪmɪleɪt/ *vt* aufnehmen; (*integrate*) assimilieren

assist /ə'sɪst/ *vt/i* helfen (+ *dat*). **~ance** n Hilfe *f*. **~ant** a Hilfs- ● n Assistent(in) *m(f)*; (*in shop*) Verkäufer(in) *m(f)*

associat|e[1] /ə'səʊʃɪeɪt/ *vt* verbinden; (*Psych*) assoziieren ● *vi* **~ with** verkehren mit. **~ion** /-'eɪʃn/ n Verband *m*. **A~ion 'football** n Fußball *m*

associate[2] /ə'səʊʃɪət/ a assoziiert ● n Kollege *m*/-gin *f*

assort|ed /ə'sɔːtɪd/ a gemischt. **~ment** n Mischung *f*

assum|e /ə'sjuːm/ *vt* annehmen; übernehmen (*office*); **~ing that** angenommen, daß

assumption /ə'sʌmpʃn/ n Annahme *f*; **on the ~** in der Annahme (**that** daß)

assurance /ə'ʃʊərəns/ n Versicherung *f*; (*confidence*) Selbstsicherheit *f*

assure /ə'ʃʊə(r)/ *vt* versichern (**s.o.** jdm); **I ~ you [of that]** das versichere ich Ihnen. **~d** a sicher

asterisk /'æstərɪsk/ n Sternchen *nt*

astern /ə'stɜːn/ *adv* achtern

asthma /'æsmə/ n Asthma *nt*. **~tic** /-'mætɪk/ a asthmatisch

astonish /ə'stɒnɪʃ/ *vt* erstaunen. **~ing** a erstaunlich. **~ment** n Erstaunen *nt*

astound /ə'staʊnd/ *vt* in Erstaunen setzen

astray /ə'streɪ/ *adv* **go ~** verlorengehen; (*person:*) sich verlaufen; (*fig*) vom rechten Weg abkommen; **lead ~** verleiten

astride /ə'straɪd/ *adv* rittlings ● *prep* rittlings auf (+ *dat/acc*)

astringent /ə'strɪndʒənt/ a adstringierend; (*fig*) beißend

astrolog|er /ə'strɒlədʒə(r)/ n Astrologe *m*/-gin *f*. **~y** n Astrologie *f*

astronaut /'æstrənɔːt/ n Astronaut(in) *m(f)*

astronom|er /ə'strɒnəmə(r)/ n Astronom *m*. **~ical** /æstrə'nɒmɪkl/ a astronomisch. **~y** n Astronomie *f*

astute /ə'stjuːt/ *a* scharfsinnig. **~ness** *n* Scharfsinn *m*

asylum /ə'saɪləm/ *n* Asyl *nt*; **[lunatic] ~** Irrenanstalt *f*

at /ət, *betont* æt/ *prep* an (+ *dat/acc*); (*with town*) in; (*price*) zu; (*speed*) mit; **at the station** am Bahnhof; **at the beginning/end** am Anfang/Ende; **at home** zu Hause; **at John's** bei John; **at work/the hairdresser's** bei der Arbeit/beim Friseur; **at school/the office** in der Schule/im Büro; **at a party/ wedding** auf einer Party/Hochzeit; **at one o'clock** um ein Uhr; **at Christmas/ Easter** zu Weihnachten/Ostern; **at the age of** im Alter von; **not at all** gar nicht; **at times** manchmal; **two at a time** zwei auf einmal; **good/bad at languages** gut/schlecht in Sprachen

ate /et/ *see* **eat**

atheist /'eɪθɪɪst/ *n* Atheist(in) *m(f)*

athletle /'æθliːt/ *n* Athlet(in) *m(f)*. **~ic** /-'letɪk/ *a* sportlich. **~ics** /-'letɪks/ *n* Leichtathletik *f*

Atlantic /ət'læntɪk/ *a & n* **the ~ [Ocean]** der Atlantik

atlas /'ætləs/ *n* Atlas *m*

atmospherle /'ætməsfɪə(r)/ *n* Atmosphäre *f*. **~ic** /-'ferɪk/ *a* atmosphärisch

atom /'ætəm/ *n* Atom *nt*. **~ bomb** *n* Atombombe *f*

atomic /ə'tɒmɪk/ *a* Atom-

atone /ə'təʊn/ *vi* büßen (**for** für). **~ment** *n* Buße *f*

atrocious /ə'trəʊʃəs/ *a* abscheulich

atrocity /ə'trɒsəti/ *n* Greueltat *f*

attach /ə'tætʃ/ *vt* befestigen (**to** an + *dat*); beimessen (*importance*) (**to** *dat*); **be ~ed to** (*fig*) hängen an (+ *dat*)

attaché /ə'tæʃeɪ/ *n* Attaché *m*. **~ case** *n* Aktenkoffer *m*

attachment /ə'tætʃmənt/ *n* Bindung *f*; (*tool*) Zubehörteil *nt*; (*additional*) Zusatzgerät *nt*

attack /ə'tæk/ *n* Angriff *m*; (*Med*) Anfall *m* ● *vt/i* angreifen. **~er** *n* Angreifer *m*

attain /ə'teɪn/ *vt* erreichen; (*get*) erlangen. **~able** /-əbl/ *a* erreichbar

attempt /ə'tempt/ *n* Versuch *m* ● *vt* versuchen

attend /ə'tend/ *vt* anwesend sein bei; (*go regularly to*) besuchen; (*take part in*) teilnehmen an (+ *dat*); (*accompany*) begleiten; (*doctor:*) behandeln ● *vi* anwesend sein; (*pay*

attention) aufpassen; **~ to** sich kümmern um; (*in shop*) bedienen. **~ance** *n* Anwesenheit *f*; (*number*) Besucherzahl *f*. **~ant** *n* Wärter(in) *m(f)*; (*in car park*) Wächter *m*

attention /ə'tenʃn/ *n* Aufmerksamkeit *f*; **~!** (*Mil*) stillgestanden! **pay ~** aufpassen; **pay ~ to** beachten, achten auf (+ *acc*); **need ~** reparaturbedürftig sein; **for the ~ of** zu Händen von

attentive /ə'tentɪv/ *a*, **-ly** *adv* aufmerksam

attest /ə'test/ *vt/i* **~ [to]** bezeugen

attic /'ætɪk/ *n* Dachboden *m*

attire /ə'taɪə(r)/ *n* Kleidung *f* ● *vt* kleiden

attitude /'ætɪtjuːd/ *n* Haltung *f*

attorney /ə'tɜːnɪ/ *n* (*Amer: lawyer*) Rechtsanwalt *m*; **power of ~** Vollmacht *f*

attract /ə'trækt/ *vt* anziehen; erregen (*attention*); **~ s.o.'s attention** jds Aufmerksamkeit auf sich (*acc*) lenken. **~ion** /-ækʃn/ *n* Anziehungskraft *f*; (*charm*) Reiz *m*; (*thing*) Attraktion *f*. **~ive** /-tɪv/ *a*, **-ly** *adv* attraktiv

attribute[1] /'ætrɪbjuːt/ *n* Attribut *nt*

attributle[2] /ə'trɪbjuːt/ *vt* zuschreiben (**to** *dat*). **~ive** /-tɪv/ *a*, **-ly** *adv* attributiv

attrition /ə'trɪʃn/ *n* **war of ~** Zermürbungskrieg *m*

aubergine /'əʊbəʒiːn/ *n* Aubergine *f*

auburn /'ɔːbən/ *a* kastanienbraun

auction /'ɔːkʃn/ *n* Auktion *f*, Versteigerung *f* ● *vt* versteigern. **~eer** /-ʃə'nɪə(r)/ *n* Auktionator *m*

audaci|ous /ɔː'deɪʃəs/ *a*, **-ly** *adv* verwegen. **~ty** /-'dæsəti/ *n* Verwegenheit *f*; (*impudence*) Dreistigkeit *f*

audible /'ɔːdəbl/ *a*, **-bly** *adv* hörbar

audience /'ɔːdɪəns/ *n* Publikum *nt*; (*Theat, TV*) Zuschauer *pl*; (*Radio*) Zuhörer *pl*; (*meeting*) Audienz *f*

audio /'ɔːdɪəʊ/: **~ typist** *n* Phonotypistin *f*. **~'visual** *a* audiovisuell

audit /'ɔːdɪt/ *n* Bücherrevision *f* ● *vt* (*Comm*) prüfen

audition /ɔː'dɪʃn/ *n* (*Theat*) Vorsprechen *nt*; (*Mus*) Vorspielen *nt*; (*for singer*) Vorsingen *nt* ● *vi* vorsprechen; vorspielen; vorsingen

auditor /'ɔːdɪtə(r)/ *n* Buchprüfer *m*

auditorium /ɔːdɪ'tɔːrɪəm/ *n* Zuschauerraum *m*

augment /ɔːg'ment/ vt vergrößern

augur /'ɔːgə(r)/ vi ~ **well/ill** etwas/ nichts Gutes verheißen

august /ɔː'gʌst/ a hoheitsvoll

August /'ɔːgəst/ n August m

aunt /ɑːnt/ n Tante f

au pair /əʊ'peə(r)/ n ~ **[girl]** Au-pair-Mädchen nt

aura /'ɔːrə/ n Fluidum nt

auspices /'ɔːspɪsɪz/ npl (protection) Schirmherrschaft f

auspicious /ɔː'spɪʃəs/ a günstig; ⟨occasion⟩ freudig

auster|e /ɒ'stɪə(r)/ a streng; (simple) nüchtern. ~**ity** /-terətɪ/ n Strenge f; (hardship) Entbehrung f

Australia /ɒ'streɪlɪə/ n Australien nt. ~**n** a australisch ● n Australier(in) m(f)

Austria /'ɒstrɪə/ n Österreich nt. ~**n** a österreichisch ● n Österreicher(in) m(f)

authentic /ɔː'θentɪk/ a echt, authentisch. ~**ate** vt beglaubigen. ~**ity** /-'tɪsətɪ/ n Echtheit f

author /'ɔːθə(r)/ n Schriftsteller m, Autor m; (of document) Verfasser m

authoritarian /ɔːθɒrɪ'teərɪən/ a autoritär

authoritative /ɔː'θɒrɪtətɪv/ a maßgebend; **be** ~ Autorität haben

authority /ɔː'θɒrətɪ/ n Autorität f; (public) Behörde f; **in** ~ verantwortlich

authorization /ɔːθəraɪ'zeɪʃn/ n Ermächtigung f

authorize /'ɔːθəraɪz/ vt ermächtigen ⟨s.o.⟩; genehmigen ⟨sth⟩

autobi'ography /ɔːtə-/ n Autobiographie f

autocratic /ɔːtə'krætɪk/ a autokratisch

autograph /'ɔːtə-/ n Autogramm nt

automatic /ɔːtə'mætɪk/ a, **-ally** adv automatisch ● n (car) Fahrzeug nt mit Automatikgetriebe; (washing machine) Waschautomat m

automation /ɔːtə'meɪʃn/ n Automation f

automobile /'ɔːtəməbiːl/ n Auto nt

autonom|ous /ɔː'tɒnəməs/ a autonom. ~**y** n Autonomie f

autopsy /'ɔːtɒpsɪ/ n Autopsie f

autumn /'ɔːtəm/ n Herbst m. ~**al** /-'tʌmnl/ a herbstlich

auxiliary /ɔːg'zɪlɪərɪ/ a Hilfs- ● n Helfer(in) m(f), Hilfskraft f

avail /ə'veɪl/ n **to no** ~ vergeblich ● vi ~ **oneself of** Gebrauch machen von

available /ə'veɪləbl/ a verfügbar; (obtainable) erhältlich

avalanche /'ævəlɑːnʃ/ n Lawine f

avaric|e /'ævərɪs/ n Habsucht f. ~**ious** /-'rɪʃəs/ a habgierig, habsüchtig

avenge /ə'vendʒ/ vt rächen

avenue /'ævənjuː/ n Allee f

average /'ævərɪdʒ/ a Durchschnitts-, durchschnittlich ● n Durchschnitt m; **on** ~ im Durchschnitt, durchschnittlich ● vt durchschnittlich schaffen ● vi ~ **out at** im Durchschnitt ergeben

avers|e /ə'vɜːs/ a **not be** ~**e to sth** etw (dat) nicht abgeneigt sein. ~**ion** /-ɜːʃn/ n Abneigung f (**to** gegen)

avert /ə'vɜːt/ vt abwenden

aviary /'eɪvɪərɪ/ n Vogelhaus nt

aviation /eɪvɪ'eɪʃn/ n Luftfahrt f

avid /'ævɪd/ a gierig (**for** nach); (keen) eifrig

avocado /ævə'kɑːdəʊ/ n Avocado f

avoid /ə'vɔɪd/ vt vermeiden; ~ **s.o.** jdm aus dem Weg gehen. ~**able** /-əbl/ a vermeidbar. ~**ance** n Vermeidung f

await /ə'weɪt/ vt warten auf (+ acc)

awake /ə'weɪk/ a wach; **wide** ~ hellwach ● vi (pt awoke, pp awoken) erwachen

awaken /ə'weɪkn/ vt wecken ● vi erwachen. ~**ing** n Erwachen nt

award /ə'wɔːd/ n Auszeichnung f; (prize) Preis m ● vt zuerkennen (**to s.o.** dat); verleihen ⟨prize⟩

aware /ə'weə(r)/ a **become** ~ gewahr werden (**of** gen); **be** ~ **that** wissen, daß. ~**ness** n Bewußtsein nt

awash /ə'wɒʃ/ a **be** ~ unter Wasser stehen

away /ə'weɪ/ adv weg, fort; (absent) abwesend; **be** ~ nicht da sein; **far** ~ weit weg; **four kilometres** ~ vier Kilometer entfernt; **play** ~ (Sport) auswärts spielen; **go/stay** ~ weggehen/ -bleiben. ~ **game** n Auswärtsspiel nt

awe /ɔː/ n Ehrfurcht f

awful /'ɔːfl/ a, **-ly** adv furchtbar

awhile /ə'waɪl/ adv eine Weile

awkward /'ɔːkwəd/ a schwierig; (clumsy) ungeschickt; (embarrassing) peinlich; (inconvenient) ungünstig. ~**ly** adv ungeschickt; (embarrassedly) verlegen

awning /'ɔːnɪŋ/ n Markise f

awoke(n) /ə'wəʊk(ən)/ *see* **awake**

awry /ə'raɪ/ *adv* schief

axe /æks/ *n* Axt *f* ● *vt* (*pres p* **axing**) streichen; (*dismiss*) entlassen

axis /'æksɪs/ *n* (*pl* **axes** /-siːz/) Achse *f*

axle /'æksl/ *n* (*Techn*) Achse *f*

ay[e] /aɪ/ *adv* ja ● *n* Jastimme *f*

B

B /biː/ *n* (*Mus*) H *nt*

BA *abbr of* **Bachelor of Arts**

babble /'bæbl/ *vi* plappern; ⟨*stream:*⟩ plätschern

baboon /bə'buːn/ *n* Pavian *m*

baby /'beɪbɪ/ *n* Baby *nt*; (*Amer, fam*) Schätzchen *nt*

baby: ∼ **carriage** *n* (*Amer*) Kinderwagen *m*. ∼**ish** *a* kindisch. ∼**-minder** *n* Tagesmutter *f*. ∼**-sit** *vi* babysitten. ∼**-sitter** *n* Babysitter *m*

bachelor /'bætʃələ(r)/ *n* Junggeselle *m*; **B**∼ **of Arts/Science** Bakkalaureus Artium/Scientium

bacillus /bə'sɪləs/ *n* (*pl* **-lli**) Bazillus *m*

back /bæk/ *n* Rücken *m*; (*reverse*) Rückseite *f*; (*of chair*) Rückenlehne *f*; (*Sport*) Verteidiger *m*; **at**/(*Auto*) **in the** ∼ hinten; **on the** ∼ auf der Rückseite; ∼ **to front** verkehrt; **at the** ∼ **of beyond** am Ende der Welt ● *a* Hinter- ● *adv* zurück; ∼ **here/there** hier/da hinten; ∼ **at home** zu Hause; **go/pay** ∼ zurückgehen/-zahlen ● *vt* (*support*) unterstützen; (*with money*) finanzieren; (*Auto*) zurücksetzen; (*Betting*) [Geld] setzen auf (+ *acc*); (*cover the back of*) mit einer Verstärkung versehen ● *vi* (*Auto*) zurücksetzen. ∼ **down** *vi* klein beigeben. ∼ **in** *vi* rückwärts hineinfahren. ∼ **out** *vi* rückwärts hinaus-/herausfahren; (*fig*) aussteigen (**of** aus). ∼ **up** *vt* unterstützen; (*confirm*) bestätigen ● *vi* (*Auto*) zurücksetzen

back: ∼**ache** *n* Rückenschmerzen *pl*. ∼**biting** *n* gehässiges Gerede *nt*. ∼**bone** *n* Rückgrat *nt*. ∼**chat** *n* Widerrede *f*. ∼**-comb** *vt* toupieren. ∼**date** *vt* rückdatieren; ∼**dated to** rückwirkend von. ∼ '**door** *n* Hintertür *f*

backer /'bækə(r)/ *n* Geldgeber *m*

back: ∼'**fire** *vi* (*Auto*) fehlzünden; (*fig*) fehlschlagen. ∼**ground** *n* Hintergrund *m*; **family** ∼**ground** Familienverhältnisse *pl*. ∼**hand** *n* (*Sport*) Rückhand *f*. ∼'**handed** *a* ⟨*compliment*⟩ zweifelhaft. ∼'**hander** *n* (*Sport*) Rückhandschlag *m*; (*fam: bribe*) Schmiergeld *nt*

backing /'bækɪŋ/ *n* (*support*) Unterstützung *f*; (*material*) Verstärkung *f*

back: ∼**lash** *n* (*fig*) Gegenschlag *m*. ∼**log** *n* Rückstand *m* (**of** an + *dat*). ∼'**seat** *n* Rücksitz *m*. ∼**side** *n* (*fam*) Hintern *m*. ∼**stage** *adv* hinter der Bühne. ∼**stroke** *n* Rückenschwimmen *nt*. ∼**-up** *n* Unterstützung *f*; (*Amer: traffic jam*) Stau *m*

backward /'bækwəd/ *a* zurückgeblieben; ⟨*country*⟩ rückständig ● *adv* rückwärts. ∼**s** rückwärts; ∼**s and forwards** hin und her

back: ∼**water** *n* (*fig*) unberührtes Fleckchen *nt*. ∼ '**yard** *n* Hinterhof *m*; **not in my** ∼ **yard** (*fam*) nicht vor meiner Haustür

bacon /'beɪkn/ *n* [Schinken]speck *m*

bacteria /bæk'tɪərɪə/ *npl* Bakterien *pl*

bad /bæd/ *a* (**worse, worst**) schlecht; (*serious*) schwer, schlimm; (*naughty*) unartig; ∼ **language** gemeine Ausdrucksweise *f*; **feel** ∼ sich schlecht fühlen; (*feel guilty*) ein schlechtes Gewissen haben; **go** ∼ schlecht werden

bade /bæd/ *see* **bid**[2]

badge /bædʒ/ *n* Abzeichen *nt*

badger /'bædʒə(r)/ *n* Dachs *m* ● *vt* plagen

badly /'bædlɪ/ *adv* schlecht; (*seriously*) schwer; ∼ **off** schlecht gestellt; ∼ **behaved** unerzogen; **want** ∼ sich (*dat*) sehnsüchtig wünschen; **need** ∼ dringend brauchen

bad-'mannered *a* mit schlechten Manieren

badminton /'bædmɪntən/ *n* Federball *m*

bad-'tempered *a* schlecht gelaunt

baffle /'bæfl/ *vt* verblüffen

bag /bæg/ *n* Tasche *f*; (*of paper*) Tüte *f*; (*pouch*) Beutel *m*; ∼**s of** (*fam*) jede Menge ● *vt* (*fam: reserve*) in Beschlag nehmen

baggage /'bægɪdʒ/ *n* [Reise]gepäck *nt*

baggy /'bægɪ/ *a* ⟨*clothes*⟩ ausgebeult

'**bagpipes** *npl* Dudelsack *m*

bail /beɪl/ n Kaution f; **on** ~ gegen Kaution ● vt ~ **s.o. out** jdn gegen Kaution freibekommen; (fig) jdm aus der Patsche helfen. ~ **out** vt (Naut) ausschöpfen ● vi (Aviat) abspringen

bailiff /'beɪlɪf/ n Gerichtsvollzieher m; (of estate) Gutsverwalter m

bait /beɪt/ n Köder m ● vt mit einem Köder versehen; (fig: torment) reizen

bake /beɪk/ vt/i backen

baker /'beɪkə(r)/ n Bäcker m; ~**'s [shop]** Bäckerei f. ~**y** n Bäckerei f

baking /'beɪkɪŋ/ n Backen nt. ~**-powder** n Backpulver nt. ~**-tin** n Backform f

balance /'bæləns/ n (equilibrium) Gleichgewicht nt, Balance f; (scales) Waage f; (Comm) Saldo m; (outstanding sum) Restbetrag m; **[bank]** ~ Kontostand m; **in the** ~ (fig) in der Schwebe ● vt balancieren; (equalize) ausgleichen; (Comm) abschließen ⟨books⟩ ● vi balancieren; (fig & Comm) sich ausgleichen. ~**d** a ausgewogen. ~ **sheet** n Bilanz f

balcony /'bælkənɪ/ n Balkon m

bald /bɔːld/ a (-er, -est) kahl; ⟨person⟩ kahlköpfig; **go** ~ eine Glatze bekommen

balderdash /'bɔːldədæʃ/ n Unsinn m

bald|ing /'bɔːldɪŋ/ a **be** ~**ing** eine Glatze bekommen. ~**ly** adv unverblümt. ~**ness** n Kahlköpfigkeit f

bale /beɪl/ n Ballen m

baleful /'beɪlfl/ a, -**ly** adv böse

balk /bɔːlk/ vt vereiteln ● vi ~ **at** zurückschrecken vor (+ dat)

Balkans /'bɔːlknz/ npl Balkan m

ball[1] /bɔːl/ n Ball m; (Billiards, Croquet) Kugel f; (of yarn) Knäuel m & nt; **on the** ~ (fam) auf Draht

ball[2] n (dance) Ball m

ballad /'bæləd/ n Ballade f

ballast /'bæləst/ n Ballast m

ball-'bearing n Kugellager nt

ballerina /bælə'riːnə/ n Ballerina f

ballet /'bæleɪ/ m Ballett nt. ~ **dancer** n Ballettänzer(in) m(f)

ballistic /bə'lɪstɪk/ a ballistisch. ~**s** n Ballistik f

balloon /bə'luːn/ n Luftballon m; (Aviat) Ballon m

ballot /'bælət/ n [geheime] Wahl f; (on issue) [geheime] Abstimmung f. ~**-box** n Wahlurne f. ~**-paper** n Stimmzettel m

ball: ~**-point** ['pen] n Kugelschreiber m. ~**room** n Ballsaal m

balm /bɑːm/ n Balsam m

balmy /'bɑːmɪ/ a (-ier, -iest) a sanft; (fam: crazy) verrückt

Baltic /'bɔːltɪk/ a & n **the** ~ **[Sea]** die Ostsee

balustrade /bælə'streɪd/ n Balustrade f

bamboo /bæm'buː/ n Bambus m

bamboozle /bæm'buːzl/ vt (fam) übers Ohr hauen

ban /bæn/ n Verbot nt ● vt (pt/pp **banned**) verbieten

banal /bə'nɑːl/ a banal. ~**ity** /-'ælətɪ/ n Banalität f

banana /bə'nɑːnə/ n Banane f

band /bænd/ n Band nt; (stripe) Streifen m; (group) Schar f; (Mus) Kapelle f ● vi ~ **together** sich zusammenschließen

bandage /'bændɪdʒ/ n Verband m; (for support) Bandage f ● vt verbinden; bandagieren ⟨limb⟩

b. & b. abbr of **bed and breakfast**

bandit /'bændɪt/ n Bandit m

band: ~**stand** n Musikpavillon m. ~**wagon** n **jump on the** ~**wagon** (fig) sich einer erfolgreichen Sache anschließen

bandy[1] /'bændɪ/ vt (pt/pp -**ied**) wechseln ⟨words⟩

bandy[2] a (-ier, -iest) **be** ~ O-Beine haben. ~**-legged** a O-beinig

bang /bæŋ/ n (noise) Knall m; (blow) Schlag m ● adv **go** ~ knallen ● int bums! peng! ● vt knallen; (shut noisily) zuknallen; (strike) schlagen auf (+ acc); ~ **one's head** sich (dat) den Kopf stoßen (**on** an + acc) ● vi schlagen; ⟨door:⟩ zuknallen

banger /'bæŋə(r)/ n (firework) Knallfrosch m; (fam: sausage) Wurst f; **old** ~ (fam: car) Klapperkiste f

bangle /'bæŋgl/ n Armreifen m

banish /'bænɪʃ/ vt verbannen

banisters /'bænɪstəz/ npl [Treppen]geländer nt

banjo /'bændʒəʊ/ n Banjo nt

bank[1] /bæŋk/ n (of river) Ufer nt; (slope) Hang m ● vi (Aviat) in die Kurve gehen

bank[2] n Bank f ● vt einzahlen; ~ **with** ein Konto haben bei. ~ **on** vt sich verlassen auf (+ acc)

'bank account n Bankkonto nt

banker /'bæŋkə(r)/ n Bankier m

bank: ∼ **'holiday** n gesetzlicher Feiertag m. ∼**ing** n Bankwesen nt. ∼**note** n Banknote f

bankrupt /'bæŋkrʌpt/ a bankrott; **go** ∼ bankrott machen ● n Bankrotteur m ● vt bankrott machen. ∼**cy** n Bankrott m

banner /'bænə(r)/ n Banner nt; (carried by demonstrators) Transparent nt, Spruchband nt

banns /bænz/ npl (Relig) Aufgebot nt

banquet /'bæŋkwɪt/ n Bankett nt

banter /'bæntə(r)/ n Spöttelei f

bap /bæp/ n weiches Brötchen nt

baptism /'bæptɪzm/ n Taufe f

Baptist /'bæptɪst/ n Baptist(in) m(f)

baptize /bæp'taɪz/ vt taufen

bar /bɑː(r)/ n Stange f; (of cage) [Gitter]stab m; (of gold) Barren m; (of chocolate) Tafel f; (of soap) Stück nt; (long) Riegel m; (café) Bar f; (counter) Theke f; (Mus) Takt m; (fig: obstacle) Hindernis nt; **parallel** ∼**s** (Sport) Barren m; **be called to the** ∼ (Jur) als plädierender Anwalt zugelassen werden; **behind** ∼**s** (fam) hinter Gittern ● vt (pt/pp barred) versperren ⟨way, door⟩; ausschließen ⟨person⟩ ● prep außer; ∼ **none** ohne Ausnahme

barbarian /bɑː'beərɪən/ n Barbar m

barbar|ic /bɑː'bærɪk/ a barbarisch. ∼**ity** n Barbarei f. ∼**ous** /'bɑːbərəs/ a barbarisch

barbecue /'bɑːbɪkjuː/ n Grill m; (party) Grillfest nt ● vt [im Freien] grillen

barbed /'bɑːbd/ a ∼ **wire** Stacheldraht m

barber /'bɑːbə(r)/ n [Herren]friseur m

barbiturate /bɑː'bɪtjʊrət/ n Barbiturat nt

'bar code n Strichkode m

bare /beə(r)/ a (-r, -st) nackt, bloß; ⟨tree⟩ kahl; (empty) leer; (mere) bloß ● vt entblößen; fletschen ⟨teeth⟩

bare: ∼**back** adv ohne Sattel. ∼**faced** a schamlos. ∼**foot** adv barfuß. ∼'**headed** a mit unbedecktem Kopf

barely /'beəlɪ/ adv kaum

bargain /'bɑːgɪn/ n (agreement) Geschäft nt; (good buy) Gelegenheitskauf m; **into the** ∼ noch dazu; **make a** ∼ sich einigen ● vi handeln; (haggle) feilschen; ∼ **for** (expect) rechnen mit

barge /bɑːdʒ/ n Lastkahn m; (towed) Schleppkahn m ● vi ∼ **in** (fam) hereinplatzen

baritone /'bærɪtəʊn/ n Bariton m

bark[1] /bɑːk/ n (of tree) Rinde f

bark[2] n Bellen nt ● vi bellen

barley /'bɑːlɪ/ n Gerste f

bar: ∼**maid** n Schankmädchen nt. ∼**man** Barmann m

barmy /'bɑːmɪ/ a (fam) verrückt

barn /bɑːn/ n Scheune f

barometer /bə'rɒmɪtə(r)/ n Barometer nt

baron /'bærn/ n Baron m. ∼**ess** n Baronin f

baroque /bə'rɒk/ a barock ● n Barock nt

barracks /'bærəks/ npl Kaserne f

barrage /'bærɑːʒ/ n (in river) Wehr nt; (Mil) Sperrfeuer nt; (fig) Hagel m

barrel /'bærl/ n Faß nt; (of gun) Lauf m; (of cannon) Rohr nt. ∼**-organ** n Drehorgel f

barren /'bærn/ a unfruchtbar; ⟨landscape⟩ öde

barricade /'bærɪˈkeɪd/ n Barrikade f ● vt verbarrikadieren

barrier /'bærɪə(r)/ n Barriere f; (across road) Schranke f; (Rail) Sperre f; (fig) Hindernis nt

barring /'bɑːrɪŋ/ prep ∼ **accidents** wenn alles gutgeht

barrister /'bærɪstə(r)/ n [plädierender] Rechtsanwalt m

barrow /'bærəʊ/ n Karre f, Karren m. ∼ **boy** n Straßenhändler m

barter /'bɑːtə(r)/ vt tauschen (**for** gegen)

base /beɪs/ n Fuß m; (fig) Basis f; (Mil) Stützpunkt m ● a gemein; ⟨metal⟩ unedel ● vt stützen (**on** auf + acc); **be** ∼**d on** basieren auf (+ dat)

base: ∼**ball** n Baseball m. ∼**less** a unbegründet. ∼**ment** n Kellergeschoß nt. ∼**ment flat** n Kellerwohnung f

bash /bæʃ/ n Schlag m; **have a** ∼! (fam) probier es mal! ● vt hauen; (dent) einbeulen; ∼**ed in** verbeult

bashful /'bæʃfl/ a, -**ly** adv schüchtern

basic /'beɪsɪk/ a Grund-; (fundamental) grundlegend; (essential) wesentlich; (unadorned) einfach; **the** ∼**s** das Wesentliche. ∼**ally** adv grundsätzlich

basil /'bæzɪl/ n Basilikum nt

basilica /bə'zɪlɪkə/ n Basilika f

basin /'beɪsn/ n Becken nt; (for washing) Waschbecken nt; (for food) Schüssel f

basis /'beɪsɪs/ n (pl -**ses** /-siːz/) Basis f

bask /bɑːsk/ vi sich sonnen

basket /'bɑːskɪt/ n Korb m. ∼**ball** n Basketball m

Basle /bɑːl/ n Basel nt

bass /beɪs/ a Baß-; ∼ **voice** Baßstimme f ● n Baß m; (person) Bassist m

bassoon /bə'suːn/ n Fagott nt

bastard /'bɑːstəd/ n (sl) Schuft m

baste[1] /beɪst/ vt (sew) heften

baste[2] vt (Culin) begießen

bastion /'bæstɪən/ n Bastion f

bat[1] /bæt/ n Schläger m; **off one's own ∼** (fam) auf eigene Faust ● vt (pt/pp **batted**) schlagen; **not ∼ an eyelid** (fig) nicht mit der Wimper zucken

bat[2] n (Zool) Fledermaus f

batch /bætʃ/ n (of people) Gruppe f; (of papers) Stoß m; (of goods) Sendung f; (of bread) Schub m

bated /'beɪtɪd/ a **with ∼ breath** mit angehaltenem Atem

bath /bɑːθ/ n (pl ∼**s** /bɑːðz/) Bad nt; (tub) Badewanne f; ∼**s** pl Badeanstalt f; **have a ∼** baden ● vt/i baden

bathe /beɪð/ n Bad nt ● vt/i baden. ∼**r** n Badende(r) m/f

bathing /'beɪðɪŋ/ n Baden nt. ∼**-cap** n Bademütze f. ∼**-costume** n Badeanzug m

bath: ∼**-mat** n Bademattef. ∼**robe** n (Amer) Bademantel m. ∼**room** n Badezimmer nt. ∼**-towel** n Badetuch nt

baton /'bætn/ n (Mus) Taktstock m; (Mil) Stab m

battalion /bə'tælɪən/ n Bataillon nt

batten /'bætn/ n Latte f

batter /'bætə(r)/ n (Culin) flüssiger Teig m ● vt schlagen. ∼**ed** a ⟨car⟩ verbeult; ⟨wife⟩ mißhandelt

battery /'bætərɪ/ n Batterie f

battle /'bætl/ n Schlacht f; (fig) Kampf m ● vi (fig) kämpfen (**for** um)

battle: ∼**axe** n (fam) Drachen m. ∼**field** n Schlachtfeld nt. ∼**ship** n Schlachtschiff nt

batty /'bætɪ/ a (fam) verrückt

Bavaria /bə'veərɪə/ n Bayern nt. ∼**n** a bayrisch ● n Bayer(in) m(f)

bawdy /'bɔːdɪ/ a (-ier, -iest) derb

bawl /bɔːl/ vt/i brüllen

bay[1] /beɪ/ n (Geog) Bucht f; (Archit) Erker m

bay[2] n **keep at ∼** fernhalten

bay[3] n (horse) Braune(r) m

bay[4] n (Bot) [echter] Lorbeer m. ∼**-leaf** n Lorbeerblatt nt

bayonet /'beɪənet/ n Bajonett nt

bay 'window n Erkerfenster nt

bazaar /bə'zɑː(r)/ n Basar m

BC abbr (**before Christ**) v. Chr.

be /biː/ vi (pres **am, are, is**, pl **are**; pt **was**, pl **were**; pp **been**) sein; (lie) liegen; (stand) stehen; (cost) kosten; **he is a teacher** er ist Lehrer; **be quiet!** sei still! **I am cold/hot** mir ist kalt/heiß; **how are you?** wie geht es Ihnen? **I am well** mir geht es gut; **there is/are** es gibt; **what do you want to be?** was willst du werden? **I have been to Vienna** ich bin in Wien gewesen; **has the postman been?** war der Briefträger schon da? **it's hot, isn't it?** es ist heiß, nicht [wahr]? **you are coming too, aren't you?** du kommst mit, nicht [wahr]? **it's yours, is it?** das gehört also Ihnen? **yes he is/I am** ja; (negating previous statement) doch; **three and three are six** drei und drei macht sechs ● v aux ∼ **reading/going** lesen/ gehen; **I am coming/staying** ich komme/bleibe; **what is he doing?** was macht er? **I am being lazy** ich faulenze; **I was thinking of you** ich dachte an dich; **you were going to ...** du wolltest ...; **I am to stay** ich soll bleiben; **you are not to ...** du darfst nicht ...; **you are to do that immediately** das mußt du sofort machen ● passive werden; **be attacked/deceived** überfallen/betrogen werden

beach /biːtʃ/ n Strand m. ∼**wear** n Strandkleidung f

beacon /'biːkn/ n Leuchtfeuer nt; (Naut, Aviat) Bake f

bead /biːd/ n Perle f

beak /biːk/ n Schnabel m

beaker /'biːkə(r)/ n Becher m

beam /biːm/ n Balken m; (of light) Strahl m ● vi strahlen. ∼**ing** a [freude]strahlend

bean /biːn/ n Bohne f; **spill the ∼s** (fam) alles ausplaudern

bear[1] /beə(r)/ n Bär m

bear[2] vt/i (pt **bore**, pp **borne**) tragen; (endure) ertragen; gebären ⟨child⟩; ∼ **right** sich rechts halten. ∼**able** /-əbl/ a erträglich

beard /bɪəd/ n Bart m. ∼**ed** a bärtig

bearer /'beərə(r)/ n Träger m; (of news, cheque) Überbringer m; (of passport) Inhaber(in) m(f)

bearing /'beərɪŋ/ n Haltung f; (Techn) Lager nt; **have a ∼ on** von Belang sein für; **get one's ∼s** sich orientieren; **lose one's ~s** die Orientierung verlieren

beast /bi:st/ n Tier nt; (fam: person) Biest nt

beastly /'bi:stlɪ/ a (-ier, -iest) (fam) scheußlich; ⟨person⟩ gemein

beat /bi:t/ n Schlag m; (of policeman) Runde f; (rhythm) Takt m ● vt/i (pt **beat**, pp **beaten**) schlagen; (thrash) verprügeln; klopfen ⟨carpet⟩; (hammer) hämmern (**on** an + acc); ~ **a retreat** (Mil) sich zurückziehen; ~ **it!** (fam) hau ab! **it ~s me** (fam) das begreife ich nicht. ~ **up** vt zusammenschlagen

beat|en /'bi:tn/ a **off the ~en track** abseits. ~**ing** n Prügel pl

beautician /bju:'tɪʃn/ n Kosmetikerin f

beauti|ful /'bju:tɪfl/ a, -**ly** adv schön. ~**fy** /-faɪ/ vt (pt/pp -**ied**) verschönern

beauty /'bju:tɪ/ n Schönheit f. ~ **parlour** n Kosmetiksalon m. ~ **spot** n Schönheitsfleck m; (place) landschaftlich besonders reizvolle Stelle f

beaver /'bi:və(r)/ n Biber m

became /bɪ'keɪm/ see **become**

because /bɪ'kɒz/ conj weil ● adv ~ **of** wegen (+ gen)

beckon /'bekn/ vt/i ~ [**to**] herbeiwinken

becom|e /bɪ'kʌm/ vt/i (pt **became**, pp **become**) werden. ~**ing** a ⟨clothes⟩ kleidsam

bed /bed/ n Bett nt; (layer) Schicht f; (of flowers) Beet nt; **in** ~ im Bett; **go to** ~ ins od zu Bett gehen; ~ **and breakfast** Zimmer mit Frühstück. ~**clothes** npl, ~**ding** n Bettzeug nt

bedlam /'bedləm/ n Chaos nt

'**bedpan** n Bettpfanne f

bedraggled /bɪ'dræɡld/ a naß und verschmutzt

bed: ~**ridden** a bettlägerig. ~**room** n Schlafzimmer nt

'**bedside** n **at his** ~ an seinem Bett. ~ '**lamp** n Nachttischlampe f. ~ '**rug** n Bettvorleger m. ~ '**table** n Nachttisch m

bed: ~'**sitter** n, ~-'**sitting-room** n Wohnschlafzimmer nt. ~**spread** n Tagesdecke f. ~**time** n **at** ~**time** vor dem Schlafengehen

bee /bi:/ n Biene f

beech /bi:tʃ/ n Buche f

beef /bi:f/ n Rindfleisch nt. ~**burger** n Hamburger m

bee: ~**hive** n Bienenstock m. ~-**keeper** n Imker(in) m(f). ~-**keeping** n Bienenzucht f. ~-**line** n **make a** ~-**line for** (fam) zusteuern auf (+ acc)

been /bi:n/ see **be**

beer /bɪə(r)/ n Bier nt

beet /bi:t/ n (Amer: beetroot) rote Bete f; [**sugar**] ~ Zuckerrübe f

beetle /'bi:tl/ n Käfer m

'**beetroot** n rote Bete f

before /bɪ'fɔ:(r)/ prep vor (+ dat/ acc); **the day** ~ **yesterday** vorgestern; ~ **long** bald ● adv vorher; (already) schon; **never** ~ noch nie; ~ **that** davor ● conj (time) ehe, bevor. ~**hand** adv vorher, im voraus

befriend /bɪ'frend/ vt sich anfreunden mit

beg /beg/ v (pt/pp **begged**) ● vi betteln ● vt (entreat) anflehen; (ask) bitten (**for** um)

began /bɪ'gæn/ see **begin**

beggar /'begə(r)/ n Bettler(in) m(f); (fam) Kerl m

begin /bɪ'gɪn/ vt/i (pt **began**, pp **begun**, pres p **beginning**) anfangen, beginnen; **to** ~ **with** anfangs. ~**ner** n Anfänger(in) m(f). ~**ning** n Anfang m, Beginn m

begonia /bɪ'gəʊnɪə/ n Begonie f

begrudge /bɪ'grʌdʒ/ vt mißgönnen

beguile /bɪ'gaɪl/ vt betören

begun /bɪ'gʌn/ see **begin**

behalf /bɪ'hɑ:f/ n **on** ~ **of** im Namen von; **on my** ~ meinetwegen

behave /bɪ'heɪv/ vi sich verhalten; ~ **oneself** sich benehmen

behaviour /bɪ'heɪvjə(r)/ n Verhalten nt; **good/bad** ~ gutes/schlechtes Benehmen nt; ~ **pattern** Verhaltensweise f

behead /bɪ'hed/ vt enthaupten

beheld /bɪ'held/ see **behold**

behind /bɪ'haɪnd/ prep hinter (+ dat/ acc); **be** ~ **sth** hinter etw (dat) stecken ● adv hinten; (late) im Rückstand; **a long way** ~ weit zurück; **in the car** ~ im Wagen dahinter ● n (fam) Hintern m. ~**hand** adv im Rückstand

behold /bɪ'həʊld/ vt (pt/pp **beheld**) (liter) sehen

beholden /bɪ'həʊldn/ a verbunden (**to** dat)

beige /beɪʒ/ a beige

being /'bi:ɪŋ/ n Dasein nt; **living** ~ Lebewesen nt; **come into** ~ entstehen

belated /bɪ'leɪtɪd/ a, -**ly** adv verspätet

belch /beltʃ/ vi rülpsen ● vt ~ **out** ausstoßen ⟨smoke⟩

belfry /'belfrɪ/ n Glockenstube f; ⟨tower⟩ Glockenturm m

Belgian /'beldʒən/ a belgisch ● n Belgier(in) m(f)

Belgium /'beldʒəm/ n Belgien nt

belief /bɪ'li:f/ n Glaube m

believable /bɪ'li:vəbl/ a glaubhaft

believe /bɪ'li:v/ vt/i glauben (**s.o.** jdm; **in** an + acc). ~**r** n ⟨Relig⟩ Gläubige(r) m/f

belittle /bɪ'lɪtl/ vt herabsetzen

bell /bel/ n Glocke f; ⟨on door⟩ Klingel f

belligerent /bɪ'lɪdʒərənt/ a kriegführend; ⟨aggressive⟩ streitlustig

bellow /'beləʊ/ vt/i brüllen

bellows /'beləʊz/ npl Blasebalg m

belly /'belɪ/ n Bauch m

belong /bɪ'lɒŋ/ vi gehören (**to** dat); ⟨be member⟩ angehören (**to** dat). ~**ings** npl Sachen pl

beloved /bɪ'lʌvɪd/ a geliebt ● n Geliebte(r) m/f

below /bɪ'ləʊ/ prep unter (+ dat/acc) ● adv unten; ⟨Naut⟩ unter Deck

belt /belt/ n Gürtel m; ⟨area⟩ Zone f; ⟨Techn⟩ [Treib]riemen m ● vi ⟨fam: rush⟩ rasen ● vt ⟨fam: hit⟩ hauen

bemused /bɪ'mju:zd/ a verwirrt

bench /bentʃ/ n Bank f; ⟨work-⟩ Werkbank f; **the B~** ⟨Jur⟩ ≈ die Richter pl

bend /bend/ n Biegung f; ⟨in road⟩ Kurve f; **round the ~** ⟨fam⟩ verrückt ● v ⟨pt/pp bent⟩ ● vt biegen; beugen ⟨arm, leg⟩ ● vi sich bücken; ⟨thing:⟩ sich biegen; ⟨road:⟩ eine Biegung machen. ~ **down** vi sich bücken. ~ **over** vi sich vornüberbeugen

beneath /bɪ'ni:θ/ prep unter (+ dat/ acc); ~ **him** ⟨fig⟩ unter seiner Würde; ~ **contempt** unter aller Würde ● adv darunter

benediction /benɪ'dɪkʃn/ n ⟨Relig⟩ Segen m

benefactor /'benɪfæktə(r)/ n Wohltäter(in) m(f)

beneficial /benɪ'fɪʃl/ a nützlich

beneficiary /benɪ'fɪʃərɪ/ n Begünstigte(r) m/f

benefit /'benɪfɪt/ n Vorteil m; ⟨allowance⟩ Unterstützung f; ⟨insurance⟩ Leistung f; **sickness ~** Krankengeld nt ● v ⟨pt/pp -**fited**, pres p -**fiting**⟩ ● vt nützen (+ dat) ● vi profitieren (**from** von)

benevolen|ce /bɪ'nevələns/ n Wohlwollen nt. ~**t** a, -**ly** adv wohlwollend

benign /bɪ'naɪn/ a, -**ly** adv gütig; ⟨Med⟩ gutartig

bent /bent/ see **bend** ● a ⟨person⟩ gebeugt; ⟨distorted⟩ verbogen; ⟨fam: dishonest⟩ korrupt; **be ~ on doing sth** darauf erpicht sein, etw zu tun ● n Hang m, Neigung f (**for** zu); **artistic ~** künstlerische Ader f

be|queath /bɪ'kwi:ð/ vt vermachen (**to** dat). ~**quest** /-'kwest/ n Vermächtnis nt

bereave|d /bɪ'ri:vd/ n **the ~d** pl die Hinterbliebenen. ~**ment** n Trauerfall m; ⟨state⟩ Trauer f

bereft /bɪ'reft/ a ~ **of** beraubt (+ gen)

beret /'bereɪ/ n Baskenmütze f

Berne /bɜ:n/ n Bern nt

berry /'berɪ/ n Beere f

berserk /bə'sɜ:k/ a **go ~** wild werden

berth /bɜ:θ/ n ⟨on ship⟩ [Schlaf]koje f; ⟨ship's anchorage⟩ Liegeplatz m; **give a wide ~ to** ⟨fam⟩ einen großen Bogen machen um ● vi anlegen

beseech /bɪ'si:tʃ/ vt ⟨pt/pp **beseeched** or **besought**⟩ anflehen

beside /bɪ'saɪd/ prep neben (+ dat/ acc); ~ **oneself** außer sich ⟨dat⟩

besides /bɪ'saɪdz/ prep außer (+ dat) ● adv außerdem

besiege /bɪ'si:dʒ/ vt belagern

besought /bɪ'sɔ:t/ see **beseech**

bespoke /bɪ'spəʊk/ a ⟨suit⟩ maßgeschneidert

best /best/ a & n beste(r,s); **the ~** der/die/das Beste; **at ~** bestenfalls; **all the ~!** alles Gute! **do one's ~** sein Bestes tun; **the ~ part of a year** fast ein Jahr; **to the ~ of my knowledge** soviel ich weiß; **make the ~ of it** das Beste daraus machen ● adv am besten; **as I could** so gut ich konnte. ~ '**man** n ≈ Trauzeuge m

bestow /bɪ'stəʊ/ vt schenken (**on** dat)

best seller n Bestseller m

bet /bet/ n Wette f ● v ⟨pt/pp bet or **betted**⟩ ● vt ~ **s.o. £5** mit jdm um £5 wetten ● vi wetten; ~ **on** [Geld] setzen auf (+ acc)

betray /bɪ'treɪ/ vt verraten. ~**al** n Verrat m

better /'betə(r)/ a besser; **get ~** sich bessern; ⟨after illness⟩ sich erholen ● adv besser; ~ **off** besser dran; ~ **not** lieber nicht; **all the ~** um so besser; **the sooner the ~** je eher, desto besser;

think ~ of sth sich eines Besseren besinnen; **you'd ~ stay** du bleibst am besten hier • *vt* verbessern; (*do better than*) übertreffen; **~ oneself** sich verbessern

'**betting shop** *n* Wettbüro *nt*

between /bɪ'twiːn/ *prep* zwischen (+ *dat/acc*); **~ you and me** unter uns; **~ us** (*together*) zusammen • *adv* **[in] ~** dazwischen

beverage /'bevərɪdʒ/ *n* Getränk *nt*

bevy /'bevɪ/ *n* Schar *f*

beware /bɪ'weə(r)/ *vi* sich in acht nehmen (**of** vor + *dat*); **~ of the dog!** Vorsicht, bissiger Hund!

bewilder /bɪ'wɪldə(r)/ *vt* verwirren. **~ment** *n* Verwirrung *f*

bewitch /bɪ'wɪtʃ/ *vt* verzaubern; (*fig*) bezaubern

beyond /bɪ'jɒnd/ *prep* über (+ *acc*) ... hinaus; (*further*) weiter als; **~ reach** außer Reichweite; **~ doubt** ohne jeden Zweifel; **it's ~ me** (*fam*) das geht über meinen Horizont • *adv* darüber hinaus

bias /'baɪəs/ *n* Voreingenommenheit *f*; (*preference*) Vorliebe *f*; (*Jur*) Befangenheit *f*; **cut on the ~** schräg geschnitten • *vt* (*pt/pp* **biased**) (*influence*) beeinflussen. **~ed** *a* voreingenommen; (*Jur*) befangen

bib /bɪb/ *n* Lätzchen *nt*

Bible /'baɪbl/ *n* Bibel *f*

biblical /'bɪblɪkl/ *a* biblisch

bibliography /bɪblɪ'ɒgrəfɪ/ *n* Bibliographie *f*

bicarbonate /baɪ'kɑːbəneɪt/ *n* **~ of soda** doppeltkohlensaures Natron *nt*

bicker /'bɪkə(r)/ *vi* sich zanken

bicycle /'baɪsɪkl/ *n* Fahrrad *nt* • *vi* mit dem Rad fahren

bid[1] /bɪd/ *n* Gebot *nt*; (*attempt*) Versuch *m* • *vt/i* (*pt/pp* **bid**, *pres p* **bidding**) bieten (**for** auf + *acc*); (*Cards*) reizen

bid[2] *vt* (*pt* **bade** *or* **bid**, *pp* **bidden** *or* **bid**, *pres p* **bidding**) (*liter*) heißen; **~ s.o. welcome** jdn willkommen heißen

bidder /'bɪdə(r)/ *n* Bieter(in) *m(f)*

bide /baɪd/ *vt* **~ one's time** den richtigen Moment abwarten

biennial /baɪ'enɪəl/ *a* zweijährlich; (*lasting two years*) zweijährig

bier /bɪə(r)/ *n* [Toten]bahre *f*

bifocals /baɪ'fəʊklz/ *npl* **[pair of] ~** Bifokalbrille *f*

big /bɪg/ *a* (**bigger, biggest**) groß • *adv* **talk ~** (*fam*) angeben

bigamist /'bɪgəmɪst/ *n* Bigamist *m*. **~y** *n* Bigamie *f*

big-'headed *a* (*fam*) eingebildet

bigot /'bɪgət/ *n* Eiferer *m*. **~ed** *a* engstirnig

'**bigwig** *n* (*fam*) hohes Tier *nt*

bike /baɪk/ *n* (*fam*) [Fahr]rad *nt*

bikini /bɪ'kiːnɪ/ *n* Bikini *m*

bilberry /'bɪlbərɪ/ *n* Heidelbeere *f*

bile /baɪl/ *n* Galle *f*

bilingual /baɪ'lɪŋgwəl/ *a* zweisprachig

bilious /'bɪljəs/ *a* (*Med*) **~ attack** verdorbener Magen *m*

bill[1] /bɪl/ *n* Rechnung *f*; (*poster*) Plakat *nt*; (*Pol*) Gesetzentwurf *m*; (*Amer: note*) Banknote *f*; **~ of exchange** Wechsel *m* • *vt* eine Rechnung schicken (+ *dat*)

bill[2] *n* (*beak*) Schnabel *m*

billet /'bɪlɪt/ *n* (*Mil*) Quartier *nt* • *vt* (*pt/pp* **billeted**) einquartieren (**on** bei)

'**billfold** *n* (*Amer*) Brieftasche *f*

billiards /'bɪljədz/ *n* Billard *nt*

billion /'bɪljən/ *n* (*thousand million*) Milliarde *f*; (*million million*) Billion *f*

billy-goat /'bɪlɪ-/ *n* Ziegenbock *m*

bin /bɪn/ *n* Mülleimer *m*; (*for bread*) Kasten *m*

bind /baɪnd/ *vt* (*pt/pp* **bound**) binden (**to** an + *acc*); (*bandage*) verbinden; (*Jur*) verpflichten; (*cover the edge of*) einfassen. **~ing** *a* verbindlich • *n* Einband *m*; (*braid*) Borte *f*; (*on ski*) Bindung *f*

binge /bɪndʒ/ *n* (*fam*) **go on the ~** eine Sauftour machen

binoculars /bɪ'nɒkjʊləz/ *npl* **[pair of] ~** Fernglas *nt*

bio'chemistry /baɪəʊ-/ *n* Biochemie *f*. **~degradable** /-dɪ'greɪdəbl/ *a* biologisch abbaubar

biograph|er /baɪ'ɒgrəfə(r)/ *n* Biograph(in) *m(f)*. **~y** *n* Biographie *f*

biological /baɪə'lɒdʒɪkl/ *a* biologisch

biolog|ist /baɪ'ɒlədʒɪst/ *n* Biologe *m*. **~y** *n* Biologie *f*

birch /bɜːtʃ/ *n* Birke *f*; (*whip*) Rute *f*

bird /bɜːd/ *n* Vogel *m*; (*fam: girl*) Mädchen *nt*; **kill two ~s with one stone** zwei Fliegen mit einer Klappe schlagen

Biro (P) /'baɪrəʊ/ *n* Kugelschreiber *m*

birth /bɜːθ/ *n* Geburt *f*

birth: **~ certificate** *n* Geburtsurkunde *f*. **~-control** *n* Geburtenregelung *f*. **~day** *n* Geburtstag *m*.

~**mark** n Muttermal nt. ~**rate** n Geburtenziffer f. ~**right** n Geburtsrecht nt

biscuit /ˈbɪskɪt/ n Keks m

bisect /baɪˈsekt/ vt halbieren

bishop /ˈbɪʃəp/ n Bischof m; (Chess) Läufer m

bit¹ /bɪt/ n Stückchen nt; (for horse) Gebiß nt; (Techn) Bohreinsatz m; **a** ~ ein bißchen; ~ **by** ~ nach und nach; **a** ~ **of bread** ein bißchen Brot; **do one's** ~ sein Teil tun

bit² see **bite**

bitch /bɪtʃ/ n Hündin f; (sl) Luder nt. ~**y** a gehässig

bit|e /baɪt/ n Biß m; **[insect]** ~ Stich m; (mouthful) Bissen m ● vt/i (pt **bit**, pp **bitten**) beißen; ⟨insect:⟩ stechen; kauen ⟨one's nails⟩. ~**ing** a beißend

bitter /ˈbɪtə(r)/ a, **-ly** adv bitter; **cry** ~**ly** bitterlich weinen; ~**ly cold** bitterkalt ● n bitteres Bier nt. ~**ness** n Bitterkeit f

bitty /ˈbɪtɪ/ a zusammengestoppelt

bizarre /bɪˈzɑː(r)/ a bizarr

blab /blæb/ vi (pt/pp **blabbed**) alles ausplaudern

black /blæk/ a (**-er, -est**) schwarz; **be** ~ **and blue** grün und blau sein ● n Schwarz nt; (person) Schwarze(r) m/f ● vt schwärzen; boykottieren ⟨goods⟩. ~ **out** vt verdunkeln ● vi (lose consciousness) das Bewußtsein verlieren

black: ~**berry** n Brombeere f. ~**bird** n Amsel f. ~**board** n (Sch) [Wand]tafel f. ~'**currant** n schwarze Johannisbeere f

blacken vt/i schwärzen

black: ~ '**eye** n blaues Auge nt. **B**~ '**Forest** n Schwarzwald m. ~ '**ice** n Glatteis nt. ~**leg** n Streikbrecher m. ~**list** vt auf die schwarze Liste setzen. ~**mail** n Erpressung f ● vt erpressen. ~**mailer** n Erpresser(in) m(f). ~'**market** n schwarzer Markt m. ~**-out** n Verdunkelung f; **have a** ~**-out** (Med) das Bewußtsein verlieren. ~'**pudding** n Blutwurst f. ~**smith** n [Huf]schmied m

bladder /ˈblædə(r)/ n (Anat) Blase f

blade /bleɪd/ n Klinge f; (of grass) Halm m

blame /bleɪm/ n Schuld f ● vt die Schuld geben (+ dat); **no one is to** ~ keiner ist schuld daran. ~**less** a schuldlos

blanch /blɑːntʃ/ vi blaß werden ● vt (Culin) blanchieren

blancmange /bləˈmɒnʒ/ n Pudding m

bland /blænd/ a (**-er, -est**) mild

blank /blæŋk/ a leer; ⟨look⟩ ausdruckslos ● n Lücke f; (cartridge) Platzpatrone f. ~ '**cheque** n Blankoscheck m

blanket /ˈblæŋkɪt/ n Decke f; **wet** ~ (fam) Spielverderber(in) m(f)

blank '**verse** n Blankvers m

blare /bleə(r)/ vt/i schmettern

blasé /ˈblɑːzeɪ/ a blasiert

blaspheme /blæsˈfiːm/ vi lästern

blasphem|ous /ˈblæsfəməs/ a [gottes]lästerlich. ~**y** n [Gottes]lästerung f

blast /blɑːst/ n (gust) Luftstoß m; (sound) Stoß m ● vt sprengen ● int (sl) verdammt. ~**ed** a (sl) verdammt

blast: ~**-furnace** n Hochofen m. ~**-off** n (of missile) Start m

blatant /ˈbleɪtənt/ a offensichtlich

blaze /bleɪz/ n Feuer nt ● vi brennen

blazer /ˈbleɪzə(r)/ n Blazer m

bleach /bliːtʃ/ n Bleichmittel nt ● vt/i bleichen

bleak /bliːk/ a (**-er, -est**) öde; (fig) trostlos

bleary-eyed /ˈblɪərɪ-/ a mit trüben/ (on waking up) verschlafenen Augen

bleat /bliːt/ vi blöken; ⟨goat:⟩ meckern

bleed /bliːd/ v (pt/pp **bled**) ● vi bluten ● vt entlüften ⟨radiator⟩

bleep /bliːp/ n Piepton m ● vi piepsen ● vt mit dem Piepser rufen. ~**er** n Piepser m

blemish /ˈblemɪʃ/ n Makel m

blend /blend/ n Mischung f ● vt mischen ● vi sich vermischen. ~**er** n (Culin) Mixer m

bless /bles/ vt segnen. ~**ed** /ˈblesɪd/ a heilig; (sl) verflixt. ~**ing** n Segen m

blew /bluː/ see **blow**¹

blight /blaɪt/ n (Bot) Brand m ● vt (spoil) vereiteln

blind /blaɪnd/ a blind; ⟨corner⟩ unübersichtlich; ~ **man/woman** Blinde(r) m/f ● n **[roller]** ~ Rouleau nt ● vt blenden

blind: ~ '**alley** n Sackgasse f. ~**fold** a & adv mit verbundenen Augen ● n Augenbinde f ● vt die Augen verbinden (+ dat). ~**ly** adv blindlings. ~**ness** n Blindheit f

blink /blɪŋk/ vi blinzeln; ⟨light:⟩ blinken

blinkers /'blɪŋkəz/ npl Scheuklappen pl

bliss /blɪs/ n Glückseligkeit f. ~ful a glücklich

blister /'blɪstə(r)/ n (Med) Blase f • vi ⟨paint:⟩ Blasen werfen

blitz /blɪts/ n Luftangriff m; (fam) Großaktion f

blizzard /'blɪzəd/ n Schneesturm m

bloated /'bləʊtɪd/ a aufgedunsen

blob /blɒb/ n Klecks m

bloc /blɒk/ n (Pol) Block m

block /blɒk/ n Block m; (of wood) Klotz m; (of flats) [Wohn]block m • vt blockieren. ~ up vt zustopfen

blockade /blɒ'keɪd/ n Blockade f • vt blockieren

blockage /'blɒkɪdʒ/ n Verstopfung f

block: ~head n (fam) Dummkopf m. ~ 'letters npl Blockschrift f

bloke /bləʊk/ n (fam) Kerl m

blonde /blɒnd/ a blond • n Blondine f

blood /blʌd/ n Blut nt

blood: ~ count n Blutbild nt. ~-curdling a markerschütternd. ~ donor n Blutspender m. ~ group n Blutgruppe f. ~hound n Bluthund m. ~-poisoning n Blutvergiftung f. ~ pressure n Blutdruck m. ~ relative n Blutsverwandte(r) m/f. ~shed n Blutvergießen nt. ~shot a blutunterlaufen. ~ sports npl Jagdsport m. ~-stained a blutbefleckt. ~stream n Blutbahn f. ~ test n Blutprobe f. ~thirsty a blutdürstig. ~ transfusion n Blutübertragung f. ~-vessel n Blutgefäß nt

bloody /'blʌdɪ/ a (-ier, -iest) blutig; (sl) verdammt. ~-'minded a (sl) stur

bloom /bluːm/ n Blüte f • vi blühen

bloomer /'bluːmə(r)/ n (fam) Schnitzer m. ~ing a (fam) verdammt

blossom /'blɒsəm/ n Blüte f • vi blühen. ~ out vi (fig) aufblühen

blot /blɒt/ n [Tinten]klecks m; (fig) Fleck m • vt (pt/pp blotted) löschen. ~ out vt (fig) auslöschen

blotch /blɒtʃ/ n Fleck m. ~y a fleckig

'blotting-paper n Löschpapier nt

blouse /blaʊz/ n Bluse f

blow[1] /bləʊ/ n Schlag m

blow[2] v (pt **blew**, pp **blown**) • vt blasen; (fam: squander) verpulvern; ~ one's nose sich (dat) die Nase putzen • vi blasen; ⟨fuse:⟩ durchbrennen. ~ away vt wegblasen • vi wegfliegen. ~ down vt umwehen • vi umfallen. ~ out vt (extinguish) ausblasen. ~ over vi umfallen; (fig: die down) vorübergehen. ~ up vt (inflate) aufblasen; (enlarge) vergrößern; (shatter by explosion) sprengen • vi explodieren

blow: ~-dry vt fönen. ~fly n Schmeißfliege f. ~lamp n Lötlampe f

blown /bləʊn/ see **blow**[2]

'blowtorch n (Amer) Lötlampe f

blowy /'bləʊɪ/ a windig

bludgeon /'blʌdʒn/ vt (fig) zwingen

blue /bluː/ a (-r, -st) blau; **feel** ~ deprimiert sein • n Blau nt; **have the** ~s deprimiert sein; **out of the** ~ aus heiterem Himmel

blue: ~bell n Sternhyazinthe f. ~berry n Heidelbeere f. ~bottle n Schmeißfliege f. ~ film n Pornofilm m. ~print n (fig) Entwurf m

bluff /blʌf/ n Bluff m • vi bluffen

blunder /'blʌndə(r)/ n Schnitzer m • vi einen Schnitzer machen

blunt /blʌnt/ a stumpf; ⟨person⟩ geradeheraus. ~ly adv unverblümt, geradeheraus

blur /blɜː(r)/ n **it's all a** ~ alles ist verschwommen • vt (pt/pp **blurred**) verschwommen machen; ~red verschwommen

blurb /blɜːb/ n Klappentext m

blurt /blɜːt/ vt ~ out herausplatzen mit

blush /blʌʃ/ n Erröten nt • vi erröten

bluster /'blʌstə(r)/ n Großtuerei f. ~y a windig

boar /bɔː(r)/ n Eber m

board /bɔːd/ n Brett nt; (for notices) schwarzes Brett nt; (committee) Ausschuß m; (of directors) Vorstand m; **on** ~ an Bord; **full** ~ Vollpension f; ~ **and lodging** Unterkunft und Verpflegung pl; **go by the** ~ (fam) unter den Tisch fallen • vt einsteigen in (+ acc); (Naut, Aviat) besteigen • vi an Bord gehen; ~ **with** in Pension wohnen bei. ~ up vt mit Brettern verschlagen

boarder /'bɔːdə(r)/ n Pensionsgast m; (Sch) Internatsschüler(in) m(f)

board: ~-**game** n Brettspiel nt. ~**ing-house** n Pension f. ~**ing-school** n Internat nt

boast /bəʊst/ vt sich rühmen (+ gen) ● vi prahlen (**about** mit). ~**ful** a, -**ly** adv prahlerisch

boat /bəʊt/ n Boot nt; (ship) Schiff nt. ~**er** n (hat) flacher Strohhut m

bob[1] /bɒb/ n Bubikopf m ● vi (pt/pp **bobbed**) (curtsy) knicksen; ~ **up and down** sich auf und ab bewegen

bobbin /'bɒbɪn/ n Spule f

'bob-sleigh n Bob m

bode /bəʊd/ vi ~ **well/ill** etwas/ nichts Gutes verheißen

bodice /'bɒdɪs/ n Mieder nt

bodily /'bɒdɪlɪ/ a körperlich ● adv (forcibly) mit Gewalt

body /'bɒdɪ/ n Körper m; (corpse) Leiche f; (corporation) Körperschaft f; **the main** ~ der Hauptanteil. ~**guard** n Leibwächter m. ~**work** n (Auto) Karosserie f

bog /bɒg/ n Sumpf m ● vt (pt/pp **bogged**) **get** ~**ged down** steckenbleiben

boggle /'bɒgl/ vi **the mind** ~**s** es ist kaum vorstellbar

bogus /'bəʊgəs/ a falsch

boil[1] /bɔɪl/ n Furunkel m

boil[2] n **bring/come to the** ~ zum Kochen bringen/kommen ● vt/i kochen; ~**ed potatoes** Salzkartoffeln pl. ~ **down** vi (fig) hinauslaufen (**to** auf + acc). ~ **over** vi überkochen. ~ **up** vt aufkochen

boiler /'bɔɪlə(r)/ n Heizkessel m. ~**suit** n Overall m

'boiling point n Siedepunkt m

boisterous /'bɔɪstərəs/ a übermütig

bold /bəʊld/ a (-er, -est), -**ly** adv kühn; (Typ) fett. ~**ness** n Kühnheit f

bollard /'bɒla:d/ n Poller m

bolster /'bəʊlstə(r)/ n Nackenrolle f ● vt ~ **up** Mut machen (+ dat)

bolt /bəʊlt/ n Riegel m; (Techn) Bolzen m; **nuts and** ~**s** Schrauben und Muttern pl ● vt schrauben (**to** an + acc); verriegeln (door); hinunterschlingen (food) ● vi abhauen; (horse) durchgehen ● adv ~ **upright** kerzengerade

bomb /bɒm/ n Bombe f ● vt bombardieren

bombard /bɒm'ba:d/ vt beschießen; (fig) bombardieren

bombastic /bɒm'bæstɪk/ a bombastisch

bomb|er /'bɒmə(r)/ n (Aviat) Bomber m; (person) Bombenleger(in) m(f). ~**shell** n **be a** ~**shell** (fig) wie eine Bombe einschlagen

bond /bɒnd/ n (fig) Band nt; (Comm) Obligation f; **be in** ~ unter Zollverschluß stehen

bondage /'bɒndɪdʒ/ n (fig) Sklaverei f

bone /bəʊn/ n Knochen m; (of fish) Gräte f ● vt von den Knochen lösen (meat); entgräten (fish). ~-'**dry** a knochentrocken

bonfire /'bɒn-/ n Gartenfeuer nt; (celebratory) Freudenfeuer nt

bonnet /'bɒnɪt/ n Haube f

bonus /'bəʊnəs/ n Prämie f; (gratuity) Gratifikation f; (fig) Plus nt

bony /'bəʊnɪ/ a (-ier, -iest) knochig; (fish) grätig

boo /bu:/ int buh! ● vt ausbuhen ● vi buhen

boob /bu:b/ n (fam: mistake) Schnitzer m ● vi (fam) einen Schnitzer machen

book /bʊk/ n Buch nt; (of tickets) Heft nt; **keep the** ~**s** (Comm) die Bücher führen ● vt/i buchen; (reserve) [vor]bestellen; (for offence) aufschreiben. ~**able** /-əbl/ a im Vorverkauf erhältlich

book: ~**case** n Bücherregal nt. ~-**ends** npl Buchstützen pl. ~**ing-office** n Fahrkartenschalter m. ~**keeping** n Buchführung f. ~**let** n Broschüre f. ~**maker** n Buchmacher m. ~**mark** n Lesezeichen nt. ~**seller** n Buchhändler(in) m(f). ~**shop** n Buchhandlung f. ~**stall** n Bücherstand m. ~**worm** n Bücherwurm m

boom /bu:m/ n (Comm) Hochkonjunktur f; (upturn) Aufschwung m ● vi dröhnen; (fig) blühen

boon /bu:n/ n Segen m

boor /bʊə(r)/ n Flegel m. ~**ish** a flegelhaft

boost /bu:st/ n Auftrieb m ● vt Auftrieb geben (+ dat). ~**er** n (Med) Nachimpfung f

boot /bu:t/ n Stiefel m; (Auto) Kofferraum m

booth /bu:ð/ n Bude f; (cubicle) Kabine f

booty /'bu:tɪ/ n Beute f

booze /bu:z/ n (fam) Alkohol m ● vi (fam) saufen

border /'bɔːdə(r)/ n Rand m; (frontier) Grenze f; (in garden) Rabatte f ● vi ~ **on** grenzen an (+ acc). ~**line** n Grenzlinie f. ~**line case** n Grenzfall m

bore¹ /bɔː(r)/ see **bear**²

bore² vt/i (Techn) bohren

bor|e³ n (of gun) Kaliber nt; (person) langweiliger Mensch m; (thing) langweilige Sache f ● vt langweilen; be ~**ed** sich langweilen. ~**edom** n Langeweile f. ~**ing** a langweilig

born /bɔːn/ pp be ~ geboren werden ● a geboren

borne /bɔːn/ see **bear**²

borough /'bʌrə/ n Stadtgemeinde f

borrow /'bɒrəʊ/ vt [sich (dat)] borgen od leihen (**from** von)

bosom /'bʊzm/ n Busen m

boss /bɒs/ n (fam) Chef m ● vt herumkommandieren. ~**y** a herrschsüchtig

botanical /bə'tænɪkl/ a botanisch

botan|ist /'bɒtənɪst/ n Botaniker(in) m(f). ~**y** n Botanik f

botch /bɒtʃ/ vt verpfuschen

both /bəʊθ/ a & pron beide; ~ [**of**] **the children** beide Kinder; ~ **of them** beide [von ihnen] ● adv ~ **men and women** sowohl Männer als auch Frauen

bother /'bɒðə(r)/ n Mühe f; (minor trouble) Ärger m ● int (fam) verflixt! ● vt belästigen; (disturb) stören ● vi sich kümmern (**about** um); **don't** ~ nicht nötig

bottle /'bɒtl/ n Flasche f ● vt auf Flaschen abfüllen; (preserve) einmachen. ~ **up** vt (fig) in sich (dat) aufstauen

bottle: ~**-neck** n (fig) Engpaß m. ~**-opener** n Flaschenöffner m

bottom /'bɒtəm/ a unterste(r,s) ● n (of container) Boden m; (of river) Grund m; (of page, hill) Fuß m; (buttocks) Hintern m; **at the** ~ unten; **get to the** ~ **of sth** (fig) hinter etw (acc) kommen. ~**less** a bodenlos

bough /baʊ/ n Ast m

bought /bɔːt/ see **buy**

boulder /'bəʊldə(r)/ n Felsblock m

bounce /baʊns/ vi [auf]springen; ⟨cheque:⟩ (fam) nicht gedeckt sein ● vt aufspringen lassen ⟨ball⟩

bouncer /'baʊnsə(r)/ n (fam) Rausschmeißer m

bouncing /'baʊnsɪŋ/ a ~ **baby** strammer Säugling m

bound¹ /baʊnd/ n Sprung m ● vi springen

bound² see **bind** ● a ~ **for** ⟨ship⟩ mit Kurs auf (+ acc); **be** ~ **to do sth** etw bestimmt machen; (obliged) verpflichtet sein, etw zu machen

boundary /'baʊndərɪ/ n Grenze f

'**boundless** a grenzenlos

bounds /baʊndz/ npl (fig) Grenzen pl; **out of** ~ verboten

bouquet /bʊ'keɪ/ n [Blumen]strauß m; (of wine) Bukett nt

bourgeois /'bʊəʒwɑː/ a (pej) spießbürgerlich

bout /baʊt/ n (Med) Anfall m; (Sport) Kampf m

bow¹ /bəʊ/ n (weapon & Mus) Bogen m; (knot) Schleife f

bow² /baʊ/ n Verbeugung f ● vi sich verbeugen ● vt neigen ⟨head⟩

bow³ /baʊ/ n (Naut) Bug m

bowel /'baʊəl/ n Darm m; ~ **movement** Stuhlgang m. ~**s** pl Eingeweide pl; (digestion) Verdauung f

bowl¹ /bəʊl/ n Schüssel f; (shallow) Schale f; (of pipe) Kopf m; (of spoon) Schöpfteil m

bowl² n (ball) Kugel f ● vt/i werfen. ~ **over** vt umwerfen

bow-legged /bəʊ'legd/ a O-beinig

bowler¹ /'bəʊlə(r)/ n (Sport) Werfer m

bowler² n ~ [**hat**] Melone f

bowling /'bəʊlɪŋ/ n Kegeln nt. ~**-alley** n Kegelbahn f

bowls /bəʊlz/ n Bowlsspiel nt

bow-'tie /bəʊ-/ n Fliege f

box¹ /bɒks/ n Schachtel f; (wooden) Kiste f; (cardboard) Karton m; (Theat) Loge f

box² vt/i (Sport) boxen; ~ **s.o.'s ears** jdn ohrfeigen

box|er /'bɒksə(r)/ n Boxer m. ~**ing** n Boxen nt. **B~ing Day** n zweiter Weihnachtstag m

box: ~**-office** n (Theat) Kasse f. ~**-room** n Abstellraum m

boy /bɔɪ/ n Junge m

boycott /'bɔɪkɒt/ n Boykott m ● vt boykottieren

boy: ~**friend** n Freund m. ~**ish** a jungenhaft

bra /brɑː/ n BH m

brace /breɪs/ n Strebe f, Stütze f; (dental) Zahnspange f; ~**s** npl Hosenträger mpl ● vt ~ **oneself** sich stemmen (**against** gegen); (fig) sich gefaßt machen (**for** auf + acc)

bracelet /'breɪslɪt/ *n* Armband *nt*

bracing /'breɪsɪŋ/ *a* stärkend

bracken /'brækn/ *n* Farnkraut *nt*

bracket /'brækɪt/ *n* Konsole *f*; (*group*) Gruppe *f*; (*Typ*) **round/ square** ∼**s** runde/eckige Klammern ● *vt* einklammern

brag /bræg/ *vi* (*pt/pp* **bragged**) prahlen (**about** mit)

braid /breɪd/ *n* Borte *f*

braille /breɪl/ *n* Blindenschrift *f*

brain /breɪn/ *n* Gehirn *nt*; ∼**s** (*fig*) Intelligenz *f*

brain: ∼**child** *n* geistiges Produkt *nt*. ∼**less** *a* dumm. ∼**wash** *vt* einer Gehirnwäsche unterziehen. ∼**wave** *n* Geistesblitz *m*

brainy /'breɪnɪ/ *a* (**-ier, -iest**) klug

braise /breɪz/ *vt* schmoren

brake /breɪk/ *n* Bremse *f* ● *vt/i* bremsen. ∼**-light** *n* Bremslicht *nt*

bramble /'bræmbl/ *n* Brombeerstrauch *m*

bran /bræn/ *n* Kleie *f*

branch /brɑːntʃ/ *n* Ast *m*; (*fig*) Zweig *m*; (*Comm*) Zweigstelle *f*; (*shop*) Filiale *f* ● *vi* sich gabeln. ∼ **off** *vi* abzweigen. ∼ **out** *vi* ∼ **out into** sich verlegen auf (+ *acc*)

brand /brænd/ *n* Marke *f*; (*on animal*) Brandzeichen *nt* ● *vt* mit dem Brandeisen zeichnen ⟨*animal*⟩; (*fig*) brandmarken als

brandish /'brændɪʃ/ *vt* schwingen

brand-'new *a* nagelneu

brandy /'brændɪ/ *n* Weinbrand *m*

brash /bræʃ/ *a* naßforsch

brass /brɑːs/ *n* Messing *nt*; (*Mus*) Blech *nt*; **get down to** ∼ **tacks** (*fam*) zur Sache kommen; **top** ∼ (*fam*) hohe Tiere *pl*. ∼ **band** *n* Blaskapelle *f*

brassiere /'bræzɪə(r)/ *n* Büstenhalter *m*

brassy /'brɑːsɪ/ *a* (**-ier, -iest**) (*fam*) ordinär

brat /bræt/ *n* (*pej*) Balg *nt*

bravado /brə'vɑːdəʊ/ *n* Forschheit *f*

brave /breɪv/ *a* (**-r, -st**), **-ly** *adv* tapfer ● *vt* die Stirn bieten (+ *dat*). ∼**ry** /-ərɪ/ *n* Tapferkeit *f*

bravo /brɑː'vəʊ/ *int* bravo!

brawl /brɔːl/ *n* Schlägerei *f* ● *vi* sich schlagen

brawn /brɔːn/ *n* (*Culin*) Sülze *f*

brawny /'brɔːnɪ/ *a* muskulös

bray /breɪ/ *vi* iahen

brazen /'breɪzn/ *a* unverschämt

brazier /'breɪzɪə(r)/ *n* Kohlenbecken *nt*

Brazil /brə'zɪl/ *n* Brasilien *nt*. ∼**ian** *a* brasilianisch. ∼ **nut** *n* Paranuß *f*

breach /briːtʃ/ *n* Bruch *m*; (*Mil & fig*) Bresche *f*; ∼ **of contract** Vertragsbruch *m* ● *vt* durchbrechen; brechen ⟨contract⟩

bread /bred/ *n* Brot *nt*; **slice of** ∼ **and butter** Butterbrot *nt*

bread: ∼**crumbs** *npl* Brotkrümel *pl*; (*Culin*) Paniermehl *nt*. ∼**line** *n* **be on the** ∼**line** gerade genug zum Leben haben

breadth /bredθ/ *n* Breite *f*

'bread-winner *n* Brotverdiener *m*

break /breɪk/ *n* Bruch *m*; (*interval*) Pause *f*; (*interruption*) Unterbrechung *f*; (*fam: chance*) Chance *f* ● *v* (*pt* **broke**, *pp* **broken**) ● *vt* brechen; (*smash*) zerbrechen; (*damage*) kaputtmachen (*fam*); (*interrupt*) unterbrechen; ∼ **one's arm** sich (*dat*) den Arm brechen ● *vi* brechen; ⟨day:⟩ anbrechen; ⟨storm:⟩ losbrechen; ⟨thing:⟩ kaputtgehen (*fam*); ⟨rope, thread:⟩ reißen; ⟨news:⟩ bekanntwerden; **his voice is** ∼**ing** er ist im Stimmbruch. ∼ **away** *vi* sich losreißen (*fig*) sich absetzen (**from** von). ∼ **down** *vi* zusammenbrechen; (*Techn*) eine Panne haben; ⟨negotiations:⟩ scheitern ● *vt* aufbrechen ⟨door⟩; aufgliedern ⟨figures⟩. ∼ **in** *vi* einbrechen. ∼ **off** *vt/i* abbrechen; lösen ⟨engagement⟩. ∼ **out** *vi* ausbrechen. ∼ **up** *vt* zerbrechen ● *vi* ⟨crowd:⟩ sich zerstreuen; ⟨marriage, couple:⟩ auseinandergehen; (*Sch*) Ferien bekommen

break|able /'breɪkəbl/ *a* zerbrechlich. ∼**age** /-ɪdʒ/ *n* Bruch *m*. ∼**down** *n* (*Techn*) Zusammenbruch *m*; (*of figures*) Aufgliederung *f*. ∼**er** *n* (*wave*) Brecher *m*

breakfast /'brekfəst/ *n* Frühstück *nt*

break: ∼**through** *n* Durchbruch *m*. ∼**water** *n* Buhne *f*

breast /brest/ *n* Brust *f*. ∼**bone** *n* Brustbein *nt*. ∼**-feed** *vt* stillen. ∼**-stroke** *n* Brustschwimmen *nt*

breath /breθ/ *n* Atem *m*; **out of** ∼ außer Atem; **under one's** ∼ vor sich (*acc*) hin

breathalyse /'breθəlaɪz/ *vt* ins Röhrchen blasen lassen. ∼**r (P)** *n* Röhrchen *nt*. ∼**r test** *n* Alcotest (P) *m*

breathe /briːð/ *vt/i* atmen. ∼ **in** *vt/i* einatmen. ∼ **out** *vt/i* ausatmen

breath|er /'briːðə(r)/ n Atempause f. ~ing n Atmen nt

breath /'breθ-/: ~less a atemlos. ~-taking a atemberaubend. ~ test n Alcotest (P) m

bred /bred/ see **breed**

breeches /'brɪtʃɪz/ npl Kniehose f; (for riding) Reithose f

breed /briːd/ n Rasse f ● v (pt/pp **bred**) ● vt züchten; (give rise to) erzeugen ● vi sich vermehren. ~er n Züchter m. ~ing n Zucht f; (fig) [gute] Lebensart f

breez|e /briːz/ n Lüftchen nt; (Naut) Brise f. ~y a [leicht] windig

brevity /'brevɪtɪ/ n Kürze f

brew /bruː/ n Gebräu nt ● vt brauen; kochen (tea) ● vi (fig) sich zusammenbrauen. ~er n Brauer m. ~ery n Brauerei f

bribe /braɪb/ n (money) Bestechungsgeld nt ● vt bestechen. ~ry /-ərɪ/ n Bestechung f

brick /brɪk/ n Ziegelstein m, Backstein m ● vt ~ **up** zumauern

'bricklayer n Maurer m

bridal /'braɪdl/ a Braut-

bride /braɪd/ n Braut f. ~groom n Bräutigam m. ~smaid n Brautjungfer f

bridge[1] /brɪdʒ/ n Brücke f; (of nose) Nasenrücken m; (of spectacles) Steg m ● vt (fig) überbrücken

bridge[2] n (Cards) Bridge nt

bridle /'braɪdl/ n Zaum m. ~-path n Reitweg m

brief[1] /briːf/ a (-er, -est) kurz; **be** ~ ⟨person:⟩ sich kurz fassen

brief[2] n Instruktionen pl; (Jur: case) Mandat nt ● vt Instruktionen geben (+ dat); (Jur) beauftragen. ~case n Aktentasche f

brief|ing /'briːfɪŋ/ n Informationsgespräch nt. ~ly adv kurz. ~ness n Kürze f

briefs /briːfs/ npl Slip m

brigad|e /brɪ'geɪd/ n Brigade f. ~ier /-ə'dɪə(r)/ n Brigadegeneral m

bright /braɪt/ a (-er, -est), **-ly** adv hell; ⟨day⟩ heiter; ~ **red** hellrot

bright|en /'braɪtn/ v ~**en [up]** ● vt aufheitern ● vi sich aufheitern. ~ness n Helligkeit f

brilliance /'brɪljəns/ n Glanz m; (of person) Genialität f

brilliant /'brɪljənt/ a, **-ly** adv glänzend; ⟨person⟩ genial

brim /brɪm/ n Rand m; (of hat) Krempe f ● vi (pt/pp **brimmed**) ~ **over** überfließen

brine /braɪn/ n Salzwasser nt; (Culin) [Salz]lake f

bring /brɪŋ/ vt (pt/pp **brought**) bringen; ~ **them with you** bring sie mit. ~ **about** vt verursachen. ~ **along** vt mitbringen. ~ **back** vt zurückbringen. ~ **down** vt herunterbringen; senken ⟨price⟩. ~ **off** vt vollbringen. ~ **on** vt (cause) verursachen. ~ **out** vt herausbringen. ~ **round** vt vorbeibringen; (persuade) überreden; wieder zum Bewußtsein bringen ⟨unconscious person⟩. ~ **up** vt heraufbringen; (vomit) erbrechen; aufziehen ⟨children⟩; erwähnen ⟨question⟩

brink /brɪŋk/ n Rand m

brisk /brɪsk/ a (-er, -est), **-ly** adv lebhaft; (quick) schnell

brist|le /'brɪsl/ n Borste f. ~ly a borstig

Brit|ain /'brɪtn/ n Großbritannien nt. ~ish a britisch; **the** ~ish die Briten pl. ~on n Brite m/Britin f

Brittany /'brɪtənɪ/ n die Bretagne

brittle /'brɪtl/ a brüchig, spröde

broach /brəʊtʃ/ vt anzapfen; anschneiden ⟨subject⟩

broad /brɔːd/ a (-er, -est) breit; ⟨hint⟩ deutlich; **in** ~ **daylight** am hellichten Tag. ~ **beans** npl dicke Bohnen pl

'broadcast n Sendung f ● vt/i (pt/pp **-cast**) senden. ~er n Rundfunk- und Fernsehpersönlichkeit f. ~ing n Funk und Fernsehen pl

broaden /'brɔːdn/ vt verbreitern; (fig) erweitern ● vi sich verbreitern

broadly /'brɔːdlɪ/ adv breit; ~ **speaking** allgemein gesagt

broad'minded a tolerant

brocade /brə'keɪd/ n Brokat m

broccoli /'brɒkəlɪ/ n inv Brokkoli pl

brochure /'brəʊʃə(r)/ n Broschüre f

brogue /brəʊg/ n (shoe) Wanderschuh m; **Irish** ~ irischer Akzent m

broke /brəʊk/ see **break** ● a (fam) pleite

broken /'brəʊkn/ see **break** ● a zerbrochen, (fam) kaputt; ~ **English** gebrochenes Englisch nt. ~-**hearted** a untröstlich

broker /'brəʊkə(r)/ n Makler m

brolly /'brɒlɪ/ n (fam) Schirm m

bronchitis /brɒŋ'kaɪtɪs/ n Bronchitis f

bronze /brɒnz/ n Bronze f
brooch /brəʊtʃ/ n Brosche f
brood /bru:d/ n Brut f ● vi brüten;
(fig) grübeln
brook[1] /brʊk/ n Bach m
brook[2] vt dulden
broom /bru:m/ n Besen m; (Bot)
Ginster m. **~stick** n Besenstiel m
broth /brɒθ/ n Brühe f
brothel /'brɒθl/ n Bordell nt
brother /'brʌðə(r)/ n Bruder m
brother: ~-in-law n (pl **-s-in-law**)
Schwager m. **~ly** a brüderlich
brought /brɔ:t/ see **bring**
brow /braʊ/ n Augenbraue f;
(forehead) Stirn f; (of hill) [Berg]-
kuppe f
'**browbeat** vt (pt **-beat**, pp **-beaten**)
einschüchtern
brown /braʊn/ a (**-er, -est**) braun; **~
'paper** Packpapier nt ● n Braun nt ● vt
bräunen ● vi braun werden
Brownie /'braʊnɪ/ n Wichtel m
browse /braʊz/ vi (read) schmökern; (in shop) sich umsehen
bruise /bru:z/ n blauer Fleck m ● vt
beschädigen (fruit); **~ one's arm** sich
(dat) den Arm quetschen
brunch /brʌntʃ/ n Brunch m
brunette /bru:'net/ n Brünette f
Brunswick /'brʌnzwɪk/ n Braunschweig nt
brunt /brʌnt/ n **the ~ of** die volle
Wucht (+ gen)
brush /brʌʃ/ n Bürste f; (with
handle) Handfeger m; (for paint, pastry) Pinsel m; (bushes) Unterholz nt;
(fig: conflict) Zusammenstoß m ● vt
bürsten; putzen (teeth); **~ against**
streifen [gegen]; **~ aside** (fig) abtun. **~ off** vt abbürsten; (reject)
zurückweisen. **~ up** vt/i (fig) **~up
[on]** auffrischen
brusque /brʊsk/ a, **-ly** adv brüsk
Brussels /'brʌslz/ n Brüssel nt. **~
sprouts** npl Rosenkohl m
brutal /'bru:tl/ a, **-ly** adv brutal.
~ity /-'tælətɪ/ n Brutalität f
brute /bru:t/ n Unmensch m. **~
force** n rohe Gewalt f
B.Sc. abbr of **Bachelor of Science**
bubble /'bʌbl/ n [Luft]blase f ● vi
sprudeln
buck[1] /bʌk/ n (deer & Gym) Bock m;
(rabbit) Rammler m ● vi (horse:)
bocken. **~ up** vi (fam) sich aufheitern; (hurry) sich beeilen
buck[2] n (Amer, fam) Dollar m

buck[3] n **pass the ~** die Verantwortung
abschieben
bucket /'bʌkɪt/ n Eimer m
buckle /'bʌkl/ n Schnalle f ● vt
zuschnallen ● vi sich verbiegen
bud /bʌd/ n Knospe f ● vi (pt/pp
budded) knospen
Buddhis|m /'bʊdɪzm/ n Buddhismus
m. **~t** a buddhistisch ● n Bud-
dhist(in) m(f)
buddy /'bʌdɪ/ n (fam) Freund m
budge /bʌdʒ/ vt bewegen ● vi sich
[von der Stelle] rühren
budgerigar /'bʌdʒərɪɡɑ:(r)/ n
Wellensittich m
budget /'bʌdʒɪt/ n Budget nt; (Pol)
Haushaltsplan m; (money available)
Etat m ● vi (pt/pp **budgeted**) **~ for
sth** etw einkalkulieren
buff /bʌf/ a (colour) sandfarben ● n
Sandfarbe f; (Amer, fam) Fan m ● vt
polieren
buffalo /'bʌfələʊ/ n (inv or pl **-es**)
Büffel m
buffer /'bʌfə(r)/ n (Rail) Puffer m;
old ~ (fam) alter Knacker m; **~ zone**
Pufferzone f
buffet[1] /'bʊfeɪ/ n Büfett nt; (on
station) Imbißstube f
buffet[2] /'bʌfɪt/ vt (pt/pp **buffeted**)
hin und her werfen
buffoon /bə'fu:n/ n Narr m
bug /bʌɡ/ n Wanze f; (fam: virus) Bazillus m; (fam: device) Abhörgerät nt,
(fam) Wanze f ● vt (pt/pp **bugged**)
(fam) verwanzen (room); abhören (telephone); (Amer: annoy) ärgern
buggy /'bʌɡɪ/ n [Kinder]sportwagen
m
bugle /'bju:ɡl/ n Signalhorn m
build /bɪld/ n (of person) Körperbau
m ● vt/i (pt/pp **built**) bauen. **~ on** vt
anbauen (**to** an + acc). **~ up** vt aufbauen ● vi zunehmen; (traffic:) sich
stauen
builder /'bɪldə(r)/ n Bauunter-
nehmer m
building /'bɪldɪŋ/ n Gebäude nt. **~
site** n Baustelle f. **~ society** n Bau-
sparkasse f
built /bɪlt/ see **build**. **~-in** a eingebaut. **~-in 'cupboard** n Einbauschrank m. **~-up area** n
bebautes Gebiet nt; (Auto) geschlossene Ortschaft f
bulb /bʌlb/ n [Blumen]zwiebel f;
(Electr) [Glüh]birne f
bulbous /'bʌlbəs/ a bauchig

Bulgaria /bʌl'geərɪə/ n Bulgarien nt
bulg|e /bʌldʒ/ n Ausbauchung f ● vi
sich ausbauchen. **~ing** a prall; ⟨eyes⟩
hervorquellend; **~ing with** prall gefüllt mit
bulk /bʌlk/ n Masse f; ⟨greater part⟩
Hauptteil m; **in ~** en gros; ⟨loose⟩ lose.
~y a sperrig; ⟨large⟩ massig
bull /bʊl/ n Bulle m, Stier m
'bulldog n Bulldogge f
'bulldozer /'bʊldəʊzə(r)/ n Planier-
raupe f
bullet /'bʊlɪt/ n Kugel f
bulletin /'bʊlɪtɪn/ n Bulletin nt
'bullet-proof a kugelsicher
'bullfight n Stierkampf m. **~er** n
Stierkämpfer m
'bullfinch n Dompfaff m
bullion /'bʊlɪən/ n **gold ~** Barrengold
nt
bullock /'bʊlək/ n Ochse m
bull: ~ring n Stierkampfarena f.
~'s-eye n **score a ~'s-eye** ins
Schwarze treffen
bully /'bʊlɪ/ n Tyrann m ● vt tyrannisieren
bum¹ /bʌm/ n ⟨sl⟩ Hintern m
bum² n ⟨Amer, fam⟩ Landstreicher m
bumble-bee /'bʌmbl-/ n Hummel f
bump /bʌmp/ n Bums m; ⟨swelling⟩
Beule f; ⟨in road⟩ holperige Stelle f
● vt stoßen; **~ into** stoßen gegen;
⟨meet⟩ zufällig treffen. **~ off** vt ⟨fam⟩
um die Ecke bringen
bumper /'bʌmpə(r)/ a Rekord- ● n
⟨Auto⟩ Stoßstange f
bumpkin /'bʌmpkɪn/ n **country ~**
Tölpel m
bumptious /'bʌmpʃəs/ a aufgeblasen
bumpy /'bʌmpɪ/ a holperig
bun /bʌn/ n Milchbrötchen nt; ⟨hair⟩
[Haar]knoten m
bunch /bʌntʃ/ n ⟨of flowers⟩ Strauß
m; ⟨of radishes, keys⟩ Bund m; ⟨of
people⟩ Gruppe f; **~ of grapes** [ganze]
Weintraube f
bundle /'bʌndl/ n Bündel nt ● vt **~
[up]** bündeln
bung /bʌŋ/ vt ⟨fam⟩ ⟨throw⟩
schmeißen. **~ up** vt ⟨fam⟩ verstopfen
bungalow /'bʌŋgələʊ/ n Bungalow
m
bungle /'bʌŋgl/ vt verpfuschen
bunion /'bʌnjən/ n ⟨Med⟩ Ballen m
bunk /bʌŋk/ n [Schlaf]koje f.
~-beds npl Etagenbett nt
bunker /'bʌŋkə(r)/ n Bunker m

bunkum /'bʌŋkəm/ n Quatsch m
bunny /'bʌnɪ/ n ⟨fam⟩ Kaninchen nt
buoy /bɔɪ/ n Boje f. **~ up** vt ⟨fig⟩
stärken
buoyan|cy /'bɔɪənsɪ/ n Auftrieb m.
~t a **be ~t** schwimmen; ⟨water:⟩ gut
tragen
burden /'bɜːdn/ n Last f ● vt belasten. **~some** /-səm/ a lästig
bureau /'bjʊərəʊ/ n (pl **-x** /-əʊz/ or
~s) ⟨desk⟩ Sekretär m; ⟨office⟩ Büro nt
bureaucracy /bjʊə'rɒkrəsɪ/ n Bürokratie f
bureaucrat /'bjʊərəkræt/ n Büro-
krat m. **~ic** /-'krætɪk/ a büro-
kratisch
burger /'bɜːgə(r)/ n Hamburger m
burglar /'bɜːglə(r)/ n Einbrecher m.
~ alarm n Alarmanlage f
burglar|ize /'bɜːglərɑɪz/ vt ⟨Amer⟩
einbrechen in (+ acc). **~y** n Einbruch m
burgle /'bɜːgl/ vt einbrechen in
(+ acc); **they have been ~d** bei ihnen
ist eingebrochen worden
Burgundy /'bɜːgəndɪ/ n Burgund nt;
b~ ⟨wine⟩ Burgunder m
burial /'berɪəl/ n Begräbnis nt
burlesque /bɜː'lesk/ n Burleske f
burly /'bɜːlɪ/ a (**-ier, -iest**) stämmig
Burm|a /'bɜːmə/ n Birma nt. **~ese**
/-'miːz/ a birmanisch
burn /bɜːn/ n Verbrennung f; ⟨on
skin⟩ Brandwunde f; ⟨on material⟩
Brandstelle f ● v (pt/pp **burnt** or
burned) ● vt verbrennen ● vi brennen;
⟨food:⟩ anbrennen. **~ down** vt/i
niederbrennen
burnish /'bɜːnɪʃ/ vt polieren
burnt /bɜːnt/ see **burn**
burp /bɜːp/ vi ⟨fam⟩ aufstoßen
burrow /'bʌrəʊ/ n Bau m ● vi
wühlen
bursar /'bɜːsə(r)/ n Rechnungs-
führer m. **~y** n Stipendium nt
burst /bɜːst/ n Bruch m; ⟨surge⟩ Ausbruch m ● v (pt/pp **burst**) ● vt platzen
machen ● vi platzen; ⟨bud:⟩ aufgehen;
~ into tears in Tränen ausbrechen
bury /'berɪ/ vt (pt/pp **-ied**) begraben;
⟨hide⟩ vergraben
bus /bʌs/ n [Auto]bus m ● vt/i (pt/pp
bussed) mit dem Bus fahren
bush /bʊʃ/ n Strauch m; ⟨land⟩
Busch m. **~y** a (**-ier, -iest**) buschig
busily /'bɪzɪlɪ/ adv eifrig
business /'bɪznɪs/ n Angelegenheit f;
⟨Comm⟩ Geschäft nt; **on ~** ge-
schäftlich; **he has no ~ to** er hat kein

Recht, zu; **mind one's own ~** sich um seine eigenen Angelegenheiten kümmern; **that's none of your ~** das geht Sie nichts an. **~-like** a geschäftsmäßig. **~man** n Geschäftsmann m

busker /'bʌskə(r)/ n Straßenmusikant m

'bus-stop n Bushaltestelle f

bust¹ /bʌst/ n Büste f. **~ size** n Oberweite f

bust² a (fam) kaputt; **go ~** pleite machen ● v (pt/pp busted or bust) (fam) ● vt kaputtmachen ● vi kaputtgehen

bustl|e /'bʌsl/ n Betrieb m, Getriebe nt ● vi **~e about** geschäftig hin und her laufen. **~ing** a belebt

'bust-up n (fam) Streit m, Krach m

busy /'bɪzɪ/ a (-ier, -iest) beschäftigt; ⟨day⟩ voll; ⟨street⟩ belebt; (with traffic) stark befahren; (Amer Teleph) besetzt; **be ~** zu tun haben ● vt **~ oneself** sich beschäftigen (**with** mit)

'busybody n Wichtigtuer(in) m(f)

but /bʌt/ a, unbetont bət/ conj aber; (after negative) sondern ● prep außer (+ dat); **~ for** (without) ohne (+ acc); **the last ~ one** der/die/das vorletzte; **the next ~ one** der/die/ das übernächste ● adv nur

butcher /'bʊtʃə(r)/ n Fleischer m, Metzger m; **~'s [shop]** Fleischerei f, Metzgerei f ● vt [ab]schlachten

butler /'bʌtlə(r)/ n Butler m

butt /bʌt/ n (of gun) [Gewehr]kolben m; (fig: target) Zielscheibe f; (of cigarette) Stummel m; (for water) Regentonne f ● vt mit dem Kopf stoßen ● vi **~ in** unterbrechen

butter /'bʌtə(r)/ n Butter f ● vt mit Butter bestreichen. **~ up** vt (fam) schmeicheln (+ dat)

butter: ~cup a Butterblume f, Hahnenfuß m. **~fly** n Schmetterling m

buttocks /'bʌtəks/ npl Gesäß nt

button /'bʌtn/ n Knopf m ● vt **~ [up]** zuknöpfen ● vi geknöpft werden. **~hole** n Knopfloch m

buttress /'bʌtrɪs/ n Strebepfeiler m; **flying ~** Strebebogen m

buxom /'bʌksəm/ a drall

buy /baɪ/ n Kauf m ● vt (pt/pp bought) kaufen. **~er** n Käufer(in) m(f)

buzz /bʌz/ n Summen nt ● vi summen. **~ off** vi (fam) abhauen

buzzard /'bʌzəd/ n Bussard m

buzzer /'bʌzə(r)/ n Summer m

by /baɪ/ prep (close to) bei; (next to) neben (+ dat/acc); (past) an (+ dat) ... vorbei; (to the extent of) um (+ acc); (at the latest) bis; (by means of) durch; **by Mozart/Dickens** von Mozart/Dickens; **~ oneself** allein; **~ the sea** am Meer; **~ car/bus** mit dem Auto/Bus; **~ sea** mit dem Schiff; **~ day/night** bei Tag/Nacht; **~ the hour** pro Stunde; **~ the metre** meterweise; **six metres ~ four** sechs mal vier Meter; **win ~ a length** mit einer Länge Vorsprung gewinnen; **miss the train ~ a minute** den Zug um eine Minute verpassen ● adv **~ and ~** mit der Zeit; **~ and large** im großen und ganzen; **put ~** beiseite legen; **go/pass ~** vorbeigehen

bye /baɪ/ int (fam) tschüs

by: ~-election n Nachwahl f. **~gone** a vergangen. **~-law** n Verordnung f. **~pass** n Umgehungsstraße f; (Med) Bypass m ● vt umfahren. **~-product** n Nebenprodukt nt. **~-road** n Nebenstraße f. **~stander** n Zuschauer(in) m(f)

Byzantine /bɪ'zæntaɪn/ a byzantinisch

C

cab /kæb/ n Taxi nt; (of lorry, train) Führerhaus nt

cabaret /'kæbəreɪ/ n Kabarett nt

cabbage /'kæbɪdʒ/ n Kohl m

cabin /'kæbɪn/ n Kabine f; (hut) Hütte f

cabinet /'kæbɪnɪt/ n Schrank m; **[display]** ~ Vitrine f; (TV, Radio) Gehäuse nt; **C~** (Pol) Kabinett nt. **~-maker** n Möbeltischler m

cable /'keɪbl/ n Kabel nt; (rope) Tau nt. **~ 'railway** n Seilbahn f. **~ 'television** n Kabelfernsehen nt

cache /kæʃ/ n Versteck nt; **~ of arms** Waffenlager nt

cackle /'kækl/ vi gackern

cactus /'kæktəs/ n (pl -ti /-taɪ/ or -tuses) Kaktus m

caddie /'kædɪ/ n Caddie m

caddy /'kædɪ/ n **[tea-]** ~ Teedose f

cadet /kə'det/ n Kadett m

cadge /kædʒ/ vt/i (fam) schnorren

Caesarean /sɪ'zeərɪən/ a & n **~ [section]** Kaiserschnitt m

café /'kæfeɪ/ n Café nt

cafeteria /kæfə'tɪərɪə/ n Selbstbe-dienungsrestaurant nt

caffeine /'kæfi:n/ n Koffein nt

cage /keɪdʒ/ n Käfig m

cagey /'keɪdʒɪ/ a (fam) **be** ~ mit der Sprache nicht herauswollen

cajole /kə'dʒəʊl/ vt gut zureden (+ dat)

cake /keɪk/ n Kuchen m; (of soap) Stück nt. ~**d** a verkrustet (**with** mit)

calamity /kə'læmətɪ/ n Katastrophe f

calcium /'kælsɪəm/ n Kalzium nt

calculat|e /'kælkjʊleɪt/ vt be-rechnen; (estimate) kalkulieren. ~**ing** a (fig) berechnend. ~**ion** /-'leɪʃn/ n Rechnung f, Kalkulation f. ~**or** n Rechner m

calendar /'kælɪndə(r)/ n Kalender m

calf[1] /kɑ:f/ n (pl **calves**) Kalb nt

calf[2] n (pl **calves**) (Anat) Wade f

calibre /'kælɪbə(r)/ n Kaliber nt

calico /'kælɪkəʊ/ n Kattun m

call /kɔ:l/ n Ruf m; (Teleph) Anruf m; (visit) Besuch m; **be on** ~ ⟨doctor:⟩ Be-reitschaftsdienst haben ● vt rufen; (Te-leph) anrufen; (wake) wecken; ausrufen ⟨strike⟩; (name) nennen; **be** ~**ed** heißen ● vi rufen; ~ **[in** or **round]** vorbei-kommen. ~ **back** vt zurückrufen ● vi noch einmal vorbeikommen. ~ **for** vt rufen nach; (demand) verlangen; (fetch) abholen. ~ **off** vt zurück-rufen ⟨dog⟩; (cancel) absagen. ~ **on** vt bitten (**for** um); (appeal to) appellieren an (+ acc); (visit) besuchen. ~ **out** vt rufen; aufrufen ⟨names⟩ ● vi rufen. ~ **up** vt (Mil) einberufen; (Teleph) anrufen

call: ~**-box** n Telefonzelle f. ~**er** n Besucher m; (Teleph) Anrufer m. ~**ing** n Berufung f

callous /'kæləs/ a gefühllos

'call-up n (Mil) Einberufung f

calm /kɑ:m/ a (**-er, -est**), **-ly** adv ruhig ● n Ruhe f ● vt ~ **[down]** beruhigen ● vi ~ **down** sich beruhigen. ~**ness** n Ruhe f; (of sea) Stille f

calorie /'kælərɪ/ n Kalorie f

calves /kɑ:vz/ npl see **calf**[1] & [2]

camber /'kæmbə(r)/ n Wölbung f

came /keɪm/ see **come**

camel /'kæml/ n Kamel nt

camera /'kæmərə/ n Kamera f. ~**-man** n Kameramann m

camouflage /'kæməflɑ:ʒ/ n Tar-nung f ● vt tarnen

camp /kæmp/ n Lager nt ● vi campen; (Mil) kampieren

campaign /kæm'peɪn/ n Feldzug m; (Comm, Pol) Kampagne f ● vi kämpfen; (Pol) im Wahlkampf ar-beiten

camp: ~**-bed** n Feldbett nt. ~**er** n Camper m; (Auto) Wohnmobil nt. ~**ing** n Camping nt. ~**site** n Cam-pingplatz m

campus /'kæmpəs/ n (pl **-puses**) (Univ) Campus m

can[1] /kæn/ n (for petrol) Kanister m; (tin) Dose f, Büchse f; **a** ~ **of beer** eine Dose Bier ● vt in Dosen od Büchsen konservieren

can[2] /kæn, unbetont kən/ v aux (pres **can**; pt **could**) können; **I cannot/can't go** ich kann nicht gehen; **he could not go** er konnte nicht gehen; **if I could go** wenn ich gehen könnte

Canad|a /'kænədə/ n Kanada nt. ~**ian** /kə'neɪdɪən/ a kanadisch ● n Kanadier(in) m(f)

canal /kə'næl/ n Kanal m

Canaries /kə'neərɪz/ npl Kanarische Inseln pl

canary /kə'neərɪ/ n Kanarienvogel m

cancel /'kænsl/ vt/i (pt/pp **cancelled**) absagen; entwerten ⟨stamp⟩; (annul) rückgängig machen; (Comm) stor-nieren; abbestellen ⟨newspaper⟩; **be** ~**led** ausfallen. ~**lation** /-ə'leɪʃn/ n Absage f

cancer /'kænsə(r)/ n, & (Astr) **C**~ Krebs m. ~**ous** /-rəs/ a krebsig

candelabra /kændə'lɑ:brə/ n Arm-leuchter m

candid /'kændɪd/ a, **-ly** adv offen

candidate /'kændɪdət/ n Kan-didat(in) m(f)

candied /'kændɪd/ a kandiert

candle /'kændl/ n Kerze f. ~**stick** n Kerzenständer m, Leuchter m

candour /'kændə(r)/ n Offenheit f

candy /'kændɪ/ n (Amer) Süßig-keiten pl; **[piece of]** ~ Bonbon m. ~**floss** /-flɒs/ n Zuckerwatte f

cane /keɪn/ n Rohr nt; (stick) Stock m ● vt mit dem Stock züchtigen

canine /'keɪnaɪn/ a Hunde-. ~ **tooth** n Eckzahn m

canister /'kænɪstə(r)/ n Blechdose f

cannabis /'kænəbɪs/ n Haschisch nt

canned /kænd/ a Dosen-, Büchsen-; ~ **music** (fam) Musik f aus der Kon-serve

cannibal /'kænɪbl/ *n* Kannibale *m*. ∼**ism** *n* Kannibalismus *m*

cannon /'kænən/ *n inv* Kanone *f*. ∼**-ball** *n* Kanonenkugel *f*

cannot /'kænɒt/ *see* **can**²

canny /'kænɪ/ *a* schlau

canoe /kə'nu:/ *n* Paddelboot *nt*; (*Sport*) Kanu *nt* ● *vi* paddeln; (*Sport*) Kanu fahren

canon /'kænən/ *n* Kanon *m*; (*person*) Kanonikus *m*. ∼**ize** /-aɪz/ *vt* kanonisieren

'**can-opener** *n* Dosenöffner *m*, Büchsenöffner *m*

canopy /'kænəpɪ/ *n* Baldachin *m*

cant /kænt/ *n* Heuchelei *f*

can't /kɑ:nt/ = **cannot**. *See* **can**²

cantankerous /kæn'tæŋkərəs/ *a* zänkisch

canteen /kæn'ti:n/ *n* Kantine *f*; ∼ **of cutlery** Besteckkasten *m*

canter /'kæntə(r)/ *n* Kanter *m* ● *vi* kantern

canvas /'kænvəs/ *n* Segeltuch *nt*; (*Art*) Leinwand *f*; (*painting*) Gemälde *nt*

canvass /'kænvəs/ *vi* um Stimmen werben

canyon /'kænjən/ *n* Cañon *m*

cap /kæp/ *n* Kappe *f*, Mütze *f*; (*nurse's*) Haube *f*; (*top, lid*) Verschluß *m* ● *vt* (*pt/pp* **capped**) (*fig*) übertreffen

capability /keɪpə'bɪlətɪ/ *n* Fähigkeit *f*

capable /'keɪpəbl/ *a*, **-bly** *adv* fähig; **be** ∼ **of doing sth** fähig sein, etw zu tun

capacity /kə'pæsətɪ/ *n* Fassungsvermögen *nt*; (*ability*) Fähigkeit *f*; **in my** ∼ **as** in meiner Eigenschaft als

cape¹ /keɪp/ *n* (*cloak*) Cape *nt*

cape² *n* (*Geog*) Kap *nt*

caper¹ /'keɪpə(r)/ *vi* herumspringen

caper² *n* (*Culin*) Kaper *f*

capital /'kæpɪtl/ *a* (*letter*) groß ● *n* (*town*) Hauptstadt *f*; (*money*) Kapital *nt*; (*letter*) Großbuchstabe *m*

capital|ism /'kæpɪtəlɪzm/ *n* Kapitalismus *m*. ∼**ist** /-ɪst/ *a* kapitalistisch ● *n* Kapitalist *m*. ∼**ize** /-aɪz/ *vi* ∼**ize on** (*fig*) Kapital schlagen aus. ∼ '**letter** *n* Großbuchstabe *m*. ∼ '**punishment** *n* Todesstrafe *f*

capitulat|e /kə'pɪtjʊleɪt/ *vi* kapitulieren. ∼**ion** /-'leɪʃn/ *n* Kapitulation *f*

capricious /kə'prɪʃəs/ *a* launisch

Capricorn /'kæprɪkɔ:n/ *n* (*Astr*) Steinbock *m*

capsize /kæp'saɪz/ *vi* kentern ● *vt* zum Kentern bringen

capsule /'kæpsjʊl/ *n* Kapsel *f*

captain /'kæptɪn/ *n* Kapitän *m*; (*Mil*) Hauptmann *m* ● *vt* anführen (*team*)

caption /'kæpʃn/ *n* Überschrift *f*; (*of illustration*) Bildtext *m*

captivate /'kæptɪveɪt/ *vt* bezaubern

captiv|e /'kæptɪv/ *a* **hold/take** ∼**e** gefangenhalten/-nehmen ● *n* Gefangene(r) *m/f*. ∼**ity** /-'tɪvətɪ/ *n* Gefangenschaft *f*

capture /'kæptʃə(r)/ *n* Gefangennahme *f* ● *vt* gefangennehmen; [ein]fangen (*animal*); (*Mil*) einnehmen (*town*)

car /kɑ:(r)/ *n* Auto *nt*, Wagen *m*; **by** ∼ mit dem Auto *od* Wagen

carafe /kə'ræf/ *n* Karaffe *f*

caramel /'kærəmel/ *n* Karamel *m*

carat /'kærət/ *n* Karat *nt*

caravan /'kærəvæn/ *n* Wohnwagen *m*; (*procession*) Karawane *f*

carbohydrate /kɑ:bə'haɪdreɪt/ *n* Kohlenhydrat *nt*

carbon /'kɑ:bən/ *n* Kohlenstoff *m*; (*paper*) Kohlepapier *nt*; (*copy*) Durchschlag *m*

carbon: ∼ **copy** *n* Durchschlag *m*. ∼ **di'oxide** *n* Kohlendioxyd *nt*; (*in drink*) Kohlensäure *f*. ∼ **paper** *n* Kohlepapier *nt*

carburettor /kɑ:bjʊ'retə(r)/ *n* Vergaser *m*

carcass /'kɑ:kəs/ *n* Kadaver *m*

card /kɑ:d/ *n* Karte *f*

'**cardboard** *n* Pappe *f*, Karton *m*. ∼ '**box** *n* Pappschachtel *f*; (*large*) [Papp]karton *m*

'**card-game** *n* Kartenspiel *nt*

cardiac /'kɑ:dɪæk/ *a* Herz-

cardigan /'kɑ:dɪgən/ *n* Strickjacke *f*

cardinal /'kɑ:dɪnl/ *a* Kardinal-; ∼ **number** Kardinalzahl *f* ● *n* (*Relig*) Kardinal *m*

card 'index *n* Kartei *f*

care /keə(r)/ *n* Sorgfalt *f*; (*caution*) Vorsicht *f*; (*protection*) Obhut *f*; (*looking after*) Pflege *f*; (*worry*) Sorge *f*; ∼ **of** (*on letter abbr* **c/o**) bei; **take** ∼ vorsichtig sein; **take into** ∼ in Pflege nehmen; **take** ∼ **of** sich kümmern um ● *vi* ∼ **about** sich kümmern um; ∼ **for** (*like*) mögen; (*look after*) betreuen; **I don't** ∼ das ist mir gleich

career /kəˈrɪə(r)/ n Laufbahn f; (*profession*) Beruf m ● vi rasen

care: ~**free** a sorglos. ~**ful** a, **-ly** adv sorgfältig; (*cautious*) vorsichtig. ~**less** a, **-ly** adv nachlässig. ~**lessness** n Nachlässigkeit f

caress /kəˈres/ n Liebkosung f ● vt liebkosen

'**caretaker** n Hausmeister m

'**car ferry** n Autofähre f

cargo /ˈkɑːgəʊ/ n (pl **-es**) Ladung f

Caribbean /kærɪˈbiːən/ n **the** ~ die Karibik

caricature /ˈkærɪkətjʊə(r)/ n Karikatur f ● vt karikieren

caring /ˈkeərɪŋ/ a (*parent*) liebevoll; (*profession, attitude*) sozial

carnage /ˈkɑːnɪdʒ/ n Gemetzel nt

carnal /ˈkɑːnl/ a fleischlich

carnation /kɑːˈneɪʃn/ n Nelke f

carnival /ˈkɑːnɪvl/ n Karneval m

carnivorous /kɑːˈnɪvərəs/ a fleischfressend

carol /ˈkærl/ n **[Christmas]** ~ Weihnachtslied nt

carp[1] /kɑːp/ n inv Karpfen m

carp[2] vi nörgeln; ~ **at** herumnörgeln an (+ dat)

'**car park** n Parkplatz m; (*multistorey*) Parkhaus nt; (*underground*) Tiefgarage f

carpent|er /ˈkɑːpɪntə(r)/ n Zimmermann m; (*joiner*) Tischler m. ~**ry** n Tischlerei f

carpet /ˈkɑːpɪt/ n Teppich m ● vt mit Teppich auslegen

carriage /ˈkærɪdʒ/ n Kutsche f; (*Rail*) Wagen m; (*of goods*) Beförderung f; (*cost*) Frachtkosten pl; (*bearing*) Haltung f. ~**way** n Fahrbahn f

carrier /ˈkærɪə(r)/ n Träger(in) m(f); (*Comm*) Spediteur m; ~**[-bag]** Tragetasche f

carrot /ˈkærət/ n Möhre f, Karotte f

carry /ˈkærɪ/ vt/i (pt/pp **-ied**) tragen; **be carried away** (*fam*) hingerissen sein. ~ **off** vt wegtragen; gewinnen (*prize*). ~ **on** vi weitermachen; ~ **on at** (*fam*) herumnörgeln an (+ dat); ~ **on with** (*fam*) eine Affäre haben mit ● vt führen; (*continue*) fortführen. ~ **out** vt hinaus-/heraustragen; (*perform*) ausführen

'**carry-cot** n Babytragetasche f

cart /kɑːt/ n Karren m; **put the** ~ **before the horse** das Pferd beim

Schwanz aufzäumen ● vt karren; (*fam: carry*) schleppen

cartilage /ˈkɑːtɪlɪdʒ/ n (*Anat*) Knorpel m

carton /ˈkɑːtn/ n [Papp]karton m; (*for drink*) Tüte f; (*of cream, yoghurt*) Becher m

cartoon /kɑːˈtuːn/ n Karikatur f; (*joke*) Witzzeichnung f; (*strip*) Comic Strips pl; (*film*) Zeichentrickfilm m; (*Art*) Karton m. ~**ist** n Karikaturist m

cartridge /ˈkɑːtrɪdʒ/ n Patrone f; (*for film, typewriter ribbon*) Kassette f; (*of record player*) Tonabnehmer m

carve /kɑːv/ vt schnitzen; (*in stone*) hauen; (*Culin*) aufschneiden

carving /ˈkɑːvɪŋ/ n Schnitzerei f. ~**-knife** n Tranchiermesser nt

'**car wash** n Autowäsche f; (*place*) Autowaschanlage f

case[1] /keɪs/ n Fall m; **in any** ~ auf jeden Fall; **just in** ~ für alle Fälle; **in** ~ **he comes** falls er kommt

case[2] n Kasten m; (*crate*) Kiste f; (*for spectacles*) Etui nt; (*suitcase*) Koffer m; (*for display*) Vitrine f

cash /kæʃ/ n Bargeld nt; **pay [in]** ~ [in] bar bezahlen; ~ **on delivery** per Nachnahme ● vt einlösen (*cheque*). ~ **desk** n Kasse f

cashier /kæˈʃɪə(r)/ n Kassierer(in) m(f)

'**cash register** n Registrierkasse f

casino /kəˈsiːnəʊ/ n Kasino nt

cask /kɑːsk/ n Faß nt

casket /ˈkɑːskɪt/ n Kasten m; (*Amer: coffin*) Sarg m

casserole /ˈkæsərəʊl/ n Schmortopf m; (*stew*) Eintopf m

cassette /kəˈset/ n Kassette f. ~ **recorder** n Kassettenrecorder m

cast /kɑːst/ n (*throw*) Wurf m; (*mould*) Form f; (*model*) Abguß m; (*Theat*) Besetzung f; **[plaster]** ~ (*Med*) Gipsverband m ● vt (pt/pp **cast**) (*throw*) werfen; (*shed*) abwerfen; abgeben (*vote*); gießen (*metal*); (*Theat*) besetzen (*role*); ~ **a glance at** einen Blick werfen auf (+ acc). ~ **off** vi (*Naut*) ablegen ● vt (*Knitting*) abketten. ~ **on** vt (*Knitting*) anschlagen

castanets /kæstəˈnets/ npl Kastagnetten pl

castaway /ˈkɑːstəweɪ/ n Schiffbrüchige(r) m/f

caste /kɑːst/ n Kaste f

cast 'iron n Gußeisen nt
cast-'iron a gußeisern
castle /'kɑːsl/ n Schloß nt; (fortified) Burg f; (Chess) Turm m
'cast-offs npl abgelegte Kleidung f
castor /'kɑːstə(r)/ n (wheel) [Lauf]rolle f
'castor sugar n Streuzucker m
castrat|e /kæ'streɪt/ vt kastrieren. **~ion** /-eɪʃn/ n Kastration f
casual /'kæzʊəl/ a, **-ly** adv (chance) zufällig; (offhand) lässig; (informal) zwanglos; (not permanent) Gelegenheits-; **~ wear** Freizeitbekleidung f
casualty /'kæzʊəltɪ/ n [Todes]opfer nt; (injured person) Verletzte(r) m/f; **~ [department]** Unfallstation f
cat /kæt/ n Katze f
catalogue /'kætəlɒg/ n Katalog m • vt katalogisieren
catalyst /'kætəlɪst/ n (Chem & fig) Katalysator m
catalytic /kætə'lɪtɪk/ a **~ converter** (Auto) Katalysator m
catapult /'kætəpʌlt/ n Katapult nt • vt katapultieren
cataract /'kætərækt/ n (Med) grauer Star m
catarrh /kə'tɑː(r)/ n Katarrh m
catastroph|e /kə'tæstrəfɪ/ n Katastrophe f. **~ic** /kætə'strɒfɪk/ a katastrophal
catch /kætʃ/ n (of fish) Fang m; (fastener) Verschluß m; (on door) Klinke f; (fam: snag) Haken m (fam) • v (pt/pp caught) • vt fangen; (be in time for) erreichen; (travel by) fahren mit; bekommen (illness); **~ a cold** sich erkälten; **~ sight of** erblicken; **~ s.o. stealing** jdn beim Stehlen erwischen; **~ one's finger in the door** sich (dat) den Finger in der Tür [ein]klemmen • vi (burn) anbrennen; (get stuck) klemmen. **~ on** vi (fam) (understand) kapieren; (become popular) sich durchsetzen. **~ up** vt einholen • vi aufholen; **~ up with** einholen (s.o.); nachholen (work)
catching /'kætʃɪŋ/ a ansteckend
catch: ~-phrase n, **~word** n Schlagwort m
catchy /'kætʃɪ/ a (-ier, -iest) einprägsam
catechism /'kætɪkɪzm/ n Katechismus m
categor|ical /kætɪ'gɒrɪkl/ a, **-ly** adv kategorisch. **~y** /'kætɪgərɪ/ n Kategorie f

cater /'keɪtə(r)/ vi **~ for** beköstigen; (firm:) das Essen liefern für (party); (fig) eingestellt sein auf (+ acc). **~ing** n (trade) Gaststättengewerbe nt
caterpillar /'kætəpɪlə(r)/ n Raupe f
cathedral /kə'θiːdrl/ n Dom m, Kathedrale f
Catholic /'kæθəlɪk/ a katholisch • n Katholik(in) m(f). **C~ism** /kə-'θɒlɪsɪzm/ n Katholizismus m
catkin /'kætkɪn/ n (Bot) Kätzchen nt
cattle /'kætl/ npl Vieh nt
catty /'kætɪ/ a (-ier, -iest) boshaft
caught /kɔːt/ see **catch**
cauldron /'kɔːldrən/ n [großer] Kessel m
cauliflower /'kɒlɪ-/ n Blumenkohl m
cause /kɔːz/ n Ursache f; (reason) Grund m; **good ~** gute Sache f • vt verursachen; **~ s.o. to do sth** jdn veranlassen, etw zu tun
'causeway n [Insel]damm m
caustic /'kɔːstɪk/ a ätzend; (fig) beißend
cauterize /'kɔːtəraɪz/ vt kauterisieren
caution /'kɔːʃn/ n Vorsicht f; (warning) Verwarnung f • vt (Jur) verwarnen
cautious /'kɔːʃəs/ a, **-ly** adv vorsichtig
cavalry /'kævəlrɪ/ n Kavallerie f
cave /keɪv/ n Höhle f • vi **~ in** einstürzen
cavern /'kævən/ n Höhle f
caviare /'kævɪɑː(r)/ n Kaviar m
caving /'keɪvɪŋ/ n Höhlenforschung f
cavity /'kævətɪ/ n Hohlraum m; (in tooth) Loch nt
cavort /kə'vɔːt/ vi tollen
cease /siːs/ n **without ~** unaufhörlich • vt/i aufhören. **~-fire** n Waffenruhe f. **~less** a, **-ly** adv unaufhörlich
cedar /'siːdə(r)/ n Zeder f
cede /siːd/ vt abtreten (**to** an + acc)
ceiling /'siːlɪŋ/ n [Zimmer]decke f; (fig) oberste Grenze f
celebrat|e /'selɪbreɪt/ vt/i feiern. **~ed** a berühmt (**for** wegen). **~ion** /-'breɪʃn/ n Feier f
celebrity /sɪ'lebrətɪ/ n Berühmtheit f
celery /'selərɪ/ n [Stangen]sellerie m & f
celiba|cy /'selɪbəsɪ/ n Zölibat nt. **~te** a **be ~te** im Zölibat leben
cell /sel/ n Zelle f

cellar /'selə(r)/ n Keller m
cellist /'tʃelɪst/ n Cellist(in) m(f)
cello /'tʃeləu/ n Cello nt
Celsius /'selsɪəs/ a Celsius
Celt /kelt/ n Kelte m/Keltin f. ~**ic** a keltisch
cement /sɪ'ment/ n Zement m; (adhesive) Kitt m ● vt zementieren; (stick) kitten
cemetery /'semətrɪ/ n Friedhof m
censor /'sensə(r)/ n Zensor m ● vt zensieren. ~**ship** n Zensur f
censure /'senʃə(r)/ n Tadel m ● vt tadeln
census /'sensəs/ n Volkszählung f
cent /sent/ n (coin) Cent m
centenary /sen'tiːnərɪ/ n, (Amer) **centennial** /sen'tenɪəl/ n Hundertjahrfeier f
center /'sentə(r)/ n (Amer) = **centre**
centi|grade /'sentɪ-/ a Celsius-; **5°** ~ 5° Celsius. ~**metre** m Zentimeter m & nt. ~**pede** /-piːd/ n Tausendfüßler m
central /'sentrl/ a, **-ly** adv zentral. ~ '**heating** n Zentralheizung f. ~**ize** vt zentralisieren. ~ **reser'vation** n (Auto) Mittelstreifen m
centre /'sentə(r)/ n Zentrum nt; (middle) Mitte f ● v (pt/pp **centred**) ● vt zentrieren; ~ **on** (fig) sich drehen um. ~-'**forward** n Mittelstürmer m
centrifugal /sentrɪ'fjuːgl/ a ~ **force** Fliehkraft f
century /'sentʃərɪ/ n Jahrhundert nt
ceramic /sɪ'ræmɪk/ a Keramik-. ~**s** n Keramik f
cereal /'sɪərɪəl/ n Getreide nt; (breakfast food) Frühstücksflocken pl
cerebral /'serɪbrl/ a Gehirn-
ceremon|ial /serɪ'məunɪəl/ a, **-ly** adv zeremoniell, feierlich ● n Zeremoniell nt. ~**ious** /-ɪəs/ a, **-ly** adv formell
ceremony /'serɪmənɪ/ n Zeremonie f, Feier f; **without** ~ ohne weitere Umstände
certain /'sɜːtn/ a sicher; (not named) gewiß; **for** ~ mit Bestimmtheit; **make** ~ (check) sich vergewissern (**that** daß); (ensure) dafür sorgen (**that** daß); **he is** ~ **to win** er wird ganz bestimmt siegen. ~**ly** adv bestimmt, sicher; ~**ly not!** auf keinen Fall! ~**ty** n Sicherheit f, Gewißheit f; **it's a** ~**ty** es ist sicher
certificate /sə'tɪfɪkət/ n Bescheinigung f; (Jur) Urkunde f; (Sch) Zeugnis nt

certify /'sɜːtɪfaɪ/ vt (pt/pp **-ied**) bescheinigen; (declare insane) für geisteskrank erklären
cessation /se'seɪʃn/ n Ende nt
cesspool /'ses-/ n Senkgrube f
cf abbr (compare) vgl
chafe /tʃeɪf/ vt wund reiben
chaff /tʃɑːf/ n Spreu f
chaffinch /'tʃæfɪntʃ/ n Buchfink m
chain /tʃeɪn/ n Kette f ● vt ketten (**to** an + acc). ~ **up** vt anketten
chain: ~ **re'action** n Kettenreaktion f. ~-**smoker** n Kettenraucher m. ~ **store** n Kettenladen m
chair /tʃeə(r)/ n Stuhl m; (Univ) Lehrstuhl m ● vt den Vorsitz führen bei. ~-**lift** n Sessellift m. ~**man** n Vorsitzende(r) m/f
chalet /'ʃæleɪ/ n Chalet nt
chalice /'tʃælɪs/ n (Relig) Kelch m
chalk /tʃɔːk/ n Kreide f. ~**y** a kreidig
challeng|e /'tʃælɪndʒ/ n Herausforderung f; (Mil) Anruf m ● vt herausfordern; (Mil) anrufen; (fig) anfechten (statement). ~**er** n Herausforderer m. ~**ing** a herausfordernd; (demanding) anspruchsvoll
chamber /'tʃeɪmbə(r)/ n Kammer f; ~**s** pl (Jur) [Anwalts]büro nt; **C**~ **of Commerce** Handelskammer f
chamber: ~**maid** n Zimmermädchen nt. ~ **music** n Kammermusik f. ~-**pot** n Nachttopf m
chamois[1] /'ʃæmwɑː/ n inv (animal) Gemse f
chamois[2] /'ʃæmɪ/-' n ~[-**leather**] Ledertuch nt
champagne /ʃæm'peɪn/ n Champagner m
champion /'tʃæmpɪən/ n (Sport) Meister(in) m(f); (of cause) Verfechter m ● vt sich einsetzen für. ~**ship** n (Sport) Meisterschaft f
chance /tʃɑːns/ n Zufall m; (prospect) Chancen pl; (likelihood) Aussicht f; (opportunity) Gelegenheit f; **by** ~ zufällig; **take a** ~ ein Risiko eingehen; **give s.o. a** ~ jdm eine Chance geben ● attrib zufällig ● vt ~ **it** es riskieren
chancellor /'tʃɑːnsələ(r)/ n Kanzler m; (Univ) Rektor m; **C**~ **of the Exchequer** Schatzkanzler m
chancy /'tʃɑːnsɪ/ a riskant
chandelier /ʃændə'lɪə(r)/ n Kronleuchter m
change /tʃeɪndʒ/ n Veränderung f; (alteration) Änderung f; (money)

Wechselgeld nt; **for a** ~ zur Abwechslung • vt wechseln; (alter) ändern; (exchange) umtauschen (**for** gegen); (transform) verwandeln; trocken legen ⟨baby⟩; ~ **one's clothes** sich umziehen; ~ **trains** umsteigen • vi sich verändern; (~ clothes) sich umziehen; (~ trains) umsteigen; **all** ~! alles aussteigen!

changeable /'tʃeɪndʒəbl/ a wechselhaft

'**changing-room** n Umkleideraum m

channel /'tʃænl/ n Rinne f; (Radio, TV) Kanal m; (fig) Weg m; **the [English] C**~ der Ärmelkanal; **the C**~ **Islands** die Kanalinseln • vt (pt/pp **channelled**) leiten; (fig) lenken

chant /tʃɑːnt/ n liturgischer Gesang m • vt singen; ⟨demonstrators:⟩ skandieren

chao|s /'keɪɒs/ n Chaos nt. ~**tic** /-'ɒtɪk/ a chaotisch

chap /tʃæp/ n (fam) Kerl m

chapel /'tʃæpl/ n Kapelle f

chaperon /'ʃæpərəʊn/ n Anstandsdame f • vt begleiten

chaplain /'tʃæplɪn/ n Geistliche(r) m

chapped /tʃæpt/ a ⟨skin⟩ aufgesprungen

chapter /'tʃæptə(r)/ n Kapitel nt

char¹ /tʃɑː(r)/ n (fam) Putzfrau f

char² vt (pt/pp **charred**) (burn) verkohlen

character /'kærɪktə(r)/ n Charakter m; (in novel, play) Gestalt f; (Typ) Schriftzeichen nt; **out of** ~ uncharakteristisch; **quite a** ~ (fam) ein Original

characteristic /kærɪktə'rɪstɪk/ a, -**ally** adv charakteristisch (**of** für) • n Merkmal nt

characterize /'kærɪktəraɪz/ vt charakterisieren

charade /ʃə'rɑːd/ n Scharade f

charcoal /'tʃɑː-/ n Holzkohle f

charge /tʃɑːdʒ/ n (price) Gebühr f; (Electr) Ladung f; (attack) Angriff m; (Jur) Anklage f; **free of** ~ kostenlos; **be in** ~ verantwortlich sein (**of** für); **take** ~ die Aufsicht übernehmen (**of** über + acc) • vt berechnen ⟨fee⟩; (Electr) laden; (attack) angreifen; (Jur) anklagen (**with** gen); ~ **s.o. for sth** jdm etw berechnen • vi (attack) angreifen

chariot /'tʃærɪət/ n Wagen m

charisma /kə'rɪzmə/ n Charisma nt. ~**tic** /kæriz'mætɪk/ a charismatisch

charitable /'tʃærɪtəbl/ a wohltätig; (kind) wohlwollend

charity /'tʃærətɪ/ n Nächstenliebe f; (organization) wohltätige Einrichtung f; **for** ~ für Wohltätigkeitszwecke; **live on** ~ von Almosen leben

charlatan /'ʃɑːlətən/ n Scharlatan m

charm /tʃɑːm/ n Reiz m; (of person) Charme f; (object) Amulett nt • vt bezaubern. ~**ing** a, -**ly** adv reizend; ⟨person, smile⟩ charmant

chart /tʃɑːt/ n Karte f; (table) Tabelle f

charter /'tʃɑːtə(r)/ n ~ **[flight]** Charterflug m • vt chartern; ~**ed accountant** Wirtschaftsprüfer(in) m(f)

charwoman /'tʃɑː-/ n Putzfrau f

chase /tʃeɪs/ n Verfolgungsjagd f • vt jagen, verfolgen. ~ **away** or **off** vt wegjagen

chasm /'kæzm/ n Kluft f

chassis /'ʃæsɪ/ n (pl **chassis** /-sɪz/) Chassis nt

chaste /tʃeɪst/ a keusch

chastise /tʃæ'staɪz/ vt züchtigen

chastity /'tʃæstətɪ/ n Keuschheit f

chat /tʃæt/ n Plauderei f; **have a** ~ **with** plaudern mit • vi (pt/pp **chatted**) plaudern. ~ **show** n Talk-Show f

chatter /'tʃætə(r)/ n Geschwätz nt • vi schwatzen; ⟨child:⟩ plappern; ⟨teeth:⟩ klappern. ~**box** n (fam) Plappermaul nt

chatty /'tʃætɪ/ a (-**ier**, -**iest**) geschwätzig

chauffeur /'ʃəʊfə(r)/ n Chauffeur m

chauvin|ism /'ʃəʊvɪnɪzm/ n Chauvinismus m. ~**ist** n Chauvinist m; **male** ~**ist** (fam) Chauvi m

cheap /tʃiːp/ a & adv (-**er**, -**est**), -**ly** adv billig. ~**en** vt entwürdigen; ~**en oneself** sich erniedrigen

cheat /tʃiːt/ n Betrüger(in) m(f); (at games) Mogler m • vt betrügen • vi (at games) mogeln (fam)

check¹ /tʃek/ a (squared) kariert • n Karo nt

check² n Überprüfung f; (inspection) Kontrolle f; (Chess) Schach nt; (Amer: bill) Rechnung f; (Amer: cheque) Scheck m; (Amer: tick) Haken m; **keep a** ~ **on** kontrollieren • vt [über]prüfen; (inspect) kontrollieren; (restrain) hemmen; (stop) aufhalten • vi [go and] nachsehen. ~ **in** vi sich anmelden; (Aviat) einchecken • vt abfertigen; einchecken. ~ **out** vi sich abmelden.

~ **up** vi prüfen, kontrollieren; ~ **up on** überprüfen

check|ed /tʃekt/ a kariert. ~**ers** n (Amer) Damespiel nt

check: ~**mate** int schachmatt! ~**-out** n Kasse f. ~**room** n (Amer) Garderobe f. ~**-up** n (Med) [Kontroll]untersuchung f

cheek /tʃiːk/ n Backe f; (impudence) Frechheit f. ~**y** a, **-ily** adv frech

cheep /tʃiːp/ vi piepen

cheer /tʃɪə(r)/ n Beifallsruf m; **three** ~**s** ein dreifaches Hoch (**for** auf + acc); ~**s!** prost! (goodbye) tschüs! ● vt zujubeln (+ dat) ● vi jubeln. ~ **up** vt aufmuntern; aufheitern ● vi munterer werden. ~**ful** a, **-ly** adv fröhlich. ~**fulness** n Fröhlichkeit f

cheerio /tʃɪərɪ'əʊ/ int (fam) tschüs!

'**cheerless** a trostlos

cheese /tʃiːz/ n Käse m. ~**cake** n Käsekuchen m

cheetah /'tʃiːtə/ n Gepard m

chef /ʃef/ n Koch m

chemical /'kemɪkl/ a, **-ly** adv chemisch ● n Chemikalie f

chemist /'kemɪst/ n (pharmacist) Apotheker(in) m(f); (scientist) Chemiker(in) m(f); ~'**s [shop]** Drogerie f; (dispensing) Apotheke f. ~**ry** n Chemie f

cheque /tʃek/ n Scheck m. ~**-book** n Scheckbuch nt. ~ **card** n Scheckkarte f

cherish /'tʃerɪʃ/ vt lieben; (fig) hegen

cherry /'tʃerɪ/ n Kirsche f ● attrib Kirsch-

cherub /'tʃerəb/ n Engelchen nt

chess /tʃes/ n Schach nt

chess: ~**board** n Schachbrett nt. ~**-man** n Schachfigur f

chest /tʃest/ n Brust f; (box) Truhe f

chestnut /'tʃesnʌt/ n Eßkastanie f, Marone f; (horse-) [Roß]kastanie f

chest of 'drawers n Kommode f

chew /tʃuː/ vt kauen. ~**ing-gum** n Kaugummi m

chic /ʃiːk/ a schick

chick /tʃɪk/ n Küken nt

chicken /'tʃɪkɪn/ n Huhn nt ● attrib Hühner- ● a (fam) feige ● vi ~ **out** (fam) kneifen. ~**pox** n Windpocken pl

chicory /'tʃɪkərɪ/ n Chicorée f; (in coffee) Zichorie f

chief /tʃiːf/ a Haupt- ● n Chef m; (of tribe) Häuptling m. ~**ly** adv hauptsächlich

chilblain /'tʃɪlbleɪn/ n Frostbeule f

child /tʃaɪld/ n (pl ~**ren**) Kind nt

child: ~**birth** n Geburt f. ~**hood** n Kindheit f. ~**ish** a kindisch. ~**less** a kinderlos. ~**like** a kindlich. ~**-minder** n Tagesmutter f

children /'tʃɪldrən/ npl see **child**

Chile /'tʃɪlɪ/ n Chile nt

chill /tʃɪl/ n Kälte f; (illness) Erkältung f ● vt kühlen

chilli /'tʃɪlɪ/ n (pl -es) Chili m

chilly /'tʃɪlɪ/ a kühl; **I felt** ~ mich fröstelte [es]

chime /tʃaɪm/ vi läuten; (clock:) schlagen

chimney /'tʃɪmnɪ/ n Schornstein m. ~**-pot** n Schornsteinaufsatz m. ~**-sweep** n Schornsteinfeger m

chimpanzee /tʃɪmpæn'ziː/ n Schimpanse m

chin /tʃɪn/ n Kinn nt

china /'tʃaɪnə/ n Porzellan nt

Chin|a n China nt. ~**ese** /-'niːz/ a chinesisch ● n (Lang) Chinesisch nt; **the** ~**ese** pl die Chinesen. ~**ese 'lantern** n Lampion m

chink[1] /tʃɪŋk/ n (slit) Ritze f

chink[2] n Geklirr nt ● vi klirren; (coins:) klimpern

chip /tʃɪp/ n (fragment) Span m; (in china, paintwork) angeschlagene Stelle f; (Computing, Gambling) Chip m; ~**s** pl (Culin) Pommes frites pl; (Amer: crisps) Chips pl ● vt (pt/pp **chipped**) (damage) anschlagen. ~**ped** a angeschlagen

chiropod|ist /kɪ'rɒpədɪst/ n Fußpfleger(in) m(f). ~**y** n Fußpflege f

chirp /tʃɜːp/ vi zwitschern; (cricket:) zirpen. ~**y** a (fam) munter

chisel /'tʃɪzl/ n Meißel m ● vt/i (pt/pp **chiselled**) meißeln

chit /tʃɪt/ n Zettel m

chival|rous /'ʃɪvlrəs/ a, **-ly** adv ritterlich. ~**ry** n Ritterlichkeit f

chives /tʃaɪvz/ npl Schnittlauch m

chlorine /'klɔːriːn/ n Chlor nt

chloroform /'klɒrəfɔːm/ n Chloroform nt

chocolate /'tʃɒkələt/ n Schokolade f; (sweet) Praline f

choice /tʃɔɪs/ n Wahl f; (variety) Auswahl f ● a auserlesen

choir /'kwaɪə(r)/ n Chor m. ~**boy** n Chorknabe m

choke /tʃəʊk/ n (Auto) Choke m ● vt würgen; (to death) erwürgen ● vi

sich verschlucken; ~ **on** [fast] ersticken an (+ *dat*)
cholera /'kɒlərə/ n Cholera f
cholesterol /kə'lestərɒl/ n Cholesterin *nt*
choose /tʃu:z/ vt/i (pt **chose**, pp
chosen) wählen; (*select*) sich (*dat*) aussuchen; ~ **to do/go** [freiwillig] tun/
gehen; **as you** ~ wie Sie wollen
choos[e]y /'tʃu:zɪ/ a (*fam*) wählerisch
chop /tʃɒp/ n (*blow*) Hieb m; (*Culin*)
Kotelett *nt* ● vt (pt/pp **chopped**)
hacken. ~ **down** vt abhacken; fällen
⟨*tree*⟩. ~ **off** vt abhacken
chop|per /'tʃɒpə(r)/ n Beil *nt*; (*fam*)
Hubschrauber m. ~**py** a kabbelig
'chopsticks *npl* Eßstäbchen *pl*
choral /'kɔ:rəl/ a Chor-; ~ **society**
Gesangverein m
chord /kɔ:d/ n (*Mus*) Akkord m
chore /tʃɔ:(r)/ n lästige Pflicht f;
[household] ~s Hausarbeit f
choreography /kɒrɪ'ɒgrəfɪ/ n Choreographie f
chortle /'tʃɔ:tl/ vi [vor Lachen]
glucksen
chorus /'kɔ:rəs/ n Chor m; (*of song*)
Refrain m
chose, chosen /tʃəʊz, 'tʃəʊzn/ see
choose
Christ /kraɪst/ n Christus m
christen /'krɪsn/ vt taufen. ~**ing** n
Taufe f
Christian /'krɪstʃən/ a christlich ● n
Christ(in) m(f). ~**ity** /-stɪ'ænətɪ/ n
Christentum *nt*. ~ **name** n Vorname
m
Christmas /'krɪsməs/ n Weihnachten *nt*. ~ **card** n Weihnachts-
karte f. ~ **'Day** n erster Weih-
nachtstag m. ~ **'Eve** n Heilig-
abend m. ~ **tree** n Weihnachtsbaum m
chrome /krəʊm/ n, **chromium**
/'krəʊmɪəm/ n Chrom *nt*
chromosome /'krəʊməsəʊm/ n
Chromosom *nt*
chronic /'krɒnɪk/ a chronisch
chronicle /'krɒnɪkl/ n Chronik f
chronological /krɒnə'lɒdʒɪkl/ a, **-ly**
adv chronologisch
chrysalis /'krɪsəlɪs/ n Puppe f
chrysanthemum /krɪ'sænθəməm/
n Chrysantheme f
chubby /'tʃʌbɪ/ a (**-ier, -iest**) mollig
chuck /tʃʌk/ vt (*fam*) schmeißen. ~
out vt (*fam*) rausschmeißen

chuckle /'tʃʌkl/ vi in sich (*acc*)
hineinlachen
chum /tʃʌm/ n Freund(in) m(f)
chunk /tʃʌŋk/ n Stück *nt*
church /tʃɜ:tʃ/ n Kirche f. ~**yard** n
Friedhof m
churlish /'tʃɜ:lɪʃ/ a unhöflich
churn /tʃɜ:n/ n Butterfaß *nt*; (*for
milk*) Milchkanne f ● vt ~ **out** am
laufenden Band produzieren
chute /ʃu:t/ n Rutsche f; (*for rubbish*) Müllschlucker m
CID *abbr* (**Criminal Investigation Department**) Kripo f
cider /'saɪdə(r)/ n Apfelwein m
cigar /sɪ'gɑ:(r)/ n Zigarre f
cigarette /sɪgə'ret/ n Zigarette f
cine-camera /'sɪnɪ-/ n Filmkamera f
cinema /'sɪnɪmə/ n Kino *nt*
cinnamon /'sɪnəmən/ n Zimt m
cipher /'saɪfə(r)/ n (*code*) Chiffre f;
(*numeral*) Ziffer f; (*fig*) Null f
circle /'sɜ:kl/ n Kreis m; (*Theat*) Rang
m ● vt umkreisen ● vi kreisen
circuit /'sɜ:kɪt/ n Runde f; (*race-
track*) Rennbahn f; (*Electr*) Strom-
kreis m. ~**ous** /sə'kju:ɪtəs/ a ~
route Um- weg m
circular /'sɜ:kjʊlə(r)/ a kreisförmig
● n Rundschreiben *nt*. ~ **'saw** n
Kreissäge f. ~ **'tour** n Rundfahrt f
circulat|e /'sɜ:kjʊleɪt/ vt in Umlauf
setzen ● vi zirkulieren. ~**ion**
/-'leɪʃn/ n Kreislauf m; (*of newspaper*) Auflage f
circumcis|e /'sɜ:kəmsaɪz/ vt be-
schneiden. ~**ion** /-'sɪʒn/ n Be-
schneidung f
circumference /sə'kʌmfərəns/ n
Umfang m
circumspect /'sɜ:kəmspekt/ a, **-ly**
adv umsichtig
circumstance /'sɜ:kəmstəns/ n Um-
stand m; ~**s** pl Umstände *pl*;
(*financial*) Verhältnisse *pl*
circus /'sɜ:kəs/ n Zirkus m
CIS *abbr* (**Commonwealth of Independent States**) GUS f
cistern /'sɪstən/ n (*tank*) Wasser-
behälter m; (*of WC*) Spülkasten m
cite /saɪt/ vt zitieren
citizen /'sɪtɪzn/ n Bürger(in) m(f).
~**ship** n Staatsangehörigkeit f
citrus /'sɪtrəs/ n ~ **[fruit]** Zitrusfrucht
f
city /'sɪtɪ/ n [Groß]stadt f

civic /'sɪvɪk/ a Bürger-
civil /'sɪvl/ a bürgerlich; ⟨aviation, defence⟩ zivil; (polite) höflich. ~ **engi'neering** n Hoch- und Tiefbau m
civilian /sɪ'vɪljən/ a Zivil-; **in ~ clothes** in Zivil ● n Zivilist m
civility /sɪ'vɪlətɪ/ n Höflichkeit f
civiliz|ation /sɪvəlar'zeɪʃn/ n Zivilisation f. ~**e** /'sɪvəlaɪz/ vt zivilisieren
civil: ~ **'servant** n Beamte(r) m/ Beamtin f. **C~ 'Service** n Staatsdienst m
clad /klæd/ a gekleidet (**in** in + acc)
claim /kleɪm/ n Anspruch m; (application) Antrag m; (demand) Forderung f; (assertion) Behauptung f ● vt beanspruchen; (apply for) beantragen; (demand) fordern; (assert) behaupten; (collect) abholen. ~**ant** n Antragsteller m
clairvoyant /kleə'vɔɪənt/ n Hellseher(in) m(f)
clam /klæm/ n Klaffmuschel f
clamber /'klæmbə(r)/ vi klettern
clammy /'klæmɪ/ a (-ier, -iest) feucht
clamour /'klæmə(r)/ n Geschrei nt ● vi ~ **for** schreien nach
clamp /klæmp/ n Klammer f ● vt [ein]spannen ● vi (fam) ~ **down** durchgreifen; ~ **down on** vorgehen gegen
clan /klæn/ n Clan m
clandestine /klæn'destɪn/ a geheim
clang /klæŋ/ n Schmettern nt. ~**er** n (fam) Schnitzer m
clank /klæŋk/ vi klirren
clap /klæp/ n **give s.o. a** ~ jdm Beifall klatschen; ~ **of thunder** Donnerschlag m ● vt/i (pt/pp **clapped**) Beifall klatschen (+ dat); ~ **one's hands** [in die Hände] klatschen
claret /'klærət/ n roter Bordeaux m
clari|fication /klærɪfɪ'keɪʃn/ n Klärung f. ~**fy** /'klærɪfaɪ/ vt/i (pt/pp -**ied**) klären
clarinet /klærɪ'net/ n Klarinette f
clarity /'klærətɪ/ n Klarheit f
clash /klæʃ/ n Geklirr nt; (fig) Konflikt m ● vi klirren; ⟨colours:⟩ sich beißen; ⟨events:⟩ ungünstig zusammenfallen
clasp /klɑːsp/ n Verschluß m ● vt ergreifen; (hold) halten
class /klɑːs/ n Klasse f; **first/second** ~ erster/zweiter Klasse ● vt einordnen
classic /'klæsɪk/ a klassisch ● n Klassiker m; ~**s** pl (Univ) Altphilologie f. ~**al** a klassisch

classi|fication /klæsɪfɪ'keɪʃn/ n Klassifikation f. ~**fy** /'klæsɪfaɪ/ vt (pt/pp -**ied**) klassifizieren
'classroom n Klassenzimmer nt
classy /'klɑːsɪ/ a (-ier, -iest) (fam) schick
clatter /'klætə(r)/ n Geklapper nt ● vi klappern
clause /klɔːz/ n Klausel f; (Gram) Satzteil m
claustrophobia /klɔːstrə'fəʊbɪə/ n Klaustrophobie f, (fam) Platzangst f
claw /klɔː/ n Kralle f; (of bird of prey & Techn) Klaue f; (of crab, lobster) Schere f ● vt kratzen
clay /kleɪ/ n Lehm m; (pottery) Ton m
clean /kliːn/ a (-er, -est) sauber ● adv glatt ● vt saubermachen; putzen ⟨shoes, windows⟩; ~ **one's teeth** sich (dat) die Zähne putzen; **have sth** ~**ed** etw reinigen lassen. ~ **up** vt saubermachen
cleaner /'kliːnə(r)/ n Putzfrau f; (substance) Reinigungsmittel nt; **[dry]** ~**'s** chemische Reinigung f
cleanliness /'klenlɪnɪs/ n Sauberkeit f
cleanse /klenz/ vt reinigen. ~**r** n Reinigungsmittel nt
clean-shaven a glattrasiert
cleansing cream /'klenz-/ n Reinigungscreme f
clear /klɪə(r)/ a (-er, -est), -**ly** adv klar; (obvious) eindeutig; (distinct) deutlich; ⟨conscience⟩ rein; (without obstacles) frei; **make sth** ~ etw klarmachen (**to** dat) ● adv **stand** ~ zurücktreten; **keep** ~ **of** aus dem Wege gehen (+ dat) ● vt räumen; abräumen ⟨table⟩; (acquit) freisprechen; (authorize) genehmigen; (jump over) überspringen; ~ **one's throat** sich räuspern ● vi ⟨fog:⟩ sich auflösen. ~ **away** vt wegräumen. ~ **off** vi (fam) abhauen. ~ **out** vt ausräumen ● vi (fam) abhauen. ~ **up** vt (tidy) aufräumen; (solve) aufklären ● vi ⟨weather:⟩ sich aufklären
clearance /'klɪərəns/ n Räumung f; (authorization) Genehmigung f; (customs) [Zoll]abfertigung f; (Techn) Spielraum m. ~ **sale** n Räumungsverkauf m
clear|ing /'klɪərɪŋ/ n Lichtung f. ~**way** n (Auto) Straße f mit Halteverbot
cleavage /'kliːvɪdʒ/ n Spaltung f; (woman's) Dekolleté nt
clef /klef/ n Notenschlüssel m

cleft /kleft/ n Spalte f

clemen|cy /'klemənsɪ/ n Milde f. ~t a mild

clench /klentʃ/ vt ~ one's fist die Faust ballen; ~ one's teeth die Zähne zusammenbeißen

clergy /'klɜːdʒɪ/ npl Geistlichkeit f. ~man n Geistliche(r) m

cleric /'klerɪk/ n Geistliche(r) m. ~al a Schreib-; (Relig) geistlich

clerk /klɑːk, Amer: klɜːk/ n Büroangestellte(r) m/f; (Amer: shop assistant) Verkäufer(in) m(f)

clever /'klevə(r)/ a (-er, -est), -ly adv klug; (skilful) geschickt

cliché /'kliːʃeɪ/ n Klischee nt

click /klɪk/ vi klicken

client /'klaɪənt/ n Kunde m/Kundin f; (Jur) Klient(in) m(f)

clientele /kliːɒn'tel/ n Kundschaft f

cliff /klɪf/ n Kliff nt

climat|e /'klaɪmət/ n Klima nt. ~ic /-'mætɪk/ a klimatisch

climax /'klaɪmæks/ n Höhepunkt m

climb /klaɪm/ n Aufstieg m ● vt besteigen (mountain); steigen auf (+ acc) ⟨ladder, tree⟩ ● vi klettern; (rise) steigen; ⟨road:⟩ ansteigen. ~ down vi hinunter-/herunterklettern; (from ladder, tree) heruntersteigen; (fam) nachgeben.

climber /'klaɪmə(r)/ n Bergsteiger m; (plant) Kletterpflanze f

clinch /klɪntʃ/ vt perfekt machen ⟨deal⟩ ● vi (boxing) clinchen

cling /klɪŋ/ vi (pt/pp clung) sich klammern (to an + acc); (stick) haften (to an + dat). ~ film n Sichtfolie f mit Hafteffekt

clinic /'klɪnɪk/ n Klinik f. ~al a, -ly adv klinisch

clink /klɪŋk/ n Klirren nt; (fam: prison) Knast m ● vi klirren

clip[1] /klɪp/ n Klammer f; (jewellery) Klipp m ● vt (pt/pp clipped) anklammern (to an + acc)

clip[2] n (extract) Ausschnitt m ● vt schneiden; knipsen (ticket). ~board n Klemmbrett nt. ~pers npl Schere f. ~ping n (extract) Ausschnitt m

clique /kliːk/ n Clique f

cloak /kləʊk/ n Umhang m. ~room n Garderobe f; (toilet) Toilette f

clobber /'klɒbə(r)/ n (fam) Zeug nt ● vt (fam: hit, defeat) schlagen

clock /klɒk/ n Uhr f; (fam: speedometer) Tacho m ● vi ~ in/out stechen

clock: ~ tower n Uhrenturm m. ~wise a & adv im Uhrzeigersinn. ~work n Uhrwerk nt; (of toy) Aufziehmechanismus m; like ~work (fam) wie am Schnürchen

clod /klɒd/ n Klumpen m

clog /klɒg/ n Holzschuh m ● vt/i (pt/pp clogged) ~ [up] verstopfen

cloister /'klɔɪstə(r)/ n Kreuzgang m

close[1] /kləʊs/ a (-r, -st) nah[e] (to dat); ⟨friend⟩ eng; ⟨weather⟩ schwül; have a ~ shave (fam) mit knapper Not davonkommen ● adv nahe; ~ by nicht weit weg ● n (street) Sackgasse f

close[2] /kləʊz/ n Ende nt; draw to a ~ sich dem Ende nähern ● vt zumachen, schließen; (bring to an end) beenden, sperren ⟨road⟩ ● vi sich schließen; ⟨shop:⟩ schließen, zumachen; (end) enden. ~ down vt schließen; stilllegen ⟨factory⟩ ● vi schließen; ⟨factory:⟩ stillgelegt werden

closed 'shop /kləʊzd-/ n ≈ Gewerkschaftszwang m

closely /'kləʊslɪ/ adv eng, nah[e]; (with attention) genau

close season /kləʊs-/ n Schonzeit f

closet /'klɒzɪt/ n (Amer) Schrank m

close-up /'kləʊs-/ n Nahaufnahme f

closure /'kləʊʒə(r)/ n Schließung f; (of factory) Stillegung f; (of road) Sperrung f

clot /klɒt/ n [Blut]gerinnsel nt; (fam: idiot) Trottel m ● vi (pt/pp clotted) ⟨blood:⟩ gerinnen

cloth /klɒθ/ n Tuch nt

clothe /kləʊð/ vt kleiden

clothes /kləʊðz/ npl Kleider pl. ~-brush n Kleiderbürste f. ~-line n Wäscheleine f

clothing /'kləʊðɪŋ/ n Kleidung f

cloud /klaʊd/ n Wolke f ● vi ~ over sich bewölken. ~burst n Wolkenbruch m

cloudy /'klaʊdɪ/ a (-ier, -iest) wolkig, bewölkt; ⟨liquid⟩ trübe

clout /klaʊt/ n (fam) Schlag m; (influence) Einfluß m ● vt (fam) hauen

clove /kləʊv/ n [Gewürz]nelke f; ~ of garlic Knoblauchzehe f

clover /'kləʊvə(r)/ n Klee m. ~ leaf n Kleeblatt nt

clown /klaʊn/ n Clown m ● vi ~ [about] herumalbern

club /klʌb/ n Klub m; (weapon) Keule f; (Sport) Schläger m; ~s pl (Cards) Kreuz nt, Treff nt ● v (pt/pp clubbed)

● *vt* knüppeln ● *vi* ~ **together** zusammenlegen

cluck /klʌk/ *vi* glucken

clue /klu:/ *n* Anhaltspunkt *m*; (*in crossword*) Frage *f*; **I haven't a** ~ (*fam*) ich habe keine Ahnung

clump /klʌmp/ *n* Gruppe *f*

clumsiness /'klʌmzɪnɪs/ *n* Ungeschicklichkeit *f*

clumsy /'klʌmzɪ/ *a* (**-ier, -iest**), **-ily** *adv* ungeschickt; (*unwieldy*) unförmig

clung /klʌŋ/ *see* **cling**

cluster /'klʌstə(r)/ *n* Gruppe *f*; (*of flowers*) Büschel *nt* ● *vi* sich scharen (**round** um)

clutch /klʌtʃ/ *n* Griff *m*; (*Auto*) Kupplung *f*; **be in s.o.'s** ~**es** (*fam*) in jds Klauen sein ● *vt* festhalten; (*grab*) ergreifen ● *vi* ~ **at** greifen nach

clutter /'klʌtə(r)/ *n* Kram *m* ● *vt* ~ **[up]** vollstopfen

c/o *abbr* (**care of**) bei

coach /kəʊtʃ/ *n* [Reise]bus *m*; (*Rail*) Wagen *m*; (*horse-drawn*) Kutsche *f*; (*Sport*) Trainer *m* ● *vt* Nachhilfestunden geben (+ *dat*); (*Sport*) trainieren

coagulate /kəʊ'ægjʊleɪt/ *vi* gerinnen

coal /kəʊl/ *n* Kohle *f*

coalition /kəʊə'lɪʃn/ *n* Koalition *f*

'coal-mine *n* Kohlenbergwerk *nt*

coarse /kɔ:s/ *a* (**-r, -st**), **-ly** *adv* grob

coast /kəʊst/ *n* Küste *f* ● *vi* (*freewheel*) im Freilauf fahren; (*Auto*) im Leerlauf fahren. ~**al** *a* Küsten-. ~**er** *n* (*mat*) Untersatz *m*

coast: ~**guard** *n* Küstenwache *f*. ~**line** *n* Küste *f*

coat /kəʊt/ *n* Mantel *m*; (*of animal*) Fell *nt*; (*of paint*) Anstrich *m*; ~ **of arms** Wappen *nt* ● *vt* überziehen; (*with paint*) [an]streichen. ~**- hanger** *n* Kleiderbügel *m*. ~**-hook** *n* Kleiderhaken *m*

coating /'kəʊtɪŋ/ *n* Überzug *m*, Schicht *f*; (*of paint*) Anstrich *m*

coax /kəʊks/ *vt* gut zureden (+ *dat*)

cob /kɒb/ *n* (*of corn*) [Mais]kolben *m*

cobble¹ /'kɒbl/ *n* Kopfstein *m*; ~**s** *pl* Kopfsteinpflaster *nt*

cobble² *vt* flicken. ~**r** *m* Schuster *m*

'cobblestones *npl* = **cobbles**

cobweb /'kɒb-/ *n* Spinnengewebe *nt*

cocaine /kəʊ'keɪn/ *n* Kokain *nt*

cock /kɒk/ *n* Hahn *m*; (*any male bird*) Männchen *nt* ● *vt* ⟨*animal:*⟩ ~ **its ears** die Ohren spitzen; ~ **the gun** den Hahn

spannen. ~**-and-'bull story** *n* (*fam*) Lügengeschichte *f*

cockerel /'kɒkərəl/ *n* [junger] Hahn *m*

cock-'eyed *a* (*fam*) schief; (*absurd*) verrückt

cockle /'kɒkl/ *n* Herzmuschel *f*

cockney /'kɒknɪ/ *n* (*dialect*) Cockney *nt*; (*person*) Cockney *m*

cock: ~**pit** *n* (*Aviat*) Cockpit *nt*. ~**roach** /-rəʊtʃ/ *n* Küchenschabe *f*. ~**tail** *n* Cocktail *m*. ~**-up** *n* (*sl*) **make a** ~**-up** Mist bauen (**of** bei)

cocky /'kɒkɪ/ *a* (**-ier, -iest**) (*fam*) eingebildet

cocoa /'kəʊkəʊ/ *n* Kakao *m*

coconut /'kəʊkənʌt/ *n* Kokosnuß *f*

cocoon /kə'ku:n/ *n* Kokon *m*

cod /kɒd/ *n* *inv* Kabeljau *m*

COD *abbr* (**cash on delivery**) per Nachnahme

coddle /'kɒdl/ *vt* verhätscheln

code /kəʊd/ *n* Kode *m*; (*Computing*) Code *m*; (*set of rules*) Kodex *m*. ~**d** *a* verschlüsselt

coedu'cational /kəʊ-/ *a* gemischt. ~ **school** *n* Koedukationsschule *f*

coerc|e /kəʊ'ɜ:s/ *vt* zwingen. ~**ion** /-'ɜ:ʃn/ *n* Zwang *m*

coe'xist *vi* koexistieren. ~**ence** *n* Koexistenz *f*

coffee /'kɒfɪ/ *n* Kaffee *m*

coffee: ~**-grinder** *n* Kaffeemühle *f*. ~**-pot** *n* Kaffeekanne *f*. ~**-table** *n* Couchtisch *m*

coffin /'kɒfɪn/ *n* Sarg *m*

cog /kɒg/ *n* (*Techn*) Zahn *m*

cogent /'kəʊdʒənt/ *a* überzeugend

cog-wheel *n* Zahnrad *nt*

cohabit /kəʊ'hæbɪt/ *vi* (*Jur*) zusammenleben

coherent /kəʊ'hɪərənt/ *a* zusammenhängend; (*comprehensible*) verständlich

coil /kɔɪl/ *n* Rolle *f*; (*Electr*) Spule *f*; (*one ring*) Windung *f* ● *vt* ~ **[up]** zusammenrollen

coin /kɔɪn/ *n* Münze *f* ● *vt* prägen

coincide /kəʊɪn'saɪd/ *vi* zusammenfallen; (*agree*) übereinstimmen

coinciden|ce /kəʊ'ɪnsɪdəns/ *n* Zufall *m*. ~**tal** /-'dentl/ *a*, **-ly** *adv* zufällig

coke /kəʊk/ *n* Koks *m*

Coke (P) *n* (*drink*) Cola *f*

colander /'kʌləndə(r)/ *n* (*Culin*) Durchschlag *m*

cold /kəʊld/ *a* (**-er, -est**) kalt; **I am** *or* **feel** ~ mir ist kalt ● *n* Kälte *f*; (*Med*) Erkältung *f*

cold: ~-'**blooded** *a* kaltblütig.
~-'**hearted** *a* kaltherzig. ~**ly** *adv*
(*fig*) kalt, kühl. ~**ness** *n* Kälte *f*
coleslaw /'kəʊlslɔː/ *n* Krautsalat *m*
colic /'kɒlɪk/ *n* Kolik *f*
collaborat|e /kə'læbəreɪt/ *vi* zu-
sammenarbeiten (**with** mit); ~**e on
sth** mitarbeiten bei etw. ~**ion**
/-'reɪʃn/ *n* Zusammenarbeit *f*, Mit-
arbeit *f*; (*with enemy*) Kollaboration
f. ~**or** *n* Mitarbeiter(in) *m*(*f*); Kol-
laborateur *m*
collaps|e /kə'læps/ *n* Zusam-
menbruch *m*; Einsturz *m* ● *vi* zusammenbrechen; ⟨*roof, building:*⟩
einstürzen. ~**ible** *a* zusammen-
klappbar
collar /'kɒlə(r)/ *n* Kragen *m*; (*for
animal*) Halsband *nt*. ~-**bone** *n*
Schlüsselbein *nt*
colleague /'kɒliːg/ *n* Kollege *m*/
Kollegin *f*
collect /kə'lekt/ *vt* sammeln; (*fetch*)
abholen; einsammeln ⟨*tickets*⟩; einziehen ⟨*taxes*⟩ ● *vi* sich [an]sammeln
● *adv* **call** ~ (*Amer*) ein R-Gespräch
führen. ~**ed** /-ɪd/ *a* gesammelt;
(*calm*) gefaßt
collection /kə'lekʃn/ *n* Sammlung *f*;
(*in church*) Kollekte *f*; (*of post*) Lee-
rung *f*; (*designer's*) Kollektion *f*
collective /kə'lektɪv/ *a* gemeinsam;
(*Pol*) kollektiv. ~ '**noun** *n* Kollek-
tivum *nt*
collector /kə'lektə(r)/ *n* Samm-
ler(in) *m*(*f*)
college /'kɒlɪdʒ/ *n* College *nt*
collide /kə'laɪd/ *vi* zusammenstoßen
colliery /'kɒlɪərɪ/ *n* Kohlengrube *f*
collision /kə'lɪʒn/ *n* Zusammenstoß
m
colloquial /kə'ləʊkwɪəl/ *a*, **-ly**
adv umgangssprachlich. ~**ism** *n*
umgangssprachlicher Ausdruck *m*
Cologne /kə'ləʊn/ *n* Köln *nt*
colon /'kəʊlən/ *n* Doppelpunkt *m*;
(*Anat*) Dickdarm *m*
colonel /'kɜːnl/ *n* Oberst *m*
colonial /kə'ləʊnɪəl/ *a* Kolonial-
colon|ize /'kɒlənaɪz/ *vt* koloni-
sieren. ~**y** *n* Kolonie *f*
colossal /kə'lɒsl/ *a* riesig
colour /'kʌlə(r)/ *n* Farbe *f*; (*complexion*) Gesichtsfarbe *f*; (*race*) Hautfarbe
f; ~**s** *pl* (*flag*) Fahne *f*; **off** ~ (*fam*)
nicht ganz auf der Höhe ● *vt* färben;
~ [**in**] ausmalen ● *vi* (*blush*) erröten

colour: ~ **bar** *n* Rassenschranke *f*.
~-**blind** *a* farbenblind. ~**ed** *a* farbig
● *n* (*person*) Farbige(r) *m*/*f*. ~-**fast** *a*
farbecht. ~ **film** *n* Farbfilm *m*. ~**ful**
a farbenfroh. ~**less** *a* farblos. ~
photo[graph] *n* Farbaufnahme *f*. ~
television *n* Farbfernsehen *nt*
colt /kəʊlt/ *n* junger Hengst *m*
column /'kɒləm/ *n* Säule *f*; (*of sol-
diers, figures*) Kolonne *f*; (*Typ*) Spalte
f; (*Journ*) Kolumne *f*. ~**ist** /-nɪst/ *n*
Kolumnist *m*
coma /'kəʊmə/ *n* Koma *nt*
comb /kəʊm/ *n* Kamm *m* ● *vt* kämmen; (*search*) absuchen; ~ **one's hair**
sich (*dat*) [die Haare] kämmen
combat /'kɒmbæt/ *n* Kampf *m* ● *vt*
(*pt/pp* **combated**) bekämpfen
combination /kɒmbɪ'neɪʃn/ *n* Verbindung *f*; (*for lock*) Kombination *f*
combine[1] /kəm'baɪn/ *vt* verbinden
● *vi* sich verbinden; ⟨*people:*⟩ sich
zusammenschließen
combine[2] /'kɒmbaɪn/ *n* (*Comm*) Konzern *m*. ~ [**harvester**] *n* Mäh-
drescher *m*
combustion /kəm'bʌstʃn/ *n* Verbrennung *f*
come /kʌm/ *vi* (*pt* **came**, *pp* **come**)
kommen; (*reach*) reichen (**to** an + *acc*);
that ~**s to £10** das macht £10; ~ **into
money** zu Geld kommen; ~ **true** wahr
werden; ~ **in two sizes** in zwei Größen
erhältlich sein; **the years to** ~ die
kommenden Jahre; **how** ~? (*fam*) wie
das? ~ **about** *vi* geschehen. ~ **across**
vi herüberkommen; (*fam*) klar
werden ● *vt* stoßen auf (+ *acc*). ~
apart *vi* sich auseinandernehmen
lassen; (*accidentally*) auseinandergehen. ~ **away** *vi* weggehen; ⟨*thing:*⟩ abgehen. ~
back *vi* zurückkommen. ~ **by**
vi vorbeikommen ● *vt* (*obtain*)
bekommen. ~ **in** *vi* hereinkommen.
~ **off** *vi* abgehen; (*take place*)
stattfinden; (*succeed*) klappen (*fam*).
~ **out** *vi* herauskommen; ⟨*book:*⟩
erscheinen; ⟨*stain:*⟩ herausgehen. ~
round *vi* vorbeikommen; (*after
fainting*) [wieder] zu sich kommen;
(*change one's mind*) sich umstimmen
lassen. ~ **to** *vi* [wieder] zu sich kommen. ~ **up** *vi* heraufkommen;
⟨*plant:*⟩ aufgehen; (*reach*) reichen (**to**
bis); ~ **up with** sich (*dat*) einfallen
lassen
'**come-back** *n* Comeback *nt*

comedian /kə'miːdɪən/ n Komiker m

'**come-down** n Rückschritt m

comedy /'kɒmədɪ/ n Komödie f

comet /'kɒmɪt/ n Komet m

come-uppance /kʌm'ʌpəns/ n **get one's** ∼ (fam) sein Fett abkriegen

comfort /'kʌmfət/ n Bequemlichkeit f; (consolation) Trost m ● vt trösten

comfortable /'kʌmfətəbl/ a, -**bly** adv bequem

'**comfort station** n (Amer) öffentliche Toilette f

comfy /'kʌmfɪ/ a (fam) bequem

comic /'kɒmɪk/ a komisch ● n Komiker m; (periodical) Comic-Heft nt. ∼**al** a, -**ly** adv komisch. ∼ **strip** n Comic Strips pl

coming /'kʌmɪŋ/ a kommend ● n Kommen nt; ∼**s and goings** Kommen und Gehen nt

comma /'kɒmə/ n Komma nt

command /kə'mɑːnd/ n Befehl m; (Mil) Kommando nt; (mastery) Beherrschung f ● vt befehlen (+ dat); kommandieren (army)

commandeer /kɒmən'dɪə(r)/ vt beschlagnahmen

command|er /kə'mɑːndə(r)/ n Befehlshaber m; (of unit) Kommandeur m; (of ship) Kommandant m. ∼**ing** a (view) beherrschend. ∼**ing officer** n Befehlshaber m. ∼**ment** n Gebot nt

commemorat|e /kə'meməreɪt/ vt gedenken (+ gen). ∼**ion** /-'reɪʃn/ n Gedenken nt. ∼**ive** /-ɪv/ a Gedenk-

commence /kə'mens/ vt/i anfangen, beginnen. ∼**ment** n Anfang m, Beginn m

commend /kə'mend/ vt loben; (recommend) empfehlen (**to** dat). ∼**able** /-əbl/ a lobenswert. ∼**ation** /kɒmen'deɪʃn/ n Lob nt

commensurate /kə'menʃərət/ a angemessen; **be** ∼ **with** entsprechen (+ dat)

comment /'kɒment/ n Bemerkung f; **no** ∼! kein Kommentar! ● vi sich äußern (**on** zu); ∼ **on** (Journ) kommentieren

commentary /'kɒməntrɪ/ n Kommentar m; [**running**] ∼ (Radio, TV) Reportage f

commentator /'kɒmənteɪtə(r)/ n Kommentator m; (Sport) Reporter m

commerce /'kɒmɜːs/ n Handel m

commercial /kə'mɜːʃl/ a, -**ly** adv kommerziell ● n (Radio, TV) Werbespot m. ∼**ize** vt kommerzialisieren

commiserate /kə'mɪzəreɪt/ vi sein Mitleid ausdrücken (**with** dat)

commission /kə'mɪʃn/ n (order for work) Auftrag m; (body of people) Kommission f; (payment) Provision f; (Mil) [Offiziers]patent nt; **out of** ∼ außer Betrieb ● vt beauftragen (s.o.); in Auftrag geben (thing); (Mil) zum Offizier ernennen

commissionaire /kəmɪʃə'neə(r)/ n Portier m

commissioner /kə'mɪʃənə(r)/ n Kommissar m; ∼ **for oaths** Notar m

commit /kə'mɪt/ vt (pt/pp com-**mitted**) begehen; (entrust) anvertrauen (**to** dat); (consign) einweisen (**to** in + acc); ∼ **oneself** sich festlegen; (involve oneself) sich engagieren; ∼ **sth to memory** sich (dat) etw einprägen. ∼**ment** n Verpflichtung f; (involvement) Engagement nt. ∼**ted** a engagiert

committee /kə'mɪtɪ/ n Ausschuß m, Komitee nt

commodity /kə'mɒdətɪ/ n Ware f

common /'kɒmən/ a (-**er**, -**est**) gemeinsam; (frequent) häufig; (ordinary) gewöhnlich; (vulgar) ordinär ● n Gemeindeland nt; **have in** ∼ gemeinsam haben; **House of C**∼**s** Unterhaus nt. ∼**er** n Bürgerliche(r) m/f

common: ∼'**law** n Gewohnheitsrecht nt. ∼**ly** adv allgemein. **C**∼ '**Market** n Gemeinsamer Markt m. ∼**place** a häufig. ∼**room** n Aufenthaltsraum m. ∼ '**sense** n gesunder Menschenverstand m

commotion /kə'məʊʃn/ n Tumult m

communal /'kɒmjʊnl/ a gemeinschaftlich

communicable /kə'mjuːnɪkəbl/ a (disease) übertragbar

communicate /kə'mjuːnɪkeɪt/ vt mitteilen (**to** dat); übertragen (disease) ● vi sich verständigen; (be in touch) Verbindung haben

communication /kəmjuːnɪ'keɪʃn/ n Verständigung f; (contact) Verbindung f; (of disease) Übertragung f; (message) Mitteilung f; ∼**s** pl (technology) Nachrichtenwesen nt. ∼ **cord** n Notbremse f

communicative /kə'mjuːnɪkətɪv/ a mitteilsam

Communion /kə'mju:nɪən/ n **[Holy]** ∼ das [heilige] Abendmahl; (*Roman Catholic*) die [heilige] Kommunion

communiqué /kə'mju:nɪkeɪ/ n Kommuniqué nt

Communis|m /'kɒmjʊnɪzm/ n Kommunismus m. ∼**t** /-ɪst/ a kommunistisch ● n Kommunist(in) m(f)

community /kə'mju:nətɪ/ n Gemeinschaft f; **local** ∼ Gemeinde f. ∼ **centre** n Gemeinschaftszentrum nt

commute /kə'mju:t/ vi pendeln ● vt (*Jur*) umwandeln. ∼**r** n Pendler(in) m(f)

compact[1] /kɒm'pækt/ a kompakt

compact[2] /'kɒmpækt/ n Puderdose f. ∼ **disc** n CD f

companion /kəm'pænjən/ n Begleiter(in) m(f). ∼**ship** n Gesellschaft f

company /'kʌmpənɪ/ n Gesellschaft f; (*firm*) Firma f; (*Mil*) Kompanie f; (*fam: guests*) Besuch m. ∼ **car** n Firmenwagen m

comparable /'kɒmpərəbl/ a vergleichbar

comparative /kəm'pærətɪv/ a vergleichend; (*relative*) relativ ● n (*Gram*) Komparativ m. ∼**ly** adv verhältnismäßig

compare /kəm'peə(r)/ vt vergleichen (**with/to** mit) ● vi sich vergleichen lassen

comparison /kəm'pærɪsn/ n Vergleich m

compartment /kəm'pɑ:tmənt/ n Fach nt; (*Rail*) Abteil nt

compass /'kʌmpəs/ n Kompaß m. ∼**es** npl **pair of** ∼**es** Zirkel m

compassion /kəm'pæʃn/ n Mitleid nt. ∼**ate** /-'ʃənət/ a mitfühlend

compatible /kəm'pætəbl/ a vereinbar; ⟨*drugs*⟩ verträglich; (*Techn*) kompatibel; **be** ∼ ⟨*people:*⟩ [gut] zueinander passen

compatriot /kəm'pætrɪət/ n Landsmann m/-männin f

compel /kəm'pel/ vt (pt/pp **compelled**) zwingen

compensat|e /'kɒmpənseɪt/ vt entschädigen ● vi ∼**e for** (*fig*) ausgleichen. ∼**ion** /-'seɪʃn/ n Entschädigung f; (*fig*) Ausgleich m

compère /'kɒmpeə(r)/ n Conférencier m

compete /kəm'pi:t/ vi konkurrieren; (*take part*) teilnehmen (**in** an + dat)

competen|ce /'kɒmpɪtəns/ n Tüchtigkeit f; (*ability*) Fähigkeit f; (*Jur*) Kompetenz f. ∼**t** a tüchtig; fähig; (*Jur*) kompetent

competition /kɒmpə'tɪʃn/ n Konkurrenz f; (*contest*) Wettbewerb m; (*in newspaper*) Preisausschreiben nt

competitive /kəm'petətɪv/ a (*Comm*) konkurrenzfähig

competitor /kəm'petɪtə(r)/ n Teilnehmer m; (*Comm*) Konkurrent m

compile /kəm'paɪl/ vt zusammenstellen; verfassen ⟨*dictionary*⟩

complacen|cy /kəm'pleɪsənsɪ/ n Selbstzufriedenheit f. ∼**t** a, -**ly** adv selbstzufrieden

complain /kəm'pleɪn/ vi klagen (**about/of** über + acc); (*formally*) sich beschweren. ∼**t** n Klage f; (*formal*) Beschwerde f; (*Med*) Leiden nt

complement[1] /'kɒmplɪmənt/ n Ergänzung f; **full** ∼ volle Anzahl f

complement[2] /'kɒmplɪment/ vt ergänzen; ∼ **each other** sich ergänzen. ∼**ary** /-'mentərɪ/ a sich ergänzend; **be** ∼**ary** sich ergänzen

complete /kəm'pli:t/ a vollständig; (*finished*) fertig; (*utter*) völlig ● vt vervollständigen; (*finish*) abschließen; (*fill in*) ausfüllen. ∼**ly** adv völlig

completion /kəm'pli:ʃn/ n Vervollständigung f; (*end*) Abschluß m

complex /'kɒmpleks/ a komplex ● n Komplex m

complexion /kəm'plekʃn/ n Teint m; (*colour*) Gesichtsfarbe f; (*fig*) Aspekt m

complexity /kəm'pleksətɪ/ n Komplexität f

compliance /kəm'plaɪəns/ n Einverständnis nt; **in** ∼ **with** gemäß (+ dat)

complicat|e /'kɒmplɪkeɪt/ vt komplizieren. ∼**ed** a kompliziert. ∼**ion** /-'keɪʃn/ n Komplikation f

complicity /kəm'plɪsətɪ/ n Mittäterschaft f

compliment /'kɒmplɪmənt/ n Kompliment nt; ∼**s** pl Grüße pl ● vt ein Kompliment machen (+ dat). ∼**ary** /-'mentərɪ/ a schmeichelhaft; (*given free*) Frei-

comply /kəm'plaɪ/ vi (pt/pp -**ied**) ∼ **with** nachkommen (+ dat)

component /kəm'pəʊnənt/ a & n ∼ **[part]** Bestandteil m, Teil nt

compose /kəm'pəʊz/ vt verfassen; (Mus) komponieren; ~ **oneself** sich fassen; **be ~d of** sich zusammensetzen aus. ~**d** a (calm) gefaßt. ~**r** n Komponist m

composition /kɒmpə'zɪʃn/ n Komposition f; (essay) Aufsatz m

compost /'kɒmpɒst/ n Kompost m

composure /kəm'pəʊzə(r)/ n Fassung f

compound[1] /kəm'paʊnd/ vt (make worse) verschlimmern

compound[2] /'kɒmpaʊnd/ a zusammengesetzt; (fracture) kompliziert ● n (Chem) Verbindung f; (Gram) Kompositum nt; (enclosure) Einfriedigung f. ~ 'interest n Zinseszins m

comprehen|d /kɒmprɪ'hend/ vt begreifen, verstehen; (include) umfassen. ~**sible** a, -**bly** adv verständlich. ~**sion** /-'henʃn/ n Verständnis nt

comprehensive /kɒmprɪ'hensɪv/ a & n umfassend; ~ **[school]** Gesamtschule f. ~ **insurance** n (Auto) Vollkaskoversicherung f

compress[1] /'kɒmpres/ n Kompresse f

compress[2] /kəm'pres/ vt zusammenpressen; ~**ed air** Druckluft f

comprise /kəm'praɪz/ vt umfassen, bestehen aus

compromise /'kɒmprəmaɪz/ n Kompromiß m ● vt kompromittieren (person) ● vi einen Kompromiß schließen

compuls|ion /kəm'pʌlʃn/ n Zwang m. ~**ive** /-sɪv/ a zwanghaft; ~**ive eating** Eßzwang m. ~**ory** /-sərɪ/ a obligatorisch; ~**ory subject** Pflichtfach nt

compunction /kəm'pʌŋkʃn/ n Gewissensbisse pl

comput|er /kəm'pju:tə(r)/ n Computer m. ~**erize** vt computerisieren (data); auf Computer umstellen (firm). ~**ing** n Computertechnik f

comrade /'kɒmreɪd/ n Kamerad m; (Pol) Genosse m/Genossin f. ~**ship** n Kameradschaft f

con[1] /kɒn/ see **pro**

con[2] n (fam) Schwindel m ● vt (pt/pp **conned**) (fam) beschwindeln

concave /'kɒŋkeɪv/ a konkav

conceal /kən'si:l/ vt verstecken; (keep secret) verheimlichen

concede /kən'si:d/ vt zugeben; (give up) aufgeben

conceit /kən'si:t/ n Einbildung f. ~**ed** a eingebildet

conceivable /kən'si:vəbl/ a denkbar

conceive /kən'si:v/ vt (Biol) empfangen; (fig) sich (dat) ausdenken ● vi schwanger werden. ~ **of** (fig) sich (dat) vorstellen

concentrat|e /'kɒnsəntreɪt/ vt konzentrieren ● vi sich konzentrieren. ~**ion** /-'treɪʃn/ n Konzentration f. ~**ion camp** n Konzentrationslager nt

concept /'kɒnsept/ n Begriff m. ~**ion** /kən'sepʃn/ n Empfängnis f; (idea) Vorstellung f

concern /kən'sɜ:n/ n Angelegenheit f; (worry) Sorge f; (Comm) Unternehmen nt ● vt (be about, affect) betreffen; (worry) kümmern; **be ~ed about** besorgt sein um; ~ **oneself with** sich beschäftigen mit; **as far as I am ~ed** was mich angeht od betrifft. ~**ing** prep bezüglich (+ gen)

concert /'kɒnsət/ n Konzert nt; **in ~** im Chor. ~**ed** /kən'sɜ:tɪd/ a gemeinsam

concertina /kɒnsə'ti:nə/ n Konzertina f

'concert-master n (Amer) Konzertmeister m

concerto /kən'tʃeətəʊ/ n Konzert nt

concession /kən'seʃn/ n Zugeständnis nt; (Comm) Konzession f; (reduction) Ermäßigung f. ~**ary** a (reduced) ermäßigt

conciliation /kənsɪlɪ'eɪʃn/ n Schlichtung f

concise /kən'saɪs/ a, -**ly** adv kurz

conclude /kən'klu:d/ vt/i schließen

conclusion /kən'klu:ʒn/ n Schluß m; **in ~** abschließend, zum Schluß

conclusive /kən'klu:sɪv/ a schlüssig

concoct /kən'kɒkt/ vt zusammenstellen; (fig) fabrizieren. ~**ion** /-ɒkʃn/ n Zusammenstellung f; (drink) Gebräu nt

concourse /'kɒŋkɔ:s/ n Halle f

concrete /'kɒŋkri:t/ a konkret ● n Beton m ● vt betonieren

concur /kən'kɜ:(r)/ vi (pt/pp **concurred**) übereinstimmen

concurrently /kən'kʌrəntlɪ/ adv gleichzeitig

concussion /kən'kʌʃn/ n Gehirnerschütterung f

condemn /kən'dem/ vt verurteilen; (*declare unfit*) für untauglich erklären. ～**ation** /kɒndem'neɪʃn/ n Verurteilung f

condensation /kɒnden'seɪʃn/ n Kondensation f

condense /kən'dens/ vt zusammenfassen; (*Phys*) kondensieren ● vi sich kondensieren. ～**d milk** n Kondensmilch f

condescend /kɒndɪ'send/ vi sich herablassen (**to** zu). ～**ing** a, **-ly** adv herablassend

condiment /'kɒndɪmənt/ n Gewürz nt

condition /kən'dɪʃn/ n Bedingung f; (*state*) Zustand m; ～**s** pl Verhältnisse pl; **on** ～ **that** unter der Bedingung, daß ● vt (*Psych*) konditionieren. ～**al** a bedingt; **be** ～**al on** abhängen von ● n (*Gram*) Konditional m. ～**er** n Haarkur f; (*for fabrics*) Weichspüler m

condolences /kən'dəʊlənsɪz/ npl Beileid nt

condom /'kɒndəm/ n Kondom nt

condominium /kɒndə'mɪnɪəm/ n (*Amer*) Eigentumswohnung f

condone /kən'dəʊn/ vt hinwegsehen über (+ acc)

conducive /kən'djuːsɪv/ a förderlich (**to** dat)

conduct[1] /'kɒndʌkt/ n Verhalten nt; (*Sch*) Betragen nt

conduct[2] /kən'dʌkt/ vt führen; (*Phys*) leiten; (*Mus*) dirigieren. ～**or** n Dirigent m; (*of bus*) Schaffner m; (*Phys*) Leiter m. ～**ress** n Schaffnerin f

cone /kəʊn/ n Kegel m; (*Bot*) Zapfen m; (*for ice-cream*) [Eis]tüte f; (*Auto*) Leitkegel m

confectioner /kən'fekʃənə(r)/ n Konditor m. ～**y** n Süßwaren pl

confederation /kənfedə'reɪʃn/ n Bund m; (*Pol*) Konföderation f

confer /kən'fɜː(r)/ v (pt/pp **conferred**) ● vt verleihen (**on** dat) ● vi sich beraten

conference /'kɒnfərəns/ n Konferenz f

confess /kən'fes/ vt/i gestehen; (*Relig*) beichten. ～**ion** /-eʃn/ n Geständnis nt; (*Relig*) Beichte f. ～**ional** /-eʃənəl/ n Beichtstuhl m. ～**or** n Beichtvater m

confetti /kən'fetɪ/ n Konfetti nt

confide /kən'faɪd/ vt anvertrauen ● vi ～ **in s.o.** sich jdm anvertrauen

confidence /'kɒnfɪdəns/ n (*trust*) Vertrauen nt; (*self-assurance*) Selbstvertrauen nt; (*secret*) Geheimnis nt; **in** ～ im Vertrauen. ～ **trick** n Schwindel m

confident /'kɒnfɪdənt/ a, **-ly** adv zuversichtlich; (*self-assured*) selbstsicher

confidential /kɒnfɪ'denʃl/ a, **-ly** adv vertraulich

confine /kən'faɪn/ vt beschränken; (*keep shut up*) einsperren; ～ **oneself to** sich beschränken auf (+ acc); **be ～d to bed** das Bett hüten müssen. ～**d** a (*narrow*) eng. ～**ment** n Haft f

confines /'kɒnfaɪnz/ npl Grenzen pl

confirm /kən'fɜːm/ vt bestätigen; (*Relig*) konfirmieren; (*Roman Catholic*) firmen. ～**ation** /kɒnfə'meɪʃn/ n Bestätigung f; Konfirmation f; Firmung f. ～**ed** a ～**ed bachelor** eingefleischter Junggeselle m

confiscat|e /'kɒnfɪskeɪt/ vt beschlagnahmen. ～**ion** /-'keɪʃn/ n Beschlagnahme f

conflict[1] /'kɒnflɪkt/ n Konflikt m

conflict[2] /kən'flɪkt/ vi im Widerspruch stehen (**with** zu). ～**ing** a widersprüchlich

conform /kən'fɔːm/ vi (*person:*) sich anpassen; (*thing:*) entsprechen (**to** dat). ～**ist** n Konformist m

confounded /kən'faʊndɪd/ a (*fam*) verflixt

confront /kən'frʌnt/ vt konfrontieren. ～**ation** /kɒnfrən'teɪʃn/ n Konfrontation f

confus|e /kən'fjuːz/ vt verwirren; (*mistake for*) verwechseln (**with** mit). ～**ing** a verwirrend. ～**ion** /-juːʒn/ n Verwirrung f; (*muddle*) Durcheinander nt

congeal /kən'dʒiːl/ vi fest werden; (*blood:*) gerinnen

congenial /kən'dʒiːnɪəl/ a angenehm

congenital /kən'dʒenɪtl/ a angeboren

congest|ed /kən'dʒestɪd/ a verstopft; (*with people*) überfüllt. ～**ion** /-estʃn/ n Verstopfung f; Überfüllung f

congratulat|e /kən'grætjʊleɪt/ vt gratulieren (+ dat) (**on** zu). ～**ions** /-'leɪʃnz/ npl Glückwünsche pl; ～**ions!** [ich] gratuliere!

congregat|e /'kɒngrɪgeɪt/ vi sich versammeln. **∼ion** /-'geɪʃn/ n (Relig) Gemeinde f

congress /'kɒngres/ n Kongreß m. **∼man** n Kongreßabgeordnete(r) m

conical /'kɒnɪkl/ a kegelförmig

conifer /'kɒnɪfə(r)/ n Nadelbaum m

conjecture /kən'dʒektʃə(r)/ n Mutmaßung f ● vt/i mutmaßen

conjugal /'kɒndʒʊgl/ a ehelich

conjugat|e /'kɒndʒʊgeɪt/ vt konjugieren. **∼ion** /-'geɪʃn/ n Konjugation f

conjunction /kən'dʒʌŋkʃn/ n Konjunktion f; **in ∼ with** zusammen mit

conjunctivitis /kəndʒʌŋktɪ'vaɪtɪs/ n Bindehautentzündung f

conjur|e /'kʌndʒə(r)/ vi zaubern ● vt **∼e up** heraufbeschwören. **∼or** n Zauberkünstler m

conk /kɒŋk/ vi **∼ out** (fam) ⟨machine:⟩ kaputtgehen; ⟨person:⟩ zusammenklappen

conker /'kɒŋkə(r)/ n (fam) [Roß]kastanie f

'con-man n (fam) Schwindler m

connect /kə'nekt/ vt verbinden (**to** mit); (Electr) anschließen (**to** an + acc) ● vi verbunden sein; ⟨train:⟩ Anschluß haben (**with** an + acc); **be ∼ed with** zu tun haben mit; (be related to) verwandt sein mit

connection /kə'nekʃn/ n Verbindung f; (Rail, Electr) Anschluß m; **in ∼ with** in Zusammenhang mit. **∼s** npl Beziehungen pl

conniv|ance /kə'naɪvəns/ n stillschweigende Duldung f. **∼e** vi **∼e at** stillschweigend dulden

connoisseur /kɒnə'sɜ:(r)/ n Kenner m

connotation /kɒnə'teɪʃn/ n Assoziation f

conquer /'kɒŋkə(r)/ vt erobern; (fig) besiegen. **∼or** n Eroberer m

conquest /'kɒŋkwest/ n Eroberung f

conscience /'kɒnʃəns/ n Gewissen nt

conscientious /kɒnʃɪ'enʃəs/ a, -ly adv gewissenhaft. **∼ ob'jector** n Kriegsdienstverweigerer m

conscious /'kɒnʃəs/ a, -ly adv bewußt; **[fully]** ∼ bei [vollem] Bewußtsein; **be/become ∼ of sth** sich (dat) etw (gen) bewußt sein/werden. **∼ness** n Bewußtsein nt

conscript[1] /'kɒnskrɪpt/ n Einberufene(r) m

conscript[2] /kən'skrɪpt/ vt einberufen. **∼ion** /-ɪpʃn/ n allgemeine Wehrpflicht f

consecrat|e /'kɒnsɪkreɪt/ vt weihen; einweihen ⟨church⟩. **∼ion** /-'kreɪʃn/ n Weihe f; Einweihung f

consecutive /kən'sekjʊtɪv/ a aufeinanderfolgend. **∼ly** adv fortlaufend

consensus /kən'sensəs/ n Übereinstimmung f

consent /kən'sent/ n Einwilligung f, Zustimmung f ● vi einwilligen (**to** in + acc), zustimmen (**to** dat)

consequen|ce /'kɒnsɪkwəns/ n Folge f; (importance) Bedeutung f. **∼t** a daraus folgend. **∼tly** adv folglich

conservation /kɒnsə'veɪʃn/ n Erhaltung f, Bewahrung f. **∼ist** n Umweltschützer m

conservative /kən'sɜ:vətɪv/ a konservativ; ⟨estimate⟩ vorsichtig. **C∼** (Pol) a konservativ ● n Konservative(r) m/f

conservatory /kən'sɜ:vətrɪ/ n Wintergarten m

conserve /kən'sɜ:v/ vt erhalten, bewahren; sparen ⟨energy⟩

consider /kən'sɪdə(r)/ vt erwägen; (think over) sich (dat) überlegen; (take into account) berücksichtigen; (regard as) betrachten als; **∼ doing sth** erwägen, etw zu tun. **∼able** /-əbl/ a, **-bly** adv erheblich

consider|ate /kən'sɪdərət/ a, **-ly** adv rücksichtsvoll. **∼ation** /-'reɪʃn/ n Erwägung f; (thoughtfulness) Rücksicht f; (payment) Entgelt nt; **take into ∼ation** berücksichtigen. **∼ing** prep wenn man bedenkt (**that** daß); **∼ing the circumstances** unter den Umständen

consign /kən'saɪn/ vt übergeben (**to** dat). **∼ment** n Lieferung f

consist /kən'sɪst/ vi **∼ of** bestehen aus

consisten|cy /kən'sɪstənsɪ/ n Konsequenz f; (density) Konsistenz f. **∼t** a konsequent; (unchanging) gleichbleibend; **be ∼t with** entsprechen (+ dat). **∼tly** adv konsequent; (constantly) ständig

consolation /kɒnsə'leɪʃn/ n Trost m. **∼ prize** n Trostpreis m

console /kən'səʊl/ vt trösten

consolidate /kən'sɒlɪdeɪt/ vt konsolidieren

consonant /'kɒnsənənt/ n Konsonant m

consort /'kɒnsɔːt/ n Gemahl(in) m(f)

conspicuous /kən'spɪkjʊəs/ a auffällig

conspiracy /kən'spɪrəsɪ/ n Verschwörung f

conspire /kən'spaɪə(r)/ vi sich verschwören

constable /'kʌnstəbl/ n Polizist m

constant /'kɒnstənt/ a, **-ly** adv beständig; (continuous) ständig

constellation /kɒnstə'leɪʃn/ n Sternbild nt

consternation /kɒnstə'neɪʃn/ n Bestürzung f

constipat|ed /'kɒnstɪpeɪtɪd/ a verstopft. ~**ion** /-'peɪʃn/ n Verstopfung f

constituency /kən'stɪtjʊənsɪ/ n Wahlkreis m

constituent /kən'stɪtjʊənt/ n Bestandteil m; (Pol) Wähler(in) m(f)

constitut|e /'kɒnstɪtjuːt/ vt bilden. ~**ion** /-'tjuːʃn/ n (Pol) Verfassung f; (of person) Konstitution f. ~**ional** /-'tjuːʃənl/ a Verfassungs- ● n Verdauungsspaziergang m

constrain /kən'streɪn/ vt zwingen. ~**t** n Zwang m; (restriction) Beschränkung f; (strained manner) Gezwungenheit f

constrict /kən'strɪkt/ vt einengen

construct /kən'strʌkt/ vt bauen. ~**ion** /-ʌkʃn/ n Bau m; (Gram) Konstruktion f; (interpretation) Deutung f; **under** ~**ion** im Bau. ~**ive** /-ɪv/ a konstruktiv

construe /kən'struː/ vt deuten

consul /'kɒnsl/ n Konsul m. ~**ate** /'kɒnsjʊlət/ n Konsulat nt

consult /kən'sʌlt/ vt [um Rat] fragen; konsultieren 〈doctor〉; nachschlagen in (+ dat) 〈book〉. ~**ant** n Berater m; (Med) Chefarzt m. ~**ation** /kɒnsl'teɪʃn/ n Beratung f; (Med) Konsultation f

consume /kən'sjuːm/ vt verzehren; (use) verbrauchen. ~**r** n Verbraucher m. ~**r goods** npl Konsumgüter pl

consummat|e /'kɒnsəmeɪt/ vt vollziehen. ~**ion** /-'meɪʃn/ n Vollzug m

consumption /kən'sʌmpʃn/ n Konsum m; (use) Verbrauch m

contact /'kɒntækt/ n Kontakt m; (person) Kontaktperson f ● vt sich in Verbindung setzen mit. ~ '**lenses** npl Kontaktlinsen pl

contagious /kən'teɪdʒəs/ a direkt übertragbar

contain /kən'teɪn/ vt enthalten; (control) beherrschen. ~**er** n Behälter m; (Comm) Container m

contaminat|e /kən'tæmɪneɪt/ vt verseuchen. ~**ion** /-'neɪʃn/ n Verseuchung f

contemplat|e /'kɒntəmpleɪt/ vt betrachten; (meditate) nachdenken über (+ acc); ~**e doing sth** daran denken, etw zu tun. ~**ion** /-'pleɪʃn/ n Betrachtung f; Nachdenken nt

contemporary /kən'tempərərɪ/ a zeitgenössisch ● n Zeitgenosse m/ -genossin f

contempt /kən'tempt/ n Verachtung f; **beneath** ~ verabscheuungswürdig; ~ **of court** Mißachtung f des Gerichts. ~**ible** /-əbl/ a verachtenswert. ~**uous** /-tjʊəs/ a, **-ly** adv verächtlich

contend /kən'tend/ vi kämpfen (**with** mit) ● vt (assert) behaupten. ~**er** n Bewerber(in) m(f); (Sport) Wettkämpfer(in) m(f)

content[1] /'kɒntent/ n & **contents** pl Inhalt m

content[2] /kən'tent/ a zufrieden ● n **to one's heart's** ~ nach Herzenslust ● vt ~ **oneself** sich begnügen (**with** mit). ~**ed** a, **-ly** adv zufrieden

contention /kən'tenʃn/ n (assertion) Behauptung f

contentment /kən'tentmənt/ n Zufriedenheit f

contest[1] /'kɒntest/ n Kampf m; (competition) Wettbewerb m

contest[2] /kən'test/ vt (dispute) bestreiten; (Jur) anfechten; (Pol) kandidieren in (+ dat). ~**ant** n Teilnehmer m

context /'kɒntekst/ n Zusammenhang m

continent /'kɒntɪnənt/ n Kontinent m

continental /kɒntɪ'nentl/ a Kontinental-. ~ **breakfast** n kleines Frühstück nt. ~ **quilt** n Daunendecke f

contingen|cy /kən'tɪndʒənsɪ/ n Eventualität f. ~**t** a **be** ~**t upon** abhängen von ● n (Mil) Kontingent nt

continual /kən'tɪnjʊəl/ a, **-ly** adv dauernd

continuation /kəntɪnjʊ'eɪʃn/ *n* Fortsetzung *f*

continue /kən'tɪnju:/ *vt* fortsetzen; ~ **doing** *or* **to do sth** fortfahren, etw zu tun; **to be ~d** Fortsetzung folgt • *vi* weitergehen; (*doing sth*) weitermachen; (*speaking*) fortfahren; ⟨*weather:*⟩ anhalten

continuity /kɒntɪ'nju:ətɪ/ *n* Kontinuität *f*

continuous /kən'tɪnjʊəs/ *a*, **-ly** *adv* anhaltend, ununterbrochen

contort /kən'tɔ:t/ *vt* verzerren. ~**ion** /-'ɔ:ʃn/ *n* Verzerrung *f*

contour /'kɒntʊə(r)/ *n* Kontur *f*; (*line*) Höhenlinie *f*

contraband /'kɒntrəbænd/ *n* Schmuggelware *f*

contracep|tion /kɒntrə'sepʃn/ *n* Empfängnisverhütung *f*. ~**tive** /-tɪv/ *a* empfängnisverhütend • *n* Empfängnisverhütungsmittel *nt*

contract[1] /'kɒntrækt/ *n* Vertrag *m*

contract[2] /kən'trækt/ *vi* sich zusammenziehen • *vt* zusammenziehen; sich (*dat*) zuziehen ⟨*illness*⟩. ~**ion** /-ækʃn/ *n* Zusammenziehung *f*; (*abbreviation*) Abkürzung *f*; (*in childbirth*) Wehe *f*. ~**or** *n* Unternehmer *m*

contradict /kɒntrə'dɪkt/ *vt* widersprechen (+ *dat*). ~**ion** /-ɪkʃn/ *n* Widerspruch *m*. ~**ory** *a* widersprüchlich

contra-flow /'kɒntrə-/ *n* Umleitung *f* [auf die entgegengesetzte Fahrbahn]

contralto /kən'træltəʊ/ *n* Alt *m*; (*singer*) Altistin *f*

contraption /kən'træpʃn/ *n* (*fam*) Apparat *m*

contrary[1] /'kɒntrərɪ/ *a* & *adv* entgegengesetzt; ~ **to** entgegen (+ *dat*) • *n* Gegenteil *nt*; **on the ~** im Gegenteil

contrary[2] /kən'treərɪ/ *a* widerspenstig

contrast[1] /'kɒntrɑ:st/ *n* Kontrast *m*

contrast[2] /kən'trɑ:st/ *vt* gegenüberstellen (**with** *dat*) • *vi* einen Kontrast bilden (**with** zu). ~**ing** *a* gegensätzlich; ⟨*colour*⟩ Kontrast-

contraven|e /kɒntrə'vi:n/ *vt* verstoßen gegen. ~**tion** /-'venʃn/ *n* Verstoß *m* (**of** gegen)

contribut|e /kən'trɪbju:t/ *vt/i* beitragen; beisteuern ⟨*money*⟩; (*donate*) spenden. ~**ion** /kɒntrɪ'bju:ʃn/ *n* Beitrag *m*; (*donation*) Spende *f*. ~**or** *n* Beitragende(r) *m/f*

contrite /kən'traɪt/ *a* reuig

contrivance /kən'traɪvəns/ *n* Vorrichtung *f*

contrive /kən'traɪv/ *vt* verfertigen; ~ **to do sth** es fertigbringen, etw zu tun

control /kən'trəʊl/ *n* Kontrolle *f*; (*mastery*) Beherrschung *f*; (*Techn*) Regler *m*; ~**s** *pl* (*of car, plane*) Steuerung *f*; **get out of** ~ außer Kontrolle geraten • *vt* (*pt/pp* **controlled**) kontrollieren; (*restrain*) unter Kontrolle halten; ~ **oneself** sich beherrschen

controvers|ial /kɒntrə'vɜ:ʃl/ *a* umstritten. ~**y** /'kɒntrəvɜ:sɪ/ *n* Kontroverse *f*

conundrum /kə'nʌndrəm/ *n* Rätsel *nt*

conurbation /kɒnɜ:'beɪʃn/ *n* Ballungsgebiet *nt*

convalesce /kɒnvə'les/ *vi* sich erholen. ~**nce** *n* Erholung *f*

convalescent /kɒnvə'lesnt/ *a* **be** ~ noch erholungsbedürftig sein. ~ **home** *n* Erholungsheim *nt*

convector /kən'vektə(r)/ *n* ~ **[heater]** Konvektor *m*

convene /kən'vi:n/ *vt* einberufen • *vi* sich versammeln

convenience /kən'vi:nɪəns/ *n* Bequemlichkeit *f*; **[public]** ~ öffentliche Toilette *f*; **with all modern ~s** mit allem Komfort

convenient /kən'vi:nɪənt/ *a*, **-ly** *adv* günstig; **be ~ for s.o.** jdm gelegen sein *od* jdm passen; **if it is ~ [for you]** wenn es Ihnen paßt

convent /'kɒnvənt/ *n* [Nonnen]kloster *nt*

convention /kən'venʃn/ *n* (*custom*) Brauch *m*, Sitte *f*; (*agreement*) Konvention *f*; (*assembly*) Tagung *f*. ~**al** *a*, **-ly** *adv* konventionell

converge /kən'vɜ:dʒ/ *vi* zusammenlaufen

conversant /kən'vɜ:sənt/ *a* ~ **with** vertraut mit

conversation /kɒnvə'seɪʃn/ *n* Gespräch *nt*; (*Sch*) Konversation *f*

converse[1] /kən'vɜ:s/ *vi* sich unterhalten

converse[2] /'kɒnvɜ:s/ *n* Gegenteil *nt*. ~**ly** *adv* umgekehrt

conversion /kən'vɜ:ʃn/ *n* Umbau *m*; (*Relig*) Bekehrung *f*; (*calculation*) Umrechnung *f*

convert[1] /'kɒnvɜ:t/ *n* Bekehrte(r) *m/f*, Konvertit *m*

convert² /kən'vɜːt/ vt bekehren ⟨person⟩; (change) umwandeln (**into** in + acc); umbauen ⟨building⟩; (calculate) umrechnen; (Techn) umstellen. ~**ible** /-əbl/ a verwandelbar ● n (Auto) Kabriolett nt

convex /'kɒnveks/ a konvex

convey /kən'veɪ/ vt befördern; vermitteln ⟨idea, message⟩. ~**ance** n Beförderung f; ⟨vehicle⟩ Beförderungsmittel nt. ~**or belt** n Förderband nt

convict¹ /'kɒnvɪkt/ n Sträfling m

convict² /kən'vɪkt/ vt verurteilen (**of** wegen). ~**ion** /-ɪkʃn/ n Verurteilung f; (belief) Überzeugung f; **previous** ~**ion** Vorstrafe f

convinc|e /kən'vɪns/ vt überzeugen. ~**ing** a, **-ly** adv überzeugend

convivial /kən'vɪvɪəl/ a gesellig

convoluted /'kɒnvəluːtɪd/ a verschlungen; (fig) verwickelt

convoy /'kɒnvɔɪ/ n Konvoi m

convuls|e /kən'vʌls/ vt be ~ed sich krümmen (**with** vor + dat). ~**ion** /-ʌlʃn/ n Krampf m

coo /kuː/ vi gurren

cook /kʊk/ n Koch m/Köchin f ● vt/i kochen; **is it** ~**ed?** ist es gar? ~ **the books** (fam) die Bilanz frisieren. ~**book** n (Amer) Kochbuch nt

cooker /'kʊkə(r)/ n [Koch]herd m; (apple) Kochapfel m. ~**y** n Kochen nt. ~**y book** n Kochbuch nt

cookie /'kʊkɪ/ n (Amer) Keks m

cool /kuːl/ a (**-er, -est**), **-ly** adv kühl ● n Kühle f ● vt kühlen ● vi abkühlen. ~**-box** n Kühlbox f. ~**ness** n Kühle f

coop /kuːp/ n [Hühner]stall m ● vt ~ **up** einsperren

co-operat|e /kəʊ'ɒpəreɪt/ vi zusammenarbeiten. ~**ion** /-'reɪʃn/ n Kooperation f

co-operative /kəʊ'ɒpərətɪv/ a hilfsbereit ● n Genossenschaft f

co-opt /kəʊ'ɒpt/ vt hinzuwählen

co-ordinat|e /kəʊ'ɔːdɪneɪt/ vt koordinieren. ~**ion** /-'neɪʃn/ n Koordination f

cop /kɒp/ n (fam) Polizist m

cope /kəʊp/ vi (fam) zurechtkommen; ~ **with** fertig werden mit

copious /'kəʊpɪəs/ a reichlich

copper¹ /'kɒpə(r)/ n Kupfer nt; ~**s** pl Kleingeld nt ● a kupfern

copper² n (fam) Polizist m

copper 'beech n Blutbuche f

coppice /'kɒpɪs/ n, **copse** /kɒps/ n Gehölz nt

copulate /'kɒpjʊleɪt/ vi sich begatten

copy /'kɒpɪ/ n Kopie f; (book) Exemplar nt ● vt (pt/pp **-ied**) kopieren; (imitate) nachahmen; (Sch) abschreiben

copy: ~**right** n Copyright nt. ~**-writer** n Texter m

coral /'kɒrl/ n Koralle f

cord /kɔːd/ n Schnur f; (fabric) Cordsamt m; ~**s** pl Cordhose f

cordial /'kɔːdɪəl/ a, **-ly** adv herzlich ● n Fruchtsirup m

cordon /'kɔːdn/ n Kordon m ● vt ~ **off** absperren

corduroy /'kɔːdərɔɪ/ n Cordsamt m

core /kɔː(r)/ n Kern m; (of apple, pear) Kerngehäuse nt

cork /kɔːk/ n Kork m; (for bottle) Korken m. ~**screw** n Korkenzieher m

corn¹ /kɔːn/ n Korn nt; (Amer: maize) Mais m

corn² n (Med) Hühnerauge nt

cornea /'kɔːnɪə/ n Hornhaut f

corned beef /kɔːnd'biːf/ n Corned beef nt

corner /'kɔːnə(r)/ n Ecke f; (bend) Kurve f; (football) Eckball m ● vt (fig) in die Enge treiben; (Comm) monopolisieren ⟨market⟩. ~**stone** n Eckstein m

cornet /'kɔːnɪt/ n (Mus) Kornett nt; (for ice-cream) [Eis]tüte f

corn: ~**flour** n, (Amer) ~**starch** n Stärkemehl nt

corny /'kɔːnɪ/ a (fam) abgedroschen

coronary /'kɒrənərɪ/ a & n ~ **[thrombosis]** Koronarthrombose f

coronation /kɒrə'neɪʃn/ n Krönung f

coroner /'kɒrənə(r)/ n Beamte(r) m, der verdächtige Todesfälle untersucht

coronet /'kɒrənet/ n Adelskrone f

corporal¹ /'kɔːpərəl/ n (Mil) Stabsunteroffizier m

corporal² a körperlich; ~ **punishment** körperliche Züchtigung f

corporate /'kɔːpərət/ a gemeinschaftlich

corporation /kɔːpə'reɪʃn/ n Körperschaft f; (of town) Stadtverwaltung f

corps /kɔː(r)/ n (pl **corps** /kɔːz/) Korps nt

corpse /kɔːps/ n Leiche f

corpulent /'kɔːpjʊlənt/ a korpulent

corpuscle /'kɔ:pʌsl/ n Blutkörperchen nt

correct /kə'rekt/ a, **-ly** adv richtig; (proper) korrekt ● vt verbessern; (Sch, Typ) korrigieren. ~**ion** /-ekʃn/ n Verbesserung f; (Typ) Korrektur f

correlation /kɒrə'leɪʃn/ n Wechselbeziehung f

correspond /kɒrɪ'spɒnd/ vi entsprechen (**to** dat); ⟨two things:⟩ sich entsprechen; (write) korrespondieren. ~**ence** n Briefwechsel m; (Comm) Korrespondenz f. ~**ent** n Korrespondent(in) m(f). ~**ing** a, **-ly** adv entsprechend

corridor /'kɒrɪdɔ:(r)/ n Gang m; (Pol, Aviat) Korridor m

corroborate /kə'rɒbəreɪt/ vt bestätigen

corro|de /kə'rəʊd/ vt zerfressen ● vi rosten. ~**sion** /-'rəʊʒn/ n Korrosion f

corrugated /'kɒrəgeɪtɪd/ a gewellt. ~ **iron** n Wellblech nt

corrupt /kə'rʌpt/ a korrupt ● vt korrumpieren; (spoil) verderben. ~**ion** /-ʌpʃn/ n Korruption f

corset /'kɔ:sɪt/ n & **-s** pl Korsett nt

Corsica /'kɔ:sɪkə/ n Korsika nt

cortège /kɔ:'teɪʒ/ n **[funeral]** ~ Leichenzug m

cosh /kɒʃ/ n Totschläger m

cosmetic /kɒz'metɪk/ a kosmetisch ● n ~**s** pl Kosmetik pl

cosmic /'kɒzmɪk/ a kosmisch

cosmonaut /'kɒzmənɔ:t/ n Kosmonaut(in) m(f)

cosmopolitan /kɒzmə'pɒlɪtən/ a kosmopolitisch

cosmos /'kɒzmɒs/ n Kosmos m

cosset /'kɒsɪt/ vt verhätscheln

cost /kɒst/ n Kosten pl; ~**s** pl (Jur) Kosten; **at all** ~**s** um jeden Preis; **I learnt to my** ~ es ist mich teuer zu stehen gekommen ● vt (pt/pp **cost**) kosten; **it** ~ **me £20** es hat mich £20 gekostet ● vt (pt/pp **costed**) ~ **[out]** die Kosten kalkulieren für

costly /'kɒstlɪ/ a (**-ier, -iest**) teuer

cost: ~ **of 'living** n Lebenshaltungskosten pl. ~ **price** n Selbstkostenpreis m

costume /'kɒstjuːm/ n Kostüm nt; (national) Tracht f. ~ **jewellery** n Modeschmuck m

cosy /'kəʊzɪ/ a (**-ier, -iest**) gemütlich ● n (tea-, egg-) Wärmer m

cot /kɒt/ n Kinderbett nt; (Amer: camp-bed) Feldbett nt

cottage /'kɒtɪdʒ/ n Häuschen nt. ~ 'cheese n Hüttenkäse m

cotton /'kɒtn/ n Baumwolle f; (thread) Nähgarn nt ● a baumwollen ● vi ~ **on** (fam) kapieren

cotton 'wool n Watte f

couch /kaʊtʃ/ n Liege f

couchette /ku:'ʃet/ n (Rail) Liegeplatz m

cough /kɒf/ n Husten m ● vi husten. ~ **up** vt/i husten; (fam: pay) blechen

'cough mixture n Hustensaft m

could /kʊd, unbetont kəd/ see **can**[2]

council /'kaʊnsl/ n Rat m; (Admin) Stadtverwaltung f; (rural) Gemeindeverwaltung f. ~ **house** n ≈ Sozialwohnung f

councillor /'kaʊnsələ(r)/ n Stadtverordnete(r) m/f

'council tax n Gemeindesteuer f

counsel /'kaʊnsl/ n Rat m; (Jur) Anwalt m ● vt (pt/pp **counselled**) beraten. ~**lor** n Berater(in) m(f)

count[1] /kaʊnt/ n Graf m

count[2] n Zählung f; **keep** ~ zählen ● vt/i zählen. ~ **on** vt rechnen auf (+ acc)

countenance /'kaʊntənəns/ n Gesicht nt ● vt dulden

counter[1] /'kaʊntə(r)/ n (in shop) Ladentisch m; (in bank) Schalter m; (in café) Theke f; (Games) Spielmarke f

counter[2] adv ~ **to** gegen (+ acc) ● a Gegen- ● vt/i kontern

counter'act vt entgegenwirken (+ dat)

'counter-attack n Gegenangriff m

counter-'espionage n Spionageabwehr f

'counterfeit /-fɪt/ a gefälscht ● n Fälschung f ● vt fälschen

'counterfoil n Kontrollabschnitt m

'counterpart n Gegenstück nt

counter-pro'ductive a **be** ~ das Gegenteil bewirken

'countersign vt gegenzeichnen

countess /'kaʊntɪs/ n Gräfin f

countless /'kaʊntlɪs/ a unzählig

countrified /'kʌntrɪfaɪd/ a ländlich

country /'kʌntrɪ/ n Land nt; (native land) Heimat f; (countryside) Landschaft f; **in the** ~ auf dem Lande. ~**man** n **[fellow]** ~**man** Landsmann m. ~**side** n Landschaft f

county /'kaʊntɪ/ n Grafschaft f

coup /kuː/ n (Pol) Staatsstreich m

couple /'kʌpl/ n Paar nt; **a ~ of** (two) zwei ● vt verbinden; (Rail) koppeln

coupon /'kuːpɒn/ n Kupon m; (voucher) Gutschein m; (entry form) Schein m

courage /'kʌrɪdʒ/ n Mut m. **~ous** /kə'reɪdʒəs/ a, **-ly** adv mutig

courgettes /kʊə'ʒets/ npl Zucchini pl

courier /'kʊrɪə(r)/ n Bote m; (diplomatic) Kurier m; (for tourists) Reiseleiter(in) m(f)

course /kɔːs/ n (Naut, Sch) Kurs m; (Culin) Gang m; (for golf) Platz m; **~ of treatment** (Med) Kur f; **of ~** natürlich, selbstverständlich; **in the ~ of** im Lauf[e] (+ gen)

court /kɔːt/ n Hof m; (Sport) Platz m; (Jur) Gericht nt ● vt werben um; herausfordern ⟨danger⟩

courteous /'kɜːtɪəs/ a, **-ly** adv höflich

courtesy /'kɜːtəsɪ/ n Höflichkeit f

court: ~ 'martial n (pl **~s martial**) Militärgericht nt. **~ shoes** npl Pumps pl. **~yard** n Hof m

cousin /'kʌzn/ n Vetter m, Cousin m; (female) Kusine f

cove /kəʊv/ n kleine Bucht f

cover /'kʌvə(r)/ n Decke f; (of cushion) Bezug m; (of umbrella) Hülle f; (of typewriter) Haube f; (of book, lid) Deckel m; (of magazine) Umschlag m; (protection) Deckung f, Schutz m; **take ~** Deckung nehmen; **under separate ~** mit getrennter Post ● vt bedecken; beziehen ⟨cushion⟩; decken ⟨costs, needs⟩; zurücklegen ⟨distance⟩; (Journ) berichten über (+ acc); (insure) versichern. **~ up** vt zudecken; (fig) vertuschen

coverage /'kʌvərɪdʒ/ n (Journ) Berichterstattung f (**of** über + acc)

cover: ~ charge n Gedeck nt. **~ing** n Decke f; (for floor) Belag m. **~-up** n Vertuschung f

covet /'kʌvɪt/ vt begehren

cow /kaʊ/ n Kuh f

coward /'kaʊəd/ n Feigling m. **~ice** /-ɪs/ n Feigheit f. **~ly** a feige

'cowboy n Cowboy m; (fam) unsolider Handwerker m

cower /'kaʊə(r)/ vi sich [ängstlich] ducken

'cowshed n Kuhstall m

cox /kɒks/ n, **coxswain** /'kɒksn/ n Steuermann m

coy /kɔɪ/ a (**-er, -est**) gespielt schüchtern

crab /kræb/ n Krabbe f. **~-apple** n Holzapfel m

crack /kræk/ n Riß m; (in china, glass) Sprung m; (noise) Knall m; (fam: joke) Witz m; (fam: attempt) Versuch m ● a (fam) erstklassig ● vt knacken ⟨nut, code⟩; einen Sprung machen in (+ acc) ⟨china, glass⟩; (fam) reißen ⟨joke⟩; (fam) lösen ⟨problem⟩ ● vi ⟨china, glass:⟩ springen; ⟨whip:⟩ knallen. **~ down** vi (fam) durchgreifen

cracked /krækt/ a gesprungen; ⟨rib⟩ angebrochen; (fam: crazy) verrückt

cracker /'krækə(r)/ n (biscuit) Kräcker m; (firework) Knallkörper m; **[Christmas] ~** Knallbonbon m. **~s** a **be ~s** (fam) einen Knacks haben

crackle /'krækl/ vi knistern

cradle /'kreɪdl/ n Wiege f

craft¹ /krɑːft/ n inv (boat) [Wasser]fahrzeug nt

craft² n Handwerk nt; (technique) Fertigkeit f. **~sman** n Handwerker m

crafty /'krɑːftɪ/ a (**-ier, -iest**), **-ily** adv gerissen

crag /kræg/ n Felszacken m. **~gy** a felsig; ⟨face⟩ kantig

cram /kræm/ v (pt/pp **crammed**) ● vt hineinstopfen (**into** in + acc); vollstopfen (**with** mit) ● vi (for exams) pauken

cramp /kræmp/ n Krampf m. **~ed** a eng

crampon /'kræmpən/ n Steigeisen nt

cranberry /'krænbərɪ/ n (Culin) Preiselbeere f

crane /kreɪn/ n Kran m; (bird) Kranich m ● vt **~ one's neck** den Hals recken

crank¹ /kræŋk/ n (fam) Exzentriker m

crank² n (Techn) Kurbel f. **~shaft** n Kurbelwelle f

cranky /'kræŋkɪ/ a exzentrisch; (Amer: irritable) reizbar

cranny /'krænɪ/ n Ritze f

crash /kræʃ/ n (noise) Krach m; (Auto) Zusammenstoß m; (Aviat) Absturz m ● vi krachen (**into** gegen); ⟨cars:⟩ zusammenstoßen; ⟨plane:⟩ abstürzen ● vt einen Unfall haben mit ⟨car⟩

crash: ~ course n Schnellkurs m. **~-helmet** n Sturzhelm m. **~-landing** n Bruchlandung f

crate 329 **crooked**

crate /kreɪt/ n Kiste f
crater /'kreɪtə(r)/ n Krater m
cravat /krə'væt/ n Halstuch nt
crav|e /kreɪv/ vi ~e for sich sehnen nach. ~ing n Gelüst nt
crawl /krɔ:l/ n (Swimming) Kraul nt; **do the ~** kraulen; **at a ~** im Kriechtempo ● vi kriechen; ⟨baby:⟩ krabbeln; ~ **with** wimmeln von. ~er **lane** n (Auto) Kriechspur f
crayon /'kreɪən/ n Wachsstift m; (pencil) Buntstift m
craze /kreɪz/ n Mode f
crazy /'kreɪzɪ/ a (-ier, -iest) verrückt; **be ~ about** verrückt sein nach
creak /kri:k/ n Knarren nt ● vi knarren
cream /kri:m/ n Sahne f; (Cosmetic, Med, Culin) Creme f ● a (colour) cremefarben ● vt (Culin) cremig rühren. ~ '**cheese** n ≈ Quark m. ~**y** a sahnig; (smooth) cremig
crease /kri:s/ n Falte f; (unwanted) Knitterfalte f ● vt falten; (accidentally) zerknittern ● vi knittern. ~-**resistant** a knitterfrei
creat|e /kri:'eɪt/ vt schaffen. ~**ion** /-'eɪʃn/ n Schöpfung f. ~**ive** /-tɪv/ a schöpferisch. ~**or** n Schöpfer m
creature /'kri:tʃə(r)/ n Geschöpf nt
crèche /kreʃ/ n Kinderkrippe f
credentials /krɪ'denʃlz/ npl Beglaubigungsschreiben nt
credibility /kredə'bɪlətɪ/ n Glaubwürdigkeit f
credible /'kredəbl/ a glaubwürdig
credit /'kredɪt/ n Kredit m; (honour) Ehre f ● vt glauben; ~ **s.o. with sth** (Comm) jdm etw gutschreiben; (fig) jdm etw zuschreiben. ~**able** /-əbl/ a lobenswert
credit: ~ **card** n Kreditkarte f. ~**or** n Gläubiger m
creed /kri:d/ n Glaubensbekenntnis nt
creek /kri:k/ n enge Bucht f; (Amer: stream) Bach m
creep /kri:p/ vi (pt/pp **crept**) schleichen ● n (fam) fieser Kerl m; **it gives me the ~s** es ist mir unheimlich. ~**er** n Kletterpflanze f. ~**y** a gruselig
cremat|e /krɪ'meɪt/ vt einäschern. ~**ion** /-eɪʃn/ n Einäscherung f
crematorium /kremə'tɔ:rɪəm/ n Krematorium nt
crêpe /kreɪp/ n Krepp m. ~ **paper** n Kreppapier nt
crept /krept/ see **creep**

crescent /'kresənt/ n Halbmond m
cress /kres/ n Kresse f
crest /krest/ n Kamm m; (coat of arms) Wappen nt
Crete /kri:t/ n Kreta nt
crevasse /krɪ'væs/ n [Gletscher]-spalte f
crevice /'krevɪs/ n Spalte f
crew /kru:/ n Besatzung f; (gang) Bande f. ~ **cut** n Bürstenschnitt m
crib[1] /krɪb/ n Krippe f
crib[2] vt/i (pt/pp **cribbed**) (fam) abschreiben
crick /krɪk/ n ~ **in the neck** steifes Genick nt
cricket[1] /'krɪkɪt/ n (insect) Grille f
cricket[2] n Kricket nt. ~**er** n Kricketspieler m
crime /kraɪm/ n Verbrechen nt; (rate) Kriminalität f
criminal /'krɪmɪnl/ a kriminell, verbrecherisch; ⟨law, court⟩ Straf- ● n Verbrecher m
crimson /'krɪmzn/ a purpurrot
cringe /krɪndʒ/ vi sich [ängstlich] ducken
crinkle /'krɪŋkl/ vt/i knittern
cripple /'krɪpl/ n Krüppel m ● vt zum Krüppel machen; (fig) lahmlegen. ~**d** a verkrüppelt
crisis /'kraɪsɪs/ n (pl -**ses** /-si:z/) Krise f
crisp /krɪsp/ a (-er, -est) knusprig. ~**bread** n Knäckebrot nt. ~**s** npl Chips pl
criss-cross /'krɪs-/ a schräg gekreuzt
criterion /kraɪ'tɪərɪən/ n (pl -**ria** /-rɪə/) Kriterium nt
critic /'krɪtɪk/ n Kritiker m. ~**al** a kritisch. ~**ally** adv kritisch; ~**ally ill** schwer krank
criticism /'krɪtɪsɪzm/ n Kritik f
criticize /'krɪtɪsaɪz/ vt kritisieren
croak /krəʊk/ vi krächzen; ⟨frog:⟩ quaken
crochet /'krəʊʃeɪ/ n Häkelarbeit f ● vt/i häkeln. ~-**hook** n Häkelnadel f
crock /krɒk/ n (fam) **old ~** (person) Wrack m; (car) Klapperkiste f
crockery /'krɒkərɪ/ n Geschirr nt
crocodile /'krɒkədaɪl/ n Krokodil nt
crocus /'krəʊkəs/ n (pl -**es**) Krokus m
crony /'krəʊnɪ/ n Kumpel m
crook /krʊk/ n (stick) Stab m; (fam: criminal) Schwindler m, Gauner m
crooked /'krʊkɪd/ a schief; (bent) krumm; (fam: dishonest) unehrlich

crop /krɒp/ n Feldfrucht f; (harvest) Ernte f; (of bird) Kropf m ● v (pt/pp cropped) ● vt stutzen ● vi ~ up (fam) zur Sprache kommen; (occur) dazwischenkommen

croquet /'krəʊeɪ/ n Krocket nt

croquette /krəʊ'ket/ n Krokette f

cross /krɒs/ a, -ly adv (annoyed) böse (with auf + acc); talk at ~ purposes aneinander vorbeireden ● n Kreuz nt; (Bot, Zool) Kreuzung f; on the ~ schräg ● vt kreuzen (cheque, animals); überqueren (road); ~ oneself sich bekreuzigen; ~ one's arms die Arme verschränken; ~ one's legs die Beine übereinanderschlagen; keep one's fingers ~ed for s.o. jdm die Daumen drücken; it ~ed my mind es fiel mir ein ● vi (go across) hinübergehen/-fahren; (lines:) sich kreuzen. ~ out vt durchstreichen

cross: ~bar n Querlatte f; (on bicycle) Stange f. ~-'country n (Sport) Crosslauf m. ~-ex'amine vt ins Kreuzverhör nehmen. ~-exami'nation n Kreuzverhör m. ~-'eyed a schielend; be ~-eyed schielen. ~fire n Kreuzfeuer nt. ~ing n Übergang m; (sea journey) Überfahrt f. ~-'reference n Querverweis m. ~roads n [Straßen]kreuzung f. ~-'section n Querschnitt m. ~-stitch n Kreuzstich m. ~wise adv quer. ~word n ~word [puzzle] Kreuzworträtsel nt

crotchet /'krɒtʃɪt/ n Viertelnote f

crotchety /'krɒtʃɪtɪ/ a griesgrämig

crouch /kraʊtʃ/ vi kauern

crow /krəʊ/ n Krähe f; as the ~ flies Luftlinie ● vi krähen. ~bar n Brechstange f

crowd /kraʊd/ n [Menschen]menge f ● vi sich drängen. ~ed /'kraʊdɪd/ a [gedrängt] voll

crown /kraʊn/ n Krone f ● vt krönen; überkronen (tooth)

crucial /'kru:ʃl/ a höchst wichtig; (decisive) entscheidend (to für)

crucifix /'kru:sɪfɪks/ n Kruzifix nt

crucif|ixion /kru:sɪ'fɪkʃn/ n Kreuzigung f. ~y /'kru:sɪfaɪ/ vt (pt/pp -ied) kreuzigen

crude /kru:d/ a (-r, -st) (raw) roh

cruel /'kru:əl/ a (crueller, cruellest), -ly adv grausam (to gegen). ~ty n Grausamkeit f; ~ty to animals Tierquälerei f

cruis|e /kru:z/ n Kreuzfahrt f ● vi kreuzen; (car:) fahren. ~er n (Mil) Kreuzer m; (motor boat) Kajütboot nt. ~ing speed n Reisegeschwindigkeit f

crumb /krʌm/ n Krümel m

crumb|le /'krʌmbl/ vt/i krümeln; (collapse) einstürzen. ~ly a krümelig

crumple /'krʌmpl/ vt zerknittern ● vi knittern

crunch /krʌntʃ/ n (fam) when it comes to the ~ wenn es [wirklich] drauf ankommt ● vt mampfen ● vi knirschen

crusade /kru:'seɪd/ n Kreuzzug m; (fig) Kampagne f. ~r n Kreuzfahrer m; (fig) Kämpfer m

crush /krʌʃ/ n (crowd) Gedränge nt ● vt zerquetschen; zerknittern (clothes); (fig: subdue) niederschlagen

crust /krʌst/ n Kruste f

crutch /krʌtʃ/ n Krücke f

crux /krʌks/ n (fig) springender Punkt m

cry /kraɪ/ n Ruf m; (shout) Schrei m; a far ~ from (fig) weit entfernt von ● vi (pt/pp cried) (weep) weinen; (baby:) schreien; (call) rufen

crypt /krɪpt/ n Krypta f. ~ic a rätselhaft

crystal /'krɪstl/ n Kristall m; (glass) Kristall nt. ~lize vi [sich] kristallisieren

cub /kʌb/ n (Zool) Junge(s) nt; C~ [Scout] Wölfling m

Cuba /'kju:bə/ n Kuba nt

cubby-hole /'kʌbɪ-/ n Fach nt

cub|e /kju:b/ n Würfel m. ~ic a Kubik-

cubicle /'kju:bɪkl/ n Kabine f

cuckoo /'kʊku:/ n Kuckuck m. ~ clock n Kuckucksuhr f

cucumber /'kju:kʌmbə(r)/ n Gurke f

cuddl|e /'kʌdl/ vt herzen ● vi ~e up to sich kuscheln an (+ acc). ~y a kuschelig. ~y 'toy n Plüschtier nt

cudgel /'kʌdʒl/ n Knüppel m

cue[1] /kju:/ n Stichwort nt

cue[2] n (Billiards) Queue nt

cuff /kʌf/ n Manschette f; (Amer: turn-up) [Hosen]aufschlag m; (blow) Klaps m; off the ~ (fam) aus dem Stegreif ● vt einen Klaps geben (+ dat). ~-link n Manschettenknopf m

cul-de-sac /'kʌldəsæk/ n Sackgasse f

culinary /'kʌlmərɪ/ a kulinarisch
cull /kʌl/ vt pflücken ⟨flowers⟩; (kill)
ausmerzen
culminat|e /'kʌlmɪneɪt/ vi gipfeln
(**in** in + dat). **~ion** /-'neɪʃn/ n Gip-
felpunkt m
culottes /kju:'lɒts/ npl Hosenrock m
culprit /'kʌlprɪt/ n Täter m
cult /kʌlt/ n Kult m
cultivate /'kʌltɪveɪt/ vt anbauen
⟨crop⟩; bebauen ⟨land⟩
cultural /'kʌltʃərəl/ a kulturell
culture /'kʌltʃə(r)/ n Kultur f. **~d** a
kultiviert
cumbersome /'kʌmbəsəm/ a hin-
derlich; (unwieldy) unhandlich
cumulative /'kju:mjʊlətɪv/ a kumu-
lativ
cunning /'kʌnɪŋ/ a listig ● n List f
cup /kʌp/ n Tasse f; (prize) Pokal m
cupboard /'kʌbəd/ n Schrank m
Cup 'Final n Pokalendspiel nt
Cupid /'kju:pɪd/ n Amor m
curable /'kjʊərəbl/ a heilbar
curate /'kjʊərət/ n Vikar m; (Roman
Catholic) Kaplan m
curator /kjʊə'reɪtə(r)/ n Kustos m
curb /kɜ:b/ vt zügeln
curdle /'kɜ:dl/ vi gerinnen
cure /kjʊə(r)/ n [Heil]mittel nt ● vt
heilen; (salt) pökeln; (smoke) räu-
chern; gerben ⟨skin⟩
curfew /'kɜ:fju:/ n Ausgangssperre f
curio /'kjʊərɪəʊ/ n Kuriosität f
curiosity /kjʊərɪ'ɒsətɪ/ n Neugier f;
(object) Kuriosität f
curious /'kjʊərɪəs/ a, -ly adv neugierig; (strange) merkwürdig, seltsam
curl /kɜ:l/ n Locke f ● vt locken ● vi
sich locken. **~ up** vi sich zusammenrollen
curler /'kɜ:lə(r)/ n Lockenwickler m
curly /'kɜ:lɪ/ a (-ier, -iest) lockig
currant /'kʌrənt/ n (dried) Korinthe
f
currency /'kʌrənsɪ/ n Geläufigkeit f;
(money) Währung f; **foreign ~**
Devisen pl
current /'kʌrənt/ a augenblicklich,
gegenwärtig; (in general use) geläufig, gebräuchlich ● n Strömung f;
(Electr) Strom m. **~ affairs or
events** npl Aktuelle(s) nt. **~ly** adv
zur Zeit
curriculum /kə'rɪkjʊləm/ n Lehrplan m. **~ vitae** /-'vi:taɪ/ n Lebens-
lauf m

curry /'kʌrɪ/ n Curry nt & m; (meal)
Currygericht nt ● vt (pt/pp -ied) **~
favour** sich einschmeicheln (**with** bei)
curse /kɜ:s/ n Fluch m ● vt ver-
fluchen ● vi fluchen
cursory /'kɜ:sərɪ/ a flüchtig
curt /kɜ:t/ a, -ly adv barsch
curtail /kɜ:'teɪl/ vt abkürzen
curtain /'kɜ:tn/ n Vorhang m
curtsy /'kɜ:tsɪ/ n Knicks m ● vi (pt/
pp -ied) knicksen
curve /kɜ:v/ n Kurve f ● vi einen
Bogen machen; **~ to the right/left**
nach rechts/links biegen. **~d** a gebogen
cushion /'kʊʃn/ n Kissen nt ● vt
dämpfen; (protect) beschützen
cushy /'kʊʃɪ/ a (-ier, -iest) (fam)
bequem
custard /'kʌstəd/ n Vanillesoße f
custodian /kʌ'stəʊdɪən/ n Hüter m
custody /'kʌstədɪ/ n Obhut f; (of
child) Sorgerecht nt; (imprisonment)
Haft f
custom /'kʌstəm/ n Brauch m;
(habit) Gewohnheit f; (Comm) Kundschaft f. **~ary** a üblich; (habitual) gewohnt. **~er** n Kunde m/Kundin f
customs /'kʌstəmz/ npl Zoll m. **~
officer** n Zollbeamte(r) m
cut /kʌt/ n Schnitt m; (Med) Schnitt-
wunde f; (reduction) Kürzung f; (in
price) Senkung f; **~ [of meat]**
[Fleisch]stück nt ● vt/i (pt/pp cut, pres
p cutting) schneiden; (mow) mähen;
abheben ⟨cards⟩; (reduce) kürzen;
senken ⟨price⟩; **~ one's finger** sich in
den Finger schneiden; **~ s.o.'s hair** jdm
die Haare schneiden; **~ short** abkürzen. **~ back** vt zurückschneiden;
(fig) einschränken, kürzen. **~ down**
vt fällen; (fig) einschränken. **~ off** vt
abschneiden; (disconnect) abstellen;
be ~ off (Teleph) unterbrochen
werden. **~ out** vt ausschneiden; (delete) streichen; **be ~ out for** (fam)
geeignet sein zu. **~ up** vt zerschneiden; (slice) aufschneiden
'cut-back n Kürzung f, Einschränkung f
cute /kju:t/ a (-r, -st) (fam) niedlich
cut 'glass n Kristall nt
cuticle /'kju:tɪkl/ n Nagelhaut f
cutlery /'kʌtlərɪ/ n Besteck nt
cutlet /'kʌtlɪt/ n Kotelett nt
'cut-price a verbilligt
cutting /'kʌtɪŋ/ a ⟨remark⟩ bissig ● n
(from newspaper) Ausschnitt m; (of
plant) Ableger m

CV abbr of **curriculum vitae**

cyclamen /'sɪkləmən/ n Alpenveilchen nt

cycl|e /'saɪkl/ n Zyklus m; (bicycle) [Fahr]rad nt ● vi mit dem Rad fahren. ∼**ing** n Radfahren nt. ∼**ist** n Radfahrer(in) m(f)

cyclone /'saɪkləʊn/ n Wirbelsturm m

cylind|er /'sɪlɪndə(r)/ n Zylinder m. ∼**rical** /-'lɪndrɪkl/ a zylindrisch

cymbals /'sɪmblz/ npl (Mus) Becken nt

cynic /'sɪnɪk/ n Zyniker m. ∼**al** a, **-ly** adv zynisch. ∼**ism** /-sɪzm/ n Zynismus m

cypress /'saɪprəs/ n Zypresse f

Cyprus /'saɪprəs/ n Zypern nt

cyst /sɪst/ n Zyste f. ∼**itis** /-'taɪtɪs/ n Blasenentzündung f

Czech /tʃek/ a tschechisch ● n Tscheche m/Tschechin f

Czechoslovak /tʃekə'sləʊvæk/ a tschechoslowakisch. ∼**ia** /-'vækɪə/ n die Tschechoslowakei. ∼**ian** /-'vækɪən/ a tschechoslowakisch

D

dab /dæb/ n Tupfer m; (of butter) Klecks m; **a ∼ of** ein bißchen ● vt (pt/pp **dabbed**) abtupfen; betupfen (**with** mit)

dabble /'dæbl/ vi ∼ **in sth** (fig) sich nebenbei mit etw befassen

dachshund /'dækshʊnd/ n Dackel m

dad[dy] /'dæd[i]/ n (fam) Vati m

daddy-'long-legs n [Kohl]schnake f; (Amer: spider) Weberknecht m

daffodil /'dæfədɪl/ n Osterglocke f, gelbe Narzisse f

daft /dɑ:ft/ a (-er, -est) dumm

dagger /'dægə(r)/ n Dolch m; (Typ) Kreuz nt; **be at ∼s drawn** (fam) auf Kriegsfuß stehen

dahlia /'deɪlɪə/ n Dahlie f

daily /'deɪlɪ/ a & adv täglich ● n (newspaper) Tageszeitung f; (fam: cleaner) Putzfrau f

dainty /'deɪntɪ/ a (-ier, -iest) zierlich

dairy /'deərɪ/ n Molkerei f; (shop) Milchgeschäft nt. ∼ **cow** n Milchkuh f. ∼ **products** pl Milchprodukte pl

dais /'deɪɪs/ n Podium nt

daisy /'deɪzɪ/ n Gänseblümchen nt

dale /deɪl/ n (liter) Tal nt

dally /'dælɪ/ vi (pt/pp **-ied**) trödeln

dam /dæm/ n [Stau]damm m ● vt (pt/pp **dammed**) eindämmen

damag|e /'dæmɪdʒ/ n Schaden m (**to** an + dat); ∼**es** pl (Jur) Schadenersatz m ● vt beschädigen; (fig) beeinträchtigen. ∼**ing** a schädlich

damask /'dæməsk/ n Damast m

dame /deɪm/ n (liter) Dame f; (Amer sl) Weib nt

damn /dæm/ a, int & adv (fam) verdammt ● int **I don't care** or **give a ∼** (fam) ich schere mich einen Dreck darum ● vt verdammen. ∼**ation** /-'neɪʃn/ n Verdammnis f ● int (fam) verdammt!

damp /dæmp/ a (-er, -est) feucht ● n Feuchtigkeit f ● vt = **dampen**

damp|en vt anfeuchten; (fig) dämpfen. ∼**ness** n Feuchtigkeit f

dance /dɑ:ns/ n Tanz m; (function) Tanzveranstaltung f ● vt/i tanzen. ∼**-hall** n Tanzlokal nt. ∼ **music** n Tanzmusik f

dancer /'dɑ:nsə(r)/ n Tänzer(in) m(f)

dandelion /'dændɪlaɪən/ n Löwenzahn m

dandruff /'dændrʌf/ n Schuppen pl

Dane /deɪn/ n Däne m/Dänin f; **Great ∼** [deutsche] Dogge f

danger /'deɪndʒə(r)/ n Gefahr f; **in/ out of ∼** in/außer Gefahr. ∼**ous** /-rəs/ a, **-ly** adv gefährlich; ∼**ously ill** schwer erkrankt

dangle /'dæŋgl/ vi baumeln ● vt baumeln lassen

Danish /'deɪnɪʃ/ a dänisch. ∼ **'pastry** n Hefeteilchen nt, Plunderstück nt

dank /dæŋk/ a (-er, -est) naßkalt

Danube /'dænju:b/ n Donau f

dare /deə(r)/ n Mutprobe f ● vt/i (challenge) herausfordern (**to** zu); ∼ **[to] do sth** [es] wagen, etw zu tun; **I ∼ say!** das mag wohl sein! ∼**devil** n Draufgänger m

daring /'deərɪŋ/ a verwegen ● n Verwegenheit f

dark /dɑ:k/ a (-er, -est) dunkel; ∼ **blue/brown** dunkelblau/-braun; ∼ **horse** (fig) stilles Wasser nt; **keep sth ∼** (fig) etw geheimhalten ● n Dunkelheit f; **after ∼** nach Einbruch der Dunkelheit; **in the ∼** im Dunkeln; **keep in the ∼** (fig) im dunkeln lassen

dark|en /'dɑ:kn/ vt verdunkeln ● vi dunkler werden. ∼**ness** n Dunkelheit f '**dark-room** *n* Dunkelkammer *f*

darling /'dɑ:lɪŋ/ *a* allerliebst ● *n* Liebling *m*

darn /dɑ:n/ *vt* stopfen. ∼**ing-needle** *n* Stopfnadel *f*

dart /dɑ:t/ *n* Pfeil *m*; (*Sewing*) Abnäher *m*; ∼**s** *sg* (*game*) [Wurf]-pfeil *m* ● *vi* flitzen

dash /dæʃ/ *n* (*Typ*) Gedankenstrich *m*; (*in Morse*) Strich *m*; **a** ∼ **of milk** ein Schuß Milch; **make a** ∼ losstürzen (**for** auf + *acc*) ● *vi* rennen ● *vt* schleudern. ∼ **off** *vi* losstürzen ● *vt* (*write quickly*) hinwerfen

'**dashboard** *n* Armaturenbrett *nt*

dashing /'dæʃɪŋ/ *a* schneidig

data /'deɪtə/ *npl* & *sg* Daten *pl*. ∼ **processing** *n* Datenverarbeitung *f*

date[1] /deɪt/ *n* (*fruit*) Dattel *f*

date[2] *n* Datum *nt*; (*fam*) Verabredung *f*; **to** ∼ bis heute; **out of** ∼ überholt; (*expired*) ungültig; **be up to** ∼ auf dem laufenden sein ● *vt/i* datieren; (*Amer, fam: go out with*) ausgehen mit; ∼ **back to** zurückgehen auf (+ *acc*)

dated /'deɪtɪd/ *a* altmodisch

'**date-line** *n* Datumsgrenze *f*

dative /'deɪtɪv/ *a* & *n* (*Gram*) ∼ [**case**] Dativ *m*

daub /dɔ:b/ *vt* beschmieren (**with** mit); schmieren (*paint*)

daughter /'dɔ:tə(r)/ *n* Tochter *f*. ∼**-in-law** *n* (*pl* ∼**s-in-law**) Schwiegertochter *f*

daunt /dɔ:nt/ *vt* entmutigen; **nothing** ∼**ed** unverzagt. ∼**less** *a* furchtlos

dawdle /'dɔ:dl/ *vi* trödeln

dawn /dɔ:n/ *n* Morgendämmerung *f*; **at** ∼ bei Tagesanbruch ● *vi* anbrechen; **it** ∼**ed on me** (*fig*) es ging mir auf

day /deɪ/ *n* Tag *m*; ∼ **by** ∼ Tag für Tag; ∼ **after** ∼ Tag um Tag; **these** ∼**s** heutzutage; **in those** ∼**s** zu der Zeit; **it's had its** ∼ (*fam*) es hat ausgedient

day: ∼**break** *n* **at** ∼**break** bei Tagesanbruch *m*. ∼**-dream** *n* Tagtraum *m* ● *vi* [mit offenen Augen] träumen. ∼**light** *n* Tageslicht *nt*. ∼ **re'turn** *n* (*ticket*) Tagesrückfahrkarte *f*. ∼**time** *n* **in the** ∼**time** am Tage

daze /deɪz/ *n* **in a** ∼ wie benommen. ∼**d** *a* benommen

dazzle /'dæzl/ *vt* blenden

deacon /'di:kn/ *n* Diakon *m*

dead /ded/ *a* tot; (*flower*) verwelkt; (*numb*) taub; ∼ **body** Leiche *f*; **be** ∼ **on time** auf die Minute pünktlich kommen; ∼ **centre** genau in der Mitte

● *adv* ∼ **tired** todmüde; ∼ **slow** sehr langsam; **stop** ∼ stehenbleiben ● *n* **the** ∼ *pl* die Toten; **in the** ∼ **of night** mitten in der Nacht

deaden /'dedn/ *vt* dämpfen (*sound*); betäuben (*pain*)

dead: ∼ **'end** *n* Sackgasse *f*. ∼ '**heat** *n* totes Rennen *nt*. ∼**line** *n* [letzter] Termin *m*. ∼**lock** *n* **reach** ∼**lock** (*fig*) sich festfahren

deadly /'dedlɪ/ *a* (**-ier, -iest**) tödlich; (*fam: dreary*) sterbenslangweilig; ∼ **sins** *pl* Todsünden *pl*

deaf /def/ *a* (**-er, -est**) taub; ∼ **and dumb** taubstumm. ∼**-aid** *n* Hörgerät *nt*

deaf|en /'defn/ *vt* betäuben; (*permanently*) taub machen. ∼**ening** *a* ohrenbetäubend. ∼**ness** *n* Taubheit *f*

deal /di:l/ *n* (*transaction*) Geschäft *nt*; **whose** ∼? (*Cards*) wer gibt? **a good** *or* **great** ∼ eine Menge; **get a raw** ∼ (*fam*) sehr schlecht abschneiden ● *v* (*pt/pp* **dealt** /delt/) ● *vt* (*Cards*) geben; ∼ **out** austeilen; ∼ **s.o. a blow** jdm einen Schlag versetzen ● *vi* ∼ **in** handeln mit; ∼ **with** zu tun haben mit; (*handle*) sich befassen mit; (*cope with*) fertig werden mit; (*be about*) handeln von; **that's been dealt with** das ist schon erledigt

deal|er /'di:lə(r)/ *n* Händler *m*; (*Cards*) Kartengeber *m*. ∼**ings** *npl* **have** ∼**ings with** zu tun haben mit

dean /di:n/ *n* Dekan *m*

dear /dɪə(r)/ *a* (**-er, -est**) lieb; (*expensive*) teuer; (*in letter*) liebe(r,s)/(*formal*) sehr geehrte(r,s) ● *n* Liebe(r) *m/f* ● *int* **oh** ∼! oje! ∼**ly** *adv* (*love*) sehr; (*pay*) teuer

dearth /dɜ:θ/ *n* Mangel *m* (**of** an + *dat*)

death /deθ/ *n* Tod *m*; **three** ∼**s** drei Todesfälle. ∼ **certificate** *n* Sterbeurkunde *f*. ∼ **duty** *n* Erbschaftssteuer *f*

deathly *a* ∼ **silence** Totenstille *f* ● *adv* ∼ **pale** totenblaß

death: ∼ **penalty** *n* Todesstrafe *f*. ∼**'s head** *n* Totenkopf *m*. ∼**-trap** *n* Todesfalle *f*

debar /dɪ'bɑ:(r)/ *vt* (*pt/pp* **debarred**) ausschließen

debase /dɪ'beɪs/ *vt* erniedrigen

debatable /dɪ'beɪtəbl/ *a* strittig

debate /dɪ'beɪt/ *n* Debatte *f* ● *vt/i* debattieren

debauchery /dɪˈbɔːtʃərɪ/ n Ausschweifung f

debility /dɪˈbɪlətɪ/ n Entkräftung f

debit /ˈdebɪt/ n Schuldbetrag m; ~ **[side]** Soll nt ● vt (pt/pp **debited**) (Comm) belasten; abbuchen ⟨sum⟩

debris /ˈdebriː/ n Trümmer pl

debt /det/ n Schuld f; **in** ~ verschuldet. ~**or** n Schuldner m

début /ˈdeɪbuː/ n Debüt nt

decade /ˈdekeɪd/ n Jahrzehnt nt

decaden|ce /ˈdekədəns/ n Dekadenz f. ~**t** a dekadent

decaffeinated /diːˈkæfɪneɪtɪd/ a koffeinfrei

decant /dɪˈkænt/ vt umfüllen. ~**er** n Karaffe f

decapitate /dɪˈkæpɪteɪt/ vt köpfen

decay /dɪˈkeɪ/ n Verfall m; (rot) Verwesung f; (of tooth) Zahnfäule f ● vi verfallen; (rot) verwesen; ⟨tooth:⟩ schlecht werden

decease /dɪˈsiːs/ n Ableben nt. ~**d** a verstorben ● n **the** ~**d** der/die Verstorbene

deceit /dɪˈsiːt/ n Täuschung f. ~**ful** a, **-ly** adv unaufrichtig

deceive /dɪˈsiːv/ vt täuschen; (be unfaithful to) betrügen

December /dɪˈsembə(r)/ n Dezember m

decency /ˈdiːsənsɪ/ n Anstand m

decent /ˈdiːsənt/ a, **-ly** adv anständig

decentralize /diːˈsentrəlaɪz/ vt dezentralisieren

decept|ion /dɪˈsepʃn/ n Täuschung f; (fraud) Betrug m. ~**ive** /-tɪv/ a, **-ly** adv täuschend

decibel /ˈdesɪbel/ n Dezibel nt

decide /dɪˈsaɪd/ vt entscheiden ● vi sich entscheiden (**on** für)

decided /dɪˈsaɪdɪd/ a, **-ly** adv entschieden

deciduous /dɪˈsɪdjʊəs/ a ~ **tree** Laubbaum m

decimal /ˈdesɪml/ a Dezimal- ● n Dezimalzahl f. ~ **'point** n Komma nt. ~ **system** n Dezimalsystem nt

decimate /ˈdesɪmeɪt/ vt dezimieren

decipher /dɪˈsaɪfə(r)/ vt entziffern

decision /dɪˈsɪʒn/ n Entscheidung f; (firmness) Entschlossenheit f

decisive /dɪˈsaɪsɪv/ a ausschlaggebend; (firm) entschlossen

deck¹ /dek/ vt schmücken

deck² n (Naut) Deck nt; **on** ~ an Deck; **top** ~ (of bus) Oberdeck nt; ~ **of cards**

(Amer) [Karten]spiel nt. ~**-chair** n Liegestuhl m

declaration /dekləˈreɪʃn/ n Erklärung f

declare /dɪˈkleə(r)/ vt erklären; angeben ⟨goods⟩; **anything to** ~? etwas zu verzollen?

declension /dɪˈklenʃn/ n Deklination f

decline /dɪˈklaɪn/ n Rückgang m; (in health) Verfall m ● vt ablehnen; (Gram) deklinieren ● vi ablehnen; (fall) sinken; (decrease) nachlassen

decode /diːˈkəʊd/ vt entschlüsseln

decompos|e /diːkəmˈpəʊz/ vi sich zersetzen

décor /ˈdeɪkɔː(r)/ n Ausstattung f

decorat|e /ˈdekəreɪt/ vt (adorn) schmücken; verzieren ⟨cake⟩; (paint) streichen; (wallpaper) tapezieren; (award medal to) einen Orden verleihen (+ dat). ~**ion** /-ˈreɪʃn/ n Verzierung f; (medal) Orden m; ~**ions** pl Schmuck m. ~**ive** /-rətɪv/ a dekorativ. ~**or** n **painter and** ~**or** Maler und Tapezierer m

decorous /ˈdekərəs/ a, **-ly** adv schamhaft

decorum /dɪˈkɔːrəm/ n Anstand m

decoy¹ /ˈdiːkɔɪ/ n Lockvogel m

decoy² /dɪˈkɔɪ/ vt locken

decrease¹ /ˈdiːkriːs/ n Verringerung f; (in number) Rückgang m; **be on the** ~ zurückgehen

decrease² /dɪˈkriːs/ vt verringern; herabsetzen ⟨price⟩ ● vi sich verringern; ⟨price:⟩ sinken

decree /dɪˈkriː/ n Erlaß m ● vt (pt/pp **decreed**) verordnen

decrepit /dɪˈkrepɪt/ a altersschwach

dedicat|e /ˈdedɪkeɪt/ vt widmen; (Relig) weihen. ~**ed** a hingebungsvoll; ⟨person⟩ aufopfernd. ~**ion** /-ˈkeɪʃn/ n Hingabe f; (in book) Widmung f

deduce /dɪˈdjuːs/ vt folgern (**from** aus)

deduct /dɪˈdʌkt/ vt abziehen

deduction /dɪˈdʌkʃn/ n Abzug m; (conclusion) Folgerung f

deed /diːd/ n Tat f; (Jur) Urkunde f

deem /diːm/ vt halten für

deep /diːp/ a (**-er, -est**), **-ly** adv tief; **go off the** ~ **end** (fam) auf die Palme gehen ● adv tief

deepen /ˈdiːpn/ vt vertiefen ● vi tiefer werden; (fig) sich vertiefen

deep-'freeze *n* Gefriertruhe *f*; (*upright*) Gefrierschrank *m*

deer /dɪə(r)/ *n inv* Hirsch *m*; (*roe*) Reh *nt*

deface /dɪ'feɪs/ *vt* beschädigen

defamat|ion /defə'meɪʃn/ *n* Verleumdung *f*. **~ory** /dɪ'fæmətərɪ/ *a* verleumderisch

default /dɪ'fɔːlt/ *n* (*Jur*) Nichtzahlung *f*; (*failure to appear*) Nichterscheinen *nt*; **win by ~** (*Sport*) kampflos gewinnen ● *vi* nicht zahlen; nicht erscheinen

defeat /dɪ'fiːt/ *n* Niederlage *f*; (*defeating*) Besiegung *f*; (*rejection*) Ablehnung *f* ● *vt* besiegen; ablehnen; (*frustrate*) vereiteln

defect[1] /dɪ'fekt/ *vi* (*Pol*) überlaufen

defect[2] /'diːfekt/ *n* Fehler *m*; (*Techn*) Defekt *m*. **~ive** /dɪ'fektɪv/ *a* fehlerhaft; (*Techn*) schadhaft

defence /dɪ'fens/ *n* Verteidigung *f*. **~less** *a* wehrlos

defend /dɪ'fend/ *vt* verteidigen; (*justify*) rechtfertigen. **~ant** *n* (*Jur*) Beklagte(r) *m/f*; (*in criminal court*) Angeklagte(r) *m/f*

defensive /dɪ'fensɪv/ *a* defensiv ● *n* Defensive *f*

defer /dɪ'fɜː(r)/ *vt* (*pt/pp* **deferred**) (*postpone*) aufschieben; **~ to s.o.** sich jdm fügen

deferen|ce /'defərəns/ *n* Ehrerbietung *f*. **~tial** /-'renʃl/ *a*, **-ly** *adv* ehrerbietig

defian|ce /dɪ'faɪəns/ *n* Trotz *m*; **in ~ce of** zum Trotz (+ *dat*). **~t** *a*, **-ly** *adv* aufsässig

deficien|cy /dɪ'fɪʃənsɪ/ *n* Mangel *m*. **~t** *a* mangelhaft; **he is ~t in ...** ihm mangelt es an ... (*dat*)

deficit /'defɪsɪt/ *n* Defizit *nt*

defile /dɪ'faɪl/ *vt* (*fig*) schänden

define /dɪ'faɪn/ *vt* bestimmen; definieren (*word*)

definite /'defɪnɪt/ *a*, **-ly** *adv* bestimmt; (*certain*) sicher

definition /defɪ'nɪʃn/ *n* Definition *f*; (*Phot*, *TV*) Schärfe *f*

definitive /dɪ'fɪnətɪv/ *a* endgültig; (*authoritative*) maßgeblich

deflat|e /dɪ'fleɪt/ *vt* die Luft auslassen aus. **~ion** /-eɪʃn/ *n* (*Comm*) Deflation *f*

deflect /dɪ'flekt/ *vt* ablenken

deform|ed /dɪ'fɔːmd/ *a* mißgebildet. **~ity** *n* Mißbildung *f*

defraud /dɪ'frɔːd/ *vt* betrügen (**of** um)

defray /dɪ'freɪ/ *vt* bestreiten

defrost /diː'frɒst/ *vt* entfrosten; abtauen (*fridge*); auftauen (*food*)

deft /deft/ *a* (**-er, -est**), **-ly** *adv* geschickt. **~ness** *n* Geschicklichkeit *f*

defunct /dɪ'fʌŋkt/ *a* aufgelöst; (*law*) außer Kraft gesetzt

defuse /diː'fjuːz/ *vt* entschärfen

defy /dɪ'faɪ/ *vt* (*pt/pp* **-ied**) trotzen (+ *dat*); widerstehen (+ *dat*) (*attempt*)

degenerate[1] /dɪ'dʒenəreɪt/ *vi* degenerieren; **~ into** (*fig*) ausarten in (+ *acc*)

degenerate[2] /dɪ'dʒenərət/ *a* degeneriert

degrading /dɪ'greɪdɪŋ/ *a* entwürdigend

degree /dɪ'griː/ *n* Grad *m*; (*Univ*) akademischer Grad *m*; **20 ~s** 20 Grad

dehydrate /diː'haɪdreɪt/ *vt* Wasser entziehen (+ *dat*). **~d** /-ɪd/ *a* ausgetrocknet

de-ice /diː'aɪs/ *vt* enteisen

deign /deɪn/ *vi* **~ to do sth** sich herablassen, etw zu tun

deity /'diːɪtɪ/ *n* Gottheit *f*

dejected /dɪ'dʒektɪd/ *a*, **-ly** *adv* niedergeschlagen

delay /dɪ'leɪ/ *n* Verzögerung *f*; (*of train, aircraft*) Verspätung *f*; **without ~** unverzüglich ● *vt* aufhalten; (*postpone*) aufschieben; **be ~ed** (*person:*) aufgehalten werden; (*train, aircraft:*) Verspätung haben ● *vi* zögern

delegate[1] /'delɪgət/ *n* Delegierte(r) *m/f*

delegat|e[2] /'delɪgeɪt/ *vt* delegieren. **~ion** /-'geɪʃn/ *n* Delegation *f*

delet|e /dɪ'liːt/ *vt* streichen. **~ion** /-iːʃn/ *n* Streichung *f*

deliberate[1] /dɪ'lɪbərət/ *a*, **-ly** *adv* absichtlich; (*slow*) bedächtig

deliberat|e[2] /dɪ'lɪbəreɪt/ *vt/i* überlegen. **~ion** /-'reɪʃn/ *n* Überlegung *f*; **with ~ion** mit Bedacht

delicacy /'delɪkəsɪ/ *n* Feinheit *f*; Zartheit *f*; (*food*) Delikatesse *f*

delicate /'delɪkət/ *a* fein; (*fabric, health*) zart; (*situation*) heikel; (*mechanism*) empfindlich

delicatessen /delɪkə'tesn/ *n* Delikatessengeschäft *nt*

delicious /dɪ'lɪʃəs/ *a* köstlich

delight /dɪ'laɪt/ *n* Freude *f* ● *vt* entzücken ● *vi* **~ in** sich erfreuen an

(+ *dat*). **~ed** *a* hocherfreut; **be ~ed** sich sehr freuen. **~ful** *a* reizend

delinquen|cy /dɪˈlɪŋkwənsɪ/ *n* Kriminalität *f*. **~t** *a* straffällig ● *n* Straffällige(r) *m/f*

deli|rious /dɪˈlɪrɪəs/ *a* **be ~rious** im Delirium sein. **~rium** /-rɪəm/ *n* Delirium *nt*

deliver /dɪˈlɪvə(r)/ *vt* liefern; zustellen ⟨*post, newspaper*⟩; halten ⟨*speech*⟩; überbringen ⟨*message*⟩; versetzen ⟨*blow*⟩; ⟨*set free*⟩ befreien; **~ a baby** ein Kind zur Welt bringen. **~ance** *n* Erlösung *f*. **~y** *n* Lieferung *f*; (*of post*) Zustellung *f*; (*Med*) Entbindung *f*; **cash on ~y** per Nachnahme

delta /ˈdeltə/ *n* Delta *nt*

delude /dɪˈluːd/ *vt* täuschen; **~ oneself** sich (*dat*) Illusionen machen

deluge /ˈdeljuːdʒ/ *n* Flut *f*; (*heavy rain*) schwerer Guß *m* ● *vt* überschwemmen

delusion /dɪˈluːʒn/ *n* Täuschung *f*

de luxe /dəˈlʌks/ *a* Luxus-

delve /delv/ *vi* hineingreifen (**into** in + *acc*); (*fig*) eingehen (**into** auf + *acc*)

demand /dɪˈmɑːnd/ *n* Forderung *f*; (*Comm*) Nachfrage *f*; **in ~** gefragt; **on ~** auf Verlangen ● *vt* verlangen, fordern (**of/from** von). **~ing** *a* anspruchsvoll

demarcation /diːmɑːˈkeɪʃn/ *n* Abgrenzung *f*

demean /dɪˈmiːn/ *vt* **~ oneself** sich erniedrigen

demeanour /dɪˈmiːnə(r)/ *n* Verhalten *nt*

demented /dɪˈmentɪd/ *a* verrückt

demise /dɪˈmaɪz/ *n* Tod *m*

demister /diːˈmɪstə(r)/ *n* (*Auto*) Defroster *m*

demo /ˈdeməʊ/ *n* (*pl* **~s**) (*fam*) Demonstration *f*

demobilize /diːˈməʊbɪlaɪz/ *vt* (*Mil*) entlassen

democracy /dɪˈmɒkrəsɪ/ *n* Demokratie *f*

democrat /ˈdeməkræt/ *n* Demokrat *m*. **~ic** /-ˈkrætɪk/ *a*, **-ally** *adv* demokratisch

demo|lish /dɪˈmɒlɪʃ/ *vt* abbrechen; (*destroy*) zerstören. **~lition** /deməˈlɪʃn/ *n* Abbruch *m*

demon /ˈdiːmən/ *n* Dämon *m*

demonstrat|e /ˈdemənstreɪt/ *vt* beweisen; vorführen ⟨*appliance*⟩ ● *vi* (*Pol*) demonstrieren. **~ion**

/-ˈstreɪʃn/ *n* Vorführung *f*; (*Pol*) Demonstration *f*

demonstrative /dɪˈmɒnstrətɪv/ *a* (*Gram*) demonstrativ; **be ~** seine Gefühle zeigen

demonstrator /ˈdemənstreɪtə(r)/ *n* Vorführer *m*; (*Pol*) Demonstrant *m*

demoralize /dɪˈmɒrəlaɪz/ *vt* demoralisieren

demote /dɪˈməʊt/ *vt* degradieren

demure /dɪˈmjʊə(r)/ *a*, **-ly** *adv* sittsam

den /den/ *n* Höhle *f*; (*room*) Bude *f*

denial /dɪˈnaɪəl/ *n* Leugnen *nt*; **official ~** Dementi *nt*

denigrate /ˈdenɪgreɪt/ *vt* herabsetzen

denim /ˈdenɪm/ *n* Jeansstoff *m*; **~s** *pl* Jeans *pl*

Denmark /ˈdenmɑːk/ *n* Dänemark *nt*

denomination /dɪnɒmɪˈneɪʃn/ *n* (*Relig*) Konfession *f*; (*money*) Nennwert *m*

denote /dɪˈnəʊt/ *vt* bezeichnen

denounce /dɪˈnaʊns/ *vt* denunzieren; (*condemn*) verurteilen

dens|e /dens/ *a* (**-r, -st**), **-ly** *adv* dicht; (*fam: stupid*) blöd[e]. **~ity** *n* Dichte *f*

dent /dent/ *n* Delle *f*, Beule *f* ● *vt* einbeulen; **~ed** /-ɪd/ verbeult

dental /ˈdentl/ *a* Zahn-; ⟨*treatment*⟩ zahnärztlich. **~ floss** /flɒs/ *n* Zahnseide *f*. **~ surgeon** *n* Zahnarzt *m*

dentist /ˈdentɪst/ *n* Zahnarzt *m* / -ärztin *f*. **~ry** *n* Zahnmedizin *f*

denture /ˈdentʃə(r)/ *n* Zahnprothese *f*; **~s** *pl* künstliches Gebiß *nt*

denude /dɪˈnjuːd/ *vt* entblößen

denunciation /dɪnʌnsɪˈeɪʃn/ *n* Denunziation *f*; (*condemnation*) Verurteilung *f*

deny /dɪˈnaɪ/ *vt* (*pt/pp* **-ied**) leugnen; (*officially*) dementieren; **~ s.o. sth** jdm etw verweigern

deodorant /diːˈəʊdərənt/ *n* Deodorant *nt*

depart /dɪˈpɑːt/ *vi* abfahren; (*Aviat*) abfliegen; (*go away*) weggehen/-fahren; (*deviate*) abweichen (**from** von)

department /dɪˈpɑːtmənt/ *n* Abteilung *f*; (*Pol*) Ministerium *nt*. **~ store** *n* Kaufhaus *nt*

departure /dɪˈpɑːtʃə(r)/ *n* Abfahrt *f*; (*Aviat*) Abflug *m*; (*from rule*) Abweichung *f*; **new ~** Neuerung *f*

depend /dɪˈpend/ *vi* abhängen (**on** von); (*rely*) sich verlassen (**on** auf

+ *acc*); **it all** ∼s das kommt darauf an.
∼**able** /-əbl/ *a* zuverlässig. ∼**ant** *n*
Abhängige(r) *m/f.* ∼**ence** *n* Abhängigkeit *f.* ∼**ent** *a* abhängig (**on**
von)

depict /dɪ'pɪkt/ *vt* darstellen

depilatory /dɪ'pɪlətərɪ/ *n* Enthaarungsmittel *nt*

deplete /dɪ'pli:t/ *vt* verringern

deplor|able /dɪ'plɔ:rəbl/ *a* bedauerlich. ∼**e** *vt* bedauern

deploy /dɪ'plɔɪ/ *vt* (*Mil*) einsetzen
● *vi* sich aufstellen

depopulate /di:'pɒpjʊleɪt/ *vt* entvölkern

deport /dɪ'pɔ:t/ *vt* deportieren,
ausweisen. ∼**ation** /di:pɔ:'teɪʃn/ *n*
Ausweisung*f*

deportment /dɪ'pɔ:tmənt/ *n* Haltung*f*

depose /dɪ'pəʊz/ *vt* absetzen

deposit /dɪ'pɒzɪt/ *n* Anzahlung *f*;
(*against damage*) Kaution *f*; (*on
bottle*) Pfand *nt*; (*sediment*) Bodensatz *m*; (*Geol*) Ablagerung *f* ● *vt* (*pt/
pp* **deposited**) legen; (*for safety*) deponieren; (*Geol*) ablagern. ∼ **account**
n Sparkonto *nt*

depot /'depəʊ/ *n* Depot *nt*; (*Amer:
railway station*) Bahnhof *m*

deprav|e /dɪ'preɪv/ *vt* verderben.
∼**ed** *a* verkommen. ∼**ity** /-'prævətɪ/
n Verderbtheit*f*

deprecate /'deprəkeɪt/ *vt* mißbilligen

depreciat|e /dɪ'pri:ʃeɪt/ *vi* an Wert
verlieren. ∼**ion** /-'eɪʃn/ *n* Wertminderung*f*; (*Comm*) Abschreibung
f

depress /dɪ'pres/ *vt* deprimieren;
(*press down*) herunterdrücken. ∼**ed**
a deprimiert; ∼**ed area** Notstandsgebiet *nt*. ∼**ing** *a* deprimierend. ∼**ion** /-eʃn/ *n* Vertiefung *f*;
(*Med*) Depression*f*; (*Meteorol*) Tief *nt*

deprivation /deprɪ'veɪʃn/ *n* Entbehrung*f*

deprive /dɪ'praɪv/ *vt* entziehen; ∼
s.o. of sth jdm etw entziehen. ∼**d** *a* benachteiligt

depth /depθ/ *n* Tiefe *f*; **in** ∼ gründlich; **in the** ∼**s of winter** im tiefsten
Winter

deputation /depjʊ'teɪʃn/ *n* Abordnung*f*

deputize /'depjʊtaɪz/ *vi* ∼ **for** vertreten

deputy /'depjʊtɪ/ *n* Stellvertreter *m*
● *attrib* stellvertretend

derail /dɪ'reɪl/ *vt* **be** ∼**ed** entgleisen.
∼**ment** *n* Entgleisung*f*

deranged /dɪ'reɪndʒd/ *a* geistesgestört

derelict /'derəlɪkt/ *a* verfallen;
(*abandoned*) verlassen

deri|de /dɪ'raɪd/ *vt* verhöhnen.
∼**sion** /-'rɪʒn/ *n* Hohn *m*

derisive /dɪ'raɪsɪv/ *a*, **-ly** *adv*
höhnisch

derisory /dɪ'raɪsərɪ/ *a* höhnisch;
⟨*offer*⟩ lächerlich

derivation /derɪ'veɪʃn/ *n* Ableitung
f

derivative /dɪ'rɪvətɪv/ *a* abgeleitet
● *n* Ableitung*f*

derive /dɪ'raɪv/ *vt/i* (*obtain*) gewinnen (**from** aus); **be** ∼**d from**
⟨*word:*⟩ hergeleitet sein aus

dermatologist /dɜ:mə'tɒlədʒɪst/ *n*
Hautarzt *m* /-ärztin*f*

derogatory /dɪ'rɒgətrɪ/ *a* abfällig

derrick /'derɪk/ *n* Bohrturm *m*

derv /dɜ:v/ *n* Diesel[kraftstoff] *m*

descend /dɪ'send/ *vt/i* hinunter-/
heruntergehen; ⟨*vehicle, lift:*⟩ hinunter-/herunterfahren; **be** ∼**ed from**
abstammen von. ∼**ant** *n* Nachkomme
m

descent /dɪ'sent/ *n* Abstieg *m*; (*lineage*) Abstammung*f*

describe /dɪ'skraɪb/ *vt* beschreiben

descrip|tion /dɪ'skrɪpʃn/ *n* Beschreibung *f*; (*sort*) Art *f*. ∼**tive**
/-tɪv/ *a* beschreibend; (*vivid*) anschaulich

desecrat|e /'desɪkreɪt/ *vt* entweihen. ∼**ion** /-'kreɪʃn/ *n* Entweihung*f*

desert[1] /'dezət/ *n* Wüste *f* ● *a* Wüsten-; ∼ **island** verlassene Insel*f*

desert[2] /dɪ'zɜ:t/ *vt* verlassen ● *vi*
desertieren. ∼**ed** *a* verlassen. ∼**er** *n*
(*Mil*) Deserteur *m*. ∼**ion** /-ɜ:ʃn/ *n*
Fahnenflucht*f*

deserts /dɪ'zɜ:ts/ *npl* **get one's** ∼
seinen verdienten Lohn bekommen

deserv|e /dɪ'zɜ:v/ *vt* verdienen.
∼**edly** /-ɪdlɪ/ *adv* verdientermaßen.
∼**ing** *a* verdienstvoll; ∼**ing cause**
guter Zweck *m*

design /dɪ'zaɪn/ *n* Entwurf *m*; (*pattern*) Muster *nt*; (*construction*) Konstruktion *f*; (*aim*) Absicht *f* ● *vt*
entwerfen; (*construct*) konstruieren;
be ∼**ed for** bestimmt sein für

designat|e /'dezɪgneɪt/ vt bezeichnen; (*appoint*) ernennen. ∼**ion** /-'neɪʃn/ n Bezeichnung f

designer /dɪ'zaɪnə(r)/ n Designer m; (*Techn*) Konstrukteur m; (*Theat*) Bühnenbildner m

desirable /dɪ'zaɪrəbl/ a wünschenswert; (*sexually*) begehrenswert

desire /dɪ'zaɪə(r)/ n Wunsch m; (*longing*) Verlangen nt (**for** nach); (*sexual*) Begierde f ● vt [sich (*dat*)] wünschen; (*sexually*) be- gehren

desk /desk/ n Schreibtisch m; (*Sch*) Pult nt; (*Comm*) Kasse f; (*in hotel*) Rezeption f

desolat|e /'desələt/ a trostlos. ∼**ion** /-'leɪʃn/ n Trostlosigkeit f

despair /dɪ'speə(r)/ n Verzweiflung f; **in** ∼ verzweifelt ● vi verzweifeln

desperat|e /'despərət/ a, **-ly** adv verzweifelt; (*urgent*) dringend; **be** ∼**e** ⟨*criminal:*⟩ zum Äußersten entschlossen sein; **be** ∼**e for** dringend brauchen. ∼**ion** /-'reɪʃn/ n Verzweiflung f; **in** ∼**ion** aus Verzweiflung

despicable /dɪ'spɪkəbl/ a verachtenswert

despise /dɪ'spaɪz/ vt verachten

despite /dɪ'spaɪt/ prep trotz (+ gen)

despondent /dɪ'spɒndənt/ a niedergeschlagen

despot /'despɒt/ n Despot m

dessert /dɪ'zɜːt/ n Dessert nt, Nachtisch m. ∼ **spoon** n Dessertlöffel m

destination /destɪ'neɪʃn/ n [Reise]ziel nt; (*of goods*) Bestimmungsort m

destine /'destɪn/ vt bestimmen

destiny /'destɪnɪ/ n Schicksal nt

destitute /'destɪtjuːt/ a völlig mittellos

destroy /dɪ'strɔɪ/ vt zerstören; (*totally*) vernichten. ∼**er** n (*Naut*) Zerstörer m

destruc|tion /dɪ'strʌkʃn/ n Zerstörung f; Vernichtung f. **-tive** /-tɪv/ a zerstörerisch; (*fig*) destruktiv

detach /dɪ'tætʃ/ vt abnehmen; (*tear off*) abtrennen. ∼**able** /-əbl/ a abnehmbar. ∼**ed** a (*fig*) distanziert; ∼**ed house** Einzelhaus nt

detachment /dɪ'tætʃmənt/ n Distanz f; (*objectivity*) Abstand m; (*Mil*) Sonderkommando nt

detail /'diːteɪl/ n Einzelheit f, Detail nt; **in** ∼ ausführlich ● vt einzeln aufführen; (*Mil*) abkommandieren. ∼**ed** a ausführlich

detain /dɪ'teɪn/ vt aufhalten; ⟨*police:*⟩ in Haft behalten; (*take into custody*) in Haft nehmen. ∼**ee** /diːteɪ'niː/ n Häftling m

detect /dɪ'tekt/ vt entdecken; (*perceive*) wahrnehmen. ∼**ion** /-ekʃn/ n Entdeckung f

detective /dɪ'tektɪv/ n Detektiv m. ∼ **story** n Detektivroman m

detector /dɪ'tektə(r)/ n Suchgerät nt; (*for metal*) Metalldetektor m

detention /dɪ'tenʃn/ n Haft f; (*Sch*) Nachsitzen nt

deter /dɪ'tɜː(r)/ vt (pt/pp **deterred**) abschrecken; (*prevent*) abhalten

detergent /dɪ'tɜːdʒənt/ n Waschmittel nt

deteriorat|e /dɪ'tɪərɪəreɪt/ vi sich verschlechtern. ∼**ion** /-'reɪʃn/ n Verschlechterung f

determination /dɪtɜːmɪ'neɪʃn/ n Entschlossenheit f

determine /dɪ'tɜːmɪn/ vt bestimmen; ∼ **to** (*resolve*) sich entschließen zu. ∼**d** a entschlossen

deterrent /dɪ'terənt/ n Abschreckungsmittel nt

detest /dɪ'test/ vt verabscheuen. ∼**able** /-əbl/ a abscheulich

detonat|e /'detəneɪt/ vt zünden ● vi explodieren. ∼**or** n Zünder m

detour /'diːtʊə(r)/ n Umweg m; (*for traffic*) Umleitung f

detract /dɪ'trækt/ vi ∼ **from** beeinträchtigen

detriment /'detrɪmənt/ n **to the** ∼ zum Schaden (**of** gen). ∼**al** /-'mentl/ a schädlich (**to** dat)

deuce /djuːs/ n (*Tennis*) Einstand m

devaluation /diːvæljʊ'eɪʃn/ n Abwertung f

de'value vt abwerten ⟨*currency*⟩

devastat|e /'devəsteɪt/ vt verwüsten. ∼**ed** /-ɪd/ a (*fam*) erschüttert. ∼**ing** a verheerend. ∼**ion** /-'steɪʃn/ n Verwüstung f

develop /dɪ'veləp/ vt entwickeln; bekommen ⟨*illness*⟩; erschließen ⟨*area*⟩ ● vi sich entwickeln (**into** zu). ∼**er** n **[property]** ∼**er** Bodenspekulant m

de'veloping country n Entwicklungsland nt

development /dɪ'veləpmənt/ n Entwicklung f

deviant /'di:vɪənt/ *a* abweichend

deviat|e /'di:vɪeɪt/ *vi* abweichen. **~ion** /-'eɪʃn/ *n* Abweichung *f*

device /dɪ'vaɪs/ *n* Gerät *nt*; (*fig*) Mittel *nt*; **leave s.o. to his own ~s** jdn sich (*dat*) selbst überlassen

devil /'devl/ *n* Teufel *m*. **~ish** *a* teuflisch

devious /'di:vɪəs/ *a* verschlagen; **~ route** Umweg *m*

devise /dɪ'vaɪz/ *vt* sich (*dat*) ausdenken

devoid /dɪ'vɔɪd/ *a* **~ of** ohne

devolution /di:və'lu:ʃn/ *n* Dezentralisierung *f*; (*of power*) Übertragung *f*

devot|e /dɪ'vəʊt/ *vt* widmen (**to** *dat*). **~ed** *a*, **-ly** *adv* ergeben; ⟨*care*⟩ liebevoll; **be ~ed to s.o.** sehr an jdm hängen. **~ee** /devə'ti:/ *n* Anhänger(in) *m(f)*

devotion /dɪ'vəʊʃn/ *n* Hingabe *f*; **~s** *pl* (*Relig*) Andacht *f*

devour /dɪ'vaʊə(r)/ *vt* verschlingen

devout /dɪ'vaʊt/ *a* fromm

dew /dju:/ *n* Tau *m*

dexterity /dek'sterətɪ/ *n* Geschicklichkeit *f*

diabet|es /daɪə'bi:ti:z/ *n* Zuckerkrankheit *f*. **~ic** /-'betɪk/ *a* zuckerkrank ● *n* Zuckerkranke(r) *m/f*, Diabetiker(in) *m(f)*

diabolical /daɪə'bɒlɪkl/ *a* teuflisch

diagnose /daɪəg'nəʊz/ *vt* diagnostizieren

diagnosis /daɪəg'nəʊsɪs/ *n* (*pl* **-oses** /-si:z/) Diagnose *f*

diagonal /daɪ'ægənl/ *a*, **-ly** *adv* diagonal ● *n* Diagonale *f*

diagram /'daɪəgræm/ *n* Diagramm *nt*

dial /'daɪəl/ *n* (*of clock*) Zifferblatt *nt*; (*Techn*) Skala *f*; (*Teleph*) Wählscheibe *f* ● *vt/i* (*pt/pp* **dialled**) (*Teleph*) wählen; **~ direct** durchwählen

dialect /'daɪəlekt/ *n* Dialekt *m*

dialling /'daɪəlɪŋ/ **~ code** *n* Vorwahlnummer *f*. **~ tone** *n* Amtszeichen *nt*

dialogue /'daɪəlɒg/ *n* Dialog *m*

'dial tone *n* (*Amer, Teleph*) Amtszeichen *nt*

diameter /daɪ'æmɪtə(r)/ *n* Durchmesser *m*

diametrically /daɪə'metrɪkəlɪ/ *adv* **~ opposed** genau entgegengesetzt (**to** *dat*)

diamond /'daɪəmənd/ *n* Diamant *m*; (*cut*) Brillant *m*; (*shape*) Raute *f*; **~s** *pl* (*Cards*) Karo *nt*

diaper /'daɪəpə(r)/ *n* (*Amer*) Windel *f*

diaphragm /'daɪəfræm/ *n* (*Anat*) Zwerchfell *nt*; (*Phot*) Blende *f*

diarrhoea /daɪə'ri:ə/ *n* Durchfall *m*

diary /'daɪərɪ/ *n* Tagebuch *nt*; (*for appointments*) [Termin]kalender *m*

dice /daɪs/ *n inv* Würfel *m* ● *vt* (*Culin*) in Würfel schneiden

dicey /'daɪsɪ/ *a* (*fam*) riskant

dictat|e /dɪk'teɪt/ *vt/i* diktieren. **~ion** /-eɪʃn/ *n* Diktat *nt*

dictator /dɪk'teɪtə(r)/ *n* Diktator *m*. **~ial** /-tə'tɔ:rɪəl/ *a* diktatorisch. **~ship** *n* Diktatur *f*

diction /'dɪkʃn/ *n* Aussprache *f*

dictionary /'dɪkʃənrɪ/ *n* Wörterbuch *nt*

did /dɪd/ *see* **do**

didactic /dɪ'dæktɪk/ *a* didaktisch

diddle /'dɪdl/ *vt* (*fam*) übers Ohr hauen

didn't /'dɪdnt/ = **did not**

die[1] /daɪ/ *n* (*Techn*) Prägestempel *m*; (*metal mould*) Gußform *f*

die[2] *vi* (*pres p* **dying**) sterben (**of** an + *dat*); ⟨*plant, animal:*⟩ eingehen; ⟨*flower:*⟩ verwelken; **be dying to do sth** (*fam*) darauf brennen, etw zu tun; **be dying for sth** (*fam*) sich nach etw sehnen. **~ down** *vi* nachlassen; ⟨*fire:*⟩ herunterbrennen. **~ out** *vi* aussterben

diesel /'di:zl/ *n* Diesel *m*. **~ engine** *n* Dieselmotor *m*

diet /'daɪət/ *n* Kost *f*; (*restricted*) Diät *f*; (*for slimming*) Schlankheitskur *f*; **be on a ~** diät leben; eine Schlankheitskur machen ● *vi* diät leben; eine Schlankheitskur machen

dietician /daɪə'tɪʃn/ *n* Diätassistent(in) *m(f)*

differ /'dɪfə(r)/ *vi* sich unterscheiden; (*disagree*) verschiedener Meinung sein

differen|ce /'dɪfrəns/ *n* Unterschied *m*; (*disagreement*) Meinungsverschiedenheit *f*. **~t** *a* andere(r,s); (*various*) verschiedene; **be ~t** anders sein (**from** als)

differential /dɪfə'renʃl/ *a* Differential- ● *n* Unterschied *m*; (*Techn*) Differential *nt*

differentiate /dɪfə'renʃɪeɪt/ *vt/i* unterscheiden (**between** zwischen + *dat*)

differently /'dɪfrəntlɪ/ *adv* anders

difficult /'dɪfɪkəlt/ *a* schwierig, schwer. **~y** *n* Schwierigkeit *f*

diffiden|ce /'dɪfɪdəns/ *n* Zaghaftig-keit *f*. **∼t** *a* zaghaft

diffuse¹ /dɪ'fjuːs/ *a* ausgebreitet; (*wordy*) langatmig

diffuse² /dɪ'fjuːz/ *vt* (*Phys*) streuen

dig /dɪg/ *n* (*poke*) Stoß *m*; (*remark*) spitze Bemerkung *f*; (*Archaeol*) Aus-grabung *f*; **∼s** *pl* (*fam*) möbliertes Zimmer *nt* ● *vt/i* (*pt/pp* **dug**, *pres p* **dig-ging**) graben; umgraben ⟨*garden*⟩; **∼ s.o. in the ribs** jdm einen Rippenstoß geben. **∼ out** *vt* ausgraben. **∼ up** *vt* ausgraben; umgraben ⟨*garden*⟩; aufreißen ⟨*street*⟩

digest¹ /'daɪdʒest/ *n* Kurzfassung *f*

digest² /dɪ'dʒest/ *vt* verdauen. **∼ible** *a* verdaulich. **∼ion** /-estʃn/ *n* Ver-dauung *f*

digger /'dɪgə(r)/ *n* (*Techn*) Bagger *m*

digit /'dɪdʒɪt/ *n* Ziffer *f*; (*finger*) Fin-ger *m*; (*toe*) Zehe *f*

digital /'dɪdʒɪtl/ *a* Digital-; **∼ clock** Digitaluhr *f*

dignified /'dɪgnɪfaɪd/ *a* würdevoll

dignitary /'dɪgnɪtərɪ/ *n* Würden-träger *m*

dignity /'dɪgnɪtɪ/ *n* Würde *f*

digress /daɪ'gres/ *vi* abschweifen. **∼ion** /-eʃn/ *n* Abschweifung *f*

dike /daɪk/ *n* Deich *m*; (*ditch*) Graben *m*

dilapidated /dɪ'læpɪdeɪtɪd/ *a* bau-fällig

dilate /daɪ'leɪt/ *vt* erweitern ● *vi* sich erweitern

dilatory /'dɪlətərɪ/ *a* langsam

dilemma /dɪ'lemə/ *n* Dilemma *nt*

dilettante /dɪlɪ'tæntɪ/ *n* Dilet-tant(in) *m*(*f*)

diligen|ce /'dɪlɪdʒəns/ *n* Fleiß *m*. **∼t** *a*, **-ly** *adv* fleißig

dill /dɪl/ *n* Dill *m*

dilly-dally /'dɪlɪdælɪ/ *vi* (*pt/pp* **-ied**) (*fam*) trödeln

dilute /daɪ'luːt/ *vt* verdünnen

dim /dɪm/ *a* (**dimmer, dimmest**), **-ly** *adv* (*weak*) schwach; (*dark*) trüb[e]; (*indistinct*) undeutlich; (*fam: stupid*) dumm, (*fam*) doof ● *v* (*pt/pp* **dimmed**) ● *vt* dämpfen ● *vi* schwächer werden

dime /daɪm/ *n* (*Amer*) Zehncentstück *nt*

dimension /daɪ'menʃn/ *n* Dimen-sion *f*; **∼s** *pl* Maße *pl*

diminish /dɪ'mɪnɪʃ/ *vt* verringern ● *vi* sich verringern

diminutive /dɪ'mɪnjʊtɪv/ *a* winzig ● *n* Verkleinerungsform *f*

dimple /'dɪmpl/ *n* Grübchen *nt*

din /dɪn/ *n* Krach *m*, Getöse *nt*

dine /daɪn/ *vi* speisen. **∼r** *n* Spei-sende(r) *m*/*f*; (*Amer: restaurant*) Eßlokal *nt*

dinghy /'dɪŋgɪ/ *n* Dinghi *nt*; (*inflat-able*) Schlauchboot *nt*

dingy /'dɪndʒɪ/ *a* (**-ier, -iest**) trübe

dining /'daɪnɪŋ/: **∼-car** *n* Speise-wagen *m*. **∼-room** *n* Eßzimmer *nt*. **∼-table** *n* Eßtisch *m*

dinner /'dɪnə(r)/ *n* Abendessen *nt*; (*at midday*) Mittagessen *nt*; (*formal*) Essen *nt*. **∼-jacket** *n* Smoking *m*

dinosaur /'daɪnəsɔː(r)/ *n* Dino-saurier *m*

dint /dɪnt/ *n* **by ∼ of** durch (+ *acc*)

diocese /'daɪəsɪs/ *n* Diözese *f*

dip /dɪp/ *n* (*in ground*) Senke *f*; (*Culin*) Dip *m*; **go for a ∼** kurz schwimmen gehen ● *v* (*pt/pp* **dipped**) *vt* [ein]tauchen; **∼ one's headlights** (*Auto*) [die Scheinwerfer] abblenden ● *vi* sich senken

diphtheria /dɪf'θɪərɪə/ *n* Diphtherie *f*

diphthong /'dɪfθɒŋ/ *n* Diphthong *m*

diploma /dɪ'pləʊmə/ *n* Diplom *nt*

diplomacy /dɪ'pləʊməsɪ/ *n* Diplo-matie *f*

diplomat /'dɪpləmæt/ *n* Diplomat *m*. **∼ic** /-'mætɪk/ *a*, **-ally** *adv* di-plomatisch

'dip-stick *n* (*Auto*) Ölmeßstab *m*

dire /'daɪə(r)/ *a* (**-r, -st**) bitter; ⟨*situ-ation, consequences*⟩ furchtbar

direct /dɪ'rekt/ *a* & *adv* direkt ● *vt* (*aim*) richten (**at** auf / (*fig*) an + *acc*); (*control*) leiten; (*order*) anweisen; **∼ s.o.** (*show the way*) jdm den Weg sagen; **∼ a film/play** bei einem Film/ Theaterstück Regie führen. **∼ 'cur-rent** *n* Gleichstrom *m*

direction /dɪ'rekʃn/ *n* Richtung *f*; (*control*) Leitung *f*; (*of play, film*) Regie *f*; **∼s** *pl* Anweisungen *pl*; **∼s for use** Gebrauchsanweisung *f*

directly /dɪ'rektlɪ/ *adv* direkt; (*at once*) sofort ● *conj* (*fam*) sobald

director /dɪ'rektə(r)/ *n* (*Comm*) Di-rektor *m*; (*of play, film*) Regisseur *m*

directory /dɪ'rektərɪ/ *n* Verzeichnis *nt*; (*Teleph*) Telefonbuch *nt*

dirt /dɜːt/ *n* Schmutz *m*; (*soil*) Erde *f*; **∼ cheap** (*fam*) spottbillig

dirty /'dɜːtɪ/ *a* (**-ier, -iest**) schmutzig ● *vt* schmutzig machen

dis|a'bility /dɪs-/ n Behinderung f. **~abled** /dɪ'seɪbld/ a [körper]behindert

disad'van|tage n Nachteil m; **at a ~tage** im Nachteil. **~taged** a benachteiligt. **~'tageous** a nachteilig

disaf'fected a unzufrieden; (*disloyal*) illoyal

disa'gree vi nicht übereinstimmen (**with** mit); **I ~** ich bin anderer Meinung; **we ~** wir sind verschiedener Meinung; **oysters ~ with me** Austern bekommen mir nicht

disa'greeable a unangenehm

disa'greement n Meinungsverschiedenheit f

disap'pear vi verschwinden. **~ance** n Verschwinden nt

disap'point vt enttäuschen. **~ment** n Enttäuschung f

disap'proval n Mißbilligung f

disap'prove vi dagegen sein; **~ of** mißbilligen

dis'arm vt entwaffnen ● vi (*Mil*) abrüsten. **~ament** n Abrüstung f. **~ing** a entwaffnend

disar'ray n Unordnung f

disast|er /dɪ'zɑ:stə(r)/ n Katastrophe f; (*accident*) Unglück nt. **~rous** /-rəs/ a katastrophal

dis'band vt auflösen ● vi sich auflösen

disbe'lief n Ungläubigkeit f; **in ~** ungläubig

disc /dɪsk/ n Scheibe f; (*record*) [Schall]platte f; (*CD*) CD f

discard /dɪ'skɑ:d/ vt ablegen; (*throw away*) wegwerfen

discern /dɪ'sɜ:n/ vt wahrnehmen. **~ible** a wahrnehmbar. **~ing** a anspruchsvoll

'discharge¹ n Ausstoßen nt; (*Naut, Electr*) Entladung f; (*dismissal*) Entlassung f; (*Jur*) Freispruch m; (*Med*) Ausfluß m

dis'charge² vt ausstoßen; (*Naut, Electr*) entladen; (*dismiss*) entlassen; (*Jur*) freisprechen ⟨*accused*⟩; **~ a duty** sich einer Pflicht entledigen

disciple /dɪ'saɪpl/ n Jünger m; (*fig*) Schüler m

disciplinary /'dɪsɪplɪnərɪ/ a disziplinarisch

discipline /'dɪsɪplɪn/ n Disziplin f ● vt Disziplin beibringen (+ dat); (*punish*) bestrafen

'disc jockey n Diskjockey m

dis'claim vt abstreiten. **~er** n Verzichterklärung f

dis'clos|e vt enthüllen. **~ure** n Enthüllung f

disco /'dɪskəʊ/ n (*fam*) Disko f

dis'colour vt verfärben ● vi sich verfärben

dis'comfort n Beschwerden pl; (*fig*) Unbehagen nt

disconcert /dɪskən'sɜ:t/ vt aus der Fassung bringen

discon'nect vt trennen; (*Electr*) ausschalten; (*cut supply*) abstellen

disconsolate /dɪs'kɒnsələt/ a untröstlich

discon'tent n Unzufriedenheit f. **~ed** a unzufrieden

discon'tinue vt einstellen; (*Comm*) nicht mehr herstellen

'discord n Zwietracht f; (*Mus & fig*) Mißklang m. **~ant** /dɪ'skɔ:dənt/ a **~ant note** Mißklang m

discothèque /'dɪskətek/ n Diskothek f

'discount¹ n Rabatt m

dis'count² vt außer acht lassen

dis'courage vt entmutigen; (*dissuade*) abraten (+ dat)

'discourse n Rede f

dis'courteous a, **-ly** adv unhöflich

discover /dɪ'skʌvə(r)/ vt entdecken. **~y** n Entdeckung f

dis'credit n Mißkredit m ● vt in Mißkredit bringen

discreet /dɪ'skri:t/ a, **-ly** adv diskret

discrepancy /dɪ'skrepənsɪ/ n Diskrepanz f

discretion /dɪ'skreʃn/ n Diskretion f; (*judgement*) Ermessen nt

discriminat|e /dɪ'skrɪmɪneɪt/ vi unterscheiden (**between** zwischen + dat); **~e against** diskriminieren. **~ing** a anspruchsvoll. **~ion** /-'neɪʃn/ n Diskriminierung f; (*quality*) Urteilskraft f

discus /'dɪskəs/ n Diskus m

discuss /dɪ'skʌs/ vt besprechen; (*examine critically*) diskutieren. **~ion** /-ʌʃn/ n Besprechung f; Diskussion f

disdain /dɪs'deɪn/ n Verachtung f ● vt verachten. **~ful** a verächtlich

disease /dɪ'zi:z/ n Krankheit f. **~d** a krank

disem'bark vi an Land gehen

disen'chant vt ernüchtern. **~ment** n Ernüchterung f

disen'gage vt losmachen; **~ the clutch** (*Auto*) auskuppeln

disen'tangle vt entwirren
dis'favour n Ungnade f; (disapproval) Mißfallen nt
dis'figure vt entstellen
dis'gorge vt ausspeien
dis'grace n Schande f; **in ~** in Ungnade ● vt Schande machen (+ dat). **~ful** a schändlich
disgruntled /dɪsˈɡrʌntld/ a verstimmt
disguise /dɪsˈɡaɪz/ n Verkleidung f; **in ~** verkleidet ● vt verkleiden; verstellen ⟨voice⟩; (conceal) verhehlen
disgust /dɪsˈɡʌst/ n Ekel m; **in ~** empört ● vt anekeln; (appal) empören. **~ing** a eklig; (appalling) abscheulich
dish /dɪʃ/ n Schüssel f; (shallow) Schale f; (small) Schälchen nt; (food) Gericht nt. **~ out** vt austeilen. **~ up** vt auftragen
'dishcloth n Spültuch nt
dis'hearten vt entmutigen. **~ing** a entmutigend
dishevelled /dɪˈʃevld/ a zerzaust
dis'honest a, **-ly** adv unehrlich. **~y** n Unehrlichkeit f
dis'honour n Schande f ● vt entehren; nicht honorieren ⟨cheque⟩. **~able** a, **-bly** adv unehrenhaft
'dishwasher n Geschirrspülmaschine f
disil'lusion vt ernüchtern. **~ment** n Ernüchterung f
disin'fect vt desinfizieren. **~ant** n Desinfektionsmittel nt
disin'herit vt enterben
dis'integrate vi zerfallen
dis'interested a unvoreingenommen; (uninterested) uninteressiert
dis'jointed a unzusammenhängend
disk /dɪsk/ n = **disc**
dis'like n Abneigung f ● vt nicht mögen
dislocate /ˈdɪsləkeɪt/ vt ausrenken; **~ one's shoulder** sich (dat) den Arm auskugeln
dis'lodge vt entfernen
dis'loyal a, **-ly** adv illoyal. **~ty** n Illoyalität f
dismal /ˈdɪzməl/ a trüb[e]; ⟨person⟩ trübselig; (fam: poor) kläglich
dismantle /dɪsˈmæntl/ vt auseinandernehmen; (take down) abbauen
dis'may n Bestürzung f. **~ed** a bestürzt

dis'miss vt entlassen; (reject) zurückweisen. **~al** n Entlassung f; Zurückweisung f
dis'mount vi absteigen
diso'bedien|ce n Ungehorsam m. **~t** a ungehorsam
diso'bey vt/i nicht gehorchen (+ dat); nicht befolgen ⟨rule⟩
dis'order n Unordnung f; (Med) Störung f. **~ly** a unordentlich; **~ly conduct** ungebührliches Benehmen nt
dis'organized a unorganisiert
dis'orientate vt verwirren; **be ~d** die Orientierung verloren haben
dis'own vt verleugnen
disparaging /dɪˈspærɪdʒɪŋ/ a, **-ly** adv abschätzig
disparity /dɪˈspærətɪ/ n Ungleichheit f
dispassionate /dɪˈspæʃənət/ a, **-ly** adv gelassen; (impartial) unparteiisch
dispatch /dɪˈspætʃ/ n (Comm) Versand m; (Mil) Nachricht f; (report) Bericht m; **with ~** prompt ● vt [ab]senden; (deal with) erledigen; (kill) töten. **~-rider** n Meldefahrer m
dispel /dɪˈspel/ vt (pt/pp **dispelled**) vertreiben
dispensable /dɪˈspensəbl/ a entbehrlich
dispensary /dɪˈspensərɪ/ n Apotheke f
dispense /dɪˈspens/ vt austeilen; **~ with** verzichten auf (+ acc). **~r** n Apotheker(in) m(f); (device) Automat m
dispers|al /dɪˈspɜːsl/ n Zerstreuung f. **~e** /dɪˈspɜːs/ vt zerstreuen ● vi sich zerstreuen
dispirited /dɪˈspɪrɪtɪd/ a entmutigt
dis'place vt verschieben; **~d person** Vertriebene(r) m/f
display /dɪˈspleɪ/ n Ausstellung f; (Comm) Auslage f; (performance) Vorführung f ● vt zeigen; ausstellen ⟨goods⟩
dis'please vt mißfallen (+ dat)
dis'pleasure n Mißfallen nt
disposable /dɪˈspəʊzəbl/ a Wegwerf-; ⟨income⟩ verfügbar
disposal /dɪˈspəʊzl/ n Beseitigung f; **be at s.o.'s ~** jdm zur Verfügung stehen
dispose /dɪˈspəʊz/ vi **~ of** beseitigen; (deal with) erledigen; **be well ~d** wohlgesinnt sein (**to** dat)
disposition /dɪspəˈzɪʃn/ n Veranlagung f; (nature) Wesensart f

disproportionate /dɪsprə'pɔːʃənət/ *a*, **-ly** *adv* unverhältnismäßig

dis'prove *vt* widerlegen

dispute /dɪ'spjuːt/ *n* Disput *m*; (*quarrel*) Streit *m* ● *vt* bestreiten

disqualifi'cation *n* Disqualifikation *f*

dis'qualify *vt* disqualifizieren; ~ **s.o. from driving** jdm den Führerschein entziehen

disquieting /dɪs'kwaɪətɪŋ/ *a* beunruhigend

disre'gard *n* Nichtbeachtung *f* ● *vt* nicht beachten, ignorieren

disre'pair *n* **fall into** ~ verfallen

dis'reputable *a* verrufen

disre'pute *n* Verruf *m*

disre'spect *n* Respektlosigkeit *f*. ~**ful** *a*, **-ly** *adv* respektlos

disrupt /dɪs'rʌpt/ *vt* stören. ~**ion** /-'ʌpʃn/ *n* Störung *f*. ~**ive** /-tɪv/ *a* störend

dissatis'faction *n* Unzufriedenheit *f*

dis'satisfied *a* unzufrieden

dissect /dɪ'sekt/ *vt* zergliedern; (*Med*) sezieren. ~**ion** /-ekʃn/ *n* Zergliederung *f*; (*Med*) Sektion *f*

disseminat|e /dɪ'semɪneɪt/ *vt* verbreiten. ~**ion** /-'neɪʃn/ *n* Verbreitung *f*

dissent /dɪ'sent/ *n* Nichtübereinstimmung *f* ● *vi* nicht übereinstimmen

dissertation /dɪsə'teɪʃn/ *n* Dissertation *f*

dis'service *n* schlechter Dienst *m*

dissident /'dɪsɪdənt/ *n* Dissident *m*

dis'similar *a* unähnlich (**to** *dat*)

dissociate /dɪ'səʊʃɪeɪt/ *vt* trennen; ~ **oneself** sich distanzieren (**from** von)

dissolute /'dɪsəluːt/ *a* zügellos; ⟨*life*⟩ ausschweifend

dissolution /dɪsə'luːʃn/ *n* Auflösung *f*

dissolve /dɪ'zɒlv/ *vt* auflösen ● *vi* sich auflösen

dissuade /dɪ'sweɪd/ *vt* abbringen (**from** von)

distance /'dɪstəns/ *n* Entfernung *f*; **long/short** ~ lange/kurze Strecke *f*; **in the/from a** ~ in/aus der Ferne

distant /'dɪstənt/ *a* fern; (*aloof*) kühl; ⟨*relative*⟩ entfernt

dis'taste *n* Abneigung *f*. ~**ful** *a* unangenehm

distend /dɪ'stend/ *vi* sich [auf] blähen

distil /dɪ'stɪl/ *vt* (*pt/pp* **distilled**) brennen; (*Chem*) destillieren. ~**lation** /-'leɪʃn/ *n* Destillation *f*. ~**lery** /-ərɪ/ *n* Brennerei *f*

distinct /dɪ'stɪŋkt/ *a* deutlich; (*different*) verschieden. ~**ion** /-ɪŋkʃn/ *n* Unterschied *m*; (*Sch*) Auszeichnung *f*. ~**ive** /-tɪv/ *a* kennzeichnend; (*unmistakable*) unverwechselbar. ~**ly** *adv* deutlich

distinguish /dɪ'stɪŋgwɪʃ/ *vt/i* unterscheiden; (*make out*) erkennen; ~ **oneself** sich auszeichnen. ~**ed** *a* angesehen; ⟨*appearance*⟩ distinguiert

distort /dɪ'stɔːt/ *vt* verzerren; (*fig*) verdrehen. ~**ion** /-ɔːʃn/ *n* Verzerrung *f*; (*fig*) Verdrehung *f*

distract /dɪ'strækt/ *vt* ablenken. ~**ed** /-ɪd/ *a* [völlig] aufgelöst. ~**ion** /-ækʃn/ *n* Ablenkung *f*; (*despair*) Verzweiflung *f*

distraught /dɪ'strɔːt/ *a* [völlig] aufgelöst

distress /dɪ'stres/ *n* Kummer *m*; (*pain*) Schmerz *m*; (*poverty, danger*) Not *f* ● *vt* Kummer/Schmerz bereiten (+ *dat*); (*sadden*) bekümmern; (*shock*) erschüttern. ~**ing** *a* schmerzlich; (*shocking*) erschütternd. ~ **signal** *n* Notsignal *nt*

distribut|e /dɪ'strɪbjuːt/ *vt* verteilen; (*Comm*) vertreiben. ~**ion** /-'bjuːʃn/ *n* Verteilung *f*; Vertrieb *m*. ~**or** *n* Verteiler *m*

district /'dɪstrɪkt/ *n* Gegend *f*; (*Admin*) Bezirk *m*. ~ **nurse** *n* Gemeindeschwester *f*

dis'trust *n* Mißtrauen *nt* ● *vt* mißtrauen (+ *dat*). ~**ful** *a* mißtrauisch

disturb /dɪ'stɜːb/ *vt* stören; (*perturb*) beunruhigen; (*touch*) anrühren. ~**ance** *n* Unruhe *f*; (*interruption*) Störung *f*. ~**ed** *a* beunruhigt; **[mentally]** ~**ed** geistig gestört. ~**ing** *a* beunruhigend

dis'used *a* stillgelegt; (*empty*) leer

ditch /dɪtʃ/ *n* Graben *m* ● *vt* (*fam: abandon*) fallenlassen ⟨*plan*⟩; wegschmeißen ⟨*thing*⟩

dither /'dɪðə(r)/ *vi* zaudern

ditto /'dɪtəʊ/ *n* dito; (*fam*) ebenfalls

divan /dɪ'væn/ *n* Polsterbett *nt*

dive /daɪv/ *n* [Kopf]sprung *m*; (*Aviat*) Sturzflug *m*; (*fam: place*) Spelunke *f* ● *vi* einen Kopfsprung machen; (*when in water*) tauchen;

(*Aviat*) einen Sturzflug machen; (*fam: rush*) stürzen

diver /'daɪvə(r)/ n Taucher m; (*Sport*) [Kunst]springer m

diver|ge /daɪ'vɜːdʒ/ vi auseinandergehen. **∼gent** /-ənt/ a abweichend

diverse /daɪ'vɜːs/ a verschieden

diversify /daɪ'vɜːsɪfaɪ/ vt/i (*pt/pp* **-ied**) variieren; (*Comm*) diversifizieren

diversion /daɪ'vɜːʃn/ n Umleitung f; (*distraction*) Ablenkung f

diversity /daɪ'vɜːsətɪ/ n Vielfalt f

divert /daɪ'vɜːt/ vt umleiten; ablenken ⟨*attention*⟩; (*entertain*) unterhalten

divest /daɪ'vest/ vt sich entledigen (*of* + *gen*); (*fig*) entkleiden

divide /dɪ'vaɪd/ vt teilen; (*separate*) trennen; (*Math*) dividieren (**by** durch)● vi sich teilen

dividend /'dɪvɪdend/ n Dividende f

divine /dɪ'vaɪn/ a göttlich

diving /'daɪvɪŋ/ n (*Sport*) Kunstspringen nt. **∼-board** n Sprungbrett nt. **∼-suit** n Taucheranzug m

divinity /dɪ'vɪnətɪ/ n Göttlichkeit f; (*subject*) Theologie f

divisible /dɪ'vɪzɪbl/ a teilbar (**by** durch)

division /dɪ'vɪʒn/ n Teilung f; (*separation*) Trennung f; (*Math, Mil*) Division f; (*Parl*) Hammelsprung m; (*line*) Trennlinie f; (*group*) Abteilung f

divorce /dɪ'vɔːs/ n Scheidung f● vt sich scheiden lassen von. **∼d** a geschieden; **get ∼d** sich scheiden lassen

divorcee /dɪvɔː'siː/ n Geschiedene(r) m/f

divulge /daɪ'vʌldʒ/ vt preisgeben

DIY abbr of **do-it-yourself**

dizziness /'dɪzɪnɪs/ n Schwindel m

dizzy /'dɪzɪ/ a (**-ier, -iest**) schwindlig; **I feel ∼** mir ist schwindlig

do /duː/ n (pl **dos** or **do's**) (*fam*) Veranstaltung f● v (3 sg pres tense **does**; pt **did**; pp **done**) ● vt/i tun, machen; (*be suitable*) passen; (*be enough*) reichen, genügen; (*cook*) kochen; (*clean*) putzen; (*Sch: study*) durchnehmen; (*fam: cheat*) beschwindeln (**out of** um); **do without** auskommen ohne; **do away with** abschaffen; **be done** (*Culin*) gar sein; **well done** gut gemacht! (*Culin*) gut durchgebraten; **done in** (*fam*) kaputt, fertig; **done for** (*fam*) verloren, erledigt; **do the flowers** die Blumen arrangieren; **do the potatoes** die Kartoffeln schälen; **do the washing up** abwaschen, spülen; **do one's hair** sich frisieren; **do well/badly** gut/schlecht abschneiden; **how is he doing?** wie geht es ihm? **this won't do** das geht nicht; **are you doing anything today?** haben Sie heute etwas vor? **I could do with a spanner** ich könnte einen Schraubenschlüssel gebrauchen ● v aux **do you speak German?** sprechen Sie deutsch? **yes, I do** ja; (*emphatic*) doch; **no, I don't** nein; **I don't smoke** ich rauche nicht; **don't you/doesn't he?** nicht [wahr]? **so do I** ich auch; **do come in** kommen Sie doch herein; **how do you do?** guten Tag. **do in** vt (*fam*) um die Ecke bringen. **do up** vt (*fasten*) zumachen; (*renovate*) renovieren; (*wrap*) einpacken

docile /'dəʊsaɪl/ a fügsam

dock[1] /dɒk/ n (*Jur*) Anklagebank f

dock[2] n Dock nt ● vi anlegen, docken ● vt docken. **∼er** n Hafenarbeiter m. **∼yard** n Werft f

doctor /'dɒktə(r)/ n Arzt m/Ärztin f; (*Univ*) Doktor m ● vt kastrieren; (*spay*) sterilisieren. **∼ate** /-ət/ n Doktorwürde f

doctrine /'dɒktrɪn/ n Lehre f, Doktrin f

document /'dɒkjʊmənt/ n Dokument nt. **∼ary** /-'mentərɪ/ a Dokumentar- ● n Dokumentarbericht m; (*film*) Dokumentarfilm m

doddery /'dɒdərɪ/ a (*fam*) tatterig

dodge /dɒdʒ/ n (*fam*) Trick m, Kniff m ● vt/i ausweichen (+ *dat*); **∼ out of the way** zur Seite springen

dodgems /'dɒdʒəmz/ npl Autoskooter pl

dodgy /'dɒdʒɪ/ a (**-ier, -iest**) (*fam*) (*awkward*) knifflig; (*dubious*) zweifelhaft

doe /dəʊ/ n Ricke f; (*rabbit*) [Kaninchen]weibchen nt

does /dʌz/ see **do**

doesn't /'dʌznt/ = **does not**

dog /dɒg/ n Hund m ● vt (pt/pp **dogged**) verfolgen

dog: ∼-biscuit n Hundekuchen m. **∼-collar** n Hundehalsband nt; (*Relig, fam*) Kragen m eines Geistlichen. **∼-eared** a **be ∼-eared** Eselsohren haben

dogged /'dɒgɪd/ a, **-ly** adv beharrlich

dogma /'dɒgmə/ n Dogma nt. **∼tic** /-'mætɪk/ a dogmatisch

'dogsbody n (fam) Mädchen nt für alles

doily /'dɔɪlɪ/ n Deckchen nt

do-it-yourself /duːɪtjə'self/ n Heimwerken nt. ~ **shop** n Heimwerkerladen m

doldrums /'dɒldrəmz/ npl **be in the** ~ niedergeschlagen sein; ⟨business:⟩ darniederliegen

dole /dəʊl/ n (fam) Stempelgeld nt; **be on the** ~ arbeitslos sein ● vt ~ **out** austeilen

doleful /'dəʊlfl/ a, **-ly** adv trauervoll

doll /dɒl/ n Puppe f ● vt (fam) ~ **oneself up** sich herausputzen

dollar /'dɒlə(r)/ n Dollar m

dollop /'dɒləp/ n (fam) Klecks m

dolphin /'dɒlfɪn/ n Delphin m

domain /də'meɪn/ n Gebiet nt

dome /dəʊm/ n Kuppel m

domestic /də'mestɪk/ a häuslich; (Pol) Innen-; (Comm) Binnen-. ~ **animal** n Haustier nt

domesticated /də'mestɪkeɪtɪd/ a häuslich; ⟨animal⟩ zahm

domestic: ~ **flight** n Inlandflug m. ~ **'servant** Hausangestellte(r) m/f

dominant /'dɒmɪnənt/ a vorherrschend

dominat|e /'dɒmɪneɪt/ vt beherrschen ● vi dominieren; ~**e over** beherrschen. ~**ion** /-'neɪʃn/ n Vorherrschaft f

domineer /dɒmɪ'nɪə(r)/ vi ~ **over** tyrannisieren. ~**ing** a herrschsüchtig

dominion /də'mɪnjən/ n Herrschaft f

domino /'dɒmɪnəʊ/ n (pl **-es**) Dominostein m; ~**es** sg (game) Domino nt

don[1] /dɒn/ vt (pt/pp **donned**) (liter) anziehen

don[2] n [Universitäts]dozent m

donat|e /dəʊ'neɪt/ vt spenden. ~**ion** /-eɪʃn/ n Spende f

done /dʌn/ see **do**

donkey /'dɒŋkɪ/ n Esel m; ~**'s years** (fam) eine Ewigkeit. ~**-work** n Routinearbeit f

donor /'dəʊnə(r)/ n Spender(in) m(f)

don't /dəʊnt/ = **do not**

doodle /'duːdl/ vi kritzeln

doom /duːm/ n Schicksal nt; (ruin) Verhängnis nt ● vt **be** ~**ed to failure** zum Scheitern verurteilt sein

door /dɔː(r)/ n Tür f; **out of** ~**s** im Freien

door: ~**man** n Portier m. ~**mat** n [Fuß]abtreter m. ~**step** n Türschwelle f; **on the** ~**step** vor der Tür. ~**way** n Türöffnung f

dope /dəʊp/ n (fam) Drogen pl; (fam: information) Informationen pl; (fam: idiot) Trottel m ● vt betäuben; (Sport) dopen

dopey /'dəʊpɪ/ a (fam) benommen; (stupid) blöd[e]

dormant /'dɔːmənt/ a ruhend

dormer /'dɔːmə(r)/ n ~ **[window]** Mansardenfenster nt

dormitory /'dɔːmɪtərɪ/ n Schlafsaal m

dormouse /'dɔː-/ n Haselmaus f

dosage /'dəʊsɪdʒ/ n Dosierung f

dose /dəʊs/ n Dosis f

doss /dɒs/ vi (sl) pennen. ~**er** n Penner m. ~**-house** n Penne f

dot /dɒt/ n Punkt m; **on the** ~ pünktlich

dote /dəʊt/ vi ~ **on** vernarrt sein in (+ acc)

dotted /'dɒtɪd/ a ~ **line** punktierte Linie f; **be** ~ **with** bestreut sein mit

dotty /'dɒtɪ/ a (**-ier, -iest**) (fam) verdreht

double /'dʌbl/ a & adv doppelt; ⟨bed, chin⟩ Doppel-; ⟨flower⟩ gefüllt ● n das Doppelte; (person) Doppelgänger m; ~**s** pl (Tennis) Doppel nt; **at the** ~ im Laufschritt ● vt verdoppeln; (fold) falten ● vi sich verdoppeln. ~ **back** vi zurückgehen. ~ **up** vi sich krümmen (**with** vor + dat)

double: ~**-'bass** n Kontrabaß m. ~**-breasted** a zweireihig. ~**-'cross** vt ein Doppelspiel treiben mit. ~**-'decker** n Doppeldecker m. ~ **'Dutch** n (fam) Kauderwelsch nt. ~ **'glazing** n Doppelverglasung f. ~ **'room** n Doppelzimmer nt

doubly /'dʌblɪ/ adv doppelt

doubt /daʊt/ n Zweifel m ● vt bezweifeln. ~**ful** a, **-ly** adv zweifelhaft; (disbelieving) skeptisch. ~**less** adv zweifellos

dough /dəʊ/ n [fester] Teig m; (fam: money) Pinke f. ~**nut** n Berliner [Pfannkuchen] m, Krapfen m

douse /daʊs/ vt übergießen; ausgießen ⟨flames⟩

dove /dʌv/ n Taube f. ~**tail** n (Techn) Schwalbenschwanz m

dowdy /'daʊdɪ/ a (**-ier, -iest**) unschick

down[1] /daʊn/ n (feathers) Daunen pl

down[2] adv unten; (with movement) nach unten; **go** ~ hinuntergehen; **come** ~ herunterkommen; ~ **there** da unten; **£50** ~ £50 Anzahlung; ~**!** (to dog) Platz! ~ **with...!** nieder mit...! ● prep ~ **the road/stairs** die Straße/Treppe hinunter; ~ **the river** den Fluß abwärts; **be** ~ **the pub** (fam) in der Kneipe sein ● vt (fam) (drink) runterkippen; ~ **tools** die Arbeit niederlegen

down: ~**-and-'out** n Penner m. ~**cast** a niedergeschlagen. ~**fall** n Sturz m; (ruin) Ruin m. ~**'grade** vt niedriger einstufen. ~**-'hearted** a entmutigt. ~**'hill** adv bergab. ~ **payment** n Anzahlung f. ~**pour** n Platzregen m. ~**right** a & adv ausgesprochen. ~**'stairs** adv unten; (go) nach unten ● a /'- -/ im Erdgeschoß. ~**'stream** adv stromabwärts. ~**-to-'earth** a sachlich. ~**town** adv (Amer) im Stadtzentrum. ~**trodden** a unterdrückt. ~**ward** a nach unten; (slope) abfallend ● adv & ~**wards** abwärts, nach unten

downy /'daʊnɪ/ a (-ier, -iest) flaumig

dowry /'daʊrɪ/ n Mitgift f

doze /dəʊz/ n Nickerchen nt ● vi dösen. ~ **off** vi einnicken

dozen /'dʌzn/ n Dutzend nt

Dr abbr of **doctor**

draft[1] /drɑːft/ n Entwurf m; (Comm) Tratte f; (Amer Mil) Einberufung f ● vt entwerfen; (Amer Mil) einberufen

draft[2] n (Amer) = **draught**

drag /dræg/ n (fam) Klotz m am Bein; **in** ~ (fam) (man) als Frau gekleidet ● vt (pt/pp **dragged**) schleppen; absuchen (river). ~ **on** vi sich in die Länge ziehen

dragon /'drægən/ n Drache m. ~**-fly** n Libelle f

'drag show n Transvestitenshow f

drain /dreɪn/ n Abfluß m; (underground) Kanal m; **the** ~**s** die Kanalisation ● vt entwässern (land); ablassen (liquid); das Wasser ablassen aus (tank); abgießen (vegetables); austrinken (glass) ● vi ~ **[away]** ablaufen; **leave sth to** ~ etw abtropfen lassen

drain|age /'dreɪnɪdʒ/ n Kanalisation f; (of land) Dränage f. ~**ing board** n Abtropfbrett nt. ~**-pipe** n Abflußrohr nt

drake /dreɪk/ n Enterich m

drama /'drɑːmə/ n Drama nt; (quality) Dramatik f

dramatic /drə'mætɪk/ a, **-ally** adv dramatisch

dramat|ist /'dræmətɪst/ n Dramatiker m. ~**ize** vt für die Bühne bearbeiten; (fig) dramatisieren

drank /dræŋk/ see **drink**

drape /dreɪp/ n (Amer) Vorhang m ● vt drapieren

drastic /'dræstɪk/ a, **-ally** adv drastisch

draught /drɑːft/ n [Luft]zug m; ~**s** sg (game) Damespiel nt; **there is a** ~ es zieht

draught: ~ **beer** n Bier nt vom Faß. ~**sman** n technischer Zeichner m

draughty /'drɑːftɪ/ a zugig; **it's** ~ es zieht

draw /drɔː/ n Attraktion f; (Sport) Unentschieden nt; (in lottery) Ziehung f ● v (pt **drew**, pp **drawn**) ● vt ziehen; (attract) anziehen; zeichnen (picture); abheben (money); holen (water); ~ **the curtains** die Vorhänge zuziehen/(back) aufziehen; ~ **lots** losen (**for** um) ● vi (tea:) ziehen; (Sport) unentschieden spielen. ~ **back** vt zurückziehen ● vi (recoil) zurückweichen. ~ **in** vt einziehen ● vi einfahren; (days:) kürzer werden. ~ **out** vt herausziehen; abheben (money) ● vi ausfahren; (days:) länger werden. ~ **up** vt aufsetzen (document); herrücken (chair); ~ **oneself up** sich aufrichten ● vi [an]halten

draw: ~**back** n Nachteil m. ~**bridge** n Zugbrücke f

drawer /drɔː(r)/ n Schublade f

drawing /'drɔːɪŋ/ n Zeichnung f

drawing: ~**-board** n Reißbrett nt. ~**-pin** n Reißzwecke f. ~**-room** n Wohnzimmer nt

drawl /drɔːl/ n schleppende Aussprache f

drawn /drɔːn/ see **draw**

dread /dred/ n Furcht f (**of** vor + dat) ● vt fürchten

dreadful a, **-ly** adv fürchterlich

dream /driːm/ n Traum m ● attrib Traum- ● vt/i (pt/pp **dreamt** /dremt/ or **dreamed**) träumen (**about/of** von)

dreary /'drɪərɪ/ a (-ier, -iest) trüb[e]; (boring) langweilig

dredge /dredʒ/ vt/i baggern. ~**r** n [Naß]bagger m

dregs /dregz/ *npl* Bodensatz *m*

drench /drentʃ/ *vt* durchnässen

dress /dres/ *n* Kleid *nt*; (*clothing*) Kleidung *f* ● *vt* anziehen; (*decorate*) schmücken; (*Culin*) anmachen; (*Med*) verbinden; ~ **oneself, get** ~**ed** sich anziehen ● *vi* sich anziehen. ~ **up** *vi* sich schön anziehen; (*in disguise*) sich verkleiden (**as** als)

dress: ~ **circle** *n* (*Theat*) erster Rang *m*. ~**er** *n* (*furniture*) Anrichte *f*; (*Amer: dressing-table*) Frisiertisch *m*

dressing *n* (*Culin*) Soße *f*; (*Med*) Verband *m*

dressing: ~ '**down** *n* (*fam*) Standpauke *f*. ~**-gown** *n* Morgenmantel *m*. ~**-room** *n* Ankleidezimmer *nt*; (*Theat*) [Künstler]garderobe *f*. ~**-table** *n* Frisiertisch *m*

dress: ~**maker** *n* Schneiderin *f*. ~**making** *n* Damenschneiderei *f*. ~ **rehearsal** *n* Generalprobe *f*

dressy /'dresɪ/ *a* (**-ier, -iest**) schick

drew /druː/ *see* **draw**

dribble /'drɪbl/ *vi* sabbern; (*Sport*) dribbeln

dried /draɪd/ *a* getrocknet; ~ **fruit** Dörrobst *nt*

drier /'draɪə(r)/ *n* Trockner *m*

drift /drɪft/ *n* Abtrift *f*; (*of snow*) Schneewehe *f*; (*meaning*) Sinn *m* ● *vi* treiben; (*off course*) abtreiben; ⟨*snow:*⟩ Wehen bilden; (*fig*) ⟨*person:*⟩ sich treiben lassen; ~ **apart** ⟨*persons:*⟩ sich auseinanderleben. ~**wood** *n* Treibholz *nt*

drill /drɪl/ *n* Bohrer *m*; (*Mil*) Drill *m* ● *vt/i* bohren (**for** nach); (*Mil*) drillen

drily /'draɪlɪ/ *adv* trocken

drink /drɪŋk/ *n* Getränk *nt*; (*alcoholic*) Drink *m*; (*alcohol*) Alkohol *m*; **have a** ~ etwas trinken ● *vt/i* (*pt* **drank**, *pp* **drunk**) trinken. ~ **up** *vt/i* austrinken

drink|able /'drɪŋkəbl/ *a* trinkbar. ~**er** *n* Trinker *m*

'**drinking-water** *n* Trinkwasser *nt*

drip /drɪp/ *n* Tropfen *m*; (*drop*) Tropfen *m*; (*Med*) Tropf *m*; (*fam: person*) Niete *f* ● *vi* (*pt/pp* **dripped**) tropfen. ~**-'dry** *a* bügelfrei. ~**ping** *n* Schmalz *nt*

drive /draɪv/ *n* [Auto]fahrt *f*; (*entrance*) Einfahrt *f*; (*energy*) Elan *m*; (*Psych*) Trieb *m*; (*Pol*) Aktion *f*; (*Sport*) Treibschlag *m*; (*Techn*) Antrieb *m* ● *v* (*pt* **drove**, *pp* **driven**) ● *vt* treiben; fahren ⟨*car*⟩; (*Sport: hit*)

schlagen; (*Techn*) antreiben; ~ **s.o. mad** (*fam*) jdn verrückt machen; **what are you driving at?** (*fam*) worauf willst du hinaus? ● *vi* fahren. ~ **away** *vt* vertreiben ● *vi* abfahren. ~ **in** *vi* hinein-/hereinfahren. ~ **off** *vt* vertreiben ● *vi* abfahren. ~ **on** *vi* weiterfahren. ~ **up** *vi* vorfahren

'**drive-in** *a* ~ **cinema** Autokino *nt*

drivel /'drɪvl/ *n* (*fam*) Quatsch *m*

driven /'drɪvn/ *see* **drive**

driver /'draɪvə(r)/ *n* Fahrer(in) *m(f)*; (*of train*) Lokführer *m*

driving /'draɪvɪŋ/ *a* ⟨*rain*⟩ peitschend; ⟨*force*⟩ treibend

driving: ~ **lesson** *n* Fahrstunde *f*. ~ **licence** *n* Führerschein *m*. ~ **school** *n* Fahrschule *f*. ~ **test** Fahrprüfung *f*; **take one's** ~ **test** den Führerschein machen

drizzle /'drɪzl/ *n* Nieselregen *m* ● *vi* nieseln

drone /drəʊn/ *n* Drohne *f*; (*sound*) Brummen *nt*

droop /druːp/ *vi* herabhängen; ⟨*flowers:*⟩ die Köpfe hängen lassen

drop /drɒp/ *n* Tropfen *m*; (*fall*) Fall *m*; (*in price, temperature*) Rückgang *m* ● *v* (*pt/pp* **dropped**) ● *vt* fallen lassen; abwerfen ⟨*bomb*⟩; (*omit*) auslassen; (*give up*) aufgeben ● *vi* fallen; (*fall lower*) sinken; ⟨*wind:*⟩ nachlassen. ~ **in** *vi* vorbeikommen. ~ **off** *vt* absetzen ⟨*person*⟩ ● *vi* abfallen; (*fall asleep*) einschlafen. ~ **out** *vi* herausfallen; (*give up*) aufgeben

'**drop-out** *n* Aussteiger *m*

droppings /'drɒpɪŋz/ *npl* Kot *m*

drought /draʊt/ *n* Dürre *f*

drove /drəʊv/ *see* **drive**

droves /drəʊvz/ *npl* **in** ~ in Scharen

drown /draʊn/ *vi* ertrinken ● *vt* ertränken; übertönen ⟨*noise*⟩; **be** ~**ed** ertrinken

drowsy /'draʊzɪ/ *a* schläfrig

drudgery /'drʌdʒərɪ/ *n* Plackerei *f*

drug /drʌg/ *n* Droge *f* ● *vt* (*pt/pp* **drugged**) betäuben

drug: ~ **addict** *n* Drogenabhängige(r) *m/f*. ~**gist** *n* (*Amer*) Apotheker *m*. ~**store** *n* (*Amer*) Drogerie *f*; (*dispensing*) Apotheke *f*

drum /drʌm/ *n* Trommel *f*; (*for oil*) Tonne *f* ● *v* (*pt/pp* **drummed**) ● *vi* trommeln ● *vt* ~ **sth into s.o.** (*fam*) jdm etw einbleuen. ~**mer** *n* Trommler *m*; (*in pop-group*)

Schlagzeuger *m.* ∼**stick** *n* Trommelschlegel *m*; (*Culin*) Keule *f*

drunk /drʌŋk/ *see* **drink** ● *a* betrunken; **get** ∼ sich betrinken ● *n* Betrunkene(r) *m*

drunk\ard /'drʌŋkəd/ *n* Trinker *m.* ∼**en** *a* betrunken; ∼**en driving** Trunkenheit *f* am Steuer

dry /draɪ/ *a* (**drier, driest**) trocken ● *vt/i* trocknen; ∼ **one's eyes** sich *dat* die Tränen abwischen. ∼ **up** *vi* austrocknen; (*fig*) versiegen ● *vt* austrocknen; abtrocknen ⟨*dishes*⟩

dry: ∼-'**clean** *vt* chemisch reinigen. ∼-'**cleaner's** *n* (*shop*) chemische Reinigung *f*. ∼**ness** *n* Trockenheit *f*

dual /'dju:əl/ *a* doppelt

dual: ∼ '**carriageway** *n* ≈ Schnellstraße *f*. ∼-'**purpose** *a* zweifach verwendbar

dub /dʌb/ *vt* (*pt/pp* **dubbed**) synchronisieren ⟨*film*⟩; kopieren ⟨*tape*⟩; (*name*) nennen

dubious /'dju:bɪəs/ *a* zweifelhaft; **be** ∼ **about** Zweifel haben über (+ *acc*)

duchess /'dʌtʃɪs/ *n* Herzogin *f*

duck /dʌk/ *n* Ente *f* ● *vt* (*in water*) untertauchen; ∼ **one's head** den Kopf einziehen ● *vi* sich ducken. ∼**ling** *n* Entchen *nt*; (*Culin*) Ente *f*

duct /dʌkt/ *n* Rohr *nt*; (*Anat*) Gang *m*

dud /dʌd/ *a* (*fam*) nutzlos; ⟨*coin*⟩ falsch; ⟨*cheque*⟩ ungedeckt; ⟨*forged*⟩ gefälscht ● *n* (*fam*) (*banknote*) Blüte *f*; (*Mil: shell*) Blindgänger *m*

due /dju:/ *a* angemessen; **be** ∼ fällig sein; ⟨*baby:*⟩ erwartet werden; ⟨*train:*⟩ planmäßig ankommen; ∼ **to** (*owing to*) wegen (+ *gen*); **be** ∼ **to** zurückzuführen sein auf (+ *acc*); **in** ∼ **course** im Laufe der Zeit; ⟨*write*⟩ zu gegebener Zeit ● *adv* ∼ **west** genau westlich

duel /'dju:əl/ *n* Duell *nt*

dues /dju:z/ *npl* Gebühren *pl*

duet /dju:'et/ *n* Duo *nt*; (*vocal*) Duett *nt*

dug /dʌg/ *see* **dig**

duke /dju:k/ *n* Herzog *m*

dull /dʌl/ *a* (**-er, -est**) (*overcast, not bright*) trüb[e]; (*not shiny*) matt; ⟨*sound*⟩ dumpf; (*boring*) langweilig; ⟨*stupid*⟩ schwerfällig ● *vt* betäuben; abstumpfen ⟨*mind*⟩

duly /'dju:lɪ/ *adv* ordnungsgemäß

dumb /dʌm/ *a* (**-er, -est**) stumm; (*fam: stupid*) dumm. ∼**founded** *a* sprachlos

dummy /'dʌmɪ/ *n* (*tailor's*) [Schneider]puppe *f*; (*for baby*) Schnuller *m*; (*Comm*) Attrappe *f*

dump /dʌmp/ *n* Abfallhaufen *m*; (*for refuse*) Müllhalde *f*, Deponie *f*; (*fam: town*) Kaff *nt*; **be down in the** ∼**s** (*fam*) deprimiert sein ● *vt* abladen; (*fam: put down*) hinwerfen (**on** auf + *acc*)

dumpling /'dʌmplɪŋ/ *n* Kloß *m*, Knödel *m*

dunce /dʌns/ *n* Dummkopf *m*

dune /dju:n/ *n* Düne *f*

dung /dʌŋ/ *n* Mist *m*

dungarees /dʌŋgə'ri:z/ *npl* Latzhose *f*

dungeon /'dʌndʒən/ *n* Verlies *nt*

dunk /dʌŋk/ *vt* eintunken

duo /'dju:əʊ/ *n* Paar *nt*; (*Mus*) Duo *nt*

dupe /dju:p/ *n* Betrogene(r) *m/f* ● *vt* betrügen

duplicate[1] /'dju:plɪkət/ *a* Zweit- ● *n* Doppel *nt*; (*document*) Duplikat *nt*; **in** ∼ in doppelter Ausfertigung *f*

duplicat\e[2] /'dju:plɪkeɪt/ *vt* kopieren; (*do twice*) zweimal machen. ∼**or** *n* Vervielfältigungsapparat *m*

durable /'djʊərəbl/ *a* haltbar

duration /djʊə'reɪʃn/ *n* Dauer *f*

duress /djʊə'res/ *n* Zwang *m*

during /'djʊərɪŋ/ *prep* während (+ *gen*)

dusk /dʌsk/ *n* [Abend]dämmerung *f*

dust /dʌst/ *n* Staub *m* ● *vt* abstauben; (*sprinkle*) bestäuben (**with** mit) ● *vi* Staub wischen

dust: ∼**bin** *n* Mülltonne *f*. ∼-**cart** *n* Müllwagen *m*. ∼**er** *n* Staubtuch *nt*. ∼-**jacket** *n* Schutzumschlag *m*. ∼**man** *n* Müllmann *m*. ∼**pan** *n* Kehrschaufel *f*

dusty /'dʌstɪ/ *a* (**-ier, -iest**) staubig

Dutch /dʌtʃ/ *a* holländisch; **go** ∼ (*fam*) getrennte Kasse machen ● *n* (*Lang*) Holländisch *nt*; **the** ∼ *pl* die Holländer. ∼**man** *n* Holländer *m*

dutiable /'dju:tɪəbl/ *a* zollpflichtig

dutiful /'dju:tɪfl/ *a*, **-ly** *adv* pflichtbewußt; (*obedient*) gehorsam

duty /'dju:tɪ/ *n* Pflicht *f*; (*task*) Aufgabe *f*; (*tax*) Zoll *m*; **be on** ∼ Dienst haben. ∼-**free** *a* zollfrei

duvet /'du:veɪ/ *n* Steppdecke *f*

dwarf /dwɔ:f/ *n* (*pl* **-s** *or* **dwarves**) Zwerg *m*

dwell /dwel/ *vi* (*pt/pp* **dwelt**) (*liter*) wohnen; ∼ **on** (*fig*) verweilen bei. ∼**ing** *n* Wohnung *f*

dwindle /'dwɪndl/ *vi* abnehmen, schwinden

dye /daɪ/ *n* Farbstoff *m* ●*vt* (*pres p* **dyeing**) färben

dying /'daɪɪŋ/ *see* **die**[2]

dynamic /daɪ'næmɪk/ *a* dynamisch. ~**s** *n* Dynamik *f*

dynamite /'daɪnəmaɪt/ *n* Dynamit *nt*

dynamo /'daɪnəməʊ/ *n* Dynamo *m*

dynasty /'dɪnəstɪ/ *n* Dynastie *f*

dysentery /'dɪsəntrɪ/ *n* Ruhr *f*

dyslex|ia /dɪs'leksɪə/ *n* Legasthenie *f*. ~**ic** *a* legasthenisch; **be** ~**ic** Legastheniker sein

E

each /i:tʃ/ *a & pron* jede(r,s); (*per*) je; ~ **other** einander; **£1**~ £1 pro Person; (*for thing*) pro Stück

eager /'i:gə(r)/ *a*, **-ly** *adv* eifrig; **be** ~ **to do sth** etw gerne machen wollen. ~**ness** *n* Eifer *m*

eagle /'i:gl/ *n* Adler *m*

ear[1] /ɪə(r)/ *n* (*of corn*) Ähre *f*

ear[2] *n* Ohr *nt*. ~**ache** *n* Ohrenschmerzen *pl*. ~**-drum** *n* Trommelfell *nt*

earl /ɜ:l/ *n* Graf *m*

early /'ɜ:lɪ/ *a & adv* (**-ier, -iest**) früh; (*reply*) baldig; **be** ~ früh dran sein; ~ **in the morning** früh am Morgen

'earmark *vt* ~ **for** bestimmen für

earn /ɜ:n/ *vt* verdienen

earnest /'ɜ:nɪst/ *a*, **-ly** *adv* ernsthaft ●*n* **in** ~ im Ernst

earnings /'ɜ:nɪŋz/ *npl* Verdienst *m*

ear: ~**phones** *npl* Kopfhörer *pl*. ~**-ring** *n* Ohrring *m*; (*clip-on*) Ohrklips *m*. ~**shot** *n* **within/out of** ~**shot** in/außer Hörweite

earth /ɜ:θ/ *n* Erde *f*; (*of fox*) Bau *m*; **where/what on** ~? wo/was in aller Welt? ●*vt* (*Electr*) erden

earthenware /'ɜ:θn-/ *n* Tonwaren *pl*

earthly /'ɜ:θlɪ/ *a* irdisch; **be no** ~ **use** (*fam*) völlig nutzlos sein

'earthquake *n* Erdbeben *nt*

earthy /'ɜ:θɪ/ *a* erdig; (*coarse*) derb

earwig /'ɪəwɪg/ *n* Ohrwurm *m*

ease /i:z/ *n* Leichtigkeit *f*; **at** ~! (*Mil*) rührt euch! **be/feel ill at** ~ ein ungutes Gefühl haben ●*vt* erleichtern; lindern (*pain*) ●*vi* (*pain:*) nachlassen; (*situation:*) sich entspannen

easel /'i:zl/ *n* Staffelei *f*

easily /'i:zɪlɪ/ *adv* leicht, mit Leichtigkeit

east /i:st/ *n* Osten *m*; **to the** ~ **of** östlich von ●*a* Ost-, ost- ●*adv* nach Osten

Easter /'i:stə(r)/ *n* Ostern *nt* ●*attrib* Oster-. ~ **egg** *n* Osterei *nt*

east|erly /'i:stəlɪ/ *a* östlich. ~**ern** *a* östlich. ~**ward[s]** /-wəd[z]/ *adv* nach Osten

easy /'i:zɪ/ *a* (**-ier, -iest**) leicht; **take it** ~ (*fam*) sich schonen; **take it** ~! beruhige dich! **go** ~ **with** (*fam*) sparsam umgehen mit

easy: ~ **chair** *n* Sessel *m*. ~**'going** *a* gelassen; **too** ~**going** lässig

eat /i:t/ *vt/i* (*pt* **ate**, *pp* **eaten**) essen; (*animal:*) fressen. ~ **up** *vt* aufessen

eat|able /'i:təbl/ *a* genießbar. ~**er** *n* (*apple*) Eßapfel *m*

eau-de-Cologne /əʊdəkə'ləʊn/ *n* Kölnisch Wasser *nt*

eaves /i:vz/ *npl* Dachüberhang *m*. ~**drop** *vi* (*pt/pp* ~**dropped**) [heimlich] lauschen; ~**drop on** belauschen

ebb /eb/ *n* (*tide*) Ebbe *f*; **at a low** ~ (*fig*) auf einem Tiefstand ●*vi* zurückgehen; (*fig*) verebben

ebony /'ebənɪ/ *n* Ebenholz *nt*

ebullient /ɪ'bʌlɪənt/ *a* überschwenglich

EC *abbr* (**European Community**) EG *f*

eccentric /ɪk'sentrɪk/ *a* exzentrisch ●*n* Exzentriker *m*

ecclesiastical /ɪkliːzɪ'æstɪkl/ *a* kirchlich

echo /'ekəʊ/ *n* (*pl* **-es**) Echo *nt*, Widerhall *m* ●*v* (*pt/pp* **echoed**, *pres p* **echoing**) ●*vt* zurückwerfen; (*imitate*) nachsagen ●*vi* widerhallen (**with** von)

eclipse /ɪ'klɪps/ *n* (*Astr*) Finsternis *f* ●*vt* (*fig*) in den Schatten stellen

ecolog|ical /i:kə'lɒdʒɪkl/ *a* ökologisch. ~**y** /i:'kɒlədʒɪ/ *n* Ökologie *f*

economic /i:kə'nɒmɪk/ *a* wirtschaftlich. ~**al** *a* sparsam. ~**ally** *adv* wirtschaftlich; (*thriftily*) sparsam. ~**s** *n* Volkswirtschaft *f*

economist /ɪ'kɒnəmɪst/ *n* Volkswirt *m*; (*Univ*) Wirtschaftswissenschaftler *m*

economize /ɪ'kɒnəmaɪz/ *vi* sparen (**on** an + *dat*)

economy /ɪ'kɒnəmɪ/ *n* Wirtschaft *f*; (*thrift*) Sparsamkeit *f*

ecstasy /'ekstəsɪ/ *n* Ekstase *f*

ecstatic /ɪk'stætɪk/ *a*, **-ally** *adv* ekstatisch

ecu /'eɪkjuː/ *n* Ecu *m*

ecumenical /i:kjʊ'menɪkl/ *a* ökumenisch

eczema /'eksɪmə/ *n* Ekzem *nt*

eddy /'edɪ/ *n* Wirbel *m*

edge /edʒ/ *n* Rand *m*; (*of table, lawn*) Kante *f*; (*of knife*) Schneide *f*; **on ~** (*fam*) nervös; **have the ~ on** (*fam*) etwas besser sein als ● *vt* einfassen. **~ forward** *vi* sich nach vorn schieben

edging /'edʒɪŋ/ *n* Einfassung *f*

edgy /'edʒɪ/ *a* (*fam*) nervös

edible /'edɪbl/ *a* eßbar

edict /'i:dɪkt/ *n* Erlaß *m*

edifice /'edɪfɪs/ *n* [großes] Gebäude *nt*

edify /'edɪfaɪ/ *vt* (*pt/pp* **-ied**) erbauen. **~ing** *a* erbaulich

edit /'edɪt/ *vt* (*pt/pp* **edited**) redigieren; herausgeben ⟨*anthology, dictionary*⟩; schneiden ⟨*film, tape*⟩

edition /ɪ'dɪʃn/ *n* Ausgabe *f*; (*impression*) Auflage *f*

editor /'edɪtə(r)/ *n* Redakteur *m*; (*of anthology, dictionary*) Herausgeber *m*; (*of newspaper*) Chefredakteur *m*; (*of film*) Cutter(in) *m(f)*

editorial /edɪ'tɔ:rɪəl/ *a* redaktionell, Redaktions- ● *n* (*Journ*) Leitartikel *m*

educate /'edjʊkeɪt/ *vt* erziehen; **be ~d at X** auf die X-Schule gehen. **~d** *a* gebildet

education /edjʊ'keɪʃn/ *n* Erziehung *f*; (*culture*) Bildung *f*. **~al** *a* pädagogisch; ⟨*visit*⟩ kulturell

eel /i:l/ *n* Aal *m*

eerie /'ɪərɪ/ *a* (**-ier, -iest**) unheimlich

effect /ɪ'fekt/ *n* Wirkung *f*, Effekt *m*; **in ~** in Wirklichkeit; **take ~** in Kraft treten ● *vt* bewirken

effective /ɪ'fektɪv/ *a*, **-ly** *adv* wirksam, effektiv; (*striking*) wirkungsvoll, effektvoll; (*actual*) tatsächlich. **~ness** *n* Wirksamkeit *f*

effeminate /ɪ'femɪnət/ *a* unmännlich

effervescent /efə'vesnt/ *a* sprudelnd

efficiency /ɪ'fɪʃənsɪ/ *n* Tüchtigkeit *f*; (*of machine, organization*) Leistungsfähigkeit *f*

efficient /ɪ'fɪʃənt/ *a* tüchtig; ⟨*machine, organization*⟩ leistungsfähig; ⟨*method*⟩ rationell. **~ly** *adv* gut; ⟨*function*⟩ rationell

effigy /'efɪdʒɪ/ *n* Bildnis *nt*

effort /'efət/ *n* Anstrengung *f*; **make an ~** sich (*dat*) Mühe geben. **~less** *a*, **-ly** *adv* mühelos

effrontery /ɪ'frʌntərɪ/ *n* Unverschämtheit *f*

effusive /ɪ'fju:sɪv/ *a*, **-ly** *adv* überschwenglich

e.g. *abbr* (**exempli gratia**) z.B.

egalitarian /ɪɡælɪ'teərɪən/ *a* egalitär

egg[1] /eɡ/ *vt* **~ on** (*fam*) anstacheln

egg[2] *n* Ei *nt*. **~-cup** *n* Eierbecher *m*. **~shell** *n* Eierschale *f*. **~-timer** *n* Eieruhr *f*

ego /'i:ɡəʊ/ *n* Ich *nt*. **~centric** /-'sentrɪk/ *a* egozentrisch. **~ism** *n* Egoismus *m*. **~ist** *n* Egoist *m*. **~tism** *n* Ichbezogenheit *f*. **~tist** *n* ichbezogener Mensch *m*

Egypt /'i:dʒɪpt/ *n* Ägypten *nt*. **~ian** /ɪ'dʒɪpʃn/ *a* ägyptisch ● *n* Ägypter(in) *m(f)*

eiderdown /'aɪdə-/ *n* (*quilt*) Daunendecke *f*

eigh|t /eɪt/ *a* acht ● *n* Acht *f*; (*boat*) Achter *m*. **~'teen** *a* achtzehn. **~'teenth** *a* achtzehnte(r,s)

eighth /eɪtθ/ *a* achte(r,s) ● *n* Achtel *nt*

eightieth /'eɪtɪɪθ/ *a* achtzigste(r,s)

eighty /'eɪtɪ/ *a* achtzig

either /'aɪðə(r)/ *a & pron* ~ **[of them]** einer von [den] beiden; (*both*) beide; **on ~ side** auf beiden Seiten ● *adv* **I don't ~** ich auch nicht ● *conj* **~... or** entweder... oder

eject /ɪ'dʒekt/ *vt* hinauswerfen

eke /i:k/ *vt* **~ out** strecken; (*increase*) ergänzen; **~ out a living** sich kümmerlich durchschlagen

elaborate[1] /ɪ'læbərət/ *a*, **-ly** *adv* kunstvoll; (*fig*) kompliziert

elaborate[2] /ɪ'læbəreɪt/ *vi* ausführlicher sein; **~ on** näher ausführen

elapse /ɪ'læps/ *vi* vergehen

elastic /ɪ'læstɪk/ *a* elastisch ● *n* Gummiband *nt*. **~ 'band** *n* Gummiband *nt*

elasticity /ɪlæs'tɪsətɪ/ *n* Elastizität *f*

elated /ɪ'leɪtɪd/ *a* überglücklich

elbow /'elbəʊ/ *n* Ellbogen *m*

elder[1] /'eldə(r)/ *n* Holunder *m*

eld|er[2] *a* ältere(r,s) ● *n* **the ~er** der/die Ältere. **~erly** *a* alt. **~est** *a* älteste(r, s) ● *n* **the ~est** der/die Älteste

elect /ɪ'lekt/ *a* **the president ~** der designierte Präsident ● *vt* wählen; **~ to do sth** sich dafür entscheiden, etw zu tun. **~ion** /-ekʃn/ *n* Wahl *f*

elector /ɪˈlektə(r)/ *n* Wähler(in) *m(f).* ~**al** *a* Wahl-; ~**al roll** Wählerverzeichnis *nt.* ~**ate** /-rət/ *n* Wählerschaft *f*

electric /ɪˈlektrɪk/ *a,* **-ally** *adv* elektrisch

electrical /ɪˈlektrɪkl/ *a* elektrisch; ~ **engineering** Elektrotechnik *f*

electric: ~ **'blanket** *n* Heizdecke *f.* ~ **'fire** *n* elektrischer Heizofen *m*

electrician /ɪlekˈtrɪʃn/ *n* Elektriker *m*

electricity /ɪlekˈtrɪsəti/ *n* Elektrizität *f*; *(supply)* Strom *m*

electrify /ɪˈlektrɪfaɪ/ *vt (pt/pp* **-ied)** elektrifizieren. ~**ing** *a (fig)* elektrisierend

electrocute /ɪˈlektrəkjuːt/ *vt* durch einen elektrischen Schlag töten; *(execute)* auf dem elektrischen Stuhl hinrichten

electrode /ɪˈlektrəʊd/ *n* Elektrode *f*

electron /ɪˈlektrɒn/ *n* Elektron *nt*

electronic /ɪlekˈtrɒnɪk/ *a* elektronisch. ~**s** *n* Elektronik *f*

elegance /ˈelɪɡəns/ *n* Eleganz *f*

elegant /ˈelɪɡənt/ *a,* **-ly** *adv* elegant

elegy /ˈelɪdʒɪ/ *n* Elegie *f*

element /ˈelɪmənt/ *n* Element *nt.* ~**ary** /-ˈmentərɪ/ *a* elementar

elephant /ˈelɪfənt/ *n* Elefant *m*

elevat|e /ˈelɪveɪt/ *vt* heben; *(fig)* erheben. ~**ion** /-ˈveɪʃn/ *n* Erhebung *f*

elevator /ˈelɪveɪtə(r)/ *n (Amer)* Aufzug *m,* Fahrstuhl *m*

eleven /ɪˈlevn/ *a* elf ● *n* Elf *f.* ~**th** *a* elfte(r,s); **at the** ~**th hour** *(fam)* in letzter Minute

elf /elf/ *n (pl* **elves)** Elfe *f*

elicit /ɪˈlɪsɪt/ *vt* herausbekommen

eligible /ˈelɪdʒəbl/ *a* berechtigt; ~ **young man** gute Partie *f*

eliminate /ɪˈlɪmɪneɪt/ *vt* ausschalten; *(excrete)* ausscheiden

élite /eɪˈliːt/ *n* Elite *f*

ellip|se /ɪˈlɪps/ *n* Ellipse *f.* ~**tical** *a* elliptisch

elm /elm/ *n* Ulme *f*

elocution /eləˈkjuːʃn/ *n* Sprecherziehung *f*

elongate /ˈiːlɒŋɡeɪt/ *vt* verlängern

elope /ɪˈləʊp/ *vi* durchbrennen *(fam)*

eloquen|ce /ˈeləkwəns/ *n* Beredsamkeit *f.* ~**t** *a,* **-ly** *adv* beredt

else /els/ *adv* sonst; **who** ~**?** wer sonst? **nothing** ~ sonst nichts; **or** ~ oder; *(otherwise)* sonst; **someone/ somewhere** ~ jemand/irgendwo anders; **anyone** ~ jeder andere; *(as question)* sonst noch jemand? **anything** ~ alles andere; *(as question)* sonst noch etwas? ~**where** *adv* woanders

elucidate /ɪˈluːsɪdeɪt/ *vt* erläutern

elude /ɪˈluːd/ *vt* entkommen (+ *dat*); *(avoid)* ausweichen (+ *dat*)

elusive /ɪˈluːsɪv/ *a* **be** ~ schwer zu fassen sein

emaciated /ɪˈmeɪsɪeɪtɪd/ *a* abgezehrt

emanate /ˈeməneɪt/ *vi* ausgehen **(from** von)

emancipat|ed /ɪˈmænsɪpeɪtɪd/ *a* emanzipiert. ~**ion** /-ˈpeɪʃn/ *n* Emanzipation *f*; *(of slaves)* Freilassung *f*

embalm /ɪmˈbɑːm/ *vt* einbalsamieren

embankment /ɪmˈbæŋkmənt/ *n* Böschung *f*; *(of railway)* Bahndamm *m*

embargo /emˈbɑːɡəʊ/ *n (pl* **-es)** Embargo *nt*

embark /ɪmˈbɑːk/ *vi* sich einschiffen; ~ **on** anfangen mit. ~**ation** /embɑːˈkeɪʃn/ *n* Einschiffung *f*

embarrass /ɪmˈbærəs/ *vt* in Verlegenheit bringen. ~**ed** *a* verlegen. ~**ing** *a* peinlich. ~**ment** *n* Verlegenheit *f*

embassy /ˈembəsɪ/ *n* Botschaft *f*

embedded /ɪmˈbedɪd/ *a* **be deeply** ~ **in** tief stecken in (+ *dat*)

embellish /ɪmˈbelɪʃ/ *vt* verzieren; *(fig)* ausschmücken

embers /ˈembəz/ *npl* Glut *f*

embezzle /ɪmˈbezl/ *vt* unterschlagen. ~**ment** *n* Unterschlagung *f*

embitter /ɪmˈbɪtə(r)/ *vt* verbittern

emblem /ˈembləm/ *n* Emblem *nt*

embodiment /ɪmˈbɒdɪmənt/ *n* Verkörperung *f*

embody /ɪmˈbɒdɪ/ *vt (pt/pp* **-ied)** verkörpern; *(include)* enthalten

emboss /ɪmˈbɒs/ *vt* prägen

embrace /ɪmˈbreɪs/ *n* Umarmung *f* ● *vt* umarmen; *(fig)* umfassen ● *vi* sich umarmen

embroider /ɪmˈbrɔɪdə(r)/ *vt* besticken; sticken ⟨design⟩; *(fig)* ausschmücken ● *vi* sticken. ~**y** *n* Stickerei *f*

embroil /ɪmˈbrɔɪl/ *vt* **become** ~**ed in sth** in etw *(acc)* verwickelt werden

embryo /ˈembrɪəʊ/ *n* Embryo *m*

emerald /ˈemərəld/ *n* Smaragd *m*

emer|ge /ɪ'mɜːdʒ/ vi auftauchen (**from** aus); (*become known*) sich herausstellen; (*come into being*) entstehen. **~gence** /-əns/ n Auftauchen nt; Entstehung f

emergency /ɪ'mɜːdʒənsɪ/ n Notfall m; **in an ~** im Notfall. **~ exit** n Notausgang m

emery-paper /'eməri-/ n Schmirgelpapier nt

emigrant /'emɪɡrənt/ n Auswanderer m

emigrat|e /'emɪɡreɪt/ vi auswandern. **~ion** /-'ɡreɪʃn/ n Auswanderung f

eminent /'emɪnənt/ a, **-ly** adv eminent

emission /ɪ'mɪʃn/ n Ausstrahlung f; (*of pollutant*) Emission f

emit /ɪ'mɪt/ vt (*pt/pp* **emitted**) ausstrahlen ⟨light, heat⟩; ausstoßen ⟨smoke, fumes, cry⟩

emotion /ɪ'məʊʃn/ n Gefühl nt. **~al** a emotional; **become ~al** sich erregen

emotive /ɪ'məʊtɪv/ a emotional

empath|ize /'empəθaɪz/ vi **~ize with s.o.** sich in jdn einfühlen. **~y** n Einfühlungsvermögen nt

emperor /'empərə(r)/ n Kaiser m

emphasis /'emfəsɪs/ n Betonung f

emphasize /'emfəsaɪz/ vt betonen

emphatic /ɪm'fætɪk/ a, **-ally** adv nachdrücklich

empire /'empaɪə(r)/ n Reich nt

empirical /ɪm'pɪrɪkl/ a empirisch

employ /ɪm'plɔɪ/ vt beschäftigen; (*appoint*) einstellen; (*fig*) anwenden. **~ee** /emplɔɪ'iː/ n Beschäftigte(r) m/f; (*in contrast to employer*) Arbeitnehmer m. **~er** n Arbeitgeber m. **~ment** n Beschäftigung f; (*work*) Arbeit f. **~ment agency** n Stellenvermittlung f

empower /ɪm'paʊə(r)/ vt ermächtigen

empress /'emprɪs/ n Kaiserin f

empties /'emptɪz/ npl leere Flaschen pl

emptiness /'emptɪnɪs/ n Leere f

empty /'emptɪ/ a leer ● vt leeren; ausleeren ⟨container⟩ ● vi sich leeren

emulate /'emjʊleɪt/ vt nacheifern (+ dat)

emulsion /ɪ'mʌlʃn/ n Emulsion f

enable /ɪ'neɪbl/ vt **~ s.o. to** es jdm möglich machen, zu

enact /ɪ'nækt/ vt (*Theat*) aufführen

enamel /ɪ'næml/ n Email nt; (*on teeth*) Zahnschmelz m; (*paint*) Lack m ● vt (*pt/pp* **enamelled**) emaillieren

enamoured /ɪ'næməd/ a **be ~ of** sehr angetan sein von

enchant /ɪn'tʃɑːnt/ vt bezaubern. **~ing** a bezaubernd. **~ment** n Zauber m

encircle /ɪn'sɜːkl/ vt einkreisen

enclave /'enkleɪv/ n Enklave f

enclos|e /ɪn'kləʊz/ vt einschließen; (*in letter*) beilegen (**with** dat). **~ure** /-ʒə(r)/ n (*at zoo*) Gehege nt; (*in letter*) Anlage f

encompass /ɪn'kʌmpəs/ vt umfassen

encore /'ɒŋkɔː(r)/ n Zugabe f ● int bravo!

encounter /ɪn'kaʊntə(r)/ n Begegnung f; (*battle*) Zusammenstoß m ● vt begegnen (+ dat); (*fig*) stoßen auf (+ acc)

encourag|e /ɪn'kʌrɪdʒ/ vt ermutigen; (*promote*) fördern. **~e-ment** n Ermutigung f. **~ing** a ermutigend

encroach /ɪn'krəʊtʃ/ vi **~ on** eindringen in (+ acc) ⟨land⟩; beanspruchen ⟨time⟩

encumb|er /ɪn'kʌmbə(r)/ vt belasten (**with** mit). **~rance** /-rəns/ n Belastung f

encyclopaed|ia /ɪnsaɪklə'piːdɪə/ n Enzyklopädie f, Lexikon nt. **~ic** a enzyklopädisch

end /end/ n Ende nt; (*purpose*) Zweck m; **in the ~** schließlich; **at the ~ of May** Ende Mai; **on ~** hochkant; **for days on ~** tagelang; **make ~s meet** (*fam*) [gerade] auskommen; **no ~ of** (*fam*) unheimlich viel(e) ● vt beenden ● vi enden; **~ up** in (*fam: arrive at*) landen in (+ dat)

endanger /ɪn'deɪndʒə(r)/ vt gefährden

endear|ing /ɪn'dɪərɪŋ/ a liebenswert. **~ment** n **term of ~ment** Kosewort nt

endeavour /ɪn'devə(r)/ n Bemühung f ● vi sich bemühen (**to** zu)

ending /'endɪŋ/ n Schluß m, Ende nt; (*Gram*) Endung f

endive /'endaɪv/ n Endivie f

endless /'endlɪs/ a, **-ly** adv endlos

endorse /en'dɔːs/ vt (*Comm*) indossieren; (*confirm*) bestätigen. **~ment** n (*Comm*) Indossament nt; (*fig*) Bestätigung f; (*on driving licence*) Strafvermerk m

endow /ɪnˈdaʊ/ vt stiften; **be ∼ed with** (fig) haben. ∼**ment** n Stiftung f

endur|able /ɪnˈdjʊərəbl/ a erträglich. ∼**ance** /-rəns/ n Durchhaltevermögen nt; **beyond ∼ance** unerträglich

endur|e /ɪnˈdjʊə(r)/ vt ertragen ● vi [lange] bestehen. ∼**ing** a dauernd

enemy /ˈenəmɪ/ n Feind m ● attrib feindlich

energetic /enəˈdʒetɪk/ a tatkräftig; **be ∼** voller Energie sein

energy /ˈenədʒɪ/ n Energie f

enforce /ɪnˈfɔːs/ vt durchsetzen. ∼**d** a unfreiwillig

engage /ɪnˈgeɪdʒ/ vt einstellen ⟨staff⟩; (Theat) engagieren; (Auto) einlegen ⟨gear⟩ ● vi sich beteiligen (**in** an + dat); (Techn) ineinandergreifen. ∼**d** a besetzt; ⟨person⟩ beschäftigt; ⟨to be married⟩ verlobt; **get ∼d** sich verloben (**to** mit). ∼**ment** n Verlobung f; (appointment) Verabredung f; (Mil) Gefecht nt

engaging /ɪnˈgeɪdʒɪŋ/ a einnehmend

engender /ɪnˈdʒendə(r)/ vt (fig) erzeugen

engine /ˈendʒɪn/ n Motor m; (Naut) Maschine f; (Rail) Lokomotive f; (of jet-plane) Triebwerk nt. ∼**-driver** n Lokomotivführer m

engineer /endʒɪˈnɪə(r)/ n Ingenieur m; (service, installation) Techniker m; (Naut) Maschinist m; (Amer) Lokomotivführer m ● vt (fig) organisieren. ∼**ing** n [mechanical] ∼**ing** Maschinenbau m

England /ˈɪŋglənd/ n England nt

English /ˈɪŋglɪʃ/ a englisch; **the ∼ Channel** der Ärmelkanal ● n (Lang) Englisch nt; **in ∼** auf englisch; **into ∼** ins Englische; **the ∼** pl die Engländer. ∼**man** n Engländer m. ∼**woman** n Engländerin f

engrav|e /ɪnˈgreɪv/ vt eingravieren. ∼**ing** n Stich m

engross /ɪnˈgrəʊs/ vt **be ∼ed in** vertieft sein in (+ acc)

engulf /ɪnˈgʌlf/ vt verschlingen

enhance /ɪnˈhɑːns/ vt verschönern; (fig) steigern

enigma /ɪˈnɪgmə/ n Rätsel nt. ∼**tic** /enɪgˈmætɪk/ a rätselhaft

enjoy /ɪnˈdʒɔɪ/ vt genießen; ∼ **oneself** sich amüsieren; ∼ **cooking/ paint- ing** gern kochen/malen; **I ∼ed**

it es hat mir gut gefallen/⟨food:⟩ geschmeckt. ∼**able** /-əbl/ a angenehm, nett. ∼**ment** n Vergnügen nt

enlarge /ɪnˈlɑːdʒ/ vt vergrößern ● vi ∼ **upon** sich näher auslassen über (+ acc). ∼**ment** n Vergrößerung f

enlighten /ɪnˈlaɪtn/ vt aufklären. ∼**ment** n Aufklärung f

enlist /ɪnˈlɪst/ vt (Mil) einziehen; ∼ **s.o.'s help** jdn zur Hilfe heranziehen ● vi (Mil) sich melden

enliven /ɪnˈlaɪvn/ vt beleben

enmity /ˈenmətɪ/ n Feindschaft f

enormity /ɪˈnɔːmətɪ/ n Ungeheuerlichkeit f

enormous /ɪˈnɔːməs/ a, **-ly** adv riesig

enough /ɪˈnʌf/ a, adv & n genug; **be ∼** reichen; **funnily ∼** komischerweise; **I've had ∼!** (fam) jetzt reicht's mir aber!

enquir|e /ɪnˈkwaɪə(r)/ vi sich erkundigen (**about** nach) ● vt sich erkundigen nach. ∼**y** n Erkundigung f; (investigation) Untersuchung f

enrage /ɪnˈreɪdʒ/ vt wütend machen

enrich /ɪnˈrɪtʃ/ vt bereichern; (improve) anreichern

enrol /ɪnˈrəʊl/ v (pt/pp **-rolled**) ● vt einschreiben ● vi sich einschreiben. ∼**ment** n Einschreibung f

ensemble /ɒnˈsɒmbl/ n (clothing & Mus) Ensemble nt

ensign /ˈensaɪn/ n Flagge f

enslave /ɪnˈsleɪv/ vt versklaven

ensue /ɪnˈsjuː/ vi folgen; (result) sich ergeben (**from** aus)

ensure /ɪnˈʃʊə(r)/ vt sicherstellen; ∼ **that** dafür sorgen, daß

entail /ɪnˈteɪl/ vt erforderlich machen; **what does it ∼?** was ist damit verbunden?

entangle /ɪnˈtæŋgl/ vt **get ∼d** sich verfangen (**in** in + dat); (fig) sich verstricken (**in** in + acc)

enter /ˈentə(r)/ vt eintreten/ ⟨vehicle:⟩ einfahren in (+ acc); einreisen in (+ acc) ⟨country⟩; (register) eintragen; sich anmelden zu ⟨competition⟩ ● vi eintreten; ⟨vehicle:⟩ einfahren; (Theat) auftreten; (register as competitor) sich anmelden; (take part) sich beteiligen (**in** an + dat)

enterpris|e /ˈentəpraɪz/ n Unternehmen nt; (quality) Unternehmungsgeist m. ∼**ing** a unternehmend

entertain /entəˈteɪn/ vt unterhalten; (invite) einladen; (to meal) bewirten

⟨*guest*⟩; (*fig*) in Erwägung ziehen ● *vi* unterhalten; (*have guests*) Gäste haben. ∼**er** *n* Unterhalter *m*. ∼**ment** *n* Unterhaltung *f*

enthral /ɪn'θrɔːl/ *vt* (*pt/pp* **en-thralled**) be ∼**led** gefesselt sein (**by** von)

enthuse /ɪn'θjuːz/ *vi* ∼ **over** schwärmen von

enthusias|m /ɪn'θjuːzɪæzm/ *n* Begeisterung *f*. ∼**t** *n* Enthusiast *m*. ∼**tic** /-'æstɪk/ *a*, **-ally** *adv* begeistert

entice /ɪn'taɪs/ *vt* locken. ∼**ment** *n* Anreiz *m*

entire /ɪn'taɪə(r)/ *a* ganz. ∼**ly** *adv* ganz, völlig. ∼**ty** /-rətɪ/ *n* **in its** ∼**ty** in seiner Gesamtheit

entitle /ɪn'taɪtl/ *vt* berechtigen; ∼**d** … mit dem Titel …; **be** ∼**d to sth** das Recht auf etw (*acc*) haben. ∼**ment** *n* Berechtigung *f*; (*claim*) Anspruch *m* (**to** auf + *acc*)

entity /'entɪtɪ/ *n* Wesen *nt*

entomology /entə'mɒlədʒɪ/ *n* Entomologie *f*

entourage /'ɒntʊrɑːʒ/ *n* Gefolge *nt*

entrails /'entreɪlz/ *npl* Eingeweide *pl*

entrance[1] /ɪn'trɑːns/ *vt* bezaubern

entrance[2] /'entrəns/ *n* Eintritt *m*; (*Theat*) Auftritt *m*; (*way in*) Eingang *m*; (*for vehicle*) Einfahrt *f*. ∼ **ex-amination** *n* Aufnahmeprüfung *f*. ∼ **fee** *n* Eintrittsgebühr *f*

entrant /'entrənt/ *n* Teilnehmer(in) *m*(*f*)

entreat /ɪn'triːt/ *vt* anflehen (**for** um)

entrench /ɪn'trentʃ/ *vt* **be** ∼**ed in** verwurzelt sein in (+ *dat*)

entrust /ɪn'trʌst/ *vt* ∼ **s.o. with sth,** ∼ **sth to s.o.** jdm etw anvertrauen

entry /'entrɪ/ *n* Eintritt *m*; (*into coun-try*) Einreise *f*; (*on list*) Eintrag *m*; **no** ∼ Zutritt/(*Auto*) Einfahrt verboten. ∼ **form** *n* Anmeldeformular *nt*. ∼ **visa** *n* Einreisevisum *nt*

enumerate /ɪ'njuːməreɪt/ *vt* aufzählen

enunciate /ɪ'nʌnsɪeɪt/ *vt* [deutlich] aussprechen; (*state*) vorbringen

envelop /ɪn'veləp/ *vt* (*pt/pp* **en-veloped**) einhüllen

envelope /'envələʊp/ *n* [Brief]um-schlag *m*

enviable /'envɪəbl/ *a* beneidenswert

envious /'envɪəs/ *a*, **-ly** *adv* neidisch (**of** auf + *acc*)

environment /ɪn'vaɪərənmənt/ *n* Umwelt *f*

environmental /ɪnvaɪərən'mentl/ *a* Umwelt-. ∼**ist** *n* Umweltschützer *m*. ∼**ly** *adv* ∼**ly friendly** umweltfreundlich

envisage /ɪn'vɪzɪdʒ/ *vt* sich (*dat*) vorstellen

envoy /'envɔɪ/ *n* Gesandte(r) *m*

envy /'envɪ/ *n* Neid *m* ● *vt* (*pt/pp* **-ied**) ∼ **s.o. sth** jdn um etw beneiden

enzyme /'enzaɪm/ *n* Enzym *nt*

epic /'epɪk/ *a* episch ● *n* Epos *nt*

epidemic /epɪ'demɪk/ *n* Epidemie *f*

epilep|sy /'epɪlepsɪ/ *n* Epilepsie *f*. ∼**tic** /-'leptɪk/ *a* epileptisch ● *n* Epileptiker(in) *m*(*f*)

epilogue /'epɪlɒg/ *n* Epilog *m*

episode /'epɪsəʊd/ *n* Episode *f*; (*instalment*) Folge *f*

epistle /ɪ'pɪsl/ *n* (*liter*) Brief *m*

epitaph /'epɪtɑːf/ *n* Epitaph *nt*

epithet /'epɪθet/ *n* Beiname *m*

epitom|e /ɪ'pɪtəmɪ/ *n* Inbegriff *m*. ∼**ize** *vt* verkörpern

epoch /'iːpɒk/ *n* Epoche *f*. ∼**-making** *a* epochemachend

equal /'iːkwl/ *a* gleich (**to** *dat*); **be** ∼ **to a task** einer Aufgabe gewachsen sein ● *n* Gleichgestellte(r) *m*/*f* ● *vt* (*pt/pp* **equalled**) gleichen (+ *dat*); (*fig*) gleichkommen (+ *dat*). ∼**ity** /ɪ'kwɒlətɪ/ *n* Gleichheit *f*

equalize /'iːkwəlaɪz/ *vt/i* ausgleichen. ∼**r** *n* (*Sport*) Ausgleich[streffer] *m*

equally /'iːkwəlɪ/ *adv* gleich; ⟨*divide*⟩ gleichmäßig; (*just as*) genauso

equanimity /ekwə'nɪmətɪ/ *n* Gleichmut *f*

equat|e /ɪ'kweɪt/ *vt* gleichsetzen (**with** mit). ∼**ion** /-eɪʒn/ *n* (*Math*) Gleichung *f*

equator /ɪ'kweɪtə(r)/ *n* Äquator *m*. ∼**ial** /ekwə'tɔːrɪəl/ *a* Äquator-

equestrian /ɪ'kwestrɪən/ *a* Reit-

equilibrium /iːkwɪ'lɪbrɪəm/ *n* Gleichgewicht *nt*

equinox /'iːkwɪnɒks/ *n* Tagund-nachtgleiche *f*

equip /ɪ'kwɪp/ *vt* (*pt/pp* **equipped**) ausrüsten; (*furnish*) ausstatten. ∼**ment** *n* Ausrüstung *f*; Ausstattung *f*

equitable /'ekwɪtəbl/ *a* gerecht

equity /'ekwɪtɪ/ *n* Gerechtigkeit *f*

equivalent /ɪ'kwɪvələnt/ *a* gleichwertig; (*corresponding*) entsprechend ● *n* Äquivalent *nt*; (*value*)

Gegenwert *m*; (*counterpart*) Gegenstück *nt*

equivocal /ɪˈkwɪvəkl/ *a* zweideutig

era /ˈɪərə/ *n* Ära *f*, Zeitalter *nt*

eradicate /ɪˈrædɪkeɪt/ *vt* ausrotten

erase /ɪˈreɪz/ *vt* ausradieren; (*from tape*) löschen; (*fig*) auslöschen. **~r** *n* Radiergummi *m*

erect /ɪˈrekt/ *a* aufrecht ● *vt* errichten. **~ion** /-ekʃn/ *n* Errichtung *f*; (*building*) Bau *m*; (*Biol*) Erektion *f*

ermine /ˈɜːmɪn/ *n* Hermelin *m*

ero|de /ɪˈrəʊd/ *vt* (*water:*) auswaschen; (*acid:*) angreifen. **~sion** /-əʊʒn/ *n* Erosion *f*

erotic /ɪˈrɒtɪk/ *a* erotisch. **~ism** /-tɪsɪzm/ *n* Erotik *f*

err /ɜː(r)/ *vi* sich irren; (*sin*) sündigen

errand /ˈerənd/ *n* Botengang *m*

erratic /ɪˈrætɪk/ *a* unregelmäßig; (*person*) unberechenbar

erroneous /ɪˈrəʊnɪəs/ *a* falsch; (*belief, assumption*) irrig. **~ly** *adv* fälschlich; irrigerweise

error /ˈerə(r)/ *n* Irrtum *m*; (*mistake*) Fehler *m*; **in ~** irrtümlicherweise

erudit|e /ˈerʊdaɪt/ *a* gelehrt. **~ion** /-ˈdɪʃn/ *n* Gelehrsamkeit *f*

erupt /ɪˈrʌpt/ *vi* ausbrechen. **~ion** /-ʌpʃn/ *n* Ausbruch *m*

escalat|e /ˈeskələt/ *vt/i* eskalieren. **~ion** /-ˈleɪʃn/ *n* Eskalation *f*. **~or** *n* Rolltreppe *f*

escapade /ˈeskəpeɪd/ *n* Eskapade *f*

escape /ɪˈskeɪp/ *n* Flucht *f*; (*from prison*) Ausbruch *m*; **have a narrow ~** gerade noch davonkommen ● *vi* flüchten; (*prisoner:*) ausbrechen; entkommen (**from** aus; **from s.o.** jdm); (*gas:*) entweichen ● *vt* **~ notice** unbemerkt bleiben; **the name ~s me** der Name entfällt mir

escapism /ɪˈskeɪpɪzm/ *n* Flucht *f* vor der Wirklichkeit, Eskapismus *m*

escort[1] /ˈeskɔːt/ *n* (*of person*) Begleiter *m*; (*Mil*) Eskorte *f*; **under ~** unter Bewachung

escort[2] /ɪˈskɔːt/ *vt* begleiten; (*Mil*) eskortieren

Eskimo /ˈeskɪməʊ/ *n* Eskimo *m*

esoteric /esəˈterɪk/ *a* esoterisch

especial /ɪˈspeʃl/ *a* besondere(r,s). **~ly** *adv* besonders

espionage /ˈespɪɒnɑːʒ/ *n* Spionage *f*

essay /ˈeseɪ/ *n* Aufsatz *m*

essence /ˈesns/ *n* Wesen *nt*; (*Chem, Culin*) Essenz *f*; **in ~** im wesentlichen

essential /ɪˈsenʃl/ *a* wesentlich; (*indispensable*) unentbehrlich ● *n* **the ~s** das Wesentliche; (*items*) das Nötigste. **~ly** *adv* im wesentlichen

establish /ɪˈstæblɪʃ/ *vt* gründen; (*form*) bilden; (*prove*) beweisen. **~ment** *n* (*firm*) Unternehmen *nt*

estate /ɪˈsteɪt/ *n* Gut *nt*; (*possessions*) Besitz *m*; (*after death*) Nachlaß *m*; (*housing*) [Wohn]siedlung *f*. **~ agent** *n* Immobilienmakler *m*. **~ car** *n* Kombi[wagen] *m*

esteem /ɪˈstiːm/ *n* Achtung *f* ● *vt* hochschätzen

estimate[1] /ˈestɪmət/ *n* Schätzung *f*; (*Comm*) [Kosten]voranschlag *m*; **at a rough ~** grob geschätzt

estimat|e[2] /ˈestɪmeɪt/ *vt* schätzen. **~ion** /-ˈmeɪʃn/ *n* Einschätzung *f*; (*esteem*) Achtung *f*; **in my ~ion** meiner Meinung nach

estuary /ˈestjʊərɪ/ *n* Mündung *f*

etc. /etˈsetərə/ *abbr* (**et cetera**) und so weiter, usw.

etching /ˈetʃɪŋ/ *n* Radierung *f*

eternal /ɪˈtɜːnl/ *a*, **-ly** *adv* ewig

eternity /ɪˈtɜːnətɪ/ *n* Ewigkeit *f*

ether /ˈiːθə(r)/ *n* Äther *m*

ethic /ˈeθɪk/ *n* Ethik *f*. **~al** *a* ethisch; (*morally correct*) moralisch einwandfrei. **~s** *n* Ethik *f*

Ethiopia /iːθɪˈəʊpɪə/ *n* Äthiopien *nt*

ethnic /ˈeθnɪk/ *a* ethnisch

etiquette /ˈetɪket/ *n* Etikette *f*

etymology /etɪˈmɒlədʒɪ/ *n* Etymologie *f*

eucalyptus /juːkəˈlɪptəs/ *n* Eukalyptus *m*

eulogy /ˈjuːlədʒɪ/ *n* Lobrede *f*

euphemis|m /ˈjuːfəmɪzm/ *n* Euphemismus *m*. **~tic** /-ˈmɪstɪk/ *a*, **-ally** *adv* verhüllend

euphoria /juːˈfɔːrɪə/ *n* Euphorie *f*

Euro-: /ˈjʊərəʊ-/ *pref* **~cheque** *n* Euroscheck *m*. **~passport** *n* Europaß *m*

Europe /ˈjʊərəp/ *n* Europa *nt*

European /jʊərəˈpɪən/ *a* europäisch; **~ Community** Europäische Gemeinschaft *f* ● *n* Europäer(in) *m(f)*

evacuat|e /ɪˈvækjueɪt/ *vt* evakuieren; räumen (*building, area*). **~ion** /-ˈeɪʃn/ *n* Evakuierung *f*; Räumung *f*

evade /ɪˈveɪd/ *vt* sich entziehen (+ *dat*); hinterziehen (*taxes*); **~ the issue** ausweichen

evaluate /ɪˈvæljʊeɪt/ *vt* einschätzen

evange|lical /i:væn'dʒelɪkl/ *a* evangelisch. **~list** /ɪ'vændʒəlɪst/ *n* Evangelist *m*

evaporat|e /ɪ'væpəreɪt/ *vi* verdunsten; **~ed milk** Kondensmilch *f*, Dosenmilch *f*. **~ion** /-'reɪʃn/ *n* Verdampfung *f*

evasion /ɪ'veɪʒn/ *n* Ausweichen *nt*; **~ of taxes** Steuerhinterziehung *f*

evasive /ɪ'veɪsɪv/ *a*, **-ly** *adv* ausweichend; **be ~** ausweichen

eve /i:v/ *n* (*liter*) Vorabend *m*

even /'i:vn/ *a* (*level*) eben; (*same, equal*) gleich; (*regular*) gleichmäßig; (*number*) gerade; **get ~ with** (*fam*) es jdm heimzahlen ● *adv* sogar, selbst; **~ so** trotzdem; **not ~** nicht einmal ● *vt* **~ the score** ausgleichen. **~ up** *vt* ausgleichen ● *vi* sich ausgleichen

evening /'i:vnɪŋ/ *n* Abend *m*; **this ~** heute abend; **in the ~** abends, am Abend. **~ class** *n* Abendkurs *m*

evenly /'i:vnlɪ/ *adv* gleichmäßig

event /ɪ'vent/ *n* Ereignis *nt*; (*function*) Veranstaltung *f*; (*Sport*) Wettbewerb *m*; **in the ~ of** im Falle (+ *gen*); **in the ~** wie es sich ergab. **~ful** *a* ereignisreich

eventual /ɪ'ventjʊəl/ *a* **his ~ success** der Erfolg, der ihm schließlich zuteil wurde. **~ity** /-'ælətɪ/ *n* Eventualität *f*, Fall *m*. **~ly** *adv* schließlich

ever /'evə(r)/ *adv* je[mals]; **not ~** nie; **for ~** für immer; **hardly ~** fast nie; **~ since** seitdem; **~ so** (*fam*) sehr, furchtbar (*fam*)

'evergreen *n* immergrüner Strauch *m*/(*tree*) Baum *m*

ever'lasting *a* ewig

every /'evrɪ/ *a* jede(r,s); **~ one** jede(r,s) einzelne; **~ other day** jeden zweiten Tag

every:~body *pron* jeder[mann]; alle *pl*. **~day** *a* alltäglich. **~one** *pron* jeder[mann]; alle *pl*. **~thing** *pron* alles. **~where** *adv* überall

evict /ɪ'vɪkt/ *vt* [aus der Wohnung] hinausweisen. **~ion** /-ɪkʃn/ *n* Ausweisung *f*

eviden|ce /'evɪdəns/ *n* Beweise *pl*; (*Jur*) Beweismaterial *nt*; (*testimony*) Aussage *f*; **give ~ce** aussagen. **~t** *a*, **-ly** *adv* offensichtlich

evil /'i:vl/ *a* böse ● *n* Böse *nt*

evocative /ɪ'vɒkətɪv/ *a* **be ~ of** heraufbeschwören

evoke /ɪ'vəʊk/ *vt* heraufbeschwören

evolution /i:və'lu:ʃn/ *n* Evolution *f*

evolve /ɪ'vɒlv/ *vt* entwickeln ● *vi* sich entwickeln

ewe /ju:/ *n* Schaf *nt*

exacerbate /ek'sæsəbeɪt/ *vt* verschlimmern; verschärfen (*situation*)

exact /ɪg'zækt/ *a*, **-ly** *adv* genau; **not ~ly** nicht gerade. ● *vt* erzwingen. **~ing** *a* anspruchsvoll. **~itude** /-ɪtju:d/ *n*, **~ness** *n* Genauigkeit *f*

exaggerat|e /ɪg'zædʒəreɪt/ *vt/i* übertreiben. **~ion** /-'reɪʃn/ *n* Übertreibung *f*

exalt /ɪg'zɔ:lt/ *vt* erheben; (*praise*) preisen

exam /ɪg'zæm/ *n* (*fam*) Prüfung *f*

examination /ɪgzæmɪ'neɪʃn/ *n* Untersuchung *f*; (*Sch*) Prüfung *f*

examine /ɪg'zæmɪn/ *vt* untersuchen; (*Sch*) prüfen; (*Jur*) verhören. **~r** *n* (*Sch*) Prüfer *m*

example /ɪg'zɑ:mpl/ *n* Beispiel *nt* (**of** für); **for ~** zum Beispiel; **make an ~of** ein Exempel statuieren an (+ *dat*)

exasperat|e /ɪg'zæspəreɪt/ *vt* zur Verzweiflung treiben. **~ion** /-'reɪʃn/ *n* Verzweiflung *f*

excavat|e /'ekskəveɪt/ *vt* ausschachten; (*Archaeol*) ausgraben. **~ion** /-'veɪʃn/ *n* Ausgrabung *f*

exceed /ɪk'si:d/ *vt* übersteigen. **~ingly** *adv* äußerst

excel /ɪk'sel/ *v* (*pt/pp* **excelled**) *vi* sich auszeichnen ● *vt* **~ oneself** sich selbst übertreffen

excellen|ce /'eksələns/ *n* Vorzüglichkeit *f*. **E~cy** *n* (*title*) Exzellenz *f*. **~t** *a*, **-ly** *adv* ausgezeichnet, vorzüglich

except /ɪk'sept/ *prep* außer (+ *dat*); **~ for** abgesehen von ● *vt* ausnehmen. **~ing** *prep* außer (+ *dat*)

exception /ɪk'sepʃn/ *n* Ausnahme *f*; **take ~ to** Anstoß nehmen an (+ *dat*). **~al** *a*, **-ly** *adv* außergewöhnlich

excerpt /'eksɜ:pt/ *n* Auszug *m*

excess /ɪk'ses/ *n* Übermaß *nt* (**of** an + *dat*); (*surplus*) Überschuß *m*; **~es** *pl* Exzesse *pl*; **in ~ of** über (+ *dat*)

excess 'fare /'ekses-/ *n* Nachlösegebühr *f*

excessive /ɪk'sesɪv/ *a*, **-ly** *adv* übermäßig

exchange /ɪks'tʃeɪndʒ/ *n* Austausch *m*; (*Teleph*) Fernsprechamt *nt*; (*Comm*) [Geld]wechsel *m*; **[stock] ~** Börse *f*; **in ~** dafür ● *vt* austauschen (**for** gegen); tauschen ⟨*places, greetings, money*⟩. ~ **rate** *n* Wechselkurs *m*

exchequer /ɪks'tʃekə(r)/ *n* (*Pol*) Staatskasse *f*

excise[1] /'eksaɪz/ *n* ~ **duty** Verbrauchssteuer *f*

excise[2] /ek'saɪz/ *vt* herausschneiden

excitable /ɪk'saɪtəbl/ *a* [leicht] erregbar

excit|e /ɪk'saɪt/ *vt* aufregen; (*cause*) erregen. ~**ed** *a*, -**ly** *adv* aufgeregt; **get** ~**ed** sich aufregen. ~**ement** *n* Aufregung *f*; Erregung *f*. ~**ing** *a* aufregend; ⟨*story*⟩ spannend

exclaim /ɪk'skleɪm/ *vt/i* ausrufen

exclamation /eksklə'meɪʃn/ *n* Ausruf *m*. ~ **mark** *n*, (*Amer*) ~ **point** *n* Ausrufezeichen *nt*

exclu|de /ɪk'sklu:d/ *vt* ausschließen. ~**ding** *prep* ausschließlich (+ *gen*). ~**sion** /-ʒn/ *n* Ausschluß *m*

exclusive /ɪk'sklu:sɪv/ *a*, -**ly** *adv* ausschließlich; (*select*) exklusiv; ~ **of** ausschließlich (+ *gen*)

excommunicate /ekskə'mju:nɪkeɪt/ *vt* exkommunizieren

excrement /'ekskrɪmənt/ *n* Kot *m*

excrete /ɪk'skri:t/ *vt* ausscheiden

excruciating /ɪk'skru:ʃɪeɪtɪŋ/ *a* gräßlich

excursion /ɪk'skɜ:ʃn/ *n* Ausflug *m*

excusable /ɪk'skju:zəbl/ *a* entschuldbar

excuse[1] /ɪk'skju:s/ *n* Entschuldigung *f*; (*pretext*) Ausrede *f*

excuse[2] /ɪk'skju:z/ *vt* entschuldigen; ~ **from** freistellen von; ~ **me!** Entschuldigung!

ex-di'rectory *a* **be** ~ nicht im Telefonbuch stehen

execute /'eksɪkju:t/ *vt* ausführen; (*put to death*) hinrichten

execution /eksɪ'kju:ʃn/ *n* (*see* **execute**) Ausführung *f*; Hinrichtung *f*. ~**er** *n* Scharfrichter *m*

executive /ɪg'zekjʊtɪv/ *a* leitend ● *n* leitende(r) Angestellte(r) *m/f*; (*Pol*) Exekutive *f*

executor /ɪg'zekjʊtə(r)/ *n* (*Jur*) Testamentsvollstrecker *m*

exemplary /ɪg'zemplərɪ/ *a* beispielhaft; (*as a warning*) exemplarisch

exemplify /ɪg'zemplɪfaɪ/ *vt* (*pt/pp* -**ied**) veranschaulichen

exempt /ɪg'zempt/ *a* befreit ● *vt* befreien (**from** von). ~**ion** /-empʃn/ *n* Befreiung *f*

exercise /'eksəsaɪz/ *n* Übung *f*; **physical** ~ körperliche Bewegung *f*; **take** ~ sich bewegen ● *vt* (*use*) ausüben; bewegen ⟨*horse*⟩; spazierenführen ⟨*dog*⟩ ● *vi* sich bewegen. ~ **book** *n* [Schul]heft *nt*

exert /ɪg'zɜ:t/ *vt* ausüben; ~ **oneself** sich anstrengen. ~**ion** /-ɜ:ʃn/ *n* Anstrengung *f*

exhale /eks'heɪl/ *vt/i* ausatmen

exhaust /ɪg'zɔ:st/ *n* (*Auto*) Auspuff *m*; (*pipe*) Auspuffrohr *nt*; (*fumes*) Abgase *pl* ● *vt* erschöpfen. ~**ed** *a* erschöpft. ~**ing** *a* anstrengend. ~**ion** /-ɔ:stʃn/ *n* Erschöpfung *f*. ~**ive** /-ɪv/ *a* (*fig*) erschöpfend

exhibit /ɪg'zɪbɪt/ *n* Ausstellungsstück *nt*; (*Jur*) Beweisstück *nt* ● *vt* ausstellen; (*fig*) zeigen

exhibition /eksɪ'bɪʃn/ *n* Ausstellung *f*; (*Univ*) Stipendium *nt*. ~**ist** *n* Exhibitionist(in) *m(f)*

exhibitor /ɪg'zɪbɪtə(r)/ *n* Aussteller *m*

exhilarat|ed /ɪg'zɪləreɪtɪd/ *a* beschwingt. ~**ing** *a* berauschend. ~**ion** /-'reɪʃn/ *n* Hochgefühl *nt*

exhort /ɪg'zɔ:t/ *vt* ermahnen

exhume /ɪg'zju:m/ *vt* exhumieren

exile /'eksaɪl/ *n* Exil *nt*; (*person*) im Exil Lebende(r) *m/f* ● *vt* ins Exil schicken

exist /ɪg'zɪst/ *vi* bestehen, existieren. ~**ence** /-əns/ *n* Existenz *f*; **be in** ~**ence** existieren

exit /'eksɪt/ *n* Ausgang *m*; (*Auto*) Ausfahrt *f*; (*Theat*) Abgang *m* ● *vi* (*Theat*) abgehen. ~ **visa** *n* Ausreisevisum *nt*

exonerate /ɪg'zɒnəreɪt/ *vt* entlasten

exorbitant /ɪg'zɔ:bɪtənt/ *a* übermäßig hoch

exorcize /'eksɔ:saɪz/ *vt* austreiben

exotic /ɪg'zɒtɪk/ *a* exotisch

expand /ɪk'spænd/ *vt* ausdehnen; (*explain better*) weiter ausführen ● *vi* sich ausdehnen; (*Comm*) expandieren; ~ **on** (*fig*) weiter ausführen

expans|e /ɪk'spæns/ *n* Weite *f*. ~**ion** /-ænʃn/ *n* Ausdehnung *f*; (*Techn, Pol, Comm*) Expansion *f*. ~**ive** /-ɪv/ *a* mitteilsam

expatriate /eks'pætrɪət/ *n* **be an** ~ im Ausland leben

expect /ɪk'spekt/ *vt* erwarten; (*suppose*) annehmen; **I** ~ **so** wahrscheinlich; **we** ~ **to arrive on Monday**

wir rechnen damit, daß wir am Montag ankommen

expectan|cy /ɪk'spektənsɪ/ n Erwartung f. ∼t a, **-ly** adv erwartungsvoll; ∼t **mother** werdende Mutter f

expectation /ekspek'teɪʃn/ n Erwartung f; ∼ **of life** Lebenserwartung f

expedient /ɪk'spi:dɪənt/ a zweckdienlich

expedite /'ekspɪdaɪt/ vt beschleunigen

expedition /ekspɪ'dɪʃn/ n Expedition f. ∼ary a (Mil) Expeditions-

expel /ɪk'spel/ vt (pt/pp **expelled**) ausweisen (**from** aus); (from school) von der Schule verweisen

expend /ɪk'spend/ vt aufwenden. ∼**able** /-əbl/ a entbehrlich

expenditure /ɪk'spendɪtʃə(r)/ n Ausgaben pl

expense /ɪk'spens/ n Kosten pl; **business** ∼s pl Spesen pl; **at my** ∼ auf meine Kosten; **at the** ∼ **of** (fig) auf Kosten (+ gen)

expensive /ɪk'spensɪv/ a, **-ly** adv teuer

experience /ɪk'spɪərɪəns/ n Erfahrung f; (event) Erlebnis nt ● vt erleben. ∼**d** a erfahren

experiment /ɪk'sperɪmənt/ n Versuch m, Experiment nt ● /-ment/ vi experimentieren. ∼**al** /-'mentl/ a experimentell

expert /'ekspɜ:t/ a, **-ly** adv fachmännisch ● n Fachmann m, Experte m

expertise /ekspɜ:'ti:z/ n Sachkenntnis f; (skill) Geschick nt

expire /ɪk'spaɪə(r)/ vi ablaufen

expiry /ɪk'spaɪərɪ/ n Ablauf m. ∼ **date** n Verfallsdatum nt

explain /ɪk'spleɪn/ vt erklären

explana|tion /eksplə'neɪʃn/ n Erklärung f. ∼**tory** /ɪk'splænətərɪ/ a erklärend

expletive /ɪk'spli:tɪv/ n Kraftausdruck m

explicit /ɪk'splɪsɪt/ a, **-ly** adv deutlich

explode /ɪk'spləʊd/ vi explodieren ● vt zur Explosion bringen

exploit[1] /'eksplɔɪt/ n [Helden]tat f

exploit[2] /ɪk'splɔɪt/ vt ausbeuten. ∼**ation** /eksplɔɪ'teɪʃn/ n Ausbeutung f

explora|tion /eksplə'reɪʃn/ n Erforschung f. ∼**tory** /ɪk'splɒrətərɪ/ a Probe-

explore /ɪk'splɔ:(r)/ vt erforschen. ∼**r** n Forschungsreisende(r) m

explos|ion /ɪk'spləʊʒn/ n Explosion f. ∼**ive** /-sɪv/ a explosiv ● n Sprengstoff m

exponent /ɪk'spəʊnənt/ n Vertreter m

export[1] /'ekspɔ:t/ n Export m, Ausfuhr f

export[2] /ɪk'spɔ:t/ vt exportieren, ausführen. ∼**er** n Exporteur m

expos|e /ɪk'spəʊz/ vt freilegen; (to danger) aussetzen (**to** dat); (reveal) aufdecken; (Phot) belichten. ∼**ure** /-ʒə(r)/ n Aussetzung f; (Med) Unterkühlung f; (Phot) Belichtung f; **24** ∼**ures** 24 Aufnahmen

expound /ɪk'spaʊnd/ vt erläutern

express /ɪk'spres/ a ausdrücklich; (purpose) fest ● adv (send) per Eilpost ● n (train) Schnellzug m ● vt ausdrücken. ∼**ion** /-ʃn/ n Ausdruck m. ∼**ive** /-ɪv/ a ausdrucksvoll. ∼**ly** adv ausdrücklich

expulsion /ɪk'spʌlʃn/ n Ausweisung f; (Sch) Verweisung f von der Schule

expurgate /'ekspəgeɪt/ vt zensieren

exquisite /ek'skwɪzɪt/ a erlesen

ex-'serviceman n Veteran m

extempore /ɪk'stempərɪ/ adv (speak) aus dem Stegreif

extend /ɪk'stend/ vt verlängern; (stretch out) ausstrecken; (enlarge) vergrößern ● vi sich ausdehnen; (table:) sich ausziehen lassen

extension /ɪk'stenʃn/ n Verlängerung f; (to house) Anbau m; (Teleph) Nebenanschluß m; ∼ **7** Apparat 7

extensive /ɪk'stensɪv/ a weit; (fig) umfassend. ∼**ly** adv viel

extent /ɪk'stent/ n Ausdehnung f; (scope) Ausmaß nt, Umfang m; **to a certain** ∼ in gewissem Maße

extenuating /ɪk'stenjʊeɪtɪŋ/ a mildernd

exterior /ɪk'stɪərɪə(r)/ a äußere(r,s) ● n **the** ∼ das Äußere

exterminat|e /ɪk'stɜːmɪneɪt/ vt ausrotten. ∼**ion** /-'neɪʃn/ n Ausrottung f

external /ɪk'stɜːnl/ a äußere(r,s); **for** ∼ **use only** (Med) nur äußerlich. ∼**ly** adv äußerlich

extinct /ɪk'stɪŋkt/ a ausgestorben; (volcano) erloschen. ∼**ion** /-ɪŋkʃn/ n Aussterben nt

extinguish /ɪk'stɪŋgwɪʃ/ vt löschen. ∼**er** n Feuerlöscher m

extol /ɪk'stəʊl/ vt (pt/pp **extolled**) preisen

extort /ɪk'stɔːt/ vt erpressen. **∼ion** /-ɔːʃn/ n Erpressung f

extortionate /ɪk'stɔːʃənət/ a übermäßig hoch

extra /'ekstrə/ a zusätzlich ● adv extra; (especially) besonders; **∼ strong** extrastark ● n (Theat) Statist(in) m(f); **∼s** pl Nebenkosten pl; (Auto) Extras pl

extract¹ /'ekstrækt/ n Auszug m; (Culin) Extrakt m

extract² /ɪk'strækt/ vt herausziehen; ziehen ⟨tooth⟩; (fig) erzwingen. **∼or [fan]** n Entlüfter m

extradit|e /'ekstrədaɪt/ vt ausliefern. **∼ion** /-'dɪʃn/ n (Jur) Auslieferung f

extra'marital a außerehelich

extraordinary /ɪk'strɔːdɪnərɪ/ a, **-ily** adv außerordentlich; (strange) seltsam

extravagan|ce /ɪk'strævəgəns/ n Verschwendung f; **an ∼ce** ein Luxus m. **∼t** a verschwenderisch; (exaggerated) extravagant

extrem|e /ɪk'striːm/ a äußerste(r,s); (fig) extrem ● n Extrem nt; **in the ∼e** im höchsten Grade. **∼ely** adv äußerst. **∼ist** n Extremist m

extremit|y /ɪk'stremətɪ/ n (distress) Not f; **the ∼ies** pl die Extremitäten pl

extricate /'ekstrɪkeɪt/ vt befreien

extrovert /'ekstrəvɜːt/ n extravertierter Mensch m

exuberant /ɪg'zjuːbərənt/ a überglücklich

exude /ɪg'zjuːd/ vt absondern; (fig) ausstrahlen

exult /ɪg'zʌlt/ vi frohlocken

eye /aɪ/ n Auge nt; (of needle) Öhr nt; (for hook) Öse f; **keep an ∼ on** aufpassen auf (+ acc); **see ∼ to ∼** einer Meinung sein ● vt (pt/pp **eyed**, pres p **ey[e]ing**) ansehen

eye: ∼ball n Augapfel m. **∼brow** n Augenbraue f. **∼lash** n Wimper f. **∼let** /-lɪt/ n Öse f. **∼lid** n Augenlid nt. **∼-shadow** n Lidschatten m. **∼sight** n Sehkraft f. **∼sore** n (fam) Schandfleck m. **∼-tooth** n Eckzahn m. **∼witness** n Augenzeuge m

F

fable /'feɪbl/ n Fabel f

fabric /'fæbrɪk/ n Stoff m; (fig) Gefüge nt

fabrication /fæbrɪ'keɪʃn/ n Erfindung f

fabulous /'fæbjʊləs/ a (fam) phantastisch

façade /fə'sɑːd/ n Fassade f

face /feɪs/ n Gesicht nt; (grimace) Grimasse f; (surface) Fläche f; (of clock) Zifferblatt nt; **pull ∼s** Gesichter schneiden; **in the ∼ of** angesichts (+ gen); **on the ∼ of it** allem Anschein nach ● vt/i gegenüberstehen (+ dat); **∼ north** ⟨house:⟩ nach Norden liegen; **∼ me!** sieh mich an! **∼ the fact that** sich damit abfinden, daß; **∼ up to s.o.** jdm die Stirn bieten

face: ∼-flannel n Waschlappen m. **∼less** a anonym. **∼-lift** n Gesichtsstraffung f

facet /'fæsɪt/ n Facette f; (fig) Aspekt m

facetious /fə'siːʃəs/ a, **-ly** adv spöttisch

'face value n Nennwert m

facial /'feɪʃl/ a Gesichts-

facile /'fæsaɪl/ a oberflächlich

facilitate /fə'sɪlɪteɪt/ vt erleichtern

facilit|y /fə'sɪlətɪ/ n Leichtigkeit f; (skill) Gewandtheit f; **∼ies** pl Einrichtungen pl

facing /'feɪsɪŋ/ n Besatz m

facsimile /fæk'sɪmlɪ/ n Faksimile nt

fact /fækt/ n Tatsache f; **in ∼** tatsächlich; (actually) eigentlich

faction /'fækʃn/ n Gruppe f

factor /'fæktə(r)/ n Faktor m

factory /'fæktərɪ/ n Fabrik f

factual /'fæktʃʊəl/ a, **-ly** adv sachlich

faculty /'fækəltɪ/ n Fähigkeit f; (Univ) Fakultät f

fad /fæd/ n Fimmel m

fade /feɪd/ vi verblassen; ⟨material:⟩ verbleichen; ⟨sound:⟩ abklingen; ⟨flower:⟩ verwelken. **∼ in/out** vt (Radio, TV) ein-/ausblenden

fag /fæg/ n (chore) Plage f; (fam: cigarette) Zigarette f; (Amer sl) Homosexuelle(r) m

fagged /fægd/ a **∼ out** (fam) völlig erledigt

Fahrenheit /'færənhaɪt/ a Fahrenheit

fail /feɪl/ n **without ∼** unbedingt ● vi ⟨attempt:⟩ scheitern; (grow weak) nachlassen; (break down) versagen; (in exam) durchfallen; **∼ to do sth** etw

nicht tun; **he ~ed to break the record**
es gelang ihm nicht, den Rekord zu brechen ● *vt* nicht bestehen ⟨*exam*⟩; durchfallen lassen ⟨*candidate*⟩; ⟨*disappoint*⟩
enttäuschen; **words ~ me** ich weiß
nicht, was ich sagen soll

failing /'feɪlɪŋ/ *n* Fehler *m* ● *prep* ~
that andernfalls

failure /'feɪljə(r)/ *n* Mißerfolg *m*;
(*breakdown*) Versagen *nt*; (*person*)
Versager *m*

faint /feɪnt/ *a* (**-er, -est**), **-ly** *adv*
schwach; **I feel ~** mir ist schwach ● *n*
Ohnmacht *f* ● *vi* ohnmächtig werden

faint: ~-'hearted *a* zaghaft. **~ness**
n Schwäche *f*

fair[1] /feə(r)/ *n* Jahrmarkt *m*; (*Comm*)
Messe *f*

fair[2] *a* (**-er, -est**) ⟨*hair*⟩ blond; ⟨*skin*⟩ hell;
⟨*weather*⟩ heiter; (*just*) gerecht, fair;
(*quite good*) ziemlich gut; (*Sch*) genügend; **a ~ amount** ziemlich viel ● *adv*
play ~ fair sein. **~ly** *adv* gerecht; (*rather*) ziemlich. **~ness** *n*
Blondheit *f*; Helle *f*; Gerechtigkeit *f*;
(*Sport*) Fairneß *f*

fairy /'feərɪ/ *n* Elfe *f*; **good/wicked ~**
gute/böse Fee *f*. **~ story, ~-tale** *n*
Märchen *nt*

faith /feɪθ/ *n* Glaube *m*; (*trust*) Vertrauen *nt* (**in** zu); **in good ~** in gutem
Glauben

faithful /'feɪθfl/ *a*, **-ly** *adv* treu; (*exact*)
genau; **Yours ~ly** Hochachtungsvoll.
~ness *n* Treue *f*; Genauigkeit *f*

'faith-healer *n* Gesundbeter(in)
m(*f*)

fake /feɪk/ *a* falsch ● *n* Fälschung *f*;
(*person*) Schwindler *m* ● *vt* fälschen;
(*pretend*) vortäuschen

falcon /'fɔːlkən/ *n* Falke *m*

fall /fɔːl/ *n* Fall *m*; (*heavy*) Sturz *m*;
(*in prices*) Fallen *nt*; (*Amer: autumn*)
Herbst *m*; **have a ~** fallen ● *vi* (*pt* **fell**,
pp **fallen**) fallen; (*heavily*) stürzen;
⟨*night:*⟩ anbrechen; **~ in love** sich verlieben; **~ back on** zurückgreifen auf
(+ *acc*); **~ for s.o.** (*fam*) sich in jdn verlieben; **~ for sth** (*fam*) auf etw (*acc*)
hereinfallen. **~ about** *vi* (*with laughter*) sich [vor Lachen] kringeln. **~
down** *vi* umfallen; ⟨*thing:*⟩ herun-
terfallen; ⟨*building:*⟩ einstürzen. **~
in** *vi* hineinfallen; (*collapse*) einfallen; (*Mil*) antreten; **~ in with** sich
anschließen (+ *dat*). **~ off** *vi* herun-
terfallen; (*diminish*) abnehmen. **~**

out *vi* her- ausfallen; ⟨*hair:*⟩ ausfallen; (*quarrel*) sich überwerfen. **~
over** *vi* hinfallen. **~ through** *vi*
durchfallen; ⟨*plan:*⟩ ins Wasser fallen

fallacy /'fæləsɪ/ *n* Irrtum *m*

fallible /'fæləbl/ *a* fehlbar

'fall-out *n* [radioaktiver] Niederschlag *m*

fallow /'fæləʊ/ *a* **lie ~** brachliegen

false /fɔːls/ *a* falsch; (*artificial*)
künstlich; **~ start** (*Sport*) Fehlstart *m*.
~hood *n* Unwahrheit *f*. **~ly** *adv*
falsch. **~ness** *n* Falschheit *f*

false 'teeth *npl* [künstliches] Gebiß
nt

falsify /'fɔːlsɪfaɪ/ *vt* (*pt/pp* **-ied**) fälschen; (*misrepresent*) verfälschen

falter /'fɔːltə(r)/ *vi* zögern; (*stumble*)
straucheln

fame /feɪm/ *n* Ruhm *m*. **~d** *a* berühmt

familiar /fə'mɪljə(r)/ *a* vertraut;
(*known*) bekannt; **too ~** familiär.
~ity /-lɪ'ærətɪ/ *n* Vertrautheit *f*.
~ize *vt* vertraut machen (**with** mit)

family /'fæməlɪ/ *n* Familie *f*

family: ~ al'lowance *n* Kindergeld
nt. **~ 'doctor** *n* Hausarzt *m*. **~ 'life**
n Familienleben *nt*. **~ 'planning** *n*
Familienplanung *f*. **~ 'tree** *n*
Stammbaum *m*

famine /'fæmɪn/ *n* Hungersnot *f*

famished /'fæmɪʃt/ *a* sehr hungrig

famous /'feɪməs/ *a* berühmt

fan[1] /fæn/ *n* Fächer *m*; (*Techn*) Ventilator *m* ● *v* (*pt/pp* **fanned**) ● *vt*
fächeln; **~ oneself** sich fächeln ● *vi* **~
out** sich fächerförmig ausbreiten

fan[2] *n* (*admirer*) Fan *m*

fanatic /fə'nætɪk/ *n* Fanatiker *m*.
~al *a*, **-ly** *adv* fanatisch. **~ism**
/-sɪzm/ *n* Fanatismus *m*

'fan belt *n* Keilriemen *m*

fanciful /'fænsɪfl/ *a* phantastisch;
(*imaginative*) phantasiereich

fancy /'fænsɪ/ *n* Phantasie *f*; **have a
~ to** Lust haben, zu; **I have taken a
real ~ to him** er hat es mir angetan
● *a* ausgefallen; **~ cakes and biscuits**
Feingebäck *nt* ● *vt* (*believe*) meinen;
(*imagine*) sich (*dat*) einbilden; (*fam:
want*) Lust haben auf (+ *acc*); **~ that!**
stell dir vor! (*really*) tatsächlich! **~
'dress** *n* Kostüm *nt*

fanfare /'fænfeə(r)/ *n* Fanfare *f*

fang /fæŋ/ *n* Fangzahn *m*; (*of snake*)
Giftzahn *m*

fan: ~ **heater** n Heizlüfter m. ~**light** n Oberlicht nt

fantas|ize /'fæntəsaɪz/ vi phantasieren. ~**tic** /-'tæstɪk/ a phantastisch. ~**y** n Phantasie f; (Mus) Fantasie f

far /fɑː(r)/ adv weit; (much) viel; **by** ~ bei weitem; ~ **away** weit weg; **as** ~ **as I know** soviel ich weiß; **as** ~ **as the church** bis zur Kirche ● a at the ~ **end** am anderen Ende; **the F**~ **East** der Ferne Osten

farc|e /fɑːs/ n Farce f. ~**ical** a lächerlich

fare /feə(r)/ n Fahrpreis m; (money) Fahrgeld nt; (food) Kost f; **air** ~ Flugpreis m. ~**dodger** /-dɒdʒə(r)/ n Schwarzfahrer m

farewell /feə'wel/ int (liter) lebe wohl! ● n Lebewohl nt; ~ **dinner** Abschiedsessen nt

far-'fetched a weit hergeholt; **be** ~ an den Haaren herbeigezogen sein

farm /fɑːm/ n Bauernhof m ● vi Landwirtschaft betreiben ● vt bewirtschaften (land). ~**er** n Landwirt m

farm: ~**house** n Bauernhaus nt. ~**ing** n Landwirtschaft f. ~**yard** n Hof m

far: ~**-'reaching** a weitreichend. ~**-'sighted** a (fig) umsichtig; (Amer: long-sighted) weitsichtig

fart /fɑːt/ n (vulg) Furz m ● vi (vulg) furzen

farther /'fɑːðə(r)/ adv weiter; ~ **off** weiter entfernt ● a at the ~ **end** am anderen Ende

fascinat|e /'fæsɪneɪt/ vt faszinieren. ~**ing** a faszinierend. ~**ion** /-'neɪʃn/ n Faszination f

fascis|m /'fæʃɪzm/ n Faschismus m. ~**t** n Faschist m ● a faschistisch

fashion /'fæʃn/ n Mode f; (manner) Art f ● vt machen; (mould) formen. ~**able** /-əbl/ a, **-bly** adv modisch; **be** ~**able** Mode sein

fast[1] /fɑːst/ a & adv (-er, -est) schnell; (firm) fest; (colour) waschecht; **be** ~ (clock:) vorgehen; **be** ~ **asleep** fest schlafen

fast[2] n Fasten nt ● vi fasten

'fastback n (Auto) Fließheck nt

fasten /'fɑːsn/ vt zumachen; (fix) befestigen (**to** an + dat); ~ **one's seatbelt** sich anschnallen. ~**er** n, ~**ing** n Verschluß m

fastidious /fə'stɪdɪəs/ a wählerisch; (particular) penibel

fat /fæt/ a (fatter, fattest) dick; (meat) fett ● n Fett nt

fatal /'feɪtl/ a tödlich; (error) verhängnisvoll. ~**ism** /-təlɪzm/ n Fatalismus m. ~**ist** /-təlɪst/ n Fatalist m. ~**ity** /fə'tælətɪ/ n Todesopfer nt. ~**ly** adv tödlich

fate /feɪt/ n Schicksal nt. ~**ful** a verhängnisvoll

'fat-head n (fam) Dummkopf m

father /'fɑːðə(r)/ n Vater m; **F**~ **Christmas** der Weihnachtsmann ● vt zeugen

father: ~**hood** n Vaterschaft f. ~**-in-law** n (pl ~**s-in-law**) Schwiegervater m. ~**ly** a väterlich

fathom /'fæðəm/ n (Naut) Faden m ● vt verstehen; ~ **out** ergründen

fatigue /fə'tiːg/ n Ermüdung f ● vt ermüden

fatten /'fætn/ vt mästen (animal). ~**ing** a **cream is** ~**ing** Sahne macht dick

fatty /'fætɪ/ a fett; (foods) fetthaltig

fatuous /'fætjʊəs/ a, **-ly** adv albern

faucet /'fɔːsɪt/ n (Amer) Wasserhahn m

fault /fɔːlt/ n Fehler m; (Techn) Defekt m; (Geol) Verwerfung f; **at** ~ im Unrecht; **find** ~ **with** etwas auszusetzen haben an (+ dat); **it's your** ~ du bist schuld ● vt etwas auszusetzen haben an (+ dat). ~**less** a, **-ly** adv fehlerfrei

faulty /'fɔːltɪ/ a fehlerhaft

fauna /'fɔːnə/ n Fauna f

favour /'feɪvə(r)/ n Gunst f; **I am in** ~ ich bin dafür; **do s.o. a** ~ jdm einen Gefallen tun ● vt begünstigen; (prefer) bevorzugen. ~**able** /-əbl/ a, **-bly** adv günstig; (reply) positiv

favourit|e /'feɪvərɪt/ a Lieblings- ● n Liebling m; (Sport) Favorit(in) m(f). ~**ism** n Bevorzugung f

fawn[1] /fɔːn/ a rehbraun ● n Hirschkalb nt

fawn[2] vi sich einschmeicheln (**on** bei)

fax /fæks/ n Fax nt ● vt faxen (**s.o.** jdm). ~ **machine** n Faxgerät nt

fear /fɪə(r)/ n Furcht f, Angst f (**of** vor + dat); **no** ~! (fam) keine Angst! ● vt/i fürchten

fear|ful /'fɪəfl/ a besorgt; (awful) furchtbar. ~**less** a, **-ly** adv furchtlos. ~**some** /-səm/ a furchterregend

feas|ibility /fiːzəˈbɪlətɪ/ n Durchführbarkeit f. **~ible** a durchführbar; (possible) möglich

feast /fiːst/ n Festmahl nt; (Relig) Fest nt ● vi **~ [on]** schmausen

feat /fiːt/ n Leistung f

feather /ˈfeðə(r)/ n Feder f

feature /ˈfiːtʃə(r)/ n Gesichtszug m; (quality) Merkmal nt; (Journ) Feature nt ● vt darstellen; ⟨film:⟩ in der Hauptrolle zeigen. **~ film** n Hauptfilm m

February /ˈfebrʊərɪ/ n Februar m

feckless /ˈfeklɪs/ a verantwortungslos

fed /fed/ see **feed** ● a **be ~ up** (fam) die Nase voll haben (**with** von)

federal /ˈfedərəl/ a Bundes-

federation /fedəˈreɪʃn/ n Föderation f

fee /fiː/ n Gebühr f; (professional) Honorar nt

feeble /ˈfiːbl/ a (**-r, -st**), **-bly** adv schwach

feed /fiːd/ n Futter nt; (for baby) Essen nt ● v (pt/pp **fed**) ● vt füttern; (support) ernähren; (into machine) eingeben; speisen ⟨computer⟩ ● vi sich ernähren (**on** von)

'feedback n Feedback nt

feel /fiːl/ v (pt/pp **felt**) ● vt fühlen; (experience) empfinden; (think) meinen ● vi sich fühlen; **~ soft/hard** sich weich/hart anfühlen; **I ~ hot/ill** mir ist heiß/schlecht; **I don't ~ like it** ich habe keine Lust dazu. **~er** n Fühler m. **~ing** n Gefühl nt; **no hard ~ings** nichts für ungut

feet /fiːt/ see **foot**

feign /feɪn/ vt vortäuschen

feint /feɪnt/ n Finte f

feline /ˈfiːlaɪn/ a Katzen-; (catlike) katzenartig

fell¹ /fel/ vt fällen

fell² see **fall**

fellow /ˈfeləʊ/ n (of society) Mitglied nt; (fam: man) Kerl m

fellow: ~-ˈcountryman n Landsmann m. **~ men** pl Mitmenschen pl. **~ship** n Kameradschaft f; (group) Gesellschaft f

felony /ˈfelənɪ/ n Verbrechen nt

felt¹ /felt/ see **feel**

felt² n Filz m. **~[-tipped] 'pen** n Filzstift m

female /ˈfiːmeɪl/ a weiblich ● nt Weibchen nt; (pej: woman) Weib nt

femin|ine /ˈfemɪnɪn/ a weiblich ● n (Gram) Femininum nt. **~inity** /-ˈnɪnətɪ/ n Weiblichkeit f. **~ist** a feministisch ● n Feminist(in) m(f)

fenc|e /fens/ n Zaun m; (fam: person) Hehler m ● vi (Sport) fechten ● vt **~e in** einzäunen. **~er** n Fechter m. **~ing** n Zaun m; (Sport) Fechten nt

fend /fend/ vi **~ for oneself** sich allein durchschlagen. **~ off** vt abwehren

fender /ˈfendə(r)/ n Kaminvorsetzer m; (Naut) Fender m; (Amer: wing) Kotflügel m

fennel /ˈfenl/ n Fenchel m

ferment¹ /ˈfɜːment/ n Erregung f

ferment² /fəˈment/ vi gären ● vt gären lassen. **~ation** /fɜːmenˈteɪʃn/ n Gärung f

fern /fɜːn/ n Farn m

feroc|ious /fəˈrəʊʃəs/ a wild. **~ity** /-ˈrɒsətɪ/ n Wildheit f

ferret /ˈferɪt/ n Frettchen nt

ferry /ˈferɪ/ n Fähre f ● vt **~ [across]** übersetzen

fertil|e /ˈfɜːtaɪl/ a fruchtbar. **~ity** /fɜːˈtɪlətɪ/ n Fruchtbarkeit f

fertilize /ˈfɜːtəlaɪz/ vt befruchten; düngen ⟨land⟩. **~r** n Dünger m

fervent /ˈfɜːvənt/ a leidenschaftlich

fervour /ˈfɜːvə(r)/ n Leidenschaft f

fester /ˈfestə(r)/ vi eitern

festival /ˈfestɪvl/ n Fest nt; (Mus, Theat) Festspiele pl

festiv|e /ˈfestɪv/ a festlich; **~e season** Festzeit f. **~ities** /feˈstɪvətɪz/ npl Feierlichkeiten pl

festoon /feˈstuːn/ vt behängen (**with** mit)

fetch /fetʃ/ vt holen; (collect) abholen; (be sold for) einbringen

fetching /ˈfetʃɪŋ/ a anziehend

fête /feɪt/ n Fest nt ● vt feiern

fetish /ˈfetɪʃ/ n Fetisch m

fetter /ˈfetə(r)/ vt fesseln

fettle /ˈfetl/ n **in fine ~** in bester Form

feud /fjuːd/ n Fehde f

feudal /ˈfjuːdl/ a Feudal-

fever /ˈfiːvə(r)/ n Fieber nt. **~ish** a fiebrig; (fig) fieberhaft

few /fjuː/ a (**-er, -est**) wenige; **every ~ days** alle paar Tage ● n **a ~** ein paar; **quite a ~** ziemlich viele

fiancé /frˈɒnseɪ/ n Verlobte(r) m. **fiancée** n Verlobte f

fiasco /frˈæskəʊ/ n Fiasko nt

fib /fɪb/ n kleine Lüge; **tell a ~** schwindeln

fibre /ˈfaɪbə(r)/ n Faser f

fickle /'fɪkl/ *a* unbeständig
fiction /'fɪkʃn/ *n* Erfindung *f*; **[works of]** ~ Erzählungsliteratur *f*. ~**al** *a* erfunden
fictitious /fɪk'tɪʃəs/ *a* [frei] erfunden
fiddle /'fɪdl/ *n* (*fam*) Geige *f*; (*cheating*) Schwindel *m* ● *vi* herumspielen (**with** mit) ● *vt* (*fam*) frisieren ⟨*accounts*⟩; ⟨*arrange*⟩ arrangieren
fiddly /'fɪdlɪ/ *a* knifflig
fidelity /fɪ'delətɪ/ *n* Treue *f*
fidget /'fɪdʒɪt/ *vi* zappeln. ~**y** *a* zappelig
field /fiːld/ *n* Feld *nt*; (*meadow*) Wiese *f*; (*subject*) Gebiet *nt*
field: ~ **events** *npl* Sprung- und Wurfdisziplinen *pl*. ~**-glasses** *npl* Feldstecher *m*. F~ '**Marshal** *n* Feldmarschall *m*. ~**work** *n* Feldforschung *f*
fiend /fiːnd/ *n* Teufel *m*. ~**ish** *a* teuflisch
fierce /fɪəs/ *a* (**-r, -st**), **-ly** *adv* wild; (*fig*) heftig. ~**ness** *n* Wildheit *f*; (*fig*) Heftigkeit *f*
fiery /'faɪərɪ/ *a* (**-ier, -iest**) feurig
fifteen /fɪf'tiːn/ *a* fünfzehn ● *n* Fünfzehn *f*. ~**th** *a* fünfzehnte(r,s)
fifth /fɪfθ/ *a* fünfte(r,s)
fiftieth /'fɪftɪɪθ/ *a* fünfzigste(r,s)
fifty /'fɪftɪ/ *a* fünfzig
fig /fɪg/ *n* Feige *f*
fight /faɪt/ *n* Kampf *m*; (*brawl*) Schlägerei *f*; (*between children, dogs*) Rauferei *f* ● *v* (*pt/pp* **fought**) ● *vt* kämpfen gegen; (*fig*) bekämpfen ● *vi* kämpfen; (*brawl*) sich schlagen; ⟨*children, dogs:*⟩ sich raufen. ~**er** *n* Kämpfer *m*; (*Aviat*) Jagdflugzeug *nt*. ~**ing** *n* Kampf *m*
figment /'fɪgmənt/ *n* ~ **of the imagination** Hirngespinst *nt*
figurative /'fɪgjərətɪv/ *a*, **-ly** *adv* bildlich, übertragen
figure /'fɪgə(r)/ *n* (*digit*) Ziffer *f*; (*number*) Zahl *f*; (*sum*) Summe *f*; (*carving, sculpture, woman's*) Figur *f*; (*form*) Gestalt *f*; (*illustration*) Abbildung *f*; ~ **of speech** Redefigur *f*; **good at** ~**s** gut im Rechnen ● *vi* (*appear*) erscheinen ● *vt* (*Amer: think*) glauben. ~ **out** *vt* ausrechnen
figure: ~**-head** *n* Galionsfigur *f*; (*fig*) Repräsentationsfigur *f*. ~ **skating** *n* Eiskunstlauf *m*
filament /'fɪləmənt/ *n* Faden *m*; (*Electr*) Glühfaden *m*

filch /fɪltʃ/ *vt* (*fam*) klauen
file[1] /faɪl/ *n* Akte *f*; (*for documents*) [Akten]ordner *m* ● *vt* ablegen ⟨*documents*⟩; (*Jur*) einreichen
file[2] *n* (*line*) Reihe *f*; **in single** ~ im Gänsemarsch
file[3] *n* (*Techn*) Feile *f* ● *vt* feilen
filigree /'fɪlɪgriː/ *n* Filigran *nt*
filings /'faɪlɪŋz/ *npl* Feilspäne *pl*
fill /fɪl/ *n* **eat one's** ~ sich satt essen ● *vt* füllen; plombieren ⟨*tooth*⟩ ● *vi* sich füllen. ~ **in** *vt* auffüllen; ausfüllen ⟨*form*⟩. ~ **out** *vt* ausfüllen ⟨*form*⟩. ~ **up** *vi* sich füllen ● *vt* vollfüllen; (*Auto*) volltanken; ausfüllen ⟨*form*⟩
fillet /'fɪlɪt/ *n* Filet *nt* ● *vt* (*pt/pp* **filleted**) entgräten
filling /'fɪlɪŋ/ *n* Füllung *f*; (*of tooth*) Plombe *f*. ~ **station** *n* Tankstelle *f*
filly /'fɪlɪ/ *n* junge Stute *f*
film /fɪlm/ *n* Film *m*; (*Culin*) **[cling]** ~ Klarsichtfolie *f* ● *vt/i* filmen; verfilmen ⟨*book*⟩. ~ **star** *n* Filmstar *m*
filter /'fɪltə(r)/ *n* Filter *m* ● *vt* filtern. ~ **through** *vi* durchsickern. ~ **tip** *n* Filter *m*; (*cigarette*) Filterzigarette *f*
filth /fɪlθ/ *n* Dreck *m*. ~**y** *a* (**-ier, -iest**) dreckig
fin /fɪn/ *n* Flosse *f*
final /'faɪnl/ *a* letzte(r,s); (*conclusive*) endgültig; ~ **result** Endresultat *nt* ● *n* (*Sport*) Finale *nt*, Endspiel *nt*; ~**s** *pl* (*Univ*) Abschlußprüfung *f*
finale /fɪ'nɑːlɪ/ *n* Finale *nt*
final|ist /'faɪnəlɪst/ *n* Finalist(in) *m*(*f*). ~**ity** /-'nælətɪ/ *n* Endgültigkeit *f*
final|ize /'faɪnəlaɪz/ *vt* endgültig festlegen. ~**ly** *adv* schließlich
finance /faɪ'næns/ *n* Finanz *f* ● *vt* finanzieren
financial /faɪ'nænʃl/ *a*, **-ly** *adv* finanziell
finch /fɪntʃ/ *n* Fink *m*
find /faɪnd/ *n* Fund *m* ● *vt* (*pt/pp* **found**) finden; (*establish*) feststellen; **go and** ~ holen; **try to** ~ suchen; ~ **guilty** (*Jur*) schuldig sprechen. ~ **out** *vt* herausfinden; (*learn*) erfahren ● *vi* (*enquire*) sich erkundigen
findings /'faɪndɪŋz/ *npl* Ergebnisse *pl*
fine[1] /faɪn/ *n* Geldstrafe *f* ● *vt* zu einer Geldstrafe verurteilen
fine[2] *a* (**-r, -st**), **-ly** *adv* fein; ⟨*weather*⟩ schön; **he's** ~ es geht ihm gut ● *adv* gut; **cut it** ~ (*fam*) sich (*dat*) wenig Zeit lassen. ~ **arts** *npl* schöne Künste *pl*

finery /'faɪnərɪ/ n Putz m, Staat m

finesse /fɪ'nes/ n Gewandtheit f

finger /'fɪŋgə(r)/ n Finger m ●vt anfassen

finger ~-**mark** n Fingerabdruck m. ~-**nail** n Fingernagel m. ~**print** n Fingerabdruck m. ~**tip** n Fingerspitze f; **have sth at one's** ~**tips** etw im kleinen Finger haben

finicky /'fɪnɪkɪ/ a knifflig; (choosy) wählerisch

finish /'fɪnɪʃ/ n Schluß m; (Sport) Finish nt; (line) Ziel nt; (of product) Ausführung f ●vt beenden; (use up) aufbrauchen; ~ **one's drink** austrinken; ~ **reading** zu Ende lesen ●vi fertig werden; (performance:) zu Ende sein; (runner:) durchs Ziel gehen

finite /'faɪnaɪt/ a begrenzt

Finland /'fɪnlənd/ n Finnland nt

Finn /fɪn/ n Finne m/Finnin f. ~**ish** a finnisch

fiord /fjɔːd/ n Fjord m

fir /fɜː(r)/ n Tanne f

fire /'faɪə(r)/ n Feuer nt; (forest, house) Brand m; **be on** ~ brennen; **catch** ~ Feuer fangen; **set** ~ **to** anzünden; (arsonist:) in Brand setzen; **under** ~ unter Beschuß ●vt brennen (pottery); abfeuern (shot); schießen mit (gun); (fam: dismiss) feuern ●vi schießen (**at** auf + acc); (engine:) anspringen

fire: ~ **alarm** n Feueralarm m; (apparatus) Feuermelder m. ~**arm** n Schußwaffe f. ~ **brigade** n Feuerwehr f. ~-**engine** n Löschfahrzeug nt. ~-**escape** n Feuertreppe f. ~ **extinguisher** n Feuerlöscher m. ~**man** n Feuerwehrmann m. ~**place** n Kamin m. ~**side** n **by** or **at the** ~**side** am Kamin. ~ **station** n Feuerwache f. ~**wood** n Brennholz nt. ~**work** n Feuerwerkskörper m; ~**works** pl (display) Feuerwerk nt

'**firing squad** n Erschießungskommando nt

firm[1] /fɜːm/ n Firma f

firm[2] a (-**er**, -**est**), -**ly** adv fest; (resolute) entschlossen; (strict) streng

first /fɜːst/ a & n erste(r,s); **at** ~ zuerst; **who's** ~? wer ist der erste? **at** ~ **sight** auf den ersten Blick; **for the** ~ **time** zum ersten Mal; **from the** ~ von Anfang an ●adv zuerst; (firstly) erstens

first: ~ '**aid** n Erste Hilfe. ~-'**aid kit** n Verbandkasten m. ~-**class** a erstklassig; (Rail) erster Klasse ●/-'-/ adv (travel) erster Klasse. ~ e'**dition** n Erstausgabe f. ~ '**floor** n erster Stock; (Amer: ground floor) Erdgeschoß nt. ~**ly** adv erstens. ~ **name** n Vorname m. ~-**rate** a erstklassig

fish /fɪʃ/ n Fisch m ●vt/i fischen; (with rod) angeln. ~ **out** vt herausfischen

fish: ~**bone** n Gräte f. ~**erman** n Fischer m. ~-**farm** n Fischzucht f. ~ '**finger** n Fischstäbchen nt

fishing /'fɪʃɪŋ/ n Fischerei f. ~ **boat** n Fischerboot nt. ~-**rod** n Angel[rute] f

fish: ~**monger** /-mʌŋgə(r)/ n Fischhändler m. ~-**slice** n Fischheber m. ~**y** a Fisch-; (fam: suspicious) verdächtig

fission /'fɪʃn/ n (Phys) Spaltung f

fist /fɪst/ n Faust f

fit[1] /fɪt/ n (attack) Anfall m

fit[2] a (**fitter, fittest**) (suitable) geeignet; (healthy) gesund; (Sport) fit; ~ **to eat** eßbar; **keep** ~ sich fit halten; **see** ~ es für angebracht halten (**to** zu)

fit[3] n (of clothes) Sitz m; **be a good** ~ gut passen ●v (pt/pp **fitted**) ●vi (be the right size) passen ●vt anbringen (**to** an + dat); (install) einbauen; (clothes:) passen (+ dat); ~ **with** versehen mit. ~ **in** vi hineinpassen; (adapt) sich einfügen (**with** in + acc) ●vt (accommodate) unterbringen

fit|**ful** /'fɪtfl/ a, -**ly** adv (sleep) unruhig. ~**ment** n Einrichtungsgegenstand m; (attachment) Zusatzgerät nt. ~**ness** n Eignung f; [**physical**] ~**ness** Gesundheit f; (Sport) Fitneß f. ~**ted** a eingebaut; (garment) tailliert

fitted: ~ '**carpet** n Teppichboden m. ~ '**cupboard** n Einbauschrank m. ~ '**kitchen** n Einbauküche f. ~ '**sheet** n Spannlaken nt

fitter /'fɪtə(r)/ n Monteur m

fitting /'fɪtɪŋ/ a passend ●n (of clothes) Anprobe f; (of shoes) Weite f; (Techn) Zubehörteil nt; ~**s** pl Zubehör nt. ~ **room** n Anprobekabine f

five /faɪv/ a fünf ●n Fünf f. ~**r** n Fünfpfundschein m

fix /fɪks/ n (sl: drugs) Fix m; **be in a** ~ (fam) in der Klemme sitzen ●vt befestigen (**to** an + dat); (arrange) festlegen; (repair) reparieren; (Phot) fixieren; ~ **a meal** (*Amer*) Essen machen

fixation /fɪkˈseɪʃn/ n Fixierung f

fixed /fɪkst/ a fest

fixture /ˈfɪkstʃə(r)/ n (*Sport*) Veranstaltung f; ~**s and fittings** zu einer Wohnung gehörende Einrichtungen pl

fizz /fɪz/ vi sprudeln

fizzle /ˈfɪzl/ vi ~ **out** verpuffen

fizzy /ˈfɪzɪ/ a sprudelnd. ~ **drink** n Brause[limonade] f

flabbergasted /ˈflæbəɡɑːstɪd/ a **be ~** platt sein (*fam*)

flabby /ˈflæbɪ/ a schlaff

flag[1] /flæɡ/ n Fahne f; (*Naut*) Flagge f ● vt (*pt/pp* **flagged**) ~ **down** anhalten ⟨*taxi*⟩

flag[2] vi (*pt/pp* **flagged**) ermüden

flagon /ˈflæɡən/ n Krug m

'flag-pole n Fahnenstange f

flagrant /ˈfleɪɡrənt/ a flagrant

'flagstone n [Pflaster]platte f

flair /fleə(r)/ n Begabung f

flake /fleɪk/ n Flocke f ● vi ~ **[off]** abblättern

flaky /ˈfleɪkɪ/ a blättrig. ~ **pastry** n Blätterteig m

flamboyant /flæmˈbɔɪənt/ a extravagant

flame /fleɪm/ n Flamme f

flammable /ˈflæməbl/ a feuergefährlich

flan /flæn/ n **[fruit]** ~ Obsttorte f

flank /flæŋk/ n Flanke f ● vt flankieren

flannel /ˈflænl/ n Flanell m; (*for washing*) Waschlappen m

flannelette /flænəˈlet/ n (*Tex*) Biber m

flap /flæp/ n Klappe f; **in a ~** (*fam*) aufgeregt ● v (*pt/pp* **flapped**) vi flattern; (*fam*) sich aufregen ● vt ~ **its wings** mit den Flügeln schlagen

flare /fleə(r)/ n Leuchtsignal nt. ● vi ~ **up** auflodern; (*fam: get angry*) aufbrausen. ~**d** a ⟨*garment*⟩ ausgestellt

flash /flæʃ/ n Blitz m; **in a ~** (*fam*) im Nu ● vi blitzen; (*repeatedly*) blinken; ~ **past** vorbeirasen ● vt aufleuchten lassen; ~ **one's headlights** die Lichthupe betätigen

flash: ~**back** n Rückblende f. ~**bulb** n (*Phot*) Blitzbirne f. ~**er** n (*Auto*) Blinker m. ~**light** n (*Phot*) Blitzlicht nt; (*Amer: torch*) Taschenlampe f. ~**y** a auffällig

flask /flɑːsk/ n Flasche f; (*Chem*) Kolben m; (*vacuum* ~) Thermosflasche (P) f

flat /flæt/ a (**flatter, flattest**) flach; ⟨*surface*⟩ eben; ⟨*refusal*⟩ glatt; ⟨*beer*⟩ schal; ⟨*battery*⟩ verbraucht/(*Auto*) leer; ⟨*tyre*⟩ platt; (*Mus*) **A** ~ As nt; **B** ~ B nt ● n Wohnung f; (*Mus*) Erniedrigungszeichen nt; (*fam: puncture*) Reifenpanne f

flat: ~ **'feet** npl Plattfüße pl. ~**-fish** n Plattfisch m. ~**ly** adv ⟨*refuse*⟩ glatt. ~ **rate** n Einheitspreis m

flatten /ˈflætn/ vt platt drücken

flatter /ˈflætə(r)/ vt schmeicheln (+ *dat*). ~**y** n Schmeichelei f

flat 'tyre n Reifenpanne f

flatulence /ˈflætjʊləns/ n Blähungen pl

flaunt /flɔːnt/ vt prunken mit

flautist /ˈflɔːtɪst/ n Flötist(in) m(f)

flavour /ˈfleɪvə(r)/ n Geschmack m ● vt abschmecken. ~**ing** n Aroma nt

flaw /flɔː/ n Fehler m. ~**less** a tadellos; ⟨*complexion*⟩ makellos

flax /flæks/ n Flachs m. ~**en** a flachsblond

flea /fliː/ n Floh m. ~ **market** n Flohmarkt m

fleck /flek/ n Tupfen m

fled /fled/ see **flee**

flee /fliː/ v (*pt/pp* **fled**) ● vi fliehen (**from** vor + *dat*) ● vt flüchten aus

fleece /fliːs/ n Vlies nt ● vt (*fam*) schröpfen. ~**y** a flauschig

fleet /fliːt/ n Flotte f; (*of cars*) Wagenpark m

fleeting /ˈfliːtɪŋ/ a flüchtig

Flemish /ˈflemɪʃ/ a flämisch

flesh /fleʃ/ n Fleisch nt; **in the ~** (*fam*) in Person. ~**y** a fleischig

flew /fluː/ see **fly**[2]

flex[1] /fleks/ vt anspannen ⟨*muscle*⟩

flex[2] n (*Electr*) Schnur f

flexibility /fleksəˈbɪlətɪ/ n Biegsamkeit f; (*fig*) Flexibilität f. ~**le** a biegsam; (*fig*) flexibel

'flexitime /ˈfleksɪ-/ n Gleitzeit f

flick /flɪk/ vt schnippen. ~ **through** vi schnell durchblättern

flicker /ˈflɪkə(r)/ vi flackern

flier /ˈflaɪə(r)/ n = **flyer**

flight[1] /flaɪt/ n (*fleeing*) Flucht f; **take ~** die Flucht ergreifen

flight[2] n (*flying*) Flug m; ~ **of stairs** Treppe f

flight: ~ **path** n Flugschneise f. ~ **recorder** n Flugschreiber m

flighty /ˈflaɪtɪ/ a (**-ier, -iest**) flatterhaft

flimsy /'flɪmzɪ/ a (**-ier, -iest**) dünn; ⟨excuse⟩ fadenscheinig

flinch /flɪntʃ/ vi zurückzucken

fling /flɪŋ/ n **have a ~** (fam) sich austoben ● vt (pt/pp **flung**) schleudern

flint /flɪnt/ n Feuerstein m

flip /flɪp/ vt/i schnippen; **~ through** durchblättern

flippant /'flɪpənt/ a, **-ly** adv leichtfertig

flipper /'flɪpə(r)/ n Flosse f

flirt /flɜːt/ n kokette Frau f ● vi flirten

flirtat|ion /flɜː'teɪʃn/ n Flirt m. **~i-ous** /-ʃəs/ a kokett

flit /flɪt/ vi (pt/pp **flitted**) flattern

float /fləʊt/ n Schwimmer m; (in procession) Festwagen m; (money) Wechselgeld nt ● vi ⟨thing:⟩ schwimmen; ⟨person:⟩ sich treiben lassen; (in air) schweben; (Comm) floaten

flock /flɒk/ n Herde f; (of birds) Schwarm m ● vi strömen

flog /flɒg/ vt (pt/pp **flogged**) auspeitschen; (fam: sell) verkloppen

flood /flʌd/ n Überschwemmung f; (fig) Flut f; **be in ~** ⟨river:⟩ Hochwasser führen ● vt überschwemmen ● vi ⟨river:⟩ über die Ufer treten

'floodlight n Flutlicht nt ● vt (pt/pp **floodlit**) anstrahlen

floor /flɔː(r)/ n Fußboden m; (storey) Stock m ● vt (baffle) verblüffen

floor: ~board n Dielenbrett nt. **~-cloth** n Scheuertuch nt. **~-polish** n Bohnerwachs nt. **~ show** n Kabarettvorstellung f

flop /flɒp/ n (fam) (failure) Reinfall m; (Theat) Durchfall m ● vi (pt/pp **flopped**) (fam) (fail) durchfallen; **~ down** sich plumpsen lassen

floppy /'flɒpɪ/ a schlapp. **~ 'disc** n Diskette f

flora /'flɔːrə/ n Flora f

floral /'flɔːrl/ a Blumen-

florid /'flɒrɪd/ a ⟨complexion⟩ gerötet; ⟨style⟩ blumig

florist /'flɒrɪst/ n Blumenhändler(in) m(f)

flounce /flaʊns/ n Volant m ● vi **~ out** hinausstolzieren

flounder[1] /'flaʊndə(r)/ vi zappeln

flounder[2] n (fish) Flunder f

flour /'flaʊə(r)/ n Mehl nt

flourish /'flʌrɪʃ/ n große Geste f; (scroll) Schnörkel m ● vi gedeihen; (fig) blühen ● vt schwenken

floury /'flaʊərɪ/ a mehlig

flout /flaʊt/ vt mißachten

flow /fləʊ/ n Fluß m; (of traffic, blood) Strom m ● vi fließen

flower /'flaʊə(r)/ n Blume f ● vi blühen

flower: ~-bed n Blumenbeet nt. **~ed** a geblümt. **~pot** n Blumentopf m. **~y** a blumig

flown /fləʊn/ see **fly**[2]

flu /fluː/ n (fam) Grippe f

fluctuat|e /'flʌktjʊeɪt/ vi schwanken. **~ion** /-'eɪʃn/ n Schwankung f

fluent /'fluːənt/ a, **-ly** adv fließend

fluff /flʌf/ n Fusseln pl; (down) Flaum m. **~y** a (**-ier, -iest**) flauschig

fluid /'fluːɪd/ a flüssig; (fig) veränderlich ● n Flüssigkeit f

fluke /fluːk/ n [glücklicher] Zufall m

flung /flʌŋ/ see **fling**

flunk /flʌŋk/ vt/i (Amer, fam) durchfallen (in + dat)

fluorescent /flʊə'resnt/ a fluoreszierend; **~ lighting** Neonbeleuchtung f

fluoride /'flʊəraɪd/ n Fluor nt

flurry /'flʌrɪ/ n (snow) Gestöber nt; (fig) Aufregung f

flush /flʌʃ/ n (blush) Erröten nt ● vi rot werden ● vt spülen ● a in einer Ebene (**with** mit); (fam: affluent) gut bei Kasse

flustered /'flʌstəd/ a nervös

flute /fluːt/ n Flöte f

flutter /'flʌtə(r)/ n Flattern nt ● vi flattern

flux /flʌks/ n **in a state of ~** im Fluß

fly[1] /flaɪ/ n (pl **flies**) Fliege f

fly[2] v (pt **flew**, pp **flown**) ● vi fliegen; ⟨flag:⟩ wehen; (rush) sausen ● vt fliegen; führen ⟨flag⟩

fly[3] n & **flies** pl (on trousers) Hosenschlitz m

flyer /'flaɪə(r)/ n Flieger(in) m(f); (Amer: leaflet) Flugblatt nt

flying: ~ 'buttress n Strebebogen m. **~ 'saucer** n fliegende Untertasse f. **~ 'visit** n Stippvisite f

fly: ~leaf n Vorsatzblatt nt. **~over** n Überführung f

foal /fəʊl/ n Fohlen nt

foam /fəʊm/ n Schaum m; (synthetic) Schaumstoff m ● vi schäumen. **~ 'rubber** n Schaumgummi m

fob /fɒb/ vt (pt/pp **fobbed**) **~ sth off** etw andrehen (**on s.o.** jdm); **~ s.o. off** jdn abspeisen (**with** mit)

focal /'fəʊkl/ n Brenn-

focus /'fəʊkəs/ n Brennpunkt m; **in ~** scharf eingestellt ● v (pt/pp **focused**

or **focussed)** ● *vt* einstellen (**on** auf + *acc*); (*fig*) konzentrieren (**on** auf + *acc*) ● *vi* (*fig*) sich konzentrieren (**on** auf + *acc*)

fodder /'fɒdə(r)/ *n* Futter *nt*

foe /fəʊ/ *n* Feind *m*

foetus /'fiːtəs/ *n* (*pl* **-tuses**) Fötus *m*

fog /fɒg/ *n* Nebel *m*

foggy /'fɒgɪ/ *a* (**foggier, foggiest**) neblig

'fog-horn *n* Nebelhorn *nt*

fogy /'fəʊgɪ/ *n* **old** ~ alter Knacker *m*

foible /'fɔɪbl/ *n* Eigenart *f*

foil¹ /fɔɪl/ *n* Folie *f*; (*Culin*) Alufolie *f*

foil² *vt* (*thwart*) vereiteln

foil³ *n* (*Fencing*) Florett *nt*

foist /fɔɪst/ *vt* andrehen (**on s.o.** jdm)

fold¹ /fəʊld/ *n* (*for sheep*) Pferch *m*

fold² *n* Falte *f*; (*in paper*) Kniff *m* ● *vt* falten; ~ **one's arms** die Arme verschränken ● *vi* sich falten lassen; (*fail*) eingehen. ~ **up** *vt* zusammenfalten; zusammenklappen 〈*chair*〉 ● *vi* sich zusammenfalten/ -klappen lassen; (*fam*) 〈*business:*〉 eingehen

fold|er /'fəʊldə(r)/ *n* Mappe *f*. ~**ing** *a* Klapp-

foliage /'fəʊlɪɪdʒ/ *n* Blätter *pl*; (*of tree*) Laub *nt*

folk /fəʊk/ *npl* Leute *pl*

folk: ~-**dance** *n* Volkstanz *m*. ~**lore** *n* Folklore *f*. ~-**song** *n* Volkslied *nt*

follow /'fɒləʊ/ *vt/i* folgen (+ *dat*); (*pursue*) verfolgen; (*in vehicle*) nachfahren (+ *dat*); ~ **suit** (*fig*) dasselbe tun. ~ **up** *vt* nachgehen (+ *dat*)

follow|er /'fɒləʊə(r)/ *n* Anhänger(in) *m(f)*. ~**ing** *a* folgend ● *n* Folgende(s) *nt*; (*supporters*) Anhängerschaft *f* ● *prep* im Anschluß an (+ *acc*)

folly /'fɒlɪ/ *n* Torheit *f*

fond /fɒnd/ *a* (**-er, -est**), **-ly** *adv* liebevoll; **be** ~ **of** gern haben; gern essen 〈*food*〉

fondle /'fɒndl/ *vt* liebkosen

fondness /'fɒndnɪs/ *n* Liebe *f* (**for** zu)

font /fɒnt/ *n* Taufstein *m*

food /fuːd/ *n* Essen *nt*; (*for animals*) Futter *nt*; (*groceries*) Lebensmittel *pl*

food: ~ **mixer** *n* Küchenmaschine *f*. ~ **poisoning** *n* Lebensmittelvergiftung *f*. ~ **processor** *n* Küchenmaschine *f* ~ **value** *n* Nährwert *m*

fool¹ /fuːl/ *n* (*Culin*) Fruchtcreme *f*

fool² *n* Narr *m*; **you are a** ~ du bist dumm; **make a** ~ **of oneself** sich

lächerlich machen ● *vt* hereinlegen ● *vi* ~ **around** herumalbern

'fool|hardy *a* tollkühn. ~**ish** *a*, **-ly** *adv* dumm. ~**ishness** *n* Dummheit *f*. ~**proof** *a* narrensicher

foot /fʊt/ *n* (*pl* **feet**) Fuß *m*; (*measure*) Fuß *m* (30,48 cm); (*of bed*) Fußende *nt*; **on** ~ zu Fuß; **on one's feet** auf den Beinen; **put one's** ~ **in it** (*fam*) ins Fettnäpfchen treten

foot: ~-**and**-'**mouth disease** *n* Maul- und Klauenseuche *f*. ~**ball** *n* Fußball *m*. ~**baller** *n* Fußballspieler *m*. ~**ball pools** *npl* Fußballtoto *nt*. ~-**brake** *n* Fußbremse *f*. ~-**bridge** *n* Fußgängerbrücke *f*. ~**hills** *npl* Vorgebirge *nt*. ~**hold** *n* Halt *m*. ~**ing** *n* Halt *m*; (*fig*) Basis *f*. ~**lights** *npl* Rampenlicht *nt*. ~**man** *n* Lakai *m*. ~**note** *n* Fußnote *f*. ~**path** *n* Fußweg *m*. ~**print** *n* Fußabdruck *m*. ~**step** *n* Schritt *m*; **follow in s.o.'s** ~**steps** (*fig*) in jds Fußstapfen treten. ~**stool** *n* Fußbank *f*. ~**wear** *n* Schuhwerk *nt*

for /fə(r), *betont* fɔː(r)/ *prep* für (+ *acc*); 〈*send, long*〉 nach; 〈*ask, fight*〉 um; **what** ~? wozu? ~ **supper** zum Abendessen; ~ **nothing** umsonst; ~ **all that** trotz allem; ~ **this reason** aus diesem Grund; ~ **a month** einen Monat; **I have lived here** ~ **ten years** ich wohne seit zehn Jahren hier ● *conj* denn

forage /'fɒrɪdʒ/ *n* Futter *nt* ● *vi* ~ **for** suchen nach

forbade /fə'bæd/ *see* **forbid**

forbear|ance /fɔː'beərəns/ *n* Nachsicht *f*. ~**ing** *a* nachsichtig

forbid /fə'bɪd/ *vt* (*pt* **forbade**, *pp* **forbidden**) verbieten (**s.o.** jdm). ~**ding** *a* bedrohlich; (*stern*) streng

force /fɔːs/ *n* Kraft *f*; (*of blow*) Wucht *f*; (*violence*) Gewalt *f*; **in** ~ gültig; (*in large numbers*) in großer Zahl; **come into** ~ in Kraft treten; **the** ~**s** *pl* die Streitkräfte *pl* ● *vt* zwingen; (*break open*) aufbrechen; ~ **sth on s.o.** jdm etw aufdrängen

forced /fɔːst/ *a* gezwungen; ~ **landing** *n* Notlandung *f*

force: ~-'**feed** *vt* (*pt/pp* **-fed**) zwangsernähren. ~**ful** *a*, **-ly** *adv* energisch

forceps /'fɔːseps/ *n inv* Zange *f*

forcibl|e /'fɔːsəbl/ *a* gewaltsam. ~**y** *adv* mit Gewalt

ford /fɔːd/ n Furt f ● vt durchwaten; (in vehicle) durchfahren

fore /fɔː(r)/ a vordere(r,s) ● n **to the ∼** im Vordergrund

fore: **∼arm** n Unterarm m. **∼boding** /-'bəʊdɪŋ/ n Vorahnung f. **∼cast** n Voraussage f; (for weather) Vorhersage f ● vt (pt/pp **∼cast**) voraussagen, vorhersagen. **∼court** n Vorhof m. **∼fathers** npl Vorfahren pl. **∼finger** n Zeigefinger m. **∼front** n **be in the ∼front** führend sein. **∼gone** a **be a ∼gone conclusion** von vornherein feststehen. **∼ground** n Vordergrund m. **∼head** /'fɒrɪd/ n Stirn f. **∼hand** n Vorhand f

foreign /'fɒrən/ a ausländisch; (country) fremd; **he is ∼** er ist Ausländer. **∼ currency** n Devisen pl. **∼er** n Ausländer(in) m(f). **∼ language** n Fremdsprache f

Foreign: **∼ Office** n ≈ Außenministerium nt. **∼ 'Secretary** n ≈ Außenminister m

fore: **∼leg** n Vorderbein nt. **∼man** n Vorarbeiter m. **∼most** a führend ● adv first and **∼most** zuallererst. **∼name** n Vorname m

forensic /fə'rensɪk/ a **∼ medicine** Gerichtsmedizin f

'forerunner n Vorläufer m

fore'see vt (pt **-saw**, pp **-seen**) voraussehen, vorhersehen. **∼able** /-əbl/ a **in the ∼able future** in absehbarer Zeit

'foresight n Weitblick m

forest /'fɒrɪst/ n Wald m. **∼er** n Förster m

fore'stall vt zuvorkommen (+ dat)

forestry /'fɒrɪstrɪ/ n Forstwirtschaft f

'foretaste n Vorgeschmack m

fore'tell vt (pt/pp **-told**) vorhersagen

forever /fə'revə(r)/ adv für immer

fore'warn vt vorher warnen

foreword /'fɔːwɜːd/ n Vorwort nt

forfeit /'fɔːfɪt/ n (in game) Pfand nt ● vt verwirken

forgave /fə'geɪv/ see **forgive**

forge[1] /fɔːdʒ/ vi **∼ ahead** (fig) Fortschritte machen

forge[2] n Schmiede f ● vt schmieden; (counterfeit) fälschen. **∼r** n Fälscher m. **∼ry** n Fälschung f

forget /fə'get/ vt/i (pt **-got**, pp **-gotten**) vergessen; verlernen (language, skill). **∼ful** a vergeßlich. **∼fulness** n Vergeßlichkeit f. **∼-me-not** n Vergißmeinnicht nt

forgive /fə'gɪv/ vt (pt **-gave**, pp **-given**) **∼ s.o. for sth** jdm etw vergeben od verzeihen. **∼ness** n Vergebung f, Verzeihung f

forgo /fɔː'gəʊ/ vt (pt **-went**, pp **-gone**) verzichten auf (+ acc)

forgot(ten) /fə'gɒt(n)/ see **forget**

fork /fɔːk/ n Gabel f; (in road) Gabelung f ● vi ⟨road:⟩ sich gabeln; **∼ right** rechts abzweigen. **∼ out** vt (fam) blechen

fork-lift 'truck n Gabelstapler m

forlorn /fə'lɔːn/ a verlassen; ⟨hope⟩ schwach

form /fɔːm/ n Form f; (document) Formular nt; (bench) Bank f; (Sch) Klasse f ● vt formen (**into** zu); (create) bilden ● vi sich bilden; ⟨idea:⟩ Gestalt annehmen

formal /'fɔːml/ a, **-ly** adv formell, förmlich. **∼ity** /-'mælətɪ/ n Förmlichkeit f; (requirement) Formalität f

format /'fɔːmæt/ n Format nt

formation /fɔː'meɪʃn/ n Formation f

formative /'fɔːmətɪv/ a **∼ years** Entwicklungsjahre pl

former /'fɔːmə(r)/ a ehemalig; **the ∼** der/die/das erstere. **∼ly** adv früher

formidable /'fɔːmɪdəbl/ a gewaltig

formula /'fɔːmjʊlə/ n (pl **-ae** /-liː/ or **-s**) Formel f

formulate /'fɔːmjʊleɪt/ vt formulieren

forsake /fə'seɪk/ vt (pt **-sook** /-sʊk/, pp **-saken**) verlassen

fort /fɔːt/ n (Mil) Fort nt

forte /'fɔːteɪ/ n Stärke f

forth /fɔːθ/ adv **back and ∼** hin und her; **and so ∼** und so weiter

forth: **∼'coming** a bevorstehend; (fam: communicative) mitteilsam. **∼right** a direkt. **∼'with** adv umgehend

fortieth /'fɔːtɪɪθ/ a vierzigste(r,s)

fortification /fɔːtɪfɪ'keɪʃn/ n Befestigung f

fortify /'fɔːtɪfaɪ/ vt (pt/pp **-ied**) befestigen; (fig) stärken

fortitude /'fɔːtɪtjuːd/ n Standhaftigkeit f

fortnight /'fɔːt-/ n vierzehn Tage pl. **∼ly** a vierzehntäglich ● adv alle vierzehn Tage

fortress /'fɔːtrɪs/ n Festung f

fortuitous /fɔː'tjuːɪtəs/ a, **-ly** adv zufällig

fortunate /'fɔːtʃʊnət/ a glücklich; **be ∼** Glück haben. **∼ly** adv glücklicherweise

fortune /'fɔːtʃuːn/ n Glück nt; (money) Vermögen nt. ~**-teller** n Wahrsagerin f

forty /'fɔːtɪ/ a vierzig; **have ~ winks** (fam) ein Nickerchen machen ●n Vierzig f

forum /'fɔːrəm/ n Forum nt

forward /'fɔːwəd/ adv vorwärts; (to the front) nach vorn ●a Vorwärts-; (presumptuous) anmaßend ●n (Sport) Stürmer m ●vt nachsenden ⟨letter⟩. ~**s** adv vorwärts

fossil /'fɒsl/ n Fossil nt. ~**ized** a versteinert

foster /'fɒstə(r)/ vt fördern; in Pflege nehmen ⟨child⟩. ~**-child** n Pflegekind nt. ~**-mother** n Pflegemutter f

fought /fɔːt/ see **fight**

foul /faʊl/ a (-er, -est) widerlich; ⟨language⟩ unflätig; ~ **play** (Jur) Mord m ●n (Sport) Foul nt ●vt verschmutzen; (obstruct) blockieren; (Sport) foulen. ~**-smelling** a übelriechend

found[1] /faʊnd/ see **find**

found[2] vt gründen

foundation /faʊn'deɪʃn/ n (basis) Grundlage f; ⟨charitable⟩ Stiftung f. ~**s** pl Fundament nt. ~**-stone** n Grundstein m

founder[1] /'faʊndə(r)/ n Gründer(in) m(f)

founder[2] vi ⟨ship:⟩ sinken; (fig) scheitern

foundry /'faʊndrɪ/ n Gießerei f

fountain /'faʊntɪn/ n Brunnen m. ~**-pen** n Füllfederhalter m

four /fɔː(r)/ a vier ●n Vier f

four: ~**-'poster** n Himmelbett nt. ~**some** /-səm/ n **in a ~some** zu viert. ~**'teen** a vierzehn ●n Vierzehn f. ~**'teenth** a vierzehnte(r,s)

fourth /fɔːθ/ a vierte(r,s)

fowl /faʊl/ n Geflügel nt

fox /fɒks/ n Fuchs m ●vt (puzzle) verblüffen

foyer /'fɔɪeɪ/ n Foyer nt; (in hotel) Empfangshalle f

fraction /'frækʃn/ n Bruchteil m; (Math) Bruch m

fracture /'fræktʃə(r)/ n Bruch m ●vt/i brechen

fragile /'frædʒaɪl/ a zerbrechlich

fragment /'frægmənt/ n Bruchstück nt, Fragment nt. ~**ary** a bruchstückhaft

fragran|ce /'freɪgrəns/ n Duft m. ~**t** a duftend

frail /freɪl/ a (-er, -est) gebrechlich

frame /freɪm/ n Rahmen m; (of spectacles) Gestell nt; (Anat) Körperbau m; ~ **of mind** Gemütsverfassung f ●vt einrahmen; (fig) formulieren; (sl) ein Verbrechen anhängen (+ dat). ~**work** n Gerüst nt; (fig) Gerippe nt

franc /fræŋk/ n (French, Belgian) Franc m; (Swiss) Franken m

France /frɑːns/ n Frankreich nt

franchise /'fræntʃaɪz/ n (Pol) Wahlrecht nt; (Comm) Franchise nt

frank[1] /fræŋk/ vt frankieren

frank[2] a, **-ly** adv offen

frankfurter /'fræŋkfɜːtə(r)/ n Frankfurter f

frantic /'fræntɪk/ a, **-ally** adv verzweifelt; **be ~** außer sich (dat) sein (**with** vor)

fraternal /frə'tɜːnl/ a brüderlich

fraud /frɔːd/ n Betrug m; (person) Betrüger(in) m(f). ~**ulent** /-jʊlənt/ a betrügerisch

fraught /frɔːt/ a ~ **with danger** gefahrvoll

fray[1] /freɪ/ n Kampf m

fray[2] vi ausfransen

freak /friːk/ n Mißbildung f; (person) Mißgeburt f; (phenomenon) Ausnahmeerscheinung f ●a anormal. ~**ish** a anormal

freckle /'frekl/ n Sommersprosse f. ~**d** a sommersprossig

free /friː/ a (**freer, freest**) frei; ⟨ticket, copy, time⟩ Frei-; (lavish) freigebig; ~ **[of charge]** kostenlos; **set ~** freilassen; (rescue) befreien; **you are ~ to...** es steht Ihnen frei, zu... ●vt (pt/pp **freed**) freilassen; (rescue) befreien; (disentangle) freibekommen

free: ~**dom** n Freiheit f. ~**hand** adv aus freier Hand. ~**hold** n [freier] Grundbesitz m. ~ **'kick** n Freistoß m. ~**lance** a & adv freiberuflich. ~**ly** adv frei; (voluntarily) freiwillig; (generously) großzügig. **F~mason** n Freimaurer m. **F~masonry** n Freimaurerei f. ~**-range** a ~**-range eggs** Landeier pl. ~ **'sample** n Gratisprobe f. ~**style** n Freistil m. ~**way** n (Amer) Autobahn f. ~**-'wheel** vi im Freilauf fahren

freez|e /friːz/ vt (pt **froze**, pp **frozen**) einfrieren; stoppen ⟨wages⟩ ●vi gefrieren; **it's ~ing** es friert

freez|er /'friːzə(r)/ n Gefriertruhe f; (upright) Gefrierschrank m. ~**ing** a eiskalt ●n **below ~ing** unter Null

freight /freɪt/ n Fracht f. ~er n
Frachter m. ~ **train** n (Amer) Güterzug m

French /frentʃ/ a französisch ● n
(Lang) Französisch nt; **the** ~ pl die
Franzosen

French: ~ '**beans** npl grüne Bohnen
pl. ~ '**bread** n Stangenbrot nt. ~
'**fries** npl Pommes frites pl. ~**man** n
Franzose m. ~ '**window** n Ter-
rassentür f. ~**woman** n Französin f

frenzied /'frenzɪd/ a rasend

frenzy /'frenzi/ n Raserei f

frequency /'fri:kwənsɪ/ n Häu-
figkeit f; (Phys) Frequenz f

frequent[1] /'fri:kwənt/ a, **-ly** adv häufig

frequent[2] /frɪ'kwent/ vt regelmäßig
besuchen

fresco /'freskəʊ/ n Fresko nt

fresh /freʃ/ a (**-er, -est**), **-ly** adv frisch;
(new) neu; (Amer: cheeky) frech

freshen /'freʃn/ vi (wind:) auffrischen. ~ **up** vt auffrischen ● vi sich
frisch machen

freshness /'freʃnɪs/ n Frische f

'**freshwater** a Süßwasser-

fret /fret/ vi (pt/pp **fretted**) sich
grämen. ~**ful** a weinerlich

'**fretsaw** n Laubsäge f

friar /'fraɪə(r)/ n Mönch m

friction /'frɪkʃn/ n Reibung f; (fig)
Reibereien pl

Friday /'fraɪdeɪ/ n Freitag m

fridge /frɪdʒ/ n Kühlschrank m

fried /fraɪd/ see **fry**[2] ● a gebraten; ~
egg Spiegelei nt

friend /frend/ n Freund(in) m(f).
~**liness** n Freundlichkeit f. ~**ly** a
(**-ier, -iest**) freundlich; ~**ly with** befreundet mit. ~**ship** n Freundschaft f

frieze /fri:z/ n Fries m

fright /fraɪt/ n Schreck m

frighten /'fraɪtn/ vt angst machen
(+ dat); (startle) erschrecken; be
~**ed** Angst haben (**of** vor + dat). ~**ing**
a angsterregend

frightful /'fraɪtfl/ a, **-ly** adv schrecklich

frigid /'frɪdʒɪd/ a frostig; (Psych) fri-
gide. ~**ity** /-'dʒɪdətɪ/ n Frostigkeit f;
Frigidität f

frill /frɪl/ n Rüsche f; (paper) Manschette f. ~**y** a rüschenbesetzt

fringe /frɪndʒ/ n Fransen pl; (of hair)
Pony m; (fig: edge) Rand m. ~ **be-**
nefits npl zusätzliche Leistungen pl

frisk /frɪsk/ vi herumspringen ● vt
(search) durchsuchen, (fam) filzen

frisky /'frɪskɪ/ a (**-ier, -iest**) lebhaft

fritter /'frɪtə(r)/ vt ~ [**away**] ver-
plempern (fam)

frivol|ity /frɪ'vɒlətɪ/ n Frivolität f.
~**ous** /'frɪvələs/ a, **-ly** adv frivol,
leichtfertig

frizzy /'frɪzɪ/ a kraus

fro /frəʊ/ see **to**

frock /frɒk/ n Kleid nt

frog /frɒg/ n Frosch m. ~**man** n
Froschmann m. ~**-spawn** n Frosch-
laich m

frolic /'frɒlɪk/ vi (pt/pp **frolicked**)
herumtollen

from /frɒm/ prep von (+ dat); (out
of) aus (+ dat); (according to) nach
(+ dat); ~ **Monday** ab Montag; ~ **that**
day seit dem Tag

front /frʌnt/ n Vorderseite f; (fig)
Fassade f; (of garment) Vorderteil nt;
(sea-) Strandpromenade f; (Mil, Pol,
Meteorol) Front f; **in** ~ **of** vor; **in** or **at**
the ~ vorne; **to the** ~ nach vorne ● a
vordere(r,s); (page, row) erste(r,s);
(tooth, wheel) Vorder-

frontal /'frʌntl/ a Frontal-

front: ~ '**door** n Haustür f. ~ '**gar-**
den n Vorgarten m

frontier /'frʌntɪə(r)/ n Grenze f

front-wheel '**drive** n Vorder-
radantrieb m

frost /frɒst/ n Frost m; (hoar-) Rau-
reif m; **ten degrees of** ~ zehn Grad
Kälte. ~**bite** n Erfrierung f. ~**bitten**
a erfroren

frost|ed /'frɒstɪd/ a ~**ed glass** Matt-
glas nt. ~**ing** n (Amer Culin)
Zuckerguß m. ~**y** a, **-ily** adv frostig

froth /frɒθ/ n Schaum m ● vi schäumen. ~**y** a schaumig

frown /fraʊn/ n Stirnrunzeln nt ● vi
die Stirn runzeln; ~ **on** mißbilligen

froze /frəʊz/ see **freeze**

frozen /'frəʊzn/ see **freeze** ● a gefroren; (Culin) tiefgekühlt; **I'm** ~ (fam)
mir ist eiskalt. ~ **food** n Tiefkühlkost
f

frugal /'fru:gl/ a, **-ly** adv sparsam;
(meal) frugal

fruit /fru:t/ n Frucht f; (collectively)
Obst nt. ~ **cake** n englischer [Tee]-
kuchen m

fruit|erer /'fru:tərə(r)/ n Obst-
händler m. ~**ful** a fruchtbar

fruition /fru:'ɪʃn/ n **come to** ~ sich
verwirklichen

fruit: ~ **juice** n Obstsaft m. ~**less** a, **-ly** adv fruchtlos. ~ **machine** n Spielautomat m. ~ '**salad** n Obstsalat m

fruity /'fru:tɪ/ a fruchtig

frumpy /'frʌmpɪ/ a unmodisch

frustrat|e /frʌ'streɪt/ vt vereiteln; (Psych) frustrieren. ~**ing** a frustrierend. ~**ion** /-eɪʃn/ n Frustrationf

fry[1] /fraɪ/ n inv **small** ~ (fig) kleine Fische pl

fry[2] vt/i (pt/pp **fried**) [in der Pfanne] braten. ~**ing-pan** n Bratpfanne f

fuck /fʌk/ vt/i (vulg) ficken. ~**ing** a (vulg) Scheiß-

fuddy-duddy /'fʌdɪdʌdɪ/ n (fam) verknöcherter Kerl m

fudge /fʌdʒ/ n weiche Karamellen pl

fuel /'fju:əl/ n Brennstoff m; (for car) Kraftstoff m; (for aircraft) Treibstoff m

fugitive /'fju:dʒətɪv/ n Flüchtling m

fugue /fju:g/ n (Mus) Fuge f

fulfil /fʊl'fɪl/ vt (pt/pp **-filled**) erfüllen. ~**ment** n Erfüllung f

full /fʊl/ a & adv (-er, -est) voll; (detailed) ausführlich; (skirt) weit; ~ of voll von (+ dat), voller (+ gen); **at** ~ **speed** in voller Fahrt ● n in ~ vollständig

full: ~ '**moon** n Vollmond m. ~**-scale** a (model) in Originalgröße; (rescue, alert) großangelegt. ~ '**stop** n Punkt m. ~**-time** a ganztägig ● adv ganztags

fully /'fʊlɪ/ adv völlig; (in detail) ausführlich

fulsome /'fʊlsəm/ a übertrieben

fumble /'fʌmbl/ vi herumfummeln (**with** an + dat)

fume /fju:m/ vi vor Wut schäumen

fumes /fju:mz/ npl Dämpfe pl; (from car) Abgase pl

fumigate /'fju:mɪgeɪt/ vt ausräuchern

fun /fʌn/ n Spaß m; **for** ~ aus od zum Spaß; **make** ~ **of** sich lustig machen über (+ acc); **have** ~! viel Spaß!

function /'fʌŋkʃn/ n Funktion f; (event) Veranstaltung f ● vi funktionieren; (serve) dienen (**as** als). ~**al** a zweckmäßig

fund /fʌnd/ n Fonds m; (fig) Vorrat m; ~**s** pl Geldmittel pl ● vt finanzieren

fundamental /fʌndə'mentl/ a grundlegend; (essential) wesentlich

funeral /'fju:nərl/ n Beerdigung f; (cremation) Feuerbestattung f

funeral: ~ **directors** pl, (Amer) ~ **home** n Bestattungsinstitut nt. ~ **march** n Trauermarsch m. ~ **parlour** n (Amer) Bestattungsinstitut nt. ~ **service** n Trauergottesdienst m

'**funfair** n Jahrmarkt m, Kirmes f

fungus /'fʌŋgəs/ n (pl **-gi** /-gaɪ/) Pilz m

funicular /fju:'nɪkjʊlə(r)/ n Seilbahn f

funnel /'fʌnl/ n Trichter m; (on ship, train) Schornstein m

funnily /'fʌnɪlɪ/ adv komisch; ~ **enough** komischerweise

funny /'fʌnɪ/ a (-ier, -iest) komisch. ~**-bone** n (fam) Musikantenknochen m

fur /fɜ:(r)/ n Fell nt; (for clothing) Pelz m; (in kettle) Kesselstein m. ~ '**coat** n Pelzmantel m

furious /'fjʊərɪəs/ a, **-ly** adv wütend (**with** auf + acc)

furnace /'fɜ:nɪs/ n (Techn) Ofen m

furnish /'fɜ:nɪʃ/ vt einrichten; (supply) liefern. ~**ed** a ~**ed room** möbliertes Zimmer nt. ~**ings** npl Einrichtungsgegenstände pl

furniture /'fɜ:nɪtʃə(r)/ n Möbel pl

furred /fɜ:d/ a (tongue) belegt

furrow /'fʌrəʊ/ n Furche f

furry /'fɜ:rɪ/ a (animal) Pelz-; (toy) Plüsch-

further /'fɜ:ðə(r)/ a weitere(r,s); **at the** ~ **end** am anderen Ende; **until** ~ **notice** bis auf weiteres ● adv weiter; ~ **off** weiter entfernt ● vt fördern

further: ~ **edu'cation** n Weiterbildung f. ~**'more** adv überdies

furthest /'fɜ:ðɪst/ a am weitesten entfernt ● adv am weitesten

furtive /'fɜ:tɪv/ a, **-ly** adv verstohlen

fury /'fjʊərɪ/ n Wut f

fuse[1] /fju:z/ n (of bomb) Zünder m; (cord) Zündschnur f

fuse[2] n (Electr) Sicherung f ● vt/i verschmelzen; **the lights have** ~**d** die Sicherung [für das Licht] ist durchgebrannt. ~**-box** n Sicherungskasten m

fuselage /'fju:zəlɑ:ʒ/ n (Aviat) Rumpf m

fusion /'fju:ʒn/ n Verschmelzung f, Fusion f

fuss /fʌs/ n Getue nt; **make a** ~ **of** verwöhnen; (caress) liebkosen ● vi Umstände machen

fussy /'fʌsɪ/ a (-ier, -iest) wählerisch; (particular) penibel

fusty /'fʌstɪ/ a moderig
futil|e /'fju:taɪl/ a zwecklos. ~**ity**
/-'tɪlətɪ/ n Zwecklosigkeit f
future /'fju:tʃə(r)/ a zukünftig ● n
Zukunft f; (Gram) [erstes] Futur nt;
~ **perfect** zweites Futur nt; **in** ~ in
Zukunft
futuristic /fju:tʃə'rɪstɪk/ a futuri-
stisch
fuzz /fʌz/ n **the** ~ (sl) die Bullen pl
fuzzy /'fʌzɪ/ a (-ier, -iest) ⟨hair⟩ kraus;
(blurred) verschwommen

G

gab /gæb/ n (fam) **have the gift of
the** ~ gut reden können
gabble /'gæbl/ vi schnell reden
gable /'geɪbl/ n Giebel m
gad /gæd/ vi (pt/pp **gadded**) ~ **about**
dauernd ausgehen
gadget /'gædʒɪt/ n [kleines] Gerät nt
Gaelic /'geɪlɪk/ n Gälisch nt
gaffe /gæf/ n Fauxpas m
gag /gæg/ n Knebel m; (joke) Witz m;
(Theat) Gag m ● vt (pt/pp **gagged**)
knebeln
gaiety /'geɪətɪ/ n Fröhlichkeit f
gaily /'geɪlɪ/ adv fröhlich
gain /geɪn/ n Gewinn m; (increase)
Zunahme f ● vt gewinnen; (obtain) erlangen; ~ **weight** zunehmen ● vi
⟨clock:⟩ vorgehen. ~**ful** a ~**ful employment** Erwerbstätigkeit f
gait /geɪt/ n Gang m
gala /'gɑ:lə/ n Fest nt; **swimming** ~
Schwimmfest nt ● attrib Gala-
galaxy /'gæləksɪ/ n Galaxie f; **the
G**~ die Milchstraße
gale /geɪl/ n Sturm m
gall /gɔ:l/ n Galle f; (impudence)
Frechheit f
gallant /'gælənt/ a, -ly adv tapfer;
(chivalrous) galant. ~**ry** n Tapferkeit f
'**gall-bladder** n Gallenblase f
gallery /'gælərɪ/ n Galerie f
galley /'gælɪ/ n (ship's kitchen) Kombüse f; ~ **[proof]** [Druck]fahne f
gallivant /'gælɪvænt/ vi (fam) ausgehen
gallon /'gælən/ n Gallone f (= 4,5 l;
Amer = 3,785 l)
gallop /'gæləp/ n Galopp m ● vi
galoppieren
gallows /'gæləʊz/ n Galgen m
'**gallstone** n Gallenstein m

galore /gə'lɔ:(r)/ adv in Hülle und
Fülle
galvanize /'gælvənaɪz/ vt galvanisieren
gambit /'gæmbɪt/ n Eröffnungs-
manöver nt
gamble /'gæmbl/ n (risk) Risiko nt
● vi [um Geld] spielen; ~ **on** (rely)
sich verlassen auf (+ acc). ~**r** n Spie-
ler(in) m(f)
game /geɪm/ n Spiel nt; (animals,
birds) Wild nt; ~**s** (Sch) Sport m ● a
(brave) tapfer; (willing) bereit (**for** zu).
~**keeper** n Wildhüter m
gammon /'gæmən/ n [geräucherter]
Schinken m
gamut /'gæmət/ n Skala f
gander /'gændə(r)/ n Gänserich m
gang /gæŋ/ n Bande f; (of workmen)
Kolonne f ● vi ~ **up** sich zusam-
menrotten (**on** gegen)
gangling /'gæŋglɪŋ/ a schlaksig
gangrene /'gæŋgri:n/ n Wundbrand
m
gangster /'gæŋstə(r)/ n Gangster m
gangway /'gæŋweɪ/ n Gang m;
(Naut, Aviat) Gangway f
gaol /dʒeɪl/ n Gefängnis nt ● vt ins
Gefängnis sperren. ~**er** n Ge-
fängniswärter m
gap /gæp/ n Lücke f; (interval) Pause
f; (difference) Unterschied m
gap|e /geɪp/ vi gaffen; ~**e at** an-
starren. ~**ing** a klaffend
garage /'gærɑ:ʒ/ n Garage f; (for
repairs) Werkstatt f; (for petrol)
Tankstelle f
garb /gɑ:b/ n Kleidung f
garbage /'gɑ:bɪdʒ/ n Müll m. ~ **can**
n (Amer) Mülleimer m
garbled /'gɑ:bld/ a verworren
garden /'gɑ:dn/ n Garten m; **[public]**
~**s** pl [öffentliche] Anlagen pl ● vi im
Garten arbeiten. ~**er** n Gärtner(in)
m(f). ~**ing** n Gartenarbeit f
gargle /'gɑ:gl/ n (liquid) Gurgel-
wasser nt ● vi gurgeln
gargoyle /'gɑ:gɔɪl/ n Wasserspeier
m
garish /'geərɪʃ/ a grell
garland /'gɑ:lənd/ n Girlande f
garlic /'gɑ:lɪk/ n Knoblauch m
garment /'gɑ:mənt/ n Kleidungsstück nt
garnet /'gɑ:nɪt/ n Granat m
garnish /'gɑ:nɪʃ/ n Garnierung f ● vt
garnieren
garret /'gærɪt/ n Dachstube f

garrison /'gærɪsn/ n Garnison f
garrulous /'gærʊləs/ a geschwätzig
garter /'gɑːtə(r)/ n Strumpfband nt; (Amer: suspender) Strumpfhalter m
gas /gæs/ n Gas nt; (Amer fam: petrol) Benzin nt ● v (pt/pp gassed) ● vt vergasen ● vi (fam) schwatzen. ~ cooker n Gasherd m. ~ 'fire n Gasofen m
gash /gæʃ/ n Schnitt m; (wound) klaffende Wunde f ● vt ~ one's arm sich (dat) den Arm aufschlitzen
gasket /'gæskɪt/ n (Techn) Dichtung f
gas: ~ mask n Gasmaske f. ~-meter n Gaszähler m
gasoline /'gæsəliːn/ n (Amer) Benzin nt
gasp /gɑːsp/ vi keuchen; (in surprise) hörbar die Luft einziehen
'gas station n (Amer) Tankstelle f
gastric /'gæstrɪk/ a Magen-. ~ 'flu n Darmgrippe f. ~ 'ulcer n Magengeschwür nt
gastronomy /gæ'strɒnəmɪ/ n Gastronomie f
gate /geɪt/ n Tor nt; (to field) Gatter nt; (barrier) Schranke f; (at airport) Flugsteig m
gâteau /'gætəʊ/ n Torte f
gate: ~crasher n ungeladener Gast m. ~way n Tor nt
gather /'gæðə(r)/ vt sammeln; (pick) pflücken; (conclude) folgern (from aus); (Sewing) kräuseln; ~ speed schneller werden ● vi sich versammeln; ⟨storm:⟩ sich zusammenziehen. ~ing n family ~ing Familientreffen nt
gaudy /'gɔːdɪ/ a (-ier, -iest) knallig
gauge /geɪdʒ/ n Stärke f; (Rail) Spurweite f; (device) Meßinstrument nt ● vt messen; (estimate) schätzen
gaunt /gɔːnt/ a hager
gauntlet /'gɔːntlɪt/ n run the ~ Spießruten laufen
gauze /gɔːz/ n Gaze f
gave /geɪv/ see give
gawky /'gɔːkɪ/ a (-ier, -iest) schlaksig
gawp /gɔːp/ vi (fam) glotzen; ~ at anglotzen
gay /geɪ/ a (-er, -est) fröhlich; (fam) homosexuell, (fam) schwul
gaze /geɪz/ n [langer] Blick m ● vi sehen; ~ at ansehen
gazelle /gə'zel/ n Gazelle f
GB abbr of **Great Britain**

gear /gɪə(r)/ n Ausrüstung f; (Techn) Getriebe nt; (Auto) Gang m; in ~ mit eingelegtem Gang; change ~ schalten ● vt anpassen (to dat)
gear: ~box n (Auto) Getriebe nt. ~-lever n, (Amer) ~-shift n Schalthebel m
geese /giːs/ see **goose**
geezer /'giːzə(r)/ n (sl) Typ m
gel /dʒel/ n Gel nt
gelatine /'dʒelətɪn/ n Gelatine f
gelignite /'dʒelɪgnaɪt/ n Gelatinedynamit nt
gem /dʒem/ n Juwel nt
Gemini /'dʒemɪnaɪ/ n (Astr) Zwillinge pl
gender /'dʒendə(r)/ n (Gram) Geschlecht nt
gene /dʒiːn/ n Gen nt
genealogy /dʒiːnɪ'ælədʒɪ/ n Genealogie f
general /'dʒenrəl/ a allgemein ● n General m; in ~ im allgemeinen. ~ e'lection n allgemeine Wahlen pl
generaliz|ation /dʒenrəlaɪ'zeɪʃn/ n Verallgemeinerung f. ~e /'dʒenrəlaɪz/ vi verallgemeinern
generally /'dʒenrəlɪ/ adv im allgemeinen
general prac'titioner n praktischer Arzt m
generate /'dʒenəreɪt/ vt erzeugen
generation /dʒenə'reɪʃn/ n Generation f
generator /'dʒenəreɪtə(r)/ n Generator m
generic /dʒɪ'nerɪk/ a ~ term Oberbegriff m
generosity /dʒenə'rɒsɪtɪ/ n Großzügigkeit f
generous /'dʒenərəs/ a, -ly adv großzügig
genetic /dʒɪ'netɪk/ a genetisch. ~ engineering n Gentechnologie f. ~s n Genetik f
Geneva /dʒɪ'niːvə/ n Genf nt
genial /'dʒiːnɪəl/ a, -ly adv freundlich
genitals /'dʒenɪtlz/ pl [äußere] Geschlechtsteile pl
genitive /'dʒenɪtɪv/ a & n ~ [case] Genitiv m
genius /'dʒiːnɪəs/ n (pl -uses) Genie nt; (quality) Genialität f
genocide /'dʒenəsaɪd/ n Völkermord m
genre /'ʒãrə/ n Gattung f, Genre nt
gent /dʒent/ n (fam) Herr m; the ~s sg die Herrentoilette f

genteel /dʒen'ti:l/ *a* vornehm

gentle /'dʒentl/ *a* (**-r, -st**) sanft

gentleman /'dʒentlmən/ *n* Herr *m*; (*well-mannered*) Gentleman *m*

gent|leness /'dʒentlnɪs/ *n* Sanftheit *f*. **~ly** *adv* sanft

genuine /'dʒenjʊɪn/ *a* echt; (*sincere*) aufrichtig. **~iy** *adv* (*honestly*) ehrlich

genus /'dʒiːnəs/ *n* (*Biol*) Gattung *f*

geograph|ical /dʒɪə'græfɪkl/ *a*, **-ly** *adv* geographisch. **~y** /dʒɪ'ɒgrəfɪ/ *n* Geographie *f*, Erdkunde *f*

geological /dʒɪə'lɒdʒɪkl/ *a*, **-ly** *adv* geologisch

geolog|ist /dʒɪ'ɒlədʒɪst/ *n* Geologe *m*/-gin *f*. **~y** *n* Geologie *f*

geometr|ic(al) /dʒɪə'metrɪk(l)/ *a* geometrisch. **~y** /dʒɪ'ɒmətrɪ/ *n* Geometrie *f*

geranium /dʒə'reɪnɪəm/ *n* Geranie *f*

geriatric /dʒerɪ'ætrɪk/ *a* geriatrisch ● *n* geriatrischer Patient *m*. **~s** *n* Geriatrie *f*

germ /dʒɜːm/ *n* Keim *m*; **~s** *pl* (*fam*) Bazillen *pl*

German /'dʒɜːmən/ *a* deutsch ● *n* (*person*) Deutsche(r) *m/f*; (*Lang*) Deutsch *nt*; **in ~** auf deutsch; **into ~** ins Deutsche

Germanic /dʒə'mænɪk/ *a* germanisch

German: ~ 'measles *n* Röteln *pl*. **~ 'shepherd [dog]** *n* [deutscher] Schäferhund *m*

Germany /'dʒɜːmənɪ/ *n* Deutschland *nt*

germinate /'dʒɜːmɪneɪt/ *vi* keimen

gesticulate /dʒe'stɪkjʊleɪt/ *vi* gestikulieren

gesture /'dʒestʃə(r)/ *n* Geste *f*

get /get/ *v* (*pt/pp* **got**, *pp* Amer also **gotten**, *pres p* **getting**) ● *vt* bekommen, (*fam*) kriegen; (*procure*) besorgen; (*buy*) kaufen; (*fetch*) holen; (*take*) bringen; (*on telephone*) erreichen; (*fam: understand*) kapieren; machen ⟨*meal*⟩; **~ s.o. to do sth** jdn dazu bringen, etw zu tun ● *vi* (*become*) werden; **~ to** kommen zu/nach ⟨*town*⟩; (*reach*) erreichen; **~ dressed** sich anziehen; **~ married** heiraten. **~ at** *vt* herankommen an (+*acc*); **what are you ~ting at?** worauf willst du hinaus? **~ away** *vi* (*leave*) wegkommen; (*escape*) entkommen. **~ back** *vi* zurückkommen ● *vt* (*recover*) zurückbekommen; **~ one's**

own back sich revanchieren. **~ by** *vi* vorbeikommen; (*manage*) sein Auskommen haben. **~ down** *vi* heruntersteigen; **~ down to** sich [heran]machen an (+*acc*) ● *vt* (*depress*) deprimieren. **~ in** *vi* einsteigen ● *vt* (*fetch*) hereinholen. **~ off** *vi* (*dismount*) absteigen; (*from bus*) aussteigen; (*leave*) wegkommen; (*Jur*) freigesprochen werden ● *vt* (*remove*) abbekommen. **~ on** *vi* (*mount*) aufsteigen; (*to bus*) einsteigen; (*be on good terms*) gut auskommen (**with** mit); (*make progress*) Fortschritte machen; **how are you ~ting on?** wie geht's? **~ out** *vi* herauskommen; (*of car*) aussteigen; **~ out of** (*avoid doing*) sich drücken um ● *vt* herausholen; herausbekommen ⟨*cork, stain*⟩. **~ over** *vi* hinübersteigen ● *vt* (*fig*) hinwegkommen über (+*acc*). **~ round** *vi* herumkommen; (*avoid*) umgehen; **I never ~ round to it** ich komme nie dazu ● *vt* herumkriegen. **~ through** *vi* durchkommen. **~ up** *vi* aufstehen

get: ~away *n* Flucht *f*. **~-up** *n* Aufmachung *f*

geyser /'giːzə(r)/ *n* Durchlauferhitzer *m*; (*Geol*) Geysir *m*

ghastly /'gɑːstlɪ/ *a* (**-ier, -iest**) gräßlich; (*pale*) blaß

gherkin /'gɜːkɪn/ *n* Essiggurke *f*

ghetto /'getəʊ/ *n* Getto *nt*

ghost /gəʊst/ *n* Geist *m*, Gespenst *nt*. **~ly** *a* geisterhaft

ghoulish /'guːlɪʃ/ *a* makaber

giant /'dʒaɪənt/ *n* Riese *m* ● *a* riesig

gibberish /'dʒɪbərɪʃ/ *n* Kauderwelsch *nt*

gibe /dʒaɪb/ *n* spöttische Bemerkung *f* ● *vi* spotten (**at** über +*acc*)

giblets /'dʒɪblɪts/ *npl* Geflügelklein *nt*

giddiness /'gɪdɪnɪs/ *n* Schwindel *m*

giddy /'gɪdɪ/ *a* (**-ier, -iest**) schwindlig; **I feel ~** mir ist schwindlig

gift /gɪft/ *n* Geschenk *nt*; (*to charity*) Gabe *f*; (*talent*) Begabung *f*. **~ed** /-ɪd/ *a* begabt. **~-wrap** *vt* als Geschenk einpacken

gig /gɪg/ *n* (*fam, Mus*) Gig *m*

gigantic /dʒaɪ'gæntɪk/ *a* riesig, riesengroß

giggle /'gɪgl/ *n* Kichern *nt* ● *vi* kichern

gild /gɪld/ *vt* vergolden

gills /gɪlz/ *npl* Kiemen *pl*

gilt /gɪlt/ a vergoldet ● n Vergoldung f. ~-edged a (Comm) mündelsicher

gimmick /'gɪmɪk/ n Trick m

gin /dʒɪn/ n Gin m

ginger /'dʒɪndʒə(r)/ a rotblond; ⟨cat⟩ rot ● n Ingwer m. ~bread n Pfefferkuchen m

gingerly /'dʒɪndʒəlɪ/ adv vorsichtig

gipsy /'dʒɪpsɪ/ n = **gypsy**

giraffe /dʒɪ'rɑːf/ n Giraffe f

girder /'gɜːdə(r)/ n (Techn) Träger m

girdle /'gɜːdl/ n Bindegürtel m; ⟨corset⟩ Hüfthalter m

girl /gɜːl/ n Mädchen nt; ⟨young woman⟩ junge Frau f. ~friend n Freundin f. ~ish a, -ly adv mädchenhaft

giro /'dʒaɪərəʊ/ n Giro nt; ⟨cheque⟩ Postscheck m

girth /gɜːθ/ n Umfang m; ⟨for horse⟩ Bauchgurt m

gist /dʒɪst/ n the ~ das Wesentliche

give /gɪv/ n Elastizität f ● v (pt gave, pp given) ● vt geben/⟨as present⟩ schenken (to dat); ⟨donate⟩ spenden; ⟨lecture⟩ halten; ⟨one's name⟩ angeben ● vi geben; ⟨yield⟩ nachgeben. ~ away vt verschenken; ⟨betray⟩ verraten; ⟨distribute⟩ verteilen; ~ away the bride ≈ Brautführer sein. ~ back vt zurückgeben. ~ in vt einreichen ● vi ⟨yield⟩ nachgeben. ~ off vt abgeben. ~ up vt/i aufgeben; ~ oneself up sich stellen. ~ way vi nachgeben; (Auto) die Vorfahrt beachten

given /'gɪvn/ see **give** ● a ~ name Vorname m

glacier /'glæsɪə(r)/ n Gletscher m

glad /glæd/ a froh (of über + acc). ~den /'glædn/ vt erfreuen

glade /gleɪd/ n Lichtung f

gladly /'glædlɪ/ adv gern[e]

glamorous /'glæmərəs/ a glanzvoll; ⟨film star⟩ glamourös

glamour /'glæmə(r)/ n [betörender] Glanz m

glance /glɑːns/ n [flüchtiger] Blick m ● vi ~ at einen Blick werfen auf (+ acc). ~ up vi aufblicken

gland /glænd/ n Drüse f

glandular /'glændjʊlə(r)/ a Drüsen-

glare /gleə(r)/ n grelles Licht nt; ⟨look⟩ ärgerlicher Blick m ● vi ~ at böse ansehen

glaring /'gleərɪŋ/ a grell; ⟨mistake⟩ kraß

glass /glɑːs/ n Glas nt; ⟨mirror⟩ Spiegel m; ~es pl ⟨spectacles⟩ Brille f. ~y a glasig

glaze /gleɪz/ n Glasur f ● vt verglasen; ⟨Culin, Pottery⟩ glasieren

glazier /'gleɪzɪə(r)/ n Glaser m

gleam /gliːm/ n Schein m ● vi glänzen

glean /gliːn/ vi Ähren lesen ● vt ⟨learn⟩ erfahren

glee /gliː/ n Frohlocken nt. ~ful a, -ly adv frohlockend

glen /glen/ n [enges] Tal nt

glib /glɪb/ a, -ly adv (pej) gewandt

glid|e /glaɪd/ vi gleiten; ⟨through the air⟩ schweben. ~er n Segelflugzeug nt. ~ing n Segelfliegen nt

glimmer /'glɪmə(r)/ n Glimmen nt ● vi glimmen

glimpse /glɪmps/ n catch a ~ of flüchtig sehen ● vt flüchtig sehen

glint /glɪnt/ n Blitzen nt ● vi blitzen

glisten /'glɪsn/ vi glitzern

glitter /'glɪtə(r)/ vi glitzern

gloat /gləʊt/ vi schadenfroh sein; ~ over sich weiden an (+ dat)

global /'gləʊbl/ a, -ly adv global

globe /gləʊb/ n Kugel f; ⟨map⟩ Globus m

gloom /gluːm/ n Düsterkeit f; ⟨fig⟩ Pessimismus m

gloomy /'gluːmɪ/ a (-ier, -iest), -ily adv düster; ⟨fig⟩ pessimistisch

glorif|y /'glɔːrɪfaɪ/ vt (pt/pp -ied) verherrlichen; a ~ied waitress eine bessere Kellnerin f

glorious /'glɔːrɪəs/ a herrlich; ⟨deed, hero⟩ glorreich

glory /'glɔːrɪ/ n Ruhm m; ⟨splendour⟩ Pracht f ● vi ~ in genießen

gloss /glɒs/ n Glanz m ● a Glanz- ● vi ~ over beschönigen

glossary /'glɒsərɪ/ n Glossar nt

glossy /'glɒsɪ/ a (-ier, -iest) glänzend

glove /glʌv/ n Handschuh m. ~ compartment n (Auto) Handschuhfach nt

glow /gləʊ/ n Glut f; ⟨of candle⟩ Schein m ● vi glühen; ⟨candle:⟩ scheinen. ~ing a glühend; ⟨account⟩ begeistert

glow-worm n Glühwürmchen nt

glucose /'gluːkəʊs/ n Traubenzucker m, Glukose f

glue /gluː/ n Klebstoff m ● vt (pres p gluing) kleben (to an + acc)

glum /glʌm/ a (glummer, glummest), -ly adv niedergeschlagen

glut /glʌt/ n Überfluß m (of an + dat); ~ of fruit Obstschwemme f

glutton /'glʌtn/ n Vielfraß m.
~**ous** /-əs/ a gefräßig. ~**y** n Ge-
fräßigkeit f
gnarled /nɑːld/ a knorrig; ⟨hands⟩
knotig
gnash /næʃ/ vt ~ **one's teeth** mit den
Zähnen knirschen
gnat /næt/ n Mücke f
gnaw /nɔː/ vt/i nagen (**at** an + dat)
gnome /nəʊm/ n Gnom m
go /gəʊ/ n (pl **goes**) Energie f;
⟨attempt⟩ Versuch m; **on the go** auf
Trab; **at one go** auf einmal; **it's your
go** du bist dran; **make a go of it** Erfolg
haben ● vi (pt **went**, pp **gone**) gehen;
(in vehicle) fahren; (leave) weggehen;
(on journey) abfahren; ⟨time:⟩ vergehen;
(vanish) verschwinden; (fail) versagen; (become) werden; (belong)
kommen; **go swimming/shopping**
schwimmen/einkaufen gehen; **where
are you going?** wo gehst du hin? **it's
all gone** es ist nichts mehr übrig; **I am
not going to** ich werde es nicht tun; **'to
go'** (Amer) 'zum Mitnehmen'. **go
away** vi weggehen/-fahren. **go back**
vi zurückgehen/-fahren. **go by** vi
vorbeigehen/-fahren; ⟨time:⟩ vergehen. **go down** vi hinuntergehen/
-fahren; ⟨sun, ship:⟩ untergehen;
⟨prices:⟩ fallen; ⟨temperature, swelling:⟩ zurückgehen. **go for** vt holen;
(fam: attack) losgehen auf (+ acc).
go in vi hineingehen/-fahren; **go in
for** teilnehmen an (+ dat) ⟨com-
petition⟩; (take up) sich verlegen auf
(+ acc). **go off** vi weggehen/-fahren;
⟨alarm:⟩ klingeln; ⟨gun, bomb:⟩ losgehen; (go bad) schlecht werden; **go
off well** gut verlaufen. **go on** vi
weitergehen/-fahren; (continue)
weitermachen; (talking) fortfahren;
(happen) vorgehen; **go on at** (fam)
herumnörgeln an (+ dat). **go out** vi
ausgehen; (leave) hinausgehen/
-fahren. **go over** vi hinübergehen/
-fahren ● vt (check) durchgehen.
go round vi herumgehen/-fahren;
(visit) vorbeigehen; (turn) sich drehen; (be enough) reichen. **go through**
vi durchgehen/-fahren ● vt (suffer)
durchmachen; (check) durchgehen.
go under vi untergehen; (fail)
scheitern. **go up** vi hinaufgehen/
-fahren; ⟨lift:⟩ hochfahren; ⟨prices:⟩
steigen. **go without** vt verzichten
auf (+ acc) ● vi darauf verzichten

goad /gəʊd/ vt anstacheln (**into** zu);
(taunt) reizen
'go-ahead a fortschrittlich; (enterprising) unternehmend ● n (fig)
grünes Licht nt
goal /gəʊl/ n Ziel nt; (Sport) Tor nt.
~**keeper** n Torwart m. ~**-post** n
Torpfosten m
goat /gəʊt/ n Ziege f
gobble /'gɒbl/ vt hinunterschlingen
'go-between n Vermittler(in) m(f)
goblet /'gɒblɪt/ n Pokal m; (glass)
Kelchglas nt
goblin /'gɒblɪn/ n Kobold m
God, god /gɒd/ n Gott m
god: ~**child** n Patenkind nt. ~
daughter n Patentochter f. ~**dess** n
Göttin f. ~**father** n Pate m. **G**~**-for-
saken** a gottverlassen. ~**mother** n
Patin f. ~**parents** npl Paten pl.
~**send** n Segen m. ~**son** n Paten-
sohn m
goggle /'gɒgl/ vi (fam) ~ **at** anglotzen. ~**s** npl Schutzbrille f
going /'gəʊɪŋ/ a ⟨price, rate⟩ gängig;
⟨concern⟩ gutgehend ● n **it is hard** ~
es ist schwierig; **while the** ~ **is good**
solange es noch geht. ~**s-'on** npl
[seltsame] Vorgänge pl
gold /gəʊld/ n Gold nt ● a golden
golden /'gəʊldn/ a golden. ~ **'handshake** n hohe Abfindungssumme f.
~ **'wedding** n goldene Hochzeit f
gold: ~**fish** n inv Goldfisch m.
~**-mine** n Goldgrube f. ~**-plated** a
vergoldet. ~**smith** n Goldschmied m
golf /gɒlf/ n Golf nt
golf: ~**-club** n Golfklub m;
(implement) Golfschläger m. ~
course n Golfplatz m. ~**er** n Golf-
spieler(in) m(f)
gondo|la /'gɒndələ/ n Gondel f. ~
lier /-'lɪə(r)/ n Gondoliere m
gone /gɒn/ see **go**
gong /gɒŋ/ n Gong m
good /gʊd/ a (**better, best**) gut; (well-
behaved) brav, artig; ~ **at** gut in
(+ dat); **a** ~ **deal** ziemlich viel; **as** ~ **as**
so gut wie; (almost) fast; ~ **morning/
evening** guten Morgen/Abend; ~
afternoon guten Tag; ~ **night** gute
Nacht ● n **the** ~ das Gute; **for** ~ für
immer; **do** ~ Gutes tun; **do s.o.** ~ jdm
guttun; **it's no** ~ es ist nutzlos; (hopeless) da ist nichts zu machen; **be up to
no** ~ nichts Gutes im Schilde führen
goodbye /gʊd'baɪ/ int auf Wiedersehen; (Teleph, Radio) auf Wieder-
hören

good: ~-**for-nothing** *a* nichtsnutzig ● *n* Taugenichts *m*. **G**~ 'Friday *n* Karfreitag *m*. ~-'looking *a* gutaussehend. ~-'natured *a* gutmütig

goodness /'gʊdnɪs/ *n* Güte *f*; **my** ~! du meine Güte! **thank** ~! Gott sei Dank!

goods /gʊdz/ *npl* Waren *pl*. ~ **train** *n* Güterzug *m*

good'will *n* Wohlwollen *nt*; (*Comm*) Goodwill *m*

goody /'gʊdɪ/ *n* (*fam*) Gute(r) *m/f*. ~-**goody** *n* Musterkind *nt*

gooey /'guːɪ/ *a* (*fam*) klebrig

goof /guːf/ *vi* (*fam*) einen Schnitzer machen

goose /guːs/ *n* (*pl* **geese**) Gans *f*

gooseberry /'gʊzbərɪ/ *n* Stachelbeere *f*

goose /guːs/: ~-**flesh** *n*, ~**pimples** *npl* Gänsehaut *f*

gore[1] /gɔː(r)/ *n* Blut *nt*

gore[2] *vt* mit den Hörnern aufspießen

gorge /gɔːdʒ/ *n* (*Geog*) Schlucht *f* ● *vt* ~ **oneself** sich vollessen

gorgeous /'gɔːdʒəs/ *a* prachtvoll; (*fam*) herrlich

gorilla /gə'rɪlə/ *n* Gorilla *m*

gormless /'gɔːmlɪs/ *a* (*fam*) doof

gorse /gɔːs/ *n inv* Stechginster *m*

gory /'gɔːrɪ/ *a* (**-ier, -iest**) blutig; ⟨*story*⟩ blutrünstig

gosh /gɒʃ/ *int* (*fam*) Mensch!

go-'slow *n* Bummelstreik *m*

gospel /'gɒspl/ *n* Evangelium *nt*

gossip /'gɒsɪp/ *n* Klatsch *m*; (*person*) Klatschbase *f* ● *vi* klatschen. ~**y** *a* geschwätzig

got /gɒt/ *see* **get**; **have** ~ haben; **have** ~ **to** müssen; **have** ~ **to do sth** etw tun müssen

Gothic /'gɒθɪk/ *a* gotisch

gotten /'gɒtn/ *see* **get**

gouge /gaʊdʒ/ *vt* ~ **out** aushöhlen

goulash /'guːlæʃ/ *n* Gulasch *nt*

gourmet /'gʊəmeɪ/ *n* Feinschmecker *m*

gout /gaʊt/ *n* Gicht *f*

govern /'gʌvn/ *vt/i* regieren; (*determine*) bestimmen. ~**ess** *n* Gouvernante *f*

government /'gʌvnmənt/ *n* Regierung *f*. ~**al** /-'mentl/ *a* Regierungs-

governor /'gʌvənə(r)/ *n* Gouverneur *m*; (*on board*) Vorstandsmitglied *nt*; (*of prison*) Direktor *m*; (*fam: boss*) Chef *m*

gown /gaʊn/ *n* [elegantes] Kleid *nt*; (*Univ, Jur*) Talar *m*

GP *abbr of* **general practitioner**

grab /græb/ *vt* (*pt/pp* **grabbed**) ergreifen; ~ **[hold of]** packen

grace /greɪs/ *n* Anmut *f*; (*before meal*) Tischgebet *nt*; (*Relig*) Gnade *f*; **with good** ~ mit Anstand; **say** ~ [vor dem Essen] beten; **three days'** ~ drei Tage Frist. ~**ful** *a*, **-ly** *adv* anmutig

gracious /'greɪʃəs/ *a* gnädig; (*elegant*) vornehm

grade /greɪd/ *n* Stufe *f*; (*Comm*) Güteklasse *f*; (*Sch*) Note *f*; (*Amer, Sch: class*) Klasse *f*; (*Amer*) = **gradient** ● *vt* einstufen; (*Comm*) sortieren. ~ **crossing** *n* (*Amer*) Bahnübergang *m*

gradient /'greɪdɪənt/ *n* Steigung *f*; (*downward*) Gefälle *nt*

gradual /'grædʒʊəl/ *a*, **-ly** *adv* allmählich

graduate[1] /'grædʒʊət/ *n* Akademiker(in) *m(f)*

graduate[2] /'grædʒʊeɪt/ *vi* (*Univ*) sein Examen machen. ~**d** *a* abgestuft; ⟨*container*⟩ mit Maßeinteilung

graffiti /grə'fiːtiː/ *npl* Graffiti *pl*

graft /grɑːft/ *n* (*Bot*) Pfropfreis *nt*; (*Med*) Transplantat *nt*; (*fam: hard work*) Plackerei *f* ● *vt* (*Bot*) aufpfropfen; (*Med*) übertragen

grain /greɪn/ *n* (*sand, salt, rice*) Korn *nt*; (*cereals*) Getreide *nt*; (*in wood*) Maserung *f*; **against the** ~ (*fig*) gegen den Strich

gram /græm/ *n* Gramm *nt*

grammar /'græmə(r)/ *n* Grammatik *f*. ~ **school** *n* ≈ Gymnasium *nt*

grammatical /grə'mætɪkl/ *a*, **-ly** *adv* grammatisch

granary /'grænərɪ/ *n* Getreidespeicher *m*

grand /grænd/ *a* (**-er, -est**) großartig

grandad /'grændæd/ *n* (*fam*) Opa *m*

'grandchild *n* Enkelkind *nt*

'granddaughter *n* Enkelin *f*

grandeur /'grændʒə(r)/ *n* Pracht *f*

'grandfather *n* Großvater *m*. ~ **clock** *n* Standuhr *f*

grandiose /'grændɪəʊs/ *a* grandios

grand: ~**mother** *n* Großmutter *f*. ~**parents** *npl* Großeltern *pl*. ~ **pi'ano** *n* Flügel *m*. ~**son** *n* Enkel *m*. ~**stand** *n* Tribüne *f*

granite /'grænɪt/ *n* Granit *m*

granny /'grænɪ/ *n* (*fam*) Oma *f*

grant /grɑːnt/ *n* Subvention *f*; (*Univ*) Studienbeihilfe *f* ● *vt* gewähren;

(admit) zugeben; **take sth for** ∼**ed** etw als selbstverständlich hinnehmen

granular /'grænjʊlə(r)/ a körnig

granulated /'grænjʊleɪtɪd/ a ∼ **sugar** Kristallzucker m

granule /'grænjuːl/ n Körnchen nt

grape /greɪp/ n [Wein]traube f; **bunch of** ∼**s** [ganze] Weintraube f

grapefruit /-'greɪp-/ n inv Grapefruit f, Pampelmuse f

graph /grɑːf/ n Kurvendiagramm nt

graphic /'græfɪk/ a, **-ally** adv grafisch; (vivid) anschaulich. ∼**s** n (design) grafische Gestaltung f

'**graph paper** n Millimeterpapier nt

grapple /'græpl/ vi ringen

grasp /grɑːsp/ n Griff m ● vt ergreifen; (understand) begreifen. ∼**ing** a habgierig

grass /grɑːs/ n Gras nt; (lawn) Rasen m; **at the** ∼ **roots** an der Basis. ∼**hopper** n Heuschrecke f. ∼**land** n Weideland nt

grassy /'grɑːsɪ/ a grasig

grate[1] /greɪt/ n Feuerrost m; (hearth) Kamin m

grate[2] vt (Culin) reiben; ∼ **one's teeth** mit den Zähnen knirschen

grateful /'greɪtfl/ a, **-ly** adv dankbar (**to** dat)

grater /'greɪtə(r)/ n (Culin) Reibe f

gratify /'grætɪfaɪ/ vt (pt/pp **-ied**) befriedigen. ∼**ing** a erfreulich

grating /'greɪtɪŋ/ n Gitter nt

gratis /'grɑːtɪs/ adv gratis

gratitude /'grætɪtjuːd/ n Dankbarkeit f

gratuitous /grə'tjuːɪtəs/ a (uncalled for) überflüssig

gratuity /grə'tjuːətɪ/ n (tip) Trinkgeld nt

grave[1] /greɪv/ a (**-r, -st**), **-ly** adv ernst; ∼**ly ill** schwer krank

grave[2] n Grab nt. ∼**-digger** n Totengräber m

gravel /'grævl/ n Kies m

grave: ∼**stone** n Grabstein m. ∼**yard** n Friedhof m

gravitate /'grævɪteɪt/ vi gravitieren

gravity /'grævətɪ/ n Ernst m; (force) Schwerkraft f

gravy /'greɪvɪ/ n [Braten]soße f

gray /greɪ/ a (Amer) = **grey**

graze[1] /greɪz/ vi ⟨animal:⟩ weiden

graze[2] n Schürfwunde f ● vt ⟨car⟩ streifen; ⟨knee⟩ aufschürfen

grease /griːs/ n Fett nt; (lubricant) Schmierfett nt ● vt einfetten; (lubricate) schmieren. ∼**-proof** '**paper** n Pergamentpapier nt

greasy /'griːsɪ/ a (**-ier, -iest**) fettig

great /greɪt/ a (**-er, -est**) groß; (fam: marvellous) großartig

great: ∼**-aunt** n Großtante f. **G**∼ '**Britain** n Großbritannien nt. ∼**-'grandchildren** npl Urenkel pl. ∼**-'grandfather** n Urgroßvater m. ∼**-'grandmother** n Urgroßmutter f

great|ly /'greɪtlɪ/ adv sehr. ∼**ness** n Größe f

great-'uncle n Großonkel m

Greece /griːs/ n Griechenland nt

greed /griːd/ n [Hab]gier f

greedy /'griːdɪ/ a (**-ier, -iest**), **-ily** adv gierig; **don't be** ∼ sei nicht so unbescheiden

Greek /griːk/ a griechisch ● n Grieche m/Griechin f; (Lang) Griechisch nt

green /griːn/ a (**-er, -est**) grün; (fig) unerfahren ● n Grün nt; (grass) Wiese f; ∼**s** pl Kohl m; **the G**∼**s** pl (Pol) die Grünen pl

greenery /'griːnərɪ/ n Grün nt

'**greenfly** n Blattlaus f

greengage /'griːngeɪdʒ/ n Reneklode f

green: ∼**grocer** n Obst- und Gemüsehändler m. ∼**house** n Gewächshaus nt. ∼**house effect** n Treibhauseffekt m

Greenland /'griːnlənd/ n Grönland nt

greet /griːt/ vt grüßen; (welcome) begrüßen. ∼**ing** n Gruß m; (welcome) Begrüßung f. ∼**ings card** n Glückwunschkarte f

gregarious /grɪ'geərɪəs/ a gesellig

grenade /grɪ'neɪd/ n Granate f

grew /gruː/ see **grow**

grey /greɪ/ a (**-er, -est**) grau ● n Grau nt ● vi grau werden. ∼**hound** n Windhund m

grid /grɪd/ n Gitter nt; (on map) Gitternetz nt; (Electr) Überlandleitungsnetz nt

grief /griːf/ n Trauer f; **come to** ∼ scheitern

grievance /'griːvəns/ n Beschwerde f

grieve /griːv/ vt betrüben ● vi trauern (**for** um)

grievous /'griːvəs/ a, **-ly** adv schwer

grill /grɪl/ *n* Gitter *nt*; (*Culin*) Grill *m*; **mixed** ~ Gemischtes *nt* vom Grill ● *vt/i* grillen; (*interrogate*) [streng] verhören

grille /grɪl/ *n* Gitter *nt*

grim /grɪm/ *a* (**grimmer, grimmest**), **-ly** *adv* ernst; (*determination*) verbissen

grimace /grɪ'meɪs/ *n* Grimasse *f* ● *vi* Grimassen schneiden

grime /graɪm/ *n* Schmutz *m*

grimy /'graɪmɪ/ *a* (**-ier, -iest**) schmutzig

grin /grɪn/ *n* Grinsen *nt* ● *vi* (*pt/pp* **grinned**) grinsen

grind /graɪnd/ *n* [fam: hard work] Plackerei *f* ● *vt* (*pt/pp* **ground**) mahlen; (*smooth, sharpen*) schleifen; (*Amer: mince*) durchdrehen; ~ **one's teeth** mit den Zähnen knirschen

grip /grɪp/ *n* Griff *m*; (*bag*) Reisetasche *f* ● *vt* (*pt/pp* **gripped**) ergreifen; (*hold*) festhalten; fesseln (*interest*)

gripe /graɪp/ *vi* (*sl: grumble*) meckern

gripping /'grɪpɪŋ/ *a* fesselnd

grisly /'grɪzlɪ/ *a* (**-ier, -iest**) grausig

gristle /'grɪsl/ *n* Knorpel *m*

grit /grɪt/ *n* [grober] Sand *m*; (*for roads*) Streugut *nt*; (*courage*) Mut *m* ● *vt* (*pt/pp* **gritted**) streuen (*road*); ~ **one's teeth** die Zähne zusammenbeißen

grizzle /'grɪzl/ *vi* quengeln

groan /grəʊn/ *n* Stöhnen *nt* ● *vi* stöhnen

grocer /'grəʊsə(r)/ *n* Lebensmittelhändler *m*; ~**'s [shop]** Lebensmittelgeschäft *nt*. ~**ies** *npl* Lebensmittel *pl*

groggy /'grɒgɪ/ *a* schwach; (*unsteady*) wackelig [auf den Beinen]

groin /grɔɪn/ *n* (*Anat*) Leiste *f*

groom /gru:m/ *n* Bräutigam *m*; (*for horse*) Pferdepfleger(in) *m(f)* ● *vt* striegeln (*horse*)

groove /gru:v/ *n* Rille *f*

grope /grəʊp/ *vi* tasten (**for** nach)

gross /grəʊs/ *a* (**-er, -est**) fett; (*coarse*) derb; (*glaring*) grob; (*Comm*) brutto; (*salary, weight*) Brutto- ● *n inv* Gros *nt*. ~**ly** *adv* (*very*) sehr

grotesque /grəʊ'tesk/ *a*, **-ly** *adv* grotesk

grotto /'grɒtəʊ/ *n* (*pl* **-es**) Grotte *f*

grotty /'grɒtɪ/ *a* (*fam*) mies

ground[1] /graʊnd/ *see* **grind**

ground[2] *n* Boden *m*; (*terrain*) Gelände *nt*; (*reason*) Grund *m*; (*Amer, Electr*) Erde *f*; ~**s** *pl* (*park*) Anlagen *pl*; (*of coffee*) Satz *m* ● *vi* (*ship:*) auflaufen ● *vt* aus dem Verkehr ziehen (*aircraft*); (*Amer, Electr*) erden

ground: ~ **floor** *n* Erdgeschoß *nt*. ~**ing** *n* Grundlage *f*. ~**less** *a* grundlos. ~ '**meat** *n* Hackfleisch *nt*. ~**sheet** *n* Bodenplane *f*. ~**work** *n* Vorarbeiten *pl*

group /gru:p/ *n* Gruppe *f* ● *vt* gruppieren ● *vi* sich gruppieren

grouse[1] /graʊs/ *n inv* schottisches Moorschneehuhn *nt*

grouse[2] *vi* (*fam*) meckern

grovel /'grɒvl/ *vi* (*pt/pp* **grovelled**) kriechen. ~**ling** *a* kriecherisch

grow /grəʊ/ *v* (*pt* **grew**, *pp* **grown**) ● *vi* wachsen; (*become*) werden; (*increase*) zunehmen ● *vt* anbauen; ~ **one's hair** sich (*dat*) die Haare wachsen lassen. ~ **up** *vi* aufwachsen; (*town:*) entstehen

growl /graʊl/ *n* Knurren *nt* ● *vi* knurren

grown /grəʊn/ *see* **grow**. ~-**up** *a* erwachsen ● *n* Erwachsene(r) *m/f*

growth /grəʊθ/ *n* Wachstum *nt*; (*increase*) Zunahme *f*; (*Med*) Gewächs *nt*

grub /grʌb/ *n* (*larva*) Made *f*; (*fam: food*) Essen *nt*

grubby /'grʌbɪ/ *a* (**-ier, -iest**) schmudelig

grudg|e /grʌdʒ/ *n* Groll *m*; **bear s.o. a** ~**e** einen Groll gegen jdn hegen ● *vt* ~**e s.o. sth** jdm etw mißgönnen. ~**ing** *a*, **-ly** *adv* widerwillig

gruelling /'gru:əlɪŋ/ *a* strapaziös

gruesome /'gru:səm/ *a* grausig

gruff /grʌf/ *a*, **-ly** *adv* barsch

grumble /'grʌmbl/ *vi* schimpfen (**at** mit)

grumpy /'grʌmpɪ/ *a* (**-ier, -iest**) griesgrämig

grunt /grʌnt/ *n* Grunzen *nt* ● *vi* grunzen

guarant|ee /gærən'ti:/ *n* Garantie *f*; (*document*) Garantieschein *m* ● *vt* garantieren; garantieren für (*quality, success*); (*product:*) Garantie haben. ~**or** *n* Bürge *m*

guard /ɡɑːd/ *n* Wache *f*; (*security*) Wächter *m*; (*on train*) ≈ Zugführer *m*; (*Techn*) Schutz *m*; **be on** ~ Wache stehen; **on one's** ~ auf der Hut ● *vt* bewachen; (*protect*) schützen ● *vi* ~ **against** sich hüten vor (+ *dat*). ~-**dog** *n* Wachhund *m*

guarded /'gɑːdɪd/ a vorsichtig
guardian /'gɑːdɪən/ n Vormund m
guerrilla /gəˈrɪlə/ n Guerillakämp-
fer m. ~ **warfare** n Partisanen-
krieg m
guess /ges/ n Vermutung f ● vt
erraten ● vi raten; (Amer: believe)
glauben. ~**work** n Vermutung f
guest /gest/ n Gast m. ~-**house** n
Pension f
guffaw /gʌˈfɔː/ n derbes Lachen nt
● vi derb lachen
guidance /'gaɪdəns/ n Führung f,
Leitung f; (advice) Beratung f
guide /gaɪd/ n Führer(in) m(f);
(book) Führer m; **[Girl] G~** Pfad-
finderin f ● vt führen, leiten. ~**book** n
Führer m
guided /'gaɪdɪd/ a ~ **missile** Fern-
lenkgeschoß nt; ~ **tour** Führung f
guide: ~**dog** n Blindenhund m.
~**lines** npl Richtlinien pl
guild /gɪld/ n Gilde f, Zunft f
guile /gaɪl/ n Arglist f
guillotine /'gɪləti:n/ n Guillotine f;
(for paper) Papierschneidema-
schine f
guilt /gɪlt/ n Schuld f. ~**ily** adv
schuldbewußt
guilty /'gɪltɪ/ a (-**ier, -iest**) a schuldig
(**of** gen); ⟨look⟩ schuldbewußt; ⟨con-
science⟩ schlecht
guinea-pig /'gɪnɪ-/ n Meer-
schweinchen nt; (person) Ver-
suchskaninchen nt
guise /gaɪz/ n **in the** ~ **of** in Gestalt
(+ gen)
guitar /gɪˈtɑː(r)/ n Gitarre f. ~**ist** n
Gitarrist(in) m(f)
gulf /gʌlf/ n (Geog) Golf m; (fig) Kluft
f
gull /gʌl/ n Möwe f
gullet /'gʌlɪt/ n Speiseröhre f;
(throat) Kehle f
gullible /'gʌlɪbl/ a leichtgläubig
gully /'gʌlɪ/ n Schlucht f; (drain)
Rinne f
gulp /gʌlp/ n Schluck m ● vi
schlucken ● vt ~ **down** hinunter-
schlucken
gum[1] /gʌm/ n & -**s** pl (Anat) Zahn-
fleisch nt
gum[2] n Gummi[harz] nt; (glue) Klebstoff m; (chewing-gum) Kaugummi m
● vt (pt/pp **gummed**) kleben (**to** an
+ acc). ~**boot** n Gummistiefel m
gummed /gʌmd/ see **gum**[2] ● a ⟨label⟩
gummiert

gumption /'gʌmpʃn/ n (fam) Grips
m
gun /gʌn/ n Schußwaffe f; (pistol)
Pistole f; (rifle) Gewehr nt; (cannon)
Geschütz nt ● vt (pt/pp **gunned**) ~
down niederschießen
gun: ~**fire** n Geschützfeuer nt.
~**man** bewaffneter Bandit m
gunner /'gʌnə(r)/ n Artillerist m
gun: ~**powder** n Schießpulver nt.
~**shot** n Schuß m
gurgle /'gɜːgl/ vi gluckern; (of baby)
glucksen
gush /gʌʃ/ vi strömen; (enthuse)
schwärmen (**over** von). ~ **out** vi
herausströmen
gusset /'gʌsɪt/ n Zwickel m
gust /gʌst/ n (of wind) Windstoß m;
(Naut) Bö f
gusto /'gʌstəʊ/ n **with** ~ mit
Schwung
gusty /'gʌstɪ/ a böig
gut /gʌt/ n Darm m; ~**s** pl Eingeweide
pl; (fam: courage) Schneid m ● vt (pt/
pp **gutted**) (Culin) ausnehmen; ~**ted**
by fire ausgebrannt
gutter /'gʌtə(r)/ n Rinnstein m; (fig)
Gosse f; (on roof) Dachrinne f
guttural /'gʌtərl/ a guttural
guy /gaɪ/ n (fam) Kerl m
guzzle /'gʌzl/ vt/i schlingen; (drink)
schlürfen
gym /dʒɪm/ n (fam) Turnhalle f;
(gymnastics) Turnen nt
gymnasium /dʒɪmˈneɪzɪəm/ n Turnhalle f
gymnast /'dʒɪmnæst/ n Turner(in)
m(f). ~**ics** /-'næstɪks/ n Turnen nt
gym: ~ **shoes** pl Turnschuhe pl.
~-**slip** n (Sch) Trägerkleid nt
gynaecolog|ist /gaɪnɪˈkɒlədʒɪst/ n
Frauenarzt m/-ärztin f. ~**y** n Gynä-
kologie f
gypsy /'dʒɪpsɪ/ n Zigeuner(in) m(f)
gyrate /dʒaɪəˈreɪt/ vi sich drehen

H

haberdashery /'hæbədæʃərɪ/ n
Kurzwaren pl; (Amer) Herrenmoden
pl
habit /'hæbɪt/ n Gewohnheit f;
(Relig: costume) Ordenstracht f; **be in**
the ~ die Angewohnheit haben (**of** zu)
habitable /'hæbɪtəbl/ a bewohnbar
habitat /'hæbɪtæt/ n Habitat nt

habitation /hæbɪˈteɪʃn/ n **unfit for human ~** für Wohnzwecke ungeeignet

habitual /həˈbɪtjʊəl/ a gewohnt; (*inveterate*) gewohnheitsmäßig. **~ly** adv gewohnheitsmäßig; (*constantly*) ständig

hack¹ /hæk/ n (*writer*) Schreiberling m; (*hired horse*) Mietpferd nt

hack² vt hacken; **~ to pieces** zerhacken

hackneyed /ˈhæknɪd/ a abgedroschen

'hacksaw n Metallsäge f

had /hæd/ *see* **have**

haddock /ˈhædək/ n inv Schellfisch m

haemorrhage /ˈhemərɪdʒ/ n Blutung f

haemorrhoids /ˈhemərɔɪdz/ npl Hämorrhoiden pl

hag /hæg/ n **old ~** alte Hexe f

haggard /ˈhægəd/ a abgehärmt

haggle /ˈhægl/ vi feilschen (**over** um)

hail¹ /heɪl/ vt begrüßen; herbeirufen ⟨*taxi*⟩ ● vi **~ from** kommen aus

hail² n Hagel m ● vi hageln. **~stone** n Hagelkorn nt

hair /heə(r)/ n Haar nt; **wash one's ~** sich (*dat*) die Haare waschen

hair: ~brush n Haarbürste f. **~cut** n Haarschnitt m; **have a ~cut** sich (*dat*) die Haare schneiden lassen. **~-do** n (*fam*) Frisur f. **~dresser** n Friseur m/Friseuse f. **~-drier** n Haartrockner m; (*hand-held*) Fön (P) m. **~-grip** n [Haar]klemme f. **~pin** n Haarnadel f. **~pin 'bend** n Haarnadelkurve f. **~-raising** a haarsträubend. **~-style** n Frisur f

hairy /ˈheərɪ/ a (**-ier, -iest**) behaart; (*excessively*) haarig; (*fam: frightening*) brenzlig

hake /heɪk/ n inv Seehecht m

hale /heɪl/ a **~ and hearty** gesund und munter

half /hɑːf/ n (pl **halves**) Hälfte f; **cut in ~** halbieren; **one and a ~** eineinhalb, anderthalb; **~ a dozen** ein halbes Dutzend; **~ an hour** eine halbe Stunde ● a & adv halb; **~ past two** halb drei; **[at] ~ price** zum halben Preis

half: ~-board n Halbpension f. **~-caste** n Mischling m. **~-'hearted** a lustlos. **~-'hourly** a & adv halbstündlich. **~-'mast** n **at ~-mast** auf halbmast. **~-measure** n Halbheit f. **~-'term** n schulfreie Tage nach dem halben Trimester. **~-'timbered** a Fachwerk-.

~-'time n (*Sport*) Halbzeit f. **~-'way** a **the ~-way mark/stage** die Hälfte ● adv auf halbem Weg; **get ~-way** den halben Weg zurücklegen; (*fig*) bis zur Hälfte kommen. **~-wit** n Idiot m

halibut /ˈhælɪbət/ n inv Heilbutt m

hall /hɔːl/ n Halle f; (*room*) Saal m; (*Sch*) Aula f; (*entrance*) Flur m; (*mansion*) Gutshaus nt; **~ of residence** (*Univ*) Studentenheim nt

'hallmark n [Feingehalts]stempel m; (*fig*) Kennzeichen nt (**of** für) ● vt stempeln

hallo /həˈləʊ/ int [guten] Tag! (*fam*) hallo!

Hallowe'en /hæləʊˈiːn/ n der Tag vor Allerheiligen

hallucination /həluːsɪˈneɪʃn/ n Halluzination f

halo /ˈheɪləʊ/ n (pl **-es**) Heiligenschein m; (*Astr*) Hof m

halt /hɔːlt/ n Halt m; **come to a ~** stehenbleiben; ⟨*traffic:*⟩ zum Stillstand kommen ● vi haltmachen; **~!** halt! **~ing**, a adv **-ly** zögernd

halve /hɑːv/ vt halbieren; (*reduce*) um die Hälfte reduzieren

ham /hæm/ n Schinken m

hamburger /ˈhæmbɜːgə(r)/ n Hamburger m

hamlet /ˈhæmlɪt/ n Weiler m

hammer /ˈhæmə(r)/ n Hammer m ● vt/i hämmern (**at** an + acc)

hammock /ˈhæmək/ n Hängematte f

hamper¹ /ˈhæmpə(r)/ n Picknickkorb m; **[gift] ~** Geschenkkorb m

hamper² vt behindern

hamster /ˈhæmstə(r)/ n Hamster m

hand /hænd/ n Hand f; (*of clock*) Zeiger m; (*writing*) Handschrift f; (*worker*) Arbeiter(in) m(f); (*Cards*) Blatt nt; **all ~s** (*Naut*) alle Mann; **at ~** in der Nähe; **on the one/other ~** einer-/ andererseits; **out of ~** außer Kontrolle; (*summarily*) kurzerhand; **in ~** unter Kontrolle; (*available*) verfügbar; **give s.o. a ~** jdm behilflich sein ● vt reichen (**to** dat). **~ in** vt abgeben. **~ out** vt austeilen. **~ over** vt überreichen

hand: ~bag n Handtasche f. **~book** n Handbuch m. **~brake** n Handbremse f. **~cuffs** npl Handschellen pl. **~ful** n Handvoll f; **be [quite] a ~ful** (*fam*) nicht leicht zu haben sein

handicap /ˈhændɪkæp/ n Behinderung f; (*Sport & fig*) Handikap nt.

~ped *a* **mentally/physically** ~**ped**
geistig/körperlich behindert

handi|craft /'hændıkra:ft/ *n* Basteln
nt; (*Sch*) Werken *nt*. ~**work** *n* Werk
nt

handkerchief /'hæŋkətʃıf/ *n* (*pl* ~**s**
& **-chieves**) Taschentuch *nt*

handle /'hændl/ *n* Griff *m*; (*of door*)
Klinke *f*; (*of cup*) Henkel *m*; (*of
broom*) Stiel *m*; **fly off the** ~ (*fam*)
aus der Haut fahren ● *vt* handhaben;
(*treat*) umgehen mit; (*touch*) anfassen.
~**bars** *npl* Lenkstange *f*

hand: ~-**luggage** *n* Handgepäck *nt*.
~**made** *a* handgemacht. ~-**out** *n*
Prospekt *m*; (*money*) Unterstützung
f. ~**rail** *n* Handlauf *m*. ~**shake** *n*
Händedruck *m*

handsome /'hænsəm/ *a* gutaussehend; (*generous*) großzügig; (*large*)
beträchtlich

hand: ~**stand** *n* Handstand *m*.
~**writing** *n* Handschrift *f*.
~-'**written** *a* handgeschrieben

handy /'hændı/ *a* (**-ier, -iest**) handlich; (*person*) geschickt; **have/keep** ~
griffbereit haben/halten. ~**man** *n*
[home] ~**man** Heimwerker *m*

hang /hæŋ/ *vt/i* (*pt/pp* **hung**)
hängen; ~ **wallpaper** tapezieren ● *vt*
(*pt/pp* **hanged**) hängen (*criminal*); ~
oneself sich erhängen ● *n* **get the** ~
of it (*fam*) den Dreh herauskriegen. ~
about *vi* sich herumdrücken. ~ **on**
vi sich festhalten (**to** an + *dat*); (*fam:
wait*) warten. ~ **out** *vi* heraus-
hängen; (*fam: live*) wohnen ● *vt*
draußen aufhängen (*washing*). ~ **up**
vt/i aufhängen

hangar /'hæŋə(r)/ *n* Flugzeughalle *f*

hanger /'hæŋə(r)/ *n* [Kleider]bügel
m

hang: ~-**glider** *n* Drachenflieger *m*.
~-**gliding** *n* Drachenfliegen *nt*.
~**man** *n* Henker *m*. ~**over** *n* (*fam*)
Kater *m* (*fam*). ~-**up** *n* (*fam*) Komplex *m*

hanker /'hæŋkə(r)/ *vi* ~ **after sth**
sich (*dat*) etw wünschen

hanky /'hæŋkı/ *n* (*fam*) Taschentuch *nt*

hanky-panky /hæŋkı'pæŋkı/ *n*
(*fam*) Mauscheleien *pl*

haphazard /hæp'hæzəd/ *a*, **-ly** *adv*
planlos

happen /'hæpn/ *vi* geschehen, passieren; **as it** ~**s** zufälligerweise; **I** ~**ed
to be there** ich war zufällig da; **what**

has ~**ed to him?** was ist mit ihm los?
(*become of*) was ist aus ihm geworden?
~**ing** *n* Ereignis *nt*

happi|ly /'hæpılı/ *adv* glücklich;
(*fortunately*) glücklicherweise. ~-
ness *n* Glück *nt*

happy /'hæpı/ *a* (**-ier, -iest**) glücklich.
~-**go-'lucky** *a* sorglos

harass /'hærəs/ *vt* schikanieren.
~**ed** *a* abgehetzt. ~**ment** *n* Schikane
f; (*sexual*) Belästigung *f*

harbour /'ha:bə(r)/ *n* Hafen *m*
● *vt* Unterschlupf gewähren (+ *dat*);
hegen (*grudge*)

hard /ha:d/ *a* (**-er, -est**) hart; (*difficult*)
schwer; ~ **of hearing** schwerhörig
● *adv* hart; (*work*) schwer; (*pull*)
kräftig; (*rain, snow*) stark; **think** ~!
denk mal nach! **be** ~ **up** (*fam*) knapp
bei Kasse sein; **be** ~ **done by** (*fam*)
ungerecht behandelt werden

hard: ~**back** *n* gebundene Ausgabe *f*.
~**board** *n* Hartfaserplatte *f*.
~-**boiled** *a* hartgekocht

harden /'ha:dn/ *vi* hart werden

hard-'hearted *a* hartherzig

hard|ly /'ha:dlı/ *adv* kaum; ~**ly ever**
kaum [jemals]. ~**ness** *n* Härte *f*.
~**ship** *n* Not *f*

hard: ~ '**shoulder** *n* (*Auto*) Rand-
streifen *m*. ~**ware** *n* Haushaltswa-
ren *pl*; (*Computing*) Hardware *f*.
~-'**wearing** *a* strapazierfähig.
~-'**working** *a* fleißig

hardy /'ha:dı/ *a* (**-ier, -iest**) abge-
härtet; (*plant*) winterhart

hare /heə(r)/ *n* Hase *m*. ~'**lip** *n*
Hasenscharte *f*

hark /ha:k/ *vi* ~! hört! ~ **back** *vi* ~
back to (*fig*) zurückkommen auf
(+ *acc*)

harm /ha:m/ *n* Schaden *m*; **out of** ~'**s
way** in Sicherheit; **it won't do any** ~
es kann nichts schaden ● *vt* ~ **s.o.** jdm
etwas antun. ~**ful** *a* schädlich. ~**less**
a harmlos

harmonica /ha:'mɒnıkə/ *n* Mundharmonika *f*

harmonious /ha:'məʊnıəs/ *a*, **-ly**
adv harmonisch

harmon|ize /'ha:mənaız/ *vi* (*fig*)
harmonieren. ~**y** *n* Harmonie *f*

harness /'ha:nıs/ *n* Geschirr *nt*; (*of
parachute*) Gurtwerk *nt* ● *vt* anschirren (*horse*); (*use*) nutzbar
machen

harp /ha:p/ *n* Harfe *f* ● *vi* ~ **on
[about]** (*fam*) herumreiten auf
(+ *dat*). ~**ist** *n* Harfenist(in) *m(f)*

harpoon /hɑːˈpuːn/ n Harpune f
harpsichord /ˈhɑːpsɪkɔːd/ n Cembalo nt
harrow /ˈhærəʊ/ n Egge f. ∼**ing** a grauenhaft
harsh /hɑːʃ/ a (**-er, -est**), **-ly** adv hart; ⟨voice⟩ rauh; ⟨light⟩ grell. ∼**ness** n Härte f; Rauheit f
harvest /ˈhɑːvɪst/ n Ernte f ● vt ernten
has /hæz/ see **have**
hash /hæʃ/ n (Culin) Haschee nt; **make a** ∼ **of** (fam) verpfuschen
hashish /ˈhæʃɪʃ/ n Haschisch nt
hassle /ˈhæsl/ n (fam) Ärger m ● vt schikanieren
hassock /ˈhæsək/ n Kniekissen nt
haste /heɪst/ n Eile f; **make** ∼ sich beeilen
hasten /ˈheɪsn/ vi sich beeilen (**to** zu); (go quickly) eilen ● vt beschleunigen
hasty /ˈheɪstɪ/ a (**-ier, -iest**), **-ily** adv hastig; ⟨decision⟩ voreilig
hat /hæt/ n Hut m; (knitted) Mütze f
hatch[1] /hætʃ/ n (for food) Durchreiche f; (Naut) Luke f
hatch[2] vi ∼ **[out]** ausschlüpfen ● vt ausbrüten
hatchback n (Auto) Modell nt mit Hecktür
hatchet /ˈhætʃɪt/ n Beil nt
hate /heɪt/ n Haß m ● vt hassen. ∼**ful** a abscheulich
hatred /ˈheɪtrɪd/ n Haß m
haughty /ˈhɔːtɪ/ a (**-ier, -iest**), **-ily** adv hochmütig
haul /hɔːl/ n (fish) Fang m; (loot) Beute f ● vt/i ziehen (**on** an + dat). ∼**age** /-ɪdʒ/ n Transport m. ∼**ier** /-ɪə(r)/ n Spediteur m
haunt /hɔːnt/ n Lieblingsaufenthalt m ● vt umgehen in (+ dat); **this house is** ∼**ed** in diesem Haus spukt es
have /hæv/ vt (3 sg pres tense **has**; pt/pp **had**) haben; bekommen ⟨baby⟩; holen ⟨doctor⟩; ∼ **a meal/drink** etwas essen/trinken; ∼ **lunch** zu Mittag essen; ∼ **a walk** spazierengehen; ∼ **a dream** träumen; ∼ **a rest** sich ausruhen; ∼ **a swim** schwimmen; ∼ **sth done** etw machen lassen; ∼ **sth made** sich (dat) etw machen lassen; ∼ **to do sth** etw tun müssen; ∼ **it out with** zur Rede stellen; **so I** ∼**!** tatsächlich! **he has [got] two houses** er hat zwei Häuser; **you have got the money, haven't you?** du hast das Geld, nicht [wahr]?

● v aux haben; (with verbs of motion & some others) sein; **I** ∼ **seen him** ich habe ihn gesehen; **he has never been there** er ist nie da gewesen. ∼ **on** vt (be wearing) anhaben; (dupe) anführen
haven /ˈheɪvn/ n (fig) Zuflucht f
haversack /ˈhævə-/ n Rucksack m
havoc /ˈhævək/ n Verwüstung f; **play** ∼ **with** (fig) völlig durcheinanderbringen
haw /hɔː/ see **hum**
hawk[1] /hɔːk/ n Falke m
hawk[2] vt hausieren mit. ∼**er** n Hausierer m
hawthorn /ˈhɔː-/ n Hagedorn m
hay /heɪ/ n Heu nt. ∼ **fever** n Heuschnupfen m. ∼**stack** n Heuschober m
haywire a (fam) **go** ∼ verrückt spielen; ⟨plans:⟩ über den Haufen geworfen werden
hazard /ˈhæzəd/ n Gefahr f; (risk) Risiko nt ● vt riskieren. ∼**ous** /-əs/ a gefährlich; (risky) riskant. ∼ **[warning] lights** npl (Auto) Warnblinkanlage f
haze /heɪz/ n Dunst m
hazel /ˈheɪzl/ n Haselbusch m. ∼**-nut** n Haselnuß f
hazy /ˈheɪzɪ/ a (**-ier, -iest**) dunstig; (fig) unklar
he /hiː/ pron er
head /hed/ n Kopf m; (chief) Oberhaupt nt; (of firm) Chef(in) m(f); (of school) Schulleiter(in) m(f); (on beer) Schaumkrone f; (of bed) Kopfende nt; **20** ∼ **of cattle** 20 Stück Vieh; ∼ **first** kopfüber ● vt anführen; (Sport) köpfen ⟨ball⟩ ● vi ∼ **for** zusteuern auf (+ acc). ∼**ache** n Kopfschmerzen pl. ∼**-dress** n Kopfschmuck m
head|er /ˈhedə(r)/ n Kopfball m; (dive) Kopfsprung m. ∼**ing** n Überschrift f
head: ∼**lamp** n (Auto) Scheinwerfer m. ∼**land** n Landspitze f. ∼**light** n (Auto) Scheinwerfer m. ∼**line** n Schlagzeile f. ∼**long** adv kopfüber. ∼'**master** n Schulleiter m. ∼'**mistress** n Schulleiterin f. ∼**-on** n & adv frontal. ∼**phones** npl Kopfhörer m. ∼**quarters** npl Hauptquartier nt; (Pol) Zentrale f. ∼**-rest** n Kopfstütze f. ∼**room** n lichte Höhe f. ∼**scarf** n Kopftuch nt. ∼**strong** a eigenwillig. ∼ '**waiter** n Oberkellner m. ∼**way** n **make** ∼**way**

Fortschritte machen. ~ **wind** n Gegenwind m. ~**word** n Stichwort nt

heady /'hedɪ/ a berauschend

heal /hiːl/ vt/i heilen

health /helθ/ n Gesundheit f

health: ~ **farm** n Schönheitsfarm f. ~ **foods** npl Reformkost f. ~-**food shop** n Reformhaus nt. ~ **insurance** n Krankenversicherung f

healthy /'helθɪ/ a (-**ier**, -**iest**), -**ily** adv gesund

heap /hiːp/ n Haufen m; ~**s** (fam) jede Menge ● vt ~ [**up**] häufen; ~**ed teaspoon** gehäufter Teelöffel

hear /hɪə(r)/ vt/i (pt/pp **heard**) hören; ~, ~! hört, hört! **he would not** ~ **of it** er ließ es nicht zu

hearing /'hɪərɪŋ/ n Gehör nt; (Jur) Verhandlung f. ~-**aid** n Hörgerät nt

'**hearsay** n **from** ~ vom Hörensagen

hearse /hɜːs/ n Leichenwagen m

heart /hɑːt/ n Herz nt; (courage) Mut m; ~**s** pl (Cards) Herz nt; **by** ~ auswendig

heart: ~**ache** n Kummer m. ~ **attack** n Herzanfall m. ~**beat** n Herzschlag m. ~-**break** n Leid nt. ~-**breaking** a herzzerreißend. ~-**broken** a untröstlich. ~**burn** n Sodbrennen nt. ~**en** vt ermutigen. ~**felt** a herzlich[st]

hearth /hɑːθ/ n Herd m; (fireplace) Kamin m. ~**rug** n Kaminvorleger m

heart|ily /'hɑːtɪlɪ/ adv herzlich; (eat) viel. ~**less** a, -**ly** adv herzlos. ~**y** a herzlich; (meal) groß; (person) burschikos

heat /hiːt/ n Hitze f; (Sport) Vorlauf m ● vt heiß machen; heizen (room). ~**ed** a geheizt; (swimming pool) beheizt; (discussion) hitzig. ~**er** n Heizgerät nt; (Auto) Heizanlage f

heath /hiːθ/ n Heide f

heathen /'hiːðn/ a heidnisch ● n Heide m/Heidin f

heather /'heðə(r)/ n Heidekraut nt

heating /'hiːtɪŋ/ n Heizung f

heat: ~-**stroke** n Hitzschlag m. ~**wave** n Hitzewelle f

heave /hiːv/ vt/i ziehen; (lift) heben; (fam: throw) schmeißen; ~ **a sigh** einen Seufzer ausstoßen

heaven /'hevn/ n Himmel m. ~**ly** a himmlisch

heavy /'hevɪ/ a (-**ier**, -**iest**), -**ily** adv schwer; (traffic, rain) stark; (sleep) tief. ~**weight** n Schwergewicht nt

Hebrew /'hiːbruː/ a hebräisch

heckle /'hekl/ vt [durch Zwischenrufe] unterbrechen. ~**r** n Zwischenrufer m

hectic /'hektɪk/ a hektisch

hedge /hedʒ/ n Hecke f ● vi (fig) ausweichen. ~**hog** n Igel m

heed /hiːd/ n **pay** ~ **to** Beachtung schenken (+ dat) ● vt beachten. ~**less** a ungeachtet (**of** gen)

heel¹ /hiːl/ n Ferse f; (of shoe) Absatz m; **down at** ~ heruntergekommen; **take to one's** ~**s** (fam) Fersengeld geben

heel² vi ~ **over** (Naut) sich auf die Seite legen

hefty /'heftɪ/ a (-**ier**, -**iest**) kräftig; (heavy) schwer

heifer /'hefə(r)/ n Färse f

height /haɪt/ n Höhe f; (of person) Größe f. ~**en** vt (fig) steigern

heir /eə(r)/ n Erbe m. ~**ess** n Erbin f. ~**loom** n Erbstück nt

held /held/ see **hold**²

helicopter /'helɪkɒptə(r)/ n Hubschrauber m

hell /hel/ n Hölle f; **go to** ~! (sl) geh zum Teufel! ● int verdammt!

hello /hə'ləʊ/ int [guten] Tag! (fam) hallo!

helm /helm/ n [Steuer]ruder nt; **at the** ~ (fig) am Ruder

helmet /'helmɪt/ n Helm m

help /help/ n Hilfe f; (employees) Hilfskräfte pl; **that's no** ~ das nützt nichts ● vt/i helfen (s.o. jdm); ~ **oneself to sth** sich (dat) etw nehmen; ~ **yourself** (at table) greif zu; **I could not** ~ **laughing** ich mußte lachen; **it cannot be** ~**ed** es läßt sich nicht ändern; **I can't** ~ **it** ich kann nichts dafür

help|er /'helpə(r)/ n Helfer(in) m(f). ~**ful** a, -**ly** adv hilfsbereit; (advice) nützlich. ~**ing** n Portion f. ~**less** a, -**ly** adv hilflos

helter-skelter /heltə'skeltə(r)/ adv holterdiepolter ● n Rutschbahn f

hem /hem/ n Saum m ● vt (pt/pp **hemmed**) säumen; ~ **in** umzingeln

hemisphere /'hemɪ-/ n Hemisphäre f

'**hem-line** n Rocklänge f

hemp /hemp/ n Hanf m

hen /hen/ n Henne f; (any female bird) Weibchen nt

hence /hens/ adv daher; **five years** ~ in fünf Jahren. ~'**forth** adv von nun an

henchman /'hentʃmən/ n (pej) Gefolgsmann m

'henpecked *a* ∼ **husband** Pantoffelheld *m*

her /hɜː(r)/ *a* ihr ●*pron* (*acc*) sie; (*dat*) ihr; **I know** ∼ ich kenne sie; **give** ∼ **the money** gib ihr das Geld

herald/'herəld/ *vt* verkünden. ∼**ry** *n* Wappenkunde *f*

herb /hɜːb/ *n* Kraut *nt*

herbaceous /hɜː'beɪʃəs/ *a* krautartig; ∼ **border** Staudenrabatte *f*

herd /hɜːd/ *n* Herde *f* ●*vt* (*tend*) hüten; (*drive*) treiben. ∼ **together** *vi* sich zusammendrängen ●*vt* zusammentreiben

here /hɪə(r)/ *adv* hier; (*to this place*) hierher; **in** ∼ hier drinnen; **come/ bring** ∼ herkommen/herbringen. ∼'**after** *adv* im folgenden. ∼'**by** *adv* hiermit

heredit|ary /hə'redɪtərɪ/ *a* erblich. ∼**y** *n* Vererbung *f*

here|sy /'herəsɪ/ *n* Ketzerei *f*. ∼**tic** *n* Ketzer(in) *m(f)*

here'with *adv* (*Comm*) beiliegend

heritage /'herɪtɪdʒ/ *n* Erbe *nt*

hermetic /hɜː'metɪk/ *a*, **-ally** *adv* hermetisch

hermit /'hɜːmɪt/ *n* Einsiedler *m*

hernia /'hɜːnɪə/ *n* Bruch *m*, Hernie *f*

hero /'hɪərəʊ/ *n* (*pl* **-es**) Held *m*

heroic /hɪ'rəʊɪk/ *a*, **-ally** *adv* heldenhaft

heroin /'herəʊɪn/ *n* Heroin *nt*

hero|ine /'herəʊɪn/ *n* Heldin *f*. ∼**ism** *n* Heldentum *nt*

heron /'hern/ *n* Reiher *m*

herring /'herɪŋ/ *n* Hering *m*; **red** ∼ (*fam*) falsche Spur *f*. ∼**bone** *n* (*pattern*) Fischgrätenmuster *nt*

hers /hɜːz/ *poss pron* ihre(r), ihrs; **a friend of** ∼ ein Freund von ihr; **that is** ∼ das gehört ihr

her'self *pron* selbst; (*refl*) sich; **by** ∼ allein

hesitant /'hezɪtənt/ *a*, **-ly** *adv* zögernd

hesitat|e /'hezɪteɪt/ *vi* zögern. ∼**ion** /-'teɪʃn/ *n* Zögern *nt*; **without** ∼**ion** ohne zu zögern

het /het/ *a* ∼ **up** (*fam*) aufgeregt

hetero'sexual /hetərəʊ-/ *a* heterosexuell

hew /hjuː/ *vt* (*pt* **hewed**, *pp* **hewed** *or* **hewn**) hauen

hexagonal /hek'sægənl/ *a* sechseckig

heyday /'heɪ-/ *n* Glanzzeit *f*

hi /haɪ/ *int* he! (*hallo*) Tag!

hiatus /haɪ'eɪtəs/ *n* (*pl* **-tuses**) Lücke *f*

hibernat|e /'haɪbəneɪt/ *vi* Winterschlaf halten. ∼**ion** /-'neɪʃn/ *n* Winterschlaf *m*

hiccup /'hɪkʌp/ *n* Hick *m*; (*fam: hitch*) Panne *f*; **have the** ∼**s** den Schluckauf haben ●*vi* hick machen

hid /hɪd/, **hidden** *see* **hide**²

hide¹ /haɪd/ *n* (*Comm*) Haut *f*; (*leather*) Leder *nt*

hide² *v* (*pt* **hid**, *pp* **hidden**) ●*vt* verstecken; (*keep secret*) verheimlichen ●*vi* sich verstecken. ∼**-and-'seek** *n* **play** ∼**-and-seek** Verstecke spielen

hideous /'hɪdɪəs/ *a*, **-ly** *adv* häßlich; (*horrible*) gräßlich

'hide-out *n* Versteck *nt*

hiding¹ /'haɪdɪŋ/ *n* (*fam*) **give s.o. a** ∼ jdn verdreschen

hiding² *n* **go into** ∼ untertauchen

hierarchy /'haɪərɑːkɪ/ *n* Hierarchie *f*

hieroglyphics /haɪərə'glɪfɪks/ *npl* Hieroglyphen *pl*

higgledy-piggledy /hɪgldɪ'pɪgldɪ/ *adv* kunterbunt durcheinander

high /haɪ/ *a* (**-er**, **-est**) hoch; *attrib* hohe(r,s); (*meat*) angegangen; (*wind*) stark; (*on drugs*) high; **it's** ∼ **time** es ist höchste Zeit ●*adv* hoch; ∼ **and low** überall ●*n* Hoch *nt*; (*temperature*) Höchsttemperatur *f*

high: ∼**brow** *a* intellektuell. ∼ **chair** *n* Kinderhochstuhl *m*. ∼-**'handed** *a* selbstherrlich. ∼-**'heeled** *a* hochhackig. ∼ **jump** *n* Hochsprung *m*

highlight *n* (*fig*) Höhepunkt *m*; ∼**s** *pl* (*in hair*) helle Strähnen *pl* ●*vt* (*emphasize*) hervorheben

highly /'haɪlɪ/ *adv* hoch; **speak** ∼ **of** loben; **think** ∼ **of** sehr schätzen. ∼-'**strung** *a* nervös

Highness /'haɪnɪs/ *n* Hoheit *f*

high: ∼-**rise** *a* ∼-**rise flats** *pl* Wohnturm *m*. ∼ **season** *n* Hochsaison *f*. ∼ **street** *n* Hauptstraße *f*. ∼ **'tide** *n* Hochwasser *nt*. ∼**way** *n* **public** ∼**way** öffentliche Straße *f*

hijack /'haɪdʒæk/ *vt* entführen. ∼**er** *n* Entführer *m*

hike /haɪk/ *n* Wanderung *f* ●*vi* wandern. ∼**r** *n* Wanderer *m*

hilarious /hɪ'leərɪəs/ *a* sehr komisch

hill /hɪl/ *n* Berg *m*; (*mound*) Hügel *m*; (*slope*) Hang *m*

hill: ∼-**billy** *n* (*Amer*) Hinterwäldler *m*. ∼**side** *n* Hang *m*. ∼**ya** hügelig

hilt /hɪlt/ *n* Griff *m*; **to the** ∼ (*fam*) voll und ganz

him /hɪm/ *pron* (*acc*) ihn; (*dat*) ihm;
I know ~ ich kenne ihn; **give** ~ **the
money** gib ihm das Geld. ~'**self** *pron*
selbst; (*refl*) sich; **by** ~**self** allein
hind /haɪnd/ *a* Hinter-
hind|er /'hɪndə(r)/ *vt* hindern. ~-
rance *n* Hindernis *nt*
hindsight /'haɪnd-/ *n* **with** ~ rückblickend
Hindu /'hɪnduː/ *n* Hindu *m* ● *a*
Hindu. ~**ism** *n* Hinduismus *m*
hinge /hɪndʒ/ *n* Scharnier *nt*; (*on
door*) Angel *f* ● *vi* ~ **on** (*fig*) ankommen auf (+ *acc*)
hint /hɪnt/ *n* Wink *m*, Andeutung *f*;
(*advice*) Hinweis *m*; (*trace*) Spur *f* ● *vi*
~ **at** anspielen auf (+ *acc*)
hip /hɪp/ *n* Hüfte *f*
hippie /'hɪpɪ/ *n* Hippie *m*
hip '**pocket** *n* Gesäßtasche *f*
hippopotamus /hɪpə'pɒtəməs/ *n*
(*pl* -**muses** *or* -**mi** /-maɪ/) Nilpferd *nt*
hire /'haɪə(r)/ *vt* mieten (*car*); leihen
(*suit*); einstellen (*person*); ~ **[out]** vermieten; verleihen ● *n* Mieten *nt*;
Leihen *nt*. ~-**car** *n* Leihwagen *m*
his /hɪz/ *a* sein ● *poss pron* seine(r),
seins; **a friend of** ~ ein Freund von
ihm; **that is** ~ das gehört ihm
hiss /hɪs/ *n* Zischen *nt* ● *vt/i* zischen
historian /hɪ'stɔːrɪən/ *n* Histori-
ker(in) *m(f)*
historic /hɪ'stɒrɪk/ *a* historisch. ~**al**
a, -**ly** *adv* geschichtlich, historisch
history /'hɪstərɪ/ *n* Geschichte *f*
hit /hɪt/ *n* (*blow*) Schlag *m*; (*fam: success*) Erfolg *m*; **direct** ~ Volltreffer *m*
● *vt/i* (*pt/pp* **hit**, *pres p* **hitting**) schlagen; (*knock against, collide with, affect*)
treffen; ~ **the target** das Ziel treffen; ~
on (*fig*) kommen auf (+ *acc*); ~ **it off**
gut auskommen (**with** mit); ~ **one's
head on sth** sich (*dat*) den Kopf an etw
(*dat*) stoßen
hitch /hɪtʃ/ *n* Problem *nt*; **technical**
~ Panne *f* ● *vt* festmachen (**to** an
+ *dat*); ~ **up** hochziehen; ~ **a lift** per
Anhalter fahren, (*fam*) trampen. ~-
hike *vi* per Anhalter fahren, (*fam*)
trampen. ~-**hiker** *n* Anhalter(in)
m(f)
hither /'hɪðə(r)/ *adv* hierher; ~ **and
thither** hin und her. ~'**to** *adv* bisher
hive /haɪv/ *n* Bienenstock *m*. ~ **off**
vt (*Comm*) abspalten
hoard /hɔːd/ *n* Hort *m* ● *vt* horten,
hamstern

hoarding /'hɔːdɪŋ/ *n* Bauzaun *m*;
(*with advertisements*) Reklamewand
f
hoar-frost /'hɔː-/ *n* Rauhreif *m*
hoarse /hɔːs/ *a* (**-r, -st**), -**ly** *adv* heiser.
~**ness** *n* Heiserkeit *f*
hoax /həʊks/ *n* übler Scherz *m*;
(*false alarm*) blinder Alarm *m*
hob /hɒb/ *n* Kochmulde *f*
hobble /'hɒbl/ *vi* humpeln
hobby /'hɒbɪ/ *n* Hobby *nt*. ~**horse** *n*
(*fig*) Lieblingsthema *nt*
hobnailed /'hɒb-/ *a* ~ **boots** *pl* ge-
nagelte Schuhe *pl*
hock /hɒk/ *n* [weißer] Rheinwein *m*
hockey /'hɒkɪ/ *n* Hockey *nt*
hoe /həʊ/ *n* Hacke *f* ● *vt* (*pres p* **hoe-
ing**) hacken
hog /hɒg/ *n* [Mast]schwein *nt* ● *vt*
(*pt/pp* **hogged**) (*fam*) mit Beschlag
belegen
hoist /hɔɪst/ *n* Lastenaufzug *m* ● *vt*
hochziehen; hissen (*flag*)
hold[1] /həʊld/ *n* (*Naut*) Laderaum *m*
hold[2] *n* Halt *m*; (*Sport*) Griff *m*; (*fig:
influence*) Einfluß *m*; **get** ~ **of** fassen;
(*fam: contact*) erreichen ● *v* (*pt/pp*
held) ● *vt* halten; (*container:*) fassen;
(*believe*) meinen; (*possess*) haben;
anhalten (*breath*); ~ **one's tongue** den
Mund halten ● *vi* (*rope:*) halten;
(*weather:*) sich halten; **not** ~ **with**
(*fam*) nicht einverstanden sein mit. ~
back *vt* zurückhalten ● *vi* zögern. ~
on *vi* (*wait*) warten; (*on telephone*)
am Apparat bleiben; ~ **on to** (*keep*)
behalten; (*cling to*) sich festhalten an
(+ *dat*). ~ **out** *vt* hinhalten ● *vi*
(*resist*) aushalten. ~ **up** *vt* hoch-
halten; (*delay*) aufhalten; (*rob*) überfallen
'**hold|all** *n* Reisetasche *f*. ~**er** *n* In-
haber(in) *m(f)*; (*container*) Halter *m*.
~-**up** *n* Verzögerung *f*; (*attack*)
Überfall *m*
hole /həʊl/ *n* Loch *nt*
holiday /'hɒlədeɪ/ *n* Urlaub *m*; (*Sch*)
Ferien *pl*; (*public*) Feiertag *m*; (*day
off*) freier Tag *m*; **go on** ~ in Urlaub
fahren. ~-**maker** *n* Urlauber(in)
m(f)
holiness /'həʊlɪnɪs/ *n* Heiligkeit *f*
Holland /'hɒlənd/ *n* Holland *nt*
hollow /'hɒləʊ/ *a* hohl; (*promise*)
leer ● *n* Vertiefung *f*; (*in ground*)
Mulde *f*. ~ **out** *vt* aushöhlen
holly /'hɒlɪ/ *n* Stechpalme *f*
'**hollyhock** *n* Stockrose *f*

hologram /ˈhɒləgræm/ n Hologramm nt

holster /ˈhəʊlstə(r)/ n Pistolentasche f

holy /ˈhəʊlɪ/ a (**-ier, -iest**) heilig. **H~ Ghost** or **Spirit** n Heiliger Geist m. ~ **water** n Weihwasser nt. **H~ Week** n Karwoche f

homage /ˈhɒmɪdʒ/ n Huldigung f; **pay ~ to** huldigen (+ dat)

home /həʊm/ n Zuhause nt; (house) Haus nt; (institution) Heim nt; (native land) Heimat f ● adv **at ~** zu Hause; **come/go ~** nach Hause kommen/gehen

home: ~ **ad'dress** n Heimatanschrift f. ~ **com'puter** n Heimcomputer m. ~ **game** n Heimspiel nt. ~ **help** n Haushaltshilfe f. ~**land** n Heimatland nt. ~**less** a obdachlos

homely /ˈhəʊmlɪ/ a (**-ier, -iest**) a gemütlich; (Amer: ugly) unscheinbar

home: ~-'made a selbstgemacht. **H~ Office** n Innenministerium nt. **H~ 'Secretary** n Innenminister m. ~**sick** a **be ~sick** Heimweh haben (**for** nach). ~**sickness** n Heimweh nt. ~ 'town n Heimatstadt f. ~**work** n (Sch) Hausaufgaben pl

homicide /ˈhɒmɪsaɪd/ n Totschlag m; (murder) Mord m

homoeopath|ic /həʊmɪəˈpæθɪk/ a homöopathisch. ~**y** /-ˈɒpəθɪ/ n Homöopathie f

homogeneous /hɒməˈdʒiːnɪəs/ a homogen

homo'sexual a homosexuell ● n Homosexuelle(r) m/f

honest /ˈɒnɪst/ a, **-ly** adv ehrlich. ~**y** n Ehrlichkeit f

honey /ˈhʌnɪ/ n Honig m; (fam: darling) Schatz m

honey: ~**comb** n Honigwabe f. ~**moon** n Flitterwochen pl; (journey) Hochzeitsreise f. ~**suckle** n Geißblatt nt

honk /hɒŋk/ vi hupen

honorary /ˈɒnərərɪ/ a ehrenamtlich; (member, doctorate) Ehren-

honour /ˈɒnə(r)/ n Ehre f ● vt ehren; honorieren (cheque). ~**able** /-əbl/ a, **-bly** adv ehrenhaft

hood /hʊd/ n Kapuze f; (of pram) [Klapp]verdeck nt; (over cooker) Abzugshaube f; (Auto, Amer) Kühlerhaube f

hoodlum /ˈhuːdləm/ n Rowdy m

'**hoodwink** vt (fam) reinlegen

hoof /huːf/ n (pl ~s or **hooves**) Huf m

hook /hʊk/ n Haken m; **by ~ or by crook** mit allen Mitteln ● vt festhaken (**to** an + acc)

hook|ed /hʊkt/ a ~**ed nose** Hakennase f; ~**ed on** (fam) abhängig von; (keen on) besessen von. ~**er** n (Amer, sl) Nutte f

hookey /ˈhʊkɪ/ n **play ~** (Amer, fam) schwänzen

hooligan /ˈhuːlɪgən/ n Rowdy m. ~**ism** n Rowdytum nt

hoop /huːp/ n Reifen m

hooray /hʊˈreɪ/ int & n = **hurrah**

hoot /huːt/ n Ruf m; ~**s of laughter** schallendes Gelächter nt ● vi (owl:) rufen; (car:) hupen; (jeer) johlen. ~**er** n (of factory) Sirene f; (Auto) Hupe f

hoover /ˈhuːvə(r)/ n **H~** (P) Staubsauger m ● vt/i [staub]saugen

hop[1] /hɒp/ n, & ~**s** pl Hopfen m

hop[2] n Hüpfer m; **catch s.o. on the ~** (fam) jdm ungelegen kommen ● vi (pt/pp **hopped**) hüpfen; ~ **it!** (fam) hau ab! ~ **in** vi (fam) einsteigen. ~ **out** vi (fam) aussteigen

hope /həʊp/ n Hoffnung f; (prospect) Aussicht f (**of** auf + acc) ● vt/i hoffen (**for** auf + acc); **I ~ so** hoffentlich

hope|ful /ˈhəʊpfl/ a hoffnungsvoll; **be ~ful that** hoffen, daß. ~**fully** adv hoffnungsvoll; (it is hoped) hoffentlich. ~**less** a, **-ly** adv hoffnungslos; (useless) nutzlos; (incompetent) untauglich

horde /hɔːd/ n Horde f

horizon /həˈraɪzn/ n Horizont m; **on the ~** am Horizont

horizontal /hɒrɪˈzɒntl/ a, **-ly** adv horizontal. ~ '**bar** n Reck nt

horn /hɔːn/ n Horn nt; (Auto) Hupe f

hornet /ˈhɔːnɪt/ n Hornisse f

horny /ˈhɔːnɪ/ a schwielig

horoscope /ˈhɒrəskəʊp/ n Horoskop nt

horrible /ˈhɒrɪbl/ a, **-bly** adv schrecklich

horrid /ˈhɒrɪd/ a gräßlich

horrific /həˈrɪfɪk/ a entsetzlich

horrify /ˈhɒrɪfaɪ/ vt (pt/pp **-ied**) entsetzen

horror /ˈhɒrə(r)/ n Entsetzen nt. ~ **film** n Horrorfilm m

hors-d'œuvre /ɔːˈdɜːvr/ n Vorspeise f

horse /hɔːs/ n Pferd nt

horse: ~back n on ~back zu Pferde.
~-'chestnut n [Roß]kastanie f.
~man n Reiter m. ~play n Toben nt.
~power n Pferdestärke f. ~-racing
n Pferderennen nt. ~radish n Meer-
rettich m. ~shoe n Hufeisen nt

horti'cultural /hɔːtɪ-/ a Garten-
'horticulture n Gartenbau m

hose /həʊz/ n (pipe) Schlauch m ● vt
~ down abspritzen

hosiery /'həʊʒərɪ/ n Strumpfwaren pl

hospice /'hɒspɪs/ n Heim nt; (for the
terminally ill) Sterbeklinik f

hospitable /hɒ'spɪtəbl/ a, -bly adv
gastfreundlich

hospital /'hɒspɪtl/ n Krankenhaus
nt

hospitality /hɒspɪ'tælətɪ/ n Gast-
freundschaft f

host¹ /həʊst/ n a ~ of eine Menge von
host² n Gastgeber m
host³ n (Relig) Hostie f

hostage /'hɒstɪdʒ/ n Geisel f

hostel /'hɒstl/ n [Wohn]heim nt

hostess /'həʊstɪs/ n Gastgeberin f

hostile /'hɒstaɪl/ a feindlich; (un-
friendly) feindselig

hostilit|y /hɒ'stɪlətɪ/ n Feindschaft
f; ~ies pl Feindseligkeiten pl

hot /hɒt/ a (hotter, hottest) heiß;
⟨meal⟩ warm; (spicy) scharf; I am or feel
~ mir ist heiß

'hotbed n (fig) Brutstätte f

hotchpotch /'hɒtʃpɒtʃ/ n Misch-
masch m

hotel /həʊ'tel/ n Hotel nt. ~ier
/-ɪə(r)/ n Hotelier m

hot: ~head n Hitzkopf m.
~'headed a hitzköpfig. ~house n
Treibhaus nt. ~ly adv (fig) heiß, heftig. ~plate n Tellerwärmer m; (of
cooker) Kochplatte f. ~ tap n Warm-
wasserhahn m. ~-tempered a jäh-
zornig. ~-'water bottle n
Wärmflasche f

hound /haʊnd/ n Jagdhund m ● vt
(fig) verfolgen

hour /'aʊə(r)/ n Stunde f. ~ly a & adv
stündlich; ~ly pay or rate Stun-
denlohn m

house¹ /haʊs/ n Haus nt; at my ~ bei
mir
house² /haʊz/ vt unterbringen

house³ /haʊs/: ~boat n Hausboot nt.
~breaking n Einbruch m. ~hold n
Haushalt m. ~holder n Haus-
inhaber(in) m(f). ~keeper n

Haushälterin f. ~keeping n Haus-
wirtschaft f; (money) Haushaltsgeld
nt. ~plant n Zimmerpflanze f.
~-trained a stubenrein.
~-warming n have a ~-warming
party Einstand feiern. ~wife n Haus-
frau f. ~work n Hausarbeit f

housing /'haʊzɪŋ/ n Wohnungen pl;
(Techn) Gehäuse nt. ~ estate n
Wohnsiedlung f

hovel /'hɒvl/ n elende Hütte f

hover /'hɒvə(r)/ vi schweben; (be
undecided) schwanken; (linger)
herumstehen. ~craft n Luftkissen-
fahrzeug nt

how /haʊ/ adv wie; ~ do you do?
guten Tag! ~ many wie viele; ~ much
wieviel; and ~! und ob!

how'ever adv (in question) wie;
(nevertheless) jedoch, aber; ~ small
wie klein es auch sein mag

howl /haʊl/ n Heulen nt ● vi heulen;
⟨baby:⟩ brüllen. ~er n (fam) Schnitzer m

hub /hʌb/ n Nabe f; (fig) Mittelpunkt
m

hubbub /'hʌbʌb/ n Stimmengewirr
nt

'hub-cap n Radkappe f

huddle /'hʌdl/ vi ~ together sich
zusammendrängen

hue¹ /hjuː/ n Farbe f

hue² n ~ and cry Aufruhr m

huff /hʌf/ n in a ~ beleidigt

hug /hʌg/ n Umarmung f ● vt (pt/pp
hugged) umarmen

huge /hjuːdʒ/ a, -ly adv riesig

hulking /'hʌlkɪŋ/ a (fam) unge-
schlacht

hull /hʌl/ n (Naut) Rumpf m

hullo /hə'ləʊ/ int = hallo

hum /hʌm/ n Summen nt; Brummen
nt ● vt/i (pt/pp hummed) summen;
⟨motor:⟩ brummen; ~ and haw nicht
mit der Sprache herauswollen

human /'hjuːmən/ a menschlich ● n
Mensch m. ~ 'being n Mensch m

humane /hjuː'meɪn/ a, -ly adv
human

humanitarian /hjuːmænɪ'teərɪən/ a
humanitär

humanit|y /hjuː'mænətɪ/ n Mensch-
heit f; ~ies pl (Univ) Geisteswissenschaften pl

humble /'hʌmbl/ a (-r, -st), -bly adv
demütig ● vt demütigen

'humdrum a eintönig

humid /'hju:mɪd/ a feucht. ~ity /-'mɪdətɪ/ n Feuchtigkeit f

humiliat|e /hju:'mɪlɪeɪt/ vt demütigen. ~ion /-'eɪʃn/ n Demütigung f

humility /hju:'mɪlətɪ/ n Demut f

'humming-bird n Kolibri m

humorous /'hju:mərəs/ a, **-ly** adv humorvoll; ⟨story⟩ humoristisch

humour /'hju:mə(r)/ n Humor m; (mood) Laune f; **have a sense of ~** Humor haben ● vt ~ s.o. jdm seinen Willen lassen

hump /hʌmp/ n Buckel m; (of camel) Höcker m ● vt schleppen

hunch /hʌntʃ/ n (idea) Ahnung f

'hunch|back n Bucklige(r) m/f. ~ed a ~ed up gebeugt

hundred /'hʌndrəd/ a **one/a ~** [ein]hundert ● n Hundert nt; (written figure) Hundert f. ~th a hundertste(r,s) ● n Hundertstel nt. ~weight n ≈ Zentner m

hung /hʌŋ/ see **hang**

Hungarian /hʌŋ'geərɪən/ a ungarisch ● n Ungar(in) m(f)

Hungary /'hʌŋgərɪ/ n Ungarn nt

hunger /'hʌŋgə(r)/ n Hunger m. ~-strike n Hungerstreik m

hungry /'hʌŋgrɪ/ a (-ier, -iest), **-ily** adv hungrig; **be ~** Hunger haben

hunk /hʌŋk/ n [großes] Stück nt

hunt /hʌnt/ n Jagd f; (for criminal) Fahndung f ● vt/i jagen; fahnden nach ⟨criminal⟩; ~ **for** suchen. ~er n Jäger m; (horse) Jagdpferd nt. ~ing n Jagd f

hurdle /'hɜ:dl/ n (Sport & fig) Hürde f. ~r n Hürdenläufer(in) m(f)

hurl /hɜ:l/ vt schleudern

hurrah /hʊ'rɑ:/, **hurray** /hʊ'reɪ/ int hurra! ● n Hurra nt

hurricane /'hʌrɪkən/ n Orkan m

hurried /'hʌrɪd/ a, **-ly** adv eilig; (superficial) flüchtig

hurry ● /'hʌrɪ/ n Eile f; **be in a ~** es eilig haben ● vi (pt/pp **-ied**) sich beeilen; (go quickly) eilen. ~ **up** vi sich beeilen ● vt antreiben

hurt /hɜ:t/ n Schmerz m ● vt/i (pt/pp **hurt**) weh tun (+ dat); (injure) verletzen; (offend) kränken. ~ful a verletzend

hurtle /'hɜ:tl/ vi ~ **along** rasen

husband /'hʌzbənd/ n [Ehe]mann m

hush /hʌʃ/ n Stille f ● vt ~ **up** vertuschen. ~ed a gedämpft. ~-'hush a (fam) streng geheim

husk /hʌsk/ n Spelze f

husky /'hʌskɪ/ a (-ier, -iest) heiser; (burly) stämmig

hustle /'hʌsl/ vt drängen ● n Gedränge nt; ~ **and bustle** geschäftiges Treiben nt

hut /hʌt/ n Hütte f

hutch /hʌtʃ/ n [Kaninchen]stall m

hybrid /'haɪbrɪd/ a hybrid ● n Hybride f

hydrangea /haɪ'dreɪndʒə/ n Hortensie f

hydrant /'haɪdrənt/ n **[fire] ~** Hydrant m

hydraulic /haɪ'drɔ:lɪk/ a, **-ally** adv hydraulisch

hydrochloric /haɪdrə'klɔːrɪk/ a ~ **acid** Salzsäure f

hydroe'lectric /haɪdrəʊ-/ a hydroelektrisch. ~ **power station** n Wasserkraftwerk nt

hydrofoil /'haɪdrə-/ n Tragflügelboot nt

hydrogen /'haɪdrədʒən/ n Wasserstoff m

hyena /haɪ'i:nə/ n Hyäne f

hygien|e /'haɪdʒi:n/ n Hygiene f. ~ic /haɪ'dʒi:nɪk/ a, **-ally** adv hygienisch

hymn /hɪm/ n Kirchenlied nt. ~-book n Gesangbuch nt

hyphen /'haɪfn/ n Bindestrich m. ~ate vt mit Bindestrich schreiben

hypno|sis /hɪp'nəʊsɪs/ n Hypnose f. ~tic /-'nɒtɪk/ a hypnotisch

hypno|tism /'hɪpnətɪzm/ n Hypnotik f. ~tist /-tɪst/ n Hypnotiseur m. ~tize vt hypnotisieren

hypochondriac /haɪpə'kɒndrɪæk/ a hypochondrisch ● n Hypochonder m

hypocrisy /hɪ'pɒkrəsɪ/ n Heuchelei f

hypocrit|e /'hɪpəkrɪt/ n Heuchler(in) m(f). ~ical /-'krɪtɪkl/ a, **-ly** adv heuchlerisch

hypodermic /haɪpə'dɜːmɪk/ a & n ~ **[syringe]** Injektionsspritze f

hypothe|sis /haɪ'pɒθəsɪs/ n Hypothese f. ~tical /-ə'θetɪkl/ a, **-ly** adv hypothetisch

hyster|ia /hɪ'stɪərɪə/ n Hysterie f. ~ical /-'sterɪkl/ a, **-ly** adv hysterisch. ~ics /hɪ'sterɪks/ npl hysterischer Anfall m

I

I /aɪ/ pron ich

ice /aɪs/ n Eis nt ● vt mit Zuckerguß überziehen ⟨cake⟩

ice: ~ **age** n Eiszeit f. ~**-axe** n Eispickel m. ~**berg** /-bɜːg/ n Eisberg m. ~**box** n (Amer) Kühlschrank m. ~**-'cream** n [Speise]eis nt. ~**-'cream parlour** n Eisdiele f. ~**-cube** n Eiswürfel m

Iceland /'aɪslənd/ n Island nt

ice: ~ **'lolly** n Eis nt am Stiel. ~ **rink** n Eisbahn f

icicle /'aɪsɪkl/ n Eiszapfen m

icing /'aɪsɪŋ/ n Zuckerguß m. ~ **sugar** n Puderzucker m

icon /'aɪkɒn/ n Ikone f

icy /'aɪsɪ/ a (-ier, -iest), -ily adv eisig; ⟨road⟩ vereist

idea /aɪ'dɪə/ n Idee f; (conception) Vorstellung f; **I have no** ~! ich habe keine Ahnung!

ideal /aɪ'dɪəl/ a ideal ● n Ideal nt. ~**ism** n Idealismus m. ~**ist** n Idealist(in) m(f). ~**istic** /-'lɪstɪk/ a idealistisch. ~**ize** vt idealisieren. ~**ly** adv ideal; (in ideal circumstances) idealerweise

identical /aɪ'dentɪkl/ a identisch; ⟨twins⟩ eineiig

identi|fication /aɪdentɪfɪ'keɪʃn/ n Identifizierung f; (proof of identity) Ausweispapiere pl. ~**fy** /aɪ'dentɪfaɪ/ vt (pt/pp -ied) identifizieren

identity /aɪ'dentətɪ/ n Identität f. ~ **card** n [Personal]ausweis m

ideolog|ical /aɪdɪə'lɒdʒɪkl/ a ideologisch. ~**y** /aɪdɪ'ɒlədʒɪ/ n Ideologie f

idiom /'ɪdɪəm/ n [feste] Redewendung f. ~**atic** /-'mætɪk/ a, -**ally** adv idiomatisch

idiosyncrasy /ɪdɪə'sɪŋkrəsɪ/ n Eigenart f

idiot /'ɪdɪət/ n Idiot m. ~**ic** /-'ɒtɪk/ a idiotisch

idle /'aɪdl/ a (-r, -st), -ly adv untätig; (lazy) faul; (empty) leer; ⟨machine⟩ nicht in Betrieb ● vi faulenzen; ⟨engine:⟩ leer laufen. ~**ness** n Untätigkeit f; Faulheit f

idol /'aɪdl/ n Idol nt. ~**ize** /'aɪdəlaɪz/ vt vergöttern

idyllic /ɪ'dɪlɪk/ a idyllisch

i.e. abbr (id est) d.h.

if /ɪf/ conj wenn; (whether) ob; **as if** als ob

ignite /ɪg'naɪt/ vt entzünden ● vi sich entzünden

ignition /ɪg'nɪʃn/ n (Auto) Zündung f. ~ **key** n Zündschlüssel m

ignoramus /ɪgnə'reɪməs/ n Ignorant m

ignoran|ce /'ɪgnərəns/ n Unwissenheit f. ~**t** a unwissend; (rude) ungehobelt

ignore /ɪg'nɔː(r)/ vt ignorieren

ilk /ɪlk/ n (fam) **of that** ~ von der Sorte

ill /ɪl/ a krank; (bad) schlecht; **feel** ~ **at ease** sich unbehaglich fühlen ● adv schlecht ● n Schlechte(s) nt; (evil) Übel nt. ~**-advised** a unklug. ~**-bred** a schlecht erzogen

illegal /ɪ'liːgl/ a, -**ly** adv illegal

illegible /ɪ'ledʒəbl/ a, -**bly** adv unleserlich

illegitima|cy /ɪlɪ'dʒɪtɪməsɪ/ n Unehelichkeit f. ~**te** /-mət/ a unehelich; ⟨claim⟩ unberechtigt

illicit /ɪ'lɪsɪt/ a, -**ly** adv illegal

illitera|cy /ɪ'lɪtərəsɪ/ n Analphabetentum nt. ~**te** /-rət/ a **be** ~**te** nicht lesen und schreiben können ● n Analphabet(in) m(f)

illness /'ɪlnɪs/ n Krankheit f

illogical /ɪ'lɒdʒɪkl/ a, -**ly** adv unlogisch

ill-treat /ɪl'triːt/ vt mißhandeln. ~**ment** n Mißhandlung f

illuminat|e /ɪ'luːmɪneɪt/ vt beleuchten. ~**ing** a aufschlußreich. ~**ion** /-'neɪʃn/ n Beleuchtung f

illusion /ɪ'luːʒn/ n Illusion f; **be under the** ~ **that** sich (dat) einbilden, daß

illusory /ɪ'luːsərɪ/ a illusorisch

illustrat|e /'ɪləstreɪt/ vt illustrieren. ~**ion** /-'streɪʃn/ n Illustration f

illustrious /ɪ'lʌstrɪəs/ a berühmt

image /'ɪmɪdʒ/ n Bild nt; (statue) Standbild nt; (figure) Figur f; (exact likeness) Ebenbild nt; **[public]** ~ Image nt

imagin|able /ɪ'mædʒɪnəbl/ a vorstellbar. ~**ary** /-ərɪ/ a eingebildet

imaginat|ion /ɪmædʒɪ'neɪʃn/ n Phantasie f; (fancy) Einbildung f. ~**ive** /ɪ'mædʒɪnətɪv/ a, -**ly** adv phantasievoll; (full of ideas) einfallsreich

imagine /ɪ'mædʒɪn/ vt sich (dat) vorstellen; (wrongly) sich (dat) einbilden

im'balance n Unausgeglichenheit f

imbecile /'ɪmbəsiːl/ n Schwachsinnige(r) m/f; (pej) Idiot m

imbibe /ɪmˈbaɪb/ vt trinken; (fig) aufnehmen

imbue /ɪmˈbjuː/ vt **be ~d with** erfüllt sein von

imitat|e /ˈɪmɪteɪt/ vt nachahmen, imitieren. **~ion** /-ˈteɪʃn/ n Nachahmung f, Imitation f

immaculate /ɪˈmækjʊlət/ a, **-ly** adv tadellos; (Relig) unbefleckt

imma'terial a (unimportant) unwichtig, unwesentlich

imma'ture a unreif

immediate /ɪˈmiːdɪət/ a sofortig; (nearest) nächste(r,s). **~ly** adv sofort; **~ly next to** unmittelbar neben ● conj sobald

immemorial /ɪməˈmɔːrɪəl/ a **from time ~** seit Urzeiten

immense /ɪˈmens/ a, **-ly** adv riesig; (fam) enorm; (extreme) äußerst

immers|e /ɪˈmɜːs/ vt untertauchen; **be ~ed in** (fig) vertieft sein in (+ acc). **~ion** /-ɜːʃn/ n Untertauchen nt. **~ion heater** n Heißwasserbereiter m

immigrant /ˈɪmɪgrənt/ n Einwanderer m

immigrat|e /ˈɪmɪgreɪt/ vi einwandern. **~ion** /-ˈgreɪʃn/ n Einwanderung f

imminent /ˈɪmɪnənt/ a **be ~** unmittelbar bevorstehen

immobil|e /ɪˈməʊbaɪl/ a unbeweglich. **~ize** /-bəlaɪz/ vt (fig) lähmen; (Med) ruhigstellen

immoderate /ɪˈmɒdərət/ a übermäßig

immodest /ɪˈmɒdɪst/ a unbescheiden

immoral /ɪˈmɒrəl/ a, **-ly** adv unmoralisch. **~ity** /ɪməˈrælətɪ/ n Unmoral f

immortal /ɪˈmɔːtl/ a unsterblich. **~ity** /-ˈtælətɪ/ n Unsterblichkeit f. **~ize** vt verewigen

immovable /ɪˈmuːvəbl/ a unbeweglich; (fig) fest

immune /ɪˈmjuːn/ a immun (**to/ from** gegen). **~ system** n Abwehrsystem nt

immunity /ɪˈmjuːnətɪ/ n Immunität f

immunize /ˈɪmjʊnaɪz/ vt immunisieren

imp /ɪmp/ n Kobold m

impact /ˈɪmpækt/ n Aufprall m; (collision) Zusammenprall m; (of bomb) Einschlag m; (fig) Auswirkung f

impair /ɪmˈpeə(r)/ vt beeinträchtigen

impale /ɪmˈpeɪl/ vt aufspießen

impart /ɪmˈpɑːt/ vt übermitteln (**to** dat); vermitteln (knowledge)

im'parti|al a unparteiisch. **~'ality** n Unparteilichkeit f

im'passable a unpassierbar

impasse /æmˈpɑːs/ n (fig) Sackgasse f

impassioned /ɪmˈpæʃnd/ a leidenschaftlich

im'passive a, **-ly** adv unbeweglich

im'patien|ce n Ungeduld f. **~t** a, **-ly** adv ungeduldig

impeach /ɪmˈpiːtʃ/ vt anklagen

impeccable /ɪmˈpekəbl/ a, **-bly** adv tadellos

impede /ɪmˈpiːd/ vt behindern

impediment /ɪmˈpedɪmənt/ n Hindernis nt; (in speech) Sprachfehler m

impel /ɪmˈpel/ vt (pt/pp **impelled**) treiben; **feel ~led** sich genötigt fühlen (**to** zu)

impending /ɪmˈpendɪŋ/ a bevorstehend

impenetrable /ɪmˈpenɪtrəbl/ a undurchdringlich

imperative /ɪmˈperətɪv/ a **be ~** dringend notwendig sein ● n (Gram) Imperativ m, Befehlsform f

imper'ceptible a nicht wahrnehmbar

im'perfect a unvollkommen; (faulty) fehlerhaft ● n (Gram) Imperfekt nt. **~ion** /-ˈfekʃn/ n Unvollkommenheit f; (fault) Fehler m

imperial /ɪmˈpɪərɪəl/ a kaiserlich. **~ism** n Imperialismus m

imperil /ɪmˈperəl/ vt (pt/pp **imperilled**) gefährden

imperious /ɪmˈpɪərɪəs/ a, **-ly** adv herrisch

im'personal a unpersönlich

impersonat|e /ɪmˈpɜːsəneɪt/ vt sich ausgeben als; (Theat) nachahmen, imitieren. **~or** n Imitator m

impertinen|ce /ɪmˈpɜːtɪnəns/ n Frechheit f. **~t** a frech

imperturbable /ɪmpəˈtɜːbəbl/ a unerschütterlich

impervious /ɪmˈpɜːvɪəs/ a **~ to** (fig) unempfänglich für

impetuous /ɪmˈpetjʊəs/ a, **-ly** adv ungestüm

impetus /ˈɪmpɪtəs/ n Schwung m

impish /ˈɪmpɪʃ/ a schelmisch

implacable /ɪm'plækəbl/ a unerbittlich

im'plant¹ vt einpflanzen

'**implant**² n Implantat nt

implement¹ /'ɪmplɪmənt/ n Gerät nt

implement² /'ɪmplɪment/ vt ausführen

implicat|e /'ɪmplɪkeɪt/ vt verwickeln. ~ion /-'keɪʃn/ n Verwicklung f; ~ions pl Auswirkungen pl; **by** ~**ion** implizit

implicit /ɪm'plɪsɪt/ a, **-ly** adv unausgesprochen; (absolute) unbedingt

implore /ɪm'plɔ:(r)/ vt anflehen

imply ● vi /ɪm'plaɪ/ vt (pt/pp **-ied**) andeuten; **what are you** ~**ing?** was wollen Sie damit sagen?

impo'lite a, **-ly** adv unhöflich

import¹ /'ɪmpɔ:t/ n Import m, Einfuhr f; (importance) Wichtigkeit f; (meaning) Bedeutung f

import² /ɪm'pɔ:t/ vt importieren, einführen

importan|ce /ɪm'pɔ:tns/ n Wichtigkeit f. ~**t** a wichtig

importer /ɪm'pɔ:tə(r)/ n Importeur m

impos|e /ɪm'pəʊz/ vt auferlegen (**on** dat) ● vi sich aufdrängen (**on** dat). ~**ing** a eindrucksvoll. ~**ition** /ɪmpə'zɪʃn/ n **be an** ~**ition** eine Zumutung sein

impossi'bility n Unmöglichkeit f

im'possible a, **-bly** adv unmöglich

impostor /ɪm'pɒstə(r)/ n Betrüger(in) m(f)

impoten|ce /'ɪmpətəns/ n Machtlosigkeit f; (Med) Impotenz f. ~**t** a machtlos; (Med) impotent

impound /ɪm'paʊnd/ vt beschlagnahmen

impoverished /ɪm'pɒvərɪʃt/ a verarmt

im'practicable a undurchführbar

im'practical a unpraktisch

impre'cise a ungenau

impregnable /ɪm'pregnəbl/ a uneinnehmbar

impregnate /'ɪmpregneɪt/ vt tränken; (Biol) befruchten

im'press vt beeindrucken; ~ **sth** [**up**]**on s.o.** jdm etw einprägen

impression /ɪm'preʃn/ n Eindruck m; (imitation) Nachahmung f; (imprint) Abdruck m; (edition) Auflage f. ~**ism** n Impressionismus m

impressive /ɪm'presɪv/ a eindrucksvoll

'**imprint**¹ n Abdruck m

im'print² vt prägen; (fig) einprägen (**on** dat)

im'prison vt gefangenhalten; (put in prison) ins Gefängnis sperren

im'probable a unwahrscheinlich

impromptu /ɪm'prɒmptju:/ a improvisiert ● adv aus dem Stegreif

im'proper a, **-ly** adv inkorrekt; (indecent) unanständig

impro'priety n Unkorrektheit f

improve /ɪm'pru:v/ vt verbessern; verschönern (appearance) ● vi sich bessern; ~ [**up**]**on** übertreffen. ~**ment** /-mənt/ n Verbesserung f; (in health) Besserung f

improvise /'ɪmprəvaɪz/ vt/i improvisieren

im'prudent a unklug

impuden|ce /'ɪmpjʊdəns/ n Frechheit f. ~**t** a, **-ly** adv frech

impuls|e /'ɪmpʌls/ n Impuls m; **on** [**an**] ~**e** impulsiv. ~**ive** /-'pʌlsɪv/ a, **-ly** adv impulsiv

impunity /ɪm'pju:nətɪ/ n **with** ~ ungestraft

im'pur|e a unrein. ~**ity** n Unreinheit f; ~**ities** pl Verunreinigungen pl

impute /ɪm'pju:t/ vt zuschreiben (**to** dat)

in /ɪn/ prep in (+ dat/(into) + acc); **sit in the garden** im Garten sitzen; **go in the garden** in den Garten gehen; **in May** im Mai; **in the summer/winter** im Sommer/Winter; **in 1992** [im Jahre] 1992; **in this heat** bei dieser Hitze; **in the rain/sun** im Regen/in der Sonne; **in the evening** am Abend; **in the sky** am Himmel; **in the world** auf der Welt; **in the street** auf der Straße; **deaf in one ear** auf einem Ohr taub; **in the army** beim Militär; **in English/ German** auf englisch/deutsch; **in ink/ pencil** mit Tinte/ Bleistift; **in a soft/ loud voice** mit leiser/lauter Stimme; **in doing this, he ...** indem er das tut/ tat, ... er ● adv (at home) zu Hause; (indoors) drinnen; **he's not in yet** er ist noch nicht da; **all in** alles inbegriffen; (fam: exhausted) kaputt; **day in, day out** tagaus, tagein; **keep in with s.o.** sich mit jdm gut stellen; **have it in for s.o.** (fam) es auf jdn abgesehen haben; **let oneself in for sth** sich auf etw (acc) einlassen; **send/go in** hineinschicken/ -gehen; **come/bring in** hereinkommen/-bringen ● a (fam: in *fashion*) in ● *n* **the ins and outs** alle Einzelheiten *pl*

ina'bility *n* Unfähigkeit *f*

inac'cessible *a* unzugänglich

in'accura|cy *n* Ungenauigkeit *f*. ∼**te** *a*, **-ly** *adv* ungenau

in'ac|tive *a* untätig. ∼'**tivity** *n* Untätigkeit *f*

in'adequate *a*, **-ly** *adv* unzulänglich; **feel** ∼ sich der Situation nicht gewachsen fühlen

inad'missible *a* unzulässig

inadvertently /məd'vɜ:təntlɪ/ *adv* versehentlich

inad'visable *a* nicht ratsam

inane /ɪ'neɪn/ *a*, **-ly** *adv* albern

in'animate *a* unbelebt

in'applicable *a* nicht zutreffend

inap'propriate *a* unangebracht

inar'ticulate *a* undeutlich; **be** ∼ sich nicht gut ausdrücken können

inat'tentive *a* unaufmerksam

in'audible *a*, **-bly** *adv* unhörbar

inaugural /ɪ'nɔ:gjʊrl/ *a* Antritts-

inaugurat|e /ɪ'nɔ:gjʊreɪt/ *vt* [feierlich] in sein Amt einführen. ∼**ion** /-'reɪʃn/ *n* Amtseinführung *f*

inau'spicious *a* ungünstig

inborn /'ɪnbɔ:n/ *a* angeboren

inbred /'ɪnbred/ *a* angeboren

incalculable /ɪn'kælkjʊləbl/ *a* nicht berechenbar; (*fig*) unabsehbar

in'capable *a* unfähig; **be** ∼ **of doing sth** nicht fähig sein, etw zu tun

incapacitate /ɪnkə'pæsɪteɪt/ *vt* unfähig machen

incarcerate /ɪn'kɑ:səreɪt/ *vt* einkerkern

incarnat|e /ɪn'kɑ:nət/ *a* **the devil** ∼**e** der leibhaftige Satan. ∼**ion** /-'neɪʃn/ *n* Inkarnation *f*

incendiary /ɪn'sendɪərɪ/ *a* & *n* ∼ **[bomb]** Brandbombe *f*

incense[1] /'ɪnsens/ *n* Weihrauch *m*

incense[2] /ɪn'sens/ *vt* wütend machen

incentive /ɪn'sentɪv/ *n* Anreiz *m*

inception /ɪn'sepʃn/ *n* Beginn *m*

incessant /ɪn'sesnt/ *a*, **-ly** *adv* unaufhörlich

incest /'ɪnsest/ *n* Inzest *m*, Blutschande *f*

inch /ɪntʃ/ *n* Zoll *m* ● *vi* ∼ **forward** sich ganz langsam vorwärtsschieben

inciden|ce /'ɪnsɪdəns/ *n* Vorkommen *nt*. ∼**t** *n* Zwischenfall *m*

incidental /ɪnsɪ'dentl/ *a* nebensächlich; ⟨*remark*⟩ beiläufig; ⟨*expenses*⟩ Neben-. ∼**ly** *adv* übrigens

incinerat|e /ɪn'sɪnəreɪt/ *vt* verbrennen. ∼**or** *n* Verbrennungsofen *m*

incipient /ɪn'sɪpɪənt/ *a* angehend

incision /ɪn'sɪʒn/ *n* Einschnitt *m*

incisive /ɪn'saɪsɪv/ *a* scharfsinnig

incisor /ɪn'saɪzə(r)/ *n* Schneidezahn *m*

incite /ɪn'saɪt/ *vt* aufhetzen. ∼**ment** *n* Aufhetzung *f*

inci'vility *n* Unhöflichkeit *f*

in'clement *a* rauh

inclination /ɪnklɪ'neɪʃn/ *n* Neigung *f*

incline[1] /ɪn'klaɪn/ *vt* neigen; **be** ∼**d to do sth** dazu neigen, etw zu tun ● *vi* sich neigen

incline[2] /'ɪnklaɪn/ *n* Neigung *f*

inclu|de /ɪn'klu:d/ *vt* einschließen; (*contain*) enthalten; (*incorporate*) aufnehmen (**in** in + *acc*). ∼**ding** *prep* einschließlich (+ *gen*). ∼**sion** /-u: ʒn/ *n* Aufnahme *f*

inclusive /ɪn'klu:sɪv/ *a* Inklusiv-; ∼ **of** einschließlich (+ *gen*) ● *adv* inklusive

incognito /ɪnkɒg'ni:təʊ/ *adv* inkognito

inco'herent *a*, **-ly** *adv* zusammenhanglos; (*incomprehensible*) unverständlich

income /'ɪnkʌm/ *n* Einkommen *nt*. ∼ **tax** *n* Einkommensteuer *f*

'incoming *a* ankommend; ⟨*mail*, *call*⟩ eingehend. ∼ **tide** *n* steigende Flut *f*

in'comparable *a* unvergleichlich

incom'patible *a* unvereinbar; **be** ∼ ⟨*people:*⟩ nicht zueinander passen

in'competen|ce *n* Unfähigkeit *f*. ∼**t** *a* unfähig

incom'plete *a* unvollständig

incompre'hensible *a* unverständlich

incon'ceivable *a* undenkbar

incon'clusive *a* nicht schlüssig

incongruous /ɪn'kɒŋgrʊəs/ *a* unpassend

inconsequential /ɪnkɒnsɪ'kwenʃl/ *a* unbedeutend

incon'siderate *a* rücksichtslos

incon'sistent *a*, **-ly** *adv* widersprüchlich; (*illogical*) inkonsequent; **be** ∼ nicht übereinstimmen

inconsolable /ɪnkən'səʊləbl/ *a* untröstlich

incon'spicuous *a* unauffällig

incontinen|ce /ɪn'kɒntɪnəns/ *n* Inkontinenz *f*. ∼**t** *a* inkontinent

incon'venien|ce *n* Unannehmlichkeit *f*; (*drawback*) Nachteil *m*; **put s.o. to ~ce** jdm Umstände machen. **~t** *a*, **-ly** *adv* ungünstig; **be ~t for s.o.** jdm nicht passen

incorporate /ɪnˈkɔːpəreɪt/ *vt* aufnehmen; (*contain*) enthalten

incor'rect *a*, **-ly** *adv* inkorrekt

incorrigible /ɪnˈkɒrɪdʒəbl/ *a* unverbesserlich

incorruptible /ɪnkəˈrʌptəbl/ *a* unbestechlich

increase[1] /ˈɪnkriːs/ *n* Zunahme *f*; (*rise*) Erhöhung *f*; **be on the ~** zunehmen

increas|e[2] /ɪnˈkriːs/ *vt* vergrößern; (*raise*) erhöhen ● *vi* zunehmen; (*rise*) sich erhöhen. **~ing** *a*, **-ly** *adv* zunehmend

in'credible *a*, **-bly** *adv* unglaublich

incredulous /ɪnˈkredjʊləs/ *a* ungläubig

increment /ˈɪnkrɪmənt/ *n* Gehaltszulage *f*

incriminate /ɪnˈkrɪmɪneɪt/ *vt* (*Jur*) belasten

incubat|e /ˈɪŋkjʊbeɪt/ *vt* ausbrüten. **~ion** /-ˈbeɪʃn/ *n* Ausbrüten *nt*. **~ion period** *n* (*Med*) Inkubationszeit *f*. **~or** *n* (*for baby*) Brutkasten *m*

inculcate /ˈɪnkʌlkeɪt/ *vt* einprägen (**in** *dat*)

incumbent /ɪnˈkʌmbənt/ *a* **be ~ on s.o.** jds Pflicht sein

incur /ɪnˈkɜː(r)/ *vt* (*pt/pp* **incurred**) sich (*dat*) zuziehen; machen (*debts*)

in'curable *a*, **-bly** *adv* unheilbar

incursion /ɪnˈkɜːʃn/ *n* Einfall *m*

indebted /ɪnˈdetɪd/ *a* verpflichtet (**to** *dat*)

in'decent *a*, **-ly** *adv* unanständig

inde'cision *n* Unentschlossenheit *f*

inde'cisive *a* ergebnislos; (*person*) unentschlossen

indeed /ɪnˈdiːd/ *adv* in der Tat, tatsächlich; **yes ~!** allerdings! **~ I do** oh doch! **very much ~** sehr; **thank you very much ~** vielen herzlichen Dank

indefatigable /ɪndɪˈfætɪgəbl/ *a* unermüdlich

in'definite *a* unbestimmt. **~ly** *adv* unbegrenzt; (*postpone*) auf unbestimmte Zeit

indelible /ɪnˈdelɪbl/ *a*, **-bly** *adv* nicht zu entfernen; (*fig*) unauslöschlich

indemni|fy /ɪnˈdemnɪfaɪ/ *vt* (*pt/pp* **-ied**) versichern; (*compensate*) entschädigen. **~ty** *n* Versicherung *f*; Entschädigung *f*

indent /ɪnˈdent/ *vt* (*Typ*) einrücken. **~ation** /-ˈteɪʃn/ *n* Einrückung *f*; (*notch*) Kerbe *f*

inde'penden|ce *n* Unabhängigkeit *f*; (*self-reliance*) Selbständigkeit *f*. **~t** *a*, **-ly** *adv* unabhängig; selbständig

indescribable /ɪndɪˈskraɪbəbl/ *a*, **-bly** *adv* unbeschreiblich

indestructible /ɪndɪˈstrʌktəbl/ *a* unzerstörbar

indeterminate /ɪndɪˈtɜːmɪnət/ *a* unbestimmt

index /ˈɪndeks/ *n* Register *nt*

index: ~ card *n* Karteikarte *f*. **~ finger** *n* Zeigefinger *m*. **~-linked** *a* (*pension*) dynamisch

India /ˈɪndɪə/ *n* Indien *nt*. **~n** *a* indisch; (*American*) indianisch ● *n* Inder(in) *m(f)*; (*American*) Indianer(in) *m(f)*

Indian: ~ 'ink *n* Tusche *f*. **~ 'summer** *n* Nachsommer *m*

indicat|e /ˈɪndɪkeɪt/ *vt* zeigen; (*point at*) zeigen auf (+*acc*); (*hint*) andeuten; (*register*) anzeigen ● *vi* (*Auto*) blinken. **~ion** /-ˈkeɪʃn/ *n* Anzeichen *nt*

indicative /ɪnˈdɪkətɪv/ *a* **be ~ of** schließen lassen auf (+*acc*) ● *n* (*Gram*) Indikativ *m*

indicator /ˈɪndɪkeɪtə(r)/ *n* (*Auto*) Blinker *m*

indict /ɪnˈdaɪt/ *vt* anklagen. **~ment** *n* Anklage *f*

in'differen|ce *n* Gleichgültigkeit *f*. **~t** *a*, **-ly** *adv* gleichgültig; (*not good*) mittelmäßig

indigenous /ɪnˈdɪdʒɪnəs/ *a* einheimisch

indi'gest|ible *a* unverdaulich; (*difficult to digest*) schwerverdaulich. **~ion** *n* Magenverstimmung *f*

indigna|nt /ɪnˈdɪgnənt/ *a*, **-ly** *adv* entrüstet, empört. **~tion** /-ˈneɪʃn/ *n* Entrüstung *f*, Empörung *f*

in'dignity *n* Demütigung *f*

indi'rect *a*, **-ly** *adv* indirekt

indi'screet *a* indiskret

indis'cretion *n* Indiskretion *f*

indiscriminate /ɪndɪˈskrɪmɪnət/ *a*, **-ly** *adv* wahllos

indi'spensable *a* unentbehrlich

indisposed /ɪndɪˈspəʊzd/ *a* indisponiert

indisputable /ɪndɪˈspjuːtəbl/ *a*, **-bly** *adv* unbestreitbar

indi'stinct *a*, **-ly** *adv* undeutlich

indistinguishable /ɪndɪˈstɪŋgwɪʃəbl/ *a* **be** ~ nicht zu unterscheiden sein; (*not visible*) nicht erkennbar sein

individual /ɪndɪˈvɪdjʊəl/ *a*, **-ly** *adv* individuell; (*single*) einzeln ● *n* Individuum *nt.* ~**ity** /-ˈælətɪ/ *n* Individualität *f*

indi'visible *a* unteilbar

indoctrinate /ɪnˈdɒktrɪneɪt/ *vt* indoktrinieren

indolen|ce /ˈɪndələns/ *n* Faulheit *f.* ~**t** *a* faul

indomitable /ɪnˈdɒmɪtəbl/ *a* unbeugsam

indoor /ˈɪndɔː(r)/ *a* Innen-; (*clothes*) Haus-; (*plant*) Zimmer-; (*Sport*) Hallen-. ~**s** /-ˈdɔːz/ *adv* im Haus, drinnen; **go** ~**s** ins Haus gehen

induce /ɪnˈdjuːs/ *vt* dazu bewegen (**to** zu); (*produce*) herbeiführen. ~**ment** *n* (*incentive*) Anreiz *m*

indulge /ɪnˈdʌldʒ/ *vt* frönen (+ *dat*); verwöhnen (*child*) ● *vi* ~ **in** frönen (+ *dat*). ~**nce** /-əns/ *n* Nachgiebigkeit *f*; (*leniency*) Nachsicht *f.* ~**nt** *a* [zu] nachgiebig; nachsichtig

industrial /ɪnˈdʌstrɪəl/ *a* Industrie-; **take** ~ **action** streiken. ~**ist** *n* Industrielle(r) *m.* ~**ized** *a* industrialisiert

industr|ious /ɪnˈdʌstrɪəs/ *a*, **-ly** *adv* fleißig. ~**y** /ˈɪndəstrɪ/ *n* Industrie *f*; (*zeal*) Fleiß *m*

inebriated /ɪˈniːbrɪeɪtɪd/ *a* betrunken

in'edible *a* nicht eßbar

inef'fective *a*, **-ly** *adv* unwirksam; (*person*) untauglich

inef'fectual /ɪnɪˈfektʃʊəl/ *a* unwirksam; (*person*) untauglich

inef'ficient *a* unfähig; (*organization*) nicht leistungsfähig; (*method*) nicht rationell

in'eligible *a* nicht berechtigt

inept /ɪˈnept/ *a* ungeschickt

ine'quality *n* Ungleichheit *f*

inert /ɪˈnɜːt/ *a* unbeweglich; (*Phys*) träge. ~**ia** /ɪˈnɜːʃə/ *n* Trägheit *f*

inescapable /ɪnɪˈskeɪpəbl/ *a* unvermeidlich

inestimable /ɪnˈestɪməbl/ *a* unschätzbar

inevitab|le /ɪnˈevɪtəbl/ *a* unvermeidlich. ~**ly** *adv* zwangsläufig

ine'xact *a* ungenau

inex'cusable *a* unverzeihlich

inexhaustible /ɪnɪgˈzɔːstəbl/ *a* unerschöpflich

inexorable /ɪnˈeksərəbl/ *a* unerbittlich

inex'pensive *a*, **-ly** *adv* preiswert

inex'perience *n* Unerfahrenheit *f.* ~**d** *a* unerfahren

inexplicable /ɪnɪkˈsplɪkəbl/ *a* unerklärlich

in'fallible *a* unfehlbar

infam|ous /ˈɪnfəməs/ *a* niederträchtig; (*notorious*) berüchtigt. ~**y** *n* Niederträchtigkeit *f*

infan|cy /ˈɪnfənsɪ/ *n* frühe Kindheit *f*; (*fig*) Anfangsstadium *nt.* ~**t** *n* Kleinkind *nt.* ~**tile** *a* kindisch

infantry /ˈɪnfəntrɪ/ *n* Infanterie *f*

infatuated /ɪnˈfætʃʊeɪtɪd/ *a* vernarrt (**with** in + *acc*)

infect /ɪnˈfekt/ *vt* anstecken, infizieren; **become** ~**ed** (*wound:*) sich infizieren. ~**ion** /-ˈfekʃn/ *n* Infektion *f.* ~**ious** /-ˈfekʃəs/ *a* ansteckend

infer /ɪnˈfɜː(r)/ *vt* (*pt/pp* **inferred**) folgern (**from** aus); (*imply*) andeuten. ~**ence** /ˈɪnfərəns/ *n* Folgerung *f*

inferior /ɪnˈfɪərɪə(r)/ *a* minderwertig; (*in rank*) untergeordnet ● *n* Untergebene(r) *m/f*

inferiority /ɪnfɪərɪˈɒrətɪ/ *n* Minderwertigkeit *f.* ~ **complex** *n* Minderwertigkeitskomplex *m*

infern|al /ɪnˈfɜːnl/ *a* höllisch. ~**o** *n* flammendes Inferno *nt*

in'fer|tile *a* unfruchtbar. ~'**tility** *n* Unfruchtbarkeit *f*

infest /ɪnˈfest/ *vt* **be** ~**ed with** befallen sein von; (*place*) verseucht sein mit

infi'delity *n* Untreue *f*

infighting /ˈɪnfaɪtɪŋ/ *n* (*fig*) interne Machtkämpfe *pl*

infiltrate /ˈɪnfɪltreɪt/ *vt* infiltrieren; (*Pol*) unterwandern

infinite /ˈɪnfɪnət/ *a*, **-ly** *adv* unendlich

infinitesimal /ɪnfɪnɪˈtesɪml/ *a* unendlich klein

infinitive /ɪnˈfɪnətɪv/ *n* (*Gram*) Infinitiv *m*

infinity /ɪnˈfɪnətɪ/ *n* Unendlichkeit *f*

infirm /ɪnˈfɜːm/ *a* gebrechlich. ~**ary** *n* Krankenhaus *nt.* ~**ity** *n* Gebrechlichkeit *f*

inflame /ɪnˈfleɪm/ *vt* entzünden; **become** ~**d** sich entzünden. ~**d** *a* entzündet

in'flammable *a* feuergefährlich

inflammation /ɪnfləˈmeɪʃn/ *n* Entzündung *f*

inflammatory /ɪnˈflæmətrɪ/ *a* aufrührerisch

inflatable /ɪnˈfleɪtəbl/ *a* aufblasbar

inflat|e /ɪnˈfleɪt/ *vt* aufblasen; (*with pump*) aufpumpen. ∼**ion** /-eɪʃn/ *n* Inflation *f*. ∼**ionary** /-eɪʃənərɪ/ *a* inflationär

in'flexible *a* starr; ⟨person⟩ unbeugsam

inflexion /ɪnˈflekʃn/ *n* Tonfall *m*; (*Gram*) Flexion *f*

inflict /ɪnˈflɪkt/ *vt* zufügen (**on** *dat*); versetzen ⟨blow⟩ (**on** *dat*)

influen|ce /ˈɪnfluəns/ *n* Einfluß *m* • *vt* beeinflussen. ∼**tial** /-ˈenʃl/ *a* einflußreich

influenza /ɪnfluˈenzə/ *n* Grippe *f*

influx /ˈɪnflʌks/ *n* Zustrom *m*

inform /ɪnˈfɔːm/ *vt* benachrichtigen; (*officially*) informieren; ∼ **s.o. of sth** jdm etw mitteilen; **keep s.o. ∼ed** jdn auf dem laufenden halten • *vi* ∼ **against** denunzieren

in'for|mal *a*, **-ly** *adv* zwanglos; (*unofficial*) inoffiziell. ∼'**mality** *n* Zwanglosigkeit *f*

informant /ɪnˈfɔːmənt/ *n* Gewährsmann *m*

informat|ion /ɪnfəˈmeɪʃn/ *n* Auskunft *f*; **a piece of ∼ion** eine Auskunft. ∼**ive** /ɪnˈfɔːmətɪv/ *a* aufschlußreich; (*instructive*) lehrreich

informer /ɪnˈfɔːmə(r)/ *n* Spitzel *m*; (*Pol*) Denunziant *m*

infra-'red /ɪnfrə-/ *a* infrarot

in'frequent *a*, **-ly** *adv* selten

infringe /ɪnˈfrɪndʒ/ *vt/i* ∼ **[on]** verstoßen gegen. ∼**ment** *n* Verstoß *m*

infuriat|e /ɪnˈfjʊərɪeɪt/ *vt* wütend machen. ∼**ing** *a* ärgerlich; **he is ∼ing** er kann einen zur Raserei bringen

infusion /ɪnˈfjuːʒn/ *n* Aufguß *m*

ingenious /ɪnˈdʒiːnɪəs/ *a* erfinderisch; ⟨thing⟩ raffiniert

ingenuity /ɪndʒɪˈnjuːətɪ/ *n* Geschicklichkeit *f*

ingenuous /ɪnˈdʒenjʊəs/ *a* unschuldig

ingot /ˈɪŋgət/ *n* Barren *m*

ingrained /ɪnˈgreɪnd/ *a* eingefleischt; **be ∼** ⟨dirt:⟩ tief sitzen

ingratiate /ɪnˈgreɪʃɪeɪt/ *vt* ∼ **oneself** sich einschmeicheln (**with** bei)

in'gratitude *n* Undankbarkeit *f*

ingredient /ɪnˈgriːdɪənt/ *n* (*Culin*) Zutat *f*

ingrowing /ˈɪngrəʊɪŋ/ *a* ⟨nail⟩ eingewachsen

inhabit /ɪnˈhæbɪt/ *vt* bewohnen. ∼**ant** *n* Einwohner(in) *m(f)*

inhale /ɪnˈheɪl/ *vt/i* einatmen; (*Med & when smoking*) inhalieren

inherent /ɪnˈhɪərənt/ *a* natürlich

inherit /ɪnˈherɪt/ *vt* erben. ∼**ance** /-əns/ *n* Erbschaft *f*, Erbe *nt*

inhibit /ɪnˈhɪbɪt/ *vt* hemmen. ∼**ed** *a* gehemmt. ∼**ion** /-ˈbɪʃn/ *n* Hemmung *f*

inho'spitable *a* ungastlich

in'human *a* unmenschlich

inimitable /ɪˈnɪmɪtəbl/ *a* unnachahmlich

iniquitous /ɪˈnɪkwɪtəs/ *a* schändlich; (*unjust*) ungerecht

initial /ɪˈnɪʃl/ *a* anfänglich, Anfangs- • *n* Anfangsbuchstabe *m*; **my ∼s** meine Initialen • *vt* (*pt/pp* **initialled**) abzeichnen; (*Pol*) paraphieren. ∼**ly** *adv* anfangs, am Anfang

initiat|e /ɪˈnɪʃɪeɪt/ *vt* einführen. ∼**ion** /-ˈeɪʃn/ *n* Einführung *f*

initiative /ɪˈnɪʃətɪv/ *n* Initiative *f*

inject /ɪnˈdʒekt/ *vt* einspritzen, injizieren. ∼**ion** /-ekʃn/ *n* Spritze *f*, Injektion *f*

injunction /ɪnˈdʒʌŋkʃn/ *n* gerichtliche Verfügung *f*

injur|e /ˈɪndʒə(r)/ *vt* verletzen. ∼**y** *n* Verletzung *f*

in'justice *n* Ungerechtigkeit *f*; **do s.o. an ∼** jdm unrecht tun

ink /ɪŋk/ *n* Tinte *f*

inkling /ˈɪŋklɪŋ/ *n* Ahnung *f*

inlaid /ɪnˈleɪd/ *a* eingelegt

inland /ˈɪnlənd/ *a* Binnen- • *adv* landeinwärts. **I∼ Revenue** *n* ≈ Finanzamt *nt*

in-laws /ˈɪnlɔːz/ *npl* (*fam*) Schwiegereltern *pl*

inlay /ˈɪnleɪ/ *n* Einlegearbeit *f*

inlet /ˈɪnlet/ *n* schmale Bucht *f*; (*Techn*) Zuleitung *f*

inmate /ˈɪnmeɪt/ *n* Insasse *m*

inn /ɪn/ *n* Gasthaus *nt*

innards /ˈɪnədz/ *npl* (*fam*) Eingeweide *pl*

innate /ɪˈneɪt/ *a* angeboren

inner /ˈɪnə(r)/ *a* innere(r,s). ∼**most** *a* innerste(r,s)

'innkeeper *n* Gastwirt *m*

innocen|ce /'ɪnəsəns/ n Unschuld f. ∼t a unschuldig. ∼tly adv in aller Unschuld

innocuous /ɪ'nɒkjʊəs/ a harmlos

innovat|e /'ɪnəveɪt/ vi neu einführen. ∼ion /-'veɪʃn/ n Neuerung f. ∼or n Neuerer m

innuendo /ɪnjuː'endəʊ/ n (pl -es) [versteckte] Anspielung f

innumerable /ɪ'njuːmərəbl/ a unzählig

inoculat|e /ɪ'nɒkjʊleɪt/ vt impfen. ∼ion /-'leɪʃn/ n Impfung f

inof'fensive a harmlos

in'operable a nicht operierbar

in'opportune a unpassend

inordinate /ɪ'nɔːdɪnət/ a, -ly adv übermäßig

inor'ganic a anorganisch

'in-patient n [stationär behandelter] Krankenhauspatient m

input /'ɪnpʊt/ n Input m & nt

inquest /'ɪnkwest/ n gerichtliche Untersuchung f

inquir|e /ɪn'kwaɪə(r)/ vi sich erkundigen (about nach); ∼e into untersuchen ● vt sich erkundigen nach. ∼y n Erkundigung f; (investigation) Untersuchung f

inquisitive /ɪn'kwɪzətɪv/ a, -ly adv neugierig

inroad /'ɪnrəʊd/ n Einfall m; make ∼s into sth etw angreifen

in'sane a geisteskrank; (fig) wahnsinnig

in'sanitary a unhygienisch

in'sanity n Geisteskrankheit f

insatiable /ɪn'seɪʃəbl/ a unersättlich

inscri|be /ɪn'skraɪb/ vt eingravieren. ∼ption /-'skrɪpʃn/ n Inschrift f

inscrutable /ɪn'skruːtəbl/ a ergründlich; (expression) undurchdringlich

insect /'ɪnsekt/ n Insekt nt. ∼icide /-'sektɪsaɪd/ n Insektenvertilgungsmittel nt

inse'cur|e a nicht sicher; (fig) unsicher. ∼ity n Unsicherheit f

insemination /ɪnsemɪ'neɪʃn/ n Besamung f; (Med) Befruchtung f

in'sensible a (unconscious) bewußtlos

in'sensitive a gefühllos; ∼ to unempfindlich gegen

in'separable a untrennbar; (people) unzertrennlich

insert[1] /'ɪnsɜːt/ n Einsatz m

insert[2] /ɪn'sɜːt/ vt einfügen, einsetzen; einstecken (key); einwerfen (coin). ∼ion /-ɜːʃn/ n (insert) Einsatz m; (in text) Einfügung f

inside /ɪn'saɪd/ n Innenseite f; (of house) Innere(s) nt ● attrib Innen- ● adv innen; (indoors) drinnen; go ∼ hineingehen; come ∼ hereinkommen; ∼ out links [herum]; know sth ∼ out etw in- und auswendig kennen ● prep ∼ [of] in (+ dat/(into) + acc)

insidious /ɪn'sɪdɪəs/ a, -ly adv heimtückisch

insight /'ɪnsaɪt/ n Einblick m (into in + acc); (understanding) Einsicht f

insignia /ɪn'sɪgnɪə/ npl Insignien pl

insig'nificant a unbedeutend

insin'cere a unaufrichtig

insinuat|e /ɪn'sɪnjʊeɪt/ vt andeuten. ∼ion /-'eɪʃn/ n Andeutung f

insipid /ɪn'sɪpɪd/ a fade

insist /ɪn'sɪst/ vi darauf bestehen; ∼ on bestehen auf (+ dat) ● vt ∼ that darauf bestehen, daß. ∼ence n Bestehen nt. ∼ent a, -ly adv beharrlich; be ∼ent darauf bestehen

'insole n Einlegesohle f

insolen|ce /'ɪnsələns/ n Unverschämtheit f. ∼t a, -ly adv unverschämt

in'soluble a unlöslich; (fig) unlösbar

in'solvent a zahlungsunfähig

insomnia /ɪn'sɒmnɪə/ n Schlaflosigkeit f

inspect /ɪn'spekt/ vt inspizieren; (test) prüfen; kontrollieren (ticket). ∼ion /-ekʃn/ n Inspektion f. ∼or n Inspektor m; (of tickets) Kontrolleur m

inspiration /ɪnspə'reɪʃn/ n Inspiration f

inspire /ɪn'spaɪə(r)/ vt inspirieren; ∼ sth in s.o. jdm etw einflößen

insta'bility n Unbeständigkeit f; (of person) Labilität f

install /ɪn'stɔːl/ vt installieren; [in ein Amt] einführen (person). ∼ation /-stə'leɪʃn/ n Installation f; Amtseinführung f

instalment /ɪn'stɔːlmənt/ n (Comm) Rate f; (of serial) Fortsetzung f; (Radio, TV) Folge f

instance /'ɪnstəns/ n Fall m; (example) Beispiel nt; in the first ∼ zunächst; for ∼ zum Beispiel

instant /'ɪnstənt/ a sofortig; (*Culin*) Instant-● n Augenblick m, Moment m. ∼aneous /-'teɪnɪəs/ a unverzüglich, unmittelbar; **death was** ∼**aneous** der Tod trat sofort ein

instant 'coffee n Pulverkaffee m

instantly /'ɪnstəntlɪ/ adv sofort

instead /ɪn'sted/ adv statt dessen; ∼ **of** statt (+ gen), anstelle von; ∼ **of me** an meiner Stelle; ∼ **of going** anstatt zu gehen

'instep n Spann m, Rist m

instigat|e /'ɪnstɪgeɪt/ vt anstiften; einleiten 〈*proceedings*〉. ∼**ion** /-'geɪʃn/ n Anstiftung f; **at his** ∼**ion** auf seine Veranlassung. ∼**or** n Anstifter(in) m(f)

instil /ɪn'stɪl/ vt (pt/pp **instilled**) einprägen (**into s.o.** jdm)

instinct /'ɪnstɪŋkt/ n Instinkt m. ∼**ive** /ɪn'stɪŋktɪv/ a, **-ly** adv instinktiv

institut|e /'ɪnstɪtjuːt/ n Institut nt ● vt einführen; einleiten 〈*search*〉. ∼**ion** /-'tjuːʃn/ n Institution f; (*home*) Anstalt f

instruct /ɪn'strʌkt/ vt unterrichten; (*order*) anweisen. ∼**ion** /-ʌkʃn/ n Unterricht m; Anweisung f; ∼**ions** pl **for use** Gebrauchsanweisung f. ∼**ive** /-ɪv/ a lehrreich. ∼**or** n Lehrer(in) m(f); (*Mil*) Ausbilder m

instrument /'ɪnstrʊmənt/ n Instrument nt. ∼**al** /-'mentl/ a Instrumental-; **be** ∼**al in** eine entscheidende Rolle spielen bei

insu'bordi|nate a ungehorsam. ∼**nation** /-'neɪʃn/ n Ungehorsam m; (*Mil*) Insubordination f

in'sufferable a unerträglich

insuf'ficient a, **-ly** adv nicht genügend

insular /'ɪnsjʊlə(r)/ a (*fig*) engstirnig

insulat|e /'ɪnsjʊleɪt/ vt isolieren. ∼**ing tape** n Isolierband nt. ∼**ion** /-'leɪʃn/ n Isolierung f

insulin /'ɪnsjʊlɪn/ n Insulin nt

insult[1] /'ɪnsʌlt/ n Beleidigung f

insult[2] /ɪn'sʌlt/ vt beleidigen

insuperable /ɪn'suːpərəbl/ a unüberwindlich

insur|ance /ɪn'ʃʊərəns/ n Versicherung f. ∼**e** vt versichern

insurrection /ɪnsə'rekʃn/ n Aufstand m

intact /ɪn'tækt/ a unbeschädigt; (*complete*) vollständig

'intake n Aufnahme f

in'tangible a nicht greifbar

integral /'ɪntɪgrl/ a wesentlich

integrat|e /'ɪntɪgreɪt/ vt integrieren ● vi sich integrieren. ∼**ion** /-'greɪʃn/ n Integration f

integrity /ɪn'tegrətɪ/ n Integrität f

intellect /'ɪntəlekt/ n Intellekt m. ∼**ual** /-'lektjʊəl/ a intellektuell

intelligen|ce /ɪn'telɪdʒəns/ n Intelligenz f; (*Mil*) Nachrichtendienst m; (*information*) Meldungen pl. ∼**t** a, **-ly** adv intelligent

intelligentsia /ɪntelɪ'dʒentsɪə/ n Intelligenz f

intelligible /ɪn'telɪdʒəbl/ a verständlich

intend /ɪn'tend/ vt beabsichtigen; **be** ∼**ed for** bestimmt sein für

intense /ɪn'tens/ a intensiv; 〈*pain*〉 stark. ∼**ly** adv äußerst; 〈*study*〉 intensiv

intensi|fication /ɪntensɪfɪ'keɪʃn/ n Intensivierung f. ∼**fy** /-'faɪ/ v (pt/pp **-ied**) ● vt intensivieren ● vi zunehmen

intensity /ɪn'tensətɪ/ n Intensität f

intensive /ɪn'tensɪv/ a, **-ly** adv intensiv; **be in** ∼ **care** auf der Intensivstation sein

intent /ɪn'tent/ a, **-ly** adv aufmerksam; ∼ **on** (*absorbed in*) vertieft in (+ acc); **be** ∼ **on doing sth** fest entschlossen sein, etw zu tun ● n Absicht f; **to all** ∼**s and purposes** im Grunde

intention /ɪn'tenʃn/ n Absicht f. ∼**al** a, **-ly** adv absichtlich

inter /ɪn'tɜː(r)/ vt (pt/pp **interred**) bestatten

inter'action n Wechselwirkung f

intercede /ɪntə'siːd/ vi Fürsprache einlegen (**on behalf of** für)

intercept /ɪntə'sept/ vt abfangen

'interchange[1] n Austausch m; (*Auto*) Autobahnkreuz nt

inter'change[2] vt austauschen. ∼**able** a austauschbar

intercom /'ɪntəkɒm/ n [Gegen]sprechanlage f

'intercourse n Verkehr m; (*sexual*) Geschlechtsverkehr m

interest /'ɪntrəst/ n Interesse nt; (*Comm*) Zinsen pl; **have an** ∼ (*Comm*) beteiligt sein (**in** an + dat) ● vt interessieren; **be** ∼**ed** sich interessieren (**in** für). ∼**ing** a interessant. ∼ **rate** n Zinssatz m

interfere /ɪntə'fɪə(r)/ vi sich einmischen. ∼**nce** /-əns/ n Einmischung f; (*Radio, TV*) Störung f

interim /'ɪntərɪm/ a Zwischen-; (*temporary*) vorläufig ● n in the ~ in der Zwischenzeit

interior /ɪn'tɪərɪə(r)/ a innere(r,s), Innen- ● n Innere(s) nt

interject /ɪntə'dʒekt/ vt einwerfen. ~ion /-ekʃn/ n Interjektion f; (*remark*) Einwurf m

inter'lock vi ineinandergreifen

interloper /'ɪntələʊpə(r)/ n Eindringling m

interlude /'ɪntəlu:d/ n Pause f; (*performance*) Zwischenspiel nt

inter'marry vi untereinander heiraten; ⟨*different groups:*⟩ Mischehen schließen

intermediary /ɪntə'mi:dɪərɪ/ n Vermittler(in) m(f)

intermediate /ɪntə'mi:dɪət/ a Zwischen-

interminable /ɪn'tɜ:mɪnəbl/ a endlos [lang]

intermission /ɪntə'mɪʃn/ n Pause f

intermittent /ɪntə'mɪtənt/ a in Abständen auftretend

intern /ɪn'tɜ:n/ vt internieren

internal /ɪn'tɜ:nl/ a innere(r,s); ⟨*matter, dispute*⟩ intern. ~ly adv innerlich; ⟨*deal with*⟩ intern

inter'national a, -ly adv international ● n Länderspiel nt; (*player*) Nationalspieler(in) m(f)

internist /ɪn'tɜ:nɪst/ n (*Amer*) Internist m

internment /ɪn'tɜ:nmənt/ n Internierung f

'interplay n Wechselspiel nt

interpolate /ɪn'tɜ:pəleɪt/ vt einwerfen

interpret /ɪn'tɜ:prɪt/ vt interpretieren; auslegen ⟨*text*⟩; deuten ⟨*dream*⟩; (*translate*) dolmetschen ● vi dolmetschen. ~ation /-'teɪʃn/ n Interpretation f. ~er n Dolmetscher(in) m(f)

interre'lated a verwandt; ⟨*facts*⟩ zusammenhängend

interrogat|e /ɪn'terəgeɪt/ vt verhören. ~ion /-'geɪʃn/ n Verhör nt

interrogative /ɪntə'rɒgətɪv/ a & n ~ [pronoun] Interrogativpronomen nt

interrupt /ɪntə'rʌpt/ vt/i unterbrechen; **don't ~!** red nicht dazwischen! ~ion /-ʌpʃn/ n Unterbrechung f

intersect /ɪntə'sekt/ vi sich kreuzen; (*Geom*) sich schneiden. ~ion /-ekʃn/ n Kreuzung f

interspersed /ɪntə'spɜ:st/ a ~ with durchsetzt mit

inter'twine vi sich ineinanderschlingen

interval /'ɪntəvl/ n Abstand m; (*Theat*) Pause f; (*Mus*) Intervall nt; **at hourly ~s** alle Stunde; **bright ~s** pl Aufheiterungen pl

interven|e /ɪntə'vi:n/ vi eingreifen; (*occur*) dazwischenkommen. ~tion /-'venʃn/ n Eingreifen nt; (*Mil, Pol*) Intervention f

interview /'ɪntəvju:/ n (*Journ*) Interview nt; (*for job*) Vorstellungsgespräch nt; **go for an ~** sich vorstellen ● vt interviewen; ein Vorstellungsgespräch führen mit. ~er n Interviewer(in) m(f)

intestine /ɪn'testɪn/ n Darm m

intimacy /'ɪntɪməsɪ/ n Vertrautheit f; (*sexual*) Intimität f

intimate[1] /'ɪntɪmət/ a, -ly adv vertraut; ⟨*friend*⟩ eng; (*sexually*) intim

intimate[2] /'ɪntɪmeɪt/ vt zu verstehen geben; (*imply*) andeuten

intimidat|e /ɪn'tɪmɪdeɪt/ vt einschüchtern. ~ion /-'deɪʃn/ n Einschüchterung f

into /'ɪntə, *vor einem Vokal* 'ɪntʊ/ prep in (+ acc); **go ~ the house** ins Haus [hinein]gehen; **be ~** (*fam*) sich auskennen mit; **7 ~ 21** 21 [geteilt] durch 7

in'tolerable a unerträglich

in'toleran|ce n Intoleranz f. ~t a intolerant

intonation /ɪntə'neɪʃn/ n Tonfall m

intoxicat|ed /ɪn'tɒksɪkeɪtɪd/ a betrunken; (*fig*) berauscht. ~ion /-'keɪʃn/ n Rausch m

intractable /ɪn'træktəbl/ a widerspenstig; ⟨*problem*⟩ hartnäckig

intransigent /ɪn'trænsɪdʒənt/ a unnachgiebig

in'transitive a, -ly adv intransitiv

intravenous /ɪntrə'vi:nəs/ a, -ly adv intravenös

intrepid /ɪn'trepɪd/ a kühn, unerschrocken

intricate /'ɪntrɪkət/ a kompliziert

intrigu|e /ɪn'tri:g/ n Intrige f ● vt faszinieren ● vi intrigieren. ~ing a faszinierend

intrinsic /ɪn'trɪnsɪk/ a ~ **value** Eigenwert m

introduce /ɪntrə'dju:s/ vt vorstellen; (*bring in, insert*) einführen

introduct|ion /ɪntrə'dʌkʃn/ n Einführung f; (to person) Vorstellung f; (to book) Einleitung f. ~ory /-tərɪ/ a einleitend

introspective /ɪntrə'spektɪv/ a in sich (acc) gerichtet

introvert /'ɪntrəvɜːt/ n introvertierter Mensch m

intru|de /ɪn'truːd/ vi stören. ~der n Eindringling m. ~sion /-uːʒn/ n Störung f

intuit|ion /ɪntjuː'ɪʃn/ n Intuition f. ~ive /-'tjuːɪtɪv/ a, -ly adv intuitiv

inundate /'ɪnʌndeɪt/ vt überschwemmen

invade /ɪn'veɪd/ vt einfallen in (+ acc). ~r n Angreifer m

invalid[1] /'ɪnvəlɪd/ n Kranke(r) m/f

invalid[2] /ɪn'vælɪd/ a ungültig. ~ate vt ungültig machen

in'valuable a unschätzbar; (person) unersetzlich

in'variab|le a unveränderlich. ~ly adv immer

invasion /ɪn'veɪʒn/ n Invasion f

invective /ɪn'vektɪv/ n Beschimpfungen pl

invent /ɪn'vent/ vt erfinden. ~ion /-enʃn/ n Erfindung f. ~ive /-tɪv/ a erfinderisch. ~or n Erfinder m

inventory /'ɪnvəntrɪ/ n Bestandsliste f; **make an ~** ein Inventar aufstellen

inverse /ɪn'vɜːs/ a, -ly adv umgekehrt ● n Gegenteil nt

invert /ɪn'vɜːt/ vt umkehren. ~ed commas npl Anführungszeichen pl

invest /ɪn'vest/ vt investieren, anlegen; ~ in (fam: buy) sich (dat) zulegen

investigat|e /ɪn'vestɪgeɪt/ vt untersuchen. ~ion /-'geɪʃn/ n Untersuchung f

invest|ment /ɪn'vestmənt/ n Anlage f; **be a good ~ment** (fig) sich bezahlt machen. ~or n Kapitalanleger m

inveterate /ɪn'vetərət/ a Gewohnheits-; (liar) unverbesserlich

invidious /ɪn'vɪdɪəs/ a unerfreulich; (unfair) ungerecht

invigilate /ɪn'vɪdʒɪleɪt/ vi (Sch) Aufsicht führen

invigorate /ɪn'vɪgəreɪt/ vt beleben

invincible /ɪn'vɪnsəbl/ a unbesiegbar

inviolable /ɪn'vaɪələbl/ a unantastbar

in'visible a unsichtbar. ~ mending n Kunststopfen nt

invitation /ɪnvɪ'teɪʃn/ n Einladung f

invit|e /ɪn'vaɪt/ vt einladen. ~ing a einladend

invoice /'ɪnvɔɪs/ n Rechnung f ● vt ~ s.o. jdm eine Rechnung schicken

invoke /ɪn'vəʊk/ vt anrufen

in'voluntary a, -ily adv unwillkürlich

involve /ɪn'vɒlv/ vt beteiligen; (affect) betreffen; (implicate) verwickeln; (entail) mit sich bringen; (mean) bedeuten; **be ~d in** beteiligt sein an (+ dat); (implicated) verwickelt sein in (+ acc); **get ~d with s.o.** mit jdm einlassen. ~d a kompliziert

in'vulnerable a unverwundbar; (position) unangreifbar

inward /'ɪnwəd/ a innere(r,s). ~ly adv innerlich. ~s adv nach innen

iodine /'aɪədiːn/ n Jod nt

iota /aɪ'əʊtə/ n Jota nt; (fam) Funke m

IOU abbr (I owe you) Schuldschein m

Iran /ɪ'rɑːn/ n der Iran

Iraq /ɪ'rɑːk/ n der Irak

irascible /ɪ'ræsəbl/ a aufbrausend

irate /aɪ'reɪt/ a wütend

Ireland /'aɪələnd/ n Irland nt

iris /'aɪərɪs/ n (Anat) Regenbogenhaut f, Iris f; (Bot) Schwertlilie f

Irish /'aɪərɪʃ/ a irisch ● n **the ~** pl die Iren. ~man n Ire m. ~woman n Irin f

irk /ɜːk/ vt ärgern. ~some /-səm/ a lästig

iron /'aɪən/ a Eisen-; (fig) eisern ● n Eisen nt; (appliance) Bügeleisen nt ● vt/i bügeln. ~ out vt ausbügeln

ironic[al] /aɪ'rɒnɪk[l]/ a ironisch

ironing /'aɪənɪŋ/ n Bügeln nt; (articles) Bügelwäsche f; **do the ~** bügeln. ~-board n Bügelbrett nt

ironmonger /'-mʌŋgə(r)/ n ~'s [shop] Haushaltswarengeschäft nt

irony /'aɪərənɪ/ n Ironie f

irradiate /ɪ'reɪdɪeɪt/ vt bestrahlen

irrational /ɪ'ræʃənl/ a irrational

irreconcilable /ɪ'rekənsaɪləbl/ a unversöhnlich

irrefutable /ɪrɪ'fjuːtəbl/ a unwiderlegbar

irregular /ɪ'regjʊlə(r)/ a, -ly adv unregelmäßig; (against rules) regelwidrig. ~ity /-'lærətɪ/ n Unregelmäßigkeit f; Regelwidrigkeit f irrelevant /ɪˈrelǝvǝnt/ *a* irrelevant

irreparable /ɪˈrepǝrǝbl/ *a* unersetzlich; **be ~** nicht wiedergutzumachen sein

irreplaceable /ɪrɪˈpleɪsǝbl/ *a* unersetzlich

irrepressible /ɪrɪˈpresǝbl/ *a* unverwüstlich; **be ~** ⟨person:⟩ nicht unterzukriegen sein

irresistible /ɪrɪˈzɪstǝbl/ *a* unwiderstehlich

irresolute /ɪˈrezǝluːt/ *a* unentschlossen

irrespective /ɪrɪˈspektɪv/ *a* **~ of** ungeachtet (+ *gen*)

irresponsible /ɪrɪˈspɒnsǝbl/ *a*, **-bly** *adv* unverantwortlich; ⟨person⟩ verantwortungslos

irreverent /ɪˈrevǝrǝnt/ *a*, **-ly** *adv* respektlos

irreversible /ɪrɪˈvɜːsǝbl/ *a* unwiderruflich; (*Med*) irreversibel

irrevocable /ɪˈrevǝkǝbl/ *a*, **-bly** *adv* unwiderruflich

irrigat|e /ˈɪrɪgeɪt/ *vt* bewässern. **~ion** /-ˈgeɪʃn/ *n* Bewässerung *f*

irritability /ɪrɪtǝˈbɪlǝtɪ/ *n* Gereiztheit *f*

irritable /ˈɪrɪtǝbl/ *a* reizbar

irritant /ˈɪrɪtǝnt/ *n* Reizstoff *m*

irritat|e /ˈɪrɪteɪt/ *vt* irritieren; (*Med*) reizen. **~ion** /-ˈteɪʃn/ *n* Ärger *m*; (*Med*) Reizung *f*

is /ɪz/ *see* be

Islam /ˈɪzlɑːm/ *n* der Islam. **~ic** /-ˈlæmɪk/ *a* islamisch

island /ˈaɪlǝnd/ *n* Insel *f*. **~er** *n* Inselbewohner(in) *m(f)*

isle /aɪl/ *n* Insel *f*

isolat|e /ˈaɪsǝleɪt/ *vt* isolieren. **~ed** *a* (*remote*) abgelegen; (*single*) einzeln. **~ion** /-ˈleɪʃn/ *n* Isoliertheit *f*; (*Med*) Isolierung *f*

Israel /ˈɪzreɪl/ *n* Israel *nt*. **~i** /ɪzˈreɪlɪ/ *a* israelisch ● *n* Israeli *m/f*

issue /ˈɪʃuː/ *n* Frage *f*; (*outcome*) Ergebnis *nt*; (*of magazine, stamps*) Ausgabe *f*; (*offspring*) Nachkommen *pl*; **what is at ~?** worum geht es? **take ~ with s.o.** jdm widersprechen ● *vt* ausgeben; ausstellen ⟨passport⟩; erteilen ⟨order⟩; herausgeben ⟨book⟩; **be ~d with sth** etw erhalten ● *vi* **~ from** herausströmen aus

isthmus /ˈɪsmǝs/ *n* (*pl* **-muses**) Landenge *f*

it /ɪt/ *pron* es; (*m*) er; (*f*) sie; (*as direct object*) es; (*m*) ihn; (*f*) sie; (*as indirect object*) ihm; (*f*) ihr; **it is raining** es regnet; **it's me** ich bin's; **who is it?** wer ist da? **of/from it** davon; **with it** damit; **out of it** daraus

Italian /ɪˈtæljǝn/ *a* italienisch ● *n* Italiener(in) *m(f)*; (*Lang*) Italienisch *nt*

italic /ɪˈtælɪk/ *a* kursiv. **~s** *npl* Kursivschrift *f*; **in ~s** kursiv

Italy /ˈɪtǝlɪ/ *n* Italien *nt*

itch /ɪtʃ/ *n* Juckreiz *m*; **I have an ~** es juckt mich ● *vi* jucken; **I'm ~ing** (*fam*) es juckt mich (**to** zu). **~y** *a* **be ~y** jucken

item /ˈaɪtǝm/ *n* Gegenstand *m*; (*Comm*) Artikel *m*; (*on agenda*) Punkt *m*; (*on invoice*) Posten *m*; (*act*) Nummer *f*; **~ [of news]** Nachricht *f*. **~ize** *vt* einzeln aufführen; spezifizieren ⟨bill⟩

itinerant /aɪˈtɪnǝrǝnt/ *a* Wander-

itinerary /aɪˈtɪnǝrǝrɪ/ *n* [Reise]route *f*

its /ɪts/ *poss pron* sein; (*f*) ihr

it's /ɪts/ = it is, it has

itself /ɪtˈself/ *pron* selbst; (*refl*) sich; **by ~** von selbst; (*alone*) allein

ivory /ˈaɪvǝrɪ/ *n* Elfenbein *nt* ● *attrib* Elfenbein-

ivy /ˈaɪvɪ/ *n* Efeu *m*

J

jab /dʒæb/ *n* Stoß *m*; (*fam: injection*) Spritze *f* ● *vt* (*pt/pp* **jabbed**) stoßen

jabber /ˈdʒæbǝ(r)/ *vi* plappern

jack /dʒæk/ *n* (*Auto*) Wagenheber *m*; (*Cards*) Bube *m* ● *vt* **~ up** (*Auto*) aufbocken

jackdaw /ˈdʒækdɔː/ *n* Dohle *f*

jacket /ˈdʒækɪt/ *n* Jacke *f*; (*of book*) Schutzumschlag *m*. **~ po'tato** *n* in der Schale gebackene Kartoffel *f*

'jackpot *n* **hit the ~** das Große Los ziehen

jade /dʒeɪd/ *n* Jade *m*

jaded /ˈdʒeɪdɪd/ *a* abgespannt

jagged /ˈdʒægɪd/ *a* zackig

jail /dʒeɪl/ = gaol

jalopy /dʒǝˈlɒpɪ/ *n* (*fam*) Klapperkiste *f*

jam¹ /dʒæm/ *n* Marmelade *f*

jam² *n* Gedränge *nt*; (*Auto*) Stau *m*; (*fam: difficulty*) Klemme *f* ● *v* (*pt/pp* **jammed**) ● *vt* klemmen (**in** in + *acc*); stören ⟨broadcast⟩ ● *vi* klemmen

Jamaica /dʒǝˈmeɪkǝ/ *n* Jamaika *nt*

jangle /'dʒæŋgl/ vi klimpern ● vt klimpern mit

janitor /'dʒænɪtə(r)/ n Hausmeister m

January /'dʒænjʊərɪ/ n Januar m

Japan /dʒə'pæn/ n Japan nt. ~ese /dʒæpə'ni:z/ a japanisch ● n Japaner(in) m(f); (Lang) Japanisch nt

jar¹ /dʒɑ:(r)/ n Glas nt; (earthenware) Topf m

jar² v (pt/pp **jarred**) vi stören ● vt erschüttern

jargon /'dʒɑ:gən/ n Jargon m

jaundice /'dʒɔ:ndɪs/ n Gelbsucht f. ~d a (fig) zynisch

jaunt /dʒɔ:nt/ n Ausflug m

jaunty /'dʒɔ:ntɪ/ a (-ier, -iest), -ily adv keck

javelin /'dʒævlɪn/ n Speer m

jaw /dʒɔ:/ n Kiefer m; ~s pl Rachen m ● vi (fam) quatschen

jay /dʒeɪ/ n Eichelhäher m. ~-walker n achtloser Fußgänger m

jazz /dʒæz/ n Jazz m. ~y a knallig

jealous /'dʒeləs/ a, -ly adv eifersüchtig (of auf + acc). ~y n Eifersucht f

jeans /dʒi:nz/ npl Jeans pl

jeer /dʒɪə(r)/ n Johlen nt ● vi johlen; ~ at verhöhnen

jell /dʒel/ vi gelieren

jelly /'dʒelɪ/ n Gelee nt; (dessert) Götterspeise f. ~fish n Qualle f

jemmy /'dʒemɪ/ n Brecheisen nt

jeopar|dize /'dʒepədaɪz/ vt gefährden. ~dy /-dɪ/ n in ~dy gefährdet

jerk /dʒɜ:k/ n Ruck m ● vt stoßen; (pull) reißen ● vi rucken; (limb, muscle:) zucken. ~ily adv ruckweise. ~y a ruckartig

jersey /'dʒɜ:zɪ/ n Pullover m; (Sport) Trikot nt; (fabric) Jersey m

jest /dʒest/ n Scherz m; in ~ im Spaß ● vi scherzen

jet¹ /dʒet/ n (Miner) Jett m

jet² n (of water) [Wasser]strahl m; (nozzle) Düse f; (plane) Düsenflugzeug nt

jet: ~-'black a pechschwarz. ~ lag n Jet-lag nt. ~-pro'pelled a mit Düsenantrieb

jettison /'dʒetɪsn/ vt über Bord werfen

jetty /'dʒetɪ/ n Landesteg m; (breakwater) Buhne f

Jew /dʒu:/ n Jude m/Jüdin f

jewel /'dʒu:əl/ n Edelstein m; (fig) Juwel nt. ~ler n Juwelier m; ~ler's

[shop] Juweliergeschäft nt. ~lery n Schmuck m

Jew|ess /'dʒu:ɪs/ n Jüdin f. ~ish a jüdisch

jib /dʒɪb/ vi (pt/pp **jibbed**) (fig) sich sträuben (at gegen)

jiffy /'dʒɪfɪ/ n (fam) in a ~ in einem Augenblick

jigsaw /'dʒɪgsɔ:/ n ~ [puzzle] Puzzlespiel nt

jilt /dʒɪlt/ vt sitzenlassen

jingle /'dʒɪŋgl/ n (rhyme) Versehen nt ● vi klimpern ● vt klimpern mit

jinx /dʒɪŋks/ n (fam) it's got a ~ on it es ist verhext

jitter|s /'dʒɪtəz/ npl (fam) have the ~s nervös sein. ~y a (fam) nervös

job /dʒɒb/ n Aufgabe f; (post) Stelle f, (fam) Job m; be a ~ (fam) nicht leicht sein; it's a good ~ that es ist [nur] gut, daß. ~ centre n Arbeitsvermittlungsstelle f. ~less a arbeitslos

jockey /'dʒɒkɪ/ n Jockei m

jocular /'dʒɒkjʊlə(r)/ a, -ly adv spaßhaft

jog /dʒɒg/ n Stoß m; at a ~ im Dauerlauf ● v (pt/pp **jogged**) ● vt anstoßen; ~ s.o.'s memory jds Gedächtnis nachhelfen ● vi (Sport) joggen. ~ging n Jogging nt

john /dʒɒn/ n (Amer, fam) Klo nt

join /dʒɔɪn/ n Nahtstelle f ● vt verbinden (to mit); sich anschließen (+ dat) ⟨person⟩; (become member of) beitreten (+ dat); eintreten in (+ acc) ⟨firm⟩ ● vi ⟨roads:⟩ sich treffen. ~ in vi mitmachen. ~ up vi (Mil) Soldat werden ● vt zusammenfügen

joiner /'dʒɔɪnə(r)/ n Tischler m

joint /dʒɔɪnt/ a, -ly adv gemeinsam ● n Gelenk nt; (in wood, brickwork) Fuge f; (Culin) Braten m; (fam: bar) Lokal nt

joist /dʒɔɪst/ n Dielenbalken m

jok|e /dʒəʊk/ n Scherz m; (funny story) Witz m; (trick) Streich m ● vi scherzen. ~er n Witzbold m; (Cards) Joker m. ~ing n ~ing apart Spaß beiseite. ~ingly adv im Spaß

jollity /'dʒɒlɪtɪ/ n Lustigkeit f

jolly /'dʒɒlɪ/ a (-ier, -iest) lustig ● adv (fam) sehr

jolt /dʒəʊlt/ n Ruck m ● vt einen Ruck versetzen (+ dat) ● vi holpern

Jordan /'dʒɔ:dn/ n Jordanien nt

jostle /'dʒɒsl/ vt anrempeln ● vi drängeln

jot /dʒɒt/ n Jota nt ● vt (pt/pp **jotted**) ~ **[down]** sich (dat) notieren. ~ter n Notizblock m

journal /'dʒɜːnl/ n Zeitschrift f; (diary) Tagebuch nt. ~ese /-ə'liːz/ n Zeitungsjargon m. ~ism n Journalismus m. ~ist n Journalist(in) m(f)

journey /'dʒɜːnɪ/ n Reise f

jovial /'dʒəʊvɪəl/ a lustig

joy /dʒɔɪ/ n Freude f. ~ful a, -ly adv freudig, froh. ~ride n (fam) Spritztour f [im gestohlenen Auto]

jubil|ant /'dʒuːbɪlənt/ a überglücklich. ~ation /-'leɪʃn/ n Jubel m

jubilee /'dʒuːbɪliː/ n Jubiläum nt

Judaism /'dʒuːdeɪɪzm/ n Judentum nt

judder /'dʒʌdə(r)/ vi rucken

judge /dʒʌdʒ/ n Richter m; (of competition) Preisrichter m ● vt beurteilen; (estimate) [ein]schätzen ● vi urteilen (**by** nach). ~ment n Beurteilung f; (Jur) Urteil nt; (fig) Urteilsvermögen nt

judic|ial /dʒuː'dɪʃl/ a gerichtlich. ~iary /-ʃərɪ/ n Richterstand m. ~ious /-ʃəs/ a klug

judo /'dʒuːdəʊ/ n Judo nt

jug /dʒʌg/ n Kanne f; (small) Kännchen nt; (for water, wine) Krug m

juggernaut /'dʒʌgənɔːt/ n (fam) Riesenlaster m

juggle /'dʒʌgl/ vi jonglieren. ~r n Jongleur m

juice /dʒuːs/ n Saft m. ~ extractor n Entsafter m

juicy /'dʒuːsɪ/ a (-ier, -iest) saftig; (fam) ⟨story⟩ pikant

juke-box /'dʒuːk-/ n Musikbox f

July /dʒʊ'laɪ/ n Juli m

jumble /'dʒʌmbl/ n Durcheinander nt ● vt ~ **[up]** durcheinanderbringen. ~ **sale** n [Wohltätigkeits]basar m

jumbo /'dʒʌmbəʊ/ n ~ **[jet]** Jumbo-[-Jet] m

jump /dʒʌmp/ n Sprung m; (in prices) Anstieg m; (in horse racing) Hindernis nt ● vi springen; (start) zusammenzucken; **make s.o.** ~ jdn erschrecken; ~ **at** ⟨fig⟩ sofort zugreifen bei ⟨offer⟩; ~ **to conclusions** voreilige Schlüsse ziehen ● vt überspringen; ~ **the gun** (fig) vorschnell handeln. ~ **up** aufspringen

jumper /'dʒʌmpə(r)/ n Pullover m, Pulli m

jumpy /'dʒʌmpɪ/ a nervös

junction /'dʒʌŋkʃn/ n Kreuzung f; (Rail) Knotenpunkt m

juncture /'dʒʌŋktʃə(r)/ n **at this** ~ zu diesem Zeitpunkt

June /dʒuːn/ n Juni m

jungle /'dʒʌŋgl/ n Dschungel m

junior /'dʒuːnɪə(r)/ a jünger; (in rank) untergeordnet; (Sport) Junioren- ● n Junior m. ~ **school** n Grundschule f

juniper /'dʒuːnɪpə(r)/ n Wacholder m

junk /dʒʌŋk/ n Gerümpel nt, Trödel m

junkie /'dʒʌŋkɪ/ n (sl) Fixer m

'junk-shop n Trödelladen m

juris|diction /dʒʊərɪs'dɪkʃn/ n Gerichtsbarkeit f. ~'prudence n Rechtswissenschaft f

juror /'dʒʊərə(r)/ n Geschworene(r) m/f

jury /'dʒʊərɪ/ n **the** ~ die Geschworenen pl; (for competition) die Jury

just /dʒʌst/ a gerecht ● adv gerade; (only) nur; (simply) einfach; (exactly) genau; ~ **as tall** ebenso groß; ~ **listen!** hör doch mal! **I'm** ~ **going** ich gehe schon; ~ **put it down** stell es nur hin

justice /'dʒʌstɪs/ n Gerechtigkeit f; **do** ~ **to** gerecht werden (+ dat); **J~ of the Peace** ≈ Friedensrichter m

justifiab|le /'dʒʌstɪfaɪəbl/ a berechtigt. ~ly adv berechtigterweise

justi|fication /dʒʌstɪfɪ'keɪʃn/ n Rechtfertigung f. ~fy /'dʒʌstɪfaɪ/ vt (pt/pp -ied) rechtfertigen

justly /'dʒʌstlɪ/ adv zu Recht

jut /dʒʌt/ vi (pt/pp **jutted**) ~ **out** vorstehen

juvenile /'dʒuːvənaɪl/ a jugendlich; (childish) kindisch ● n Jugendliche(r) m/f. ~ **delinquency** n Jugendkriminalität f

juxtapose /dʒʌkstə'pəʊz/ vt nebeneinanderstellen

K

kangaroo /kæŋgə'ruː/ n Känguruh nt

karate /kə'rɑːtɪ/ n Karate nt

kebab /kɪ'bæb/ n (Culin) Spießchen nt

keel /kiːl/ n Kiel m ● vi ~ **over** umkippen; (Naut) kentern

keen /kiːn/ a (**-er, -est**) (*sharp*) scharf; (*intense*) groß; (*eager*) eifrig, begeistert; ~ **on** (*fam*) erpicht auf (+ *acc*); ~ **on s.o.** von jdm sehr angetan; **be ~ to do sth** etw gerne machen wollen. ~**ly** adv tief. ~**ness** n Eifer m, Begeisterung f

keep /kiːp/ n (*maintenance*) Unterhalt m; (*of castle*) Bergfried m; **for ~s** für immer ● v (*pt/pp* **kept**) ● vt behalten; (*store*) aufbewahren; (*not throw away*) aufheben; (*support*) unterhalten; (*detain*) aufhalten; freihalten (*seat*); halten (*promise, animals*); führen, haben (*shop*); einhalten (*law, rules*); ~ **sth hot** etw warm halten; ~ **s.o. from doing sth** jdn davon abhalten, etw zu tun; ~ **s.o. waiting** jdn warten lassen; ~ **sth to oneself** etw nicht weitersagen; **where do you ~ the sugar?** wo hast du den Zucker? ● vi (*remain*) bleiben; (*food:*) sich halten; ~ **left/right** sich links/rechts halten; ~ **doing sth** etw dauernd machen; ~ **on doing sth** etw weitermachen; ~ **in with** sich gut stellen mit. ~ **up** vi Schritt halten ● vt (*continue*) weitermachen

keep|er /ˈkiːpə(r)/ n Wärter(in) m(f). ~**ing** n Obhut f; **be in ~ing with** passen zu. ~**sake** n Andenken nt

keg /keg/ n kleines Faß nt

kennel /ˈkenl/ n Hundehütte f; ~**s** pl (*boarding*) Hundepension f; (*breeding*) Zwinger m

Kenya /ˈkenjə/ n Kenia nt

kept /kept/ see **keep**

kerb /kɜːb/ n Bordstein m

kernel /ˈkɜːnl/ n Kern m

kerosene /ˈkerəsiːn/ n (*Amer*) Petroleum nt

ketchup /ˈketʃʌp/ n Ketchup m

kettle /ˈketl/ n [Wasser]kessel m; **put the ~ on** Wasser aufsetzen; **a pretty ~ of fish** (*fam*) eine schöne Bescherung f

key /kiː/ n Schlüssel m; (*Mus*) Tonart f; (*of piano, typewriter*) Taste f ● vt ~ **in** vt eintasten

key: ~**board** n Tastatur f; (*Mus*) Klaviatur f. ~**boarder** n Taster(in) m(f). ~**hole** n Schlüsselloch nt. ~**ring** n Schlüsselring m

khaki /ˈkɑːkɪ/ a khakifarben ● n Khaki nt

kick /kɪk/ n [Fuß]tritt m; **for ~s** (*fam*) zum Spaß ● vt treten; ~ **the bucket** (*fam*) abkratzen ● vi (*animal:*) ausschlagen. ~**-off** n (*Sport*) Anstoß m

kid /kɪd/ n Kitz nt; (*fam: child*) Kind nt ● vt (*pt/pp* **kidded**) (*fam*) ~ **s.o.** jdm etwas vormachen. ~ **gloves** npl Glacéhandschuhe pl

kidnap /ˈkɪdnæp/ vt (*pt/pp* **-napped**) entführen. ~**per** n Entführer m. ~**ping** n Entführung f

kidney /ˈkɪdnɪ/ n Niere f. ~ **machine** n künstliche Niere f

kill /kɪl/ vt töten; (*fam*) totschlagen (*time*); ~ **two birds with one stone** zwei Fliegen mit einer Klappe schlagen. ~**er** n Mörder(in) m(f). ~**ing** n Tötung f; (*murder*) Mord m

ˈ**killjoy** n Spielverderber m

kiln /kɪln/ n Brennofen m

kilo /ˈkiːləʊ/ n Kilo nt

kilo /ˈkɪlə/: ~**gram** n Kilogramm nt. ~**hertz** /-hɜːts/ n Kilohertz nt. ~**metre** n Kilometer m. ~**watt** n Kilowatt nt

kilt /kɪlt/ n Schottenrock m

kin /kɪn/ n Verwandtschaft f; **next of ~** nächster Verwandter m/nächste Verwandte f

kind[1] /kaɪnd/ n Art f; (*brand, type*) Sorte f; **what ~ of car?** was für ein Auto? ~ **of** (*fam*) irgendwie

kind[2] a (**-er, -est**) nett; ~ **to animals** gut zu Tieren; ~ **regards** herzliche Grüße

kindergarten /ˈkɪndəɡɑːtn/ n Vorschule f

kindle /ˈkɪndl/ vt anzünden

kind|ly /ˈkaɪndlɪ/ a (**-ier, -iest**) nett ● adv netterweise; (*if you please*) gefälligst. ~**ness** n Güte f; (*favour*) Gefallen m

kindred /ˈkɪndrɪd/ a ~ **spirit** Gleichgesinnte(r) m/f

kinetic /kɪˈnetɪk/ a kinetisch

king /kɪŋ/ n König m; (*Draughts*) Dame f. ~**dom** n Königreich nt; (*fig & Relig*) Reich nt

king: ~**fisher** n Eisvogel m. ~**-sized** a extragroß

kink /kɪŋk/ n Knick m. ~**y** a (*fam*) pervers

kiosk /ˈkiːɒsk/ n Kiosk m

kip /kɪp/ n **have a ~** (*fam*) pennen ● vi (*pt/pp* **kipped**) (*fam*) pennen

kipper /ˈkɪpə(r)/ n Räucherhering m

kiss /kɪs/ n Kuß m ● vt/i küssen

kit /kɪt/ n Ausrüstung f; (*tools*) Werkzeug nt; (*construction ~*) Bausatz m ● vt (*pt/pp* **kitted**) ~ **out** ausrüsten. ~**bag** n Seesack m

kitchen /'kɪtʃɪn/ n Küche f ● attrib Küchen-. **~ette** /kɪtʃɪ'net/ n Kochnische f

kitchen: ~ 'garden n Gemüsegarten m. ~ 'sink n Spülbecken nt

kite /kaɪt/ n Drachen m

kith /kɪθ/ n **with ~ and kin** mit der ganzen Verwandtschaft

kitten /'kɪtn/ n Kätzchen nt

kitty /'kɪtɪ/ n (money) [gemeinsame] Kasse f

kleptomaniac /kleptə'meɪnɪæk/ n Kleptomane m/-manin f

knack /næk/ n Trick m, Dreh m

knapsack /'næp-/ n Tornister m

knead /ni:d/ vt kneten

knee /ni:/ n Knie nt. **~cap** n Kniescheibe f

kneel /ni:l/ vi (pt/pp **knelt**) knien; ~ **[down]** sich [nieder]knien

knelt /nelt/ see **kneel**

knew /nju:/ see **know**

knickers /'nɪkəz/ npl Schlüpfer m

knick-knacks /'nɪknæks/ npl Nippsachen pl

knife /naɪf/ n (pl **knives**) Messer nt ● vt einen Messerstich versetzen (+ dat); (to death) erstechen

knight /naɪt/ n Ritter m; (Chess) Springer m ● vt adeln

knit /nɪt/ vt/i (pt/pp **knitted**) stricken; ~ **one, purl one** eine rechts, eine links; ~ **one's brow** die Stirn runzeln. **~ting** n Stricken nt; (work) Strickzeug nt. **~ting-needle** n Stricknadel f. **~wear** n Strickwaren pl

knives /naɪvz/ npl see **knife**

knob /nɒb/ n Knopf m; (on door) Knauf m; (small lump) Beule f; (small piece) Stückchen nt. **~bly** a knorrig; (bony) knochig

knock /nɒk/ n Klopfen nt; (blow) Schlag m; **there was a ~ at the door** es klopfte ● vt anstoßen; (at door) klopfen an (+ acc); (fam: criticize) heruntermachen; ~ **a hole in sth** ein Loch in etw (acc) schlagen; ~ **one's head** sich (dat) den Kopf stoßen (**on** an + dat) ● vi klopfen. ~ **about** vt schlagen ● vi (fam) herumkommen. ~ **down** vt herunterwerfen; (with fist) niederschlagen; (in car) anfahren; (demolish) abreißen; (fam: reduce) herabsetzen. ~ **off** vt herunterwerfen; (fam: steal) klauen; (fam: complete quickly) hinhauen ● vi (fam: cease work) Feierabend machen. ~ **out** vt ausschlagen; (make unconscious) bewußtlos schlagen; (Boxing) k.o. schlagen. ~ **over** vt umwerfen; (in car) anfahren

knock: **~-down** a **~-down prices** Schleuderpreise pl. **~er** n Türklopfer m. **~-kneed** /-'ni:d/ a X-beinig. **~-out** n (Boxing) K.o. m

knot /nɒt/ n Knoten m ● vt (pt/pp **knotted**) knoten

knotty /'nɒtɪ/ a (-ier, -iest) (fam) verwickelt

know /nəʊ/ vt/i (pt **knew**, pp **known**) wissen; kennen (person); können (language); **get to ~** kennenlernen ● n **in the ~** (fam) im Bild

know: **~-all** n (fam) Alleswisser m. **~-how** n (fam) [Sach]kenntnis f. **~ing** a wissend. **~ingly** adv wissend; (intentionally) wissentlich

knowledge /'nɒlɪdʒ/ n Kenntnis f (**of** von/gen); (general) Wissen nt; (specialized) Kenntnisse pl. **~able** /-əbl/ a **be ~able** viel wissen

known /nəʊn/ see **know** ● a bekannt

knuckle /'nʌkl/ n [Finger]knöchel m; (Culin) Hachse f ● vi ~ **under** sich fügen; ~ **down** sich dahinterklemmen

kosher /'kəʊʃə(r)/ a koscher

kowtow /kaʊ'taʊ/ vi Kotau machen (**to** vor + dat)

kudos /'kju:dɒs/ n (fam) Prestige nt

L

lab /læb/ n (fam) Labor nt

label /'leɪbl/ n Etikett nt ● vt (pt/pp **labelled**) etikettieren

laboratory /lə'bɒrətrɪ/ n Labor nt

laborious /lə'bɔ:rɪəs/ a, **-ly** adv mühsam

labour /'leɪbə(r)/ n Arbeit f; (workers) Arbeitskräfte pl; (Med) Wehen pl; **L~** (Pol) die Labourpartei ● attrib Labour- ● vi arbeiten ● vt (fig) sich lange auslassen über (+ acc). **~er** n Arbeiter m

'labour-saving a arbeitssparend

laburnum /lə'bɜ:nəm/ n Goldregen m

labyrinth /'læbərɪnθ/ n Labyrinth nt

lace /leɪs/ n Spitze f; (of shoe) Schnürsenkel m ● vt schnüren; **~d with rum** mit einem Schuß Rum

lacerate /'læsəreɪt/ vt zerreißen

lack /læk/ *n* Mangel *m* (**of** an + *dat*)
• *vt* I ~ **the time** mir fehlt die Zeit • *vi*
be ~**ing** fehlen

lackadaisical /lækə'deızıkl/ *a* lustlos

laconic /lə'kɒnık/ *a*, **-ally** *adv*
lakonisch

lacquer /'lækə(r)/ *n* Lack *m*; (*for
hair*) [Haar]spray *m*

lad /læd/ *n* Junge *m*

ladder /'lædə(r)/ *n* Leiter *f*; (*in
fabric*) Laufmasche *f*

laden /'leıdn/ *a* beladen

ladle /'leıdl/ *n* [Schöpf]kelle *f* • *vt*
schöpfen

lady /'leıdı/ *n* Dame *f*; (*title*) Lady *f*

lady: ~**bird** *n*, (*Amer*) ~**bug** *n*
Marienkäfer *m*. ~**like** *a* damenhaft

lag¹ /læg/ *vi* (*pt/pp* **lagged**) ~ **behind**
zurückbleiben; (*fig*) nachhinken

lag² *vt* (*pt/pp* **lagged**) umwickeln
⟨*pipes*⟩

lager /'lɑːgə(r)/ *n* Lagerbier *nt*

lagoon /lə'guːn/ *n* Lagune *f*

laid /leıd/ *see* **lay**³

lain /leın/ *see* **lie**²

lair /leə(r)/ *n* Lager *nt*

laity /'leıətı/ *n* Laienstand *m*

lake /leık/ *n* See *m*

lamb /læm/ *n* Lamm *nt*

lame /leım/ *a* (**-r, -st**) lahm

lament /lə'ment/ *n* Klage *f*; (*song*)
Klagelied *nt* • *vt* beklagen • *vi*
klagen. ~**able** /'læməntəbl/ *a* be-
klagenswert

laminated /'læmıneıtıd/ *a* laminiert

lamp /læmp/ *n* Lampe *f*; (*in street*)
Laterne *f*. ~**post** *n* Laternenpfahl *m*.
~**shade** *n* Lampenschirm *m*

lance /lɑːns/ *n* Lanze *f* • *vt* (*Med*)
aufschneiden. ~-'**corporal** *n* Ge-
freite(r) *m*

land /lænd/ *n* Land *nt*; **plot of** ~
Grundstück *nt* • *vt/i* landen; ~ **s.o.
with sth** (*fam*) jdm etw aufhalsen

landing /'lændıŋ/ *n* Landung *f*; (*top
of stairs*) Treppenflur *m*. ~-**stage** *n*
Landesteg *m*

land: ~**lady** *n* Wirtin *f*. ~-**locked** *a*
~-**locked country** Binnenstaat *m*.
~**lord** *n* Wirt *m*; (*of land*) Grundbesitzer *m*; (*of building*) Haus-
besitzer *m*. ~**mark** *n* Erkennungs-
zeichen *nt*; (*fig*) Meilenstein
m. ~**owner** *n* Grundbesitzer *m*.
~**scape** /-skeıp/ *n* Landschaft *f*.
~**slide** *n* Erdrutsch *m*

lane /leın/ *n* kleine Landstraße *f*;
(*Auto*) Spur *f*; (*Sport*) Bahn *f*; '**get in**
~' (*Auto*) 'bitte einordnen'

language /'læŋgwıdʒ/ *n* Sprache *f*;
(*speech, style*) Ausdrucksweise *f*. ~
laboratory *n* Sprachlabor *nt*

languid /'læŋgwıd/ *a*, **-ly** *adv* träge

languish /'læŋgwıʃ/ *vi* schmachten

lank /læŋk/ *a* ⟨*hair*⟩ strähnig

lanky /'læŋkı/ *a* (**-ier, -iest**) schlaksig

lantern /'læntən/ *n* Laterne *f*

lap¹ /læp/ *n* Schoß *m*

lap² *n* (*Sport*) Runde *f*; (*of journey*)
Etappe *f* • *vi* (*pt/pp* **lapped**) plätschern (**against** gegen)

lap³ *vt* (*pt/pp* **lapped**) ~ **up** auf-
schlecken

lapel /lə'pel/ *n* Revers *nt*

lapse /læps/ *n* Fehler *m*; (*moral*)
Fehltritt *m*; (*of time*) Zeitspanne *f*
• *vi* (*expire*) erlöschen; ~ **into** verfallen in (+ *acc*)

larceny /'lɑːsənı/ *n* Diebstahl *m*

lard /lɑːd/ *n* [Schweine]schmalz *nt*

larder /'lɑːdə(r)/ *n* Speisekammer *f*

large /lɑːdʒ/ *a* (**-r, -st**) & *adv* groß; **by
and** ~ im großen und ganzen; **at** ~
auf freiem Fuß; (*in general*) im
allgemeinen. ~**ly** *adv* großenteils

lark¹ /lɑːk/ *n* ⟨*bird*⟩ Lerche *f*

lark² *n* (*joke*) Jux *m* • *vi* ~ **about** herumalbern

larva /'lɑːvə/ *n* (*pl* -**vae** /-viː/) Larve *f*

laryngitis /lærın'dʒaıtıs/ *n* Kehl-
kopfentzündung *f*

larynx /'lærıŋks/ *n* Kehlkopf *m*

lascivious /lə'sıvıəs/ *a* lüstern

laser /'leızə(r)/ *n* Laser *m*

lash /læʃ/ *n* Peitschenhieb *m*; (*eye-
lash*) Wimper *f* • *vt* peitschen; (*tie*)
festbinden (**to** an + *acc*). ~ **out** *vi* um
sich schlagen; (*spend*) viel Geld ausgeben (**on** für)

lashings /'læʃıŋz/ *npl* ~ **of** (*fam*) eine
Riesenmenge von

lass /læs/ *n* Mädchen *nt*

lasso /lə'suː/ *n* Lasso *nt*

last¹ /lɑːst/ *n* (*for shoe*) Leisten *m*

last² *a* & *n* letzte(r,s); ~ **night** heute *od*
gestern nacht; (*evening*) gestern abend;
at ~ endlich; **the** ~ **time** das letztemal;
for the ~ **time** zum letztenmal; **the** ~
but one der/die/das vorletzte; **that's
the** ~ **straw** (*fam*) das schlägt dem Faß
den Boden aus • *adv* zuletzt; (*last time*)
das letztemal; **do sth** ~ etw zuletzt *od*
als letztes machen; **he/she went** ~ er/
sie ging als letzter/letzte • *vi* dauern;

⟨*weather:*⟩ sich halten; ⟨*relationship:*⟩ halten. ∼**ing** *a* dauerhaft. ∼**ly** *adv* schließlich, zum Schluß

latch /lætʃ/ *n* [einfache] Klinke *f*; **on the** ∼ nicht verschlossen

late /leɪt/ *a & adv* (**-r, -st**) spät; ⟨*delayed*⟩ verspätet; ⟨*deceased*⟩ verstorben; **the** ∼**st news** die neuesten Nachrichten; **stay up** ∼ bis spät aufbleiben; **of** ∼ in letzter Zeit; **arrive** ∼ zu spät ankommen; **I am** ∼ ich komme zu spät *od* habe mich verspätet; **the train is** ∼ der Zug hat Verspätung. ∼**comer** *n* Zuspätkommende(r) *m/f*. ∼**ly** *adv* in letzter Zeit. ∼**ness** *n* Zuspätkommen *nt*; ⟨*delay*⟩ Verspätung *f*

latent /'leɪtnt/ *a* latent

later /'leɪtə(r)/ *a & adv* später; ∼ **on** nachher

lateral /'lætərəl/ *a* seitlich

lathe /leɪð/ *n* Drehbank *f*

lather /'lɑːðə(r)/ *n* [Seifen]schaum *m* ● *vt* einseifen ● *vi* schäumen

Latin /'lætɪn/ *a* lateinisch ● *n* Latein *nt*. ∼ **A'merica** *n* Lateinamerika *nt*

latitude /'lætɪtjuːd/ *n* ⟨*Geog*⟩ Breite *f*; ⟨*fig*⟩ Freiheit *f*

latter /'lætə(r)/ *a & n* **the** ∼ der/die/ das letztere. ∼**ly** *adv* in letzter Zeit

lattice /'lætɪs/ *n* Gitter *nt*

Latvia /'lætvɪə/ *n* Lettland *nt*

laudable /'lɔːdəbl/ *a* lobenswert

laugh /lɑːf/ *n* Lachen *nt*; **with a** ∼ lachend ● *vi* lachen (**at/about** über + *acc*); ∼ **at s.o.** ⟨*mock*⟩ jdn auslachen. ∼**able** /-əbl/ *a* lachhaft, lächerlich. ∼**ing-stock** *n* Gegenstand *m* des Spottes

laughter /'lɑːftə(r)/ *n* Gelächter *nt*

launch¹ /lɔːntʃ/ *n* ⟨*boat*⟩ Barkasse *f*

launch² *n* Stapellauf *m*; ⟨*of rocket*⟩ Abschuß *m*; ⟨*of product*⟩ Lancierung *f* ● *vt* vom Stapel lassen ⟨*ship*⟩; zu Wasser lassen ⟨*lifeboat*⟩; abschießen ⟨*rocket*⟩; starten ⟨*attack*⟩; ⟨*Comm*⟩ lancieren ⟨*product*⟩

launder /'lɔːndə(r)/ *vt* waschen. ∼**ette** /-'dret/ *n* Münzwäscherei *f*

laundry /'lɔːndrɪ/ *n* Wäscherei *f*; ⟨*clothes*⟩ Wäsche *f*

laurel /'lɒrl/ *n* Lorbeer *m*

lava /'lɑːvə/ *n* Lava *f*

lavatory /'lævətrɪ/ *n* Toilette *f*

lavender /'lævəndə(r)/ *n* Lavendel *m*

lavish /'lævɪʃ/ *a*, **-ly** *adv* großzügig; ⟨*wasteful*⟩ verschwenderisch; **on a** ∼

scale mit viel Aufwand ● *vt* ∼ **sth on s.o.** jdn mit etw überschütten

law /lɔː/ *n* Gesetz *nt*; ⟨*system*⟩ Recht *nt*; **study** ∼ Jura studieren; ∼ **and order** Recht und Ordnung

law: ∼**-abiding** *a* gesetzestreu. ∼**court** *n* Gerichtshof *m*. ∼**ful** *a* rechtmäßig. ∼**less** *a* gesetzlos

lawn /lɔːn/ *n* Rasen *m*. ∼**-mower** *n* Rasenmäher *m*

'law suit *n* Prozeß *m*

lawyer /'lɔːjə(r)/ *n* Rechtsanwalt *m*/ -anwältin *f*

lax /læks/ *a* lax, locker

laxative /'læksətɪv/ *n* Abführmittel *nt*

laxity /'læksətɪ/ *n* Laxheit *f*

lay¹ /leɪ/ *a* Laien-

lay² *see* **lie**²

lay³ *vt* ⟨*pt/pp* **laid**⟩ legen; decken ⟨*table*⟩; ∼ **a trap** eine Falle stellen. ∼ **down** *vt* hinlegen; festlegen ⟨*rules, conditions*⟩. ∼ **off** *vt* entlassen ⟨*workers*⟩ ● *vi* ⟨*fam: stop*⟩ aufhören. ∼ **out** *vt* hinlegen; aufbahren ⟨*corpse*⟩; anlegen ⟨*garden*⟩; ⟨*Typ*⟩ gestalten

lay: ∼**about** *n* Faulenzer *m*. ∼**-by** *n* Parkbucht *f*; ⟨*on motorway*⟩ Rastplatz *m*

layer /'leɪə(r)/ *n* Schicht *f*

layette /leɪ'et/ *n* Babyausstattung *f*

lay: ∼**man** *n* Laie *m*. ∼**out** *n* Anordnung *f*; ⟨*design*⟩ Gestaltung *f*; ⟨*Typ*⟩ Layout *nt*. ∼ **'preacher** *n* Laienprediger *m*

laze /leɪz/ *vi* ∼ **[about]** faulenzen

laziness /'leɪzɪnɪs/ *n* Faulheit *f*

lazy /'leɪzɪ/ *a* (**-ier, -iest**) faul. ∼**-bones** *n* Faulenzer *m*

lb /paʊnd/ *abbr* (**pound**) Pfd.

lead¹ /led/ *n* Blei *nt*; ⟨*of pencil*⟩ [Blei]stift]mine *f*

lead² /liːd/ *n* Führung *f*; ⟨*leash*⟩ Leine *f*; ⟨*flex*⟩ Schnur *f*; ⟨*clue*⟩ Hinweis *m*, Spur *f*; ⟨*Theat*⟩ Hauptrolle *f*; ⟨*distance ahead*⟩ Vorsprung *m*; **be in the** ∼ in Führung liegen ● *vt/i* ⟨*pt/pp* **led**⟩ führen; leiten ⟨*team*⟩; ⟨*induce*⟩ bringen; ⟨*at cards*⟩ ausspielen; ∼ **the way** vorangehen; ∼ **up to sth** ⟨*fig*⟩ etw ⟨*dat*⟩ vorangehen. ∼ **away** *vt* wegführen

leaded /'ledɪd/ *a* verbleit

leader /'liːdə(r)/ *n* Führer *m*; ⟨*of expedition, group*⟩ Leiter(in) *m(f)*; ⟨*of orchestra*⟩ Konzertmeister *m*; ⟨*in newspaper*⟩ Leitartikel *m*. ∼**ship** *n* Führung *f*; Leitung *f*

leading /'li:dɪŋ/ a führend; ~ **lady** Hauptdarstellerin f; ~ **question** Suggestivfrage f

leaf /li:f/ n (pl **leaves**) Blatt nt; (of table) Ausziehplatte f ● vi ~ **through** sth etw durchblättern. ~**let** n Merkblatt nt; (advertising) Reklameblatt nt; (political) Flugblatt nt

league /li:g/ n Liga f; **be in** ~ **with** unter einer Decke stecken mit

leak /li:k/ n (hole) undichte Stelle f; (Naut) Leck nt; (of gas) Gasausfluß m ● vi undicht sein; ⟨ship:⟩ leck sein, lecken; ⟨liquid:⟩ auslaufen; ⟨gas:⟩ ausströmen ● vt auslaufen lassen; ~ **sth to s.o.** (fig) jdm etw zuspielen. ~**y** a undicht; (Naut) leck

lean[1] /li:n/ a (-**er**, -**est**) mager

lean[2] v (pt/pp **leaned** or **leant** /lent/) ● vt lehnen (**against**/**on** an + acc) ● vi ⟨person:⟩ sich lehnen (**against**/**on** an + acc); (not be straight) sich neigen; **be** ~**ing against** lehnen an (+ dat); ~ **on s.o.** (depend) bei jdm festen Halt finden. ~ **back** vi sich zurücklehnen. ~ **forward** vi sich vorbeugen. ~ **out** vi sich hinauslehnen. ~ **over** vi sich vorbeugen

leaning /'li:nɪŋ/ a schief ● n Neigung f

leap /li:p/ n Sprung m ● vi (pt/pp **leapt** /lept/ or **leaped**) springen; **he leapt at it** (fam) er griff sofort zu. ~**-frog** n Bockspringen nt. ~ **year** n Schaltjahr nt

learn /lɜːn/ vt/i (pt/pp **learnt** or **learned**) lernen; (hear) erfahren; ~ **to swim** schwimmen lernen

learn|ed /'lɜːnɪd/ a gelehrt. ~**er** n Anfänger m; ~**er [driver]** Fahrschüler(in) m(f). ~**ing** n Gelehrsamkeit f

lease /li:s/ n Pacht f; (contract) Mietvertrag m; (Comm) Pachtvertrag m ● vt pachten; ~ **[out]** verpachten

leash /li:ʃ/ n Leine f

least /li:st/ a geringste(r,s); **have** ~ **time** am wenigsten Zeit haben ● n **the** ~ das wenigste; **at** ~ wenigstens, mindestens; **not in the** ~ nicht im geringsten ● adv am wenigsten

leather /'leðə(r)/ n Leder nt. ~**y** a ledern; (tough) zäh

leave /li:v/ n Erlaubnis f; (holiday) Urlaub m; **on** ~ auf Urlaub; **take one's** ~ sich verabschieden ● v (pt/pp **left**) ● vt lassen; (go out of, abandon) verlassen; (forget) liegenlassen; (bequeath) vermachen (**to** dat); ~ **it to me!**

überlassen Sie es mir! **there is nothing left** es ist nichts mehr übrig ● vi [weg]gehen/fahren; ⟨train, bus:⟩ abfahren. ~ **behind** vt zurücklassen; (forget) liegenlassen. ~ **out** vt liegenlassen; (leave outside) draußen lassen; (omit) auslassen

leaves /li:vz/ see **leaf**

Lebanon /'lebənən/ n Libanon m

lecherous /'letʃərəs/ a lüstern

lectern /'lektɜːn/ n [Lese]pult nt

lecture /'lektʃə(r)/ n Vortrag m; (Univ) Vorlesung f; (reproof) Strafpredigt f ● vi einen Vortrag/eine Vorlesung halten (**on** über + acc) ● vt ~ **s.o.** jdm eine Strafpredigt halten. ~**r** n Vortragende(r) m/f; (Univ) Dozent(in) m(f)

led /led/ see **lead**[2]

ledge /ledʒ/ n Leiste f; (shelf, of window) Sims m; (in rock) Vorsprung m

ledger /'ledʒə(r)/ n Hauptbuch nt

lee /li:/ n (Naut) Lee f

leech /li:tʃ/ n Blutegel m

leek /li:k/ n Stange f Porree; ~**s** pl Porree m

leer /lɪə(r)/ n anzügliches Grinsen nt ● vi anzüglich grinsen

lee|ward /'li:wəd/ adv nach Lee. ~**way** n (fig) Spielraum m

left[1] /left/ see **leave**

left[2] a linke(r,s) ● adv links; ⟨go⟩ nach links ● n linke Seite f; **on the** ~ links; **from/to the** ~ von/nach links; **the** ~ (Pol) die Linke

left: ~**-'handed** a linkshändig. ~**-'luggage [office]** n Gepäckaufbewahrung f. ~**overs** npl Reste pl. ~**-'wing** a (Pol) linke(r,s)

leg /leg/ n Bein nt; (Culin) Keule f; (of journey) Etappe f

legacy /'legəsɪ/ n Vermächtnis nt, Erbschaft f

legal /'li:gl/ a, -**ly** adv gesetzlich; ⟨matters⟩ rechtlich; ⟨documents, position⟩ Rechts-; **be** ~ [gesetzlich] erlaubt sein; **take** ~ **action** gerichtlich vorgehen

legality /lɪ'gælətɪ/ n Legalität f

legalize /'li:gəlaɪz/ vt legalisieren

legend /'ledʒənd/ n Legende f. ~**ary** a legendär

legible /'ledʒəbl/ a, -**bly** adv leserlich

legion /'li:dʒn/ n Legion f

legislat|e /'ledʒɪsleɪt/ vi Gesetze erlassen. ~**ion** /-'leɪʃn/ n Gesetzgebung f; (laws) Gesetze pl

legislat|ive /'ledʒɪslətɪv/ a gesetzgebend. ~**ure** /-leɪtʃə(r)/ n Legislative f

legitimate /lɪ'dʒɪtɪmət/ a rechtmäßig; (*justifiable*) berechtigt; ⟨*child*⟩ ehelich

leisure /'leʒə(r)/ n Freizeit f; **at your ~** wenn Sie Zeit haben. **~ly** a gemächlich

lemon /'lemən/ n Zitrone f. **~ade** /-'neɪd/ n Zitronenlimonade f

lend /lend/ vt (*pt/pp* **lent**) leihen; **~ s.o. sth** jdm etw leihen; **~ a hand** (*fam*) helfen. **~ing library** n Leihbücherei f

length /leŋθ/ n Länge f; (*piece*) Stück nt; (*of wallpaper*) Bahn f; (*of time*) Dauer f; **at ~** ausführlich; (*at last*) endlich

length|en /'leŋθən/ vt länger machen ● vi länger werden. **~ways** adv der Länge nach, längs

lengthy /'leŋθɪ/ a (-**ier, -iest**) langwierig

lenien|ce /'liːnɪəns/ n Nachsicht f. **~t** a, **-ly** adv nachsichtig

lens /lenz/ n Linse f; (*Phot*) Objektiv nt; (*of spectacles*) Glas nt

lent /lent/ *see* **lend**

Lent n Fastenzeit f

lentil /'lentl/ n (*Bot*) Linse f

Leo /'liːəʊ/ n (*Astr*) Löwe m

leopard /'lepəd/ n Leopard m

leotard /'liːətɑːd/ n Trikot nt

leper /'lepə(r)/ n Leprakranke(r) m/f; n (*Bible & fig*) Aussätzige(r) m/f

leprosy /'leprəsɪ/ n Lepra f

lesbian /'lezbɪən/ a lesbisch ● n Lesbierin f

lesion /'liːʒn/ n Verletzung f

less /les/ a, adv, n & prep weniger; **~ and ~** immer weniger; **not any the ~** um nichts weniger

lessen /'lesn/ vt verringern ● vi nachlassen; ⟨*value:*⟩ abnehmen

lesser /'lesə(r)/ a geringere(r,s)

lesson /'lesn/ n Stunde f; (*in textbook*) Lektion f; (*Relig*) Lesung f; **teach s.o. a ~** (*fig*) jdm eine Lehre erteilen

lest /lest/ conj (*liter*) damit... nicht

let /let/ vt (*pt/pp* **let**, *pres p* **letting**) lassen; (*rent*) vermieten; **'to ~'** zu vermieten'; **~ us go** gehen wir; **~ me know** Sie mir Bescheid; **~ him do it** laß ihn das machen; **just ~ him!** soll er doch! ● **~ s.o. sleep/win** jdn schlafen/gewinnen lassen; **~ oneself**

in for sth (*fam*) sich (*dat*) etw einbrocken. **~ down** vt hinunter-/herunterlassen; (*lengthen*) länger machen; **~ s.o. down** (*fam*) jdn im Stich lassen; (*disappoint*) jdn enttäuschen. **~ in** vt hereinlassen. **~ off** vt abfeuern ⟨*gun*⟩; hochgehen lassen ⟨*firework, bomb*⟩; (*emit*) ausstoßen; (*excuse from*) befreien von; (*not punish*) frei ausgehen lassen. **~ out** vt hinaus-/herauslassen; (*make larger*) auslassen. **~ through** vt durchlassen. **~ up** vi (*fam*) nachlassen

'let-down n Enttäuschung f, (*fam*) Reinfall m

lethal /'liːθl/ a tödlich

letharg|ic /lɪ'θɑːdʒɪk/ a lethargisch. **~y** /'leθədʒɪ/ n Lethargie f

letter /'letə(r)/ n Brief m; (*of alphabet*) Buchstabe m; **by ~** brieflich. **~-box** n Briefkasten m. **~-head** n Briefkopf m. **~ing** n Beschriftung f

lettuce /'letɪs/ n [Kopf]salat m

'let-up n (*fam*) Nachlassen nt

leukaemia /luː'kiːmɪə/ n Leukämie f

level /'levl/ a eben; (*horizontal*) waagerecht; (*in height*) auf gleicher Höhe; ⟨*spoonful*⟩ gestrichen; **draw ~ with** gleichziehen mit; **one's ~ best** sein möglichstes ● n Höhe f; (*fig*) Ebene f, Niveau nt; (*stage*) Stufe f; **on the ~** (*fam*) ehrlich ● vt (*pt/pp* **levelled**) einebnen; (*aim*) richten (**at** auf + *acc*)

level: ~ 'crossing n Bahnübergang m. **~-'headed** a vernünftig

lever /'liːvə(r)/ n Hebel m ● vt **~ up** mit einem Hebel anheben. **~age** /-rɪdʒ/ n Hebelkraft f

levity /'levətɪ/ n Heiterkeit f; (*frivolity*) Leichtfertigkeit f

levy /'levɪ/ vt (*pt/pp* **levied**) erheben ⟨*tax*⟩

lewd /ljuːd/ a (-**er, -est**) anstößig

liabilit|y /laɪə'bɪlətɪ/ n Haftung f; **~ies** pl Verbindlichkeiten pl

liable /'laɪəbl/ a haftbar; **be ~ to do sth** etw leicht tun können

liaise /lɪ'eɪz/ vi (*fam*) Verbindungsperson sein

liaison /lɪ'eɪzɒn/ n Verbindung f; (*affair*) Verhältnis nt

liar /'laɪə(r)/ n Lügner(in) m(f)

libel /'laɪbl/ n Verleumdung f ● vt (*pt/pp* **libelled**) verleumden. **~lous** a verleumderisch

liberal /'lɪbərl/ a, **-ly** adv tolerant; (*generous*) großzügig. **L~** a (*Pol*) liberal ● n Liberale(r) m/f

liberat|e /'lɪbəreɪt/ vt befreien. ~**ed** a ⟨woman⟩ emanzipiert. ~**ion** /-'reɪʃn/ n Befreiung f. ~**or** n Befreier m

liberty /'lɪbətɪ/ n Freiheit f; **take the** ~ **of doing sth** sich (dat) erlauben, etw zu tun; **take liberties** sich (dat) Freiheiten erlauben

Libra /'li:brə/ n (Astr) Waage f

librarian /laɪ'breərɪən/ n Bibliothekar(in) m(f)

library /'laɪbrərɪ/ n Bibliothek f

Libya /'lɪbɪə/ n Libyen nt

lice /laɪs/ see **louse**

licence /'laɪsns/ n Genehmigung f; (Comm) Lizenz f; (for TV) ≈ Fernsehgebühr f; (for driving) Führerschein m; (for alcohol) Schankkonzession f; (freedom) Freiheit f

license /'laɪsns/ vt eine Genehmigung/(Comm) Lizenz erteilen (+ dat); **be** ~**d** ⟨car:⟩ zugelassen sein; ⟨restaurant:⟩ Schankkonzession haben. ~**-plate** n Nummernschild nt

licentious /laɪ'senʃəs/ a lasterhaft

lichen /'laɪkən/ n (Bot) Flechte f

lick /lɪk/ n Lecken nt; **a** ~ **of paint** ein bißchen Farbe ● vt lecken; (fam: defeat) schlagen

lid /lɪd/ n Deckel m; (of eye) Lid nt

lie[1] /laɪ/ n Lüge f; **tell a** ~ lügen ● vi (pt/pp **lied**, pres p **lying**) lügen; ~ **to** belügen

lie[2] vi (pt **lay**, pp **lain**, pres p **lying**) liegen; **here** ~**s** ... hier ruht ... ~ **down** vi sich hinlegen

Liège /lɪ'eɪʒ/ n Lüttich nt

'lie-in n **have a** ~ [sich] ausschlafen

lieu /lju:/ n **in** ~ **of** statt (+ gen)

lieutenant /lef'tenənt/ n Oberleutnant m

life /laɪf/ n (pl **lives**) Leben nt; (biography) Biographie f; **lose one's** ~ ums Leben kommen

life: ~**belt** n Rettungsring m. ~**boat** n Rettungsboot m. ~**buoy** n Rettungsring m. ~**-guard** n Lebensretter m. ~**-jacket** n Schwimmweste f. ~**less** a leblos. ~**like** a naturgetreu. ~**line** n Rettungsleine f. ~**long** a lebenslang. ~ **preserver** n (Amer) Rettungsring m. ~**-size(d)** a ... in Lebensgröße. ~**time** n Leben nt; **in s.o.'s** ~**time** zu jds Lebzeiten; **the chance of a** ~**time** eine einmalige Gelegenheit

lift /lɪft/ n Aufzug m, Lift m; **give s.o. a** ~ jdn mitnehmen; **get a** ~ mitgenommen werden ● vt heben; aufheben ⟨restrictions⟩ ● vi ⟨fog:⟩ sich lichten. ~ **up** vt hochheben

'lift-off n Abheben nt

ligament /'lɪgəmənt/ n (Anat) Band nt

light[1] /laɪt/ a (-er, -est) (not dark) hell; ~ **blue** hellblau ● n Licht nt; (lamp) Lampe f; **in the** ~ **of** (fig) angesichts (+ gen); **have you [got] a** ~? haben Sie Feuer? ● vt (pt/pp **lit** or **lighted**) anzünden ⟨fire, cigarette⟩; anmachen ⟨lamp⟩; (illuminate) beleuchten. ~ **up** vi ⟨face:⟩ sich erhellen

light[2] a (-er, -est) (not heavy) leicht; ~ **sentence** milde Strafe f ● adv **travel** ~ mit wenig Gepäck reisen

'light-bulb n Glühbirne f

lighten[1] /'laɪtn/ vt heller machen ● vi heller werden

lighten[2] vt leichter machen ⟨load⟩

lighter /'laɪtə(r)/ n Feuerzeug nt

light: ~**-'headed** a benommen. ~**-'hearted** a unbekümmert. ~**house** n Leuchtturm m. ~**ing** n Beleuchtung f. ~**ly** adv leicht; (casually) leichthin; **get off** ~**ly** glimpflich davonkommen

lightning /'laɪtnɪŋ/ n Blitz m. ~**-conductor** n Blitzableiter m

'lightweight a leicht ● n (Boxing) Leichtgewicht nt

like[1] /laɪk/ a ähnlich; (same) gleich ● prep wie; (similar to) ähnlich (+ dat); ~ **this** so; **a man** ~ **that** so ein Mann; **what's he** ~? wie ist er denn? ● conj (fam: as) wie; (Amer: as if) als ob

like[2] vt mögen; **I should/would** ~ ich möchte; **I** ~ **the car** das Auto gefällt mir; **I** ~ **chocolate** ich esse gern Schokolade; ~ **dancing/singing** gern tanzen/singen; **I** ~ **that!** das ist ja doch die Höhe! ● n ~**s and dislikes** pl Vorlieben und Abneigungen pl

like|able /'laɪkəbl/ a sympathisch. ~**lihood** /-lɪhʊd/ n Wahrscheinlichkeit f. ~**ly** a (-ier, -iest) & adv wahrscheinlich; **not** ~**ly!** (fam) auf gar keinen Fall!

'like-minded a gleichgesinnt

liken /'laɪkən/ vt vergleichen (**to** mit)

like|ness /'laɪknɪs/ n Ähnlichkeit f. ~**wise** adv ebenso

liking /'laɪkɪŋ/ n Vorliebe f; **is it to your** ~? gefällt es Ihnen?

lilac /'laɪlək/ n Flieder m ● a fliederfarben

lily /'lɪlɪ/ n Lilie f. ~ **of the valley** n Maiglöckchen nt

limb /lɪm/ n Glied nt

limber /'lɪmbə(r)/ vi ~ **up** Lockerungsübungen machen

lime[1] /laɪm/ n (fruit) Limone f; (tree) Linde f

lime[2] n Kalk m. ~**light** n **be in the** ~**light** im Rampenlicht stehen. ~**stone** n Kalkstein m

limit /'lɪmɪt/ n Grenze f; (limitation) Beschränkung f; **that's the** ~! (fam) das ist doch die Höhe! ● vt beschränken (**to** auf + acc). ~**ation** /-ɪ'teɪʃn/ n Beschränkung f. ~**ed** a beschränkt; ~**ed company** Gesellschaft f mit beschränkter Haftung

limousine /'lɪməzi:n/ n Limousine f

limp[1] /lɪmp/ n Hinken nt; **have a** ~ hinken ● vi hinken

limp[2] a (-er, -est), -**ly** adv schlaff

limpet /'lɪmpɪt/ n **like a** ~ (fig) wie eine Klette

limpid /'lɪmpɪd/ a klar

linctus /'lɪŋktəs/ n **[cough]** ~ Hustensirup m

line[1] /laɪn/ n Linie f; (length of rope, cord) Leine f; (Teleph) Leitung f; (of writing) Zeile f; (row) Reihe f; (wrinkle) Falte f; (of business) Branche f; (Amer: queue) Schlange f; **in** ~ **with** gemäß (+ dat) ● vt säumen ⟨street⟩. ~ **up** vi sich aufstellen ● vt aufstellen

line[2] vt füttern ⟨garment⟩; (Techn) auskleiden

lineage /'lɪnɪɪdʒ/ n Herkunft f

linear /'lɪnɪə(r)/ a linear

lined[1] /laɪnd/ a (wrinkled) faltig; ⟨paper⟩ liniert

lined[2] a ⟨garment⟩ gefüttert

linen /'lɪnɪn/ n Leinen nt; (articles) Wäsche f

liner /'laɪnə(r)/ n Passagierschiff nt

linesman n (Sport) Linienrichter m

linger /'lɪŋgə(r)/ vi [zurück]bleiben

lingerie /'læʒərɪ/ n Damenunterwäsche f

linguist /'lɪŋgwɪst/ n Sprachkundige(r) m/f

linguistic /lɪŋ'gwɪstɪk/ a, -**ally** adv sprachlich. ~**s** n Linguistik f

lining /'laɪnɪŋ/ n (of garment) Futter nt; (Techn) Auskleidung f

link /lɪŋk/ n (of chain) Glied nt; (fig) Verbindung f ● vt verbinden; ~ **arms** sich unterhaken

links /lɪŋks/ n or npl Golfplatz m

lino /'laɪnəʊ/, **linoleum** /lɪ'nəʊlɪəm/ n Linoleum nt

lint /lɪnt/ n Verbandstoff m

lion /'laɪən/ n Löwe m; ~**'s share** (fig) Löwenanteil m. ~**ess** n Löwin f

lip /lɪp/ n Lippe f; (edge) Rand m; (of jug) Schnabel m

lip: ~-**reading** n Lippenlesen nt. ~-**service** n **pay** ~-**service** ein Lippenbekenntnis ablegen (**to** zu). ~**stick** n Lippenstift m

liquefy /'lɪkwɪfaɪ/ vt (pt/pp -**ied**) verflüssigen ● vi sich verflüssigen

liqueur /lɪ'kjʊə(r)/ n Likör m

liquid /'lɪkwɪd/ n Flüssigkeit f ● a flüssig

liquidat|e /'lɪkwɪdeɪt/ vt liquidieren. ~**ion** /-'deɪʃn/ n Liquidation f

liquidize /'lɪkwɪdaɪz/ vt [im Mixer] pürieren. ~**r** n (Culin) Mixer m

liquor /'lɪkə(r)/ n Alkohol m; (juice) Flüssigkeit f

liquorice /'lɪkərɪs/ n Lakritze f

'liquor store n (Amer) Spirituosengeschäft nt

lisp /lɪsp/ n Lispeln nt ● vt/i lispeln

list[1] /lɪst/ n Liste f ● vt aufführen

list[2] vi ⟨ship:⟩ Schlagseite haben

listen /'lɪsn/ vi zuhören (**to** dat); ~ **to the radio** Radio hören. ~**er** n Zuhörer(in) m(f); (Radio) Hörer(in) m(f)

listless /'lɪstlɪs/ a, -**ly** adv lustlos

lit /lɪt/ see **light**[1]

litany /'lɪtənɪ/ n Litanei f

literacy /'lɪtərəsɪ/ n Lese- und Schreibfertigkeit f

literal /'lɪtərl/ a wörtlich. ~**ly** adv buchstäblich

literary /'lɪtərərɪ/ a literarisch

literate /'lɪtərət/ a **be** ~ lesen und schreiben können

literature /'lɪtrətʃə(r)/ n Literatur f; (fam) Informationsmaterial nt

lithe /laɪð/ a geschmeidig

Lithuania /lɪθjʊ'eɪnɪə/ n Litauen nt

litigation /lɪtɪ'geɪʃn/ n Rechtsstreit m

litre /'li:tə(r)/ n Liter m & nt

litter /'lɪtə(r)/ n Abfall m; (Zool) Wurf m ● vt **be** ~**ed with** übersät sein mit. ~-**bin** n Abfalleimer m

little /'lɪtl/ a klein; (not much) wenig ● adv & n wenig; **a** ~ ein bißchen/wenig; ~ **by** ~ nach und nach

liturgy /'lɪtədʒɪ/ n Liturgie f

live[1] /laɪv/ a lebendig; ⟨ammunition⟩ scharf; ~ **broadcast** Live-Sendung f; **be** ~ (Electr) unter Strom stehen ● adv (Radio, TV) live

live[2] /lɪv/ vi leben; (reside) wohnen; ~ **up to** gerecht werden (+ dat). ~ **on** vt leben von; (eat) sich ernähren von ● vi weiterleben

liveli|hood /'laɪvlɪhʊd/ n Lebensunterhalt m. ~**ness** n Lebendigkeit f

lively /'laɪvlɪ/ a (-ier, -iest) lebhaft, lebendig

liven /'laɪvn/ v ~ **up** vt beleben ● vi lebhaft werden

liver /'lɪvə(r)/ n Leber f

lives /laɪvz/ see **life**

livestock /'laɪv-/ n Vieh nt

livid /'lɪvɪd/ a (fam) wütend

living /'lɪvɪŋ/ a lebend ● n **earn one's** ~ seinen Lebensunterhalt verdienen; **the** ~ pl die Lebenden. ~**-room** n Wohnzimmer nt

lizard /'lɪzəd/ n Eidechse f

load /ləʊd/ n Last f; (quantity) Ladung f; (Electr) Belastung f; ~**s of** (fam) jede Menge ● vt laden ⟨goods, gun⟩; beladen ⟨vehicle⟩; ~ **a camera** einen Film in eine Kamera einlegen. ~**ed** a beladen; (fam: rich) steinreich; ~**ed question** Fangfrage f

loaf[1] /ləʊf/ n (pl **loaves**) Brot nt

loaf[2] vi faulenzen

loan /ləʊn/ n Leihgabe f; (money) Darlehen nt; **on** ~ geliehen ● vt leihen (**to** dat)

loath /ləʊθ/ a **be** ~ **to do sth** etw ungern tun

loath|e /ləʊð/ vt verabscheuen. ~**ing** n Abscheu m. ~**some** a abscheulich

loaves /ləʊvz/ see **loaf**[1]

lobby /'lɒbɪ/ n Foyer nt; (anteroom) Vorraum m; (Pol) Lobby f

lobe /ləʊb/ n (of ear) Ohrläppchen nt

lobster /'lɒbstə(r)/ n Hummer m

local /'ləʊkl/ a hiesig; ⟨time, traffic⟩ Orts-; **under** ~ **anaesthetic** unter örtlicher Betäubung; **I'm not** ~ ich bin nicht von hier ● n Hiesige(r) m/f; (fam: public house) Stammkneipe f. ~ **au'thority** n Kommunalbehörde f. ~ **call** n (Teleph) Ortsgespräch nt

locality /ləʊ'kælətɪ/ n Gegend f

localized /'ləʊkəlaɪzd/ a lokalisiert

locally /'ləʊkəlɪ/ adv am Ort

locat|e /ləʊ'keɪt/ vt ausfindig machen; **be** ~**ed** sich befinden. ~**ion** /-'keɪʃn/ n Lage f; **filmed on** ~**ion** als Außenaufnahme gedreht

lock[1] /lɒk/ n (hair) Strähne f

lock[2] n (on door) Schloß nt; (on canal) Schleuse f ● vt abschließen ● vi sich abschließen lassen. ~ **in** vt einschließen. ~ **out** vt ausschließen. ~ **up** vt abschließen; einsperren ⟨person⟩ ● vi zuschließen

locker /'lɒkə(r)/ n Schließfach nt; (Mil) Spind m; (in hospital) kleiner Schrank m

locket /'lɒkɪt/ n Medaillon nt

lock: ~**-out** n Aussperrung f. ~**smith** n Schlosser m

locomotion /ləʊkə'məʊʃn/ n Fortbewegung f

locomotive /ləʊkə'məʊtɪv/ n Lokomotive f

locum /'ləʊkəm/ n Vertreter(in) m(f)

locust /'ləʊkəst/ n Heuschrecke f

lodge /lɒdʒ/ n (porter's) Pförtnerhaus nt; (masonic) Loge f ● vt (submit) einreichen; (deposit) deponieren ● vi zur Untermiete wohnen (**with** bei); (become fixed) steckenbleiben. ~**r** n Untermieter(in) m(f)

lodging /'lɒdʒɪŋ/ n Unterkunft f; ~**s** npl möbliertes Zimmer nt

loft /lɒft/ n Dachboden m

lofty /'lɒftɪ/ a (-ier, -iest) hoch; (haughty) hochmütig

log /lɒg/ n Baumstamm m; (for fire) [Holz]scheit nt; **sleep like a** ~ (fam) wie ein Murmeltier schlafen

logarithm /'lɒgərɪðm/ n Logarithmus m

'log-book n (Naut) Logbuch nt

loggerheads /'lɒgə-/ npl **be at** ~ (fam) sich in den Haaren liegen

logic /'lɒdʒɪk/ n Logik f. ~**al** a, -**ly** adv logisch

logistics /lə'dʒɪstɪks/ npl Logistik f

logo /'ləʊgəʊ/ n Symbol nt, Logo nt

loin /lɔɪn/ n (Culin) Lende f

loiter /'lɔɪtə(r)/ vi herumlungern

loll /lɒl/ vi sich lümmeln

loll|ipop /'lɒlɪpɒp/ n Lutscher m. ~**y** n Lutscher m; (fam: money) Moneten pl

London /'lʌndən/ n London nt ● attrib Londoner. ~**er** n Londoner(in) m(f)

lone /ləʊn/ a einzeln. ~**liness** n Einsamkeit f

lonely /'ləʊnlɪ/ a (**-ier, -iest**) einsam

lone|r /'ləʊnə(r)/ n Einzelgänger m. ~**some** a einsam

long[1] /lɒŋ/ a (**-er** /'lɒŋgə(r)/, **-est** /'lɒŋgɪst/) lang; ⟨journey⟩ weit; **a ~ time** lange; **a ~ way** weit; **in the ~ run** auf lange Sicht; (in the end) letzten Endes ● adv lange; **all day ~** den ganzen Tag; **not ~ ago** vor kurzem; **before ~** bald; **no ~er** nicht mehr; **as or so ~ as** solange; **so ~!** (fam) tschüs! **will you be ~?** dauert es noch lange [bei dir]? **it won't take ~** es dauert nicht lange

long[2] vi ~ **for** sich sehnen nach

long-'distance a Fern-; (Sport) Langstrecken-

longevity /lɒn'dʒevətɪ/ n Langlebigkeit f

'longhand n Langschrift f

longing /'lɒŋɪŋ/ a, **-ly** adv sehnsüchtig ● n Sehnsucht f

longitude /'lɒŋgɪtjuːd/ n (Geog) Länge f

long: ~ **jump** n Weitsprung m. ~**-life 'milk** n H-Milch f. ~**-lived** /-lɪvd/ a langlebig. ~**-range** a (Mil, Aviat) Langstrecken-; ⟨forecast⟩ langfristig. ~**-sighted** a weitsichtig. ~**-sleeved** a langärmelig. ~**-suffering** a langmütig. ~**-term** a langfristig. ~ **wave** n Langwelle f. ~**-winded** /-'wɪndɪd/ a langatmig

loo /luː/ n (fam) Klo nt

look /lʊk/ n Blick m; (appearance) Aussehen nt; **[good] ~s** pl Aussehen nt; **have a ~ at** sich (dat) ansehen; **go and have a ~** sieh mal nach ● vi sehen; (search) nachsehen; (seem) aussehen; **don't ~** sieh nicht hin; ~ **here!** hören Sie mal! ~ **at** ansehen; ~ **for** suchen; ~ **forward to** sich freuen auf (+ acc); ~ **in on** vorbeischauen bei; ~ **into** (examine) nachgehen (+ dat); ~ **like** aussehen wie; ~ **on to** ⟨room:⟩ gehen auf (+ acc); ~ **after** vt betreuen. ~ **down** vi hinuntersehen; ~ **down on s.o.** (fig) auf jdn herabsehen. ~ **out** vi hinaus-/heraussehen; (take care) aufpassen; ~ **out for** Ausschau halten nach; ~ **out!** Vorsicht! ~ **round** vi sich umsehen. ~ **up** vi aufblicken; ~ **up to s.o.** (fig) zu jdm aufsehen ● vt nachschlagen ⟨word⟩

'look-out n Wache f; (prospect) Aussicht f; **be on the ~ for** Ausschau halten nach

loom[1] /luːm/ n Webstuhl m

loom[2] vi auftauchen; (fig) sich abzeichnen

loony /'luːnɪ/ a (fam) verrückt

loop /luːp/ n Schlinge f; (in road) Schleife f; (on garment) Aufhänger m ● vt schlingen. ~**hole** n Hintertürchen nt; (in the law) Lücke f

loose /luːs/ a (**-r, -st**), **-ly** adv lose; (not tight enough) locker; (inexact) frei; **be at a ~ end** nichts zu tun haben; **set ~** freilassen; **run ~** frei herumlaufen. ~ **'change** n Kleingeld nt. ~ **'chippings** npl Rollsplit m

loosen /'luːsn/ vt lockern ● vi sich lockern

loot /luːt/ n Beute f ● vt/i plündern. ~**er** n Plünderer m

lop /lɒp/ vt (pt/pp **lopped**) stutzen. ~ **off** vt abhacken

lop'sided a schief

loquacious /lə'kweɪʃəs/ a redselig

lord /lɔːd/ n Herr m; (title) Lord m; **House of L~s** ≈ Oberhaus nt; **the L~'s Prayer** das Vaterunser; **good L~!** du liebe Zeit!

lore /lɔː(r)/ n Überlieferung f

lorry /'lɒrɪ/ n Last[kraft]wagen m

lose /luːz/ v (pt/pp **lost**) ● vt verlieren; (miss) verpassen ● vi verlieren; ⟨clock:⟩ nachgehen; **get lost** verlorengehen; ⟨person:⟩ sich verlaufen. ~**r** n Verlierer m

loss /lɒs/ n Verlust m; **be at a ~** nicht mehr weiter wissen; **be at a ~ for words** nicht wissen, was man sagen soll

lost /lɒst/ see **lose**. ~ **'property office** n Fundbüro nt

lot[1] /lɒt/ n Los nt; (at auction) Posten m; **draw ~s** losen (**for** um)

lot[2] n **the ~** alle; (everything) alles; **a ~ [of]** viel; (many) viele; **~s of** (fam) eine Menge; **it has changed a ~** es hat sich sehr verändert

lotion /'ləʊʃn/ n Lotion f

lottery /'lɒtərɪ/ n Lotterie f. ~ **ticket** n Los nt

loud /laʊd/ a (**-er, -est**), **-ly** adv laut; ⟨colours⟩ grell ● adv **[out]** ~ laut. ~**'hailer** n Megaphon nt. ~**'speaker** n Lautsprecher m

lounge /laʊndʒ/ n Wohnzimmer nt; (in hotel) Aufenthaltsraum m. ● vi sich lümmeln. ~ **suit** n Straßenanzug m

louse /laʊs/ n (pl **lice**) Laus f

lousy /'lauzɪ/ a (-ier, -iest) (fam) lausig

lout /laut/ n Flegel m, Lümmel m. ~ish a flegelhaft

lovable /'lʌvəbl/ a liebenswert

love /lʌv/ n Liebe f; (Tennis) null; in ~ verliebt ● vt lieben; ~ doing sth etw sehr gerne machen; I ~ chocolate ich esse sehr gerne Schokolade. ~-affair n Liebesverhältnis nt. ~ letter n Liebesbrief m

lovely /'lʌvlɪ/ a (-ier, -iest) schön; we had a ~ time es war sehr schön

lover /'lʌvə(r)/ n Liebhaber m

love: ~ song n Liebeslied nt. ~ story n Liebesgeschichte f

loving /'lʌvɪŋ/ a, -ly adv liebevoll

low /ləu/ a (-er, -est) niedrig; ⟨cloud, note⟩ tief; ⟨voice⟩ leise; (depressed) niedergeschlagen ● adv niedrig; ⟨fly, sing⟩ tief; ⟨speak⟩ leise; feel ~ deprimiert sein ● n (Meteorol) Tief nt; (fig) Tiefstand m

low: ~brow a geistig anspruchslos. ~-cut a ⟨dress⟩ tief ausgeschnitten

lower /'ləuə(r)/ a & adv see low ● vt niedriger machen; (let down) herunterlassen; (reduce) senken; ~ oneself sich herabwürdigen

low: ~-'fat a fettarm. ~-'grade a minderwertig. ~lands /-ləndz/ npl Tiefland nt. ~ 'tide n Ebbe f

loyal /'lɔɪəl/ a, -ly adv treu. ~ty n Treue f

lozenge /'lɒzɪndʒ/ n Pastille f

Ltd abbr (Limited)

lubricant /'lu:brɪkənt/ n Schmiermittel nt

lubricat|e /'lu:brɪkeɪt/ vt schmieren. ~ion /-'keɪʃn/ n Schmierung f

lucid /'lu:sɪd/ a klar. ~ity /-'sɪdətɪ/ n Klarheit f

luck /lʌk/ n Glück nt; bad ~ Pech nt; good ~! viel Glück! ~ily adv glücklicherweise, zum Glück

lucky /'lʌkɪ/ a (-ier, -iest) glücklich; ⟨day, number⟩ Glücks-; be ~ Glück haben; ⟨thing:⟩ Glück bringen. ~ 'charm n Amulett nt

lucrative /'lu:krətɪv/ a einträglich

ludicrous /'lu:dɪkrəs/ a lächerlich

lug /lʌg/ vt (pt/pp lugged) (fam) schleppen

luggage /'lʌgɪdʒ/ n Gepäck nt

luggage: ~-rack n Gepäckablage f. ~ trolley n Kofferkuli m. ~-van n Gepäckwagen m

lugubrious /lu:'gu:brɪəs/ a traurig

lukewarm /'lu:k-/ a lauwarm

lull /lʌl/ n Pause f ● vt ~ to sleep einschläfern

lullaby /'lʌləbaɪ/ n Wiegenlied nt

lumbago /lʌm'beɪgəu/ n Hexenschuß m

lumber /'lʌmbə(r)/ n Gerümpel nt; (Amer: timber) Bauholz m ● vt ~ s.o. with sth jdm etw aufhalsen. ~jack n (Amer) Holzfäller m

luminous /'lu:mɪnəs/ a leuchtend; be ~ leuchten

lump[1] /lʌmp/ n Klumpen m; (of sugar) Stück nt; (swelling) Beule f; (in breast) Knoten m; (tumour) Geschwulst f; a ~ in one's throat (fam) ein Kloß im Hals ● vt ~ together zusammentun

lump[2] vt ~ it (fam) sich damit abfinden

lump: ~ sugar n Würfelzucker m. ~ 'sum n Pauschalsumme f

lumpy /'lʌmpɪ/ a (-ier, -iest) klumpig

lunacy /'lu:nəsɪ/ n Wahnsinn m

lunar /'lu:nə(r)/ a Mond-

lunatic /'lu:nətɪk/ n Wahnsinnige(r) m/f

lunch /lʌntʃ/ n Mittagessen nt ● vi zu Mittag essen

luncheon /'lʌntʃn/ n Mittagessen nt. ~ meat n Frühstücksfleisch nt. ~ voucher n Essensbon m

lunch: ~-hour n Mittagspause f. ~-time n Mittagszeit f

lung /lʌŋ/ n Lungenflügel m; ~s pl Lunge f. ~ cancer n Lungenkrebs m

lunge /lʌndʒ/ vi sich stürzen (at auf + acc)

lurch[1] /lɜːtʃ/ n leave in the ~ (fam) im Stich lassen

lurch[2] vi schleudern; ⟨person:⟩ torkeln

lure /luə(r)/ n Lockung f; (bait) Köder m ● vt locken

lurid /'luərɪd/ a grell; (sensational) reißerisch

lurk /lɜːk/ vi lauern

luscious /'lʌʃəs/ a lecker, köstlich

lush /lʌʃ/ a üppig

lust /lʌst/ n Begierde f ● vi ~ after gieren nach. ~ful a lüstern

lustre /'lʌstə(r)/ n Glanz m

lusty /'lʌstɪ/ a (-ier, -iest) kräftig

lute /lu:t/ n Laute f

luxuriant /lʌg'ʒuərɪənt/ a üppig

luxurious /lʌg'ʒuərɪəs/ a, -ly adv luxuriös

luxury /'lʌkʃərɪ/ n Luxus m ● attrib Luxus-

lying /'laɪɪŋ/ see lie[1], lie[2]

lymph gland /'lɪmf-/ *n* Lymphdrüse *f*

lynch /lɪntʃ/ *vt* lynchen

lynx /lɪŋks/ *n* Luchs *m*

lyric /'lɪrɪk/ *a* lyrisch. **~al** *a* lyrisch; *(fam: enthusiastic)* schwärmerisch. **~ poetry** *n* Lyrik *f*. **~s** *npl* [Lied]text *m*

M

mac /mæk/ *n (fam)* Regenmantel *m*

macabre /mə'kɑːbr/ *a* makaber

macaroni /mækə'rəʊnɪ/ *n* Makkaroni *pl*

macaroon /mækə'ruːn/ *n* Makrone *f*

mace[1] /meɪs/ *n* Amtsstab *m*

mace[2] *n (spice)* Muskatblüte *f*

machinations /mækɪ'neɪʃnz/ *pl* Machenschaften *pl*

machine /mə'ʃiːn/ *n* Maschine *f* ● *vt* (*sew*) mit der Maschine nähen; *(Techn)* maschinell bearbeiten. **~-gun** *n* Maschinengewehr *nt*

machinery /mə'ʃiːnərɪ/ *n* Maschinerie *f*

machine tool *n* Werkzeugmaschine *f*

machinist /mə'ʃiːnɪst/ *n* Maschinist *m*; (*on sewing machine*) Maschinennäherin *f*

mackerel /'mækrl/ *n inv* Makrele *f*

mackintosh /'mækɪntɒʃ/ *n* Regenmantel *m*

mad /mæd/ *a* (**madder, maddest**) verrückt; (*dog*) tollwütig; (*fam: angry*) böse (**at** auf + *acc*)

madam /'mædəm/ *n* gnädige Frau *f*

madden /'mædn/ *vt* (*make angry*) wütend machen

made /meɪd/ *see* **make**; **~ to measure** maßgeschneidert

Madeira cake /mə'dɪərə-/ *n* Sandkuchen *m*

mad|ly /'mædlɪ/ *adv (fam)* wahnsinnig. **~man** *n* Irre(r) *m*. **~ness** *n* Wahnsinn *m*

madonna /mə'dɒnə/ *n* Madonna *f*

magazine /mægə'ziːn/ *n* Zeitschrift *f*; (*Mil, Phot*) Magazin *nt*

maggot /'mægət/ *n* Made *f*. **~y** *a* madig

Magi /'meɪdʒaɪ/ *npl* **the ~** die Heiligen Drei Könige

magic /'mædʒɪk/ *n* Zauber *m*; (*tricks*) Zauberkunst *f* ● *a* magisch; (*word, wand, flute*) Zauber-. **~al** *a* zauberhaft

magician /mə'dʒɪʃn/ *n* Zauberer *m*; (*entertainer*) Zauberkünstler *m*

magistrate /'mædʒɪstreɪt/ *n* ≈ Friedensrichter *m*

magnanim|ity /mægnə'nɪmətɪ/ *n* Großmut *f*. **~ous** /-'nænɪməs/ *a* großmütig

magnesia /mæg'niːʃə/ *n* Magnesia *f*

magnet /'mægnɪt/ *n* Magnet *m*. **~ic** /-'netɪk/ *a* magnetisch. **~ism** *n* Magnetismus *m*. **~ize** *vt* magnetisieren

magnification /mægnɪfɪ'keɪʃn/ *n* Vergrößerung *f*

magnificen|ce /mæg'nɪfɪsəns/ *n* Großartigkeit *f*. **~t** *a*, **-ly** *adv* großartig

magnify /'mægnɪfaɪ/ *vt* (*pt/pp* **-ied**) vergrößern; (*exaggerate*) übertreiben. **~ing glass** *n* Vergrößerungsglas *nt*

magnitude /'mægnɪtjuːd/ *n* Größe *f*; (*importance*) Bedeutung *f*

magpie /'mægpaɪ/ *n* Elster *f*

mahogany /mə'hɒgənɪ/ *n* Mahagoni *nt*

maid /meɪd/ *n* Dienstmädchen *nt*; (*liter: girl*) Maid *f*; **old ~** (*pej*) alte Jungfer *f*

maiden /'meɪdn/ *n* (*liter*) Maid *f* ● *a* ⟨*speech, voyage*⟩ Jungfern-. **~ 'aunt** *n* unverheiratete Tante *f*. **~ name** *n* Mädchenname *m*

mail[1] /meɪl/ *n* Kettenpanzer *m*

mail[2] *n* Post *f* ● *vt* mit der Post schicken; (*send off*) abschicken

mail: ~-bag *n* Postsack *m*. **~box** *n* (*Amer*) Briefkasten *m*. **~ing list** *n* Postversandliste *f*. **~man** *n* (*Amer*) Briefträger *m*. **~-order firm** *n* Versandhaus *nt*

maim /meɪm/ *vt* verstümmeln

main[1] /meɪn/ *n* (*water, gas, electricity*) Hauptleitung *f*

main[2] *a* Haupt- ● *n* **in the ~** im großen und ganzen

main: ~land /-lənd/ *n* Festland *nt*. **~ly** *adv* hauptsächlich. **~stay** *n* (*fig*) Stütze *f*. **~ street** *n* Hauptstraße *f*

maintain /meɪn'teɪn/ *vt* aufrechterhalten; (*keep in repair*) instand halten; (*support*) unterhalten; (*claim*) behaupten

maintenance /'meɪntənəns/ *n* Aufrechterhaltung *f*; (*care*) Instandhaltung *f*; (*allowance*) Unterhalt *m*

maisonette /meɪzə'net/ n Wohnung f [auf zwei Etagen]

maize /meɪz/ n Mais m

majestic /mə'dʒestɪk/ a, **-ally** adv majestätisch

majesty /'mædʒəstɪ/ n Majestät f

major /'meɪdʒə(r)/ a größer ● n (Mil) Major m; (Mus) Dur nt ● vi (Amer) ~ **in** als Hauptfach studieren

Majorca /mə'jɔːkə/ n Mallorca nt

majority /mə'dʒɒrətɪ/ n Mehrheit f; **in the** ~ in der Mehrzahl

major road n Hauptverkehrsstraße f

make /meɪk/ n (brand) Marke f ● v (pt/pp **made**) ● vt machen; (force) zwingen; (earn) verdienen; halten ⟨speech⟩; treffen ⟨decision⟩; erreichen ⟨destination⟩ ● vi ~ **as if to** Miene machen zu. ~ **do** vi zurechtkommen (with mit). ~ **for** vi zusteuern auf (+ acc). ~ **off** vi sich davonmachen (with mit). ~ **out** vt (distinguish) ausmachen; (write out) ausstellen; (assert) behaupten. ~ **over** vt überschreiben (to auf + acc). ~ **up** vt (constitute) bilden; (invent) erfinden; (apply cosmetics to) schminken; ~ **up one's mind** sich entschließen ● vi sich versöhnen; ~ **up for** sth etw wiedergutmachen; ~ **up for lost time** verlorene Zeit aufholen

'make-believe n Phantasie f

maker /'meɪkə(r)/ n Hersteller m

make: ~**shift** a behelfsmäßig ● n Notbehelf m. ~**-up** n Make-up nt

making /'meɪkɪŋ/ n **have the** ~**s of** das Zeug haben zu

maladjusted /mælə'dʒʌstɪd/ a verhaltensgestört

malaise /mə'leɪz/ n (fig) Unbehagen nt

male /meɪl/ a männlich ● n Mann m; (animal) Männchen nt. ~ **nurse** n Krankenpfleger m. ~ **voice 'choir** n Männerchor m

malevolen|ce /mə'levələns/ n Bosheit f. ~**t** a boshaft

malfunction /mæl'fʌŋkʃn/ n technische Störung f; (Med) Funktionsstörung f ● vi nicht richtig funktionieren

malice /'mælɪs/ n Bosheit f; **bear s.o.** ~ einen Groll gegen jdn hegen

malicious /mə'lɪʃəs/ a, **-ly** adv böswillig

malign /mə'laɪn/ vt verleumden

malignan|cy /mə'lɪgnənsɪ/ n Bösartigkeit f. ~**t** a bösartig

malinger /mə'lɪŋgə(r)/ vi simulieren, sich krank stellen. ~**er** n Simulant m

malleable /'mælɪəbl/ a formbar

mallet /'mælɪt/ n Holzhammer m

malnu'trition /mæl-/ n Unterernährung f

mal'practice n Berufsvergehen nt

malt /mɔːlt/ n Malz nt

mal'treat /mæl-/ vt mißhandeln. ~**ment** n Mißhandlung f

mammal /'mæml/ n Säugetier nt

mammoth /'mæməθ/ a riesig ● n Mammut nt

man /mæn/ n (pl **men**) Mann m; (mankind) der Mensch; (chess) Figur f; (draughts) Stein m ● vt (pt/pp **manned**) bemannen ⟨ship⟩; bedienen ⟨pump⟩; besetzen ⟨counter⟩

manacle /'mænəkl/ vt fesseln (**to** an + acc); ~**d** in Handschellen

manage /'mænɪdʒ/ vt leiten; verwalten ⟨estate⟩; (cope with) fertig werden mit; ~ **to do sth** es schaffen, etw zu tun ● vi zurechtkommen; ~ **on** auskommen mit. ~**able** /-əbl/ a ⟨tool⟩ handlich; ⟨person⟩ fügsam. ~**ment** /-mənt/ n **the** ~**ment** die Geschäftsleitung f

manager /'mænɪdʒə(r)/ n Geschäftsführer m; (of bank) Direktor m; (of estate) Verwalter m; (Sport) [Chef]trainer m. ~**ess** n Geschäftsführer(in) f. ~**ial** /-'dʒɪərɪəl/ a ~**ial staff** Führungskräfte pl

managing /'mænɪdʒɪŋ/ a ~ **director** Generaldirektor m

mandarin /'mændərɪn/ n ~ **[orange]** Mandarine f

mandat|e /'mændeɪt/ n Mandat nt. ~**ory** /-dətrɪ/ a obligatorisch

mane /meɪn/ n Mähne f

manful /'mænfl/ a, **-ly** adv mannhaft

manger /'meɪndʒə(r)/ n Krippe f

mangle[1] /'mæŋgl/ n Wringmaschine f; (for smoothing) Mangel f

mangle[2] vt (damage) verstümmeln

mango /'mæŋgəʊ/ n (pl **-es**) Mango f

mangy /'meɪndʒɪ/ a ⟨dog⟩ räudig

man: ~**'handle** vt grob behandeln ⟨person⟩. ~**hole** n Kanalschacht m. ~**hole cover** n Kanaldeckel m. ~**hood** n Mannesalter nt; (quality) Männlichkeit f. ~**-hour** n Arbeitsstunde f. ~**-hunt** n Fahndung f

man|ia /'meɪnɪə/ n Manie f. **~iac** /-ɪæk/ n Wahnsinnige(r) m/f

manicur|e /'mænɪkjʊə(r)/ n Maniküre f ● vt maniküren. **~ist** n Maniküre f

manifest /'mænɪfest/ a, **-ly** adv offensichtlich ● vt **~ itself** sich manifestieren

manifesto /mænɪ'festəʊ/ n Manifest nt

manifold /'mænɪfəʊld/ a mannigfaltig

manipulat|e /mə'nɪpjʊleɪt/ vt handhaben; (pej) manipulieren. **~ion** /-'leɪʃn/ n Manipulation f

man'kind n die Menschheit

manly /'mænlɪ/ a männlich

'man-made a künstlich. **~ fibre** n Kunstfaser f

manner /'mænə(r)/ n Weise f; (kind, behaviour) Art f; **in this ~** auf diese Weise; **[good/bad] ~s** [gute/ schlechte] Manieren pl. **~ism** n Angewohnheit f

mannish /'mænɪʃ/ a männlich

manœuvrable /mə'nu:vrəbl/ a manövrierfähig

manœuvre /mə'nu:və(r)/ n Manöver nt ● vt/i manövrieren

manor /'mænə(r)/ n Gutshof m; (house) Gutshaus nt

man: ~power n Arbeitskräfte pl. **~servant** n (pl **menservants**) Diener m

mansion /'mænʃn/ n Villa f

imanslaughter n Totschlag m

mantelpiece /'mæntl-/ n Kaminsims m & nt

manual /'mænjʊəl/ a Hand- ● n Handbuch nt

manufacture /mænjʊ'fæktʃə(r)/ vt herstellen ● n Herstellung f. **~r** n Hersteller m

manure /mə'njʊə(r)/ n Mist m

manuscript /'mænjʊskrɪpt/ n Manuskript nt

many /'menɪ/ a viele; **~ a time** oft ● n **a good/great ~** sehr viele

map /mæp/ n Landkarte f; (of town) Stadtplan m ● vt (pt/pp **mapped**) **~ out** (fig) ausarbeiten

maple /'meɪpl/ n Ahorn m

mar /mɑ:(r)/ vt (pt/pp **marred**) verderben

marathon /'mærəθən/ n Marathon m

marauding /mə'rɔ:dɪŋ/ a plündernd

marble /'mɑ:bl/ n Marmor m; (for game) Murmel f

March /mɑ:tʃ/ n März m

march n Marsch m ● vi marschieren ● vt marschieren lassen; **~ s.o. off** jdn abführen

mare /'meə(r)/ n Stute f

margarine /mɑ:dʒə'ri:n/ n Margarine f

margin /'mɑ:dʒɪn/ n Rand m; (leeway) Spielraum m; (Comm) Spanne f. **~al** a, **-ly** adv geringfügig

marigold /'mærɪgəʊld/ n Ringelblume f

marijuana /mærɪ'hwɑ:nə/ n Marihuana nt

marina /mə'ri:nə/ n Jachthafen m

marinade /mærɪ'neɪd/ n Marinade f ● vt marinieren

marine /mə'ri:n/ a Meeres- ● n Marine f; (sailor) Marineinfanterist m

marionette /mærɪə'net/ n Marionette f

marital /'mærɪtl/ a ehelich. **~ status** n Familienstand m

maritime /'mærɪtaɪm/ a See-

marjoram /'mɑ:dʒərəm/ n Majoran m

mark[1] /mɑ:k/ n (currency) Mark f

mark[2] /mɑ:k/ n Fleck m; (sign) Zeichen nt; (trace) Spur f; (target) Ziel nt; (Sch) Note f ● vt markieren; (spoil) beschädigen; (characterize) kennzeichnen; (Sch) korrigieren; (Sport) decken; **~ time** (Mil) auf der Stelle treten; (fig) abwarten; **~ my words** das [eine] will ich dir sagen. **~ out** vt markieren

marked /mɑ:kt/ a, **~ly** /-kɪdlɪ/ adv deutlich; (pronounced) ausgeprägt

marker /'mɑ:kə(r)/ n Marke f; (of exam) Korrektor(in) m(f)

market /'mɑ:kɪt/ n Markt m ● vt vertreiben; (launch) auf den Markt bringen. **~ing** n Marketing nt. **~ re-'search** n Marktforschung f

marking /'mɑ:kɪŋ/ n Markierung f; (on animal) Zeichnung f

marksman /'mɑ:ksmən/ n Scharfschütze m

marmalade /'mɑ:məleɪd/ n Orangenmarmelade f

marmot /'mɑ:mət/ n Murmeltier nt

maroon /mə'ru:n/ a dunkelrot

marooned /mə'ru:nd/ a (fig) von der Außenwelt abgeschnitten

marquee /mɑ:'ki:/ n Festzelt nt; (Amer: awning) Markise f

marquetry /'mɑ:kɪtrɪ/ n Einlege-arbeit f

marquis /'mɑ:kwɪs/ n Marquis m

marriage /'mærɪdʒ/ n Ehe f; (wedding) Hochzeit f. ∼**able** /-əbl/ a heiratsfähig

married /'mærɪd/ see **marry** ● a verheiratet. ∼ **life** n Eheleben nt

marrow /'mærəʊ/ n (Anat) Mark nt; (vegetable) Kürbis m

marr|y /'mærɪ/ vt/i (pt/pp **married**) heiraten; (unite) trauen; **get** ∼**ied** heiraten

marsh /mɑ:ʃ/ n Sumpf m

marshal /'mɑ:ʃl/ n Marschall m; (steward) Ordner m ● vt (pt/pp **marshalled**) (Mil) formieren; (fig) ordnen

marshy /'mɑ:ʃɪ/ a sumpfig

marsupial /mɑ:'su:pɪəl/ n Beuteltier nt

martial /'mɑ:ʃl/ a kriegerisch. ∼ **law** n Kriegsrecht nt

martyr /'mɑ:tə(r)/ n Märtyrer(in) m(f) ● vt zum Märtyrer machen. ∼**dom** /-dəm/ n Martyrium nt

marvel /'mɑ:vl/ n Wunder nt ● vi (pt/pp **marvelled**) staunen (**at** über + acc). ∼**lous** /-vələs/ a, **-ly** adv wunderbar

Marxis|m /'mɑ:ksɪzm/ n Marxismus m. ∼**t** a marxistisch ● n Marxist(in) m(f)

marzipan /'mɑ:zɪpæn/ n Marzipan nt

mascara /mæ'skɑ:rə/ n Wimperntusche f

mascot /'mæskət/ n Maskottchen nt

masculin|e /'mæskjʊlɪn/ a männlich ● n (Gram) Maskulinum nt. ∼**ity** /-'lɪnətɪ/ n Männlichkeit f

mash /mæʃ/ n (fam, Culin) Kartoffelpüree nt ● vt stampfen. ∼**ed potatoes** npl Kartoffelpüree nt

mask /mɑ:sk/ n Maske f ● vt maskieren

masochis|m /'mæsəkɪzm/ n Masochismus m. ∼**t** /-ɪst/ n Masochist m

mason /'meɪsn/ n Steinmetz m

Mason n Freimaurer m. ∼**ic** /mə'sɒnɪk/ a freimaurerisch

masonry /'meɪsnrɪ/ n Mauerwerk nt

masquerade /mæskə'reɪd/ n (fig) Maskerade f ● vi ∼ **as** (pose) sich ausgeben als

mass[1] /mæs/ n (Relig) Messe f

mass[2] n Masse f ● vi sich sammeln; (Mil) sich massieren

massacre /'mæsəkə(r)/ n Massaker nt ● vt niedermetzeln

massage /'mæsɑ:ʒ/ n Massage f ● vt massieren

masseu|r /mæ'sɜ:(r)/ n Masseur m. ∼**se** /-'sɜ:z/ n Masseuse f

massive /'mæsɪv/ a massiv; (huge) riesig

mass: ∼ **media** npl Massenmedien pl. ∼-**pro'duce** vt in Massenproduktion herstellen. ∼ **pro-'duction** n Massenproduktion f

mast /mɑ:st/ n Mast m

master /'mɑ:stə(r)/ n Herr m; (teacher) Lehrer m; (craftsman, artist) Meister m; (of ship) Kapitän m ● vt meistern; beherrschen ⟨language⟩

master: ∼-**key** n Hauptschlüssel m. ∼**ly** a meisterhaft. ∼-**mind** n führender Kopf m ● vt der führende Kopf sein von. ∼**piece** n Meisterwerk nt. ∼**y** n (of subject) Beherrschung f

masturbat|e /'mæstəbeɪt/ vi masturbieren. ∼**ion** /-'beɪʃn/ n Masturbation f

mat /mæt/ n Matte f; (on table) Untersatz m

match[1] /mætʃ/ n Wettkampf m; (in ball games) Spiel nt; (Tennis) Match nt; (marriage) Heirat f; **be a good** ∼ ⟨colours:⟩ gut zusammenpassen; **be no** ∼ **for s.o.** jdm nicht gewachsen sein ● vt (equal) gleichkommen (+ dat); (be like) passen zu; (find sth similar) etwas Passendes finden zu ● vi zusammenpassen

match[2] n Streichholz nt. ∼**box** n Streichholzschachtel f

matching /'mætʃɪŋ/ a [zusammen]-passend

mate[1] /meɪt/ n Kumpel m; (assistant) Gehilfe m; (Naut) Maat m; (Zool) Männchen nt; (female) Weibchen nt ● vi sich paaren ● vt paaren

mate[2] n (Chess) Matt nt

material /mə'tɪərɪəl/ n Material nt; (fabric) Stoff m; **raw** ∼**s** Rohstoffe pl ● a materiell

material|ism /mə'tɪərɪəlɪzm/ n Materialismus m. ∼**istic** /-'lɪstɪk/ a materialistisch. ∼**ize** /-laɪz/ vi sich verwirklichen

maternal /mə'tɜ:nl/ a mütterlich

maternity /mə'tɜ:nətɪ/ n Mutterschaft f. ∼ **clothes** npl Umstandskleidung f. ~ **ward** n Entbindungsstation f

matey /ˈmeɪtɪ/ a (fam) freundlich

mathematic|al /mæθəˈmætɪkl/ a, **-ly** adv mathematisch. ~**ian** /-məˈtɪʃn/ n Mathematiker(in) m(f)

mathematics /mæθəˈmætɪks/ n Mathematik f

maths /mæθs/ n (fam) Mathe f

matinée /ˈmætɪneɪ/ n (Theat) Nachmittagsvorstellung f

matriculat|e /məˈtrɪkjʊleɪt/ vi sich immatrikulieren. ~**ion** /-ˈleɪʃn/ n Immatrikulation f

matrimon|ial /mætrɪˈməʊnɪəl/ a Ehe-. ~**y** /ˈmætrɪmənɪ/ n Ehe f

matrix /ˈmeɪtrɪks/ n (pl **matrices** /-siːz/) n (Techn: mould) Matrize f

matron /ˈmeɪtrən/ n (of hospital) Oberin f; (of school) Hausmutter f. ~**ly** a matronenhaft

matt /mæt/ a matt

matted /ˈmætɪd/ a verfilzt

matter /ˈmætə(r)/ n (affair) Sache f; (pus) Eiter m; (Phys: substance) Materie f; **money** ~**s** Geldangelegenheiten pl; **as a** ~ **of fact** eigentlich; **what is the** ~? was ist los? ● vi wichtig sein; ~ **to s.o.** jdm etwas ausmachen; **it doesn't** ~ es macht nichts. ~**-of-fact** a sachlich

matting /ˈmætɪŋ/ n Matten pl

mattress /ˈmætrɪs/ n Matratze f

matur|e /məˈtjʊə(r)/ a reif; (Comm) fällig ● vi reifen; (person:) reifer werden; (Comm) fällig werden ● vt reifen lassen. ~**ity** n Reife f; (Comm) Fälligkeit f

maul /mɔːl/ vt übel zurichten

Maundy /ˈmɔːndɪ/ n ~ **Thursday** Gründonnerstag m

mauve /məʊv/ a lila

mawkish /ˈmɔːkɪʃ/ a rührselig

maxim /ˈmæksɪm/ n Maxime f

maximum /ˈmæksɪməm/ a maximal ● n (pl **-ima**) Maximum nt. ~ **speed** n Höchstgeschwindigkeit f

may /meɪ/ v aux (nur Präsens) (be allowed to) dürfen; (be possible) können; **may I come in?** darf ich reinkommen? **may he succeed** möge es ihm gelingen; **I may as well stay** am besten bleibe ich hier; **it may be true** es könnte wahr sein

May n Mai m

maybe /ˈmeɪbi:/ adv vielleicht

May Day n der Erste Mai

mayonnaise /meɪəˈneɪz/ n Mayonnaise f

mayor /ˈmeə(r)/ n Bürgermeister m. ~**ess** n Bürgermeisterin f; (wife of mayor) Frau Bürgermeister f

maze /meɪz/ n Irrgarten m; (fig) Labyrinth nt

me /mi:/ pron (acc) mich; (dat) mir; **he knows** ~ er kennt mich; **give** ~ **the money** gib mir das Geld; **it's** ~ (fam) ich bin es

meadow /ˈmedəʊ/ n Wiese f

meagre /ˈmi:gə(r)/ a dürftig

meal[1] /mi:l/ n Mahlzeit f; (food) Essen nt

meal[2] n (grain) Schrot m

mealy-mouthed /mi:lɪˈmaʊðd/ a heuchlerisch

mean[1] /mi:n/ a (**-er**, **-est**) geizig; (unkind) gemein; (poor) schäbig

mean[2] a mittlere(r,s) ● n (average) Durchschnitt m; **the golden** ~ die goldene Mitte

mean[3] vt (pt/pp **meant**) heißen; (signify) bedeuten; (intend) beabsichtigen; **I** ~ **it** das ist mein Ernst; **es well** es gut meinen; **be meant for** ⟨present:⟩ bestimmt sein für; ⟨remark:⟩ gerichtet sein an (+ acc)

meander /mɪˈændə(r)/ vi sich schlängeln; ⟨person:⟩ schlendern

meaning /ˈmi:nɪŋ/ n Bedeutung f. ~**ful** a bedeutungsvoll. ~**less** a bedeutungslos

means /mi:nz/ n Möglichkeit f, Mittel nt; ~ **of transport** Verkehrsmittel nt; **by** ~ **of** durch; **by all** ~! aber natürlich! **by no** ~ keineswegs ● npl (resources) [Geld]mittel pl. ~ **test** n Bedürftigkeitsnachweis m

meant /ment/ see **mean**[3]

'meantime n **in the** ~ in der Zwischenzeit ● adv inzwischen

'meanwhile adv inzwischen

measles /ˈmi:zlz/ n Masern pl

measly /ˈmi:zlɪ/ a (fam) mickerig

measurable /ˈmeʒərəbl/ a meßbar

measure /ˈmeʒə(r)/ n Maß nt; (action) Maßnahme f ● vt/i messen; ~ **up to** (fig) herankommen an (+ acc). ~**d** a gemessen. ~**ment** /-mənt/ n Maß nt

meat /mi:t/ n Fleisch nt. ~**ball** n (Culin) Klops m. ~ **loaf** n falscher Hase m

mechan|ic /mɪˈkænɪk/ n Mechaniker m. ~**ical** a, **-ly** adv mechanisch. ~**ical engineering** Maschinenbau

m. ~**ics** n Mechanik f ● n pl Mechanismus m

mechan|ism /'mekənɪzm/ n Mechanismus m. ~**ize** vt mechanisieren

medal /'medl/ n Orden m; (Sport) Medaille f

medallion /mɪ'dæliən/ n Medaillon nt

medallist /'medəlɪst/ n Medaillengewinner(in) m(f)

meddle /'medl/ vi sich einmischen (**in** in + acc); (tinker) herumhantieren (**with** an + acc)

media /'miːdɪə/ see **medium** ● n pl **the** ~ die Medien pl

median /'miːdɪən/ a ~ **strip** (Amer) Mittelstreifen m

mediat|e /'miːdɪeɪt/ vi vermitteln. ~**or** n Vermittler(in) m(f)

medical /'medɪkl/ a medizinisch; (treatment) ärztlich ● n ärztliche Untersuchung f. ~ **insurance** n Krankenversicherung f. ~ **student** n Medizinstudent m

medicat|ed /'medɪkeɪtɪd/ a medizinisch. ~**ion** /-'keɪʃn/ n (drugs) Medikamente pl

medicinal /mɪ'dɪsɪnl/ a medizinisch; (plant) heilkräftig

medicine /'medsən/ n Medizin f; (preparation) Medikament nt

medieval /medɪ'iːvl/ a mittelalterlich

mediocr|e /miːdɪ'əʊkə(r)/ a mittelmäßig. ~**ity** /-'ɒkrətɪ/ n Mittelmäßigkeit f

meditat|e /'medɪteɪt/ vi nachdenken (**on** über + acc); (Relig) meditieren. ~**ion** /-'teɪʃn/ n Meditation f

Mediterranean /medɪtə'reɪnɪən/ n Mittelmeer nt ● a Mittelmeer-

medium /'miːdɪəm/ a mittlere(r,s); (steak) medium; **of** ~ **size** von mittlerer Größe ● n (pl **media**) Medium nt; (means) Mittel nt ● (pl **-s**) (person) Medium nt

medium: ~**-sized** a mittelgroß. ~ **wave** n Mittelwelle f

medley /'medlɪ/ n Gemisch nt; (Mus) Potpourri nt

meek /miːk/ a (**-er**, **-est**), **-ly** adv sanftmütig; (unprotesting) widerspruchslos

meet /miːt/ v (pt/pp **met**) ● vt treffen; (by chance) begegnen (+ dat); (at station) abholen; (make the acquaintance of) kennenlernen; stoßen auf (+ acc)

(problem); bezahlen (bill); erfüllen (requirements) ● vi sich treffen; (for the first time) sich kennenlernen; ~ **with** stoßen auf (+ acc) (problem); sich treffen mit (person) ● n Jagdtreffen nt

meeting /'miːtɪŋ/ n Treffen nt; (by chance) Begegnung f; (discussion) Besprechung f; (of committee) Sitzung f; (large) Versammlung f

megalomania /megələ'meɪnɪə/ n Größenwahnsinn m

megaphone /'megəfəʊn/ n Megaphon nt

melancholy /'melənkəlɪ/ a melancholisch ● n Melancholie f

mellow /'meləʊ/ a (**-er**, **-est**) (fruit) ausgereift; (sound, person) sanft ● vi reifer werden

melodic /mɪ'lɒdɪk/ a melodisch

melodious /mɪ'ləʊdɪəs/ a melodiös

melodrama /'melə-/ n Melodrama nt. ~**tic** /-drə'mætɪk/ a, **-ally** adv melodramatisch

melody /'melədɪ/ n Melodie f

melon /'melən/ n Melone f

melt /melt/ vt/i schmelzen. ~ **down** vt einschmelzen. ~**ing-pot** n (fig) Schmelztiegel m

member /'membə(r)/ n Mitglied nt; (of family) Angehörige(r) m/f; **M~ of Parliament** Abgeordnete(r) m/f. ~**ship** n Mitgliedschaft f; (members) Mitgliederzahl f

membrane /'membreɪn/ n Membran f

memento /mɪ'mentəʊ/ n Andenken nt

memo /'meməʊ/ n Mitteilung f

memoirs /'memwɑːz/ n pl Memoiren pl

memorable /'memərəbl/ a denkwürdig

memorandum /memə'rændəm/ n Mitteilung f

memorial /mɪ'mɔːrɪəl/ n Denkmal nt. ~ **service** n Gedenkfeier f

memorize /'meməraɪz/ vt sich (dat) einprägen

memory /'memərɪ/ n Gedächtnis nt; (thing remembered) Erinnerung f; (of computer) Speicher m; **from** ~ auswendig; **in** ~ **of** zur Erinnerung an (+ acc)

men /men/ see **man**

menac|e /'menɪs/ n Drohung f; (nuisance) Plage f ● vt bedrohen. ~**ing** a, **-ly** adv drohend

mend /mend/ vt reparieren; (patch) flicken; ausbessern ⟨clothes⟩ • n **on the** ~ auf dem Weg der Besserung

'menfolk n pl Männer pl

menial /'mi:nɪəl/ a niedrig

meningitis /menɪn'dʒaɪtɪs/ n Hirnhautentzündung f, Meningitis f

menopause /'menə-/ n Wechseljahre pl

menstruat|e /'menstrʊeɪt/ vi menstruieren. ~**ion** /-'eɪʃn/ n Menstruation f

mental /'mentl/ a, -**ly** adv geistig; (fam: mad) verrückt. ~ a'**rithmetic** n Kopfrechnen nt. ~ '**illness** n Geisteskrankheit f

mentality /men'tælətɪ/ n Mentalität f

mention /'menʃn/ n Erwähnung f • vt erwähnen; **don't** ~ **it** keine Ursache; bitte

menu /'menju:/ n Speisekarte f

mercantile /'mɜːkəntaɪl/ a Handels-

mercenary /'mɜːsɪnərɪ/ a geldgierig • n Söldner m

merchandise /'mɜːtʃəndaɪz/ n Ware f

merchant /'mɜːtʃənt/ n Kaufmann m; (dealer) Händler m. ~ '**navy** n Handelsmarine f

merci|ful /'mɜːsɪfl/ a barmherzig. ~**fully** adv (fam) glücklicherweise. ~**less** a, -**ly** adv erbarmungslos

mercury /'mɜːkjʊrɪ/ n Quecksilber nt

mercy /'mɜːsɪ/ n Barmherzigkeit f, Gnade f; **be at s.o.'s** ~ jdm ausgeliefert sein

mere /mɪə(r)/ a, -**ly** adv bloß

merest /'mɪərɪst/ a kleinste(r,s)

merge /mɜːdʒ/ vi zusammenlaufen; (Comm) fusionieren • vt (Comm) zusammenschließen

merger /'mɜːdʒə(r)/ n Fusion f

meridian /mə'rɪdɪən/ n Meridian m

meringue /mə'ræŋ/ n Baiser nt

merit /'merɪt/ n Verdienst nt; (advantage) Vorzug m; (worth) Wert m • vt verdienen

mermaid /'mɜːmeɪd/ n Meerjungfrau f

merri|ly /'merɪlɪ/ adv fröhlich. ~**ment** /-mənt/ n Fröhlichkeit f; (laughter) Gelächter nt

merry /'merɪ/ a (-**ier**, -**iest**) fröhlich; ~ **Christmas!** fröhliche Weihnachten!

merry: ~**-go-round** n Karussell nt. ~**-making** n Feiern nt

mesh /meʃ/ n Masche f; (size) Maschenweite f; (fig: network) Netz nt

mesmerize /'mezməraɪz/ vt hypnotisieren. ~**d** a (fig) [wie] gebannt

mess /mes/ n Durcheinander nt; (trouble) Schwierigkeiten pl; (something spilt) Bescherung f (fam); (Mil) Messe f; **make a** ~ **of** (botch) verpfuschen • vt ~ **up** in Unordnung bringen; (botch) verpfuschen • vi ~ **about** herumalbern; (tinker) herumspielen (**with** mit)

message /'mesɪdʒ/ n Nachricht f; **give s.o. a** ~ jdm etwas ausrichten

messenger /'mesɪndʒə(r)/ n Bote m

Messiah /mɪ'saɪə/ n Messias m

Messrs /'mesəz/ n pl see **Mr**; (on letter) ~ **Smith** Firma Smith

messy /'mesɪ/ a (-**ier**, -**iest**) schmutzig; (untidy) unordentlich

met /met/ see **meet**

metabolism /mɪ'tæbəlɪzm/ n Stoffwechsel m

metal /'metl/ n Metall nt • a Metall-. ~**lic** /mɪ'tælɪk/ a metallisch. ~**lurgy** /mɪ'tælədʒɪ/ n Metallurgie f

metamorphosis /metə'mɔːfəsɪs/ n (pl -**phoses** /-si:z/) Metamorphose f

metaphor /'metəfə(r)/ n Metapher f. ~**ical** /-'fɒrɪkl/ a, -**ly** adv metaphorisch

meteor /'mi:tɪə(r)/ n Meteor m. ~**ic** /-'ɒrɪk/ a kometenhaft

meteorological /mi:tɪərə'lɒdʒɪkl/ a Wetter-

meteorolog|ist /mi:tɪə'rɒlədʒɪst/ n Meteorologe m/-gin f. ~**y** n Meteorologie f

meter¹ /'mi:tə(r)/ n Zähler m

meter² n (Amer) = **metre**

method /'meθəd/ n Methode f; (Culin) Zubereitung f

methodical /mɪ'θɒdɪkl/ a, -**ly** adv systematisch, methodisch

Methodist /'meθədɪst/ n Methodist(in) m(f)

meths /meθs/ n (fam) Brennspiritus m

methylated /'meθɪleɪtɪd/ a ~ **spirit[s]** Brennspiritus m

meticulous /mɪ'tɪkjʊləs/ a, -**ly** adv sehr genau

metre /'mi:tə(r)/ n Meter m & n; (rhythm) Versmaß nt

metric /'metrɪk/ a metrisch

metropolis /mɪ'trɒpəlɪs/ n Metropole f

metropolitan /metrə'pɒlɪtən/ *a* hauptstädtisch; (*international*) weltstädtisch

mettle /'metl/ *n* Mut *m*

mew /mju:/ *n* Miau *nt* ● *vi* miauen

Mexican /'meksɪkən/ *a* mexikanisch ● *n* Mexikaner(in) *m(f)*. '**Mexico** *n* Mexiko *nt*

miaow /mɪ'aʊ/ *n* Miau *nt* ● *vi* miauen

mice /maɪs/ *see* **mouse**

microbe /'maɪkrəʊb/ *n* Mikrobe *f*

micro /'maɪkrəʊ/: ~**chip** *n* Mikrochip *nt*. ~**computer** *n* Mikrocomputer *m*. ~**film** *n* Mikrofilm *m*. ~**phone** *n* Mikrophon *nt*. ~**processor** *n* Mikroprozessor *m*. ~**scope** /-skəʊp/ *n* Mikroskop *nt*. ~**scopic** /-'skɒpɪk/ *a* mikroskopisch. ~**wave** *n* Mikrowelle *f*. ~**wave [oven]** *n* Mikrowellenherd *m*

mid /mɪd/ *a* ~ **May** Mitte Mai; **in** ~ **air** in der Luft

midday /mɪd'deɪ/ *n* Mittag *m*

middle /'mɪdl/ *a* mittlere(r,s); **the M**~ **Ages** das Mittelalter; **the** ~ **class[es]** der Mittelstand; **the M**~ **East** der Nahe Osten ● *n* Mitte *f*; **in the** ~ **of the night** mitten in der Nacht

middle: ~**-aged** *a* mittleren Alters. ~**-class** *a* bürgerlich. ~**man** *n* (*Comm*) Zwischenhändler *m*

middling /'mɪdlɪŋ/ *a* mittelmäßig

midge /mɪdʒ/ *n* [kleine] Mücke *f*

midget /'mɪdʒɪt/ *n* Liliputaner(in) *m(f)*

Midlands /'mɪdləndz/ *npl* **the** ~ Mittelengland *n*

'**midnight** *n* Mitternacht *f*

midriff /'mɪdrɪf/ *n* (*fam*) Taille *f*

midst /mɪdst/ *n* **in the** ~ **of** mitten in (+ *dat*); **in our** ~ unter uns

mid: ~**summer** *n* Hochsommer *m*; (*solstice*) Sommersonnenwende *f*. ~**way** *adv* auf halbem Wege. ~**wife** *n* Hebamme *f*. ~**wifery** /-wɪfrɪ/ *n* Geburtshilfe *f*. ~'**winter** *n* Mitte *f* des Winters

might[1] /maɪt/ *v aux* **I** ~ vielleicht; **it** ~ **be true** es könnte wahr sein; **I** ~ **as well stay** am besten bleibe ich hier; **he asked if he** ~ **go** er fragte, ob er gehen dürfte; **you** ~ **have drowned** du hättest ertrinken können

might[2] *n* Macht *f*

mighty /'maɪtɪ/ *a* (**-ier, -iest**) mächtig

migraine /'mi:greɪn/ *n* Migräne *f*

migrant /'maɪgrənt/ *a* Wander- ● *n* (*bird*) Zugvogel *m*

migrat|e /maɪ'greɪt/ *vi* abwandern; ⟨*birds:*⟩ ziehen. ~**ion** /-'greɪʃn/ *n* Wanderung *f*; (*of birds*) Zug *m*

mike /maɪk/ *n* (*fam*) Mikrophon *nt*

mild /maɪld/ *a* (**-er, -est**) mild

mildew /'mɪldju:/ *n* Schimmel *m*; (*Bot*) Mehltau *m*

mild|ly /'maɪldlɪ/ *adv* leicht; **to put it** ~**ly** gelinde gesagt. ~**ness** *n* Milde *f*

mile /maɪl/ *n* Meile *f* (= *1,6 km*); ~**s too big** (*fam*) viel zu groß

mile|age /-ɪdʒ/ *n* Meilenzahl *f*; (*of car*) Meilenstand *m*. ~**stone** *n* Meilenstein *m*

militant /'mɪlɪtənt/ *a* militant

military /'mɪlɪtrɪ/ *a* militärisch. ~ **service** *n* Wehrdienst *m*

militate /'mɪlɪteɪt/ *vi* ~ **against** sprechen gegen

militia /mɪ'lɪʃə/ *n* Miliz *f*

milk /mɪlk/ *n* Milch *f* ● *vt* melken

milk: ~**man** *n* Milchmann *m*. ~ **shake** *n* Milchmixgetränk *nt*

milky /'mɪlkɪ/ *a* (**-ier, -iest**) milchig. **M**~ **Way** *n* (*Astr*) Milchstraße *f*

mill /mɪl/ *n* Mühle *f*; (*factory*) Fabrik *f* ● *vt/i* mahlen; (*Techn*) fräsen. ~ **about,** ~ **around** *vi* umherlaufen

millennium /mɪ'lenɪəm/ *n* Jahrtausend *nt*

miller /'mɪlə(r)/ *n* Müller *m*

millet /'mɪlɪt/ *n* Hirse *f*

milli|gram /'mɪlɪ-/ *n* Milligramm *nt*. ~**metre** *n* Millimeter *m* & *nt*

milliner /'mɪlɪnə(r)/ *n* Modistin *f*; (*man*) Hutmacher *m*. ~**y** *n* Damenhüte *pl*

million /'mɪljən/ *n* Million *f*; **a** ~ **pounds** eine Million Pfund. ~**aire** /-'neə(r)/ *n* Millionär(in) *m(f)*

'**millstone** *n* Mühlstein *m*

mime /maɪm/ *n* Pantomime *f* ● *vt* pantomimisch darstellen

mimic /'mɪmɪk/ *n* Imitator *m* ● *vt* (*pt/pp* **mimicked**) nachahmen. ~**ry** *n* Nachahmung *f*

mimosa /mɪ'məʊzə/ *n* Mimose *f*

mince /mɪns/ *n* Hackfleisch *nt* ● *vt* (*Culin*) durchdrehen; **not** ~ **words** kein Blatt vor den Mund nehmen

mince: ~**meat** *n* Masse *f* aus Korinthen, Zitronat *usw*; **make** ~**meat of** (*fig*) vernichtend schlagen. ~'**pie** *n* mit 'mincemeat' gefülltes Pastetchen *nt*

mincer /'mɪnsə(r)/ *n* Fleischwolf *m*

mind /maɪnd/ n Geist m; (sanity) Verstand m; **to my** ~ meiner Meinung nach; **give s.o. a piece of one's** ~ jdm gehörig die Meinung sagen; **make up one's** ~ sich entschließen; **be out of one's** ~ nicht bei Verstand sein; **have sth in** ~ etw im Sinn haben; **bear sth in** ~ an etw (acc) denken; **have a good** ~ **to** große Lust haben, zu; **I have changed my** ~ ich habe es mir anders überlegt • vt aufpassen auf (+ acc); **I don't** ~ **the noise** der Lärm stört mich nicht; ~ **the step!** Achtung Stufe! • vi (care) sich kümmern (**about** um); **I don't** ~ mir macht es nichts aus; **never** ~**!** macht nichts! **do you** ~ **if?** haben Sie etwas dagegen, wenn? ~ **out** vi aufpassen

mind|ful a ~**ful of** eingedenk (+ gen). ~**less** a geistlos

mine[1] /maɪn/ poss pron meine(r), meins; **a friend of** ~ ein Freund von mir; **that is** ~ das gehört mir

mine[2] n Bergwerk nt; (explosive) Mine f • vt abbauen; (Mil) verminen. ~ **detector** n Minensuchgerät nt. ~**field** n Minenfeld nt

miner /ˈmaɪnə(r)/ n Bergarbeiter m

mineral /ˈmɪnərl/ n Mineral nt. ~**ogy** /-ˈrælədʒɪ/ n Mineralogie f. ~ **water** n Mineralwasser nt

minesweeper /ˈmaɪn-/ n Minenräumboot nt

mingle /ˈmɪŋgl/ vi ~ **with** sich mischen unter (+ acc)

miniature /ˈmɪnɪtʃə(r)/ a Klein- • n Miniatur f

mini|bus /ˈmɪnɪ-/ n Kleinbus m. ~**cab** n Taxi nt

minim /ˈmɪnɪm/ n (Mus) halbe Note f

minim|al /ˈmɪnɪməl/ a minimal. ~**ize** vt auf ein Minimum reduzieren. ~**um** n (pl -**ima**) Minimum nt • a Mindest-

mining /ˈmaɪnɪŋ/ n Bergbau m

miniskirt /ˈmɪnɪ-/ n Minirock m

minist|er /ˈmɪnɪstə(r)/ n Minister m; (Relig) Pastor m. ~**erial** /-ˈstɪərɪəl/ a ministeriell

ministry /ˈmɪnɪstrɪ/ n (Pol) Ministerium nt; **the** ~ (Relig) das geistliche Amt

mink /mɪŋk/ n Nerz m

minor /ˈmaɪnə(r)/ a kleiner; (less important) unbedeutend • n Minderjährige(r) m/f; (Mus) Moll nt

minority /maɪˈnɒrətɪ/ n Minderheit f; (age) Minderjährigkeit f

minor road n Nebenstraße f

mint[1] /mɪnt/ n Münzstätte f • a (stamp) postfrisch; **in** ~ **condition** wie neu • vt prägen

mint[2] n (herb) Minze f; (sweet) Pfefferminzbonbon m & nt

minuet /mɪnjʊˈet/ n Menuett nt

minus /ˈmaɪnəs/ prep minus, weniger; (fam: without) ohne • n ~ **[sign]** Minuszeichen nt

minute[1] /ˈmɪnɪt/ n Minute f; **in a** ~ (shortly) gleich; ~**s** pl (of meeting) Protokoll nt

minute[2] /maɪˈnjuːt/ a winzig; (precise) genau

mirac|le /ˈmɪrəkl/ n Wunder nt. ~**ulous** /-ˈrækjʊləs/ a wunderbar

mirage /ˈmɪrɑːʒ/ n Fata Morgana f

mire /ˈmaɪə(r)/ n Morast m

mirror /ˈmɪrə(r)/ n Spiegel m • vt widerspiegeln

mirth /mɜːθ/ n Heiterkeit f

misad'venture /mɪs-/ n Mißgeschick nt

misanthropist /mɪˈzænθrəpɪst/ n Menschenfeind m

misappre'hension n Mißverständnis nt; **be under a** ~ sich irren

misbe'hav|e vi sich schlecht benehmen. ~**iour** n schlechtes Benehmen nt

mis'calcu|late vt falsch berechnen • vi sich verrechnen. ~**'lation** n Fehlkalkulation f

'miscarriage n Fehlgeburt f; ~ **of justice** Justizirrtum m. **mis'carry** vi eine Fehlgeburt haben

miscellaneous /mɪsəˈleɪnɪəs/ a vermischt

mischief /ˈmɪstʃɪf/ n Unfug m; (harm) Schaden m

mischievous /ˈmɪstʃɪvəs/ a, -**ly** adv schelmisch; (malicious) boshaft

miscon'ception n falsche Vorstellung f

mis'conduct n unkorrektes Verhalten nt; (adultery) Ehebruch m

miscon'strue vt mißdeuten

mis'deed n Missetat f

misde'meanour n Missetat f

miser /ˈmaɪzə(r)/ n Geizhals m

miserable /ˈmɪzrəbl/ a, -**bly** adv unglücklich; (wretched) elend

miserly /ˈmaɪzəlɪ/ adv geizig

misery /ˈmɪzərɪ/ n Elend nt; (fam: person) Miesepeter m

mis'fire vi fehlzünden; (go wrong) fehlschlagen

'**misfit** n Außenseiter(in) m(f)
mis'fortune n Unglück nt
mis'givings npl Bedenken pl
mis'guided a töricht
mishap /'mıshæp/ n Mißgeschick nt
misin'form vt falsch unterrichten
misin'terpret vt mißdeuten
mis'judge vt falsch beurteilen; (estimate wrongly) falsch einschätzen
mis'lay vt (pt/pp **-laid**) verlegen
mis'lead vt (pt/pp **-led**) irreführen.
~**ing** a irreführend
mis'manage vt schlecht verwalten.
~**ment** n Mißwirtschaft f
misnomer /mıs'nəʊmə(r)/ n Fehlbezeichnung f
'**misprint** n Druckfehler m
mis'quote vt falsch zitieren
misrepre'sent vt falsch darstellen
miss /mıs/ n Fehltreffer m ● vt verpassen; (fail to hit or find) verfehlen; (fail to attend) versäumen; (fail to notice) übersehen; (feel the loss of) vermissen ● vi (fail to hit) nicht treffen. ~ **out** vt auslassen
Miss n (pl **-es**) Fräulein nt
misshapen /mıs'ʃeıpən/ a mißgestaltet
missile /'mısaıl/ n [Wurf]geschoß nt; (Mil) Rakete f
missing /'mısıŋ/ a fehlend; (lost) verschwunden; (Mil) vermißt; **be** ~ fehlen
mission /'mıʃn/ n Auftrag m; (Mil) Einsatz m; (Relig) Mission f
missionary /'mıʃənrı/ n Missionar(in) m(f)
mis'spell vt (pt/pp **-spelt** or **-spelled**) falsch schreiben
mist /mıst/ n Dunst m; (fog) Nebel m; (on window) Beschlag m ● vi ~ **up** beschlagen
mistake /mı'steık/ n Fehler m; **by** ~ aus Versehen ● vt (pt **mistook**, pp **mistaken**) mißverstehen; ~ **for** verwechseln mit
mistaken /mı'steıkən/ a falsch; **be** ~ sich irren; ~ **identity** Verwechslung f. ~**ly** adv irrtümlicherweise
mistletoe /'mısltəʊ/ n Mistel f
mistress /'mıstrıs/ n Herrin f; (teacher) Lehrerin f; (lover) Geliebte f
mis'trust n Mißtrauen nt ● vt mißtrauen (+ dat)
misty /'mıstı/ a (**-ier, -iest**) dunstig; (foggy) neblig; (fig) unklar

misunder'stand vt (pt/pp **-stood**) mißverstehen. ~**ing** n Mißverständnis nt
misuse[1] /mıs'ju:z/ vt mißbrauchen
misuse[2] /mıs'ju:s/ n Mißbrauch m
mite /maıt/ n (Zool) Milbe f; **little** ~ (child) kleines Ding nt
mitigat|e /'mıtıgeıt/ vt mildern. ~**ing** a mildernd
mitten /'mıtn/ n Fausthandschuh m
mix /mıks/ n Mischung f ● vt mischen ● vi sich mischen; ~ **with** (associate with) verkehren mit. ~ **up** vt mischen; (muddle) durcheinanderbringen; (mistake for) verwechseln (**with** mit)
mixed /mıkst/ a gemischt; **be** ~ **up** durcheinander sein
mixer /'mıksə(r)/ n Mischmaschine f; (Culin) Küchenmaschine f
mixture /'mıkstʃə(r)/ n Mischung f; (medicine) Mixtur f; (Culin) Teig m
'**mix-up** n Durcheinander nt; (confusion) Verwirrung f; (mistake) Verwechslung f
moan /məʊn/ n Stöhnen nt ● vi stöhnen; (complain) jammern
moat /məʊt/ n Burggraben m
mob /mɒb/ n Horde f; (rabble) Pöbel m; (fam: gang) Bande f ● vt (pt/pp **mobbed**) herfallen über (+ acc); belagern ⟨celebrity⟩
mobile /'məʊbaıl/ a beweglich ● n Mobile nt. ~ '**home** n Wohnwagen m
mobility /mə'bılətı/ n Beweglichkeit f
mobi|lization /məʊbılaı'zeıʃn/ n Mobilisierung f. ~**lize** /'məʊbılaız/ vt mobilisieren
mocha /'mɒkə/ n Mokka m
mock /mɒk/ a Schein- ● vt verspotten ● vi spotten. ~**ery** n Spott m
'**mock-up** n Modell nt
modal /'məʊdl/ a ~ **auxiliary** Modalverb nt
mode /məʊd/ n Art und] Weise f; (fashion) Mode f
model /'mɒdl/ n Modell nt; (example) Vorbild nt; **[fashion]** ~ Mannequin nt ● a Modell-; (exemplary) Muster- ● v (pt/pp **modelled**) ● vt formen, modellieren; vorführen ⟨clothes⟩ ● vi Mannequin sein; (for artist) Modell stehen
moderate[1] /'mɒdəreıt/ vt mäßigen ● vi sich mäßigen

moderate² /'mɒdərət/ a mäßig; ⟨opinion⟩ gemäßigt ● n (Pol) Gemäßigte(r) m/f. ~ly adv mäßig; (fairly) einigermaßen

moderation /mɒdə'reɪʃn/ n Mäßigung f; **in** ~ mit Maß[en]

modern /'mɒdn/ a modern. ~ize vt modernisieren. ~ **languages** npl neuere Sprachen pl

modest /'mɒdɪst/ a bescheiden; (decorous) schamhaft. ~y n Bescheidenheit f

modicum /'mɒdɪkəm/ n **a** ~ **of** ein bißchen

modif|ication /mɒdɪfɪ'keɪʃn/ n Abänderung f. ~y /'mɒdɪfaɪ/ vt (pt/pp -fied) abändern

modulate /'mɒdjʊleɪt/ vt/i modulieren

moist /mɔɪst/ a (-er, -est) feucht

moisten /'mɔɪsn/ vt befeuchten

moistur|e /'mɔɪstʃə(r)/ n Feuchtigkeit f. ~izer n Feuchtigkeitscreme f

molar /'məʊlə(r)/ n Backenzahn m

molasses /mə'læsɪz/ n (Amer) Sirup m

mole¹ /məʊl/ n Leberfleck m

mole² n (Zool) Maulwurf m

mole³ n (breakwater) Mole f

molecule /'mɒlɪkjuːl/ n Molekül nt

'molehill n Maulwurfshaufen m

molest /mə'lest/ vt belästigen

mollify /'mɒlɪfaɪ/ vt (pt/pp -ied) besänftigen

mollusc /'mɒləsk/ n Weichtier nt

mollycoddle /'mɒlɪkɒdl/ vt verzärteln

molten /'məʊltən/ a geschmolzen

mom /mɒm/ n (Amer fam) Mutti f

moment /'məʊmənt/ n Moment m, Augenblick m; **at the** ~ im Augenblick, augenblicklich. ~ary a vorübergehend

momentous /mə'mentəs/ a bedeutsam

momentum /mə'mentəm/ n Schwung m

monarch /'mɒnək/ n Monarch(in) m(f). ~y n Monarchie f

monast|ery /'mɒnəstrɪ/ n Kloster nt. ~ic /mə'næstɪk/ a Kloster-

Monday /'mʌndeɪ/ n Montag m

money /'mʌnɪ/ n Geld nt

money: ~-**box** n Sparbüchse f. ~-**lender** n Geldverleiher m. ~ **order** n Zahlungsanweisung f

mongrel /'mʌŋgrəl/ n Promenadenmischung f

monitor /'mɒnɪtə(r)/ n (Techn) Monitor m ● vt überwachen ⟨progress⟩; abhören ⟨broadcast⟩

monk /mʌŋk/ n Mönch m

monkey /'mʌŋkɪ/ n Affe m. ~-**nut** n Erdnuß f. ~-**wrench** n (Techn) Engländer m

mono /'mɒnəʊ/ n Mono nt

monocle /'mɒnəkl/ n Monokel nt

monogram /'mɒnəgræm/ n Monogramm nt

monologue /'mɒnəlɒg/ n Monolog m

monopol|ize /mə'nɒpəlaɪz/ vt monopolisieren. ~y n Monopol nt

monosyll|abic /mɒnəsɪ'læbɪk/ a einsilbig. ~able /'mɒnəsɪləbl/ n einsilbiges Wort nt

monotone /'mɒnətəʊn/ n **in a** ~ mit monotoner Stimme

monoton|ous /mə'nɒtənəs/ a, -ly adv eintönig, monoton; (tedious) langweilig. ~y n Eintönigkeit f, Monotonie f

monsoon /mɒn'suːn/ n Monsun m

monster /'mɒnstə(r)/ n Ungeheuer nt; (cruel person) Unmensch m

monstrosity /mɒn'strɒsətɪ/ n Monstrosität f

monstrous /'mɒnstrəs/ a ungeheuer; (outrageous) ungeheuerlich

montage /mɒn'tɑːʒ/ n Montage f

month /mʌnθ/ n Monat m. ~ly a & adv monatlich ● n (periodical) Monatszeitschrift f

monument /'mɒnjʊmənt/ n Denkmal nt. ~al /-'mentl/ a (fig) monumental

moo /muː/ n Muh nt ● vi (pt/pp mooed) muhen

mooch /muːtʃ/ vi ~ **about** (fam) herumschleichen

mood /muːd/ n Laune f; **be in a good/bad** ~ gute/schlechte Laune haben

moody /'muːdɪ/ a (-ier, -iest) launisch

moon /muːn/ n Mond m; **over the** ~ (fam) überglücklich

moon: ~**light** n Mondschein m. ~**lighting** n (fam) ≈ Schwarzarbeit f. ~**lit** a mondhell

moor¹ /mʊə(r)/ n Moor nt

moor² vt (Naut) festmachen ● vi anlegen. ~**ings** npl (chains) Verankerung f; (place) Anlegestelle f

moose /muːs/ n Elch m

moot

mould

moot /muːt/ *a* **it's a ~ point** darüber läßt sich streiten ● *vt* aufwerfen ⟨*question*⟩

mop /mɒp/ *n* Mop *m*; **~ of hair** Wuschelkopf *m* ● *vt* (*pt/pp* **mopped**) wischen. **~ up** *vt* aufwischen

mope /məʊp/ *vi* Trübsal blasen

moped /'məʊped/ *n* Moped *nt*

moral /'mɒrl/ *a*, **-ly** *adv* moralisch, sittlich; (*virtuous*) tugendhaft ● *n* Moral *f*; **~s** *pl* Moral *f*

morale /mə'rɑːl/ *n* Moral *f*

morality /mə'rælətɪ/ *n* Sittlichkeit *f*

moralize /'mɒrəlaɪz/ *vi* moralisieren

morbid /'mɔːbɪd/ *a* krankhaft; (*gloomy*) trübe

more /mɔː(r)/ *a, adv & n* mehr; (*in addition*) noch; **a few ~** noch ein paar; **any ~** noch etwas; **once ~** noch einmal; **~ or less** mehr oder weniger; **some ~ tea?** noch etwas Tee? **~ interesting** interessanter; **~ [and ~]** **quickly** [immer] schneller; **no ~, thank you,** nichts mehr, danke; **no ~ bread** kein Brot mehr; **no ~ apples** keine Äpfel mehr

moreover /mɔː'rəʊvə(r)/ *adv* außerdem

morgue /mɔːg/ *n* Leichenschauhaus *nt*

moribund /'mɒrɪbʌnd/ *a* sterbend

morning /'mɔːnɪŋ/ *n* Morgen *m*; **in the ~** morgens, am Morgen; (*tomorrow*) morgen früh

Morocco /mə'rɒkəʊ/ *n* Marokko *nt*

moron /'mɔːrɒn/ *n* (*fam*) Idiot *m*

morose /mə'rəʊs/ *a*, **-ly** *adv* mürrisch

morphine /'mɔːfiːn/ *n* Morphium *nt*

Morse /mɔːs/ *n* **~ [code]** Morsealphabet *nt*

morsel /'mɔːsl/ *n* (*food*) Happen *m*

mortal /'mɔːtl/ *a* sterblich; (*fatal*) tödlich ● *n* Sterbliche(r) *m/f*. **~ity** /mɔː'tælətɪ/ *n* Sterblichkeit *f*. **~ly** *adv* tödlich

mortar /'mɔːtə(r)/ *n* Mörtel *m*

mortgage /'mɔːgɪdʒ/ *n* Hypothek *f* ● *vt* hypothekarisch belasten

mortify /'mɔːtɪfaɪ/ *vt* (*pt/pp* **-ied**) demütigen

mortuary /'mɔːtjʊərɪ/ *n* Leichenhalle *f*; (*public*) Leichenschauhaus *nt*; (*Amer: undertaker's*) Bestattungsinstitut *nt*

mosaic /məʊ'zeɪɪk/ *n* Mosaik *nt*

Moscow /'mɒskəʊ/ *n* Moskau *nt*

Moselle /məʊ'zel/ *n* Mosel *f*; (*wine*) Moselwein *m*

mosque /mɒsk/ *n* Moschee *f*

mosquito /mɒs'kiːtəʊ/ *n* (*pl* **-es**) [Stech]mücke *f*, Schnake *f*; (*tropical*) Moskito *m*

moss /mɒs/ *n* Moos *nt*. **~y** *a* moosig

most /məʊst/ *a* der/die/das meiste; (*majority*) die meisten; **for the ~ part** zum größten Teil ● *adv* am meisten; (*very*) höchst; **the ~ interesting day** der interessanteste Tag; **~ unlikely** höchst unwahrscheinlich ● *n* das meiste; **~ of them** die meisten [von ihnen]; **at [the] ~** höchstens; **~ of the time** die meiste Zeit. **~ly** *adv* meist

MOT *n* ≈ TÜV *m*

motel /məʊ'tel/ *n* Motel *nt*

moth /mɒθ/ *n* Nachtfalter *m*; **[clothes-]~** Motte *f*

moth: ~ball *n* Mottenkugel *f*. **~-eaten** *a* mottenzerfressen

mother /'mʌðə(r)/ *n* Mutter *f*; **M~'s Day** Muttertag *m* ● *vt* bemuttern

mother: ~hood *n* Mutterschaft *f*. **~-in-law** *n* (*pl* **~s-in-law**) Schwiegermutter *f*. **~land** *n* Mutterland *nt*. **~ly** *a* mütterlich. **~-of-pearl** *n* Perlmutter *f*. **~-to-be** *n* werdende Mutter *f*. **~ tongue** *n* Muttersprache *f*

mothproof /'mɒθ-/ *a* mottenfest

motif /məʊ'tiːf/ *n* Motiv *nt*

motion /'məʊʃn/ *n* Bewegung *f*; (*proposal*) Antrag *m* ● *vt/i* **~ [to] s.o.** jdm ein Zeichen geben (**to** zu). **~less** *a*, **-ly** *adv* bewegungslos

motivat|e /'məʊtɪveɪt/ *vt* motivieren. **~ion** /-'veɪʃn/ *n* Motivation *f*

motive /'məʊtɪv/ *n* Motiv *nt*

motley /'mɒtlɪ/ *a* bunt

motor /'məʊtə(r)/ *n* Motor *m*; (*car*) Auto *nt* ● *a* Motor-; (*Anat*) motorisch ● *vi* [mit dem Auto] fahren

Motorail /'məʊtəreɪl/ *n* Autozug *m*

motor: ~ bike *n* (*fam*) Motorrad *nt*. **~ boat** *n* Motorboot *nt*. **~cade** /-keɪd/ *n* (*Amer*) Autokolonne *f*. **~ car** *n* Auto *nt*, Wagen *m*. **~ cycle** *n* Motorrad *nt*. **~cyclist** *n* Motorradfahrer *m*. **~ing** *n* Autofahren *nt*. **~ist** *n* Autofahrer(in) *m(f)*. **~ize** *vt* motorisieren. **~ vehicle** *n* Kraftfahrzeug *nt*. **~way** *n* Autobahn *f*

mottled /'mɒtld/ *a* gesprenkelt

motto /'mɒtəʊ/ *n* (*pl* **-es**) Motto *nt*

mould[1] /məʊld/ *n* (*fungus*) Schimmel *m*

mould² n Form f ● vt formen (**into** zu).
~**ing** n (Archit) Fries m
mouldy /'məʊldɪ/ a schimmelig;
(fam: worthless) schäbig
moult /məʊlt/ vi (bird:) sich mau-
sern; (animal:) sich haaren
mound /maʊnd/ n Hügel m; (of
stones) Haufen m
mount¹ /maʊnt/ n Berg m
mount² n (animal) Reittier nt; (of
jewel) Fassung f; (of photo, picture)
Passepartout nt ● vt (get on) steigen auf
(+ acc); (on pedestal) montieren auf
(+ acc); besteigen ⟨horse⟩; fassen
⟨jewel⟩; aufziehen ⟨photo, picture⟩ ● vi
aufsteigen; (tension:) steigen. ~ **up** vi
sich häufen; (add up) sich anhäufen
mountain /'maʊntɪn/ n Berg m
mountaineer /maʊntɪ'nɪə(r)/ n
Bergsteiger(in) m(f). ~**ing** n Berg-
steigen nt
mountainous /'maʊntɪnəs/ a ber-
gig, gebirgig
mourn /mɔːn/ vt betrauern ● vi
trauern (**for** um). ~**er** n Trauernde(r)
m/f. ~**ful** a, -**ly** adv trauervoll. ~**ing**
n Trauer f
mouse /maʊs/ n (pl **mice**) Maus f.
~**trap** n Mausefalle f
mousse /muːs/ n Schaum m; (Culin)
Mousse f
moustache /mə'stɑːʃ/ n Schnurr-
bart m
mousy /'maʊsɪ/ a graubraun;
⟨person⟩ farblos
mouth¹ /maʊð/ vt ~ **sth** etw lautlos
mit den Lippen sagen
mouth² /maʊθ/ n Mund m; (of
animal) Maul nt; (of river) Mündung
f
mouth: ~**ful** n Mundvoll m; (bite) Bis-
sen m. ~**organ** n Mundharmonika
f. ~**piece** n Mundstück nt; (fig: person) Sprachrohr nt. ~**wash** n Mund-
wasser nt
movable /'muːvəbl/ a beweglich
move /muːv/ n Bewegung f; (fig)
Schritt m; (moving house) Umzug m;
(in board-game) Zug m; **on the** ~ (on
the go) unterwegs; **get a** ~ **on** (fam) sich beeilen
● vt bewegen; (emotionally) rühren;
(move along) rücken; (in board-game)
ziehen; (take away) wegnehmen; weg-
fahren ⟨car⟩; (rearrange) umstellen;
(transfer) versetzen ⟨person⟩; verlegen
⟨office⟩; (propose) beantragen; ~ **house**
umziehen ● vi sich bewegen; (move
house) umziehen; **don't** ~! stillhalten!

(stop) stillstehen! ~ **along** vt/i wei-
terrücken. ~ **away** vt/i wegrücken;
(move house) wegziehen. ~ **forward**
vt/i vorrücken; ⟨vehicle:⟩ vorwärts
fahren. ~ **in** vi einziehen. ~ **off** vi
⟨vehicle:⟩ losfahren. ~ **out** vi ausziehen. ~ **over** vt/i [zur Seite]
rücken. ~ **up** vi aufrücken
movement /'muːvmənt/ n Bewegung f; (Mus) Satz m; (of clock) Uhrwerk nt
movie /'muːvɪ/ n (Amer) Film m; **go
to the** ~**s** ins Kino gehen
moving /'muːvɪŋ/ a beweglich;
(touching) rührend
mow /məʊ/ vt (pt **mowed**, pp **mown**
or **mowed**) mähen. ~ **down** vt (destroy) niedermähen
mower /'məʊə(r)/ n Rasenmäher m
MP abbr see **Member of Parliament**
Mr /'mɪstə(r)/ n (pl **Messrs**) Herr m
Mrs /'mɪsɪz/ n Frau f
Ms /'mɪz/ n Frau f
much /mʌtʃ/ a, adv & n viel; **as** ~ **as**
soviel wie; **very** ~ **loved/interested**
sehr geliebt/interessiert
muck /mʌk/ n Mist m; (fam: filth)
Dreck m. ~ **about** vi herumalbern;
(tinker) herumspielen (**with** mit). ~
in vi (fam) mitmachen. ~ **out** vt aus-
misten. ~ **up** vt (fam) vermasseln;
(make dirty) schmutzig machen
mucky /'mʌkɪ/ a (-**ier**, -**iest**) dreckig
mucus /'mjuːkəs/ n Schleim m
mud /mʌd/ n Schlamm m
muddle /'mʌdl/ n Durcheinander
nt; (confusion) Verwirrung f ● vt ~
[**up**] durcheinanderbringen
muddy /'mʌdɪ/ a (-**ier**, -**iest**)
schlammig; ⟨shoes⟩ schmutzig
mudguard n Kotflügel m; (on bicycle) Schutzblech nt
muesli /'muːzlɪ/ n Müsli nt
muff /mʌf/ n Muff m
muffle /'mʌfl/ vt dämpfen ⟨sound⟩; ~
[**up**] (for warmth) einhüllen (**in** in
+ acc)
muffler /'mʌflə(r)/ n Schal m;
(Amer, Auto) Auspufftopf m
mufti /'mʌftɪ/ n **in** ~ in Zivil
mug¹ /mʌg/ n Becher m; (for beer)
Bierkrug m; (fam: face) Visage f;
(fam: simpleton) Trottel m
mug² vt (pt/pp **mugged**) überfallen.
~**ger** n Straßenräuber m. ~**ging** n
Straßenraub m
muggy /'mʌgɪ/ a (-**ier**, -**iest**) schwül
mule¹ /mjuːl/ n Maultier nt

mule² n (slipper) Pantoffel m

mull /mʌl/ vt ∼ **over** nachdenken über (+ acc)

mulled /mʌld/ a ∼ **wine** Glühwein m

multi /ˈmʌltɪ/: ∼**coloured** a vielfarbig, bunt. ∼**lingual** /-ˈlɪŋgwəl/ a mehrsprachig. ∼**national** a multinational

multiple /ˈmʌltɪpl/ a vielfach; (with pl) mehrere ● n Vielfache(s) nt

multiplication /mʌltɪplɪˈkeɪʃn/ n Multiplikation f

multiply /ˈmʌltɪplaɪ/ v (pt/pp -ied) ● vt multiplizieren (by mit) ● vi sich vermehren

multi-storey a ∼ **car park** Parkhaus nt

mum¹ /mʌm/ a keep ∼ (fam) den Mund halten

mum² n (fam) Mutti f

mumble /ˈmʌmbl/ vt/i murmeln

mummy¹ /ˈmʌmɪ/ n (fam) Mutti f

mummy² n (Archaeol) Mumie f

mumps /mʌmps/ n Mumps m

munch /mʌntʃ/ vt/i mampfen

mundane /mʌnˈdeɪn/ a banal; (worldly) weltlich

municipal /mjuːˈnɪsɪpl/ a städtisch

munitions /mjuːˈnɪʃnz/ npl Kriegsmaterial nt

mural /ˈmjʊərəl/ n Wandgemälde nt

murder /ˈmɜːdə(r)/ n Mord m ● vt ermorden; (fam: ruin) verhunzen. ∼**er** n Mörder m. ∼**ess** n Mörderin f. ∼**ous** /-rəs/ a mörderisch

murky /ˈmɜːkɪ/ a (-ier, -iest) düster

murmur /ˈmɜːmə(r)/ n Murmeln nt ● vt/i murmeln

muscle /ˈmʌsl/ n Muskel m

muscular /ˈmʌskjʊlə(r)/ a Muskel-; (strong) muskulös

muse /mjuːz/ vi nachsinnen (on über + acc)

museum /mjuːˈzɪəm/ n Museum nt

mush /mʌʃ/ n Brei m

mushroom /ˈmʌʃrʊm/ n [eßbarer] Pilz m, esp Champignon m ● vi (fig) wie Pilze aus dem Boden schießen

mushy /ˈmʌʃɪ/ a breiig

music /ˈmjuːzɪk/ n Musik f; (written) Noten pl; **set to** ∼ vertonen

musical /ˈmjuːzɪkl/ a musikalisch ● n Musical nt. ∼ **box** n Spieldose f. ∼ **instrument** n Musikinstrument nt

music-hall n Varieté nt

musician /mjuːˈzɪʃn/ n Musiker(in) m(f)

music-stand n Notenständer m

Muslim /ˈmʊzlɪm/ a mohammedanisch ● n Mohammedaner(in) m(f)

muslin /ˈmʌzlɪn/ n Musselin m

mussel /ˈmʌsl/ n [Mies]muschel f

must /mʌst/ v aux (nur Präsens) müssen; (with negative) dürfen ● n a ∼ (fam) ein Muß nt

mustard /ˈmʌstəd/ n Senf m

muster /ˈmʌstə(r)/ vt versammeln; aufbringen (strength) ● vi sich versammeln

musty /ˈmʌstɪ/ a (-ier, -iest) muffig

mutation /mjuːˈteɪʃn/ n Veränderung f; (Biol) Mutation f

mute /mjuːt/ a stumm

muted /ˈmjuːtɪd/ a gedämpft

mutilat|e /ˈmjuːtɪleɪt/ vt verstümmeln. ∼**ion** /-ˈleɪʃn/ n Verstümmelung f

mutin|ous /ˈmjuːtɪnəs/ a meuterisch. ∼**y** n Meuterei f ● vi (pt/pp -ied) meutern

mutter /ˈmʌtə(r)/ n Murmeln nt ● vt/i murmeln

mutton /ˈmʌtn/ n Hammelfleisch nt

mutual /ˈmjuːtjʊəl/ a gegenseitig; (fam: common) gemeinsam. ∼**ly** adv gegenseitig

muzzle /ˈmʌzl/ n (of animal) Schnauze f; (of firearm) Mündung f; (for dog) Maulkorb m ● vt einen Maulkorb anlegen (+ dat)

my /maɪ/ a mein

myopic /maɪˈɒpɪk/ a kurzsichtig

myself /maɪˈself/ pron selbst; (refl) mich; **by** ∼ allein; **I thought to** ∼ ich habe mir gedacht

mysterious /mɪˈstɪərɪəs/ a, -ly adv geheimnisvoll; (puzzling) mysteriös, rätselhaft

mystery /ˈmɪstərɪ/ n Geheimnis nt; (puzzle) Rätsel nt; ∼ **[story]** Krimi m

mysti|c[al] /ˈmɪstɪk[l]/ a mystisch. ∼**cism** /-sɪzm/ n Mystik f

mystification /mɪstɪfɪˈkeɪʃn/ n Verwunderung f

mystified /ˈmɪstɪfaɪd/ a be ∼ vor einem Rätsel stehen

mystique /mɪˈstiːk/ n geheimnisvoller Zauber m

myth /mɪθ/ n Mythos m; (fam: untruth) Märchen nt. ∼**ical** a mythisch; (fig) erfunden

mythology /mɪˈθɒlədʒɪ/ n Mythologie f

N

nab /næb/ vt (pt/pp **nabbed**) (fam) erwischen

nag[1] /næg/ n (horse) Gaul m

nag[2] vt/i (pt/pp **nagged**) herumnörgeln (**s.o.** an jdm). **~ging** a (pain) nagend ● n Nörgelei f

nail /neɪl/ n (Anat, Techn) Nagel m; **on the ~** (fam) sofort ● vt nageln (**to** an + acc). **~ down** vt festnageln; (close) zunageln

nail: **~-brush** n Nagelbürste f. **~-file** n Nagelfeile f. **~ polish** n Nagellack m. **~ scissors** npl Nagelschere f. **~ varnish** n Nagellack m

naive /naɪˈiːv/ a, **-ly** adv naiv. **~ty** /-ətɪ/ n Naivität f

naked /ˈneɪkɪd/ a nackt; (flame) offen; **with the ~ eye** mit bloßem Auge. **~ness** n Nacktheit f

name /neɪm/ n Name m; (reputation) Ruf m; **by ~** dem Namen nach; **by the ~ of** namens; **call s.o. ~s** (fam) jdn beschimpfen ● vt nennen; (give a name to) einen Namen geben (+ dat); (announce publicly) den Namen bekanntgeben von. **~less** a namenlos. **~ly** adv nämlich

name: **~-plate** n Namensschild nt. **~sake** n Namensvetter m/ Namensschwester f

nanny /ˈnænɪ/ n Kindermädchen nt. **~-goat** n Ziege f

nap /næp/ n Nickerchen nt; **have a ~** ein Nickerchen machen ● vi **catch s.o. ~ping** jdn überrumpeln

nape /neɪp/ n ~ **[of the neck]** Nacken m

napkin /ˈnæpkɪn/ n Serviette f; (for baby) Windel f

nappy /ˈnæpɪ/ n Windel f

narcotic /nɑːˈkɒtɪk/ a betäubend ● n Narkotikum nt; (drug) Rauschgift nt

narrat|e /nəˈreɪt/ vt erzählen. **~ion** /-eɪʃn/ n Erzählung f

narrative /ˈnærətɪv/ a erzählend ● n Erzählung f

narrator /nəˈreɪtə(r)/ n Erzähler(in) m(f)

narrow /ˈnærəʊ/ a (**-er, -est**) schmal; (restricted) eng; (margin, majority) knapp; (fig) beschränkt; **have a ~ escape**, adv **~ly escape** mit knapper Not davonkommen ● vi sich verengen. **~-ˈminded** a engstirnig

nasal /ˈneɪzl/ a nasal; (Med & Anat) Nasen-

nastily /ˈnɑːstɪlɪ/ adv boshaft

nasturtium /nəˈstɜːʃəm/ n Kapuzinerkresse f

nasty /ˈnɑːstɪ/ a (**-ier, -iest**) übel; (unpleasant) unangenehm; (unkind) boshaft; (serious) schlimm; **turn ~** gemein werden

nation /ˈneɪʃn/ n Nation f; (people) Volk nt

national /ˈnæʃənl/ a national; (newspaper) überregional; (campaign) landesweit ● n Staatsbürger(in) m(f)

national: **~ ˈanthem** n Nationalhymne f. **N~ ˈHealth Service** n staatlicher Gesundheitsdienst m. **N~ Inˈsurance** n Sozialversicherung f

nationalism /ˈnæʃənəlɪzm/ n Nationalismus m

nationality /næʃəˈnælətɪ/ n Staatsangehörigkeit f

national|ization /næʃənəlaɪˈzeɪʃn/ n Verstaatlichung f. **~ize** /ˈnæʃənə- laɪz/ vt verstaatlichen. **~ly** /ˈnæʃə- nəlɪ/ adv landesweit

ˈnation-wide a landesweit

native /ˈneɪtɪv/ a einheimisch; (innate) angeboren ● n Eingeborene(r) m/f; (local inhabitant) Einheimische(r) m/f; **a ~ of Vienna** ein gebürtiger Wiener

native: **~ ˈland** n Heimatland nt. **~ ˈlanguage** n Muttersprache f

Nativity /nəˈtɪvətɪ/ n **the ~** Christi Geburt f. **~ play** n Krippenspiel nt

natter /ˈnætə(r)/ n **have a ~** (fam) einen Schwatz halten ● vi (fam) schwatzen

natural /ˈnætʃrəl/ a, **-ly** adv natürlich; **~[-coloured]** naturfarben

natural: **~ ˈgas** n Erdgas nt. **~ ˈhistory** n Naturkunde f

naturalist /ˈnætʃrəlɪst/ n Naturforscher m

natural|ization /nætʃrəlaɪˈzeɪʃn/ n Einbürgerung f. **~ize** /ˈnætʃrəlaɪz/ vt einbürgern

nature /ˈneɪtʃə(r)/ n Natur f; (kind) Art f; **by ~** von Natur aus. **~ reserve** n Naturschutzgebiet nt

naturism /ˈneɪtʃərɪzm/ n Freikörperkultur f

naught /nɔːt/ n = **nought**

naughty /'nɔːtɪ/ a (-**ier**, -**iest**), -**ily** adv
unartig; (*slightly indecent*) gewagt
nausea /'nɔːzɪə/ n Übelkeit f
nause|ate /'nɔːzɪeɪt/ vt anekeln.
~**ating** a ekelhaft. ~**ous** /-ɪəs/ a
I feel ~**ous** mir ist übel
nautical /'nɔːtɪkl/ a nautisch. ~
mile n Seemeile f
naval /'neɪvl/ a Marine-
nave /neɪv/ n Kirchenschiff nt
navel /'neɪvl/ n Nabel m
navigable /'nævɪgəbl/ a schiffbar
navigat|e /'nævɪgeɪt/ vi navigieren
● vt befahren ⟨river⟩. ~**ion** /-'geɪʃn/
n Navigation f. ~**or** n Navigator m
navvy /'nævɪ/ n Straßenarbeiter m
navy /'neɪvɪ/ n [Kriegs]marine f ● a
~ **[blue]** marineblau
near /nɪə(r)/ a (-**er**, -**est**) nah[e]; **the**
~**est bank** die nächste Bank ● adv
nahe; ~ **by** nicht weit weg; ~ **at hand**
in der Nähe; **draw** ~ sich nähern
● prep nahe an (+ dat/acc); in der Nähe
von; ~ **to tears** den Tränen nahe; **go** ~
[to] sth nahe an etw (acc) herangehen
● vt sich nähern (+ dat)
near: ~**by** a nahegelegen. ~**ly** adv
fast, beinahe; **not** ~**ly** bei weitem
nicht. ~**ness** n Nähe f. ~ **side** n
Beifahrerseite f. ~-**sighted** a
(*Amer*) kurzsichtig
neat /niːt/ a (-**er**, -**est**), -**ly** adv adrett;
(*tidy*) ordentlich; (*clever*) geschickt;
(*undiluted*) pur. ~**ness** n Ordentlichkeit f
necessarily /'nesəserəlɪ/ adv not-
wendigerweise; **not** ~ nicht unbedingt
necessary /'nesəsərɪ/ a nötig, notwendig
necessit|ate /nɪ'sesɪteɪt/ vt not-
wendig machen. ~**y** n Notwendigkeit f; **she works from** ~**y** sie
arbeitet, weil sie es nötig hat
neck /nek/ n Hals m; ~ **and** ~ Kopf
an Kopf
necklace /'neklɪs/ n Halskette f
neck: ~**line** n Halsausschnitt m.
~**tie** n Schlips m
nectar /'nektə(r)/ n Nektar m
née /neɪ/ a ~ **Brett** geborene Brett
need /niːd/ n Bedürfnis nt; (*misfortune*) Not f; **be in** ~ Not leiden; **be
in** ~ **of** brauchen; **in case of** ~ notfalls;
if ~ **be** wenn nötig; **there is a** ~ **for** es
besteht ein Bedarf an (+ dat); **there is
no** ~ **for that** das ist nicht nötig; **there
is no** ~ **for you to go** du brauchst

nicht zu gehen ● vt brauchen; **you** ~
not go du brauchst nicht zu gehen; ~ **I
come?** muß ich kommen? **I** ~ **to know**
ich muß es wissen; **it** ~**s to be done** es
muß gemacht werden
needle /'niːdl/ n Nadel f ● vt (*annoy*)
ärgern
needless /'niːdlɪs/ a, -**ly** adv unnötig;
~ **to say** selbstverständlich, natürlich
'**needlework** n Nadelarbeit f
needy /'niːdɪ/ a (-**ier**, -**iest**) bedürftig
negation /nɪ'geɪʃn/ n Verneinung f
negative /'negətɪv/ a negativ ● n
Verneinung f; (*photo*) Negativ nt
neglect /nɪ'glekt/ n Vernach-
lässigung f; **state of** ~ verwahrloster
Zustand m ● vt vernachlässigen; (*omit*)
versäumen (**to** zu). ~**ed** a verwahrlost. ~**ful** a nachlässig; **be** ~**ful
of** vernachlässigen
negligen|ce /'neglɪdʒəns/ n Nach-
lässigkeit f; (*Jur*) Fahrlässigkeit f.
~**t** a, -**ly** adv nachlässig; (*Jur*) fahr-
lässig
negligible /'neglɪdʒəbl/ a unbedeutend
negotiable /nɪ'gəʊʃəbl/ a ⟨road⟩ befahrbar; (*Comm*) unverbindlich; **not**
~ nicht übertragbar
negotiat|e /nɪ'gəʊʃɪeɪt/ vt aus-
handeln; (*Auto*) nehmen ⟨bend⟩ ● vi
verhandeln. ~**ion** /-'eɪʃn/ n Verhandlung f. ~**or** n Unterhändler(in)
m(f)
Negro /'niːgrəʊ/ a Neger- ● n (pl -**es**)
Neger m
neigh /neɪ/ vi wiehern
neighbour /'neɪbə(r)/ n Nachbar(in)
m(f). ~**hood** n Nachbarschaft f; **in
the** ~**hood of** in der Nähe von; (*fig*)
um ... herum. ~**ing** a Nachbar-. ~**ly**
a [gut]nachbarlich
neither /'naɪðə(r)/ a & pron keine-
(r,s) [von beiden] ● adv ~ ... **nor**
weder ... noch ● conj auch nicht
neon /'niːɒn/ n Neon nt. ~ **light** n
Neonlicht nt
nephew /'nevjuː/ n Neffe m
nepotism /'nepətɪzm/ n Vettern-
wirtschaft f
nerve /nɜːv/ n Nerv m; (*fam: courage*) Mut m; (*fam: impudence*)
Frechheit f; **lose one's** ~ den Mut
verlieren. ~-**racking** a nerven-
aufreibend
nervous /'nɜːvəs/ a, -**ly** adv (*afraid*)
ängstlich; (*highly-strung*) nervös;
(*Anat, Med*) Nerven-; **be** ~ Angst

haben. ~ 'breakdown n Nerven-
zusammenbruch m. ~ness Ängst-
lichkeit f; (Med) Nervosität f
nervy /'nɜːvɪ/ a (-ier, -iest) nervös;
(Amer: impudent) frech
nest /nest/ n Nest nt ● vi nisten.
~-egg n Notgroschen m
nestle /'nesl/ vi sich schmiegen
(against an + acc)
net¹ /net/ n Netz nt; (curtain) Store m
● vt (pt/pp netted) (catch) [mit dem
Netz] fangen
net² a netto; (salary, weight) Netto- ● vt
(pt/pp netted) netto einnehmen;
(yield) einbringen
'netball n l Korbball m
Netherlands /'neðələndz/ npl the ~
die Niederlande pl
netting /'netɪŋ/ n [wire] ~ Maschendraht m
nettle /'netl/ n Nessel f
'network n Netz nt
neuralgia /njʊə'rældʒə/ n Neuralgie
f
neurolog|ist /njʊə'rɒlədʒɪst/ n
Neurologe m/-gin f. ~y n Neurologie
f
neur|osis /njʊə'rəʊsɪs/ n (pl -oses
/-siːz/) Neurose f. ~otic /-'rɒtɪk/ a
neurotisch
neuter /'njuːtə(r)/ a (Gram) sächlich
● n (Gram) Neutrum nt ● vt
kastrieren; (spay) sterilisieren
neutral /'njuːtrl/ a neutral ● n in ~
(Auto) im Leerlauf. ~ity /-'trælətɪ/ n
Neutralität f. ~ize vt neutralisieren
never /'nevə(r)/ adv nie, niemals;
(fam: not) nicht; ~ mind macht
nichts; well I ~! ja so was! ~-ending
a endlos
nevertheless /nevəðə'les/ adv
dennoch, trotzdem
new /njuː/ a (-er, -est) neu
new: ~born a neugeboren. ~comer
n Neuankömmling m. ~fangled
/-'fæŋgld/ a (pej) neumodisch.
~-laid a frisch gelegt
'newly adv frisch. ~-weds npl
jungverheiratetes Paar nt
new: ~ 'moon n Neumond m.
~ness n Neuheit f
news /njuːz/ n Nachricht f; (Radio,
TV) Nachrichten pl; piece of ~
Neuigkeit f
news: ~agent n Zeitungshändler m.
~ bulletin n Nachrichtensendung f.
~caster n Nachrichtensprecher(in)
m(f). ~flash n Kurzmeldung f.

~letter n Mitteilungsblatt nt.
~paper n Zeitung f; (material)
Zeitungspapier m. ~reader n
Nachrichtensprecher(in) m(f)
newt /njuːt/ n Molch m
New: ~ Year's 'Day n Neujahr nt. ~
Year's 'Eve n Silvester nt. ~ Zealand /'ziːlənd/ n Neuseeland nt
next /nekst/ a & n nächste(r,s);
who's ~? wer kommt als nächster
dran? the ~ best das nächstbeste; ~
door nebenan; my ~ of kin mein
nächster Verwandter; ~ to nothing
fast gar nichts; the week after ~
übernächste Woche ● adv als nächstes;
~ to neben
NHS abbr see National Health Service
nib /nɪb/ n Feder f
nibble /'nɪbl/ vt/i knabbern (at an
+ dat)
nice /naɪs/ a (-r, -st) nett; (day,
weather) schön; (food) gut; (distinction)
fein. ~ly adv nett; (well) gut. ~ties
/'naɪsətɪz/ npl Feinheiten pl
niche /niːʃ/ n Nische f; (fig) Platz m
nick /nɪk/ n Kerbe f; (fam: prison)
Knast m; (fam: police station) Revier
nt; in the ~ of time (fam) gerade noch
rechtzeitig; in good ~ (fam) in gutem
Zustand ● vt einkerben; (steal) klauen;
(fam: arrest) schnappen
nickel /'nɪkl/ n Nickel nt; (Amer)
Fünfcentstück nt
'nickname n Spitzname m
nicotine /'nɪkətiːn/ n Nikotin nt
niece /niːs/ n Nichte f
Nigeria /naɪ'dʒɪərɪə/ n Nigeria nt.
~n a nigerianisch ● n Nigeria-
ner(in) m(f)
niggardly /'nɪgədlɪ/ a knauserig
niggling /'nɪglɪŋ/ a gering; (petty)
kleinlich; (pain) quälend
night /naɪt/ n Nacht f; (evening)
Abend m; at ~ nachts; Monday ~
Montag nacht/abend
night: ~cap n Schlafmütze f; (drink)
Schlaftrunk m. ~-club n Nachtklub
m. ~-dress n Nachthemd nt. ~fall n
at ~fall bei Einbruch der Dunkelheit.
~-gown n, (fam) ~ie /'naɪtɪ/ n
Nachthemd nt
nightingale /'naɪtɪŋgeɪl/ n Nachtigall f
night: ~-life n Nachtleben nt. ~ly a
nächtlich ● adv jede Nacht. ~mare
n Alptraum m. ~shade n (Bot)
deadly ~shade Tollkirsche f.

∼**-time** n **at** ∼**-time** bei Nacht.
∼**-'watchman** n Nachtwächter m
nil /nɪl/ n null
nimble /'nɪmbl/ a (**-r, -st**), **-bly** adv
flink
nine /naɪn/ a neun ● n Neun f.
∼**'teen** a neunzehn. ∼**'teenth** a
neunzehnte(r,s)
ninetieth /'naɪntɪɪθ/ a neunzigste-
(r,s)
ninety /'naɪntɪ/ a neunzig
ninth /naɪnθ/ a neunte(r,s)
nip /nɪp/ n Kniff m; (bite) Biß m ● vt
kneifen; (bite) beißen; ∼ **in the bud**
(fig) im Keim ersticken ● vi (fam: run)
laufen
nipple /'nɪpl/ n Brustwarze f; (Amer:
on bottle) Sauger m
nippy /'nɪpɪ/ a (**-ier, -iest**) (fam) (cold)
frisch; (quick) flink
nitrate /'naɪtreɪt/ n Nitrat nt
nitrogen /'naɪtrədʒən/ n Stickstoff
m
nitwit /'nɪtwɪt/ n (fam) Dummkopf
m
no /nəʊ/ adv nein ● n (pl **noes**) Nein
nt ● a kein(e); (pl) keine; **in no time**
[sehr] schnell; **no parking/smoking**
Parken/Rauchen verboten; **no one** =
nobody
nobility /nəʊ'bɪlətɪ/ n Adel m
noble /'nəʊbl/ a (**-r, -st**) edel; (aris-
tocratic) adlig. ∼**man** n Adlige(r) m
nobody /'nəʊbədɪ/ pron niemand,
keiner; **he knows** ∼ er kennt nie-
manden od keinen ● n **a** ∼ ein Niemand m
nocturnal /nɒk'tɜːnl/ a nächtlich;
〈animal, bird〉 Nacht-
nod /nɒd/ n Nicken nt ● v (pt/pp
nodded) ● vi nicken ● vt ∼ **one's head**
mit dem Kopf nicken. ∼ **off** vi einnicken
nodule /'nɒdjuːl/ n Knötchen nt
noise /nɔɪz/ n Geräusch nt; (loud)
Lärm m. ∼**less** a, **-ly** adv geräuschlos
noisy /'nɔɪzɪ/ a (**-ier, -iest**), **-ily** adv
laut; 〈eater〉 geräuschvoll
nomad /'nəʊmæd/ n Nomade m.
∼**ic** /-'mædɪk/ a nomadisch; 〈life,
tribe〉 Nomaden-
nominal /'nɒmɪnl/ a, **-ly** adv nominell
nominat|e /'nɒmɪneɪt/ vt nomi-
nieren, aufstellen; (appoint) ernennen. ∼**ion** /-'neɪʃn/ n Nominierung
f; Ernennung f

nominative /'nɒmɪnətɪv/ a & n
(Gram) ∼ [**case**] Nominativ m
nonchalant /'nɒnʃələnt/ a, **-ly** adv
nonchalant; 〈gesture〉 lässig
non-com'missioned /nɒn-/ a ∼
officer Unteroffizier m
non-com'mittal /nɒn-/ a unverbindlich;
be ∼ sich nicht festlegen
nondescript /'nɒndɪskrɪpt/ a unbe-
stimmbar; 〈person〉 unscheinbar
none /nʌn/ pron keine(r)/keins; ∼
of us keiner von uns; ∼ **of it/this**
nichts davon ● adv ∼ **too** nicht gerade;
∼ **too soon** [um] keine Minute zu früh;
∼ **the wiser** um nichts klüger; ∼ **the
less** dennoch
nonentity /nɒ'nentətɪ/ n Null f
non-ex'istent a nichtvorhanden;
be ∼ nicht vorhanden sein
non-'fiction n Sachliteratur f
non-'iron a bügelfrei
nonplussed /nɒn'plʌst/ a verblüfft
nonsens|e /'nɒnsəns/ n Unsinn m.
∼**ical** /-'sensɪkl/ a unsinnig
non-'smoker n Nichtraucher m;
(compartment) Nichtraucherabteil
nt
non-'stop adv ununterbrochen; 〈fly〉
nonstop; ∼ **'flight** Nonstopflug m
non-'swimmer n Nichtschwimmer
m
non-'violent a gewaltlos
noodles /'nuːdlz/ npl Bandnudeln pl
nook /nʊk/ n Eckchen nt, Winkel m
noon /nuːn/ n Mittag m; **at** ∼ um 12
Uhr mittags
noose /nuːs/ n Schlinge f
nor /nɔː(r)/ adv noch ● conj auch
nicht
Nordic /'nɔːdɪk/ a nordisch
norm /nɔːm/ n Norm f
normal /'nɔːml/ a normal. ∼**ity**
/-'mælətɪ/ n Normalität f. ∼**ly** adv
normal; (usually) normalerweise
north /nɔːθ/ n Norden m; **to the** ∼
of nördlich von ● a Nord-, nord- ● adv
nach Norden
north: N∼ **America** n Nordamerika
nt. ∼**-east** a Nordost- ● n Nordosten
m
norther|ly /'nɔːðəlɪ/ a nördlich. ∼**n**
a nördlich. **N**∼**n Ireland** n Nord-
irland nt
north: N∼ **'Pole** n Nordpol m. **N**∼
'Sea n Nordsee f. ∼**ward[s]**
/-wəd[z]/ adv nach Norden. ∼**-west**
a Nordwest- ● n Nordwesten m

Nor|way /'nɔ:weɪ/ n Norwegen nt. **∼wegian** /-'wi:dʒn/ a norwegisch ● n Norweger(in) m(f)

nose /nəʊz/ n Nase f ● vi **∼ about** herumschnüffeln

nose: **∼bleed** n Nasenbluten nt. **∼dive** n (Aviat) Sturzflug m

nostalg|ia /nɒ'stældʒɪə/ n Nostalgie f. **∼ic** a nostalgisch

nostril /'nɒstrəl/ n Nasenloch nt; (of horse) Nüster f

nosy /'nəʊzɪ/ a (**-ier, -iest**) (fam) neugierig

not /nɒt/ adv nicht; **∼ a** kein(e); **if ∼** wenn nicht; **∼ at all** gar nicht; **∼ a bit** kein bißchen; **∼ even** nicht mal; **∼ yet** noch nicht; **he is ∼ a German** er ist kein Deutscher

notab|le /'nəʊtəbl/ a bedeutend; (remarkable) bemerkenswert. **∼ly** adv insbesondere

notary /'nəʊtərɪ/ n **∼ 'public /** Notar

notation /nəʊ'teɪʃn/ n Notation f; (Mus) Notenschrift f

notch /nɒtʃ/ n Kerbe f. **∼ up** vt (score) erzielen

note /nəʊt/ n (written comment) Notiz f, Anmerkung f; (short letter) Briefchen nt, Zettel m; (bank∼) Banknote f, Schein m; (Mus) Note f; (sound) Ton m; (on piano) Taste f; **eighth/quarter ∼** (Amer) Achtel-/ Viertelnote f; **half/whole ∼** (Amer) halbe/ganze Note f; **of ∼** von Bedeutung; **make a ∼ of** notieren ● vt beachten; (notice) bemerken (**that** daß). **∼ down** vt notieren

'notebook n Notizbuch nt

noted /nəʊtɪd/ a bekannt (**for** für)

note: **∼paper** n Briefpapier nt. **∼worthy** a beachtenswert

nothing /'nʌθɪŋ/ n, pron & adv nichts; **for ∼** umsonst; **∼ but** nichts als; **∼ much** nicht viel; **∼ interesting** nichts Interessantes; **it's ∼ to do with you** das geht dich nichts an

notice /'nəʊtɪs/ n (on board) Anschlag m, Bekanntmachung f; (announcement) Anzeige f; (review) Kritik f; (termination of lease, employment) Kündigung f; [**advance**] **∼** Bescheid m; **give [in one's] ∼** kündigen; **give s.o. ∼** jdm kündigen; **take no ∼ of** keine Notiz nehmen von; **take no ∼!** ignoriere es! ● vt bemerken. **∼able** /-əbl/ a, **-bly** adv merklich. **∼-board** n Anschlagbrett nt

noti|fication /nəʊtɪfɪ'keɪʃn/ n Benachrichtigung f. **∼fy** /'nəʊtɪfaɪ/ vt (pt/pp **-ied**) benachrichtigen

notion /'nəʊʃn/ n Idee f; **∼s** pl (Amer: haberdashery) Kurzwaren pl

notorious /nəʊ'tɔ:rɪəs/ a berüchtigt

notwith'standing prep trotz (+ gen) ● adv trotzdem, dennoch

nought /nɔ:t/ n Null f

noun /naʊn/ n Substantiv nt

nourish /'nʌrɪʃ/ vt nähren. **∼ing** a nahrhaft. **∼ment** n Nahrung f

novel /'nɒvl/ a neu[artig] ● n Roman m. **∼ist** n Romanschriftsteller(in) m(f). **∼ty** n Neuheit f; **∼ties** pl kleine Geschenkartikel pl

November /nəʊ'vembə(r)/ n November m

novice /'nɒvɪs/ n Neuling m; (Relig) Novize m/Novizin f

now /naʊ/ adv & conj jetzt; **∼ [that]** jetzt, wo; **just ∼** gerade, eben; **right ∼** sofort; **∼ and again** hin und wieder; **now, now!** na, na!

'nowadays adv heutzutage

nowhere /'nəʊ-/ adv nirgendwo, nirgends

noxious /'nɒkʃəs/ a schädlich

nozzle /'nɒzl/ n Düse f

nuance /'nju:ɑ̃s/ n Nuance f

nuclear /'nju:klɪə(r)/ a Kern-. **∼ de'terrent** n nukleares Abschreckungsmittel nt

nucleus /'nju:klɪəs/ n (pl **-lei** -lɪaɪ/) Kern m

nude /nju:d/ a nackt ● n (Art) Akt m; **in the ∼** nackt

nudge /nʌdʒ/ n Stups m ● vt stupsen

nud|ist /'nju:dɪst/ n Nudist m. **∼ity** n Nacktheit f

nugget /'nʌgɪt/ n [Gold]klumpen m

nuisance /'nju:sns/ n Ärgernis nt; (pest) Plage f; **be a ∼** ärgerlich sein; ⟨person:⟩ lästig sein; **what a ∼!** wie ärgerlich!

null /nʌl/ a **∼ and void** null und nichtig. **∼ify** /'nʌlɪfaɪ/ vt (pt/pp **-ied**) für nichtig erklären

numb /nʌm/ a gefühllos, taub; **∼ with cold** taub vor Kälte ● vt betäuben

number /'nʌmbə(r)/ n Nummer f; (amount) Anzahl f; (Math) Zahl f ● vt numerieren; (include) zählen (**among** zu). **∼-plate** n Nummernschild nt

numeral /'nju:mərl/ n Ziffer f

numerate /'nju:mərət/ a **be ∼** rechnen können

numerical /nju:'merɪkl/ *a*, **-ly** *adv* numerisch; **in ~ order** zahlenmäßig geordnet

numerous /'nju:mərəs/ *a* zahlreich

nun /nʌn/ *n* Nonne *f*

nuptial /'nʌpʃl/ *a* Hochzeits-. **~s** *npl* (*Amer*) Hochzeit *f*

nurse /nɜ:s/ *n* [Kranken]schwester *f*; (*male*) Krankenpfleger *m*; **children's ~** Kindermädchen *nt* ● *vt* pflegen. **~maid** *n* Kindermädchen *nt*

nursery /'nɜ:sərɪ/ *n* Kinderzimmer *nt*; (*Hort*) Gärtnerei *f*; **[day] ~** Kindertagesstätte *f*. **~ rhyme** *n* Kinderreim *m*. **~ school** *n* Kindergarten *m*

nursing /'nɜ:sɪŋ/ *n* Krankenpflege *f*. **~ home** *n* Pflegeheim *nt*

nurture /'nɜ:tʃə(r)/ *vt* nähren; (*fig*) hegen

nut /nʌt/ *n* Nuß *f*; (*Techn*) [Schrauben]mutter *f*; (*fam: head*) Birne *f* (*fam*); **be ~s** (*fam*) spinnen (*fam*). **~crackers** *npl* Nußknacker *m*. **~meg** *n* Muskat *m*

nutrient /'nju:trɪənt/ *n* Nährstoff *m*

nutrit|ion /nju:'trɪʃn/ *n* Ernährung *f*. **~ious** /-ʃəs/ *a* nahrhaft

'nutshell *n* Nußschale *f*; **in a ~** (*fig*) kurz gesagt

nuzzle /'nʌzl/ *vt* beschnüffeln

nylon /'naɪlɒn/ *n* Nylon *nt*; **~s** *pl* Nylonstrümpfe *pl*

nymph /nɪmf/ *n* Nymphe *f*

O

O /əʊ/ *n* (*Teleph*) null

oaf /əʊf/ *n* (*pl* **oafs**) Trottel *m*

oak /əʊk/ *n* Eiche *f* ● *attrib* Eichen-

OAP *abbr* (**old-age pensioner**) Rentner(in) *m(f)*

oar /ɔ:(r)/ *n* Ruder *nt*. **~sman** *n* Ruderer *m*

oasis /əʊ'eɪsɪs/ *n* (*pl* **oases** /-si:z/) Oase *f*

oath /əʊθ/ *n* Eid *m*; (*swear-word*) Fluch *m*

oatmeal /'əʊt-/ *n* Hafermehl *nt*

oats /əʊts/ *npl* Hafer *m*; (*Culin*) **[rolled] ~** Haferflocken *pl*

obedien|ce /ə'bi:dɪəns/ *n* Gehorsam *m*. **~t** *a*, **-ly** *adv* gehorsam

obes|e /əʊ'bi:s/ *a* fettleibig. **~ity** *n* Fettleibigkeit *f*

obey /ə'beɪ/ *vt/i* gehorchen (+ *dat*); befolgen ⟨*instructions, rules*⟩

obituary /ə'bɪtjʊərɪ/ *n* Nachruf *m*; (*notice*) Todesanzeige *f*

object¹ /'ɒbdʒɪkt/ *n* Gegenstand *m*; (*aim*) Zweck *m*; (*intention*) Absicht *f*; (*Gram*) Objekt *nt*; **money is no ~** Geld spielt keine Rolle

object² /əb'dʒekt/ *vi* Einspruch erheben (**to** gegen); (*be against*) etwas dagegen haben

objection /əb'dʒekʃn/ *n* Einwand *m*; **have no ~** nichts dagegen haben. **~able** /-əbl/ *a* anstößig; ⟨*person*⟩ unangenehm

objectiv|e /əb'dʒektɪv/ *a*, **-ly** *adv* objektiv ● *n* Ziel *nt*. **~ity** /-'tɪvətɪ/ *n* Objektivität *f*

objector /əb'dʒektə(r)/ *n* Gegner *m*

obligation /ɒblɪ'geɪʃn/ *n* Pflicht *f*; **be under an ~** verpflichtet sein; **without ~** unverbindlich

obligatory /ə'blɪgətrɪ/ *a* obligatorisch; **be ~** Vorschrift sein

oblig|e /ə'blaɪdʒ/ *vt* verpflichten; (*compel*) zwingen; (*do a small service*) einen Gefallen tun (+ *dat*); **much ~ed!** vielen Dank! **~ing** *a* entgegenkommend

oblique /ə'bli:k/ *a* schräg; ⟨*angle*⟩ schief; (*fig*) indirekt. **~ stroke** *n* Schrägstrich *m*

obliterate /ə'blɪtəreɪt/ *vt* auslöschen

oblivion /ə'blɪvɪən/ *n* Vergessenheit *f*

oblivious /ə'blɪvɪəs/ *a* **be ~** sich (*dat*) nicht bewußt sein (**of** *or* **to** *gen*)

oblong /'ɒblɒŋ/ *a* rechteckig ● *n* Rechteck *nt*

obnoxious /əb'nɒkʃəs/ *a* widerlich

oboe /'əʊbəʊ/ *n* Oboe *f*

obscen|e /əb'si:n/ *a* obszön; (*atrocious*) abscheulich. **~ity** /-'senətɪ/ *n* Obszönität *f*; Abscheulichkeit *f*

obscur|e /əb'skjʊə(r)/ *a* dunkel; (*unknown*) unbekannt ● *vt* verdecken; (*confuse*) verwischen. **~ity** *n* Dunkelheit *f*; Unbekanntheit *f*

obsequious /əb'si:kwɪəs/ *a* unterwürfig

observa|nce /əb'zɜ:vns/ *n* (*of custom*) Einhaltung *f*. **~nt** *a* aufmerksam. **~tion** /ɒbzə'veɪʃn/ *n* Beobachtung *f*; (*remark*) Bemerkung *f*

observatory /əb'zɜ:vətrɪ/ *n* Sternwarte *f*; (*weather*) Wetterwarte *f*

observe /əb'zɜːv/ vt beobachten; (say, notice) bemerken; (keep, celebrate) feiern; (obey) einhalten. ~r n Beobachter m

obsess /əb'ses/ vt **be ~ed by** besessen sein von. ~**ion** /-eʃn/ n Besessenheit f; (persistent idea) fixe Idee f. ~**ive** /-ɪv/ a, **-ly** adv zwanghaft

obsolete /'ɒbsəliːt/ a veraltet

obstacle /'ɒbstəkl/ n Hindernis nt

obstetrician /ɒbstə'trɪʃn/ n Geburtshelfer m. **obstetrics** /-'stetrɪks/ n Geburtshilfe f

obstina|cy /'ɒbstɪnəsɪ/ n Starrsinn m. ~**te** /-nət/ a, **-ly** adv starrsinnig; (refusal) hartnäckig

obstreperous /əb'strepərəs/ a widerspenstig

obstruct /əb'strʌkt/ vt blockieren; (hinder) behindern. ~**ion** /-ʌkʃn/ n Blockierung f; Behinderung f; (obstacle) Hindernis nt. ~**ive** /-ɪv/ a **be ~ive** Schwierigkeiten bereiten

obtain /əb'teɪn/ vt erhalten, bekommen ● vi gelten. ~**able** /-əbl/ a erhältlich

obtrusive /əb'truːsɪv/ a aufdringlich; (thing) auffällig

obtuse /əb'tjuːs/ a (Geom) stumpf; (stupid) begriffsstutzig

obviate /'ɒbvɪeɪt/ vt beseitigen

obvious /'ɒbvɪəs/ a, **-ly** adv offensichtlich, offenbar

occasion /ə'keɪʒn/ n Gelegenheit f; (time) Mal nt; (event) Ereignis nt; (cause) Anlaß m, Grund m; **on ~** gelegentlich, hin und wieder; **on the ~ of** anläßlich (+ gen) ● vt veranlassen

occasional /ə'keɪʒənl/ a gelegentlich; **he has the ~ glass of wine** er trinkt gelegentlich ein Glas Wein. ~**ly** adv gelegentlich, hin und wieder

occult /ɒ'kʌlt/ a okkult

occupant /'ɒkjʊpənt/ n Bewohner(in) m(f); (of vehicle) Insasse m

occupation /ɒkjʊ'peɪʃn/ n Beschäftigung f; (job) Beruf m; (Mil) Besetzung f; (period) Besatzung f. ~**al** a Berufs-. ~**al therapy** n Beschäftigungstherapie f

occupier /'ɒkjʊpaɪə(r)/ n Bewohner(in) m(f)

occupy /'ɒkjʊpaɪ/ vt (pt/pp **occupied**) besetzen (seat, (Mil) country); einnehmen (space); in Anspruch nehmen (time); (live in) bewohnen; (fig)

bekleiden (office); (keep busy) beschäftigen; ~ **oneself** sich beschäftigen

occur /ə'kɜː(r)/ vi (pt/pp **occurred**) geschehen; (exist) vorkommen, auftreten; **it ~red to me that** es fiel mir ein, daß. **occurrence** /ə'kʌrəns/ n Auftreten nt; (event) Ereignis nt

ocean /'əʊʃn/ n Ozean m

o'clock /ə'klɒk/ adv **[at] 7 ~** [um] 7 Uhr

octagonal /ɒk'tægənl/ a achteckig

octave /'ɒktɪv/ n (Mus) Oktave f

October /ɒk'təʊbə(r)/ n Oktober m

octopus /'ɒktəpəs/ n (pl **-puses**) Tintenfisch m

odd /ɒd/ a (**-er, -est**) seltsam, merkwürdig; (number) ungerade; (not of set) einzeln; **forty ~** über vierzig; **~ jobs** Gelegenheitsarbeiten pl; **the ~ one out** die Ausnahme; **at ~ moments** zwischendurch; **have the ~ glass of wine** gelegentlich ein Glas Wein trinken

odd|ity /'ɒdɪtɪ/ n Kuriosität f. ~**ly** adv merkwürdig; ~**ly enough** merkwürdigerweise. ~**ment** n (of fabric) Rest m

odds /ɒdz/ npl (chances) Chancen pl; **at ~** uneinig; **~ and ends** Kleinkram m; **it makes no ~** es spielt keine Rolle

ode /əʊd/ n Ode f

odious /'əʊdɪəs/ a widerlich, abscheulich

odour /'əʊdə(r)/ n Geruch m. ~**less** a geruchlos

oesophagus /iː'sɒfəgəs/ n Speiseröhre f

of /ɒv, unbetont əv/ prep von (+ dat); (made of) aus (+ dat); **the two of us** wir zwei; **a child of three** ein dreijähriges Kind; **the fourth of January** der vierte Januar; **a pound of butter** ein Pfund Butter; **a cup of tea/coffee** eine Tasse Tee/Kaffee; **a bottle of wine** eine Flasche Wein; **half of it** die Hälfte davon; **the whole of the room** das ganze Zimmer

off /ɒf/ prep von (+ dat); **£10 ~ the price** £10 Nachlaß; **~ the coast** vor der Küste; **get ~ the ladder/bus** von der Leiter/aus dem Bus steigen; **take/ leave the lid ~ the saucepan** den Topf abdecken/nicht zudecken ● adv weg; (button, lid, handle) ab; (light) aus; (brake) los; (machine) abgeschaltet; (tap) zu; (on appliance) **'off'** 'aus'; **2 kilometres ~** 2 Kilometer entfernt; **a**

long way ~ weit weg; (*time*) noch lange hin; **~ and on** hin und wieder; **with his hat/coat ~** ohne Hut/Mantel; **with the light/lid ~** ohne Licht/Deckel; **20% ~** 20% Nachlaß; **be ~** (*leave*) [weg]gehen; (*Sport*) starten; ⟨*food*⟩ schlecht; (*all gone*) alle sein; **be better/ worse ~** besser/schlechter dran sein; **be well ~** gut dran sein; (*financially*) wohlhabend sein; **have a day ~** einen freien Tag haben; **go/ drive ~** weggehen/ -fahren; **turn/take sth ~** etw abdrehen/-nehmen

offal /'ɒfl/ *n* (*Culin*) Innereien *pl*

offence /ə'fens/ *n* (*illegal act*) Vergehen *nt*; **give/take ~** Anstoß erregen/nehmen (**at** an + *dat*)

offend /ə'fend/ *vt* beleidigen. **~er** *n* (*Jur*) Straftäter *m*

offensive /ə'fensɪv/ *a* anstößig; (*Mil*, *Sport*) offensiv ● *n* Offensive *f*

offer /'ɒfə(r)/ *n* Angebot *nt*; **on special ~** im Sonderangebot ● *vt* anbieten (**to** *dat*); leisten ⟨*resistance*⟩; **~ s.o. sth** jdm etw anbieten; **~ to do sth** sich anbieten, etw zu tun. **~ing** *n* Gabe *f*

off'hand *a* brüsk; (*casual*) lässig ● *adv* so ohne weiteres

office /'ɒfɪs/ *n* Büro *nt*; (*post*) Amt *nt*; **in ~** im Amt; **~ hours** *pl* Dienststunden *pl*

officer /'ɒfɪsə(r)/ *n* Offizier *m*; (*official*) Beamte(r) *m*/Beamtin *f*; (*police*) Polizeibeamte(r) *m*/ -beamtin *f*

official /ə'fɪʃl/ *a* offiziell, amtlich ● *n* Beamte(r) *m*/Beamtin *f*; (*Sport*) Funktionär *m*. **~ly** *adv* offiziell

officiate /ə'fɪʃɪeɪt/ *vi* amtieren

officious /ə'fɪʃəs/ *a*, **-ly** *adv* übereifrig

'offing *n* **in the ~** in Aussicht

'off-licence *n* Wein- und Spirituosenhandlung *f*

off-'load *vt* ausladen

'off-putting *a* (*fam*) abstoßend

off'set *vt* (*pt/pp* **-set**, *pres p* **-setting**) ausgleichen

'offshoot *n* Schößling *m*; (*fig*) Zweig *m*

'offshore *a* offshore-. **~ rig** *n* Bohrinsel *f*

off'side *a* (*Sport*) abseits

'offspring *n* Nachwuchs *m*

off'stage *adv* hinter den Kulissen

off-'white *a* fast weiß

often /'ɒfn/ *adv* oft; **every so ~** von Zeit zu Zeit

ogle /'əʊgl/ *vt* beäugeln

ogre /'əʊgə(r)/ *n* Menschenfresser *m*

oh /əʊ/ *int* oh! ach! **oh dear!** o weh!

oil /ɔɪl/ *n* Öl *nt*; (*petroleum*) Erdöl *nt* ● *vt* ölen

oil: ~cloth *n* Wachstuch *nt*. **~field** *n* Ölfeld *nt*. **~-painting** *n* Ölgemälde *nt*. **~ refinery** *n* [Erd]ölraffinerie *f*. **~skins** *npl* Ölzeug *nt*. **~-slick** *n* Ölteppich *m*. **~-tanker** *n* Öltanker *m*. **~ well** *n* Ölquelle *f*

oily /'ɔɪlɪ/ *a* (**-ier, -iest**) ölig

ointment /'ɔɪntmənt/ *n* Salbe *f*

OK /əʊ'keɪ/ *a* & *int* (*fam*) in Ordnung; okay ● *adv* (*well*) gut ● *vt* (*auch* **okay**) (*pt/pp* **okayed**) genehmigen

old /əʊld/ *a* (**-er, -est**) alt; (*former*) ehemalig

old: ~ 'age *n* Alter *nt*. **~-age 'pensioner** *n* Rentner(in) *m*(*f*). **~ boy** *n* ehemaliger Schüler. **~-'fashioned** *a* altmodisch. **~ girl** *n* ehemalige Schülerin *f*. **~ 'maid** *n* alte Jungfer *f*

olive /'ɒlɪv/ *n* Olive *f*; (*colour*) Oliv *nt* ● *a* olivgrün. **~ branch** *n* Ölzweig *m*; (*fig*) Friedensangebot *nt*. **~ 'oil** *n* Olivenöl *nt*

Olympic /ə'lɪmpɪk/ *a* olympisch ● *n* **the ~s** die Olympischen Spiele *pl*

omelette /'ɒmlɪt/ *n* Omelett *nt*

omen /'əʊmən/ *n* Omen *nt*

ominous /'ɒmɪnəs/ *a* bedrohlich

omission /ə'mɪʃn/ *n* Auslassung *f*; (*failure to do*) Unterlassung *f*

omit /ə'mɪt/ *vt* (*pt/pp* **omitted**) auslassen; **~ to do sth** es unterlassen, etw zu tun

omnipotent /ɒm'nɪpətənt/ *a* allmächtig

on /ɒn/ *prep* auf (+ *dat*/(*on to*) + *acc*); (*on vertical surface*) an (+ *dat*/(*on to*) + *acc*); (*about*) über (+ *acc*); **on Monday** [am] Montag; **on Mondays** montags; **on the first of May** am ersten Mai; **on arriving** als ich ankam; **on one's finger** am Finger; **on the right/left** rechts/links; **on the Rhine/Thames** am Rhein/an der Themse; **on the radio/television** im Radio/Fernsehen; **on the bus/train** im Bus/Zug; **go on the bus/train** mit dem Bus/Zug fahren; **get on the bus/train** in den Bus/Zug einsteigen; **on me** (*with me*) bei mir; **it's on me** (*fam*) das spendiere ich ● *adv* (*further on*) weiter; (*switched on*) an; ⟨*brake*⟩ angezogen; ⟨*machine*⟩ angeschaltet; (*on appliance*) **'on'** 'ein'; **with/without his hat/coat**

on mit/ohne Hut/Mantel; **with/ without the lid on** mit/ohne Deckel; **be on** ⟨*film:*⟩ laufen; ⟨*event:*⟩ stattfinden; **be on at** (*fam*) bedrängen (**zu** to); **it's not on** (*fam*) das geht nicht; **on and on** immer weiter; **on and off** hin und wieder; **and so on** und so weiter; *later on* später; **move/drive on** weitergehen/-fahren; **stick/sew on** ankleben/-nähen

once /wʌns/ *adv* einmal; (*formerly*) früher; **at** ~ sofort; (*at the same time*) gleichzeitig; ~ **and for all** ein für allemal ● *conj* wenn; (*with past tense*) als. ~**-over** *n* (*fam*) **give s.o./sth the** ~**-over** sich (*dat*) jdn/etw kurz ansehen

'**oncoming** *a* ~ **traffic** Gegenverkehr *m*

one /wʌn/ *a* ein(e); (*only*) einzig; **not** ~ kein(e); ~ **day/evening** eines Tages/Abends ● *n* Eins *f* ● *pron* eine(r)/eins; (*impersonal*) man; **which** ~ welche(r,s); ~ **another** einander; ~ **by** ~ einzeln; ~ **never knows** man kann nie wissen

one: ~**-eyed** *a* einäugig. ~**-parent** '**family** *n* Einelternfamilie *f*. ~'**self** *pron* selbst; (*refl*) sich; **by** ~**self** allein. ~**-sided** *a* einseitig. ~**-way** *a* ⟨*street*⟩ Einbahn-; ⟨*ticket*⟩ einfach

onion /'ʌnjən/ *n* Zwiebel *f*

'**onlooker** *n* Zuschauer(in) *m*(*f*)

only /'əʊnlɪ/ *a* einzige(r,s)ᵀ; **an** ~ **child** ein Einzelkind *nt* ● *adv & conj* nur; ~ **just** gerade erst; (*barely*) gerade noch

'**onset** *n* Beginn *m*; (*of winter*) Einsetzen *nt*

'**onslaught** /'ɒnslɔ:t/ *n* heftiger Angriff *m*

onus /'əʊnəs/ *n* **the** ~ **is on me** es liegt an mir (**to** zu)

onward[s] /'ɒnwəd[z]/ *adv* vorwärts; **from then** ~ von der Zeit an

ooze /u:z/ *vi* sickern

opal /'əʊpl/ *n* Opal *m*

opaque /əʊ'peɪk/ *a* undurchsichtig

open /'əʊpən/ *a*, **-ly** *adv* offen; **be** ~ ⟨*shop:*⟩ geöffnet sein; **in the** ~ **air** im Freien ● *n* **in the** ~ im Freien ● *vt* öffnen, aufmachen; (*start, set up*) eröffnen ● *vi* sich öffnen; ⟨*flower:*⟩ aufgehen; ⟨*shop:*⟩ öffnen, aufmachen; (*be started*) eröffnet werden. ~ **up** *vt* öffnen, aufmachen; (*fig*) eröffnen ● *vi* sich öffnen; sich eröffnen

open: ~**-air** '**swimming pool** *n* Freibad *nt*. ~ **day** *n* Tag *m* der offenen Tür

opener /'əʊpənə(r)/ *n* Öffner *m*

opening /'əʊpənɪŋ/ *n* Öffnung *f*; (*beginning*) Eröffnung *f*; (*job*) Einstiegsmöglichkeit *f*. ~ **hours** *npl* Öffnungszeiten *pl*

open: ~**-'minded** *a* aufgeschlossen. ~**-plan** *a* ~**-plan office** Großraumbüro *nt*. ~ '**sandwich** *n* belegtes Brot *nt*

opera /'ɒpərə/ *n* Oper *f*

operable /'ɒpərəbl/ *a* operierbar

opera: ~**-glasses** *npl* Opernglas *nt*. ~**-house** *n* Opernhaus *nt*. ~**-singer** *n* Opernsänger(in) *m*(*f*)

operate /'ɒpəreɪt/ *vt* bedienen ⟨*machine, lift*⟩; betätigen ⟨*lever, brake*⟩; (*fig: run*) betreiben ● *vi* (*Techn*) funktionieren; (*be in action*) in Betrieb sein; (*Mil & fig*) operieren; ~ **[on]** (*Med*) operieren

operatic /ɒpə'rætɪk/ *a* Opern-

operation /ɒpə'reɪʃn/ *n* (*see* **operate**) Bedienung *f*; Betätigung *f*; Operation *f*; **in** ~ (*Techn*) in Betrieb; **come into** ~ (*fig*) in Kraft treten; **have an** ~ (*Med*) operiert werden. ~**al** *a* **be** ~**al** in Betrieb sein; ⟨*law:*⟩ in Kraft sein

operative /'ɒpərətɪv/ *a* wirksam

operator /'ɒpəreɪtə(r)/ *n* (*user*) Bedienungsperson *f*; (*Teleph*) Vermittlung *f*

operetta /ɒpə'retə/ *n* Operette *f*

opinion /ə'pɪnjən/ *n* Meinung *f*; **in my** ~ meiner Meinung nach. ~**ated** *a* rechthaberisch

opium /'əʊpɪəm/ *n* Opium *nt*

opponent /ə'pəʊnənt/ *n* Gegner(in) *m*(*f*)

opportun|e /'ɒpətju:n/ *a* günstig. ~**ist** /-'tju:nɪst/ *a* opportunistisch ● *n* Opportunist *m*

opportunity /ɒpə'tju:nətɪ/ *n* Gelegenheit *f*

oppos|e /ə'pəʊz/ *vt* Widerstand leisten (+ *dat*); (*argue against*) sprechen gegen; **be** ~**ed to sth** gegen etw sein; **as** ~**ed to** im Gegensatz zu. ~**ing** *a* gegnerisch; (*opposite*) entgegengesetzt

opposite /'ɒpəzɪt/ *a* entgegengesetzt; ⟨*house, side*⟩ gegenüberliegend; ~ **number** (*fig*) Gegenstück *nt*; **the** ~ **sex** das andere Geschlecht ● *n* Gegenteil *nt* ● *adv* gegenüber ● *prep* gegenüber (+ *dat*)

opposition /ɒpə'zɪʃn/ *n* Widerstand *m*; (*Pol*) Opposition *f*

oppress /ə'pres/ vt unterdrücken. ∼**ion** /-eʃn/ n Unterdrückung f. ∼**ive** /-ɪv/ a tyrannisch; ⟨heat⟩ drückend. ∼**or** n Unterdrücker m

opt /ɒpt/ vi ∼ **for** sich entscheiden für; ∼ **out** ausscheiden (**of** aus)

optical /'ɒptɪkl/ a optisch; ∼ **illusion** optische Täuschung f

optician /ɒp'tɪʃn/ n Optiker m

optics /'ɒptɪks/ n Optik f

optimis|m /'ɒptɪmɪzm/ n Optimismus m. ∼**t** /-mɪst/ n Optimist m. ∼**tic** /-'mɪstɪk/ a, **-ally** adv optimistisch

optimum /'ɒptɪməm/ a optimal ● n (pl **-ima**) Optimum nt

option /'ɒpʃn/ n Wahl f; (Comm) Option f. ∼**al** a auf Wunsch erhältlich; ⟨subject⟩ wahlfrei; ∼**al extras** pl Extras pl

opu|lence /'ɒpjʊləns/ n Prunk m; (wealth) Reichtum m. ∼**lent** a prunkvoll; (wealthy) sehr reich

or /ɔ:(r)/ conj oder; (after negative) noch; **or [else]** sonst; **in a year or two** in ein bis zwei Jahren

oracle /'ɒrəkl/ n Orakel nt

oral /'ɔ:rl/ a, **-ly** adv mündlich; (Med) oral ● n (fam) Mündliche(s) nt

orange /'ɒrɪndʒ/ n Apfelsine f, Orange f; (colour) Orange nt ● a orangefarben. ∼**ade** /-'dʒeɪd/ n Orangeade f

oration /ə'reɪʃn/ n Rede f

orator /'ɒrətə(r)/ n Redner m

oratorio /ɒrə'tɔ:rɪəʊ/ n Oratorium nt

oratory /'ɒrətərɪ/ n Redekunst f

orbit /'ɔ:bɪt/ n Umlaufbahn f ● vt umkreisen. ∼**al** a ∼**al road** Ringstraße f

orchard /'ɔ:tʃəd/ n Obstgarten m

orches|tra /'ɔ:kɪstrə/ n Orchester nt. ∼**tral** /-'kestrəl/ a Orchester-. ∼**trate** vt orchestrieren

orchid /'ɔ:kɪd/ n Orchidee f

ordain /ɔ:'deɪn/ vt bestimmen; (Relig) ordinieren

ordeal /ɔ:'di:l/ n (fig) Qual f

order /'ɔ:də(r)/ n Ordnung f; (sequence) Reihenfolge f; (condition) Zustand m; (command) Befehl m; (in restaurant) Bestellung f; (Comm) Auftrag m; (Relig, medal) Orden m; **out of** ∼ ⟨machine⟩ außer Betrieb; **in** ∼ **that** damit; **in** ∼ **to help** um zu helfen; **take holy** ∼**s** Geistlicher werden ● vt (put in ∼) ordnen; (command) befehlen

(+ dat); (Comm, in restaurant) bestellen; (prescribe) verordnen

orderly /'ɔ:dəlɪ/ a ordentlich; (not unruly) friedlich ● n (Mil, Med) Sanitäter m

ordinary /'ɔ:dɪnərɪ/ a gewöhnlich, normal; ⟨meeting⟩ ordentlich

ordination /ɔ:dɪ'neɪʃn/ n (Relig) Ordination f

ore /ɔ:(r)/ n Erz nt

organ /'ɔ:gən/ n (Biol & fig) Organ nt; (Mus) Orgel f

organic /ɔ:'gænɪk/ a, **-ally** adv organisch; (without chemicals) biodynamisch; ⟨crop⟩ biologisch angebaut; ⟨food⟩ Bio-; ∼**ally grown** biologisch angebaut. ∼ **farm** Biohof m. ∼ **farming** n biologischer Anbau m

organism /'ɔ:gənɪzm/ n Organismus m

organist /'ɔ:gənɪst/ n Organist m

organization /ɔ:gənaɪ'zeɪʃn/ n Organisation f

organize /'ɔ:gənaɪz/ vt organisieren; veranstalten ⟨event⟩. ∼**r** n Organisator m; Veranstalter m

orgasm /'ɔ:gæzm/ n Orgasmus m

orgy /'ɔ:dʒɪ/ n Orgie f

Orient /'ɔ:rɪənt/ n Orient m. **o**∼**al** /-'entl/ a orientalisch; ∼**al carpet** Orientteppich m ● n Orientale m/ Orientalin f

orient|ate /'ɔ:rɪənteɪt/ vt ∼**ate oneself** sich orientieren. ∼**ation** /-'teɪʃn/ n Orientierung f

orifice /'ɒrɪfɪs/ n Öffnung f

origin /'ɒrɪdʒɪn/ n Ursprung m; (of person, goods) Herkunft f

original /ə'rɪdʒənl/ a ursprünglich; (not copied) original; (new) originell ● n Original nt. ∼**ity** /-'nælətɪ/ n Originalität f. ∼**ly** adv ursprünglich

originat|e /ə'rɪdʒɪneɪt/ vi entstehen ● vt hervorbringen. ∼**or** n Urheber m

ornament /'ɔ:nəmənt/ n Ziergegenstand m; (decoration) Verzierung f. ∼**al** /-'mentl/ a dekorativ. ∼**ation** /-'teɪʃn/ n Verzierung f

ornate /ɔ:'neɪt/ a reich verziert

ornithology /ɔ:nɪ'θɒlədʒɪ/ n Vogelkunde f

orphan /'ɔ:fn/ n Waisenkind nt, Waise f ● vt zur Waise machen; ∼**ed** verwaist. ∼**age** /-ɪdʒ/ n Waisenhaus nt

orthodox /'ɔ:θədɒks/ a orthodox

orthography /ɔ:'θɒɡrəfɪ/ *n* Recht-schreibung *f*
orthopaedic /ɔ:θə'pi:dɪk/ *a* ortho-pädisch
oscillate /'ɒsɪleɪt/ *vi* schwingen
ostensible /ɒ'stensəbl/ *a*, **-bly** *adv* angeblich
ostentat|ion /ɒsten'teɪʃn/ *n* Prot-zerei *f* (*fam*). **~ious** /-ʃəs/ *a* protzig (*fam*)
osteopath /'ɒstɪəpæθ/ *n* Osteopath *m*
ostracize /'ɒstrəsaɪz/ *vt* ächten
ostrich /'ɒstrɪtʃ/ *n* Strauß *m*
other /'ʌðə(r)/ *a, pron & n* andere(r, s); **the ~ [one]** der/die/das andere; **the ~ two** die zwei anderen; **two ~s** zwei andere; (*more*) noch zwei; **no ~s** sonst keine; **any ~ questions?** sonst noch Fragen? **every ~ day** jeden zwei-ten Tag; **the ~ day** neulich; **the ~ evening** neulich abends; **someone/ something or ~** irgend jemand/etwas ● *adv* anders; **~ than him** außer ihm; **somehow/somewhere or ~** irgend-wie/irgendwo
otherwise *adv* sonst; (*differently*) anders
otter /'ɒtə(r)/ *n* Otter *m*
ouch /aʊtʃ/ *int* autsch
ought /ɔ:t/ *v aux* **I/we ~ to stay** ich sollte/wir sollten eigentlich bleiben; **he ~ not to have done it** er hätte es nicht machen sollen; **that ~ to be enough** das sollte eigentlich genügen
ounce /aʊns/ *n* Unze *f* (*28,35 g*)
our /aʊə(r)/ *a* unser
ours /'aʊəz/ *poss pron* unsere(r,s); **a friend of ~** ein Freund von uns; **that is ~** das gehört uns
ourselves /aʊə'selvz/ *pron* selbst; (*refl*) uns; **by ~** allein
oust /aʊst/ *vt* entfernen
out /aʊt/ *adv* (*not at home*) weg; (*out-side*) draußen; (*not alight*) aus; (*un-conscious*) bewußtlos; **be ~** ⟨*sun.*⟩ scheinen; ⟨*flower:*⟩ blühen; ⟨*workers:*⟩ streiken; ⟨*calculation:*⟩ nicht stimmen; (*Sport*) aus sein; (*fig: not feasible*) nicht in Frage kommen; **~ and about** un-terwegs; **have it ~ with s.o.** (*fam*) jdn zur Rede stellen; **get ~!** (*fam*) raus! **~ with it!** (*fam*) heraus damit! **go/send ~** hinausgehen/-schicken; **come/ bring ~** herauskommen/-bringen ● *prep* **~ of** aus (+ *dat*); **go ~ of the door** zur Tür hinausgehen; **be ~ of bed/the room** nicht im Bett/im Zimmer sein; **~ of breath/ danger** außer Atem/Gefahr; **~ of work** ar-beitslos; **nine ~ of ten** neun von zehn; **be ~ of sugar/bread** keinen Zucker/ kein Brot mehr haben ● *prep* aus (+ *dat*); **go ~ the door** zur Tür hinaus-gehen

out'bid *vt* (*pt/pp* **-bid**, *pres p* **-bidding**) überbieten
'outboard *a* **~ motor** Außen-bordmotor *m*
'outbreak *n* Ausbruch *m*
'outbuilding *n* Nebengebäude *nt*
'outburst *n* Ausbruch *m*
'outcast *n* Ausgestoßene(r) *m/f*
'outcome *n* Ergebnis *nt*
'outcry *n* Aufschrei *m* [der Ent-rüstung]
out'dated *a* überholt
out'do *vt* (*pt* **-did**, *pp* **-done**) über-treffen, übertrumpfen
'outdoor *a* ⟨*life, sports*⟩ im Freien; **~ shoes** *pl* Straßenschuhe *pl*; **~ swim-ming pool** Freibad *nt*
out'doors *adv* draußen; **go ~** nach draußen gehen
'outer *a* äußere(r,s)
'outfit *n* Ausstattung *f*; (*clothes*) En-semble *nt*; (*fam: organization*) Be-trieb *m*; (*fam*) Laden *m*. **~ter** *n* **men's ~ter's** Herrenbekleidungs-geschäft *nt*
'outgoing *a* ausscheidend; ⟨*mail*⟩ ausgehend; (*sociable*) kontakt-freudig. **~s** *npl* Ausgaben *pl*
out'grow *vt* (*pt* **-grew**, *pp* **-grown**) herauswachsen aus
'outhouse *n* Nebengebäude *nt*
outing /'aʊtɪŋ/ *n* Ausflug *m*
outlandish /aʊt'lændɪʃ/ *a* un-gewöhnlich
'outlaw *n* Geächtete(r) *m/f* ● *vt* ächten
'outlay *n* Auslagen *pl*
'outlet *n* Abzug *m*; (*for water*) Abfluß *m*; (*fig*) Ventil *nt*; (*Comm*) Ab-satzmöglichkeit *f*
'outline *n* Umriß *m*; (*summary*) kurze Darstellung *f* ● *vt* umreißen
out'live *vt* überleben
'outlook *n* Aussicht *f*; (*future prospect*) Aussichten *pl*; (*attitude*) Einstellung *f*
'outlying *a* entlegen; **~ areas** *pl* Außengebiete *pl*
out'moded *a* überholt
out'number *vt* zahlenmäßig über-legen sein (+ *dat*)

'**out-patient** *n* ambulanter Patient *m*; **~s' department** Ambulanz *f*

'**outpost** *n* Vorposten *m*

'**output** *n* Leistung *f*, Produktion *f*

'**outrage** *n* Greueltat *f*; (*fig*) Skandal *m*; (*indignation*) Empörung *f* ● *vt* empören. **~ous** /-'reɪdʒəs/ *a* empörend

'**outright**¹ *a* völlig, total; (*refusal*) glatt

out'**right**² *adv* ganz; (*at once*) sofort; (*frankly*) offen

'**outset** *n* Anfang *m*; **from the ~** von Anfang an

'**outside**¹ *a* äußere(r,s); **~ wall** Außenwand *f* ● *n* Außenseite *f*; **from the ~** von außen; **at the ~** höchstens

out'**side**² *adv* außen; (*out of doors*) draußen; **go ~** nach draußen gehen ● *prep* außerhalb (+ *gen*); (*in front of*) vor (+ *dat/acc*)

out'**sider** *n* Außenseiter *m*

'**outsize** *a* übergroß

'**outskirts** *npl* Rand *m*

out'**spoken** *a* offen; **be ~** kein Blatt vor den Mund nehmen

out'**standing** *a* hervorragend; (*conspicuous*) bemerkenswert; (*not settled*) unerledigt; (*Comm*) ausstehend

'**outstretched** *a* ausgestreckt

out'**strip** *vt* (*pt/pp* **-stripped**) davonlaufen (+ *dat*); (*fig*) übertreffen

out'**vote** *vt* überstimmen

'**outward** /-wəd/ *a* äußerlich; **~ journey** Hinreise *f* ● *adv* nach außen; **be ~ bound** (*ship:*) auslaufen. **~ly** *adv* nach außen hin, äußerlich. **~s** *adv* nach außen

out'**weigh** *vt* überwiegen

out'**wit** *vt* (*pt/pp* **-witted**) überlisten

oval /'əʊvl/ *a* oval ● *n* Oval *nt*

ovary /'əʊvərɪ/ *n* (*Anat*) Eierstock *m*

ovation /əʊ'veɪʃn/ *n* Ovation *f*

oven /'ʌvn/ *n* Backofen *m*. **~-ready** *a* bratfertig

over /'əʊvə(r)/ *prep* über (+ *acc/dat*); **~ dinner** beim Essen; **~ the weekend** übers Wochenende; **~ the phone** am Telefon; **~ the page** auf der nächsten Seite; **all ~ Germany** in ganz Deutschland; (*travel*) durch ganz Deutschland; **all ~ the place** (*fam*) überall ● *adv* (*remaining*) übrig; (*ended*) zu Ende; **~ again** noch einmal; **~ and ~** immer wieder; **~ here/there** hier/da drüben; **all ~** (*everywhere*) überall; **it's all ~** es ist vorbei; **I ache all ~** mir tut alles weh; **go/drive ~**

hinübergehen/-fahren; **come/bring ~** herüberkommen/-bringen; **turn ~** herumdrehen

overall¹ /'əʊvərɔːl/ *n* Kittel *m*; **~s** *pl* Overall *m*

overall² /əʊvər'ɔːl/ *a* gesamt; (*general*) allgemein ● *adv* insgesamt

over'**awe** *vt* (*fig*) überwältigen

over'**balance** *vi* das Gleichgewicht verlieren

over'**bearing** *a* herrisch

'**overboard** *adv* (*Naut*) über Bord

'**overcast** *a* bedeckt

over'**charge** *vt* **~ s.o.** jdm zu viel berechnen ● *vi* zu viel verlangen

'**overcoat** *n* Mantel *m*

over'**come** *vt* (*pt* **-came**, *pp* **-come**) überwinden; **be ~ by** überwältigt werden von

over'**crowded** *a* überfüllt

over'**do** *vt* (*pt* **-did**, *pp* **-done**) übertreiben; (*cook too long*) zu lange kochen; **~ it** (*fam: do too much*) sich übernehmen

'**overdose** *n* Überdosis *f*

'**overdraft** *n* [Konto]überziehung *f*; **have an ~** sein Konto überzogen haben

over'**draw** *vt* (*pt* **-drew**, *pp* **-drawn**) (*Comm*) überziehen

over'**due** *a* überfällig

over'**estimate** *vt* überschätzen

'**overflow**¹ *n* Überschuß *m*; (*outlet*) Überlauf *m*

over'**flow**² *vi* überlaufen

over'**grown** *a* (*garden*) überwachsen

'**overhang**¹ *n* Überhang *m*

over'**hang**² *vt/i* (*pt/pp* **-hung**) überhängen (über + *acc*)

'**overhaul**¹ *n* Überholung *f*

over'**haul**² *vt* (*Techn*) überholen

over'**head**¹ *adv* oben

'**overhead**² *a* Ober-; (*ceiling*) Decken-. **~s** *npl* allgemeine Unkosten *pl*

over'**hear** *vt* (*pt/pp* **-heard**) mit anhören (*conversation*); **I overheard him saying it** ich hörte zufällig, wie er das sagte

over'**heat** *vi* zu heiß werden ● *vt* zu stark erhitzen

over'**joyed** *a* überglücklich

'**overland** *a & adv* /-'-'-/ auf dem Landweg; **~ route** Landroute *f*

over'**lap** *v* (*pt/pp* **-lapped**) ● *vi* sich überschneiden ● *vt* überlappen

over'**leaf** *adv* umseitig

over'load vt überladen; (*Electr*) überlasten

'**overlook**[1] n (*Amer*) Aussichtspunkt m

over'look[2] vt überblicken; (*fail to see, ignore*) übersehen

overly /'əʊvəlɪ/ adv übermäßig

over'night[1] adv über Nacht; **stay ~** übernachten

'**overnight**[2] a Nacht-; **~ stay** Übernachtung f

'**overpass** n Überführung f

over'pay vt (*pt/pp* **-paid**) überbezahlen

over'populated a übervölkert

over'power vt überwältigen. **~ing** a überwältigend

over'priced a zu teuer

overpro'duce vt überproduzieren

over'rate vt überschätzen. **~d** a überbewertet

over'reach vt **~ oneself** sich übernehmen

overre'act vi überreagieren. **~ion** n Überreaktion f

over'rid|e vt (*pt* **-rode**, *pp* **-ridden**) sich hinwegsetzen über (+ *acc*). **~ing** a Haupt-

over'rule vt ablehnen; **we were ~d** wir wurden überstimmt

over'run vt (*pt* **-ran**, *pp* **-run**, *pres p* **-running**) überrennen; überschreiten ⟨*time*⟩; **be ~ with** überlaufen sein von

over'seas[1] adv in Übersee; **go ~** nach Übersee gehen

'**overseas**[2] a Übersee-

over'see vt (*pt* **-saw**, *pp* **-seen**) beaufsichtigen

'**overseer** /-sɪə(r)/ n Aufseher m

over'shadow vt überschatten

over'shoot vt (*pt/pp* **-shot**) hinausschießen über (+ *acc*)

'**oversight** n Versehen nt

over'sleep vi (*pt/pp* **-slept**) [sich] verschlafen

over'step vt (*pt/pp* **-stepped**) überschreiten

over'strain vt überanstrengen

overt /əʊ'vɜːt/ a offen

over'tak|e vt/i (*pt* **-took**, *pp* **-taken**) überholen. **~ing** n Überholen nt; **no ~ing** Überholverbot nt

over'tax vt zu hoch besteuern; (*fig*) überfordern

'**overthrow**[1] n (*Pol*) Sturz m

over'throw[2] vt (*pt* **-threw**, *pp* **-thrown**) (*Pol*) stürzen

'**overtime** n Überstunden pl ● adv **work ~** Überstunden machen

over'tired a übermüdet

'**overtone** n (*fig*) Unterton m

overture /'əʊvətjʊə(r)/ n (*Mus*) Ouvertüre f; **~s** pl (*fig*) Annäherungsversuche pl

over'turn vt umstoßen ● vi umkippen

over'weight a übergewichtig; **be ~** Übergewicht haben

overwhelm /-'welm/ vt überwältigen. **~ing** a überwältigend

over'work n Überarbeitung f ● vt überfordern ● vi sich überarbeiten

over'wrought a überreizt

ovulation /ɒvjʊ'leɪʃn/ n Eisprung m

ow|e /əʊ/ vt schulden/(*fig*) verdanken (**[to]** **s.o.** jdm); **~e s.o. sth** jdm etw schuldig sein; **be ~ing** ⟨*money:*⟩ ausstehen. '**~ing to** prep wegen (+ *gen*)

owl /aʊl/ n Eule f

own[1] /əʊn/ a & pron eigen; **it's my ~** es gehört mir; **a car of my ~** mein eigenes Auto; **on one's ~** allein; **hold one's ~** sich behaupten; **get one's ~ back** (*fam*) sich revanchieren

own[2] vt besitzen; (*confess*) zugeben; **I don't ~ it** es gehört mir nicht. **~ up** vi es zugeben

owner /'əʊnə(r)/ n Eigentümer(in) m(f), Besitzer(in) m(f); (*of shop*) Inhaber(in) m(f). **~ship** n Besitz m

ox /ɒks/ n (*pl* **oxen**) Ochse m

oxide /'ɒksaɪd/ n Oxyd nt

oxygen /'ɒksɪdʒən/ n Sauerstoff m

oyster /'ɔɪstə(r)/ n Auster f

ozone /'əʊzəʊn/ n Ozon nt. **~-'friendly** a ≈ ohne FCKW. **~ layer** n Ozonschicht f

P

pace /peɪs/ n Schritt m; (*speed*) Tempo nt; **keep ~ with** Schritt halten mit ● vi **~ up and down** auf und ab gehen. **~-maker** n (*Sport & Med*) Schrittmacher m

Pacific /pə'sɪfɪk/ a & n **the ~ [Ocean]** der Pazifik

pacifier /'pæsɪfaɪə(r)/ n (*Amer*) Schnuller m

pacifist /'pæsɪfɪst/ n Pazifist m

pacify /'pæsɪfaɪ/ vt (*pt/pp* **-ied**) beruhigen

pack /pæk/ n Packung f; (*Mil*) Tornister m; (*of cards*) [Karten]spiel nt;

(*gang*) Bande *f*; (*of hounds*) Meute *f*; (*of wolves*) Rudel *nt*; **a ~ of lies** ein Haufen Lügen ● *vt/i* packen; einpacken ⟨*article*⟩; **be ~ed** (*crowded*) [gedrängt] voll sein; **send s.o. ~ing** (*fam*) jdn wegschicken. **~ up** *vt* einpacken ● *vi* (*fam*) ⟨*machine:*⟩ kaputtgehen; ⟨*person:*⟩ einpacken (*fam*)

package /'pækɪdʒ/ *n* Paket *nt* ● *vt* verpacken. **~ holiday** *n* Pauschalreise *f*

packed 'lunch *n* Lunchpaket *nt*

packet /'pækɪt/ *n* Päckchen *nt*; **cost a ~** (*fam*) einen Haufen Geld kosten

packing /'pækɪŋ/ *n* Verpackung *f*

pact /pækt/ *n* Pakt *m*

pad[1] /pæd/ *n* Polster *nt*; (*for writing*) [Schreib]block *m*; (*fam: home*) Wohnung *f* ● *vt* (*pt/pp* **padded**) polstern

pad[2] *vi* (*pt/pp* **padded**) tappen

padding /'pædɪŋ/ *n* Polsterung *f*; (*in written work*) Füllwerk *nt*

paddle[1] /'pædl/ *n* Paddel *nt* ● *vt* (*row*) paddeln

paddle[2] *vi* waten

paddock /'pædək/ *n* Koppel *f*

padlock /'pædlɒk/ *n* Vorhängeschloß *nt* ● *vt* mit einem Vorhängeschloß verschließen

paediatrician /pi:dɪə'trɪʃn/ *n* Kinderarzt *m*/-ärztin *f*

pagan /'peɪgən/ *a* heidnisch ● *n* Heide *m*/Heidin *f*

page[1] /peɪdʒ/ *n* Seite *f*

page[2] *n* (*boy*) Page *m* ● *vt* ausrufen ⟨*person*⟩

pageant /'pædʒənt/ *n* Festzug *m*. **~ry** *n* Prunk *m*

paid /peɪd/ *see* **pay** ● *a* bezahlt; **put ~ to** (*fam*) zunichte machen

pail /peɪl/ *n* Eimer *m*

pain /peɪn/ *n* Schmerz *m*; **be in ~** Schmerzen haben; **take ~s** sich (*dat*) Mühe geben; **~ in the neck** (*fam*) Nervensäge *f* ● *vt* (*fig*) schmerzen

pain: ~ful *a* schmerzhaft; (*fig*) schmerzlich. **~-killer** *n* schmerzstillendes Mittel *nt*. **~less** *a*, **-ly** *adv* schmerzlos

painstaking /'peɪnzteɪkɪŋ/ *a* sorgfältig

paint /peɪnt/ *n* Farbe *f* ● *vt/i* streichen; ⟨*artist:*⟩ malen. **~brush** *n* Pinsel *m*. **~er** *n* Maler *m*; (*decorator*) Anstreicher *m*. **~ing** *n* Malerei *f*; (*picture*) Gemälde *nt*

pair /peə(r)/ *n* Paar *nt*; **~ of trousers** Hose *f*; **~ of scissors** Schere *f* ● *vt* paaren ● *vi* **~ off** Paare bilden

pajamas /pə'dʒɑːməz/ *npl* (*Amer*) Schlafanzug *m*

Pakistan /pɑːkɪ'stɑːn/ *n* Pakistan *nt*. **~i** *a* pakistanisch ● *n* Pakistaner(in) *m(f)*

pal /pæl/ *n* Freund(in) *m(f)*

palace /'pælɪs/ *n* Palast *m*

palatable /'pælətəbl/ *a* schmackhaft

palate /'pælət/ *n* Gaumen *m*

palatial /pə'leɪʃl/ *a* palastartig

palaver /pə'lɑːvə(r)/ *n* (*fam: fuss*) Theater *nt* (*fam*)

pale[1] /peɪl/ *n* (*stake*) Pfahl *m*; **beyond the ~** (*fam*) unmöglich

pale[2] *a* (**-r, -st**) blaß ● *vi* blaß werden. **~ness** *n* Blässe *f*

Palestin|e /'pælɪstaɪn/ *n* Palästina *nt*. **~ian** /pælə'stɪnɪən/ *a* palästinensisch ● *n* Palästinenser(in) *m(f)*

palette /'pælɪt/ *n* Palette *f*

pall /pɔːl/ *n* Sargtuch *nt*; (*fig*) Decke *f* ● *vi* an Reiz verlieren

pall|id /'pælɪd/ *a* bleich. **~or** *n* Blässe *f*

palm /pɑːm/ *n* Handfläche *f*; (*tree, symbol*) Palme *f* ● *vt* **~ sth off on s.o.** jdm etw andrehen. **P~ 'Sunday** *n* Palmsonntag *m*

palpable /'pælpəbl/ *a* tastbar; (*perceptible*) spürbar

palpitat|e /'pælpɪteɪt/ *vi* klopfen. **~ions** /-'teɪʃnz/ *npl* Herzklopfen *nt*

paltry /'pɔːltrɪ/ *a* (**-ier, -iest**) armselig

pamper /'pæmpə(r)/ *vt* verwöhnen

pamphlet /'pæmflɪt/ *n* Broschüre *f*

pan /pæn/ *n* Pfanne *f*; (*saucepan*) Topf *m*; (*of scales*) Schale *f* ● *vt* (*pt/pp* **panned**) (*fam*) verreißen

panacea /pænə'siːə/ *n* Allheilmittel *nt*

panache /pə'næʃ/ *n* Schwung *m*

pancake *n* Pfannkuchen *m*

pancreas /'pæŋkrɪəs/ *n* Bauchspeicheldrüse *f*

panda /'pændə/ *n* Panda *m*. **~ car** *n* Streifenwagen *m*

pandemonium /pændɪ'məʊnɪəm/ *n* Höllenlärm *m*

pander /'pændə(r)/ *vi* **~ to s.o.** jdm zu sehr nachgeben

pane /peɪn/ *n* [Glas]scheibe *f*

panel /'pænl/ *n* Tafel *f*, Platte *f*; **~ of experts** Expertenrunde *f*; **~ of judges** Jury *f*. **~ling** *n* Täfelung *f*

pang /pæŋ/ n ~s **of hunger** Hungergefühl nt; ~s **of conscience** Gewissensbisse pl

panic /'pænɪk/ n Panik f ● vi (pt/pp **panicked**) in Panik geraten. ~**-stricken** a von Panik ergriffen

panoram|a /pænə'rɑ:mə/ n Panorama nt. ~**ic** /-'ræmɪk/ a Panorama-

pansy /'pænzɪ/ n Stiefmütterchen nt

pant /pænt/ vi keuchen; ⟨dog:⟩ hecheln

pantechnicon /pæn'teknɪkən/ n Möbelwagen m

panther /'pænθə(r)/ n Panther m

panties /'pæntɪz/ npl [Damen]slip m

pantomime /'pæntəmaɪm/ n [zu Weihnachten aufgeführte] Märchenvorstellung f

pantry /'pæntrɪ/ n Speisekammer f

pants /pænts/ npl Unterhose f; (woman's) Schlüpfer m; (trousers) Hose f

'pantyhose n (Amer) Strumpfhose f

papal /'peɪpl/ a päpstlich

paper /'peɪpə(r)/ n Papier nt; (wall~) Tapete f; (newspaper) Zeitung f; (exam ~) Testbogen m; (exam) Klausur f; (treatise) Referat nt; ~s pl (documents) Unterlagen pl; (for identification) [Ausweis]papiere pl; **on** ~ schriftlich ● vt tapezieren

paper: ~**back** n Taschenbuch nt. ~**-clip** n Büroklammer f. ~**knife** n Brieföffner m. ~**weight** n Briefbeschwerer m. ~**work** n Schreibarbeit f

par /pɑ:(r)/ n (Golf) Par nt; **on a** ~ gleichwertig (**with** dat); **feel below** ~ sich nicht ganz auf der Höhe fühlen

parable /'pærəbl/ n Gleichnis nt

parachut|e /'pærəʃu:t/ n Fallschirm m ● vi [mit dem Fallschirm] abspringen. ~**ist** n Fallschirmspringer m

parade /pə'reɪd/ n Parade f; (procession) Festzug m ● vi marschieren ● vt (show off) zur Schau stellen

paradise /'pærədaɪs/ n Paradies nt

paradox /'pærədɒks/ n Paradox nt. ~**ical** /-'dɒksɪkl/ paradox

paraffin /'pærəfɪn/ n Paraffin nt

paragon /'pærəgən/ n ~ **of virtue** Ausbund m der Tugend

paragraph /'pærəgrɑ:f/ n Absatz m

parallel /'pærəlel/ a & adv parallel ● n (Geog) Breitenkreis m; (fig) Parallele f

paralyse /'pærəlaɪz/ vt lähmen; (fig) lahmlegen

paralysis /pə'ræləsɪs/ n (pl **-ses** /-si:z/) Lähmung f

paramount /'pærəmaʊnt/ a überragend; **be** ~ vorgehen

paranoid /'pærənɔɪd/ a [krankhaft] mißtrauisch

parapet /'pærəpɪt/ n Brüstung f

paraphernalia /pærəfə'neɪlɪə/ n Kram m

paraphrase /'pærəfreɪz/ n Umschreibung f ● vt umschreiben

paraplegic /pærə'pli:dʒɪk/ a querschnittsgelähmt ● n Querschnittsgelähmte(r) m/f

parasite /'pærəsaɪt/ n Parasit m, Schmarotzer m

parasol /'pærəsɒl/ n Sonnenschirm m

paratrooper /'pærətru:pə(r)/ n Fallschirmjäger m

parcel /'pɑ:sl/ n Paket nt

parch /pɑ:tʃ/ vt austrocknen; **be** ~**ed** ⟨person:⟩ einen furchtbaren Durst haben

parchment /'pɑ:tʃmənt/ n Pergament nt

pardon /'pɑ:dn/ n Verzeihung f; (Jur) Begnadigung f; ~? (fam) bitte? **I beg your** ~ wie bitte? (sorry) Verzeihung! ● vt verzeihen; (Jur) begnadigen

pare /peə(r)/ vt (peel) schälen

parent /'peərənt/ n Elternteil m; ~**s** pl Eltern pl. ~**al** /pə'rentl/ a elterlich

parenthesis /pə'renθəsɪs/ n (pl **-ses** /-si:z/) Klammer f

parish /'pærɪʃ/ n Gemeinde f. ~**ioner** /pə'rɪʃənə(r)/ n Gemeindemitglied nt

parity /'pærətɪ/ n Gleichheit f

park /pɑ:k/ n Park m ● vt/i parken

parking /'pɑ:kɪŋ/ n Parken nt; **'no** ~' 'Parken verboten'. ~**-lot** n (Amer) Parkplatz m. ~**-meter** n Parkuhr f. ~ **space** n Parkplatz m

parliament /'pɑ:ləmənt/ n Parlament nt. ~**ary** /-'mentərɪ/ a parlamentarisch

parlour /'pɑ:lə(r)/ n Wohnzimmer nt

parochial /pə'rəʊkɪəl/ a Gemeinde-; (fig) beschränkt

parody /'pærədɪ/ n Parodie f ● vt (pt/pp **-ied**) parodieren

parole /pə'rəʊl/ n **on** ~ auf Bewährung

paroxysm /'pærəksɪzm/ n Anfall m

parquet /'pɑ:keɪ/ n ~ **floor** Parkett nt

parrot /'pærət/ n Papagei m

parry /'pærɪ/ vt (pt/pp **-ied**) abwehren ⟨blow⟩; (Fencing) parieren

parsimonious /pɑːsɪ'məʊnɪəs/ a geizig

parsley /'pɑːslɪ/ n Petersilie f

parsnip /'pɑːsnɪp/ n Pastinake f

parson /'pɑːsn/ n Pfarrer m

part /pɑːt/ n Teil m; (Techn) Teil nt; (area) Gegend f; (Theat) Rolle f; (Mus) Part m; **spare** ∼ Ersatzteil nt; **for my** ∼ meinerseits; **on the** ∼ **of** von Seiten (+ gen); **take s.o.'s** ∼ für jdn Partei ergreifen; **take** ∼ **in** teilnehmen an (+ dat) ● adv teils ● vt trennen; scheiteln ⟨hair⟩ ● vi ⟨people:⟩ sich trennen; ∼ **with** sich trennen von

partake /pɑː'teɪk/ vt (pt **-took**, pp **-taken**) teilnehmen; ∼ **of** ⟨eat⟩ zu sich nehmen

part-ex'change n **take in** ∼ in Zahlung nehmen

partial /'pɑːʃl/ a Teil-; **be** ∼ **to** mögen. ∼**ity** /pɑːʃɪ'ælətɪ/ n Voreingenommenheit f; (liking) Vorliebe f. ∼**ly** adv teilweise

particip|ant /pɑː'tɪsɪpənt/ n Teilnehmer(in) m(f). ∼**ate** /-peɪt/ vi teilnehmen (**in** an + dat). ∼**ation** /-'peɪʃn/ n Teilnahme f

participle /'pɑːtɪsɪpl/ n Partizip nt; **present/past** ∼ erstes/zweites Partizip nt

particle /'pɑːtɪkl/ n Körnchen nt; (Phys) Partikel nt; (Gram) Partikel f

particular /pə'tɪkjʊlə(r)/ a besondere(r,s); (precise) genau; (fastidious) penibel; **in** ∼ besonders. ∼**ly** adv besonders. ∼**s** npl nähere Angaben pl

parting /'pɑːtɪŋ/ n Abschied m; (in hair) Scheitel m ● attrib Abschieds-

partition /pɑː'tɪʃn/ n Trennwand f; (Pol) Teilung f ● vt teilen. ∼ **off** vt abtrennen

partly /'pɑːtlɪ/ adv teilweise

partner /'pɑːtnə(r)/ n Partner(in) m(f); (Comm) Teilhaber m. ∼**ship** n Partnerschaft f; (Comm) Teilhaberschaft f

partridge /'pɑːtrɪdʒ/ n Rebhuhn nt

part-'time a & adv Teilzeit-; **be** or **work** ∼ Teilzeitarbeit machen

party /'pɑːtɪ/ n Party f, Fest nt; (group) Gruppe f; (Pol, Jur) Partei f; **be** ∼ **to** sich beteiligen an (+ dat)

'party line[1] n (Teleph) Gemeinschaftsanschluß m

party 'line[2] n (Pol) Parteilinie f

pass /pɑːs/ n Ausweis m; (Geog, Sport) Paß m; (Sch) ≈ ausreichend; **get a** ∼ bestehen ● vt vorbeigehen/ -fahren an (+ dat); (overtake) überholen; (hand) reichen; (Sport) abgeben, abspielen; (approve) annehmen; (exceed) übersteigen; bestehen ⟨exam⟩; machen ⟨remark⟩; fällen ⟨judgement⟩; (Jur) verhängen ⟨sentence⟩; ∼ **water** Wasser lassen; ∼ **the time** sich (dat) die Zeit vertreiben; ∼ **sth off as sth** etw als etw ausgeben; ∼ **one's hand over sth** mit der Hand über etw (acc) fahren ● vi vorbeigehen/-fahren; (get by) vorbeikommen; (overtake) überholen; ⟨time:⟩ vergehen; ⟨in exam⟩ bestehen; **let sth** ∼ (fig) etw übergehen; **[I]** ∼! [ich] passe! ∼ **away** vi sterben. ∼ **down** vt herunterreichen; (fig) weitergeben. ∼ **out** vi ohnmächtig werden. ∼ **round** vt herumreichen. ∼ **up** vt heraufreichen; (fam: miss) vorübergehen lassen

passable /'pɑːsəbl/ a ⟨road⟩ befahrbar; (satisfactory) passabel

passage /'pæsɪdʒ/ n Durchgang m; (corridor) Gang m; (voyage) Überfahrt f; (in book) Passage f

passenger /'pæsɪndʒə(r)/ n Fahrgast m; (Naut, Aviat) Passagier m; (in car) Mitfahrer m. ∼ **seat** n Beifahrersitz m

passer-by /pɑːsə'baɪ/ n (pl **-s-by**) Passant(in) m(f)

'passing place n Ausweichstelle f

passion /'pæʃn/ n Leidenschaft f. ∼**ate** /-ət/ a, **-ly** adv leidenschaftlich

passive /'pæsɪv/ a passiv ● n Passiv nt

Passover /'pɑːsəʊvə(r)/ n Passah nt

pass: ∼port n [Reise]paß m. ∼**word** n Kennwort nt; (Mil) Losung f

past /pɑːst/ a vergangene(r,s); (former) ehemalig; **in the** ∼ **few days** in den letzten paar Tagen; **that's all** ∼ das ist jetzt vorbei ● n Vergangenheit f ● prep an (+ dat) … vorbei; (after) nach; **at ten** ∼ **two** um zehn nach zwei ● adv vorbei; **go/come** ∼ vorbeigehen/-kommen

pasta /'pæstə/ n Nudeln pl

paste /peɪst/ n Brei m; (dough) Teig m; (fish-, meat-) Paste f; (adhesive) Kleister m; (jewellery) Straß m ● vt kleistern

pastel /'pæstl/ n Pastellfarbe f; (crayon) Pastellstift m; (drawing) Pastell nt ● attrib Pastell-

pasteurize /'pɑːstʃəraɪz/ vt pasteurisieren

pastille /'pæstɪl/ n Pastille f
pastime /'pɑːstaɪm/ n Zeitvertreib m
pastoral /'pɑːstərl/ a ländlich; ⟨care⟩ seelsorgerisch
pastr|y /'peɪstrɪ/ n Teig m; **cakes and ∼ies** Kuchen und Gebäck
pasture /'pɑːstʃə(r)/ n Weide f
pasty[1] /'peɪstɪ/ n Pastete f
pasty[2] /'peɪstɪ/ a blaß, (fam) käsig
pat /pæt/ n Klaps m; (of butter) Stückchen nt ● adv **have sth off ∼** etw aus dem Effeff können ● vt (pt/pp **patted**) tätscheln; **∼ s.o. on the back** jdm auf die Schulter klopfen
patch /pætʃ/ n Flicken m; (spot) Fleck m; **not a ∼ on** (fam) gar nicht zu vergleichen mit ● vt flicken. **∼ up** vt [zusammen]flicken; beilegen ⟨quarrel⟩
patchy /'pætʃɪ/ a ungleichmäßig
pâté /'pæteɪ/ n Pastete f
patent /'peɪtnt/ a, **-ly** adv offensichtlich ● n Patent nt ● vt patentieren. **∼ leather** n Lackleder nt
patern|al /pə'tɜːnl/ a väterlich. **∼ity** n Vaterschaft f
path /pɑːθ/ n (pl **∼s** /pɑːðz/) [Fuß]weg m, Pfad m; (orbit, track) Bahn f; (fig) Weg m
pathetic /pə'θetɪk/ a mitleiderregend; ⟨attempt⟩ erbärmlich
patholog|ical /pæθə'lɒdʒɪkl/ a pathologisch. **∼ist** /pə'θɒlədʒɪst/ n Pathologe m
pathos /'peɪθɒs/ n Rührseligkeit f
patience /'peɪʃns/ n Geduld f; (game) Patience f
patient /'peɪʃnt/ a, **-ly** adv geduldig ● n Patient(in) m(f)
patio /'pætɪəʊ/ n Terrasse f
patriot /'pætrɪət/ n Patriot(in) m(f). **∼ic** /-'ɒtɪk/ a patriotisch. **∼ism** n Patriotismus m
patrol /pə'trəʊl/ n Patrouille f ● vt/i patrouillieren [in (+ dat)]; ⟨police:⟩ auf Streife gehen/fahren [in (+ dat)]. **∼ car** n Streifenwagen m
patron /'peɪtrən/ n Gönner m; (of charity) Schirmherr m; (of the arts) Mäzen m; (customer) Kunde m/Kundin f; (Theat) Besucher m. **∼age** /'pætrənɪdʒ/ n Schirmherrschaft f
patroniz|e /'pætrənaɪz/ vt (fig) herablassend behandeln. **∼ing** a, **-ly** adv gönnerhaft
patter[1] /'pætə(r)/ n Getrippel nt; (of rain) Plätschern nt ● vi trippeln; plätschern

patter[2] n (speech) Gerede nt
pattern /'pætn/ n Muster nt
paunch /pɔːntʃ/ n [Schmer]bauch m
pauper /'pɔːpə(r)/ n Arme(r) m/f
pause /pɔːz/ n Pause f ● vi innehalten
pave /peɪv/ vt pflastern; **∼ the way** den Weg bereiten (**for** dat). **∼ment** n Bürgersteig m
pavilion /pə'vɪljən/ n Pavillon m; (Sport) Klubhaus nt
paw /pɔː/ n Pfote f; (of large animal) Pranke f, Tatze f
pawn[1] /pɔːn/ n (Chess) Bauer m; (fig) Schachfigur f
pawn[2] vt verpfänden ● n **in ∼** verpfändet. **∼broker** n Pfandleiher m. **∼shop** n Pfandhaus nt
pay /peɪ/ n Lohn m; (salary) Gehalt nt; **be in the ∼ of** bezahlt werden von ● v (pt/pp **paid**) ● vt bezahlen; zahlen ⟨money⟩; **∼ s.o. a visit** jdm einen Besuch abstatten; **∼ s.o. a compliment** jdm ein Kompliment machen ● vi zahlen; (be profitable) sich bezahlt machen; (fig) sich lohnen; **∼ for sth** etw bezahlen. **∼ back** vt zurückzahlen. **∼ in** vt einzahlen. **∼ off** vt abzahlen ⟨debt⟩ ● vi (fig) sich auszahlen. **∼ up** vi zahlen
payable /'peɪəbl/ a zahlbar; **make ∼ to** ausstellen auf (+ acc)
payee /peɪ'iː/ n [Zahlungs]empfänger m
payment /'peɪmənt/ n Bezahlung f; (amount) Zahlung f
pay: ∼ packet n Lohntüte f; **∼ phone** n Münzfernsprecher m
pea /piː/ n Erbse f
peace /piːs/ n Frieden m; **for my ∼ of mind** zu meiner eigenen Beruhigung
peace|able /'piːsəbl/ a friedlich. **∼ful** a, **-ly** adv friedlich. **∼maker** n Friedensstifter m
peach /piːtʃ/ n Pfirsich m
peacock /'piːkɒk/ n Pfau m
peak /piːk/ n Gipfel m; (fig) Höhepunkt m. **∼ed 'cap** n Schirmmütze f. **∼ hours** npl Hauptbelastungszeit f; (for traffic) Hauptverkehrszeit f
peaky /'piːkɪ/ a kränklich
peal /piːl/ n (of bells) Glockengeläut nt; **∼s of laughter** schallendes Gelächter nt
peanut[1] n Erdnuß f; **for ∼s** (fam) für einen Apfel und ein Ei
pear /peə(r)/ n Birne f

pearl /pɜ:l/ *n* Perle *f*

peasant /'peznt/ *n* Bauer *m*

peat /pi:t/ *n* Torf *m*

pebble /'pebl/ *n* Kieselstein *m*

peck /pek/ *n* Schnabelhieb *m*; (*kiss*) flüchtiger Kuß *m* ● *vt/i* picken/(*nip*) hacken (**at** nach). **~ing order** *n* Hackordnung *f*

peckish /'pekɪʃ/ *a* **be ~** (*fam*) Hunger haben

peculiar /pɪ'kju:lɪə(r)/ *a* eigenartig, seltsam; **~ to** eigentümlich (+*dat*). **~ity** /-'ærətɪ/ *n* Eigenart *f*

pedal /'pedl/ *n* Pedal *nt* ● *vt* fahren ⟨*bicycle*⟩ ● *vi* treten. **~ bin** *n* Treteimer *m*

pedantic /pɪ'dæntɪk/ *a*, **-ally** *adv* pedantisch

peddle /'pedl/ *vt* handeln mit

pedestal /'pedɪstl/ *n* Sockel *m*

pedestrian /pɪ'destrɪən/ *n* Fußgänger(in) *m(f)* ● *a* (*fig*) prosaisch. **~ 'crossing** *n* Fußgängerüberweg *m*. **~ 'precinct** *n* Fußgängerzone *f*

pedicure /'pedɪkjʊə(r)/ *n* Pediküre *f*

pedigree /'pedɪgri:/ *n* Stammbaum *m* ● *attrib* ⟨*animal*⟩ Rasse-

pedlar /'pedlə(r)/ *n* Hausierer *m*

pee /pi:/ *vi* (*pt/pp* **peed**) (*fam*) pinkeln

peek /pi:k/ *vi* (*fam*) gucken

peel /pi:l/ *n* Schale *f* ● *vt* schälen ● *vi* ⟨*skin:*⟩ sich schälen; ⟨*paint:*⟩ abblättern. **~ings** *npl* Schalen *pl*

peep /pi:p/ *n* kurzer Blick *m* ● *vi* gucken. **~-hole** *n* Guckloch *nt*. **P~ing 'Tom** *n* (*fam*) Spanner *m*

peer[1] /pɪə(r)/ *vi* **~ at** forschend ansehen

peer[2] *n* Peer *m*; **his ~s** *pl* seinesgleichen

peev|ed /pi:vd/ *a* (*fam*) ärgerlich. **~ish** *a* reizbar

peg /peg/ *n* (*hook*) Haken *m*; (*for tent*) Pflock *m*, Hering *m*; (*for clothes*) [Wäsche]klammer *f*; **off the ~** (*fam*) von der Stange ● *vt* (*pt/pp* **pegged**) anpflocken; anklammern ⟨*washing*⟩

pejorative /pɪ'dʒɒrətɪv/ *a*, **-ly** *adv* abwertend

pelican /'pelɪkən/ *n* Pelikan *m*

pellet /'pelɪt/ *n* Kügelchen *nt*

pelt[1] /pelt/ *n* ⟨*skin*⟩ Pelz *m*, Fell *nt*

pelt[2] *vt* bewerfen ● *vi* (*fam: run fast*) rasen; **~ [down]** ⟨*rain:*⟩ [hernieder]-prasseln

pelvis /'pelvɪs/ *n* (*Anat*) Becken *nt*

pen[1] /pen/ *n* (*for animals*) Hürde *f*

pen[2] *n* Federhalter *m*; (*ball-point*) Kugelschreiber *m*

penal /'pi:nl/ *a* Straf-. **~ize** *vt* bestrafen; (*fig*) benachteiligen

penalty /'penltɪ/ *n* Strafe *f*; (*fine*) Geldstrafe *f*; (*Sport*) Strafstoß *m*; (*Football*) Elfmeter *m*

penance /'penəns/ *n* Buße *f*

pence /pens/ *see* **penny**

pencil /'pensɪl/ *n* Bleistift *m* ● *vt* (*pt/pp* **pencilled**) mit Bleistift schreiben. **~-sharpener** *n* Bleistiftspitzer *m*

pendant /'pendənt/ *n* Anhänger *m*

pending /'pendɪŋ/ *a* unerledigt ● *prep* bis zu

pendulum /'pendjʊləm/ *n* Pendel *nt*

penetrat|e /'penɪtreɪt/ *vt* durchdringen; **~e [into]** eindringen in (+*acc*). **~ing** *a* durchdringend. **~ion** /-'treɪʃn/ *n* Durchdringen *nt*

'penfriend *n* Brieffreund(in) *m(f)*

penguin /'peŋgwɪn/ *n* Pinguin *m*

penicillin /penɪ'sɪlɪn/ *n* Penizillin *nt*

peninsula /pə'nɪnsʊlə/ *n* Halbinsel *f*

penis /'pi:nɪs/ *n* Penis *m*

peniten|ce /'penɪtəns/ *n* Reue *f*. **~t** *a* reuig ● *n* Büßer *m*

penitentiary /penɪ'tenʃərɪ/ *n* (*Amer*) Gefängnis *nt*

pen: **~knife** *n* Taschenmesser *nt*. **~-name** *n* Pseudonym *nt*

pennant /'penənt/ *n* Wimpel *m*

penniless /'penɪlɪs/ *a* mittellos

penny /'penɪ/ *n* (*pl* **pence**; *single coins* **pennies**) Penny *m*; (*Amer*) Centstück *nt*; **spend a ~** (*fam*) mal verschwinden; **the ~'s dropped** (*fam*) der Groschen ist gefallen

pension /'penʃn/ *n* Rente *f*; (*of civil servant*) Pension *f*. **~er** *n* Rentner(in) *m(f)*; Pensionär(in) *m(f)*

pensive /'pensɪv/ *a* nachdenklich

Pentecost /'pentɪkɒst/ *n* Pfingsten *nt*

pent-up /'pentʌp/ *a* angestaut

penultimate /pe'nʌltɪmət/ *a* vorletzte(r,s)

penury /'penjʊrɪ/ *n* Armut *f*

peony /'pɪənɪ/ *n* Pfingstrose *f*

people /'pi:pl/ *npl* Leute *pl*, Menschen *pl*; (*citizens*) Bevölkerung *f*; **the ~** das Volk; **English ~** die Engländer; **~ say** man sagt; **for four ~** für vier Personen ● *vt* bevölkern

pep /pep/ *n* (*fam*) Schwung *m*

pepper /'pepə(r)/ *n* Pfeffer *m*; (*vegetable*) Paprika *m* ● *vt* (*Culin*) pfeffern

pepper: ∼**corn** n Pfefferkorn nt. ∼**mint** n Pfefferminz nt; (Bot) Pfefferminze f. ∼**pot** n Pfefferstreuer m

per /pɜː(r)/ prep pro; ∼ **cent** Prozent nt

perceive /pə'siːv/ vt wahrnehmen

percentage /pə'sentɪdʒ/ n Prozentsatz m; (part) Teil m

perceptible /pə'septəbl/ a wahrnehmbar

percept|ion /pə'sepʃn/ n Wahrnehmung f. ∼**ive** /-tɪv/ a feinsinnig

perch¹ /pɜːtʃ/ n Stange f ● vi (bird:) sich niederlassen

perch² n inv (fish) Barsch m

percolat|e /'pɜːkəleɪt/ vi durchsickern. ∼**or** n Kaffeemaschine f

percussion /pə'kʌʃn/ n Schlagzeug nt. ∼ **instrument** n Schlaginstrument nt

peremptory /pə'remptərɪ/ a herrisch

perennial /pə'renɪəl/ a (problem) immer wiederkehrend ● n (Bot) mehrjährige Pflanze f

perfect¹ /'pɜːfɪkt/ a perfekt, vollkommen; (fam: utter) völlig ● n (Gram) Perfekt nt

perfect² /pə'fekt/ vt vervollkommnen. ∼**ion** /-ekʃn/ n Vollkommenheit f; **to** ∼**ion** perfekt

perfectly /'pɜːfɪktlɪ/ adv perfekt; (completely) vollkommen, völlig

perforate /'pɜːfəreɪt/ vt perforieren; (make a hole in) durchlöchern. ∼**d** a perforiert

perform /pə'fɔːm/ vt ausführen; erfüllen (duty); (Theat) aufführen (play); spielen (role) ● vi (Theat) auftreten; (Techn) laufen. ∼**ance** n Aufführung f; (at theatre, cinema) Vorstellung f; (Techn) Leistung f. ∼**er** n Künstler(in) m(f)

perfume /'pɜːfjuːm/ n Parfüm nt; (smell) Duft m

perfunctory /pə'fʌŋktərɪ/ a flüchtig

perhaps /pə'hæps/ adv vielleicht

peril /'perəl/ n Gefahr f. ∼**ous** /-əs/ a gefährlich

perimeter /pə'rɪmɪtə(r)/ n [äußere] Grenze f; (Geom) Umfang m

period /'pɪərɪəd/ n Periode f; (Sch) Stunde f; (full stop) Punkt m ● attrib (costume) zeitgenössisch; (furniture) antik. ∼**ic** /-'ɒdɪk/ a, **-ally** adv periodisch. ∼**ical** /-'ɒdɪkl/ n Zeitschrift f

peripher|al /pə'rɪfərl/ a nebensächlich. ∼**y** n Peripherie f

periscope /'perɪskəʊp/ n Periskop nt

perish /'perɪʃ/ vi (rubber:) verrotten; (food:) verderben; (die) ums Leben kommen. ∼**able** /-əbl/ a leicht verderblich. ∼**ing** a (fam: cold) eiskalt

perjur|e /'pɜːdʒə(r)/ vt ∼**e oneself** einen Meineid leisten. ∼**y** n Meineid m

perk¹ /pɜːk/ n (fam) [Sonder]vergünstigung f

perk² vi ∼ **up** munter werden

perky /'pɜːkɪ/ a munter

perm /pɜːm/ n Dauerwelle f ● vt ∼ **s.o.'s hair** jdm eine Dauerwelle machen

permanent /'pɜːmənənt/ a ständig; (job, address) fest. ∼**ly** adv ständig; (work, live) dauernd, permanent; (employed) fest

permeable /'pɜːmɪəbl/ a durchlässig

permeate /'pɜːmɪeɪt/ vt durchdringen

permissible /pə'mɪsəbl/ a erlaubt

permission /pə'mɪʃn/ n Erlaubnis f

permissive /pə'mɪsɪv/ a (society) permissiv

permit¹ /pə'mɪt/ vt (pt/pp **-mitted**) erlauben (**s.o.** jdm); ∼ **me!** gestatten Sie!

permit² /'pɜːmɪt/ n Genehmigung f

pernicious /pə'nɪʃəs/ a schädlich; (Med) perniziös

perpendicular /pɜːpən'dɪkjʊlə(r)/ a senkrecht ● n Senkrechte f

perpetrat|e /'pɜːpɪtreɪt/ vt begehen. ∼**or** n Täter m

perpetual /pə'petjʊəl/ a, **-ly** adv ständig, dauernd

perpetuate /pə'petjʊeɪt/ vt bewahren; verewigen (error)

perplex /pə'pleks/ vt verblüffen. ∼**ed** a verblüfft. ∼**ity** n Verblüffung f

persecut|e /'pɜːsɪkjuːt/ vt verfolgen. ∼**ion** /-'kjuːʃn/ n Verfolgung f

perseverance /pɜːsɪ'vɪərəns/ n Ausdauer f

persever|e /pɜːsɪ'vɪə(r)/ vi beharrlich weitermachen. ∼**ing** a ausdauernd

Persia /'pɜːʃə/ n Persien nt

Persian /'pɜːʃn/ a persisch; (cat, carpet) Perser-

persist /pə'sɪst/ vi beharrlich weitermachen; (continue) anhalten;

⟨*view:*⟩ weiter bestehen; ~ **in doing
sth** dabei bleiben, etw zu tun. ~**ence**
n Beharrlichkeit *f.* ~**ent** *a*, **-ly** *adv*
beharrlich; (*continuous*) anhaltend
person /'pɜːsn/ *n* Person *f*; **in** ~ persönlich
personal /'pɜːsənl/ *a*, **-ly** *adv* persönlich. ~ **'hygiene** *n* Körperpflege *f*
personality /pɜːsə'næləti/ *n* Per-
sönlichkeit *f*
personify /pə'sɒnɪfaɪ/ *vt* (*pt/pp* **-ied**)
personifizieren, verkörpern
personnel /pɜːsə'nel/ *n* Personal *nt*
perspective /pə'spektɪv/ *n* Per-
spektive *f*
perspicacious /pɜːspɪ'keɪʃəs/ *a*
scharfsichtig
persp|iration /pə:spɪ'reɪʃn/ *n*
Schweiß *m.* ~**ire** /-'spaɪə(r)/ *vi*
schwitzen
persua|de /pə'sweɪd/ *vt* überreden;
(*convince*) überzeugen. ~**sion**
/-eɪʒn/ *n* Überredung *f*; (*powers of
*~*sion*) Überredungskunst *f*; (*belief*)
Glaubensrichtung *f*
persuasive /pə'sweɪsɪv/ *a*, **-ly** *adv*
beredsam; (*convincing*) überzeugend
pert /pɜːt/ *a*, **-ly** *adv* keß
pertain /pə'teɪn/ *vi* ~ **to** betreffen;
(*belong*) gehören zu
pertinent /'pɜːtɪnənt/ *a* relevant (**to**
für)
perturb /pə'tɜːb/ *vt* beunruhigen
peruse /pə'ruːz/ *vt* lesen
perva|de /pə'veɪd/ *vt* durchdringen.
~**sive** /-sɪv/ *a* durchdringend
pervers|e /pə'vɜːs/ *a* eigensinnig.
~**ion** /-ɜːʃn/ *n* Perversion *f*
pervert[1] /pə'vɜːt/ *vt* verdrehen; verführen ⟨*person*⟩
pervert[2] /'pɜːvɜːt/ *n* Perverse(r) *m*
perverted /pə'vɜːtɪd/ *a* abartig
pessimis|m /'pesɪmɪzm/ *n* Pessi-
mismus *m.* ~**t** /-mɪst/ *n* Pessimist *m.*
~**tic** /-'mɪstɪk/ *a*, **-ally** *adv* pessimistisch
pest /pest/ *n* Schädling *m*; (*fam: person*) Nervensäge *f*
pester /'pestə(r)/ *vt* belästigen; ~
s.o. for sth jdm wegen etw in den
Ohren liegen
pesticide /'pestɪsaɪd/ *n* Schäd-
lingsbekämpfungsmittel *nt*
pet /pet/ *n* Haustier *nt*; (*favourite*)
Liebling *m* ● *vt* (*pt/pp* **petted**) liebkosen
petal /'petl/ *n* Blütenblatt *nt*

peter /'piːtə(r)/ *vi* ~ **out** allmählich
aufhören; ⟨*stream:*⟩ versickern
petite /pə'tiːt/ *a* klein und zierlich
petition /pə'tɪʃn/ *n* Bittschrift *f* ● *vt*
eine Bittschrift richten an (+ *acc*)
pet 'name *n* Kosename *m*
petrif|y /'petrɪfaɪ/ *vt/i* (*pt/pp* **-ied**)
versteinern; ~**ied** (*frightened*) vor
Angst wie versteinert
petrol /'petrl/ *n* Benzin *nt*
petroleum /pɪ'trəʊlɪəm/ *n* Petroleum *nt*
petrol: ~**-pump** *n* Zapfsäule *f.* ~
station *n* Tankstelle *f.* ~ **tank** *n*
Benzintank *m*
pet shop *n* Tierhandlung *f*
petticoat /'petɪkəʊt/ *n* Unterrock *m*
petty /'peti/ *a* (**-ier, -iest**) kleinlich. ~
'cash *n* Portokasse *f*
petulant /'petjʊlənt/ *a* gekränkt
pew /pjuː/ *n* [Kirchen]bank *f*
pewter /'pjuːtə(r)/ *n* Zinn *nt*
phantom /'fæntəm/ *n* Gespenst *nt*
pharmaceutical /fɑːmə'sjuːtɪkl/ *a*
pharmazeutisch
pharmac|ist /'fɑːməsɪst/ *n* Apothe-
ker(in) *m(f).* ~**y** *n* Pharmazie *f*;
(*shop*) Apotheke *f*
phase /feɪz/ *n* Phase *f* ● *vt* ~ **in/out**
allmählich einführen/abbauen
Ph.D. (*abbr of* **Doctor of Philosophy**)
Dr. phil.
pheasant /'feznt/ *n* Fasan *m*
phenomen|al /fɪ'nɒmɪnl/ *a* phäno-
menal. ~**on** *n* (*pl* **-na**) Phänomen *nt*
phial /'faɪəl/ *n* Fläschchen *nt*
philanderer /fɪ'lændərə(r)/ *n* Ver-
führer *m*
philanthrop|ic /fɪlən'θrɒpɪk/ *a* men-
schenfreundlich. ~**ist** /fɪ'læn-
θrəpɪst/ *n* Philanthrop *m*
philately /fɪ'lætəlɪ/ *n* Philatelie *f*,
Briefmarkenkunde *f*
philharmonic /fɪlɑː'mɒnɪk/ *n* (*orchestra*) Philharmoniker *pl*
Philippines /'fɪlɪpiːnz/ *npl* Philip-
pinen *pl*
philistine /'fɪlɪstaɪn/ *n* Banause *m*
philosoph|er /fɪ'lɒsəfə(r)/ *n* Philo-
soph *m.* ~**ical** /fɪlə'sɒfɪkl/ *a*, **-ly** *adv*
philosophisch. ~**y** *n* Philosophie *f*
phlegm /flem/ *n* (*Med*) Schleim *m*
phlegmatic /fleg'mætɪk/ *a* phlegmatisch
phobia /'fəʊbɪə/ *n* Phobie *f*
phone /fəʊn/ *n* Telefon *nt*; **be on the
** ~ Telefon haben; (*be phoning*) telefonieren ● *vt* anrufen ● *vi* telefonieren.

potter[1] /'pɒtə(r)/ *vi* ~ **[about]** herumwerkeln

potter[2] *n* Töpfer(in) *m(f)*. ~**y** *n* Töpferei *f*; (*articles*) Töpferwaren *pl*

potty /'pɒtɪ/ *a* (**-ier, -iest**) (*fam*) verrückt ● *n* Töpfchen *nt*

pouch /paʊtʃ/ *n* Beutel *m*

pouffe /puːf/ *n* Sitzkissen *nt*

poultry /'pəʊltrɪ/ *n* Geflügel *nt*

pounce /paʊns/ *vi* zuschlagen; ~ **on** sich stürzen auf (+ *acc*)

pound[1] /paʊnd/ *n* (*money & 0,454 kg*) Pfund *nt*

pound[2] *vt* hämmern ● *vi* ⟨*heart:*⟩ hämmern; (*run heavily*) stampfen

pour /pɔː(r)/ *vt* gießen; einschenken ⟨*drink*⟩ ● *vi* strömen; (*with rain*) gießen. ~ **out** *vi* ausströmen ● *vt* ausschütten; einschenken ⟨*drink*⟩

pout /paʊt/ *vi* einen Schmollmund machen

poverty /'pɒvətɪ/ *n* Armut *f*

powder /'paʊdə(r)/ *n* Pulver *nt*; (*cosmetic*) Puder *m* ● *vt* pudern. ~**y** *a* pulverig

power /'paʊə(r)/ *n* Macht *f*; (*strength*) Kraft *f*; (*Electr*) Strom *m*; (*nuclear*) Energie *f*; (*Math*) Potenz *f*. ~ **cut** *n* Stromsperre *f*. ~**ed** *a* betrieben (**by** mit); ~**ed by electricity** mit Elektroantrieb. ~**ful** *a* mächtig; (*strong*) stark. ~**less** *a* machtlos. ~**-station** *n* Kraftwerk *nt*

practicable /'præktɪkəbl/ *a* durchführbar, praktikabel

practical /'præktɪkl/ *a*, **-ly** *adv* praktisch. ~ '**joke** *n* Streich *m*

practice /'præktɪs/ *n* Praxis *f*; (*custom*) Brauch *m*; (*habit*) Gewohnheit *f*; (*exercise*) Übung *f*; (*Sport*) Training *nt*; **in** ~ (*in reality*) in der Praxis; **out of** ~ außer Übung; **put into** ~ ausführen

practise /'præktɪs/ *vt* üben; (*carry out*) praktizieren; ausüben ⟨*profession*⟩ ● *vi* üben; ⟨*doctor:*⟩ praktizieren. ~**d** *a* geübt

pragmatic /præg'mætɪk/ *a*, ~**ally** *adv* pragmatisch

praise /preɪz/ *n* Lob *nt* ● *vt* loben. ~**worthy** *a* lobenswert

pram /præm/ *n* Kinderwagen *m*

prance /prɑːns/ *vi* herumhüpfen; ⟨*horse:*⟩ tänzeln

prank /præŋk/ *n* Streich *m*

prattle /'prætl/ *vi* plappern

prawn /prɔːn/ *n* Garnele *f*, Krabbe *f*. ~ '**cocktail** *n* Krabbencocktail *m*

pray /preɪ/ *vi* beten. ~**er** /preə(r)/ *n* Gebet *nt*; ~**ers** *pl* (*service*) Andacht *f*

preach /priːtʃ/ *vt/i* predigen. ~**er** *n* Prediger *m*

preamble /prɪ'æmbl/ *n* Einleitung *f*

pre-ar'range /priː-/ *vt* im voraus arrangieren

precarious /prɪ'keərɪəs/ *a*, **-ly** *adv* unsicher

precaution /prɪ'kɔːʃn/ *n* Vorsichtsmaßnahme *f*; **as a** ~ zur Vorsicht. ~**ary** *a* Vorsichts-

precede /prɪ'siːd/ *vt* vorangehen (+ *dat*)

preceden|ce /'presɪdəns/ *n* Vorrang *m*. ~**t** *n* Präzedenzfall *m*

preceding /prɪ'siːdɪŋ/ *a* vorhergehend

precinct /'priːsɪŋkt/ *n* Bereich *m*; (*traffic-free*) Fußgängerzone *f*; (*Amer: district*) Bezirk *m*

precious /'preʃəs/ *a* kostbar; ⟨*style*⟩ preziös ● *adv* (*fam*) ~ **little** recht wenig

precipice /'presɪpɪs/ *n* Steilabfall *m*

precipitate[1] /prɪ'sɪpɪtət/ *a* voreilig

precipitat|e[2] /prɪ'sɪpɪteɪt/ *vt* schleudern; (*fig: accelerate*) beschleunigen. ~**ion** /-'teɪʃn/ *n* (*Meteorol*) Niederschlag *m*

précis /'preɪsiː/ *n* (*pl* **précis** /-siːz/) Zusammenfassung *f*

precis|e /prɪ'saɪs/ *a*, **-ly** *adv* genau. ~**ion** /-'sɪʒn/ *n* Genauigkeit *f*

preclude /prɪ'kluːd/ *vt* ausschließen

precocious /prɪ'kəʊʃəs/ *a* frühreif

pre|con'ceived /priː-/ *a* vorgefaßt. ~**con'ception** *n* vorgefaßte Meinung *f*

precursor /priː'kɜːsə(r)/ *n* Vorläufer *m*

predator /'predətə(r)/ *n* Raubtier *nt*

predecessor /'priːdɪsesə(r)/ *n* Vorgänger(in) *m(f)*

predicament /prɪ'dɪkəmənt/ *n* Zwangslage *f*

predicat|e /'predɪkət/ *n* (*Gram*) Prädikat *nt*. ~**ive** /prɪ'dɪkətɪv/ *a*, **-ly** *adv* prädikativ

predict /prɪ'dɪkt/ *vt* voraussagen. ~**able** /-əbl/ *a* voraussehbar; ⟨*person*⟩ berechenbar. ~**ion** /-'dɪkʃn/ *n* Voraussage *f*

pre'domin|ant /prɪ-/ *a* vorherrschend. ~**antly** *adv* hauptsächlich, überwiegend. ~**ate** *vi* vorherrschen

pre-'eminent /priː-/ *a* hervorragend

pre-empt /priː'empt/ vt zuvorkommen (+ dat)

preen /priːn/ vt putzen; ~ **oneself** (fig) selbstgefällig tun

pre|fab /'priːfæb/ n (fam) [einfaches] Fertighaus nt. ~'**fabricated** a vorgefertigt

preface /'prefɪs/ n Vorwort nt

prefect /'priːfekt/ n Präfekt m

prefer /prɪ'fɜː(r)/ vt (pt/pp **preferred**) vorziehen; **I ~ to walk** ich gehe lieber zu Fuß; **I ~ wine** ich trinke lieber Wein

prefera|ble /'prefərəbl/ a **be ~ble** vorzuziehen sein (**to** dat). ~**bly** adv vorzugsweise

preferen|ce /'prefərəns/ n Vorzug m. ~**tial** /-'renʃl/ a bevorzugt

prefix /'priːfɪks/ n Vorsilbe f

pregnan|cy /'pregnənsɪ/ n Schwangerschaft f. ~**t** a schwanger; ⟨animal⟩ trächtig

prehi'storic /priː-/ a prähistorisch

prejudice /'predʒʊdɪs/ n Vorurteil nt; (bias) Voreingenommenheit f ● vt einnehmen (**against** gegen). ~**d** a voreingenommen

preliminary /prɪ'lɪmɪnərɪ/ a Vor-

prelude /'prelju:d/ n Vorspiel nt

pre-'marital a vorehelich

premature /'premətjʊə(r)/ a vorzeitig; ⟨birth⟩ Früh-. ~**ly** adv zu früh

pre'meditated /priː-/ a vorsätzlich

premier /'premɪə(r)/ a führend ● n (Pol) Premier[minister] m

première /'premɪeə(r)/ n Premiere f

premises /'premɪsɪz/ npl Räumlichkeiten pl; **on the ~** im Haus

premiss /'premɪs/ n Prämisse f

premium /'priːmɪəm/ n Prämie f; **be at a ~** hoch im Kurs stehen

premonition /premə'nɪʃn/ n Vorahnung f

preoccupied /prɪ'ɒkjʊpaɪd/ a [in Gedanken] beschäftigt

prep /prep/ n (Sch) Hausaufgaben pl

pre-'packed /priː-/ a abgepackt

preparation /prepə'reɪʃn/ n Vorbereitung f; (substance) Präparat nt

preparatory /prɪ'pærətrɪ/ a Vor- ● adv ~ **to** vor (+ dat)

prepare /prɪ'peə(r)/ vt vorbereiten; anrichten ⟨meal⟩ ● vi sich vorbereiten (**for** auf + acc); ~**d to** bereit zu

pre'pay /priː-/ vt (pt/pp **-paid**) im voraus bezahlen

preposition /prepə'zɪʃn/ n Präposition f

prepossessing /priːpə'zesɪŋ/ a ansprechend

preposterous /prɪ'pɒstərəs/ a absurd

prerequisite /priː'rekwɪzɪt/ n Voraussetzung f

prerogative /prɪ'rɒgətɪv/ n Vorrecht nt

Presbyterian /prezbɪ'tɪərɪən/ a presbyterianisch ● n Presbyterianer(in) m(f)

prescribe /prɪ'skraɪb/ vt vorschreiben; (Med) verschreiben

prescription /prɪ'skrɪpʃn/ n (Med) Rezept nt

presence /'prezns/ n Anwesenheit f, Gegenwart f; ~ **of mind** Geistesgegenwart f

present[1] /'preznt/ a gegenwärtig; **be ~** anwesend sein; (occur) vorkommen ● n Gegenwart f; (Gram) Präsens nt; **at ~** zur Zeit; **for the ~** vorläufig

present[2] n (gift) Geschenk nt

present[3] /prɪ'zent/ vt überreichen; (show) zeigen; vorlegen ⟨cheque⟩; (introduce) vorstellen; ~ **s.o. with sth** jdm etw überreichen. ~**able** /-əbl/ a **be ~able** sich zeigen lassen können

presentation /prezn'teɪʃn/ n Überreichung f. ~ **ceremony** n Verleihungszeremonie f

presently /'prezntlɪ/ adv nachher; (Amer: now) zur Zeit

preservation /prezə'veɪʃn/ n Erhaltung f

preservative /prɪ'zɜːvətɪv/ n Konservierungsmittel nt

preserve /prɪ'zɜːv/ vt erhalten; (Culin) einmachen; ⟨bottle⟩ einmachen ● n (Hunting & fig) Revier nt; (jam) Konfitüre f

preside /prɪ'zaɪd/ vi den Vorsitz haben (**over** bei)

presidency /'prezɪdənsɪ/ n Präsidentschaft f

president /'prezɪdənt/ n Präsident m; (Amer: chairman) Vorsitzende(r) m/f. ~**ial** /-'denʃl/ a Präsidenten-; ⟨election⟩ Präsidentschafts-

press /pres/ n Presse f ● vt/i drücken; drücken auf (+ acc) ⟨button⟩; pressen ⟨flower⟩; (iron) bügeln; (urge) bedrängen; ~ **for** drängen auf (+ acc); **be ~ed for time** in Zeitdruck sein. ~ **on** vi weitergehen/-fahren; (fig) weitermachen

press: ~ **cutting** n Zeitungsausschnitt m. ~**ing** a dringend. ~**-stud**

n Druckknopf *m*. **~-up** *n* Liegestütz *m*

pressure /'preʃə(r)/ *n* Druck *m*
● *vt* = **pressurize**. **~-cooker** *n* Schnellkochtopf *m*. **~ group** *n* Interessengruppe *f*

pressurize /'preʃəraɪz/ *vt* Druck ausüben auf (+ *acc*). **~d** *a* Druck-

prestig|e /pre'sti:ʒ/ *n* Prestige *nt*. **~ious** /-'stɪdʒəs/ *a* Prestige-

presumably /prɪ'zju:məblɪ/ *adv* vermutlich

presume /prɪ'zju:m/ *vt* vermuten; **~ to do sth** sich (*dat*) anmaßen, etw zu tun ● *vi* **~ on** ausnutzen

presumpt|ion /prɪ'zʌmpʃn/ *n* Vermutung *f*; (*boldness*) Anmaßung *f*. **~uous** /-'zʌmptjʊəs/ *a*, **-ly** *adv* anmaßend

presup'pose /pri:-/ *vt* voraussetzen

pretence /prɪ'tens/ *n* Verstellung *f*; (*pretext*) Vorwand *m*; **it's all ~** das ist alles gespielt

pretend /prɪ'tend/ *vt* (*claim*) vorgeben; **~ that** so tun, als ob; **~ to be** sich ausgeben als

pretentious /prɪ'tenʃəs/ *a* protzig

pretext /'pri:tekst/ *n* Vorwand *m*

pretty /'prɪtɪ/ *a* (**-ier, -iest**), **~ily** *adv* hübsch ● *adv* (*fam:fairly*) ziemlich

pretzel /'pretsl/ *n* Brezel *f*

prevail /prɪ'veɪl/ *vi* siegen; (*custom:*) vorherrschen; **~ on s.o. to do sth** jdn dazu bringen, etw zu tun

prevalen|ce /'prevələns/ *n* Häufigkeit *f*. **~t** *a* vorherrschend

prevent /prɪ'vent/ *vt* verhindern, verhüten; **~ s.o. [from] doing sth** jdn daran hindern, etw zu tun. **~able** /-əbl/ *a* vermeidbar. **~ion** /-enʃn/ *n* Verhinderung *f*, Verhütung *f*. **~ive** /-ɪv/ *a* vorbeugend

preview /'pri:vju:/ *n* Voraufführung *f*

previous /'pri:vɪəs/ *a* vorhergehend; **~ to** vor (+ *dat*). **~ly** *adv* vorher, früher

pre-'war /pri:-/ *a* Vorkriegs-

prey /preɪ/ *n* Beute *f*; **bird of ~** Raubvogel *m* ● *vi* **~ on** Jagd machen auf (+ *acc*); **~ on s.o.'s mind** jdm schwer auf der Seele liegen

price /praɪs/ *n* Preis *m* ● *vt* (*Comm*) auszeichnen. **~less** *a* unschätzbar; (*fig*) unbezahlbar

prick /prɪk/ *n* Stich *m* ● *vt/i* stechen; **~ up one's ears** die Ohren spitzen

prickl|e /'prɪkl/ *n* Stachel *m*; (*thorn*) Dorn *m*. **~y** *a* stachelig; (*sensation*) stechend

pride /praɪd/ *n* Stolz *m*; (*arrogance*) Hochmut *m*; (*of lions*) Rudel *nt* ● *vt* **~ oneself on** stolz sein auf (+ *acc*)

priest /pri:st/ *n* Priester *m*

prig /prɪg/ *n* Tugendbold *m*

prim /prɪm/ *a* (**primmer, primmest**) prüde

primarily /'praɪmərɪlɪ/ *adv* hauptsächlich, in erster Linie

primary /'praɪmərɪ/ *a* Haupt-. **~ school** *n* Grundschule *f*

prime[1] /praɪm/ *a* Haupt-; (*first-rate*) erstklassig ● *n* **be in one's ~** in den besten Jahren sein

prime[2] *vt* scharf machen (*bomb*); grundieren (*surface*); (*fig*) instruieren

Prime Minister /praɪ'mɪnɪstə(r)/ *n* Premierminister(in) *m*(*f*)

primeval /praɪ'mi:vl/ *a* Ur-

primitive /'prɪmɪtɪv/ *a* primitiv

primrose /'prɪmrəʊz/ *n* gelbe Schlüsselblume *f*

prince /prɪns/ *n* Prinz *m*

princess /prɪn'ses/ *n* Prinzessin *f*

principal /'prɪnsəpl/ *a* Haupt- ● *n* (*Sch*) Rektor(in) *m*(*f*)

principality /prɪnsɪ'pælətɪ/ *n* Fürstentum *nt*

principally /'prɪnsəplɪ/ *adv* hauptsächlich

principle /'prɪnsəpl/ *n* Prinzip *nt*, Grundsatz *m*; **in/on ~** im/aus Prinzip

print /prɪnt/ *n* Druck *m*; (*Phot*) Abzug *m*; **in ~** gedruckt; (*available*) erhältlich; **out of ~** vergriffen ● *vt* drucken; (*write in capitals*) in Druckschrift schreiben; (*Computing*) ausdrucken; (*Phot*) abziehen. **~ed matter** *n* Drucksache *f*

print|er /'prɪntə(r)/ *n* Drucker *m*. **~ing** *n* Druck *m*

'printout *n* (*Computing*) Ausdruck *m*

prior /'praɪə(r)/ *a* frühere(r,s); **~ to** vor (+ *dat*)

priority /praɪ'ɒrətɪ/ *n* Priorität *f*, Vorrang *m*; (*matter*) vordringliche Sache *f*

prise /praɪz/ *vt* **~ open/up** aufstemmen/hochstemmen

prism /'prɪzm/ *n* Prisma *nt*

prison /'prɪzn/ *n* Gefängnis *nt*. **~er** *n* Gefangene(r) *m*/*f*

pristine /'prɪsti:n/ *a* tadellos

privacy /'prɪvəsɪ/ n Privatsphäre f; **have no** ～ nie für sich sein

private /'praɪvət/ a, **-ly** adv privat; (confidential) vertraulich; ⟨car, secretary, school⟩ Privat- ● n (Mil) [einfacher] Soldat m; **in** ～ privat; (confidentially) vertraulich

privation /praɪ'veɪʃn/ n Entbehrung f

privatize /'praɪvətaɪz/ vt privatisieren

privilege /'prɪvəlɪdʒ/ n Privileg nt. ～**d** a privilegiert

privy /'prɪvɪ/ a **be** ～ **to** wissen

prize /praɪz/ n Preis m ● vt schätzen. ～**-giving** n Preisverleihung f. ～**-winner** n Preisgewinner(in) m(f)

pro /prəʊ/ n (fam) Profi m; **the** ～**s and cons** das Für und Wider

probability /prɒbə'bɪlətɪ/ n Wahrscheinlichkeit f

probable /'prɒbəbl/ a, **-bly** adv wahrscheinlich

probation /prə'beɪʃn/ n (Jur) Bewährung f. ～**ary** a Probe-; ～**ary period** Probezeit f

probe /prəʊb/ n Sonde f; (fig: investigation) Untersuchung f ● vt/i ～ **[into]** untersuchen

problem /'prɒbləm/ n Problem nt; (Math) Textaufgabe f. ～**atic** /-'mætɪk/ a problematisch

procedure /prə'siːdʒə(r)/ n Verfahren nt

proceed /prə'siːd/ vi gehen; (in vehicle) fahren; (continue) weitergehen/-fahren; (speaking) fortfahren; (act) verfahren ● vt ～ **to do sth** anfangen, etw zu tun

proceedings /prə'siːdɪŋz/ npl Verfahren nt; (Jur) Prozeß m

proceeds /'prəʊsiːdz/ npl Erlös m

process /'prəʊses/ n Prozeß m; (procedure) Verfahren nt; **in the** ～ dabei ● vt verarbeiten; (Admin) bearbeiten; (Phot) entwickeln

procession /prə'seʃn/ n Umzug m, Prozession f

proclaim /prə'kleɪm/ vt ausrufen

proclamation /prɒklə'meɪʃn/ n Proklamation f

procure /prə'kjʊə(r)/ vt beschaffen

prod /prɒd/ n Stoß m ● vt stoßen; (fig) einen Stoß geben (+ dat)

prodigal /'prɒdɪgl/ a verschwenderisch

prodigious /prə'dɪdʒəs/ a gewaltig

prodigy /'prɒdɪdʒɪ/ n **[infant]** ～ Wunderkind nt

produce[1] /'prɒdjuːs/ n landwirtschaftliche Erzeugnisse pl

produce[2] /prə'djuːs/ vt erzeugen, produzieren; (manufacture) herstellen; (bring out) hervorholen; (cause) hervorrufen; inszenieren ⟨play⟩; (Radio, TV) redigieren. ～**r** n Erzeuger m, Produzent m; Hersteller m; (Theat) Regisseur m; (Radio, TV) Redakteur(in) m(f)

product /'prɒdʌkt/ n Erzeugnis nt, Produkt nt. ～**ion** /prə'dʌkʃn/ n Produktion f; (Theat) Inszenierung f

productiv|e /prə'dʌktɪv/ a produktiv; (land, talks) fruchtbar. ～**ity** /-'tɪvətɪ/ n Produktivität f

profan|e /prə'feɪn/ a weltlich; (blasphemous) [gottes]lästerlich. ～**ity** /-'fænətɪ/ n (oath) Fluch m

profess /prə'fes/ vt behaupten; bekennen ⟨faith⟩

profession /prə'feʃn/ n Beruf m. ～**al** a, **-ly** adv beruflich; (not amateur) Berufs-; (expert) fachmännisch; (Sport) professionell ● n Fachmann m; (Sport) Profi m

professor /prə'fesə(r)/ n Professor m

proficien|cy /prə'fɪʃnsɪ/ n Können nt. ～**t** a **be** ～**t in** beherrschen

profile /'prəʊfaɪl/ n Profil nt; (character study) Porträt nt

profit /'prɒfɪt/ n Gewinn m, Profit m ● vi ～ **from** profitieren von. ～**able** /-əbl/ a, **-bly** adv gewinnbringend; (fig) nutzbringend

profound /prə'faʊnd/ a, **-ly** adv tief

profus|e /prə'fjuːs/ a, **-ly** adv üppig; (fig) überschwenglich. ～**ion** /-juːʒn/ n **in** ～**ion** in großer Fülle

progeny /'prɒdʒənɪ/ n Nachkommenschaft f

program /'prəʊgræm/ n Programm nt ● vt (pt/pp **programmed**) programmieren

programme /'prəʊgræm/ n Programm nt; (Radio, TV) Sendung f. ～**r** n (Computing) Programmierer(in) m(f)

progress[1] /'prəʊgres/ n Vorankommen nt; (fig) Fortschritt m; **in** ～ im Gange; **make** ～ (fig) Fortschritte machen

progress[2] /prə'gres/ vi vorankommen; (fig) fortschreiten. ～**ion**

/-eʃn/ n Folge f; (development) Entwicklung f

progressive /prə'gresɪv/ a fortschrittlich; (disease) fortschreitend. ~ly adv zunehmend

prohibit /prə'hɪbɪt/ vt verbieten (s.o. jdm). ~ive /-ɪv/ a unerschwinglich

project¹ /'prɒdʒekt/ n Projekt nt; (Sch) Arbeit f

project² /prə'dʒekt/ vt projizieren (film); (plan) planen ● vi (jut out) vorstehen

projectile /prə'dʒektaɪl/ n Geschoß nt

projector /prə'dʒektə(r)/ n Projektor m

proletariat /prəʊlɪ'teərɪət/ n Proletariat nt

prolific /prə'lɪfɪk/ a fruchtbar; (fig) produktiv

prologue /'prəʊlɒg/ n Prolog m

prolong /prə'lɒŋ/ vt verlängern

promenade /prɒmə'nɑːd/ n Promenade f ● vi spazierengehen

prominent /'prɒmɪnənt/ a vorstehend; (important) prominent; (conspicuous) auffällig; (place) gut sichtbar

promiscu|ity /prɒmɪ'skjuːətɪ/ n Promiskuität f. ~ous /prə'mɪskjʊəs/ a be ~ous häufig den Partner wechseln

promis|e /'prɒmɪs/ n Versprechen nt ● vt/i versprechen (s.o. jdm); the P~ed Land das Gelobte Land. ~ing a vielversprechend

promot|e /prə'məʊt/ vt befördern; (advance) fördern; (publicize) Reklame machen für; **be ~ed** (Sport) aufsteigen. ~ion /-əʊʃn/ n Beförderung f; (Sport) Aufstieg m; (Comm) Reklame f

prompt /prɒmpt/ a prompt, unverzüglich; (punctual) pünktlich ● adv pünktlich ● vt/i veranlassen (to, zu); (Theat) soufflieren (+ dat). ~er n Souffleur m/Souffleuse f. ~ly adv prompt

prone /prəʊn/ a **be/lie ~** auf dem Bauch liegen; **be ~ to** neigen zu; **be ~ to do sth** dazu neigen, etw zu tun

prong /prɒŋ/ n Zinke f

pronoun /'prəʊnaʊn/ n Fürwort nt, Pronomen nt

pronounce /prə'naʊns/ vt aussprechen; (declare) erklären. ~d a ausgeprägt; (noticeable) deutlich. ~ment n Erklärung f

pronunciation /prənʌnsɪ'eɪʃn/ n Aussprache f

proof /pruːf/ n Beweis m; (Typ) Korrekturbogen m ● a ~ **against water/ theft** wasserfest/diebessicher. ~-reader n Korrektor m

prop¹ /prɒp/ n Stütze f ● vt (pt/pp propped) ~ **open** offenhalten; ~ **against** (lean) lehnen an (+ acc). ~ **up** vt stützen

prop² n (Theat, fam) Requisit nt

propaganda /prɒpə'gændə/ n Propaganda f

propagate /'prɒpəgeɪt/ vt vermehren; (fig) verbreiten, propagieren

propel /prə'pel/ vt (pt/pp propelled) [an]treiben. ~ler n Propeller m. ~ling 'pencil n Drehbleistift m

propensity /prə'pensətɪ/ n Neigung f (**for** zu)

proper /'prɒpə(r)/ a, -ly adv richtig; (decent) anständig. ~ 'name, ~ 'noun n Eigenname m

property /'prɒpətɪ/ n Eigentum nt; (quality) Eigenschaft f; (Theat) Requisit nt; (land) [Grund]besitz m; (house) Haus nt. ~ **market** n Immobilienmarkt m

prophecy /'prɒfəsɪ/ n Prophezeiung f

prophesy /'prɒfɪsaɪ/ vt (pt/pp -ied) prophezeien

prophet /'prɒfɪt/ n Prophet m. ~ic /prə'fetɪk/ a prophetisch

proportion /prə'pɔːʃn/ n Verhältnis nt; (share) Teil m; ~s pl Proportionen; (dimensions) Maße. ~al a, -ly adv proportional

proposal /prə'pəʊzl/ n Vorschlag m; (of marriage) [Heirats]antrag m

propose /prə'pəʊz/ vt vorschlagen; (intend) vorhaben; einbringen (motion); ausbringen (toast) ● vi einen Heiratsantrag machen

proposition /prɒpə'zɪʃn/ n Vorschlag m

propound /prə'paʊnd/ vt darlegen

proprietor /prə'praɪətə(r)/ n Inhaber(in) m(f)

propriety /prə'praɪətɪ/ n Korrektheit f; (decorum) Anstand m

propulsion /prə'pʌlʃn/ n Antrieb m

prosaic /prə'zeɪɪk/ a prosaisch

prose /prəʊz/ n Prosa f

prosecut|e /'prɒsɪkjuːt/ vt strafrechtlich verfolgen. ~ion /-'kjuːʃn/ n strafrechtliche Verfolgung f; **the**

~**ion** die Anklage. ~**or** n **[Public] P~or** Staatsanwalt m

prospect[1] /'prɒspekt/ n Aussicht f

prospect[2] /prə'spekt/ vi suchen (**for** nach)

prospect|ive /prə'spektɪv/ a (future) zukünftig. ~**or** n Prospektor m

prospectus /prə'spektəs/ n Prospekt m

prosper /'prɒspə(r)/ vi gedeihen, florieren; ⟨person⟩ Erfolg haben. ~**ity** /-'sperətɪ/ n Wohlstand m

prosperous /'prɒspərəs/ a wohlhabend

prostitut|e /'prɒstɪtjuːt/ n Prostituierte f. ~**ion** /-'tjuːʃn/ n Prostitution f

prostrate /'prɒstreɪt/ a ausgestreckt; ~ **with grief** (fig) vor Kummer gebrochen

protagonist /prəʊ'tægənɪst/ n Kämpfer m; (fig) Protagonist m

protect /prə'tekt/ vt schützen (**from** vor + dat); beschützen ⟨person⟩. ~**ion** /-ekʃn/ n Schutz m. ~**ive** /-ɪv/ a Schutz-; (fig) beschützend. ~**or** n Beschützer m

protégé /'prɒtɪʒeɪ/ n Schützling m, Protegé m

protein /'prəʊtiːn/ n Eiweiß nt

protest[1] /'prəʊtest/ n Protest m

protest[2] /prə'test/ vi protestieren

Protestant /'prɒtɪstənt/ a protestantisch, evangelisch ● n Protestant(in) m(f), Evangelische(r) m/f

protester /prə'testə(r)/ n Protestierende(r) m/f

protocol /'prəʊtəkɒl/ n Protokoll nt

prototype /'prəʊtə-/ n Prototyp m

protract /prə'trækt/ vt verlängern. ~**or** n Winkelmesser m

protrude /prə'truːd/ vi [her]vorstehen

proud /praʊd/ a, -**ly** adv stolz (**of** auf + acc)

prove /pruːv/ vt beweisen ● vi ~ **to be** sich erweisen als

proverb /'prɒvɜːb/ n Sprichwort nt. ~**ial** /prə'vɜːbɪəl/ a sprichwörtlich

provide /prə'vaɪd/ vt zur Verfügung stellen; spenden ⟨shade⟩; ~ **s.o. with sth** jdn mit etw versorgen od versehen ● vi ~ **for** sorgen für

provided /prə'vaɪdɪd/ conj ~ **[that]** vorausgesetzt [daß]

providen|ce /'prɒvɪdəns/ n Vorsehung f. ~**tial** /-'denʃl/ a **be** ~**tial** ein Glück sein

providing /prə'vaɪdɪŋ/ conj = **provided**

provinc|e /'prɒvɪns/ n Provinz f; (fig) Bereich m. ~**ial** /prə'vɪnʃl/ a provinziell

provision /prə'vɪʒn/ n Versorgung f (**of** mit); ~**s** pl Lebensmittel pl. ~**al** a, -**ly** adv vorläufig

proviso /prə'vaɪzəʊ/ n Vorbehalt m

provocat|ion /prɒvə'keɪʃn/ n Provokation f. ~**ive** /prə'vɒkətɪv/ a, -**ly** adv provozierend; (sexually) aufreizend

provoke /prə'vəʊk/ vt provozieren; (cause) hervorrufen

prow /praʊ/ n Bug m

prowess /'praʊɪs/ n Kraft f

prowl /praʊl/ vi herumschleichen ● n **be on the** ~ herumschleichen

proximity /prɒk'sɪmətɪ/ n Nähe f

proxy /'prɒksɪ/ n Stellvertreter(in) m(f); (power) Vollmacht f

prude /pruːd/ n **be a** ~ prüde sein

pruden|ce /'pruːdns/ n Umsicht f. ~**t** a, -**ly** adv umsichtig; (wise) klug

prudish /'pruːdɪʃ/ a prüde

prune[1] /pruːn/ n Backpflaume f

prune[2] vt beschneiden

pry /praɪ/ vi (pt/pp **pried**) neugierig sein

psalm /sɑːm/ n Psalm m

pseudonym /'sjuːdənɪm/ n Pseudonym nt

psychiatric /saɪkɪ'ætrɪk/ a psychiatrisch

psychiatr|ist /saɪ'kaɪətrɪst/ n Psychiater(in) m(f). ~**y** n Psychiatrie f

psychic /'saɪkɪk/ a übersinnlich; **I'm not** ~ ich kann nicht hellsehen

psycho|'analyse /saɪkəʊ-/ vt psychoanalysieren. ~**a'nalysis** n Psychoanalyse f. ~**'analyst** Psychoanalytiker(in) m(f)

psychological /saɪkə'lɒdʒɪkl/ a, -**ly** adv psychologisch; ⟨illness⟩ psychisch

psycholog|ist /saɪ'kɒlədʒɪst/ n Psychologe m/-login f. ~**y** n Psychologie f

psychopath /'saɪkəpæθ/ n Psychopath(in) m(f)

PTO abbr (**please turn over**) b.w.

pub /pʌb/ n (fam) Kneipe f

puberty /'pjuːbətɪ/ n Pubertät f

public /'pʌblɪk/ a, -**ly** adv öffentlich; **make** ~ publik machen ● n **the** ~ die Öffentlichkeit; **in** ~ in aller Öffentlichkeit

publican /'pʌblɪkən/ n [Gast]wirt m

publication /pʌblɪ'keɪʃn/ n Veröffentlichung f
public: ~ con'venience n öffentliche Toilette f. ~ 'holiday n gesetzlicher Feiertag m. ~ 'house n [Gast]wirtschaft f
publicity /pʌb'lɪsətɪ/ n Publicity f; (advertising) Reklame f
publicize /'pʌblɪsaɪz/ vt Reklame machen für
public: ~ 'library n öffentliche Bücherei f. ~ 'school n Privatschule f; (Amer) staatliche Schule f. ~-'spirited a be ~-spirited Gemeinsinn haben. ~ 'transport n öffentliche Verkehrsmittel pl
publish /'pʌblɪʃ/ vt veröffentlichen. ~er n Verleger(in) m(f); (firm) Verlag m. ~ing n Verlagswesen nt
pucker /'pʌkə(r)/ vt kräuseln
pudding /'pʊdɪŋ/ n Pudding m; (course) Nachtisch m
puddle /'pʌdl/ n Pfütze f
puerile /'pjʊəraɪl/ a kindisch
puff /pʌf/ n (of wind) Hauch m; (of smoke) Wölkchen nt; (for powder) Quaste f ● vt blasen, pusten; ~ out ausstoßen. ● vi keuchen; ~ at paffen an (+ dat) 〈pipe〉. ~ed a (out of breath) aus der Puste. ~ pastry n Blätterteig m
puffy /'pʌfɪ/ a geschwollen
pugnacious /pʌg'neɪʃəs/ a, -ly adv aggressiv
pull /pʊl/ n Zug m; (jerk) Ruck m; (fam: influence) Einfluß m ● vt ziehen; ziehen an (+ dat) 〈rope〉; ~ a muscle sich (dat) einen Muskel zerren; ~ oneself together sich zusammennehmen; ~ one's weight tüchtig mitarbeiten; ~ s.o.'s leg (fam) jdn auf den Arm nehmen. ~ down vt herunterziehen; (demolish) abreißen. ~ in vt hereinziehen ● vi (Auto) einscheren. ~ off vt abziehen; (fam) schaffen. ~ out vt herausziehen ● vi (Auto) ausscheren. ~ through vt durchziehen ● vi (recover) durchkommen. ~ up vt herausziehen; ausziehen 〈plant〉; (reprimand) zurechtweisen ● vi (Auto) anhalten
pulley /'pʊlɪ/ n (Techn) Rolle f
pullover /'pʊləʊvə(r)/ n Pullover m
pulp /pʌlp/ n Brei m; (of fruit) [Frucht]fleisch nt
pulpit /'pʊlpɪt/ n Kanzel f
pulsate /pʌl'seɪt/ vi pulsieren

pulse /pʌls/ n Puls m
pulses /'pʌlsɪz/ npl Hülsenfrüchte pl
pulverize /'pʌlvəraɪz/ vt pulverisieren
pumice /'pʌmɪs/ n Bimsstein m
pummel /'pʌml/ vt (pt/pp pummelled) mit den Fäusten bearbeiten
pump /pʌmp/ n Pumpe f ● vt pumpen; (fam) aushorchen. ~ up vt hochpumpen; (inflate) aufpumpen
pumpkin /'pʌmpkɪn/ n Kürbis m
pun /pʌn/ n Wortspiel nt
punch[1] /pʌntʃ/ n Faustschlag m; (device) Locher m ● vt boxen; lochen 〈ticket〉; stanzen 〈hole〉
punch[2] n (drink) Bowle f
punch: ~ line n Pointe f. ~-up n Schlägerei f
punctual /'pʌŋktjʊəl/ a, -ly adv pünktlich. ~ity /-'ælətɪ/ n Pünktlichkeit f
punctuat|e /'pʌŋktjʊeɪt/ vt mit Satzzeichen versehen. ~ion /-'eɪʃn/ n Interpunktion f. ~ion mark n Satzzeichen nt
puncture /'pʌŋktʃə(r)/ n Loch nt; (tyre) Reifenpanne f ● vt durchstechen
pundit /'pʌndɪt/ n Experte m
pungent /'pʌndʒənt/ a scharf
punish /'pʌnɪʃ/ vt bestrafen. ~able /-əbl/ a strafbar. ~ment n Strafe f
punitive /'pju:nɪtɪv/ a Straf-
punnet /'pʌnɪt/ n Körbchen nt
punt /pʌnt/ n (boat) Stechkahn m
punter /'pʌntə(r)/ n (gambler) Wetter m; (client) Kunde m
puny /'pju:nɪ/ a (-ier, -iest) mickerig
pup /pʌp/ n = **puppy**
pupil /'pju:pl/ n Schüler(in) m(f); (of eye) Pupille f
puppet /'pʌpɪt/ n Puppe f; (fig) Marionette f
puppy /'pʌpɪ/ n junger Hund m
purchase /'pɜ:tʃəs/ n Kauf m; (leverage) Hebelkraft f ● vt kaufen. ~r n Käufer m
pure /pjʊə(r)/ a (-r, -st), -ly adv rein
purée /'pjʊəreɪ/ n Püree nt, Brei m
purgatory /'pɜ:gətrɪ/ n (Relig) Fegefeuer nt; (fig) Hölle f
purge /pɜ:dʒ/ n (Pol) Säuberungsaktion f ● vt reinigen; (Pol) säubern
puri|fication /pjʊərɪfɪ'keɪʃn/ n Reinigung f. ~fy /'pjʊərɪfaɪ/ vt (pt/pp -ied) reinigen

puritanical /pjʊərɪ'tænɪkl/ a puritanisch

purity /'pjʊərɪtɪ/ n Reinheit f

purl /pɜːl/ n (Knitting) linke Masche f ● vt/i links stricken

purple /'pɜːpl/ a [dunkel]lila

purport /pə'pɔːt/ vt vorgeben

purpose /'pɜːpəs/ n Zweck m; (intention) Absicht f; (determination) Entschlossenheit f; **on** ~ absichtlich; **to no** ~ unnützerweise. ~**ful** a, **-ly** adv entschlossen. ~**ly** adv absichtlich

purr /pɜː(r)/ vi schnurren

purse /pɜːs/ n Portemonnaie nt; (Amer: handbag) Handtasche f ● vt schürzen ⟨lips⟩

pursue /pə'sjuː/ vt verfolgen; (fig) nachgehen (+ dat). ~**r** /-ə(r)/ n Verfolger m

pursuit /pə'sjuːt/ n Verfolgung f; Jagd f; (pastime) Beschäftigung f; **in** ~ hinterher

pus /pʌs/ n Eiter m

push /pʊʃ/ n Stoß m, (fam) Schubs m; **get the** ~ (fam) hinausfliegen ● vt/i schieben; (press) drücken; (roughly) stoßen; **be** ~**ed for time** (fam) unter Zeitdruck stehen. ~ **off** vt hinunterstoßen ● vi (fam: leave) abhauen. ~ **on** vi (continue) weitergehen/-fahren; (with activity) weitermachen. ~ **up** vt hochschieben; hochtreiben ⟨price⟩

push: ~**-button** n Druckknopf m. ~**-chair** n [Kinder]sportwagen m. ~**-over** n (fam) Kinderspiel nt. ~**-up** n (Amer) Liegestütz m

pushy /'pʊʃɪ/ a (fam) aufdringlich

puss /pʊs/ n, **pussy** /'pʊsɪ/ n Miezef

put /pʊt/ vt (pt/pp **put**, pres p **putting**) tun; (place) setzen; (upright) stellen; (flat) legen; (express) ausdrücken; (say) sagen; (estimate) schätzen (**at** auf + acc); ~ **aside** or **by** beiseite legen; ~ **one's foot down** (fam) energisch werden; (Auto) Gas geben ● vi ~ **to sea** auslaufen ● a **stay** ~ dableiben. ~ **away** vt wegräumen. ~ **back** vt wieder hinsetzen/-stellen/-legen; zurückstellen ⟨clock⟩. ~ **down** vt hinsetzen/-stellen/-legen; (suppress) niederschlagen; (kill) töten; (write) niederschreiben; (attribute) zuschreiben (**to** dat). ~ **forward** vt vorbringen; vorstellen ⟨clock⟩. ~ **in** vt hineinsetzen/-stellen/-legen; (insert) einstecken; (submit) einreichen ● vi ~ **in for** beantragen. ~

off vt ausmachen ⟨light⟩; (postpone) verschieben; ~ **s.o. off** jdn abbestellen; (disconcert) jdn aus der Fassung bringen; ~ **s.o. off sth** jdm etw verleiden. ~ **on** vt anziehen ⟨clothes, brake⟩; sich (dat) aufsetzen ⟨hat⟩; (Culin) aufsetzen; anmachen ⟨light⟩; aufführen ⟨play⟩; annehmen ⟨accent⟩; ~ **on weight** zunehmen. ~ **out** vt hinaussetzen/-stellen/-legen; ausmachen ⟨fire, light⟩; ausstrecken ⟨hand⟩; (disconcert) aus der Fassung bringen; ~ **s.o./oneself out** jdm/sich Umstände machen. ~ **through** vt durchstecken; (Teleph) verbinden (**to** mit). ~ **up** vt errichten ⟨building⟩; aufschlagen ⟨tent⟩; aufspannen ⟨umbrella⟩; anschlagen ⟨notice⟩; erhöhen ⟨price⟩; unterbringen ⟨guest⟩; ~ **s.o. up to sth** jdn zu etw anstiften ● vi (at hotel) absteigen in (+ dat); ~ **up with sth** sich (dat) etw bieten lassen

putrefy /'pjuːtrɪfaɪ/ vi (pt/pp **-ied**) verwesen

putrid /'pjuːtrɪd/ faulig

putty /'pʌtɪ/ n Kitt m

put-up /'pʊtʌp/ a **a** ~ **job** ein abgekartetes Spiel nt

puzzl|e /'pʌzl/ n Rätsel nt; (jig-saw) Puzzlespiel nt ● vt **it** ~**es me** es ist mir rätselhaft ● vi ~**e over** sich (dat) den Kopf zerbrechen über (+ acc). ~**ing** a rätselhaft

pyjamas /pə'dʒɑːməz/ npl Schlafanzug m

pylon /'paɪlən/ n Mast m

pyramid /'pɪrəmɪd/ n Pyramide f

python /'paɪθn/ n Pythonschlange f

Q

quack[1] /kwæk/ n Quaken nt ● vi quaken

quack[2] n (doctor) Quacksalber m

quad /kwɒd/ n (fam: court) Hof m; ~**s** pl = **quadruplets**

quadrangle /'kwɒdræŋgl/ n Viereck nt; (court) Hof m

quadruped /'kwɒdrʊped/ n Vierfüßer m

quadruple /'kwɒdrʊpl/ a vierfach ● vt vervierfachen ● vi sich vervierfachen. ~**ts** /-plɪts/ npl Vierlinge pl

quagmire /'kwɒgmaɪə(r)/ n Sumpf m

quaint /kweɪnt/ a (**-er, -est**) malerisch; (*odd*) putzig

quake /kweɪk/ n (*fam*) Erdbeben nt ● vi beben; (*with fear*) zittern

Quaker /'kweɪkə(r)/ n Quäker(in) m(f)

qualif|ication /kwɒlɪfɪ'keɪʃn/ n Qualifikation f; (*reservation*) Einschränkung f. ~**ied** /-faɪd/ a qualifiziert; (*trained*) ausgebildet; (*limited*) bedingt

qualify /'kwɒlɪfaɪ/ v (*pt/pp* **-ied**) ● vt qualifizieren; (*entitle*) berechtigen; (*limit*) einschränken ● vi sich qualifizieren

quality /'kwɒlətɪ/ n Qualität f; (*characteristic*) Eigenschaft f

qualm /kwɑːm/ n Bedenken pl

quandary /'kwɒndərɪ/ n Dilemma nt

quantity /'kwɒntətɪ/ n Quantität f, Menge f; **in** ~ in großen Mengen

quarantine /'kwɒrəntiːn/ n Quarantäne f

quarrel /'kwɒrl/ n Streit m ● vi (*pt/pp* **quarrelled**) sich streiten. ~**some** a streitsüchtig

quarry[1] /'kwɒrɪ/ n (*prey*) Beute f

quarry[2] n Steinbruch m

quart /kwɔːt/ n Quart nt

quarter /'kwɔːtə(r)/ n Viertel nt; (*of year*) Vierteljahr nt; (*Amer*) 25-Cent-Stück nt; ~**s** pl Quartier nt; **at [a]** ~ **to six** um Viertel vor sechs; **from all** ~**s** aus allen Richtungen ● vt vierteln; (*Mil*) einquartieren (**on** bei). ~-'**final** n Viertelfinale nt

quarterly /'kwɔːtəlɪ/ a & adv vierteljährlich

quartet /kwɔː'tet/ n Quartett nt

quartz /kwɔːts/ n Quarz m. ~ **watch** n Quarzuhr f

quash /kwɒʃ/ vt aufheben; niederschlagen ⟨*rebellion*⟩

quaver /'kweɪvə(r)/ n (*Mus*) Achtelnote f ● vi zittern

quay /kiː/ n Kai m

queasy /'kwiːzɪ/ a **I feel** ~ mir ist übel

queen /kwiːn/ n Königin f; (*Cards, Chess*) Dame f

queer /kwɪə(r)/ a (**-er, -est**) eigenartig; (*dubious*) zweifelhaft; (*ill*) unwohl; (*fam: homosexual*) schwul ● n (*fam*) Schwule(r) m

quell /kwel/ vt unterdrücken

quench /kwentʃ/ vt löschen

query /'kwɪərɪ/ n Frage f; (*question mark*) Fragezeichen nt ● vt (*pt/pp* **-ied**) in Frage stellen; reklamieren ⟨*bill*⟩

quest /kwest/ n Suche f (**for** nach)

question /'kwestʃn/ n Frage f; (*for discussion*) Thema nt; **out of the** ~ ausgeschlossen; **without** ~ ohne Frage; **the person in** ~ die fragliche Person ● vt in Frage stellen; ~ **s.o.** jdn ausfragen; ⟨*police:*⟩ jdn verhören. ~**able** /-əbl/ a zweifelhaft. ~ **mark** n Fragezeichen nt

questionnaire /kwestʃə'neə(r)/ n Fragebogen m

queue /kjuː/ n Schlange f ● vi ~ [**up**] Schlange stehen, sich anstellen (**for** nach)

quibble /'kwɪbl/ vi Haarspalterei treiben

quick /kwɪk/ a (**-er, -est**), **-ly** adv schnell; **be** ~! mach schnell! **have a** ~ **meal** schnell etwas essen ● adv schnell ● n **cut to the** ~ (*fig*) bis ins Mark getroffen. ~**en** vt beschleunigen ● vi sich beschleunigen

quick: ~**sand** n Treibsand m. ~**-tempered** a aufbrausend

quid /kwɪd/ n inv (*fam*) Pfund nt

quiet /'kwaɪət/ a (**-er, -est**), **-ly** adv still; (*calm*) ruhig; ⟨*soft*⟩ leise; **keep** ~ **about** (*fam*) nichts sagen von ● n Stille f; Ruhe f; **on the** ~ heimlich

quiet|en /'kwaɪətn/ vt beruhigen ● vi ~**en down** ruhig werden. ~**ness** n (*see* **quiet**) Stille f; Ruhe f

quill /kwɪl/ n Feder f; (*spine*) Stachel m

quilt /kwɪlt/ n Steppdecke f. ~**ed** a Stepp-

quince /kwɪns/ n Quitte f

quins /kwɪnz/ npl (*fam*) = **quintuplets**

quintet /kwɪn'tet/ n Quintett nt

quintuplets /'kwɪntjʊplɪts/ npl Fünflinge pl

quip /kwɪp/ n Scherz m ● vi (*pt/pp* **quipped**) scherzen

quirk /kwɜːk/ n Eigenart f

quit /kwɪt/ v (*pt/pp* **quitted** or **quit**) ● vt verlassen; (*give up*) aufgeben; ~ **doing sth** aufhören, etw zu tun ● vi gehen; **give s.o. notice to** ~ jdm die Wohnung kündigen

quite /kwaɪt/ adv ganz; (*really*) wirklich; ~ [**so**]! genau! ~ **a few** ziemlich viele

quits /kwɪts/ a quitt

quiver /'kwɪvə(r)/ vi zittern

quiz /kwɪz/ n Quiz nt ● vt (*pt/pp* **quizzed**) ausfragen. ~**zical** a, **-ly** adv fragend

quorum /'kwɔːrəm/ n have a ~ beschlußfähig sein
quota /'kwəʊtə/ n Anteil m; (Comm) Kontingent nt
quotation /kwəʊ'teɪʃn/ n Zitat nt; (price) Kostenvoranschlag m; (of shares) Notierung f. ~ marks npl Anführungszeichen pl
quote /kwəʊt/ n (fam) = **quotation;** **in ~s** in Anführungszeichen ● vt/i zitieren

R

rabbi /'ræbaɪ/ n Rabbiner m; (title) Rabbi m
rabbit /'ræbɪt/ n Kaninchen nt
rabble /'ræbl/ n the ~ der Pöbel
rabid /'ræbɪd/ a fanatisch; (animal) tollwütig
rabies /'reɪbiːz/ n Tollwut f
race[1] /reɪs/ n Rasse f
race[2] n Rennen nt; (fig) Wettlauf m ● vi [am Rennen] teilnehmen; (athlete, horse:) laufen; (fam: rush) rasen ● vt um die Wette laufen mit; an einem Rennen teilnehmen lassen (horse)
race: ~**course** n Rennbahn f. ~**horse** n Rennpferd nt. ~-**track** n Rennbahn f
racial /'reɪʃl/ a, -**ly** adv rassisch; (discrimination, minority) Rassen-
racing /'reɪsɪŋ/ n Rennsport m; (horse-) Pferderennen nt. ~ **car** n Rennwagen m. ~ **driver** n Rennfahrer m
racis|m /'reɪsɪzm/ n Rassismus m. ~**t** /-ɪst/ a rassistisch ● n Rassist m
rack[1] /ræk/ n Ständer m; (for plates) Gestell nt ● vt ~ one's brains sich (dat) den Kopf zerbrechen
rack[2] n go to ~ and ruin verfallen; (fig) herunterkommen
racket[1] /'rækɪt/ n (Sport) Schläger m
racket[2] n (din) Krach m; (swindle) Schwindelgeschäft nt
racy /'reɪsɪ/ a (-ier, -iest) schwungvoll; (risqué) gewagt
radar /'reɪdɑː(r)/ n Radar m
radian|ce /'reɪdɪəns/ n Strahlen nt. ~**t** a, -**ly** adv strahlend
radiat|e /'reɪdɪeɪt/ vt ausstrahlen ● vi (heat:) ausgestrahlt werden; (roads:) strahlenförmig ausgehen. ~**ion** /-'eɪʃn/ n Strahlung f
radiator /'reɪdɪeɪtə(r)/ n Heizkörper m; (Auto) Kühler m

radical /'rædɪkl/ a, -**ly** adv radikal ● n Radikale(r) m/f
radio /'reɪdɪəʊ/ n Radio nt; **by** ~ über Funk ● vt funken (message)
radio|'active a radioaktiv. ~**ac'tivity** n Radioaktivität f
radiography /reɪdɪ'ɒgrəfɪ/ n Röntgenographie f
'radio ham n Hobbyfunker m
radio'therapy n Strahlenbehandlung f
radish /'rædɪʃ/ n Radieschen nt
radius /'reɪdɪəs/ n (pl -**dii** /-dɪaɪ/) Radius m, Halbmesser m
raffle /'ræfl/ n Tombola f ● vt verlosen
raft /rɑːft/ n Floß nt
rafter /'rɑːftə(r)/ n Dachsparren m
rag[1] /ræg/ n Lumpen m; (pej: newspaper) Käseblatt nt; **in ~s** in Lumpen
rag[2] vt (pt/pp ragged) (fam) aufziehen
rage /reɪdʒ/ n Wut f; **all the** ~ (fam) der letzte Schrei ● vi rasen; (storm:) toben
ragged /'rægɪd/ a zerlumpt; (edge) ausgefranst
raid /reɪd/ n Überfall m; (Mil) Angriff m; (police) Razzia f ● vt überfallen; (Mil) angreifen; (police:) eine Razzia durchführen in (+ dat); (break in) eindringen in (+ acc). ~**er** n Eindringling m; (of bank) Bankräuber m
rail /reɪl/ n Schiene f; (pole) Stange f; (hand~) Handlauf m; (Naut) Reling f; **by** ~ mit der Bahn
railings /'reɪlɪŋz/ npl Geländer nt
'railroad n (Amer) = **railway**
'railway n [Eisen]bahn f. ~**man** n Eisenbahner m. ~ **station** n Bahnhof m
rain /reɪn/ n Regen m ● vi regnen
rain: ~**bow** n Regenbogen m. ~**check** n (Amer) **take a ~check on** aufschieben. ~**coat** n Regenmantel m. ~**fall** n Niederschlag m
rainy /'reɪnɪ/ a (-ier, -iest) regnerisch
raise /reɪz/ n (Amer) Lohnerhöhung f ● vt erheben; (upright) aufrichten; (make higher) erhöhen; (lift) [hoch]heben; lüften (hat); [auf]ziehen (children, animals); aufwerfen (question); aufbringen (money)
raisin /'reɪzn/ n Rosine f
rake /reɪk/ n Harke f, Rechen m ● vt harken, rechen. ~ **up** vt zusammenharken; (fam) wieder aufrühren
'rake-off n (fam) Prozente pl

rally /'rælɪ/ n Versammlung f; (Auto) Rallye f; (Tennis) Ballwechsel m ● vt sammeln ● vi sich sammeln; (recover strength) sich erholen

ram /ræm/ n Schafbock m; (Astr) Widder m ● vt (pt/pp rammed) rammen

rambl|e /'ræmbl/ n Wanderung f ● vi wandern; (in speech) irrereden. **~er** n Wanderer m; (rose) Kletterrose f. **~ing** a weitschweifig; (club) Wander-

ramp /ræmp/ n Rampe f; (Aviat) Gangway f

rampage¹ /'ræmpeɪdʒ/ n **be/go on the ~** randalieren

rampage² /ræm'peɪdʒ/ vi randalieren

rampant /'ræmpənt/ a weit verbreitet; (in heraldry) aufgerichtet

rampart /'ræmpɑːt/ n Wall m

ramshackle /'ræmʃækl/ a baufällig

ran /ræn/ see **run**

ranch /rɑːntʃ/ n Ranch f

rancid /'rænsɪd/ a ranzig

rancour /'ræŋkə(r)/ n Groll m

random /'rændəm/ a willkürlich; **a ~ sample** eine Stichprobe ● n **at ~** aufs Geratewohl; (choose) willkürlich

randy /'rændɪ/ a (-ier, -iest) (fam) geil

rang /ræŋ/ see **ring²**

range /reɪndʒ/ n Serie f, Reihe f; (Comm) Auswahl f, Angebot nt (of an + dat); (of mountains) Kette f; (Mus) Umfang m; (distance) Reichweite f; (for shooting) Schießplatz m; (stove) Kohlenherd m; **at a ~ of** auf eine Entfernung von ● vi reichen; **~ from...to** gehen von...bis. **~r** n Aufseher m

rank¹ /ræŋk/ n (row) Reihe f; (Mil) Rang m; (social position) Stand m; **the ~ and file** die breite Masse; **the ~s** pl die gemeinen Soldaten ● vt/i einstufen; **~ among** zählen zu

rank² a (bad) übel; (plants) üppig; (fig) kraß

ransack /'rænsæk/ vt durchwühlen; (pillage) plündern

ransom /'rænsəm/ n Lösegeld nt; **hold s.o. to ~** Lösegeld für jdn fordern

rant /rænt/ vi rasen

rap /ræp/ n Klopfen nt; (blow) Schlag m ● v (pt/pp rapped) ● vt klopfen auf (+ acc) ● vi **~ at/on** klopfen an/auf (+ acc)

rape¹ /reɪp/ n (Bot) Raps m

rape² n Vergewaltigung f ● vt vergewaltigen

rapid /'ræpɪd/ a, **-ly** adv schnell. **~ity** /rə'pɪdətɪ/ n Schnelligkeit f

rapids /'ræpɪdz/ npl Stromschnellen pl

rapist /'reɪpɪst/ n Vergewaltiger m

rapport /ræ'pɔː(r)/ n [innerer] Kontakt m

rapt /ræpt/ a, **-ly** adv gespannt; (look) andächtig; **~ in** versunken in (+ acc)

raptur|e /'ræptʃə(r)/ n Entzücken nt. **~ous** /-rəs/ a, **-ly** adv begeistert

rare¹ /reə(r)/ a (-r, -st), **-ly** adv selten

rare² a (Culin) englisch gebraten

rarefied /'reərɪfaɪd/ a dünn

rarity /'reərətɪ/ n Seltenheit f

rascal /'rɑːskl/ n Schlingel m

rash¹ /ræʃ/ n (Med) Ausschlag m

rash² a (-er, -est), **-ly** adv voreilig

rasher /'ræʃə(r)/ n Speckscheibe f

rasp /rɑːsp/ n Raspel f

raspberry /'rɑːzbərɪ/ n Himbeere f

rat /ræt/ n Ratte f; (fam: person) Schuft m; **smell a ~** (fam) Lunte riechen

rate /reɪt/ n Rate f; (speed) Tempo nt; (of payment) Satz m; (of exchange) Kurs m; **~s** pl (taxes) ≈ Grundsteuer f; **at any ~** auf jeden Fall; **at this ~** auf diese Weise ● vt einschätzen; **~ among** zählen zu ● vi **~ as** gelten als

rather /'rɑːðə(r)/ adv lieber; (fairly) ziemlich; **~!** und ob!

rati|fication /rætɪfɪ'keɪʃn/ n Ratifizierung f. **~fy** /'rætɪfaɪ/ vt (pt/pp -ied) ratifizieren

rating /'reɪtɪŋ/ n Einschätzung f; (class) Klasse f; (sailor) [einfacher] Matrose m; **~s** pl (Radio, TV) ≈ Einschaltquote f

ratio /'reɪʃɪəʊ/ n Verhältnis nt

ration /'ræʃn/ n Ration f ● vt rationieren

rational /'ræʃənl/ a, **-ly** adv rational. **~ize** /-ɪ/ vt/i rationalisieren

rat race n (fam) Konkurrenzkampf m

rattle /'rætl/ n Rasseln nt; (of china, glass) Klirren nt; (of windows) Klappern nt; (toy) Klapper f ● vi rasseln; klirren; klappern ● vt rasseln mit; (shake) schütteln. **~ off** vt herunterrasseln

rattlesnake n Klapperschlange f

raucous /'rɔːkəs/ a rauh

ravage /'rævɪdʒ/ vt verwüsten, verheeren

rave /reɪv/ *vi* toben; ~ **about** schwärmen von

raven /'reɪvn/ *n* Rabe *m*

ravenous /'rævənəs/ *a* heißhungrig

ravine /rə'viːn/ *n* Schlucht *f*

raving /'reɪvɪŋ/ *a* ~ **mad** (*fam*) total verrückt

ravishing /'rævɪʃɪŋ/ *a* hinreißend

raw /rɔː/ *a* (**-er, -est**) roh; (*not processed*) Roh-; 〈*skin*〉 wund; 〈*weather*〉 naßkalt; (*inexperienced*) unerfahren; **get a** ~ **deal** (*fam*) schlecht wegkommen. ~ **ma·terials** *npl* Rohstoffe *pl*

ray /reɪ/ *n* Strahl *m*; ~ **of hope** Hoffnungsschimmer *m*

raze /reɪz/ *vt* ~ **to the ground** dem Erdboden gleichmachen

razor /'reɪzə(r)/ *n* Rasierapparat *m*. ~ **blade** *n* Rasierklinge *f*

re /riː/ *prep* betreffs (+ *gen*)

reach /riːtʃ/ *n* Reichweite *f*; (*of river*) Strecke *f*; **within/out of** ~ in/außer Reichweite; **within easy** ~ leicht erreichbar ● *vt* erreichen; (*arrive at*) ankommen in (+ *dat*); (~ *as far as*) reichen bis zu; kommen zu 〈*decision, conclusion*〉; (*pass*) reichen ● *vi* reichen (**to** bis zu); ~ **for** greifen nach; **I can't** ~ ich komme nicht daran

re'act /rɪ-/ *vi* reagieren (**to** auf + *acc*)

re'action /rɪ-/ *n* Reaktion *f*. ~**ary** *a* reaktionär

reactor /rɪ'æktə(r)/ *n* Reaktor *m*

read /riːd/ *vt/i* (*pt/pp* **read** /red/) lesen; (*aloud*) vorlesen (**to** dat); (*Univ*) studieren; ablesen 〈*meter*〉. ~ **out** *vt* vorlesen

readable /'riːdəbl/ *a* lesbar

reader /'riːdə(r)/ *n* Leser(in) *m(f)*; (*book*) Lesebuch *nt*

readi|ly /'redɪlɪ/ *adv* bereitwillig; (*easily*) leicht. ~**ness** *n* Bereitschaft *f*; **in** ~**ness** bereit

reading /'riːdɪŋ/ *n* Lesen *nt*; (*Pol, Relig*) Lesung *f*

rea'djust /riː-/ *vt* neu einstellen ● *vi* sich umstellen (**to** auf + *acc*)

ready /'redɪ/ *a* (**-ier, -iest**) fertig; (*willing*) bereit; (*quick*) schnell; **get** ~ sich fertigmachen; (*prepare to*) sich bereitmachen

ready: ~**-'made** *a* fertig. ~ **'money** *n* Bargeld *nt*. ~**-to-'wear** *a* Konfektions-

real /rɪəl/ *a* wirklich; (*genuine*) echt; (*actual*) eigentlich ● *adv* (*Amer, fam*) echt. ~ **estate** *n* Immobilien *pl*

realis|m /'rɪəlɪzm/ *n* Realismus *m*. ~**t** /-lɪst/ *n* Realist *m*. ~**tic** /-'lɪstɪk/ *a*, **-ally** *adv* realistisch

reality /rɪ'ælətɪ/ *n* Wirklichkeit *f*, Realität *f*

realization /rɪəlaɪ'zeɪʃn/ *n* Erkenntnis *f*

realize /'rɪəlaɪz/ *vt* einsehen; (*become aware*) gewahr werden; verwirklichen 〈*hopes, plans*〉; (*Comm*) realisieren; einbringen 〈*price*〉; **I didn't** ~ das wußte ich nicht

really /'rɪəlɪ/ *adv* wirklich; (*actually*) eigentlich

realm /relm/ *n* Reich *nt*

realtor /'riːəltə(r)/ *n* (*Amer*) Immobilienmakler *m*

reap /riːp/ *vt* ernten

reap'pear /riː-/ *vi* wiederkommen

rear¹ /rɪə(r)/ *a* Hinter-; (*Auto*) Heck- ● *n* **the** ~ der hintere Teil; **from the** ~ von hinten

rear² *vt* aufziehen ● *vi* ~ **[up]** 〈*horse:*〉 sich aufbäumen

'rear-light *n* Rücklicht *nt*

re'arm /riː-/ *vi* wieder aufrüsten

rear'range /riː-/ *vt* umstellen

rear-view 'mirror *n* (*Auto*) Rückspiegel *m*

reason /'riːzn/ *n* Grund *m*; (*good sense*) Vernunft *f*; (*ability to think*) Verstand *m*; **within** ~ in vernünftigen Grenzen ● *vi* argumentieren; ~ **with** vernünftig reden mit. ~**able** /-əbl/ *a* vernünftig; (*not expensive*) preiswert. ~**ably** /-əblɪ/ *adv* (*fairly*) ziemlich

reas'sur|ance /riː-/ *n* Beruhigung *f*; Versicherung *f*. ~**e** *vt* beruhigen; ~**e s.o. of sth** jdm etw (*gen*) versichern

rebate /'riːbeɪt/ *n* Rückzahlung *f*; (*discount*) Nachlaß *m*

rebel¹ /'rebl/ *n* Rebell *m*

rebel² /rɪ'bel/ *vi* (*pt/pp* **rebelled**) rebellieren. ~**lion** /-ɪən/ *n* Rebellion *f*. ~**lious** /-ɪəs/ *a* rebellisch

re'bound¹ /rɪ-/ *vi* abprallen

'rebound² /riː-/ *n* Rückprall *m*

rebuff /rɪ'bʌf/ *n* Abweisung *f* ● *vt* abweisen; eine Abfuhr erteilen (**s.o.** jdm)

re'build /riː-/ *vt* (*pt/pp* **-built**) wieder aufbauen; (*fig*) wiederaufbauen

rebuke /rɪ'bjuːk/ *n* Tadel *m* ● *vt* tadeln

rebuttal /rɪ'bʌtl/ *n* Widerlegung *f*

recall 467 **recover**

re'call /rɪ-/ n Erinnerung f; **beyond** ∼ unwiderruflich ● vt zurückrufen; abberufen ⟨diplomat⟩; vorzeitig einberufen ⟨parliament⟩; (remember) sich erinnern an (+ acc)

recant /rɪ'kænt/ vt widerrufen

recap /'riː.kæp/ vt/i (fam) = **recapitulate**

recapitulate /riː.kə'pɪtjʊleɪt/ vt/i zusammenfassen; rekapitulieren

re'capture /riː-/ vt wieder gefangennehmen ⟨person⟩; wieder einfangen ⟨animal⟩

reced|e /rɪ'siːd/ vi zurückgehen. ∼ing a ⟨forehead, chin⟩ fliehend; ∼ing hair Stirnglatze f

receipt /rɪ'siːt/ n Quittung f; (receiving) Empfang m; ∼s pl (Comm) Einnahmen pl

receive /rɪ'siːv/ vt erhalten, bekommen; empfangen ⟨guests⟩. ∼r n (Teleph) Hörer m; (Radio, TV) Empfänger m; (of stolen goods) Hehler m

recent /'riːsənt/ a kürzlich erfolgte(r,s). ∼ly adv in letzter Zeit; (the other day) kürzlich, vor kurzem

receptacle /rɪ'septəkl/ n Behälter m

reception /rɪ'sepʃn/ n Empfang m; ∼ [desk] (in hotel) Rezeption f. ∼ist n Empfangsdame f

receptive /rɪ'septɪv/ a aufnahmefähig; ∼ to empfänglich für

recess /rɪ'ses/ n Nische f; (holiday) Ferien pl; (Amer, Sch) Pause f

recession /rɪ'seʃn/ n Rezession f

re'charge /riː-/ vt [wieder] aufladen

recipe /'resəpɪ/ n Rezept nt

recipient /rɪ'sɪpɪənt/ n Empfänger m

reciprocal /rɪ'sɪprəkl/ a gegenseitig. ∼cate /-keɪt/ vt erwidern

recital /rɪ'saɪtl/ n (of poetry, songs) Vortrag m; (on piano) Konzert nt

recite /rɪ'saɪt/ vt aufsagen; (before audience) vortragen; (list) aufzählen

reckless /'reklɪs/ a, -ly adv leichtsinnig; (careless) rücksichtslos. ∼ness n Leichtsinn m; Rücksichtslosigkeit f

reckon /'rekən/ vt rechnen; (consider) glauben ● vi ∼ on/with rechnen mit

re'claim /rɪ-/ vt zurückfordern; zurückgewinnen ⟨land⟩

reclin|e /rɪ'klaɪn/ vi liegen. ∼ing seat n Liegesitz m

recluse /rɪ'kluːs/ n Einsiedler(in) m(f)

recognition /rekəg'nɪʃn/ n Erkennen nt; (acknowledgement) Anerkennung f; in ∼ als Anerkennung (of gen); be beyond ∼ nicht wiederzuerkennen sein

recognize /'rekəgnaɪz/ vt erkennen; (know again) wiedererkennen; (acknowledge) anerkennen

re'coil /rɪ-/ vi zurückschnellen; (in fear) zurückschrecken

recollect /rekə'lekt/ vt sich erinnern an (+ acc). ∼ion /-ekʃn/ n Erinnerung f

recommend /rekə'mend/ vt empfehlen. ∼ation /-'deɪʃn/ n Empfehlung f

recompense /'rekəmpens/ n Entschädigung f ● vt entschädigen

recon|cile /'rekənsaɪl/ vt versöhnen; ∼cile oneself to sich abfinden mit. ∼ciliation /-sɪlɪ'eɪʃn/ n Versöhnung f

recon'dition /riː-/ vt generalüberholen. ∼ed engine n Austauschmotor m

reconnaissance /rɪ'kɒnɪsns/ n (Mil) Aufklärung f

reconnoitre /rekə'nɔɪtə(r)/ vi (pres p -tring) auf Erkundung ausgehen

recon'sider /riː-/ vt sich (dat) noch einmal überlegen

recon'struct /riː-/ vt wieder aufbauen; rekonstruieren ⟨crime⟩. ∼ion n Wiederaufbau m; Rekonstruktion f

record¹ /rɪ'kɔːd/ vt aufzeichnen; (register) registrieren; (on tape) aufnehmen

record² /'rekɔːd/ n Aufzeichnung f; (Jur) Protokoll nt; (Mus) [Schall]platte f; (Sport) Rekord m; ∼s pl Unterlagen pl; keep a ∼ of sich (dat) notieren; off the ∼ inoffiziell; have a [criminal] ∼ vorbestraft sein

recorder /rɪ'kɔːdə(r)/ n (Mus) Blockflöte f

recording /rɪ'kɔːdɪŋ/ n Aufzeichnung f, Aufnahme f

'record-player n Plattenspieler m

recount /rɪ'kaʊnt/ vt erzählen

re-'count¹ /riː-/ vt nachzählen

're-count² /riː-/ n (Pol) Nachzählung f

recoup /rɪ'kuːp/ vt wiedereinbringen; ausgleichen ⟨losses⟩

recourse /rɪ'kɔːs/ n have ∼ to Zuflucht nehmen zu

re-'cover /riː-/ vt neu beziehen

recover /rɪ'kʌvə(r)/ vt zurückbekommen; bergen ⟨wreck⟩ ● vi sich

erholen. ~**y** n Wiedererlangung f;
Bergung f; (of health) Erholung f

recreation /rekrɪ'eɪʃn/ n Erholung
f; (hobby) Hobby nt. ~**al** a Freizeit-;
be ~**al** erholsam sein

recrimination /rɪkrɪmɪ'neɪʃn/ n Ge-
genbeschuldigung f

recruit /rɪ'kru:t/ n (Mil) Rekrut m;
new ~ (member) neues Mitglied nt;
(worker) neuer Mitarbeiter m ● vt re-
krutieren; anwerben (staff). ~**ment** n
Rekrutierung f; Anwerbung f

rectang|le /'rektæŋgl/ n Rechteck
nt. ~**ular** /-'tæŋgjʊlə(r)/ a rechteckig

rectify /'rektɪfaɪ/ vt (pt/pp -**ied**) be-
richtigen

rector /'rektə(r)/ n Pfarrer m; (Univ)
Rektor m. ~**y** n Pfarrhaus nt

recuperat|e /rɪ'kju:pəreɪt/ vi sich
erholen. ~**ion** /-'reɪʃn/ n Erholung f

recur /rɪ'kɜ:(r)/ vi (pt/pp **recurred**)
sich wiederholen; (illness:) wieder-
kehren

recurren|ce /rɪ'kʌrəns/ n Wieder-
kehr f. ~**t** a wiederkehrend

recycle /ri:'saɪkl/ vt wieder-
verwerten. ~**d paper** n
Umweltschutzpapier nt

red /red/ a (**redder, reddest**) rot ● n
Rot nt. ~'**currant** n rote Johannisbeere f

redd|en /'redn/ vt röten ● vi rot
werden. ~**ish** a rötlich

re'decorate /ri:-/ vt renovieren;
(paint) neu streichen; (wallpaper)
neu tapezieren

redeem /rɪ'di:m/ vt einlösen; (Relig)
erlösen

redemption /rɪ'dempʃn/ n Erlösung f

rede'ploy /ri:-/ vt an anderer Stelle
einsetzen

red: ~**-haired** a rothaarig. ~-
'**handed** a **catch s.o.** ~**-handed** jdn
auf frischer Tat ertappen. ~ '**herring**
n falsche Spur f. ~**-hot** a glühend
heiß. R~ '**Indian** n Indianer(in
m(f)

redi'rect /ri:-/ vt nachsenden (letter); umleiten (traffic)

red: ~ '**light** n (Auto) rote Ampel f.
~**ness** n Röte f

re'do /ri:-/ vt (pt -**did**, pp -**done**) noch
einmal machen

re'double /ri:-/ vt verdoppeln

redress /rɪ'dres/ n Entschädigung f
● vt wiedergutmachen; wiederherstellen (balance)

red 'tape n (fam) Bürokratie f

reduc|e /rɪ'dju:s/ vt verringern, ver-
mindern; (in size) verkleinern; er-
mäßigen (costs); herabsetzen (price,
goods); (Culin) einkochen lassen.
~**tion** /-'dʌkʃn/ n Verringerung f;
(in price) Ermäßigung f; (in size) Ver-
kleinerung f

redundan|cy /rɪ'dʌndənsɪ/ n Be-
schäftigungslosigkeit f; (payment)
Abfindung f. ~**t** a überflüssig; **make**
~**t** entlassen; **be made** ~**t** be-
schäftigungslos werden

reed /ri:d/ n [Schilf]rohr nt; ~**s** pl
Schilf nt

reef /ri:f/ n Riff nt

reek /ri:k/ vi riechen (**of** nach)

reel /ri:l/ n Rolle f, Spule f ● vi (stagger) taumeln ● vt ~ **off** (fig) herunterrasseln

refectory /rɪ'fektərɪ/ n Refektorium
nt; (Univ) Mensa f

refer /rɪ'fɜ:(r)/ v (pt/pp **referred**) ● vt
verweisen (**to** an + acc); übergeben,
weiterleiten (matter) (**to** an + acc) ● vi
~ **to** sich beziehen auf (+ acc); (mention) erwähnen; (concern) betreffen;
(consult) sich wenden an (+ acc);
nachschlagen in (+ dat) (book); **are
you** ~**ring to me?** meinen Sie mich?

referee /refə'ri:/ n Schiedsrichter
m; (Boxing) Ringrichter m; (for job)
Referenz f ● vt/i (pt/pp **refereed**)
Schiedsrichter/Ringrichter sein (bei)

reference /'refərəns/ n Erwähnung
f; (in book) Verweis m; (for job) Referenz f; (Comm) '**your** ~' 'Ihr Zeichen';
with ~ **to** in bezug auf (+ acc); (in letter) unter Bezugnahme auf (+ acc);
make [a] ~ **to** erwähnen. ~ **book** n
Nachschlagewerk nt. ~ **number** n
Aktenzeichen nt

referendum /refə'rendəm/ n Volks-
abstimmung f

re'fill[1] /ri:-/ vt nachfüllen

'**refill**[2] /ri:-/ n (for pen) Ersatzmine f

refine /rɪ'faɪn/ vt raffinieren. ~**d** a
fein, vornehm. ~**ment** n Vor-
nehmheit f; (Techn) Verfeinerung f.
~**ry** /-ərɪ/ n Raffinerie f

reflect /rɪ'flekt/ vt reflektieren;
(mirror:) [wider]spiegeln; **be** ~**ed in**
sich spiegeln in (+ dat) ● vi nachdenken (**on** über + acc); ~ **badly upon
s.o.** (fig) jdn in ein schlechtes
Licht stellen. ~**ion** /-ekʃn/ n Refle-
xion f; (image) Spiegelbild nt; **on**
~**ion** nach nochmaliger Überlegung.

reflective

rejoin

∼ive /-ɪv/ a, -ly adv nachdenklich.
∼or n Rückstrahler m

reflex /'riːfleks/ n Reflex m ● attrib
Reflex-

reflexive /rɪ'fleksɪv/ a reflexiv

reform /rɪ'fɔːm/ n Reform f ● vt re-
formieren ● vi sich bessern. R∼
ation /refə'meɪʃn/ n (Relig)
Reformation f. ∼er n Reformer m;
(Relig) Reformator m

refract /rɪ'frækt/ vt (Phys) brechen

refrain¹ /rɪ'freɪn/ n Refrain m

refrain² vi ∼ from doing sth etw nicht
tun

refresh /rɪ'freʃ/ vt erfrischen. ∼ing
a erfrischend. ∼ments npl Erfri-
schungen pl

refrigerat|e /rɪ'frɪdʒəreɪt/ vt küh-
len. ∼or n Kühlschrank m

re'fuel /riː-/ v (pt/pp -fuelled) vt/i
auftanken

refuge /'refjuːdʒ/ n Zuflucht f; take
∼ in Zuflucht nehmen in (+ dat)

refugee /refjʊ'dʒiː/ n Flüchtling m

'refund¹ /riː-/ get a ∼ sein Geld
zurückbekommen

re'fund² /rɪ-/ vt zurückerstatten

refurbish /riː'fɜːbɪʃ/ vt renovieren

refusal /rɪ'fjuːzl/ n (see refuse¹) Ablehnung f; Weigerung f

refuse¹ /rɪ'fjuːz/ vt ablehnen; (not
grant) verweigern; ∼ to do sth sich
weigern, etw zu tun ● vi ablehnen; sich
weigern

refuse² /'refjuːs/ n Müll m, Abfall m.
∼ collection n Müllabfuhr f

refute /rɪ'fjuːt/ vt widerlegen

re'gain /rɪ-/ vt wiedergewinnen

regal /'riːgl/ a, -ly adv königlich

regalia /rɪ'geɪlɪə/ npl Insignien pl

regard /rɪ'gɑːd/ n (heed) Rücksicht f;
(respect) Achtung f; ∼s pl Grüße pl;
with ∼ to in bezug auf (+ acc) ● vt ansehen, betrachten (as als); as ∼s in bezug auf (+ acc). ∼ing prep bezüglich
(+ gen). ∼less adv ohne Rücksicht
(of auf + acc)

regatta /rɪ'gætə/ n Regatta f

regenerate /rɪ'dʒenəreɪt/ vt regenerieren ● vi sich regenerieren

regime /reɪ'ʒiːm/ n Regime nt

regiment /'redʒɪmənt/ n Regiment
nt. ∼al /-'mentl/ a Regiments-.
∼ation /-'teɪʃn/ n Reglementierung
f

region /'riːdʒən/ n Region f; in the ∼
of (fig) ungefähr. ∼al a, -ly adv
regional

register /'redʒɪstə(r)/ n Register
nt; (Sch) Anwesenheitsliste f ● vt
registrieren; (report) anmelden;
einschreiben ⟨letter⟩; aufgeben ⟨lug-
gage⟩ ● vi (report) sich anmelden; it
didn't ∼ (fig) ich habe es nicht re-
gistriert

registrar /redʒɪ'strɑː(r)/ n Stan-
desbeamte(r) m

registration /redʒɪ'streɪʃn/ n Regi-
strierung f; Anmeldung f. ∼ number n Autonummer f

registry office /'redʒɪstrɪ-/ n
Standesamt nt

regret /rɪ'gret/ n Bedauern nt ● vt
(pt/pp regretted) bedauern. ∼fully
adv mit Bedauern

regrettab|le /rɪ'gretəbl/ a be-
dauerlich. ∼ly adv bedauer-
licherweise

regular /'regjʊlə(r)/ a, -ly adv regelmäßig; (usual) üblich; (Mil) Berufs-
● n Berufssoldat m; (in pub) Stammgast
m; (in shop) Stammkunde m. ∼ity
/-'lærətɪ/ n Regelmäßigkeit f

regulat|e /'regjʊleɪt/ vt regulieren.
∼ion /-'leɪʃn/ n (rule) Vorschrift f

rehabilitat|e /riːhə'bɪlɪteɪt/ vt
rehabilitieren. ∼ion /-'teɪʃn/ n
Rehabilitation f

rehears|al /rɪ'hɜːsl/ n (Theat) Probe
f. ∼e vt proben

reign /reɪn/ n Herrschaft f ● vi herrschen, regieren

reimburse /riːɪm'bɜːs/ vt ∼ s.o. for
sth jdm etw zurückerstatten

rein /reɪn/ n Zügel m

reincarnation /riːɪnkɑː'neɪʃn/ n
Reinkarnation f, Wiedergeburt f

reindeer /'reɪndɪə(r)/ n inv Rentier
nt

reinforce /riːɪn'fɔːs/ vt verstärken.
∼d 'concrete n Stahlbeton m.
∼ment n Verstärkung f; send ∼-
ments Verstärkung schicken

reinstate /riːɪn'steɪt/ vt wieder-
einstellen; (to office) wiedereinsetzen

reiterate /riː'ɪtəreɪt/ vt wiederholen

reject /rɪ'dʒekt/ vt ablehnen. ∼ion
/-'ekʃn/ n Ablehnung f

rejects /'riːdʒekts/ npl (Comm) Aus-
schußware f

rejoic|e /rɪ'dʒɔɪs/ vi (liter) sich
freuen. ∼ing n Freude f

re'join /rɪ-/ vt sich wieder anschließen (+ dat); wieder beitreten
(+ dat) ⟨club, party⟩; (answer) erwidern

rejuvenate /rɪ'dʒu:vəneɪt/ vt verjüngen

relapse /rɪ'læps/ n Rückfall m ● vi einen Rückfall erleiden

relate /rɪ'leɪt/ vt (tell) erzählen; (connect) verbinden ● vi zusammenhängen (**to** mit). ~**d** a verwandt (**to** mit)

relation /rɪ'leɪʃn/ n Beziehung f; (person) Verwandte(r) m/f. ~**ship** n Beziehung f; (link) Verbindung f; (blood tie) Verwandtschaft f; (affair) Verhältnis nt

relative /'relətɪv/ n Verwandte(r) m/ f ● a relativ; (Gram) Relativ-. ~**ly** adv relativ, verhältnismäßig

relax /rɪ'læks/ vt lockern, entspannen ● vi sich lockern, sich entspannen. ~**ation** /-'seɪʃn/ n Entspannung f. ~**ing** a entspannend

relay[1] /ri:'leɪ/ vt (pt/pp -**layed**) weitergeben; (Radio, TV) übertragen

relay[2] /'ri:leɪ/ n (Electr) Relais nt; **work in** ~**s** sich bei der Arbeit ablösen. ~ [**race**] n Staffel f

release /rɪ'li:s/ n Freilassung f, Entlassung f; (Techn) Auslöser m ● vt freilassen; (let go of) loslassen; (Techn) auslösen; veröffentlichen ⟨information⟩

relegate /'relɪgeɪt/ vt verbannen; **be** ~**d** (Sport) absteigen

relent /rɪ'lent/ vi nachgeben. ~**less** a, -**ly** adv erbarmungslos; (unceasing) unaufhörlich

relevan|ce /'reləvəns/ n Relevanz f. ~**t** a relevant (**to** für)

reliab|ility /rɪlaɪə'bɪlətɪ/ n Zuverlässigkeit f. ~**le** /-'laɪəbl/ a, -**ly** adv zuverlässig

relian|ce /rɪ'laɪəns/ n Abhängigkeit f (**on** von). ~**t** a angewiesen (**on** auf + acc)

relic /'relɪk/ n Überbleibsel nt; (Relig) Reliquie f

relief /rɪ'li:f/ n Erleichterung f; (assistance) Hilfe f; (distraction) Abwechslung f; (replacement) Ablösung f; (Art) Relief nt; **in** ~ im Relief. ~ **map** n Reliefkarte f. ~ **train** n Entlastungszug m

relieve /rɪ'li:v/ vt erleichtern; (take over from) ablösen; ~ **of** entlasten von

religion /rɪ'lɪdʒən/ n Religion f

religious /rɪ'lɪdʒəs/ a religiös. ~**ly** adv (conscientiously) gewissenhaft

relinquish /rɪ'lɪŋkwɪʃ/ vt loslassen; (give up) aufgeben

relish /'relɪʃ/ n Genuß m; (Culin) Würze f ● vt genießen

relo'**cate** /ri:-/ vt verlegen

reluctan|ce /rɪ'lʌktəns/ n Widerstreben nt. ~**t** a widerstrebend; **be** ~**t** zögern (**to** zu). ~**tly** adv ungern, widerstrebend

rely /rɪ'laɪ/ vi (pt/pp -**ied**) ~ **on** sich verlassen auf (+ acc); (be dependent on) angewiesen sein auf (+ acc)

remain /rɪ'meɪn/ vi bleiben; (be left) übrigbleiben. ~**der** n Rest m. ~**ing** a restlich. ~**s** npl Reste pl; [**mortal**] ~**s** [sterbliche] Überreste pl

remand /rɪ'mɑ:nd/ n **on** ~ in Untersuchungshaft ● vt ~ **in custody** in Untersuchungshaft schicken

remark /rɪ'mɑ:k/ n Bemerkung f ● vt bemerken. ~**able** /-əbl/ a, -**bly** adv bemerkenswert

re'**marry** /ri:-/ vi wieder heiraten

remedial /rɪ'mi:dɪəl/ a Hilfs-; (Med) Heil-

remedy /'remədɪ/ n [Heil]mittel nt (**for** gegen); (fig) Abhilfe f ● vt (pt/pp -**ied**) abhelfen (+ dat); beheben ⟨fault⟩

rememb|er /rɪ'membə(r)/ vt sich erinnern an (+ acc); ~**er to do sth** daran denken, etw zu tun; ~**er me to him** grüßen Sie ihn von mir ● vi sich erinnern. ~**rance** n Erinnerung f

remind /rɪ'maɪnd/ vt erinnern (**of** an + acc). ~**er** n Andenken nt; (letter, warning) Mahnung f

reminisce /remɪ'nɪs/ vi sich seinen Erinnerungen hingeben. ~**nces** /-ənsɪs/ npl Erinnerungen pl. ~**nt** a **be** ~**nt of** erinnern an (+ acc)

remiss /rɪ'mɪs/ a nachlässig

remission /rɪ'mɪʃn/ n Nachlaß m; (of sentence) [Straf]erlaß m; (Med) Remission f

remit /rɪ'mɪt/ vt (pt/pp **remitted**) überweisen ⟨money⟩. ~**tance** n Überweisung f

remnant /'remnənt/ n Rest m

remonstrate /'remənstreɪt/ vi protestieren; ~ **with s.o.** jdm Vorhaltungen machen

remorse /rɪ'mɔ:s/ n Reue f. ~**ful** a, -**ly** adv reumütig. ~**less** a, -**ly** adv unerbittlich

remote /rɪ'məʊt/ a fern; (isolated) abgelegen; (slight) gering. ~ **con**-'**trol** n Fernsteuerung f; (for TV) Fernbedienung f. ~-**con**'**trolled** a ferngesteuert; fernbedient

remotely /rɪ'məʊtlɪ/ *adv* entfernt; **not** ~ nicht im entferntesten

re'movable /rɪ-/ *a* abnehmbar

removal /rɪ'muːvl/ *n* Entfernung *f*; (*from house*) Umzug *m*. ~ **van** *n* Möbelwagen *m*

remove /rɪ'muːv/ *vt* entfernen; (*take off*) abnehmen; (*take out*) herausnehmen

remunerat|e /rɪ'mjuːnəreɪt/ *vt* bezahlen. ~**ion** /-'reɪʃn/ *n* Bezahlung *f*. ~**ive** /-ətɪv/ *a* einträglich

render /'rendə(r)/ *vt* machen; erweisen ⟨*service*⟩; (*translate*) wiedergeben; (*Mus*) vortragen

renegade /'renɪgeɪd/ *n* Abtrünnige(r) *m/f*

renew /rɪ'njuː/ *vt* erneuern; verlängern ⟨*contract*⟩. ~**al** *n* Erneuerung *f*; Verlängerung *f*

renounce /rɪ'naʊns/ *vt* verzichten auf (+ *acc*); (*Relig*) abschwören (+ *dat*)

renovat|e /'renəveɪt/ *vt* renovieren. ~**ion** /-'veɪʃn/ *n* Renovierung *f*

renown /rɪ'naʊn/ *n* Ruf *m*. ~**ed** *a* berühmt

rent /rent/ *n* Miete *f* ●*vt* mieten; (*hire*) leihen; ~ **[out]** vermieten; verleihen. ~**al** *n* Mietgebühr *f*; Leihgebühr *f*

renunciation /rɪnʌnsɪ'eɪʃn/ *n* Verzicht *m*

re'open /riː-/ *vt/i* wieder aufmachen

re'organize /riː-/ *vt* reorganisieren

rep /rep/ *n* (*fam*) Vertreter *m*

repair /rɪ'peə(r)/ *n* Reparatur *f*; **in good/bad** ~ in gutem/schlechtem Zustand ●*vt* reparieren

repartee /repɑː'tiː/ *n* **piece of** ~ schlagfertige Antwort *f*

repatriat|e /riː'pætrɪeɪt/ *vt* repatriieren. ~**ion** /-'eɪʃn/ *n* Repatriierung *f*

re'pay /riː-/ *vt* (*pt/pp* **-paid**) zurückzahlen; ~ **s.o. for sth** jdm etw zurückzahlen. ~**ment** *n* Rückzahlung *f*

repeal /rɪ'piːl/ *n* Aufhebung *f* ●*vt* aufheben

repeat /rɪ'piːt/ *n* Wiederholung *f* ●*vt/i* wiederholen; ~ **after me** sprechen Sie mir nach. ~**ed** *a*, **-ly** *adv* wiederholt

repel /rɪ'pel/ *vt* (*pt/pp* **repelled**) abwehren; (*fig*) abstoßen. ~**lent** *a* abstoßend

repent /rɪ'pent/ *vi* Reue zeigen. ~**ance** *n* Reue *f*. ~**ant** *a* reuig

repercussions /riːpə'kʌʃnz/ *npl* Auswirkungen *pl*

repertoire /'repətwɑː(r)/ *n* Repertoire *nt*

repertory /'repətrɪ/ *n* Repertoire *nt*

repetit|ion /repɪ'tɪʃn/ *n* Wiederholung *f*. ~**ive** /rɪ'petɪtɪv/ *a* eintönig

re'place /rɪ-/ *vt* zurücktun; (*take the place of*) ersetzen; (*exchange*) austauschen, auswechseln. ~**ment** *n* Ersatz *m*. ~**ment part** *n* Ersatzteil *nt*

'**replay** /riː-/ *n* (*Sport*) Wiederholungsspiel *nt*; **[action]** ~ Wiederholung *f*

replenish /rɪ'plenɪʃ/ *vt* auffüllen ⟨*stocks*⟩; (*refill*) nachfüllen

replete /rɪ'pliːt/ *a* gesättigt

replica /'replɪkə/ *n* Nachbildung *f*

reply /rɪ'plaɪ/ *n* Antwort *f* (**to** auf + *acc*) ●*vt/i* (*pt/pp* **replied**) antworten

report /rɪ'pɔːt/ *n* Bericht *m*; (*Sch*) Zeugnis *nt*; (*rumour*) Gerücht *nt*; (*of gun*) Knall *m* ●*vt* berichten; (*notify*) melden; ~ **s.o. to the police** jdn anzeigen ●*vi* berichten (**on** über + *acc*); (*present oneself*) sich melden (**to** bei). ~**er** *n* Reporter(in) *m(f)*

repose /rɪ'pəʊz/ *n* Ruhe *f*

repos'sess /riː-/ *vt* wieder in Besitz nehmen

reprehensible /reprɪ'hensəbl/ *a* tadelnswert

represent /reprɪ'zent/ *vt* darstellen; (*act for*) vertreten, repräsentieren. ~**ation** /-'teɪʃn/ *n* Darstellung *f*; **make** ~**ations to** vorstellig werden bei

representative /reprɪ'zentətɪv/ *a* repräsentativ (**of** für) ●*n* Bevollmächtigte(r) *m/f*; (*Comm*) Vertreter(in) *m(f)*; (*Amer, Pol*) Abgeordnete(r) *m/f*

repress /rɪ'pres/ *vt* unterdrücken. ~**ion** /-eʃn/ *n* Unterdrückung *f*. ~**ive** /-ɪv/ *a* repressiv

reprieve /rɪ'priːv/ *n* Begnadigung *f*; (*postponement*) Strafaufschub *m*; (*fig*) Gnadenfrist *f* ●*vt* begnadigen

reprimand /'reprɪmɑːnd/ *n* Tadel *m* ●*vt* tadeln

'**reprint**[1] /riː-/ *n* Nachdruck *m*

re'print[2] /riː-/ *vt* neu auflegen

reprisal /rɪ'praɪzl/ *n* Vergeltungsmaßnahme *f*

reproach /rɪ'prəʊtʃ/ n Vorwurf m
● vt Vorwürfe pl machen (+ dat).
~ful a, -ly adv vorwurfsvoll
repro'duc|e /riː-/ vt wiedergeben,
reproduzieren ● vi sich fortpflanzen.
~tion /-'dʌkʃn/ n Reproduktion f;
(Biol) Fortpflanzung f. ~tion furniture n Stilmöbel pl. ~tive
/-'dʌktɪv/ a Fortpflanzungs-
reprove /rɪ'pruːv/ vt tadeln
reptile /'reptaɪl/ n Reptil nt
republic /rɪ'pʌblɪk/ n Republik f.
~an a republikanisch ● n Re-
publikaner(in) m(f)
repudiate /rɪ'pjuːdɪeɪt/ vt zurückweisen
repugnan|ce /rɪ'pʌɡnəns/ n Wider-
wille m. ~t a widerlich
repuls|e /rɪ'pʌls/ vt abwehren; (fig)
abweisen. ~ion /-ʌlʃn/ n Widerwille
m. ~ive /-ɪv/ a abstoßend, widerlich
reputable /'repjʊtəbl/ a ⟨firm⟩ von
gutem Ruf; (respectable) anständig
reputation /repjʊ'teɪʃn/ n Ruf m
repute /rɪ'pjuːt/ n Ruf m. ~d /-ɪd/ a,
-ly adv angeblich
request /rɪ'kwest/ n Bitte f ● vt
bitten. ~ stop n Bedarfshaltestelle f
require /rɪ'kwaɪə(r)/ vt (need) brauchen; (demand) erfordern; **be ~d to
do sth** etw tun müssen. ~ment n Bedürfnis nt; (condition) Erfordernis nt
requisite /'rekwɪzɪt/ a erforderlich
● n **toilet/travel ~s** pl Toiletten-/
Reiseartikel pl
requisition /rekwɪ'zɪʃn/ n ~ **[order]**
Anforderung f ● vt anfordern
re'sale /riː-/ n Weiterverkauf m
rescind /rɪ'sɪnd/ vt aufheben
rescue /'reskjuː/ n Rettung f ● vt
retten. ~r n Retter m
research /rɪ'sɜːtʃ/ n Forschung f ● vt
erforschen; (Journ) recherchieren
● vi ~ **into** erforschen. ~er n Forscher m; (Journ) Rechercheur m
resem|blance /rɪ'zembləns/ n Ähn-
lichkeit f. ~ble /-bl/ vt ähneln
(+ dat)
resent /rɪ'zent/ vt übelnehmen;
einen Groll hegen gegen ⟨person⟩.
~ful a, -ly adv verbittert. ~ment n
Groll m
reservation /rezə'veɪʃn/ n Reservie-
rung f; (doubt) Vorbehalt m; (enclosure) Reservat nt
reserve /rɪ'zɜːv/ n Reserve f; (for
animals) Reservat nt; (Sport) Re-
servespieler(in) m(f) ● vt reservieren; ⟨client:⟩ reservieren lassen;

(keep) aufheben; sich (dat) vor-
behalten ⟨right⟩. ~d a reserviert
reservoir /'rezəvwɑː(r)/ n Reservoir
nt
re'shape /riː-/ vt umformen
re'shuffle /riː-/ n (Pol) Umbildung f
● vt (Pol) umbilden
reside /rɪ'zaɪd/ vi wohnen
residence /'rezɪdəns/ n Wohnsitz m;
(official) Residenz f; (stay) Aufenthalt m. ~ **permit** n Aufent-
haltsgenehmigung f
resident /'rezɪdənt/ a ansässig (**in** in
+ dat); ⟨housekeeper, nurse⟩ im Haus
wohnend ● n Bewohner(in) m(f); (of
street) Anwohner m. ~ial /-'denʃl/ a
Wohn-
residue /'rezɪdjuː/ n Rest m; (Chem)
Rückstand m
resign /rɪ'zaɪn/ vt ~ **oneself to** sich
abfinden mit ● vi kündigen; (from
public office) zurücktreten. ~ation
/rezɪɡ'neɪʃn/ n Resignation f; (from
job) Kündigung f; Rücktritt m. ~ed
a, -ly adv resigniert
resilient /rɪ'zɪlɪənt/ a federnd; (fig)
widerstandsfähig
resin /'rezɪn/ n Harz nt
resist /rɪ'zɪst/ vt/i sich widersetzen
(+ dat); (fig) widerstehen (+ dat).
~ance n Widerstand m. ~ant a
widerstandsfähig
resolut|e /'rezəluːt/ a, -ly adv ent-
schlossen. ~ion /-'luːʃn/ n Entschlossenheit f; (intention) Vorsatz
m; (Pol) Resolution f
resolve /rɪ'zɒlv/ n Entschlossenheit
f; (decision) Beschluß m ● vt
beschließen; (solve) lösen. ~d a entschlossen
resonan|ce /'rezənəns/ n Resonanz
f. ~t a klangvoll
resort /rɪ'zɔːt/ n (place) Urlaubsort
m; **as a last ~** wenn alles andere
fehlschlägt ● vi ~ **to** (fig) greifen zu
resound /rɪ'zaʊnd/ vi widerhallen.
~ing a widerhallend; (loud) laut;
(notable) groß
resource /rɪ'sɔːs/ n ~s pl Ressourcen
pl. ~ful a findig. ~fulness n Fin-
digkeit f
respect /rɪ'spekt/ n Respekt m, Achtung f (**for** vor + dat); (aspect) Hinsicht f; **with ~ to** in bezug auf (+ acc)
● vt respektieren, achten
respectability /rɪspektə'bɪlətɪ/ n
(see **respectable**) Ehrbarkeit f; An-
ständigkeit f

respect|able /rɪ'spektəbl/ *a*, **-bly**
adv ehrbar; (*decent*) anständig; (*considerable*) ansehnlich. ∼**ful** *a*, **-ly** *adv*
respektvoll

respective /rɪ'spektɪv/ *a* jeweilig.
∼**ly** *adv* beziehungsweise

respiration /respə'reɪʃn/ *n* Atmung
f

respite /'respaɪt/ *n* [Ruhe]pause *f*;
(*delay*) Aufschub *m*

resplendent /rɪ'splendənt/ *a* glänzend

respond /rɪ'spɒnd/ *vi* antworten;
(*react*) reagieren (**to** auf + *acc*);
⟨*patient:*⟩ ansprechen (**to** auf + *acc*)

response /rɪ'spɒns/ *n* Antwort *f*;
Reaktion *f*

responsibility /rɪspɒnsɪ'bɪlətɪ/ *n*
Verantwortung *f*; (*duty*) Verpflichtung *f*

responsib|le /rɪ'spɒnsəbl/ *a* verantwortlich; (*trustworthy*) verantwortungsvoll. ∼**ly** *adv* verantwortungsbewußt

responsive /rɪ'spɒnsɪv/ *a* **be** ∼
reagieren

rest[1] /rest/ *n* Ruhe *f*; (*holiday*) Erholung *f*; (*interval & Mus*) Pause *f*;
have a ∼ eine Pause machen; (*rest*)
sich ausruhen ● *vt* ausruhen; (*lean*)
lehnen (**on** an/auf + *acc*) ● *vi* ruhen;
(*have a rest*) sich ausruhen

rest[2] *n* **the** ∼ der Rest; (*people*) die
Übrigen *pl* ● *vi* **it** ∼**s with you** es ist an
Ihnen (**to** zu)

restaurant /'restərɒnt/ *n* Restaurant *nt*, Gaststätte *f*. ∼ **car** *n* Speisewagen *m*

restful /'restfl/ *a* erholsam

restitution /restɪ'tjuːʃn/ *n* Entschädigung *f*; (*return*) Rückgabe *f*

restive /'restɪv/ *a* unruhig

restless /'restlɪs/ *a*, **-ly** *adv* unruhig

restoration /restə'reɪʃn/ *n* (*of building*) Restaurierung *f*

restore /rɪ'stɔː(r)/ *vt* wiederherstellen; restaurieren ⟨*building*⟩;
(*give back*) zurückgeben

restrain /rɪ'streɪn/ *vt* zurückhalten;
∼ **oneself** sich beherrschen. ∼**ed** *a*
zurückhaltend. ∼**t** *n* Zurückhaltung
f

restrict /rɪ'strɪkt/ *vt* einschränken;
∼ **to** beschränken auf (+ *acc*). ∼**ion**
/-ɪkʃn/ *n* Einschränkung *f*; Beschränkung *f*. ∼**ive** /-ɪv/ *a* einschränkend

'rest room *n* (*Amer*) Toilette *f*

result /rɪ'zʌlt/ *n* Ergebnis *nt*,
Resultat *nt*; (*consequence*) Folge *f*; **as
a** ∼ als Folge (**of** *gen*) ● *vi* sich ergeben
(**from** aus); ∼ **in** enden in (+ *dat*); (*lead
to*) führen zu

resume /rɪ'zjuːm/ *vt* wiederaufnehmen; wieder einnehmen
⟨*seat*⟩ ● *vi* wieder beginnen

résumé /'rezʊmeɪ/ *n* Zusammenfassung *f*

resumption /rɪ'zʌmpʃn/ *n* Wiederaufnahme *f*

resurgence /rɪ'sɜːdʒəns/ *n* Wiederaufleben *nt*

resurrect /rezə'rekt/ *vt* (*fig*) wiederbeleben. ∼**ion** /-ekʃn/ *n* **the
R**∼**ion** (*Relig*) die Auferstehung

resuscitat|e /rɪ'sʌsɪteɪt/ *vt* wiederbeleben. ∼**ion** /-'teɪʃn/ *n* Wiederbelebung *f*

retail /'riːteɪl/ *n* Einzelhandel *m*
● *a* Einzelhandels- ● *adv* im Einzelhandel ● *vt* im Einzelhandel verkaufen ● *vi* ∼ **at** im Einzelhandel
kosten. ∼**er** *n* Einzelhändler *m*. ∼
price *n* Ladenpreis *m*

retain /rɪ'teɪn/ *vt* behalten

retaliat|e /rɪ'tælɪeɪt/ *vi* zurückschlagen. ∼**ion** /-'eɪʃn/ *n* Vergeltung
f; **in** ∼**ion** als Vergeltung

retarded /rɪ'tɑːdɪd/ *a* zurückgeblieben

retentive /rɪ'tentɪv/ *a* ⟨*memory*⟩ gut

reticen|ce /'retɪsns/ *n* Zurückhaltung *f*. ∼**t** *a* zurückhaltend

retina /'retɪnə/ *n* Netzhaut *f*

retinue /'retɪnjuː/ *n* Gefolge *nt*

retire /rɪ'taɪə(r)/ *vi* in den Ruhestand
treten; (*withdraw*) sich zurückziehen. ∼**d** *a* im Ruhestand. ∼**ment**
n Ruhestand *m*; **since my** ∼**ment** seit
ich nicht mehr arbeite

retiring /rɪ'taɪərɪŋ/ *a* zurückhaltend

retort /rɪ'tɔːt/ *n* scharfe Erwiderung
f; (*Chem*) Retorte *f* ● *vt* scharf erwidern

re'touch /riː-/ *vt* (*Phot*) retuschieren

re'trace /rɪ-/ *vt* zurückverfolgen; ∼
one's steps denselben Weg zurückgehen

retract /rɪ'trækt/ *vt* einziehen; zurücknehmen ⟨*remark*⟩ ● *vi* widerrufen

re'train /riː-/ *vt* umschulen ● *vi*
umgeschult werden

retreat /rɪ'triːt/ *n* Rückzug *m*; (*place*)
Zufluchtsort *m* ● *vi* sich zurückziehen

re'trial /ri:-/ n Wiederaufnahme-verfahren nt

retribution /retrɪ'bju:ʃn/ n Vergeltung f

retrieve /rɪ'tri:v/ vt zurückholen; (from wreckage) bergen; (Computing) wiederauffinden; (dog:) apportieren

retrograde /'retrəgreɪd/ a rückschrittlich

retrospect /'retrəspekt/ n in ~ rückblickend. ~ive /-ɪv/ a, -ly adv rückwirkend; (looking back) rückblickend

return /rɪ'tɜ:n/ n Rückkehr f; (giving back) Rückgabe f; (Comm) Ertrag m; (ticket) Rückfahrkarte f; (Aviat) Rückflugschein m; by ~ [of post] postwendend; in ~ dafür; in ~ for für; many happy ~s! herzlichen Glückwunsch zum Geburtstag! ● vi zurückgehen/-fahren; (come back) zurückkommen ● vt zurückgeben; (put back) zurückstellen/-legen; (send back) zurückschicken; (elect) wählen

return: ~ **flight** n Rückflug m. ~ **match** n Rückspiel nt. ~ **ticket** n Rückfahrkarte f; (Aviat) Rückflugschein m

reunion /ri:'ju:nɪən/ n Wiedervereinigung f; (social gathering) Treffen nt

reunite /ri:ju:'naɪt/ vt wiedervereinigen ● vi sich wiedervereinigen

re'us|able /ri:-/ a wiederverwendbar. ~e vt wiederverwenden

rev /rev/ n (Auto, fam) Umdrehung f ● vt/i ~ [up] den Motor auf Touren bringen

reveal /rɪ'vi:l/ vt zum Vorschein bringen; (fig) enthüllen. ~ing a (fig) aufschlußreich

revel /'revl/ vi (pt/pp revelled) ~ in sth etw genießen

revelation /revə'leɪʃn/ n Offenbarung f, Enthüllung f

revelry /'revlrɪ/ n Lustbarkeit f

revenge /rɪ'vendʒ/ n Rache f; (fig & Sport) Revanche f ● vt rächen

revenue /'revənju:/ n [Staats]-einnahmen pl

reverberate /rɪ'vɜ:bəreɪt/ vi nachhallen

revere /rɪ'vɪə(r)/ vt verehren. ~nce /'revərəns/ n Ehrfurcht f

Reverend /'revərənd/ a the ~ X Pfarrer X; (Catholic) Hochwürden X

reverent /'revərənt/ a, -ly adv ehrfürchtig

reverie /'revərɪ/ n Träumerei f

revers /rɪ'vɪə/ n (pl revers /-z/) Revers nt

reversal /rɪ'vɜ:sl/ n Umkehrung f

reverse /rɪ'vɜ:s/ a umgekehrt ● n Gegenteil nt; (back) Rückseite f; (Auto) Rückwärtsgang m ● vt umkehren; (Auto) zurücksetzen; ~ the charges (Teleph) ein R-Gespräch führen ● vi zurücksetzen

revert /rɪ'vɜ:t/ vi ~ to zurückfallen an (+ acc); zurückkommen auf (+ acc) (topic)

review /rɪ'vju:/ n Rückblick m (of auf + acc); (re-examination) Überprüfung f; (Mil) Truppenschau f; (of book, play) Kritik f, Rezension f ● vt zurückblicken auf (+ acc); überprüfen (situation); (Mil) besichtigen; kritisieren, rezensieren (book, play). ~er n Kritiker m, Rezensent m

revile /rɪ'vaɪl/ vt verunglimpfen

revis|e /rɪ'vaɪz/ vt revidieren; (for exam) wiederholen. ~ion /-'vɪʒn/ n Revision f; Wiederholung f

revival /rɪ'vaɪvl/ n Wiederbelebung f

revive /rɪ'vaɪv/ vt wiederbeleben; (fig) wieder aufleben lassen ● vi wieder aufleben

revoke /rɪ'vəʊk/ vt aufheben; widerrufen (command, decision)

revolt /rɪ'vəʊlt/ n Aufstand m ● vi rebellieren ● vt anwidern. ~ing a widerlich, eklig

revolution /revə'lu:ʃn/ n Revolution f; (Auto) Umdrehung f. ~ary /-ərɪ/ a revolutionär. ~ize vt revolutionieren

revolve /rɪ'vɒlv/ vi sich drehen; ~ around kreisen um

revolv|er /rɪ'vɒlvə(r)/ n Revolver m. ~ing a Dreh-

revue /rɪ'vju:/ n Revue f; (satirical) Kabarett nt

revulsion /rɪ'vʌlʃn/ n Abscheu m

reward /rɪ'wɔ:d/ n Belohnung f ● vt belohnen. ~ing a lohnend

re'write /ri:-/ vt (pt rewrote, pp rewritten) noch einmal [neu] schreiben; (alter) umschreiben

rhapsody /'ræpsədɪ/ n Rhapsodie f

rhetoric /'retərɪk/ n Rhetorik f. ~al /rɪ'tɒrɪkl/ a rhetorisch

rheuma|tic /ru:'mætɪk/ a rheumatisch. ~tism /'ru:mətɪzm/ n Rheumatismus m, Rheuma nt

Rhine /raɪn/ n Rhein m
rhinoceros /raɪˈnɒsərəs/ n Nashorn nt, Rhinozeros nt
rhubarb /ˈruːbɑːb/ n Rhabarber m
rhyme /raɪm/ n Reim m ● vt reimen ● vi sich reimen
rhythm /ˈrɪðm/ n Rhythmus m. ~**ic[al]** a, **-ally** adv rhythmisch
rib /rɪb/ n Rippe f ● vt (pt/pp **ribbed**) (fam) aufziehen (fam)
ribald /ˈrɪbld/ a derb
ribbon /ˈrɪbən/ n Band nt; (for typewriter) Farbband nt; **in ~s** in Fetzen
rice /raɪs/ n Reis m
rich /rɪtʃ/ a (**-er, -est**), **-ly** adv reich; ⟨food⟩ gehaltvoll; ⟨heavy⟩ schwer ● n **the ~** pl die Reichen; **~es** pl Reichtum m
rickets /ˈrɪkɪts/ n Rachitis f
rickety /ˈrɪkəti/ a wackelig
ricochet /ˈrɪkəʃeɪ/ vi abprallen
rid /rɪd/ vt (pt/pp **rid**, pres p **ridding**) befreien (**of** von); **get ~ of** loswerden
riddance /ˈrɪdns/ n **good ~!** auf Nimmerwiedersehen!
ridden /ˈrɪdn/ see **ride**
riddle /ˈrɪdl/ n Rätsel nt
riddled /ˈrɪdld/ a **~ with** durchlöchert mit
ride /raɪd/ n Ritt m; (in vehicle) Fahrt f; **take s.o. for a ~** (fam) jdn reinlegen ● v (pt **rode**, pp **ridden**) ● vt reiten ⟨horse⟩; fahren mit ⟨bicycle⟩ ● vi reiten; (in vehicle) fahren. ~**r** n Reiter(in) m(f); (on bicycle) Fahrer(in) m(f); (in document) Zusatzklausel f
ridge /rɪdʒ/ n Erhebung f; (on roof) First m; (of mountain) Grat m, Kamm m; (of high pressure) Hochdruckkeil m
ridicule /ˈrɪdɪkjuːl/ n Spott m ● vt verspotten, spotten über (+ acc)
ridiculous /rɪˈdɪkjʊləs/ a, **-ly** adv lächerlich
riding /ˈraɪdɪŋ/ n Reiten nt ● attrib Reit-
rife /raɪf/ a **be ~** weit verbreitet sein
riff-raff /ˈrɪfræf/ n Gesindel nt
rifle /ˈraɪfl/ n Gewehr nt ● vt plündern; ~ **through** durchwühlen
rift /rɪft/ n Spalt m; (fig) Riß m
rig[1] /rɪg/ n Ölbohrturm m; (at sea) Bohrinsel f ● vt (pt/pp **rigged**) ~ **out** ausrüsten; ~ **up** aufbauen
rig[2] vt (pt/pp **rigged**) manipulieren
right /raɪt/ a richtig; (not left) rechte(r,s); **be ~** ⟨person:⟩ recht haben; ⟨clock:⟩ richtig gehen; **put ~** wieder in

Ordnung bringen; (fig) richtigstellen; **that's ~!** das stimmt! ● adv richtig; (directly) direkt; (completely) ganz; (not left) rechts; ⟨go⟩ nach rechts; ~ **away** sofort ● n Recht nt; (not left) rechte Seite f; **on the ~** rechts; **from/to the ~** von/nach rechts; **be in the ~** recht haben; **by ~s** eigentlich; **the R~** (Pol) die Rechte. ~ **angle** n rechter Winkel m
righteous /ˈraɪtʃəs/ a rechtschaffen
rightful /ˈraɪtfl/ a, **-ly** adv rechtmäßig
right: ~**-handed** a rechtshändig. ~**-hand** ˈman n (fig) rechte Hand f
rightly /ˈraɪtli/ adv mit Recht
right: ~ **of way** n Durchgangsrecht nt; (path) öffentlicher Fußweg m; (Auto) Vorfahrt f. ~**-ˈwing** a (Pol) rechte(r,s)
rigid /ˈrɪdʒɪd/ a starr; (strict) streng. ~**ity** /-ˈdʒɪdəti/ n Starrheit f; Strenge f
rigmarole /ˈrɪgmərəʊl/ n Geschwätz nt; (procedure) Prozedur f
rigorous /ˈrɪgərəs/ a, **-ly** adv streng
rigour /ˈrɪgə(r)/ n Strenge f
rile /raɪl/ vt (fam) ärgern
rim /rɪm/ n Rand m; (of wheel) Felge f
rind /raɪnd/ n (on fruit) Schale f; (on cheese) Rinde f; (on bacon) Schwarte f
ring[1] /rɪŋ/ n Ring m; (for circus) Manege f; **stand in a ~** im Kreis stehen ● vt umringen; ~ **in red** rot einkreisen
ring[2] n Klingeln nt; **give s.o. a ~** (Teleph) jdn anrufen ● v (pt **rang**, pp **rung**) ● vt läuten; ~ **[up]** (Teleph) anrufen ● vi läuten, klingeln. ~ **back** vt/i (Teleph) zurückrufen. ~ **off** vi (Teleph) auflegen
ring: ~**leader** n Rädelsführer m. ~ **road** n Umgehungsstraße f
rink /rɪŋk/ n Eisbahn f
rinse /rɪns/ n Spülung f; (hair colour) Tönung f ● vt spülen; tönen ⟨hair⟩. ~ **off** vt abspülen
riot /ˈraɪət/ n Aufruhr m; ~**s** pl Unruhen pl; ~ **of colours** bunte Farbenpracht f; **run ~** randalieren ● vi randalieren. ~**er** n Randalierer m. ~**ous** /-əs/ a aufrührerisch; (boisterous) wild
rip /rɪp/ n Riß m ● vt/i (pt/pp **ripped**) zerreißen; ~ **open** aufreißen. ~ **off** vt (fam) neppen
ripe /raɪp/ a (**-r, -st**) reif
ripen /ˈraɪpn/ vi reifen ● vt reifen lassen

ripeness /'raɪpnɪs/ n Reife f

'**rip-off** n (fam) Nepp m

ripple /'rɪpl/ n kleine Welle f ● vt kräuseln ● vi sich kräuseln

rise /raɪz/ n Anstieg m; (fig) Aufstieg m; (increase) Zunahme f; (in wages) Lohnerhöhung f; (in salary) Gehaltserhöhung f; **give ∼ to** Anlaß geben zu ● vi (pt **rose,** pp **risen**) steigen; (ground:) ansteigen; (sun, dough:) aufgehen; (river:) entspringen; (get up) aufstehen; (fig) aufsteigen (**to** zu); (rebel) sich erheben; (court:) sich vertagen. ∼**r** n **early ∼r** Frühaufsteher m

rising /'raɪzɪŋ/ a steigend; (sun) aufgehend; **the ∼ generation** die heranwachsende Generation ● n (revolt) Aufstand m

risk /rɪsk/ n Risiko nt; **at one's own ∼** auf eigene Gefahr ● vt riskieren

risky /'rɪskɪ/ a (**-ier, -iest**) riskant

risqué /'rɪskeɪ/ a gewagt

rissole /'rɪsəʊl/ n Frikadelle f

rite /raɪt/ n Ritus m; **last ∼s** Letzte Ölung f

ritual /'rɪtjʊəl/ a rituell ● n Ritual nt

rival /'raɪvl/ a rivalisierend ● n Rivale m/Rivalin f; ∼**s** pl (Comm) Konkurrenten pl ● vt (pt/pp **rivalled**) gleichkommen (+ dat); (compete with) rivalisieren mit. ∼**ry** n Rivalität f; (Comm) Konkurrenzkampf m

river /'rɪvə(r)/ n Fluß m. ∼**-bed** n Flußbett nt

rivet /'rɪvɪt/ n Niete f ● vt [ver]nieten; ∼**ed by** (fig) gefesselt von

road /rəʊd/ n Straße f; (fig) Weg m

road: ∼-block n Straßensperre f. ∼**-hog** n (fam) Straßenschreck m. ∼**-map** n Straßenkarte f. ∼ **safety** n Verkehrssicherheit f. ∼ **sense** n Verkehrssinn m. ∼**side** n Straßenrand m. ∼**way** n Fahrbahn f. ∼**works** npl Straßenarbeiten pl. ∼**worthy** a verkehrssicher

roam /rəʊm/ vi wandern

roar /rɔ:(r)/ n Gebrüll nt; ∼**s of laughter** schallendes Gelächter nt ● vi brüllen; (with laughter) schallend lachen. ∼**ing** a (fire) prasselnd; **do a ∼ing trade** (fam) ein Bombengeschäft machen

roast /rəʊst/ a gebraten, Brat-; ∼ **beef/pork** Rinder-/Schweinebraten m ● n Braten m ● vt/i braten; rösten (coffee, chestnuts)

rob /rɒb/ vt (pt/pp **robbed**) berauben (**of** gen); ausrauben (bank). ∼**ber** n Räuber m. ∼**bery** n Raub m

robe /rəʊb/ n Robe f; (Amer: bathrobe) Bademantel m

robin /'rɒbɪn/ n Rotkehlchen nt

robot /'rəʊbɒt/ n Roboter m

robust /rəʊ'bʌst/ a robust

rock[1] /rɒk/ n Fels m; **stick of ∼** Zuckerstange f; **on the ∼s** (ship) aufgelaufen; (marriage) kaputt; (drink) mit Eis

rock[2] vt/i schaukeln

rock[3] n (Mus) Rock m

rock-'bottom n Tiefpunkt m

rockery /'rɒkərɪ/ n Steingarten m

rocket /'rɒkɪt/ n Rakete f ● vi in die Höhe schießen

rocking: ∼-chair n Schaukelstuhl m. ∼**-horse** n Schaukelpferd nt

rocky /'rɒkɪ/ a (**-ier, -iest**) felsig; (unsteady) wackelig

rod /rɒd/ n Stab m; (stick) Rute f; (for fishing) Angel[rute] f

rode /rəʊd/ see **ride**

rodent /'rəʊdnt/ n Nagetier nt

roe[1] /rəʊ/ n Rogen m; (soft) Milch f

roe[2] n (pl **roe** or **roes**) ∼**[-deer]** Reh nt

rogue /rəʊg/ n Gauner m

role /rəʊl/ n Rolle f

roll /rəʊl/ n Rolle f; (bread) Brötchen nt; (list) Liste f; (of drum) Wirbel m ● vi rollen; **be ∼ing in money** (fam) Geld wie Heu haben ● vt rollen; walzen (lawn); ausrollen (pastry). ∼ **over** vi sich auf die andere Seite rollen. ∼ **up** vt aufrollen; hochkrempeln (sleeves) ● vi (fam) auftauchen

'**roll-call** n Namensaufruf m; (Mil) Appell m

roller /'rəʊlə(r)/ n Rolle f; (lawn, road) Walze f; (hair) Lockenwickler m. ∼ **blind** n Rollo nt. ∼**-coaster** n Berg-und-Talbahn f. ∼**-skate** n Rollschuh m

'**rolling-pin** n Teigrolle f

Roman /'rəʊmən/ a römisch ● n Römer(in) m(f)

romance /rə'mæns/ n Romantik f; (love-affair) Romanze f; (book) Liebesgeschichte f

Romania /rəʊ'meɪnɪə/ n Rumänien nt. ∼**n** a rumänisch ● n Rumäne m/ -nin f

romantic /rəʊ'mæntɪk/ a, **-ally** adv romantisch. ∼**ism** /-tɪsɪzm/ n Romantik f

Rome /rəʊm/ n Rom nt

romp /rɒmp/ n Tollen nt ● vi [herum]tollen. ∼**ers** npl Strampelhöschen nt

roof /ru:f/ *n* Dach *nt*; (*of mouth*) Gaumen *m* ● *vt* ~ **over** überdachen. ~-**rack** *n* Dachgepäckträger *m*. ~-**top** *n* Dach *nt*

rook /rʊk/ *n* Saatkrähe *f*; (*Chess*) Turm *m* ● *vt* (*fam: swindle*) schröpfen

room /ru:m/ *n* Zimmer *nt*; (*for functions*) Saal *m*; (*space*) Platz *m*. ~**y** *a* geräumig

roost /ru:st/ *n* Hühnerstange *f* ● *vi* schlafen

root[1] /ru:t/ *n* Wurzel *f*; **take** ~ anwachsen ● *vi* Wurzeln schlagen. ~ **out** *vt* (*fig*) ausrotten

root[2] *vi* ~ **about** wühlen; ~ **for s.o.** (*Amer, fam*) für jdn sein

rope /rəʊp/ *n* Seil *nt*; **know the** ~**s** (*fam*) sich auskennen. ~ **in** *vt* (*fam*) einspannen

rope-'**ladder** *n* Strickleiter *f*

rosary /'rəʊzərɪ/ *n* Rosenkranz *m*

rose[1] /rəʊz/ *n* Rose *f*; (*of watering-can*) Brause *f*

rose[2] *see* **rise**

rosemary /'rəʊzmərɪ/ *n* Rosmarin *m*

rosette /rəʊ'zet/ *n* Rosette *f*

roster /'rɒstə(r)/ *n* Dienstplan *m*

rostrum /'rɒstrəm/ *n* Podest *nt*, Podium *nt*

rosy /'rəʊzɪ/ *a* (-**ier**, -**iest**) rosig

rot /rɒt/ *n* Fäulnis *f*; (*fam: nonsense*) Quatsch *m* ● *vi* (*pt/pp* **rotted**) [ver]faulen

rota /'rəʊtə/ *n* Dienstplan *m*

rotary /'rəʊtərɪ/ *a* Dreh-; (*Techn*) Rotations-

rotat|**e** /rəʊ'teɪt/ *vt* drehen; im Wechsel anbauen (*crops*) ● *vi* sich drehen; (*Techn*) rotieren. ~**ion** /-eɪʃn/ *n* Drehung *f*; (*of crops*) Fruchtfolge *f*; **in** ~**ion** im Wechsel

rote /rəʊt/ *n* **by** ~ auswendig

rotten /'rɒtn/ *a* faul; (*fam*) mies; (*person*) fies

rotund /rəʊ'tʌnd/ *a* rundlich

rough /rʌf/ *a* (-**er**, -**est**) rauh; (*uneven*) uneben; (*coarse, not gentle*) grob; (*brutal*) roh; (*turbulent*) stürmisch; (*approximate*) ungefähr ● *adv* **sleep** ~ im Freien übernachten; **play** ~ holzen ● *n* **do sth in** ~ etw ins unreine schreiben ● *vt* ~ **it** primitiv leben. ~ **out** *vt* im Groben entwerfen

roughage /'rʌfɪdʒ/ *n* Ballaststoffe *pl*

rough '**draft** *n* grober Entwurf *m*

rough|**ly** /'rʌflɪ/ *adv* (*see* **rough**) rauh; grob; roh; ungefähr. ~**ness** *n* Rauheit *f*

'**rough paper** *n* Konzeptpapier *nt*

round /raʊnd/ *a* (-**er**, -**est**) rund ● *n* Runde *f*; (*slice*) Scheibe *f*; **do one's** ~**s** seine Runde machen ● *prep* um (+ *acc*); ~ **the clock** rund um die Uhr ● *adv* **all** ~ ringsherum; ~ **and** ~ im Kreis; **ask s.o.** ~ jdn einladen; **turn/look** ~ sich umdrehen/umsehen ● *vt* biegen um (*corner*) ● *vi* ~ **on s.o.** jdn anfahren. ~ **off** *vt* abrunden. ~ **up** *vt* aufrunden; zusammentreiben (*animals*); festnehmen (*criminals*)

roundabout /'raʊndəbaʊt/ *a* ~ **route** Umweg *m* ● *n* Karussell *nt*; (*for traffic*) Kreisverkehr *m*

round: ~-'**shouldered** *a* mit einem runden Rücken. ~ '**trip** *n* Rundreise *f*

rous|**e** /raʊz/ *vt* wecken; (*fig*) erregen. ~**ing** *a* mitreißend

route /ru:t/ *n* Route *f*; (*of bus*) Linie *f*

routine /ru:'ti:n/ *a*, -**ly** *adv* routinemäßig ● *n* Routine *f*; (*Theat*) Nummer *f*

roux /ru:/ *n* Mehlschwitze *f*

rove /rəʊv/ *vi* wandern

row[1] /rəʊ/ *n* (*line*) Reihe *f*; **in a** ~ (*one after the other*) nacheinander

row[2] *vt/i* rudern

row[3] /raʊ/ *n* (*fam*) Krach *m* ● *vi* (*fam*) sich streiten

rowan /'rəʊən/ *n* Eberesche *f*

rowdy /'raʊdɪ/ *a* (-**ier**, -**iest**) laut

rowing boat /'rəʊɪŋ-/ *n* Ruderboot *nt*

royal /'rɔɪəl/ *a*, -**ly** *adv* königlich

royalt|**y** /'rɔɪəltɪ/ *n* Königtum *nt*; (*persons*) Mitglieder *pl* der königlichen Familie; -**ies** *pl* (*payments*) Tantiemen *pl*

rub /rʌb/ *n* **give sth a** ~ etw reiben/ (*polish*) polieren ● *vt* (*pt/pp* **rubbed**) reiben; (*polish*) polieren; **don't** ~ **it in** (*fam*) reib es mir nicht unter die Nase. ~ **off** *vt* abreiben ● *vi* abgehen; ~ **off on** abfärben auf (+ *acc*). ~ **out** *vt* ausradieren

rubber /'rʌbə(r)/ *n* Gummi *m*; (*eraser*) Radiergummi *m*. ~ **band** *n* Gummiband *nt*. ~**y** *a* gummiartig

rubbish /'rʌbɪʃ/ *n* Abfall *m*, Müll *m*; (*fam: nonsense*) Quatsch *m*; (*fam: junk*) Plunder *m*, Kram *m* ● *vt* (*fam*) schlechtmachen. ~ **bin** *n* Mülleimer *m*, Abfalleimer *m*. ~ **dump** *n* Abfallhaufen *m*; (*official*) Müllhalde *f*

rubble /'rʌbl/ n Trümmer pl, Schutt m

ruby /'ru:bɪ/ n Rubin m

rucksack /'rʌksæk/ n Rucksack m

rudder /'rʌdə(r)/ n [Steuer]ruder nt

ruddy /'rʌdɪ/ a (-ier, -iest) rötlich; (sl) verdammt

rude /ru:d/ a (-r, -st), -ly adv unhöflich; (improper) unanständig. ~ness n Unhöflichkeit f

rudiment /'ru:dɪmənt/ n ~s pl Anfangsgründe pl. ~ary /-'mentərɪ/ a elementar; (Biol) rudimentär

rueful /'ru:fl/ a, -ly adv reumütig

ruffian /'rʌfɪən/ n Rüpel m

ruffle /'rʌfl/ n Rüsche f ● vt zerzausen

rug /rʌg/ n Vorleger m, [kleiner] Teppich m; (blanket) Decke f

rugged /'rʌgɪd/ a ⟨coastline⟩ zerklüftet

ruin /'ru:ɪn/ n Ruine f; (fig) Ruin m ● vt ruinieren. ~ous /-əs/ a ruinös

rule /ru:l/ n Regel f; (control) Herrschaft f; (government) Regierung f; (for measuring) Lineal nt; **as a** ~ in der Regel ● vt regieren, herrschen über (+ acc); (fig) beherrschen; (decide) entscheiden; ziehen ⟨line⟩ ● vi regieren, herrschen. ~ **out** vt ausschließen

ruled /ru:ld/ a ⟨paper⟩ liniert

ruler /'ru:lə(r)/ n Herrscher(in) m(f); (measure) Lineal nt

ruling /'ru:lɪŋ/ a herrschend; ⟨factor⟩ entscheidend; (Pol) regierend ● n Entscheidung f

rum /rʌm/ n Rum m

rumble /'rʌmbl/ n Grollen nt ● vi grollen; ⟨stomach:⟩ knurren

ruminant /'ru:mɪnənt/ n Wiederkäuer m

rummage /'rʌmɪdʒ/ vi wühlen; ~ **through** durchwühlen

rummy /'rʌmɪ/ n Rommé nt

rumour /'ru:mə(r)/ n Gerücht nt ● vt **it is** ~**ed that** es geht das Gerücht, daß

rump /rʌmp/ n Hinterteil nt. ~ **steak** n Rumpsteak nt

rumpus /'rʌmpəs/ n (fam) Spektakel m

run /rʌn/ n Lauf m; (journey) Fahrt f; (series) Serie f, Reihe f; (Theat) Laufzeit f; (Skiing) Abfahrt f; (enclosure) Auslauf m; (Amer: ladder) Laufmasche f; **at a** ~ im Laufschritt; ~ **of bad luck** Pechsträhne f; **be on the** ~ flüchtig sein; **have the** ~ **of sth** etw zu seiner freien Verfügung haben; **in**

the long ~ auf lange Sicht ● v (pt ran, pp run, pres p running) ● vi laufen; (flow) fließen; ⟨eyes:⟩ tränen; ⟨bus:⟩ verkehren, fahren; ⟨colours:⟩ [ab]färben; (in election) kandidieren; ~ **across s.o./sth** auf jdn/etw stoßen ● vt laufen lassen; einlaufen lassen ⟨bath⟩; (manage) führen, leiten; (drive) fahren; eingehen ⟨risk⟩; (Journ) bringen ⟨article⟩; ~ **one's hand over sth** mit der Hand über etw (acc) fahren. ~ **away** vi weglaufen. ~ **down** vi hinunter-/herunterlaufen; ⟨clockwork:⟩ ablaufen; ⟨stocks:⟩ sich verringern ● vt (run over) überfahren; (reduce) verringern; (fam: criticize) heruntermachen. ~ **in** vi hinein-/hereinlaufen. ~ **off** vi weglaufen ● vt abziehen ⟨copies⟩. ~ **out** vi hinaus-/herauslaufen; ⟨supplies, money:⟩ ausgehen; **I've** ~ **out of sugar** ich habe keinen Zucker mehr. ~ **over** vi hinüber-/herüberlaufen; (overflow) überlaufen ● vt überfahren. ~ **through** vi durchlaufen. ~ **up** vi hinauf-/herauflaufen; (towards) hinlaufen ● vt machen ⟨debts⟩; auflaufen lassen ⟨bill⟩; (sew) schnell nähen

'runaway n Ausreißer m

run-'down a ⟨area⟩ verkommen

rung[1] /rʌŋ/ n (of ladder) Sprosse f

rung[2] see **ring**[2]

runner /'rʌnə(r)/ n Läufer m; (Bot) Ausläufer m; (on sledge) Kufe f. ~ **bean** n Stangenbohne f. ~**-up** n Zweite(r) m/f

running /'rʌnɪŋ/ a laufend; ⟨water⟩ fließend; **four times** ~ viermal nacheinander ● n Laufen nt; (management) Führung f, Leitung f; **be/not be in the** ~ eine/keine Chance haben. ~ **'commentary** n fortlaufender Kommentar m

runny /'rʌnɪ/ a flüssig

run: ~**-of-the-'mill** a gewöhnlich. ~**-up** n (Sport) Anlauf m; (to election) Zeit f vor der Wahl. ~**way** n Start- und Landebahn f, Piste f

rupture /'rʌptʃə(r)/ n Bruch m ● vt/i brechen; ~ **oneself** sich (dat) einen Bruch heben

rural /'rʊərəl/ a ländlich

ruse /ru:z/ n List f

rush[1] /rʌʃ/ n (Bot) Binse f

rush[2] n Hetze f; **in a** ~ in Eile ● vi sich hetzen; (run) rasen; ⟨water:⟩ rauschen

● *vt* hetzen, drängen; ~ **s.o. to hospital** jdn schnellstens ins Krankenhaus bringen. ~**-hour** *n* Hauptverkehrszeit *f*, Stoßzeit *f*

rusk /rʌsk/ *n* Zwieback *m*

Russia /'rʌʃə/ *n* Rußland *nt*. ~**n** *a* russisch ● *n* Russe *m*/Russin *f*; (*Lang*) Russisch *nt*

rust /rʌst/ *n* Rost *m* ● *vi* rosten

rustic /'rʌstɪk/ *a* bäuerlich; ⟨*furniture*⟩ rustikal

rustle /'rʌsl/ *vi* rascheln ● *vt* rascheln mit; (*Amer*) stehlen ⟨*cattle*⟩. ~ **up** *vt* (*fam*) improvisieren

'**rustproof** *a* rostfrei

rusty /'rʌstɪ/ *a* (**-ier, -iest**) rostig

rut /rʌt/ *n* Furche *f*; **be in a** ~ (*fam*) aus dem alten Trott nicht herauskommen

ruthless /'ru:θlɪs/ *a*, **-ly** *adv* rücksichtslos. ~**ness** *n* Rücksichtslosigkeit *f*

rye /raɪ/ *n* Roggen *m*

S

sabbath /'sæbəθ/ *n* Sabbat *m*

sabbatical /sə'bætɪkl/ *n* (*Univ*) Forschungsurlaub *m*

sabot|age /'sæbətɑ:ʒ/ *n* Sabotage *f* ● *vt* sabotieren. ~**eur** /-'tɜ:(r)/ *n* Saboteur *m*

sachet /'sæʃeɪ/ *n* Beutel *m*; (*scented*) Kissen *nt*

sack[1] /sæk/ *vt* (*plunder*) plündern

sack[2] *n* Sack *m*; **get the** ~ (*fam*) rausgeschmissen werden ● *vt* (*fam*) rausschmeißen. ~**ing** *n* Sackleinen *nt*; (*fam: dismissal*) Rausschmiß *m*

sacrament /'sækrəmənt/ *n* Sakrament *nt*

sacred /'seɪkrɪd/ *a* heilig

sacrifice /'sækrɪfaɪs/ *n* Opfer *nt* ● *vt* opfern

sacrilege /'sækrɪlɪdʒ/ *n* Sakrileg *nt*

sad /sæd/ *a* (**sadder, saddest**) traurig; ⟨*loss, death*⟩ schmerzlich. ~**den** *vt* traurig machen

saddle /'sædl/ *n* Sattel *m* ● *vt* satteln; ~ **s.o. with sth** (*fam*) jdm etw aufhalsen

sadis|m /'seɪdɪzm/ *n* Sadismus *m*. ~**t** /-dɪst/ *n* Sadist *m*. ~**tic** /sə'dɪstɪk/ *a*, **-ally** *adv* sadistisch

sad|ly /'sædlɪ/ *adv* traurig; (*unfortunately*) leider. ~**ness** *n* Traurigkeit *f*

safe /seɪf/ *a* (**-r, -st**) sicher; ⟨*journey*⟩ gut; (*not dangerous*) ungefährlich; ~ **and sound** gesund und wohlbehalten ● *n* Safe *m*. ~**guard** *n* Schutz *m* ● *vt* schützen. ~**ly** *adv* sicher; ⟨*arrive*⟩ gut

safety /'seɪftɪ/ *n* Sicherheit *f*. ~**-belt** *n* Sicherheitsgurt *m*. ~**-pin** *n* Sicherheitsnadel *f*. ~**-valve** *n* [Sicherheits]ventil *nt*

sag /sæg/ *vi* (*pt/pp* **sagged**) durchhängen

saga /'sɑ:gə/ *n* Saga *f*; (*fig*) Geschichte *f*

sage[1] /seɪdʒ/ *n* (*herb*) Salbei *m*

sage[2] *a* weise ● *n* Weise(r) *m*

Sagittarius /sædʒɪ'teərɪəs/ *n* (*Astr*) Schütze *m*

said /sed/ *see* **say**

sail /seɪl/ *n* Segel *nt*; (*trip*) Segelfahrt *f* ● *vi* segeln; (*on liner*) fahren; (*leave*) abfahren (**for** nach) ● *vt* segeln mit

'**sailboard** *n* Surfbrett *nt*. ~**ing** *n* Windsurfen *nt*

sailing /'seɪlɪŋ/ *n* Segelsport *m*. ~**-boat** *n* Segelboot *nt*. ~**-ship** *n* Segelschiff *nt*

sailor /'seɪlə(r)/ *n* Seemann *m*; (*in navy*) Matrose *m*

saint /seɪnt/ *n* Heilige(r) *m*/*f*. ~**ly** *a* heilig

sake /seɪk/ *n* **for the** ~ **of ...** um ... (*gen*) willen; **for my/your** ~ um meinet-/deinetwillen

salad /'sæləd/ *n* Salat *m*. ~ **cream** *n* ≈ Mayonnaise *f*. ~**-dressing** *n* Salatsoße *f*

salary /'sælərɪ/ *n* Gehalt *nt*

sale /seɪl/ *n* Verkauf *m*; (*event*) Basar *m*; (*at reduced prices*) Schlußverkauf *m*; **for** ~ zu verkaufen

sales|man *n* Verkäufer *m*. ~**woman** *n* Verkäuferin *f*

salient /'seɪlɪənt/ *a* wichtigste(r,s)

saliva /sə'laɪvə/ *n* Speichel *m*

sallow /'sæləʊ/ *a* (**-er, -est**) bleich

salmon /'sæmən/ *n* Lachs *m*. ~**-pink** *a* lachsrosa

saloon /sə'lu:n/ *n* Salon *m*; (*Auto*) Limousine *f*; (*Amer: bar*) Wirtschaft *f*

salt /sɔ:lt/ *n* Salz *nt* ● *a* salzig; ⟨*water, meat*⟩ Salz- ● *vt* salzen; (*cure*) pökeln; streuen ⟨*road*⟩. ~**-cellar** *n* Salzfaß *nt*. ~ '**water** *n* Salzwasser *nt*. ~**y** *a* salzig

salutary /'sæljʊtərɪ/ *a* heilsam

salute /sə'luːt/ n (*Mil*) Gruß m ● vt/i (*Mil*) grüßen

salvage /'sælvɪdʒ/ n (*Naut*) Bergung f ● vt bergen

salvation /sæl'veɪʃn/ n Rettung f; (*Relig*) Heil nt. **S~** '**Army** n Heilsarmee f

salvo /'sælvəʊ/ n Salve f

same /seɪm/ a & pron die ~ der/die/das gleiche; (*pl*) die gleichen; (*identical*) der-/die-/dasselbe; (*pl*) dieselben ● adv **the ~** gleich; **all the ~** trotzdem; **the ~ to you** gleichfalls

sample /'sɑːmpl/ n Probe f; (*Comm*) Muster nt ● vt probieren, kosten

sanatorium /sænə'tɔːrɪəm/ n Sanatorium nt

sanctify /'sæŋktɪfaɪ/ vt (pt/pp -**fied**) heiligen

sanctimonious /sæŋktɪ'məʊnɪəs/ a, -**ly** adv frömmlerisch

sanction /'sæŋkʃn/ n Sanktion f ● vt sanktionieren

sanctity /'sæŋktətɪ/ n Heiligkeit f

sanctuary /'sæŋktjʊərɪ/ n (*Relig*) Heiligtum nt; (*refuge*) Zuflucht f; (*for wildlife*) Tierschutzgebiet nt

sand /sænd/ n Sand m ● vt ~ [**down**] [ab]schmirgeln

sandal /'sændl/ n Sandale f

sand: ~**bank** n Sandbank f. ~**paper** n Sandpapier nt ● vt [ab]schmirgeln. ~-**pit** n Sandkasten m

sandwich /'sænwɪdʒ/ n ≈ belegtes Brot nt; Sandwich m ● vt ~**ed between** eingeklemmt zwischen

sandy /'sændɪ/ a (-**ier**, -**iest**) sandig; (*beach, soil*) Sand-; (*hair*) rotblond

sane /seɪn/ a (-**r**, -**st**) geistig normal; (*sensible*) vernünftig

sang /sæŋ/ see **sing**

sanitary /'sænɪtərɪ/ a hygienisch; (*system*) sanitär. ~ **napkin** n (*Amer*), ~ **towel** n [Damen]binde f

sanitation /sænɪ'teɪʃn/ n Kanalisation und Abfallbeseitigung pl

sanity /'sænətɪ/ n [gesunder] Verstand m

sank /sæŋk/ see **sink**

sap /sæp/ n (*Bot*) Saft m ● vt (pt/pp **sapped**) schwächen

sapphire /'sæfaɪə(r)/ n Saphir m

sarcas|m /'sɑːkæzm/ n Sarkasmus m. ~**tic** /-'kæstɪk/ a, -**ally** adv sarkastisch

sardine /sɑː'diːn/ n Sardine f

Sardinia /sɑː'dɪnɪə/ n Sardinien nt

sardonic /sɑː'dɒnɪk/ a, -**ally** adv höhnisch; (*smile*) sardonisch

sash /sæʃ/ n Schärpe f

sat /sæt/ see **sit**

satanic /sə'tænɪk/ a satanisch

satchel /'sætʃl/ n Ranzen m

satellite /'sætəlaɪt/ n Satellit m. ~ **dish** n Satellitenschüssel f. ~ **television** n Satellitenfernsehen nt

satin /'sætɪn/ n Satin m

satire /'sætaɪə(r)/ n Satire f

satirical /sə'tɪrɪkl/ a, -**ly** adv satirisch

satir|ist /'sætərɪst/ n Satiriker(in) m(f). ~**ize** vt satirisch darstellen; (*book:*) eine Satire sein auf (+ acc)

satisfaction /sætɪs'fækʃn/ n Befriedigung f; **to my ~** zu meiner Zufriedenheit

satisfactory /sætɪs'fæktərɪ/ a, -**ily** adv zufriedenstellend

satisf|y /'sætɪsfaɪ/ vt (pt/pp -**fied**) befriedigen; zufriedenstellen (*customer*); (*convince*) überzeugen; **be ~ied** zufrieden sein. ~**ying** a befriedigend; (*meal*) sättigend

saturat|e /'sætʃəreɪt/ vt durchtränken; (*Chem & fig*) sättigen. ~**ed** a durchnäßt; (*fat*) gesättigt

Saturday /'sætədeɪ/ n Samstag m, Sonnabend m

sauce /sɔːs/ n Soße f; (*cheek*) Frechheit f. ~**pan** n Kochtopf m

saucer /'sɔːsə(r)/ n Untertasse f

saucy /'sɔːsɪ/ a (-**ier**, -**iest**) frech

Saudi Arabia /saʊdɪə'reɪbɪə/ n Saudi-Arabien nt

sauna /'sɔːnə/ n Sauna f

saunter /'sɔːntə(r)/ vi schlendern

sausage /'sɒsɪdʒ/ n Wurst f

savage /'sævɪdʒ/ a wild; (*fierce*) scharf; (*brutal*) brutal ● n Wilde(r) m/f ● vt anfallen. ~**ry** n Brutalität f

save /seɪv/ n (*Sport*) Abwehr f ● vt retten (**from** vor + dat); (*keep*) aufheben; (*not waste*) sparen; (*collect*) sammeln; (*avoid*) ersparen; (*Sport*) verhindern (*goal*) ● vi ~ [**up**] sparen ● prep außer (+ dat), mit Ausnahme (+ gen)

saver /'seɪvə(r)/ n Sparer m

saving /'seɪvɪŋ/ n (*see* **save**) Rettung f; Sparen nt; Ersparnis f; ~**s** pl (*money*) Ersparnisse pl. ~**s account** n Sparkonto nt. ~**s bank** n Sparkasse f

saviour /'seɪvjə(r)/ n Retter m

savour /'seɪvə(r)/ n Geschmack m ● vt auskosten. ~**y** a herzhaft, würzig; (*fig*) angenehm saw¹ /sɔ:/ *see* **see**¹

saw² *n* Säge *f* ● *vt/i* (*pt* **sawed**, *pp* **sawn** *or* **sawed**) sägen. ∼**dust** *n* Sägemehl *nt*

saxophone /'sæksəfəʊn/ *n* Saxophon *nt*

say /seɪ/ *n* Mitspracherecht *nt*; **have one's** ∼ seine Meinung sagen ● *vt/i* (*pt/pp* **said**) sagen; sprechen ⟨*prayer*⟩; **that is to** ∼ das heißt; **that goes without** ∼**ing** das versteht sich von selbst; **when all is said and done** letzten Endes; **I** ∼**!** (*attracting attention*) hallo! ∼**ing** *n* Redensart *f*

scab /skæb/ *n* Schorf *m*; (*pej*) Streikbrecher *m*

scaffold /'skæfəld/ *n* Schafott *nt*. ∼**ing** *n* Gerüst *nt*

scald /skɔ:ld/ *vt* verbrühen

scale¹ /skeɪl/ *n* (*of fish*) Schuppe *f*

scale² *n* Skala *f*; (*Mus*) Tonleiter *f*; (*ratio*) Maßstab *m*; **on a grand** ∼ in großem Stil ● *vt* (*climb*) erklettern. ∼ **down** *vt* verkleinern

scales /skeɪlz/ *npl* (*for weighing*) Waage *f*

scalp /skælp/ *n* Kopfhaut *f* ● *vt* skalpieren

scalpel /'skælpl/ *n* Skalpell *nt*

scam /skæm/ *n* (*fam*) Schwindel *m*

scamper /'skæmpə(r)/ *vi* huschen

scan /skæn/ *n* (*Med*) Szintigramm *nt* ● *v* (*pt/pp* **scanned**) ● *vt* absuchen; (*quickly*) flüchtig ansehen; (*Med*) szintigraphisch untersuchen ● *vi* ⟨*poetry:*⟩ das richtige Versmaß haben

scandal /'skændl/ *n* Skandal *m*; (*gossip*) Skandalgeschichten *pl*. ∼**ize** /-dəlaɪz/ *vt* schockieren. ∼**ous** /-əs/ *a* skandalös

Scandinavia /skændɪ'neɪvɪə/ *n* Skandinavien *nt*. ∼**n** *a* skandinavisch ● *n* Skandinavier(in) *m(f)*

scant /skænt/ *a* wenig

scanty /'skæntɪ/ *a* (**-ier, -iest**), **-ily** *adv* spärlich; ⟨*clothing*⟩ knapp

scapegoat /'skeɪp-/ *n* Sündenbock *m*

scar /skɑ:(r)/ *n* Narbe *f* ● *vt* (*pt/pp* **scarred**) eine Narbe hinterlassen auf (+ *dat*)

scarc|e /skeəs/ *a* (**-r, -st**) knapp; **make oneself** ∼**e** (*fam*) sich aus dem Staub machen. ∼**ely** *adv* kaum. ∼**ity** *n* Knappheit *f*

scare /skeə(r)/ *n* Schreck *m*; (*panic*) [allgemeine] Panik *f*; (*bomb* ∼) Bombendrohung *f* ● *vt* Angst

machen (+ *dat*); **be** ∼**d** Angst haben (**of** vor + *dat*)

'**scarecrow** *n* Vogelscheuche *f*

scarf /skɑ:f/ *n* (*pl* **scarves**) Schal *m*; (*square*) Tuch *nt*

scarlet /'skɑ:lət/ *a* scharlachrot. ∼ '**fever** *n* Scharlach *m*

scary /'skeərɪ/ *a* unheimlich

scathing /'skeɪðɪŋ/ *a* bissig

scatter /'skætə(r)/ *vt* verstreuen; (*disperse*) zerstreuen ● *vi* sich zerstreuen. ∼**-brained** *a* (*fam*) schusselig. ∼**ed** *a* verstreut; ⟨*showers*⟩ vereinzelt

scatty /'skætɪ/ *a* (**-ier, -iest**) (*fam*) verrückt

scavenge /'skævɪndʒ/ *vi* [im Abfall] Nahrung suchen; ⟨*animal:*⟩ Aas fressen. ∼**r** *n* Aasfresser *m*

scenario /sɪ'nɑ:rɪəʊ/ *n* Szenario *nt*

scene /si:n/ *n* Szene *f*; (*sight*) Anblick *m*; (*place of event*) Schauplatz *m*; **behind the** ∼**s** hinter den Kulissen; ∼ **of the crime** Tatort *m*

scenery /'si:nərɪ/ *n* Landschaft *f*; (*Theat*) Szenerie *f*

scenic /'si:nɪk/ *a* landschaftlich schön; (*Theat*) Bühnen-

scent /sent/ *n* Duft *m*; (*trail*) Fährte *f*; (*perfume*) Parfüm *nt*. ∼**ed** *a* parfümiert

sceptic|al /'skeptɪkl/ *a*, **-ly** *adv* skeptisch. ∼**ism** /-tɪsɪzm/ *n* Skepsis *f*

schedule /'ʃedju:l/ *n* Programm *nt*; (*of work*) Zeitplan *m*; (*timetable*) Fahrplan *m*; **behind** ∼ im Rückstand; **according to** ∼ planmäßig ● *vt* planen. ∼**d flight** *n* Linienflug *m*

scheme /ski:m/ *n* Programm *nt*; (*plan*) Plan *m*; (*plot*) Komplott *nt* ● *vi* Ränke schmieden

schizophren|ia /skɪtsə'fri:nɪə/ *n* Schizophrenie *f*. ∼**ic** /-'frenɪk/ *a* schizophren

scholar /'skɒlə(r)/ *n* Gelehrte(r) *m/f*. ∼**ly** *a* gelehrt. ∼**ship** *n* Gelehrtheit *f*; (*grant*) Stipendium *nt*

school /sku:l/ *n* Schule *f*; (*Univ*) Fakultät *f* ● *vt* schulen; dressieren ⟨*animal*⟩

school: ∼**boy** *n* Schüler *m*. ∼**girl** *n* Schülerin *f*. ∼**ing** *n* Schulbildung *f*. ∼**master** *n* Lehrer *m*. ∼**mistress** *n* Lehrerin *f*. ∼**teacher** *n* Lehrer(in) *m(f)*

sciatica /saɪ'ætɪkə/ *n* Ischias *m*

scien|ce /'saɪəns/ *n* Wissenschaft *f*. ∼**tific** /-'tɪfɪk/ *a* wissenschaftlich. ∼**tist** *n* Wissenschaftler *m*

scintillating /'sɪntɪleɪtɪŋ/ a sprühend

scissors /'sɪzəz/ npl Schere f; **a pair of** ∼ eine Schere

scoff[1] /skɒf/ vi ∼ **at** spotten über (+ acc)

scoff[2] vt (fam) verschlingen

scold /skəʊld/ vt ausschimpfen

scoop /sku:p/ n Schaufel f; (Culin) Portionierer m; (Journ) Exklusivmeldung f ● vt ∼ **out** aushöhlen; (remove) auslöffeln; ∼ **up** schaufeln; schöpfen ⟨liquid⟩

scoot /sku:t/ vi (fam) rasen. ∼er n Roller m

scope /skəʊp/ n Bereich m; (opportunity) Möglichkeiten pl

scorch /skɔːtʃ/ vt versengen. ∼ing a glühend heiß

score /skɔː(r)/ n [Spiel]stand m; (individual) Punktzahl f; (Mus) Partitur f; (Cinema) Filmmusik f; **a** ∼ **[of]** (twenty) zwanzig; **keep [the]** ∼ zählen; (written) aufschreiben; **on that** ∼ was das betrifft ● vt erzielen; schießen ⟨goal⟩; (cut) einritzen ● vi Punkte erzielen; (Sport) ein Tor schießen; (keep score) Punkte zählen. ∼r n Punktezähler m; (of goals) Torschütze m

scorn /skɔːn/ n Verachtung f ● vt verachten. ∼ful a, -ly adv verächtlich

Scorpio /'skɔːpɪəʊ/ n (Astr) Skorpion m

scorpion /'skɔːpɪən/ n Skorpion m

Scot /skɒt/ n Schotte m/Schottin f

Scotch /skɒtʃ/ a schottisch ● n (whisky) Scotch m

scotch vt unterbinden

scot-'free a **get off** ∼ straffrei ausgehen

Scot|land /'skɒtlənd/ n Schottland nt. ∼s, ∼tish a schottisch

scoundrel /'skaʊndrl/ n Schurke m

scour[1] /'skaʊə(r)/ vt (search) absuchen

scour[2] vt (clean) scheuern

scourge /skɜːdʒ/ n Geißel f

scout /skaʊt/ n (Mil) Kundschafter m ● vi ∼ **for** Ausschau halten nach

Scout n **[Boy]** ∼ Pfadfinder m

scowl /skaʊl/ n böser Gesichtsausdruck m ● vi ein böses Gesicht machen

scraggy /'skrægɪ/ a (-ier, -iest) (pej) dürr, hager

scram /skræm/ vi (fam) abhauen

scramble /'skræmbl/ n Gerangel nt ● vi klettern; ∼ **for** sich drängen nach

● vt (Teleph) verschlüsseln. ∼d **'egg[s]** n[pl] Rührei nt

scrap[1] /skræp/ n (fam: fight) Rauferei f ● vi sich raufen

scrap[2] n Stückchen nt; (metal) Schrott m; ∼s pl Reste; **not a** ∼ kein bißchen ● vt (pt/pp **scrapped**) aufgeben

'scrap-book n Sammelalbum nt

scrape /skreɪp/ vt schaben; (clean) abkratzen; (damage) [ver]schrammen. ∼ **through** vi gerade noch durchkommen. ∼ **together** vt zusammenkriegen

scraper /'skreɪpə(r)/ n Kratzer m

'scrap iron n Alteisen nt

scrappy /'skræpɪ/ a lückenhaft

'scrap-yard n Schrottplatz m

scratch /skrætʃ/ n Kratzer m; **start from** ∼ von vorne anfangen; **not be up to** ∼ zu wünschen übriglassen ● vt/i kratzen; (damage) zerkratzen

scrawl /skrɔːl/ n Gekrakel nt ● vt/i krakeln

scrawny /'skrɔːnɪ/ a (-ier, -iest) (pej) dürr, hager

scream /skriːm/ n Schrei m ● vt/i schreien

screech /skriːtʃ/ n Kreischen nt ● vt/i kreischen

screen /skriːn/ n Schirm m; (Cinema) Leinwand f; (TV) Bildschirm m ● vt schützen; (conceal) verdecken; vorführen ⟨film⟩; (examine) überprüfen; (Med) untersuchen. ∼ing n (Med) Reihenuntersuchung f. ∼play n Drehbuch nt

screw /skruː/ n Schraube f ● vt schrauben. ∼ **up** vt festschrauben; (crumple) zusammenknüllen; zusammenkneifen ⟨eyes⟩; (sl: bungle) vermasseln; ∼ **up one's courage** seinen Mut zusammennehmen

'screwdriver n Schraubenzieher m

screwy /'skruːɪ/ a (-ier, -iest) (fam) verrückt

scribble /'skrɪbl/ n Gekritzel nt ● vt/i kritzeln

script /skrɪpt/ n Schrift f; (of speech, play) Text m; (Radio, TV) Skript nt; (of film) Drehbuch nt

Scripture /'skrɪptʃə(r)/ n (Sch) Religion f; **the** ∼s pl die Heilige Schrift f

scroll /skrəʊl/ n Schriftrolle f; (decoration) Volute f

scrounge /skraʊndʒ/ vt/i schnorren. ∼r n Schnorrer m

scrub[1] /skrʌb/ n (land) Buschland nt, Gestrüpp nt

scrub[2] *vt/i* (*pt/pp* **scrubbed**) schrubben; (*fam: cancel*) absagen; fallenlassen ⟨*plan*⟩

scruff /skrʌf/ *n* **by the** ~ **of the neck** beim Genick

scruffy /'skrʌfɪ/ *a* (**-ier, -iest**) vergammelt

scrum /skrʌm/ *n* Gedränge *nt*

scruple /'skru:pl/ *n* Skrupel *m*

scrupulous /'skru:pjʊləs/ *a*, **-ly** *adv* gewissenhaft

scrutin|ize /'skru:tɪnaɪz/ *vt* [genau] ansehen. ~**y** *n* (*look*) prüfender Blick *m*

scuff /skʌf/ *vt* abstoßen

scuffle /'skʌfl/ *n* Handgemenge *nt*

scullery /'skʌlərɪ/ *n* Spülküche *f*

sculpt|or /'skʌlptə(r)/ *n* Bildhauer(in) *m(f)*. ~**ure** /-tʃə(r)/ *n* Bildhauerei *f*; (*piece of work*) Skulptur *f*, Plastik *f*

scum /skʌm/ *n* Schmutzschicht *f*; (*people*) Abschaum *m*

scurrilous /'skʌrɪləs/ *a* niederträchtig

scurry /'skʌrɪ/ *vi* (*pt/pp* **-ied**) huschen

scuttle[1] /'skʌtl/ *n* Kohleneimer *m*

scuttle[2] *vt* versenken ⟨*ship*⟩

scuttle[3] *vi* schnell krabbeln

scythe /saɪð/ *n* Sense *f*

sea /si:/ *n* Meer *nt*, See *f*; **at** ~ auf See; **by** ~ mit dem Schiff. ~**board** *n* Küste *f*. ~**food** *n* Meeresfrüchte *pl*. ~**gull** *n* Möwe *f*

seal[1] /si:l/ *n* (*Zool*) Seehund *m*

seal[2] *n* Siegel *nt*; (*Techn*) Dichtung *f* ● *vt* versiegeln; (*Techn*) abdichten; (*fig*) besiegeln. ~ **off** *vt* abriegeln

sea-level *n* Meeresspiegel *m*

seam /si:m/ *n* Naht *f*; (*of coal*) Flöz *nt*

seaman *n* Seemann *m*; (*sailor*) Matrose *m*

seamless /'si:mlɪs/ *a* nahtlos

seance /'seɪɑ:ns/ *n* spiritistische Sitzung *f*

sea: ~**plane** *n* Wasserflugzeug *nt*. ~**port** *n* Seehafen *m*

search /sɜ:tʃ/ *n* Suche *f*; (*official*) Durchsuchung *f* ● *vt* durchsuchen; absuchen ⟨*area*⟩ ● *vi* suchen (**for** nach). ~**ing** *a* prüfend, forschend

search: ~**light** *n* [Such]scheinwerfer *m*. ~-**party** *n* Suchmannschaft *f*

sea: ~**sick** *a* seekrank. ~**side** *n* **at/to the** ~**side** am/ans Meer

season /'si:zn/ *n* Jahreszeit *f*; (*social, tourist, sporting*) Saison *f* ● *vt* (*flavour*) würzen. ~**able** /-əbl/ *a* der Jahreszeit gemäß. ~**al** *a* Saison-. ~**ing** *n* Gewürze *pl*

season ticket *n* Dauerkarte *f*

seat /si:t/ *n* Sitz *m*; (*place*) Sitzplatz *m*; (*bottom*) Hintern *m*; **take a** ~ Platz nehmen ● *vt* setzen; (*have seats for*) Sitzplätze bieten (+ *dat*); **remain** ~**ed** sitzen bleiben. ~-**belt** *n* Sicherheitsgurt *m*; **fasten one's** ~-**belt** sich anschnallen

sea: ~**weed** *n* [See]tang *m.* ~-**worthy** *a* seetüchtig

secateurs /sekə'tɜ:z/ *npl* Gartenschere *f*

seclu|de /sɪ'klu:d/ *vt* absondern. ~**ded** *a* abgelegen. ~**sion** /-ʒn/ *n* Zurückgezogenheit *f*

second[1] /sɪ'kɒnd/ *vt* (*transfer*) [vorübergehend] versetzen

second[2] /'sekənd/ *a* zweite(r,s); **on** ~ **thoughts** nach weiterer Überlegung ● *n* Sekunde *f*; (*Sport*) Sekundant *m*; ~**s** *pl* (*goods*) Waren zweiter Wahl; **the** ~ der/die/das zweite ● *adv* (*in race*) an zweiter Stelle ● *vt* unterstützen ⟨*proposal*⟩

secondary /'sekəndrɪ/ *a* zweitrangig; (*Phys*) Sekundär-. ~ **school** *n* höhere Schule *f*

second: ~-**best** *a* zweitbeste(r,s). ~-**class** *adv* ⟨*travel, send*⟩ zweiter Klasse. ~-**class** *a* zweitklassig

second hand *n* (*on clock*) Sekundenzeiger *m*

second-'hand *a* gebraucht ● *adv* aus zweiter Hand

secondly /'sekəndlɪ/ *adv* zweitens

second-'rate *a* zweitklassig

secrecy /'si:krəsɪ/ *n* Heimlichkeit *f*

secret /'si:krɪt/ *a* geheim; ⟨*agent, police*⟩ Geheim-; ⟨*drinker, lover*⟩ heimlich ● *n* Geheimnis *nt*

secretarial /sekrə'teərɪəl/ *a* Sekretärinnen-; ⟨*work, staff*⟩ Sekretariats-

secretary /'sekrətərɪ/ *n* Sekretär(in) *m(f)*

secret|e /sɪ'kri:t/ *vt* absondern. ~**ion** /-i:ʃn/ *n* Absonderung *f*

secretive /'si:krətɪv/ *a* geheimtuerisch. ~**ness** *n* Heimlichtuerei *f*

secretly /'si:krɪtlɪ/ *adv* heimlich

sect /sekt/ *n* Sekte *f*

section /'sekʃn/ *n* Teil *m*; (*of text*) Abschnitt *m*; (*of firm*) Abteilung *f*; (*of organization*) Sektion *f*

sector /'sektə(r)/ *n* Sektor *m*

secular /'sekjʊlə(r)/ *a* weltlich

secure /sɪ'kjʊə(r)/ *a*, **-ly** *adv* sicher; (*firm*) fest; (*emotionally*) geborgen ● *vt* sichern; (*fasten*) festmachen; (*obtain*) sich (*dat*) sichern

securit|y /sɪ'kjʊərətɪ/ *n* Sicherheit *f*; (*emotional*) Geborgenheit *f*; **~ies** *pl* Wertpapiere *pl*; (*Fin*) Effekten *pl*

sedan /sɪ'dæn/ *n* (*Amer*) Limousine *f*

sedate[1] /sɪ'deɪt/ *a*, **-ly** *adv* gesetzt

sedate[2] *vt* sedieren

sedation /sɪ'deɪʃn/ *n* Sedierung *f*; **be under** ~ sediert sein

sedative /'sedətɪv/ *a* beruhigend ● *n* Beruhigungsmittel *nt*

sedentary /'sedəntərɪ/ *a* sitzend

sediment /'sedɪmənt/ *n* [Boden]satz *m*

seduce /sɪ'dju:s/ *vt* verführen

seduct|ion /sɪ'dʌkʃn/ *n* Verführung *f*. **~ive** /-tɪv/ *a*, **-ly** *adv* verführerisch

see[1] /si:/ *v* (*pt* **saw**, *pp* **seen**) ● *vt* sehen; (*understand*) einsehen; (*imagine*) sich (*dat*) vorstellen; (*escort*) begleiten; **go and** ~ nachsehen; (*visit*) besuchen; ~ **you later!** bis nachher! **~ing that** da ● *vi* sehen; (*check*) nachsehen; ~ **about** sich kümmern um. ~ **off** *vt* verabschieden; (*chase away*) vertreiben. ~ **through** *vi* durchsehen ● *vt* (*fig*) ~ **through s.o.** jdn durchschauen

see[2] *n* (*Relig*) Bistum *nt*

seed /si:d/ *n* Samen *m*; (*of grape*) Kern *m*; (*fig*) Saat *f*; (*Tennis*) gesetzter Spieler *m*; **go to** ~ Samen bilden; (*fig*) herunterkommen. **~ed** *a* (*Tennis*) gesetzt. **~ling** *n* Sämling *m*

seedy /'si:dɪ/ *a* (**-ier, -iest**) schäbig; (*area*) heruntergekommen

seek /si:k/ *vt* (*pt/pp* **sought**) suchen

seem /si:m/ *vi* scheinen. **~ingly** *adv* scheinbar

seemly /'si:mlɪ/ *a* schicklich

seen /si:n/ *see* **see**[1]

seep /si:p/ *vi* sickern

see-saw /'si:sɔ:/ *n* Wippe *f*

seethe /si:ð/ *vi* ~ **with anger** vor Wut schäumen

'see-through *a* durchsichtig

segment /'segmənt/ *n* Teil *m*; (*of worm*) Segment *nt*; (*of orange*) Spalte *f*

segregat|e /'segrɪgeɪt/ *vt* trennen. **~ion** /-'geɪʃn/ *n* Trennung *f*

seize /si:z/ *vt* ergreifen; (*Jur*) beschlagnahmen; ~ **s.o. by the arm** jdn

am Arm packen. ~ **up** *vi* (*Techn*) sich festfressen

seizure /'si:ʒə(r)/ *n* (*Jur*) Beschlagnahme *f*; (*Med*) Anfall *m*

seldom /'seldəm/ *adv* selten

select /sɪ'lekt/ *a* ausgewählt; (*exclusive*) exklusiv ● *vt* auswählen; aufstellen ⟨team⟩. **~ion** /-ekʃn/ *n* Auswahl *f*. **~ive** /-ɪv/ *a*, **-ly** *adv* selektiv; (*choosy*) wählerisch

self /self/ *n* (*pl* **selves**) Ich *nt*

self: **~-ad'dressed** *a* adressiert. **~-ad'hesive** *a* selbstklebend. **~-as-'surance** *n* Selbstsicherheit *f*. **~-as-'sured** *a* selbstsicher. **~-'catering** *n* Selbstversorgung *f*. **~-'centred** *a* egozentrisch. **~-'confidence** *n* Selbstbewußtsein *nt*, Selbstvertrauen *nt*. **~-'confident** *a* selbstbewußt. **~-'conscious** *a* befangen. **~-con'tained** *a* ⟨flat⟩ abgeschlossen. **~-con'trol** *n* Selbstbeherrschung *f*. **~-de'fence** *n* Selbstverteidigung *f*; (*Jur*) Notwehr *f*. **~-de'nial** *n* Selbstverleugnung *f*. **~-determi'nation** *n* Selbstbestimmung *f*. **~-em'ployed** *a* selbständig. **~-e'steem** *n* Selbstachtung *f*. **~-'evident** *a* offensichtlich. **~-'governing** *a* selbstverwaltet. **~-'help** *n* Selbsthilfe *f*. **~-in-'dulgent** *a* maßlos. **~-'interest** *n* Eigennutz *m*

self|ish /'selfɪʃ/ *a*, **-ly** *adv* egoistisch, selbstsüchtig. **~less** *a*, **-ly** *adv* selbstlos

self: **~-'pity** *n* Selbstmitleid *nt*. **~-'portrait** *n* Selbstporträt *nt*. **~-pos'sessed** *a* selbstbeherrscht. **~-preser'vation** *n* Selbsterhaltung *f*. **~-re'spect** *n* Selbstachtung *f*. **~-'righteous** *a* selbstgerecht. **~-'sacrifice** *n* Selbstaufopferung *f*. **~-'satisfied** *a* selbstgefällig. **~-'service** *n* Selbstbedienung *f* ● *attrib* Selbstbedienungs-. **~-'sufficient** *a* selbständig. **~-'willed** *a* eigenwillig

sell /sel/ *v* (*pt/pp* **sold**) ● *vt* verkaufen; **be sold out** ausverkauft sein ● *vi* sich verkaufen. ~ **off** *vt* verkaufen

seller /'selə(r)/ *n* Verkäufer *m*

Sellotape (P) /'seləʊ-/ *n* ≈ Tesafilm (P) *m*

'sell-out *n* **be a** ~ ausverkauft sein; (*fam: betrayal*) Verrat sein

selves /selvz/ *see* **self**

semblance /'sembləns/ *n* Anschein *m*

semen /'si:mən/ n (Anat) Samen m

semester /sɪ'mestə(r)/ n (Amer) Semester nt

semi|breve /'semɪbri:v/ n (Mus) ganze Note f. ~**circle** n Halbkreis m. ~**'circular** a halbkreisförmig. ~**'colon** n Semikolon nt. ~**-de'tached** a & n ~**-detached [house]** Doppelhaushälfte f. ~**'final** n Halbfinale nt

seminar /'semɪnɑ:(r)/ n Seminar nt. ~**y** /-nərɪ/ n Priesterseminar nt

'semitone n (Mus) Halbton m

semolina /semə'li:nə/ n Grieß m

senat|e /'senət/ n Senat m. ~**or** n Senator m

send /send/ vt/i (pt/pp **sent**) schicken; ~ **one's regards** grüßen lassen; ~ **for** kommen lassen ⟨person⟩; sich ⟨dat⟩ schicken lassen ⟨thing⟩. ~**er** n Absender m. ~**-off** n Verabschiedung f

senil|e /'si:naɪl/ a senil. ~**ity** /sɪ'nɪlətɪ/ n Senilität f

senior /'si:nɪə(r)/ a älter; (in rank) höher ● n Ältere(r) m/f; (in rank) Vorgesetzte(r) m/f. ~ **'citizen** n Senior(in) m(f)

seniority /si:nɪ'ɒrətɪ/ n höheres Alter nt; (in rank) höherer Rang m

sensation /sen'seɪʃn/ n Sensation f; (feeling) Gefühl nt. ~**al** a, **-ly** adv sensationell

sense /sens/ n Sinn m; (feeling) Gefühl nt; (common ~) Verstand m; **in a ~** in gewisser Hinsicht; **make** ~ Sinn ergeben ● vt spüren. ~**less** a, **-ly** adv sinnlos; (unconscious) bewußtlos

sensible /'sensəbl/ a, **-bly** adv vernünftig; (suitable) zweckmäßig

sensitiv|e /'sensətɪv/ a, **-ly** adv empfindlich; (understanding) einfühlsam. ~**ity** /-'tɪvətɪ/ n Empfindlichkeit f

sensory /'sensərɪ/ a Sinnes-

sensual /'sensjʊəl/ a sinnlich. ~**ity** /-'ælətɪ/ n Sinnlichkeit f

sensuous /'sensjʊəs/ a sinnlich

sent /sent/ see **send**

sentence /'sentəns/ n Satz m; (Jur) Urteil nt; (punishment) Strafe f ● vt verurteilen

sentiment /'sentɪmənt/ n Gefühl nt; (opinion) Meinung f; (sentimentality) Sentimentalität f. ~**al** a /-'mentl/ a sentimental. ~**ality** /-'tælətɪ/ n Sentimentalität f

sentry /'sentrɪ/ n Wache f

separable /'sepərəbl/ a trennbar

separate[1] /'sepərət/ a, **-ly** adv getrennt, separat

separat|e[2] /'sepəreɪt/ vt trennen ● vi sich trennen. ~**ion** /-'reɪʃn/ n Trennung f

September /sep'tembə(r)/ n September m

septic /'septɪk/ a vereitert; **go** ~ vereitern

sequel /'si:kwl/ n Folge f; (fig) Nachspiel nt

sequence /'si:kwəns/ n Reihenfolge f

sequin /'si:kwɪn/ n Paillette f

serenade /serə'neɪd/ n Ständchen nt ● vt ~ **s.o.** jdm ein Ständchen bringen

seren|e /sɪ'ri:n/ a, **-ly** adv gelassen. ~**ity** /-'renətɪ/ n Gelassenheit f

sergeant /'sɑ:dʒənt/ n (Mil) Feldwebel m; (in police) Polizeimeister m

serial /'sɪərɪəl/ n Fortsetzungsgeschichte f; (Radio, TV) Serie f. ~**ize** vt in Fortsetzungen veröffentlichen/ (Radio, TV) senden

series /'sɪərɪz/ n inv Serie f

serious /'sɪərɪəs/ a, **-ly** adv ernst; (illness, error) schwer. ~**ness** n Ernst m

sermon /'sɜ:mən/ n Predigt f

serpent /'sɜ:pənt/ n Schlange f

serrated /se'reɪtɪd/ a gezackt

serum /'sɪərəm/ n Serum nt

servant /'sɜ:vənt/ n Diener(in) m(f)

serve /sɜ:v/ n (Tennis) Aufschlag m ● vt dienen (+ dat); bedienen ⟨customer, guest⟩; servieren ⟨food⟩; (Jur) zustellen (**on s.o.** jdm); verbüßen ⟨sentence⟩; ~ **its purpose** seinen Zweck erfüllen; **it** ~**s you right!** das geschieht dir recht! ~**s** two für zwei Personen ● vi dienen; (Tennis) aufschlagen

service /'sɜ:vɪs/ n Dienst m; (Relig) Gottesdienst m; (in shop, restaurant) Bedienung f; (transport) Verbindung f; (maintenance) Wartung f; (set of crockery) Service nt; (Tennis) Aufschlag m; ~**s** pl Dienstleistungen pl; (on motorway) Tankstelle und Raststätte f; **in the** ~**s** beim Militär; **be of** ~ nützlich sein; **out of/in** ~ ⟨machine:⟩ außer/in Betrieb ● vt (Techn) warten. ~**able** /-əbl/ a nützlich; (durable) haltbar

service: ~ **area** n Tankstelle und Raststätte f. ~ **charge** n Bedienungszuschlag m. ~**man** n Soldat m. ~ **station** n Tankstelle f

serviette /sɜ:vɪ'et/ n Serviette f

servile /'sɜːvaɪl/ *a* unterwürfig
session /'seʃn/ *n* Sitzung *f*; (*Univ*) Studienjahr *nt*
set /set/ *n* Satz *m*; (*of crockery*) Service *nt*; (*of cutlery*) Garnitur *f*; (*TV, Radio*) Apparat *m*; (*Math*) Menge *f*; (*Theat*) Bühnenbild *nt*; (*Cinema*) Szenenaufbau *m*; (*of people*) Kreis *m*; **shampoo and ~** Waschen und Legen ● *a* (*ready*) fertig, bereit; (*rigid*) fest; ⟨*book*⟩ vorgeschrieben; **be ~ on doing sth** entschlossen sein, etw zu tun; **be ~ in one's ways** in seinen Gewohnheiten festgefahren sein ● *v* (*pt/pp* **set**, *pres p* **setting**) ● *vt* setzen; (*adjust*) einstellen; stellen ⟨*task, alarm clock*⟩; festsetzen, festlegen ⟨*date, limit*⟩; aufgeben ⟨*homework*⟩; zusammenstellen ⟨*questions*⟩; [ein]fassen ⟨*gem*⟩; einrichten ⟨*bone*⟩; legen ⟨*hair*⟩; decken ⟨*table*⟩ ● *vi* ⟨*sun:*⟩ untergehen; (*become hard*) fest werden; **~ about sth** sich an etw (*acc*) machen; **~ about doing sth** sich daranmachen, etw zu tun. **~ back** *vt* zurücksetzen; (*hold up*) aufhalten; (*fam: cost*) kosten. **~ off** *vi* losgehen; (*in vehicle*) losfahren ● *vt* auslösen ⟨*alarm*⟩; explodieren lassen ⟨*bomb*⟩. **~ out** *vi* losgehen; (*in vehicle*) losfahren; **~ out to do sth** sich vornehmen, etw zu tun ● *vt* auslegen; (*state*) darlegen. **~ up** *vt* aufbauen; (*fig*) gründen
set 'meal *n* Menü *nt*
settee /se'tiː/ *n* Sofa *nt*, Couch *f*
setting /'setɪŋ/ *n* Rahmen *m*; (*surroundings*) Umgebung *f*; (*of sun*) Untergang *m*; (*of jewel*) Fassung *f*
settle /'setl/ *vt* (*decide*) entscheiden; (*agree*) regeln; (*fix*) festsetzen; (*calm*) beruhigen; (*pay*) bezahlen ● *vi* sich niederlassen; ⟨*snow, dust:*⟩ liegenbleiben; (*subside*) sich senken; ⟨*sediment:*⟩ sich absetzen. **~ down** *vi* sich beruhigen; (*permanently*) seßhaft werden. **~ up** *vi* abrechnen
settlement /'setlmənt/ *n* (*see* **settle**) Entscheidung *f*; Regelung *f*; Bezahlung *f*; (*Jur*) Vergleich *m*; (*colony*) Siedlung *f*
settler /'setlə(r)/ *n* Siedler *m*
'set-to *n* (*fam*) Streit *m*
'set-up *n* System *nt*
seven /'sevn/ *a* sieben. **~'teen** *a* siebzehn. **~'teenth** *a* siebzehnte(r,s)
seventh /'sevnθ/ *a* siebte(r,s)
seventieth /'sevntiɪθ/ *a* siebzigste(r,s)
seventy /'sevnti/ *a* siebzig

sever /'sevə(r)/ *vt* durchtrennen; abbrechen ⟨*relations*⟩
several /'sevrl/ *a & pron* mehrere, einige
sever|e /sɪ'vɪə(r)/ *a* (**-r, -st**), **-ly** *adv* streng; ⟨*pain*⟩ stark; ⟨*illness*⟩ schwer. **~ity** /-'verəti/ *n* Strenge *f*; Schwere *f*
sew /səʊ/ *vt/i* (*pt* **sewed**, *pp* **sewn** or **sewed**) nähen. **~ up** *vt* zunähen
sewage /'suːɪdʒ/ *n* Abwasser *nt*
sewer /'suːə(r)/ *n* Abwasserkanal *m*
sewing /'səʊɪŋ/ *n* Nähen *nt*; (*work*) Näharbeit *f*. **~ machine** *n* Nähmaschine *f*
sewn /səʊn/ *see* **sew**
sex /seks/ *n* Geschlecht *nt*; (*sexuality, intercourse*) Sex *m*. **~ist** *a* sexistisch. **~ offender** *n* Triebverbrecher *m*
sexual /'seksjʊəl/ *a*, **-ly** *adv* sexuell. **~ 'intercourse** *n* Geschlechtsverkehr *m*
sexuality /seksjʊ'æləti/ *n* Sexualität *f*
sexy /'seksi/ *a* (**-ier, -iest**) sexy
shabby /'ʃæbi/ *a* (**-ier, -iest**), **-ily** *adv* schäbig
shack /ʃæk/ *n* Hütte *f*
shackles /'ʃæklz/ *npl* Fesseln *pl*
shade /ʃeɪd/ *n* Schatten *m*; (*of colour*) [Farb]ton *m*; (*for lamp*) [Lampen]schirm *m*; (*Amer: window-blind*) Jalousie *f* ● *vt* beschatten; (*draw lines on*) schattieren
shadow /'ʃædəʊ/ *n* Schatten *m* ● *vt* (*follow*) beschatten. **~y** *a* schattenhaft
shady /'ʃeɪdi/ *a* (**-ier, -iest**) schattig; (*fam: disreputable*) zwielichtig
shaft /ʃɑːft/ *n* Schaft *m*; (*Techn*) Welle *f*; (*of light*) Strahl *m*; (*of lift*) Schacht *m*; **~s** *pl* (*of cart*) Gabeldeichsel *f*
shaggy /'ʃægi/ *a* (**-ier, -iest**) zottig
shake /ʃeɪk/ *n* Schütteln *nt* ● *v* (*pt* **shook**, *pp* **shaken**) ● *vt* schütteln; (*cause to tremble, shock*) erschüttern; **~ hands with s.o.** jdm die Hand geben ● *vi* wackeln; (*tremble*) zittern. **~ off** *vt* abschütteln
shaky /'ʃeɪki/ *a* (**-ier, -iest**) wackelig; ⟨*hand, voice*⟩ zittrig
shall /ʃæl/ *v aux* **I ~ go** ich werde gehen; **we ~ see** wir werden sehen; **what ~ I do?** was soll ich machen? **I'll come too, ~ I?** ich komme mit, ja? **thou shalt not kill** (*liter*) du sollst nicht töten

shallow /'ʃæləʊ/ a (**-er, -est**) seicht; ⟨dish⟩ flach; (fig) oberflächlich

sham /ʃæm/ a unecht ● n Heuchelei f; (person) Heuchler(in) m(f) ● vt (pt/pp **shammed**) vortäuschen

shambles /'ʃæmblz/ n Durcheinander nt

shame /ʃeɪm/ n Scham f; (disgrace) Schande f; **be a ~** schade sein; **what a ~!** wie schade! **~-faced** a betreten

shame|ful /'ʃeɪmfl/ a, **-ly** adv schändlich. **~less** a, **-ly** adv schamlos

shampoo /ʃæm'pu:/ n Shampoo nt ● vt schamponieren

shandy /'ʃændɪ/ n Radler m

shan't /ʃɑ:nt/ = **shall not**

shape /ʃeɪp/ a (figure) Gestalt f; **take ~** Gestalt annehmen ● vt formen (**into** zu) ● vi **~ up** sich entwickeln. **~less** a formlos; ⟨clothing⟩ unförmig

shapely /'ʃeɪplɪ/ a (**-ier, -iest**) wohlgeformt

share /ʃeə(r)/ n [An]teil m; (Comm) Aktie f ● vt/i teilen. **~holder** n Aktionär(in) m(f)

shark /ʃɑ:k/ n Hai[fisch] m

sharp /ʃɑ:p/ a (**-er, -est**), **-ly** adv scharf; (pointed) spitz; (severe) heftig; (sudden) steil; (alert) clever; (unscrupulous) gerissen ● adv scharf; (Mus) zu hoch; **at six o'clock ~** Punkt sechs Uhr; **look ~!** beeil dich! ● n (Mus) Kreuz nt. **~en** vt schärfen; [an]spitzen ⟨pencil⟩

shatter /'ʃætə(r)/ vt zertrümmern; (fig) zerstören; **be ~ed** ⟨person:⟩ erschüttert sein ● vi zersplittern

shave /ʃeɪv/ n Rasur f; **have a ~** sich rasieren ● vt rasieren ● vi sich rasieren. **~r** n Rasierapparat m

shaving /'ʃeɪvɪŋ/ n Rasieren nt. **~-brush** n Rasierpinsel m

shawl /ʃɔ:l/ n Schultertuch nt

she /ʃi:/ pron sie

sheaf /ʃi:f/ n (pl **sheaves**) Garbe f; (of papers) Bündel nt

shear /ʃɪə(r)/ vt (pt **sheared**, pp **shorn** or **sheared**) scheren

shears /ʃɪəz/ npl [große] Schere f

sheath /ʃi:θ/ n (pl **~s** /ʃi:ðz/) Scheide f

sheaves /ʃi:vz/ see **sheaf**

shed[1] /ʃed/ n Schuppen m; (for cattle) Stall m

shed[2] vt (pt/pp **shed**, pres p **shedding**) verlieren; vergießen ⟨blood, tears⟩; **~ light on** Licht bringen in (+ acc)

sheen /ʃi:n/ n Glanz m

sheep /ʃi:p/ n inv Schaf nt. **~-dog** n Hütehund m

sheepish /'ʃi:pɪʃ/ a, **-ly** adv verlegen

'sheepskin n Schaffell nt

sheer /ʃɪə(r)/ a rein; (steep) steil; (transparent) hauchdünn ● adv steil

sheet /ʃi:t/ n Laken nt, Bettuch nt; (of paper) Blatt nt; (of glass, metal) Platte f

sheikh /ʃeɪk/ n Scheich m

shelf /ʃelf/ n (pl **shelves**) Brett nt, Bord nt; (set of shelves) Regal nt

shell /ʃel/ n Schale f; (of snail) Haus nt; (of tortoise) Panzer m; (on beach) Muschel f; (of unfinished building) Rohbau m; (Mil) Granate f ● vt pellen; enthülsen ⟨peas⟩; (Mil) [mit Granaten] beschießen. **~ out** vi (fam) blechen

'shellfish n inv Schalentiere pl; (Culin) Meeresfrüchte pl

shelter /'ʃeltə(r)/ n Schutz m; (air-raid ~) Luftschutzraum m ● vt schützen (**from** vor + dat) ● vi sich unterstellen. **~ed** a geschützt; ⟨life⟩ behütet

shelve /ʃelv/ vt auf Eis legen; (abandon) aufgeben ● vi ⟨slope:⟩ abfallen

shelves /ʃelvz/ see **shelf**

shelving /'ʃelvɪŋ/ n (shelves) Regale pl

shepherd /'ʃepəd/ n Schäfer m; (Relig) Hirte m ● vt führen. **~ess** n Schäferin f. **~'s pie** n Auflauf m aus mit Kartoffelbrei bedecktem Hackfleisch

sherry /'ʃerɪ/ n Sherry m

shield /ʃi:ld/ n Schild m; (for eyes) Schirm m; (Techn & fig) Schutz m ● vt schützen (**from** vor + dat)

shift /ʃɪft/ n Verschiebung f; (at work) Schicht f; **make ~** sich (dat) behelfen (**with** mit) ● vt rücken; (take away) wegnehmen; (rearrange) umstellen; schieben ⟨blame⟩ (**on to** auf + acc) ● vi sich verschieben; (fam: move quickly) rasen

'shift work n Schichtarbeit f

shifty /'ʃɪftɪ/ a (**-ier, -iest**) (pej) verschlagen

shilly-shally /'ʃɪlɪʃælɪ/ vi fackeln (fam)

shimmer /'ʃɪmə(r)/ n Schimmer m ● vi schimmern

shin /ʃɪn/ n Schienbein nt

shine /ʃaɪn/ n Glanz m ● v (pt/pp **shone**) ● vi leuchten; (reflect light) glänzen; ⟨*sun:*⟩ scheinen ● *vt* ~ **a light on** beleuchten

shingle /'ʃɪŋgl/ *n* (*pebbles*) Kiesel *pl*

shingles /'ʃɪŋglz/ *n* (*Med*) Gürtelrose *f*

shiny /'ʃaɪnɪ/ *a* (**-ier, -iest**) glänzend

ship /ʃɪp/ *n* Schiff *nt* ● *vt* (*pt/pp* **shipped**) verschiffen

ship: ~**building** *n* Schiffbau *m*. ~**ment** *n* Sendung *f*. ~**per** *n* Spediteur *m*. ~**ping** *n* Versand *m*; (*traffic*) Schiffahrt *f*. ~**shape** *a* & *adv* in Ordnung. ~**wreck** *n* Schiffbruch *m*. ~**wrecked** *a* schiffbrüchig. ~**yard** *n* Werft *f*

shirk /ʃɜːk/ *vt* sich drücken vor (+ *dat*). ~**er** *n* Drückeberger *m*

shirt /ʃɜːt/ *n* [Ober]hemd *nt*; (*for woman*) Hemdbluse *f*

shit /ʃɪt/ *n* (*vulg*) Scheiße *f* ● *vi* (*pt/pp* **shit**) (*vulg*) scheißen

shiver /'ʃɪvə(r)/ *n* Schauder *m* ● *vi* zittern

shoal /ʃəʊl/ *n* (*of fish*) Schwarm *m*

shock /ʃɒk/ *n* Schock *m*; (*Electr*) Schlag *m*; (*impact*) Erschütterung *f* ● *vt* einen Schock versetzen (+ *dat*); (*scandalize*) schockieren. ~**ing** *a* schockierend; (*fam: dreadful*) fürchterlich

shod /ʃɒd/ *see* **shoe**

shoddy /'ʃɒdɪ/ *a* (**-ier, -iest**) minderwertig

shoe /ʃuː/ *n* Schuh *m*; (*of horse*) Hufeisen *nt* ● *vt* (*pt/pp* **shod**, *pres p* **shoeing**) beschlagen ⟨*horse*⟩

shoe: ~**horn** *n* Schuhanzieher *m*. ~**lace** *n* Schnürsenkel *m*. ~**maker** *n* Schuhmacher *m*. ~**string** *n* **on a** ~**string** (*fam*) mit ganz wenig Geld

shone /ʃɒn/ *see* **shine**

shoo /ʃuː/ *vt* scheuchen ● *int* sch!

shook /ʃʊk/ *see* **shake**

shoot /ʃuːt/ *n* (*Bot*) Trieb *m*; (*hunt*) Jagd *f* ● *v* (*pt/pp* **shot**) ● *vt* schießen; (*kill*) erschießen; drehen ⟨*film*⟩ ● *vi* schießen. ~ **down** *vt* abschießen. ~ **out** *vi* (*rush*) herausschießen. ~ **up** *vi* (*grow*) in die Höhe schießen; ⟨*prices:*⟩ schnellen

'shooting-range *n* Schießstand *m*

shop /ʃɒp/ *n* Laden *m*, Geschäft *nt*; (*workshop*) Werkstatt *f*; **talk** ~ (*fam*) fachsimpeln ● *vi* (*pt/pp* **shopped**, *pres p* **shopping**) einkaufen; **go** ~**ping** einkaufen gehen

shop: ~ **assistant** *n* Verkäufer(in) *m*(*f*). ~**keeper** *n* Ladenbesitzer(in)

m(*f*). ~**lifter** *n* Ladendieb *m*. ~**lifting** *n* Ladendiebstahl *m*

shopping /'ʃɒpɪŋ/ *n* Einkaufen *nt*; (*articles*) Einkäufe *pl*; **do the** ~ einkaufen. ~ **bag** *n* Einkaufstasche *f*. ~ **centre** *n* Einkaufszentrum *nt*. ~ **trolley** *n* Einkaufswagen *m*

shop: ~**'steward** *n* [gewerkschaftlicher] Vertrauensmann *m*. ~**'window** *n* Schaufenster *nt*

shore /ʃɔː(r)/ *n* Strand *m*; (*of lake*) Ufer *nt*

shorn /ʃɔːn/ *see* **shear**

short /ʃɔːt/ *a* (**-er, -est**) kurz; ⟨*person*⟩ klein; (*curt*) schroff; **a** ~ **time ago** vor kurzem; **be** ~ **of** ... zuwenig ... haben; **be in** ~ **supply** knapp sein ● *adv* kurz; (*abruptly*) plötzlich; (*curtly*) kurz angebunden; **in** ~ kurzum; ~ **of** (*except*) außer; **go** ~ Mangel leiden; **stop** ~ **of doing sth** davor zurückschrecken, etw zu tun

shortage /'ʃɔːtɪdʒ/ *n* Mangel *m* (**of** an + *dat*); (*scarcity*) Knappheit *f*

short: ~**bread** *n* ≈ Mürbekekse *pl*. ~ **'circuit** *n* Kurzschluß *m*. ~**coming** *n* Fehler *m*. ~ **'cut** *n* Abkürzung *f*

shorten /'ʃɔːtn/ *vt* [ab]kürzen; kürzer machen ⟨*garment*⟩

short: ~**hand** *n* Kurzschrift *f*, Stenographie *f*. ~**'handed** *a* **be** ~**handed** zuwenig Personal haben. ~**hand 'typist** *n* Stenotypistin *f*. ~ **list** *n* engere Auswahl *f*. ~**-lived** /-lɪvd/ *a* kurzlebig

short|ly /'ʃɔːtlɪ/ *adv* in Kürze; ~**ly before/after** kurz vorher/danach. ~**ness** *n* Kürze *f*; (*of person*) Kleinheit *f*

shorts /ʃɔːts/ *npl* kurze Hose *f*, Shorts *pl*

short: ~**'sighted** *a* kurzsichtig. ~**-sleeved** *a* kurzärmelig. ~**-'staffed** *a* **be** ~**-staffed** zuwenig Personal haben. ~ **'story** *n* Kurzgeschichte *f*. ~**-'tempered** *a* aufbrausend. ~**-term** *a* kurzfristig. ~ **wave** *n* Kurzwelle *f*

shot /ʃɒt/ *see* **shoot** ● *n* Schuß *m*; (*pellets*) Schrot *m*; (*person*) Schütze *m*; (*Phot*) Aufnahme *f*; (*injection*) Spritze *f*; (*fam: attempt*) Versuch *m*; **like a** ~ (*fam*) sofort. ~**gun** *n* Schrotflinte *f*. ~**-putting** *n* (*Sport*) Kugelstoßen *nt*

should /ʃʊd/ *v aux* **you** ~ **go** du solltest gehen; **I** ~ **have seen him** ich hätte ihn sehen sollen; **I** ~ **like** ich möchte;

this ∼ **be enough** das müßte eigentlich reichen; **if he** ∼ **be there** falls er da
sein sollte
shoulder /'ʃəʊldə(r)/ n Schulter f
● vt schultern; (fig) auf sich (acc)
nehmen. ∼**-blade** n Schulterblatt nt.
∼**-strap** n Tragriemen m; (on
garment) Träger m
shout /ʃaʊt/ n Schrei m ● vt/i
schreien. ∼ **down** vt niederschreien
shouting /'ʃaʊtɪŋ/ n Geschrei nt
shove /ʃʌv/ n Stoß m; (fam) Schubs
m ● vt stoßen; (fam) schubsen; (fam:
put) tun ● vi drängeln. ∼ **off** vi
(fam) abhauen
shovel /'ʃʌvl/ n Schaufel f ● vt (pt/
pp **shovelled**) schaufeln
show /ʃəʊ/ n (display) Pracht f; (exhibition) Ausstellung f, Schau f;
(performance) Vorstellung f; (Theat,
TV) Show f; **on** ∼ ausgestellt ● v (pt
showed, pp **shown**) ● vt zeigen; (put
on display) ausstellen; vorführen ⟨film⟩
● vi sichtbar sein; ⟨film:⟩ gezeigt
werden. ∼ **in** vt hereinführen. ∼ **off**
vi (fam) angeben ● vt vorführen;
(flaunt) angeben mit. ∼ **up** vi
[deutlich] zu sehen sein; (fam: arrive) auftauchen ● vt deutlich
zeigen; (fam: embarrass) blamieren
'**show-down** n Entscheidungs-
kampf m
shower /'ʃaʊə(r)/ n Dusche f; (of
rain) Schauer m; **have a** ∼ duschen
● vt ∼ **with** überschütten mit ● vi duschen. ∼**proof** a regendicht. ∼**y** a
regnerisch
'**show-jumping** n Springreiten nt
shown /ʃəʊn/ see **show**
show: ∼**-off** n Angeber(in) m(f).
∼**-piece** n Paradestück nt. ∼**room** n
Ausstellungsraum m
showy /'ʃəʊɪ/ a protzig
shrank /ʃræŋk/ see **shrink**
shred /ʃred/ n Fetzen m; (fig) Spur
f ● vt (pt/pp **shredded**) zerkleinern;
(Culin) schnitzeln. ∼**der** n Reißwolf
m; (Culin) Schnitzelwerk nt
shrewd /ʃruːd/ a (-er, -est), -ly adv
klug. ∼**ness** n Klugheit f
shriek /ʃriːk/ n Schrei m ● vt/i
schreien
shrift /ʃrɪft/ n **give s.o. short** ∼ jdn
kurz abfertigen
shrill /ʃrɪl/ a, -y adv schrill
shrimp /ʃrɪmp/ n Garnele f, Krabbe f
shrine /ʃraɪn/ n Heiligtum nt

shrink /ʃrɪŋk/ vi (pt **shrank**, pp
shrunk) schrumpfen; ⟨garment:⟩ einlaufen; (draw back) zurückschrecken
(**from** vor + dat)
shrivel /'ʃrɪvl/ vi (pt/pp **shrivelled**)
verschrumpeln
shroud /ʃraʊd/ n Leichentuch nt;
(fig) Schleier m
Shrove /ʃrəʊv/ n ∼ '**Tuesday** Fast-
nachtsdienstag m
shrub /ʃrʌb/ n Strauch m
shrug /ʃrʌg/ n Achselzucken nt ● vt/
i (pt/pp **shrugged**) ∼ **[one's shoul-
ders]** die Achseln zucken
shrunk /ʃrʌŋk/ see **shrink**. ∼**en** a ge-
schrumpft
shudder /'ʃʌdə(r)/ n Schauder m
● vi schaudern; (tremble) zittern
shuffle /'ʃʌfl/ vi schlurfen ● vt mischen ⟨cards⟩
shun /ʃʌn/ vt (pt/pp **shunned**) meiden
shunt /ʃʌnt/ vt rangieren
shush /ʃʊʃ/ int sch!
shut /ʃʌt/ v (pt/pp **shut**, pres p **shut-
ting**) ● vt zumachen, schließen; ∼
one's finger in the door sich (dat) den
Finger in der Tür einklemmen ● vi sich
schließen; ⟨shop:⟩ schließen, zumachen.
∼ **down** vt schließen; stillegen
⟨factory⟩ ● vi schließen; ⟨factory:⟩
stillgelegt werden. ∼ **up** vt abschließen; (lock in) einsperren ● vi
(fam) den Mund halten
'**shut-down** n Stillegung f
shutter /'ʃʌtə(r)/ n [Fenster]laden
m; (Phot) Verschluß m
shuttle /'ʃʌtl/ n (Tex) Schiffchen nt
● vi pendeln
shuttle: ∼**cock** n Federball m. ∼ **service** n Pendelverkehr m
shy /ʃaɪ/ a (-er, -est), -ly adv schüchtern; (timid) scheu ● vi (pt/pp **shied**)
⟨horse:⟩ scheuen. ∼**ness** n Schüch-
ternheit f
Siamese /saɪə'miːz/ a siamesisch
siblings /'sɪblɪŋz/ npl Geschwister pl
Sicily /'sɪsɪlɪ/ n Sizilien nt
sick /sɪk/ a krank; ⟨humour⟩
makaber; **be** ∼ (vomit) sich übergeben; **be** ∼ **of sth** (fam) etw satt
haben; **I feel** ∼ mir ist schlecht
sicken /'sɪkn/ vt anwidern ● vi **be**
∼**ing for something** krank werden
sickle /'sɪkl/ n Sichel f
sick|ly /'sɪklɪ/ a (-ier, -iest) kränklich.
∼**ness** n Krankheit f; (vomiting) Erbrechen nt

'**sick-room** *n* Krankenzimmer *nt*
side /saɪd/ *n* Seite *f*; **on the ~** (*as side-line*) nebenbei; **~ by ~** nebeneinander; (*fig*) Seite an Seite; **take ~s** Partei ergreifen (**with** für); **to be on the safe ~** vorsichtshalber ● *attrib* Seiten- (*gun*) Partei ergreifen für
side: ~board *n* Anrichte *f*. **~burns** *npl* Koteletten *pl*. **~-effect** *n* Nebenwirkung *f*. **~lights** *npl* Standlicht *nt*. **~line** *n* Nebenbeschäftigung *f*. **~-show** *n* Nebenattraktion *f*. **~-step** *vt* ausweichen (+ *dat*). **~-track** *vt* ablenken. **~walk** *n* (*Amer*) Bürgersteig *m*. **~ways** *adv* seitwärts
siding /'saɪdɪŋ/ *n* Abstellgleis *nt*
sidle /'saɪdl/ *vi* sich heranschleichen (**up to** an + *acc*)
siege /si:dʒ/ *n* Belagerung *f*; (*by police*) Umstellung *f*
sieve /sɪv/ *n* Sieb *nt* ● *vt* sieben
sift /sɪft/ *vt* sieben; (*fig*) durchsehen
sigh /saɪ/ *n* Seufzer *m* ● *vi* seufzen
sight /saɪt/ *n* Sicht *f*; (*faculty*) Sehvermögen *nt*; (*spectacle*) Anblick *m*; (*on gun*) Visier *nt*; **~s** *pl* Sehenswürdigkeiten *pl*; **at first ~** auf den ersten Blick; **within/out of ~** in/außer Sicht; **lose ~ of** aus dem Auge verlieren; **know by ~** vom Sehen kennen; **have bad ~** schlechte Augen haben ● *vt* sichten
'**sightseeing** *n* **go ~** die Sehenswürdigkeiten besichtigen
sign /saɪn/ *n* Zeichen *nt*; (*notice*) Schild *nt* ● *vt/i* unterschreiben; (*author, artist:*) signieren. **~ on** *vi* (*as unemployed*) sich arbeitslos melden; (*Mil*) sich verpflichten
signal /'sɪgnl/ *n* Signal *nt* ● *vt/i* (*pt/pp* **signalled**) signalisieren; **~ to s.o.** jdm ein Signal geben (**to** zu). **~-box** *n* Stellwerk *nt*
signature /'sɪgnətʃə(r)/ *n* Unterschrift *f*; (*of artist*) Signatur *f*. **~ tune** *n* Kennmelodie *f*
signet-ring /'sɪgnɪt-/ *n* Siegelring *m*
significan|ce /sɪg'nɪfɪkəns/ *n* Bedeutung *f*. **~t** *a*, **-ly** *adv* bedeutungsvoll; (*important*) bedeutend
signify /'sɪgnɪfaɪ/ *vt* (*pt/pp* **-ied**) bedeuten
signpost /'saɪn-/ *n* Wegweiser *m*
silence /'saɪləns/ *n* Stille *f*; (*of person*) Schweigen *nt* ● *vt* zum Schweigen bringen. **~r** *n* (*on gun*)

Schalldämpfer *m*; (*Auto*) Auspufftopf *m*
silent /'saɪlənt/ *a*, **-ly** *adv* still; (*without speaking*) schweigend; **remain ~** schweigen. **~ film** *n* Stummfilm *m*
silhouette /sɪlu:'et/ *n* Silhouette *f*; (*picture*) Schattenriß *m* ● *vt* **be ~d** sich als Silhouette abheben
silicon /'sɪlɪkən/ *n* Silizium *nt*
silk /sɪlk/ *n* Seide *f* ● *attrib* Seiden-. **~worm** *n* Seidenraupe *f*
silky /'sɪlkɪ/ *a* (**-ier, -iest**) seidig
sill /sɪl/ *n* Sims *m* & *nt*
silly /'sɪlɪ/ *a* (**-ier, -iest**) dumm, albern
silo /'saɪləʊ/ *n* Silo *m*
silt /sɪlt/ *n* Schlick *m*
silver /'sɪlvə(r)/ *a* silbern; (*coin, paper*) Silber- ● *n* Silber *nt*
silver: ~-plated *a* versilbert. **~ware** *n* Silber *nt*. **~ 'wedding** *n* Silberhochzeit *f*
similar /'sɪmɪlə(r)/ *a*, **-ly** *adv* ähnlich. **~ity** /-'lærətɪ/ *n* Ähnlichkeit *f*
simile /'sɪmɪlɪ/ *n* Vergleich *m*
simmer /'sɪmə(r)/ *vi* leise kochen, ziehen ● *vt* ziehen lassen
simple /'sɪmpl/ *a* (**-r, -st**) einfach; (*person*) einfältig. **~-'minded** *a* einfältig. **~ton** /'sɪmpltən/ *n* Einfaltspinsel *m*
simplicity /sɪm'plɪsətɪ/ *n* Einfachheit *f*
simpli|fication /sɪmplɪfɪ'keɪʃn/ *n* Vereinfachung *f*. **~fy** /'sɪmplɪfaɪ/ *vt* (*pt/pp* **-ied**) vereinfachen
simply /'sɪmplɪ/ *adv* einfach
simulat|e /'sɪmjʊleɪt/ *vt* vortäuschen; (*Techn*) simulieren. **~ion** /-'leɪʃn/ *n* Vortäuschung *f*; Simulation *f*
simultaneous /sɪml'teɪnɪəs/ *a*, **-ly** *adv* gleichzeitig; (*interpreting*) Simultan-
sin /sɪn/ *n* Sünde *f* ● *vi* (*pt/pp* **sinned**) sündigen
since /sɪns/ *prep* seit (+ *dat*) ● *adv* seitdem ● *conj* seit; (*because*) da
sincere /sɪn'sɪə(r)/ *a* aufrichtig; (*heartfelt*) herzlich. **~ly** *adv* aufrichtig; **Yours ~ly** Mit freundlichen Grüßen
sincerity /sɪn'serətɪ/ *n* Aufrichtigkeit *f*
sinew /'sɪnju:/ *n* Sehne *f*
sinful /'sɪnfl/ *a* sündhaft
sing /sɪŋ/ *vt/i* (*pt* **sang**, *pp* **sung**) singen

singe /sɪndʒ/ vt (pres p **singeing**) versengen

singer /'sɪŋə(r)/ n Sänger(in) m(f)

single /'sɪŋgl/ a einzeln; (one only) einzig; (unmarried) ledig; ⟨ticket⟩ einfach; ⟨room, bed⟩ Einzel-. ● n ⟨ticket⟩ einfache Fahrkarte f; ⟨record⟩ Single f; ~s pl (Tennis) Einzel nt ● vt ~ out auswählen

single: ~-**breasted** a einreihig. ~-**handed** a & adv allein. ~-**minded** a zielstrebig. ~ **'parent** n Alleinerziehende(r) m/f

singlet /'sɪŋglɪt/ n Unterhemd nt

singly /'sɪŋglɪ/ adv einzeln

singular /'sɪŋgjʊlə(r)/ a eigenartig; (Gram) im Singular ● n Singular m. ~**ly** adv außerordentlich

sinister /'sɪnɪstə(r)/ a finster

sink /sɪŋk/ n Spülbecken nt ● v (pt **sank**, pp **sunk**) ● vi sinken ● vt versenken ⟨ship⟩; senken ⟨shaft⟩. ~ **in** vi einsinken; (fam: be understood) kapiert werden

'sink unit n Spüle f

sinner /'sɪnə(r)/ n Sünder(in) m(f)

sinus /'saɪnəs/ n Nebenhöhle f

sip /sɪp/ n Schlückchen nt ● vt (pt/pp **sipped**) in kleinen Schlucken trinken

siphon /'saɪfn/ n ⟨bottle⟩ Siphon m. ~ **off** vt mit einem Saugheber ablassen

sir /sɜː(r)/ n mein Herr; **S**~ ⟨title⟩ Sir; **Dear S**~**s** Sehr geehrte Herren

siren /'saɪrən/ n Sirene f

sissy /'sɪsɪ/ n Waschlappen m

sister /'sɪstə(r)/ n Schwester f; (nurse) Oberschwester f. ~-**in-law** n (pl ~**s-in-law**) Schwägerin f. ~**ly** a schwesterlich

sit /sɪt/ v (pt/pp **sat**, pres p **sitting**) ● vi sitzen; (sit down) sich setzen; ⟨committee:⟩ tagen ● vt setzen; machen ⟨exam⟩. ~ **back** vi sich zurücklehnen. ~ **down** vi sich setzen. ~ **up** vi [aufrecht] sitzen; (rise) sich aufsetzen; (not slouch) gerade sitzen; (stay up) aufbleiben

site /saɪt/ n Gelände nt; (for camping) Platz m; (Archaeol) Stätte f ● vt legen

sitting /'sɪtɪŋ/ n Sitzung f; (for meals) Schub m

situat|e /'sɪtjʊeɪt/ vt legen; **be** ~**ed** liegen. ~**ion** /-'eɪʃn/ n Lage f; (circumstances) Situation f; (job) Stelle f

six /sɪks/ a sechs. ~**teen** a sechzehn. ~**teenth** a sechzehnte(r,s)

sixth /sɪksθ/ a sechste(r,s)

sixtieth /'sɪkstɪɪθ/ a sechzigste(r,s)

sixty /'sɪkstɪ/ a sechzig

size /saɪz/ n Größe f ● vt ~ **up** (fam) taxieren

sizeable /'saɪzəbl/ a ziemlich groß

sizzle /'sɪzl/ vi brutzeln

skate[1] /skeɪt/ n inv (fish) Rochen m

skate[2] n Schlittschuh m; (roller-) Rollschuh m ● vi Schlittschuh/Rollschuh laufen. ~**r** n Eisläufer(in) m(f); Rollschuhläufer(in) m(f)

skating /'skeɪtɪŋ/ n Eislaufen nt. ~-**rink** n Eisbahn f

skeleton /'skelɪtn/ n Skelett nt. ~ **'key** n Dietrich m. ~ **'staff** n Minimalbesetzung f

sketch /sketʃ/ n Skizze f; (Theat) Sketch m ● vt skizzieren

sketchy /'sketʃɪ/ a (-ier, -iest), -**ily** adv skizzenhaft

skew /skjuː/ n **on the** ~ schräg

skewer /'skjʊə(r)/ n [Brat]spieß m

ski /skiː/ n Ski m ● vi (pt/pp **skied**, pres p **skiing**) Ski fahren or laufen

skid /skɪd/ n Schleudern nt ● vi (pt/pp **skidded**) schleudern

skier /'skiːə(r)/ n Skiläufer(in) m(f)

skiing /'skiːɪŋ/ n Skilaufen nt

skilful /'skɪlfl/ a, -**ly** adv geschickt

skill /skɪl/ n Geschick nt. ~**ed** a geschickt; (trained) ausgebildet

skim /skɪm/ vt (pt/pp **skimmed**) entrahmen ⟨milk⟩. ~ **off** vt abschöpfen. ~ **through** vt überfliegen

skimp /skɪmp/ vi sparen an (+ dat)

skimpy /'skɪmpɪ/ a (-ier, -iest) knapp

skin /skɪn/ n Haut f; (on fruit) Schale f ● vt (pt/pp **skinned**) häuten; schälen ⟨fruit⟩

skin: ~-**deep** a oberflächlich. ~-**diving** n Sporttauchen nt

skinflint /'skɪnflɪnt/ n Geizhals m

skinny /'skɪnɪ/ a (-ier, -iest) dünn

skip[1] /skɪp/ n Container m

skip[2] n Hüpfer m ● v (pt/pp **skipped**) vi hüpfen; (with rope) seilspringen ● vt überspringen

skipper /'skɪpə(r)/ n Kapitän m

'skipping-rope n Sprungseil nt

skirmish /'skɜːmɪʃ/ n Gefecht nt

skirt /skɜːt/ n Rock m ● vt herumgehen um

skit /skɪt/ n parodistischer Sketch m

skittle /'skɪtl/ n Kegel m

skive /skaɪv/ vi (fam) blaumachen

skulk /skʌlk/ vi lauern

skull /skʌl/ n Schädel m

skunk /skʌŋk/ n Stinktier nt

sky /skaɪ/ n Himmel m. **~light** n Dachluke f. **~scraper** n Wolkenkratzer m

slab /slæb/ n Platte f; (slice) Scheibe f; (of chocolate) Tafel f

slack /slæk/ a (**-er, -est**) schlaff, locker; (person) nachlässig; (Comm) flau ● vi bummeln

slacken /'slækn/ vi sich lockern; (diminish) nachlassen; (speed:) sich verringern ● vt lockern; (diminish) verringern

slacks /slæks/ npl Hose f

slag /slæg/ n Schlacke f

slain /sleɪn/ see **slay**

slake /sleɪk/ vt löschen

slam /slæm/ v (pt/pp **slammed**) ● vt zuschlagen; (put) knallen (fam); (fam: criticize) verreißen ● vi zuschlagen

slander /'slɑ:ndə(r)/ n Verleumdung f ● vt verleumden. **~ous** /-rəs/ a verleumderisch

slang /slæŋ/ n Slang m. **~y** a salopp

slant /slɑ:nt/ n Schräge f; **on the ~** schräg ● vt abschrägen; (fig) färben (report) ● vi sich neigen

slap /slæp/ n Schlag m ● vt (pt/pp **slapped**) schlagen; (put) knallen (fam) ● adv direkt

slap: ~dash a (fam) schludrig. **~-up** a (fam) toll

slash /slæʃ/ n Schlitz m ● vt aufschlitzen; [drastisch] reduzieren (prices)

slat /slæt/ n Latte f

slate /sleɪt/ n Schiefer m ● vt (fam) heruntermachen; verreißen (performance)

slaughter /'slɔ:tə(r)/ n Schlachten nt; (massacre) Gemetzel nt ● vt schlachten; abschlachten. **~house** n Schlachthaus nt

Slav /slɑ:v/ a slawisch ● n Slawe m/ Slawin f

slave /sleɪv/ n Sklave m/Sklavin f ● vi ~ **[away]** schuften. **~-driver** n Leuteschinder m

slav|ery /'sleɪvəri/ n Sklaverei f. **~ish** a, **-ly** adv sklavisch

Slavonic /slə'vɒnɪk/ a slawisch

slay /sleɪ/ vt (pt **slew**, pp **slain**) ermorden

sleazy /'sli:zɪ/ a (**-ier, -iest**) schäbig

sledge /sledʒ/ n Schlitten m. **~-hammer** n Vorschlaghammer m

sleek /sli:k/ a (**-er, -est**) seidig; (wellfed) wohlgenährt

sleep /sli:p/ n Schlaf m; **go to ~** einschlafen; **put to ~** einschläfern ● v (pt/ pp **slept**) ● vi schlafen ● vt (accommodate) Unterkunft bieten für. **~er** n Schläfer(in) m(f); (Rail) Schlafwagen m; (on track) Schwelle f

sleeping: ~-bag n Schlafsack m. **~-car** n Schlafwagen m. **~-pill** n Schlaftablette f

sleep: ~less a schlaflos. **~-walking** n Schlafwandeln nt

sleepy /'sli:pɪ/ a (**-ier, -iest**), **-ily** adv schläfrig

sleet /sli:t/ n Schneeregen m ● vi **it is ~ing** es gibt Schneeregen

sleeve /sli:v/ n Ärmel m; (for record) Hülle f. **~less** a ärmellos

sleigh /sleɪ/ n [Pferde]schlitten m

sleight /slaɪt/ n ~ **of hand** Taschenspielerei f

slender /'slendə(r)/ a schlank; (fig) gering

slept /slept/ see **sleep**

sleuth /slu:θ/ n Detektiv m

slew¹ /slu:/ vi schwenken

slew² see **slay**

slice /slaɪs/ n Scheibe f ● vt in Scheiben schneiden; **~d bread** Schnittbrot nt

slick /slɪk/ a clever ● n (of oil) Ölteppich m

slid|e /slaɪd/ n Rutschbahn f; (for hair) Spange f; (Phot) Dia n ● v (pt/ pp **slid**) ● vi rutschen ● vt schieben. **~ing** a gleitend; (door, seat) Schiebe-

slight /slaɪt/ a (**-er, -est**), **-ly** adv leicht; (importance) gering; (acquaintance) flüchtig; (slender) schlank; **not in the ~est** nicht im geringsten; **~ly better** ein bißchen besser ● vt kränken, beleidigen ● n Beleidigung f

slim /slɪm/ a (**slimmer, slimmest**) schlank; (volume) schmal; (fig) gering ● vi eine Schlankheitskur machen

slim|e /slaɪm/ n Schleim m. **~y** a schleimig

sling /slɪŋ/ n (Med) Schlinge f ● vt (pt/pp **slung**) (fam) schmeißen

slip /slɪp/ n (mistake) Fehler m, (fam) Patzer m; (petticoat) Unterrock m; (for pillow) Bezug m; (paper) Zettel m; **give s.o. the ~** (fam) jdm entwischen; **~ of the tongue** Versprecher m ● v (pt/pp **slipped**) ● vi rutschen; (fall) ausrutschen; (go quickly) schlüpfen; (decline) nachlassen ● vt schieben; **~ s.o.'s mind** jdm entfallen. **~ away** vi sich fortschleichen;

∼ **barrier** *n* Schallmauer *f*. ∼**less** *a*, **-ly** *adv* lautlos

soundly /'saʊndlɪ/ *adv* solide; ⟨*sleep*⟩ fest; ⟨*defeat*⟩ vernichtend

'**soundproof** *a* schalldicht

soup /su:p/ *n* Suppe *f*. ∼**ed-up** *a* (*fam*) ⟨*engine*⟩ frisiert

soup: ∼**-plate** *n* Suppenteller *m*. ∼**-spoon** *n* Suppenlöffel *m*

sour /'saʊə(r)/ *a* (**-er, -est**) sauer; (*bad-tempered*) griesgrämig, verdrießlich

source /sɔ:s/ *n* Quelle *f*

south /saʊθ/ *n* Süden *m*; **to the** ∼ **of** südlich von ● *a* Süd-, süd- ● *adv* nach Süden

south: S∼ '**Africa** *n* Südafrika *nt*. S∼ A'**merica** *n* Südamerika *nt*. ∼-'**east** *n* Südosten *m*

southerly /'sʌðəlɪ/ *a* südlich

southern /'sʌðən/ *a* südlich

South 'Pole *n* Südpol *m*

'**southward[s]** /-wəd[z]/ *adv* nach Süden

souvenir /su:və'nɪə(r)/ *n* Andenken *nt*, Souvenir *nt*

sovereign /'sɒvrɪn/ *a* souverän ● *n* Souverän *m*. ∼**ty** *n* Souveränität *f*

Soviet /'səʊvɪət/ *a* sowjetisch; ∼ **Union** Sowjetunion *f*

sow[1] /saʊ/ *n* Sau *f*

sow[2] /səʊ/ *vt* (*pt* **sowed**, *pp* **sown** or **sowed**) säen

soya /'sɔɪə/ *n* ∼ **bean** Sojabohne *f*

spa /spɑ:/ *n* Heilbad *nt*

space /speɪs/ *n* Raum *m*; (*gap*) Platz *m*; (*Astr*) Weltraum *m*; **leave/clear a** ∼ Platz lassen/schaffen ● *vt* ∼ [**out**] [in Abständen] verteilen

space: ∼**craft** *n* Raumfahrzeug *nt*. ∼**ship** *n* Raumschiff *nt*

spacious /'speɪʃəs/ *a* geräumig

spade /speɪd/ *n* Spaten *m*; (*for child*) Schaufel *f*; ∼**s** *pl* (*Cards*) Pik *nt*; **call a** ∼ **a** ∼ das Kind beim rechten Namen nennen. ∼**work** *n* Vorarbeit *f*

Spain /speɪn/ *n* Spanien *nt*

span[1] /spæn/ *n* Spanne *f*; (*of arch*) Spannweite *f* ● *vt* (*pt/pp* **spanned**) überspannen; umspannen ⟨*time*⟩

span[2] *see* **spick**

Span|iard /'spænjəd/ *n* Spanier(in) *m(f)*. ∼**ish** *a* spanisch ● *n* (*Lang*) Spanisch *nt*; **the** ∼**ish** *pl* die Spanier

spank /spæŋk/ *vt* verhauen

spanner /'spænə(r)/ *n* Schraubenschlüssel *m*

spar /spɑ:(r)/ *vi* (*pt/pp* **sparred**) (*Sport*) sparren; (*argue*) sich zanken

spare /speə(r)/ *a* (*surplus*) übrig; (*additional*) zusätzlich; ⟨*seat, time*⟩ frei; ⟨*room*⟩ Gäste-; ⟨*bed, cup*⟩ Extra- ● *n* (*part*) Ersatzteil *nt* ● *vt* ersparen; (*not hurt*) verschonen; (*do without*) entbehren; (*afford to give*) erübrigen; **to** ∼ (*surplus*) übrig. ∼ '**wheel** *n* Reserverad *nt*

sparing /'speərɪŋ/ *a*, **-ly** *adv* sparsam

spark /spɑ:k/ *n* Funke *m* ● *vt* ∼ **off** zünden; (*fig*) auslösen. ∼**ing-plug** *n* (*Auto*) Zündkerze *f*

sparkl|e /'spɑ:kl/ *n* Funkeln *nt* ● *vi* funkeln. ∼**ing** *a* funkelnd; ⟨*wine*⟩ Schaum-

sparrow /'spærəʊ/ *n* Spatz *m*

sparse /spɑ:s/ *a* spärlich. ∼**ly** *adv* spärlich; ⟨*populated*⟩ dünn

Spartan /'spɑ:tn/ *a* spartanisch

spasm /'spæzm/ *n* Anfall *m*; (*cramp*) Krampf *m*. ∼**odic** /-'mɒdɪk/ *a*, **-ally** *adv* sporadisch; (*Med*) krampfartig

spastic /'spæstɪk/ *a* spastisch [gelähmt] ● *n* Spastiker(in) *m(f)*

spat /spæt/ *see* **spit**[2]

spate /speɪt/ *n* Flut *f*; (*series*) Serie *f*; **be in full** ∼ Hochwasser führen

spatial /'speɪʃl/ *a* räumlich

spatter /'spætə(r)/ *vt* spritzen; ∼ **with** bespritzen mit

spatula /'spætjʊlə/ *n* Spachtel *m*; (*Med*) Spatel *m*

spawn /spɔ:n/ *n* Laich *m* ● *vi* laichen ● *vt* (*fig*) hervorbringen

spay /speɪ/ *vt* sterilisieren

speak /spi:k/ *v* (*pt* **spoke**, *pp* **spoken**) ● *vi* sprechen (**to** mit); ∼**ing!** (*Teleph*) am Apparat! ● *vt* sprechen; sagen ⟨*truth*⟩. ∼ **up** *vi* lauter sprechen; ∼ **up for oneself** seine Meinung äußern

speaker /'spi:kə(r)/ *n* Sprecher(in) *m(f)*; (*in public*) Redner(in) *m(f)*; (*loudspeaker*) Lautsprecher *m*

spear /spɪə(r)/ *n* Speer *m* ● *vt* aufspießen. ∼**head** *vt* (*fig*) anführen

spec /spek/ *n* **on** ∼ (*fam*) auf gut Glück

special /'speʃl/ *a* besondere(r,s), speziell. ∼**ist** *n* Spezialist *m*; (*Med*) Facharzt *m*/-ärztin *f*. ∼**ity** /-ʃɪ'ælətɪ/ *n* Spezialität *f*

special|ize /'speʃəlaɪz/ *vi* sich spezialisieren (**in** auf + *acc*). ∼**ly** *adv* speziell; (*particularly*) besonders

species /'spi:ʃi:z/ *n* Art *f*

specific /spə'sɪfɪk/ *a* bestimmt; (*precise*) genau; (*Phys*) spezifisch. ∼**ally** *adv* ausdrücklich

specification /spesɪfɪ'keɪʃn/ n & ~s pl genaue Angaben pl

specify /'spesɪfaɪ/ vt (pt/pp -ied) [genau] angeben

specimen /'spesɪmən/ n Exemplar nt; (sample) Probe f; (of urine) Urinprobe f

speck /spek/ n Fleck m; (particle) Teilchen nt

speckled /'spekld/ a gesprenkelt

specs /speks/ npl (fam) Brille f

spectacle /'spektəkl/ n (show) Schauspiel nt; (sight) Anblick m. ~s npl Brille f

spectacular /spek'tækjʊlə(r)/ a spektakulär

spectator /spek'teɪtə(r)/ n Zuschauer(in) m(f)

spectre /'spektə(r)/ n Gespenst nt; (fig) Schreckgespenst nt

spectrum /'spektrəm/ n (pl -tra) Spektrum nt

speculat|e /'spekjʊleɪt/ vi spekulieren. ~ion /-'leɪʃn/ n Spekulation f. ~or n Spekulant m

sped /sped/ see **speed**

speech /spiːtʃ/ n Sprache f; (address) Rede f. ~less a sprachlos

speed /spiːd/ n Geschwindigkeit f; (rapidity) Schnelligkeit f; (gear) Gang m; **at** ~ mit hoher Geschwindigkeit ● vi (pt/pp sped) schnell fahren ● (pt/pp speeded) (go too fast) zu schnell fahren. ~ **up** (pt/pp speeded up) ● vt beschleunigen ● vi schneller werden; (vehicle:) schneller fahren

speed: ~**boat** n Rennboot nt. ~**ing** n Geschwindigkeitsüberschreitung f. ~ **limit** n Geschwindigkeitsbeschränkung f

speedometer /spiː'dɒmɪtə(r)/ n Tachometer m

speedy /'spiːdɪ/ a (-ier, -iest), -ily adv schnell

spell[1] /spel/ n Weile f; (of weather) Periode f

spell[2] v (pt/pp spelled or spelt) ● vt schreiben; (aloud) buchstabieren; (fig: mean) bedeuten ● vi richtig schreiben; (aloud) buchstabieren. ~ **out** vt buchstabieren; (fig) genau erklären

spell[3] n Zauber m; (words) Zauberspruch m. ~**bound** a wie verzaubert

spelling /'spelɪŋ/ n Schreibweise f; (orthography) Rechtschreibung f

spelt /spelt/ see **spell**[2]

spend /spend/ vt/i (pt/pp spent) ausgeben; verbringen (time)

spent /spent/ see **spend**

sperm /spɜːm/ n Samen m

spew /spjuː/ vt speien

spher|e /sfɪə(r)/ n Kugel f; (fig) Sphäre f. ~**ical** /'sferɪkl/ a kugelförmig

spice /spaɪs/ n Gewürz nt; (fig) Würze f

spick /spɪk/ a ~ **and span** blitzsauber

spicy /'spaɪsɪ/ a würzig, pikant

spider /'spaɪdə(r)/ n Spinne f

spik|e /spaɪk/ n Spitze f; (Bot, Zool) Stachel m; (on shoe) Spike m. ~**y** a stachelig

spill /spɪl/ v (pt/pp spilt or spilled) ● vt verschütten; vergießen (blood) ● vi überlaufen

spin /spɪn/ v (pt/pp spun, pres p spinning) ● vt drehen; spinnen (wool); schleudern (washing) ● vi sich drehen. ~ **out** vt in die Länge ziehen

spinach /'spɪnɪdʒ/ n Spinat m

spinal /'spaɪnl/ a Rückgrat-. ~ '**cord** n Rückenmark nt

spindl|e /'spɪndl/ n Spindel f. ~**y** a spindeldürr

spin-'drier n Wäscheschleuder f

spine /spaɪn/ n Rückgrat nt; (of book) [Buch]rücken m; (Bot, Zool) Stachel m. ~**less** a (fig) rückgratlos

spinning /'spɪnɪŋ/ n Spinnen nt. ~**-wheel** n Spinnrad nt

'spin-off n Nebenprodukt nt

spinster /'spɪnstə(r)/ n ledige Frau f

spiral /'spaɪrl/ a spiralig ● n Spirale f ● vi (pt/pp spiralled) sich hochwinden; (smoke:) in einer Spirale aufsteigen. ~ '**staircase** n Wendeltreppe f

spire /'spaɪə(r)/ n Turmspitze f

spirit /'spɪrɪt/ n Geist m; (courage) Mut m; ~**s** pl (alcohol) Spirituosen pl; **in high** ~**s** in gehobener Stimmung; **in low** ~**s** niedergedrückt. ~ **away** vt verschwinden lassen

spirited /'spɪrɪtɪd/ a lebhaft; (courageous) beherzt

spirit: ~**-level** n Wasserwaage f. ~ **stove** n Spirituskocher m

spiritual /'spɪrɪtjʊəl/ a geistig; (Relig) geistlich. ~**ism** n /-ɪzm/ n Spiritismus m. ~**ist** /-ɪst/ a spiritistisch ● n Spiritist m

spit[1] /spɪt/ n (for roasting) [Brat]spieß m

spit² n Spucke f ● vt/i (pt/pp **spat**, pres p **spitting**) spucken; ⟨cat:⟩ fauchen; ⟨fat:⟩ spritzen; **it's ~ting with rain** es tröpfelt; **be the ~ting image of s.o.** jdm wie aus dem Gesicht geschnitten sein

spite /spaɪt/ n Boshaftigkeit f; **in ~ of** trotz (+ gen) ● vt ärgern. **~ful** a, **-ly** adv gehässig

spittle /'spɪtl/ n Spucke f

splash /splæʃ/ n Platschen nt; (fam: drop) Schuß m; **~ of colour** Farbfleck m ● vt spritzen; **~ s.o. with sth** jdn mit etw bespritzen ● vi spritzen. **~ about** vi planschen

spleen /spli:n/ n Milz f

splendid /'splendɪd/ a herrlich, großartig

splendour /'splendə(r)/ n Pracht f

splint /splɪnt/ n (Med) Schiene f

splinter /'splɪntə(r)/ n Splitter m ● vi zersplittern

split /splɪt/ n Spaltung f; (Pol) Bruch m; (tear) Riß m ● v (pt/pp **split**, pres p **splitting**) ● vt spalten; (share) teilen; (tear) zerreißen; **~ one's sides** sich kaputtlachen ● vi sich spalten; (tear) zerreißen; **~ on s.o.** (fam) jdn verpfeifen. **~ up** vt aufteilen ● vi ⟨couple:⟩ sich trennen

splutter /'splʌtə(r)/ vi prusten

spoil /spɔɪl/ n **~s** pl Beute f ● v (pt/pp **spoilt** or **spoiled**) ● vt verderben; verwöhnen ⟨person⟩ ● vi verderben. **~-sport** n Spielverderber m

spoke¹ /spəʊk/ n Speiche f

spoke², **spoken** /'spəʊkn/ see **speak**

spokesman n Sprecher m

sponge /spʌndʒ/ n Schwamm m ● vt abwaschen ● vi **~ on** schmarotzen bei. **~-bag** n Waschbeutel m. **~-cake** n Biskuitkuchen m

spong|er /'spʌndʒə(r)/ n Schmarotzer m. **~y** a schwammig

sponsor /'spɒnsə(r)/ n Sponsor m; (god-parent) Pate m/Patin f; (for membership) Bürge m ● vt sponsern; bürgen für

spontaneous /spɒn'teɪnɪəs/ a, **-ly** adv spontan

spoof /spu:f/ n (fam) Parodie f

spooky /'spu:kɪ/ a (-ier, -iest) (fam) gespenstisch

spool /spu:l/ n Spule f

spoon /spu:n/ n Löffel m ● vt löffeln. **~-feed** vt (pt/pp **-fed**) (fig) alles vorkauen (+ dat). **~ful** n Löffel m

sporadic /spə'rædɪk/ a, **-ally** adv sporadisch

sport /spɔ:t/ n Sport m; (amusement) Spaß m ● vt [stolz] tragen. **~ing** a sportlich; **a ~ing chance** eine faire Chance

sports: **~ car** n Sportwagen m. **~ coat** n, **~ jacket** n Sakko m. **~man** n Sportler m. **~woman** n Sportlerin f

sporty /'spɔ:tɪ/ a (-ier, -iest) sportlich

spot /spɒt/ n Fleck m; (place) Stelle f; (dot) Punkt m; (drop) Tropfen m; (pimple) Pickel m; **~s** pl (rash) Ausschlag m; **a ~ of** (fam) ein bißchen; **on the ~** auf der Stelle; **be in a tight ~** (fam) in der Klemme sitzen ● vt (pt/pp **spotted**) entdecken

spot: **~ 'check** n Stichprobe f. **~less** a makellos; (fam: very clean) blitzsauber. **~light** n Scheinwerfer m; (fig) Rampenlicht nt

spotted /'spɒtɪd/ a gepunktet

spotty /'spɒtɪ/ a (-ier, -iest) fleckig; (pimply) pickelig

spouse /spaʊz/ n Gatte m/Gattin f

spout /spaʊt/ n Schnabel m, Tülle f ● vi schießen (**from** aus)

sprain /spreɪn/ n Verstauchung f ● vt verstauchen

sprang /spræŋ/ see **spring**²

sprat /spræt/ n Sprotte f

sprawl /sprɔ:l/ vi sich ausstrecken; (fall) der Länge nach hinfallen

spray¹ /spreɪ/ n (of flowers) Strauß m

spray² n Sprühnebel m; (from sea) Gischt m; (device) Spritze f; (container) Sprühdose f; (preparation) Spray nt ● vt spritzen; (with aerosol) sprühen

spread /spred/ n Verbreitung f; (paste) Aufstrich m; (fam: feast) Festessen nt ● v (pt/pp **spread**) ● vt ausbreiten; streichen ⟨butter, jam⟩; bestreichen ⟨bread, surface⟩; streuen ⟨sand, manure⟩; verbreiten ⟨news, disease⟩; verteilen ⟨payments⟩ ● vi sich ausbreiten. **~ out** vt ausbreiten; (space out) verteilen ● vi sich verteilen

spree /spri:/ n (fam) **go on a shopping ~** groß einkaufen gehen

sprig /sprɪg/ n Zweig m

sprightly /'spraɪtlɪ/ a (-ier, -iest) rüstig

spring¹ /sprɪŋ/ n Frühling m ● attrib Frühlings-

spring² n (jump) Sprung m; (water) Quelle f; (device) Feder f; (elasticity) Elastizität f ● v (pt **sprang**, pp **sprung**) ● vi springen; (arise) entspringen

(**from** *dat*) ● *vt* ~ **sth on s.o.** jdn mit etw überfallen
spring: ~**board** *n* Sprungbrett *nt.* ~-'**cleaning** *n* Frühjahrsputz *m.* ~**time** *n* Frühling *m*
sprinkl|e /'sprɪŋkl/ *vt* sprengen; (*scatter*) streuen; bestreuen ⟨surface⟩. ~**er** *n* Sprinkler *m*; (*Hort*) Sprenger *m.* ~**ing** *n* dünne Schicht *f*
sprint /sprɪnt/ *n* Sprint *m* ● *vi* rennen; (*Sport*) sprinten. ~**er** *n* Kurzstreckenläufer(in) *m(f)*
sprout /spraʊt/ *n* Trieb *m*; [**Brussels**] ~**s** *pl* Rosenkohl *m* ● *vi* sprießen
spruce /spruːs/ *a* gepflegt ● *n* Fichte *f*
sprung /sprʌŋ/ *see* **spring²** ● *a* gefedert
spry /spraɪ/ *a* (**-er, -est**) rüstig
spud /spʌd/ *n* (*fam*) Kartoffel *f*
spun /spʌn/ *see* **spin**
spur /spɜː(r)/ *n* Sporn *m*; (*stimulus*) Ansporn *m*; (*road*) Nebenstraße *f*; **on the ~ of the moment** ganz spontan ● *vt* (*pt/pp* **spurred**) ~ [**on**] (*fig*) anspornen
spurious /'spjʊərɪəs/ *a*, **-ly** *adv* falsch
spurn /spɜːn/ *vt* verschmähen
spurt /spɜːt/ *n* Strahl *m*; (*Sport*) Spurt *m*; **put on a ~** spurten ● *vi* spritzen
spy /spaɪ/ *n* Spion(in) *m(f)* ● *vi* spionieren; ~ **on s.o.** jdm nachspionieren ● *vt* (*fam: see*) sehen. ~ **out** *vt* auskundschaften
spying /'spaɪɪŋ/ *n* Spionage *f*
squabble /'skwɒbl/ *n* Zank *m* ● *vi* sich zanken
squad /skwɒd/ *n* Gruppe *f*; (*Sport*) Mannschaft *f*
squadron /'skwɒdrən/ *n* (*Mil*) Geschwader *nt*
squalid /'skwɒlɪd/ *a*, **-ly** *adv* schmutzig
squall /skwɔːl/ *n* Bö *f* ● *vi* brüllen
squalor /'skwɒlə(r)/ *n* Schmutz *m*
squander /'skwɒndə(r)/ *vt* vergeuden
square /skweə(r)/ *a* quadratisch; ⟨metre, mile⟩ Quadrat-; ⟨meal⟩ anständig; **all ~** (*fam*) quitt ● *n* Quadrat *nt*; (*area*) Platz *m*; (*on chessboard*) Feld *nt* ● *vt* (*settle*) klären; (*Math*) quadrieren ● *vi* (*agree*) übereinstimmen
squash /skwɒʃ/ *n* Gedränge *nt*; (*drink*) Fruchtsaftgetränk *nt*; (*Sport*) Squash *nt* ● *vt* zerquetschen; (*suppress*) niederschlagen. ~**y** *a* weich

squat /skwɒt/ *a* gedrungen ● *n* (*fam*) besetztes Haus *nt* ● *vi* (*pt/pp* **squatted**) hocken; ~ **in a house** ein Haus besetzen. ~**ter** *n* Hausbesetzer *m*
squawk /skwɔːk/ *vi* krächzen
squeak /skwiːk/ *n* Quieken *nt*; (*of hinge, brakes*) Quietschen *nt* ● *vi* quieken; quietschen
squeal /skwiːl/ *n* Schrei *m*; (*screech*) Kreischen *nt* ● *vi* schreien; kreischen
squeamish /'skwiːmɪʃ/ *a* empfindlich
squeeze /skwiːz/ *n* Druck *m*; (*crush*) Gedränge *nt* ● *vt* drücken; (*to get juice*) ausdrücken; (*force*) zwängen; (*fam: extort*) herauspressen (**from** aus) ● *vi* ~ **in/out** sich hinein-/hinauszwängen
squelch /skweltʃ/ *vi* quatschen
squid /skwɪd/ *n* Tintenfisch *m*
squiggle /'skwɪgl/ *n* Schnörkel *m*
squint /skwɪnt/ *n* Schielen *nt* ● *vi* schielen
squire /'skwaɪə(r)/ *n* Gutsherr *m*
squirm /skwɜːm/ *vi* sich winden
squirrel /'skwɪrl/ *n* Eichhörnchen *nt*
squirt /skwɜːt/ *n* Spritzer *m* ● *vt/i* spritzen
St *abbr* (**Saint**) St.; (**Street**) Str.
stab /stæb/ *n* Stich *m*; (*fam: attempt*) Versuch *m* ● *vt* (*pt/pp* **stabbed**) stechen; (*to death*) erstechen
stability /stə'bɪlətɪ/ *n* Stabilität *f*
stabilize /'steɪbɪlaɪz/ *vt* stabilisieren ● *vi* sich stabilisieren
stable¹ /'steɪbl/ *a* (**-r, -st**) stabil
stable² *n* Stall *m*; (*establishment*) Reitstall *m*
stack /stæk/ *n* Stapel *m*; (*of chimney*) Schornstein *m*; (*fam: large quantity*) Haufen *m* ● *vt* stapeln
stadium /'steɪdɪəm/ *n* Stadion *nt*
staff /stɑːf/ *n* (*stick & Mil*) Stab *m* ● (*& pl*) (*employees*) Personal *nt*; (*Sch*) Lehrkräfte *pl* ● *vt* mit Personal besetzen. ~-**room** *n* (*Sch*) Lehrerzimmer *nt*
stag /stæg/ *n* Hirsch *m*
stage /steɪdʒ/ *n* Bühne *f*; (*in journey*) Etappe *f*; (*in process*) Stadium *nt*; **by** *or* **in** ~**s** in Etappen ● *vt* aufführen; (*arrange*) veranstalten
stage: ~ **door** *n* Bühneneingang *m.* ~ **fright** *n* Lampenfieber *nt*
stagger /'stægə(r)/ *vi* taumeln ● *vt* staffeln ⟨holidays⟩; versetzt anordnen ⟨seats⟩; **I was** ~**ed** es hat mir die

Sprache verschlagen. ~**ing** a unglaublich

stagnant /'stægnənt/ a stehend; (*fig*) stagnierend

stagnat|e /stæg'neɪt/ vi (*fig*) stagnieren. ~**ion** /-'neɪʃn/ n Stagnation f

staid /steɪd/ a gesetzt

stain /steɪn/ n Fleck m; (*for wood*) Beize f ● vt färben; beizen (*wood*); (*fig*) beflecken; ~**ed glass** farbiges Glas nt. ~**less** a fleckenlos; (*steel*) rostfrei. ~ **remover** n Fleckentferner m

stair /steə(r)/ n Stufe f; ~**s** pl Treppe f. ~**case** n Treppe f

stake /steɪk/ n Pfahl m; (*wager*) Einsatz m; (*Comm*) Anteil m; **be at** ~ auf dem Spiel stehen ● vt [an einem Pfahl] anbinden; (*wager*) setzen; ~ **a claim to sth** Anspruch auf etw (*acc*) erheben

stale /steɪl/ a (**-r, -st**) alt; (*air*) verbraucht. ~**mate** n Patt nt

stalk[1] /stɔːk/ n Stiel m, Stengel m

stalk[2] vt pirschen auf (+ *acc*) ● vi stolzieren

stall /stɔːl/ n Stand m; ~**s** pl (*Theat*) Parkett nt ● vi (*engine:*) stehenbleiben; (*fig*) ausweichen ● vt abwürgen (*engine*)

stallion /'stæljən/ n Hengst m

stalwart /'stɔːlwət/ a treu ● n treuer Anhänger m

stamina /'stæmɪnə/ n Ausdauer f

stammer /'stæmə(r)/ n Stottern nt ● vt/i stottern

stamp /stæmp/ n Stempel m; (*postage* ~) [Brief]marke f ● vt stempeln; (*impress*) prägen; (*put postage on*) frankieren; ~ **one's feet** mit den Füßen stampfen ● vi stampfen. ~ **out** vt [aus]stanzen; (*fig*) ausmerzen

stampede /stæm'piːd/ n wilde Flucht f; (*fam*) Ansturm m ● vi in Panik fliehen

stance /stɑːns/ n Haltung f

stand /stænd/ n Stand m; (*rack*) Ständer m; (*pedestal*) Sockel m; (*Sport*) Tribüne f; (*fig*) Einstellung f ● v (*pt/pp* **stood**) ● vi stehen; (*rise*) aufstehen; (*be candidate*) kandidieren; (*stay valid*) gültig bleiben; ~ **still** stillstehen; ~ **firm** (*fig*) festbleiben; ~ **together** zusammenhalten; ~ **to lose/ gain** gewinnen/verlieren können; ~ **to reason** logisch sein; ~ **in for** vertreten; ~ **for** (*mean*) bedeuten; **I won't** ~ **for that** das lasse ich mir nicht bieten

● vt stellen; (*withstand*) standhalten (+ *dat*); (*endure*) ertragen; vertragen (*climate*); (*put up with*) aushalten; haben (*chance*); ~ **one's ground** nicht nachgeben; ~ **the test of time** sich bewähren; ~ **s.o. a beer** jdm ein Bier spendieren; **I can't** ~ **her** (*fam*) ich kann sie nicht ausstehen. ~ **by** vi danebenstehen; (*be ready*) sich bereithalten ● vt ~ **by s.o.** (*fig*) zu jdm stehen. ~ **down** vi (*retire*) zurücktreten. ~ **out** vi hervorstehen; (*fig*) herausragen. ~ **up** vi aufstehen; ~ **up for** eintreten für; ~ **up to** sich wehren gegen

standard /'stændəd/ a Normal-; **be** ~ **practice** allgemein üblich sein ● n Maßstab m; (*Techn*) Norm f; (*level*) Niveau nt; (*flag*) Standarte f; ~**s** pl (*morals*) Prinzipien pl; ~ **of living** Lebensstandard m. ~**ize** vt standardisieren; (*Techn*) normen

standard lamp n Stehlampe f

stand-in n Ersatz m

standing /'stændɪŋ/ a (*erect*) stehend; (*permanent*) ständig ● n Rang m; (*duration*) Dauer f. ~ **order** n Dauerauftrag m. ~**room** n Stehplätze pl

stand: ~**offish** /stænd'ɒfɪʃ/ a distanziert. ~**point** n Standpunkt m. ~**still** n Stillstand m; **come to a** ~**still** zum Stillstand kommen

stank /stæŋk/ *see* **stink**

staple[1] /'steɪpl/ a Grund- ● n (*product*) Haupterzeugnis nt

staple[2] n Heftklammer f ● vt heften. ~**r** n Heftmaschine f

star /stɑː(r)/ n Stern m; (*asterisk*) Sternchen nt; (*Theat, Sport*) Star m ● vi (*pt/pp* **starred**) die Hauptrolle spielen

starboard /'stɑːbəd/ n Steuerbord nt

starch /stɑːtʃ/ n Stärke f ● vt stärken. ~**y** a stärkehaltig; (*fig*) steif

stare /steə(r)/ n Starren nt ● vi starren; ~ **at** anstarren

starfish n Seestern m

stark /stɑːk/ a (**-er, -est**) scharf; (*contrast*) kraß ● adv ~ **naked** splitternackt

starling /'stɑːlɪŋ/ n Star m

starlit a sternhell

starry /'stɑːrɪ/ a sternklar

start /stɑːt/ n Anfang m, Beginn m; (*departure*) Aufbruch m; (*Sport*) Start m; **from the** ~ von Anfang an;

for a ~ erstens ● *vi* anfangen, beginnen; (*set out*) aufbrechen; ⟨*engine:*⟩ anspringen; (*Auto, Sport*) starten; (*jump*) aufschrecken; **to** ~ **with** zuerst ● *vt* anfangen, beginnen; (*cause*) verursachen; (*found*) gründen; starten ⟨*car, race*⟩; in Umlauf setzen ⟨*rumour*⟩. ~**er** *n* (*Culin*) Vorspeise *f*; (*Auto, Sport*) Starter *m*. ~**ing-point** *n* Ausgangspunkt *m*

startle /'stɑːtl/ *vt* erschrecken

starvation /stɑːˈveɪʃn/ *n* Verhungern *nt*

starve /stɑːv/ *vi* hungern; (*to death*) verhungern ● *vt* verhungern lassen

stash /stæʃ/ *vt* (*fam*) ~ **[away]** beiseite schaffen

state /steɪt/ *n* Zustand *m*; (*grand style*) Prunk *m*; (*Pol*) Staat *m*; ~ **of play** Spielstand *m*; **be in a** ~ ⟨*person:*⟩ aufgeregt sein; **lie in** ~ feierlich aufgebahrt sein ● *attrib* Staats-, staatlich ● *vt* erklären; (*speci- fy*) angeben. ~**-aided** *a* staatlich gefördert. ~**less** *a* staatenlos

stately /'steɪtlɪ/ *a* (**-ier, -iest**) stattlich. ~ **'home** *n* Schloß *nt*

statement /'steɪtmənt/ *n* Erklärung *f*; (*Jur*) Aussage *f*; (*Banking*) Auszug *m*

'statesman *n* Staatsmann *m*

static /'stætɪk/ *a* statisch; **remain** ~ unverändert bleiben

station /'steɪʃn/ *n* Bahnhof *m*; (*police*) Wache *f*; (*radio*) Sender *m*; (*space, weather*) Station *f*; (*Mil*) Posten *m*; (*status*) Rang *m* ● *vt* stationieren; (*post*) postieren. ~**ary** /-ərɪ/ *a* stehend; **be** ~**ary** stehen

stationer /'steɪʃənə(r)/ *n* ~'**s [shop]** Schreibwarengeschäft *nt*. ~**y** *n* Briefpapier *nt*; (*writing-materials*) Schreibwaren *pl*

'station-wagon *n* (*Amer*) Kombi[wagen] *m*

statistic /stəˈtɪstɪk/ *n* statistische Tatsache *f*. ~**al** *a*, **-ly** *adv* statistisch. ~**s** *n* & *pl* Statistik *f*

statue /'stætjuː/ *n* Statue *f*

stature /'stætʃə(r)/ *n* Statur *f*; (*fig*) Format *nt*

status /'steɪtəs/ *n* Status *m*, Rang *m*. ~ **symbol** *n* Statussymbol *nt*

statut|e /'stætjuːt/ *n* Statut *nt*. ~**ory** *a* gesetzlich

staunch /stɔːntʃ/ *a* (**-er, -est**), **-ly** *adv* treu

stave /steɪv/ *vt* ~ **off** abwenden

stay /steɪ/ *n* Aufenthalt *m* ● *vi* bleiben; (*reside*) wohnen; ~ **the night** übernachten; ~ **put** dableiben ● *vt* ~ **the course** durchhalten. ~ **away** *vi* wegbleiben. ~ **behind** *vi* zurückbleiben. ~ **in** *vi* zu Hause bleiben; (*Sch*) nachsitzen. ~ **up** *vi* oben bleiben; (*upright*) stehen bleiben; (*on wall*) hängen bleiben; ⟨*person:*⟩ aufbleiben

stead /sted/ *n* **in his** ~ an seiner Stelle; **stand s.o. in good** ~ jdm zustatten kommen. ~**fast** *a*, **-ly** *adv* standhaft

steadily /'stedɪlɪ/ *adv* fest; (*continually*) stetig

steady /'stedɪ/ *a* (**-ier, -iest**) fest; (*not wobbly*) stabil; ⟨*hand*⟩ ruhig; (*regular*) regelmäßig; (*dependable*) zuverlässig

steak /steɪk/ *n* Steak *nt*

steal /stiːl/ *vt/i* (*pt* **stole**, *pp* **stolen**) stehlen (**from** *dat*). ~ **in/out** *vi* sich hinein-/hinausstehlen

stealth /stelθ/ *n* Heimlichkeit *f*; **by** ~ heimlich. ~**y** *a* heimlich

steam /stiːm/ *n* Dampf *m*; **under one's own** ~ (*fam*) aus eigener Kraft ● *vt* (*Culin*) dämpfen, dünsten ● *vi* dampfen. ~ **up** *vi* beschlagen

'steam-engine *n* Dampfmaschine *f*; (*Rail*) Dampflokomotive *f*

steamer /'stiːmə(r)/ *n* Dampfer *m*

'steamroller *n* Dampfwalze *f*

steamy /'stiːmɪ/ *a* dampfig

steel /stiːl/ *n* Stahl *m* ● *vt* ~ **oneself** allen Mut zusammennehmen

steep[1] /stiːp/ *vt* (*soak*) einweichen

steep[2] *a*, **-ly** *adv* steil; (*fam: exorbitant*) gesalzen

steeple /'stiːpl/ *n* Kirchturm *m*. ~**chase** *n* Hindernisrennen *nt*

steer /stɪə(r)/ *vt/i* steuern; ~ **clear of s.o./sth** jdm/etw aus dem Weg gehen. ~**ing** *n* (*Auto*) Steuerung *f*. ~**ing-wheel** *n* Lenkrad *nt*

stem[1] /stem/ *n* Stiel *m*; (*of word*) Stamm *m* ● *vi* (*pt/pp* **stemmed**) ~ **from** zurückzuführen sein auf (+ *acc*)

stem[2] *vt* (*pt/pp* **stemmed**) eindämmen; stillen ⟨*bleeding*⟩

stench /stentʃ/ *n* Gestank *m*

stencil /'stensl/ *n* Schablone *f*; (*for typing*) Matrize *f*

step /step/ *n* Schritt *m*; (*stair*) Stufe *f*; ~**s** *pl* (*ladder*) Trittleiter *f*; **in** ~ im Schritt; ~ **by** ~ Schritt für Schritt; **take** ~**s** (*fig*) Schritte unternehmen ● *vi* (*pt/pp* **stepped**) treten; ~ **in** (*fig*) eingreifen; ~ **into s.o.'s shoes** an jds

Stelle treten; ∼ **out of line** aus der Reihe tanzen. ∼ **up** *vi* hinaufsteigen ● *vt* (*increase*) erhöhen, steigern; verstärken ⟨*efforts*⟩

step: ∼**brother** *n* Stiefbruder *m*. ∼**child** *n* Stiefkind *nt*. ∼**daughter** *n* Stieftochter *f*. ∼**father** *n* Stiefvater *m*. ∼**ladder** *n* Trittleiter *f*. ∼**mother** *n* Stiefmutter *f*

'**stepping-stone** *n* Trittstein *m*; (*fig*) Sprungbrett *nt*

step: ∼**sister** *n* Stiefschwester *f*. ∼**son** *n* Stiefsohn *m*

stereo /'steriəʊ/ *n* Stereo *nt*; (*equipment*) Stereoanlage *f*; **in** ∼ stereo. ∼**phonic** /-'fɒnɪk/ *a* stereophon

stereotype /'steriətaɪp/ *n* stereotype Figur *f*. ∼**d** *a* stereotyp

steril|e /'steraɪl/ *a* steril. ∼**ity** /stə'rɪlətɪ/ *n* Sterilität *f*

steriliz|ation /sterəlaɪ'zeɪʃn/ *n* Sterilisation *f*. ∼**e** *vt* sterilisieren

sterling /'stɜːlɪŋ/ *a* Sterling-; (*fig*) gediegen ● *n* Sterling *m*

stern[1] /stɜːn/ *a* (**-er**, **-est**), **-ly** *adv* streng

stern[2] *n* (*of boat*) Heck *nt*

stew /stjuː/ *n* Eintopf *m*; **in a** ∼ (*fam*) aufgeregt ● *vt/i* schmoren; ∼**ed fruit** Kompott *nt*

steward /'stjuːəd/ *n* Ordner *m*; (*on ship, aircraft*) Steward *m*. ∼**ess** *n* Stewardeß *f*

stick[1] /stɪk/ *n* Stock *m*; (*of chalk*) Stück *nt*; (*of rhubarb*) Stange *f*; (*Sport*) Schläger *m*

stick[2] *v* (*pt/pp* **stuck**) ● *vt* stecken; (*stab*) stechen; (*glue*) kleben; (*fam: put*) tun; (*fam: endure*) aushalten ● *vi* stecken; (*adhere*) kleben, haften (**to** an + *dat*); (*jam*) klemmen; ∼ **to sth** (*fig*) bei etw bleiben; ∼ **at it** (*fam*) dranbleiben; ∼ **at nothing** (*fam*) vor nichts zurückschrecken; ∼ **up for** (*fam*) eintreten für; **be stuck** nicht weiterkönnen; ⟨*vehicle:*⟩ festsitzen, festgefahren sein; ⟨*drawer:*⟩ klemmen; **be stuck with sth** (*fam*) etw am Hals haben. ∼ **out** *vi* abstehen; ⟨*project*⟩ vorstehen ● *vt* (*fam*) hinausstrecken; herausstrecken ⟨*tongue*⟩

sticker /'stɪkə(r)/ *n* Aufkleber *m*

'**sticking plaster** *n* Heftpflaster *nt*

stickler /'stɪklə(r)/ *n* **be a** ∼ **for** es sehr genau nehmen mit

sticky /'stɪkɪ/ *a* (**-ier**, **-iest**) klebrig; (*adhesive*) Klebe-

stiff /stɪf/ *a* (**-er**, **-est**), **-ly** *adv* steif; ⟨*brush*⟩ hart; ⟨*dough*⟩ fest; (*difficult*) schwierig; ⟨*penalty*⟩ schwer; **be bored** ∼ (*fam*) sich zu Tode langweilen. ∼**en** *vt* steif machen ● *vi* steif werden. ∼**ness** *n* Steifheit *f*

stifl|e /'staɪfl/ *vt* ersticken; (*fig*) unterdrücken. ∼**ing** *a* **be** ∼**ing** zum Ersticken sein

stigma /'stɪgmə/ *n* Stigma *nt*

stile /staɪl/ *n* Zauntritt *m*

stiletto /stɪ'letəʊ/ *n* Stilett *nt*; (*heel*) Bleistiftabsatz *m*

still[1] /stɪl/ *n* Destillierapparat *m*

still[2] *a* still; ⟨*drink*⟩ ohne Kohlensäure; **keep** ∼ stillhalten; **stand** ∼ stillstehen ● *n* Stille *f* ● *adv* noch; (*emphatic*) immer noch; (*nevertheless*) trotzdem; ∼ **not** immer noch nicht

'**stillborn** *a* totgeboren

still 'life *n* Stilleben *nt*

stilted /'stɪltɪd/ *a* gestelzt, geschraubt

stilts /stɪlts/ *npl* Stelzen *pl*

stimulant /'stɪmjʊlənt/ *n* Anregungsmittel *nt*

stimulat|e /'stɪmjʊleɪt/ *vt* anregen. ∼**ion** /-'leɪʃn/ *n* Anregung *f*

stimulus /'stɪmjʊləs/ *n* (*pl* **-li** /-laɪ/) Reiz *m*

sting /stɪŋ/ *n* Stich *m*; (*from nettle, jellyfish*) Brennen *nt*; (*organ*) Stachel *m* ● *v* (*pt/pp* **stung**) ● *vt* stechen ● *vi* brennen; ⟨*insect:*⟩ stechen. ∼**ing nettle** *n* Brennessel *f*

stingy /'stɪndʒɪ/ *a* (**-ier**, **-iest**) geizig, (*fam*) knauserig

stink /stɪŋk/ *n* Gestank *m* ● *vi* (*pt* **stank**, *pp* **stunk**) stinken (**of** nach)

stint /stɪnt/ *n* Pensum *nt* ● *vi* ∼ **on** sparen an (+ *dat*)

stipulat|e /'stɪpjʊleɪt/ *vt* vorschreiben. ∼**ion** /-'leɪʃn/ *n* Bedingung *f*

stir /stɜː(r)/ *n* (*commotion*) Aufregung *f* ● *v* (*pt/pp* **stirred**) *vt* rühren ● *vi* sich rühren

stirrup /'stɪrəp/ *n* Steigbügel *m*

stitch /stɪtʃ/ *n* Stich *m*; (*Knitting*) Masche *f*; (*pain*) Seitenstechen *nt*; **be in** ∼**es** (*fam*) sich kaputtlachen ● *vt* nähen

stoat /stəʊt/ *n* Hermelin *nt*

stock /stɒk/ *n* Vorrat *m* (**of** an + *dat*); (*in shop*) [Waren]bestand *m*; (*livestock*) Vieh *nt*; (*lineage*) Abstammung *f*; (*Finance*) Wertpapiere *pl*; (*Culin*) Brühe *f*; (*plant*) Levkoje *f*; **in/out of** ∼ vorrätig/ nicht vorrätig; **take** ∼ (*fig*) Bilanz ziehen ● *a* Standard- ● *vt* ⟨*shop:*⟩ führen;

auffüllen ⟨*shelves*⟩. ∼ **up** *vi* sich eindecken (**with** mit)
stock: ∼**broker** *n* Börsenmakler *m.*
∼ **cube** *n* Brühwürfel *m*. **S**∼ **Ex-**
change *n* Börse *f*
stocking /'stɒkɪŋ/ *n* Strumpf *m*
stockist /'stɒkɪst/ *n* Händler *m*
stock: ∼ **market** *n* Börse *f*. ∼**pile** *vt*
horten; anhäufen ⟨*weapons*⟩. ∼-
'**still** *a* bewegungslos. ∼**taking** *n*
(*Comm*) Inventur *f*
stocky /'stɒkɪ/ *a* (**-ier, -iest**)
untersetzt
stodgy /'stɒdʒɪ/ *a* pappig [und
schwer verdaulich]
stoical /'stəʊɪkl/ *a*, **-ly** *adv* stoisch
stoke /stəʊk/ *vt* heizen
stole[1] /stəʊl/ *n* Stola *f*
stole[2]**, stolen** /'stəʊln/ *see* **steal**
stolid /'stɒlɪd/ *a*, **-ly** *adv* stur
stomach /'stʌmək/ *n* Magen *m* ● *vt*
vertragen. ∼-**ache** *n* Magen-
schmerzen *pl*
stone /stəʊn/ *n* Stein *m*; (*weight*)
6,35 kg ● *a* steinern; ⟨*wall, Age*⟩
Stein-. ● *vt* mit Steinen bewerfen;
entsteinen ⟨*fruit*⟩. ∼-**cold** *a* eiskalt. ∼-'**deaf** *n* (*fam*) stocktaub
stony /'stəʊnɪ/ *a* steinig
stood /stʊd/ *see* **stand**
stool /stuːl/ *n* Hocker *m*
stoop /stuːp/ *n* **walk with a** ∼ gebeugt gehen ● *vi* sich bücken; (*fig*) sich
erniedrigen
stop /stɒp/ *n* Halt *m*; (*break*) Pause
f; (*for bus*) Haltestelle *f*; (*for train*)
Station *f*; (*Gram*) Punkt *m*; (*on*
organ) Register *nt*; **come to a** ∼
stehenbleiben; **put a** ∼ **to sth** etw unterbinden ● *v* (*pt/pp* **stopped**) ● *vt* anhalten, stoppen; (*switch off*) abstellen;
(*plug, block*) zustopfen; (*prevent*)
verhindern; ∼ **s.o. doing sth** jdn daran
hindern, etw zu tun; ∼ **doing sth** aufhören, etw zu tun; ∼ **that!** hör auf damit! laß das sein! ● *vi* anhalten; (*cease*)
aufhören; ⟨*clock:*⟩ stehenbleiben; (*fam:*
stay) bleiben (**with** bei) ● *int* halt!
stopp!
stop: ∼**gap** *n* Notlösung *f*. ∼**over** *n*
Zwischenaufenthalt *m*; (*Aviat*) Zwi-
schenlandung *f*
stoppage /'stɒpɪdʒ/ *n* Unterbrechung *f*; (*strike*) Streik *m*; (*de-*
duction) Abzug *m*
stopper /'stɒpə(r)/ *n* Stöpsel *m*
stop: ∼-**press** *n* letzte Meldungen *pl*.
∼-**watch** *n* Stoppuhr *f*

storage /'stɔːrɪdʒ/ *n* Aufbewahrung
f; (*in warehouse*) Lagerung *f*; (*Com-*
puting) Speicherung *f*
store /stɔː(r)/ *n* (*stock*) Vorrat *m*;
(*shop*) Laden *m*; (*department* ∼)
Kaufhaus *nt*; (*depot*) Lager *nt*; **in** ∼
auf Lager; **put in** ∼ lagern; **set great** ∼
by großen Wert legen auf (+ *acc*); **be in**
∼ **for s.o.** (*fig*) jdm bevorstehen ● *vt*
aufbewahren; (*in warehouse*) lagern;
(*Computing*) speichern. ∼-**room** *n*
Lagerraum *m*
storey /'stɔːrɪ/ *n* Stockwerk *nt*
stork /stɔːk/ *n* Storch *m*
storm /stɔːm/ *n* Sturm *m*; (*with thun-*
der) Gewitter *nt* ● *vt/i* stürmen. ∼**y** *a*
stürmisch
story /'stɔːrɪ/ *n* Geschichte *f*; (*in*
newspaper) Artikel *m*; (*fam: lie*)
Märchen *nt*
stout /staʊt/ *a* (**-er, -est**) beleibt;
(*strong*) fest
stove /stəʊv/ *n* Ofen *m*; (*for cooking*)
Herd *m*
stow /stəʊ/ *vt* verstauen. ∼**away** *n*
blinder Passagier *m*
straddle /'strædl/ *vt* rittlings sitzen
auf (+ *dat*); (*standing*) mit ge-
spreizten Beinen stehen über (+ *dat*)
straggl|e /'strægl/ *vi* hinter-
herhinken. ∼**er** *n* Nachzügler *m*. ∼**y**
a strähnig
straight /streɪt/ *a* (**-er, -est**) gerade;
(*direct*) direkt; (*clear*) klar; ⟨*hair*⟩ glatt;
⟨*drink*⟩ pur; **be** ∼ (*tidy*) in Ordnung sein
● *adv* gerade; (*directly*) direkt, ge-
radewegs; (*clearly*) klar; ∼ **away** sofort;
∼ **on** *or* **ahead** geradeaus; ∼ **out** (*fig*)
geradeheraus; **go** ∼ (*fam*) ein ehr-
liches Leben führen; **put sth** ∼ etw in
Ordnung bringen; **sit/stand up** ∼ ge-
radesitzen/-stehen
straighten /'streɪtn/ *vt* gerade-
machen; (*put straight*) gerade-
richten ● *vi* gerade werden; ∼ **[up]**
⟨*person:*⟩ sich aufrichten. ∼ **out** *vt* ge-
radebiegen
straight'forward *a* offen; (*simple*)
einfach
strain[1] /streɪn/ *n* Rasse *f*; (*Bot*) Sorte
f; (*of virus*) Art *f*
strain[2] *n* Belastung *f*; ∼**s** *pl* (*of music*)
Klänge *pl* ● *vt* belasten; (*overexert*)
überanstrengen; (*injure*) zerren
⟨*muscle*⟩; (*Culin*) durchseihen; abgießen
⟨*vegetables*⟩ ● *vi* sich anstrengen. ∼**ed**
a ⟨*relations*⟩ gespannt. ∼**er** *n* Sieb *nt*

strait /streɪt/ n Meerenge f; **in dire ~s** in großen Nöten. **~-jacket** n Zwangsjacke f. **~-'laced** a puritanisch

strand[1] /strænd/ n (of thread) Faden m; (of beads) Kette f; (of hair) Strähne f

strand[2] vt **be ~ed** festsitzen

strange /streɪndʒ/ a (**-r, -st**) fremd; (odd) seltsam, merkwürdig. **~r** n Fremde(r) m/f

strangely /'streɪndʒlɪ/ adv seltsam, merkwürdig; **~ enough** seltsamerweise

strangle /'stræŋgl/ vt erwürgen; (fig) unterdrücken

strangulation /stræŋgjʊ'leɪʃn/ n Erwürgen nt

strap /stræp/ n Riemen m; (for safety) Gurt m; (to grasp in vehicle) Halteriemen m; (of watch) Armband nt; (shoulder-) Träger m ● vt (pt/pp **strapped**) schnallen; **~ in** or **down** festschnallen

strapping /'stræpɪŋ/ a stramm

strata /'strɑːtə/ npl see **stratum**

stratagem /'strætədʒəm/ n Kriegslist f

strategic /strə'tiːdʒɪk/ a, **-ally** adv strategisch

strategy /'strætədʒɪ/ n Strategie f

stratum /'strɑːtəm/ n (pl **strata**) Schicht f

straw /strɔː/ n Stroh nt; (single piece, drinking) Strohhalm m; **that's the last ~** jetzt reicht's aber

strawberry /'strɔːbərɪ/ n Erdbeere f

stray /streɪ/ a streunend ● n streunendes Tier nt ● vi sich verirren; (deviate) abweichen

streak /striːk/ n Streifen m; (in hair) Strähne f; (fig: trait) Zug m ● vi flitzen. **~y** a streifig; (bacon) durchwachsen

stream /striːm/ n Bach m; (flow) Strom m; (current) Strömung f; (Sch) Parallelzug m ● vi strömen; **~ in/out** hinaus-/herausströmen

streamer /'striːmə(r)/ n Luftschlange f; (flag) Wimpel m

streamline vt (fig) rationalisieren. **~d** a stromlinienförmig

street /striːt/ n Straße f. **~car** n (Amer) Straßenbahn f. **~ lamp** n Straßenlaterne f

strength /streŋθ/ n Stärke f; (power) Kraft f; **on the ~ of** auf Grund (+ gen). **~en** vt stärken; (reinforce) verstärken

strenuous /'strenjʊəs/ a anstrengend

stress /stres/ n (emphasis) Betonung f; (strain) Belastung f; (mental) Streß m ● vt betonen; (put a strain on) belasten. **~ful** a stressig (fam)

stretch /stretʃ/ n (of road) Strecke f; (elasticity) Elastizität f; **at a ~** ohne Unterbrechung; **a long ~** eine lange Zeit; **have a ~** sich strecken ● vt strecken; (widen) dehnen; (spread) ausbreiten; fordern (person); **~ one's legs** sich (dat) die Beine vertreten ● vi sich erstrecken; (become wider) sich dehnen; (person:) sich strecken. **~er** n Tragbahre f

strew /struː/ vt (pp **strewn** or **strewed**) streuen

stricken /'strɪkn/ a betroffen; **~ with** heimgesucht von

strict /strɪkt/ a (**-er, -est**), **-ly** adv streng; **~ly speaking** strenggenommen

stride /straɪd/ n [großer] Schritt m; **make great ~s** (fig) große Fortschritte machen; **take sth in one's ~** mit etw gut fertig werden ● vi (pt **strode**, pp **stridden**) [mit großen Schritten] gehen

strident /'straɪdnt/ a, **-ly** adv schrill; (colour) grell

strife /straɪf/ n Streit m

strike /straɪk/ n Streik m; (Mil) Angriff m; **be on ~** streiken ● v (pt/pp **struck**) ● vt schlagen; (knock against, collide with) treffen; prägen (coin); anzünden (match); stoßen auf (+ acc) (oil, gold); abbrechen (camp); (delete) streichen; (impress) beeindrucken; (occur to) einfallen (+ dat); (Mil) angreifen; **~ s.o. a blow** jdm einen Schlag versetzen ● vi treffen; (lightning:) einschlagen; (clock:) schlagen; (attack) zuschlagen; (workers:) streiken; **~ lucky** Glück haben. **~-breaker** n Streikbrecher m

striker /'straɪkə(r)/ n Streikende(r) m/f

striking /'straɪkɪŋ/ a auffallend

string /strɪŋ/ n Schnur f; (thin) Bindfaden m; (of musical instrument, racket) Saite f; (of bow) Sehne f; (of pearls) Kette f; **the ~s** (Mus) die Streicher pl; **pull ~s** (fam) seine Beziehungen spielen lassen, Fäden ziehen ● vt (pt/pp **strung**) (thread) aufziehen (beads). **~ed** a (Mus) Saiten-; (played with bow) Streich-

stringent /'strɪndʒnt/ a streng

strip /strɪp/ n Streifen m • v (pt/pp **stripped**) • vt ablösen; ausziehen ⟨clothes⟩; abziehen ⟨bed⟩; abbeizen ⟨wood, furniture⟩; auseinandernehmen ⟨machine⟩; (deprive) berauben (**of** gen); **~ sth off sth** etw von etw entfernen • vi (undress) sich ausziehen. **~ club** n Stripteaselokal nt

stripe /straɪp/ n Streifen m. **~d** a gestreift

'striplight n Neonröhre f

stripper /'strɪpə(r)/ n Stripperin f; (male) Stripper m

strip-'tease n Striptease m

strive /straɪv/ vi (pt **strove**, pp **striven**) sich bemühen (**to** zu); **~ for** streben nach

strode /strəʊd/ see **stride**

stroke[1] /strəʊk/ n Schlag m; (of pen) Strich m; (Swimming) Zug m; (style) Stil m; (Med) Schlaganfall m; **~ of luck** Glücksfall m; **put s.o. off his ~** jdn aus dem Konzept bringen

stroke[2] • vt streicheln

stroll /strəʊl/ n Spaziergang m, (fam) Bummel m • vi spazieren, (fam) bummeln. **~er** n (Amer: pushchair) [Kinder]sportwagen m

strong /strɒŋ/ a (-**er** /-gə(r)/, -**est** /-gɪst/), -**ly** adv stark; (powerful, healthy) kräftig; (severe) streng; (sturdy) stabil; (convincing) gut

strong: ~-box n Geldkassette f. **~hold** n Festung f; (fig) Hochburg f. **~-'minded** a willensstark. **~-room** n Tresorraum m

stroppy /'strɒpɪ/ a widerspenstig

strove /strəʊv/ see **strive**

struck /strʌk/ see **strike**

structural /'strʌktʃərl/ a, -**ly** adv baulich

structure /'strʌktʃə(r)/ n Struktur f; (building) Bau m

struggle /'strʌgl/ n Kampf m; **with a ~** mit Mühe • vi kämpfen; **~ for breath** nach Atem ringen; **~ to do sth** sich abmühen, etw zu tun; **~ to one's feet** mühsam aufstehen

strum /strʌm/ v (pt/pp **strummed**) • vt klimpern auf (+ dat) • vi klimpern

strung /strʌŋ/ see **string**

strut[1] /strʌt/ n Strebe f

strut[2] vi (pt/pp **strutted**) stolzieren

stub /stʌb/ n Stummel m; (counterfoil) Abschnitt m • vt (pt/pp **stubbed**) **~ one's toe** sich (dat) den Zeh stoßen (**on** an + dat). **~ out** vt ausdrücken ⟨cigarette⟩

stubb|le /'stʌbl/ n Stoppeln pl. **~ly** a stoppelig

stubborn /'stʌbən/ a, -**ly** adv starrsinnig; ⟨refusal⟩ hartnäckig

stubby /'stʌbɪ/ a (-**ier**, -**iest**) kurz und dick

stucco /'stʌkəʊ/ n Stuck m

stuck /stʌk/ see **stick**[2]. **~-'up** a (fam) hochnäsig

stud[1] /stʌd/ n Nagel m; (on clothes) Niete f; (for collar) Kragenknopf m; (for ear) Ohrstecker m

stud[2] n (of horses) Gestüt nt

student /'stju:dnt/ n Student(in) m(f); (Sch) Schüler(in) m(f). **~ nurse** n Lernschwester f

studied /'stʌdɪd/ a gewollt

studio /'stju:dɪəʊ/ n Studio nt; (for artist) Atelier nt

studious /'stju:dɪəs/ a lerneifrig; (earnest) ernsthaft

stud|y /'stʌdɪ/ n Studie f; (room) Studierzimmer nt; (investigation) Untersuchung f; **~ies** pl Studium nt • v (pt/pp **studied**) • vt studieren; (examine) untersuchen • vi lernen; (at university) studieren

stuff /stʌf/ n Stoff m; (fam: things) Zeug nt • vt vollstopfen; (with padding, Culin) füllen; ausstopfen ⟨animal⟩; **~ sth into sth** etw in etw (acc) [hinein]stopfen. **~ing** n Füllung f

stuffy /'stʌfɪ/ a (-**ier**, -**iest**) stickig; (old-fashioned) spießig

stumbl|e /'stʌmbl/ vi stolpern; **~e across** zufällig stoßen auf (+ acc). **~ing-block** n Hindernis nt

stump /stʌmp/ n Stumpf m • **~ up** vt/i (fam) blechen. **~ed** a (fam) überfragt

stun /stʌn/ vt (pt/pp **stunned**) betäuben; **~ned by** (fig) wie betäubt von

stung /stʌŋ/ see **sting**

stunk /stʌŋk/ see **stink**

stunning /'stʌnɪŋ/ a (fam) toll

stunt[1] /stʌnt/ n (fam) Kunststück nt

stunt[2] vt hemmen. **~ed** a verkümmert

stupendous /stju:'pendəs/ a, -**ly** adv enorm

stupid /'stju:pɪd/ a dumm. **~ity** /-'pɪdətɪ/ n Dummheit f. **~ly** adv dumm; **~ly [enough]** dummerweise

stupor /'stju:pə(r)/ n Benommenheit f

sturdy /'stɜ:dɪ/ a (-**ier**, -**iest**) stämmig; ⟨furniture⟩ stabil; ⟨shoes⟩ fest

stutter /'stʌtə(r)/ n Stottern nt ● vt/i stottern

sty[1] /staɪ/ n (pl **sties**) Schweinestall m

sty[2], **stye** n (pl **styes**) (Med) Gerstenkorn nt

style /staɪl/ n Stil m; (fashion) Mode f; (sort) Art f; (hair~) Frisur f; **in ~** in großem Stil

stylish /'staɪlɪʃ/ a, **-ly** adv stilvoll

stylist /'staɪlɪst/ n Friseur m/Friseuse f. **~ic** /-'lɪstɪk/ a, **-ally** adv stilistisch

stylized /'staɪlaɪzd/ a stilisiert

stylus /'staɪləs/ n (on record-player) Nadel f

suave /swɑːv/ a (pej) gewandt

sub'conscious /sʌb-/ a, **-ly** adv unterbewußt ● n Unterbewußtsein nt

subcon'tract vt [vertraglich] weitervergeben (**to** an + acc)

'subdivi|de vt unterteilen. **~sion** n Unterteilung f

subdue /səb'djuː/ vt unterwerfen; (make quieter) beruhigen. **~d** a gedämpft; (person) still

subject[1] /'sʌbdʒɪkt/ a **be ~ to sth** etw (dat) unterworfen sein ● n Staatsbürger(in) m(f); (of ruler) Untertan m; (theme) Thema nt; (of investigation) Gegenstand m; (Sch) Fach nt; (Gram) Subjekt nt

subject[2] /səb'dʒekt/ vt unterwerfen (**to** dat); (expose) aussetzen (**to** dat)

subjective /səb'dʒektɪv/ a, **-ly** adv subjektiv

subjugate /'sʌbdʒʊgeɪt/ vt unterjochen

subjunctive /səb'dʒʌŋktɪv/ n Konjunktiv m

sub'let vt (pt/pp **-let**) untervermieten

sublime /sə'blaɪm/ a, **-ly** adv erhaben

subliminal /sʌ'blɪmɪnl/ a unterschwellig

sub-ma'chine-gun n Maschinenpistole f

subma'rine n Unterseeboot nt

submerge /səb'mɜːdʒ/ vt untertauchen; **be ~d** unter Wasser stehen ● vi tauchen

submiss|ion /səb'mɪʃn/ n Unterwerfung f. **~ive** /-sɪv/ a gehorsam; (pej) unterwürfig

submit /səb'mɪt/ v (pt/pp **-mitted**, pres p **-mitting**) ● vt vorlegen (**to** dat); (hand in) einreichen ● vi sich unterwerfen (**to** dat)

subordinate[1] /sə'bɔːdɪnət/ a untergeordnet ● n Untergebene(r) m/f

subordinate[2] /sə'bɔːdɪneɪt/ vt unterordnen (**to** dat)

subscribe /səb'skraɪb/ vi spenden; **~ to** (fig) sich anschließen (+ dat); abonnieren (newspaper). **~r** n Spender m; Abonnent m

subscription /səb'skrɪpʃn/ n (to club) [Mitglieds]beitrag m; (to newspaper) Abonnement nt; **by ~** mit Spenden

subsequent /'sʌbsɪkwənt/ a, **-ly** adv folgend; (later) später

subservient /səb'sɜːvɪənt/ a, **-ly** adv untergeordnet; (servile) unterwürfig

subside /səb'saɪd/ vi sinken; (ground:) sich senken; (storm:) nachlassen

subsidiary /səb'sɪdɪərɪ/ a untergeordnet ● n Tochtergesellschaft f

subsid|ize /'sʌbsɪdaɪz/ vt subventionieren. **~y** n Subvention f

subsist /səb'sɪst/ vi leben (**on** von). **~ence** n Existenz f

substance /'sʌbstəns/ n Substanz f

sub'standard a unzulänglich; (goods) minderwertig

substantial /səb'stænʃl/ a solide; (meal) reichhaltig; (considerable) beträchtlich. **~ly** adv solide; (essentially) im wesentlichen

substantiate /səb'stænʃɪeɪt/ vt erhärten

substitut|e /'sʌbstɪtjuːt/ n Ersatz m; (Sport) Ersatzspieler(in) m(f) ● vt **~e A for B** B durch A ersetzen ● vi **~e for s.o.** jdn vertreten. **~ion** /-'tjuːʃn/ n Ersetzung f

subterfuge /'sʌbtəfjuːdʒ/ n List f

subterranean /sʌbtə'reɪnɪən/ a unterirdisch

'subtitle n Untertitel m

subtle /'sʌtl/ a (**-r, -st**), **-tly** adv fein; (fig) subtil

subtract /səb'trækt/ vt abziehen, subtrahieren. **~ion** /-ækʃn/ n Subtraktion f

suburb /'sʌbɜːb/ n Vorort m; **in the ~s** am Stadtrand. **~an** /sə'bɜːbən/ a Vorort-; (pej) spießig. **~ia** /sə'bɜː-bɪə/ n die Vororte pl

subversive /səb'vɜːsɪv/ a subversiv

'subway n Unterführung f; (Amer: railway) U-Bahn f

succeed /sək'siːd/ vi Erfolg haben; (plan:) gelingen; (follow) nachfolgen (+ dat); **I ~ed** es ist mir gelungen; **he ~ed in escaping** es gelang ihm zu entkommen ● *vt* folgen (+ *dat*). ~**ing** *a* folgend

success /sək'ses/ *n* Erfolg *m*. ~**ful** *a*, **-ly** *adv* erfolgreich

succession /sək'seʃn/ *n* Folge *f*; (*series*) Serie *f*; (*to title, office*) Nachfolge *f*; (*to throne*) Thronfolge *f*; **in** ~ hintereinander

successive /sək'sesɪv/ *a* aufeinanderfolgend. ~**ly** *adv* hintereinander

successor /sək'sesə(r)/ *n* Nachfolger(in) *m(f)*

succinct /sək'sɪŋkt/ *a*, **-ly** *adv* prägnant

succulent /'sʌkjʊlənt/ *a* saftig

succumb /sə'kʌm/ *vi* erliegen (**to** *dat*)

such /sʌtʃ/ *a* solche(r,s); ~ **a book** ein solches *od* solch ein Buch; ~ **a thing** so etwas; ~ **a long time** so lange; **there is no ~ thing** das gibt es gar nicht; **there is no ~ person** eine solche Person gibt es nicht ● *pron* **as** ~ als solche(r,s); (*strictly speaking*) an sich; ~ **as** wie [zum Beispiel]; **and** ~ und dergleichen. ~**like** *pron* (*fam*) dergleichen

suck /sʌk/ *vt/i* saugen; lutschen ⟨*sweet*⟩. ~ **up** *vt* aufsaugen ● *vi* ~ **up to s.o.** (*fam*) sich bei jdm einschmeicheln

sucker /'sʌkə(r)/ *n* (*Bot*) Ausläufer *m*; (*fam: person*) Dumme(r) *m/f*

suckle /'sʌkl/ *vt* säugen

suction /'sʌkʃn/ *n* Saugwirkung *f*

sudden /'sʌdn/ *a*, **-ly** *adv* plötzlich; (*abrupt*) jäh ● *n* **all of a** ~ auf einmal

sue /su:/ *vt* (*pres p* **suing**) verklagen (**for** auf + *acc*) ● *vi* klagen

suede /sweɪd/ *n* Wildleder *nt*

suet /'su:ɪt/ *n* [Nieren]talg *m*

suffer /'sʌfə(r)/ *vi* leiden (**from** an + *dat*) ● *vt* erleiden; (*tolerate*) dulden. ~**ance** /-əns/ *n* **on** ~**ance** bloß geduldet. ~**ing** *n* Leiden *nt*

suffice /sə'faɪs/ *vi* genügen

sufficient /sə'fɪʃnt/ *a*, **-ly** *adv* genug, genügend; **be** ~ genügen

suffix /'sʌfɪks/ *n* Nachsilbe *f*

suffocat|e /'sʌfəkeɪt/ *vt/i* ersticken. ~**ion** /-'keɪʃn/ *n* Ersticken *nt*

sugar /'ʃʊgə(r)/ *n* Zucker *m* ● *vt* zuckern; (*fig*) versüßen. ~ **basin**, ~-**bowl** *n* Zuckerschale *f*. ~**y** *a* süß; (*fig*) süßlich

suggest /sə'dʒest/ *vt* vorschlagen; (*indicate, insinuate*) andeuten. ~**ion** /-estʃn/ *n* Vorschlag *m*; Andeutung *f*;

(*trace*) Spur *f*. ~**ive** /-ɪv/ *a*, **-ly** *adv* anzüglich; **be** ~**ive of** schließen lassen auf (+ *acc*)

suicidal /su:ɪ'saɪdl/ *a* selbstmörderisch

suicide /'su:ɪsaɪd/ *n* Selbstmord *m*

suit /su:t/ *n* Anzug *m*; (*woman's*) Kostüm *nt*; (*Cards*) Farbe *f*; (*Jur*) Prozeß *m*; **follow** ~ (*fig*) das Gleiche tun ● *vt* (*adapt*) anpassen (**to** *dat*); (*be convenient for*) passen (+ *dat*); (*go with*) passen zu; ⟨*clothing:*⟩ stehen (**s.o.** jdm); **be** ~**ed for** geeignet sein für; ~ **yourself!** wie du willst!

suit|able /'su:təbl/ *a* geeignet; (*convenient*) passend; (*appropriate*) angemessen; (*for weather, activity*) zweckmäßig. ~**ably** *adv* angemessen; zweckmäßig

'suitcase *n* Koffer *m*

suite /swi:t/ *n* Suite *f*; (*of furniture*) Garnitur *f*

sulk /sʌlk/ *vi* schmollen. ~**y** *a* schmollend

sullen /'sʌlən/ *a*, **-ly** *adv* mürrisch

sulphur /'sʌlfə(r)/ *n* Schwefel *m*. ~**ic** /-'fjʊərɪk/ *a* ~**ic acid** Schwefelsäure *f*

sultana /sʌl'tɑ:nə/ *n* Sultanine *f*

sultry /'sʌltrɪ/ *a* (**-ier, -iest**) ⟨*weather*⟩ schwül

sum /sʌm/ *n* Summe *f*; (*Sch*) Rechenaufgabe *f* ● *vt/i* (*pt/pp* **summed**) ~ **up** zusammenfassen; (*assess*) einschätzen

summar|ize /'sʌməraɪz/ *vt* zusammenfassen. ~**y** *n* Zusammenfassung *f* ● *a*, **-ily** *adv* summarisch; ⟨*dismissal*⟩ fristlos

summer /'sʌmə(r)/ *n* Sommer *m*. ~-**house** *n* [Garten]laube *f*. ~**time** *n* Sommer *m*

summery /'sʌmərɪ/ *a* sommerlich

summit /'sʌmɪt/ *n* Gipfel *m*. ~ **conference** *n* Gipfelkonferenz *f*

summon /'sʌmən/ *vt* rufen; holen ⟨*help*⟩; (*Jur*) vorladen. ~ **up** *vt* aufbringen

summons /'sʌmənz/ *n* (*Jur*) Vorladung *f* ● *vt* vorladen

sump /sʌmp/ *n* (*Auto*) Ölwanne *f*

sumptuous /'sʌmptjʊəs/ *a*, **-ly** *adv* prunkvoll; ⟨*meal*⟩ üppig

sun /sʌn/ *n* Sonne *f* ● *vt* (*pt/pp* **sunned**) ~ **oneself** sich sonnen

sun: ~**bathe** *vi* sich sonnen. ~-**bed** *n* Sonnenbank *f*. ~**burn** *n* Sonnenbrand *m*

sundae /'sʌndeɪ/ *n* Eisbecher *m*

Sunday 509 **surly**

Sunday /'sʌndeɪ/ n Sonntag m
'sundial n Sonnenuhr f
sundry /'sʌndrɪ/ a verschiedene pl;
all and ~ alle pl
'sunflower n Sonnenblume f
sung /sʌŋ/ see sing
'sun-glasses npl Sonnenbrille f
sunk /sʌŋk/ see sink
sunken /'sʌŋkn/ a gesunken; ⟨eyes⟩
eingefallen
sunny /'sʌnɪ/ a (-ier, -iest) sonnig
sun: ~rise n Sonnenaufgang m.
~-roof n (Auto) Schiebedach nt.
~set n Sonnenuntergang m. ~
shade n Sonnenschirm m. ~shine n
Sonnenschein m. ~stroke n Sonnen-
stich m. ~-tan n [Sonnen]bräune f.
~-tanned a braun[gebrannt].
~-tan oil n Sonnenöl nt
super /'su:pə(r)/ a (fam) prima, toll
superb /sʊ'pɜːb/ a erstklassig
supercilious /su:pə'sɪlɪəs/ a überlegen
superficial /su:pə'fɪʃl/ a, -ly adv
oberflächlich
superfluous /sʊ'pɜːflʊəs/ a überflüssig
super'human a übermenschlich
superintendent /su:pərɪn'tendənt/
n (of police) Kommissar m
superior /su:'pɪərɪə(r)/ a überlegen;
(in rank) höher ● n Vorgesetzte(r)
m/f. ~ity /-'ɒrətɪ/ n Überlegenheit f
superlative /su:'pɜːlətɪv/ a un-
übertrefflich ● n Superlativ m
'superman n Übermensch m
'supermarket n Supermarkt m
super'natural a übernatürlich
'superpower n Supermacht f
supersede /su:pə'si:d/ vt ersetzen
super'sonic a Überschall-
superstiti|on /su:pə'stɪʃn/ n Aber-
glaube m. ~ous /-'stɪʃəs/ a, -ly adv
abergläubisch
supervis|e /'su:pəvaɪz/ vt be-
aufsichtigen; überwachen ⟨work⟩.
~ion /-'vɪʒn/ n Aufsicht f; Überwachung f. ~or n Aufseher(in) m(f)
supper /'sʌpə(r)/ n Abendessen nt
supple /'sʌpl/ a geschmeidig
supplement /'sʌplɪmənt/ n Ergänzung f; (addition) Zusatz m; (to
fare) Zuschlag m; (book) Er-
gänzungsband m; (to newspaper)
Beilage f ● vt ergänzen. ~ary
/-'mentərɪ/ a zusätzlich
supplier /sə'plaɪə(r)/ n Lieferant m

supply /sə'plaɪ/ n Vorrat m; supplies
pl (Mil) Nachschub m ● vt (pt/pp -ied)
liefern; ~ s.o. with sth jdn mit etw
versorgen
support /sə'pɔːt/ n Stütze f; (fig)
Unterstützung f ● vt stützen; (bear
weight of) tragen; (keep) ernähren;
(give money to) unterstützen; (speak
in favour of) befürworten; (Sport)
Fan sein von. ~er n Anhänger(in)
m(f); (Sport) Fan m. ~ive /-ɪv/ a be
~ive [to s.o.] [jdm] eine große Stütze
sein
suppose /sə'pəʊz/ vt annehmen;
(presume) vermuten; (imagine) sich
(dat) vorstellen; be ~d to do sth
etw tun sollen; not be ~d to (fam)
nicht dürfen; I ~ so vermutlich. ~dly
/-ɪdlɪ/ adv angeblich
supposition /sʌpə'zɪʃn/ n Vermutung f
suppository /sʌ'pɒzɪtrɪ/ n Zäpfchen
nt
suppress /sə'pres/ vt unterdrücken.
~ion /-eʃn/ n Unterdrückung f
supremacy /su:'preməsɪ/ n Vorherr-
schaft f
supreme /su:'priːm/ a höchste(r,s);
⟨court⟩ oberste(r,s)
surcharge /'sɜːtʃɑːdʒ/ n Zuschlag m
sure /ʃʊə(r)/ a (-r, -st) sicher; make
~ sich vergewissern (of gen);
(check) nachprüfen; be ~ to do it sieh
zu, daß du es tust ● adv (Amer, fam)
klar; ~ enough tatsächlich. ~ly adv
sicher; (for emphasis) doch; (Amer:
gladly) gern
surety /'ʃʊərətɪ/ n Bürgschaft f;
stand ~ for bürgen für
surf /sɜːf/ n Brandung f
surface /'sɜːfɪs/ n Oberfläche f ● vi
(emerge) auftauchen. ~ mail n by ~
mail auf dem Land-/Seeweg
'surfboard n Surfbrett nt
surfeit /'sɜːfɪt/ n Übermaß nt
surfing /'sɜːfɪŋ/ n Surfen nt
surge /sɜːdʒ/ n (of sea) Branden nt;
(fig) Welle f ● vi branden; ~ forward
nach vorn drängen
surgeon /'sɜːdʒən/ n Chirurg(in)
m(f)
surgery /'sɜːdʒərɪ/ n Chirurgie f;
(place) Praxis f; (room) Sprechzimmer nt; (hours) Sprechstunde f;
have ~ operiert werden
surgical /'sɜːdʒɪkl/ a, -ly adv
chirurgisch
surly /'sɜːlɪ/ a (-ier, -iest) mürrisch

surmise /sə'maɪz/ vt mutmaßen
surmount /sə'maʊnt/ vt überwinden
surname /'sɜːneɪm/ n Nachname m
surpass /sə'pɑːs/ vt übertreffen
surplus /'sɜːpləs/ a überschüssig; **be ~ to requirements** nicht benötigt werden ● n Überschuß m (**of** an + dat)
surpris|e /sə'praɪz/ n Überraschung f ● vt überraschen; **be ~ed** sich wundern (**at** über + acc). **~ing** a, **-ly** adv überraschend
surrender /sə'rendə(r)/ n Kapitulation f ● vi sich ergeben; (Mil) kapitulieren ● vt aufgeben
surreptitious /sʌrəp'tɪʃəs/ a, **-ly** adv heimlich, verstohlen
surrogate /'sʌrəgət/ n Ersatz m. **~ 'mother** n Leihmutter f
surround /sə'raʊnd/ vt umgeben; (encircle) umzingeln; **~ed by** umgeben von. **~ing** a umliegend. **~ings** npl Umgebung f
surveillance /sə'veɪləns/ n Überwachung f; **be under ~** überwacht werden
survey[1] /'sɜːveɪ/ n Überblick m; (poll) Umfrage f; (investigation) Untersuchung f; (of land) Vermessung f; (of house) Gutachten nt
survey[2] /sə'veɪ/ vt betrachten; vermessen (land); begutachten (building). **~or** n Landvermesser m; Gutachter m
survival /sə'vaɪvl/ n Überleben nt; (of tradition) Fortbestand m
surviv|e /sə'vaɪv/ vt überleben ● vi überleben; (tradition:) erhalten bleiben. **~or** n Überlebende(r) m/f; **be a ~or** (fam) nicht unterzukriegen sein
susceptible /sə'septəbl/ a empfänglich; (Med) anfällig (**to** für)
suspect[1] /sə'spekt/ vt verdächtigen; (assume) vermuten; **he ~s nothing** er ahnt nichts
suspect[2] /'sʌspekt/ a verdächtig ● n Verdächtige(r) m/f
suspend /sə'spend/ vt aufhängen; (stop) [vorläufig] einstellen; (from duty) vorläufig beurlauben. **~er belt** n Strumpfbandgürtel m. **~ers** npl Strumpfbänder pl; (Amer: braces) Hosenträger pl
suspense /sə'spens/ n Spannung f
suspension /sə'spenʃn/ n (Auto) Federung f. **~ bridge** n Hängebrücke f

suspici|on /sə'spɪʃn/ n Verdacht m; (mistrust) Mißtrauen nt; (trace) Spur f. **~ous** /-ɪʃəs/ a, **-ly** adv mißtrauisch; (arousing suspicion) verdächtig
sustain /sə'steɪn/ vt tragen; (fig) aufrechterhalten; erhalten (life); erleiden (injury)
sustenance /'sʌstɪnəns/ n Nahrung f
swab /swɒb/ n (Med) Tupfer m; (specimen) Abstrich m
swagger /'swægə(r)/ vi stolzieren
swallow[1] /'swɒləʊ/ vt/i schlucken. **~ up** vt verschlucken; verschlingen (resources)
swallow[2] n (bird) Schwalbe f
swam /swæm/ see **swim**
swamp /swɒmp/ n Sumpf m ● vt überschwemmen. **~y** a sumpfig
swan /swɒn/ n Schwan m
swank /swæŋk/ vi (fam) angeben
swap /swɒp/ n (fam) Tausch m ● vt/i (pt/pp **swapped**) (fam) tauschen (**for** gegen)
swarm /swɔːm/ n Schwarm m ● vi schwärmen; **be ~ing with** wimmeln von
swarthy /'swɔːðɪ/ a (**-ier, -iest**) dunkel
swastika /'swɒstɪkə/ n Hakenkreuz nt
swat /swɒt/ vt (pt/pp **swatted**) totschlagen
sway /sweɪ/ n (fig) Herrschaft f ● vi schwanken; (gently) sich wiegen ● vt wiegen; (influence) beeinflussen
swear /sweə(r)/ v (pt **swore**, pp **sworn**) ● vt schwören ● vi schwören (**by** auf + acc); (curse) fluchen. **~-word** n Kraftausdruck m
sweat /swet/ n Schweiß m ● vi schwitzen
sweater /'swetə(r)/ n Pullover m
sweaty /'swetɪ/ a verschwitzt
swede /swiːd/ n Kohlrübe f
Swed|e n Schwede m/-din f. **~en** n Schweden nt. **~ish** a schwedisch
sweep /swiːp/ n Schornsteinfeger m; (curve) Bogen m; (movement) ausholende Bewegung f; **make a clean ~** (fig) gründlich aufräumen ● v (pt/pp **swept**) ● vt fegen, kehren ● vi (go swiftly) rauschen; (wind:) fegen. **~ up** vt zusammenfegen/-kehren
sweeping /'swiːpɪŋ/ a ausholend; (statement) pauschal; (changes) weitreichend

sweet /swi:t/ a (**-er, -est**) süß; **have a ∼ tooth** gern Süßes mögen ● n Bonbon m & nt; (dessert) Nachtisch m. **∼ corn** n [Zucker]mais m

sweeten /'swi:tn/ vt süßen. **∼er** n Süßstoff m; (fam: bribe) Schmiergeld nt

sweet: ∼heart n Schatz m. **∼-shop** n Süßwarenladen m. **∼ness** n Süße f. **∼ 'pea** n Wicke f

swell /swel/ n Dünung f ● v (pt **swelled**, pp **swollen** or **swelled**) ● vi [an]schwellen; ⟨sails:⟩ sich blähen; ⟨wood:⟩ aufquellen ● vt anschwellen lassen; (increase) vergrößern. **∼ing** n Schwellung f

swelter /'sweltə(r)/ vi schwitzen

swept /swept/ see **sweep**

swerve /swɜ:v/ vi einen Bogen machen

swift /swɪft/ a (**-er, -est**), **-ly** adv schnell

swig /swɪg/ n (fam) Schluck m, Zug m ● vt (pt/pp **swigged**) (fam) [herunter]kippen

swill /swɪl/ n (for pigs) Schweinefutter nt ● vt ∼ [**out**] [aus]spülen

swim /swɪm/ n **have a ∼** schwimmen ● vi (pt **swam**, pp **swum**) schwimmen; **my head is ∼ming** mir dreht sich der Kopf. **∼mer** n Schwimmer(in) m(f)

swimming /'swɪmɪŋ/ n Schwimmen nt. **∼-baths** npl Schwimmbad nt. **∼-pool** n Schwimmbecken nt; (private) Swimmingpool m

'swim-suit n Badeanzug m

swindle /'swɪndl/ n Schwindel m, Betrug m ● vt betrügen. **∼r** n Schwindler m

swine /swaɪn/ n Schwein nt

swing /swɪŋ/ n Schwung m; (shift) Schwenk m; (seat) Schaukel f; **in full ∼** in vollem Gange ● v (pt/pp **swung**) ● vi schwingen; (on swing) schaukeln; (sway) schwanken; (dangle) baumeln; (turn) schwenken ● vt schwingen; (influence) beeinflussen. **∼-'door** n Schwingtür f

swingeing /'swɪndʒɪŋ/ a hart; (fig) drastisch

swipe /swaɪp/ n (fam) Schlag m ● vt (fam) knallen; (steal) klauen

swirl /swɜ:l/ n Wirbel m ● vt/i wirbeln

swish /swɪʃ/ a (fam) schick ● vi zischen

Swiss /swɪs/ a Schweizer, schweizerisch ● n Schweizer(in) m(f); **the ∼**

pl die Schweizer. **∼ 'roll** n Biskuitrolle f

switch /swɪtʃ/ n Schalter m; (change) Wechsel m; (Amer, Rail) Weiche f ● vt wechseln; (exchange) tauschen ● vi wechseln; **∼ to** umstellen auf (+ acc). **∼ off** vt ausschalten; abschalten ⟨engine⟩. **∼ on** vt einschalten, anschalten

switch: ∼back n Achterbahn f. **∼board** n [Telefon]zentrale f

Switzerland /'swɪtsələnd/ n die Schweiz

swivel /'swɪvl/ v (pt/pp **swivelled**) ● vt drehen ● vi sich drehen

swollen /'swəʊlən/ see **swell** ● a geschwollen. **∼-'headed** a eingebildet

swoop /swu:p/ n Sturzflug m; (by police) Razzia f ● vi ∼ **down** herabstoßen

sword /sɔ:d/ n Schwert nt

swore /swɔ:(r)/ see **swear**

sworn /swɔ:n/ see **swear**

swot /swɒt/ n (fam) Streber m ● vt/i (pt/pp **swotted**) (fam) büffeln

swum /swʌm/ see **swim**

swung /swʌŋ/ see **swing**

syllable /'sɪləbl/ n Silbe f

syllabus /'sɪləbəs/ n Lehrplan m; (for exam) Studienplan m

symbol /'sɪmbəl/ n Symbol nt (**of** für). **∼ic** /-'bɒlɪk/ a, **-ally** adv symbolisch. **∼ism** /-ɪzm/ n Symbolik f. **∼ize** vt symbolisieren

symmetr|ical /sɪ'metrɪkl/ a, **-ly** adv symmetrisch. **∼y** /'sɪmətrɪ/ n Symmetrie f

sympathetic /sɪmpə'θetɪk/ a, **-ally** adv mitfühlend; (likeable) sympathisch

sympathize /'sɪmpəθaɪz/ vi mitfühlen. **∼r** n (Pol) Sympathisant m

sympathy /'sɪmpəθɪ/ n Mitgefühl nt; (condolences) Beileid nt

symphony /'sɪmfənɪ/ n Sinfonie f

symptom /'sɪmptəm/ n Symptom nt. **∼atic** /-'mætɪk/ a symptomatisch (**of** für)

synagogue /'sɪnəgɒg/ n Synagoge f

synchronize /'sɪŋkrənaɪz/ vt synchronisieren

syndicate /'sɪndɪkət/ n Syndikat nt

syndrome /'sɪndrəʊm/ n Syndrom nt

synonym /'sɪnənɪm/ n Synonym nt. **∼ous** /-'nɒnɪməs/ a, **-ly** adv synonym

synopsis /sɪ'nɒpsɪs/ n (pl **-opses** /-si:z/) Zusammenfassung f; (of opera, ballet) Inhaltsangabe f

syntax /'sɪntæks/ n Syntax f

synthesis /'sɪnθəsɪs/ n (pl **-ses** /-si:z/) Synthese f

synthetic /sɪn'θetɪk/ a synthetisch ● n Kunststoff m

Syria /'sɪrɪə/ n Syrien nt

syringe /sɪ'rɪndʒ/ n Spritze f ● vt spritzen; ausspritzen ⟨ears⟩

syrup /'sɪrəp/ n Sirup m

system /'sɪstəm/ n System nt. ~**atic** /-'mætɪk/ a, **-ally** adv systematisch

T

tab /tæb/ n (projecting) Zunge f; ⟨with name⟩ Namensschild nt; (loop) Aufhänger m; **keep** ~**s on** (fam) [genau] beobachten; **pick up the** ~ (fam) bezahlen

tabby /'tæbɪ/ n getigerte Katze f

table /'teɪbl/ n Tisch m; (list) Tabelle f; **at [the]** ~ bei Tisch ● vt einbringen. ~**-cloth** n Tischdecke f, Tischtuch nt. ~**spoon** n Servierlöffel m

tablet /'tæblɪt/ n Tablette f; (of soap) Stück nt; (slab) Tafel f

'table tennis n Tischtennis nt

tabloid /'tæblɔɪd/ n kleinformatige Zeitung f; (pej) Boulevardzeitung f

taboo /tə'bu:/ a tabu ● n Tabu nt

tacit /'tæsɪt/ a, **-ly** adv stillschweigend

taciturn /'tæsɪtɜ:n/ a wortkarg

tack /tæk/ n (nail) Stift m; (stitch) Heftstich m; (Naut & fig) Kurs m ● vt festnageln; (sew) heften ● vi (Naut) kreuzen

tackle /'tækl/ n Ausrüstung f ● vt angehen

tacky /'tækɪ/ a klebrig

tact /tækt/ n Takt m, Taktgefühl nt. ~**ful** a, **-ly** adv taktvoll

tactic|al /'tæktɪkl/ a, **-ly** adv taktisch. ~**s** npl Taktik f

tactless /'tæktlɪs/ a, **-ly** adv taktlos. ~**ness** n Taktlosigkeit f

tadpole /'tædpəʊl/ n Kaulquappe f

tag[1] /tæg/ n (label) Schild nt ● vi (pt/pp **tagged**) ~**along** mitkommen

tag[2] n (game) Fangen nt

tail /teɪl/ n Schwanz m; ~**s** pl (tailcoat) Frack m; **heads or** ~**s?** Kopf oder Zahl? ● vt (fam:follow) beschatten ● vi ~**off** zurückgehen

tail: ~**back** n Rückstau m. ~**coat** n Frack m. ~**-end** n Ende nt. ~**light** n Rücklicht nt

tailor /'teɪlə(r)/ n Schneider m. ~**-made** a maßgeschneidert

'tail wind n Rückenwind m

taint /teɪnt/ vt verderben

take /teɪk/ v (pt **took**, pp **taken**) ● vt nehmen; (with one) mitnehmen; (take to a place) bringen; (steal) stehlen; (win) gewinnen; (capture) einnehmen; (require) brauchen; (last) dauern; (teach) geben; machen ⟨exam, subject, holiday, photograph⟩; messen ⟨pulse, temperature⟩; ~ **s.o. home** jdn nach Hause bringen; ~ **sth to the cleaner's** etw in die Reinigung bringen; ~ **s.o. prisoner** jdn gefangennehmen; **be** ~**n ill** krank werden; ~ **sth calmly** etw gelassen aufnehmen ● vi ⟨plant:⟩ angehen; ~ **after s.o.** jdm nachschlagen; (in looks) jdm ähnlich sehen; ~ **to** (like) mögen; (as a habit) sich (dat) angewöhnen. ~ **away** vt wegbringen; (remove) wegnehmen; (subtract) abziehen; **'to** ~ **away'** 'zum Mitnehmen'. ~ **back** vt zurücknehmen; (return) zurückbringen. ~ **down** vt herunternehmen; (remove) abnehmen; (write down) aufschreiben. ~ **in** vt hineinbringen; (bring indoors) hereinholen; (to one's home) aufnehmen; (understand) begreifen; (deceive) hereinlegen; (make smaller) enger machen. ~ **off** vt abnehmen; ablegen ⟨coat⟩; sich (dat) ausziehen ⟨clothes⟩; (deduct) abziehen; (mimic) nachmachen; ~ **time off** sich (dat) frei nehmen; ~ **oneself off** [fort]gehen ● vi (Aviat) starten. ~ **on** vt annehmen; (undertake) übernehmen; (engage) einstellen; (as opponent) antreten gegen. ~ **out** vt hinausbringen; (for pleasure) ausgehen mit; ausführen ⟨dog⟩; (remove) herausnehmen; (withdraw) abheben ⟨money⟩; (from library) ausleihen; ~ **out a subscription to sth** etw abonnieren; ~ **it out on s.o.** (fam) seinen Ärger an jdm auslassen. ~ **over** vt hinüberbringen; übernehmen ⟨firm, control⟩ ● vi ~ **over from s.o.** jdn ablösen. ~ **up** vt hinaufbringen; annehmen ⟨offer⟩; ergreifen ⟨profession⟩; sich (dat) zulegen ⟨hobby⟩; in Anspruch nehmen ⟨time⟩; einnehmen ⟨space⟩; aufreißen ⟨floorboards⟩; ~ **sth up with s.o.** mit jdm über etw (acc) sprechen ● vi ~ **up with s.o.** sich mit jdm einlassen

take: ~**-away** n Essen nt zum Mitnehmen; (*restaurant*) Restaurant nt mit Straßenverkauf. ~**-off** n (*Aviat*) Start m, Abflug m. ~**-over** n Übernahme f

takings /'teɪkɪŋz/ npl Einnahmen pl

talcum /'tælkəm/ n ~ **[powder]** Körperpuder m

tale /teɪl/ n Geschichte f

talent /'tælənt/ n Talent nt. ~**ed** a talentiert

talk /tɔːk/ n Gespräch nt; (*lecture*) Vortrag m; **make small** ~ Konversation machen ● vi reden, sprechen **(to/with** mit) ● vt reden; ~ **s.o. into sth** jdn zu etw überreden. ~ **over** vt besprechen

talkative /'tɔːkətɪv/ a gesprächig

'**talking-to** n Standpauke f

tall /tɔːl/ a (**-er, -est**) groß; ⟨building, tree⟩ hoch; **that's a** ~ **order** das ist ziemlich viel verlangt. ~**boy** n hohe Kommode f. ~ '**story** n übertriebene Geschichte f

tally /'tælɪ/ n **keep a** ~ **of** Buch führen über (+ acc) ● vi übereinstimmen

talon /'tælən/ n Klaue f

tambourine /tæmbə'riːn/ n Tamburin nt

tame /teɪm/ a (**-r, -st**), **-ly** adv zahm; (*dull*) lahm (*fam*) ● vt zähmen. ~**r** n Dompteur m

tamper /'tæmpə(r)/ vi ~ **with** sich (*dat*) zu schaffen machen an (+ *dat*)

tampon /'tæmpɒn/ n Tampon m

tan /tæn/ a gelbbraun ● n Gelbbraun nt; (*from sun*) Bräune f ● v (*pt/pp* **tanned**) ● vt gerben ⟨hide⟩ ● vi braun werden

tang /tæŋ/ n herber Geschmack m; (*smell*) herber Geruch m

tangent /'tændʒənt/ n Tangente f; **go off at a** ~ (*fam*) vom Thema abschweifen

tangible /'tændʒɪbl/ a greifbar

tangle /'tæŋgl/ n Gewirr nt; (*in hair*) Verfilzung f ● vt ~ **[up]** verheddern ● vi sich verheddern

tango /'tæŋgəʊ/ n Tango m

tank /tæŋk/ n Tank m; (*Mil*) Panzer m

tankard /'tæŋkəd/ n Krug m

tanker /'tæŋkə(r)/ n Tanker m; (*lorry*) Tank[last]wagen m

tantaliz|e /'tæntəlaɪz/ vt quälen. ~**ing** a verlockend

tantamount /'tæntəmaʊnt/ a **be** ~ **to** gleichbedeutend sein mit

tantrum /'tæntrəm/ n Wutanfall m

tap /tæp/ n Hahn m; (*knock*) Klopfen nt; **on** ~ zur Verfügung ● v (*pt/pp* **tapped**) ● vt klopfen an (+ *acc*); anzapfen ⟨barrel, tree⟩; erschließen ⟨resources⟩; abhören ⟨telephone⟩ ● vi klopfen. ~**dance** n Step[tanz] m ● vi Step tanzen, steppen

tape /teɪp/ n Band nt; (*adhesive*) Klebstreifen m; (*for recording*) Tonband nt ● vt mit Klebstreifen zukleben; (*record*) auf Band aufnehmen

'**tape-measure** n Bandmaß nt

taper /'teɪpə(r)/ n dünne Wachskerze f ● vi sich verjüngen

'**tape recorder** n Tonbandgerät nt

tapestry /'tæpɪstrɪ/ n Gobelinstickerei f

'**tapeworm** n Bandwurm m

'**tap water** n Leitungswasser nt

tar /tɑː(r)/ n Teer m ● vt (*pt/pp* **tarred**) teeren

tardy /'tɑːdɪ/ a (**-ier, -iest**) langsam; (*late*) spät

target /'tɑːgɪt/ n Ziel nt; (*board*) [Ziel]scheibe f

tariff /'tærɪf/ n Tarif m; (*duty*) Zoll m

tarnish /'tɑːnɪʃ/ vi anlaufen

tarpaulin /tɑː'pɔːlɪn/ n Plane f

tarragon /'tærəgən/ n Estragon m

tart¹ /tɑːt/ a (**-er, -est**) sauer; (*fig*) scharf

tart² n *l* Obstkuchen m; (*individual*) Törtchen nt; (*sl: prostitute*) Nutte f ● vt ~ **oneself up** (*fam*) sich auftakeln

tartan /'tɑːtn/ n Schottenmuster nt; (*cloth*) Schottenstoff m ● attrib schottisch kariert

tartar /'tɑːtə(r)/ n (*on teeth*) Zahnstein m

tartar '**sauce** /tɑːtə-/ n ≈ Remouladensoße f

task /tɑːsk/ n Aufgabe f; **take s.o. to** ~ jdm Vorhaltungen machen. ~ **force** n Sonderkommando nt

tassel /'tæsl/ n Quaste f

taste /teɪst/ n Geschmack m; (*sample*) Kostprobe f ● vt kosten, probieren; schmecken ⟨flavour⟩ ● vi schmecken (**of** nach). ~**ful** a, **-ly** adv (*fig*) geschmackvoll. ~**less** a, **-ly** adv geschmacklos

tasty /'teɪstɪ/ a (**-ier, -iest**) lecker, schmackhaft

tat /tæt/ see **tit**²

tatter|ed /'tætəd/ a zerlumpt; ⟨pages⟩ zerfleddert. ~**s** npl **in** ~**s** in Fetzen

tattoo¹ /tə'tu:/ n Tätowierung f ● vt tätowieren

tattoo² n (Mil) Zapfenstreich m

tatty /'tætɪ/ a (**-ier, -iest**) schäbig; ⟨book⟩ zerfleddert

taught /tɔ:t/ see **teach**

taunt /tɔ:nt/ n höhnische Bemerkung f ● vt verhöhnen

Taurus /'tɔ:rəs/ n (Astr) Stier m

taut /tɔ:t/ a straff

tavern /'tævən/ n (liter) Schenke f

tawdry /'tɔ:drɪ/ a (**-ier, -iest**) billig und geschmacklos

tawny /'tɔ:nɪ/ a gelbbraun

tax /tæks/ n Steuer f ● vt besteuern; (fig) strapazieren; ~ **with** beschuldigen (+ gen). ~**able** /-əbl/ a steuerpflichtig. ~**ation** /-'seɪʃn/ n Besteuerung f. ~**-free** a steuerfrei

taxi /'tæksɪ/ n Taxi nt ● vi (pt/pp **taxied**, pres p **taxiing**) ⟨aircraft:⟩ rollen. ~ **driver** n Taxifahrer m. ~ **rank** n Taxistand m

'taxpayer n Steuerzahler m

tea /ti:/ n Tee m. ~**-bag** n Teebeutel m. ~**-break** n Teepause f

teach /ti:tʃ/ vt/i (pt/pp **taught**) unterrichten; ~ **s.o. sth** jdm etw beibringen. ~**er** n Lehrer(in) m(f)

tea: ~**-cloth** n (for drying) Geschirrtuch nt. ~**cup** n Teetasse f

teak /ti:k/ n Teakholz nt

team /ti:m/ n Mannschaft f; (fig) Team nt; (of animals) Gespann nt ● vi ~ **up** sich zusammentun

'team-work n Teamarbeit f

'teapot n Teekanne f

tear¹ /teə(r)/ n Riß m ● v (pt **tore**, pp **torn**) ● vt reißen; (damage) zerreißen; ~ **open** aufreißen; ~ **oneself away** sich losreißen ● vi [zer]reißen; (run) rasen. ~ **up** vt zerreißen

tear² /tɪə(r)/ n Träne f. ~**ful** a weinend. ~**fully** adv unter Tränen. ~**-gas** n Tränengas nt

tease /ti:z/ vt necken

tea: ~**-set** n Teeservice nt. ~ **shop** n Café nt. ~**spoon** n Teelöffel m. ~**-strainer** n Teesieb nt

teat /ti:t/ n Zitze f; (on bottle) Sauger m

'tea-towel n Geschirrtuch nt

technical /'teknɪkl/ a technisch; (specialized) fachlich. ~**ity** /-'kælətɪ/ n technisches Detail nt; (Jur) Formfehler m. ~**ly** adv technisch; (strictly) streng genommen. ~ **term** n Fachausdruck m

technician /tek'nɪʃn/ n Techniker m

technique /tek'ni:k/ n Technik f

technological /teknə'lɒdʒɪkl/ a, **-ly** adv technologisch

technology /tek'nɒlədʒɪ/ n Technologie f

teddy /'tedɪ/ n ~ **[bear]** Teddybär m

tedious /'ti:dɪəs/ a langweilig

tedium /'ti:dɪəm/ n Langeweile f

teem /ti:m/ vi (rain) in Strömen gießen; **be ~ing with** (full of) wimmeln von

teenage /'ti:neɪdʒ/ a Teenager-; ~ **boy/girl** Junge m/Mädchen nt im Teenageralter. ~**r** n Teenager m

teens /ti:nz/ npl **the ~** die Teenagerjahre pl

teeny /'ti:nɪ/ a (**-ier, -iest**) winzig

teeter /'ti:tə(r)/ vi schwanken

teeth /ti:θ/ see **tooth**

teeth|e /ti:ð/ vi zahnen. ~**ing troubles** npl (fig) Anfangsschwierigkeiten pl

teetotal /ti:'təʊtl/ a abstinent. ~**ler** n Abstinenzler m

telecommunications /telɪkəmju:nɪ-'keɪʃnz/ npl Fernmeldewesen n

telegram /'telɪgræm/ n Telegramm nt

telegraph /'telɪgrɑ:f/ n Telegraf m. ~**ic** /-'græfɪk/ a telegrafisch. ~ **pole** n Telegrafenmast m

telepathy /tɪ'lepəθɪ/ n Telepathie f; **by ~** telepathisch

telephone /'telɪfəʊn/ n Telefon nt; **be on the ~** Telefon haben; (be telephoning) telefonieren ● vt anrufen ● vi telefonieren

telephone: ~ **book** n Telefonbuch nt. ~ **booth** n, ~ **box** n Telefonzelle f. ~ **directory** n Telefonbuch nt. ~ **number** n Telefonnummer f

telephonist /tɪ'lefənɪst/ n Telefonist(in) m(f)

tele'photo /telɪ-/ a ~ **lens** Teleobjektiv nt

teleprinter /telɪ-/ n Fernschreiber m

telescop|e /'telɪskəʊp/ n Teleskop nt, Fernrohr nt. ~**ic** /-'skɒpɪk/ a teleskopisch; (collapsible) ausziehbar

televise /'telɪvaɪz/ vt im Fernsehen übertragen

television /'telɪvɪʒn/ n Fernsehen nt; **watch ~** fernsehen. ~ **set** n Fernsehapparat m, Fernseher m

telex /'teleks/ n Telex nt ● vt telexen

tell /tel/ *vt/i* (*pt/pp* **told**) sagen (**s.o.** jdm); (*relate*) erzählen; (*know*) wissen; (*distinguish*) erkennen; ∼ **the time** die Uhr lesen; **time will** ∼ das wird man erst sehen; **his age is beginning to** ∼ sein Alter macht sich bemerkbar; **don't** ∼ **me** sag es mir nicht; **you mustn't** ∼ du darfst nichts sagen. ∼ **off** *vt* ausschimpfen

teller /'telə(r)/ *n* (*cashier*) Kassierer(in) *m(f)*

telly /'telɪ/ *n* (*fam*) = **television**

temerity /tɪ'merətɪ/ *n* Kühnheit *f*

temp /temp/ *n* (*fam*) Aushilfssekretärin *f*

temper *n* /'tempə(r)/ *n* (*disposition*) Naturell *nt*; (*mood*) Laune *f*; (*anger*) Wut *f*; **lose one's** ∼ wütend werden ● *vt* (*fig*) mäßigen

temperament /'temprəmənt/ *n* Temperament *nt*. ∼**al** /-'mentl/ *a* temperamentvoll; (*moody*) launisch

temperance /'tempərəns/ *n* Mäßigung *f*; (*abstinence*) Abstinenz *f*

temperate /'tempərət/ *a* gemäßigt

temperature /'temprətʃə(r)/ *n* Temperatur *f*; **have** *or* **run a** ∼ Fieber haben

tempest /'tempɪst/ *n* Sturm *m*. ∼**uous** /-'pestjʊəs/ *a* stürmisch

template /'templɪt/ *n* Schablone *f*

temple *n* /'templ/ *n* Tempel *m*

temple *n* (*Anat*) Schläfe *f*

tempo /'tempəʊ/ *n* Tempo *nt*

temporary /'tempərərɪ/ *a*, **-ily** *adv* vorübergehend; (*measure, building*) provisorisch

tempt /tempt/ *vt* verleiten; (*Relig*) versuchen; herausfordern (*fate*); (*entice*) [ver]locken; **be** ∼**ed** versucht sein (**to** zu); **I am** ∼**ed by it** es lockt mich. ∼**ation** /-'teɪʃn/ *n* Versuchung *f*. ∼**ing** *a* verlockend

ten /ten/ *a* zehn

tenable /'tenəbl/ *a* (*fig*) haltbar

tenaci|ous /tɪ'neɪʃəs/ *a*, **-ly** *adv* hartnäckig. ∼**ty** /-'næsətɪ/ *n* Hartnäckigkeit *f*

tenant /'tenənt/ *n* Mieter(in) *m(f)*; (*Comm*) Pächter(in) *m(f)*

tend *n* /tend/ *vt* (*look after*) sich kümmern um

tend *n* *vi* ∼ **to do sth** dazu neigen, etw zu tun

tendency /'tendənsɪ/ *n* Tendenz *f*; (*inclination*) Neigung *f*

tender *n* /'tendə(r)/ *n* (*Comm*) Angebot *nt*; **legal** ∼ gesetzliches Zahlungsmittel *nt* ● *vt* anbieten; einreichen (*resignation*)

tender *n* *a* zart; (*loving*) zärtlich; (*painful*) empfindlich. ∼**ly** *adv* zärtlich. ∼**ness** *n* Zartheit *f*; Zärtlichkeit *f*

tendon /'tendən/ *n* Sehne *f*

tenement /'tenəmənt/ *n* Mietshaus *nt*

tenet /'tenɪt/ *n* Grundsatz *m*

tenner /'tenə(r)/ *n* (*fam*) Zehnpfundschein *m*

tennis /'tenɪs/ *n* Tennis *nt*. ∼**-court** *n* Tennisplatz *m*

tenor /'tenə(r)/ *n* Tenor *m*

tense *n* /tens/ *n* (*Gram*) Zeit *f*

tense *n* *a* (**-r, -st**) gespannt ● *vt* anspannen (*muscle*)

tension /'tenʃn/ *n* Spannung *f*

tent /tent/ *n* Zelt *nt*

tentacle /'tentəkl/ *n* Fangarm *m*

tentative /'tentətɪv/ *a*, **-ly** *adv* vorläufig; (*hesitant*) zaghaft

tenterhooks /'tentəhʊks/ *npl* **be on** ∼ wie auf glühenden Kohlen sitzen

tenth /tenθ/ *a* zehnte(r,s) ● *n* Zehntel *nt*

tenuous /'tenjʊəs/ *a* (*fig*) schwach

tepid /'tepɪd/ *a* lauwarm

term /tɜːm/ *n* Zeitraum *m*; (*Sch*) ≈ Halbjahr *nt*; (*Univ*) **I** Semester *nt*; (*expression*) Ausdruck *m*; ∼**s** *pl* (*conditions*) Bedingungen *pl*; ∼ **of office** Amtszeit *f*; **in the short/long** ∼ kurz-/langfristig; **be on good/bad** ∼**s** gut/nicht gut miteinander auskommen; **come to** ∼**s with** sich abfinden mit

terminal /'tɜːmɪnl/ *a* End-; (*Med*) unheilbar ● *n* (*Aviat*) Terminal *m*; (*of bus*) Endstation *f*; (*on battery*) Pol *m*; (*Computing*) Terminal *nt*

terminat|e /'tɜːmɪneɪt/ *vt* beenden; lösen (*contract*); unterbrechen (*pregnancy*) ● *vi* enden. ∼**ion** /-'neɪʃn/ *n* Beendigung *f*; (*Med*) Schwangerschaftsabbruch *m*

terminology /tɜːmɪ'nɒlədʒɪ/ *n* Terminologie *f*

terminus /'tɜːmɪnəs/ *n* (*pl* **-ni** /-naɪ/) Endstation *f*

terrace /'terəs/ *n* Terrasse *f*; (*houses*) Häuserreihe *f*; **the** ∼**s** (*Sport*) die [Steh]ränge *pl*. ∼**d house** *n* Reihenhaus *nt*

terrain /te'reɪn/ *n* Gelände *nt*

terrible /'terəbl/ *a*, **-bly** *adv* schrecklich

terrier /'terɪə(r)/ *n* Terrier *m*

terrific /təˈrɪfɪk/ a (fam) (excellent)
sagenhaft; (huge) riesig

terri|fy /ˈterɪfaɪ/ vt (pt/pp -ied) angst
machen (+dat); **be** ~**fied** Angst
haben. ~**fying** a furchterregend

territorial /terɪˈtɔːrɪəl/ a Territorial-

territory /ˈterɪtərɪ/ n Gebiet nt

terror /ˈterə(r)/ n [panische] Angst f;
(Pol) Terror m. ~**ism** /-ɪzm/ n Ter-
rorismus m. ~**ist** /-ɪst/ n Terrorist
m. ~**ize** vt terrorisieren

terse /tɜːs/ a, **-ly** adv kurz, knapp

test /test/ n Test m; (Sch) Klas-
senarbeit f; **put to the** ~ auf die Probe
stellen ● vt prüfen; (examine) untersuchen (**for** auf + acc)

testament /ˈtestəmənt/ n Testament
nt; **Old/New T**~ Altes/Neues Testament nt

testicle /ˈtestɪkl/ n Hoden m

testify /ˈtestɪfaɪ/ v (pt/pp -ied) ● vt
beweisen; ~ **that** bezeugen, daß ● vi
aussagen; ~ **to** bezeugen

testimonial /testɪˈməʊnɪəl/ n Zeugnis nt

testimony /ˈtestɪmənɪ/ n Aussage f

'test-tube n Reagenzglas nt. ~
'**baby** n (fam) Retortenbaby nt

testy /ˈtestɪ/ a gereizt

tetanus /ˈtetənəs/ n Tetanus m

tetchy /ˈtetʃɪ/ a gereizt

tether /ˈteðə(r)/ n **be at the end of
one's** ~ am Ende seiner Kraft sein ● vt
anbinden

text /tekst/ n Text m. ~**book** n
Lehrbuch nt

textile /ˈtekstaɪl/ a Textil- ● n ~**s** pl
Textilien pl

texture /ˈtekstʃə(r)/ n Be-
schaffenheit f; (Tex) Struktur f

Thai /taɪ/ a thailändisch. ~**land** n
Thailand nt

Thames /temz/ n Themse f

than /ðən, betont ðæn/ conj als; **older**
~ **me** älter als ich

thank /θæŋk/ vt danken (+dat); ~
you [very much] danke [schön]. ~**ful**
a, **-ly** adv dankbar. ~**less** a undankbar

thanks /θæŋks/ npl Dank m; ~!
(fam) danke! ~ **to** dank (+dat or gen)

that /ðæt/ a & pron (pl **those**) der/
die/das; (pl) die; ~ **one** der/die/das
da; **I'll take** ~ ich nehme den/die/das;
I don't like those die mag ich nicht; ~ **is**
das heißt; **is** ~ **you?** bist du es? **who
is** ~? wer ist da? **with/after** ~ damit/
danach; **like** ~ so; **a man like** ~ so ein

Mann; ~ **is why** deshalb; ~'**s it!** genau!
all ~ **I know** alles was ich weiß; **the
day** ~ **I saw him** an dem Tag, als ich
ihn sah ● adv so; ~ **good/hot** so gut/
heiß ● conj daß

thatch /θætʃ/ n Strohdach nt. ~**ed** a
strohgedeckt

thaw /θɔː/ n Tauwetter nt ● vt/i auftauen; **it's** ~**ing** es taut

the /ðə, vor einem Vokal ðiː/ def art
der/die/das; (pl) die; **play** ~ **piano/
violin** Klavier/Geige spielen ● adv ~
more ~ **better** je mehr, desto besser;
all ~ **better** um so besser

theatre /ˈθɪətə(r)/ n Theater nt;
(Med) Operationssaal m

theatrical /θɪˈætrɪkl/ a Theater-;
(showy) theatralisch

theft /θeft/ n Diebstahl m

their /ðeə(r)/ a ihr

theirs /ðeəz/ poss pron ihre(r), ihrs;
a friend of ~ ein Freund von ihnen;
those are ~ die gehören ihnen

them /ðem/ pron (acc) sie; (dat)
ihnen; **I know** ~ ich kenne sie; **give** ~
the money gib ihnen das Geld

theme /θiːm/ n Thema nt

them'selves pron selbst; (refl) sich;
by ~ allein

then /ðen/ adv dann; (at that time in
past) damals; **by** ~ bis dahin; **since** ~
seitdem; **before** ~ vorher; **from** ~ **on**
von da an; **now and** ~ dann und wann;
there and ~ auf der Stelle ● a damalig

theolog|ian /θɪəˈləʊdʒɪən/ n Theo-
loge m. ~**y** /-ˈɒlədʒɪ/ n Theologie f

theorem /ˈθɪərəm/ n Lehrsatz m

theoretical /θɪəˈretɪkl/ a, **-ly** adv
theoretisch

theory /ˈθɪərɪ/ n Theorie f; **in** ~
theoretisch

therapeutic /θerəˈpjuːtɪk/ a thera-
peutisch

therap|ist /ˈθerəpɪst/ n Thera-
peut(in) m(f). ~**y** n Therapie f

there /ðeə(r)/ adv da; (with
movement) dahin, dorthin; **down/up**
~ da unten/oben; ~ **is/are** da ist/sind;
(in existence) es gibt; ~ **he/she is** da ist
er/sie; **send/take** ~ hinschicken/
-bringen ● int **there, there!** nun, nun!

there: ~**abouts** adv da [in der Nähe];
or ~**abouts** (roughly) ungefähr.
~'**after** adv danach. ~**by** adv dadurch. ~**fore** /-fɔː(r)/ adv deshalb,
also

thermal /ˈθɜːml/ a Thermal-; ~
'**underwear** n Thermowäsche f

thermometer /θə'mɒmɪtə(r)/ n
Thermometer nt

Thermos (P) /'θɜːməs/ n ~ **[flask]**
Thermosflasche (P)f

thermostat /'θɜːməstæt/ n Thermostat m

these /ðiːz/ see **this**

thesis /'θiːsɪs/ n (pl **-ses** /-siːz/) Dissertation f; (proposition) These f

they /ðeɪ/ pron sie; ~ **say** (generalizing) man sagt

thick /θɪk/ a (-**er**, -**est**), -**ly** adv dick; (dense) dicht; ⟨liquid⟩ dickflüssig; (fam: stupid) dumm ● adv dick ● n **in the ~ of** mitten in (+ dat). ~**en** vt dicker machen; eindicken ⟨sauce⟩ ● vi dicker werden; ⟨fog:⟩ dichter werden; ⟨plot:⟩ kompliziert werden. ~**ness** n Dicke f; Dichte f; Dickflüssigkeit f

thick: ~**set** a untersetzt. ~-'**skinned** a (fam) dickfellig

thief /θiːf/ n (pl **thieves**) Dieb(in) m(f)

thieving /'θiːvɪŋ/ a diebisch ● n Stehlen nt

thigh /θaɪ/ n Oberschenkel m

thimble /'θɪmbl/ n Fingerhut m

thin /θɪn/ a (**thinner**, **thinnest**), -**ly** adv dünn ● adv dünn ● v (pt/pp **thinned**) ● vt verdünnen ⟨liquid⟩ ● vi sich lichten. ~ **out** vt ausdünnen

thing /θɪŋ/ n Ding nt; (subject, affair) Sache f; ~**s** pl (belongings) Sachen pl; **for one** ~ erstens; **the right** ~ das Richtige; **just the** ~! genau das Richtige! **how are** ~**s?** wie geht's? **the latest** ~ (fam) der letzte Schrei; **the best** ~ **would be** am besten wäre es

think /θɪŋk/ vt/i (pt/pp **thought**) denken (**about/of** an + acc); (believe) meinen; (consider) nachdenken; (regard as) halten für; **I** ~ **so** ich glaube schon; **what do you** ~? was meinen Sie? **what do you** ~ **of it?** was halten Sie davon? ~ **better of it** es sich (dat) anders überlegen. ~ **over** vt sich (dat) überlegen. ~ **up** vt sich (dat) ausdenken

third /θɜːd/ a dritte(r,s) ● n Drittel nt. ~**ly** adv drittens. ~-**rate** a drittrangig

thirst /θɜːst/ n Durst m. ~**y** a, -**ily** adv durstig; **be** ~**y** Durst haben

thirteen /θɜː'tiːn/ a dreizehn. ~**th** a dreizehnte(r,s)

thirtieth /'θɜːtɪɪθ/ a dreißigste(r,s)

thirty /'θɜːtɪ/ a dreißig

this /ðɪs/ a (pl **these**) diese(r,s); (pl) diese; ~ **one** diese(r,s) da; **I'll take** ~ ich nehme diesen/diese/dieses; ~ **evening/morning** heute abend/morgen; **these days** heutzutage ● pron (pl **these**) das, dies[es]; (pl) die, diese; ~ **and that** dies und das; ~ **or that** dieses oder das das; **like** ~ so; ~ **is Peter** das ist Peter; (Teleph) hier [spricht] Peter; **who is** ~? wer ist das? (Teleph, Amer) wer ist am Apparat?

thistle /'θɪsl/ n Distel f

thorn /θɔːn/ n Dorn m. ~**y** a dornig

thorough /'θʌrə/ a gründlich

thorough: ~**bred** n reinrassiges Tier nt; (horse) Rassepferd nt. ~**fare** n Durchgangsstraße f; **'no** ~**fare'** 'keine Durchfahrt'

thorough|ly /'θʌrəlɪ/ adv gründlich; (completely) völlig; ~ (extremely) äußerst. ~**ness** n Gründlichkeit f

those /ðəʊz/ see **that**

though /ðəʊ/ conj obgleich, obwohl; **as** ~ als ob ● adv (fam) doch

thought /θɔːt/ see **think** ● n Gedanke m; (thinking) Denken nt. ~**ful** a, -**ly** adv nachdenklich; (considerate) rücksichtsvoll. ~**less** a, -**ly** adv gedankenlos

thousand /'θaʊznd/ a **one/a** ~ [ein]tausend ● n Tausend nt; ~**s of** Tausende von. ~**th** a tausendste(r,s) ● n Tausendstel nt

thrash /θræʃ/ vt verprügeln; (defeat) [vernichtend] schlagen. ~ **about** vi sich herumwerfen; ⟨fish:⟩ zappeln. ~ **out** vt ausdiskutieren

thread /θred/ n Faden m; (of screw) Gewinde nt ● vt einfädeln; auffädeln ⟨beads⟩; ~ **one's way through** sich schlängeln durch. ~**bare** a fadenscheinig

threat /θret/ n Drohung f; (danger) Bedrohung f

threaten /'θretn/ vt drohen (+ dat); (with weapon) bedrohen; ~ **to do sth** drohen, etw zu tun; ~ **s.o. with sth** jdm etw androhen ● vi drohen. ~**ing** a, -**ly** adv drohend; (ominous) bedrohlich

three /θriː/ a drei. ~**fold** a & adv dreifach. ~**some** /-səm/ n Trio nt

thresh /θreʃ/ vt dreschen

threshold /'θreʃəʊld/ n Schwelle f

threw /θruː/ see **throw**

thrift /θrɪft/ n Sparsamkeit f. ~**y** a sparsam

thrill /θrɪl/ n Erregung f; (fam) Nervenkitzel m ● vt (excite) erregen;

be ∼ed with sich sehr freuen über (+ *acc*). ∼er *n* Thriller *m.* ∼ing *a* erregend

thrive /θraɪv/ *vi* (*pt* **thrived** *or* **throve**, *pp* **thrived** *or* **thriven** /'θrɪvn/) gedeihen (**on** bei); ⟨*business:*⟩ florieren

throat /θrəʊt/ *n* Hals *m;* **sore** ∼ Halsschmerzen *pl;* **cut s.o.'s** ∼ jdm die Kehle durchschneiden

throb /θrɒb/ *n* Pochen *nt* ● *vi* (*pt/pp* **throbbed**) pochen; ⟨*vibrate*⟩ vibrieren

throes /θrəʊz/ *npl* **in the** ∼ **of** ⟨*fig*⟩ mitten in (+ *dat*)

thrombosis /θrɒm'bəʊsɪs/ *n* Thrombose *f*

throne /θrəʊn/ *n* Thron *m*

throng /θrɒŋ/ *n* Menge *f*

throttle /'θrɒtl/ *vt* erdrosseln

through /θruː/ *prep* durch (+ *acc*); ⟨*during*⟩ während (+ *gen*); ⟨*Amer: up to & including*⟩ bis einschließlich ● *adv* durch; **all** ∼ die ganze Zeit; ∼ **and** ∼ durch und durch; **wet** ∼ durch und durch naß; **read sth** ∼ etw durchlesen; **let/walk** ∼ durchlassen/ -gehen ● *a* ⟨*train*⟩ durchgehend; **be** ∼ ⟨*finished*⟩ fertig sein; ⟨*Teleph*⟩ durch sein

throughout /θruː'aʊt/ *prep* ∼ **the country** im ganzen Land; ∼ **the night** die Nacht durch ● *adv* ganz; ⟨*time*⟩ die ganze Zeit

throve /θrəʊv/ *see* **thrive**

throw /θrəʊ/ *n* Wurf *m* ● *vt* (*pt* **threw**, *pp* **thrown**) werfen; schütten ⟨*liquid*⟩; betätigen ⟨*switch*⟩; abwerfen ⟨*rider*⟩; ⟨*fam: disconcert*⟩ aus der Fassung bringen; (*fam*) geben ⟨*party*⟩; ∼ **sth to s.o.** jdm etw zuwerfen; ∼ **sth at s.o.** etw nach jdm werfen; ⟨*pelt with*⟩ jdn mit etw bewerfen. ∼ **away** *vt* werfen. ∼ **out** *vt* hinauswerfen; ⟨∼ *away*⟩ wegwerfen; verwerfen ⟨*plan*⟩. ∼ **up** *vt* hochwerfen ● *vi* (*fam*) sich übergeben

'**throw-away** *a* Wegwerf-

thrush /θrʌʃ/ *n* Drossel *f*

thrust /θrʌst/ *n* Stoß *m;* ⟨*Phys*⟩ Schub *m* ● *vt* (*pt/pp* **thrust**) stoßen; ⟨*insert*⟩ stecken; ∼ **[up]on** aufbürden ⟨*s.o.* jdm⟩

thud /θʌd/ *n* dumpfer Schlag *m*

thug /θʌg/ *n* Schläger *m*

thumb /θʌm/ *n* Daumen *m;* **rule of** ∼ Faustregel *f;* **under s.o.'s** ∼ unter jds Fuchtel ● *vt* ∼ **a lift** (*fam*) per Anhalter fahren. ∼-**index** *n* Daumenregister *nt.* ∼**tack** *n* ⟨*Amer*⟩ Reißzwecke *f*

thump /θʌmp/ *n* Schlag *m;* ⟨*noise*⟩ dumpfer Schlag *m* ● *vt* schlagen ● *vi* hämmern (**on** an/auf + *acc*); ⟨*heart:*⟩ pochen

thunder /'θʌndə(r)/ *n* Donner *m* ● *vi* donnern. ∼**clap** *n* Donnerschlag *m.* ∼**storm** *n* Gewitter *nt.* ∼**y** *a* gewittrig

Thursday /'θɜːzdeɪ/ *n* Donnerstag *m*

thus /ðʌs/ *adv* so

thwart /θwɔːt/ *vt* vereiteln; ∼ **s.o.** jdm einen Strich durch die Rechnung machen

thyme /taɪm/ *n* Thymian *m*

thyroid /'θaɪrɔɪd/ *n* Schilddrüse *f*

tiara /tɪ'ɑːrə/ *n* Diadem *nt*

tick[1] /tɪk/ *n* **on** ∼ (*fam*) auf Pump

tick[2] *n* ⟨*sound*⟩ Ticken *nt;* ⟨*mark*⟩ Häkchen *nt;* ⟨*fam: instant*⟩ Sekunde *f* ● *vi* ticken ● *vt* abhaken. ∼ **off** *vt* abhaken; (*fam*) rüffeln. ∼ **over** *vi* ⟨*engine:*⟩ im Leerlauf laufen

ticket /'tɪkɪt/ *n* Karte *f;* ⟨*for bus, train*⟩ Fahrschein *m;* ⟨*Aviat*⟩ Flugschein *m;* ⟨*for lottery*⟩ Los *nt;* ⟨*for article deposited*⟩ Schein *m;* ⟨*label*⟩ Schild *nt;* ⟨*for library*⟩ Lesekarte *f;* ⟨*fine*⟩ Strafzettel *m.* ∼-**collector** *n* Fahrkartenkontrolleur *m.* ∼-**office** *n* Fahrkartenschalter *m;* ⟨*for entry*⟩ Kasse *f*

tick|le /'tɪkl/ *n* Kitzeln *nt* ● *vt/i* kitzeln. ∼**lish** /'tɪklɪʃ/ *a* kitzlig

tidal /'taɪdl/ *a* ⟨*river, harbour*⟩ Tide-. ∼ **wave** *n* Flutwelle *f*

tiddly-winks /'tɪdlɪwɪŋks/ *n* Flohspiel *nt*

tide /taɪd/ *n* Gezeiten *pl;* ⟨*of events*⟩ Strom *m;* **the** ∼ **is in/out** es ist Flut/ Ebbe ● *vt* ∼ **s.o. over** jdm über die Runden helfen

tidiness /'taɪdɪnɪs/ *n* Ordentlichkeit *f*

tidy /'taɪdɪ/ *a* (-**ier**, -**iest**), -**ily** *adv* ordentlich ● *vt* ∼ **[up]** aufräumen; ∼ **oneself up** sich zurechtmachen

tie /taɪ/ *n* Krawatte *f,* Schlips *m;* ⟨*cord*⟩ Schnur *f;* ⟨*fig: bond*⟩ Band *nt;* ⟨*restriction*⟩ Bindung *f;* ⟨*Sport*⟩ Unentschieden *nt;* ⟨*in competition*⟩ Punktgleichheit *f* ● *v* (*pres p* **tying**) ● *vt* binden; machen ⟨*knot*⟩ ● *vi* ⟨*Sport*⟩ unentschieden spielen; ⟨*have equal scores, votes*⟩ punktgleich sein; ∼ **in with** passen zu. ∼ **up** *vt* festbinden; verschnüren ⟨*parcel*⟩; fesseln ⟨*person*⟩; **be** ∼**d up** (*busy*) beschäftigt sein

tier /tɪə(r)/ n Stufe f; (of cake) Etage f; (in stadium) Rang m

tiff /tɪf/ n Streit m, (fam) Krach m

tiger /'taɪgə(r)/ n Tiger m

tight /taɪt/ a (-er, -est), **-ly** adv fest; (taut) straff; ⟨clothes⟩ eng; ⟨control⟩ streng; (fam: drunk) blau; **in a ~ corner** (fam) in der Klemme ● adv fest

tighten /'taɪtn/ vt festerziehen; straffen ⟨rope⟩; anziehen ⟨screw⟩; verschärfen ⟨control⟩ ● vi sich spannen

tight: ~-'fisted a knauserig. **~rope** n Hochseil nt

tights /taɪts/ npl Strumpfhose f

tile /taɪl/ n Fliese f; (on wall) Kachel f; (on roof) [Dach]ziegel m ● vt mit Fliesen auslegen; kacheln ⟨wall⟩; decken ⟨roof⟩

till¹ /tɪl/ prep & conj = **until**

till² n Kasse f

tiller /'tɪlə(r)/ n Ruderpinne f

tilt /tɪlt/ n Neigung f; **at full ~** mit voller Wucht ● vt kippen; [zur Seite] neigen ⟨head⟩ ● vi sich neigen

timber /'tɪmbə(r)/ n [Nutz]holz nt

time /taɪm/ n Zeit f; (occasion) Mal nt; (rhythm) Takt m; **~s** (Math) mal; **at any ~** jederzeit; **this ~** dieses Mal, diesmal; **at ~s** manchmal; **~ and again** immer wieder; **two at a ~** zwei auf einmal; **on ~** pünktlich; **in ~** rechtzeitig; (eventually) mit der Zeit; **in no ~** im Handumdrehen; **in a year's ~** in einem Jahr; **behind ~** verspätet; **behind the ~s** rückständig; **for the ~ being** vorläufig; **what is the ~?** wie spät ist es? wieviel Uhr ist es? **by the ~ we arrive** bis wir ankommen; **did you have a nice ~?** hat es dir gut gefallen? **have a good ~!** viel Vergnügen! ● vt stoppen ⟨race⟩; **be well ~d** gut abgepaßt sein

time: ~ bomb n Zeitbombe f. **~-lag** n Zeitdifferenz f. **~less** a zeitlos. **~ly** a rechtzeitig. **~-switch** n Zeitschalter m. **~table** n Fahrplan m; (Sch) Stundenplan m

timid /'tɪmɪd/ a, **-ly** adv scheu; (hesitant) zaghaft

timing /'taɪmɪŋ/ n Wahl f des richtigen Zeitpunkts; (Sport, Techn) Timing nt

tin /tɪn/ n Zinn nt; (container) Dose f ● vt (pt/pp **tinned**) in Dosen od Büchsen konservieren. **~ foil** n Stanniol nt; (Culin) Alufolie f

tinge /tɪndʒ/ n Hauch m ● vt **~d with** mit einer Spur von

tingle /'tɪŋgl/ vi kribbeln

tinker /'tɪŋkə(r)/ vi herumbasteln (**with** an + dat)

tinkle /'tɪŋkl/ n Klingeln nt ● vi klingeln

tinned /tɪnd/ a Dosen-, Büchsen-

'tin opener n Dosen-/Büchsenöffner m

'tinpot a (pej) ⟨firm⟩ schäbig

tinsel /'tɪnsl/ n Lametta nt

tint /tɪnt/ n Farbton m ● vt tönen

tiny /'taɪnɪ/ a (-ier, -iest) winzig

tip¹ /tɪp/ n Spitze f

tip² n (money) Trinkgeld nt; (advice) Rat m, (fam) Tip m; (for rubbish) Müllhalde f ● v (pt/pp **tipped**) ● vt (tilt) kippen; (reward) Trinkgeld geben (**s.o.** jdm) ● vi kippen. **~ off** vt **~ s.o. off** jdm einen Hinweis geben. **~ out** vt auskippen. **~ over** vt/i umkippen

'tip-off n Hinweis m

tipped /tɪpt/ a Filter-

tipsy /'tɪpsɪ/ a (fam) beschwipst

tiptoe /'tɪptəʊ/ n **on ~** auf Zehenspitzen

tiptop /tɪp'tɒp/ a (fam) erstklassig

tire /'taɪə(r)/ vt/i ermüden. **~d** a müde; **be ~d of sth** etw satt haben; **~d out** [völlig] erschöpft. **~less** a, **-ly** adv unermüdlich. **~some** /-səm/ a lästig

tiring /'taɪərɪŋ/ a ermüdend

tissue /'tɪʃuː/ n Gewebe nt; (handkerchief) Papiertaschentuch nt. **~-paper** n Seidenpapier nt

tit¹ /tɪt/ n (bird) Meise f

tit² n **~ for tat** wie du mir, so ich dir

'titbit n Leckerbissen m

titillate /'tɪtɪleɪt/ vt erregen

title /'taɪtl/ n Titel m. **~-role** n Titelrolle f

tittle-tattle /'tɪtltætl/ n Klatsch m

titular /'tɪtjʊlə(r)/ a nominell

to /tu:, unbetont tə/ prep zu (+ dat); (with place, direction) nach; (to cinema, theatre) in (+ acc); (to wedding, party) auf (+ acc); ⟨address, send, fasten⟩ an (+ acc); (per) pro; (up to, until) bis; **to the station** zum Bahnhof; **to Germany/Switzerland** nach Deutschland/in die Schweiz; **to the toilet/one's room** auf die Toilette/sein Zimmer; **to the office/an exhibition** ins Büro/in eine Ausstellung; **to university** auf die Universität; **twenty/quarter to eight** zwanzig/Viertel vor acht; **5 to 6 pounds** 5 bis 6 Pfund; **to the end** bis zum Schluß; **to this day** bis heute; **to the best of my knowledge**

nach meinem besten Wissen; **give/say sth to s.o.** jdm etw geben/sagen; **go/ come to s.o.** zu jdm gehen/kommen; **I've never been to Berlin** ich war noch nie in Berlin; **there's nothing to it** es ist nichts dabei ● *verbal constructions* **to go** gehen; **to stay** bleiben; **learn to swim** schwimmen lernen; **want to/ have to go** gehen wollen/müssen; **be easy/difficult to forget** leicht/schwer zu vergessen sein; **too ill/tired to go** zu krank/ müde, um zu gehen; **he did it to annoy me** er tat es, um mich zu ärgern; **you have to** du mußt; **I don't want to** ich will nicht; **I'd love to** gern; **I forgot to** ich habe es vergessen; **he wants to be a teacher** er will Lehrer werden; **live to be 90** 90 werden; **he was the last to arrive** er kam als letzter; **to be honest** ehrlich gesagt ● *adv* **pull to** anlehnen; **to and fro** hin und her

toad /təʊd/ *n* Kröte *f*. **~stool** *n* Giftpilz *m*

toast /təʊst/ *n* Toast *m* ● *vt* toasten ⟨bread⟩; ⟨drink a ~ to⟩ trinken auf (+ acc). **~er** *n* Toaster *m*

tobacco /tə'bækəʊ/ *n* Tabak *m*. **~nist's [shop]** *n* Tabakladen *m*

toboggan /tə'bɒgən/ *n* Schlitten *m* ● *vi* Schlitten fahren

today /tə'deɪ/ *n* & *adv* heute; **~ week** heute in einer Woche; **~'s paper** die heutige Zeitung

toddler /'tɒdlə(r)/ *n* Kleinkind *nt*

to-do /tə'du:/ *n* (*fam*) Getue *nt*, Theater *nt*

toe /təʊ/ *n* Zeh *m*; ⟨of footwear⟩ Spitze *f* ● *vt* **~ the line** spuren. **~nail** *n* Zehennagel *m*

toffee /'tɒfɪ/ *n* Karamelbonbon *m* & *nt*

together /tə'geðə(r)/ *adv* zusammen; ⟨at the same time⟩ gleichzeitig

toil /tɔɪl/ *n* [harte] Arbeit *f* ● *vi* schwer arbeiten

toilet /'tɔɪlɪt/ *n* Toilette *f*. **~ bag** *n* Kulturbeutel *m*. **~ paper** *n* Toilettenpapier *nt*

toiletries /'tɔɪlɪtrɪz/ *npl* Toilettenartikel *pl*

toilet: ~ roll *n* Rolle *f* Toilettenpapier. **~ water** *n* Toilettenwasser *nt*

token /'təʊkən/ *n* Zeichen *nt*; ⟨counter⟩ Marke *f*; ⟨voucher⟩ Gutschein *m* ● *attrib* symbolisch

told /təʊld/ *see* **tell** ● *a* **all ~** insgesamt

tolerable /'tɒlərəbl/ *a*, **-bly** *adv* erträglich; (*not bad*) leidlich

toleran|ce /'tɒlərəns/ *n* Toleranz *f*. **~t** *a*, **-ly** *adv* tolerant

tolerate /'tɒləreɪt/ *vt* dulden, tolerieren; (*bear*) ertragen

toll¹ /təʊl/ *n* Gebühr *f*; (*for road*) Maut *f* (*Aust*); **death ~** Zahl *f* der Todesopfer; **take a heavy ~** einen hohen Tribut fordern

toll² *vi* läuten

tom /tɒm/ *n* (*cat*) Kater *m*

tomato /tə'mɑ:təʊ/ *n* (*pl* **-es**) Tomate *f*. **~ purée** *n* Tomatenmark *nt*

tomb /tu:m/ *n* Grabmal *nt*

'tomboy *n* Wildfang *m*

'tombstone *n* Grabstein *m*

'tom-cat *n* Kater *m*

tome /təʊm/ *n* dicker Band *m*

tomfoolery /tɒm'fu:lərɪ/ *n* Blödsinn *m*

tomorrow /tə'mɒrəʊ/ *n* & *adv* morgen; **~ morning** morgen früh; **the day after ~** übermorgen; **see you ~!** bis morgen!

ton /tʌn/ *n* Tonne *f*; **~s of** (*fam*) jede Menge

tone /təʊn/ *n* Ton *m*; (*colour*) Farbton *m* ● *vt* **~ down** dämpfen; (*fig*) mäßigen. **~ up** *vt* kräftigen; straffen ⟨muscles⟩

tongs /tɒŋz/ *npl* Zange *f*

tongue /tʌŋ/ *n* Zunge *f*; **~ in cheek** (*fam*) nicht ernst. **~-twister** *n* Zungenbrecher *m*

tonic /'tɒnɪk/ *n* Tonikum *nt*; (*for hair*) Haarwasser *nt*; (*fig*) Wohltat *f*; **~ [water]** Tonic *nt*

tonight /tə'naɪt/ *n* & *adv* heute nacht; (*evening*) heute abend

tonne /tʌn/ *n* Tonne *f*

tonsil /'tɒnsl/ *n* (*Anat*) Mandel *f*. **~litis** /-sə'laɪtɪs/ *n* Mandelentzündung *f*

too /tu:/ *adv* zu; (*also*) auch; **~ much/ little** zuviel/zuwenig

took /tʊk/ *see* **take**

tool /tu:l/ *n* Werkzeug *nt*; (*for gardening*) Gerät *nt*

toot /tu:t/ *n* Hupsignal *nt* ● *vi* tuten; (*Auto*) hupen

tooth /tu:θ/ *n* (*pl* **teeth**) Zahn *m*

tooth: ~ache *n* Zahnschmerzen *pl*. **~brush** *n* Zahnbürste *f*. **~less** *a* zahnlos. **~paste** *n* Zahnpasta *f*. **~pick** *n* Zahnstocher *m*

top¹ /tɒp/ *n* (*toy*) Kreisel *m*

top[2] *n* oberer Teil *m*; (*apex*) Spitze *f*; (*summit*) Gipfel *m*; (*Sch*) Erste(r) *m/f*; (*top part or half*) Oberteil *nt*; (*head*) Kopfende *nt*; (*of road*) oberes Ende *nt*; (*upper surface*) Oberfläche *f*; (*lid*) Deckel *m*; (*of bottle*) Verschluß *m*; (*garment*) Top *nt*; **at the/on ~** oben; **on ~ of** oben auf (+ *dat/acc*); **on ~ of that** (*besides*) obendrein; **from ~ to bottom** von oben bis unten ● *a* oberste(r,s); (*highest*) höchste(r,s); (*best*) beste(r,s) ● *vt* (*pt/pp* **topped**) an erster Stelle stehen auf (+ *dat*) (*list*); (*exceed*) übersteigen; (*remove the ~ of*) die Spitze abschneiden von. **~ up** *vt* nachfüllen, auffüllen

top: **~ 'hat** *n* Zylinder[hut] *m*. **~-heavy** *a* kopflastig

topic /'tɒpɪk/ *n* Thema *nt*. **~al** *a* aktuell

top: **~less** *a* & *adv* oben ohne. **~most** *a* oberste(r,s)

topple /'tɒpl/ *vt/i* umstürzen. **~ off** *vi* stürzen

top-'secret *a* streng geheim

topsy-turvy /tɒpsɪ'tɜːvɪ/ *adv* völlig durcheinander

torch /tɔːtʃ/ *n* Taschenlampe *f*; (*flaming*) Fackel *f*

tore /tɔː(r)/ *see* **tear**[1]

torment[1] /'tɔːment/ *n* Qual *f*

torment[2] /tɔː'ment/ *vt* quälen

torn /tɔːn/ *see* **tear**[1] ● *a* zerrissen

tornado /tɔː'neɪdəʊ/ *n* (*pl* **-es**) Wirbelsturm *m*

torpedo /tɔː'piːdəʊ/ *n* (*pl* **-es**) Torpedo *m* ● *vt* torpedieren

torrent /'tɒrənt/ *n* reißender Strom *m*. **~ial** /tə'renʃl/ *a* (*rain*) wolkenbruchartig

torso /'tɔːsəʊ/ *n* Rumpf *m*; (*Art*) Torso *m*

tortoise /'tɔːtəs/ *n* Schildkröte *f*. **~shell** *n* Schildpatt *nt*

tortuous /'tɔːtjʊəs/ *a* verschlungen; (*fig*) umständlich

torture /'tɔːtʃə(r)/ *n* Folter *f*; (*fig*) Qual *f* ● *vt* foltern; (*fig*) quälen

toss /tɒs/ *vt* werfen; (*into the air*) hochwerfen; (*shake*) schütteln; (*unseat*) abwerfen; mischen (*salad*); wenden (*pancake*); **~ a coin** mit einer Münze losen ● *vi* **~ and turn** (*in bed*) sich [schlaflos] im Bett wälzen. **~ up** *vi* [mit einer Münze] losen

tot[1] /tɒt/ *n* kleines Kind *nt*; (*fam: of liquor*) Gläschen *nt*

tot[2] *vt* (*pt/pp* **totted**) **~ up** (*fam*) zusammenzählen

total /'təʊtl/ *a* gesamt; (*complete*) völlig, total ● *n* Gesamtzahl *f*; (*sum*) Gesamtsumme *f* ● *vt* (*pt/pp* **totalled**) zusammenzählen; (*amount to*) sich belaufen auf (+ *acc*)

totalitarian /təʊtælɪ'teərɪən/ *a* totalitär

totally /'təʊtəlɪ/ *adv* völlig, total

totter /'tɒtə(r)/ *vi* taumeln; (*rock*) schwanken. **~y** *a* wackelig

touch /tʌtʃ/ *n* Berührung *f*; (*sense*) Tastsinn *m*; (*Mus*) Anschlag *m*; (*contact*) Kontakt *m*; (*trace*) Spur *f*; (*fig*) Anflug *m*; **get/be in ~** sich in Verbindung setzen/in Verbindung stehen (**with** mit) ● *vt* berühren; (*get hold of*) anfassen; (*lightly*) tippen auf/ an (+ *acc*); (*brush against*) streifen [gegen]; (*reach*) erreichen; (*equal*) herankommen an (+ *acc*); (*fig: move*) rühren; anrühren (*food, subject*); **don't ~ that!** faß das nicht an! ● *vi* sich berühren; **~ on** (*fig*) berühren. **~ down** *vi* (*Aviat*) landen. **~ up** *vt* ausbessern

touch|ing /'tʌtʃɪŋ/ *a* rührend. **~y** *a* empfindlich; (*subject*) heikel

tough /tʌf/ *a* (**-er, -est**) zäh; (*severe, harsh*) hart; (*difficult*) schwierig; (*durable*) strapazierfähig

toughen /'tʌfn/ *vt* härten; **~ up** abhärten

tour /tʊə(r)/ *n* Reise *f*, Tour *f*; (*of building, town*) Besichtigung *f*; (*Theat, Sport*) Tournee *f*; (*of duty*) Dienstzeit *f* ● *vt* fahren durch; besichtigen (*building*) ● *vi* herumreisen

touris|m /'tʊərɪzm/ *n* Tourismus *m*, Fremdenverkehr *m*. **~t** /-rɪst/ *n* Tourist(in) *m(f)* ● *attrib* Touristen-. **~t office** *n* Fremdenverkehrsbüro *nt*

tournament /'tʊənəmənt/ *n* Turnier *nt*

'tour operator *n* Reiseveranstalter *m*

tousle /'taʊzl/ *vt* zerzausen

tout /taʊt/ *n* Anreißer *m*; (*ticket ~*) Kartenschwarzhändler *m* ● *vi* **~ for customers** Kunden werben

tow /təʊ/ *n* **give s.o./a car a ~** jdn/ein Auto abschleppen; **'on ~'** 'wird geschleppt'; **in ~** (*fam*) im Schlepptau ● *vt* schleppen; ziehen (*trailer*). **~ away** *vt* abschleppen

toward[s] /tə'wɔːd(z)/ *prep* zu (+ *dat*); (*with time*) gegen (+ *acc*); (*with respect to*) gegenüber (+ *dat*)

towel /'tauəl/ *n* Handtuch *nt*. ~**ling** *n* (*Tex*) Frottee *nt*

tower /'tauə(r)/ *n* Turm *m* ● *vi* ~ **above** überragen. ~ **block** *n* Hochhaus *nt*. ~**ing** *a* hochragend

town /taun/ *n* Stadt *f*. ~ '**hall** *n* Rathaus *nt*

tow: ~-**path** *n* Treidelpfad *m*. ~-**rope** *n* Abschleppseil *nt*

toxic /'tɒksɪk/ *a* giftig. ~ '**waste** *n* Giftmüll *m*

toxin /'tɒksɪn/ *n* Gift *nt*

toy /tɔɪ/ *n* Spielzeug *nt* ● *vi* ~ **with** spielen mit; stochern in (+ *dat*) ⟨*food*⟩. ~**shop** *n* Spielwarengeschäft *nt*

trac|e /treɪs/ *n* Spur *f* ● *vt* folgen (+ *dat*); (*find*) finden; (*draw*) zeichnen; (*with tracing-paper*) durchpausen. ~**ing-paper** *n* Pauspapier *nt*

track /træk/ *n* Spur *f*; (*path*) [unbefestigter] Weg *m*; (*Sport*) Bahn *f*; (*Rail*) Gleis *nt*; **keep** ~ **of** im Auge behalten ● *vt* verfolgen. ~ **down** *vt* aufspüren; (*find*) finden

'**tracksuit** *n* Trainingsanzug *m*

tract[1] /trækt/ *n* (*land*) Gebiet *nt*

tract[2] *n* (*pamphlet*) [Flug]schrift *f*

tractor /'træktə(r)/ *n* Traktor *m*

trade /treɪd/ *n* Handel *m*; (*line of business*) Gewerbe *nt*; (*business*) Geschäft *nt*; (*craft*) Handwerk *nt*; **by** ~ von Beruf ● *vt* tauschen; ~ **in** (*give in part exchange*) in Zahlung geben ● *vi* handeln (**in** mit)

'**trade mark** *n* Warenzeichen *nt*

trader /'treɪdə(r)/ *n* Händler *m*

trade: ~ '**union** *n* Gewerkschaft *f*. ~ '**unionist** *n* Gewerkschaftler(in) *m(f)*

trading /'treɪdɪŋ/ *n* Handel *m*. ~ **estate** *n* Gewerbegebiet *nt*. ~ **stamp** *n* Rabattmarke *f*

tradition /trə'dɪʃn/ *n* Tradition *f*. ~**al** *a*, -**ly** *adv* traditionell

traffic /'træfɪk/ *n* Verkehr *m*; (*trading*) Handel *m* ● *vi* handeln (**in** mit)

traffic: ~ **circle** *n* (*Amer*) Kreisverkehr *m*. ~ **jam** *n* [Verkehrs]stau *m*. ~ **lights** *npl* [Verkehrs]ampel *f*. ~ **warden** *n* ≈ Hilfspolizist *m*; (*woman*) Politesse *f*

tragedy /'trædʒədɪ/ *n* Tragödie *f*

tragic /'trædʒɪk/ *a*, -**ally** *adv* tragisch

trail /treɪl/ *n* Spur *f*; (*path*) Weg *m*, Pfad *m* ● *vi* schleifen; ⟨*plant:*⟩ sich ranken; ~ **[behind]** zurückbleiben; (*Sport*) zurückliegen ● *vt* verfolgen, folgen (+ *dat*); (*drag*) schleifen

trailer /'treɪlə(r)/ *n* (*Auto*) Anhänger *m*; (*Amer: caravan*) Wohnwagen *m*; (*film*) Vorschau *f*

train /treɪn/ *n* Zug *m*; (*of dress*) Schleppe *f*; ~ **of thought** Gedankengang *m* ● *vt* ausbilden; (*Sport*) trainieren; (*aim*) richten auf (+ *acc*); erziehen ⟨*child*⟩; abrichten/(*to do tricks*) dressieren ⟨*animal*⟩; ziehen ⟨*plant*⟩ ● *vi* eine Ausbildung machen; (*Sport*) trainieren. ~**ed** *a* ausgebildet

trainee /treɪ'niː/ *n* Auszubildende(r) *m/f*; (*Techn*) Praktikant(in) *m(f)*

train|er /'treɪnə(r)/ *n* (*Sport*) Trainer *m*; (*in circus*) Dompteur *m*; ~**ers** *pl* Trainingsschuhe *pl*. ~**ing** *n* Ausbildung *f*; (*Sport*) Training *nt*; (*of animals*) Dressur *f*

traipse /treɪps/ *vi* (*fam*) latschen

trait /treɪt/ *n* Eigenschaft *f*

traitor /'treɪtə(r)/ *n* Verräter *m*

tram /træm/ *n* Straßenbahn *f*. ~-**lines** *npl* Straßenbahnschienen *pl*

tramp /træmp/ *n* Landstreicher *m*; (*hike*) Wanderung *f* ● *vi* stapfen; (*walk*) marschieren

trample /'træmpl/ *vt/i* trampeln (**on** auf + *acc*)

trampoline /'træmpəliːn/ *n* Trampolin *nt*

trance /trɑːns/ *n* Trance *f*

tranquil /'træŋkwɪl/ *a* ruhig. ~**lity** /-'kwɪlətɪ/ *n* Ruhe *f*

tranquillizer /'træŋkwɪlaɪzə(r)/ *n* Beruhigungsmittel *nt*

transact /træn'zækt/ *vt* abschließen. ~**ion** /-ækʃn/ *n* Transaktion *f*

transcend /træn'send/ *vt* übersteigen

transcript /'trænskrɪpt/ *n* Abschrift *f*; (*of official proceedings*) Protokoll *nt*. ~**ion** /-'skrɪpʃn/ *n* Abschrift *f*

transept /'trænsept/ *n* Querschiff *nt*

transfer[1] /'trænsfɜː(r)/ *n* (*see* **transfer**[2]) Übertragung *f*; Verlegung *f*; Versetzung *f*; Überweisung *f*; (*Sport*) Transfer *m*; (*design*) Abziehbild *nt*

transfer[2] /træns'fɜː(r)/ *v* (*pt/pp* **transferred**) ● *vt* übertragen; verlegen ⟨*firm, prisoners*⟩; versetzen ⟨*employee*⟩; überweisen ⟨*money*⟩; (*Sport*) transferieren ● *vi* [über]wechseln; (*when* *travelling*) umsteigen. ∼**able** /-əbl/ *a* übertragbar

transform /træns'fɔ:m/ *vt* verwandeln. ∼**ation** /-fə'meɪʃn/ *n* Verwandlung *f*. ∼**er** *n* Transformator *m*

transfusion /træns'fju:ʒn/ *n* Transfusion *f*

transient /'trænzɪənt/ *a* kurzlebig; ⟨*life*⟩ kurz

transistor /træn'zɪstə(r)/ *n* Transistor *m*

transit /'trænsɪt/ *n* Transit *m*; (*of goods*) Transport *m*; **in** ∼ ⟨*goods*⟩ auf dem Transport

transition /træn'sɪʒn/ *n* Übergang *m*. ∼**al** *a* Übergangs-

transitive /'trænsɪtɪv/ *a*, **-ly** *adv* transitiv

transitory /'trænsɪtərɪ/ *a* vergänglich; ⟨*life*⟩ kurz

translat|e /træns'leɪt/ *vt* übersetzen. ∼**ion** /-'leɪʃn/ *n* Übersetzung *f*. ∼**or** *n* Übersetzer(in) *m*(*f*)

translucent /trænz'lu:snt/ *a* durchscheinend

transmission /trænz'mɪʃn/ *n* Übertragung *f*

transmit /trænz'mɪt/ *vt* (*pt/pp* **transmitted**) übertragen. ∼**ter** *n* Sender *m*

transparen|cy /træns'pærənsɪ/ *n* (*Phot*) Dia *nt*. ∼**t** *a* durchsichtig

transpire /træn'spaɪə(r)/ *vi* sich herausstellen; (*fam: happen*) passieren

transplant[1] /'trænsplɑ:nt/ *n* Verpflanzung *f*, Transplantation *f*

transplant[2] /træns'plɑ:nt/ *vt* umpflanzen; (*Med*) verpflanzen

transport[1] /'trænspɔ:t/ *n* Transport *m*

transport[2] /træn'spɔ:t/ *vt* transportieren. ∼**ation** /-'teɪʃn/ *n* Transport *m*

transpose /træns'pəʊz/ *vt* umstellen

transvestite /træns'vestaɪt/ *n* Transvestit *m*

trap /træp/ *n* Falle *f*; (*fam: mouth*) Klappe *f*; **pony and** ∼ Einspänner *m* ● *vt* (*pt/pp* **trapped**) [mit einer Falle] fangen; (*jam*) einklemmen; **be** ∼**ped** festsitzen; (*shut in*) eingeschlossen sein; (*cut off*) abgeschnitten sein. ∼'**door** *n* Falltür *f*

trapeze /trə'pi:z/ *n* Trapez *nt*

trash /træʃ/ *n* Schund *m*; (*rubbish*) Abfall *m*; (*nonsense*) Quatsch *m*.

∼**can** *n* (*Amer*) Mülleimer *m*. ∼**y** *a* Schund-

trauma /'trɔ:mə/ *n* Trauma *nt*. ∼**tic** /-'mætɪk/ *a* traumatisch

travel /'trævl/ *n* Reisen *nt* ● *v* (*pt/pp* **travelled**) ● *vi* reisen; (*go in vehicle*) fahren; ⟨*light, sound:*⟩ sich fortpflanzen; (*Techn*) sich bewegen ● *vt* bereisen; fahren ⟨*distance*⟩. ∼ **agency** *n* Reisebüro *nt*. ∼ **agent** *n* Reisebürokaufmann *m*

traveller /'trævələ(r)/ *n* Reisende(r) *m/f*; (*Comm*) Vertreter *m*; ∼**s** *pl* (*gypsies*) Zigeuner *pl*. ∼'**s cheque** *n* Reisescheck *m*

trawler /'trɔ:lə(r)/ *n* Fischdampfer *m*

tray /treɪ/ *n* Tablett *nt*; (*for baking*) [Back]blech *nt*; (*for documents*) Ablagekorb *m*

treacher|ous /'tretʃərəs/ *a* treulos; (*dangerous, deceptive*) tückisch. ∼**y** *n* Verrat *m*

treacle /'tri:kl/ *n* Sirup *m*

tread /tred/ *n* Schritt *m*; (*step*) Stufe *f*; (*of tyre*) Profil *nt* ● *v* (*pt* **trod**, *pp* **trodden**) ● *vi* (*walk*) gehen; ∼ **on/in** treten auf/in (+ *acc*) ● *vt* treten

treason /'tri:zn/ *n* Verrat *m*

treasure /'treʒə(r)/ *n* Schatz *m* ● *vt* in Ehren halten. ∼**r** *n* Kassenwart *m*

treasury /'treʒərɪ/ *n* Schatzkammer *f*; **the T**∼ das Finanzministerium

treat /tri:t/ *n* [besonderes] Vergnügen *nt*; **give s.o. a** ∼ jdm etwas Besonderes bieten ● *vt* behandeln; ∼ **s.o. to sth** jdm etw spendieren

treatise /'tri:tɪz/ *n* Abhandlung *f*

treatment /'tri:tmənt/ *n* Behandlung *f*

treaty /'tri:tɪ/ *n* Vertrag *m*

treble /'trebl/ *a* dreifach; ∼ **the amount** dreimal soviel ● *n* (*Mus*) Diskant *m*; (*voice*) Sopran *m* ● *vt* verdreifachen ● *vi* sich verdreifachen. ∼ **clef** *n* Violinschlüssel *m*

tree /tri:/ *n* Baum *m*

trek /trek/ *n* Marsch *m* ● *vi* (*pt/pp* **trekked**) latschen

trellis /'trelɪs/ *n* Gitter *nt*

tremble /'trembl/ *vi* zittern

tremendous /trɪ'mendəs/ *a*, **-ly** *adv* gewaltig; (*fam: excellent*) großartig

tremor /'tremə(r)/ *n* Zittern *nt*; **[earth]** ∼ Beben *nt*

trench /trentʃ/ *n* Graben *m*; (*Mil*) Schützengraben *m*

trend /trend/ *n* Tendenz *f*; (*fashion*) Trend *m*. ∼**y** *a* (**-ier, -iest**) (*fam*) modisch

trepidation /trepɪ'deɪʃn/ *n* Beklommenheit *f*

trespass /'trespəs/ *vi* ∼ **on** unerlaubt betreten. ∼**er** *n* Unbefugte(r) *m/f*

trial /'traɪəl/ *n* (*Jur*) [Gerichts]-verfahren *nt*, Prozeß *m*; (*test*) Probe *f*; (*ordeal*) Prüfung *f*; **be on** ∼ auf Probe sein; (*Jur*) angeklagt sein (**for** wegen); **by** ∼ **and error** durch Probieren

triang|le /'traɪæŋgl/ *n* Dreieck *nt*; (*Mus*) Triangel *m*. ∼**ular** /-'æŋgjʊlə(r)/ *a* dreieckig

tribe /traɪb/ *n* Stamm *m*

tribulation /trɪbjʊ'leɪʃn/ *n* Kummer *m*

tribunal /traɪ'bjuːnl/ *n* Schiedsgericht *nt*

tributary /'trɪbjʊtərɪ/ *n* Nebenfluß *m*

tribute /'trɪbjuːt/ *n* Tribut *m*; **pay** ∼ Tribut zollen (**to** *dat*)

trice /traɪs/ *n* **in a** ∼ im Nu

trick /trɪk/ *n* Trick *m*; (*joke*) Streich *m*; (*Cards*) Stich *m*; (*feat of skill*) Kunststück *nt*; **that should do the** ∼ (*fam*) damit dürfte es klappen ● *vt* täuschen, (*fam*) hereinlegen

trickle /'trɪkl/ *vi* rinnen

trick|ster /'trɪkstə(r)/ *n* Schwindler *m*. ∼**y** *a* (**-ier, -iest**) *a* schwierig

tricycle /'traɪsɪkl/ *n* Dreirad *nt*

tried /traɪd/ *see* **try**

trif|le /'traɪfl/ *n* Kleinigkeit *f*; (*Culin*) Trifle *nt*. ∼**ing** *a* unbedeutend

trigger /'trɪgə(r)/ *n* Abzug *m*; (*fig*) Auslöser *m* ● *vt* ∼ [**off**] auslösen

trigonometry /trɪgə'nɒmɪtrɪ/ *n* Trigonometrie *f*

trim /trɪm/ *a* (**trimmer, trimmest**) gepflegt ● *n* (*cut*) Nachschneiden *nt*; (*decoration*) Verzierung *f*; (*condition*) Zustand *m* ● *vt* schneiden; (*decorate*) besetzen; (*Naut*) trimmen. ∼**ming** *n* Besatz *m*; ∼**mings** *pl* (*accessories*) Zubehör *nt*; (*decorations*) Verzierungen *pl*; **with all the** ∼**mings** mit allem Drum und Dran

Trinity /'trɪnɪtɪ/ *n* **the [Holy]** ∼ die [Heilige] Dreieinigkeit *f*

trinket /'trɪŋkɪt/ *n* Schmuckgegenstand *m*

trio /'triːəʊ/ *n* Trio *nt*

trip /trɪp/ *n* Reise *f*; (*excursion*) Ausflug *m* ● *v* (*pt/pp* **tripped**) ● *vt* ∼ **s.o.**

up jdm ein Bein stellen ● *vi* stolpern (**on/over** über + *acc*)

tripe /traɪp/ *n* Kaldaunen *pl*; (*nonsense*) Quatsch *m*

triple /'trɪpl/ *a* dreifach ● *vt* verdreifachen ● *vi* sich verdreifachen

triplets /'trɪplɪts/ *npl* Drillinge *pl*

triplicate /'trɪplɪkət/ *n* **in** ∼ in dreifacher Ausfertigung

tripod /'traɪpɒd/ *n* Stativ *nt*

tripper /'trɪpə(r)/ *n* Ausflügler *m*

trite /traɪt/ *a* banal

triumph /'traɪʌmf/ *n* Triumph *m* ● *vi* triumphieren (**over** über + *acc*). ∼**ant** /-'ʌmfnt/ *a*, **-ly** *adv* triumphierend

trivial /'trɪvɪəl/ *a* belanglos. ∼**ity** /-'ælətɪ/ *n* Belanglosigkeit *f*

trod, trodden /trɒd, 'trɒdn/ *see* **tread**

trolley /'trɒlɪ/ *n* (*for serving food*) Servierwagen *m*; (*for shopping*) Einkaufswagen *m*; (*for luggage*) Kofferkuli *m*; (*Amer: tram*) Straßenbahn *f*. ∼ **bus** *n* O-Bus *m*

trombone /trɒm'bəʊn/ *n* Posaune *f*

troop /truːp/ *n* Schar *f*; ∼**s** *pl* Truppen *pl* ● *vi* ∼ **in/out** hinein-/hinausströmen

trophy /'trəʊfɪ/ *n* Trophäe *f*; (*in competition*) ≈ Pokal *m*

tropic /'trɒpɪk/ *n* Wendekreis *m*; ∼**s** *pl* Tropen *pl*. ∼**al** *a* tropisch; ⟨*fruit*⟩ Süd-

trot /trɒt/ *n* Trab *m* ● *vi* (*pt/pp* **trotted**) traben

trouble /'trʌbl/ *n* Ärger *m*; (*difficulties*) Schwierigkeiten *pl*; (*inconvenience*) Mühe *f*; (*conflict*) Unruhe *f*; (*Med*) Beschwerden *pl*; (*Techn*) Probleme *pl*; **get into** ∼ Ärger bekommen; **take** ∼ sich (*dat*) Mühe geben ● *vt* (*disturb*) stören; (*worry*) beunruhigen ● *vi* sich bemühen. ∼**-maker** *n* Unruhestifter *m*. ∼**some** /-səm/ *a* schwierig; ⟨*flies, cough*⟩ lästig

trough /trɒf/ *n* Trog *m*

trounce /traʊns/ *vt* vernichtend schlagen; (*thrash*) verprügeln

troupe /truːp/ *n* Truppe *f*

trousers /'traʊzəz/ *npl* Hose *f*

trousseau /'truːsəʊ/ *n* Aussteuer *f*

trout /traʊt/ *n inv* Forelle *f*

trowel /'traʊəl/ *n* Kelle *f*; (*for gardening*) Pflanzkelle *f*

truant /'truːənt/ *n* **play** ∼ die Schule schwänzen

truce /truːs/ n Waffenstillstand m

truck /trʌk/ n Last[kraft]wagen m; (Rail) Güterwagen m

truculent /'trʌkjʊlənt/ a aufsässig

trudge /trʌdʒ/ n [mühseliger] Marsch m ● vi latschen

true /truː/ a (-r, -st) wahr; (loyal) treu; (genuine) echt; **come** ~ in Erfüllung gehen; **is that** ~? stimmt das?

truism /'truːɪzm/ n Binsenwahrheit f

truly /'truːlɪ/ adv wirklich; (faithfully) treu; **Yours** ~ Hochachtungsvoll

trump /trʌmp/ n (Cards) Trumpf m ● vt übertrumpfen. ~ **up** vt (fam) erfinden

trumpet /'trʌmpɪt/ n Trompete f. ~**er** n Trompeter m

truncheon /'trʌntʃn/ n Schlagstock m

trundle /'trʌndl/ vt/i rollen

trunk /trʌŋk/ n [Baum]stamm m; (body) Rumpf m; (of elephant) Rüssel m; (for travelling) [Übersee]koffer m; (for storage) Truhe f; (Amer: of car) Kofferraum m; ~s pl Badehose f

truss /trʌs/ n (Med) Bruchband nt

trust /trʌst/ n Vertrauen nt; (group of companies) Trust m; (organization) Treuhandgesellschaft f; (charitable) Stiftung f ● vt trauen (+ dat), vertrauen (+ dat); (hope) hoffen ● vi vertrauen (in/to auf + acc)

trustee /trʌsˈtiː/ n Treuhänder m

'trust|ful /'trʌstfl/ a, -ly adv vertrauensvoll. ~**ing** a vertrauensvoll. ~**worthy** a vertrauenswürdig

truth /truːθ/ n (pl -s /truːðz/) Wahrheit f. ~**ful** a, -ly adv ehrlich

try /traɪ/ n Versuch m ● v (pt/pp **tried**) ● vt versuchen; (sample, taste) probieren; (be a strain on) anstrengen; (Jur) vor Gericht stellen; verhandeln 〈case〉 ● vi versuchen; (make an effort) sich bemühen. ~ **on** vt anprobieren; aufprobieren 〈hat〉. ~ **out** vt ausprobieren

trying /'traɪɪŋ/ a schwierig

T-shirt /'tiː-/ n T-Shirt nt

tub /tʌb/ n Kübel m; (carton) Becher m; (bath) Wanne f

tuba /'tjuːbə/ n (Mus) Tuba f

tubby /'tʌbɪ/ a (-ier, -iest) rundlich

tube /tjuːb/ n Röhre f; (pipe) Rohr nt; (flexible) Schlauch m; (of toothpaste) Tube f; (Rail, fam) U-Bahn f

tuber /'tjuːbə(r)/ n Knolle f

tuberculosis /tjuːbɜːkjʊˈləʊsɪs/ n Tuberkulose f

tubing /'tjuːbɪŋ/ n Schlauch m

tubular /'tjuːbjʊlə(r)/ a röhrenförmig

tuck /tʌk/ n Saum m; (decorative) Biese f ● vt (put) stecken. ~ **in** vt hineinstecken; ~ **s.o. in** jdn zudecken ● vi (fam: eat) zulangen. ~ **up** vt hochkrempeln 〈sleeves〉; (in bed) zudecken

Tuesday /'tjuːzdeɪ/ n Dienstag m

tuft /tʌft/ n Büschel nt

tug /tʌg/ n Ruck m; (Naut) Schleppdampfer m ● v (pt/pp **tugged**) ● vt ziehen ● vi zerren (**at** an + dat). ~ **of war** n Tauziehen nt

tuition /tjuːˈɪʃn/ n Unterricht m

tulip /'tjuːlɪp/ n Tulpe f

tumble /'tʌmbl/ n Sturz m ● vi fallen; ~ **to sth** (fam) etw kapieren. ~**down** a verfallen. ~**-drier** n Wäschetrockner m

tumbler /'tʌmblə(r)/ n Glas nt

tummy /'tʌmɪ/ n (fam) Magen m; (abdomen) Bauch m

tumour /'tjuːmə(r)/ n Geschwulst f, Tumor m

tumult /'tjuːmʌlt/ n Tumult m. ~**uous** /-'mʌltjʊəs/ a stürmisch

tuna /'tjuːnə/ n Thunfisch m

tune /tjuːn/ n Melodie f; **out of** ~ 〈instrument〉 verstimmt; **to the** ~ **of** (fam) in Höhe von ● vt stimmen; (Techn) einstellen. ~ **in** vt einstellen ● vi ~ **in to a station** einen Sender einstellen. ~ **up** vi (Mus) stimmen

tuneful /'tjuːnfl/ a melodisch

tunic /'tjuːnɪk/ n (Mil) Uniformjacke f; (Sch) Trägerkleid nt

Tunisia /tjuːˈnɪzɪə/ n Tunesien nt

tunnel /'tʌnl/ n Tunnel m ● vi (pt/pp **tunnelled**) einen Tunnel graben

turban /'tɜːbən/ n Turban m

turbine /'tɜːbaɪn/ n Turbine f

turbot /'tɜːbət/ n Steinbutt m

turbulen|ce /'tɜːbjʊləns/ n Turbulenz f. ~**t** a stürmisch

tureen /tjʊəˈriːn/ n Terrine f

turf /tɜːf/ n Rasen m; (segment) Rasenstück nt. ~ **out** vt (fam) rausschmeißen

'turf accountant n Buchmacher m

Turk /tɜːk/ n Türke m/Türkin f

turkey /'tɜːkɪ/ n Pute f, Truthahn m

Turk|ey n die Türkei. ~**ish** a türkisch

turmoil /'tɜːmɔɪl/ n Aufruhr m; (confusion) Durcheinander nt

turn /tɜːn/ n (*rotation*) Drehung f; (*in road*) Kurve f; (*change of direction*) Wende f; (*short walk*) Runde f; (*Theat*) Nummer f; (*fam: attack*) Anfall m; **do s.o. a good ~** jdm einen guten Dienst erweisen; **take ~s** sich abwechseln; **in ~** der Reihe nach; **out of ~** außer der Reihe; **it's your ~** du bist an der Reihe ● vt drehen; (*~ over*) wenden; (*reverse*) umdrehen; (*Techn*) drechseln ⟨wood⟩; **~ the page** umblättern; **~ the corner** um die Ecke biegen ● vi sich drehen; (*~ round*) sich umdrehen; ⟨car:⟩ wenden; ⟨leaves:⟩ sich färben; ⟨weather:⟩ umschlagen; (*become*) werden; **~ right/left** nach rechts/links abbiegen; **~ to s.o.** sich an jdn wenden; **have ~ed against s.o.** gegen jdn sein. **~ away** vt abweisen ● vi sich abwenden. **~ down** vt herunterschlagen ⟨collar⟩; herunterdrehen ⟨heat, gas⟩; leiser stellen ⟨sound⟩; (*reject*) ablehnen; abweisen ⟨person⟩. **~ in** vt einschlagen ⟨edges⟩ ● vi ⟨car:⟩ einbiegen; (*fam: go to bed*) ins Bett gehen. **~ off** vt zudrehen ⟨tap⟩; ausschalten ⟨light, radio⟩; abstellen ⟨water, gas, engine, machine⟩ ● vi abbiegen. **~ on** vt aufdrehen ⟨tap⟩; einschalten ⟨light, radio⟩; anstellen ⟨water, gas, engine, machine⟩. **~ out** vt (*expel*) vertreiben, (*fam*) hinauswerfen; ausschalten ⟨light⟩; abdrehen ⟨gas⟩; (*produce*) produzieren; (*empty*) ausleeren; [gründlich] aufräumen ⟨room, cupboard⟩ ● vi (*go out*) hinausgehen; (*transpire*) sich herausstellen; **~ out well/badly** gut/schlecht gehen. **~ over** vt umdrehen ● vi sich umdrehen. **~ up** vt hochschlagen ⟨collar⟩; aufdrehen ⟨heat, gas⟩; lauter stellen ⟨sound, radio⟩ ● vi auftauchen

turning /'tɜːnɪŋ/ n Abzweigung f. **~-point** n Wendepunkt m

turnip /'tɜːnɪp/ n weiße Rübe f

turn: **~-out** n (*of people*) Teilnahme f, Beteiligung f; (*of goods*) Produktion f. **~over** n (*Comm*) Umsatz m; (*of staff*) Personalwechsel m. **~pike** n (*Amer*) gebührenpflichtige Autobahn f. **~stile** n Drehkreuz nt. **~table** n Drehscheibe f; (*on record-player*) Plattenteller m. **~-up** n [Hosen]aufschlag m

turpentine /'tɜːpəntaɪn/ n Terpentin nt

turquoise /'tɜːkwɔɪz/ a türkis[farben] ● n (*gem*) Türkis m

turret /'tʌrɪt/ n Türmchen nt

turtle /'tɜːtl/ n Seeschildkröte f

tusk /tʌsk/ n Stoßzahn m

tussle /'tʌsl/ n Balgerei f; (*fig*) Streit m ● vi sich balgen

tutor /'tjuːtə(r)/ n [Privat]lehrer m

tuxedo /tʌk'siːdəʊ/ n (*Amer*) Smoking m

TV abbr of **television**

twaddle /'twɒdl/ n Geschwätz nt

twang /twæŋ/ n (*in voice*) Näseln nt ● vt zupfen

tweed /twiːd/ n Tweed m

tweezers /'twiːzəz/ npl Pinzette f

twelfth /twelfθ/ a zwölfte(r,s)

twelve /twelv/ a zwölf

twentieth /'twentɪɪθ/ a zwanzigste(r,s)

twenty /'twentɪ/ a zwanzig

twerp /twɜːp/ n (*fam*) Trottel m

twice /twaɪs/ adv zweimal

twiddle /'twɪdl/ vt drehen an (+ dat)

twig[1] /twɪg/ n Zweig m

twig[2] vt/i (pt/pp **twigged**) (*fam*) kapieren

twilight /'twaɪ-/ n Dämmerlicht nt

twin /twɪn/ n Zwilling m ● attrib Zwillings-. **~ beds** npl zwei Einzelbetten pl

twine /twaɪn/ n Bindfaden m ● vi sich winden; ⟨plant:⟩ sich ranken

twinge /twɪndʒ/ n Stechen nt; **~ of conscience** Gewissensbisse pl

twinkle /'twɪŋkl/ n Funkeln nt ● vi funkeln

twin 'town n Partnerstadt f

twirl /twɜːl/ vt/i herumwirbeln

twist /twɪst/ n Drehung f; (*curve*) Kurve f; (*unexpected occurrence*) überraschende Wendung f ● vt drehen; (*distort*) verdrehen; (*fam: swindle*) beschummeln; **~ one's ankle** sich (dat) den Knöchel verrenken ● vi sich drehen; ⟨road:⟩ sich winden. **~er** n (*fam*) Schwindler m

twit /twɪt/ n (*fam*) Trottel m

twitch /twɪtʃ/ n Zucken nt ● vi zucken

twitter /'twɪtə(r)/ n Zwitschern nt ● vi zwitschern

two /tuː/ a zwei

two: **~-faced** a falsch. **~-piece** a zweiteilig. **~some** /-səm/ n Paar nt. **~-way** a **~-way traffic** Gegenverkehr m

tycoon /taɪ'kuːn/ n Magnat m

tying /'taɪɪŋ/ *see* **tie**

type /taɪp/ *n* Art *f*, Sorte *f*; (*person*) Typ *m*; (*printing*) Type *f* ● *vt* mit der Maschine schreiben, (*fam*) tippen ● *vi* maschineschreiben, (*fam*) tippen. **~writer** *n* Schreibmaschine *f*. **~written** *a* maschinegeschrieben

typhoid /'taɪfɔɪd/ *n* Typhus *m*

typical /'tɪpɪkl/ *a*, **-ly** *adv* typisch (**of** für)

typify /'tɪpɪfaɪ/ *vt* (*pt/pp* **-ied**) typisch sein für

typing /'taɪpɪŋ/ *n* Maschineschreiben *nt*. **~ paper** *n* Schreibmaschinenpapier *nt*

typist /'taɪpɪst/ *n* Schreibkraft *f*

typography /taɪ'pɒgrəfɪ/ *n* Typographie *f*

tyrannical /tɪ'rænɪkl/ *a* tyrannisch

tyranny /'tɪrənɪ/ *n* Tyrannei *f*

tyrant /'taɪrənt/ *n* Tyrann *m*

tyre /'taɪə(r)/ *n* Reifen *m*

U

ubiquitous /ju:'bɪkwɪtəs/ *a* allgegenwärtig; **be ~** überall zu finden sein

udder /'ʌdə(r)/ *n* Euter *nt*

ugl|iness /'ʌglɪnɪs/ *n* Häßlichkeit *f*. **~y** *a* (**-ier, -iest**) häßlich; (*nasty*) übel

UK *abbr see* **United Kingdom**

ulcer /'ʌlsə(r)/ *n* Geschwür *nt*

ulterior /ʌl'tɪərɪə(r)/ *a* **~ motive** Hintergedanke *m*

ultimate /'ʌltɪmət/ *a* letzte(r,s); (*final*) endgültig; (*fundamental*) grundlegend, eigentlich. **~ly** *adv* schließlich

ultimatum /ʌltɪ'meɪtəm/ *n* Ultimatum *nt*

ultrasound /'ʌltrə-/ *n* (*Med*) Ultraschall *m*

ultra'violet *a* ultraviolett

umbilical /ʌm'bɪlɪkl/ *a* **~ cord** Nabelschnur *f*

umbrella /ʌm'brelə/ *n* [Regen]-schirm *m*

umpire /'ʌmpaɪə(r)/ *n* Schiedsrichter *m* ● *vt/i* Schiedsrichter sein (bei)

umpteen /ʌmp'ti:n/ *a* (*fam*) zig. **~th** *a* (*fam*) zigste(r,s); **for the ~th time** zum zigsten Mal

un'able /ʌn-/ *a* **be ~ to do sth** etw nicht tun können

una'bridged *a* ungekürzt

unac'companied *a* ohne Begleitung; (*luggage*) unbegleitet

unac'countabl|e *a* unerklärlich. **~y** *adv* unerklärlicherweise

unac'customed *a* ungewohnt; **be ~ to sth** etw nicht gewohnt sein

una'dulterated *a* unverfälscht, rein; (*utter*) völlig

un'aided *a* ohne fremde Hilfe

unalloyed /ʌnə'lɔɪd/ *a* (*fig*) ungetrübt

unanimity /ju:nə'nɪmətɪ/ *n* Einstimmigkeit *f*

unanimous /ju:'nænɪməs/ *a*, **-ly** *adv* einmütig; (*vote, decision*) einstimmig

un'armed *a* unbewaffnet; **~ combat** Kampf *m* ohne Waffen

unas'suming *a* bescheiden

unat'tached *a* nicht befestigt; (*person*) ungebunden

unat'tended *a* unbeaufsichtigt

un'authorized *a* unbefugt

una'voidable *a* unvermeidlich

una'ware *a* **be ~ of sth** sich (*dat*) etw (*gen*) nicht bewußt sein. **~s** /-eəz/ *adv* **catch s.o. ~s** jdn überraschen

un'balanced *a* unausgewogen; (*mentally*) unausgeglichen

un'bearable *a*, **-bly** *adv* unerträglich

unbeat|able /ʌn'bi:təbl/ *a* unschlagbar. **~en** *a* ungeschlagen; (*record*) ungebrochen

unbeknown /ʌnbɪ'nəʊn/ *a* (*fam*) **~ to me** ohne mein Wissen

unbe'lievable *a* unglaublich

un'bend *vi* (*pt/pp* **-bent**) (*relax*) aus sich herausgehen

un'biased *a* unvoreingenommen

un'block *vt* frei machen

un'bolt *vt* aufriegeln

un'breakable *a* unzerbrechlich

unbridled /ʌn'braɪdld/ *a* ungezügelt

un'burden *vt* **~ oneself** (*fig*) sich aussprechen

un'button *vt* aufknöpfen

uncalled-for /ʌn'kɔ:ldfɔ:(r)/ *a* unangebracht

un'canny *a* unheimlich

un'ceasing *a* unaufhörlich

uncere'monious *a*, **-ly** *adv* formlos; (*abrupt*) brüsk

un'certain *a* (*doubtful*) ungewiß; (*origins*) unbestimmt; **be ~** nicht sicher sein; **in no ~ terms** ganz eindeutig. **~ty** *n* Ungewißheit *f*

un'changed *a* unverändert

un'charitable *a* lieblos

uncle /'ʌŋkl/ *n* Onkel *m*

un'comfortable *a*, **-bly** *adv* unbequem; **feel** ~ (*fig*) sich nicht wohl fühlen

un'common *a* ungewöhnlich

un'compromising *a* kompromißlos

uncon'ditional *a*, **-ly** *adv* bedingungslos

un'conscious *a* bewußtlos; (*unintended*) unbewußt; **be** ~ **of sth** sich (*dat*) etw (*gen*) nicht bewußt sein. ~**ly** *adv* unbewußt

uncon'ventional *a* unkonventionell

unco'operative *a* nicht hilfsbereit

un'cork *vt* entkorken

uncouth /ʌn'kuːθ/ *a* ungehobelt

un'cover *vt* aufdecken

unctuous /'ʌŋktjʊəs/ *a*, **-ly** *adv* salbungsvoll

unde'cided *a* unentschlossen; (*not settled*) nicht entschieden

undeniable /ʌndɪ'naɪəbl/ *a*, **-bly** *adv* unbestreitbar

under /'ʌndə(r)/ *prep* unter (+ *dat*/*acc*); ~ **it** darunter; ~ **there** da drunter; ~ **repair** in Reparatur; ~ **construction** im Bau; ~ **age** minderjährig; ~ **way** unterwegs; (*fig*) im Gange ● *adv* darunter

'undercarriage *n* (*Aviat*) Fahrwerk *nt*, Fahrgestell *nt*

'underclothes *npl* Unterwäsche *f*

under'cover *a* geheim

'undercurrent *n* Unterströmung *f*; (*fig*) Unterton *m*

under'cut *vt* (*pt/pp* **-cut**) (*Comm*) unterbieten

'underdog *n* Unterlegene(r) *m*

under'done *a* nicht gar; (*rare*) nicht durchgebraten

under'estimate *vt* unterschätzen

under'fed *a* unterernährt

under'foot *adv* am Boden; **trample** ~ zertrampeln

under'go *vt* (*pt* **-went**, *pp* **-gone**) durchmachen; sich unterziehen (+ *dat*) ⟨*operation, treatment*⟩; ~ **repairs** repariert werden

under'graduate *n* Student(in) *m*(*f*)

under'ground[1] *adv* unter der Erde; ⟨*mining*⟩ unter Tage

'underground[2] *a* unterirdisch; (*secret*) Untergrund- ● *n* (*railway*) U-Bahn *f*. ~ **car park** *n* Tiefgarage *f*

'undergrowth *n* Unterholz *nt*

'underhand *a* hinterhältig

'underlay *n* Unterlage *f*

under'lie *vt* (*pt* **-lay**, *pp* **-lain**, *pres p* **-lying**) (*fig*) zugrundeliegen (+ *dat*)

under'line *vt* unterstreichen

underling /'ʌndəlɪŋ/ *n* (*pej*) Untergebene(r) *m*/*f*

under'lying *a* (*fig*) eigentlich

under'mine *vt* (*fig*) unterminieren, untergraben

underneath /ʌndə'niːθ/ *prep* unter (+ *dat*/*acc*); ~ **it** darunter ● *adv* darunter

'underpants *npl* Unterhose *f*

'underpass *n* Unterführung *f*

under'privileged *a* unterprivilegiert

under'rate *vt* unterschätzen

'underseal *n* (*Auto*) Unterbodenschutz *m*

'undershirt *n* (*Amer*) Unterhemd *nt*

understaffed /-'stɑːft/ *a* unterbesetzt

under'stand *vt*/*i* (*pt/pp* **-stood**) verstehen; **I** ~ **that ...** (*have heard*) ich habe gehört, daß ... ~**able** /-əbl/ *a* verständlich. ~**ably** /-əblɪ/ *adv* verständlicherweise

under'standing *a* verständnisvoll ● *n* Verständnis *nt*; (*agreement*) Vereinbarung *f*; **reach an** ~ sich verständigen; **on the** ~ **that** unter der Voraussetzung, daß

'understatement *n* Untertreibung *f*

'understudy *n* (*Theat*) Ersatzspieler(in) *m*(*f*)

under'take *vt* (*pt* **-took**, *pp* **-taken**) unternehmen; ~ **to do sth** sich verpflichten, etw zu tun

'undertaker *n* Leichenbestatter *m*; **[firm of]** ~**s** Bestattungsinstitut *nt*

under'taking *n* Unternehmen *nt*; (*promise*) Versprechen *nt*

'undertone *n* (*fig*) Unterton *m*; **in an** ~ mit gedämpfter Stimme

under'value *vt* unterbewerten

'underwater[1] *a* Unterwasser-

under'water[2] *adv* unter Wasser

'underwear *n* Unterwäsche *f*

under'weight *a* untergewichtig; **be** ~ Untergewicht haben

'underworld *n* Unterwelt *f*

'underwriter *n* Versicherer *m*

unde'sirable *a* unerwünscht

undies /'ʌndɪz/ *npl* (*fam*) [Damen]-unterwäsche *f*

un'dignified *a* würdelos

un'do vt (pt **-did**, pp **-done**) aufmachen; (fig) ungeschehen machen; (ruin) zunichte machen

un'done a offen; (not accomplished) unerledigt

un'doubted a unzweifelhaft. ~ly adv zweifellos

un'dress vt ausziehen; **get ~ed** sich ausziehen ● vi sich ausziehen

un'due a übermäßig

undulating /'ʌndjʊleɪtɪŋ/ a Wellen-; ⟨country⟩ wellig

un'duly adv übermäßig

un'dying a ewig

un'earth vt ausgraben; (fig) zutage bringen. ~ly a unheimlich; **at an ~ly hour** (fam) in aller Herrgottsfrühe

un'eas|e n Unbehagen nt. ~y a unbehaglich; **I feel ~y** mir ist unbehaglich zumute

un'eatable a ungenießbar

uneco'nomic a, **-ally** adv unwirtschaftlich

uneco'nomical a verschwenderisch

unem'ployed a arbeitslos ● npl **the ~** die Arbeitslosen

unem'ployment n Arbeitslosigkeit f. **~ benefit** n Arbeitslosenunterstützung f

un'ending a endlos

un'equal a unterschiedlich; ⟨struggle⟩ ungleich; **be ~ to a task** einer Aufgabe nicht gewachsen sein. ~ly adv ungleichmäßig

unequivocal /ʌnɪ'kwɪvəkl/ a, **-ly** adv eindeutig

unerring /ʌn'ɜːrɪŋ/ a unfehlbar

un'ethical a unmoralisch; **be ~** gegen das Berufsethos verstoßen

un'even a uneben; (unequal) ungleich; (not regular) ungleichmäßig; ⟨number⟩ ungerade. ~ly adv ungleichmäßig

unex'pected a, **-ly** adv unerwartet

un'failing a nie versagend

un'fair a, **-ly** adv ungerecht, unfair. ~ness n Ungerechtigkeit f

un'faithful a untreu

unfa'miliar a ungewohnt; (unknown) unbekannt

un'fasten vt aufmachen; (detach) losmachen

un'favourable a ungünstig

un'feeling a gefühllos

un'finished a unvollendet; ⟨business⟩ unerledigt

un'fit a ungeeignet; (incompetent) unfähig; (Sport) nicht fit; **~ for work** arbeitsunfähig

unflinching /ʌn'flɪntʃɪŋ/ a unerschrocken

un'fold vt auseinanderfalten, entfalten; (spread out) ausbreiten ● vi sich entfalten

unfore'seen a unvorhergesehen

unforgettable /ʌnfə'getəbl/ a unvergeßlich

unforgivable /ʌnfə'gɪvəbl/ a unverzeihlich

un'fortunate a unglücklich; (unfavourable) ungünstig; (regrettable) bedauerlich; **be ~** ⟨person:⟩ Pech haben. ~ly adv leider

un'founded a unbegründet

unfurl /ʌn'fɜːl/ vt entrollen ● vi sich entrollen

un'furnished a unmöbliert

ungainly /ʌn'geɪnlɪ/ a unbeholfen

ungodly /ʌn'gɒdlɪ/ a gottlos; **at an ~ hour** (fam) in aller Herrgottsfrühe

un'grateful a, **-ly** adv undankbar

un'happi|ly adv unglücklich; (unfortunately) leider. ~ness n Kummer m

un'happy a unglücklich; (not content) unzufrieden

un'harmed a unverletzt

un'healthy a ungesund

un'hook vt vom Haken nehmen; aufhaken ⟨dress⟩

un'hurt a unverletzt

unhy'gienic a unhygienisch

unicorn /'juːnɪkɔːn/ n Einhorn nt

unification /juːnɪfɪ'keɪʃn/ n Einigung f

uniform /'juːnɪfɔːm/ a, **-ly** adv einheitlich ● n Uniform f

unify /'juːnɪfaɪ/ vt (pt/pp **-ied**) einigen

uni'lateral /juːnɪ-/ a, **-ly** adv einseitig

uni'maginable a unvorstellbar

unim'portant a unwichtig

unin'habited a unbewohnt

unin'tentional a, **-ly** adv unabsichtlich

union /'juːnɪən/ n Vereinigung f; (Pol) Union f; (trade ~) Gewerkschaft f. ~ist n (Pol) Unionist m

unique /juː'niːk/ a einzigartig. ~ly adv einmalig

unison /'juːnɪsn/ n **in ~** einstimmig

unit /'juːnɪt/ n Einheit f; (Math) Einer m; (of furniture) Teil nt, Element nt

unite /juːˈnaɪt/ vt vereinigen ● vi sich vereinigen

united /juːˈnaɪtɪd/ a einig. **U~ 'Kingdom** n Vereinigtes Königreich nt. **U~ 'Nations** pl Vereinte Nationen pl. **U~ States [of America]** Vereinigte Staaten pl [von Amerika]

unity /ˈjuːnətɪ/ n Einheit f; (harmony) Einigkeit f

universal /juːnɪˈvɜːsl/ a, **-ly** adv allgemein

universe /ˈjuːnɪvɜːs/ n [Welt]all nt, Universum nt

university /juːnɪˈvɜːsətɪ/ n Universität f ● attrib Universitäts-

un'just a, **-ly** adv ungerecht

unkempt /ʌnˈkempt/ a ungepflegt

un'kind a, **-ly** adv unfreundlich; (harsh) häßlich. **~ness** n Unfreundlichkeit f; Häßlichkeit f

un'known a unbekannt

un'lawful a, **-ly** adv gesetzwidrig

unleaded /ʌnˈledɪd/ a bleifrei

un'leash vt (fig) entfesseln

unless /ənˈles/ conj wenn ... nicht; **~ I am mistaken** wenn ich mich nicht irre

un'like a nicht ähnlich, unähnlich; (not the same) ungleich ● prep im Gegensatz zu (+ dat)

un'likely a unwahrscheinlich

un'limited a unbegrenzt

un'load vt entladen; ausladen (luggage)

un'lock vt aufschließen

un'lucky a unglücklich; (day, number) Unglücks-; **be ~** Pech haben; (thing:) Unglück bringen

un'manned a unbemannt

un'married a unverheiratet. **~ 'mother** n ledige Mutter f

un'mask vt (fig) entlarven

unmistakable /ʌnmɪˈsteɪkəbl/ a, **-bly** adv unverkennbar

un'mitigated a vollkommen

un'natural a, **-ly** adv unnatürlich; (not normal) nicht normal

un'necessary a, **-ily** adv unnötig

un'noticed a unbemerkt

unob'tainable a nicht erhältlich

unob'trusive a, **-ly** adv unaufdringlich; (thing:) unauffällig

unof'ficial a, **-ly** adv inoffiziell

un'pack vt/i auspacken

un'paid a unbezahlt

un'palatable a ungenießbar

un'paralleled a beispiellos

un'pick vt auftrennen

un'pleasant a, **-ly** adv unangenehm. **~ness** n (bad feeling) Ärger m

un'plug vt (pt/pp **-plugged**) den Stecker herausziehen von

un'popular a unbeliebt

un'precedented a beispiellos

unpre'dictable a unberechenbar

unpre'meditated a nicht vorsätzlich

unpre'pared a nicht vorbereitet

unprepos'sessing a wenig attraktiv

unpre'tentious a bescheiden

un'principled a skrupellos

unpro'fessional a **be ~** gegen das Berufsethos verstoßen; (Sport) unsportlich sein

un'profitable a unrentabel

un'qualified a unqualifiziert; (fig: absolute) uneingeschränkt

un'questionable a unbezweifelbar; (right) unbestreitbar

unravel /ʌnˈrævl/ vt (pt/pp **-ravelled**) entwirren; (Knitting) aufziehen

un'real a unwirklich

un'reasonable a unvernünftig; **be ~** zuviel verlangen

unre'lated a unzusammenhängend; **be ~** nicht verwandt sein; (events:) nicht miteinander zusammenhängen

unre'liable a unzuverlässig

unrequited /ʌnrɪˈkwaɪtɪd/ a unerwidert

unreservedly /ʌnrɪˈzɜːvɪdlɪ/ adv uneingeschränkt; (frankly) offen

un'rest n Unruhen pl

un'rivalled a unübertroffen

un'roll vt aufrollen ● vi sich aufrollen

unruly /ʌnˈruːlɪ/ a ungebärdig

un'safe a nicht sicher

un'said a ungesagt

un'salted a ungesalzen

unsatis'factory a unbefriedigend

un'savoury a unangenehm; (fig) unerfreulich

unscathed /ʌnˈskeɪθd/ a unversehrt

un'screw vt abschrauben

un'scrupulous a skrupellos

un'seemly a unschicklich

un'selfish a selbstlos

un'settled a ungeklärt; (weather) unbeständig; (bill) unbezahlt

unshakeable /ʌnˈʃeɪkəbl/ a unerschütterlich

unshaven /ʌnˈʃeɪvn/ a unrasiert

unsightly /ʌnˈsaɪtlɪ/ a unansehnlich

un'skilled a ungelernt; ⟨work⟩ unqualifiziert

un'sociable a ungesellig

unso'phisticated a einfach

un'sound a krank, nicht gesund; ⟨building⟩ nicht sicher; ⟨advice⟩ unzuverlässig; ⟨reasoning⟩ nicht stichhaltig; **of ~ mind** unzurechnungsfähig

unspeakable /ʌn'spiːkəbl/ a unbeschreiblich

un'stable a nicht stabil; (mentally) labil

un'steady a, **-ily** adv unsicher; (wobbly) wackelig

un'stuck a **come ~** sich lösen; (fam: fail) scheitern

unsuc'cessful a, **-ly** adv erfolglos; **be ~** keinen Erfolg haben

un'suitable a ungeeignet; (inappropriate) unpassend; (for weather, activity) unzweckmäßig

unsu'specting a ahnungslos

un'sweetened a ungesüßt

unthinkable /ʌn'θɪŋkəbl/ a unvorstellbar

un'tidiness n Unordentlichkeit f

un'tidy a, **-ily** adv unordentlich

un'tie vt aufbinden; losbinden ⟨person, boat, horse⟩

until /ən'tɪl/ prep bis (+ acc); **not ~** erst; **~ the evening** bis zum Abend; **~ his arrival** bis zu seiner Ankunft ● conj bis; **not ~** erst wenn; (in past) erst als

untimely /ʌn'taɪmlɪ/ a ungelegen; (premature) vorzeitig

un'tiring a unermüdlich

un'told a unermeßlich

unto'ward a ungünstig; (unseemly) ungehörig; **if nothing ~ happens** wenn nichts dazwischenkommt

un'true a unwahr; **that's ~** das ist nicht wahr

unused[1] /ʌn'juːzd/ a unbenutzt; (not utilized) ungenutzt

unused[2] /ʌn'juːst/ a **be ~ to sth** etw nicht gewohnt sein

un'usual a, **-ly** adv ungewöhnlich

un'veil vt enthüllen

un'versed a nicht bewandert (**in** in + dat)

un'wanted a unerwünscht

un'warranted a ungerechtfertigt

un'welcome a unwillkommen

un'well a **be** or **feel ~** sich nicht wohl fühlen

unwieldy /ʌn'wiːldɪ/ a sperrig

un'willing a, **-ly** adv widerwillig; **be ~ to do sth** etw nicht tun wollen

un'wind v (pt/pp **unwound**) ● vt abwickeln ● vi sich abwickeln; (fam: relax) sich entspannen

un'wise a, **-ly** adv unklug

unwitting /ʌn'wɪtɪŋ/ a, **-ly** adv unwissentlich

un'worthy a unwürdig

un'wrap vt (pt/pp **-wrapped**) auswickeln; auspacken ⟨present⟩

un'written a ungeschrieben

up /ʌp/ adv oben; (with movement) nach oben; (not in bed) auf; ⟨collar⟩ hochgeklappt; ⟨road⟩ aufgerissen; ⟨price⟩ gestiegen; ⟨curtains⟩ aufgehängt; ⟨shelves⟩ angebracht; ⟨notice⟩ angeschlagen; ⟨tent⟩ aufgebaut; ⟨building⟩ gebaut; **be up for sale** zu verkaufen sein; **up there** da oben; **up to** (as far as) bis; **time's up** die Zeit ist um; **what's up?** (fam) was ist los? **what's he up to?** (fam) was hat er vor? **I don't feel up to it** ich fühle mich dem nicht gewachsen; **be one up on s.o.** (fam) jdm etwas voraushaben; **go up** hinaufgehen; **come up** heraufkommen ● prep **be up on sth** [oben] auf etw ⟨dat⟩ sein; **up the mountain** oben am Berg; (movement) den Berg hinauf; **be up the tree** oben im Baum sein; **up the road** die Straße entlang; **up the river** stromaufwärts; **go up the stairs** die Treppe hinaufgehen; **be up the pub** (fam) in der Kneipe sein

'upbringing n Erziehung f

up'date vt auf den neuesten Stand bringen

up'grade vt aufstufen

upheaval /ʌp'hiːvl/ n Unruhe f; (Pol) Umbruch m

up'hill a (fig) mühsam ● adv bergauf

up'hold vt (pt/pp **upheld**) unterstützen; bestätigen ⟨verdict⟩

upholster /ʌp'həʊlstə(r)/ vt polstern. **~er** n Polsterer m. **~y** n Polsterung f

'upkeep n Unterhalt m

up-'market a anspruchsvoll

upon /ə'pɒn/ prep auf (+ dat/acc)

upper /'ʌpə(r)/ a obere(r,s); ⟨deck, jaw, lip⟩ Ober-; **have the ~ hand** die Oberhand haben ● n (of shoe) Obermaterial nt

upper: **~ circle** n zweiter Rang m. **~ class** n Oberschicht f. **~most** a oberste(r,s)

'upright a aufrecht ● n Pfosten m

'**uprising** *n* Aufstand *m*
'**uproar** *n* Aufruhr *m*
up'**root** *vt* entwurzeln
up'**set**[1] *vt* ⟨*pt/pp* upset, *pres p* up-
setting⟩ umstoßen; (*spill*) verschütten;
durcheinanderbringen ⟨*plan*⟩; (*distress*)
erschüttern; ⟨*food:*⟩ nicht bekommen
(+ *dat*); **get ~ about sth** sich über etw
(*acc*) aufregen; **be very ~** sehr bestürzt
sein
'**upset**[2] *n* Aufregung *f*; **have a stomach ~** einen verdorbenen Magen
haben
'**upshot** *n* Ergebnis *nt*
upside '**down** *adv* verkehrt herum;
turn ~ umdrehen
up'**stairs**[1] *adv* oben; ⟨*go*⟩ nach oben
'**upstairs**[2] *a* im Obergeschoß
'**upstart** *n* Emporkömmling *m*
up'**stream** *adv* stromaufwärts
'**upsurge** *n* Zunahme *f*
'**uptake** *n* **slow on the ~** schwer von
Begriff; **be quick on the ~** schnell begreifen
up'**tight** *a* nervös
'**upturn** *n* Aufschwung *m*
upward /'ʌpwəd/ *a* nach oben;
⟨*movement*⟩ Aufwärts-; **~ slope** Steigung *f* ● **~[s]** aufwärts, nach oben
uranium /jʊ'reɪnɪəm/ *n* Uran *nt*
urban /'ɜːbən/ *a* städtisch
urbane /ɜː'beɪn/ *a* weltmännisch
urge /ɜːdʒ/ *n* Trieb *m*, Drang *m* ● *vt*
drängen; **~ on** antreiben
urgen|cy /'ɜːdʒənsɪ/ *n* Dringlichkeit
f. **~t** *a*, **-ly** *adv* dringend
urinate /'jʊərɪneɪt/ *vi* urinieren
urine /'jʊərɪn/ *n* Urin *m*, Harn *m*
urn /ɜːn/ *n* Urne *f*; (*for tea*) Teema-
schine *f*
us /ʌs/ *pron* uns; **it's us** wir sind es
US[A] *abbr* USA *pl*
usable /'juːzəbl/ *a* brauchbar
usage /'juːzɪdʒ/ *n* Brauch *m*; (*of
word*) [Sprach]gebrauch *m*
use[1] /juːs/ *n* (*see* **use**[2]) Benutzung *f*;
Verwendung *f*; Gebrauch *m*; **be of ~**
nützlich sein; **be of no ~** nichts
nützen; **make ~ of** Gebrauch machen
von; (*exploit*) ausnutzen; **it is no ~** es
hat keinen Zweck; **what's the ~?**
wozu?
use[2] /juːz/ *vt* benutzen ⟨*implement,
room, lift*⟩; verwenden ⟨*ingredient,
method, book, money*⟩; gebrauchen
⟨*words, force, brains*⟩; **~ [up]** aufbrauchen

used[1] /juːzd/ *a* benutzt; ⟨*car*⟩ Ge-
braucht-
used[2] /juːst/ *pt/pp* **be ~ to sth** an etw
(*acc*) gewöhnt sein; **get ~ to** sich gewöhnen an (+ *acc*); **he ~ to say** er hat
immer gesagt; **he ~ to live here** er hat
früher hier gewohnt
useful /'juːsfl/ *a* nützlich. **~ness** *n*
Nützlichkeit *f*
useless /'juːslɪs/ *a* nutzlos; (*not usable*) unbrauchbar; (*pointless*)
zwecklos
user /'juːzə(r)/ *n* Benutzer(in) *m(f)*.
~-'friendly *a* benutzerfreundlich
usher /'ʌʃə(r)/ *n* Platzanweiser *m*;
(*in court*) Gerichtsdiener *m* ● *vt* **~ in**
hineinführen
usherette /ʌʃə'ret/ *n* Platzanweise-
rin *f*
USSR *abbr* UdSSR *f*
usual /'juːʒəl/ *a* üblich. **~ly** *adv*
gewöhnlich
usurp /juː'zɜːp/ *vt* sich (*dat*) wider-
rechtlich aneignen
utensil /juː'tensl/ *n* Gerät *nt*
uterus /'juːtərəs/ *n* Gebärmutter *f*
utilitarian /juːtɪlɪ'teərɪən/ *a* zweckmäßig
utility /juː'tɪlətɪ/ *a* Gebrauchs- ● *n*
Nutzen *m*. **~ room** *n* Waschküche *f*
utiliz|ation /juːtɪlaɪ'zeɪʃn/ *n* Nut-
zung *f*. **~e** /'juːtɪlaɪz/ *vt* nutzen
utmost /'ʌtməʊst/ *a* äußerste(r,s),
größte(r,s) ● *n* **do one's ~** sein
möglichstes tun
utter[1] /'ʌtə(r)/ *a*, **-ly** *adv* völlig
utter[2] *vt* von sich geben ⟨*sigh, sound*⟩;
sagen ⟨*word*⟩. **~ance** /-əns/ *n*
Äußerung *f*
U-turn /'juː-/ *n* (*fig*) Kehrtwendung
f; '**no ~s'** (*Auto*) 'Wenden verboten'

V

vacan|cy /'veɪkənsɪ/ *n* (*job*) freie
Stelle *f*; (*room*) freies Zimmer *nt*; '**no
~cies'** 'belegt'. **~t** *a* frei; ⟨*look*⟩ [ge-
danken]leer
vacate /və'keɪt/ *vt* räumen
vacation /və'keɪʃn/ *n* (*Univ & Amer*)
Ferien *pl*
vaccinat|e /'væksɪneɪt/ *vt* impfen.
~ion /-'neɪʃn/ *n* Impfung *f*
vaccine /'væksiːn/ *n* Impfstoff *m*
vacuum /'vækjʊəm/ *n* Vakuum *nt*,
luftleerer Raum *m* ● *vt* saugen.
~ cleaner *n* Staubsauger *m*.

~ **flask** *n* Thermosflasche (P) *f.*
~-**packed** *a* vakuumverpackt
vagaries /'veɪgərɪz/ *npl* Launen *pl*
vagina /və'dʒaɪnə/ *n* (*Anat*) Scheide
f
vagrant /'veɪgrənt/ *n* Landstreicher
m
vague /veɪg/ *a* (**-r, -st**), **-ly** *adv* vage;
⟨*outline*⟩ verschwommen
vain /veɪn/ *a* (**-er, -est**) eitel; ⟨*hope,
attempt*⟩ vergeblich; **in** ~ vergeblich.
~**ly** *adv* vergeblich
vale /veɪl/ *n* (*liter*) Tal *nt*
valet /'væleɪ/ *n* Kammerdiener *m*
valiant /'vælɪənt/ *a*, **-ly** *adv* tapfer
valid /'vælɪd/ *a* gültig; ⟨*claim*⟩ berechtigt; ⟨*argument*⟩ stichhaltig;
⟨*reason*⟩ triftig. ~**ate** *vt* (*confirm*) bestätigen. ~**ity** /və'lɪdətɪ/ *n* Gül-
tigkeit *f*
valley /'vælɪ/ *n* Tal *nt*
valour /'vælə(r)/ *n* Tapferkeit *f*
valuable /'væljʊəbl/ *a* wertvoll. ~**s**
npl Wertsachen *pl*
valuation /væljʊ'eɪʃn/ *n* Schätzung
f
value /'vælju:/ *n* Wert *m*; (*usefulness*)
Nutzen *m* ● *vt* schätzen. ~ '**added
tax** *n* Mehrwertsteuer *f*
valve /vælv/ *n* Ventil *nt*; (*Anat*)
Klappe *f*; (*Electr*) Röhre *f*
vampire /'væmpaɪə(r)/ *n* Vampir *m*
van /væn/ *n* Lieferwagen *m*
vandal /'vændl/ *n* Rowdy *m*. ~**ism**
/-ɪzm/ *n* mutwillige Zerstörung *f*.
~**ize** *vt* demolieren
vanilla /və'nɪlə/ *n* Vanille *f*
vanish /'vænɪʃ/ *vi* verschwinden
vanity /'vænətɪ/ *n* Eitelkeit *f.* ~ **bag**
n Kosmetiktäschchen *nt*
vantage-point /'vɑːntɪdʒ-/ *n* Aussichtspunkt *m*
vapour /'veɪpə(r)/ *n* Dampf *m*
variable /'veərɪəbl/ *a* unbeständig;
(*Math*) variabel; (*adjustable*) re-
gulierbar
variance /'veərɪəns/ *n* **be at** ~ nicht
übereinstimmen
variant /'veərɪənt/ *n* Variante *f*
variation /veərɪ'eɪʃn/ *n* Variation *f*;
(*difference*) Unterschied *m*
varicose /'værɪkəʊs/ *a* ~ **veins** *pl*
Krampfadern *pl*
varied /'veərɪd/ *a* vielseitig; ⟨*diet*⟩
abwechslungsreich
variety /və'raɪətɪ/ *n* Abwechslung *f*;
(*quantity*) Vielfalt *f*; (*Comm*) Auswahl *f*; (*type*) Art *f*; (*Bot*) Abart *f*;
(*Theat*) Varieté *nt*

various /'veərɪəs/ *a* verschiedene.
~**ly** *adv* unterschiedlich
varnish /'vɑːnɪʃ/ *n* Lack *m* ● *vt*
lackieren
vary /'veərɪ/ *v* (*pt/pp* **-ied**) ● *vi* sich
ändern; (*be different*) verschieden
sein ● *vt* [ver]ändern; (*add variety to*)
abwechslungsreicher gestalten. ~-
ing *a* wechselnd; (*different*) unterschiedlich
vase /vɑːz/ *n* Vase *f*
vast /vɑːst/ *a* riesig; ⟨*expanse*⟩ weit.
~**ly** *adv* gewaltig
vat /væt/ *n* Bottich *m*
VAT /viːeɪ'tiː, væt/ *abbr* (**value added
tax**) Mehrwertsteuer *f,* MwSt.
vault[1] /vɔːlt/ *n* (*roof*) Gewölbe *nt*; (*in
bank*) Tresor *m*; (*tomb*) Gruft *f*
vault[2] *n* Sprung *m* ● *vt/i* ~ [**over**]
springen über
VDU *abbr* (**visual display unit**) Bildschirmgerät *nt*
veal /viːl/ *n* Kalbfleisch *nt* ● *attrib*
Kalbs-
veer /vɪə(r)/ *vi* sich drehen; (*Naut*)
abdrehen; (*Auto*) ausscheren
vegetable /'vedʒtəbl/ *n* Gemüse *nt*;
~**s** *pl* Gemüse *nt* ● *attrib* Gemüse-; ⟨*oil,
fat*⟩ Pflanzen-
vegetarian /vedʒɪ'teərɪən/ *a* vegeta-
risch ● *n* Vegetarier(in) *m(f)*
vegetat|e /'vedʒɪteɪt/ *vi* dahin-
vegetieren. ~**ion** /-'teɪʃn/ *n* Vegetation *f*
vehemen|ce /'viːəməns/ *n* Heftig-
keit *f.* ~**t** *a*, **-ly** *adv* heftig
vehicle /'viːɪkl/ *n* Fahrzeug *nt*; (*fig:
medium*) Mittel *nt*
veil /veɪl/ *n* Schleier *m* ● *vt* verschleiern
vein /veɪn/ *n* Ader *f*; (*mood*) Stimmung *f*; (*manner*) Art *f*; ~**s and
arteries** Venen und Arterien. ~**ed** *a*
geädert
Velcro (P) /'velkrəʊ/ *n* ~ **fastening**
Klettverschluß *m*
velocity /vɪ'lɒsətɪ/ *n* Geschwindigkeit *f*
velvet /'velvɪt/ *n* Samt *m*. ~**y** *a* sam-
tig
vending-machine /'vendɪŋ-/ *n*
[Verkaufs]automat *m*
vendor /'vendə(r)/ *n* Verkäufer(in)
m(f)
veneer /və'nɪə(r)/ *n* Furnier *nt*; (*fig*)
Tünche *f.* ~**ed** *a* furniert
venerable /'venərəbl/ *a* ehrwürdig

venereal /vɪ'nɪərɪəl/ a ~ **disease** Geschlechtskrankheit f

Venetian /və'ni:ʃn/ a venezianisch. **v~ blind** n Jalousie f

vengeance /'vendʒəns/ n Rache f; **with a ~** (fam) gewaltig

Venice /'venɪs/ n Venedig nt

venison /'venɪsn/ n (Culin) Wild nt

venom /'venəm/ n Gift nt; (fig) Haß m. ~**ous** /-əs/ a giftig

vent[1] /vent/ n Öffnung f; (fig) Ventil nt; **give ~ to** Luft machen (+ dat) ● vt Luft machen (+ dat)

vent[2] n (in jacket) Schlitz m

ventilat|e /'ventɪleɪt/ vt belüften. ~**ion** /-'leɪʃn/ n Belüftung f; (installation) Lüftung f. ~**or** n Lüftungsvorrichtung f; (Med) Beatmungsgerät nt

ventriloquist /ven'trɪləkwɪst/ n Bauchredner m

venture /'ventʃə(r)/ n Unternehmung f ● vt wagen ● vi sich wagen

venue /'venju:/ n Treffpunkt m; (for event) Veranstaltungsort m

veranda /və'rændə/ n Veranda f

verb /vɜ:b/ n Verb nt. ~**al** a, **-ly** adv mündlich; (Gram) verbal

verbatim /vɜ:'beɪtɪm/ a & adv [wort]wörtlich

verbose /vɜ:'bəʊs/ a weitschweifig

verdict /'vɜ:dɪkt/ n Urteil nt

verge /vɜ:dʒ/ n Rand m; **be on the ~ of doing sth** im Begriff sein, etw zu tun ● vi ~ **on** (fig) grenzen an (+ acc)

verger /'vɜ:dʒə(r)/ n Küster m

verify /'verɪfaɪ/ vt (pt/pp **-ied**) überprüfen; (confirm) bestätigen

vermin /'vɜ:mɪn/ n Ungeziefer nt

vermouth /'vɜ:məθ/ n Wermut m

vernacular /və'nækjʊlə(r)/ n Landessprache f

versatil|e /'vɜ:sətaɪl/ a vielseitig. ~**ity** /-'tɪlətɪ/ n Vielseitigkeit f

verse /vɜ:s/ n Strophe f; (of Bible) Vers m; (poetry) Lyrik f

version /'vɜ:ʃn/ n Version f; (translation) Übersetzung f; (model) Modell nt

versus /'vɜ:səs/ prep gegen (+ acc)

vertebra /'vɜ:tɪbrə/ n (pl **-brae** /-bri:/) (Anat) Wirbel m

vertical /'vɜ:tɪkl/ a, **-ly** adv senkrecht ● n Senkrechte f

vertigo /'vɜ:tɪgəʊ/ n (Med) Schwindel m

verve /vɜ:v/ n Schwung m

very /'verɪ/ adv sehr; ~ **much** sehr; (quantity) sehr viel; ~ **little** sehr wenig; ~ **probably** höchstwahrscheinlich; **at the ~ most** allerhöchstens ● a (mere) bloß; **the ~ first** der/die/das allererste; **the ~ thing** genau das Richtige; **at the ~ end/beginning** ganz am Ende/Anfang; **only a ~ little** nur ein ganz kleines bißchen

vessel /'vesl/ n Schiff nt; (receptacle & Anat) Gefäß nt

vest /vest/ n [Unter]hemd nt; (Amer: waistcoat) Weste f ● vt ~ **sth in s.o.** jdm etw verleihen; **have a ~ed interest in sth** ein persönliches Interesse an etw (dat) haben

vestige /'vestɪdʒ/ n Spur f

vestment /'vestmənt/ n (Relig) Gewand nt

vestry /'vestrɪ/ n Sakristei f

vet /vet/ n Tierarzt m/-ärztin f ● vt (pt/pp **vetted**) überprüfen

veteran /'vetərən/ n Veteran m. ~ **car** n Oldtimer m

veterinary /'vetərɪnərɪ/ a tierärztlich. ~ **surgeon** n Tierarzt m /-ärztin f

veto /'vi:təʊ/ n (pl **-es**) Veto nt ● vt sein Veto einlegen gegen

vex /veks/ vt ärgern. ~**ation** /-'seɪʃn/ n Ärger m. ~**ed** a verärgert; ~**ed question** vieldiskutierte Frage f

VHF abbr (**very high frequency**) UKW

via /'vaɪə/ prep über (+ acc)

viable /'vaɪəbl/ a lebensfähig; (fig) realisierbar; (firm) rentabel

viaduct /'vaɪədʌkt/ n Viadukt nt

vibrant /'vaɪbrənt/ a (fig) lebhaft

vibrat|e /vaɪ'breɪt/ vi vibrieren. ~**ion** /-'breɪʃn/ n Vibrieren nt

vicar /'vɪkə(r)/ n Pfarrer m. ~**age** /-rɪdʒ/ n Pfarrhaus nt

vicarious /vɪ'keərɪəs/ a nachempfunden

vice[1] /vaɪs/ n Laster nt

vice[2] n (Techn) Schraubstock m

vice 'chairman n stellvertretender Vorsitzender m

vice 'president n Vizepräsident m

vice versa /vaɪsɪ'vɜ:sə/ adv umgekehrt

vicinity /vɪ'sɪnətɪ/ n Umgebung f; **in the ~ of** in der Nähe von

vicious /'vɪʃəs/ a, **-ly** adv boshaft; (animal) bösartig. ~ **'circle** n Teufelskreis m

victim /'vɪktɪm/ n Opfer nt. ~**ize** vt schikanieren

victor /'vɪktə(r)/ n Sieger m
victor|ious /vɪk'tɔːrɪəs/ a siegreich.
~**y** /'vɪktərɪ/ n Sieg m
video /'vɪdɪəʊ/ n Video nt; (recorder)
Videorecorder m ● attrib Video- ● vt
[auf Videoband] aufnehmen
video: ~ **cas'sette** n Videokassette
f. ~ **game** n Videospiel nt. ~ **'nasty**
n Horrorvideo nt. ~ **recorder** n
Videorecorder m
vie /vaɪ/ vi (pres p **vying**) wetteifern
Vienn|a /vɪ'enə/ n Wien nt. ~**ese**
/vɪə'niːz/ a Wiener
view /vjuː/ n Sicht f; (scene) Aussicht
f, Blick m; (picture, opinion) Ansicht
f; **in my** ~ meiner Ansicht nach; **in** ~
of angesichts (+ gen); **keep/have sth
in** ~ etw im Auge behalten/haben; **be
on** ~ besichtigt werden können ● vt
sich (dat) ansehen; besichtigen ⟨house⟩;
(consider) betrachten ● vi (TV) fernsehen. ~**er** n (TV) Zuschauer(in)
m(f); (Phot) Diabetrachter m
view: ~**finder** n (Phot) Sucher m.
~**point** n Standpunkt m
vigil /'vɪdʒɪl/ n Wache f
vigilan|ce /'vɪdʒɪləns/ n Wach-
samkeit f. ~**t** a, -**ly** adv wachsam
vigorous /'vɪgərəs/ a, -**ly** adv kräftig;
(fig) heftig
vigour /'vɪgə(r)/ n Kraft f; (fig) Heftigkeit f
vile /vaɪl/ a abscheulich
villa /'vɪlə/ n (for holidays) Ferien-
haus nt
village /'vɪlɪdʒ/ n Dorf nt. ~**r** n
Dorfbewohner(in) m(f)
villain /'vɪlən/ n Schurke m; (in
story) Bösewicht m
vim /vɪm/ n (fam) Schwung m
vindicat|e /'vɪndɪkeɪt/ vt recht-
fertigen. ~**ion** /-'keɪʃn/ n Recht-
fertigung f
vindictive /vɪn'dɪktɪv/ a nach-
tragend
vine /vaɪn/ n Weinrebe f
vinegar /'vɪnɪgə(r)/ n Essig m
vineyard /'vɪnjɑːd/ n Weinberg m
vintage /'vɪntɪdʒ/ a erlesen ● n
(year) Jahrgang m. ~ **'car** n Oldtimer
m
viola /vɪ'əʊlə/ n (Mus) Bratsche f
violat|e /'vaɪəleɪt/ vt verletzen;
(break) brechen; (disturb) stören;
(defile) schänden. ~**ion** /-'leɪʃn/ n
Verletzung f; Schändung f
violen|ce /'vaɪələns/ n Gewalt f;
(fig) Heftigkeit f. ~**t** a gewalttätig;

(fig) heftig. ~**tly** adv brutal; (fig)
heftig
violet /'vaɪələt/ a violett ● n (flower)
Veilchen nt
violin /vaɪə'lɪn/ n Geige f, Violine f.
~**ist** n Geiger(in) m(f)
VIP abbr (**very important person**) Pro-
minente(r) m/f
viper /'vaɪpə(r)/ n Kreuzotter f; (fig)
Schlange f
virgin /'vɜːdʒɪn/ a unberührt ● n
Jungfrau f. ~**ity** /-'dʒɪnətɪ/ n Unschuld f
Virgo /'vɜːgəʊ/ n (Astr) Jungfrau f
viril|e /'vɪraɪl/ a männlich. ~**ity**
/-'rɪlətɪ/ n Männlichkeit f
virtual /'vɜːtjʊəl/ a **a** ~ ... praktisch
ein ... ~**ly** adv praktisch
virtu|e /'vɜːtjuː/ n Tugend f; (ad-
vantage) Vorteil m; **by** or **in** ~**e of** auf
Grund (+ gen)
virtuoso /vɜːtjʊ'əʊzəʊ/ n (pl -**si** /-ziː/)
Virtuose m
virtuous /'vɜːtjʊəs/ a tugendhaft
virulent /'vɪrʊlənt/ a bösartig;
⟨poison⟩ stark; (fig) scharf
virus /'vaɪərəs/ n Virus nt
visa /'viːzə/ n Visum nt
vis-à-vis /viːzɑː'viː/ adv & prep
gegenüber (+ dat)
viscous /'vɪskəs/ a dickflüssig
visibility /vɪzə'bɪlətɪ/ n Sichtbarkeit
f; (Meteorol) Sichtweite f
visible /'vɪzəbl/ a, -**bly** adv sichtbar
vision /'vɪʒn/ n Vision f; (sight) Sehkraft f; (foresight) Weitblick m
visit /'vɪzɪt/ n Besuch m ● vt besuchen; besichtigen ⟨town, building⟩.
~**ing hours** npl Besuchszeiten pl.
~**or** n Besucher(in) m(f); (in hotel)
Gast m; **have** ~**ors** Besuch haben
visor /'vaɪzə(r)/ n Schirm m; (on
helmet) Visier nt; (Auto) [Sonnen]-
blende f
vista /'vɪstə/ n Aussicht f
visual /'vɪzjʊəl/ a, -**ly** adv visuell; ~**ly
handicapped** sehbehindert. ~ **aids**
npl Anschauungsmaterial nt. ~ **dis-
'play unit** n Bildschirmgerät nt
visualize /'vɪzjʊəlaɪz/ vt sich (dat)
vorstellen
vital /'vaɪtl/ a unbedingt notwendig;
(essential to life) lebenswichtig.
~**ity** /vaɪ'tælətɪ/ n Vitalität f. ~**ly**
/'vaɪtəlɪ/ adv äußerst
vitamin /'vɪtəmɪn/ n Vitamin nt

vitreous /'vɪtrɪəs/ a glasartig; ⟨enamel⟩ Glas-

vivaci|ous /vɪ'veɪʃəs/ a, **-ly** adv lebhaft. ∼**ty** /-'væsətɪ/ n Lebhaftigkeit f

vivid /'vɪvɪd/ a, **-ly** adv lebhaft; ⟨description⟩ lebendig

vixen /'vɪksn/ n Füchsin f

vocabulary /və'kæbjʊlərɪ/ n Wortschatz m; (list) Vokabelverzeichnis nt; **learn** ∼ Vokabeln lernen

vocal /'vəʊkl/ a, **-ly** adv stimmlich; (vociferous) lautstark. ∼ **cords** npl Stimmbänder pl

vocalist /'vəʊkəlɪst/ n Sänger(in) m(f)

vocation /və'keɪʃn/ n Berufung f. ∼**al** a Berufs-

vociferous /və'sɪfərəs/ a lautstark

vodka /'vɒdkə/ n Wodka m

vogue /vəʊg/ n Mode f; **in** ∼ in Mode

voice /vɔɪs/ n Stimme f ● vt zum Ausdruck bringen

void /vɔɪd/ a leer; (not valid) ungültig; ∼ **of** ohne ● n Leere f

volatile /'vɒlətaɪl/ a flüchtig; ⟨person⟩ sprunghaft

volcanic /vɒl'kænɪk/ a vulkanisch

volcano /vɒl'keɪnəʊ/ n Vulkan m

volition /və'lɪʃn/ n **of one's own** ∼ aus eigenem Willen

volley /'vɒlɪ/ n (of gunfire) Salve f; (Tennis) Volley m

volt /vəʊlt/ n Volt nt. ∼**age** /-ɪdʒ/ n (Electr) Spannung f

voluble /'vɒljʊbl/ a, **-bly** adv redselig; ⟨protest⟩ wortreich

volume /'vɒljuːm/ n (book) Band m; (Geom) Rauminhalt m; (amount) Ausmaß nt; (Radio, TV) Lautstärke f. ∼ **control** n Lautstärkeregler m

voluntary /'vɒləntərɪ/ a, **-ily** adv freiwillig

volunteer /vɒlən'tɪə(r)/ n Freiwillige(r) m/f ● vt anbieten; geben ⟨information⟩ ● vi sich freiwillig melden

voluptuous /və'lʌptjʊəs/ a sinnlich

vomit /'vɒmɪt/ n Erbrochene(s) nt ● vt erbrechen ● vi sich übergeben

voracious /və'reɪʃəs/ a gefräßig; ⟨appetite⟩ unbändig

vot|e /vəʊt/ n Stimme f; (ballot) Abstimmung f; (right) Wahlrecht nt; **take a** ∼**e on** abstimmen über (+ acc) ● vi abstimmen; (in election) wählen ● vt ∼**e s.o. president** jdn zum Präsidenten wählen. ∼**er** n Wähler(in) m(f)

vouch /vaʊtʃ/ vi ∼ **for** sich verbürgen für. ∼**er** n Gutschein m

vow /vaʊ/ n Gelöbnis nt; (Relig) Gelübde nt ● vt geloben

vowel /'vaʊəl/ n Vokal m

voyage /'vɔɪdʒ/ n Seereise f; (in space) Reise f, Flug m

vulgar /'vʌlgə(r)/ a vulgär, ordinär. ∼**ity** /-'gærətɪ/ n Vulgarität f

vulnerable /'vʌlnərəbl/ a verwundbar

vulture /'vʌltʃə(r)/ n Geier m

vying /'vaɪɪŋ/ see **vie**

W

wad /wɒd/ n Bausch m; (bundle) Bündel nt. ∼**ding** n Wattierung f

waddle /'wɒdl/ vi watscheln

wade /weɪd/ vi waten; ∼ **through** (fam) sich durchackern durch ⟨book⟩

wafer /'weɪfə(r)/ n Waffel f; (Relig) Hostie f

waffle[1] /'wɒfl/ vi (fam) schwafeln

waffle[2] n (Culin) Waffel f

waft /wɒft/ vt/i wehen

wag /wæg/ v (pt/pp **wagged**) ● vt wedeln mit; ∼ **one's finger at s.o.** jdm mit dem Finger drohen ● vi wedeln

wage[1] /weɪdʒ/ vt führen

wage[2] n, & ∼**s** pl Lohn m. ∼ **packet** n Lohntüte f

wager /'weɪdʒə(r)/ n Wette f

waggle /'wægl/ vt wackeln mit ● vi wackeln

wagon /'wægən/ n Wagen m; (Rail) Waggon m

wail /weɪl/ n [klagender] Schrei m ● vi heulen; (lament) klagen

waist /weɪst/ n Taille f. ∼**coat** /'weɪskəʊt/ n Weste f. ∼**line** n Taille f

wait /weɪt/ n Wartezeit f; **lie in** ∼ **for** auflauern (+ dat) ● vi warten (**for** auf + acc); (at table) servieren; ∼ **on** bedienen ● vt ∼ **one's turn** warten, bis man an der Reihe ist

waiter /'weɪtə(r)/ n Kellner m; ∼! Herr Ober!

waiting: ∼**-list** n Warteliste f. ∼**-room** n Warteraum m; (doctor's) Wartezimmer nt

waitress /'weɪtrɪs/ n Kellnerin f

waive /weɪv/ vt verzichten auf (+ acc)

wake[1] /weɪk/ *n* Totenwache *f* ● *v* (*pt* **woke**, *pp* **woken**) ~ **[up]** ● *vt* [auf]wecken ● *vi* aufwachen

wake[2] *n* (*Naut*) Kielwasser *nt*; **in the** ~ **of** im Gefolge (+ *gen*)

waken /'weɪkn/ *vt* [auf]wecken ● *vi* aufwachen

Wales /weɪlz/ *n* Wales *nt*

walk /wɔːk/ *n* Spaziergang *m*; (*gait*) Gang *m*; (*path*) Weg *m*; **go for a** ~ spazierengehen ● *vi* gehen; (*not ride*) laufen, zu Fuß gehen; (*ramble*) wandern; **learn to** ~ laufen lernen ● *vt* ausführen ⟨*dog*⟩. ~ **out** *vi* hinausgehen; ⟨*workers:*⟩ in den Streik treten; ~ **out on s.o.** jdn verlassen

walker /'wɔːkə(r)/ *n* Spaziergänger(in) *m*(*f*); (*rambler*) Wanderer *m*/Wanderin *f*

walking /'wɔːkɪŋ/ *n* Gehen *nt*; (*rambling*) Wandern *nt*. ~**-stick** *n* Spazierstock *m*

walk: ~**-out** *n* Streik *m*. ~**-over** *n* (*fig*) leichter Sieg *m*

wall /wɔːl/ *n* Wand *f*; (*external*) Mauer *f*; **go to the** ~ (*fam*) eingehen; **drive s.o. up the** ~ (*fam*) jdn auf die Palme bringen ● *vt* ~ **up** zumauern

wallet /'wɒlɪt/ *n* Brieftasche *f*

'**wallflower** *n* Goldlack *m*

wallop /'wɒləp/ *n* (*fam*) Schlag *m* ● *vt* (*pt/pp* **walloped**) (*fam*) schlagen

wallow /'wɒləʊ/ *vi* sich wälzen; (*fig*) schwelgen

'**wallpaper** *n* Tapete *f* ● *vt* tapezieren

walnut /'wɔːlnʌt/ *n* Walnuß *f*

waltz /wɔːlts/ *n* Walzer *m* ● *vi* Walzer tanzen; **come** ~**ing up** (*fam*) angetanzt kommen

wan /wɒn/ *a* bleich

wand /wɒnd/ *n* Zauberstab *m*

wander /'wɒndə(r)/ *vi* umherwandern, (*fam*) bummeln; (*fig: digress*) abschweifen. ~ **about** *vi* umherwandern. ~**lust** *n* Fernweh *nt*

wane /weɪn/ *n* **be on the** ~ schwinden; ⟨*moon:*⟩ abnehmen ● *vi* schwinden; abnehmen

wangle /'wæŋgl/ *vt* (*fam*) organisieren

want /wɒnt/ *n* Mangel *m* (**of** an + *dat*); (*hardship*) Not *f*; (*desire*) Bedürfnis *nt* ● *vt* wollen; (*need*) brauchen; ~ **[to have] sth** etw haben wollen; ~ **to do sth** etw tun wollen; **we** ~ **to stay** wir wollen bleiben; **I** ~ **you to go** ich will, daß du gehst; **it** ~**s painting** es

müßte gestrichen werden; **you** ~ **to learn to swim** du solltest schwimmen lernen ● *vi* **he doesn't** ~ **for anything** ihm fehlt es an nichts. ~**ed** *a* gesucht. ~**ing** *a* **be** ~**ing** fehlen; **he is** ~**ing in** ihm fehlt es an (+ *dat*)

wanton /'wɒntən/ *a*, **-ly** *adv* mutwillig

war /wɔː(r)/ *n* Krieg *m*; **be at** ~ sich im Krieg befinden

ward /wɔːd/ *n* [Kranken]saal *m*; (*unit*) Station *f*; (*of town*) Wahlbezirk *m*; (*child*) Mündel *nt* ● *vt* ~ **off** abwehren

warden /'wɔːdn/ *n* Heimleiter(in) *m*(*f*); (*of youth hostel*) Herbergsvater *m*; (*supervisor*) Aufseher(in) *m*(*f*)

warder /'wɔːdə(r)/ *n* Wärter(in) *m*(*f*)

wardrobe /'wɔːdrəʊb/ *n* Kleiderschrank *m*; (*clothes*) Garderobe *f*

warehouse /'weəhaʊs/ *n* Lager *nt*; (*building*) Lagerhaus *nt*

wares /weəz/ *npl* Waren *pl*

war: ~**fare** *n* Krieg *m*. ~**head** *n* Sprengkopf *m*. ~**like** *a* kriegerisch

warm /wɔːm/ *a* (**-er**, **-est**), **-ly** *adv* warm; (*welcome*) herzlich; **I am** ~ mir ist warm ● *vt* wärmen. ~ **up** *vt* aufwärmen ● *vi* warm werden; (*Sport*) sich aufwärmen. ~**-hearted** *a* warmherzig

warmth /wɔːmθ/ *n* Wärme *f*

warn /wɔːn/ *vt* warnen (**of** vor + *dat*). ~**ing** *n* Warnung *f*; (*advance notice*) Vorwarnung *f*; (*caution*) Verwarnung *f*

warp /wɔːp/ *vt* verbiegen ● *vi* sich verziehen

'**war-path** *n* **on the** ~ auf dem Kriegspfad

warrant /'wɒrənt/ *n* (*for arrest*) Haftbefehl *m*; (*for search*) Durchsuchungsbefehl *m* ● *vt* (*justify*) rechtfertigen; (*guarantee*) garantieren

warranty /'wɒrəntɪ/ *n* Garantie *f*

warrior /'wɒrɪə(r)/ *n* Krieger *m*

'**warship** *n* Kriegsschiff *nt*

wart /wɔːt/ *n* Warze *f*

'**wartime** *n* Kriegszeit *f*

wary /'weərɪ/ *a* (**-ier**, **-iest**), **-ily** *adv* vorsichtig; (*suspicious*) mißtrauisch

was /wɒz/ *see* **be**

wash /wɒʃ/ *n* Wäsche *f*; (*Naut*) Wellen *pl*; **have a** ~ sich waschen ● *vt* waschen; spülen ⟨*dishes*⟩; aufwischen ⟨*floor*⟩; (*flow over*) bespülen; ~ **one's**

hands sich (dat) die Hände waschen ● vi sich waschen; ⟨fabric:⟩ sich waschen lassen. ~ **out** vt auswaschen; ausspülen ⟨mouth⟩. ~ **up** vt abwaschen, spülen ● vi (Amer) sich waschen

washable /ˈwɒʃəbl/ a waschbar

wash: ~-**basin** n Waschbecken nt. ~**cloth** n (Amer) Waschlappen m

washed ˈ**out** a ⟨faded⟩ verwaschen; ⟨tired⟩ abgespannt

washer /ˈwɒʃə(r)/ n (Techn) Dichtungsring m; ⟨machine⟩ Waschmaschine f

washing /ˈwɒʃɪŋ/ n Wäsche f. ~-**machine** n Waschmaschine f. ~-**powder** n Waschpulver nt. ~-ˈ**up** n Abwasch m; **do the** ~-**up** abwaschen, spülen. ~-ˈ**up liquid** n Spülmittel nt

wash: ~-**out** n Pleite f; ⟨person⟩ Niete f. ~-**room** n Waschraum m

wasp /wɒsp/ n Wespe f

wastage /ˈweɪstɪdʒ/ n Schwund m

waste /weɪst/ n Verschwendung f; ⟨rubbish⟩ Abfall m; ~s pl Öde f; ~ **of time** Zeitverschwendung f ● a ⟨product⟩ Abfall-; **lay** ~ verwüsten ● vt verschwenden ● vi ~ **away** immer mehr abmagern

waste: ~-**di**ˈ**sposal unit** n Müllzerkleinerer m. ~**ful** a verschwenderisch. ~**land** n Ödland nt. ~ ˈ**paper** n Altpapier nt. ~-ˈ**paper basket** n Papierkorb m

watch /wɒtʃ/ n Wache f; ⟨timepiece⟩ [Armband]uhr f; **be on the** ~ aufpassen ● vt beobachten; sich (dat) ansehen ⟨film, match⟩; ⟨be careful of, look after⟩ achten auf (+ acc); ~ **television** fernsehen ● vi zusehen. ~ **out** vi Ausschau halten (**for** nach); ⟨be careful⟩ aufpassen

watch: ~-**dog** n Wachhund m. ~**ful** a, -**ly** adv wachsam. ~**maker** n Uhrmacher m. ~**man** n Wachmann m. ~-**strap** n Uhrarmband nt. ~-**tower** n Wachturm m. ~**word** n Parole f

water /ˈwɔːtə(r)/ n Wasser nt; ~s pl Gewässer nt ● vt gießen ⟨garden, plant⟩; ⟨dilute⟩ verdünnen; ⟨give drink to⟩ tränken ● vi ⟨eyes:⟩ tränen; **my mouth was** ~**ing** mir lief das Wasser im Munde zusammen. ~ **down** vt verwässern

water: ~-**colour** n Wasserfarbe f; ⟨painting⟩ Aquarell nt. ~**cress** n Brunnenkresse f. ~**fall** n Wasserfall m

ˈ**watering-can** n Gießkanne f

water: ~-**lily** n Seerose f. ~**logged** a **be** ~**logged** ⟨ground:⟩ unter Wasser stehen. ~-**main** n Hauptwasserleitung f. ~**mark** n Wasserzeichen nt. ~ **polo** n Wasserball m. ~-**power** n Wasserkraft f. ~**proof** a wasserdicht. ~**shed** n Wasserscheide f; ⟨fig⟩ Wendepunkt m. ~-**skiing** n Wasserskilaufen nt. ~**tight** a wasserdicht. ~**way** n Wasserstraße f

watery /ˈwɔːtərɪ/ a wäßrig

watt /wɒt/ n Watt nt

wave /weɪv/ n Welle f; ⟨gesture⟩ Handbewegung f; ⟨as greeting⟩ Winken nt ● vt winken mit; ⟨brandish⟩ schwingen; ⟨threateningly⟩ drohen mit; wellen ⟨hair⟩; ~ **one's hand** winken ● vi winken (**to** dat); ⟨flag:⟩ wehen. ~**length** n Wellenlänge f

waver /ˈweɪvə(r)/ vi schwanken

wavy /ˈweɪvɪ/ a wellig

wax[1] /wæks/ vi ⟨moon:⟩ zunehmen; ⟨fig: become⟩ werden

wax[2] n Wachs nt; ⟨in ear⟩ Schmalz nt ● vt wachsen. ~**works** n Wachsfigurenkabinett nt

way /weɪ/ n Weg m; ⟨direction⟩ Richtung f; ⟨respect⟩ Hinsicht f; ⟨manner⟩ Art f; ⟨method⟩ Weise f; ~s pl Gewohnheiten pl; **in the** ~ im Weg; **on the** ~ auf dem Weg (**to** nach/zu); ⟨under way⟩ unterwegs; **a little/long** ~ ein kleines/ganzes Stück; **a long** ~ **off** weit weg; **this** ~ hierher; ⟨like this⟩ so; **which** ~ in welche Richtung; ⟨how⟩ wie; **by the** ~ übrigens; **in some** ~s in gewisser Hinsicht; **either** ~ so oder so; **in this** ~ auf diese Weise; **in a** ~ in gewisser Weise; **in a bad** ~ ⟨person⟩ in schlechter Verfassung; **lead the** ~ vorausgehen; **make** ~ Platz machen (**for** dat); '**give** ~' (Auto) 'Vorfahrt beachten'; **go out of one's** ~ ⟨fig⟩ sich (dat) besondere Mühe geben (**to** zu); **get one's [own]** ~ seinen Willen durchsetzen ● adv weit; ~ **behind** weit zurück. ~ ˈ**in** n Eingang m

wayˈ**lay** vt (pt/pp -**laid**) überfallen; ⟨fam: intercept⟩ abfangen

way ˈ**out** n Ausgang m; ⟨fig⟩ Ausweg m

way-ˈ**out** a ⟨fam⟩ verrückt

wayward /ˈweɪwəd/ a eigenwillig

WC abbr WC nt

we /wi:/ *pron* wir

weak /wi:k/ *a* (**-er, -est**), **-ly** *adv*
schwach; ⟨*liquid*⟩ dünn. **~en** *vt* schwächen ● *vi* schwächer werden. **~ling**
n Schwächling *m*. **~ness** *n* Schwäche *f*

wealth /welθ/ *n* Reichtum *m*; (*fig*)
Fülle *f* (**of** an + *dat*). **~y** *a* (**-ier, -iest**)
reich

wean /wi:n/ *vt* entwöhnen

weapon /'wepən/ *n* Waffe *f*

wear /weə(r)/ *n* (*clothing*) Kleidung
f; **~ and tear** Abnutzung *f*, Verschleiß
m ● *v* (*pt* **wore**, *pp* **worn**) ● *vt* tragen;
(*damage*) abnutzen; **~ a hole in sth** etw
durchwetzen; **what shall I ~?** was soll
ich anziehen? ● *vi* sich abnutzen; (*last*)
halten. **~ off** *vi* abgehen; ⟨*effect:*⟩
nachlassen. **~ out** *vt* abnutzen;
(*exhaust*) erschöpfen ● *vi* sich abnutzen

wearable /'weərəbl/ *a* tragbar

weary /'wɪərɪ/ *a* (**-ier, -iest**), **-ily** *adv*
müde ● *v* (*pt/pp* **wearied**) ● *vt* ermüden ● *vi* **~ of sth** etw (*gen*)
überdrüssig werden

weasel /'wi:zl/ *n* Wiesel *nt*

weather /'weðə(r)/ *n* Wetter *nt*; **in
this ~** bei diesem Wetter; **under the ~**
(*fam*) nicht ganz auf dem Posten ● *vt*
abwettern ⟨*storm*⟩; (*fig*) überstehen

weather: **~-beaten** *a* verwittert;
wettergegerbt ⟨*face*⟩. **~cock** *n*
Wetterhahn *m*. **~ forecast** *n*
Wettervorhersage *f*. **~-vane** *n* Wet-
terfahne *f*

weave¹ /wi:v/ *vi* (*pt/pp* **weaved**)
sich schlängeln (**through** durch)

weave² *n* (*Tex*) Bindung *f* ● *vt* (*pt*
wove, *pp* **woven**) weben; (*plait*)
flechten; (*fig*) einflechten (**in** in + *acc*).
~r *n* Weber *m*

web /web/ *n* Netz *nt*. **~bed feet** *npl*
Schwimmfüße *pl*

wed /wed/ *vt/i* (*pt/pp* **wedded**)
heiraten. **~ding** *n* Hochzeit *f*; (*ceremony*) Trauung *f*

wedding: **~ day** *n* Hochzeitstag *m*.
~ dress *n* Hochzeitskleid *nt*. **~-ring**
n Ehering *m*, Trauring *m*

wedge /wedʒ/ *n* Keil *m*; (*of cheese*)
[keilförmiges] Stück *nt* ● *vt* fest-
klemmen

wedlock /'wedlɒk/ *n* (*liter*) Ehe *f*; **in/
out of ~** ehelich/unehelich

Wednesday /'wenzdeɪ/ *n* Mittwoch
m

wee /wi:/ *a* (*fam*) klein ● *vi* Pipi
machen

weed /wi:d/ *n* & **~s** *pl* Unkraut *nt*
● *vt/i* jäten. **~ out** *vt* (*fig*) aussieben

'weed-killer *n* Unkrautver-
tilgungsmittel *nt*

weedy /'wi:dɪ/ *a* (*fam*) spillerig

week /wi:k/ *n* Woche *f*. **~day** *n*
Wochentag *m*. **~end** *n* Wochenende
nt

weekly /'wi:klɪ/ *a* & *adv* wöchentlich ● *n* Wochenzeitschrift *f*

weep /wi:p/ *vi* (*pt/pp* **wept**) weinen.
~ing willow *n* Trauerweide *f*

weigh /weɪ/ *vt/i* wiegen; **~ anchor**
den Anker lichten. **~ down** *vt* (*fig*)
niederdrücken. **~ up** *vt* (*fig*) abwägen

weight /weɪt/ *n* Gewicht *nt*; **put on/
lose ~** zunehmen/abnehmen. **~ing** *n*
(*allowance*) Zulage *f*

weight: **~lessness** *n* Schwere-
losigkeit *f*. **~-lifting** *n* Gewicht-
heben *nt*

weighty /'weɪtɪ/ *a* (**-ier, -iest**)
schwer; (*important*) gewichtig

weir /wɪə(r)/ *n* Wehr *nt*

weird /wɪəd/ *a* (**-er, -est**) unheimlich;
(*bizarre*) bizarr

welcome /'welkəm/ *a* willkommen;
you're ~! nichts zu danken! **you're ~
to have it** das können Sie gerne haben
● *n* Willkommen *nt* ● *vt* begrüßen

weld /weld/ *vt* schweißen. **~er** *n*
Schweißer *m*

welfare /'welfeə(r)/ *n* Wohl *nt*;
(*Admin*) Fürsorge *f*. **W~ State** *n*
Wohlfahrtsstaat *m*

well¹ /wel/ *n* Brunnen *m*; (*oil* **~**) Quelle
f; (*of staircase*) Treppenhaus *nt*

well² *adv* (**better, best**) gut; **as ~** auch;
as ~ as (*in addition*) sowohl … als
auch; **~ done!** gut gemacht! ● *a* gesund; **he is not ~** es geht ihm nicht gut;
get ~ soon! gute Besserung! ● *int* nun,
na

well: **~-behaved** *a* artig. **~-being** *n*
Wohl *nt*. **~-bred** *a* wohlerzogen.
~-heeled *a* (*fam*) gut betucht

wellingtons /'welɪŋtənz/ *npl* Gummistiefel *pl*

well: **~-known** *a* bekannt.
~-meaning *a* wohlmeinend.
~-meant *a* gutgemeint. **~-off** *a*
wohlhabend; **be ~-off** gut dran sein.
~-read *a* belesen. **~-to-do** *a*
wohlhabend

Welsh /welʃ/ a walisisch ● n (Lang) Walisisch nt; **the** ~ pl die Waliser. ~**man** n Waliser m. ~ **rabbit** n überbackenes Käsebrot nt

went /went/ see **go**

wept /wept/ see **weep**

were /wɜː(r)/ see **be**

west /west/ n Westen m; **to the** ~ **of** westlich von ● a West-, west- ● adv nach Westen; **go** ~ (fam) flötengehen. ~**erly** a westlich. ~**ern** a westlich ● n Western m

West: ~ '**Germany** n Westdeutschland nt. ~ '**Indian** a westindisch ● n Westinder(in) m(f). ~ '**Indies** /-'ındız/ npl Westindische Inseln pl

'**westward[s]** /-wəd[z]/ adv nach Westen

wet /wet/ a (**wetter, wettest**) naß; ⟨fam: person⟩ weichlich, lasch; '~ **paint**' 'frisch gestrichen' ● vt (pt/pp **wet** or **wetted**) naß machen. ~ '**blanket** n Spaßverderber m

whack /wæk/ n (fam) Schlag m ● vt (fam) schlagen. ~**ed** a (fam) kaputt

whale /weɪl/ n Wal m; **have a** ~ **of a time** (fam) sich toll amüsieren

wharf /wɔːf/ n Kai m

what /wɒt/ pron & int was; ~ **for?** wozu? ~ **is it like?** wie ist es? ~ **is your name?** wie ist Ihr Name? ~ **is the weather like?** wie ist das Wetter? ~'**s he talking about?** wovon redet er? ● a welche(r,s); ~ **kind of a** was für ein(e); **at** ~ **time?** um wieviel Uhr?

what'ever a [egal] welche(r,s) ● pron was ... auch; ~ **is it?** was ist das bloß? ~ **he does** was er auch tut; ~ **happens** was auch geschieht; **nothing** ~ überhaupt nichts

whatso'ever pron & a ≈ **whatever**

wheat /wiːt/ n Weizen m

wheedle /'wiːdl/ vt gut zureden (+ dat); ~ **sth out of s.o.** jdm etw ablocken

wheel /wiːl/ n Rad nt; (pottery) Töpferscheibe f; (steering ~) Lenkrad nt; **at the** ~ am Steuer ● vt (push) schieben ● vi kehrtmachen; (circle) kreisen

wheel: ~**barrow** n Schubkarre f. ~**chair** n Rollstuhl m. ~**clamp** n Parkkralle f

wheeze /wiːz/ vi keuchen

when /wen/ adv wann; **the day** ~ der Tag, an dem ● conj wenn; (in the past) als; (although) wo ... doch; ~

swimming/reading beim Schwimmen/Lesen

whence /wens/ adv (liter) woher

when'ever conj & adv [immer] wenn; (at whatever time) wann immer; ~ **did it happen?** wann ist das bloß passiert?

where /weə(r)/ adv & conj wo; ~ **[to]** wohin; ~ **[from]** woher

whereabouts[1] /weərə'baʊts/ adv wo
'**whereabouts**[2] n Verbleib m; (of person) Aufenthaltsort m

where'as conj während; (in contrast) wohingegen

where'by adv wodurch

whereu'pon adv worauf[hin]

wher'ever conj & adv wo immer; (to whatever place) wohin immer; (from whatever place) woher immer; (everywhere) überall wo; ~ **is he?** wo ist er bloß? ~ **possible** wenn irgend möglich

whet /wet/ vt (pt/pp **whetted**) wetzen; anregen ⟨appetite⟩

whether /'weðə(r)/ conj ob

which /wɪtʃ/ a & pron welche(r,s); ~ **one** welche(r,s) ● rel pron der/die/das, (pl) die; (after clause) was; **after** ~ wonach; **on** ~ worauf

which'ever a & pron [egal] welche(r,s); ~ **it is** was es auch ist

whiff /wɪf/ n Hauch m

while /waɪl/ n Weile f; **a long** ~ lange; **be worth** ~ sich lohnen; **it's worth my** ~ es lohnt sich für mich ● conj während; (as long as) solange; (although) obgleich ● vt ~ **away** sich (dat) vertreiben

whilst /waɪlst/ conj während

whim /wɪm/ n Laune f

whimper /'wɪmpə(r)/ vi wimmern; ⟨dog:⟩ winseln

whimsical /'wɪmzɪkl/ a skurril

whine /waɪn/ n Winseln nt ● vi winseln

whip /wɪp/ n Peitsche f; (Pol) Einpeitscher m ● vt (pt/pp **whipped**) peitschen; (Culin) schlagen; (snatch) reißen; (fam: steal) klauen. ~ **up** vt (incite) anheizen; (fam) schnell hinzaubern ⟨meal⟩. ~**ped 'cream** n Schlagsahne f

whirl /wɜːl/ n Wirbel m; **I am in a** ~ mir schwirrt der Kopf ● vt/i wirbeln. ~**pool** n Strudel m. ~**wind** n Wirbelwind m

whirr /wɜː(r)/ vi surren

whisk /wɪsk/ n (Culin) Schneebesen m ● vt (Culin) schlagen. ~ **away** vt wegreißen

whisker /'wɪskə(r)/ *n* Schnurrhaar
nt; ~s *pl* (*on man's cheek*) Backenbart
m
whisky /'wɪskɪ/ *n* Whisky *m*
whisper /'wɪspə(r)/ *n* Flüstern *nt*;
(*rumour*) Gerücht *nt*; **in a** ~ im
Flüsterton● *vt/i* flüstern
whistle /'wɪsl/ *n* Pfiff *m*;
(*instrument*) Pfeife *f* ● *vt/i* pfeifen
white /waɪt/ *a* (**-r, -st**) weiß ● *n* Weiß
nt; (*of egg*) Eiweiß *nt*; (*person*) Weiße(r)
m/f
white: ~ **'coffee** *n* Kaffee *m* mit
Milch. ~-'**collar worker** *n* Ange-
stellte(r) *m*. ~ '**lie** *n* Notlüge *f*
whiten /'waɪtn/ *vt* weiß machen ● *vi*
weiß werden
whiteness /'waɪtnɪs/ *n* Weiß *nt*
'**whitewash** *n* Tünche *f*; (*fig*)
Schönfärberei *f* ● *vt* tünchen
Whitsun /'wɪtsn/ *n* Pfingsten *nt*
whittle /'wɪtl/ *vt* ~ **down** reduzieren;
kürzen ⟨*list*⟩
whiz[z] /wɪz/ *vi* (*pt/pp* **whizzed**)
zischen. ~-**kid** *n* (*fam*) Senk-
rechtstarter *m*
who /hu:/ *pron* wer; (*acc*) wen; (*dat*)
wem ● *rel pron* der/die/das, (*pl*) die
who'ever *pron* wer [immer]; ~ **he is**
wer er auch ist; ~ **is it?** wer ist das
bloß?
whole /həʊl/ *a* ganz; ⟨*truth*⟩ voll ● *n*
Ganze(s) *nt*; **as a** ~ als Ganzes; **on the**
~ im großen und ganzen; **the** ~ **lot**
alle; (*everything*) alles; **the** ~ **of Ger-**
many ganz Deutschland; **the** ~ **time**
die ganze Zeit
whole: ~**food** *n* Vollwertkost *f*.
~-'**hearted** *a* rückhaltlos. ~**meal** *a*
Vollkorn-
'**wholesale** *a* Großhandels- ● *adv*
en gros; (*fig*) in Bausch und Bogen.
~**r** *n* Großhändler *m*
wholesome /'həʊlsəm/ *a* gesund
wholly /'həʊlɪ/ *adv* völlig
whom /hu:m/ *pron* wen; **to** ~ wem
● *rel pron* den/die/das, (*pl*) die; (*dat*)
dem/der/dem, (*pl*) denen
whooping cough /'hu:pɪŋ-/ *n*
Keuchhusten *m*
whopping /'wɒpɪŋ/ *a* (*fam*) Riesen-
whore /hɔ:(r)/ *n* Hure *f*
whose /hu:z/ *pron* wessen; ~ **is**
that? wem gehört das? ● *rel pron*
dessen/deren/dessen, (*pl*) deren
why /waɪ/ *adv* warum; (*for what*
purpose) wozu; **that's** ~ darum ● *int*
na

wick /wɪk/ *n* Docht *m*
wicked /'wɪkɪd/ *a* böse; (*mischiev-*
ous) frech, boshaft
wicker /'wɪkə(r)/ *n* Korbgeflecht *nt*
● *attrib* Korb-
wide /waɪd/ *a* (**-r, -st**) weit; (*broad*)
breit; (*fig*) groß; **be** ~ (*far from target*)
danebengehen ● *adv* weit; (*off target*)
daneben; ~ **awake** hellwach; **far and**
~ weit und breit. ~**ly** *adv* weit;
⟨*known, accepted*⟩ weithin; ⟨*differ*⟩
stark
widen /'waɪdn/ *vt* verbreitern; (*fig*)
erweitern ● *vi* sich verbreitern
'**widespread** *a* weitverbreitet
widow /'wɪdəʊ/ *n* Witwe *f*. ~**ed** *a*
verwitwet. ~**er** *n* Witwer *m*
width /wɪdθ/ *n* Weite *f*; (*breadth*)
Breite *f*
wield /wi:ld/ *vt* schwingen; ausüben
⟨*power*⟩
wife /waɪf/ *n* (*pl* **wives**) [Ehe]frau *f*
wig /wɪg/ *n* Perücke *f*
wiggle /'wɪgl/ *vi* wackeln ● *vt*
wackeln mit
wild /waɪld/ *a* (**-er, -est**), **-ly** *adv* wild;
⟨*animal*⟩ wildlebend; ⟨*flower*⟩ wild-
wachsend; (*furious*) wütend; **be** ~
about (*keen on*) wild sein auf (+ *acc*)
● *adv* wild; **run** ~ frei herumlaufen ● *n*
in the ~ wild; **the** ~**s** *pl* die Wildnis *f*
'**wildcat strike** *n* wilder Streik *m*
wilderness /'wɪldənɪs/ *n* Wildnis *f*;
(*desert*) Wüste *f*
wild: ~-'**goose chase** *n* aus-
sichtslose Suche *f*. ~**life** *n* Tierwelt *f*
wilful /'wɪlfl/ *a*, **-ly** *adv* mutwillig;
(*self-willed*) eigenwillig
will[1] /wɪl/ *v aux* wollen; (*forming*
future tense) werden; **he** ~ **arrive to-**
morrow er wird morgen kommen; ~
you go? gehst du? **you** ~ **be back**
soon, won't you? du kommst doch
bald wieder, nicht? **he** ~ **be there,**
won't he? er wird doch da sein? **she** ~
be there by now sie wird jetzt schon
da sein; ~ **you be quiet!** willst du wohl
ruhig sein! ~ **you have some wine?**
möchten Sie Wein? **the engine won't**
start der Motor will nicht anspringen
will[2] *n* Wille *m*; (*document*) Testament
nt
willing /'wɪlɪŋ/ *a* willig; (*eager*)
bereitwillig; **be** ~ bereit sein. ~**ly** *adv*
bereitwillig; (*gladly*) gern. ~**ness** *n*
Bereitwilligkeit *f*
willow /'wɪləʊ/ *n* Weide *f*
'**will-power** *n* Willenskraft *f*

willy-'nilly *adv* wohl oder übel

wilt /wɪlt/ *vi* welk werden, welken

wily /'waɪlɪ/ *a* (**-ier, -iest**) listig

wimp /wɪmp/ *n* Schwächling *m*

win /wɪn/ *n* Sieg *m*; **have a ~** gewinnen ● *v* (*pt/pp* **won**; *pres p* **winning**) ● *vt* gewinnen; bekommen ⟨*scholarship*⟩ ● *vi* gewinnen; (*in battle*) siegen. **~ over** *vt* auf seine Seite bringen

wince /wɪns/ *vi* zusammenzucken

winch /wɪntʃ/ *n* Winde *f* ● *vt* **~ up** hochwinden

wind[1] /wɪnd/ *n* Wind *m*; (*breath*) Atem *m*; (*fam: flatulence*) Blähungen *pl*; **have the ~ up** (*fam*) Angst haben ● *vt* **~ s.o.** jdm den Atem nehmen

wind[2] /waɪnd/ *v* (*pt/pp* **wound**) ● *vt* (*wrap*) wickeln; (*move by turning*) kurbeln; aufziehen ⟨*clock*⟩ ● *vi* ⟨*road:*⟩ sich winden. **~ up** *vt* aufziehen ⟨*clock*⟩; schließen ⟨*proceedings*⟩

wind /wɪnd/: **~fall** *n* unerwarteter Glücksfall *m*; **~falls** *pl* (*fruit*) Fallobst *nt*. **~ instrument** *n* Blasinstrument *nt*. **~mill** *n* Windmühle *f*

window /'wɪndəʊ/ *n* Fenster *nt*; (*of shop*) Schaufenster *nt*

window: **~-box** *n* Blumenkasten *m*. **~-cleaner** *n* Fensterputzer *m*. **~-dresser** *n* Schaufensterdekorateur(in) *m(f)*. **~-dressing** *n* Schaufensterdekoration *f*; (*fig*) Schönfärberei *f*. **~-pane** *n* Fensterscheibe *f*. **~-shopping** *n* Schaufensterbummel *m*. **~-sill** *n* Fensterbrett *nt*

'windpipe *n* Luftröhre *f*

'windscreen *n*, (*Amer*) **'windshield** *n* Windschutzscheibe *f*. **~ washer** *n* Scheibenwaschanlage *f*. **~-wiper** *n* Scheibenwischer *m*

wind: **~surfing** *n* Windsurfen *nt*. **~swept** *a* windgepeitscht; ⟨*person*⟩ zersaust

windy /'wɪndɪ/ *a* (**-ier, -iest**) windig; **be ~** (*fam*) Angst haben

wine /waɪn/ *n* Wein *m*

wine: **~-bar** *n* Weinstube *f*. **~glass** *n* Weinglas *nt*. **~-list** *n* Weinkarte *f*

winery /'waɪnərɪ/ *n* (*Amer*) Weingut *nt*

'wine-tasting *n* Weinprobe *f*

'wing /wɪŋ/ *n* Flügel *m*; (*Auto*) Kotflügel *m*; **~s** *pl* (*Theat*) Kulissen *pl*

wink /wɪŋk/ *n* Zwinkern *nt*; **not sleep a ~** kein Auge zutun ● *vi* zwinkern; ⟨*light:*⟩ blinken

winner /'wɪnə(r)/ *n* Gewinner(in) *m(f)*; (*Sport*) Sieger(in) *m(f)*

winning /'wɪnɪŋ/ *a* siegreich; ⟨*smile*⟩ gewinnend. **~-post** *n* Zielpfosten *m*. **~s** *npl* Gewinn *m*

winter /'wɪntə(r)/ *n* Winter *m*. **~ry** *a* winterlich

wipe /waɪp/ *n* **give sth a ~** etw abwischen ● *vt* abwischen; aufwischen ⟨*floor*⟩; (*dry*) abtrocknen. **~ off** *vt* abwischen; (*erase*) auslöschen. **~ out** *vt* (*cancel*) löschen; (*destroy*) ausrotten. **~ up** *vt* aufwischen; abtrocknen ⟨*dishes*⟩

wire /'waɪə(r)/ *n* Draht *m*. **~-haired** *a* rauhhaarig

wireless /'waɪəlɪs/ *n* Radio *nt*

wire 'netting *n* Maschendraht *m*

wiring /'waɪərɪŋ/ *n* [elektrische] Leitungen *pl*

wiry /'waɪərɪ/ *a* (**-ier, -iest**) drahtig

wisdom /'wɪzdəm/ *n* Weisheit *f*; (*prudence*) Klugheit *f*. **~ tooth** *n* Weisheitszahn *m*

wise /waɪz/ *a* (**-r, -st**), **-ly** *adv* weise; (*prudent*) klug

wish /wɪʃ/ *n* Wunsch *m* ● *vt* wünschen; **~ s.o. well** jdm alles Gute wünschen; **I ~ you could stay** ich wünschte, du könntest hierbleiben ● *vi* sich (*dat*) etwas wünschen. **~ful** *a* **~ful thinking** Wunschdenken *nt*

wishy-washy /'wɪʃɪwɒʃɪ/ *a* labberig; ⟨*colour*⟩ verwaschen; ⟨*person*⟩ lasch

wisp /wɪsp/ *n* Büschel *nt*; (*of hair*) Strähne *f*; (*of smoke*) Fahne *f*

wisteria /wɪs'tɪərɪə/ *n* Glyzinie *f*

wistful /'wɪstfl/ *a*, **-ly** *adv* wehmütig

wit /wɪt/ *n* Geist *m*, Witz *m*; (*intelligence*) Verstand *m*; (*person*) geistreicher Mensch *m*; **be at one's ~s' end** sich (*dat*) keinen Rat mehr wissen; **scared out of one's ~s** zu Tode erschrocken

witch /wɪtʃ/ *n* Hexe *f*. **~craft** *n* Hexerei *f*. **~-hunt** *n* Hexenjagd *f*

with /wɪð/ *prep* mit (+ *dat*); **~ fear/ cold** vor Angst/Kälte; **~ it** damit; **I'm going ~ you** ich gehe mit; **take it ~ you** nimm es mit; **I haven't got it ~ me** ich habe es nicht bei mir; **I'm not ~ you** (*fam*) ich komme nicht mit

with'draw *v* (*pt* **-drew**, *pp* **-drawn**) ● *vt* zurückziehen; abheben ⟨*money*⟩ ● *vi* sich zurückziehen. **~al** *n* Zurückziehen *nt*; (*of money*) Abhebung *f*; (*from drugs*) Entzug *m*. ~**al symptoms** *npl* Entzugserscheinungen *pl*

with'drawn *see* **withdraw** ● *a* ⟨*person*⟩ verschlossen

wither /'wɪðə(r)/ *vi* [ver]welken

with'hold *vt* (*pt/pp* -**held**) vorenthalten (**from s.o.** jdm)

with'in *prep* innerhalb (+ *gen*); ~ **the law** im Rahmen des Gesetzes ● *adv* innen

with'out *prep* ohne (+ *acc*); ~ **my noticing it** ohne daß ich es merkte

with'stand *vt* (*pt/pp* -**stood**) standhalten (+ *dat*)

witness /'wɪtnɪs/ *n* Zeuge *m*/Zeugin *f*; (*evidence*) Zeugnis *nt* ● *vt* Zeuge/ Zeugin sein (+ *gen*); bestätigen ⟨*signature*⟩. ~**box** *n*, (*Amer*) ~**stand** *n* Zeugenstand *m*

witticism /'wɪtɪsɪzm/ *n* geistreicher Ausspruch *m*

wittingly /'wɪtɪŋlɪ/ *adv* wissentlich

witty /'wɪtɪ/ *a* (-**ier,** -**iest**) witzig, geistreich

wives /waɪvz/ *see* **wife**

wizard /'wɪzəd/ *n* Zauberer *m*. ~**ry** *n* Zauberei *f*

wizened /'wɪznd/ *a* verhutzelt

wobb|le /'wɒbl/ *vi* wackeln. ~**ly** *a* wackelig

woe /wəʊ/ *n* (*liter*) Jammer *m*; ~ **is me!** wehe mir!

woke, woken /wəʊk, 'wəʊkn/ *see* **wake**[1]

wolf /wʊlf/ *n* (*pl* **wolves** /wʊlvz/) Wolf *m* ● *vt* ~ [**down**] hinunterschlingen

woman /'wʊmən/ *n* (*pl* **women**) Frau *f*. ~**izer** *n* Schürzenjäger *m*. ~**ly** *a* fraulich

womb /wuːm/ *n* Gebärmutter *f*

women /'wɪmɪn/ *npl see* **woman**; **W**~**'s Libber** /'lɪbə(r)/ *n* Frauenrechtlerin *f*. **W**~**'s Liberation** *n* Frauenbewegung *f*

won /wʌn/ *see* **win**

wonder /'wʌndə(r)/ *n* Wunder *nt*; (*surprise*) Staunen *nt* ● *vt/i* sich fragen; (*be surprised*) sich wundern; **I** ~ da frage ich mich; **I** ~ **whether she is ill** ob sie wohl krank ist? ~**ful** *a*, **-ly** *adv* wunderbar

won't /wəʊnt/ = **will not**

woo /wuː/ *vt* (*liter*) werben um; (*fig*) umwerben

wood /wʊd/ *n* Holz *nt*; (*forest*) Wald *m*; **touch** ~**!** unberufen!

wood: ~**cut** *n* Holzschnitt *m*. ~**ed** /-ɪd/ *a* bewaldet. ~**en** *a* Holz-; (*fig*) hölzern. ~**pecker** *n* Specht *m*. ~**wind** *n* Holzbläser *pl*. ~**work** *n* (*wooden parts*) Holzteile *pl*; (*craft*) Tischlerei *f*. ~**worm** *n* Holzwurm *m*. ~**y** *a* holzig

wool /wʊl/ *n* Wolle *f* ● *attrib* Woll-. ~**len** *a* wollen. ~**lens** *npl* Wollsachen *pl*

woolly /'wʊlɪ/ *a* (-**ier,** -**iest**) wollig; (*fig*) unklar

word /wɜːd/ *n* Wort *nt*; (*news*) Nachricht *f*; **by** ~ **of mouth** mündlich; **have a** ~ **with** sprechen mit; **have** ~**s** einen Wortwechsel haben. ~**ing** *n* Wortlaut *m*. ~ **processor** *n* Textverarbeitungssystem *nt*

wore /wɔː(r)/ *see* **wear**

work /wɜːk/ *n* Arbeit *f*; (*Art, Literature*) Werk *nt*; ~**s** *pl* (*factory, mechanism*) Werk *nt*; **at** ~ bei der Arbeit; **out of** ~ arbeitslos ● *vi* arbeiten; ⟨*machine, system:*⟩ funktionieren; (*have effect*) wirken; (*study*) lernen; **it won't** ~ (*fig*) es klappt nicht ● *vt* arbeiten lassen; bedienen ⟨*machine*⟩; betätigen ⟨*lever*⟩; ~ **one's way through sth** sich durch etw hindurcharbeiten. ~ **off** *vt* abarbeiten. ~ **out** *vt* ausrechnen; (*solve*) lösen ● *vi* gutgehen, (*fam*) klappen. ~ **up** *vt* aufbauen; sich (*dat*) holen ⟨*appetite*⟩; **get** ~**ed up** sich aufregen

workable /'wɜːkəbl/ *a* (*feasible*) durchführbar

workaholic /wɜːkə'hɒlɪk/ *n* arbeitswütiger Mensch *m*

worker /'wɜːkə(r)/ *n* Arbeiter(in) *m*(*f*)

working /'wɜːkɪŋ/ *a* berufstätig; ⟨*day, clothes*⟩ Arbeits-; **be in** ~ **order** funktionieren. ~ '**class** *n* Arbeiterklasse *f*. ~**class** *a* Arbeiter-; **be** ~**class** zur Arbeiterklasse gehören

work: ~**man** *n* Arbeiter *m*; (*craftsman*) Handwerker *m*. ~**manship** *n* Arbeit *f*. ~**out** *n* [Fitneß]training *nt*. ~**shop** *n* Werkstatt *f*

world /wɜːld/ *n* Welt *f*; **in the** ~ auf der Welt; **a** ~ **of difference** ein himmelweiter Unterschied; **think the** ~ **of s.o.** große Stücke auf jdn halten. ~**ly** *a* weltlich; ⟨*person*⟩ weltlich gesinnt. ~**wide** *a & adv* /-'-/ weltweit

worm /wɜːm/ *n* Wurm *m* ● *vt* ~ **one's way into s.o.'s confidence** sich in jds

Vertrauen einschleichen. ~**-eaten** *a* wurmstichig

worn /wɔːn/ *see* **wear** ● *a* abgetragen. ~**-out** *a* abgetragen; ⟨*carpet*⟩ abgenutzt; ⟨*person*⟩ erschöpft

worried /'wʌrɪd/ *a* besorgt

worry /'wʌrɪ/ *n* Sorge *f* ● *v* (*pt/pp* **worried**) ● *vt* beunruhigen, Sorgen machen (+*dat*); ⟨*bother*⟩ stören ● *vi* sich beunruhigen, sich (*dat*) Sorgen machen. ~**ing** *a* beunruhigend

worse /wɜːs/ *a* & *adv* schlechter; ⟨*more serious*⟩ schlimmer ● *n* Schlechtere(s) *nt*; Schlimmere(s) *nt*

worsen /'wɜːsn/ *vt* verschlechtern ● *vi* sich verschlechtern

worship /'wɜːʃɪp/ *n* Anbetung *f*; ⟨*service*⟩ Gottesdienst *m*; **Your/His W~** Euer/Seine Ehren ● *v* (*pt/pp* **-shipped**) ● *vt* anbeten ● *vi* am Gottesdienst teilnehmen

worst /wɜːst/ *a* schlechteste(r,s) ⟨*most serious*⟩ schlimmste(r,s) ● *adv* am schlechtesten; am schlimmsten ● *n* **the** ~ das Schlimmste; **get the** ~ **of it** den kürzeren ziehen

worsted /'wʊstɪd/ *n* Kammgarn *m*

worth /wɜːθ/ *n* Wert *m*; **£10's** ~ **of petrol** Benzin für £10 ● *a* **be** ~ **£5** £5 wert sein; **be** ~ **it** (*fig*) sich lohnen. ~**less** *a* wertlos. ~**while** *a* lohnend

worthy /'wɜːðɪ/ *a* würdig

would /wʊd/ *v aux* **I** ~ **do it** ich würde es tun, ich täte es; ~ **you go?** würdest du gehen? **he said he** ~**n't** er sagte, er würde es nicht tun; **what** ~ **you like?** was möchten Sie?

wound¹ /wuːnd/ *n* Wunde *f* ● *vt* verwunden

wound² /waʊnd/ *see* **wind²**

wove, woven /wəʊv, 'wəʊvn/ *see* **weave²**

wrangle /'ræŋgl/ *n* Streit *m* ● *vi* sich streiten

wrap /ræp/ *n* Umhang *m* ● *vt* (*pt/pp* **wrapped**) ~ **[up]** wickeln; einpacken ⟨*present*⟩ ● *vi* ~ **up warmly** sich warm einpacken; **be** ~**ped up in** (*fig*) aufgehen in (+*dat*). ~**per** *n* Hülle *f*. ~**p-ing** *n* Verpackung *f*. ~**ping paper** *n* Einwickelpapier *nt*

wrath /rɒθ/ *n* Zorn *m*

wreak /riːk/ *vt* ~ **havoc** Verwüstungen anrichten

wreath /riːθ/ *n* (*pl* ~**s** /-ðz/) Kranz *m*

wreck /rek/ *n* Wrack *nt* ● *vt* zerstören; zunichte machen ⟨*plans*⟩; zerrütten ⟨*marriage*⟩. ~**age** /-ɪdʒ/ *n* Wrackteile *pl*; (*fig*) Trümmer *pl*

wren /ren/ *n* Zaunkönig *m*

wrench /rentʃ/ *n* Ruck *m*; ⟨*tool*⟩ Schraubenschlüssel *m*; **be a** ~ (*fig*) weh tun ● *vt* reißen; ~ **sth from s.o.** jdm etw entreißen

wrest /rest/ *vt* entwinden (**from s.o.** jdm)

wrestl|e /'resl/ *vi* ringen. ~**er** *n* Ringer *m*. ~**ing** *n* Ringen *nt*

wretch /retʃ/ *n* Kreatur *f*. ~**ed** /-ɪd/ *a* elend; ⟨*very bad*⟩ erbärmlich

wriggle /'rɪgl/ *n* Zappeln *nt* ● *vi* zappeln; ⟨*move forward*⟩ sich schlängeln; ~ **out of sth** (*fam*) sich vor etw (*dat*) drücken

wring /rɪŋ/ *vt* (*pt/pp* **wrung**) wringen; (~ **out**) auswringen; umdrehen ⟨*neck*⟩; ringen ⟨*hands*⟩; **be** ~**ing wet** tropfnaß sein

wrinkle /'rɪŋkl/ *n* Falte *f*; (*on skin*) Runzel *f* ● *vt* kräuseln ● *vi* sich kräuseln, sich falten. ~**d** *a* runzlig

wrist /rɪst/ *n* Handgelenk *nt*. ~**-watch** *n* Armbanduhr *f*

writ /rɪt/ *n* (*Jur*) Verfügung *f*

write /raɪt/ *vt/i* (*pt* **wrote**, *pp* **written**, *pres p* **writing**) schreiben. ~ **down** *vt* aufschreiben. ~ **off** *vt* abschreiben; zu Schrott fahren ⟨*car*⟩

'write-off *n* ≈ Totalschaden *m*

writer /'raɪtə(r)/ *n* Schreiber(in) *m(f)*; (*author*) Schriftsteller(in) *m(f)*

'write-up *n* Bericht *m*; (*review*) Kritik *f*

writhe /raɪð/ *vi* sich winden

writing /'raɪtɪŋ/ *n* Schreiben *nt*; (*handwriting*) Schrift *f*; **in** ~ schriftlich. ~**-paper** *n* Schreibpapier *nt*

written /'rɪtn/ *see* **write**

wrong /rɒŋ/ *a*, **-ly** *adv* falsch; (*morally*) unrecht; (*not just*) ungerecht; **be** ~ nicht stimmen; ⟨*person:*⟩ unrecht haben; **what's** ~? was ist los? ● *adv* falsch; **go** ~ ⟨*person:*⟩ etwas falsch machen; ⟨*machine:*⟩ kaputtgehen; ⟨*plan:*⟩ schiefgehen ● *n* Unrecht *nt* ● *vt* Unrecht tun (+*dat*). ~**ful** *a* ungerechtfertigt. ~**fully** *adv* ⟨*accuse*⟩ zu Unrecht

wrote /rəʊt/ *see* **write**

wrought 'iron /rɔːt-/ *n* Schmiedeeisen *nt* ● *attrib* schmiedeeisern

wrung /rʌŋ/ *see* **wring**

wry /raɪ/ *a* (**-er, -est**) ironisch; ⟨*humour*⟩ trocken

X

xerox (P) /'zɪərɒks/ *vt* fotokopieren
Xmas /'krɪsməs, 'eksməs/ *n* (*fam*) Weihnachten *nt*
'**X-ray** *n* (*picture*) Röntgenaufnahme *f*; ∼**s** *pl* Röntgenstrahlen *pl*; **have an** ∼ geröntgt werden ● *vt* röntgen; durchleuchten ⟨*luggage*⟩

Y

yacht /jɒt/ *n* Jacht *f*; (*for racing*) Segelboot *nt*. ∼**ing** *n* Segeln *nt*
yank /jæŋk/ *vt* (*fam*) reißen
Yank *n* (*fam*) Amerikaner(in) *m(f)*, (*fam*) Ami *m*
yap /jæp/ *vi* (*pt/pp* **yapped**) ⟨*dog:*⟩ kläffen
yard¹ /jɑːd/ *n* Hof *m*; (*for storage*) Lager *nt*
yard² *n* Yard *nt* (= 0,91 m). ∼**stick** *n* (*fig*) Maßstab *m*
yarn /jɑːn/ *n* Garn *nt*; (*fam: tale*) Geschichte *f*
yawn /jɔːn/ *n* Gähnen *nt* ● *vi* gähnen. ∼**ing** *a* gähnend
year /jɪə(r)/ *n* Jahr *nt*; (*of wine*) Jahrgang *m*; **for** ∼**s** jahrelang. ∼**-book** *n* Jahrbuch *nt*. ∼**ly** *a & adv* jährlich
yearn /jɜːn/ *vi* sich sehnen (**for** nach). ∼**ing** *n* Sehnsucht *f*
yeast /jiːst/ *n* Hefe *f*
yell /jel/ *n* Schrei *m* ● *vi* schreien
yellow /'jeləʊ/ *a* gelb ● *n* Gelb *nt*. ∼**ish** *a* gelblich
yelp /jelp/ *vi* jaulen
yen /jen/ *n* Wunsch *m* (**for** nach)
yes /jes/ *adv* ja; (*contradicting*) doch ● *n* Ja *nt*
yesterday /'jestədeɪ/ *n & adv* gestern; ∼'**s paper** die gestrige Zeitung; **the day before** ∼ vorgestern
yet /jet/ *adv* noch; (*in question*) schon; (*nevertheless*) doch; **as** ∼ bisher; **not** ∼ noch nicht; **the best** ∼ das bisher beste ● *conj* doch
yew /juː/ *n* Eibe *f*
Yiddish /'jɪdɪʃ/ *n* Jiddisch *nt*

yield /jiːld/ *n* Ertrag *m* ● *vt* bringen; abwerfen ⟨*profit*⟩ ● *vi* nachgeben; (*Amer, Auto*) die Vorfahrt beachten
yodel /'jəʊdl/ *vi* (*pt/pp* **yodelled**) jodeln
yoga /'jəʊgə/ *n* Yoga *m*
yoghurt /'jɒgət/ *n* Joghurt *m*
yoke /jəʊk/ *n* Joch *nt*; (*of garment*) Passe *f*
yokel /'jəʊkl/ *n* Bauerntölpel *m*
yolk /jəʊk/ *n* Dotter *m*, Eigelb *nt*
yonder /'jɒndə(r)/ *adv* (*liter*) dort drüben
you /juː/ *pron* du; (*acc*) dich; (*dat*) dir; (*pl*) ihr; (*acc, dat*) euch; (*formal*) (*nom & acc, sg & pl*) Sie; (*dat, sg & pl*) Ihnen; (*one*) man; (*acc*) einen; (*dat*) einem; **all of** ∼ ihr/Sie alle; **I know** ∼ ich kenne dich/euch/Sie; **I'll give** ∼ **the money** ich gebe dir/euch/Ihnen das Geld; **it does** ∼ **good** es tut gut; **it's bad for** ∼ es ist ungesund
young /jʌŋ/ *a* (**-er** /-gə(r)/, **-est** /-gɪst/) jung ● *npl* (*animals*) Junge *pl*; **the** ∼ die Jugend *f*. ∼**ster** *n* Jugendliche(r) *m/f*; (*child*) Kleine(r) *m/f*
your /jɔː(r)/ *a* dein; (*pl*) euer; (*formal*) Ihr
yours /jɔːz/ *poss pron* deine(r), deins; (*pl*) eure(r), euers; (*formal, sg & pl*) Ihre(r), Ihr[e]s; **a friend of** ∼ ein Freund von dir/Ihnen/euch; **that is** ∼ das gehört dir/Ihnen/euch
your'self *pron* (*pl* **-selves**) selbst; (*refl*) dich; (*dat*) dir; (*pl*) euch; (*formal*) sich; **by** ∼ allein
youth /juːθ/ *n* (*pl* **youths** /-ðz/ Jugend *f*; (*boy*) Jugendliche(r) *m*. ∼**ful** *a* jugendlich. ∼ **hostel** *n* Jugendherberge *f*
Yugoslav /'juːgəslɑːv/ *a* jugoslawisch. ∼**ia** /-'slɑːvɪə/ *n* Jugoslawien *nt*

Z

zany /'zeɪnɪ/ *a* (**-ier, -iest**) närrisch, verrückt
zeal /ziːl/ *n* Eifer *m*
zealous /'zeləs/ *a*, **-ly** *adv* eifrig
zebra /'zebrə/ *n* Zebra *nt*. ∼'**crossing** *n* Zebrastreifen *m*
zenith /'zenɪθ/ *n* Zenit *m*; (*fig*) Gipfel *m*
zero /'zɪərəʊ/ *n* Null *f*
zest /zest/ *n* Begeisterung *f*

zigzag /'zɪgzæg/ n Zickzack m ● vi (*pt/pp* -**zagged**) im Zickzack laufen/ (*in vehicle*) fahren

zinc /zɪŋk/ n Zink nt

zip /zɪp/ n ~ **[fastener]** Reißverschluß m ● vt ~ **[up]** den Reißverschluß zuziehen an (+ *dat*)

'**Zip code** n (*Amer*) Postleitzahl f

zipper /'zɪpə(r)/ n Reißverschluß m

zither /'zɪðə(r)/ n Zither f

zodiac /'zəʊdɪæk/ n Tierkreis m

zombie /'zɒmbɪ/ n (*fam*) **like a ~** ganz benommen

zone /zəʊn/ n Zone f

zoo /zu:/ n Zoo m

zoological /zəʊə'lɒdʒɪkl/ a zoologisch

zoolog|ist /zəʊ'ɒlədʒɪst/ n Zoologe m/ -gin f. ~**y** Zoologie f

zoom /zu:m/ vi sausen. ~ **lens** n Zoomobjektiv nt

Englische unregelmäßige Verben

Ein Sternchen (*) weist darauf hin, daß die korrekte Form von der jeweiligen Bedeutung abhängt.

Infinitive *Infinitiv*	Past Tense *Präteritum*	Past Participle *2. Partizip*
arise	arose	arisen
awake	awoke	awoken
be	was *sg*, were *pl*	been
bear	bore	borne
beat	beat	beaten
become	became	become
begin	began	begun
behold	beheld	beheld
bend	bent	bent
beseech	beseeched, besought	beseeched, besought
bet	bet, betted	bet, betted
bid	*bade, bid	*bidden, bid
bind	bound	bound
bite	bit	bitten
bleed	bled	bled
blow	blew	blown
break	broke	broken
breed	bred	bred
bring	brought	brought
build	built	built
burn	burnt, burned	burnt, burned
burst	burst	burst
bust	busted, bust	busted, bust
buy	bought	bought
cast	cast	cast
catch	caught	caught
choose	chose	chosen
cling	clung	clung
come	came	come
cost	*cost, costed	*cost, costed
creep	crept	crept
cut	cut	cut
deal	dealt	dealt
dig	dug	dug
do	did	done
draw	drew	drawn
dream	dreamt, dreamed	dreamt, dreamed
drink	drank	drunk
drive	drove	driven
dwell	dwelt	dwelt
eat	ate	eaten
fall	fell	fallen
feed	fed	fed
feel	felt	felt
fight	fought	fought
find	found	found
flee	fled	fled

Infinitive *Infinitiv*	Past Tense *Präteritum*	Past Participle *2. Partizip*
fling	flung	flung
fly	flew	flown
forbid	forbade	forbidden
forget	forgot	forgotten
forgive	forgave	forgiven
forsake	forsook	forsaken
freeze	froze	frozen
get	got	got, (*Amer also*) gotten
give	gave	given
go	went	gone
grind	ground	ground
grow	grew	grown
hang	*hung, hanged	*hung, hanged
have	had	had
hear	heard	heard
hew	hewed	hewed, hewn
hide	hid	hidden
hit	hit	hit
hold	held	held
hurt	hurt	hurt
keep	kept	kept
kneel	knelt	knelt
know	knew	known
lay	laid	laid
lead	led	led
lean	leaned, lent	leaned, lent
leap	leapt, leaped	leapt, leaped
learn	learnt, learned	learnt, learned
leave	left	left
lend	lent	lent
let	let	let
lie²	lay	lain
light	lit, lighted	lit, lighted
lose	lost	lost
make	made	made
mean	meant	meant
meet	met	met
mow	mowed	mown, mowed
overhang	overhung	overhung
pay	paid	paid
put	put	put
quit	quitted, quit	quitted, quit
read /ri:d/	read /red/	read /red/
rid	rid	rid
ride	rode	ridden
ring²	rang	rung
rise	rose	risen
run	ran	run
saw	sawed	sawn, sawed
say	said	said
see	saw	seen
seek	sought	sought
sell	sold	sold
send	sent	sent

Infinitive *Infinitiv*	Past Tense *Präteritum*	Past Participle *2. Partizip*
set	set	set
sew	sewed	sewn, sewed
shake	shook	shaken
shear	sheared	shorn, sheared
shed	shed	shed
shine	shone	shone
shit	shit	shit
shoe	shod	shod
shoot	shot	shot
show	showed	shown
shrink	shrank	shrunk
shut	shut	shut
sing	sang	sung
sink	sank	sunk
sit	sat	sat
slay	slew	slain
sleep	slept	slept
slide	slid	slid
sling	slung	slung
slit	slit	slit
smell	smelt, smelled	smelt, smelled
sow	sowed	sown, sowed
speak	spoke	spoken
speed	*sped, speeded	*sped, speeded
spell	spelled, spelt	spelled, spelt
spend	spent	spent
spill	spilt, spilled	spilt, spilled
spin	spun	spun
spit	spat	spat
split	split	split
spoil	spoilt, spoiled	spoilt, spoiled
spread	spread	spread
spring	sprang	sprung
stand	stood	stood
steal	stole	stolen
stick	stuck	stuck
sting	stung	stung
stink	stank	stunk
strew	strewed	strewn, strewed
stride	strode	stridden
strike	struck	struck
string	strung	strung
strive	strove	striven
swear	swore	sworn
sweep	swept	swept
swell	swelled	swollen, swelled
swim	swam	swum
swing	swung	swung
take	took	taken
teach	taught	taught
tear	tore	torn
tell	told	told
think	thought	thought
thrive	thrived, throve	thrived, thriven
throw	threw	thrown

Infinitive *Infinitiv*	Past Tense *Präteritum*	Past Participle *2. Partizip*
thrust	thrust	thrust
tread	trod	trodden
understand	understood	understood
undo	undid	undone
wake	woke	woken
wear	wore	worn
weave[2]	wove	woven
weep	wept	wept
wet	wet, wetted	wet, wetted
win	won	won
wind[2] /waɪnd/	wound /waʊnd/	wound /waʊnd/
wring	wrung	wrung
write	wrote	written

Phonetic symbols used for German words

a	Hand	hant	ŋ	lang	laŋ
aː	Bahn	baːn	o	moral	mo'raːl
ɐ	Ober	'oːbɐ	oː	Boot	boːt
ɐ̯	Uhr	uːɐ̯	ọ	Foyer	fọa'jeː
ã	Conférencier	kõferã'sieː	õ	Konkurs	kõ'kʊrs
ãː	Abonnement	abɔnə'mãː	õː	Ballon	ba'lõː
ai̯	weit	vai̯t	ɔ	Post	pɔst
au̯	Haut	hau̯t	ø	Ökonom	øko'noːm
b	Ball	bal	øː	Öl	øːl
ç	ich	ɪç	œ	göttlich	'gœtlɪç
d	dann	dan	ɔy	heute	'hɔytə
dʒ	Gin	dʒɪn	p	Pakt	pakt
e	Metall	me'tal	r	Rast	rast
eː	Beet	beːt	s	Hast	hast
ɛ	mästen	'mɛstən	ʃ	Schal	ʃaːl
ɛː	wählen	'vɛːlən	t	Tal	taːl
ẽː	Cousin	ku'zẽː	ts	Zahl	tsaːl
ə	Nase	'naːzə	tʃ	Couch	kau̯tʃ
f	Faß	fas	u	kulant	ku'lant
g	Gast	gast	uː	Hut	huːt
h	haben	'haːbən	u̯	aktuell	ak'tu̯ɛl
i	Rivale	ri'vaːlə	ʊ	Pult	pʊlt
iː	viel	fiːl	v	was	vas
i̯	Aktion	ak'tsi̯oːn	x	Bach	bax
ɪ	Birke	'bɪrkə	y	Physik	fy'ziːk
j	ja	jaː	yː	Rübe	'ryːbə
k	kalt	kalt	ỹ	Nuance	'nỹãːsə
l	Last	last	ʏ	Fülle	'fʏlə
m	Mast	mast	z	Nase	'naːzə
n	Naht	naːt	ʒ	Regime	re'ʒiːm

ʔ Glottal stop, e.g. Koordination /koʔɔrdina'tsi̯oːn/.
ː Length sign after a vowel, e.g. Chrom /kroːm/.
' Stress mark before stressed syllable, e.g. Balkon /bal'kõː/.

Die für das Englische verwendeten Zeichen der Lautschrift

ɑː	barn	bɑːn	l	lot	lɒt
ɑ̃	nuance	'njuːɑ̃s	m	mat	mæt
æ	fat	fæt	n	not	nɒt
æ̃	lingerie	'læʒərɪ	ŋ	sing	sɪŋ
aɪ	fine	faɪn	ɒ	got	gɒt
aʊ	now	naʊ	ɔː	paw	pɔː
b	bat	bæt	ɔɪ	boil	bɔɪl
d	dog	dɒg	p	pet	pet
dʒ	jam	dʒæm	r	rat	ræt
e	met	met	s	sip	sɪp
eɪ	fate	feɪt	ʃ	ship	ʃɪp
eə	fairy	'feərɪ	t	tip	tɪp
əʊ	goat	gəʊt	tʃ	chin	tʃɪn
ə	ago	ə'gəʊ	θ	thin	θɪn
ɜː	fur	fɜː(r)	ð	the	ðə
f	fat	fæt	uː	boot	buːt
g	good	gʊd	ʊ	book	bʊk
h	hat	hæt	ʊə	tourism	'tʊərɪzm
ɪ	bit, happy	bɪt, 'hæpɪ	ʌ	dug	dʌg
ɪə	near	nɪə(r)	v	van	væn
iː	meet	miːt	w	win	wɪn
j	yet	jet	z	zip	zɪp
k	kit	kɪt	ʒ	vision	'vɪʒn

ː bezeichnet Länge des vorhergehenden Vokals, z. B. boot [buːt].
ˈ Betonung, steht unmittelbar vor einer betonten Silbe, z. B. ago [ə'gəʊ].
(r) Ein „r" in runden Klammern wird nur gesprochen, wenn im Text-
zusammenhang ein Vokal unmittelbar folgt, z. B. fire /'faɪə(r); fire at
/'faɪər æt/.

Guide to German pronunciation

Consonants are pronounced as in English with the following exceptions:

b	as	p	
d	as	t	*at the end of a word or syllable*
g	as	k	

ch   as in Scottish lo<u>ch</u> *after a, o, u, au*

         like an exaggerated h as in <u>h</u>uge

                 after i, e, ä, ö, ü, eu, ei

-chs	as	x	(as in bo<u>x</u>)
-ig	as	-ich /ɪç/	*when a suffix*
j	as	y	(as in <u>y</u>es)
ps			
			the p is pronounced
pn			
qu	as	k + v	
s	as	z	(as in <u>z</u>ero) *at the beginning of a word*
	as	s	(as in bu<u>s</u>) *at the end of a word or syllable, before a consonant, or when doubled*
sch	as	sh	
sp	as	shp	*at the beginning of a*
st	as	sht	*word*
v	as f		(as in <u>f</u>or)
	as v		(as in <u>v</u>ery) *within a word*
w	as	v	(as in <u>v</u>ery)
z	as	ts	

Vowels are approximately as follows:

a	short	as	u	(as in b<u>u</u>t)
	long	as	a	(as in c<u>ar</u>)
e	short	as	e	(as in p<u>e</u>n)
	long	as	a	(as in p<u>a</u>per)
i	short	as	i	(as in b<u>i</u>t)
	long	as	ee	(as in qu<u>ee</u>n)
o	short	as	o	(as in h<u>o</u>t)
	long	as	o	(as in p<u>o</u>pe)

u	short	as	oo	(as in f<u>oo</u>t)
	long	as	oo	(as in b<u>oo</u>t)

Vowels are always short before a double consonant, and long when followed by an h or when double

ie	is pronounced ee			(as in k<u>ee</u>p)

Diphthongs

au		as	ow	(as in h<u>ow</u>)
ei ai		as	y	(as in m<u>y</u>)
eu äu		as	oy	(as in b<u>oy</u>)

German irregular verbs

1st, 2nd and 3rd person present are given after the infinitive, and past subjunctive after the past indicative, where there is a change of vowel or any other irregularity.

Compound verbs are only given if they do not take the same forms as the corresponding simple verb, e.g. *befehlen*, or if there is no corresponding simple verb, e.g. *bewegen*.

An asterisk (*) indicates a verb which is also conjugated regularly.

Infinitive *Infinitiv*	Past Tense *Präteritum*	Past Participle 2. *Partizip*
abwägen	wog (wöge) ab	abgewogen
ausbedingen	bedang (bedänge) aus	ausbedungen
*backen (du bäckst, er bäckt)	buk (büke)	gebacken
befehlen (du befiehlst, er befiehlt)	befahl (beföhle, befähle)	befohlen
beginnen	begann (begänne)	begonnen
beißen (du/er beißt)	biß (bisse)	gebissen
bergen (du birgst, er birgt)	barg (bärge)	geborgen
bersten (du/er birst)	barst (bärste)	geborsten
bewegen²	bewog (bewöge)	bewogen
biegen	bog (böge)	gebogen
bieten	bot (böte)	geboten
binden	band (bände)	gebunden
bitten	bat (bäte)	gebeten
blasen (du/er bläst)	blies	geblasen
bleiben	blieb	geblieben
*bleichen	blich	geblichen
braten (du brätst, er brät)	briet	gebraten
brechen (du brichst, er bricht)	brach (bräche)	gebrochen
brennen	brannte (brennte)	gebrannt
bringen	brachte (brächte)	gebracht
denken	dachte (dächte)	gedacht
dreschen (du drischst, er drischt)	drosch (drösche)	gedroschen
dringen	drang (dränge)	gedrungen
dürfen (ich/er darf, du darfst)	durfte (dürfte)	gedurft
empfehlen (du empfiehlst, er empfiehlt)	empfahl (empföhle)	empfohlen
erlöschen (du erlischst, er erlischt)	erlosch (erlösche)	erloschen
*erschallen	erscholl (erschölle)	erschollen
*erschrecken (du erschrickst, er erschrickt)	erschrak (erschräke)	erschrocken

Infinitive *Infinitiv*	Past Tense *Präteritum*	Past Participle *2. Partizip*
erwägen	erwog (erwöge)	erwogen
essen (du/er ißt)	aß (äße)	gegessen
fahren (du fährst, er fährt)	fuhr (führe)	gefahren
fallen (du fällst, er fällt)	fiel	gefallen
fangen (du fängst, er fängt)	fing	gefangen
fechten (du fichtst, er ficht)	focht (föchte)	gefochten
finden	fand (fände)	gefunden
flechten (du flichtst, er flicht)	flocht (flöchte)	geflochten
fliegen	flog (flöge)	geflogen
fliehen	floh (flöhe)	geflohen
fließen (du/er fließt)	floß (flösse)	geflossen
fressen (du/er frißt)	fraß (fräße)	gefressen
frieren	fror (fröre)	gefroren
*gären	gor (göre)	gegoren
gebären (du gebierst, sie gebiert)	gebar (gebäre)	geboren
geben (du gibst, er gibt)	gab (gäbe)	gegeben
gedeihen	gedieh	gediehen
gehen	ging	gegangen
gelingen	gelang (gelänge)	gelungen
gelten (du giltst, er gilt)	galt (gölte, gälte)	gegolten
genesen (du/er genest)	genas (genäse)	genesen
genießen (du/er genießt)	genoß (genösse)	genossen
geschehen (es geschieht)	geschah (geschähe)	geschehen
gewinnen	gewann (gewönne, gewänne)	gewonnen
gießen (du/er gießt)	goß (gösse)	gegossen
gleichen	glich	geglichen
gleiten	glitt	geglitten
glimmen	glomm (glömme)	geglommen
graben (du gräbst, er gräbt)	grub (grübe)	gegraben
greifen	griff	gegriffen
haben (du hast, er hat)	hatte (hätte)	gehabt
halten (du hältst, er hält)	hielt	gehalten
hängen[2]	hing	gehangen
hauen	haute	gehauen
heben	hob (höbe)	gehoben
heißen (du/er heißt)	hieß	geheißen
helfen (du hilfst, er hilft)	half (hülfe)	geholfen
kennen	kannte (kennte)	gekannt
klingen	klang (klänge)	geklungen
kneifen	kniff	gekniffen
kommen	kam (käme)	gekommen
können (ich/er kann, du kannst)	konnte (könnte)	gekonnt
kriechen	kroch (kröche)	gekrochen
laden (du lädst, er lädt)	lud (lüde)	geladen
lassen (du/er läßt)	ließ	gelassen
laufen (du läufst, er läuft)	lief	gelaufen

Infinitive *Infinitiv*	Past Tense *Präteritum*	Past Participle *2. Partizip*
leiden	litt	gelitten
leihen	lieh	geliehen
lesen (du/er liest)	las (läse)	gelesen
liegen	lag (läge)	gelegen
lügen	log (löge)	gelogen
mahlen	mahlte	gemahlen
meiden	mied	gemieden
melken	molk (mölke)	gemolken
messen (du/er mißt)	maß (mäße)	gemessen
mißlingen	mißlang (mißlänge)	mißlungen
mögen (ich/er mag, du magst)	mochte (möchte)	gemocht
müssen (ich/er muß, du mußt)	mußte (müßte)	gemußt
nehmen (du nimmst, er nimmt)	nahm (nähme)	genommen
nennen	nannte (nennte)	genannt
pfeifen	pfiff	gepfiffen
preisen (du/er preist)	pries	gepriesen
quellen (du quillst, er quillt)	quoll (quölle)	gequollen
raten (du rätst, er rät)	riet	geraten
reiben	rieb	gerieben
reißen (du/er reißt)	riß	gerissen
reiten	ritt	geritten
rennen	rannte (rennte)	gerannt
riechen	roch (röche)	gerochen
ringen	rang (ränge)	gerungen
rinnen	rann (ränne)	geronnen
rufen	rief	gerufen
*salzen (du/er salzt)	salzte	gesalzen
saufen (du säufst, er säuft)	soff (söffe)	gesoffen
*saugen	sog (söge)	gesogen
schaffen[1]	schuf (schüfe)	geschaffen
scheiden	schied	geschieden
scheinen	schien	geschienen
scheißen (du/er scheißt)	schiß	geschissen
schelten (du schiltst, er schilt)	schalt (schölte)	gescholten
scheren[1]	schor (schöre)	geschoren
schieben	schob (schöbe)	geschoben
schießen (du/er schießt)	schoß (schösse)	geschossen
schinden	schindete	geschunden
schlafen (du schläfst, er schläft)	schlief	geschlafen
schlagen (du schlägst, er schlägt)	schlug (schlüge)	geschlagen
schleichen	schlich	geschlichen
schleifen[2]	schliff	geschliffen
schließen (du/er schließt)	schloß (schlösse)	geschlossen
schlingen	schlang (schlänge)	geschlungen

Infinitive *Infinitiv*	Past Tense *Präteritum*	Past Participle 2. *Partizip*
schmeißen (du/er schmeißt)	schmiß (schmisse)	geschmissen
schmelzen (du/er schmilzt)	schmolz (schmölze)	geschmolzen
schneiden	schnitt	geschnitten
*schrecken (du schrickst, er schrickt)	schrak (schräke)	geschreckt
schreiben	schrieb	geschrieben
schreien	schrie	geschrie[e]n
schreiten	schritt	geschritten
schweigen	schwieg	geschwiegen
schwellen (du schwillst, er schwillt)	schwoll (schwölle)	geschwollen
schwimmen	schwamm (schwömme)	geschwommen
schwinden	schwand (schwände)	geschwunden
schwingen	schwang (schwänge)	geschwungen
schwören	schwor (schwüre)	geschworen
sehen (du siehst, er sieht)	sah (sähe)	gesehen
sein (ich bin, du bist, er ist, wir sind, ihr seid, sie sind)	war (wäre)	gewesen
senden[1]	sandte (sendete)	gesandt
sieden	sott (sötte)	gesotten
singen	sang (sänge)	gesungen
sinken	sank (sänke)	gesunken
sinnen	sann (sänne)	gesonnen
sitzen (du/er sitzt)	saß (säße)	gesessen
sollen (ich/er soll, du sollst)	sollte	gesollt
*spalten	spaltete	gespalten
speien	spie	gespie[e]n
spinnen	spann (spönne, spänne)	gesponnen
sprechen (du sprichst, er spricht)	sprach (spräche)	gesprochen
sprießen (du/er sprießt)	sproß (sprösse)	gesprossen
springen	sprang (spränge)	gesprungen
stechen (du stichst, er sticht)	stach (stäche)	gestochen
stehen	stand (stünde, stände)	gestanden
stehlen (du stiehlst, er stiehlt)	stahl (stähle)	gestohlen
steigen	stieg	gestiegen
sterben (du stirbst, er stirbt)	starb (stürbe)	gestorben
stinken	stank (stänke)	gestunken
stoßen (du/er stößt)	stieß	gestoßen
streichen	strich	gestrichen
streiten	stritt	gestritten
tragen (du trägst, er trägt)	trug (trüge)	getragen
treffen (du triffst, er trifft)	traf (träfe)	getroffen

Infinitive *Infinitiv*	Past Tense *Präteritum*	Past Participle *2. Partizip*
treiben	trieb	getrieben
treten (du trittst, er tritt)	trat (träte)	getreten
*triefen	troff (tröffe)	getroffen
trinken	trank (tränke)	getrunken
trügen	trog (tröge)	getrogen
tun (du tust, er tut)	tat (täte)	getan
verderben (du verdirbst, er verdirbt)	verdarb (verdürbe)	verdorben
vergessen (du/er vergißt)	vergaß (vergäße)	vergessen
verlieren	verlor (verlöre)	verloren
verschleißen (du/er verschleißt)	verschliß	verschlissen
verzeihen	verzieh	verziehen
wachsen[1] (du/er wächst)	wuchs (wüchse)	gewachsen
waschen (du wäschst, er wäscht)	wusch (wüsche)	gewaschen
weichen[2]	wich	gewichen
weisen (du/er weist)	wies	gewiesen
*wenden[2]	wandte (wendete)	gewandt
werben (du wirbst, er wirbt)	warb (würbe)	geworben
werden (du wirst, er wird)	wurde (würde)	geworden
werfen (du wirfst, er wirft)	warf (würfe)	geworfen
wiegen[1]	wog (wöge)	gewogen
winden	wand (wände)	gewunden
wissen (ich/er weiß, du weißt)	wußte (wüßte)	gewußt
wollen (ich/er will, du willst)	wollte	gewollt
wringen	wrang (wränge)	gewrungen
ziehen	zog (zöge)	gezogen
zwingen	zwang (zwänge)	gezwungen